THE
NUMB
O
n
Blues
HITS

THE Billboard® BOOK OF NUMBER ONE Rhythm & Blues HITS

ADAM WHITE AND FRED BRONSON

BILLBOARD BOOKS
An imprint of Watson-Guptill Publications/New York

Edited by Paul Lukas
Cover and interior design by Bob Fillie, Graphiti Graphics
Graphic production by Hector Campbell

First published by Billboard Books, an imprint of Watson-Guptill Publications, a division of BPI Communications, L.P., 1515 Broadway, New York, NY 10036

Library of Congress Cataloging-in-Publication Data
White, Adam
The Billboard book of number one rhythm & blues hits / Adam White and Fred Bronson
p. cm.
ISBN 0-8230-8285-7
1. Rhythm and blues music—Discography. I. Bronson, Fred. II. Billboard (Cincinnati, Ohio : 1963) III. Title. IV. Title: Billboard book of number 1 rhythm & blues hits.
ML156.4.B6W55 1993
016.781643'0266—dc20 93-13336

Manufactured in the United States of America

First printing, 1993

1 2 3 4 5 6 7 8 9 / 99 98 97 96 95 94 93

To James Jamerson, Benny Benjamin, and Earl Van Dyke

CONTENTS

Numerical references are to entry numbers, not page numbers.

1965

1966

1967

33	Tell It Like It Is	*Aaron Neville*
34	Are You Lonely for Me	*Freddie Scott*
35	Love Is Here and Now You're Gone	*The Supremes*
36	I Never Loved a Man (The Way I Love You)	*Aretha Franklin*
37	Jimmy Mack	*Martha and the Vandellas*
38	Respect	*Aretha Franklin*
39	I Was Made to Love Her	*Stevie Wonder*
40	Make Me Yours	*Bettye Swann*
41	Baby, I Love You	*Aretha Franklin*
42	Cold Sweat	*James Brown*
43	Funky Broadway	*Wilson Pickett*
44	(Your Love Keeps Lifting Me) Higher and Higher	*Jackie Wilson*
45	Soul Man	*Sam & Dave*
46	I Heard It Through the Grapevine	*Gladys Knight & the Pips*

1968

47	I Second That Emotion	*Smokey Robinson and the Miracles*
48	Chain of Fools	*Aretha Franklin*
49	I Wish It Would Rain	*The Temptations*
50	We're a Winner	*The Impressions*
51	(Sittin' On) The Dock of the Bay	*Otis Redding*
52	(Sweet Sweet Baby) Since You've Been Gone	*Aretha Franklin*
53	I Got the Feelin'	*James Brown*
54	Cowboys to Girls	*The Intruders*
55	Tighten Up	*Archie Bell and the Drells*
56	Shoo-Be-Doo-Be-Doo-Da-Day	*Stevie Wonder*
57	Ain't Nothing Like the Real Thing	*Marvin Gaye and Tammi Terrell*
58	Think	*Aretha Franklin*
59	I Could Never Love Another (After Loving You)	*The Temptations*
60	Grazing in the Grass	*Hugh Masekela*
61	Stay in My Corner	*The Dells*
62	You're All I Need to Get By	*Marvin Gaye and Tammi Terrell*
63	Say It Loud—I'm Black and I'm Proud (Part 1)	*James Brown*
64	Hey, Western Union Man	*Jerry Butler*
65	Who's Making Love	*Johnnie Taylor*
66	I Heard It Through the Grapevine	*Marvin Gaye*

1969

67	Can I Change My Mind	*Tyrone Davis*
68	Everyday People	*Sly & the Family Stone*
69	Give It Up Or Turnit a Loose	*James Brown*
70	Run Away Child, Running Wild	*The Temptations*
71	Only the Strong Survive	*Jerry Butler*
72	It's Your Thing	*The Isley Brothers*
73	The Chokin' Kind	*Joe Simon*
74	Too Busy Thinking About My Baby	*Marvin Gaye*

75 What Does It Take (To Win Your Love) — *Jr. Walker & the All Stars*
76 Mother Popcorn (You Got to Have a Mother for Me) (Part 1) — *James Brown*
77 Choice of Colors — *The Impressions*
78 Share Your Love with Me — *Aretha Franklin*
79 Oh, What a Night — *The Dells*
80 I Can't Get Next to You — *The Temptations*
81 Baby, I'm for Real — *The Originals*
82 Someday We'll Be Together — *Diana Ross and the Supremes*

1970

83 I Want You Back — *The Jackson 5*
84 Thank You (Falettin Me Be Mice Elf Again) — *Sly & the Family Stone*
85 Rainy Night in Georgia — *Brook Benton*
86 Call Me — *Aretha Franklin*
87 ABC — *The Jackson 5*
88 Turn Back the Hands of Time — *Tyrone Davis*
89 Love on a Two-Way Street — *The Moments*
90 The Love You Save — *The Jackson 5*
91 Signed, Sealed, Delivered, I'm Yours — *Stevie Wonder*
92 Don't Play That Song (You Lied) — *Aretha Franklin*
93 Ain't No Mountain High Enough — *Diana Ross*
94 I'll Be There — *The Jackson 5*
95 Super Bad (Part 1 & Part 2) — *James Brown*
96 The Tears of a Clown — *Smokey Robinson and the Miracles*
97 Stoned Love — *The Supremes*

1971

98 Groove Me — *King Floyd*
99 If I Were Your Woman — *Gladys Knight & the Pips*
100 (Do The) Push and Pull, Part 1 — *Rufus Thomas*
101 Jody's Got Your Girl and Gone — *Johnnie Taylor*
102 Just My Imagination (Running Away With Me) — *The Temptations*
103 What's Going On — *Marvin Gaye*
104 Never Can Say Goodbye — *The Jackson 5*
105 Bridge over Troubled Water — *Aretha Franklin*
106 Want Ads — *The Honey Cone*
107 Don't Knock My Love (Part 1) — *Wilson Pickett*
108 Mr. Big Stuff — *Jean Knight*
109 Hot Pants (She Got to Use What She Got to Get What She Wants) (Part 1) — *James Brown*
110 Mercy Mercy Me (The Ecology) — *Marvin Gaye*
111 Spanish Harlem — *Aretha Franklin*
112 Stick-Up — *The Honey Cone*
113 Make It Funky — *James Brown*
114 Thin Line Between Love & Hate — *The Persuaders*
115 Trapped by a Thing Called Love — *Denise LaSalle*
116 Inner City Blues (Make Me Wanna Holler) — *Marvin Gaye*
117 Have You Seen Her — *The Chi-Lites*
118 Family Affair — *Sly & the Family Stone*

1972

119 Let's Stay Together — *Al Green*
120 Talking Loud and Saying Nothing (Part 1) — *James Brown*
121 I Gotcha — *Joe Tex*
122 In the Rain — *The Dramatics*
123 Day Dreaming — *Aretha Franklin*
124 I'll Take You There — *The Staple Singers*
125 Oh Girl — *The Chi-Lites*
126 Woman's Gotta Have it — *Bobby Womack*
127 Lean on Me — *Bill Withers*
128 Outa-Space — *Billy Preston*
129 (If Loving You Is Wrong) I Don't Want to Be Right — *Luther Ingram*
130 Where Is the Love — *Roberta Flack and Donny Hathaway*
131 I'm Still in Love with You — *Al Green*
132 Power of Love — *Joe Simon*
133 Back Stabbers — *The O'Jays*
134 Get on the Good Foot — *James Brown*
135 I'll Be Around — *The Spinners*
136 If You Don't Know Me by Now — *Harold Melvin and the Blue Notes*
137 You Ought to Be with Me — *Al Green*
138 Me and Mrs. Jones — *Billy Paul*

1973

139 Superstition — *Stevie Wonder*
140 Why Can't We Live Together — *Timmy Thomas*
141 Could It Be I'm Falling in Love — *The Spinners*
142 Love Train — *The O'Jays*
143 Neither One of Us (Wants to Be the First to Say Goodbye) — *Gladys Knight & the Pips*
144 Masterpiece — *The Temptations*
145 Pillow Talk — *Sylvia*
146 Funky Worm — *The Ohio Players*
147 Leaving Me — *The Independents*
148 I'm Gonna Love You Just a Little More Baby — *Barry White*
149 One of a Kind (Love Affair) — *The Spinners*
150 Doing It to Death — *Fred Wesley and the J.B.'s*
151 I Believe in You (You Believe in Me) — *Johnnie Taylor*
152 Angel — *Aretha Franklin*
153 Let's Get It On — *Marvin Gaye*
154 Higher Ground — *Stevie Wonder*
155 Keep on Truckin' (Part 1) — *Eddie Kendricks*
156 Midnight Train to Georgia — *Gladys Knight & the Pips*
157 Space Race — *Billy Preston*
158 The Love I Lost — *Harold Melvin and the Blue Notes*
159 If You're Ready (Come Go with Me) — *The Staple Singers*
160 Living for the City — *Stevie Wonder*

1974

161	Until You Come Back to Me (That's What I'm Gonna Do)	*Aretha Franklin*
162	I've Got to Use My Imagination	*Gladys Knight & the Pips*
163	Livin' for You	*Al Green*
164	Let Your Hair Down	*The Temptations*
165	Boogie Down	*Eddie Kendricks*
166	Mighty Love	*The Spinners*
167	Lookin' for a Love	*Bobby Womack*
168	Best Thing That Ever Happened to Me	*Gladys Knight & the Pips*
169	TSOP (The Sound Of Philadelphia)	*MFSB featuring the Three Degrees*
170	The Payback (Part 1)	*James Brown*
171	Dancing Machine	*The Jackson 5*
172	I'm in Love	*Aretha Franklin*
173	Be Thankful for What You Got	*William DeVaughn*
174	Hollywood Swinging	*Kool & the Gang*
175	Sideshow	*Blue Magic*
176	Finally Got Myself Together (I'm a Changed Man)	*The Impressions*
177	Rock Your Baby	*George McCrae*
178	My Thang	*James Brown*
179	Feel Like Makin' Love	*Roberta Flack*
180	Can't Get Enough of Your Love, Babe	*Barry White*
181	You Haven't Done Nothin'	*Stevie Wonder*
182	Papa Don't Take No Mess	*James Brown*
183	Do It ('Til You're Satisfied)	*B.T. Express*
184	Higher Plane	*Kool & the Gang*
185	Let's Straighten It Out	*Latimore*
186	Woman to Woman	*Shirley Brown*
187	I Feel a Song (In My Heart)	*Gladys Knight & the Pips*
188	You Got the Love	*Rufus featuring Chaka Khan*
189	She's Gone	*Tavares*
190	Boogie on Reggae Woman	*Stevie Wonder*

1975

191	Kung Fu Fighting	*Carl Douglas*
192	You're the First, the Last, My Everything	*Barry White*
193	Fire	*The Ohio Players*
194	Happy People	*The Temptations*
195	I Belong to You	*Love Unlimited*
196	Lady Marmalade	*LaBelle*
197	Shame, Shame, Shame	*Shirley & Company*
198	Express	*B.T. Express*
199	Supernatural Thing (Part 1)	*Ben E. King*
200	Shining Star	*Earth, Wind & Fire*
201	Shoeshine Boy	*Eddie Kendricks*
202	L-O-V-E (Love)	*Al Green*
203	Shakey Ground	*The Temptations*
204	What Am I Gonna Do with You	*Barry White*
205	Get Down, Get Down (Get on the Floor)	*Joe Simon*
206	Baby That's Backatcha	*Smokey Robinson*

1976

255	Just to Be Close to You	*The Commodores*
256	The Rubberband Man	*The Spinners*
257	Message In Our Music	*The O'Jays*
258	Love Ballad	*L.T.D.*
259	You Don't Have to Be a Star (To Be in My Show)	*Marilyn McCoo and Billy Davis, Jr.*
260	Dazz	*Brick*
261	Car Wash	*Rose Royce*

1977

262	Darlin' Darlin' Baby (Sweet, Tender, Love)	*The O'Jays*
263	I Wish	*Stevie Wonder*
264	Don't Leave Me This Way	*Thelma Houston*
265	I've Got Love on My Mind	*Natalie Cole*
266	Tryin' to Love Two	*William Bell*
267	At Midnight (My Love Will Lift You Up)	*Rufus featuring Chaka Khan*
268	The Pride (Part 1)	*The Isley Brothers*
269	Got to Give It Up (Part 1)	*Marvin Gaye*
270	Whodunit	*Tavares*
271	Sir Duke	*Stevie Wonder*
272	Break It to Me Gently	*Aretha Franklin*
273	Best of My Love	*The Emotions*
274	Easy	*The Commodores*
275	Slide	*Slave*
276	Strawberry Letter 23	*The Brothers Johnson*
277	Float On	*The Floaters*
278	Keep It Comin' Love	*KC and the Sunshine Band*
279	It's Ecstacy When You Lay Down Next to Me	*Barry White*
280	(Every Time I Turn Around) Back in Love Again	*L.T.D.*
281	Serpentine Fire	*Earth, Wind & Fire*

1978

282	Ffun	*Con Funk Shun*
283	Our Love	*Natalie Cole*
284	Theme Song from "Which Way Is Up"	*Stargard*
285	Too Hot Ta Trot	*The Commodores*
286	It's You That I Need	*Enchantment*
287	Flash Light	*Parliament*
288	Bootzilla	*Bootsy's Rubber Band*
289	The Closer I Get to You	*Roberta Flack with Donny Hathaway*
290	Too Much, Too Little, Too Late	*Johnny Mathis and Deniece Williams*
291	Take Me to the Next Phase (Part 1)	*The Isley Brothers*
292	Use Ta Be My Girl	*The O'Jays*
293	Stuff Like That	*Quincy Jones*
294	Close the Door	*Teddy Pendergrass*
295	You and I	*Rick James*
296	Boogie Oogie Oogie	*A Taste of Honey*
297	Three Times a Lady	*The Commodores*
298	Get Off	*Foxy*

299	Holding On (When Love Is Gone)	*L.T.D.*
300	Got to Get You into My Life	*Earth, Wind & Fire*
301	One Nation under a Groove (Part 1)	*Funkadelic*
302	I'm Every Woman	*Chaka Khan*
303	Le Freak	*Chic*

1979

304	Got to Be Real	*Cheryl Lynn*
305	September	*Earth, Wind & Fire*
306	Aqua Boogie	*Parliament*
307	Bustin' Loose Part 1	*Chuck Brown and the Soul Searchers*
308	I Got My Mind Made Up (You Can Get It Girl)	*Instant Funk*
309	He's the Greatest Dancer	*Sister Sledge*
310	Disco Nights (Rock-Freak)	*GQ*
311	Reunited	*Peaches and Herb*
312	I Wanna Be with You (Part 1)	*The Isley Brothers*
313	Ain't No Stoppin' Us Now	*McFadden & Whitehead*
314	We Are Family	*Sister Sledge*
315	Ring My Bell	*Anita Ward*
316	Bad Girls	*Donna Summer*
317	Good Times	*Chic*
318	Don't Stop 'Til You Get Enough	*Michael Jackson*
319	(not just) Knee Deep Part 1	*Funkadelic*
320	Ladies Night	*Kool & the Gang*
321	Still	*The Commodores*
322	I Wanna Be Your Lover	*Prince*
323	Do You Love What You Feel	*Rufus and Chaka*

1980

324	Rock with You	*Michael Jackson*
325	The Second Time Around	*Shalamar*
326	Special Lady	*Ray, Goodman & Brown*
327	And the Beat Goes On	*The Whispers*
328	Stomp!	*The Brothers Johnson*
329	Don't Say Goodnight (It's Time for Love) (Parts 1 & 2)	*The Isley Brothers*
330	Let's Get Serious	*Jermaine Jackson*
331	Take Your Time (Do It Right)	*The S.O.S. Band*
332	One in a Million You	*Larry Graham*
333	Upside Down	*Diana Ross*
334	Give Me the Night	*George Benson*
335	Funkin' for Jamaica (N.Y.)	*Tom Browne*
336	Master Blaster (Jammin')	*Stevie Wonder*
337	Celebration	*Kool & the Gang*

1981

338	Fantastic Voyage	*Lakeside*
339	Burn Rubber (Why You Wanna Hurt Me)	*The Gap Band*

340	Don't Stop the Music	*Yarbrough & Peoples*
341	Being with You	*Smokey Robinson*
342	Sukiyaki	*A Taste of Honey*
343	A Woman Needs Love (Just Like You Do)	*Ray Parker Jr. & Raydio*
344	What Cha' Gonna Do for Me	*Chaka Khan*
345	Give It to Me Baby	*Rick James*
346	Double Dutch Bus	*Frankie Smith*
347	I'm in Love	*Evelyn King*
348	Endless Love	*Diana Ross and Lionel Richie*
349	When She Was My Girl	*The Four Tops*
350	Never Too Much	*Luther Vandross*
351	I Heard It Through the Grapevine	*Roger*
352	Take My Heart (You Can Have It If You Want It)	*Kool & the Gang*
353	Let's Groove	*Earth, Wind & Fire*

1982

354	Turn Your Love Around	*George Benson*
355	I Can't Go for That (No Can Do)	*Daryl Hall and John Oates*
356	Call Me	*Skyy*
357	That Girl	*Stevie Wonder*
358	If It Ain't One Thing...It's Another	*Richard "Dimples" Fields*
359	It's Gonna Take a Miracle	*Deniece Williams*
360	Let It Whip	*The Dazz Band*
361	Early in The Morning	*The Gap Band*
362	And I'm Telling You I'm Not Going	*Jennifer Holliday*
363	Dance Floor	*Zapp*
364	Jump to It	*Aretha Franklin*
365	Love Come Down	*Evelyn King*
366	Sexual Healing	*Marvin Gaye*

1983

367	The Girl Is Mine	*Michael Jackson/Paul McCartney*
368	Outstanding	*The Gap Band*
369	Billie Jean	*Michael Jackson*
370	Atomic Dog	*George Clinton*
371	Candy Girl	*New Edition*
372	Beat It	*Michael Jackson*
373	Save the Overtime (For Me)	*Gladys Knight & the Pips*
374	Juicy Fruit	*Mtume*
375	She Works Hard for the Money	*Donna Summer*
376	Get it Right	*Aretha Franklin*
377	Cold Blooded	*Rick James*
378	Ain't Nobody	*Rufus and Chaka Khan*
379	All Night Long (All Night)	*Lionel Richie*
380	Time Will Reveal	*DeBarge*

1984

381	Joanna	*Kool & the Gang*
382	If Only You Knew	*Patti LaBelle*
383	Encore	*Cheryl Lynn*
384	Somebody's Watching Me	*Rockwell*
385	She's Strange	*Cameo*
386	Hello	*Lionel Richie*
387	Don't Waste Your Time	*Yarbrough & Peoples*
388	Let's Hear It for the Boy	*Deniece Williams*
389	Lovelite	*O'Bryan*
390	When Doves Cry	*Prince*
391	Ghostbusters	*Ray Parker Jr.*
392	Caribbean Queen (No More Love on the Run)	*Billy Ocean*
393	Let's Go Crazy	*Prince and the Revolution*
394	I Just Called to Say I Love You	*Stevie Wonder*
395	I Feel for You	*Chaka Khan*
396	Cool It Now	*New Edition*
397	Solid	*Ashford & Simpson*
398	Operator	*Midnight Star*

1985

399	Gotta Get You Home Tonight	*Eugene Wilde*
400	Mr. Telephone Man	*New Edition*
401	Missing You	*Diana Ross*
402	Nightshift	*The Commodores*
403	Back in Stride	*Maze featuring Frankie Beverly*
404	Rhythm of the Night	*DeBarge*
405	We Are the World	*USA for Africa*
406	Fresh	*Kool & the Gang*
407	You Give Good Love	*Whitney Houston*
408	Rock Me Tonight (For Old Times Sake)	*Freddie Jackson*
409	Hangin' on a String (Contemplating)	*Loose Ends*
410	Save Your Love (For #1)	*Rene & Angela*
411	Freeway of Love	*Aretha Franklin*
412	Saving All My Love for You	*Whitney Houston*
413	Cherish	*Kool & the Gang*
414	Oh Sheila	*Ready For The World*
415	You Are My Lady	*Freddie Jackson*
416	Part-Time Lover	*Stevie Wonder*
417	Caravan of Love	*Isley/Jasper/Isley*
418	Don't Say No Tonight	*Eugene Wilde*

1986

419	Say You, Say Me	*Lionel Richie*
420	That's What Friends Are For	*Dionne Warwick & Friends*
421	Do Me Baby	*Meli'sa Morgan*
422	How Will I Know	*Whitney Houston*

423	Your Smile	*Rene & Angela*
424	What Have You Done for Me Lately	*Janet Jackson*
425	Kiss	*Prince and the Revolution*
426	I Have Learned to Respect the Power of Love	*Stephanie Mills*
427	On My Own	*Patti LaBelle and Michael McDonald*
428	Nasty	*Janet Jackson*
429	There'll Be Sad Songs (To Make You Cry)	*Billy Ocean*
430	Who's Johnny	*El DeBarge*
431	Rumors	*Timex Social Club*
432	Closer than Close	*Jean Carne*
433	Do You Get Enough Love	*Shirley Jones*
434	Love Zone	*Billy Ocean*
435	Ain't Nothin' Goin' On but the Rent	*Gwen Guthrie*
436	(Pop, Pop, Pop, Pop) Goes My Mind	*Levert*
437	The Rain	*Oran "Juice" Jones*
438	Word Up	*Cameo*
439	Shake You Down	*Gregory Abbott*
440	A Little Bit More	*Melba Moore with Freddie Jackson*
441	Tasty Love	*Freddie Jackson*
442	Love You Down	*Ready For The World*
443	Girlfriend	*Bobby Brown*

1987

444	Control	*Janet Jackson*
445	Stop to Love	*Luther Vandross*
446	Candy	*Cameo*
447	Falling	*Melba Moore*
448	Have You Ever Loved Somebody	*Freddie Jackson*
449	Slow Down	*Loose Ends*
450	Let's Wait Awhile	*Janet Jackson*
451	Looking for a New Love	*Jody Watley*
452	Sign `O' the Times	*Prince*
453	Don't Disturb This Groove	*The System*
454	There's Nothing Better Than Love	*Luther Vandross with Gregory Hines*
455	Always	*Atlantic Starr*
456	Head to Toe	*Lisa Lisa and Cult Jam*
457	Rock Steady	*The Whispers*
458	Diamonds	*Herb Alpert*
459	I Feel Good All Over	*Stephanie Mills*
460	Fake	*Alexander O'Neal*
461	The Pleasure Principle	*Janet Jackson*
462	Jam Tonight	*Freddie Jackson*
463	Casanova	*Levert*
464	Love Is a House	*The Force M.D.'s*
465	I Just Can't Stop Loving You	*Michael Jackson with Siedah Garrett*
466	I Need Love	*L.L. Cool J*
467	Lost in Emotion	*Lisa Lisa and Cult Jam*
468	(You're Puttin') A Rush on Me	*Stephanie Mills*
469	Bad	*Michael Jackson*
470	Lovin' You	*The O'Jays*

471	Angel	*Angela Winbush*
472	Skeletons	*Stevie Wonder*
473	System of Survival	*Earth, Wind & Fire*
474	I Want to Be Your Man	*Roger*
475	The Way You Make Me Feel	*Michael Jackson*

1988

476	Love Overboard	*Gladys Knight & the Pips*
477	I Want Her	*Keith Sweat*
478	Girlfriend	*Pebbles*
479	You Will Know	*Stevie Wonder*
480	Fishnet	*Morris Day*
481	Man in the Mirror	*Michael Jackson*
482	Wishing Well	*Terence Trent D'Arby*
483	Ooo La La La	*Teena Marie*
484	Get Outta My Dreams, Get into My Car	*Billy Ocean*
485	Da'Butt	*E.U.*
486	Nite and Day	*Al B. Sure!*
487	Mercedes Boy	*Pebbles*
488	Just Got Paid	*Johnny Kemp*
489	Little Walter	*Tony! Toni! Toné!*
490	One More Try	*George Michael*
491	Joy	*Teddy Pendergrass*
492	Paradise	*Sade*
493	Roses Are Red	*The Mac Band featuring the McCampbell Brothers*
495	Off on Your Own (Girl)	*Al B. Sure!*
496	Loosey's Rap	*Rick James featuring Roxanne Shante*
497	Nice 'N' Slow	*Freddie Jackson*
498	Another Part of Me	*Michael Jackson*
499	She's on the Left	*Jeffrey Osborne*
500	Addicted to You	*Levert*
501	My Prerogative	*Bobby Brown*
502	The Way You Love Me	*Karyn White*
503	Any Love	*Luther Vandross*
504	Giving You the Best That I Got	*Anita Baker*
505	Thanks for My Child	*Cheryl Pepsii Riley*
506	Hey Lover	*Freddie Jackson*
507	Dial My Heart	*The Boys*
508	Everything I Miss at Home	*Cherrelle*
509	Tumblin' Down	*Ziggy Marley and the Melody Makers*

1989

510	Oasis	*Roberta Flack*
511	Superwoman	*Karyn White*
512	Can You Stand the Rain	*New Edition*
513	Dreamin'	*Vanessa Williams*
514	Just Because	*Anita Baker*
515	Just Coolin'	*Levert featuring Heavy D*
516	Closer than Friends	*Surface*

517 Lucky Charm — *The Boys*
518 Girl I Got My Eyes on You — *Today*
519 Every Little Step — *Bobby Brown*
520 Love Saw It — *Karyn White*
521 Real Love — *Jody Watley*
522 Start of a Romance — *Skyy*
523 My First Love — *Atlantic Starr*
524 Miss You Like Crazy — *Natalie Cole*
525 Me Myself and I — *De La Soul*
526 Have You Had Your Love Today — *The O'Jays*
527 Show and Tell — *Peabo Bryson*
528 Keep on Movin' — *Soul II Soul featuring Caron Wheeler*
529 Turned Away — *Chuckii Booker*
530 Shower Me with Your Love — *Surface*
531 On Our Own — *Bobby Brown*
532 Batdance — *Prince*
533 Something in the Way (You Make Me Feel) — *Stephanie Mills*
534 It's No Crime — *Babyface*
535 My Fantasy — *Teddy Riley featuring Guy*
536 Remember (The First Time) — *Eric Gable*
537 Can't Get Over You — *Maze featuring Frankie Beverly*
538 Back To Life (However Do You Want Me) — *Soul II Soul featuring Caron Wheeler*
539 Miss You Much — *Janet Jackson*
540 Baby Come to Me — *Regina Belle*
541 You Are My Everything — *Surface*
542 Don't Take It Personal — *Jermaine Jackson*
543 Home — *Stephanie Mills*
544 Here and Now — *Luther Vandross*
545 Ain't Nuthin' in the World — *Miki Howard*
546 All of My Love — *The Gap Band*

1990

547 Tender Lover — *Babyface*
548 Rhythm Nation — *Janet Jackson*
549 I'll Be Good to You — *Quincy Jones featuring Ray Charles and Chaka Khan*
550 Make It Like It Was — *Regina Belle*
551 Real Love — *Skyy*
552 It's Gonna Be Alright — *Ruby Turner*
553 Where Do We Go from Here — *Stacy Lattisaw with Johnny Gill*
554 Escapade — *Janet Jackson*
555 The Secret Garden (Sweet Seduction Suite) — *Quincy Jones featuring Barry White, Al B. Sure!, James Ingram, and El DeBarge*
556 All Around the World — *Lisa Stansfield*
557 Spread My Wings — *Troop*
558 Ready or Not — *After 7*
559 Poison — *Bell Biv DeVoe*
560 Rub You the Right Way — *Johnny Gill*
561 Hold On — *En Vogue*
562 The Blues — *Tony! Toni! Toné!*
563 Tomorrow (A Better You, A Better Me) — *Quincy Jones with Tevin Campbell*

INTRODUCTION

The awesome combustion of the Four Tops and the Motown house band in "I Can't Help Myself." The redemptive optimism of Chic's "Good Times." The unstoppable locomotion of Aretha Franklin and the Muscle Shoals magicians in "(Sweet Sweet Baby) Since You've Been Gone." The unimpeachable logic of "I'll Take You There" by the Staple Singers.

For reasons such as these, *The Billboard Book of Number One Rhythm & Blues Hits* was written. Not because it can capture or adequately reflect the power and passion of this magnificent music—a choice between listening to the records or reading about them is no contest—but because it can celebrate and respect the people who made it.

Here is a quarter-century of rhythm & blues, represented by every single that topped the *Billboard* R&B charts between 1965 and 1990. The book starts when it does for two reasons: The magazine didn't publish any rhythm & blues charts between the end of November 1963 and the beginning of January 1965, and those that it did publish in the early '60s were rather odd.

During the 1940s and '50s, the *Billboard* charts defined both the music and the era—although by the end of the '50s, there were such Number One anomalies as David Seville's "Witch Doctor." That trend continued into the new decade: R&B chart-toppers in '63, for instance, included Paul & Paula's "Hey Paula" and Jimmy Gilmer's "Sugar Shack." Among others on the R&B charts at that time: Ray Stevens, Jan & Dean, Lesley Gore.

Billboard returned to credible coverage in its issue dated January 30, 1965, with a top 40 R&B singles chart (ruled by the Temptations' "My Girl") and a top 10 album list (topped by the Supremes' *Where Did Our Love Go*). That week, and "My Girl," is the kick-off point for this book; the final week covered herein is December 22, 1990.

The magazine's chart format has stayed generally constant since 1965, aside from small changes in depth (expanding to 50 positions in 1966, and to 100 in 1973) and name (switching to "soul" in 1969, to "black" in 1982, and back to "R&B" in 1990). Meanwhile, the chart methodology—using retail store and radio airplay reports—has changed and improved over the years; today, it's more accurate than ever.

This book's format is similar to the one employed in previous volumes covering *Billboard*'s pop and country music charts, telling some of the stories behind each hit. In many cases, this has been done with fresh interviews, to affirm previously published history or to obtain new insights. An artist's career details may be downplayed (this isn't really intended as an encyclopedia) in favor of information about a specific Number One. And of course, every participant in each of these records has a different point of view. Each is valid. With luck, the ones included here approach the truth.

In particular, recognition for musicians and songwriters behind the hits is common to many of the anecdotes, even though these folks stand in the shadow of more celebrated names. But the music of Motown, for instance, couldn't have happened the way it did without James Jamerson, Benny Benjamin, and Earl Van Dyke.

Likewise, it's impossible to imagine how different many of Aretha's records would have been without Jimmy Johnson or Roger Hawkins, King Curtis or Spooner Oldham, or how James Brown could have worked his alchemy without Fred Wesley or Jabo Starks, Jimmy Nolen or Maceo Parker.

The only thing more impossible to imagine? How twentieth-century popular music would have sounded without the extraordinary contributions of rhythm & blues. About these 583 Number One examples of that art: read, listen, enjoy.

ACKNOWLEDGMENTS

To tell the stories of these songs and these recordings, we enlisted the help of hundreds of people. And so, firstly, thanks are due to all the singers, musicians, songwriters, arrangers, and producers who made themselves available to talk about their recent or distant past with patience, grace, humor, and attention to detail.

Many other people gave enthusiastic, dedicated support for which we're grateful. Harry Weinger unstintingly shared his insights and expertise about James Brown, ensuring the accuracy of these entries and, in many cases, lending a hand with the writing. He, in turn, had assistance from onetime Brown associate Alan Leeds and from many former JB musicians.

Harry's resources covered a number of other artists, including Kool & the Gang, but—just as importantly—his own passion for this music and its *true* history was inspirational. Likewise, the help of two vital figures in rhythm & blues, Al Bell and Curtis Mayfield, encouraged us to "keep the faith."

Yo! to Sean Ross, another R&B patriot. His perspective (and humor) influenced the book, as did his help in writing the entries about Al Green, Earth, Wind & Fire, Sister Sledge, L.T.D., Con Funk Shun, and the Parliafunkadelicament crew.

A formidable thank you to research assistant *extraordinaire* Brian Carroll. A former writer for Dick Clark and Casey Kasem, Brian conducted over 150 interviews with artists, songwriters, producers, and record label personnel. His insight into music and knowledge of artists and their repertoires added to the depth of information in these pages.

Grateful thanks to researchers Jim Richliano and Brett Atwood, who also conducted interviews used in these pages, and to Marcia Rovins for additional research. Brady L. Benton of Peer Music also gave many hours of his time to uncovering information that proved to be of much value.

This book's contents are a vivid testimony to the willingness of so many people to talk about three decades of Number One records. But some sources did more: opening their Rolodex files, suggesting leads, doing detective work on our behalf, sharing information and insights from diaries, collections, notes, and related memorabilia. They include Bob Fisher, Louis Iacueo, Chris Poole, John Thorogood, and Alan Warner.

A citation goes to Allan Slutsky (Dr. Licks), whose help was invaluable and whose biography of the late James Jamerson, *Standing in the Shadows of Motown*, stands as a fitting tribute to the bassist and his fellow Motown musicians. Special mention is also due to the late Jay Lasker, who was always generous with anecdotes and information about his remarkable past.

Many authors and journalists have written about rhythm & blues over the past 30 years, often profoundly. Without their pioneering efforts, this volume would have been much the poorer—if it would have existed at all. The most valuable of these sources are mostly identified within each of the book's individual entries. Among others were the essential Record Research chronicles of Joel Whitburn (especially *Top R&B Singles 1942–1988*), *Atlantic Records: A Discography* by Michel Ruppli, *Chicago Soul* by Robert Pruter, *The Sound of Philadelphia* by Tony Cummings, *The Guinness Book of Rock Stars* by Dafydd Rees and Luke Crampton, *Dreamgirl* by Mary Wilson, *The Encyclopedia of Pop, Rock and Soul* by Irwin Stambler, *The Penguin Encyclopedia of Popular Music*, edited by Donald Clarke, *The Faber Companion to 20th-Century Popular Music* by Phil Hardy and Dave Laing, and two by Sharon Davis, *I Heard It Through the Grapevine* and *Motown: The History*.

Britain's *Blues & Soul* and *Black Music* were the first to publish anything meaningful about many R&B artists and records. To these magazines and their contributors—including John Abbey, David Nathan, Clive Richardson, Cliff White, Tony Cummings, Sharon Davis, Geoff Brown—grateful thanks.

Still more who assisted: Marylou Badeaux, Malcolm and Poli Cecil, Cleveland Brown, Lisa Maldonado, Cary Mansfield, Bob Pruter, Todd Mayfield, Tom Noonan, Fred Goodman, Juggy Gayles, Leo Sacks, Louie Dorado, Larry Klein, Mark Young, Dennis Clark, Jim Zoller, Steve Nelson, Guy Aoki, Pam Miller-Algar, Rob Younes, Ted Cordes, Bill Derby, Susan Sackett, Dorothee Wilk, John Hendricks, Gloria Jones, Bob Killbourn, Jeff Tarry, Bill Holland, Ray Passman, Nancy Farbman, Jim Fishel, Fred Frank, Keith Harris, Wolfgang Spahr, Gordon Frewin, Adam Yeldham, Joe Tarsia, Paul Sexton, Walt Love, Charles Macmillan, Terry West, Logan Anderson, Aynne Price, William Bell, Gene Sculatti, David Knight, Eugene Record, Roger Armstrong, Irv Lichtman, John Pidgeon, Robin Gosden, Andy McKaie, Steve Hoffman, Jeremy Silver.

At BMI, thanks to Robbin Ahrold, Phil Graham, Pat Baird, Leslie Morgan, Stacy Nick, and Caroline Davis; at ASCAP, James Fisher, Paul Harrigan, and Michael Donovan; at MUSICbase, Dan Allen.

Thanks to Barry Despenza and Billy Davis, who helped chronicle Chicago's contributions to the music in this book, and to Stuart Grundy, for his insightful Norman Whitfield interview.

Before, during, and after the detective work and the writing, the burden fell on the people at Billboard Books. Paul Lukas was the most patient, cool-headed, and attentive editor any authors could have. Thanks, Paul. Additional appreciation is due to Tad Lathrop and Fred Weiler, for key contributions along the way. And of course the book wouldn't look as fine as it does if not for the superb book design and layout work of Bob Fillie.

Family support is always appreciated. Thanks to Anne White, Irving Bronson, and Bea Goldman for being constant sources of love and support.

Finally, thanks to journalists and editors—present and past—at *Billboard* magazine. Their reporting, dedication and insights over the years were implicitly and explicitly vital, helping and sustaining us. We hope they enjoy *The Billboard Book of Number One Rhythm & Blues Hits*.

ADAM WHITE AND FRED BRONSON
August 1993

THE Billboard BOOK OF

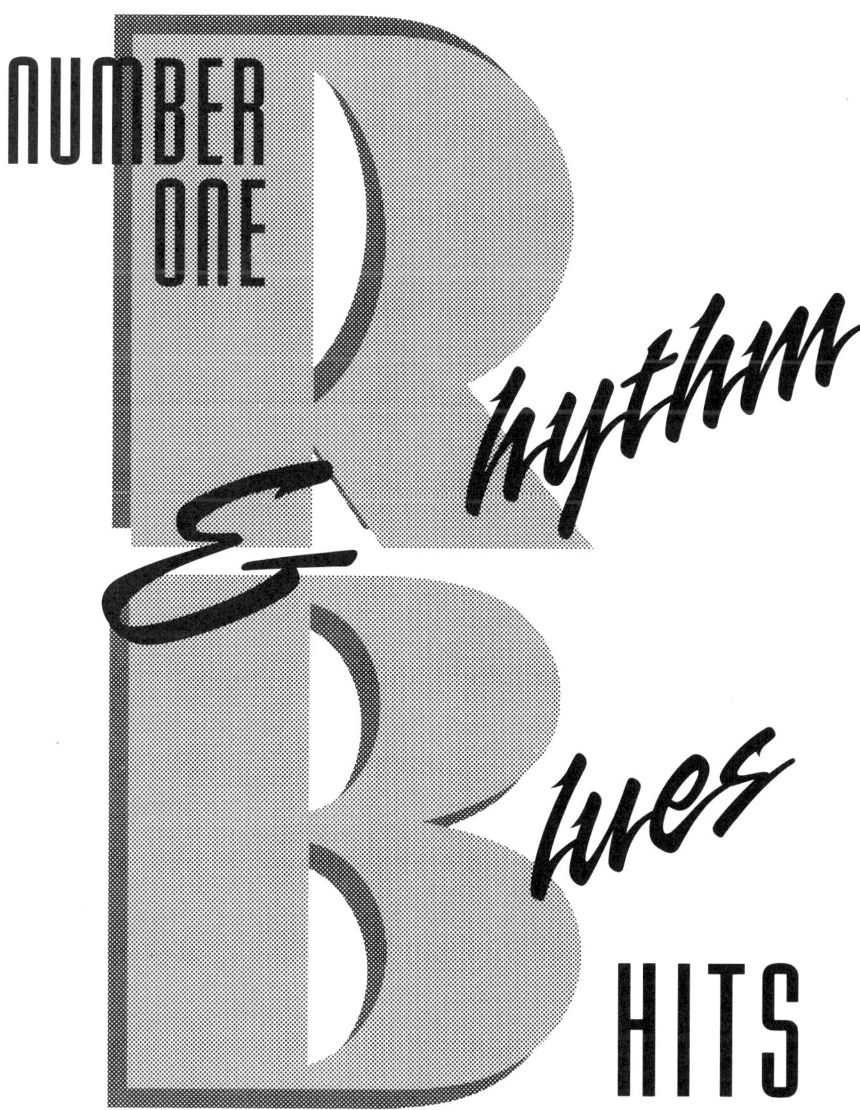

1

MY GIRL

The Temptations

GORDY 7038
WRITERS: WILLIAM "SMOKEY" ROBINSON, RONALD WHITE
PRODUCERS: WILLIAM "SMOKEY" ROBINSON, RONALD WHITE
January 30, 1965 (6 weeks)

More than a hit record, "My Girl" was a touchstone.

For William "Smokey" Robinson, it became a signature song, perfectly evoking his timeless lyrical and melodic touch. For the Temptations, it propelled them—for the first time—to the peak of the pop charts. For David Ruffin, it was his first lead on a Temptations single, affirming the Midas potential of the singer's sandpaper-and-honey style.

Robinson composed "My Girl" with Ron White, one of the Miracles, when the group was on the road in 1964. "We had the Temptations on a package tour with us," he told *Black Music* magazine. "We were doing quite a lot of dates and 'My Girl' was written in New York at the Apollo Theater. I was at the piano and Ronnie White came down...and we kind of worked out the words and everything.

"I was going in different directions with the Temptations at that time because Paul Williams and Eddie Kendricks had done all the lead vocalizing at that point, and I knew David was a dynamic singer. We wanted to try some songs with David [as] lead and 'My Girl' was the very first one."

In Detroit, Robinson cut the track with Motown's studio cadre, the Funk Brothers. James Jamerson gave "My Girl" its heartbeat bass, Robert White played the ascending guitar introduction, and Paul Riser wrote the charts. "All of Smokey's mechanics had to be right," Riser explains. "He would first of all sit at the piano and play his little songs as plain and clear as he could, and sing them as clear as he could. It would just be piano and voice that I would have to work from."

Riser's talent gave "My Girl" its texture, the strings of the Detroit Symphony Orchestra providing sweet counterpoint to David Ruffin's rough-hewn lead. Like so many at Motown, he worked instinctively, although he was a classically-trained musician. "It wasn't like I'd sit down and map it out, this note is perfect for this spot, this voicing is perfect for that spot. I would just do it," he says.

The Temptations—Ruffin, Williams, Kendricks, Melvin Franklin, and Otis Williams—added their vocal parts in the closing weeks of 1964. "Smokey is one of those people whose songs have a ring of truth to them," comments bass voice Franklin. "If you're singing that song—and you have the kind of voices like the Temptations—it's easy to believe it will make it."

At Motown, the Temptations had been striving since 1961 to make it. The company's A&R chief then, William (Mickey) Stevenson, says, "They were our demo cutters, our background singers. Whatever I wanted to do with a song or whenever I had an idea, I'd call the Temps. Every time they touched something, it would have color to it. They didn't care who the song was for. With that kind of spirit, they had to end up a winner."

SHOTGUN

Jr. Walker and the All Stars

SOUL 35008
WRITER: AUTRY DEWALT
PRODUCERS: BERRY GORDY JR., LAWRENCE HORN
March 13, 1965 (4 weeks)

General Motors never produced a vehicle as roadworthy as Jr. Walker and the All Stars—and Motown never produced a star as casual about making records as Jr. Walker.

"I guess he figured being in the studio was a gamble," says Lamont Dozier, who helped forge Walker's "(I'm A) Road Runner" smash in 1966, "and he needed to be out there on the road, picking up the money. That was a sure thing, right? He could see it in his hand, not like waiting six months for a royalty check."

Another Motown producer, Johnny Bristol, remembers that he used to have studio time booked, "and Junior would call me from Indiana and say, 'Look, this guy called me at the last minute and I have to go make this money. I'll be there tomorrow, can you set it up for tomorrow?' "

Walker obviously showed up for the late-'64 session that led to "Shotgun." It was the first popular evidence of his shrieking sax style, double-barreled vocals, and roadtested All Stars, featuring Willie Woods on guitar, Vic Thomas on organ, and James Graves on drums. Walker (née Autry DeWalt) has said he wrote the tune after "watching a couple of kids doing this different kind of dance in a club."

Berry Gordy Jr. caught an early version of "Shotgun," according to the late Earl Van Dyke, the keyboard player who directed Motown's session band. "Berry went ape," recalled Van Dyke. "He heard it, he *felt* it—but then he said, 'Well, it's got to be cleaned up,' because Junior had tried to cut it with his group.

The Temptations

Berry said, 'We can't put that out,' so he had to infiltrate staff musicians into Junior's band. That's Benny Benjamin on drums and James Jamerson on bass. Some things I had to go behind Vic Thomas and overdub. The guitars were Joe Messina and Eddie Willis."

Johnny Bristol affirms, "Junior's guys were basically a road band. I'm sure they could be recorded in the studio, but it was a lot more expedient and professional to use the guys at the company, Earl Van Dyke, James Jamerson, and so on." For "Shotgun," Motown engineer Lawrence Horn shared production credits with Berry Gordy.

In the early '60s, Bristol and partner Jackey Beavers performed at the same nightclub as Walker in Battle Creek, Michigan. "Jackey and I sang on weekends, and Junior's was the band," Bristol elaborates. "It was the El Grotto Bar, affectionately known as 'the Bloody Corner,' because someone got bloody every weekend, except us, thank God. The place was constantly packed. Junior could play blues, jazz, rock, and definitely soul."

3

GOT TO GET YOU OFF MY MIND

Solomon Burke

ATLANTIC 2276
WRITER: SOLOMON BURKE
PRODUCER: JERRY WEXLER
April 3, 1965 (3 weeks)

Billboard's own Paul Ackerman helped Solomon Burke make the connection that transformed him from a substandard balladeer in the '50s to the big-voiced soul shaker of the '60s.

Ackerman, music editor of the magazine for 30 years, was profoundly knowledgeable about American popular music, and passionate about country & western and the blues. When Jerry Wexler was a reporter at *Billboard* in 1948–1951, before he joined Atlantic Records, the two men were colleagues and close friends.

"Paul's the one who pulled my coat to Solomon Burke," recounts Wexler. "He kept saying, 'Man, if

Solomon ever gets loose, you've got to sign him.' I guess he knew Solomon from his records on Apollo. He also pulled my coat to the song that was Solomon's first hit, 'Just Out of Reach,' which was a country song on 4 Star Records."

Burke, a onetime boy preacher in his Philadelphia hometown, had been recording for Apollo, where owner Bess Berman viewed him as a potential Harry Belafonte. No dice; his fortunes changed only when he signed to Atlantic, in 1960.

Country by birth, "Just Out Of Reach" was pure soul when adopted by Burke. It became an R&B and pop chart success in 1961, first link in an Atlantic chain of hits that included "Cry to Me," "If You Need Me," and "You're Good for Me" over the next three years.

Most of these hits were produced by Wexler and Bert Berns, separately or together, but Berns eventually fell out with Burke. "And," says Wexler, "when it came to the session I had in mind to do with 'Tonight's the Night' and 'Got to Get You Off My Mind,' Bert said, 'I'm finished with this guy.' I mean, he walked out on me, so I said, 'That's fine, who cares?' And I did it myself."

The Berns/Burke breakup wasn't the singer's only fracture—he was getting divorced, and "Got to Get You Off My Mind" was telling some painful home truths. "I wrote it coming back on the train from Los Angeles," Burke told Dave (Daddy Cool) Booth in *Goldmine*. "Earlier that day, I'd sat in a meeting with Sam Cooke and his manager, and then learned that Sam had been killed. It was a double shot. I didn't take the plane because I needed time to think."

Cooke was slain on December 11, 1964. Six weeks later, Burke, Wexler, and arranger Gene Page were in New York cutting "Got to Get You Off My Mind," its warm vocals and rolling rhythm suffused with Cooke's spirit. Musicians on the date included Ernie Hayes (piano), Eric Gale, Bob Bushnell, and Bill Suyker (guitars), Panama Francis (drums), David Adams (bass), Sam "The Man" Taylor (tenor sax), and Seldon Powell (baritone sax). Dee Dee Warwick and Cissy Houston were among the backup singers.

"Eighty percent of the songs I recorded during the '60s were about me," Burke explained to Booth. "You could hear those records and know what was going on in my love life, my family life, and how long it took me to grow up."

The fruitless wedlock that inspired Burke to write "Got to Get You off My Mind" produced another hit, too. "My mother told me that the marriage was wrong," he recalled. "She said, 'I told you, fool, I told you.' I was standing onstage at the Apollo Theater and I had just been informed that my wife had just smashed all the windows in my limousine and shot up all the tires. I had to go on, and we made up 'The Price' right there on stage."

4

WE'RE GONNA MAKE IT

Little Milton

CHECKER 1105

WRITERS: BILLY DAVIS, CARL SMITH, RAYNARD MINER, GENE BARGE

PRODUCER: BILLY DAVIS

May 1, 1965 (3 weeks)

"When I first started working with Little Milton," declares Billy Davis, onetime A&R chief of Chess Records, "he was like the Midwest version of Bobby 'Blue' Bland." True enough. Bland's brash rhythm & bluesology influenced hundreds of '60s singers, just as Sam Cooke's smoother, gospel-rooted purity shaped the style of hundreds more.

Oliver Sain helped bring Milton Campbell Jr. to Chess in 1961. A Mississippi musician with connections to the likes of Howlin' Wolf and Sonny Boy Williamson, Sain served as Milton's bandleader around that time. When Billy Davis became involved, he sought to broaden the singer's audience. "I tried to put Milton in more of a pop-blues bag than the country-blues bag he had been in," he says.

Chess songwriters Raynard Miner and Carl Smith [see 11—"Rescue Me," 44—"Higher And Higher"] were enlisted. "When artists came up to Chicago to be recorded," states Davis, "I would put the writers to work, to try to come up with material. I gave them ideas, they would come back to me, and we'd work on songs until they were finished."

One such idea was "We're Gonna Make It," which Milton cut at the Chess studios on February 16, 1965. "I remember not knowing whether I liked it or not," Davis says, "but I came to the conclusion that, well, it was different. A little more poppy, maybe a step further than I wanted to go, but maybe not."

Company principal Leonard Chess evidently had some doubts, too. "Leonard looked at me," says Davis, "and sort of frowned, like 'What is this, what are you doing to my blues artist?' But the whole time I was there, he never second-guessed me too much—we had an uncanny relationship—and they went with it."

The session featured Milton on guitar as well as vocals, and the Chess house band, which included Leonard Caston (piano), Sonny Thompson (organ), Louis Satterfield (bass), Pete Cosey and Gerald Sims (guitars), Charles Stepney (vibes), and Maurice White (drums). Gene Barge played tenor sax and directed the horn section. The arranger was Phil Wright.

Everything was cut live. Says Davis: "Milton was kind of pleased with the session. He'd never been

Little Milton

surrounded with this type of big band. He knew what we were trying to do, and he was 100 percent on board."

Moreover, the song's lyrics were in tune with the times, offering a civil-rights metaphor echoing Curtis Mayfield's "Keep On Pushing" from the year before. "It was not intended as that," notes Davis, "although I was aware of the possibility. When you listen to the lyrics, you're back down to earth: 'Here we are, living in poverty, we've got each other and we're gonna make it.' "

5

I'LL BE DOGGONE

Marvin Gaye

TAMLA 54112
WRITERS: WILLIAM "SMOKEY" ROBINSON, PETE MOORE, MARV TARPLIN
PRODUCER: WILLIAM "SMOKEY" ROBINSON
May 22, 1965 (1 week)

Marvin Gaye co-wrote his first three hit records—"Stubborn Kind of Fellow," "Hitch Hike," and "Pride and Joy"—and was among the very few Motown artists to do so. Not even Stevie Wonder could match that achievement.

Yet at the time, Gaye made light of his composing skills. Discussing "Hitch Hike," for example, during a '60s interview, he said, "My sister was doing the dance, going back and forth, like someone on an expressway or something, making the gyrations with her hands—only her hands. So I sort of made a song out of it...It wasn't really difficult, I think anybody could do it."

Whether or not the singer took writing seriously, Motown called the commercial shots after "Pride and Joy." Every Gaye single bar one featured other people's material, and that state of affairs didn't change until 1971.

But Gaye *was* the perfect interpreter. Nick Ashford, who co-authored Gaye's chart-topping duets with Tammi Terrell, says, "Marvin could take what you thought was a so-so lyric and after he did it, you'd ask, 'Oh, did I write that?' He had that about him." Smokey Robinson felt the same way, judging by comments in his autobiography: "He'd interpret my material like he'd written it himself, improvising and improving the original concept."

Robinson, of course, helped create some of Gaye's most compelling hits—"I'll Be Doggone" was the first—with guitarist Marv Tarplin and members of the Miracles, including Warren (Pete) Moore. "Smokey and I would primarily do the lyrics, and Marv was the musical part," explains Moore. "Marv

Marvin Gaye

used to come up with a lot of licks and melodies, and when Smokey and I heard one we liked, we would follow up and write a song to it."

"I'll Be Doggone" was one such inspiration. "Back in those days, we had 24-hour access to the Motown studio," says Moore, "so we went in as soon as we possibly could after writing. We liked the ideas to stay fresh in our mind and keep the momentum going."

Motown's studio core—leader Earl Van Dyke on keyboards, Benny Benjamin on drums, James Jamerson on bass, and Robert White, Joe Messina, and Eddie Willis on guitars—added their own momentum, and respected Gaye to boot. The late Van Dyke explained, "Marvin had put out an album, *When I'm Alone I Cry,* which was the kind of thing he liked to do. He loved jazz, he was a good jazz drummer. And basically, all the staff musicians at Motown were jazz musicians."

In fact, Gaye's first labors for Motown were behind the scenes, playing drums—on tour and on record—for the Miracles, the Marvelettes and others. He joined the company through Harvey Fuqua, the onetime member of the Moonglows who had recruited Gaye to a late edition of that group. When Fuqua and partner Gwen Gordy sold their Tri-Phi label to Gwen's brother, Berry Gordy, in 1963, Marvin came with the package.

6

BACK IN MY ARMS AGAIN

The Supremes

MOTOWN 1075
WRITERS: BRIAN HOLLAND, LAMONT DOZIER, EDDIE HOLLAND
PRODUCERS: BRIAN HOLLAND, LAMONT DOZIER
May 29, 1965 (1 week)

Just five records transformed Motown between August 1964 and June 1965. Each one—"Where Did Our Love Go," "Baby Love," "Come See About Me," "Stop! In the Name of Love," and "Back in My Arms Again"—bore the same machine-stamped name from the Motor City: the Supremes.

Five consecutive Number One hits. The music industry knew that Berry Gordy's company already had some pop chart credentials. It recognized that the Supremes' records were an innovative, intoxicating blend of rhythm & blues and pop. And it realized that the group's sound—and look—represented a strikingly new level of sophistication for black female singers.

But what really blew the industry off its feet, and what really sprinkled the magic dust over Gordy's two-story bungalow at 2648 West Grand Boulevard, was the sheer audacity of that achievement: *five consecutive Number One hits.*

"You have to remember that we did not know what we were doing," declares Lamont Dozier, one of the alchemists responsible for Motown's explosive development. "We were just going on pure instinct and feeling. There were really no rule books."

"Back in My Arms Again" was the fifth spell cast by Dozier and the Holland brothers, Eddie and Brian, for the Supremes. Eddie wrote the song's central theme of romance repossessed, but Dozier claims credit for the girl-talk touch where lead vocalist Diana Ross discusses the advice dispensed by Mary Wilson and Florence Ballard. "That was my line," he says, "and Eddie surrounded the rest of the story with his lyrics."

The Supremes laid down their vocals in Detroit on the first day of December 1964. The instrumental track was propelled by James Jamerson's thunderous bass, Mike Terry's guttural saxophone, and James Gittens's ringing vibes. The studio was disarmingly small. "We did a lot of tracking, mainly because there wasn't enough space," said Earl Van Dyke, the late Motown bandleader. For one Holland/Dozier/Holland session, the room was jammed with musicians. "They had to put the strings on a platform, up against the wall. That day, Berry father's told him he needed a larger studio."

The Supremes

Holland/Dozier/Holland's creative authority with the Supremes was in sharp contrast to the group's early, hitless years. Back in those days, the recording process brought the assorted singers and musicians together in the Motown studio. "By '63 and early '64, we were pretty much doing it to tracks," says Mary Wilson. "Sometimes it would be just a piano, it wouldn't be a full track. They had just started over-dubbing at that time, just come out of recording with the full band."

That was a significant change, which vested more power with the producers—especially Holland/Dozier/Holland—and helped advance Motown towards the big breakthrough. In 1964 and '65, however, Berry Gordy's original family spirit still shone through.

"It was such a small community," explains Wilson, "that when a song was finished and the producers felt really great about it, they'd run around and call everybody in the studio. You'd have the Temps and Marvin Gaye and the Supremes and the Marvelettes all in the studio listening to it, and we'd take the records home and pass them out around the projects."

7

I CAN'T HELP MYSELF

The Four Tops

MOTOWN 1076
WRITERS: BRIAN HOLLAND, LAMONT DOZIER, EDDIE HOLLAND
PRODUCERS: BRIAN HOLLAND, LAMONT DOZIER
June 5, 1965 (9 weeks)

For Motown, "I Can't Help Myself" was the drive-away smash of 1965. Shipped from the Detroit assembly line on April 23, it accelerated onto the floor of *Billboard*'s R&B showrooms during the second week of May. By the beginning of June, it was the top-selling model.

Admittedly, the design wasn't entirely new. Just as Steve Cropper had reshaped "In the Midnight Hour" into another vehicle [see 30—"Knock on Wood"], the Motown team behind "I Can't Help Myself" borrowed from one of their earlier productions for the Supremes: "Where Did Our Love Go." Lamont Dozier is quick to point out that the two songs use the same chords. He remembers starting to create "I Can't Help Myself" at the piano one day while fooling around—after a couple of drinks—with the melody of the earlier tune. The similarity wasn't intentional. "It just happened that way," he says. Hence, the title.

Dozier and the Holland brothers were superior craftsmen, and often improvisational. "Most of the time we cut the tracks first, because we didn't have the lyrics finished," he explains. "I would collaborate with Edward on the lyric, he'd had something to start from, and Brian would give him melodies for the entire song."

Each member of the trio brought different strengths to the creative process, and it was all by instinct, not training. "It's by the grace of God that those things sold, because we were really guessing," says Dozier. That included final mixing of the records, although Berry Gordy was influential in that process.

Instinct also fueled Motown's session band, dubbed the Funk Brothers. "It was like having your own rhythm section," describes Dozier. "We'd go in with the guys, and Brian or I would be on the piano to get the basic feeling across, and they would follow. It didn't take us a long time to communicate, so we were able to get a lot of songs like that done."

When signed to Motown in 1963, the Four Tops—Levi Stubbs, Abdul "Duke" Fakir, Renaldo Benson, and Lawrence Payton—were the most professional singers on the young company's books. Theirs was a slick cabaret act, polished during the '50s by opening for Della Reese, Count Basie, Brook Benton, and, especially, Billy Eckstine.

The quartet had a prior link with Berry Gordy. When first formed in Detroit, the group included Roquel (Billy) Davis; after they signed to Chess Records, he opted for a songwriting career. Just a few years later, Davis became Gordy's partner in composing Jackie Wilson's breakthrough hits.

8

IN THE MIDNIGHT HOUR

Wilson Pickett

ATLANTIC 2289
WRITERS: WILSON PICKETT, STEVE CROPPER
PRODUCERS: JIM STEWART, JERRY WEXLER
August 7, 1965 (1 week)

Time was running out for Wilson Pickett at Atlantic Records in the spring of 1965. He had been signed to the label for about a year, and the temperature was frigid: His first single had reached number 124 on the Billboard charts, colder than his previous releases on the diminutive Double L label.

A second single had turned to ice on contact with the market, despite the credentials of writers Barry Mann and Cynthia Weil and producer Bert Berns. "I couldn't find anybody after Bert for Wilson," explains Jerry Wexler, who was Atlantic's A&R sorcerer in those years. "So he and I would get together. And it would never be right. He didn't like the songs I had, you know, procured, and I didn't like the songs he was suggesting.

"So his manager—a tough little Italian guy—called me one day. He said, 'Hey, you-know-what or get off the pot.' So I said, 'You're right, we've been dicking around for a year now, and he deserves something.' Then I got the brainstorm to take him to Stax."

Stax meant Memphis, where Jim Stewart's close-knit crew had just been impressing the hell out of Atlantic with the breakthrough sessions on Otis Redding. Wexler and Pickett jetted there on May 11, 1965. "Jim picked Jerry and Wilson up at the airport," recalls Steve Cropper, the Stax house band's linchpin guitarist at the time, who doubled as a member of Booker T. and the MGs.

"We all met at the hotel, and Jim and Jerry went off to have a meeting or get something to eat or whatever. When they came back, we played them 'In The Midnight Hour' and 'Don't Fight It.' They couldn't believe in a couple of hours we had written two songs. We cut the next day and they were gone, that was it."

The historic date was Memphis magic stirred by Wexler's alchemy. The musicians on hand were Cropper on guitar, Donald "Duck" Dunn on electric bass,

Al Jackson Jr. on drums, and Joe Hall on piano; the horn section comprised Wayne Jackson (trumpet), Floyd Newman (baritone saxophone), Andrew Love, and Charles "Packy" Axton (both tenor sax).

"Wexler got the best out of the session," affirms Cropper. "For 'Midnight Hour,' I had written another, slightly different guitar part. Jerry was really wanting to emphasize this new jerk beat, the dance, and that's why I started playing the 2/4 thing, and Al and I started laying that back, you know."

The Atlantic executive had his eye on the target, by Cropper's account: "He said, 'Take out all the fancy licks and embellishments, so we can get into that dance thing.' It was real funny watching him, this New York Jewish fellow dancing around the room. It was kind of comical, but it pulled the groove out of us. And, of course, Pickett, his performance goes without saying."

The two-and-a-half blowtorching minutes of "In the Midnight Hour" changed Pickett's life—and that of Stax, too. "It really did open us up to a different way of thinking," Cropper states, "and we used that delayed backbeat thing—where one is on, and two and four is a little behind—we used that on a lot of records."

9

PAPA'S GOT A BRAND NEW BAG (PART 1)

James Brown

KING 5999
WRITER: JAMES BROWN
PRODUCER: JAMES BROWN
August 14, 1965 (8 weeks)

A new bag, a new horizon, stretching farther than the eye could see in February 1965, when James Brown recorded "Papa's Got a Brand New Bag." Beyond the skyline, out of sight, was his unimaginable influence on music, an unexpected stature in politics, an unassailable ministry in black American culture, and an unforgiving judiciary.

It was the singer's first new side for King Records in more than a year. He had been with the label since 1956's seismic "Please Please Please," but fell out with monarch Syd Nathan over material made in '64 for Smash Records, a Mercury subsidiary.

With King and Mercury at a legal standoff, Brown may have begun to sympathize with underdog Nathan. In February 1965, he and his band went into Arthur Smith's studio in Charlotte, North Carolina. "I think we had been playing in Greensboro," says drummer Melvin Parker. "We didn't stay overnight anywhere after playing the tune, we just did it and kept on going."

James Brown

Brown himself told Harry Weinger, "Now, I come up with a slang, 'Papa's Got a Brand New Bag.' Music is written on two-and-fo'. On the upbeat. But you see, when you think of something, you pat your foot. That's on the downbeat. And you pat your hand in church, that's on the downbeat. See? So I put the music on the downbeat. And then it's on one-and-three, not two-and-fo', in anticipation." He adds, "That's what everybody felt. Now, right away, I got a new bag going."

Playing with Brown at the record's epicenter were Parker on drums; his younger brother, Maceo, on baritone sax; Nat Jones on organ and doubling on alto sax; and Sam Thomas or Bernard Odum on bass. A signature role also belonged to guitarist Jimmy Nolen, a blues player who had previously cut solo material for Federal and Specialty, among others. He had just joined Brown's band in 1965, but was to make an eternal mark with his arresting, jingling guitar scratch on "Papa's Got a Brand New Bag."

The horn section included tenor men St. Clair Pinckney, Eldee Williams, and Al Clark, trumpeters Joe Dupars, Ron Tooley, and Levi Rasbury, and Wilmer Milton on trombone.

Nevertheless, this revolution in sound didn't thrill King Records at first. The label received the seven-minute take—with *two* Maceo Parker sax solos—and brought it down to a tight two minutes for the single's topside. It also speeded up the track, adding echo and reverb.

Ron Lenhoff, whose work became a key part of the James Brown sound, was a King engineer when "Papa" was delivered. He remembers, "The original tape was so bad—muffled—that when Syd Nathan heard it, he exclaimed, 'My God, I can't put that out!' I had to edit it, and EQ it section by section. It took two days."

10

I WANT TO (DO EVERYTHING FOR YOU)

Joe Tex

DIAL 4016
WRITER: JOE TEX
PRODUCER: BUDDY KILLEN
October 9, 1965 (3 weeks)

His producer was a country music publisher. He made many of his hits in Nashville. And Roger Miller's gutstring guitar was used at the session that produced his first major chart success. "He wanted to be a country singer," says Buddy Killen, the producer who was that music publisher. "That's why he called himself Joe Tex."

Killen first heard about Joseph Arrington Jr. (as Tex was born) while he was on his honeymoon. "I was down in Daytona Beach," he explains, when his assistant at Tree Music, Jerry Crutchfield, called. "Jerry said, 'Buddy, you've got to get back up here. There's a guy here, I don't know, but there's something awfully special about him. And he's black.' "

When Killen got back to Nashville, he saw for himself what Crutchfield meant. "Joe came in and sat down at the piano—he could just play with two fingers—and started singing 'With the Devil on My Shoulder,' or whatever it was. He just knocked me out."

Yet Killen couldn't excite record companies about Tex. "Nobody in Nashville understood that kind of thing, so I started my own label, Dial Records." Even then, Tex didn't happen, and in 1964 he wanted out.

Killen agreed, but only if one last session couldn't produce a hit. He booked time at the Fame studios in Muscle Shoals on November 6, 1964. "Joe brought his bass player and, I believe, even his drummer. I took some of the musicians from Nashville, as well as Roger Miller's gutstring guitar. We worked about seven hours on a song called 'Fresh Out of Tears.'

"We just wore everyone out," Killen remembers. Nobody had high hopes for another song cut that night, "Hold What You've Got," either. Yet once he was back in Nashville, Killen struck lucky. "I started editing 'Hold What You've Got,' cutting a piece here and a piece there. I found one chorus that held together all the way, and every time it came to the chorus, we used that same piece throughout the whole song."

Killen had spliced his way to a hit, aided by a Dial distribution deal with Atlantic. Tex followed up with a further six top 20 R&B hits before '65 turned to '66. Among them was "I Want To (Do Everything for You)," made in Nashville with Buddy Killen's discreet, two-step production process. "Through the years, Joe would come in and bring his [road] band, and I'd have to use them sometimes. It was just amazing how bad they were.

"So when he left, I'd have my own group standing by. The only thing I'd use on the tape would be his performance. I just replaced all the music that we put on there. And then he'd tell me, 'Man, what did you do? When I left there, it was awful. It didn't sound like that.' "

11

RESCUE ME

Fontella Bass

CHECKER 1120
WRITERS: CARL SMITH, RAYNARD MINER
PRODUCERS: BILLY DAVIS, CARL SMITH, RAYNARD MINER
October 30, 1965 (4 weeks)

With or without Fontella Bass, "Rescue Me" boasted the hottest bass line to blow out of Chicago in all of 1965. The drummer on the date, Maurice White, endorses that view. "The track was a smash by itself," he says.

White played on "Rescue Me" and scores of other Windy City recordings at that time, 10 years before he directed Earth Wind & Fire to the summit. His fellow Chess musicians included Louis Satterfield (bass), Leonard Caston (piano), Sonny Thompson (organ), Charles Stepney (vibes), and Gerald Sims and Pete Cosey (guitars). They were the heartbeat of Chess as the label was cresting the new wave of '60s rhythm & blues.

"Our competition was really Motown," says White. "We were out of Chicago, so we were very competitive. We created this sound in the studio. We would just work things out, rhythm-wise, until we got it together; then we'd record. A lot of times, we wouldn't do but a few takes."

"Rescue Me" typified the new Chess: built on a bedrock of Satterfield's bass and White's drums, powered by Gene Barge's horn section, and propelled by the call-and-response of singer and background vocalists. Producer Billy Davis gives arranger Phil Wright a lot of credit for the sound. "He learned how to respect a rhythm section, and recognized when to let it happen."

Fontella, daughter of gospel star Martha Bass, made her move to Chess in 1964 after several years performing with bluesman Little Milton [see 4—"We're Gonna Make It"] and bandleader Oliver Sain. Davis remembers Sain bringing Bass by car from St. Louis, her hometown. "She sang live for me in the studio. She had lungs, a wonderful sound, although she also had a tendency to do everything that way—powerful, stretch straight out and knock 'em dead. No finesse, forget about phrasing and all those other things like dynamics. If dynamics weren't in the melody, forget it."

"Rescue Me" was created over an August 1965 weekend by Chess staff writers Carl Smith and Raynard Miner, working in the studio with Wright and Bass. "It wasn't that I thought it was a great song, but it had those elements that I thought were great," recalls Davis. "It hit a groove and stayed there." As the track was being cut, he was out among the musicians, rather than in the control room. "I would usually tell the engineer when to fade the song, but on this particular take, an idea came to me: not to fade it right away, but to milk the groove even longer.

"So I went around the studio and tapped each musician on the shoulder to make him stop. At first they thought 'What the hell's he doing?' I almost had to go after Leonard Caston's hands! But when we played that back, everyone said, 'That's it.' We did another couple of takes, but that *was* it."

12

AIN'T THAT PECULIAR

Marvin Gaye

TAMLA 54122
WRITERS: WARREN MOORE, WILLIAM "SMOKEY" ROBINSON, BOBBY ROGERS, MARV TARPLIN
PRODUCER: WILLIAM "SMOKEY" ROBINSON
November 27, 1965 (1 week)

Berry Gordy shipped his most popular artists to Britain and France in the spring of 1965, to coincide with the launch of the Tamla-Motown label through the company's European licensee, EMI Records.

This particular Motortown Revue featured Martha and the Vandellas, Stevie Wonder, the Supremes, and the bill-topping Miracles, all backed by Earl Van Dyke and the Soul Brothers. An incandescent caravan, it visited a dozen cities during March and April, generating critical kudos but light crowds.

The tour was also the backdrop for at least one hit record. The Miracles' longtime guitarist, Marv Tarplin, came up with the melody for "Ain't That Peculiar" while on the road in England. Smokey Robinson, together with fellow Miracles Warren (Pete) Moore and Bobby Rogers, capitalized on Tarplin's riff—which was itself influenced, he said, by Bill Doggett's 1956 instrumental, "Honky Tonk"—to create one of Marvin Gaye's most hyperkinetic singles.

"Willie Shorter was doing all our rhythm charts in those days," explains Moore, "so Smokey and I got together with William and played the basic melody for him. He came up with the rhythm arrangements and the lead sheets. We'd cut the rhythms and voices a couple of days later, then bring in Paul Riser to do the string arrangements."

The late Earl Van Dyke, leader of Motown's incomparable studio band, added, "Willie was a good piano player and an exceptional arranger, and he could copy anything. By Smokey playing a little piano, and Marv Tarplin with him, that helped quite a bit. Marv would put it on tape, and Willie would take it from there. Smokey knew when he came in what he was looking for."

Tarplin had worked for the Miracles since late 1958, touring and recording with the group. His skills as a guitarist ranged from the ebullient ("I'll Be Doggone") to the exquisite ("The Tracks Of My Tears").

For his part, Marvin Gaye would lay down vocals tracks with flair and imagination. "That's what was so great about working with Marvin," Robinson said subsequently. "I'd show him a song one time and I knew he would sing it even better than the way I envisaged it.

"I think you should explain the basics, the melody and the lyrics, but other than that, lay down no restrictions. He'd always do something unexpected and wonderful. He sounded like he knew it before I even showed it to him."

Even while interpreting other people's material, Gaye worked on his own enigmatic agenda. "He would always get on the piano first, while the engineers were setting the mikes up," recalls Sylvia Moy, who co-wrote "It Takes Two," Gaye's successful union with Kim Weston. "He had this piece that he was working on. He called it his concerto, and I often wonder where it is now and whether it will surface at some time or other. It was a real masterpiece."

13

I GOT YOU (I FEEL GOOD)

James Brown

KING 6015
WRITER: JAMES BROWN
PRODUCER: JAMES BROWN
December 4, 1965 (6 weeks)

New York, Hollywood, Miami. The song that stands as the Godfather of Soul's universal signature ("Mr. Brown, how do you feel...?") traveled through a few capitals before attaining its lofty status. He recorded "I Got You" at Manhattan's Bell Sound in September 1964 for his Fair Deal production company, leasing the tune to Smash Records as part of his "Out of Sight" album.

Accompanying him at the session were Brown bandmembers Bobby Byrd (organ), Bernard Odum (bass), and Nat Jones (alto sax), together with the Parker brothers, Melvin (drums) and Maceo (tenor and baritone sax).

It was a crisp, jazz-flecked treatment—with no guitars—of a song born more than two years earlier. On that occasion, it was called "I Found You," energized by a singer in Brown's live revue, Yvonne Fair. "When I cut it myself, I just changed the lyric slightly," he wrote in his autobiography, *The Godfather Of Soul* (Macmillan, 1986). "She did a good job on the song, right down to the holler."

Brown's '64 model of "I Got You" fell victim to the legal dispute between Smash and King Records, his primary label [see 9—"Papa's Got a Brand New Bag"]. It was to have been a single release that fall, but King went to court to block release of all the Smash material.

Ironically, Brown and his manager, Ben Bart of Universal Attractions, had planned a multimedia campaign for "I Got You." The singer taped a cameo appearance in *Ski Party*, a Hollywood beach-party flick featuring Frankie Avalon, and did a couple of lip-sync performances on television's *Where the Action Is.*

When the Smash 45 was canceled, the momentum had already begun. Onetime disc jockey Alan Leeds, who was later employed by Brown, remembers dubbing "I Got You" off the TV and getting it aired on WANT-AM in Richmond, Virginia. He recalls: "*Boom!* The request lines lit up, stores wanted to order it—and Ben Bart called to say, 'Keep playing it, it'll help ticket sales.' "

The snafu didn't deter Brown, who took the opportunity to make the song over, emphasizing the screams on the downbeat. The first version had been "too sharp," he told Bruce Pilato, a Gannett wire service reporter. Brown continued, "I was sleeping one night in Jacksonville, Florida, and I called my band director, Nat Jones. I said, 'Nat, this song is too hip.'

"And he said, 'What do you mean?' And I said, 'It's too sharp. We're taking some of the funk out of it and making it too jazz. And the groove is really laid-back funk.' So I went into Criteria Studio in Miami, and a good friend of mine, Henry Stone, got my time for me."

The time was in studio B, the date was May 6, 1965, and "I Got You (I Feel Good)" turned out to be the first gold disc cut at Mack Emerman's Criteria. Packing the room for the regrooved tune were some players from the earlier take—the Parkers on drums and tenor sax, Jones on organ and alto sax, and Odum on bass—plus guitarists Alphonso "Country" Kellum and Jimmy Nolen and tenor saxmen Al Clark, Eldee Williams, and St. Clair Pinckney.

"Mr. Brown, how do you feel...?"

14

A SWEET WOMAN LIKE YOU

Joe Tex

DIAL 4022
WRITER: JOE TEX
PRODUCER: BUDDY KILLEN
January 8, 1966 (1 week)

Joe Tex cut "A Sweet Woman Like You" in Memphis in late October 1965. The single—exemplary Southern soul, with its rough-hewn rhythm track and imploring horns—became his seventh release to reach Billboard's R&B top 20, and his second Number One.

Whether recording in Memphis, New York, or Nashville, Tex usually took members of his own band into the studio. The nucleus included Leroy Hadley on guitar, Clyde Williams on drums, and J. Alfred Cook on bass. But producer Buddy Killen says he often overdubbed parts cut later with other musicians, because Tex's players were suited for the road, not the recording studio [see 10—"I Want To (Do Everything for You)"].

"In the early days, some of the people were musicians I had right here at Tree," Killen elaborates. "People like Kelso Herston or Ronnie Wilkins, who were close friends and good musicians. We'd just go in and replace those tracks with them, rather than take them into the studio at the time we were recording. But there were all kinds of different ways. Nothing was always the same—we used every trick in the world to cut a hit."

Tex was prepared for the recording process, according to Killen. "He would write the songs, and we would go over them, set the sessions, and go into

Joe Tex

the studio. Joe was so clever, he heard arrangements in his head." He also had what Killen calls "an innate sense" of songwriting. "If he'd get a little bit dry of ideas, Joe would go to the bus station, get a newspaper, and sit there, listening to what people were saying. He'd go to the barber's shop, get his hair cut, or just sit there and read newspapers and talk to people. He'd get ideas right off the street, then go home and write them."

Jerry Wexler of Atlantic Records, which marketed and distributed Killen's Dial label, played a vital role, too. "I'd cut a record and send it to him, or call on the phone and play it it for him. He'd say, 'Buddy, I think so-and-so.' Jerry was a great guide—when he would approve it, I knew it was in the groove.

"The funny thing was, the more R&B a record was, the more records it sold. If I'd try one of those slick kind of things with Joe, we'd just lose sales. For example, 'Show Me,' wasn't that big a seller, probably 300,000 or 400,000 records. But 'I Gotcha' sold over three million. So the slicker it got, the less records it sold."

Tex himself said he preferred downtempo material. "Through to 'Skinny Legs' in '68, I had always stayed with those slow ballads," he told *Blues & Soul* in 1977. "I feel more comfortable when I'm talking a little, singing a little, and doing my little bit of rap. You see, I don't sing well and I know it. By rapping, I have a different way of getting over to my people."

15

UPTIGHT (EVERYTHING'S ALRIGHT)

Stevie Wonder

TAMLA 54124
WRITERS: HENRY COSBY, SYLVIA MOY, STEVIE WONDER
PRODUCERS: HENRY COSBY, WILLIAM STEVENSON
January 22, 1966 (5 weeks)

Did Motown Records come close to dropping Stevie Wonder for a few awkward moments in 1965? His record sales were declining, his voice was changing, and at the time, none of the record company's producers appeared to know what to do with him.

Songwriter Sylvia Moy remembers a meeting that year where A&R chief William (Mickey) Stevenson was reviewing the Motown roster. "They would go through the list of artists, and give assignments to the various producers," she says. When they reached Wonder's name, volunteers were sought. None came forward.

Just two years earlier, Little Stevie Wonder had been an industry phenomenon: the first artist to reach Number One on three *Billboard* charts simultaneously. In August 1963, his helium-pumped single of "Fingertips Part 2" had topped the R&B and pop rankings, while *The 12 Year Old Genius Recorded Live* was the nation's top album.

Steveland Morris certainly had extraordinary gifts. The "little nappy-headed boy," as he would later refer to himself, sang and played drums, bongos, piano, organ, and harmonica. Ron White, a member of the Miracles, helped bring the youngster to Berry Gordy's attention around 1960, and the Motown president helped shape his image as Little Stevie Wonder.

Yet after "Fingertips," marketing the teenager's talents was tough. His album sales slumped, his singles slipped. Clarence Paul, who had been guiding Wonder up to that point, confirms the dire straits described by Sylvia Moy. "I had exclusive production on Stevie, but we were cold. I didn't have no hits, I couldn't think of nothing, and he couldn't think of nothing."

Then "Uptight (Everything's Alright)" put Wonder's career back on track. Moy says she had sought to work with him after that A&R meeting. "I had a bag of songs at the time, but I told Stevie, 'I want you to play everything, all of the little ditties you have, play them for me.' He went through everything. He said, 'That's all I have,' and I thought I was going to have start working from my bag.

"I asked him, 'Are you sure you don't have anything else?' He said, 'No, not really, although I have got this one thing.' He started singing and playing, 'Everything is alright, uptight,' and that was as much as he had. I said, 'That's it, let's work with that.' "

By Moy's account, Wonder laid down the song's chords, she worked with the vocal melody and the lyrics, and Hank Cosby created the arrangement. "I would stand in the control room," she says, "Stevie would be at the mike in the studio, and I would sing the song to him with the lyric. He would be listening on his headset to one line ahead, and singing the previous line, without missing a beat or a note."

And maybe the prospect of dropping Wonder had been a mirage after all. "Sylvia may have gotten that feeling," recalls Mickey Stevenson. "We would slow down on certain artists, only because we weren't sure of what direction to go—but would never release the artist. That's out."

16

BABY SCRATCH MY BACK

Slim Harpo

EXCELLO 2273
WRITER: JAMES ISAAC MOORE
PRODUCER: J. D. MILLER
February 26, 1966 (2 weeks)

Motown and Atlantic were the R&B chart goliaths of 1966, occupying the high ground for more than nine months that year. But Ernie Young's diminutive Excello Records felled the giants for a couple of weeks, thanks to the 50,000 watts of Nashville powerhouse WLAC.

Young used the station nightly to advertise his label's releases and his mail-order business, Ernie's Record Mart. The clear-channel station was heard in 38 states, and 98% of Young's sales were by mail. "The only thing we had was WLAC," declares J. D. (Jay) Miller, who recorded Slim Harpo and leased the results to Excello. "There wasn't any promotion other than that."

"Baby Scratch My Back" was a throwback, mixing Harpo's blueswailing harmonica and nasal monologue over a rough, rolling rhythm foundation. "We used a lot of percussion on it," explains Miller. "We gave it a lot of feel. I've always been a big believer in percussion, because we didn't have too many real good musicians. So what we lacked in one way, we tried to make up in another."

Miller recorded "Baby Scratch My Back" at his studio in Crowley, Louisiana—about 25 miles west of Lafayette—sometime in 1965, just as he had been doing with Harpo for the previous ten years. "Fact is,

I met Harpo when he was playing harmonica for Lightnin' Slim. I thought he was one of the poorest singers I'd ever heard, but Lightnin' was trying so hard to get me to do something, because he didn't want to lose Harpo as a harmonica player."

So Miller cut Harpo at a '55 Crowley session that delivered "I'm a King Bee" and "I Got Love If You Want It." "I was in there, the studio control room, and I said, 'Can you sing it through your nose?' And that's what did it, really. It's not that he was a good singer, but he had something that caught the ear, and it was different." At this point, Harpo—born James Isaac Moore—took his professional name from the harmonica he'd been playing in Louisiana since childhood.

The musicians Miller used at Harpo sessions included Al Foreman, James Johnson, and Rudolph Richard on guitars, Rufus Thibodeaux on bass, Katie Webster on piano, and Warren Storm on drums. "Every time I recorded not only Slim, but all those Baton Rouge boys, they came with different musicians," Miller says. "It made it a little difficult to get a style, but we did all right."

When Excello released "Baby Scratch My Back" in late '65, Ernie Young harnessed the power of WLAC and station DJ John R. Richbourg. "You can tell in the type of business I operate when you've got a hit," he told *Billboard* that December. "I've got about 35 distributors around the country. When they start ordering the five-and-one [they order 500 records and get 100 free] and when the mail orders are heavy within a few days of advertising, you know you've got a hit."

17

634-5789 (SOULSVILLE, U.S.A.)

Wilson Pickett

ATLANTIC 2320
WRITERS: STEVE CROPPER, EDDIE FLOYD
PRODUCERS: JIM STEWART, STEVE CROPPER
March 12, 1966 (7 weeks)

It was just before Christmas 1965. The session in Memphis brought together two men who shared a home state—neighboring Alabama—and a bond in music. Wilson Pickett and Eddie Floyd were both members of the Falcons, and Pickett's gospel-grounded vocalizing had fronted their 1962 smash, "I Found a Love," made in Detroit for Floyd's uncle, Robert West.

The Falcons eventually scattered. Pickett consolidated his popularity with solo hits for the label co-owned by Lloyd Price, Double L Records. Floyd migrated to Washington, D.C., connecting there with Al Bell, the radio DJ who would soon advance his career further [see 30—"Knock On Wood"].

Now it was December 1965. Pickett had journeyed to Memphis, home of Stax Records, to recapture the groove that had given him "In the Midnight Hour." Floyd, a writer at Stax by this time, had been collaborating with Steve Cropper on a song entitled "634-5789."

"Eddie and I had worked on the thing and done the demo," recalls Cropper, "and were sort of happy about it. We couldn't wait for Wilson to get in to play it for him. So instead of taking him to the hotel, we brought him straight from the airport to the studio."

Cropper says he didn't really know that Floyd and Pickett had been friends for years. "So Wilson's listening to the song, and we gave him the lyrics, and he's reading them. About halfway through, he scrunches it up and throws it down, saying, 'Man, this is crap.' So here comes Eddie, flying across the room, at his throat.

"There was scuffling around, and I'm going, 'My God, if I get in the middle of this, I'm dead.' I was just shocked—I couldn't believe this was going on. Basically, they were kind of putting me on, but I was still, like, shaken. So they broke it up, and Eddie said, 'Well, I guess you don't like our song then!' "

Pickett retreated to his hotel, the Lorraine. Later, Cropper called. "I was thinking, 'What am I going to do, I've got a whole session to cut this week.' But Wilson got on the phone like nothing had taken place. So we went down there that night, and I said, 'You still wanna write?' He said, 'Yeah, I wanna write.' " With Floyd, they authored "Ninety-Nine and a Half" the same evening, which they cut, along with "634-5789," the next day, December 20, in the Stax studio.

Cropper played guitar on the session, just as he had for "In the Midnight Hour." Joining him were Duck Dunn on bass, Al Jackson Jr. on drums, and Isaac Hayes on piano, with horns provided by Wayne Jackson (trumpet), Andrew Love (tenor sax), and Floyd Newman (baritone sax). The co-producer was Stax president Jim Stewart. "Jim had a very good ear," says Cropper, "and very good taste in music. He was mainly a ballad man—Otis [Redding] and Carla [Thomas] and stuff like that—but he really strived to pull the best out of people. He was really good at that."

Wilson Pickett, meanwhile, was good at recognizing how others contributed to his success. "For all the bad press he gets," says Steve Cropper, "part of it is publicity, you know that. Of all of the [non-Stax] artists, he was the only one who ever sent the band a bonus for a job well done. I'll never forget that. He passed a little something on to the guys. That was pretty neat."

18

GET READY

The Temptations

GORDY 7049
WRITER: WILLIAM "SMOKEY" ROBINSON
PRODUCER: WILLIAM "SMOKEY" ROBINSON
April 30, 1966 (1 week)

For the most part, Motown set trends; sometimes, however, it hopped aboard them—"Mickey's Monkey" by the Miracles, for example, or "Here Comes The Judge" by Shorty Long.

Even Smokey Robinson, master of the romantic lyric, was known to indulge. For the dance floors of '64, he helped write "Come on Do the Jerk." About a year later, he created "Get Ready" to capitalize on the duck.

That was the hip dance as 1965 became '66, and Jackie Lee's "The Duck" was *the* happening record: top 20 on the national pop charts, top five in San Francisco and New York, Number One in St. Louis and New Orleans.

"Get Ready" featured the same supercharged, swirling rhythm as "The Duck," and skated into stores as Lee's record dipped. Its aggressive drive differed from Robinson's four previous hits for the Temptations, which were either tender ("My Girl," "It's Growing," "My Baby") or melancholy ("Since I Lost My Baby").

"Get Ready" also gave lead vocal chores to Eddie Kendricks for the first time on a single topside since "Girl (Why You Wanna Make Me Blue)." The hot sax break, meanwhile, showcased Motown's Norris Patterson instead of the more prevalent Mike Terry or Hank Cosby.

Otis Williams of the Temptations, writing in his biography of the group, said Robinson produced "Get Ready" around the same time that Norman Whitfield cut "Ain't Too Proud to Beg." Williams explained, "When the two songs came up at the same Quality Control meeting, the nod went to 'Get Ready.' Apparently people thought it was the stronger tune."

Lending credence to this view, Motown tagged the new Temptations album *Gettin' Ready* when it was released that June, even though "Ain't Too Proud to Beg" was part of the package. As it turned out, "Get Ready" topped the R&B charts, but fell short of the Temptations' earlier benchmark in the pop market. Williams said this guaranteed Whitfield that "Ain't Too Proud to Beg" would be the group's next release—which it was.

Smokey Robinson was never again responsible for a major Temptations hit, but "Get Ready" lasted a lot longer than the duck. A 1969 reissue in Britain became the group's first top ten hit there. Later the same year, Ella Fitzgerald recorded a version that bubbled under the Hot 100. In 1970, Rare Earth's rock remake was a major pop success.

Robinson himself included a disco revamp of "Get Ready" on his "Warm Thoughts" album, in 1979. It was also shipped as a single, but radio programmers, to their eternal credit, instead jumped all over another track from the album, "Cruisin'."

The Temptations sparked "Get Ready" into a promotional tune for CBS-TV in the fall of 1990, then laid down a new version of the song on their 1991 *Milestone* album. Of the group that cut the original, only Otis Williams and Melvin Franklin remained.

19

WHEN A MAN LOVES A WOMAN

Percy Sledge

ATLANTIC 2326
WRITERS: CALVIN LEWIS, ANDREW WRIGHT
PRODUCERS: MARLIN GREENE, QUIN IVY
May 7, 1966 (4 weeks)

When a Man Loves a Woman" was made in church. The details of the session may point to the contrary—the real venue was Quin Ivy's rough 'n' ready studio in Sheffield, Alabama—but the spiritual origins of the record are clear.

Percy Sledge himself claimed to have performed gospel music with his cousin's group before "When a Man Loves a Woman." That cousin was Jimmy Hughes, better known as an R&B soloist who recorded in Muscle Shoals in 1962–63, before it was hip to do so.

When Hughes hit the open road, his band included Calvin Lewis on electric bass, Andrew Wright on organ, Frederick Alexander on drums, and James Richard on sax. "We played behind Jimmy," recalls Lewis, "and Arthur Alexander, and then a myriad of other guys who never made it. Percy became our stand-up vocalist in about 1965.

"It was all natural talent, no training. Percy was very self-confident. Initially, he had no real desire to become professional; he was just like the rest of the guys in the band. We all loved music, and did it on weekends for extra cash." They were known as the Esquires, and played in clubs and colleges in Alabama, Mississippi, and Tennessee.

"When a Man Loves a Woman" originated with organist Wright during a Friday night gig. "He started playing the changes, the chord progressions," Lewis explains. "We all liked what he was doing, but assumed he wouldn't remember it after that night.

Next day in practice, Andrew started playing the chord progressions again, and we said, 'Let's put some words to it.' So we started doing the song—it was called 'Why Did You Leave Me' at that time—in our set over the next couple of weeks."

According to Lewis, the Esquires performed the number "for maybe a couple of months" before Quin Ivy became involved. A disc jockey and professional associate of Muscle Shoals producer Rick Hall, Ivy was looking to make a name for himself in production, too. He wanted Sledge to audition because he was starting his own studio.

"We were hopeful that maybe it would get us a big break, or at least the beginning of a big break. Andrew, Richard, and myself went with Percy into Quin's new studio. After we did some of the covers we were playing, he asked whether we had anything else, anything original. We played 'Why Did You Leave Me.' "

Ivy appeared to like the song, but later—while he was on-air at local station WLAY—got the urge for changes. "We went into a frenzy doing a rewrite," says Lewis, "but we had no objections, being young. The chords and the music per se were still the same, but the title and the storyline changed."

At Ivy's Sheffield studio, Sledge cut "When a Man Loves a Woman" at the end of 1965, with Spooner Oldham on organ, Junior Lowe on bass, Roger Hawkins on drums, and Marlin Greene, Ivy's partner, on guitar. The horn players were local recruits, and the background vocalists included a couple of girls who were schoolmates of Calvin Lewis.

Ivy sent the result to Jerry Wexler at Atlantic Records early the following year, with the help of Rick Hall. "Quin called us all excited one day," Lewis says, "to let us know that Atlantic had accepted Percy and that we had the A-side release. I had bragging rights in school that year."

20

IT'S A MAN'S MAN'S MAN'S WORLD

James Brown

KING 6035
WRITERS: JAMES BROWN, BETTY NEWSOME
PRODUCER: JAMES BROWN
June 4, 1966 (2 weeks)

The man who arranged James Brown's biggest hit of 1966 spoke of the early-hours telephone call from France: "He said he had 20,000 people or something," the late Sammy Lowe explained. "He had to do 'A Man's Man's World' four times before he could get off the stage. And he called me, woke me up about four o'clock in the morning, but I appreciated it. He was telling me, 'Mr. Lowe, you did a good arrangement there.' "

The woman who co-authored the song has a recollection that's closer to home. "I wrote the lyrics from the Bible," says Betty Newsome. "I had the idea from experiences I'd had with men in the past, bad experiences, and my relationship with James."

Brown had taped a first draft of the song in June 1964 at Chicago's Universal Studios, with a no-frills rhythm section: Melvin Parker on drums, Bernard Odum on bass, Les Buie on guitar, and Lucas "Fats" Gonder or Bobby Byrd on piano. But the legal skirmish between King Records and Smash Records [see 9—"Papa's Got a Brand New Bag"] may have exiled this recording, along with others from the time.

For her part, Newsome says that she composed "It's a Man's Man's Man's World," and that Brown "rearranged it, put things in, put things out, so I gave him co-writing credit. He didn't do it by himself."

Once a professional dancer on television, Newsome is today a born-again Christian living in New York. Harlem's Salvation and Deliverance Church, where she worships, is celebrated for its 200-member choir. She adds, "I don't believe in equal rights for women. I believe a woman has a place, a man has a place. And I was saying that whatever happens, whether he has the first word or the last word, he's nothing without a woman."

To cut the new version of "It's a Man's Man's Man's World," Brown turned to Sammy Lowe. His experience and credentials as an arranger were significant, featuring work with Sam Cooke, the Platters, and even popsters like Little Peggy March; Lowe also arranged Brown's first top twenty pop hit, "Prisoner of Love."

Brown had sent him an acetate of the tune, with instructions to prepare an arrangement for the following day, February 16, 1966. The venue was Bob Gallo's Talentmasters studio in New York; the players included Bernard Purdie on drums, Ernie Hayes on piano, Billy Butler on guitar, and Waymon Reed, Dud Bascomb, Heywood Henry, and Lamarr Wright in the horn section.

Lowe recounts, "James came in, and [after] the first time down, he said, 'That's it. I like it, that's it.' I said, 'Let's take one more, just for the heck of it.' James didn't like to keep doing numbers over and over. If he liked it, that was it. I don't know which one we took, I really don't. I did that just for safety's sake. He wanted to stop after the first one."

Just weeks after recording "It's a Man's Man's Man's World," James and his band embarked on their first overseas trek, to Europe. An entire edition of British television's hip *Ready Steady Go!* was turned over to their performance March 11, after which Brown performed two gigs in London. Call it Brown's World.

21

HOLD ON! I'M A COMIN'

Sam & Dave

STAX 189
WRITERS: ISAAC HAYES, DAVID PORTER
PRODUCERS: ISAAC HAYES, DAVID PORTER
June 18, 1966 (1 week)

This double dose of double dynamite—Sam & Dave, Isaac Hayes & David Porter—was Stax Records' first Number One in four years, an R&B smash that also gave the label its strongest pop showing since Otis Redding's "I've Been Loving You Too Long" in July 1965.

While the Redding hit was climbing the charts, Hayes and Porter were collaborating as writers for the first time. They brewed Sam & Dave's commanding "I Take What I Want," and then the pair's first R&B chart entry, "You Don't Know Like I Know."

Rapidly, the two teams locked into joyous sync. Steve Cropper, one of the creative linchpins of Stax as guitarist, composer, and de facto A&R man, recalls, "Isaac and David were pretty much hired in terms of writers at about the same time, in terms of being put on a draw so they would be around on a weekly basis and so forth."

"Hold On! I'm A Comin' " was supposedly created in five fast minutes, after Hayes had been badgering Porter to vacate the bathroom. Porter's through-the-door response became the song's title, and Hayes snapped together a melody on the piano after both men had finished answering nature's call.

The recording process wasn't necessarily as rapid, according to Cropper: "A lot of times the writers would come in, they would have an idea of what they wanted, but somehow we just couldn't fit that into our formula. It would be beating a dead horse until we'd say, 'Guys, you'd better let us try it our way, because we're just not making it.'

"We'd always give them a shot to get what they wanted first, and if it didn't happen, we'd change it. 'Hold On! I'm A Comin' ' was one that we definitely changed the groove on. I don't even remember how

Sam & Dave

it went the old way, but I do remember what Al and I did with it later. Just putting that 'chuck-chuck, dang-de-dang' in there switches a different groove from what they had written."

The "Al" in question was Al Jackson Jr., the extraordinary drummer who anchored most Stax recordings of the '60s and doubled as one-fourth of Booker T. and the MGs. The other three-quarters were Booker T. (Jones) on keyboards, Cropper on guitar, and Donald "Duck" Dunn on bass. These were the Stax house musicians who laid down the bedrock of "Hold On! I'm A Comin'," with Isaac Hayes on piano and David Porter on backup vocals, plus the horns of the Mar-Keys.

The single cracked Billboard's charts shortly after release (Stax had the distribution clout of Atlantic Records) on March 14, 1966. For Sam Moore and Dave Prater, the ride to the summit happened barely a year after they came to the Memphis label by way of Miami and New York.

Gospel-grounded Moore (he sang in Florida with the Melonaires) hooked up with Prater at a Miami club, the King of Hearts, around 1958. The tale is that Dave, a cook at the club, jumped up onstage while Sam was performing—and the double dynamite fuse was lit. After recording briefly for Roulette, Sam & Dave were signed to Atlantic by Jerry Wexler, who cut a deal with Stax president Jim Stewart for the pair to record there—providing the releases went out under Stewart's banner.

22

AIN'T TOO PROUD TO BEG

The Temptations

GORDY 7054
WRITERS: NORMAN WHITFIELD, EDDIE HOLLAND
PRODUCER: NORMAN WHITFIELD
June 25, 1966 (8 weeks)

When the Temptations' first release of 1966 [see 18—"Get Ready"] didn't reach the top 10 of the pop charts, Berry Gordy Jr. kept his promise to producer Norman Whitfield: that "Ain't Too Proud to Beg" would be the group's next single.

It was Gordy's practice—for he believed that competition begat champions—to pit Motown writers and producers against each other for the privilege of handling the company's top artists. And so the relative failure of "Get Ready," written and produced by William "Smokey" Robinson, delivered the Temptations to Whitfield.

With a straight eight weeks at the chart summit, "Ain't Too Proud to Beg" proved to be the group's most successful single since "My Girl." It was the first of *26* top 10 R&B hits (including ten Number Ones) that Whitfield would mastermind with them over the next eight years.

And it was the record that ratified David Ruffin as the Temptations' defining voice, at least until he was fired from the quintet in 1968. Ruffin was the perfect troubadour with the ballads of Smokey Robinson, but his syrup-and-sandpaper signature took on a new edge, a new urgency, under Whitfield.

In retrospect, the producer says "Ain't Too Proud to Beg" was "not one of my better songs, but I felt like it was part of my standard at the time. It was good and it was exciting, and I think the Temptations felt what I was trying to convey in terms of lyrical content—and it had a tremendous amount to do with who sang the song.

"There are certain people who can deliver love songs better than [those with] the more raunchy-type voice. David could give you both. That's a very rare thing, to find that kind of chemistry with a singer, and he had a tremendous amount of influence over other singers."

Whitfield had been preparing his own brand of chemistry since switching to music from professional pool in the late '5 0s. "I wasn't intrigued by producing per se—I wanted to become a writer," he explains, recalling that when he saw Smokey Robinson in Detroit with a brand-new Cadillac, "it excited me to the point to realize that a young black guy could actually do something of that nature, be a writer—and Smokey was also a singer—and really become prominent. It was quite exciting to me, and it drove me very hard from the time I entered Motown in the late '5 0s, early '60s."

Eddie Holland, co-author of "Ain't Too Proud to Beg," had hooked up with Berry Gordy before Whitfield. He sang the demos of Gordy's songs for Jackie Wilson, enjoyed a hit of his own ("Jamie") in 1962, and then evolved into one of Motown's linchpin songwriters.

23

LET'S GO GET STONED

Ray Charles

ABC/TRC 10808
WRITERS: VALERIE SIMPSON, NICKOLAS ASHFORD, JO ARMSTEAD
PRODUCER: JOE ADAMS
July 23, 1966 (1 week)

For Ray Charles, "Let's Go Get Stoned" was the *58th* hit record in an awe-inspiring chart chronology that began in 1949. For Nick Ashford and Valerie Simpson, "Let's Go Get Stoned" was their career breakthrough.

At the time, the pair were staff writers for the publishing arm of New York's Scepter/Wand Records. They had met at the White Rock Baptist Church in Harlem—he was 21, she 17—and blended their mutual interests in music and songwriting.

Working with partner Joshie Jo Armstead, Ashford and Simpson were prolific. Betty Everett, Doris Troy, Chuck Jackson and Maxine Brown, the Shirelles, and Mitty Collier were among those who cut their songs. Nothing was a major R&B hit, although Tina Britt's frenetic "The Real Thing" came close in 1965.

Making a living was uppermost in the trio's minds. Ashford recalls, "Ed Silvers, our publisher, had given us an office to work in, this music room, so we had been trying to write something all day." Adds Simpson, "We were trying to get this advance at the end of the week, you know, so we'd have some money."

Yet the creative juices weren't flowing. "We couldn't come up with anything," says Ashford, "and so I guess I said, 'Let's go get stoned.' I meant, just go have a drink, so we started laughing out the door, singing 'Let's go get stoned.'

"The next day, we came in and Ed asked, 'You got anything?' We said, 'Yeah, we've got this great song,' and I started ad-libbing the title, and Val picked it up and we just kind of made it up. Ed said, 'Y'all joking, but if you finish this, I bet I can get a record with Ray Charles.' "

They didn't take Silvers seriously, but Charles evidently did, cutting "Let's Go Get Stoned" in California on December 5, 1965. The studio was the singer's own, RPM International, in Los Angeles; the date featured members of his band and a few session musicians; the producer was Joe Adams, Charles's personal manager.

Charles wasn't the only artist interested in the song—at least one other version (by the Coasters) was made the same year—but his was the only one that mattered: a chaotic, compelling ramble in the spirit of Brother Ray.

Released as a single in May of 1966, "Let's Go Get Stoned" tripped its way to the top by the time summer rolled around. Ashford remembers walking down Lenox Avenue in Harlem, hearing the song blaring from a radio in—where else?—a neighborhood bar. "It was my most thrilling moment as a songwriter," he says.

Ray Charles

24

BLOWIN' IN THE WIND

Stevie Wonder

TAMLA 54136
WRITER: BOB DYLAN
PRODUCER: CLARENCE PAUL
August 27, 1966 (1 week)

In the spirit of the civil rights movement, Berry Gordy Jr. believed in self-help. So it was rare for his company to select a song by a non-Motown writer for the topside of an important single release. Nevertheless, Stevie Wonder's *soul*ful interpretation—with the help of Clarence Paul—of "Blowin' in the Wind" was the right message at the right time.

"Stevie has always been concerned about what's happening in the world, and he was concerned then," says Paul, who was Wonder's producer in the early '60s, as well as assistant A&R director at Motown. "I sung that song to him one day, and he loved it."

Wonder wasn't alone. Sam Cooke, for one, was inspired by "Blowin' in the Wind" to pen "A Change Is Gonna Come," his most powerful work. Cooke's manager, J. W. Alexander, told author Peter Guralnick, "[Sam] said, 'Alex, I got to write something. Here's a white boy writing a song like this...' "

Cooke would likely have heard Dylan's song in the summer of '63, when a version by Peter, Paul & Mary rose to number two on the *Billboard* Hot 100. Clarence Paul also would have caught it then—especially as a song he co-wrote for Stevie Wonder ("Fingertips Part 2") was holding Peter, Paul & Mary out of Number One.

Wonder began featuring "Blowin' in the Wind" in his live show for "maybe a couple of years before he recorded it," according to Paul. "We did it onstage a lot, and the requests were the reason Stevie went in and cut it."

The session was done in Detroit—probably some time in 1965—using the regular Motown studio band, with Earl Van Dyke providing the bluesy piano underlay. Clarence Paul's counterpoint vocals made for the same powerful effect on disc that they did in concert. "The reason I was on it onstage," Paul laughs, "is because of the lyrics. I was leading Stevie in because he didn't know the second verse. That's how it got started, and he said, 'Man, keep doing that,' so we put it in the song."

Paul was no slouch as a vocalist. "I had a couple of records out myself before I went to Motown," he says. "I had one called 'I Need Your Lovin',' then Roy Hamilton covered my record and knocked me out of the charts. The flipside was a tune called 'I'll Be by Your Side.' They turned it over—and then Hank Ballard covered that. So I started writing, because those were expensive demos I was putting out for everybody!"

As a writer, producer, and A&R man, Paul steered Wonder through his remarkable but sometimes unfocused early years at Motown. In those days, Wonder worked hard and fast. "The producers had more to say than the artist," admits Paul, "so we just went in and did things, and the artist came in and overdubbed. That was just about the system."

25

YOU CAN'T HURRY LOVE

The Supremes

MOTOWN 1097
WRITERS: BRIAN HOLLAND,
LAMONT DOZIER, EDDIE HOLLAND
PRODUCERS: BRIAN HOLLAND, LAMONT DOZIER
September 3, 1966 (2 weeks)

As clear, compact and compelling a single as the Supremes would ever make, "You Can't Hurry Love" was their first R&B Number One in more than a year. Pumped full of hooks—James Jamerson's pounding bass line, Robert White's ringing guitar chords, the Supremes' tight, melodic harmonies on the chorus—the record was Berry Gordy's machine at its commercial peak. "Berry was a great believer in hooks," understates Lamont Dozier, the song's co-writer with Eddie and Brian Holland.

"He would come into the studio, and everybody would feel a little anxiety. If [the recording] was unfinished, he would just smile and walk out. But the feeling that everyone got, I can remember. It was just like your old man coming in and checking your homework."

The Supremes probably taped their vocals for "You Can't Hurry Love" in Detroit on June 14, 1966, at a session sandwiched between concert engagements in San Francisco and Toronto. By this time, the group had been at the top of their game for two straight years; their itineraries were crammed with concert and television dates, personal appearances, and overseas tours.

Time in the Motown studios was at a premium, and Lamont Dozier recalls that instructing the trio in their harmony parts was time-consuming. "It wasn't as if you had so many tracks to lay different sets of vocals on," he says. "We put more emphasis on the music and the band, to make sure that was fat.

"Harmonywise, the reason [the Supremes] got started singing in unison most of the time is because it was just taking up a lot of time to teach them the parts. When they were on the road and had to come in and learn three or four songs, it would get very tedious. I came up with this system of just singing either very close two-part harmony or just unison, so you'd get the feeling of a haunting little thing in the background."

Diana Ross, Mary Wilson, and Florence Ballard evidently learned to work swiftly. "You usually got what you needed within two takes," says Dozier. "Those people were so talented and intuitive, they had a lot of that raw instinct about how to sell a song. I don't know where they learned it from, it was just natural talent. Having that natural talent made our job easier."

Motown's studio musicians made that job easier, too. The crew included Jamerson, White, drummer Benny Benjamin, and bandleader Earl Van Dyke, who usually played piano or organ. In Allan Slutsky's biography of Jamerson, *Standing in the Shadows of Motown* (Dr. Licks/Hal Leonard, 1989), Van Dyke said, "When Robert and I played parts in unison, we played so close and tight that a lot of times, they would stop the session in the middle of a tune and say, 'I can't hear the piano' or 'I can't hear the guitar,' because they couldn't separate us—like on 'You Can't Hurry Love.' "

26

LAND OF 1,000 DANCES

Wilson Pickett

ATLANTIC 2348
WRITERS: CHRIS KENNER, ANTOINE (FATS) DOMINO
PRODUCERS: JERRY WEXLER, RICK HALL
September 17, 1966 (1 week)

A 30-year-old party animal, "Land Of 1,000 Dances" has been appropriated by everyone from Bill Haley to Ted Nugent, from Little Richard to Jimi Hendrix, from Tom Jones to the J. Geils Band—and from Wilson Pickett '66 to Wilson Pickett '88.

The original was created by New Orleans writer/performer Chris Kenner, who based the song on "Children, Go Where I Send You," an old spiritual. "It was inspired by the dance tunes going around," Kenner told British author John Broven. He recorded the tune in 1962 for Instant Records, with an Allen Toussaint arrangement.

Kenner already had a couple of successful copyrights to his name: "Sick and Tired," a hit for Fats Domino, and "I Like It Like That," a smash recorded by the writer himself. Domino was said to have acquired a share in "Land of 1,000 Dances" in return for cutting it, but Kenner's original became the hit in 1963.

Next up were Cannibal and the Headhunters. This quartet of Latino rockers from East Los Angeles kicked their version higher up the charts than Kenner's, and added the neanderthal "na na-na-na" chant to the introduction.

Wilson Pickett joined the party on May 11, 1966. It marked a change of venue for the singer. His previous hits for Atlantic were made in Memphis, but producer Jerry Wexler wanted to switch. He chose Rick Hall's Fame facility in Muscle Shoals, Alabama.

Pickett started work there on Sunday, May 8. At Wexler's instruction, Hall had rounded up "the best musicians available," including Chips Moman and Jimmy Johnson (guitars), Spooner Oldham (keyboards), Roger Hawkins (drums), and Tommy Cogbill (bass). He also imported the Memphis Horns: Charlie Chalmers and Andrew Love (tenor sax), Wayne Jackson (trumpet), and Floyd Newman (baritone sax).

This electric combo tackled 11 tunes, according to the Atlantic files, with "Land of 1,000 Dances" cut on May 11. Music historian Peter Guralnick advises that Junior Lowe brewed the bass on that particular track, while Roger Hawkins pile-drived the drums.

"Wilson was a pro, and very soulful," affirms writer George Jackson, who helped pen "Mini-Skirt Minnie" and "A Man and a Half" for Pickett. "He could go in the studio and sing his heart out, if he liked the song. That's one thing about Wilson: If he didn't like the song, he wouldn't cut it."

Pickett evidently liked "Land of 1,000 Dances," and the public agreed. It became his first release to reach the top 10 of *Billboard*'s pop charts, in early September 1966. Twenty-two years later, the singer returned to the same landscape. His '88 remake was featured in the Dan Aykroyd/John Candy movie *The Great Outdoors*—in a party scene, of course—and Atlantic released the soundtrack. The session reunited Pickett with another blast from his past—the producer was Steve Cropper.

27

BEAUTY IS ONLY SKIN DEEP

The Temptations

GORDY 7055
WRITERS: NORMAN WHITFIELD, EDDIE HOLLAND
PRODUCER: NORMAN WHITFIELD
September 24, 1966 (5 weeks)

As a songwriter, Norman Whitfield's first significant royalty check would have been for "Pride and Joy," created with Marvin Gaye and Mickey Stevenson. As a producer, his first projects at

Motown were by Kim Weston ("Love Me All the Way") and the Temptations ("The Further You Look, the Less You See").

Stevenson and Janie Bradford were among Whitfield's earliest writing partners, followed by Eddie Holland. When the Temptations' "Beauty Is Only Skin Deep" followed "Ain't Too Proud to Beg" to the summit, Norman's stock as a composer *and* producer turned to blue-chip.

"In dealing with Eddie Holland, I found a tremendous amount of new areas for myself in terms of development," says Whitfield, "because he is a very thorough writer. He's just as thorough in dealing with the artist as in overdubbing that artist on a tune. I'd go so far as to say he's a perfectionist. A lot of that rubbed off on me."

Yet Whitfield calls himself "a much more earthy person" than Holland in songwriting. "And I don't think I'm totally R&B. I listened to other people's records to expand my limited exposure to music, but I would also listen to absorb and try to understand why a record was a hit—and to more or less make the ingredients a part of my repertoire, without stealing."

Holland was a fast worker, by Whitfield's account. "We had two different types of philosophies in terms of dealing with lyric writing. I'm a person that deals with the punch line first, and I always think the punch line is the key to the song. If you have the actual hook, I think you can build around it to create that monster [hit] you're looking for."

The hook of "Beauty Is Only Skin Deep" was a powerful punch, underscored by David Ruffin's heart-rending lead and the Temptations' ebullient harmonies. The group cut the song in Detroit around the middle of 1966, anchored by Motown's master of the shuffle beat, Richard "Pistol" Allen, on drums, and James Jamerson on bass.

Paul Riser, who was the arranger for much of Whitfield's work, remembers, "Norman was a feel person. He would just go into the studio with maybe a bass line and build his whole song around that bass line. He really was a master rhythm producer, building from the ground up."

Another recollection comes from Billie Jean Brown, onetime head of Motown's quality control department. In *The Motown Story* (Scribners, 1985), by Don Waller, she told of a dispute between her and the Temptations. "They were just furious. And I got called into Mr. Gordy's office and there were all the Tempts. They were really upset because they thought I'd made the wrong choice—that the record I'd chosen to put out was not going to be a hit.

"So Mr. Gordy asked me to bring it to him and asked me to bring this other record they wanted out. And we played the both of 'em and the record I wanted went out. It was 'Beauty's Only Skin Deep.' " Brown concludes, "If you're gonna be *that* wrong..."

28

REACH OUT I'LL BE THERE

The Four Tops

MOTOWN 1098
WRITERS: BRIAN HOLLAND, LAMONT DOZIER, EDDIE HOLLAND
PRODUCERS: BRIAN HOLLAND, LAMONT DOZIER
October 29, 1966 (2 weeks)

Like great movies, great records create their own worlds. And in the '60s, Detroit was popular music's Hollywood. With direction by Holland/Dozier/Holland, the leading man of the Four Tops gave the performances of his life: "Seven Rooms of Gloom," "Bernadette," "Standing in the Shadows of Love," and, of course, "Reach Out I'll Be There."

Levi Stubbs had the voice, and the urgency, needed for the quartet's recordings with Holland/Dozier/Holland. "Everybody thought so," affirms Lamont Dozier, "even the guys—Larry and Obie and Duke." They were Levi's fellow Tops—Payton and Benson and Fakir, respectively.

Stubbs even wanted Payton front and center for their 1965 box office giant, "I Can't Help Myself," according to Dozier. "Lawrence said, 'No way, man, you have got to sing this song.' His voice was lighter. But these guys, they're business, they don't care who sings the lead and everything. All they wanted what was best for the song."

What was best for "Reach Out I'll Be There" was Stubbs's stentorian passion, and a wide-screen instrumental track that redefined the boundaries of Motown's urban-pop process. Dozier recalls how those sessions were handled: "At first we would start out with Benny [Benjamin] on the drums, 'Here is the way the beat is going to go,' and then we'd get to [James] Jamerson, 'The bass line goes like this.'

"Or if it wasn't really a bass line, like on 'Reach Out I'll Be There,' something that was a little sparser, then he would follow the chords, because the chords would be moving fast sometimes."

Holland/Dozier/Holland were adding their own depth and innovation. Like "I Hear a Symphony" by the Supremes, "Reach Out I'll Be There" reflected diverse influences. "Our folks played classical music a lot," says Dozier. "My aunt, she played classical piano. All I heard around the house was Chopin and Debussy and stuff like that. That's when we weren't singing gospel songs."

With classical and jazz backgrounds of their own, Motown's in-house musicians could handle this. "Classics are my first love, actually," says Paul Riser, who handled string arrangements for Holland/Dozier/

The Four Tops

Holland. "I would have been a classical musician if it weren't for the uncertainty and prejudice at that particular time."

For "Reach Out I'll Be There" and other Motown pinnacles, players from the Detroit Symphony Orchestra would be crammed into the Motown studios. "The rhythm track would be there," explains Riser, "and we'd just overlay the strings and horns."

By several accounts, the Four Tops cut their vocal parts for "Reach Out I'll Be There" in short order. "I think we did that in one take," Duke Fakir told Jeff Tamarkin of *Goldmine*. "It seemed like the bigger the tune, the simpler it was for us to do. They were simple and they stuck with us right away." On another occasion, Fakir said, "I couldn't stand the song when I first heard it. I thought it was too different. I didn't go for it until the first time I heard it on the radio."

The record was "so different from anything anybody had ever heard before," says Lamont Dozier. "It had so many different moods and changes. I mean, what was this? R&B? Pop? It was the talk of the music industry at the time."

29

LOVE IS A HURTIN' THING

Lou Rawls

CAPITOL 5709
WRITERS: DAVE LINDEN, BEN RALEIGH
PRODUCER: DAVID AXELROD
November 12, 1966 (1 week)

Is the night at its darkest just before dawn? Lou Rawls may not have looked like an asset to Capitol Records in 1965, five years into his label contract. *Black and Blue* was the singer's only charted release, and that at the bottom of *Billboard*'s album rankings.

Songwriter Ben Raleigh says there was even talk that the record company was going to drop Rawls. "They told me Capitol was on the verge of letting him go, because he had done records that sounded very good, but hadn't been able to get anything in the nature of a hit."

The dawn broke in 1966, first, with a smash album (*Lou Rawls Live!*), which captured the excitement of the singer's showmanship in concert, and then with a smash single, "Love Is a Hurtin' Thing," which reached the top 20 of the pop charts as well as the R&B apex. By year's end, the boss baritone was asking $5,000 a concert, plus 50 percent of the gross over $10,000. Six years earlier, Rawls had been singing in a Los Angeles coffee house for $10 a night.

Raleigh co-authored "Love Is a Hurtin' Thing" after being asked for material by Capitol producer David Axelrod. The two men were talking about another song at the label's Hollywood headquarters one day, Raleigh recalls. "We chatted for a minute and I had my hand on the door, when Dave said, 'Ben, d'you ever hear a singer named Lou Rawls?' I replied, 'Yeah, I've heard him, I think he's very good.' Dave said, 'Well, I've got an album session coming up on him. Would you want to write something for it?' "

Raleigh's previous work had gained some R&B acceptance, notably "That's How Heartaches Are Made" by Baby Washington. After he and Dave Linden wrote "Love Is a Hurtin' Thing," Axelrod sent the song to Rawls' manager, J. W. Alexander. Raleigh and his partner had each contributed to the music and lyrics; it was their first collaboration, and Linden sang on the demo which Alexander heard.

Axelrod cut the song with Rawls at Capitol's Los Angeles studios, with a slow-burn arrangement by H. B. Barnum. "He wrote an introduction that captivated you from the first note," says Raleigh. "I have to give him credit, he was a terrific arranger."

The rhythm section included Earl Palmer on drums, Barney Kessel on guitar, Gerald Wiggins on piano, and Jimmy Bond on bass. Palmer, who played on many of Fats Domino's classic hits, certainly knew Rawls—the two had played together in California during the late '5 0s.

"Everybody came over to me at the session," adds Raleigh, "and said, 'Did you write that?' I was surprised that the thing stood out that much. I thought it was a good song, but didn't realize it was that good. So it became the single release, and Lou's first hit."

30

KNOCK ON WOOD

Eddie Floyd

STAX 194
WRITERS: STEVE CROPPER, EDDIE FLOYD
PRODUCER: JIM STEWART
November 19, 1966 (1 week)

The president of Stax Records, Jim Stewart, put "Knock on Wood" into suspended animation for nine months, according to Steve Cropper, because it sounded too much like Wilson Pickett's "In the Midnight Hour" [see 8].

Eddie Floyd

Cropper co-wrote both songs—anthems for a generation of soul bands—and played lead guitar on the '65 Memphis sessions that hatched them. "One intro is backwards from the other," he admits, "but one melody starts on the four, and the other starts on the one." That difference didn't convince Stewart, who declined to release Eddie Floyd's recording until the year after "In the Midnight Hour" climbed to Number One.

Another Stax insider, Al Bell, was also a believer in "Knock on Wood." Bell had joined the company in 1965 after a spell as an influential DJ on Washington's WUST and as a partner in Safice Records, a local label. Safice's primary artist (and a co-owner) was Eddie Floyd, who switched to Stax when Bell did. "That was part of the understanding I had with Jim—that I would come, but I wanted emphasis placed on Eddie," says Bell.

Floyd came from Montgomery, Alabama, but he carved out credentials for himself in Detroit as a member of the gospel/soul shouters the Falcons. Their 1962 hit, "I Found a Love," featured impassioned lead vocals by another member: Wilson Pickett. Floyd told *Blues & Soul*, "We quit the Falcons on the spot the day Wilson made his decision to go solo."

Once he got to Stax, Floyd worked initially as a songwriter, collaborating with Steve Cropper and Al Bell on tunes for Carla Thomas, Wilson Pickett [see 17—"634-5789"], and Otis Redding.

"Knock on Wood" (which may even have been intended first for Redding) was crafted in the middle of a Memphis storm. Cropper explains: "The song came when we wanted to write something about superstition, about a rabbit's foot and good luck, that kind of thing. And one of us came up with that old phrase, 'Knock on Wood.' " The lyric's line about thunder and lightning was sparked by exactly that. "It was a pretty big storm that night," he says.

To help with the arrangement for "Knock on Wood," Cropper recruited the Mar-Keys' horn player, Wayne Jackson, who was gigging that evening in West Memphis. "I called him on his last break and said, 'When you get through, can you come over and listen to this thing, 'cause I think we've got a real winner.' So when we went in to the studio the next day, we had the whole thing ready to go."

Backing Floyd were Cropper and fellow Stax linchpins Booker T. Jones (keyboards), Duck Dunn (bass), and Al Jackson Jr. (drums), with Isaac Hayes on piano and the Mar-Keys on horns. Singing backup were David Porter—the voice echoing Floyd—and Quincy Billops of the Premiers.

"Knock on Wood" was Eddie Floyd's most successful record, but not an instant smash. "In its early stages, it was being rejected by radio," says Al Bell. "I decided that if there was anyplace it had a shot, it was Washington. That's where we had the relationships, where Eddie had a strong base." Bell booked into a Rhode Island Avenue hotel and spent two weeks working radio stations between D.C. and Baltimore. "At the end of that, the record was taking off."

31

YOU KEEP ME HANGIN' ON

The Supremes

MOTOWN 1101
WRITERS: BRIAN HOLLAND, LAMONT DOZIER, EDDIE HOLLAND
PRODUCERS: BRIAN HOLLAND, LAMONT DOZIER
November 26, 1966 (4 weeks)

Motown Records conscripted nine singles for the top of the R&B charts in 1966, from "Uptight (Everything's Alright)" in January to "(I Know) I'm Losing You" in December. As "Ain't Too Proud to Beg" marched to Number One in the middle of the year, the Supremes were readying "You Keep Me Hangin' On" to capture the peak position in the fall.

The group added their vocals to the song's instrumental track during the last day of June that year. "We cut three or four of these songs at one time," says Lamont Dozier. "We didn't know, but later on, trying to remember, we found that we had cut several hit tunes at the same session."

Thus, it wasn't immediately obvious which would be the singles. "We had no idea," Dozier continues, "we were just shooting from the hip, a gut reaction. If it felt good and it stood up and we could remember it a couple of days later, we figured that we'd done our job. Almost all the time we cut the tracks first, because we didn't have the lyrics finished. I would collaborate with Edward on the lyric—he'd had something to start from—and Brian would give him melodies for the entire song."

The Supremes would often add lead and harmonies to an unsweetened, basic track, which only encouraged them further to fill the vacuum with their vocals. "That's correct," says Dozier. "But although it sounded sparse, there were quite a few instruments used as far as rhythm [was concerned]. In several cases, we used to use three or four guitars, mainly because we wanted to fatten up the rhythm.

"We didn't have certain echo and sophistication we have today, so we discovered that the more instruments—even if the guys only played units and all the same licks together—only enhanced the sound, gave us a more dynamic sound."

Arrangements were done with similar disregard for the rules. "They were basically head arrangements," says Dozier. "Most of the time, Hank Cosby just wrote what we played on the piano, wrote out the structure. He would look at what we were playing or take it from a tape of the song and the chords, and we would show him on the piano how we wanted the chords voiced so you would get the same sound. That was very important."

As their success rate snowballed, Holland/Dozier/Holland grew bolder. They made "You Keep Me Hangin' On" and "Reach Out I'll Be There" at around the same time—and both records pushed forward the team's creative boundaries. "We were trying to open up to different things," says Dozier. "That's why we loved what John [Lennon] and Paul [McCartney] were doing. There weren't too many people we really respected; we respected them because of their freeness."

The versatility of Motown's studio musicians underpinned the Holland/Dozier/Holland innovations. "Sometimes we would have a couple of basses in there: stand-up and electric," Dozier explains. "We tried all sorts of things; a lot were done manually, with hammers and nails, literally bringing chains that you pulled trucks and cars with into the session to get a certain sound."

32

(I KNOW) I'M LOSING YOU

The Temptations

GORDY 7057
WRITERS: CORNELIUS GRANT,
EDDIE HOLLAND, NORMAN WHITFIELD
PRODUCER: NORMAN WHITFIELD
December 24, 1966 (2 weeks)

For the Temptations, "(I Know) I'm Losing You" capped an extraordinary year. They monopolized the R&B singles charts in '66 with four consecutive Number One records, shutting out the competition for a total of 16 weeks. They also performed strongly on the album charts, where *Gettin' Ready* spent six weeks at the summit.

The Temptations' guitarist, Cornelius Grant, contributed to "(I Know) I'm Losing You" as writer and musician: That's his guitar that ignites the record (and which was sampled a quarter-century later in Son of Bazerk's top 10 rap hit, "Change the Style").

Norman Whitfield recognized a good guitarist when he heard one. In 1968, he recruited Detroit session man Dennis Coffey for the Temptations' own change of style, "Cloud Nine." Thus, Coffey became one of the first players to bring a wah-wah pedal into rhythm and blues.

"After being there for a while," said the late Motown session chief Earl Van Dyke, "you learned every producer's style. So when the musicians came into the studio and asked who was producing that day, they would say, 'Well, it's Norman Whitfield.' The guys would know, 'OK, pull out the wah-wahs, pull out the crybabies.' If Berry came in, we knew to put that shit up. If Holland/Dozier came in, we knew we had to have a heavy beat."

Whitfield feels he drew "that little extra something" out of the Motown players, "even though these were the same musicians that Smokey was using, and Mickey Stevenson, Berry Gordy himself, Holland/Dozier/Holland, Hank Cosby. We had a set format in terms of the guys we would use. They were so great and so versatile, and came up with all those different sounds. We all at some point have taken our hats off to the musicians—these guys were in there with us, they really appreciated what we were doing."

Their versatility was vital, according to Whitfield. "We only knew about what we were creating," he says, "but they were able to play the top 40, the top 10, maybe jazz in some cases, gospel music. By them having such a large repertoire, we could ask for just about anything."

If Whitfield's expertise was in the tracks, co-writer Eddie Holland's skill was with the lyric. "We knew that women love to hear guys pleading, begging, confessing, and basically admitting they'd made mistakes," wrote Otis Williams of the Temptations in his autobiography, *Temptations* (Putnam, 1988). "After all, it works so well in real life."

Williams wanted Holland's insights. " 'Eddie,' I said one day, 'you have to tell me how you do it.' 'Otis, the greatest thing you can do is sit and listen to women talk,' he answered. 'Every once in a while, one of them will say something, and I say to myself, "I'll use that," and I go home and write it down.' "

33

TELL IT LIKE IT IS

Aaron Neville

PARLO 101
WRITERS: GEORGE DAVIS,
LEE DIAMOND
PRODUCER: GEORGE DAVIS
January 7, 1967 (5 weeks)

Aaron Neville's melancholy, rural ballad was in sharp contrast to the Motor City grit of the Temptations' smash it displaced. Little wonder: "Tell It Like It Is" came from the South.

New Orleans–born Neville had seen R&B chart action in 1960 with Minit Records, but had lost his commercial luster by the middle of the decade. "He was kind of disgusted because he couldn't get a record deal," recalls George Davis, the veteran musician who helped reverse the singer's fortunes.

Davis knew Aaron and brother Art Neville when they were teenagers, and he was a founder member of the Hawketts, whose "Mardi Gras Mambo" was a defining moment of the circa-1954 Crescent City sound. Art joined the combo after their original singer was fired, according to Davis. "Aaron wasn't singing professionally at that point, like Art was, although he aspired to. Eventually he was recorded by Allen Toussaint, but didn't do as well as they expected, so they cut his contract." When Davis became a partner with saxman Alvin (Red) Tyler and former teacher Warren Parker in a new recording venture, Aaron became their first artist.

"Tell It Like It Is" began life in the hands of local bandleader Lee Diamond, with whom Davis wrote. Diamond, also known as Wilbert Smith, was one of Little Richard's Upsetters and drew a paycheck as a member of King Records's house band. Davis explains, "Lee brought the hook 'round to my house and said, 'Look, I think this is going to be a good song,' although he just had the title at that time. He left town for a while, and I got working on it."

The outcome was one of four sides recorded at Cosimo Matassa's New Orleans studio during 1965. "It was six instruments, three background singers, and I was the arranger," remembers Davis. The record's mood-setting piano was played by Willie Tee, with Davis on baritone sax and Tyler on tenor, Emery Thomas on trumpet, Albert "June" Gardner on drums, and "Deacon" John Moore on guitar. Davis, Tyler, and Tami Lynn sang backup.

Neville himself needed only modest coaching. "Aaron was a writer's dream and very easy to work with," describes Davis, "but you had to sort of contain him. He had such control over his instrument that you had to tell him to slow down, not to oversing. Tell him, 'Maybe don't open the window so wide.' "

Davis took the results first to record companies in New Orleans, then to major labels in New York. "Everybody turned it down," he says, and 1965 turned into 1966. "So finally we came back to New Orleans, and pressed up 2,000 records, to see about getting play ourselves. We went over to local radio stations—and the next thing we knew, two months later, it was a gold record."

After Parlo Records, according to Davis, "the whole scene just about crashed" in the Crescent City. "We were the last successful company," he says. The widespread popularity of "Tell It Like It Is" had ensured that Cosimo Matassa—who ran a New Orleans distributorship, as well as a studio—was paid by other wholesalers, who were anxious to have the hit. "But there was nothing coming after that," Davis tells, "so naturally all of the [local labels] crashed. [Cosimo] was our only distributor who was doing something nationwide."

34

ARE YOU LONELY FOR ME

Freddie Scott

SHOUT 307
WRITER: BERT BERNS
PRODUCER: BERT BERNS
February 11, 1967 (4 weeks)

Losers *can* be winners. Big-voiced Freddie Scott from Rhode Island failed to impress the crowd during one of the Apollo Theater's legendary amateur nights, but providence helped him to build a career in music anyway.

First, as a songwriter. Scott labored for the Screen Gems/Columbia music publishing shop in the early '60s, his copyrights waxed by Tommy Hunt, Gene Chandler, and Paul Anka, among others. Later, his deep-throated rendition of Carole King and Gerry Goffin's melancholy "Hey Girl" was an R&B jewel in a song catalog that tended toward the vanilla.

Composer, musician, producer, and occasional recording artist Bertrand Russell Berns, on the other hand, "never played a major ninth or a major seventh that even hinted at vanilla," affirms Garry Sherman. He was a longtime Berns associate and the man who arranged "Hey Girl" and "Are You Lonely for Me," Freddie Scott's two biggest hits.

"Bert was the most focused R&B person I ever worked with," Sherman explains. "He was so funky, he felt the pulse—the R&B essence—whenever he would sing a song to you or play a guitar."

As a writer and producer, Berns (also known as Bert Russell) helped to create a breathtaking body of work, including "Twist and Shout" by the Isley Brothers, "Everybody Needs Somebody to Love" by Solomon Burke, "Cry Baby" by Garnet Mimms, "Under the Boardwalk" by the Drifters, and "Piece of My Heart" by Erma Franklin.

A nervous man with a vain streak, he was also a tough taskmaster. Sherman recalls that Freddie Scott—signed to Berns's Shout Records in 1966—spent hours in the studio working on "Are You Lonely for Me," his label debut. "Bert did way over 100 takes with Freddie," he says, "to make him get that R&B perspective he knew so well. Freddie respected him, and although Bert pushed him, he stayed the course.

"With Bert, everything was geared to soul and the guts of human emotion: the use of baritone sax way down at the bottom, the guitar sound, the voicings I would choose for the horns—it was just totally R&B. He would communicate with me musically, and one-on-one with the artist. Sometimes he'd get really annoyed and be very guttural in his attitude, and extract a guttural attitude from these R&B people, who had grown up in the streets."

Berns and Sherman employed a regular roll call of New York artisans, among them drummer Gary Chester, pianist Paul Griffin, and guitarist Eric Gale. On backup, there were the heaven-made harmonies of Cissy Houston and her group. Sherman thinks that "Are You Lonely for Me" was cut at Manhattan's A&R studios with engineer Phil Ramone, although album credits of the time suggest it was Mirasound, with Brooks Arthur and Phil Macey at the desk.

The single was Shout Records' highest-charted hit, sandblasted from a quarry of soulful releases during 1966–67 by Donald Height, Erma Franklin, and the Exciters, among others. On December 31, 1967, less than a year after his song topped the R&B charts, in New York, Berns died of a heart attack at age 38.

35

LOVE IS HERE AND NOW YOU'RE GONE

The Supremes

MOTOWN 1103
WRITERS: BRIAN HOLLAND, LAMONT DOZIER, EDDIE HOLLAND
PRODUCERS: BRIAN HOLLAND, LAMONT DOZIER
March 11, 1967 (2 weeks)

Long before transplanting its heart to Los Angeles from Detroit, Motown was active in California. Producers Hal Davis and Marc Gordon had opened a West Coast office for the company in the early '60s, recruiting and recording a number of acts there. One of them was Brenda Holloway; another would have been the 5th Dimension (then known as the Versatiles), but for Berry Gordy's turndown.

The Supremes went Hollywood in 1966, going on '67. The trio recorded the title song of an Anthony Quinn movie called *The Happening,* which put Holland/Dozier/Holland into collaboration with composer Frank DeVol.

The crack Motown writing/production team worked on the track in Los Angeles, according to Dozier. "We did it at the Columbia studios, the big room on Sunset [Boulevard] where they used to do film scores," he recalls.

Dozier believes the session also yielded "Love Is Here and Now You're Gone." He says, "We had about 60 musicians, so we made sure we had four songs. The whole thing was a totally different sound for us." The orchestrations were handled by arranger Gene Page, who frequently worked on the West Coast.

Shipped as a single on January 11, 1967, "Love Is Here and Now You're Gone" certainly sounded like Diana Ross in Hollywood. It featured dramatic, semi-spoken segments which could have been torn from the soundtrack of a Hepburn or Bacall movie. That same month, by coincidence, Ross and the Supremes recorded material for a never-released album of songs associated with Walt Disney films.

As producers verging on directors, Lamont Dozier and Brian Holland helped make Diana Ross resemble the actress she would become. "I liked to cut her beneath her key," Dozier says, "because she got more of a sultry thing than nasal." They also recorded Ross's lead vocals fast, to keep an edge to her sound before she knew the song too well.

"You can call it 'edge,' " advised the late Earl Van Dyke, leader of the Motown studio crew known as the Funk Brothers, "but she never liked to do a lot of takes. She had that prima donna shit going then. You know how that is."

Comments Dozier, "Diana was always a thorough professional. If she heard something [wrong], you wouldn't have to stop her, she'd stop herself and say, 'I'll do that again.' Once she was into it, she liked to go from beginning to end without stopping. She may have felt it wasn't necessary to do it over. She would do it if you pressed the issue, but we found out that it was—like Earl said—best to get it over with, rather than cause yourself a lot of headaches."

36

I NEVER LOVED A MAN (THE WAY I LOVE YOU)

Aretha Franklin

ATLANTIC 2386
WRITER: RONNIE SHANNON
PRODUCER: JERRY WEXLER
March 25, 1967 (7 weeks)

It was a party crowd at the Hotel St. Regis in New York on January 10, 1967. Radio personality Bill Gavin was presenting his annual "record man of the year" award. The chandeliered room bulged with music industry swamis—Mitch Miller, Ahmet and Nesuhi Ertegun, Russ Sanjek, *Billboard*'s Paul Ackerman—who had paid $12 each to lunch and to toast.

The honoree was Jerry Wexler of Atlantic Records, the onetime U.S. Customs inspector who—*shazam!*—became a magician of rhythm & blues. Exactly two weeks later, far from the sophisticated salons of the St. Regis, he helped ignite the career of America's greatest female soul singer.

Aretha Franklin, raised in church and schooled on the road with her reverend father, first caught Wexler's attention with her 1956 release, "Precious

Lord." Ten years on, those gospel connections brought her to Atlantic Records through Louise Bishop, wife of influential disc jockey Jimmy Bishop and a gospel DJ in her own right.

"Her on-air name was Louise Williams," says Wexler, "but she was Louise Bishop. When Aretha would go around to different towns—even though she had been in a pop context for five years on Columbia—she still felt more comfortable with her old friends from the gospel world."

Aretha signed to Atlantic in October 1966. There was no creative agenda dictated in negotiations between the label, Franklin, and Ted White, her husband and manager. Wexler recalls, "I said to her, 'I'll bring you some songs, you bring me some songs, and we'll agree. And in the case of a tie, you win.' "

One of the possibilities was "I Never Loved a Man," authored by Ronnie Shannon. "Aretha's husband at that time asked me to write a song for her," he explains. "Being my first big opportunity to write for a well-known artist, best results were very important. The idea was to write an original soul message. Not knowing exactly where to begin, I decided to let vivid imagination be my guide."

"I Never Loved a Man" came to life in the most storied soul session of the '60s. Franklin, White, Wexler, and engineer Tom Dowd traveled to Rick Hall's Fame studios in Muscle Shoals towards the end of January 1967. The rhythm section featured Hall's favorite sons—Jimmy Johnson on rhythm guitar, Roger Hawkins on drums, Spooner Oldham on organ—plus Tommy Cogbill on bass and Chips Moman on lead guitar, the latter pair drafted from Memphis.

Southern white boys, with a graying New Yorker in charge. Wexler had turned 50 at the St. Regis shindig two weeks earlier; Franklin was two months shy of 25. Yet when she hit the piano's keys in that cluttered studio, she made sense of songwriter Shannon's meandering demo. Age became irrelevant—Aretha simply melted the divide.

Yet the session didn't pass without problems. There was a fracas involving Ted White and one of the musicians, then a heated exchange—chronicled by Peter Guralnick in *Sweet Soul Music* (Harper & Row, 1986)—between White and Rick Hall. Consequently, Aretha and spouse quit town, leaving Wexler with just one completed song.

Returning to New York, the producer added background vocals to "I Never Loved a Man" and began shipping acetates to DJs. The music hit like a hurricane. Stations clamored for finished pressings, forcing the producer to tailor another track—fast—for the flip. Within moments of its release on February 10, 1967, "I Never Loved a Man" became Atlantic's fastest-breaking single of the decade. And put the world on notice that Aretha Franklin had arrived.

37

JIMMY MACK

Martha & the Vandellas

GORDY 7058
WRITERS: BRIAN HOLLAND, LAMONT DOZIER, EDDIE HOLLAND
PRODUCERS: BRIAN HOLLAND, LAMONT DOZIER
May 13, 1967 (1 week)

Take three young women, gather them together as a group with a distinctive, resonant lead vocalist, and then put them alongside three young men who are developing their songwriting and producing partnership. The outcome: three consecutive hit records, which help to establish the career of the vocal trio and the synergy of the writing/production team.

Martha and the Vandellas—not the Supremes—were the first Motown act to benefit from the Midas touch of Lamont Dozier, Brian Holland, and Eddie Holland. "Come and Get These Memories," "Heat Wave," and "Quicksand" were major hits in 1963, the year before "Where Did Our Love Go" focused the world's attention on that other female threesome from the Motor City.

Yet within three years, Reeves and her Vandellas (Rosalind Ashford and Betty Kelly) were said to be frustrated over how the Supremes were hogging the headlines, the top of the charts, *and* the attention of Holland/Dozier/Holland. They wanted some respect from Motown.

"I remember that Berry was looking for something for Martha," says Dozier, "because her career was on a downward slope. She was very unhappy about it, so she went to him and said, 'What's happening? I'm not getting the songs, and things are just at a standstill.' "

Gordy called for action, Dozier recollects. "He said, 'Pull everything out of the can and let's see.' " At first, the Motown president was not impressed, and it wasn't until more tapes were retrieved from the vaults that he thought he heard a hit. It was "Jimmy Mack," recorded around June 1964 (the same time as "Dancing in the Street") but consigned to the shelf by the head of quality control, Billie Jean King.

"I don't know whether she didn't like the song," Dozier continues, "or whether she just didn't feel it was worth anything. Berry said, 'You mean this has been sitting in the can? Get this thing ready to go out right away. This is a damn hit record.' "

Events may not have happened precisely that way. "Jimmy Mack" was first slotted into Martha and the Vandellas' *Watchout!* album, released in November 1966. Then it received some support from radio—

Martha & the Vandellas

Motown later took out an advertisement in *Billboard* thanking stations in Boston and Cleveland "for bringing this record to our attention"—and was shipped as a single on February 3, 1967.

Dozier says he was gratified by the outcome because the song was "my inspiration and my original idea," written after he met the mother of another successful composer, Ronnie Mack, during a music industry awards dinner. Mack had authored the Chiffons' 1963 smash, "He's So Fine," but died soon afterwards; his mother was there to collect the accolade.

"Jimmy Mack" featured a decidedly '64 groove, but that was part of its charm. Nothing was altered from Martha and the group's original recording, which, says Dozier, was already the model of simplicity. "I just showed Earl [Van Dyke] the melody and the feeling of the thing, and showed [James] Jamerson the bass line idea, and that was that."

38

RESPECT

Aretha Franklin

ATLANTIC 2403
WRITER: OTIS REDDING
PRODUCER: JERRY WEXLER
May 20, 1967 (8 weeks)

"That girl done stole my song," Otis Redding told producer Jerry Wexler, just before Aretha Franklin's version of "Respect" was released.

He was not wrong. The two-and-a-half minutes of pure dynamite propelled Aretha to the center of the universe in 1967—or at least, to the galactic intersection of rhythm & blues and race relations. Her "Respect" commanded the nation's attention during a turbulence described by *Ebony* writer David Llorens as "the summer of 'Retha, Rap, and Revolt!"

Otis Redding had written the song a couple of years earlier, after a conversation with Stax drummer Al Jackson Jr. produced a punch line about respect. Recorded in Memphis, it became a top five R&B hit late in 1965. Franklin heard and liked his original ("It's something we all identify with in terms of our personal dignity," she said later) and cut her version in New York on February 14, 1967.

Present in the Atlantic studios were the same Muscle Shoals rhythm team that had energized her first recording for the label [see 36—"I Never Loved A Man"] just three weeks earlier: Jimmy Johnson on guitar, Roger Hawkins on drums, Tommy Cogbill on bass, Spooner Oldham on organ. Also, saxmen King Curtis and Charlie Chalmers on tenor, Willie Bridges on baritone, and Melvin Lastie on cornet were present.

Aretha and Carolyn Franklin created the midsong breakdown, including the celebrated "sock-it-to-me-sock-it-to-me" answerback. Carolyn was important to her older sister "in every respect," according to Jerry Wexler. "Aretha was very family-oriented," he says. Also taking part in the call-and-response of "Respect" was her other sister, Erma.

"There was a fabulous atmosphere in the room," recalls Arif Mardin, who, together with engineer Tom Dowd, lent production assistance to Wexler during the Franklin sessions. "It was almost like making a finished record that night, and that's it."

Moreover, it was a collective atmosphere, which Mardin says helped to produce the idea for the key change with King Curtis's tenor solo—borrowed from Sam & Dave's "When Something Is Wrong with My Baby." He explains, "We were doing a King Curtis album [*The Great Memphis Hits*] that afternoon or the day before, whatever, and we had those changes.

"When we went to the solo on 'Respect,' either Tommy or I said, 'Why don't we use those same changes?' That would constitute a key change, and then from the F sharp to the G again—there you go, the first chord of the song. We did it, and it fit. All of a sudden in the middle of C major, you jump to F sharp minor, which is really a jarring shift, but somehow Curtis made it work."

Less than a month later, Atlantic packaged "Respect" into Aretha's debut album for the label. Her first hit, "I Never Loved a Man (The Way I Love You)," was still in the R&B top ten, but the radio reaction to her version of Otis Redding's song was uncontainable. Atlantic rushed it as a single. "Stock and DJ copies are on the way to you now," Jerry Wexler stressed in a telegram to the company's distributors. "Run!"

39

I WAS MADE TO LOVE HER

Stevie Wonder

TAMLA 54151
WRITERS: HENRY COSBY, LULA MAE HARDAWAY, SYLVIA MOY, STEVIE WONDER
PRODUCER: HENRY COSBY
July 15, 1967 (4 weeks)

Stevie Wonder was 16 when he cut "I Was Made to Love Her," and it showed. Maturing as a vocalist, he was evidently becoming more comfortable with lyrics of love. "He began to take more of an active part with the vocal melody and the lyric," Sylvia Moy explains.

Moy was co-writer of three of Wonder's top ten R&B hits in 1966: "Uptight (Everything's Alright),"

"Nothing's Too Good for My Baby," and "With a Child's Heart." She says, "Stevie began to grow and grow, which was very fortunate, and he began to find out more about himself, which was very good."

In writing lyrics for "I Was Made to Love Her," Moy drew from her own family background. "The song was really about my mom and dad," she says. "My mother was from Arkansas, and it was based on stories I heard from them. Stevie just locked right into it—but then creative people are so sensitive, you can express a story to them and they can absorb it."

Producer Henry Cosby may have helped Wonder absorb something else for "I Was Made To Love Her." By one account, Cosby took him to a Baptist church in Detroit to hear the preacher's shouting and screaming, hoping the teenager would be influenced—as apparently he was—to imitate that fever pitch for his own singing.

When he was laying down vocal tracks, Moy adds, Wonder wanted company. "I guess it was his blindness. With other singers, you'd have to put people out of the studio, because it would get ridiculous and you'd never get the vocals done. But Stevie was different; he had to feel the presence of people. If there were none around, his vocal was just dead. Oft times, I had to go outside and just stop people who were passing to bring them in, so Stevie could feel their presence. Once we got that, he could fire into that feeling."

"I Was Made to Love Her" was also notable for Wonder's front-and-center harmonica work. He had been downplaying the instrument—or so it appeared—while striving to shed his "Little" Stevie identity, so this record marked its full reinstatement.

"He was getting very tired of the 'Little Stevie Wonder' thing," confirms songwriter and recording artist Lee Garrett, who first met Wonder at the Michigan School for the Blind in Lansing and later collaborated with him [see 91—"Signed, Sealed, Delivered," 330—"Let's Get Serious"].

"I remember one time in particular, we were doing a show together, and the MC called out, 'Little Stevie Wonder.' Stevie exploded: 'Little! Little! Little Stevie Wonder! I'm not going on that fucking stage, I'm not Little Stevie Wonder!' I put my hand on Stevie's shoulder, and said, 'That's OK, you've got to let *them* grow out of it.' "

40

MAKE ME YOURS

Bettye Swann

MONEY 126
WRITER: BETTY JEAN CHAMPION
PRODUCER: ARTHUR WRIGHT
July 22, 1967 (2 weeks)

Sisters were increasingly doin' it for themselves in the mid-'60s, but seldom enough to break the male monopoly of the R&B summit. Louisiana's Bettye Swann was one of the few females to reach Number One during 1965–69, and to do so with a song of her own.

Swann, born in Shreveport as Betty Jean Champion, sang in high school with a group. At age 19, she relocated to Los Angeles in hopes of making a record, and at age 20—on her birthday, in fact, October 24—she signed with Money Records.

The company was operated by John Dolphin, a key figure in the Los Angeles black music business,

Bettye Swann

and his wife, Ruth. In the heart of the ghetto, Dolphin's Record Store on Vernon and Central was a hip location in the '50s, made hipper still by disc jockey Dick (Huggie Boy) Hugg broadcasting over station KRKD from a small booth in the storefront window.

In 1965, Money Records was hot with the Larks ("The Jerk") and Bettye Swann's initial chart excursion, "Don't Wait Too Long." Arranger and producer Arthur Wright had worked with Swann on that hit, and they reunited for "Make Me Yours." He recalls, "We spent two or three days on the song, at my office. Bettye liked to sing a lot of words, so I put music around the words so that it didn't sound too busy.

"We had a copyist who played a piano line that I hummed to him, and when I heard it, I said, 'That'll be the hook.' So we added rhythm, piano and vibes played together, and bass. The theme of the music was the bass line and the piano/vibe line."

The recording session was done in Los Angeles at Audio Arts, with musicians whom Wright says he used constantly: James Carmichael on piano, Bob West on bass, Charles Wright and Les Buie on guitars, and Abraham Mills on drums. "Vibes would have been Roy Ayers, Alton Hammond or Gary Coleman," adds Wright. Playing sax were John Williams (baritone) and Jackie Kelso (tenor); the horn section also included Melvin Moore and Freddie Hill on trumpet, and John Ewing on trombone. A local group contributed backup vocals.

Several of the sidemen went on to success in their own right, Carmichael as producer of all the Commodores and Lionel Richie hits, West as a writer for the Jackson 5 [see 94—"I'll Be There"], and Wright as leader of the Watts 103rd Street Rhythm Band.

Wright remembers Swann as a shy, capable artist who liked to be prepared. "She wanted to be involved in every part of the record, and we had a good time. The only problem was that high note where she comes back into the song after the sax break. She didn't like to sing high notes."

41

BABY, I LOVE YOU

Aretha Franklin

ATLANTIC 2427
WRITER: RONNIE SHANNON
PRODUCER: JERRY WEXLER
August 26, 1967 (2 weeks)

On Friday, June 23, 1967, the hottest room in all Manhattan was on the second floor of 1841 Broadway. Aretha Franklin was in the Atlantic studios with producer Jerry Wexler, recording what would be her third and fourth Number One hits, "Baby, I Love You" and "Chain of Fools," respectively.

It was hot outside, too. Aretha's "Respect" had been raising the nation's temperature since April that year, while her debut LP for Atlantic, *I Never Loved a Man the Way I Love You,* had been scorching *Billboard's* R&B charts since March.

The singer was busy in the studio all week, working with Wexler and his assistants, arranger Arif Mardin, and engineer Tom Dowd. In addition to new material, she cut several evergreens, including "Never Let Me Go" and "You Are My Sunshine." The rhythm section comprised Jimmy Johnson and Joe South (guitars), Tommy Cogbill (bass), Roger Hawkins (drums), Spooner Oldham (electric piano), and Truman Thomas (organ).

Handling backup vocals were Aretha's sisters, Carolyn and Erma, and the Sweet Inspirations: Cissy Houston, Sylvia Shemwell, Myrna Smith, and Estelle Brown. The horn section was King Curtis and Charlie Chalmers on tenor sax, Willie Bridges on baritone sax, Tony Studd on trombone, and Melvin Lastie on trumpet.

The man responsible for the horn charts was Arif Mardin. "With Aretha," he says, "it's very easy to write sweetening parts, strings or horns, because her vocal intensity and dynamics dictate what you have to do. You have to put that string pad or horn pad under, and you have to punctuate with her. You can't drown her, because she's live."

"Baby, I Love You" was written by Ronnie Shannon, author of Franklin's first fireball, "I Never Loved a Man (The Way I Love You)." The choice of material was often a collaborative effort with her producer. "Aretha brought in a majority of the songs," says Jerry Wexler. "It would maybe turn out to be 60/40 or even 70/30."

Franklin spoke about making "Baby, I Love You" and about the Atlantic studio in Mark Bego's *The Queen of Soul* (Robert Hale, 1989). "It was big enough for the rhythm section, but intimate enough for the vocals," she said. "Those sessions were a lot of fun, and there was a lot of good food coming in and out of the studio. Lots of burgers, fries, milk shakes. In between takes, we would sit and chat, whoever was producing, Jerry or Arif. They'd be enjoying those burgers so much I couldn't wait until mine came!"

Mardin remembers the food ("Aretha orders steak without salt!") and, of course, the Atlantic studio. "It was a fabulous room—not huge, but still you could do 15 strings. The ceiling wasn't too high. The room had columns; sometimes the conductor couldn't see part of it. And the drum sound was great."

"Baby, I Love You" was not only Aretha's third consecutive chart-topper, but also her third straight single to reach the top 10 of the pop charts, and third Atlantic release to be certified gold.

42

COLD SWEAT (PART 1)

James Brown

KING 6110
WRITERS: JAMES BROWN, ALFRED ELLIS
PRODUCER: JAMES BROWN
September 9, 1967 (3 weeks)

Funky, funky Broadway... "I wrote 'Cold Sweat' because Wilson Pickett and Dyke—you remember Dyke and the Blazers from Arizona—they tried to get into my thing," James Brown told writer Tom Terrell. "Before I let them do it, I 'broke out in a cold sweat...' "

It was Brown's most significant record—innovative, influential, incendiary—and, perhaps not by coincidence, was made with a new bandleader, Alfred "Pee Wee" Ellis. A tenor sax player schooled in jazz, Ellis had recorded with Brown from the previous June. In February '67, he stepped to the fore.

"I was riding the bus, writing a lot, playing the shows," Ellis outlined to Harry Weinger. "That's all there was. James called me in to his dressing room after a gig. He grunted the rhythm, a bass line, to me. I wrote the rhythm down on a piece of paper. There were no notes; I had to translate it. I made some sort of graphic of where the notes should be."

Maceo! Come on, now... The tenor sax break of "Cold Sweat," as powerful as a call to arms, was the work of Maceo Parker, just loose from Uncle Sam's grip. "The whole thing happened *then*, on the spot," explained Ellis. "The solos happened because James told them to play a solo. I didn't write any of them in. The guys looked to me when the changes were going to happen, and I got them from James.

"There was a lot to go by from James. You got a sense of a musical palette from hearing him, from seeing his body movement, facial expressions, seeing him dance, and from being up there with the band, seeing his audience. So you get a picture of that, and you write it."

Give the drummer some! On the skins, Clyde Stubblefield served as one of two Brown regulars in 1967; the other was John "Jabo" Starks. "Cold Sweat" was Stubblefield's first hit with the combo. "I just sit down and strike up something that goes along with what's going down," he told Weinger. "Then Brown says, 'Well, that's the way we're gonna record it.' "

Helping Stubblefield out was bass player Bernard Odum, while Alphonso Kellum and Jimmy Nolen on guitars, St. Clair Pinckney on baritone sax, Eldee Williams on tenor, Levi Rasbury on trombone, and Waymond Reed and Joe Dupars on trumpets completed the lineup. Bandleader Ellis played alto sax on the date.

"Cold Sweat" was an up-tempo, reworked version of a slow blues on 1962's *James Brown and His Famous Flames Tour the U.S.A.* album. It was also indebted to "So What," a key track on Miles Davis's *Kind of Blue* (at that historic New York recording session in 1959, Davis had secured fine solos from his own hot band: John Coltrane, Cannonball Adderley, and Bill Evans).

James Brown made *his* milestone in May 1967 at the Cincinnati studios of King Records, where it became engineer Ron Lenhoff's first recording session with him. He recalls, "For 'Cold Sweat,' we made a record right then and there: set up, got it down, mixed it to mono, mastered it, got it ready for the street. People nowadays can't believe it, but that's how it was done."

43

FUNKY BROADWAY

Wilson Pickett

ATLANTIC 2430
WRITER: ARLESTER CHRISTIAN
PRODUCER: JERRY WEXLER
September 30, 1967 (1 week)

For all the custom-written material Wilson Pickett cut in the '60s, he never seemed unwilling to tackle the hits of others.

The biggest pop success of Pickett's career, for example, had been to the charts twice before [see 26—"Land of 1,000 Dances"]. Later, he boldly reshaped the Beatles ("Hey Jude"), Motown ("You Keep Me Hanging On"), and even bubblegum ("Sugar Sugar").

During February 1967 sessions in Muscle Shoals, Alabama, Pickett not only remade "I Found a Love," his 1962 hit with the Falcons, but also grabbed Arlester Christian's "Funky Broadway."

In this, he was timely: The original version of "Funky Broadway" by Dyke and the Blazers was then about to crack *Billboard*'s R&B top 50. Arlester Christian was Dyke, and his "Broadway" was breaking for Original Sound Records, which had acquired the 45 from a smalltime label in Phoenix.

Pickett molded his chrome-finished model—crisper and more commercial than the original—with the Muscle Shoals regulars. They included Jimmy Johnson and Chips Moman on guitars, Tommy Cogbill on bass, Roger Hawkins on drums, and Spooner Oldham on keyboards. Gene "Bowlegs" Miller, Floyd Newman, Charlie Chalmers, and Jimmy Mitchell were the horn section; Chalmers handled the record's tenor sax solo.

For all his "Wicked Pickett" reputation, singer and sidemen got along. "He interacted very well with them because they were all Southerners," asserts Jerry Wexler, explaining the notion of Southern solidarity with a reference from the memoirs of writer Willie Morris, *North Toward Home*: "[Morris] is taking a taxi in New York with another friend of his from the South. The cab driver is going 'the fuckin' boogies this' and 'the fuckin' boogies that,' and Morris leaned over and tapped him on the shoulder. He says, 'Enough of that, you're talking about my kin.' "

Wexler continues, "There's this great general picture abroad of Klansmen in sheets, and burning crosses, and nooses and so on. But Southern whites and blacks have a certain kinship that's much more real than [that of] liberal New Yorkers who read Max Reiner, and who only come into contact with blacks at a fundraiser, or when their kitchen is being cleaned."

"Funky Broadway" was first an album cut on *The Sound of Wilson Pickett*, slotted there while Atlantic Records worked another number ("Soul Dance Number Three") from the same Muscle Shoals sessions. Yet within two weeks of the LP's arrival at R&B radio, DJs were clamoring for "Funky Broadway" and Atlantic rush-released it as a single.

The two-time winner was Arlester Christian: His song spent more than two-thirds of 1967 among the R&B best-sellers. Dyke and the Blazers peaked inside the top 20 in June during their six-month chart run. Pickett's version debuted right after theirs left the top 50, and cruised all the way to the summit during its three-month stay.

44

(YOUR LOVE KEEPS LIFTING ME) HIGHER AND HIGHER

Jackie Wilson

BRUNSWICK 55336
WRITERS: CARL SMITH, RAYNARD MINER, GARY JACKSON, BILLY DAVIS
PRODUCER: CARL DAVIS
October 7, 1967 (1 week)

Fuel-injected by moonlighting Motown musicians and machine-tooled in the Windy City by producer Carl Davis, "Higher and Higher" accelerated onto the charts in 1967 to become Jackie Wilson's biggest record in years.

The song was originally written by Billy Davis, Raynard Miner, and Carl Smith, and was recorded in 1967 by the Dells. "But before we could release it on them," says Davis, who was then A&R head of Chess Records, "I remember being in my office and someone called me and said, 'Did you hear Jackie Wilson's

Jackie Wilson

new record? It sounds like the same song you guys did with the Dells.'

"I said, 'No, it couldn't be.' So I got a copy of the record, and sure enough, it was the same song, same hook, same message. There were a few lyrics changed. I said, 'Wow, how did this happen?' " To find out, Davis checked with Miner and Smith. "A fellow named Gary Jackson had just started coming around and wanted to be one of our staff writers.

"Carl and Raynard took a liking to Gary and thought he might be able to add to that group." They gave Jackson a share in several copyrights, including "Higher and Higher," with Davis's agreement. "I said, 'OK, let's do it, I'll take my name off.'"

A subsequent rewrite of the song by Jackson ended up at Brunswick Records, where label boss Nat Tarnopol and producer Carl Davis thought it right for Jackie Wilson. "Man, he heard the track and he flipped," says Sonny Saunders, who was the arranger. "Sometimes an artist has a little trouble getting into a song, or forgetting a line, or whatever. This guy, he just ate the song to bits."

No surprise, considering that some of Detroit's finest were playing what Wilson heard: James Jamerson on bass, Robert White on guitar, Richard "Pistol" Allen on drums, Johnny Griffith on keyboards. These were card-carrying members of the Funk Brothers, Motown's studio band. "We would have three or four of the guys come over from Detroit, lay a few tracks for a couple of days, and go back home," says Saunders, who recalls the "Higher and Higher" session taking place at the Columbia studios in Chicago.

Saunders also tells that drummer Allen fired the shot that made the track work. "We were playing around with this thing for about half an hour and the groove wasn't quite there. So Pistol says, 'Hey, Sonny, man, try this out for a second.' I said, 'What are you going to do?' He says, 'Just count it down,' and he double-timed the rhythm. Everybody knew immediately—that was it!"

"Higher and Higher" took off soon after that July 7, 1967 session—and Billy Davis told producer Carl Davis to let it fly. "I said, 'Look, Carl, tell Nat [Tarnopol] that you guys have apparently redone the song, and it's apparently a hit. So I'm willing to share it with you." A deal was made.

And so Billy Davis (nee Tyran Carlo) was reteamed with Jackie Wilson, the singer for whom he had co-written—with Berry Gordy—such career-making hits as "Reet Petite," "To Be Loved," and "Lonely Teardrops."

45

SOUL MAN

Sam & Dave

STAX 231

WRITERS: ISAAC HAYES, DAVID PORTER

PRODUCERS: ISAAC HAYES, DAVID PORTER

October 14, 1967 (7 weeks)

The guitar signature that ignites "Soul Man" may be Stax Records's most instantly recognizable lead-in. But grab this, too: "It was probably the most unique record in terms of marrying a dance groove with a song with a message," contends Steve Cropper, who was the guitarist behind that lead-in.

"It was the all-'round song that fit in every category. It had the intro, it had the performance, it had the uniqueness of the song, it was different. It went to three verses before going to any kind of bridge!"

Al Bell, a key executive and songwriter at Stax in those days, shares Cropper's perspective. "We had unique artists, and what was evolving was a great, unique blend of writers who, once they got in tune with those artists and a direction was set, could write tailor-made songs for them.

"But it was a matter of getting that kind of chemistry going with that writing group, 'cause there were a lot of writers in there. Some never got a chance to get their recognition, who were like farm club writers, if you will, fighting to get in position."

Isaac Hayes and David Porter were two who did get recognition as writers and, later, producers. Their working style was different than that of label president Jim Stewart, or Steve Cropper. "I think maybe, because of Isaac's jazz influence, there might have been a little more polish, musically," says the guitarist.

"David was not a musician; he's a singer. He's got a great ear and all that. David even sang background on a lot of the records, on a lot of the things he wrote. He had records out on his own originally." So did Hayes, who connected with Stax when playing in a band fronted by saxman Floyd Newman of the Mar-Keys.

The musicians on "Soul Man" included Cropper, Hayes on piano, Al Jackson Jr. on drums, and Donald "Duck" Dunn on bass, as well as the Stax horn section. By this time, Hayes's creative and production skills were accelerating. Dunn told music historian Rob Bowman, "All those counterpoint things, those pieces that fit together, that was Isaac."

The guitar and bass parts of "Soul Man" were rooted in "Bo Diddley," said Dunn in praise of Hayes. "He's got everything moving around. It works. It just knocked me out. When he did it that day, I said, 'Isaac, son of a bitch, he knows what he's doing.' "

There were other admirers, north of Memphis. "Soul Man" caught the attention of such Motor City magicians as Lamont Dozier, whose own work with the Supremes and the Four Tops was far more burnished. "I loved Sam & Dave for that funk, that old gospel sound," Dozier declares. "They just left the raw edges, they didn't polish it. That's what made it fun to me, because it was just raw talent. Dave, with that rough exterior...man, you liked the grittiness and the street type of thing. No polish, just here it is."

For Sam & Dave, "Soul Man" was their peak. The pair's career and personal relations eventually deteriorated, ending in a series of splits, reunions, and, ultimately, lawsuits. Prater died on April 11, 1988, in an auto accident.

For the man with the guitar, "Soul Man" lived on. Steve Cropper (as well as Duck Dunn) played on a 1978 recording of the song by the Blues Brothers, John Belushi and Dan Aykroyd, which grooved into the top 20 of the Hot 100 the following year. Less commendable was Sam Moore's own 1986 remake with Lou Reed, for a movie soundtrack.

46

I HEARD IT THROUGH THE GRAPEVINE

Gladys Knight & the Pips

SOUL 35039
WRITERS: NORMAN WHITFIELD,
BARRETT STRONG
PRODUCER: NORMAN WHITFIELD
December 2, 1967 (6 weeks)

Motown could be tough for artists like Gladys Knight & the Pips, the Isley Brothers, and Chuck Jackson, who joined the company with track records of their own. Each had their own distinct style and hits on the scoreboard. Did they want to sound like every other player at 2648 West Grand Boulevard?

The Pips (as they were originally known), from Atlanta, fashioned their identity in 1961 with "Every Beat of My Heart," an arresting ballad on Vee-Jay Records that hit Number One R&B before Motown hit its stride.

When Berry Gordy came calling, the group—featuring Gladys Knight, her brother Merald, and cousins Edward Patten and William Guest—had enjoyed three other hits. The quartet took a vote on whether to join Motown. "The guys voted to sign," Knight said years later. "I voted 'no.' I got out-voted."

At first, her reservations appeared to have been justified. Producer Norman Whitfield says the company *did* have problems finding the right material for the group. "They were becoming a little frustrated at the time," he declares. "There were many records cut, but nothing seemed to have that breakthrough potential."

With Whitfield, their luck changed. He had laboratory-tested "I Heard It Through the Grapevine" on three other acts—the Miracles, the Isley Brothers, and Marvin Gaye—but none was released. This time, the producer had apparently found the right match. "They were probably the most co-operative group I've ever dealt with in the studio," he comments, "and I really wanted to get a hit on them."

The song's co-author, Barrett Strong, recalls when it was written. "We just got together," he says, "and I came up with a little idea on the piano, the bassline figure, and we thought it was a great idea. I had thought of this title because I'd heard people say it so much—but nobody had ever written a song about it."

Strong believes that the Miracles were the first to record "I Heard It Through the Grapevine" in 1965 or '66, followed by the Isley Brothers. Knight and Gaye cut it on separate

Gladys Knight & the Pips

occasions in 1967. Her version with the Pips was brash, gospel-rooted and gloriously percussive; Gaye's was dark, anguished, and unsettling.

The late Earl Van Dyke, leader of the Motown studio band, said barely a month separated the Knight and Gaye sessions—and that the group's came first. "We looked up, and it was Norman's session. We said, 'Well, what is this shit? We just cut this.' He said, 'Now we're going to do it a different way.' And I remember Norman telling us, 'Forget what we did on Gladys.' If I'm not mistaken, I played Wurlitzer electric piano on Marvin. On Gladys, I played acoustic piano."

If Van Dyke was on form, fellow musician Benny Benjamin was not. Motown's ace drummer—anchor of 100 hits—was falling victim to his heroin addiction. The recording session for Knight's "Grapevine" was, according to Van Dyke, "when they really realized Benny was down and out." Another drummer, Uriel Jones, was brought in. "Benny just didn't have the stamina, so they used them together: Benny for pickups and Uriel to keep time."

47

I SECOND THAT EMOTION

Smokey Robinson & the Miracles

TAMLA 54159
WRITERS: WILLIAM "SMOKEY" ROBINSON, AL CLEVELAND
PRODUCERS: WILLIAM "SMOKEY" ROBINSON, AL CLEVELAND
January 13, 1968 (1 week)

A slip of the tongue produced the third Number One of the Miracles' career, and their first since "You've Really Got a Hold on Me" hit the top in 1963.

"I Second That Emotion" was the group's follow-up to "More Love," which Robinson wrote for his wife, Claudette, after the death of prematurely-born twins. Battling the blues, he went Christmas shopping in downtown Detroit with friend and Motown colleague Al Cleveland.

"Hudson's was hip, the biggest and best department store in downtown Detroit," Robinson recalled in his autobiography, *Inside My Life* (McGraw-Hill, 1989). "The holiday hustle and bustle—merry decorations, folks piled up with packages—got me to feeling a little better. I avoided the toys and baby department, heading straight for the jewelry counter."

There, he selected pearls for Claudette and hoped aloud that she would like them. "I second that emotion," Cleveland said, according to Robinson. The two men laughed at the verbal slip, but it stayed in Smokey's thoughts after they left Hudson's. "That afternoon we wrote the song," he declared.

Judging by Robinson's chronology, "I Second That Emotion" was composed in December 1967. The record was released the following October, and blazed a trail to the soul summit and the top five of the Hot 100. Only one previous single by the Miracles had done better in the pop market: 1960's "Shop Around."

Robinson was often inspired to reshape an expression or saying into a compelling lyric. "I've always known there are no new words," he said once. "There are no new notes, there are no new chords, so I've gotta use those some old tools and make it come out differently. And it happens! It starts from a spoken phrase or a billboard sign or a few notes of a melody. It happens in my sleep. It got to the point where I'd dream a song and jump up in the middle of the night to jot it down or tape it because I thought it was wonderful—and then in the morning, I'd realize it was nothing."

For a couple of years, Al Cleveland turned out to be a potent (and critically overlooked) partner for Smokey. After "I Second That Emotion," the pair wrote *seven* of the next eight Miracles hits, including "If You Can Want," "Special Occasion," and "Baby, Baby Don't Cry." All but one reached the R&B top ten.

In 1970–71, Cleveland collaborated with Marvin Gaye on material for his *What's Going On* album, including the title track. Later still, after leaving Motown, Cleveland formed his own label in Pittsburgh, dubbed Hitsburgh Records. There, he recorded a new line-up of the Miracles, featuring original member Bobby Rogers.

48

CHAIN OF FOOLS

Aretha Franklin

ATLANTIC 2464
WRITER: DON COVAY
PRODUCER: JERRY WEXLER
January 20, 1968 (4 weeks)

"You see, we all hung around Atlantic," explains Don Covay. "It was like a family."

When Aretha Franklin pumped 50,000 volts of electricity into his song, "Chain of Fools," in 1967, Covay had belonged to Atlantic's extended family for some years. He was friendly with their favorite sons—Wilson Pickett, Solomon Burke, Otis Redding—and father figure Jerry Wexler.

The origin of "Chain of Fools" dates back to Covay's youth. "I really knew nothing about writing then," he says. "I was doing gospel music, and it just kind of came to me, singing to my brothers and sisters: 'chain, chain, chain.' Later, I started conjuring with those ideas."

Later still, Covay joined Atlantic. He remembers receiving a call from Wexler. "He said, 'Otis would like to work with you.' I was on the road, and I remember thinking, 'I've got to have this situation together when I see Otis.' "

Wexler phoned again: Redding would be at Atlantic tomorrow. Could Covay meet him there? And so "Chain of Fools" was prepared. "I made the demo with me and my guitar real quick, overdubbed my voice three or four times. I took it to Jerry's office. We were playing the song, and Otis was saying, 'That's a smash! Oh man, that sounds like Pop Staples.'

"All of a sudden, Wexler came in: 'Hey, man, hey, what's that?' I said, 'Well, I just finished the song, it's great for Otis.' He said, 'Hey, man, Aretha needs to hear this.' And all of a sudden, she was there. 'It sounds fantastic,' she said. '*That's* what I need.' "

Franklin and Wexler wasted no time in recording "Chain of Fools," according to the songwriter. "At Atlantic at that time, when they liked something, they did it in a few days." Redding didn't seem to mind. "When we left that day," Covay says, "Otis and I were writing songs all the way down in the elevator."

"Chains of Fools" was cut at Atlantic's New York studios on June 23, 1967. Wexler had imported the magicians of Muscle Shoals, including Jimmy Johnson (guitar), Tommy Cogbill (bass), Roger Hawkins (drums), and Truman Thomas (organ). Sax sovereign Curtis Ousley played tenor, as did Charlie Chalmers; Willie Bridges blew baritone sax, and Melvin Lastie played cornet.

Later, Joe South's mesmerizing guitar intro was overdubbed. "He tuned the low E string of the guitar to a low C," recalls Arif Mardin, who assisted with the production. "Wexler loves those things, of course." Mardin was also in charge of the record's backing vocals, featuring Erma and Carolyn Franklin, the Sweet Inspirations, and Ellie Greenwich.

"Jerry Wexler was to me a great instrument of recognizing what was a good song and a bad song," concludes Don Covay, who says he was lucky that Aretha liked his work. "She's the greatest pop singer of our time. It was an honor."

Covay had earned it. "You learn one thing," he says, "you've got to be quick to work with soul artists—they're warm kind of people, reaching for the soul. When they say something, you've got to catch it."

In particular, Covay recognizes the importance of a hook. "I could have written, 'Chain of Love,' but no, I had to say something that immediately gets your attention. Otherwise, [listeners] might not let me get to the first verse."

49

I WISH IT WOULD RAIN

The Temptations

GORDY 7068
WRITERS: NORMAN WHITFIELD, BARRETT STRONG, ROGER PENZABENE
PRODUCER: NORMAN WHITFIELD
February 17, 1968 (3 weeks)

"I Wish It Would Rain" was the first of 16 Temptations hits, including five Number Ones, that Norman Whitfield was to write with Barrett Strong. In fact, the pair grew into one of Motown's most prolific, powerful partnerships, who carved almost as many milestones as Lamont Dozier and the Holland brothers, Eddie and Brian.

Even before he teamed up with Whitfield, Barrett Strong had credentials as Motown's first successful solo artist: His recording of "Money (That's What I Want)" was an R&B smash in 1960. Then Strong left Detroit for a few years, joining the A&R staff of Vee-Jay Records in Chicago and working with the Dells [see 61—"Stay in My Corner"].

By 1966, Barrett was back in the Motor City. He began writing with Whitfield, Roger Penzabene and the Temptations' guitarist, Cornelius Grant, on material cut by Jimmy Ruffin, the Isley Brothers, and Gladys Knight & the Pips.

Strong says "I Wish It Would Rain" started with a different set of lyrics and another title, "At the End of a Long, Hard Working Day." He recalls, "The melody and some of the lyrics came first, then Norman recorded the track and came up with the lyric for 'I Wish It Would Rain.' Sometimes when you do a song, you never really stay satisfied with that particular topic. You try to search for something better."

Better, and also deeply poignant. The song's third writer, Roger Penzabene, contributed real life to the lyric. "It was a true story," says Melvin Franklin, the Temptations' bass singer. "Roger's wife, whom he loved very much, was unfaithful to him—and he committed suicide because of it. He never got to know that it was a gold record."

"I Wish It Would Rain" demonstrated Norman Whitfield's confident grasp of what was commercial for the Temptations. "There's a tremendous amount of adrenalin that starts to flow when you're on a roll," he says. "The magic starts to come out of the fingers, the ears, the eyes, the mouth. It's worth much more than money when you're into that kind of thing, especially when you have good songs.

"Those songs were not your mainstream-type R&B songs. There were a million groups and a million different-type R&B singers and stuff—but the Tempta-

The Temptations

tions were always classified with the Beatles and the Rolling Stones, those kind of acts, because they were able to walk through many trends."

"I Wish It Would Rain" thundered to Number One in just five weeks, arresting the top slot at the same time that the Temptations' *In A Mellow Mood* was the best-selling title on the R&B album charts.

Later the same year, a version of "I Wish It Would Rain" by Gladys Knight & the Pips—also produced by Norman Whitfield—was released as a single, and reached the R&B top 20. Later still, the song attracted Ike & Tina Turner, the Faces (a U.K. top 10 hit in 1973), and Aretha Franklin, among others.

50

WE'RE A WINNER

The Impressions

ABC 11022
WRITER: CURTIS MAYFIELD
PRODUCER: JOHNNY PATE
March 9, 1968 (1 week)

While others crossed over, the Impressions stayed close to the community. Curtis Mayfield's songs, using the language and metaphors of the civil rights movement, captured the hopes and aspirations of an era: "Keep on Pushing," "People Get Ready," and—a few months before Dr. Martin Luther King's death—"We're a Winner."

"We may not have been the biggest group," says Mayfield of the Impressions, "but we were always respected for our ability to speak in terms of current events, and reach the heart as to what's going on. We were very innocent, we were nothing but kids ourselves. We observed, we felt, we had love in our hearts, and we needed to express so many, many things about the surroundings of our lives."

In 1968, Curtis and his compadres, Sam Gooden and Fred Cash, were resolutely movin' on up. "We're a Winner" was their *19th* R&B hit since the Impressions had become a trio five years earlier, and their most successful single since 1965's "People Get Ready."

It also remains one of Mayfield's favorite compositions. "I actually dreamed that song. I got up late in the night and put parts of the song on tape. Then during the [next] day, I wrote the rest and put it together."

With producer/arranger Johnny Pate, the Impressions usually worked at Chicago's RCA-Victor and Universal studios. "We did most of our recording at Universal," says Mayfield. "That was by Johnny's choice. When I found myself in the business with Vee-Jay Records, they were using Universal. Everybody was more or less in Universal.

"I would come in, and Johnny would prior to that day have written or laid out his arrangements to match my songs. If there were any changes [to the instrumental tracks] needed, that's where I would discuss and make them through Johnny. Sometimes I'd have to get out there in the studio itself and let them know through chord changes on my guitar or sing or whatever to dictate what I needed."

Guitarist Phil Upchurch, too, was a studio catalyst. "His work and what he has lent through his own ideas and his own talent are so fruitful, I can't even tell you," comments Mayfield. "We go back so far and we have done so many records where he has brilliantly come up with other little movements that have helped me."

Rounding out the rhythm section on "We're a Winner" were drummer Billy Griffin and bass player Lenny Brown, while Johnny Pate directed the horn and string sections. The record's "live" atmosphere came from a crowd in the studio audibly fronted ("All right now, sock it to me baby") by Audrey Thomas, wife of the Impressions' then-manager, Eddie Thomas.

"I just wanted the feel of people there because of the statement and the inspiration that was needed," recalls Mayfield. "They kind of carried on, with a little gospel feeling, and it sort of locked in with the movement of equality that we were going through during those years."

51

(SITTIN' ON) THE DOCK OF THE BAY

Otis Redding

VOLT 157

WRITERS: STEVE CROPPER, OTIS REDDING

PRODUCER: STEVE CROPPER

March 16, 1968 (3 weeks)

The posthumous release of "(Sittin' On) The Dock of the Bay" gave Otis Redding what he had been denied during his life: a crossover smash commensurate with his creativity, charisma, and influence. Released on Stax Records's Volt subsidiary, the 45 reached Number One on the Hot 100 and fueled his most successful album, *The Dock of the Bay*.

The irony—or injustice—was not lost on Jerry Wexler at Atlantic Records, the company that helped build Stax into an R&B powerhouse. Says Wexler, "They talk about the great lies: 'the check is in the mail,' and so on. The greatest lie in our culture is, 'Man, I used to buy Ray Charles's and Otis Redding's records before anybody else on my block.' They're all full of shit, because I've got the sales figures to prove it."

Not one of Otis Redding's R&B hits between 1963 and 1967 found a foothold in the top 20 of the pop charts, despite his growing reputation as an artist who could stand shoulder to shoulder with greats like Ray Charles, Sam Cooke, and James Brown. In 1966, Wexler told *Billboard* that Redding had the potential "to be the next Ray Charles."

"Otis and I spent a lot of time talking about his image and how he was perceived," says former Stax president Al Bell, who had first met Redding while booking concert dates in Memphis. "We started moving him into some kind of folk singer image, which might advance him to where we would get more than just Southern black radio play. We were getting some New York play and some D.C. play, but it still wasn't quite there."

Bell continues, "We were talking about this folk song [idea] and about writing folk songs, or songs we could call folk songs. And I'm sure that 'Dock of the Bay' came out of that kind of thinking, because it was a departure from the type of songs Otis had been writing."

Redding reportedly composed "(Sittin' On) The Dock of the Bay" near oceanside Sausalito, after his mesmerizing turn at California's Monterey Pop Festival in June 1967. Later, he shaped the song with Steve Cropper, and they cut it in Memphis on December 6–7 with the Stax session crew; Cropper played acoustic and electric guitar on the date.

"I don't recall having been around an artist that worked as hard in recording and writing as Otis Redding," declares Al Bell. "He was obsessed, obsessed." The singer, together with the MGs and producer Jim Stewart, "would be virtually locked in the studio for days. And that was back when it was mono, one track—it was take after take after take.

"I remember in the back of that studio, I'd come in there many times when Otis would be recording and go back to where he was. There was sweat on the floor, and he was stripped down to his trousers or shorts or whatever, just [soaked in] perspiration. He'd be singing the last take as strong and as profound as the first one. You talk about chemistry, you talk about magnetism—that was the epitome of that when it comes to our music, and this art form."

52

(SWEET SWEET BABY) SINCE YOU'VE BEEN GONE

Aretha Franklin

ATLANTIC 2486

WRITERS: ARETHA FRANKLIN, TED WHITE

PRODUCER: JERRY WEXLER

April 6, 1968 (3 weeks)

Just three weeks after "(Sweet Sweet Baby) Since You've Been Gone" became Aretha Franklin's fifth gold single, Atlantic Records held a press conference on April 25 in New York to announce her new recording contract.

The deal replaced the singer's October 1966 pact, which still had several years to run. Negotiated by Atlantic's Jerry Wexler and Franklin's manager/husband, Ted White, it was said to contain one of the largest royalty guarantees given to a recording artist at the time. Asked to reveal the amount, the erudite Wexler responded that to do so would be "in gross bad taste."

Aretha was obviously on a roll. In one week alone, "Since You've Been Gone" sold 450,000 copies. The LP from which it levitated, *Lady Soul*, was near the peak of *Billboard*'s album charts, sharing a top five berth with Otis Redding's *The Dock of the Bay*.

The locomotive power of "Since You've Been Gone" was stoked at Atlantic's New York studios in December 1967, during two days of recording in the middle of the month. Four of the session's six sides were selected for *Lady Soul*. Jerry Wexler airlifted in the Muscle Shoals squad for the date, including guitarists Jimmy Johnson, Joe South, and Bobby Womack; Roger Hawkins on drums; Tommy Cogbill on bass; and Spooner Oldham on electric keyboards. Aretha played piano. King Curtis, Seldon Powell, and Frank Wess were on tenor sax; Haywood Henry handled baritone sax; Melvin Lastie, Joe Newman, and Bernie Glow were on trumpet; Tony Studd blew bass trombone.

Vocalizing in back were Erma and Carolyn Franklin, with the Sweet Inspirations. "We had been singing gospel together all our lives," explains Erma Franklin, "so we were used to singing together. It was just an extension of what we'd already been doing—we never dreamed it would go to the heights that it did."

As youngsters, the Franklin sisters had the best tutors, including the Rev. James Cleveland. "He used to direct my father's choir," says Erma, "and he stayed on us to practice together all the time, too."

The Atlantic sessions were fun, by Erma's account. "It was all live, in living color," she laughs. "We'd be there for maybe 12 to 14 hours sometimes, half the night, so they just sent food in. Everybody who was there knew each other and were friends and everything."

Fun aside, Aretha's talent was formidable, and her sidemen knew it. They were "practically awestruck," according to Wexler. "They got humble. They were some talented musicians—and some feisty assholes, too. But she just swept everything in front of her."

True enough. "Since You've Been Gone" was released one year after Aretha's Atlantic debut. In the space of that year, five of her 45s had trampled their way up the R&B charts, and four of them had locked up the summit for a total of 21 weeks. In exceedingly good taste, those numbers.

Aretha Franklin

53

I GOT THE FEELIN'

James Brown

KING 6155
WRITER: JAMES BROWN
PRODUCER: JAMES BROWN
April 27, 1968 (2 weeks)

James Brown was in Los Angeles at the beginning in 1968, raising television's temperature with appearances on *Hollywood Palace* and other ephemera. Within three months, he would be using television to help cool down a nation.

This was to be the most turbulent year of Brown's life, although there were few hints of that in January when he and his band pulled up at 15456 Cabrito Road in Van Nuys, California, and trooped into the Vox Recording Studio. The session was to produce as quirky, wicked, and intricate a record as he would ever make.

"I Got the Feelin' " came together without overdubs. It was live for 10 takes, until the musicians—Brown's regular touring crew—got the horn chops and tricky rhythms in unison, just right.

Pee Wee Ellis was directing the James Brown Orchestra this day: Bernard Odum (bass), Clyde Stubblefield (drums), "Country" Kellum and Jimmy Nolen (guitars), Waymon Reed and Joe Dupars (trumpets), Levi Rasbury (trombone), Maceo Parker (tenor sax), and St. Clair Pinckney (baritone sax). Ellis himself played alto sax.

James Brown

Stubblefield's drums on "I Got the Feelin' " took time, practice, and some nudging from the boss. On the master tape, Brown's instructions are audible ("No, it's uh-uhhh-*owww*"), and he actually went so far as to pick up the sticks and hit the tom-tom. "Oh, he *tried* to tell me what to play," says Stubblefield.

"It was a different kind of thing," agrees Ellis. "The band had started to gel, and we were feeling very unified. We were getting into our own thing, and starting to stretch. That's why this is so intricate.

"I had developed a policy of section rehearsals, separate for the horn players and the rhythm section players, to give them a sense of self-pride. And I gave them more complex things to play, so they felt they could do things that were away from their normal selves.

"James was very rhythmic, punctuated; the whole level of a recording would go up just by his presence. The word 'feelin' '—the way he says it, *'feelin' '*—told me what to tell the band to play. What the band did was a reflection of what he did."

"I Got the Feelin' " was released in March 1968, amid a whirlwind of events. Syd Nathan of King Records, the man who, in Brown's words, "gave this poor country boy from Georgia the vehicle to do everything he'd ever dreamed of doing," had died at the beginning of the month. Little Willie John, fellow King artist and a Brown inspiration, died March 27. And Dr. Martin Luther King was slain April 3.

In the assassination's aftermath, James Brown hit the airwaves. In Boston, he performed a live television concert that helped keep anger off the streets; in Washington, D.C., he made personal appearances on television and radio to cool the riotous climate. Dr. King was "our hero," Brown said. "We have an obligation to try to fulfill his dream of true brotherhood. You can't do that with violence."

54

COWBOYS TO GIRLS

The Intruders

GAMBLE 214
WRITERS: KENNY GAMBLE, LEON HUFF
PRODUCERS: KENNY GAMBLE, LEON HUFF
May 11, 1968 (1 week)

A Pennsylvania businessman took a gamble in 1966, and helped two local musicians to build a foundation for their dreams—and, eventually, to create one of the most innovative musical workshops in the history of rhythm & blues. The Sound of Philadelphia owed its start to a clothing merchant.

Some years earlier, a Trailways bus had carried Leon Huff from Camden, New Jersey, to New York. He became a versatile session pianist, a gun-for-hire acquainted with several writers in the Brill Building and with various producers, including Jerry Leiber and Mike Stoller.

Later, Huff toiled in Philadelphia's Cameo-Parkway pop factory, where he met fellow songwriter and musician Kenny Gamble. "The first time we came into any real contact was when I was hired as pianist for one of their sessions for Cameo," Huff explained to Tony Cummings in *The Sound of Philadelphia* (Methuen, 1975).

Gamble and Huff began to collaborate. "I suppose we started writing together because we just had the feeling—the second sense—that told us we had something special to give each other," Gamble said. "Once we wrote together, we just we had to produce together. We had to take the initiative. Nothing much else was happening for us."

The pair planned their own label. "We scuffled around trying to raise some capital to start the venture off, and eventually this clothing manufacturer Ben Krass put up a little bit of money," said Gamble. "But we *had* to be right on the first shot. We called the label Excel Records and the act we recorded were the Intruders."

The group—Eugene Daughtry, Phil Terry, Robert Edwards, "Little" Sonny Brown—was schooled in street-sharp doo-wop harmonies, and popular around Philadelphia. Phil Terry told Cummings, "We were singing ballads with a kind of slickness in the production that the public wanted. But what really got the Intruders and Gamble away was Little Sonny's voice." It sounded flat, Terry admitted, "but it's not really flat. It's that difference that made us successful."

"(We'll Be) United" was the Intruders' first hit in the summer of '66—by then, the Excel name had been changed to Gamble—and was followed by "Devil with an Angel's Smile" and "Together." Most were recorded at the Cameo studio on South Broad Street.

"We were feeling around," Kenny Gamble said, "looking for our own sound. We knew the kids weren't buying the old primitive kind of R&B anymore, they wanted something more sophisticated. So we were using strings, vibes, big orchestrations. But it took us some time to find the right blend."

Among the musicians who helped pinpoint the sound were arranger Bobby Martin and players Norman Harris and Roland Chambers (guitars), Earl Young (drums), and Ronnie Baker (bass). Huff himself played piano at many of the sessions. "At last people began to hear our records and say, 'Yeah, but it don't have the same groove as Motown.' Now they accepted what *we* were doing."

55

TIGHTEN UP

Archie Bell & the Drells

ATLANTIC 2478
WRITERS: BILLY BUTLER, ARCHIE BELL
PRODUCER: SKIPPER LEE FRAZIER
May 18, 1968 (2 weeks)

See who's driving the white Cadillac with the hit record in the trunk? That's disc jockey Skipper Lee Frazier from radio station KCOH in Houston. See the box of 45s he's taking out of the car? That's the "Tighten Up"!

Archie Bell and the Drells danced their way onto the national charts in 1968, thanks to Frazier, producer Huey Meaux, and a hot soul combo from the Lone Star state.

As the top jock on KCOH, Skipper Lee was at the center of Houston's music scene in the '60s, managing local musicians and recording some for his own label, Ovid. One of those bands was the TSU (for Texas Southern University) Toronados, led by Leroy Lewis. Another was the Drells, featuring Archie Bell, Billy Butler, James Wise, and Willie Parnell. When Frazier put them all together, the result was the hippest dance hit since "Funky Broadway."

"The TSU Toronados had been performing the music for 'Tighten Up' instrumentally in the different clubs," Frazier explains, "and they got a good response to it. So I told them, 'Hey, let's put some lyrics to it and let Archie Bell and the Drells do it.' "

The Toronados cut their "Tighten Up" instrumental track at Doyle Jones's eight-track studio in Houston. The band featured guitarists Cal and Will Thomas, Jerry Jenkins on bass, Dwight Burns on drums, and Robert Sanders on organ, with Clarence Harper, Nelson Mills, and leader Leroy Lewis on horns. "That studio was state-of-the-art at the time," recalls Jenkins, "but there was no booth for the singer. He just stood in the middle of the floor. It was, 'Go play and y'all come and sing.' "

The Drells' vocals took some perfecting. "At that particular time," recalls Frazier, "James Brown had a record out, he was saying, 'Give the drummer some.' Well, we stayed up 'til three o'clock in the morning trying to get Archie to say 'Tighten up on the drums.' The music was already there, so he had to come in—boom!—at the right place."

Frazier issued "Tighten Up" in 1967 on Ovid. "What I was doing was peddling out of the trunk of my car, running to these one-stops, leaving a box of 45s. When I was a disc jockey, I was playing the other side, 'Dog Eat Dog.' I had a DJ working with me, and she said, 'You're playing the wrong side.' I said, 'No, no, that's the side.' She said, 'You listen to me.' "

Frazier's partner was right: "Tighten Up" turned into a Texas-sized hit and—eventually—a national success after influential producer Huey Meaux tipped Atlantic Records, which soon picked up the record for distribution. And so the spotlight fell on the Drells. "They used to do a thing called the Monkey," says Frazier. "James Wise could squat down and act just like a monkey, scratch his side and everything. Archie would say, 'Look at that monkey, climb that tree, monkey,' and James would take that microphone like he was climbing a tree. That's what really attracted me to this group."

56

SHOO-BE-DOO-BE-DOO-DA-DAY

Stevie Wonder

TAMLA 54165
WRITERS: HENRY COSBY, SYLVIA MOY, STEVIE WONDER
PRODUCER: HENRY COSBY
June 1, 1968 (1 week)

Like his fellow artists at Motown, Stevie Wonder was a product of the company's highly efficient studio system. At this system's peak, the producers called most of the creative shots, the "quality control" department chose the songs most suitable for singles, and Berry Gordy Jr. had the final cut.

*Un*like his fellow artists, Stevie Wonder was involved in writing most of his '60s hits. Between the release of "Uptight (Everything's Alright)" in November 1965 and "Yester-Me, Yester-You, Yesterday" in September 1969, he placed 13 singles in *Billboard*'s R&B top 10, and co-wrote seven of them. Only Smokey Robinson outperformed him in this respect.

Sylvia Moy and Henry (Hank) Cosby were Wonder's most frequent collaborators. He would often lay down the chords of a song, while also contributing its title and/or part of its lyric. Moy would handle the vocal melody and the rest of the lyrics. Cosby (who co-composed Wonder's very first hit, "Fingertips Part 2") would shape the arrangement and work out the instrumental track with the studio musicians. On a few occasions, Wonder's mother, Lula Mae Hardaway, received a writer's credit [see 39—"I Was Made to Love Her"].

Wonder created "Shoo-Be-Doo-Be-Doo-Da-Day," his only R&B Number One of 1968, with Moy and Cosby. "That was really Stevie's title," Moy recounts. "And he was always a little upset because he was saying 'Shoo-Be-Doo-Be-Doo-*Don*-Day,' and it came up 'Da-Day' [on the label copy of the record].

"At that point, we had really more or less run out of titles, and I think that the song's message was like a little scat. It says something and then it doesn't, and yet it says a lot."

The fluid funk of "Shoo-Be-Doo-Be-Doo-Da-Day" displayed Wonder's interest in the clavinet, and perhaps the beginnings of his independence from the Motown studio system. "I had the confidence that something good was gonna happen, but I didn't know when," he told David Breskin years later. "And then...it began to happen."

Later in 1968, Wonder experimented with an entirely instrumental album, *Eivets Rednow*, showcasing his harmonica and clavinet skills. Evidently, Motown didn't know how to promote the project—or didn't want to—because it failed to chart when released that December.

Fifteen months later, the company still couldn't handle their superstar's enthusiasm for new technology. When *Stevie Wonder Live* was trucked to stores in March 1970, the sleeve included a telling misprint: Wonder's clavinet solo on "Shoo-Be-Doo-Be-Doo-Da-Day" was listed as a *clarinet* solo.

57

AIN'T NOTHING LIKE THE REAL THING

Marvin Gaye & Tammi Terrell

TAMLA 54163
WRITERS: NICKOLAS ASHFORD, VALERIE SIMPSON
PRODUCERS: NICKOLAS ASHFORD, VALERIE SIMPSON
June 8, 1968 (1 week)

It's showtime on a summer night in 1983. During the last concert tour of his life, Marvin Gaye is about to perform several songs he made famous with the late Tammi Terrell 15 years earlier. "Give her a big round of applause," he urges the audience. "She'll hear you."

Gaye's voice alone would have carried to where she was. Together, Marvin and Tammi had been the sweet songbirds of Motown. "They were perfect," declares Johnny Bristol, who co-produced (with Harvey Fuqua) "Ain't No Mountain High Enough" and "Your Precious Love," the pair's initial hits. "The sound of their two voices together was better than any of the other duets Marvin had done, it was just so distinctive."

Terrell had joined Motown in 1965 at age 19, after several years of recording for other labels, and singing with Jerry Butler and James Brown. Every one of Marvin and Tammi's nine major hits was written by Nick Ashford and Valerie Simpson, a New York

Marvin Gaye and Tammi Terrell

twosome who connected with Motown after success with Ray Charles [see 23—"Let's Go Get Stoned"].

They were so New York, in fact, that they never moved to Detroit. "That gave us a little one-upmanship, because we would fly in and stay for a week, 10 days," says Simpson. "They gave us a music room, but we did most of our work at home. We would fly there with the material and let them review it."

When it came to "Ain't Nothing Like the Real Thing," the pair decided they wanted to produce the record themselves, recalls Johnny Bristol, "which was understandable, because they were fantastic." Motown's response: to have Bristol and Harvey Fuqua *and* Ashford and Simpson record separate versions of the song with Marvin and Tammi.

The final decision was to be made at one of the company's quality control meetings. "I was so nervous," Ashford remembers. "Val wasn't with me, and I'd never been to a quality control meeting before. Berry was right there at the middle of the table. Beads of sweat must have been popping out of my head! So there was this silence after our record was played, and then Berry said, 'I don't think we need to vote on this one. Let's just send it out right away.' "

Bristol's recollections are different, although he acknowledges that Gordy encouraged competition. "We had our own material that we had done on Marvin and Tammi, so there was competition insofar as Ashford and Simpson producing those songs, and us producing different songs, but theirs won out. We didn't produce the same songs."

Aretha Franklin

ATLANTIC 2518
WRITERS: ARETHA FRANKLIN, TED WHITE
PRODUCER: JERRY WEXLER
June 15, 1968 (3 weeks)

Lady Soul was wowing Europe when "Think" was released at the beginning of May 1968. She hit Paris like a hurricane ("C'est la nouvelle reine du blues," declared one critic) and recorded a live album at the city's Olympia Theatre on the evening of May 7. Five days later, she lifted the roof of London's Hammersmith Odeon with an equally dynamic show.

"The near-hysteria at the last concert at Hammersmith," declared a *Blues & Soul* review, "rivalled, if not surpassed, the reaction to the last concerts here by Otis Redding and the more recent Sam & Dave/Arthur Conley tour."

In the recording studio, Aretha Franklin had some of the best musicians available; on the road, that wasn't always the case. "When Aretha started and the politics were controlled by her husband [Ted White] at that time," observes Jerry Wexler, "her husband had control of a band led by some friend of his, a bebop trumpet player from Detroit. I don't know what the hell they were—second-rate jazzmen—but they were horrible."

Arranger Arif Mardin remembers that bandleader, too. "He would forget the charts, and things like that," he says. Nevertheless, Wexler acknowledges that Ted White never tried to get those musicians into the studio with Aretha. "They only played behind her on her gigs," he says, "and I was never interfered with. I was able to use all the best players."

Aretha's husband's influence extended beyond the choice of touring musicians—he shared the songwriter credits on "Think," just as he did on her previous Number One, "(Sweet Sweet Baby) Since You've Been Gone," and on "Dr. Feelgood (Love Is A Serious Business)," a transcendental track from her first Atlantic album.

"Think" was recorded in New York at the Atlantic studios on April 15, 1968. Aretha played piano on the track, with support from Spooner Oldham (organ), Roger Hawkins (drums), Tommy Cogbill and Jimmy Johnson (guitars), and Jerry Jemmott (bass).

The horn players, like the rhythm section, were imported from Memphis: Wayne Jackson (trumpet), Andrew Love and Charles Chalmers (tenor saxes), and Floyd Newman and Willie Bridges (baritone saxes). The background vocalists were the Sweet Inspirations.

Jerry Wexler recalls one highlight from the session—how bassman Cogbill spiced up the instrumentation with some guitar overdubs, which kick in as the song changes key. "After we finished [the track], Tommy said, 'There's like a little obligato I can do, a guitar obligato—listen to this.' I said, 'That's great, go ahead and do it.' Now, you listen to it carefully and if it isn't what I'm telling you, it's a damned close cousin: it's 'Dixie.' "

Twelve years later, "Think" made a surprise comeback by way of Hollywood. In John Belushi and Dan Aykroyd's *The Blues Brothers*, Aretha appeared as a soul food restaurant owner, advising her screen husband against rejoining Jake and Elwood Blues in their band ("You'd better *think*"). She sang a version of the song that almost matched the drive of the original—and was infinitely more entertaining than the automobile mayhem of the movie's climax.

59

I COULD NEVER LOVE ANOTHER (AFTER LOVING YOU)

The Temptations

GORDY 7072
WRITERS: NORMAN WHITFIELD, BARRETT STRONG, ROGER PENZABENE
PRODUCER: NORMAN WHITFIELD
July 6, 1968 (1 week)

It happened in Cleveland, Ohio, just before "I Could Never Love Another (After Loving You)" climbed to Number One: The Temptations fired David Ruffin.

"We drew up a legal document, which Melvin Franklin, Eddie Kendricks, Paul Williams, and I signed," wrote Otis Williams in his autobiography and history of the group, *Temptations* (Putnam, 1988). "It basically stated that David Ruffin was being relieved of all further responsibilities to the Temptations."

And so it was that "I Could Never Love Another" became the group's last single featuring Ruffin's heartbreaking lead. The song was written by Norman Whitfield and Barrett Strong with Roger Penzabene, a collaboration that had delivered the Temptations' previous smash [see 49—"I Wish It Would Rain"]. Strong recalls, "Roger was a nice person, and he had great ideas." He was also a victim, compelled by a miserable love life to commit suicide at the end of that year.

Probably recorded in Detroit at the beginning of '68, "I Could Never Love Another" was released in April in sync with the Temptations' ninth album, *Wish It Would Rain*. By the end of June, with the LP topping the R&B charts, Ruffin's ego pushed the group to the breaking point.

"I was fired in Cleveland after a show because I kept insisting I wanted to know what I was earning," Ruffin declared in an October press statement. Unintentionally, he affirmed the vanity that drove him out of the Temptations. "We are preparing to appeal to the Supreme Court," he said.

David Ruffin was not Motown's only headache that summer. Eddie Holland, Brian Holland, and Lamont Dozier had quit, and sued over royalties. Martha Reeves was in dispute with the company. And there were even rumors that Eddie Kendricks and Paul Williams were going to follow Ruffin out of the Temptations.

A senior Motown executive, Michael Roshkind, refuted such speculation. "David is a strong personality, multi-talented, and a great performer, so naturally he has made close friends in the group," he told *Billboard*. "But it's an ever-changing situation. To date, [the Temptations] are all together and have reached an understanding."

Such rifts would have been inconceivable 10 years earlier, when Ruffin was unknown. "He was brought up to Detroit by Eddie Bush, a guy who called himself David's manager at the time," says Billy Davis, who produced and wrote Ruffin's early singles for Anna and Checkmate in 1961–62. "David was like a shy kid, willing to do whatever you asked him to do. He could really sing, he always had that ability, and he could also dance very well." Nonetheless, even as "I Could Never Love Another (After Loving You)" was topping the R&B charts, he was out of a job.

60

GRAZING IN THE GRASS

Hugh Masekela

UNI 55066
WRITER: PHILEMON HOU
PRODUCER: STEWART LEVINE
July 13, 1968 (4 weeks)

"Get off my lawn, you bastard!" Producer Stewart Levine recalls hearing that command on an obscure African recording ("Mr. Bull No. 5") found by trumpeter Hugh Masekela during a trip to Zambia in the '60s. "It had this little guitar riff on it, and a cowbell," he explains. "The record started with this yell, as if the person were talking to a cow, then the guitar lick would come in."

It evidently made an impression. Masekela, Levine and actor/singer Philemon Hou reshaped "Mr. Bull No. 5" into "Grazing in the Grass," with all the locomotion of a loose-screwed steam engine rattling down a railroad track. "And the whole thing took half an hour," says the producer.

Originally from South Africa, Masekela met Levine while both attended the Manhattan School of Music in 1961. They became friends, then partners in Chisa Productions, through which Masekela's music was released in America.

He had two albums through Uni Records and was preparing a third, but the vibe wasn't good. "They wanted an African Herb Alpert," claims Levine, "and we were at odds with them. We more or less finished the album, and Uni heard it. They weren't thrilled, said we owed them another track.

"We were in the studio, finishing up, and I said to Hugh, 'We'd better do another song.' He said, 'Well, what do we do?' " And so, "Grazing in the Grass" was born, inspired by the curious recording from Zambia.

Philemon Hou delivered the melody. "We were cutting the rhythm track, figuring we'd come up with the tune later. Phil, who was not really a musician, hummed that line—and it just seemed to be the right melody at the right time."

Hugh Masekela

The session took place at Gold Star, the Hollywood studio used for a number of Phil Spector's "wall of sound" epics. "I liked the sound of the room," declares Levine. "It was very small, but it just had a great acoustical feel to it. There was an old beat-up desk, which the engineer used to kick when it went wrong."

Levine says the musicians behind Masekela included Bruce Langhorne on guitar ("a great folk and rock player"), Al Abreu on alto sax ("he had a lot to do with the record's sound"), and William Henderson on piano. "Basically, it was Hugh's band, plus a friend, Bruce, on guitar," says the producer. "That guitar was important, gave it an authentic feel."

"Grazing in the Grass" was "a bit of a spoof," Levine admits. "It was, 'You want another song, Uni? Here's a song.' But [label executive] Russ Regan, to his credit, said, 'This is a smash.' And about eight weeks later, the record was Number One."

Which probably only deepened the company's determination to make Masekela an African Alpert. "It was the kiss of death in a certain way," agrees Levine. "Before that, Hugh's career was moving along nicely, the albums were selling—and suddenly he becomes this pop star. 'Grazing' was a great piece of work, but we came out of jazz and were into doing lots of different things."

61

STAY IN MY CORNER

The Dells

CADET 5612
WRITERS: WADE FLEMONS, BOBBY MILLER, BARRETT STRONG
PRODUCER: BOBBY MILLER
August 10, 1968 (3 weeks)

"We've been blessed," declares Chuck Barksdale, a founding member of the Dells.

True enough. Few other groups have maintained as many original members. Few other groups have seen their life story told by Hollywood (*The Five Heartbeats*, directed by Robert Townsend). And *no* other group has a career spanning four decades of *Billboard*'s rhythm & blues charts, from the '50s ("Oh What a Nite") to the '90s ("A Heart Is a House for Love").

Clearly, the Dells have had help. According to Barksdale, those who deserve credit include Harvey Fuqua of the Moonglows, who gave them vocal training; Kirk Stewart, who taught them to sing jazz; Bobby Miller, who produced their finest '60s hits; and Charles Stepney, who arranged those same hits.

The Dells first waxed "Stay in My Corner" in 1964, 11 years after forming (as the El Rays) in Chicago. They were under contract to Vee-Jay Records, and their lineup comprised bassman Barksdale, tenors Johnny Carter and Verne Allison, baritone Michael McGill, and another baritone, Marvin Junior, who sang lead.

Barksdale says the group was encouraged to help Vee-Jay A&R chief Calvin Carter develop the company's roster of talent. "We used to have a little makeshift writing team," he remembers. "It helped us create a feel that was modeled after Motown, because Barrett Strong had come from Detroit and brought a lot of that musical influence over to Chicago. Bobby Miller was an out-of-tune guitar plucker who was aspiring to learn." And Flemons was a writer/performer who created a 1958 hit for himself on Vee-Jay, "Here I Stand."

Barksdale recalls that the idea for "Stay in My Corner" came from Flemons, that Miller shaped the lyrics, and that Strong made various contributions. The original Vee-Jay version was a top 30 R&B success in June 1965, and the song became a fixture of the Dells' live act. A couple of years later, they were looking for material to record in the wake of "O-o, I Love You," their first hit for that other pillar of Chicago music, Chess Records.

"We needed another song to fill up some space on the album," explains Barksdale. "We already had the charts for 'Stay in My Corner,' so Charles Stepney just took it and augmented it with strings, and so on."

Recorded at Chess in January 1968, the new model of "Stay in My Corner" was a six-minute masterwork, as bold as anything produced by Motown or Phil Spector. The white heat of the Dells' doo-wop harmonies was fused with Marvin Junior's powerful, soulful lead and Johnny Carter's laser-sharp falsetto. Behind them was the musicianship of Phil Upchurch on guitar, Louis Satterfield on bass, and Morris Jennings on drums; the string section featured members of the Chicago Symphony Orchestra.

Chess lifted the song from the Dells' *There Is* album, pressing the full six minutes and 10 seconds onto a Cadet single in June. "We went to England and Germany," says Barksdale, "and by the time we got back, reporters were coming up to us, wanting to know how we felt about having a major hit. We said, 'What are you talking about?' By the time we got to sit down with the record company, it was busting open the top 20."

62

YOU'RE ALL I NEED TO GET BY

Marvin Gaye & Tammi Terrell

TAMLA 54169
WRITERS: NICKOLAS ASHFORD, VALERIE SIMPSON
PRODUCERS: NICKOLAS ASHFORD, VALERIE SIMPSON
August 31, 1968 (5 weeks)

Marvin Gaye, a restless spirit, seemed to find sanctuary (or, at least, satisfaction) in his Tammi Terrell duets and in the teamwork involved, first with Johnny Bristol and Harvey Fuqua as producers, then with Nick Ashford and Valerie Simpson [see 57—"Ain't Nothing Like the Real Thing"].

"Marvin was always cooperative with us," says Bristol. "He and Harvey were the best of friends. The four of us were like a little family thing, people who liked each other, because Harvey and Marvin and myself were married into the same family. There was a lot of kidding and laughing, which took away the tensions of recording."

Likewise, Ashford and Simpson recall those sessions as high-spirited and enjoyable. "They worked well together," tells Ashford. "They made things easy. Marvin was just full of jokes—although they weren't that funny! I used to say, 'Marvin, why don't you get some jokes that make me laugh?' "

Initially, the couple provided their songs in the form of demos. "I remember when we started, I wasn't thinking of Marvin and Tammi, I was just thinking of the songs," says Ashford. Later, the material was tailored to fit. "I would always sing Marvin's part very straight, with no frills, so I wouldn't be embarrassed when he sang."

Gaye and Terrell generally cut their vocals together, at Motown's Detroit studios. "At that time, tracks were limited," says Ashford. "If you got two good vocals, you were happy." The writers sang backup on the records; Simpson played piano. "That's the way we envisioned the song when we wrote it, so [the piano] was usually the foundation that kind of cued the feeling," she states.

The foundation—and the feeling—originated with gospel music. Ashford met Simpson in church, after all, and "You're All I Need to Get By" contains a spiritual subtext. "I had no doubt that some of our background would creep into the music," Ashford says. "So much soul comes out of the Baptist church, it's so embedded in you. You could go out any minute and turn the sweetest ballad into a gospel song if you felt real good about it."

The tragic side of these soaring pop spirituals lay in Tammi Terrell's illness. The young singer had been suffering from severe headaches, and during a 1967 show with Gaye in Virginia, she collapsed onstage. The ailment was subsequently diagnosed as a brain tumor, requiring hospitalization and frequent surgery over the next few years.

"When I learned just how sick she was, I cried," Marvin Gaye told biographer David Ritz. "Love seemed cruel to me. Love was a lie. Tammi was the victim of the violent side of love—at least that's how it felt. I have no first-hand knowledge of what really killed her, but it was a deep vibe, as though she was dying for everyone who couldn't find love."

Terrell succumbed on March 16, 1970, at age 24. The funeral service was held in Philadelphia, her hometown, at the Methodist church where she once sang in the choir. Marvin Gaye was among the mourners.

63

SAY IT LOUD—I'M BLACK AND I'M PROUD (PART 1)

James Brown

KING 6187
WRITERS: JAMES BROWN, ALFRED ELLIS
PRODUCER: JAMES BROWN
October 5, 1968 (6 weeks)

"Hail, James Brown," declared *Billboard* in an April 1968 editorial, soon after the singer went on TV and radio to help douse the flames ignited by the

James Brown

assassination of Dr. Martin Luther King. "Brown is a credit to his race, his profession and his country," the magazine wrote.

It wasn't a unanimous view. Brown was criticized by some in the black community for his patriotic rap, "America Is My Home," and for his endorsement of Democratic presidential candidate Hubert Humphrey. In *The Godfather of Soul* (Macmillan, 1986), Brown even told of a hand grenade deposited outside his hotel room the night he was due to cut "Say It Loud—I'm Black and I'm Proud." He implied that it was left by black militants.

At the time, JB was in southern California. "Say It Loud" was recorded on August 7, 1968, at the Vox studios in Van Nuys. His band had been through important personnel changes, with youngbloods replacing longtime veterans.

Bass player Bernard Odum was succeeded by Charles (Sweets) Sherrell; trumpeter Joe Dupars was replaced by Richard (Kush) Griffith; and trombone player Levi Rasbury gave way to Fred Wesley, who became "a real innovator and a real creator as an arranger," according to Brown.

"Say It Loud" was their first recording date with him. The rest of the band that night comprised Clyde Stubblefield on drums and Jimmy Nolen on guitar, and, in the horn section, trumpeter Waymon

Reed and tenor saxmen Maceo Parker and St. Clair Pinckney. Alto player Alfred "Pee Wee" Ellis was the bandleader.

The Vox studio was large: The players and James set up like a live show to be able to see each other's cues—critical for the "UNH!" intro, which begins on the original session tape without so much as a countdown. The same applied to the tune's changes and vamps, cited by Brown's screams (*"ooo-wee, you're killin' me"*). Ellis kept his eyes glued to the man, careful not to miss a hand signal or body move.

Knowing that "Say It Loud—I'm Black and I'm Proud" would be crucial to the nation's mood that summer, Brown organized the record's release within two weeks of the Vox session. Barely a week after that, on August 26, he was clarifying the song's intent to a Dallas concert audience:

"You know, one way of solving a lot of problems that we've got in this country is lettin' a person feel that they're important, feel that they're somebody. And a man can't get himself together until he knows who he is, and be proud of who he is and where he comes from.

"Now I've just recorded a tune called 'Say It Loud, I'm Black and I'm Proud.' If a man is not proud of who he is and where he comes from, he's not a man. So I want each and everyone to understand: This tune is for the good of what it means and what it can do for a man's self-pride."

Brown then asked the audience to chant along in the chorus, blacks during the "I'm black" part, "everybody" during the "proud" part. "A little love won't hurt," he added. Then he turned to the band ("you ready?") and tore the roof off. Afterward, he said, "The atmosphere seems so clean now. We can really get together now."

64

HEY, WESTERN UNION MAN

Jerry Butler

MERCURY 72850
WRITERS: KENNY GAMBLE,
LEON HUFF, JERRY BUTLER
PRODUCERS: KENNY GAMBLE, LEON HUFF
November 16, 1968 (1 week)

Call it one of music's ironies. The singer who helped to propel the Philadelphia sound into orbit, Jerry Butler, is usually associated with Chicago. That's certainly where he made his first recording, "For Your Precious Love," a 1958 soul milestone with the Impressions.

Ten years later, a solo star, Butler journeyed to Philadelphia to work with an upwardly mobile pair of writers and producers, Kenny Gamble and Leon Huff. "For most of my career up to that point," he says, "I had been the singer of ballads. 'Hey, Western Union Man' was the first kind of an uptempo tune I really had any kind of success with. It was such an awesome kind of a groove. Driving back to Chicago, my brother Billy and I played it in the car all the way home. We knew it was special."

Butler recalls meeting Gamble and Huff in 1966 in Philadelphia, where Gamble managed a club on Broad Street called Peps. "I was performing there the night that he and Huff came in and caught the show," says Butler. "They had just been successful with the Intruders, so when they introduced themselves and told me what they did, I said, 'Man, I was just listening to that record by the Intruders—what a fresh, interesting sound.'

"They returned the compliment by saying they used to come to the Uptown Theater to catch my show, and saying how it would be wonderful if we could do some things together. So the next morning, we came back to the club, around noon, sat at the piano on the stage of Peps, and started to write some songs."

Two of Butler's compositions with Gamble and Huff, "Lost" and "Never Give You Up," were R&B hits for the singer in 1968. A third was "Hey, Western Union Man," cut at Philadelphia's Cameo-Parkway studios on July 9, 1968.

Gamble and Huff produced; Bobby Martin was the arranger. "The song was kind of put together out of an idea that Kenny had, about a singing telegram," Butler explains. "Western Union telegrams have always had a fascination for people. They always open them, because they're always important, are usually urgent—and most times are bearers of bad news.

"Kenny said, 'Who is going to turn down Western Union, especially a singing Western Union, with somebody pouring their heart out?' So that was the whole concept behind the song."

The musicians were the crew that Gamble and Huff had been developing for all their Philadelphia work, according to Butler. "Bobby Martin, Thom Bell, Linda Creed—all the people who formed that nucleus that became Mighty Three Music and the Sound of Philadelphia—were there," he says. Others at the core were Norman Harris and Roland Chambers on guitars, Ronnie Baker on bass, Earl Young on drums, and Vince Montana on vibes.

"They had succeeded in duplicating, in some fashion, what Motown had done in Detroit: accumulating a group of arrangers, artists, musicians, singers and songwriters, who all kind of felt—and *were*—the energy of the sound of Philadelphia," concludes Butler. And that energy powered "Hey, Western Union Man" all the way to the top of the R&B charts.

WHO'S MAKIN' LOVE

Johnnie Taylor

STAX 0009
WRITERS: HOMER BANKS, BETTYE CRUTCHER, DON DAVIS, RAYMOND JACKSON
PRODUCER: DON DAVIS
November 23, 1968 (3 weeks)

When Otis Redding died on December 10, 1967, the torch was passed to a new generation at Stax Records, embodied by Johnnie Taylor.

Well, perhaps not to a new generation—Taylor was actually three years *older* than Otis—but certainly to a new custodian. With "Who's Makin' Love," the gospel-grounded singer from Crawfordsville, Arkansas, emerged as Stax's most successful singles artist. That hit alone became the biggest-selling release in the company's history, and Taylor followed it with 16 consecutive top 20 R&B records between 1968 and 1974. A dozen gained entry to the top ten, and three reached Number One.

"Irrespective of Otis, Johnnie's growth would also have been realized," says Al Bell, former president of Stax. "No one really inherited [Redding's] position, and I don't think anybody would have wanted it. That was a void we chose to leave empty—a space that could not be filled."

Bell knew Taylor, he says, "from the days he was singing with the Highway QCs, when they brought him into the Soul Stirrers to replace Sam [Cooke]." Johnnie signed to Cooke's Sar Records in 1960 as one of the Soul Stirrers, then recorded solo. After Cooke's death, Taylor dropped by Stax, according to Bell, "when he was visiting relatives in West Memphis. He came to talk to me, about how he hadn't really gotten his shot at Sar because Sam was so dominant, and how he really wanted to step out on his own."

Taylor really stepped out when Bell put the singer together with producer and former Motown session player Don Davis. "I was trying to develop a cross-fertilization between Memphis and Detroit," says Bell. "I was trying to get me a hybrid."

He got "Who's Makin' Love" through Davis and three Stax songwriters, Homer Banks, Bettye Crutcher, and Raymond Jackson. "Mr. Davis came and heard the song one day in the studio," recalls Banks, "and he said, 'I would love to cut that on Johnnie Taylor.' "

Banks confirms that the bold lyrics of "Who's Makin' Love" had deterred several Stax producers. "Some staff members felt the song had a little too much gospel in it. Some others thought the lyrics were, well, immoral." Neither concern bothered Davis or Taylor, however. "Johnnie pretty well knew where to take the song. With my gospel background, I knew he would get into that kind of feel." Banks's own voice can be heard on the record, shadowing Taylor's.

The basic rhythm track was cut with Stax musicians, including Steve Cropper and Raymond Jackson, as well as Davis himself. "Don played guitar," says Cropper. "There were three guitars on that. I think Don took it back to Detroit and did some overdubs, but the track was definitely cut at Stax."

Homer Banks felt it was a certain smash "because somehow it had the pulse that people would get into," he says. "The record was kind of revolutionary, pretty radical at that time." The power-packed rhythm track, Taylor's expressive vocals, and the lyric content proved a potent combination.

"I shall never forget the debates and questions we had in there [about the song]," concludes Al Bell. "Everyone was saying, 'I don't know, man, that's a pretty rough lyric.' I said, 'No, we've got to have it.' And compared to today's music, it's like Sunday school."

66

I HEARD IT THROUGH THE GRAPEVINE

Marvin Gaye

TAMLA 54176
WRITERS: NORMAN WHITFIELD, BARRETT STRONG
PRODUCER: NORMAN WHITFIELD
December 14, 1968 (7 weeks)

If anything deserved to be called the Devil's work, it was the tom-toms of Richard "Pistol" Allen in "I Heard It Through the Grapevine," resonating alongside the beat laid down by Uriel Jones, the rattlesnake tambourine of Jack Ashford, and the white heat of Marvin Gaye's voice.

Yet the recording was not, at first, judged good enough for release; only a producer's persistence reversed that decision. Norman Whitfield was that producer, and Barrett Strong his collaborator. Whitfield explains, "We took a lot of time, a lot of pain and strain to try to make it really custom. It was patterned somewhat after a Ray Charles–type feeling. It was very different than most of the Motown records, and it was something that Barrett and I were very proud of."

Whitfield is referring to Gaye's version, even though the Miracles were, in fact, the first to cut the song around 1966, followed by the Isley Brothers, then Gaye, and Gladys Knight & the Pips [see 46].

By Whitfield's account, he recorded Marvin on the song in the first half of 1967. He recalls bringing it into one of Motown's product evaluation meetings, chaired by Berry Gordy. "Brian and Eddie Holland and Lamont Dozier had a song [on Marvin] called 'Your Unchanging Love,' and they were hot at the time.

"Berry would usually give the benefit of the doubt to the person who was hot with a particular artist, or give them the edge if it was a very close vote. But the vote wasn't close at all; matter of fact, the vote was something like 37 to three in favor of 'I Heard It Through the Grapevine.' "

Nevertheless, Gordy favored "Your Unchanging Love." Whitfield comments, "It was like I came up with this mystical, magical thing out of nowhere, and it was like, 'Well, do we nourish the up-and-coming guy or do we continue to deal with our blue-chip people?' "

The producer was disappointed, but not daunted. He sought permission to cut it on another artist: "I hounded Berry until he was very angry with me." And until Gordy capitulated. So Whitfield got to produce the song on Gladys Knight & the Pips, whose version became a crossover giant. Soon afterwards, he says, the Motown chief told him, "I don't know what you've got, son, but I'm very proud of you, because you really stuck up and fought for what you really feel is a winner."

Whitfield fought for his song again in 1968, when Motown was assembling a Marvin Gaye LP. "I just wanted to get it in the album," he says. The head of quality control, Billie Jean Brown, eventually agreed: "I Heard It Through the Grapevine" was added to *In the Groove*.

Next, Chicago called. Former Motown marketing executive Phil Jones remembers hearing from E. Rodney Jones at the city's influential WVON, about a track on the album. "He told me, 'I played the record at the hop, and they went crazy. I put it on the air here last night, and the phones lit up.' "

Jones continues, "I went to quality control. Billie Jean said, 'Phil, I scraped the bottom of the can to get this.' Yet within a couple of days, Ernie Leaner at United Record Distributors [in Chicago] ordered 100,000 copies. I told Norman Whitfield, and he said, 'See, I told you, Phil, it's the tom-toms.' "

Marvin Gaye

67

CAN I CHANGE MY MIND

Tyrone Davis

DAKAR 602
WRITERS: BARRY DESPENZA, CARL WOLFOLK
PRODUCER: WILLIE HENDERSON
February 1, 1969 (3 weeks)

With its locomotive brass and spiralling guitar riff, "Can I Change My Mind" barreled onto the national best-sellers chart from Chicago and set Tyrone Davis onto a long-term career path of sophisticated soul crooning.

A Southerner transplanted to Chicago, Davis toiled as valet and chauffeur for bluesman Freddy King in the early '60s, then began singing semi-professionally at various Windy City clubs. National Casting, a steel mill, provided his day job.

After some local recording efforts, Davis was inked to ABC Records by Barry Despenza, the label's Midwest A&R director. It was Despenza who got the idea for "Can I Change My Mind," while relaxing at a South Side lounge called Peyton Place. He remembers scribbling the lyrics on a cocktail napkin even as saxman Monk Higgins was onstage.

The next day, Despenza enlisted the help of guitarist Carl Wolfolk to finish the song. "We were sitting there, playing," says Despenza, "and we finally got it to fit together, and who walks in but Tyrone. He said, 'Ooh, baby, let me have that song, it sounds great. Who's it for?' "

Despenza had been thinking of Bobby Rush, whom he had also signed to ABC. "Tyrone had horrible timing—he just couldn't keep time—so it was a toss-up between him and Bobby. But Bobby was more of a talk singer, and I knew he'd never be able to handle it, so I said, 'OK, Tyrone, the song is yours.' "

The song, yes. His deal with ABC, no longer. The label had decided to fire Despenza and let Davis go. Only the intervention of the singer's manager, Wally Roker, rescued "Can I Change My Mind." Despenza remembers, "Wally said, 'I'm going to pay for a session on Tyrone, and we'll do it on an independent label if ABC doesn't take it.' "

Davis cut the song (with a Monk Higgins arrangement) in Los Angeles at Ray Charles's Tangerine studios, "but ABC didn't want it," says Despenza. "They kept the tape but weren't going to release it."

Back in Chicago, Tyrone struck a deal with Carl Davis of Brunswick Records and began laying down material—including a fresh version of "Can I Change My Mind"—at the city's Universal studios. Willie Henderson was producing, with Quinton Joseph (drums), Floyd Morris (piano), Bernard Reed (bass), Mighty Joe Young (rhythm guitar), and Carl Wolfolk (lead guitar) among the sidemen.

There were no strings and no female background vocals on the remake. "It really was a cheaper version," says Despenza, "but that's what was called for. And that guitar sticking out there is Carl Wolfolk."

"A Woman Needs to Be Loved" was chosen as the topside of Tyrone's debut on Dakar (a Brunswick offshoot), but record buyers reacted to the flip: "Can I Change My Mind." Houston disc jockey Wild Child playlisted it after hearing his five-year-old son jamming the song at home—and his station request lines went crazy. "It shocked the hell out of Chicago when Houston came through on the other side," concludes Despenza.

68

EVERYDAY PEOPLE

Sly & the Family Stone

EPIC 10407
WRITER: SYLVESTER STEWART
PRODUCER: SLY STONE
February 22, 1969 (2 weeks)

San Francisco's got a shop that does nothing but repair automatic transmissions: That's Triple-A Transmissions at 925 Golden Gate Avenue. At Triple-A, you get a complete automatic transmission overhaul for just $99.50, with nothing down. If all your car needs is a simple adjustment, mention my name, Sylvester...uh, Sly Stone, and the cost is just $3.95."

It's commercial time at soul-formatted KSOL in Oakland, California, circa 1965. The DJ's tripped tongue reveals the true identity of a man who would soon rewrite the rules of rhythm & blues. With rock licks slammed into soul grooves, doo-wop tricks jammed into psychedelic moves, Sly & the Family Stone would emerge as one of popular music's most influential comets.

Sly salt 'n' peppered his music while riding the mid-'60s airwaves. "He would play all kinds of stuff," declares Larry Graham, who was bass player with the Family Stone. "And if you were celebrating something, Sly would sing personally to you over the air, 'cause he had a piano at the studio. So he would maybe make up a little song for you, include your name it."

The "family" coalesced in 1966 in San Francisco: Stone (keyboards), Graham (bass), Freddie Stone (guitar), Cynthia Robinson (trumpet), Greg Errico (drums), and Jerry Martini (sax). Later, pianist Rosie Stone joined. "Even before we went into the studio, we were having great success doing live shows," says Graham. "For example, Winchester Cathedral in

Sly & the Family Stone

Redwood City—people would come and check us out there, and just be knocked out. You could tell from the audience, there was something special about this band."

When they did begin recording, for Epic, Sly's experience (he had earlier produced top 40 hits by Bobby Freeman and the Beau Brummels) and the group's integrated innovation was magic. "We had creative freedom, and you could hear it in the music," says Graham. "Sly was witty with words, he would live up to his name. He had a very unique way of putting things."

"Dance to the Music" was the band's first hit, but "Everyday People" was their first *monster*, beating a path through the chart jungle with the help of a single bass note. "It was like the first time that I would be playing one note for the whole song," declares Graham. "I hadn't realized yet how my style of playing—thumping and plucking—was going to change some things musically."

Others in the band were trendsetting, too. "Greg Errico certainly had a very unique way of playing the drums," says Graham. "If you allowed him to do what he does, then you'd come up with things like 'Everyday People.' That wasn't your everyday drum beat. But with him doing what he did, and my bass part going with that, it kind of all clicked."

69

GIVE IT UP OR TURNIT A LOOSE

James Brown

KING 6213
WRITER: CHARLES BOBBITT
PRODUCER: JAMES BROWN
March 8, 1969 (2 weeks)

James Brown was *busy* in January 1969. He was publicizing a new fast-food restaurant chain, Gold Platter Inc., which bore his endorsement. America's incoming President, Richard Nixon, had invited him to play at the inaugural ball. And King Records was shipping his first single of the year, "Give It Up or Turnit a Loose."

Brown was an advocate of black capitalism, and saw Gold Platter as "dedicated to the objective of providing investment and job opportunities for members of minority races." Later that same year, he sealed a deal giving him ownership of Augusta radio station WRDW—where he had once polished shoes out front.

The singer was proud of that purchase. In his autobiography, *James Brown* (Macmillan, 1986), he wrote, "See, shining shoes has a lot of meanings for Afro-Americans, especially *this* Afro-American, because I actually did it.

"When the B'nai B'rith gave me their Humanitarian Award for 1969, I carried a shoeshine box with me to their award ceremony. 'You made it possible for me not to have to carry a shoeshine box,' I said in my speech, 'but I carried the box just the same.' " And so WDRW became part of JB Broadcasting, alongside stations in Knoxville, Tennessee, and Baltimore.

JB's primary source of economic muscle, of course, was music. He was fresh from two smash hits in late '68, "Say It Loud—I'm Black and I'm Proud" [see 63] and the blues ballad "Goodbye My Love."

"Give It Up or Turnit a Loose" was rhythmically complex, but not as taut as Brown's previous few tunes—as if the musicians doubted their destination. The weak horns in the beginning prompt his command, "Start it over again." After that, he cues them with a precise *"Hunh!"*

The session took place on October 29, 1968, at Miami's Criteria Studios. The rhythm section comprised Charles Sherrell on bass, Nate Jones on drums, and guitarists Jimmy Nolen and "Country" Kellum.

Brown exhorted his band on almost every record, and Sherrell says various studio instructions—like a "no-no-no-no-no" directed from Brown to Sherrell—weren't due to audible mistakes. He says that JB, facing the band as usual, "saw us lean into getting ready for the chord changes. But for him it wasn't the right time, and he waved us off."

"Give It Up or Turnit a Loose" was issued three months later, with a scream spliced onto the front for added excitement. Its authorship was credited to Charles Bobbit, one of Brown's managers.

Yet the song was never played the same way again. Hot-wired with a new arrangement, it stayed in the JB stage repertoire for years, unlike "Cold Sweat" or "Say It Loud—I'm Black and I'm Proud," among others. It was a favorite especially of The J.B.'s (Mark I, the Bootsy era), whose recorded studio take of the song was a highlight of Brown's *Sex Machine* LP, overdubbed applause and all.

Soon after drafting the youngbloods in March 1970, James performed a radically fresh version of "Give It Up or Turnit a Loose" onstage in Virginia. Former JB tour director Alan Leeds explained the scenario in notes with 1991's *Star Time* reissue: "I asked Brown about it afterward. 'Oh, that's my new tune,' he said. I didn't understand how a two-year-old record could be his 'new' tune, but all Brown would offer was, 'Wait until we get to Nashville tomorrow. You'll see.' "

Leeds saw when the band assembled in the Starday-King studios on April 25, 1970. "Sure enough, there were the licks I'd heard in 'Give It Up.' Only this time, the song was named 'Get Up (I Feel Like Being A) Sex Machine.' "

Once again, a simple groove had been transformed into a gold platter.

70

RUN AWAY CHILD, RUNNING WILD

The Temptations

GORDY 7084
WRITERS: NORMAN WHITFIELD, BARRETT STRONG
PRODUCER: NORMAN WHITFIELD
March 22, 1969 (2 weeks)

An earthquake rumbled under Motown Records in 1968, exposing a series of fissures in the family firm. Eddie Holland, Brian Holland, and Lamont Dozier departed in an acrimonious dispute over money. David Ruffin was fired from the Temptations. Turmoil struck Martha Reeves and the Vandellas. And the corporate atmosphere of the company's new headquarters in downtown Detroit subverted the camaraderie of its original home on West Grand Boulevard.

Yet when the dust settled, Motown finished the year with the top three records in the country (including Marvin Gaye's multi-million monster, "I Heard It Through the Grapevine") and two more in the top ten.

Instead of burying Berry Gordy's business, the '68 upheavals reshaped its work force. Norman Whitfield, for one, grew in stature—with Holland/ Dozier/ Holland gone, that was inevitable—and harnessed some of the other creative forces pulsing through popular music. The rock 'n' R&B fusion of Sly & the Family Stone influenced Whitfield, and he propelled the Temptations into their "psychedelic phase."

This coincided with David Ruffin's exit. His replacement, Dennis Edwards, had industrial-strength gravel in his voice—perfect for the declamatory, swirling currents of "Cloud Nine," Whitfield's first production with the reborn Temptations.

"His choice of instrumentation," noted the group's Otis Williams in *Temptations* (Putnam, 1988), "was also radical for Motown: heavy electric guitars using effects like wah-wah pedals, different rhythms and background-vocal arrangements where each of us sang different lines and parts, rather than doing the monolithic 'aah' and 'doo' patterns."

The guitarist whose electricity powered "Cloud Nine" was Dennis Coffey, recruited from Motown's Detroit competition, Ric Tic Records. And Whitfield began to use other Motor City players to expand his musical vocabulary, including bassist Bob Babbitt and drummer Uriel Jones. "Norman was a little ahead of his time," said Motown bandleader Earl Van Dyke.

"Cloud Nine" affirmed the promise of the producer's new direction, grabbing chart peaks in R&B and pop between December '68 and January '69—and

Motown's first Grammy award. The follow-up was even more radical, unveiled in full (clocking in at a lengthy 9:38!) on the Temptations' *Cloud Nine* album.

Whitfield's writing partner, Barrett Strong, recalls the creative process behind "Run Away Child, Running Wild": "You read about [runaways] and you hear these things as a child, as you grow up. You might know some kids in school who had these same problems, so these sort of things pop into your mind, and it just becomes a subject. That was primarily how Norman saw it; he thought this might be pretty interesting to do.

"Plus the Temps were such creative people themselves. They would say, 'Let's try this, let's try that.' They were great to work with. You see, the thing is, if you have a great producer like Norman Whitfield, who knows what he's doing, and if you have good songs and great artists, there's nothing to question."

71

ONLY THE STRONG SURVIVE

Jerry Butler

MERCURY 72898
WRITERS: KENNY GAMBLE, LEON HUFF, JERRY BUTLER
PRODUCERS: KENNY GAMBLE, LEON HUFF
April 5, 1969 (2 weeks)

The song recognized as the most successful of Jerry Butler's career—and the crown jewel of his landmark album, *The Iceman Cometh*—provokes a chuckle from the singer himself. "It was not one of the tunes from the session that we thought was going to be big," he says.

"Only the Strong Survive" was neither the lead-off song of the album nor its lead-out. "It was stuck somewhere in the middle," the singer comments. "If you've been around the record industry for a long time, you know never to stick what you feel would potentially be a hit in the middle."

Butler had cut "Only the Strong Survive" on September 8, 1968. It was done at Sigma Sound, Philadelphia, with musicians who had backed him before [see 64—"Hey, Western Union Man"]. Another song from that same session was chosen as his next single, while producers Kenny Gamble and Leon Huff assembled the album that was to be *The Iceman Cometh*.

"The unique thing is that when I took the album home and played it for my wife," recalls Butler, "the song she locked into right away was 'Only the Strong Survive.' Then there was a guy doing radio in Houston, Charlie Brown, who started playing the song every night, kind of as a sign-off, because he and his girlfriend were having some problems.

"I went down there to do an engagement—it was at Prairie View College—and the kid who picked me up at the airport wanted to know if I was going to sing 'Only the Strong Survive.' Well, I was unprepared, and I hadn't added it to my show. He said, 'If you don't sing it, you don't leave Prairie View, Texas—you're just going to be a spot of dirt here.' So we did a quick rehearsal on it, got the musicians to take a good listen to the record, and we sang it that night. Once it got started, everybody there sang it for us. That's how we discovered it."

The song itself originated from a conversation between Gamble, Huff, and Butler, which the singer recalls taking place at the Mercury Records offices in New York. "We were having a corned beef sandwich, messing around with the piano. And we got to talking about Aretha and Ray Charles and Otis Redding, because at that time the music was starting to change.

"Huff said, 'Only the strong survive,' and Kenny went, 'What a great idea for a song.' Then I said, 'You know, when I was a kid, my mother used to tell me this poem by Rudyard Kipling: "If you can keep your head while all about you/Are losing theirs and blaming it on

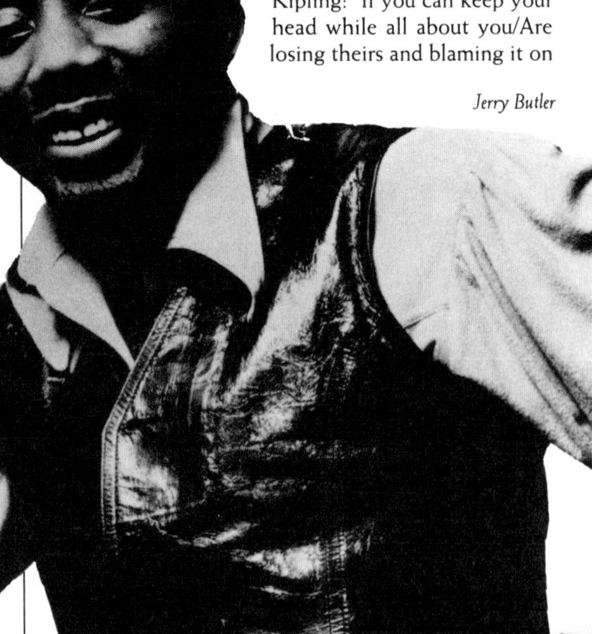

Jerry Butler

you." ' And out of that basically came the whole idea [for the song]."

Musically, Huff's contribution was vital, declares Butler. "I always used to say that Huff wrote the arrangement the way he played the piano, and all that happened then was that Bobby Martin or Thom Bell would take what he had played, and put it into different segments of the orchestra. That was why Huff was so strong, and why he could use almost any musicians to capture the sound. He was the holder of the key."

72

IT'S YOUR THING

The Isley Brothers

T-NECK 901
WRITERS: O'KELLY ISLEY,
RONALD ISLEY, RUDOLPH ISLEY
PRODUCERS: THE ISLEY BROTHERS
April 19, 1969 (4 weeks)

The week in April 1956 when Ron, Rudy, and O'Kelly Isley stepped aboard a Greyhound bus in Cincinnati, bound for New York, Little Richard's "Long Tall Sally" ruled the *Billboard* R&B charts.

Thirteen years later, to the week, the Isleys Brothers ruled the very same charts with "It's Your Thing." With its Sly Stone–influenced groove and Stax-soaked horns, the record was a watershed for the trio, and also for a couple of the Isleys' younger siblings, Ernie and Marvin.

"Basically, Ronald wrote the song," recounts Marvin, "and he came in one day and kind of showed us the idea. He said, 'When the band gets here tomorrow, I want you guys to show them the song.' So we did that."

Ernie Isley did more. "There was another bass player supposed to play," he explains, "but he didn't play with the same feeling that we had in rehearsal, so at the last minute, they said, 'Ernie, you play.' I was scared to death, but it worked." Ernie was just 17.

The session took place in January 1969 at New York's A&R Studios, with musicians from Wilson Pickett's road band, the Midnight Movers. The blistering lead guitar belonged to Charles Pitts Jr. (who later played the distinctive wah-wah guitar on Isaac Hayes's "Shaft"), the piano was in the hands of Herb Rooney (a friend of O'Kelly Isley), and the drummer was George Morland. The arrangement was handled by George Patterson, who also played alto sax.

In creating the song, lead vocalist Ron Isley was influenced by the sounds of Stax. Says Ernie, "It was a funk-licking guitar line, a funk-licking bass, a funk-licking drums. It had a little bit of everything, and 'It's your thing' was a hip saying at the time, like 'Sock it to me' or whatever. It tied in all that, as well as a little double entendre. And then it was danceable on top of that."

The record was released on the Isleys' own T-Neck label via Buddah Records, which had signed them after they left Motown in December 1968. Yet soon after "It's Your Thing" became a smash, Motown sued the group, claiming it was recorded a month before they obtained their contractual release.

Later, a judge concluded that the Isleys made a second recording of the song in January 1969, and failed to submit the original tape to Motown as agreed in their contract. The verdicts went back and forth. In the spring of 1975, a jury ruled in favor of the Isleys; in the fall, a judge reversed that result, and ordered a new trial.

Two years later, another jury accepted independent testimony that "It's Your Thing" was cut after the brothers left Motown, and ruled accordingly. Finally, a federal judge upheld that verdict and settled the case.

Ernie Isley recalls asking brother Ron why they didn't make the record at Motown. "Ronald said, 'Because it would have been done differently, with a different arrangement.' And he said that there was a certain way they wanted the song to go, and a certain direction they wanted their career to go in."

73

THE CHOKIN' KIND

Joe Simon

SOUND STAGE 7 2628
WRITER: HARLAN HOWARD
PRODUCER: JOHN RICHBOURG
May 17, 1969 (3 weeks)

One of the biggest crossover hits of the early '60s was "Busted" by Ray Charles, a country song remade into rhythm & blues. It was composed by celebrated Nashville writer Harlan Howard, whose catalog included "I Got to Pieces," "Heartaches by the Number," and "I've Got a Tiger by the Tail."

Howard had been introduced to Charles about a year before "The Chokin' Kind" was successful for Joe Simon. "Ray had sung 'Busted' in some nightclub in Nashville," he says, "and when I met him afterwards, he asked me to send him another hit. I sent him 'The Chokin' Kind.' "

Charles didn't respond, however, leaving the field clear for Joe Simon, another artist who could spin country copyrights into soul gold. Howard's only complaint about Simon's version of "The Chokin' Kind" was that he changed the mood. "I liked Joe's record and appreciated it," he says, "but something was lost in translation: my song was sad."

Simon, who was certainly capable of being melancholy, loved country music. "It's tellin' it like it is, just like in gospel music," he once declared. "It really is very close in its background to gospel." That's how he was musically raised, first in Louisiana, then in California.

The singer's first national recognition came in 1965 through "Let's Do It Over," cut with Rick Hall in Muscle Shoals. Then he signed to Sound Stage 7 Records, an imprint of Nashville's Monument label. "John Richbourg was producing Joe," recalls Howard. "He came over and wanted to hear some of my songs. I played some favorites, and he heard 'The Chokin' Kind,' and cut it with white musicians in Nashville."

True enough: Richbourg worked at Music City Recorders with such players as Tim Drummond on bass, Mac Gayden and Troy Seals on guitars, Bob Wilson on piano, and Kenny Buttrey on drums. "Nashville doesn't get much credit for making R&B and pop records," says Howard, "but there have been more than most people think."

The original of "The Chokin' Kind" was made by Waylon Jennings. "Waylon and I are close friends," tells Howard, "and he heard that song in the office while I was putting it down on a guitar one morning. 'Man,' he said, 'I want that.' "

The writer says his songs usually reflect his life. Two years before penning "The Chokin' Kind," Howard was divorced "from some lady who was a little more sophisticated than me, a little more uptown. The song was about the difference [between us] and how she tried to change me."

Joe Simon went on to record other titles by Howard, including "Baby, Don't Be Looking in My Mind" (the follow-up to "The Chokin' Kind") and another top ten hit, "Yours Love," in 1970. Says the songwriter, "John Richbourg had me come over and I'd hang out for an hour or two with Joe once in a while. He was a good singer."

74

TOO BUSY THINKING ABOUT MY BABY

Marvin Gaye

TAMLA 54181

WRITERS: NORMAN WHITFIELD, JANIE BRADFORD, BARRETT STRONG

PRODUCER: NORMAN WHITFIELD

June 7, 1969 (6 weeks)

Marvin Gaye's "I Heard It Through the Grapevine" inhabited a time and place of its own—dark, shrouded, painful—and writer/producer Norman Whitfield knew better than to attempt a second landing there. Instead, he charted a follow-up course to the lighter, brighter atmosphere of Motown's school days.

"Too Busy Thinking About My Baby" was auditioned first on the Temptations album *Gettin' Ready*. Theirs was a '66 swing treatment, its gossamer lead by Eddie Kendricks blessed with all the charm of Sam Cooke's "Wonderful World." Those were carefree days: Kendricks aching to see his girl "once I get out of class," just as Cooke had resigned himself to not being an "A student."

"That was just a lyric, basically," says songwriter Janie Bradford. "I took it to Norman, and he and Barrett came up with the melody. It was nothing special, because we all kind of hung around and wrote; whoever was there, we grabbed and worked with them and whatever."

Bradford has no cause for modesty. As co-author of "Money (That's What I Want)," she has a permanent corner in the Motown hall of fame. "Sometimes I would write at home or take a lyric to Smokey or whoever. Or if they were working on something at the office, I'd take it there."

Gaye almost certainly cut his version of "Too Busy Thinking About My Baby" during the opening weeks of 1969. Motown shipped the record in April, anxious to maintain the multi-million momentum of "I Heard It Through the Grapevine," and then designated May to be "Marvin Gaye Month."

Two albums were released at the same time: *M.P.G.*, with new material, and *Marvin Gaye and His Girls*, a repackage of duets with Mary Wells, Kim Weston, and Tammi Terrell. *M.P.G.* (for Marvin Pentz Gaye) not only yielded "Too Busy Thinking About My Baby" and another top 10 single, "That's the Way Love Is," but also became the singer's highest-charting LP of the '60s, peaking at 33 on the *Billboard* pop album chart.

For Janie Bradford, Whitfield's revival of her song came out of left field. "He cut it and said, 'I've got a surprise for you.' I didn't even know they were about to release it, he kept it quiet that long. Then when I found out what it was..."

When released on the Temptations' album in 1966, "Too Busy Thinking About My Baby" credited Bradford and Whitfield as writers; when Gaye's version was released, Barrett Strong's name was added. "That was a clerical error," explains Bradford. "We learned everything there by trial and error. You have to remember that we were all in our mid-teens and whatever. Barrett was only 27 when it started, so we had to learn a lot."

The flip of Marvin Gaye's single featured another chart-topper: "Wherever I Lay My Hat (That's My Home)." Blue-eyed soul singer Paul Young remade that song into a British Number One in 1983.

75

WHAT DOES IT TAKE (TO WIN YOUR LOVE)

Jr. Walker & the All Stars

SOUL 35062
WRITERS: JOHNNY BRISTOL, HARVEY FUQUA, VERNON BULLOCK
PRODUCERS: HARVEY FUQUA, JOHNNY BRISTOL
July 19, 1969 (2 weeks)

Jr. Walker & the All Stars blew through the R&B charts for four straight years after their first blast of buckshot [see 2—"Shotgun"] in 1965. The group's top 10 singles included "Shake and Fingerpop," "(I'm A) Road Runner," "How Sweet It Is (To Be Loved By You)," and "Come See About Me."

Jr. Walker

Their top 10 albums included *Shotgun*, *Soul Session*, and *Road Runner*, with contents closer to the grittiness of Stax than the sheen of most Motown. "You could say that," agreed Walker years later, "but I didn't pay much attention to what I was doing in that sense. I didn't pay that much attention to what people or magazines were saying, either." He didn't have the time, he explained, "because we were always steady traveling."

The producers assigned to Walker in those years were usually Brian Holland and Lamont Dozier, Johnny Bristol and Harvey Fuqua, or Berry Gordy Jr. and Lawrence Horn. "He liked to sing little riffs or something while he was playing the sax," remembers Dozier. "He had done 'Shotgun' and a few other things, but he didn't consider himself a singer."

Towards the end of 1968, Johnny Bristol—who had sung with Walker before either of them joined Motown—thought the man could use a change of pace. With Vernon Bullock, he set about crafting something sweeter than usual. "Vernon worked with me in artist development," explains Bristol, "and he was more versatile than I was on the piano. I said, 'Vernon, play this, because I've gotten as far as I can go. I want a couple of different feelings right in through here that I can't play but I can hum.' "

Those feelings turned into "What Does It Take (To Win Your Love)," a midtempo ballad unlike Walker's normal fare. "Yeah, Junior was a little hesitant," says Bristol. "He's a real 'Shotgun' kinda guy, just yell it out. I said, 'No, Junior, a little prettier, a little warmer.' And I sang harmony with him. He loved it after it was finished, it just blew him away."

The song *was* warm and pretty, kicked off by Robert White's melodic guitar signature. "That was a little thing I could play on the piano," Bristol comments. "As soon as you hear that, it's very identifiable. And what the voices are doing, that came with me taking off Junior blowing the alto sax. We just had the background vocals emphasize it."

Motown didn't immediately see the song's hit potential. During an A&R meeting, the majority vote went to a more typical Walker recipe ("Home Cookin' ") produced by Hank Cosby. Bristol's response? "I stood up confidently and said, 'Well, if you want a song that's going to sell about 200,000 or 300,000, release "Home Cookin'." But if you want a million-seller, release "What Does It Take." And Mr. Gordy said, 'Well, that's fine, John, we understand why you feel that way.' He said it with a smile—but the proof was in the pudding."

After "Home Cookin' " turned cold in its fourth chart week, Gordy took Bristol's advice. "What Does It Take (To Win Your Love)" climbed to the R&B summit *and* crossed to the Hot 100, becoming Walker's first top five pop success since "Shotgun." A little prettier, a little warmer.

76

MOTHER POPCORN (YOU GOT TO HAVE A MOTHER FOR ME) (PART 1)

James Brown

KING 6245
WRITERS: JAMES BROWN, ALFRED ELLIS
PRODUCER: JAMES BROWN
August 2, 1969 (2 weeks)

And so, "Mother Popcorn" dethroned "What Does It Take (To Win Your Love)." Jr. Walker may have gone mellow, but not James Brown. This was a nasty, sexual piece of funk two years after "Cold Sweat." And Part 2 features JB's longest scream on record.

"Mother" was Brown's codeword for a woman's big butt—a theme he'd extend in "Hot Pants (She Got to Use What She Got to Get What She Wants)," "I'm a Greedy Man" (*You got to have something to sit on/Before I carry you home*), and 1978's infamous "For Goodness Sakes, Look at Those Cakes." Alan Leeds, new to the staff of James Brown Productions in 1969, recalls, "We'd be out at a club, he'd spot a woman and say, 'Ohhh, look at that mother there.' "

The music itself was an outgrowth of "Cold Sweat." Bandleader Alfred "Pee Wee" Ellis explains, "We had one of those immediate recording sessions in Cincinnati. I was in a music store downtown to pick up supplies, the rhythm of 'Cold Sweat' going through my head. I was standing in the store, waiting for the car to pick me up for the session, and that's when I hit on 'Mother Popcorn.' "

The popcorn was *the* black dance of the moment—and every time you turned around, it seems JB was churning out a "Popcorn" record. In fact, "Mother Popcorn" was released almost simultaneously with "The Popcorn" instrumental in May 1969. And both were in the top 20 at the same time.

Pee Wee Ellis may have heard "Cold Sweat," but the tune also had more immediate origins. In January 1969, Brown cut a track called "You Got to Have a Mother for Me," which was soon scheduled as King 6223 for release in April. In the interim, JB recorded and issued "I Don't Want Nobody to Give Me Nothing (Open up the Door, I'll Get It Myself)."

That single's success—it was heading for the top three in April—pushed "You Got to Have a Mother for Me" back into the vaults, and King 6223 was cancelled. When the popcorn dance took hold, Brown re-recorded the tune, retaining the original lyrics while making sure that this time, the tempo fitted the dance. And he threw in the word "Popcorn!" every few bars for good measure.

The session took place with JB's customary band at King's Cincy studios May 13, and "Mother Popcorn" was on the charts in June. "The single was *rush*-released," says Alan Leeds. "King could turn around a single in seven days, since they owned the studio, a pressing plant, and distribution."

For his part, Pee Wee Ellis stuck around long enough to see "Mother Popcorn" hit the top, then departed. About the JB experience, he is clear: "It was a successful marriage of funk and jazz—but still *funk*...It was very gratifying to be part of a winning team. We would kick ass and take names. Our attitude was that we were the best."

77

CHOICE OF COLORS

The Impressions

CURTOM 1943
WRITER: CURTIS MAYFIELD
PRODUCER: CURTIS MAYFIELD
August 16, 1969 (1 week)

Curtis Mayfield's choice in 1968 was to launch his own label, after more than six bountiful years with ABC. In Curtom Records, he was partnered with manager Eddie Thomas and aided by fellow Impressions Fred Cash and Sam Gooden, who were named "talent coordinators."

Curtom's motto was "We're a Winner," the title of the Impressions' final Number One hit for ABC [see 50]. The new company's first Number One was "Choice of Colors."

"When you talk to all people—black, white, whatever—it may be that it gives them food for thought," declares Mayfield, "and that is really how the song came about. Asking the question first, and then going a little bit deeper in reference to what we all deal in: our teachers, our preachers, and lending food for thought."

Lyricist *and* melody maker, Mayfield frequently composed on the road. "Many times I've written songs right in that car while we were riding along," he says, offering the Impressions' first chart-topper ("It's All Right") by way of example. "My incentive to write it was listening to Fred Cash. As I spoke on inspiring things, he would just say, 'All right, well, all right. It's all right.' "

In the early days at ABC Records, the group depended on producer and arranger Johnny Pate. "I don't know how to write or read music," says Mayfield, "and my fundamentals were more or less a gift given to me. Johnny was that middle man who could help me speak the language and help me dictate to the other musicians."

Later, Donny Hathaway became a vital player, both behind the scenes (he co-arranged "Choice of Colors" with Pate) and in front (he recorded as an artist for Curtom). "Donny's talent was not only his gift, it was his training," Mayfield explains. "He was from the Howard University in Washington.

"As a kid, he was not allowed to do anything but play gospel music. And, of course, through the Howard, he went back to long-haired [classical] music; he knew it like A-B-C. Between the two and his respect for what the young kids were doing, there was nothing Donny couldn't do. He was one of those musical geniuses."

Hathaway played keyboards on "Choice of Colors," with Billy Griffin likely on drums. "Billy was part of our caravan when we worked on the road," says Mayfield. "We had gotten good enough to where we didn't need Johnny Pate to bring in the rhythm section [into the studio] anymore. We had Lenny Brown on bass, and between those two gentlemen and myself, we would always have the basics of whatever we needed rhythmically."

The Impressions' vocals were arranged by Mayfield, Cash, and Gooden. "It was quite natural, the fellas having come up in church themselves and having sung with other harmony gospel groups as youngsters," notes Mayfield. "What really began to make our sound was that we were one of the first groups who coordinated the background with the [lead] vocal itself, and we always had something of that gospel feel within our music."

78

SHARE YOUR LOVE WITH ME

Aretha Franklin

ATLANTIC 2650
WRITERS: DEADRIC MALONE, AL BRAGGS
PRODUCERS: JERRY WEXLER, TOM DOWD, ARIF MARDIN
August 23, 1969 (5 weeks)

"Aretha brought that song to me," recalls Jerry Wexler. "That's a nice record, isn't it?"

As she had done with "Respect" in 1967, Franklin reached into the past for "Share Your Love with Me." The song came from the catalog of Bobby Bland, whose original recording was a top 50 pop hit in 1964, when *Billboard* published no R&B charts. As it turned out, Lady Soul's remake became her longest-running Number One hit since "Respect."

"I believe a man can sing a woman's lyrics, and conversely," declares Wexler, "because what you do is step outside of the frame, and you let the music take it. I've done that very often. I have another theory that a lot of songs are fungible. One will work very well—if it's a great song—with another singer who you wouldn't think of it for, as long as you get the arrangement to sit comfortably."

The man who helped make the arrangement of Aretha's "Share Your Love with Me" sit comfortably was Arif Mardin. It was the first Franklin chart-topper that saw him receive equal co-producing credit with Wexler and engineer Tom Dowd. The division of labor between the three men—who had worked together with Aretha since she joined Atlantic—was "sort of pragmatic," says Wexler. "The material was my concern. Arif surely took care of a lot of the sweetening, the strings and so on. Tommy was generally helpful. Anybody was more than welcome to say anything on his mind—and very often, we would try everything."

Franklin recorded "Share Your Love with Me" at Atlantic's New York studios on January 8, 1969. The players included guitarist Jimmy Johnson, bassman David Hood, drummer Roger Hawkins, and, on electric piano, Barry Beckett.

"I love the way she sings that," says Mardin, "and she plays the piano beautifully." Franklin recorded other people's songs with some frequency. If Mardin didn't know the original, he says, "then I would make a point of not listening to that version."

The Sweet Inspirations provided the backing vocals on "Share Your Love with Me," while another Atlantic linchpin, King Curtis, played tenor sax. "Music, Curtis was all music," says Jerry Wexler. "He was brilliant—and also a wonderful guy. Of all of the musicians, he was the most ring-wise, he knew most about the music of the music business. Which meant he was pretty good at extracting advances from me.

"But I really loved him, and I also had so much respect for him as a saxophone player. He was typed as a studio honker on the Coasters' records, but he was a great jazz player. He could do Lester Young and tear your heart out."

The credit for writing "Share Your Love with Me" belongs to Al (TNT) Braggs and Deadric Malone. Braggs was a onetime gospel singer found and favored by Bobby Bland, who brought him to the attention of Don Robey, owner of Houston's Duke/Peacock Records. Braggs recorded for the label and authored another of Bland's biggest hits, "Call on Me." Deadric Malone was a pseudonym used by Don Robey when he acquired and published songs, which were often written by others.

The flipside of Aretha's "Share Your Love with Me" maintained the Houston connection: There, she featured her version of "Pledging My Love," the posthumous signature song of Duke legend Johnny Ace, and she combined it with another Ace classic, "The Clock."

79
OH, WHAT A NIGHT
The Dells

CADET 5649
WRITERS: MARVIN JUNIOR, JOHNNY FUNCHES
PRODUCER: BOBBY MILLER
September 27, 1969 (1 week)

Leonard Chess knew a good idea when he heard one, and the remake of one of the Dells' earlier recordings had been just that. It was the first Number One hit of the group's career, and Chess Records's most successful single of 1968.

"Leonard had a knack for black music," understates Chuck Barksdale, bass singer of the Dells. And so it was that Chess advised them to again visit their past: to re-record "Oh, What a Nite," their 1956 chart debut. "He remembered how monstrous a tune it had been the first time, selling in excess of...whatever. God knows, we never got paid for it, so I'll just say 'in excess of whatever.' "

The Dells cut the original of "Oh, What a Nite" for Chicago's Vee-Jay Records. The song was written by Marvin Junior and Johnny Funches, who had helped form the group (as the El Rays) several years before. The Vee-Jay release was a triple winner on *Billboard*'s R&B charts of the day, reaching number four on the best-seller lists and number five on the disc jockey and jukebox rankings.

"People say we came from the doo-wop era," Barksdale comments, "and we did. But we grew—we grew as men as well as musically, and we were singing a lot of very hip jazz things, just trying to keep food on the table."

It was through just such a jazz gig at the Club Pigalle on Chicago's North Side that Barksdale remembers meeting Charles Stepney, a vibraphone player and the leader of his own jazz trio. Later, Stepney arranged the Dells' most successful Chess recordings, "Stay in My Corner" and "Oh, What a Night" among them. "Charles had never done any arrangements of full orchestras, but he had the talent," Barksdale recalls. "He got a chance to experiment, and his experimentation won."

Likewise, producer Bobby Miller played a vital role in their career. "After Vee-Jay had closed down and we ended up at Chess, Bobby was the only one who wanted to pay any attention to us—and he had

The Dells with producer Bobby Miller

some great songs: 'O-o I Love You,' 'There Is,' 'Always Together.' No one else would give him an opportunity to record them. And we said, 'Well, here are the Dells.' "

The partnership produced the group's most commercial work. In 1968, the Dells spent 42 weeks on the R&B charts. The following year, "Oh, What a Night" helped them bring the total to 47 weeks. "We had decided to put a little monologue in front of it," recalls Barksdale, "and that seemed to work." Just a short time after the record peaked, the man who inspired the group, Leonard Chess, died of a heart attack.

In retrospect, Chuck Barksdale says Bobby Miller, Charles Stepney, and the Dells were "an indescribably delicious triangle of music that came from nobody knowing too much of anything." Oh, what a triangle.

80

I CAN'T GET NEXT TO YOU

The Temptations

GORDY 7093
WRITERS: NORMAN WHITFIELD, BARRETT STRONG
PRODUCER: NORMAN WHITFIELD
October 4, 1969 (5 weeks)

Soul 'n' social commentary served the Temptations well: Message songs such as "Cloud Nine," "Run Away Child, Running Wild," and "Don't Let the Joneses Get You Down" were among the group's biggest R&B hits during 1968–69. So were "Ball of Confusion" and "Ungena Za Ulimwengu (Unite The World)" in 1970.

But when producer Norman Whitfield wanted to hit a home run in the pop market, he turned to matters of the heart. "I Can't Get Next to You" was one such example—and it became the Temptations' first crossover Number One since 1965's "My Girl."

After Earl Van Dyke's mood-setting piano, the record showcased the lead vocal skills of *every* member of the quintet: Dennis Edwards, Melvin Franklin, Eddie Kendricks, Otis Williams, Paul Williams. "After David Ruffin left the group," recounts Barrett Strong, Whitfield's co-writer, "it was a matter of changing stock." Edwards was given the opportunity to shine ("We had to let Dennis be Dennis," says Strong), but so were his fellow Temptations.

And "I Can't Get Next to You"? "Like I said," explains Strong, "once we got caught up into the lead singers on these different songs, it became such a thing that we figured why not continue it, you know?"

One of Motown's most credentialed songwriters, Barrett Strong is also one of its most modest. He'll describe the background of a dozen blockbusters in a few, sparse sentences. "I knew Norman before I started working with him and we did 'I Heard It Through the Grapevine,' " he says. "I was into the style of music he liked, and he was into the style I liked. And for the whole period of time we were together, it worked out real smooth."

Strong was also an accomplished vocalist, and his demos set a high standard, according to Melvin Franklin. "I remember when Barrett was in the studio, singing the demo lead for us on 'Take a Look Around.' With any of the guys in the Temps, when somebody sang the song, you couldn't get anybody better than Barrett Strong to do that.

"Then the competitive urge would come up, and they'd say, 'I've got to buckle down.' Because, you see, Barrett can *sing*. He sang so good. So when it came our time to sing it, hey, we're not going to let this guy show us up!"

Norman Whitfield and Barrett Strong were often competing with themselves, too. "I Can't Get Next to You" kept Marvin Gaye's version of another of their songs, "That's the Way Love Is," out of Number One on the soul charts that October—just as Gaye's "I Heard It Through the Grapevine" had prevented the Temptations' "Cloud Nine" from reaching the summit nine months earlier.

81

BABY, I'M FOR REAL

The Originals

SOUL 35066
WRITERS: ANNA GAYE, MARVIN GAYE
PRODUCERS: MARVIN GAYE, RICHARD MORRIS
November 8, 1969 (5 weeks)

While Sly & the Family Stone ("Stand!"), the Temptations ("Run Away Child, Running Wild"), and the Isley Brothers ("It's Your Thing") were marching toward what would become the funk of the '70s, three other groups were reaching back into the past with '50s-styled harmony hits: the Impressions ("Choice of Colors"), the Dells ("Oh, What A Night"), and the Originals.

"Baby, I'm for Real" started out on *Green Grow the Lilacs*, the Originals' debut album in 1969. By then, the group—Freddie Gorman, Walter Gaines, C.P. Spencer, Hank Dixon—had been under contract to Motown for three years. "We were just singing background for most of the artists at the company," explains Gorman. "Even some of the girl groups!"

Among the Originals' hits as session voices were Jimmy Ruffin's "What Becomes of the Brokenhearted," Stevie Wonder's "For Once in My Life," and David Ruffin's "My Whole World Ended." Says Gorman, "It was really like going to school. It made our harmonies that much tighter for when we started doing things on our own. In those days, the company was really a family, and it was fun and a learning experience."

One family member was Lamont Dozier. "I had been with Motown earlier as a solo artist," says Gorman, "and had left and started doing some things with Golden World. Then I left Golden World, and at that time, Lamont and I were very good friends—and he was also friends with Walter. Walter had gotten out of the service and we talked about getting a group together, so Lamont brought me over."

The Originals' first single for Motown featured a flipside co-authored by Marvin Gaye, "Need Your Lovin' (Want You Back)." Three years later, he produced them. Gorman remarks, "Marvin being an old group guy himself [in the Moonglows], I guess it was a dream of his to do something as another group-type song. He wrote that song with that in mind, and we were fortunate enough to be available."

Paul Riser, who arranged "Baby, I'm for Real," suggests it took shape during the recording process. "I'm almost certain it started off as another song," he says, "and was taken in that direction by Marvin and Richard Morris. They'd do that a lot at Motown, rewriting songs after the music production was done."

The track was cut by Motown's stalwart rhythm team, while the eloquent strings featured members of the Detroit Symphony Orchestra, directed by Gordon Staples. "We would call a session at a particular time," Riser recounts, "and they would come in just as if they were preparing for their own concert or rehearsal."

Freddie Gorman says that when "Baby, I'm for Real" was presented to Motown, "everybody loved it. But for some reason—I guess because of the doo-wop element—they didn't feel it was time for it. So that's how it got on the album instead of being a single release from the beginning. But once the album was released, it was picked immediately by radio stations across the country."

The Originals

82

SOMEDAY WE'LL BE TOGETHER

Diana Ross & the Supremes

MOTOWN 1156
WRITERS: JACKEY BEAVERS,
JOHNNY BRISTOL, HARVEY FUQUA
PRODUCER: JOHNNY BRISTOL
December 13, 1969 (4 weeks)

The swan song of Diana Ross and the Supremes was composed a lifetime away from the showbiz glitz of Las Vegas, where the group performed their last concert together at the Frontier Hotel in January 1970.

Johnny Bristol and Jackey Beavers were young Southerners, criss-crossing the Midwest in search of success—not to mention an income—as the '50s met the '60s. "We were traveling in Jackey's car throughout various parts of Indiana and Michigan and Ohio," says Bristol, "just singing in different places in our little red bow ties. If you saw a picture, you'd die."

Billed as Johnny and Jackey, they were on the road a lot. "As a matter of fact, 'Someday We'll Be Together' was written mostly in the car as we were driving," Bristol explains. "We just remembered the melody, we wrote it a cappella, and got back [home] and finished it up."

Beavers and Bristol had become acquainted in the air force, stationed outside Detroit. "We would sing at various local clubs and stuff. Jackie and I took it a little more seriously than the other guys—they needed half a gallon of wine. We were just young guys who wanted to sing."

The two recorded their original version of "Someday We'll Be Together" in 1961 for Harvey Fuqua, who ran tiny Tri-Phi Records in Detroit with Gwen Gordy, Berry's sister. Soon afterwards, the label was merged into Motown, where Bristol became a key member of the company's cadre of songwriters and producers.

Towards the end of the '60s, Bristol thought about reviving his act with Beavers—at least on record—and he cut a new version of "Someday We'll Be Together." Hearing the song, Berry Gordy thought it ideal for Diana Ross. "At the time," says Bristol, "you didn't argue with him. The idea was a producer's dream, so I said, 'Sure, great,' and he and I went into the studio with Diana."

Yet Ross's lead—on top of harmony vocals by the Waters—didn't go smoothly. "Diana wasn't in the greatest of moods, and we weren't getting the right feeling from her," relates Bristol. "I suggested to Mr. Gordy that I go in the other booth and just sing along with her, just a little soulful thing to kind of help. He said, 'OK, great, go ahead.'

"We started off, then he stopped the tape and said, 'I've got to start over, I made a mistake.' And unbeknownst to myself and Diana, he recorded everything I did, and said, 'I'm gonna keep this, it's a smash.' And he was absolutely right."

Bristol's supportive, soulful accompaniment (over an instrumental track arranged by Wade Marcus) was the kicker to lyrics perfectly suited for a superstar act on the eve of fracture. "Someday We'll Be Together" was shipped as a single on October 14, 1969—and three weeks later, Motown announced that Diana Ross would be leaving the Supremes.

83

I WANT YOU BACK

The Jackson 5

MOTOWN 1157
WRITERS: BERRY GORDY JR., FONCE MIZELL,
FREDDIE PERREN, DEKE RICHARDS
PRODUCERS: THE CORPORATION
January 10, 1970 (4 weeks)

With planning as intense as that for any presidential campaign, Berry Gordy nominated his newest candidates for public approval in the fall of '69. Helped by the endorsement of a popular entertainer, the brothers Jackson began reaching the people in October and November. They took office in January—and the Motown torch was passed to a new generation.

With Gordy acting as campaign manager, the Jackson 5 were showcased for music industry tastemakers at the Daisy in Beverly Hills on August 11, 1969, where Diana Ross welcomed the group and their "sensational eight-year-old lead singer," Michael Jackson.

On October 18, Ross introduced the Jacksons to a national audience on ABC-TV's *The Hollywood Palace*, and they performed "I Want You Back." The record debuted on the R&B charts a few weeks later, and took over from "Someday We'll Be Together" at Number One in January 1969.

One of Berry Gordy's tireless campaign workers was Freddie Perren, who co-wrote "I Want You Back" after he and longtime schoolmate Fonce Mizell had moved to Los Angeles from Washington, D.C. In California, the pair connected with Motown producer Deke Richards.

"[Deke] said, 'There's one way to really get into things fast: Find someone who's cold and write a hit on them,' " explains Perren. "Gladys Knight at the time was cold, so we wrote this song. It just started out kind of like a track that sounded really good, so we started molding it for Gladys."

Auditioning their work, Berry Gordy had a better idea. "He said, 'We just signed these five brothers out of Gary, Indiana, and this sounds like a lively young track. Why don't you rewrite the song for them, to be like a young guys' group?' "

Later, the Motown founder offered more comment. "He said, 'I think you should do a thing that has to do with a little guy who lost his girl, who's going, like, "Whoo, baby, give me one more chance," he wants another chance.' We took that and ran with it."

Vocal work began with the Jacksons. "I knew this thing went up to a high E flat," says Perren, "and thought, 'Wow, this guy has really got to sing high to get this.' I worried about that more than anything else. Michael wasn't as outgoing or playful as the other guys. He would just stand there, we were singing the song, and all the time I was showing it to him, I was thinking, 'Can he reach these notes?' Finally, we took a try at it and he just hit it the first time."

While the Jacksons honed their vocals, the track was being sharpened. Perren and Mizell cut an electrifying piano glissando for the record's opening. "I played the gliss," says Perren, "and Fonce played the downbeat at the end of it. When Berry heard that, he said, 'OK, I know you've got it now.' "

David T. Walker, Louis Shelton and Don Peake were fretmen on the date, with Wilton Felder and Gene Pello on bass and drums, respectively; Sandra Crouch, sister of Andrae, testified on tambourine. "I was keyboards," says Perren, "and there were three guitarists. The way it starts out with the octave guitar, that's Louis. Don Peake doubled the bassline. David T. did the solo."

By this time, Perren and his partners were sure "I Want You Back" was a vote-catcher. "We took it to Berry, who was over at Don Costa's studio, with our chests sticking out. He said, 'Oh man, you guys are getting ready to blow a hit. Get the fellas back and do some more rehearsing.' So we shaped them up on it, and worked a couple more days, getting their P's and Q's, getting the I's dotted and everything. Then we were on our way."

84

THANK YOU (FALETTINME BE MICE ELF AGAIN)

Sly & the Family Stone

EPIC 10555

WRITER: SYLVESTER STEWART

PRODUCER: SLY STONE

February 7, 1970 (5 weeks)

Two years—and almost a lifetime of experience—separated Sly & the Family Stone's first Number One, "Everyday People," and their second, "Thank You (Falettinme Be Mice Elf Again)." This was a *band*, constantly driven and innovating. Its members looked within for creative inspiration, seldom playing with other musicians or guesting on other people's records.

"I can't really recall anybody influencing us other than each other," says Larry Graham, the group's foundation on bass guitar. "I was into Freddie [Stone] as a guitar player; I was into Sly as a guitar and keyboards player. They were into what I was doing as a bass player."

He continues, "Some things that you'd hear later on the records were actually created onstage, live. We would play the song pretty much like the record the first time around. Let's say we were doing 'Dance to the Music,' and everybody would do their part like it was on the record. But the second time around, you'd pretty much do what you wanted to. Which means that each night, the songs were different—we would come up with new things depending on how we felt that night, and how we were playing.

"That's what made the live shows so fiery, too, because you were always looking to stretch out and go a little bit further. The things that you would play, especially that second time around, were just straight out of the heart. And some of those things would spark ideas for new songs."

The band worked at two San Francisco studios, Golden State Recorders and Pacific High Recording, when putting ideas on tape. Another favored site, says Graham, was the Columbia facility in Los Angeles. They would cut the instrumental tracks first, then vocals, with seldom much rehearsal in either case. "That to me was one of the things that gave us such a unique sound," he says. "Everything always had like a little raw edge to it, a little roughness, not too polished.

"Everybody would get a chance to contribute, which also helped the band sound unique, and which I thought was very smart on Sly's part. He recognized that different band members had things to contribute if you let them. By today's standards, on some of the songs, we would have been considered writers."

"Thank You (Falettinme Be Mice Elf Again)" was recorded in the latter half of 1969, and followed the group's seasonal smash, "Hot Fun in the Summertime." There was to have been an album of new material, but it never released. Instead, both songs were used for a *Greatest Hits* package.

"Thank You" was the record that "really put me on the map as a bass player," says Graham. "Overall, it was just a new kind of funk, the way the wah-wahs were being used and the interaction between the guitar parts. That stuff's still funky today. 'Rhythm Nation' from Janet Jackson, that's the breakdown from 'Thank You.' "

85

RAINY NIGHT IN GEORGIA

Brook Benton

COTILLION 44057
WRITER: TONY JOE WHITE
PRODUCER: ARIF MARDIN
March 14, 1970 (1 week)

Tony Joe White remembers the first time he heard Brook Benton's "Rainy Night in Georgia." Jerry Wexler of Atlantic Records had mailed him a copy of the single. "I played it probably 50 times in 30 minutes," says White. "It was the perfect match, the perfect singer—and that's when I really started liking the song."

Wexler already liked the song, made aware of it by another writer, Donnie Fritts. Benton had joined Atlantic's Cotillion label in 1968, and Wexler was looking for suitable material. "Jerry said, 'There's this Tony Joe White song you've gotta do,' " explains producer Arif Mardin. "I said, 'Yes, sir, captain!' "

The session took place on November 5, 1969, at Miami's Criteria studios, soon after Mardin had co-produced Aretha Franklin's "Call Me" there—the record that was to dislodge "Rainy Night in Georgia" from its peak. Mardin recalls that Benton was "in fabulous voice," but not at first thrilled about White's lyrics. "He said, 'I don't want to sing a song about Georgia.' I said, 'The man isn't crazy, Brook, he wants to get out of there.' Brook replied, 'I see your point.' "

Together, Benton and Mardin painted a vivid landscape, helped by the vermilion hues of guitarist Cornell Dupree's introduction and the melancholy harmonica of Toots Thielmans. Additional texture came from Billy Carter (organ), Dave Crawford (piano), Harold Cowart (bass), and Tubby Ziegler (drums).

"We didn't really know we had a hit," says Mardin. "We were too involved. So when I played it—either the finished version or the rough mix—for Ahmet [Ertegun] and Jerry, they said, 'This sounds great.' "

It was a milestone for Tony Joe White, too. He came to prominence in 1969 with his Louisiana swamp-rock and a top 10 pop hit, "Polk Salad Annie." But he had been making music since the early '60s, and the inspiration for "Rainy Night in Georgia" came when he was fresh out of high school, driving a dumptruck for the state highway department in Marietta, Georgia. Heavy storms at night meant "we wouldn't have to work the next day," he says, "and I could stay at home and play my guitar."

Two years later, White was performing Lightnin' Hopkins and Elvis Presley tunes in Texas nightclubs, and writing songs of his own. "I did 'Rainy Night in Georgia' and 'Polk Salad Annie' in the same two-week period," he declares. "I wrote about those times in Marietta, and what I knew. I knew about rainy nights in Georgia and polk salad."

Brook Benton

White and Benton performed "Rainy Night in Georgia" for a Nashville television show in 1988. "We had never been onstage together until then," says White. "He sang, I played guitar and harmonica—and the audience gave us a standing ovation. You could see tears in people's eyes."

CALL ME

Aretha Franklin

ATLANTIC 2706
WRITER: ARETHA FRANKLIN
PRODUCERS: JERRY WEXLER,
TOM DOWD, ARIF MARDIN
March 21, 1970 (2 weeks)

To record a song inspired by a Manhattan moment, Aretha Franklin left town.

"Call Me" was made in Miami, in Studio B of the Criteria studios owned by Mack Emerman. It was the singer's first Number One not minted at the Atlantic studios in New York—and her first Number One since separating from husband Ted White.

"It's a very feminine song, a woman's point of view," says co-producer Arif Mardin. He tells what Franklin told him: that she wrote it after seeing a young couple on New York's Park Avenue, talking intensely and then parting. Each called to the other, "I love you," followed by, "call me, the moment you get there." To suit the melancholy passion of Aretha's vocal, Mardin mixed the sweetening prominently. "It had to be like that," he explains. "My string arrangement was very romantic."

The Criteria session took place on October 3, 1969, with Barry Beckett on organ, David Hood on bass, Eddie Hinton and Jimmy Johnson on guitars, and Roger Hawkins on drums. On piano, of course, was Aretha. "My theory," explains Jerry Wexler, "is that if you have a singer who can also play—and I'm putting it in those terms, I'm not talking about virtuosity—then I want him to play on that session. Because it puts him more into the game, it's part of his essence.

"If you have a great player—an Aretha Franklin, who's a great player—you surely want her there. So her sessions were almost invariably built around a piano part she had developed at home. And she would have the background singers come over, whether it was the Sweet Inspirations, or her sisters, or the other girls, and she would work out the lead vocal, the piano part, and the group part.

"She'd come into the studio with all that worked out. And there'd be the full rhythm section, they'd start playing and it was like painting by the numbers—all we had to do was fill it in. We might change it from there, you know, make some small modifications. We might even change the key occasionally. But not often."

Mardin notes how Franklin's left- and right-hand playing would dictate the rest of the rhythm section's parts. "Who can do anything else? The bass, for instance, has to either go along with it, or stay out of the way. She would sing along [with the rhythm track], too, and we would sometimes keep those vocals, even though you'd have all the room leakage, drums and so on."

Aretha's 1969 breakup with White *did* affect her work. Guitarist Jimmy Johnson told Mark Bego, author of *The Queen of Soul*, " 'Call Me' is the perfect example, I think, of some of the feelings she was having. I think she may have cried during the lyrics of that song—because she definitely had us crying."

Despite its R&B success, "Call Me" missed the pop top 10. But the record did spend more time on the Hot 100 than any Aretha hit since 1968's "(Sweet Sweet Baby) Since You've Been Gone." Truly, a long-distance call.

ABC

The Jackson 5

MOTOWN 1163
WRITERS: FREDDIE PERREN, FONCE MIZELL, DEKE RICHARDS, BERRY GORDY JR.
PRODUCERS: THE CORPORATION
April 4, 1970 (4 weeks)

Phil Jones still recalls the September 1969 staff meeting at Motown's Detroit headquarters. Berry Gordy had jetted from Los Angeles to discuss launch plans for his newest signing, the Jackson 5. "Berry came in," says Jones, who was one of the company's senior marketing executives at the time, "and he had this acetate in his hand, like a waiter would hold a tray. 'Gentlemen,' he said, 'this is apple pie.' He put it on the turntable, and it was 'I Want You Back.' "

Just a few months later, Motown released "ABC," another piece of the same tasty pie. It was prepared by identical chefs, too: The songwriting and production team dubbed "The Corporation," which comprised Gordy, Freddie Perren, Fonce Mizell, and Deke Richards.

Perren explains, "On the chorus part to 'I Want You Back,' it comes around to the end and Michael sings, *I want you back/Yeh, yeh, yeh*. The music of 'ABC' is right there. We just took that music and kept playing it. However, it wasn't that simple—it had to be fashioned into a real song. It was thought out, we didn't just get around and start singing little catchy phrases and rhyme. It was thought out to coincide with the fact that [the Jackson 5] were the age they were, and that most of their fans were still in school."

Perren, Mizell, and Richards cut the instrumental tracks at Hollywood's Sound Factory. "ABC" featured the same core of musicians used for "I Want You Back," including Perren and Mizell on keyboards. In charge of tasting the end product was Richards. "Deke was very persistent at mixing," affirms Perren.

The Corporation was nothing if not prolific. "We had rewrites and a lot of verses," Perren says. "Where a song may have had two verses, we may have written eight or ten. We would go to Berry Gordy and he would tell us what to do. Most people think he's just an executive, but he's a great writer."

Just an executive? Not Mr. Gordy, as most of his staff knew him. This man honed Motown's chart edge with a matchless mix of business smarts and first-hand creative skills. When Holland/Dozier/Holland quit the company, Gordy apparently chose a quasi-corporate identity for future teams of writers and producers.

"Deke [Richards] and Berry were in The Clan, and they had produced 'Love Child,' " says Perren. "I think that was born because H/D/H were in litigation with Motown. They probably didn't want to create any more 'superstars.' But that sounded OK to us. When I signed my contract, all it had to have was 'Motown' at the top. That's all we needed to see, so we signed it.

"If you didn't sign it, there was someone else waiting. That was our chance to get on the inside. It was the same when Deke came back and said, 'We're going to be The Corporation.' I didn't like it when the record came out—there's something about having your name on it—but the work and the pleasure was so great that it didn't really take anything away from that."

88

TURN BACK THE HANDS OF TIME

Tyrone Davis

DAKAR 616
WRITERS: JACK DANIELS, JOHNNY MOORE
PRODUCER: WILLIE HENDERSON
May 2, 1970 (2 weeks)

Chicago champ Tyrone Davis was firmly under the influence of Bobby Bland and Little Milton in the mid-'60s, when writer Jack Daniels first saw him. "He had very limited success in the early years," he says, "because people just don't gyrate to singers who imitate others."

Daniels was a partner in the 4 Brothers label, where Davis made his first recordings in 1965–66. "Tyrone at that time had just started to do a little singing in the clubs. I guess he had tasted success, or had seen it from the outside and wanted some for himself. He was really interested but didn't know what direction to go."

Barry Despenza, co-author of Davis's first national hit [see 67—"Can I Change My Mind"], deserves credit for defining that direction, according to Daniels. "Barry found that soft style that Tyrone developed," he says. In turn, Despenza credits disc jockey Big Bill Hill at Chicago station WOPA. "He told me I had Tyrone singing too hard. He said he'd never make it singing that way."

Two years after leaving 4 Brothers, Davis and Daniels were reunited for "Turn Back the Hands of Time." The songwriter and his partner, Johnny Moore, had been woodshedding in Philly with Thom Bell, Bobby Martin, and others. "In working with them, we really learned how to write, and decided to focus on songs that were easy for people to relate to. Most of those story lines revolved around love."

"Turn Back the Hands of Time" drew specifically on Daniels's personal experiences. "I had been through a very traumatic relationship with the mother of my child," he explains. "Johnny and I were so close at the time that we could feel what each other was going through. He had the original idea for the song and the chorus, and I put the lyrics to it. The lyrics related to the relationship I had just broken up from." (Moore apparently also had some personal problems, which saw him use the name of a girlfriend, Bonnie Thompson, for the initial writer credits of the song.)

The pair submitted "Turn Back the Hands of Time" to producer Carl Davis, with whom Tyrone Davis was recording. "Carl asked us to go to Tom Tom Washington to make sure of the changes and chord structures, and he wrote the arrangement. Tom got the music together, Willie Henderson handled the vocals and background."

The session employed many of the same musicians who played on "Can I Change My Mind," including Quinton Joseph on drums, Floyd Morris on piano, and Carl Wolfolk on guitar. "Barbara Acklin used to sing backup on a lot of that stuff," adds Daniels. Also on hand, he says, were Eugene Record and Robert "Squirrel" Lester from the Chi-Lites.

And Tyrone? "He's a guy who doesn't seem to be serious in real life—but he took recording very seriously," remembers Daniels. "He realized that what he was getting in that studio would be a determining factor in his success as an artist. He was a pleasure to record."

89

LOVE ON A TWO-WAY STREET

The Moments

STANG 5012
WRITERS: SYLVIA ROBINSON, BERT KEYES
PRODUCER: SYLVIA ROBINSON
May 16, 1970 (5 weeks)

It wasn't Detroit, Memphis, or even Muscle Shoals, but for a few years in the '70s, the record industry knew about Englewood, New Jersey.

The suburban township, just a few miles from Manhattan across the George Washington Bridge, was where Joe and Sylvia Robinson launched All Platinum Records in 1968. And for the next ten years or so, the label (with sister imprints Stang, Turbo, and Vibration) made a number of memorable, successful records in between scores of rough 'n' ready releases by dozens of forgettable performers.

Moreover, the Robinsons' low-fi, low-rent approach was a notable alternative to the upwardly mobile, highly polished sounds of Motown and Philadelphia International—just as the stone statues that decorated the drive of the couple's Englewood home clashed with their neighbors' more, uh, refined tastes.

"Love on a Two-Way Street" was All Platinum's first major hit, a certified-gold single that put them, and the Moments, on the map. Sylvia Robinson—who had been in the music business since the '50s [see 145—"Pillow Talk"]—and veteran arranger Bert Keyes wrote the song, cutting it first with Leslie Valentine.

After the Moments became the company's hottest act in 1969 with three consecutive top 20 records, Robinson and Keyes cut "Love on a Two-Way Street" with the group. It was, she admits today, originally intended as filler for an album.

The Moments, discovered by artist/producer Ed Townsend, signed with the Robinsons in '68. When "Love on a Two-Way Street" was made the following year, their lineup featured Billy Brown, Johnny Morgan, and Al Goodman, with Brown handling the song's brittle lead.

"All our singles made the R&B charts, but we needed something a little bigger to give us a crossover hit into pop," Goodman explained to *Black Music* in 1975. "One day Bert Keyes...brought us this song that he'd written that All Platinum had cut on another artist which hadn't sold, but which he thought could make it big with us...and he was right!"

The session took place at All Platinum's eight-track studio in Englewood, of course, and Joe Robinson says the musicians included arranger Keyes (piano), Willie Feaster (guitar), Val Burke (bass), and Arnold Ramsey (drums), otherwise known as Willie and the Mighty Magnificents. Keyes added a three-piece string section, overdubbed three times.

"Strings don't make the record," Robinson countered, when a cheeky British reporter asked him about All Platinum's low-fi sound. "It's a cushioning type of thing for us," he stressed. "If the song is not there and the performance is not there, you could put a hundred strings there and you'd have nothing." More to the point, Robinson said, was the sex appeal of the Moments. "A group has got four or five guys and you've got all the little girls in the audience."

"Love on a Two-Way Street" was released on Stang Records (Joe Robinson named the label after his Mustang) in March of 1970, and traveled one way: to Number One. It also crossed—as Al Goodman had hoped—to the top three of the pop charts.

And as the Robinsons might have hoped, the song earned a long-term ticket in their publishing catalog. Eleven summers later, a remake of "Love on a Two-Way Street" by Stacy Lattisaw parked at number two on the charts for four weeks.

90

THE LOVE YOU SAVE

The Jackson 5

MOTOWN 1166
WRITERS: FREDDIE PERREN, FONCE MIZELL, DEKE RICHARDS, BERRY GORDY JR.
PRODUCERS: THE CORPORATION
June 20, 1970 (6 weeks)

After two consecutive Number One hits and eight weeks atop *Billboard*'s soul charts, the Jackson 5 formula wasn't broke—so no one wanted to fix it.

For "The Love You Save," the group's third single, "we kept a lot of the ingredients in there," admits Freddie Perren, part of the four-man Motown team that wrote and produced as The Corporation.

"There was a little play between Jermaine and Michael, we always tried to get that in there," he says. "We found out Tito had a commercial bass voice and we would put little trick things in with him. We had a little list of things, a checklist, that we followed."

Another 25-percent stockholder in The Corporation was Berry Gordy. Perren recalls the Motown chief anticipating the next hit. " 'You've got two hot ones there,' he said. 'We have to start thinking about another single.' "

Perren, Fonce Mizell, and Deke Richards eventually kicked "The Love You Save" into shape. "We recorded our own little version of it one night," says Perren. "I didn't realize how raggedy it was, but it said what it was supposed to say, so that when some real pros got on it, they could play it right."

Those professionals included guitarists David T. Walker, Louis Shelton, and Don Peake, drummer Gene Pello, and bassman Wilton Felder. The recording session took place at the Sound Factory, Los Angeles.

Perren agrees that Michael and Jermaine carried most of the quintet's vocal weight, as does Willie Hutch, co-writer of their next hit [see 94—"I'll Be There"]. "I have some very fond memories with those young cats," he says. "They could sing, it just took a while for them to really come into their own.

"Like, Tito was not really a singer's singer, neither was Marlon. They were not what you'd call lead singers or anything like that. But they could do enough once they were formulated, and knew who sang what best. They did as well or better than all the other kids. Plus, when you're dealing with a situation where there's an age spread like that, you're going to have a few immature voices as well as mature voices—and you try to blend all of that."

Hutch also recalls the brothers as "typical kids." He explains, "They were playful, good-hearted, just genuine children, and they took direction well. I remember many times we used to have to drive them from the Motown building on Sunset to the studio. Tito would always want to ride with me, so we'd stop by the Farmer's Market to pick up some cherries and a pack of cigarettes. I'd tell him, 'I'm not buying you no cigarettes, your father won't like it.' "

91

SIGNED, SEALED, DELIVERED, I'M YOURS

Stevie Wonder

TAMLA 54196
WRITERS: STEVIE WONDER, LEE GARRETT, SYREETA WRIGHT, LULA MAE HARDAWAY
PRODUCER: STEVIE WONDER
August 1, 1970 (6 weeks)

One year before turning 21 and renegotiating his entire contractual relationship with Motown, Stevie Wonder was busy with two career firsts. He was writing and producing for a fellow Motown act, the Spinners, and taking sole charge of producing his own records.

On both projects, Wonder was collaborating with Syreeta Wright and Lee Garrett. Wright was a Motown secretary-turned-singer with whom he had become romantically involved (they later married). She had recorded a single, "I Can't Give Back the Love I Feel for You," released in 1968 amid rumors—false, as it eventually turned out—that she was actually Diana Ross's sister.

Garrett was also a singer as well as a radio DJ, who had met Wonder years earlier when both attended the Michigan School for the Blind. He remembers Wonder playing him basic tracks for "Signed, Sealed, Delivered, I'm Yours" and "It's a Shame" (the song earmarked for the Spinners) around the same time, at the star's Detroit home.

"Actually, 'It's a Shame' came first," says Garrett, "but even before I did the lyric for that, he brought me another track, and said, 'Listen to this.' Syreeta and I went into the basement, and it was kind of funny, we both started singing 'Signed, Sealed, Delivered' at the same time."

Wonder had the same idea, according to Garrett, "and from then on, we just bounced around with lyrics. I would say a verse: *Like a fool I went and stayed too long/But now I'm wondering if your love's still strong.* That felt good there, so then it was, *Ooh baby, here I am/Signed, sealed, delivered, I'm yours.*

Stevie Wonder

"Then I wanted to sing something else, and Syreeta said, 'OK, we should take it to...and then, and then, and then. OK, I said, *Then that time I went and said goodbye/Now I'm back and not ashamed to cry*. And it just went on like that, with her saying, 'And then? And then?' I would just kind of spout out the lyrics."

Garrett wasn't in the studio when the song was recorded ("I felt Motown had one Stevie Wonder, they didn't need another [blind] guy bouncing around"), but he remembers hearing the finished version and thinking of Johnnie Taylor. "That's really who we were creating it for, but Stevie said, 'Damn, I think I'll record this shit myself.' "

The Taylor connection was no accident. Even though Motown regulars like bassist James Jamerson and drummer Richard "Pistol" Allen played on "Signed, Sealed, Delivered, I'm Yours," Wonder later said he had been striving for a Memphis feel. He told David Breskin, "If Stax Records had done something with the kind of groove I liked, well...I did 'We Can Work It Out' with a Stax kind of groove."

Many at Motown didn't understand that, in Wonder's view. "I had the desire to move out of the one little thing that the musicians were in, and that Motown was in. And I wanted to do it, hey, because I liked the groove."

92

DON'T PLAY THAT SONG (YOU LIED)

Aretha Franklin

ATLANTIC 2751
WRITERS: BETTY NELSON, AHMET ERTEGUN
PRODUCERS: JERRY WEXLER, TOM DOWD, ARIF MARDIN
September 12, 1970 (3 weeks)

As the '60s gave way to the '70s, Aretha Franklin separated from husband Ted White, and traded Manhattan for Miami as a recording location.

The studio was Criteria, previously best known as the place where James Brown made "I Got You (I Feel Good)" in 1965. In fact, Atlantic Records came to favor the Florida facility so much that it leased Studio B on an annual basis, frequently referring to it as "Atlantic South."

And so in March 1970, far from frigid New York, Aretha began work there on a batch of songs that—when combined with material cut at Criteria six months earlier [see 86—"Call Me"]—would make up *Spirit in The Dark*, her ninth Atlantic album.

"Don't Play That Song (You Lied)" was one of the sides recorded that March, with Franklin on piano as well as vocals, and a group known as the Dixie Flyers handling the rhythm: Charlie Freeman on guitar, Tommy McClure on bass, Sammy Creason on drums, and Jim Dickinson and Mike Utley on keyboards. The background vocalists were Margaret Branch, Brenda Bryant, and Almeda Lattimore.

Producer Jerry Wexler was said to have found the Flyers at a Memphis blues festival. In 1969, the group played on Tony Joe White's *Continued* album; later, they recorded with other Wexler favorites, including Delaney & Bonnie, Kris Kristofferson, and Donnie Fritts.

"Don't Play That Song (You Lied)" was well-known to the Atlantic crowd, of course. It was co-authored by Ben E. King (under the name of his wife, Betty Nelson) and Atlantic co-founder Ahmet Ertegun. King recorded his original in March 1962; it was a major R&B and pop success in June of that year.

"That's a good story about cooperation," affirms Arif Mardin, who co-produced Aretha's version with Wexler and Tom Dowd. After the rhythm track was cut, Mardin and Dowd overdubbed the sweetening. "Tommy did the horns in Miami," says Mardin, "I did the strings in New York. We didn't even talk to each other."

Nor did Wexler tell his co-producers what the other was doing. In John Tobler and Stuart Grundy's *The Record Producers* (St. Martin's Press, 1982), Dowd explained, "He didn't say a thing to Arif about there being horns on 'Don't Play That Song,' but just told him that he wanted strings on it, and he didn't tell me that was happening either."

So when the finished single came out, Dowd was surprised. "I remember sitting in Miami listening to the radio and hearing it and thinking, 'When did they put those strings on that? That's where the horns are supposed to be.' " It was Wexler who had performed the alchemy, of course. "If we'd known that we were working on the song," said Dowd, "Arif would have changed the strings and I'd have changed the horns, and it wouldn't have been the same thing."

93

AIN'T NO MOUNTAIN HIGH ENOUGH

Diana Ross

MOTOWN 1169
WRITERS: NICKOLAS ASHFORD, VALERIE SIMPSON
PRODUCERS: NICKOLAS ASHFORD, VALERIE SIMPSON
October 3, 1970 (1 week)

As if rehearsing for *Lady Sings the Blues*, Diana Ross swept through her role in "Ain't No Mountain High Enough" with all the drama and majesty befitting the queen of Motown.

Just months earlier, Motown's king, Berry Gordy, had put his most skilled artisans to work. "Berry thought we would be the most innovative with her solo album," explains Nick Ashford, who wrote and produced it with partner Valerie Simpson. "We were trying to think of directions to take her. At that time, lengthy records were starting to come out: six, seven minutes.

"We didn't have any songs like that, but we wanted Diana to feel she was into new things. We thought to stretch 'Ain't No Mountain High Enough,' and we thought how sexy and silky her voice was..." Simpson interrupts: "*You* thought about how sexy her voice was."

Berry Gordy's trust in the couple was well-placed. The New Yorkers had crafted urban pop ballads to perfection for Marvin Gaye and Tammi Terrell [see 57—"Ain't Nothing Like the Real Thing" and 62—"You're All I Need to Get By"]. And since they met through a Harlem church choir, it was no surprise to hear that background in their work.

Despite Gordy's wide-screen ambitions for Diana Ross after she left the Supremes, he gave Simpson and Ashford relative independence in the recording sessions. "I must say from the time we started producing, you had total control," Simpson states. "They restricted you in terms of how long you had [to record], but as long as you stayed within those guidelines, they let you do what you wanted to do."

Ashford does remember Ross questioning the choice of "Ain't No Mountain High Enough," which had been a hit three years earlier. "She just kind of raised her eyebrows, and said, 'Marvin and Tammi already did that.' We said, 'This is especially for you.' She said, 'OK,' and just gave it all she had."

Arranger Paul Riser framed the record like a three-act play, with the singer occasionally offstage. "We cut the rhythm track in Detroit," says Riser. "The strings and horns were a little too sophisticated for the players there, so we went to New York to do it, to get the best possible performance." Simpson played piano; she and Ashford also handled backing vocals, joined by their earlier songwriting partner, Jo Armstead.

Breaking the rules of hook-conscious Motown, the finished production of "Ain't No Mountain High Enough" was inverted—the climactic chorus consumed the last two minutes of its six-minute running time.

"When we took it to Berry," recalls Ashford, "he said, 'I think it sounds good, but you're gonna have to take the back and put it up in the front.' "

Ashford and Simpson were not pleased. "Berry wouldn't release that song [as a single]," Ashford contends. "We refused to change it, and he refused to release it. He didn't release it—the disc jockeys did. They picked it up all over the country."

94

I'LL BE THERE

The Jackson 5

MOTOWN 1171

WRITERS: BERRY GORDY JR., BOB WEST, WILLIE HUTCH, HAL DAVIS

PRODUCER: HAL DAVIS

October 10, 1970 (6 weeks)

After three uptempo hits, "I'll Be There" was the Jackson 5's first ballad—and their most successful single on the Hot 100: five weeks at Number One, compared to two weeks apiece for "ABC" and "The Love You Save," and one for "I Want You Back." Not bad for a song that didn't impress Motown chairman Berry Gordy at first.

"Mr. Gordy liked the title and the track, but he didn't like the song," explains Willie Hutch, who was then asked by producer Hal Davis to rework Bob West's original composition. "Hal came to my house at about 3:45 in the morning," he says. "He felt I could get the song done."

Hutch was a writer associated with the 5th Dimension and several other West Coast R&B acts; Davis had opened Motown's Los Angeles office in the early '60s. "Willie's wife was mad at me," remembers Davis about the early-hours visit, "but I work late."

Hutch contends that the task took him about 90 minutes. "I'm a singer myself, so when I heard the track, I first just kind of hummed the melody, then I thought about it. At four o'clock in the morning, there's really not much distraction."

Hutch rewrote "I'll Be There" with two options. "One was more or less a brotherhood kind of lyric, and the other was more guy–girl," he says. "But I kept the brotherhood aspect in both songs at the beginning: *You and I must make a pact/We must bring salvation back*. I thought, 'That's good, either way it goes.' "

By eight o'clock that same morning, the writer and the producer were at Gordy's mansion. "I had both songs," says Hutch. "Berry listened for about 15 minutes, and said, 'OK, that's a smash. Set up studio time for one o'clock.' "

The instrumental track for "I'll Be There" was arranged by Bob West, the song's original author. It was cut at the Sound Factory in Los Angeles, according to onetime Motown arranger Art Wright. Among the musicians Davis favored for session work were Wright on guitar, Jimmy Bond on bass, Joe Sample on keyboards, and either Gene Pello or James Gadson on drums. On "I'll Be There," the distinctive opening featured a keyboard instrument known as the Rock-si-chord.

The studio where the Jacksons did their vocals was the Record Plant, Los Angeles. The lead was performed by Michael Jackson, who later described "I'll Be There" as "our real breakthrough song." Brother Jermaine handled the vocals at the bridge, and the group—augmented by other backup singers—contributed harmonies.

Willie Hutch remembers those sessions, too. "You know, of course, that Mr. Gordy has an entourage," he says, "and it's always with him. Everybody was standing around, so I told them, 'I've done my job, you guys have got it now,' and I was getting ready to leave. But Mr. Gordy said, 'Don't leave, I want you to dub the group in.' So I wound up doing that."

95

SUPER BAD (PART 1 & PART 2)

James Brown

KING 6329

WRITER/PRODUCER: JAMES BROWN

November 21, 1970 (2 weeks)

This was only the second recording by James Brown with his young new band, a unique, rhythmic ensemble he recruited in March 1970. Teenagers who'd been King Records sessioneers as well as a backup group for local shows with Marva Whitney and Hank Ballard, they had area gigs where they were known as the Pacesetters.

They included William "Bootsy" and Phelps "Catfish" Collins, brothers on bass and rhythm guitar, respectively. Says Bootsy, "Mr. Brown was so out of our reach...We were treated like a stepchild."

Once behind the main man, the "New Breed" (so dubbed until, more officially, becoming the J.B.'s) were anchored by two important, feet-on-the-ground vets: Bobby Byrd and Jabo Starks. Organist and singer Byrd, the soul of the entourage, schooled them in life with JB; drummer Jabo had the solid beat that rendered the whole thing seamless. "They were our heroes," says Bootsy. "At first, I couldn't get used to the fact that I was playing next to *James Brown's drummer*. Fact is, I don't think I ever got used to it."

The Pacesetters band was asked to join Brown live on stage the same night the heralded '60s band quit. No rehearsals, no run-down except salary. Backstage, the crowd restless, JB set the new band's weekly pay at $250 per man. Then he started the show.

In the weeks and months ahead, as Bootsy and Catfish remember, Brown cut the newcomers a lot of slack. If they weren't comfortable with something, they'd walk, or say what was on their mind—grounds for heavy fines, or dismissal, as their predecessors had discovered just a few months before.

One of the results: a new sound. "Get Up (I Feel Like Being A) Sex Machine" was the first lightning bolt, forged in April 1970 at the Starday/King studios at Nashville. A couple of months later, according to Alan Leeds, who was then Brown's tour director, JB went out of his way to return there, to cut "Super Bad."

The lineup that June 30 was the Collins brothers, Byrd, Starks, Johnny Griggs (congas), Robert McCollough (tenor), and Clayton Gunnells and Darryl Jamison (trumpets). "That's a hell of a groove, fellas," allows Brown, heard on the original "Super Bad" session tape. Later, as the musicians' grip on the song improves, he adds further compliments—but is also careful to caution: "See, the *down*-beat's what's happenin'."

The final result excited Brown. Alan Leeds recalls, "James came to Cincinnati on an off-day after the session. We went club-hopping, and as the entourage grew, we were invited back to Brown's suite at the Terrace Hilton. He had a stereo system set up in the room.

"He was supercharged, and started playing the acetate of 'Super Bad.' Everyone had a few drinks, some girls got up to dance, we were feeling good. The tune was slammin'. After the usual back-slapping ('Yeah, it's better than "Sex Machine," Mr. Brown'), James played it again and again and again and again, over and over throughout the night and into early morning."

96

THE TEARS OF A CLOWN

Smokey Robinson & the Miracles

TAMLA 54199

WRITERS: HENRY COSBY, WILLIAM "SMOKEY" ROBINSON, STEVIE WONDER

PRODUCERS: HENRY COSBY, WILLIAM "SMOKEY" ROBINSON

December 5, 1970 (3 weeks)

At the London offices of EMI Records in leafy Manchester Square, John Reid was looking for a hit. It was 1970, and Reid (who would later become the manager of rock superstar Elton John) was Motown's man at EMI, which marketed the company's releases in Britain.

His problem was Smokey Robinson and the Miracles. Their U.S. singles were seldom suitable for the U.K. market. In fact, the group's first major British hit didn't happen until 1969—and that was a reissue of 1965's "The Tracks of My Tears."

For help, Reid turned to Karen Spreadbury, head of the British fan club known as Motown Ad Astra.

Smokey Robinson & the Miracles

She remembers him throwing the Miracles' *Make It Happen* album across his office with a challenge: Find a single from this.

The LP, three years old at that point, mostly showcased Smokey's trademark ballads, including "The Love I Saw in You Was Just a Mirage" and "More Love." Tucked away as the last track on side two was "The Tears of a Clown." Spreadbury says, "It stuck out like a sore thumb because it was so different."

The song was originally an instrumental track created by Stevie Wonder and Motown staff producer Hank Cosby. During a Christmas party in 1966, according to Robinson, Wonder asked him to write some lyrics. "I took the tape home," he said years later, "put it on and this music is awesome, smokin'!

"But what I've got immediately is that opening: 'Bom-bom-bom, ba-da-dum-dum-dum-dum.' The circus, what else? OK, so what can I write about the circus that's going to be profound enough, heart-jerking enough for people to care? I start to search myself. Lion tamers? Acrobats? Elephants? What's touching about that?

"Then I remembered the clowns. All my life I'd known the story of Pagliacci, the most famous clown there'd ever been...the joymaker. But then, the show's over, he goes to his dressing room and he cries. He doesn't have a woman. Everybody loves him as Pagliacci the clown, but he doesn't have someone who loves him as a man."

The joymaker of Ruggiero Leoncavallo's famous opera, *Pagliacci*, had inspired Robinson before. He used the same simile in Carolyn Crawford's "My Smile Is Just a Frown (Turned Upside Down)" in 1964 and a similar motif, of course, in "The Tracks of My Tears."

As part of *Make It Happen*, "The Tears of a Clown" was released in America in the summer of '67. In London three years later, John Reid took Karen Spreadbury's advice and shipped the song as a single. By the second week of September 1970, Smokey and the Miracles were clowning around at Number One in the British charts.

Motown followed that lead soon afterwards in the States, propelling "The Tears of a Clown" to the top of the R&B charts and, one week later, to the peak of the Hot 100. "When it did go to Number One," says Spreadbury, "Smokey phoned and thanked me. So I said, 'I hope the champagne's on its way.' If you don't ask, you don't get—and I didn't get!"

97

STONED LOVE

The Supremes

MOTOWN 1172
WRITERS: FRANK WILSON, KENNY THOMAS
PRODUCER: FRANK WILSON
December 26, 1970 (1 week)

"Stoned Love" could just as easily have been titled "Rock of Ages." Composer Kenny Thomas was striving for a message of permanence in the lyrics of his song, written at a time of seismic social change.

"We had civil rights issues going on in this country," he says. "Vietnam, drugs, 'make love, not war.' But stones are forever—they don't break or come apart. Love will be here forever. It's not important about color and things of that nature."

Berry Gordy wasn't impressed. "I remember that he hated that record," says producer Frank Wilson. "He called it garbage." The Motown chieftain relented only when senior executive Barney Ales promised that every radio station in the influential RKO chain would play "Stoned Love" if Motown shipped it as a single.

Ales delivered: The release became the Supremes' biggest R&B *and* pop success since the departure of Diana Ross. Its graceful, uplifting lead vocals were those of Jean Terrell, whom Berry Gordy had first seen performing in Miami in 1968 and who officially succeeded Ross in January 1970.

Kenny Thomas was 17 when Frank Wilson heard his material on WJLB Detroit, during a teen talent contest hosted by the station's "Frantic" Ernie Durham. Wilson visited the teenager's home. "He came by and had me play several of the songs I played at the contest," says Thomas. "He asked me if I had anything else, and I said, 'Yes, there's this song I'm working on right now, that I haven't actually performed yet.' And I played 'Stoned Love.' "

Wilson was impressed, subsequently inviting Thomas to meet a member of the Supremes, on a Sunday in 1970 etched vividly in his memory. "In comes Mary Wilson—and I die," tells Thomas. "He introduces us, and she asks, 'Gee, Frank, this is a baby, what does he have?' Frank says, 'Go get him a 7-Up, he'll play it.' "

The Supreme soon shared the producer's enthusiasm, and arranger David Van DePitte was recruited. "We went down in the basement and this kid, Kenny Thomas, gets out a guitar," remembers Van DePitte. "There were only two strings, and this kid had worked out a system of binary chords that he could plunk along to, and he was singing 'Stoned Love.' "

When the track was recorded, Thomas was present. "It was at Motown on West Grand Boulevard, in a basement almost as big as a football field," he says. "David hits the baton on the podium, and the musicians play—maybe a 50-piece orchestra, strings and everything. I cried."

Jean Terrell, Mary Wilson, and Cindy Birdsong cut their vocal parts later in New York, according to Thomas, who says he flew from Detroit for the session. "Jean had to do the whole thing right about the first time, with the exception of a couple of cute riffs that were added."

When released in October 1970, "Stoned Love" listed Wilson and an enigmatic Y. Samoht as authors. "Frank added about four lines [to the song] for continuity," explains Thomas, who altered his name for fun in the manner of Stevie Wonder's "Eivets Rednow." It also hinted at one of his influences, Nina Simone. "Ynnek Samoht sounds a bit like that—the Simone part, anyway—and it became my personal tribute to her."

98

GROOVE ME

King Floyd

CHIMNEYVILLE 435
WRITER: KING FLOYD
PRODUCER: WARDELL QUEZERGUE
January 2, 1971 (4 weeks)

Southern lightning evidently strikes twice. On Sunday, May 17, 1970, the Malaco studios in Jackson, Mississippi, electrified two Number One hits: King Floyd's "Groove Me" and Jean Knight's "Mr. Big Stuff."

Both were recorded at the same session on that date, and both were testimony to the talents of Wardell Quezergue, a journeyman arranger/producer from New Orleans who brought up Floyd and Knight—and a couple of other acts—from Louisiana for a shot at the big time.

"They were artists that Wardell and a guy named Elijah Walker got together," explains Tommy Couch, whose studio it was (and still is). "We had a New Orleans week here at Malaco. They got on the bus and came on up."

Quezergue had traveled up the *Billboard* charts, too. He arranged a couple of 1965's more distinctive hits, "Teasin' You" by Willie Tee and "Iko Iko" by the Dixie Cups. He was also behind "Barefootin' " by Robert Parker, a quintessential Crescent City smash in '66.

Enter King Floyd, also from New Orleans. "I started singing when I was about 11 or 12," he told Jeff Hannusch in a *Goldmine* interview. "I used to hang out with Earl King and Willie Tee around the One Stop

Record Shop on Rampart Street. I decided back then I wanted to be a musician, and the best way for me to learn was to hang out and learn from the people that were out there doin' it."

Floyd knocked "Groove Me" into shape with the help of singer Carrollton Pierre (C.P.) Love, who had recorded for a label set up by Elijah Walker and Earl King. "Floyd was sort of the more established artist of the group," says Tommy Couch, recalling that three of them—Knight, the Barons, and a girl group—came to Jackson from New Orleans "in an old school bus." Floyd traveled by car.

The week before, the men of Malaco cut the instrumental tracks for the four acts. "We did two sides on each," says Couch. "The B side to 'Groove Me' was really the A side, 'What Our Love Needs.' We thought it was the A side because we put strings on it." The vocals were added that Sunday, May 17.

The rhythm section featured Jerry Puckett on guitar, Vernie Robbins on bass, and James Stroud on drums, with Quezergue playing keyboards. The team had played together before: behind Southern soul sister Jackie Moore in 1969, for instance, when she was signed to Atlantic Records.

On this occasion, however, Malaco couldn't interest anyone—including Atlantic—in the material. "So we decided to put out King Floyd's record ourselves," declares Couch, "and that's when we came up with the Chimneyville label." The name echoed back to the Civil War: When Northern regiments came through Jackson, "they burned the city to the ground," says the Malaco executive, "and the only thing that was left were chimneys, sticking up in the air. So they called it Chimneyville."

99

IF I WERE YOUR WOMAN

Gladys Knight & the Pips

SOUL 35078
WRITERS: GLORIA JONES,
PAM SAWYER, CLAY MCMURRAY
PRODUCER: CLAY MCMURRAY
January 23, 1971 (1 week)

A barbecue lunch washed down with champagne helped songwriters Gloria Jones and Pam Sawyer serve up Gladys Knight & the Pips' first Number One since 1967's "I Heard It Through the Grapevine." "If I Were Your Woman" even recaptured the mood of the group's pre-Motown days, when they were cutting strikingly personal ballads like "Letter Full of Tears" and "Giving Up."

Gloria Jones tells that she and Sawyer crafted the song in 30 minutes one Los Angeles afternoon. "We wanted to come up with something that was real magic. The women's liberation movement was strong at that time, but Pam and I were more romantic.

"We went around the corner and bought a barbecue meal, then champagne. We figured we would just have lunch and relax and discuss this song about how women, when they fall in love, can't hold back. The woman gives all—she can't keep anything from her man, she's willing to die for him.

"After lunch, we just started putting the song together. I came up with the melody first—which I actually wrote in thirds—and then we started putting lyrics to it. Pam and I were discussing how love is and how it can be deceiving, but we turned everything around to make it positive."

Sawyer submitted the song to Motown's Clay McMurray, who was taking over the production of Gladys and the Pips from Norman Whitfield. "Norman heard the song," Jones says, "and told Clay, 'If you record that on Gladys, you'll have a Number One record.' "

McMurray may have been convinced, but Knight was not, and Jones contends that it took Berry Gordy himself to convince her of the song's potential. Once persuaded, she recorded it in Detroit with the crack Motown musicians—that melodramatic lead guitar belongs to Robert White, according to Jones—and arranger Paul Riser.

"Paul arranged it exactly the way it was written: it was faithful to the original melody," says Jones. "The session went very well, especially with Clay as producer. He's the one who brought it off. He got the performance out of Gladys."

When "If I Were Your Woman" was first released, Jones took her composer credits under the name LaVern Ware to avoid association with her earlier adventures as a recording artist (she cut the original version of "Tainted Love"). In those days, she says, "If you were a singer, you were a singer. If you wrote songs, you were a songwriter. The only way I could get in as a writer was to use another name."

100

(DO THE) PUSH AND PULL, PART 1

Rufus Thomas

STAX 0079
WRITER: RUFUS THOMAS
PRODUCERS: AL BELL, TOM NIXON
February 6, 1971 (2 weeks)

I knew that whenever we needed a hit," declares Al Bell, onetime president of Stax Records, "we were going to get one if there was a dance being born anywhere in America. I just needed to find out where it was, how they looked when they were doing it, and tell Rufus. And he'd get a hit, whatever it was."

Rufus Thomas was, indeed, the crown prince of dance: His menagerie of steps included the dog, the funky chicken, the breakdown, the funky penguin. Bell talks about the "youthful spirit" of the man, who was 46 when "Walking the Dog" whistled its way into the top 10 of the pop charts in 1963, and 53 when "(Do The) Push and Pull" hit Number One on the R&B top 50. "Somehow or other, he was always able to connect with young people."

The former Stax chief recalls seeing teenagers dancing the push and pull in Chicago, where he was nightclubbing with Rodney Jones, the influential DJ from local powerhouse WVON. Bell and Stax colleague Tom Nixon were qualified to help Thomas turn it into a record: one year earlier, they had produced "Do the Funky Chicken," the performer's biggest hit since "Walking the Dog."

"Rufus was an artist who took a groove and wrote a song," says Bell. "He would walk into the studio, get the musicians to play, and probably not even have a song on his mind. Once they got a groove—if they didn't get a groove, he wouldn't be inspired—Rufus would start writing, and the song would come as the music was being played. He'd be in the middle of the floor, and he'd be singing whatever came to his mind that fit. And somehow or other, it would always fit."

Rufus Thomas

Tom Nixon, co-producer of "(Do The) Push and Pull," was an engineer who had been working in California with former Motown A&R director Mickey Stevenson. Bell, who brought him to Memphis, says, "Tom was brilliant, and this session with Rufus was the first time I had ever seen an engineer measuring beats per minute, because on 'Push and Pull,' Tom had a stopwatch.

"I couldn't understand for the life of me what he was doing. As it's being worked up in the studio, he's over in the corner, counting these beats. I'm saying, 'What do you mean, beats per minute? Who cares?' As long as the groove is there, put the stopwatch down." The groove *was* there, aided by arranger Carl Hampton and the Stax studio band.

Bell attributes Thomas's versatility to his background: a singer and dancer with the Rabbit Foot Minstrels revue in the '30s, a radio personality on Memphis station WDIA in the '40s. Later, his duet with daughter Carla, "Cause I Love You," was the first release to spark the historic relationship between Stax Records (then known as Satellite) and Atlantic.

"Rufus had the training and professionalism most people didn't know," Bell concludes. "Having come out of the minstrel era, working in early black radio, that's the kind of experience that's really unique."

101

JODY'S GOT YOUR GIRL AND GONE

Johnnie Taylor

STAX 0085
WRITERS: KAY BARKER,
JAMES WILSON, DON DAVIS
PRODUCER: DON DAVIS
February 20, 1971 (2 weeks)

Johnnie Taylor's first Number One [see 65—"Who's Making Love"] floored him, quite literally.

About a month after cutting the record, producer Don Davis says he ran into the singer in the lobby of Miami's Sheraton-Four Ambassadors Hotel. It was August 1968, and both men were at the annual convention of the black DJs' association, NATRA.

Taylor began berating Davis about the intense pressure of the recording session for "Who's Making Love," which had not yet been released. "I kept walking," says the producer, "and he kept taunting me. Finally, I made it to the elevator, turned around and

Johnnie Taylor

told him that the record had come out three days ago and that Chicago had ordered 35,000 copies the first day, and 70,000 the third day.

"He looked at me, and said, 'You're kidding.' Johnnie was used to selling 100,000 records nationwide, not just from one city. He said, 'Jeez,' and slid down the wall onto the floor and sat there."

"Who's Making Love" went on to sell a couple of million copies, of course, and was followed by six more Taylor-made top 10 hits between 1969 and 1970. Early the following year, "Jody's Got Your Girl and Gone" took its turn at the top.

"We didn't necessarily cut a record because we had a song," Don Davis explains. "We cut a record because we had the music." In the case of "Jody," the instrumental track was crafted first in Memphis. "It was just one of those many days when I felt these grooves, you know. We got in there and played this thing and, boy, it was just hitting and hitting and hitting." Davis, a session musician in Detroit during the '60s, played guitar fills alongside the Stax house band.

Storing the track for future use, the producer went about his business until, two months later, it was time to prepare a new Johnnie Taylor album. "It was a Friday night, and I was trying to find a title for this groove. My best friend came by, and he was trying to persuade me to go out on the town. I said, 'No, I've got to work on these records.' "

The friend, James Wilson, stuck around for a couple of hours, recalls Davis. "Finally, when he got ready to leave, he said, 'Man, I'm not going home, ain't no sense in going home, Jody's got your girl and gone.' He was talking about a conversation he was having on the telephone. I said, 'That's what this track is!' And so we sat down and wrote the song right then and there."

"Jody's Got Your Girl and Gone" was polished later with Kay Barker (a writer whom Wilson knew) and then Johnnie Taylor cut his vocals. Davis overdubbed horns at Detroit's United Sound, where he also recorded the background singers. Drafted for those tough male chants—sounding for all the world like a platoon of drill sergeants—were the Dramatics [see 122—"In the Rain"]. Theirs was also the last piece of the record. Says Davis, "They came in, did a great job, and that was it!"

102

JUST MY IMAGINATION (RUNNING AWAY WITH ME)

The Temptations

GORDY 7105

WRITERS: NORMAN WHITFIELD, BARRETT STRONG

PRODUCER: NORMAN WHITFIELD

March 6, 1971 (3 weeks)

Edward James Kendricks had leaving on his mind in 1970.

He was managing a group called the Posse ("Looking and sounding like early Temptations," reported *Billboard*), who were signed to his own label, EJK Records. He had begun talks with Motown and producer Frank Wilson about cutting solo material [see 155—"Keep on Truckin' "]. And he was experiencing friction with his fellow Temptations. "We didn't try to stop him from going and he didn't want to stay," declared the group's Otis Williams in his autobiography *Temptations* (Putnam, 1988), "so that was that."

Before Eddie ran away, there was "Just My Imagination." The song itself was a couple of years old, according to Barrett Strong, who wrote lyrics to Norman Whitfield's melodies. "The idea was shown to Norman, you know, sometime before we recorded it," he remembers. "He said, 'Not right now,' but then he came by my house one morning and said, 'Remember that idea? Well, play it.' "

Whitfield wasted no more time. " 'I am going down to the studio and I am going to record it,' " Strong recalls the producer announcing. "I had no idea how he was going to go about doing it. When I

The Temptations

heard the track and everything, it shocked me—and I thought it was great."

True enough. Eddie Kendricks's feather-light lead and the group's Jacuzzi-warm harmonies melted perfectly into Jerry Long's orchestration—tympani, banks of violins, and a harp!—underpinned by James Jamerson's strolling bass and Jack Brokensha's shimmering vibes.

"We loved the song with just the basic tracks," Otis Williams wrote, "but we were totally knocked out when we heard the finished record, with all the strings. Arranger Jerry Long, who studied in Paris and scored movies, did a wonderful job capturing the song's magical, dreamy sadness. It was, I think, Eddie's finest moment.

"We were up half the night recording the song, and when I left at six in the morning, Eddie was still putting down his vocals. Things between us were very bad, but I called him the next day to let him know I was concerned about how hard he worked and appreciated his efforts."

Kendricks was officially gone (replaced by Ricky Owens, then Damon Harris) in March 1971, the month that "Just My Imagination" held sway at Number One. "When I left the Temps," he explained afterwards, "I never expected to do so much hard work 'cause I had gotten used to having things done for me."

What Motown had done for the Temptations—and vice versa—was apparent in 1970's year-end issue of *Billboard*. The group was named "top soul LP artists of the '60s," with 13 Number One albums, and "top soul singles artists of the '60s," with nine Number One 45s. They had captured the imagination of a decade.

103
WHAT'S GOING ON
Marvin Gaye

TAMLA 54201
WRITERS: AL CLEVELAND,
MARVIN GAYE, RENALDO BENSON
PRODUCER: MARVIN GAYE
March 27, 1971 (5 weeks)

The alto sax of Eli Fountain sketched a haunting, liquid signature at the start of "What's Going On," opening the book on one of the most celebrated, influential albums in the history of rhythm & blues.

Marvin Gaye's music baffled and defied the old Motown order—Berry Gordy certainly didn't like what he heard—even as it defined the new. In particular, the album's release in May 1971 gave heart to Stevie Wonder, who turned 21 that same month and took charge of his own career.

Yet Gordy's opposition was hardly the project's first obstacle. Gaye was not popular among the producers and arrangers of Motown in 1970, according to David Van DePitte, who arranged and conducted the orchestra on "What's Going On."

"I thought he was pretty terrific, but I had never worked with him or for him prior to this project," Van DePitte tells. "Somebody said to me, 'Guess what, you're elected.' After taking a quick poll around the room, I came to find out that nobody else wanted to do it. They had all worked with Marvin before and found him to be such a pain in the fanny."

DePitte says that when took on the task, he was persuaded that Gaye had written all the songs, that everything was completed, and that he had the overall album concept. "Then as we sat down and started working on these tunes, not only did he not have a concept, but I thought it bizarre that all this material was finished but he didn't have lyrics for all of it.

"When Obie Benson showed up one night and started asking Marvin about how his tune was coming along, and when James Nyx and I would sit there hour after hour staring at each other, waiting for Marvin to show up from his basketball game or whatever the hell he was doing...then it dawned on me that there were more people involved than he had led me to believe."

Benson, one of the Four Tops, and Al Cleveland, a Motown staff writer/producer, were the original authors of "What's Going On," and had submitted a tape of the song to Gaye. Yet even though the singer wrote only two of the album's nine songs by himself, Van DePitte found a common thread in the material: "The way the tunes were laying, they were little stories, and it just kind of felt that one should flow into the next." Consequently, the arranger says he suggested the use of musical bridges between the tunes, to hang them together.

Lyrically, Gaye was affected by the social and political turmoil of the times—and by the first-hand experiences of someone close. "When my brother Frankie came home from Vietnam and began telling me stories," Gaye explained to biographer David Ritz in *Divided Soul* (McGraw Hill, 1985), "my blood started to boil. I knew I had something—an anger, an energy, an artistic point of view."

Later, when the singer delivered the single of "What's Going On," Motown officials thought the mix was terrible, like two radio stations playing simultaneously. Phil Jones, one of the company's marketing executives at the time, recalls, "Marvin said, 'OK, Phil, if you think it needs a remix. I've only remixed it 83 times.'

"So we listened to it again, and I said, 'We're going to release the damn thing like it is.' I set it up for my birthday—January 20th, 1971—and we shipped the record. Within a day, distributors were calling me back—it was a monster."

104

NEVER CAN SAY GOODBYE

The Jackson 5

MOTOWN 1179
WRITER: CLIFTON DAVIS
PRODUCER: HAL DAVIS
May 1, 1971 (3 weeks)

Thin walls at Motown's Los Angeles headquarters on Sunset Boulevard helped to bring "Never Can Say Goodbye" to the Jackson 5.

Producer Hal Davis was in his office there, trying to talk to fellow producer Jerry Marcellino. Someone was playing a piano in an adjacent room, he remembers. "I heard this melody, and it kept interrupting my ear, because the melody was a hit. I told Jerry, 'That's a hit, whatever it is.'

"I walked next door, and Clifton Davis was auditioning this tune that he wanted to bring to the publishing company. I said, 'That's a hit, can I cut it?' He said, 'Yeah, who've you got?' And I said, 'I'll cut it on the Jackson 5 right away.' He said, 'When you gonna cut it?' I said, 'Tonight.' "

Hal Davis had bragging rights on the Jacksons at that stage, having produced their biggest-selling single to date [see 94—"I'll Be There"]. Clifton Davis (no relation) was an actor and songwriter, an evangelist's son who had moved to Los Angeles. (He went on to compose another Jackson 5 success, "Lookin' Through the Windows," and eventually to star in the popular '80s television sitcom, *Amen*.)

Fast-working Hal Davis says he recorded the track for "Never Can Say Goodbye" that same night, with arranger Gene Page. He used the Sound Factory for most of his early-'70s sessions, with a cadre of Los Angeles sidemen that generally included Bob West (bass), Art Wright and David T. Walker (guitars), Joe Sample (keyboards), and Gene Pello (drums).

Two days later, Davis cut the Jackson 5 vocals. The group wasn't yet as comfortable with ballads as with uptempo tunes, but the producer asserts that their admiration for *his* vocalizing ("I was a child singer") helped smooth the task. "That's one tune they didn't give me any problems on, because they were reaching for something else. I had been to Vegas with them, and we had played the Grand

The Jackson 5

Hotel. They wanted to go adult, and 'Never Can Say Goodbye' did it for them."

Even so, Davis needed Berry Gordy's intervention to get the song released as a single—and thin walls at Motown once again came to the rescue. "The head of A&R felt the tune was a little *too* adult," explains Davis. "He said, 'Hal, we wanna keep them R&B, I don't think I'm gonna release it.'

"I got very upset, and got me a couple of shots of booze. My office was next door to Berry's, and he had a meeting in there. So I turned my stereo real loud, so all Berry could hear was 'Never Can Say Goodbye.' He came out of his office and said, 'Stop, that's a smash.' And I said, 'That's why I turned it up.' He said, 'What's the problem?' I told him, 'A&R is holding it up, it's been cut over a month and it's just been sitting in the can.' The rest was history."

105

BRIDGE OVER TROUBLED WATER

Aretha Franklin

ATLANTIC 2796
WRITER: PAUL SIMON
PRODUCERS: JERRY WEXLER, TOM DOWD, ARIF MARDIN
May 22, 1971 (2 weeks)

As the curtain rose on 1971, Atlantic Records wanted more *respect* for Aretha Franklin—at least, in the pop market.

The singer hadn't reached the top 10 of *Billboard's* Hot 100 since "The House That Jack Built"/"I Say a Little Prayer" in 1968. Likewise, her last top 10 LP was *Aretha Now*, that same year. And 1970's *Spirit in the*

Dark met with disappointing sales—the first Aretha album on Atlantic to fall short of the top 20.

So the record company was determined to return Aretha to the pop pinnacle in 1971. Its strategy included a live LP taped at San Francisco's Fillmore West, an intense schedule of public appearances elsewhere, and a little help from the Paul Simon songbook.

Simon wrote "Bridge over Troubled Water" for himself and Art Garfunkel in Los Angeles in 1969. That's also where he recorded the instrumental track, although Peter Guralnick reported in his book, *Sweet Soul Music* (Harper & Row, 1986), that there was a plan to cut it with the Stax rhythm section in Memphis.

For her part, Aretha had begun to reach in rock's repertory around 1969–70, trying songs by John Lennon and Paul McCartney, Elton John, and Robbie Robertson. She taped "Bridge over Troubled Water" (and McCartney's "The Long And Winding Road") in August 1970 at the Atlantic studios in New York.

The session featured not the customary players imported from Muscle Shoals but some of the other best musicians in the country: Billy Preston on organ, Cornell Dupree on guitar, Chuck Rainey on electric bass, Ray Lucas on drums, and, of course, King Curtis on tenor sax. "It was a slightly different band," affirms the record's co-producer, Arif Mardin. "That Curtis solo was really beautiful, and there was Aretha's fabulous background arrangement.

"She would cook dinner, the girls would come in, help with the food and everything. And as they're working in this warm atmosphere, they would go, *Why don't you/why don't you/let it be*, or whatever the part was. *Still waters run deep*. When they came to the studio, we had to learn from them, because they had the timing."

"Bridge over Troubled Water" stayed on the shelf for several months, however, while Jerry Wexler planned her 1971 shows at the Fillmore West March 5–7 and an appearance at the Grammy awards in Los Angeles on March 16. On both occasions, Franklin sang "Bridge over Troubled Water." The Grammy show, before a live television audience, created a particular impact. On March 19, Atlantic released her studio recording of the song as a single, and within four chart weeks, it soared into the top 10 of the Hot 100.

Later in the year, *Aretha Live at Fillmore West* returned Franklin to the top 10 of the pop LP charts for the first time since *Aretha Now*. Part of the album's appeal: a live recording of "Bridge over Troubled Water."

Just as the original had earned awards in 1970 for Simon & Garfunkel, so did Aretha's version gain a Grammy the following year. It was also the first of four consecutive top 10 pop hits for Aretha in 1971–72. The Queen of Soul, crowned anew.

106

WANT ADS

The Honey Cone

HOT WAX 7011
WRITERS: NORMAN JOHNSON, GREG PERRY, BARNEY PERKINS
PRODUCER: GREG PERRY
May 29, 1971 (3 weeks)

For girl-group fans, "Want Ads" was heaven on earth. It featured three young women—a cross between the Shangri-Las and the Supremes—and the guiding vision of Detroit's finest:Holland/Dozier/Holland. All this, and a lead singer whose sister was the Queen of Phil Spector's "wall of sound."

Hot Wax Records was launched in 1969 as Eddie Holland's first business venture since he quit Motown with brother Brian and partner Lamont Dozier. The label's first act was the Honey Cone, featuring Edna Wright on lead vocals.

"Eddie had heard my voice years before, unbeknownest to me," says Wright, sister of Darlene Love. "He wanted me as a single artist; I gave them the idea for a girl group. I had been out on the road with Billy Preston and the Righteous Brothers, and I didn't want to go alone again."

Wright's fellow recruits were Carolyn Willis, a close friend who had been a member of the one-hit Girlfriends, and Shelly Clark, who used to sing with the Ikettes. "While You're Out Looking for Sugar?" was the first Honey Cone success; "Want Ads" was their fourth, a million-selling crossover hit that booked space at the top of Billboard's R&B *and* pop charts.

The song was written by two members of the Hot Wax creative team, Greg Perry and Norman (General) Johnson, with Barney Perkins, an engineer at the Holland/Dozier/Holland studio. "Barney also used to work at another small studio," recalls Perry. "I went over there, we were talking and he said, 'Hey, somebody should write a song about the want ads,' because he had been looking for a job or something.

"About a week later, I was sitting at the piano and it came out! I wrote the chorus line, but it was a little different: I had said, *'Gonna put it in the want ads/I need some love for sale.'* When I told this to General, he said, 'Hey, man, you're making this girl sound like a prostitute. Change it around.' So we changed it and went from there, cut it a couple of times—and the second time, we came up with 'Wanted: young man, single and free.' "

Such adjustments were easy with an in-house studio and a regular crew of musicians [see 112—"Stick-Up"]. Initially, Perry cut "Want Ads" with Scherrie

Payne and the Glass House. "I walked into the studio to do something," says Edna Wright, "and Scherrie was doing 'Want Ads,' but it was different. The lyrics were different, and so was the chorus line. Scherrie came out and told me, 'You do it, I don't care for it.' I said, 'Are you serious?' She said, 'Yeah.'

"Greg and General went back in the studio and did it again. I think General changed a few of the lyrics on it, and Perry upped the track, made the bass lines and everything tighter and better. When I heard it again, I said, 'This is it,' put my voice on, and everyone knew it was a smash after that."

107

DON'T KNOCK MY LOVE (PART 1)

Wilson Pickett

ATLANTIC 2797
WRITERS: WILSON PICKETT, BRAD SHAPIRO
PRODUCERS: DAVE CRAWFORD, BRAD SHAPIRO
June 26, 1971 (1 week)

Somewhere in a storage room at Atlantic Records—or perhaps now in the Rock & Roll Hall of Fame—is a pair of headphones once favored by Wilson Pickett. "They were green and funky," declares Brad Shapiro, "and he didn't like singing without them."

The 'phones certainly bestowed their good luck on "Don't Knock My Love," another Pickett fireball in a career ablaze with them. Shapiro co-wrote and co-produced the song. "Jerry Wexler had put me together with Dave Crawford in some kind of nouveau combination," he says, "the black and the white producer."

It was January 1971, and the pair journeyed to Muscle Shoals Sound, the onetime casket factory converted to a recording studio. The musicians were seasoned by hitmaking: Barry Beckett on organ, Dennis Coffey and Tippy Armstrong on guitars, David Hood on bass, Roger Hawkins on drums, and a couple of Motown imports, Eddie "Bongo" Brown on congas, and Jack Ashford on tambourine. Dave Crawford played piano.

"It was the last song on the date," Shapiro tells. "They were fooling around with a riff Dennis had just started playing, and a bassline by David evolved from that. And out of the corner of my eye, I saw Pickett run into the vocal booth—because we were cutting him live—and when they got to a certain part of the riff, he started singing: *If you don't like it/don't knock it/Somebody else/might want to rock it.*"

That was all the lyric Pickett had, so as he was running it down, Shapiro says, "I got a yellow-line pad and just started writing one line after another. Nothing was prepared at all; there was no chord sheet, nothing."

Musicians and singers kept jamming, and when they took a break, Shapiro called over: " 'Pickett, look at these lyrics.' And he just jumped up and said, 'That's it!' So we came back out and the tape was running on this riff. Still nobody took a chord sheet. I just counted the bars and as [the musicians] were running down the first verse, I wrote the second verse. Then there was a little bridge part, going up to the third verse—and I handed that to him the same way."

The session over, Shapiro and Pickett headed to Atlantic's studios at 1841 Broadway. "Pickett never kept his [original] vocals," says the producer. "He would always go back to New York and do them over." Later, too, the Memphis Horns and background vocals were overdubbed.

The final mixing took some time, Shapiro admits, but no one doubted "Don't Knock My Love" was a smash. "I remember [Atlantic VP] Henry Allen telling someone, '*This* is the record,' and the first day, Detroit sold 25,000 or 30,000 copies. There was that much buzz."

To this day, Shapiro's admiration for Pickett runs deep. "I still don't know where he got the phrase, 'Don't knock my love.' He might have got it in Philadelphia; I think he showed it to Gamble and Huff, but they didn't do anything with it. Nobody ever knew how talented Pickett really was. I guess it was a distraction from the rest of his personality."

108

MR. BIG STUFF

Jean Knight

STAX 0088
WRITERS: JOE BROUSSARD, RALPH WILLIAMS, CARROL WASHINGTON
PRODUCER: WARDELL QUEZERGUE
July 3, 1971 (5 weeks)

Jean Knight of New Orleans gave Stax Records of Memphis one of their biggest hits of 1971—but the sassy, brassy single almost didn't make it past the starting gate.

"Mr. Big Stuff" was recorded at the Malaco studios in Jackson, Mississippi, on the same Sunday in 1970 that gave birth to King Floyd's certified million-seller, "Groove Me" [see 98]. Producer Wardell Quezergue and his partner, Elijah Walker, were cutting four acts for Malaco that May weekend.

"Right when we got through, we took all four of these artists to Memphis and played them for somebody at Stax," says Malaco proprietor Tommy

Jean Knight

Couch. "I don't want to call any names, but the guy listened to all four of the artists, two songs each. He said, 'It sounds good, but I don't hear any hits.' "

When Malaco launched its own Chimneyville label to release King Floyd's "What Our Love Needs," most DJs didn't hear a hit, either. It took one adventurous jock to flip the single—and "Groove Me" was on its way.

"A good friend of mine, Tim Whitsett, worked for Stax and ran the publishing company," declares Couch. "After 'Groove Me' came out and started catching on, he remembered the Jean Knight thing that was in there and insisted they take it." Even then, it was a full year between the weekend "Mr. Big Stuff" was recorded and the week it debuted on *Billboard*'s R&B charts in the spring of '71.

Jean Knight came from New Orleans, with a resume that showed she'd been produced by Huey Meaux. At the Malaco session, she sang to a rhythm track crafted earlier by the Chimneyville Express: Jerry Puckett (guitar), Vernie Robbins (bass), and James Stroud (drums), with keyboards in the hands of Wardell Quezergue, who also had a local horn section riffing to his instructions.

"Wardell was a great guy, one of the most talented arrangers of anyone I've ever seen," says Couch. "He could sit and listen to a playback in the studio while writing horn charts on another song—and point out things that he was hearing while writing that other song."

Ironically, Tommy Couch and Jean Knight played a return match—on opposite sides—14 years after "Mr. Big Stuff" hit the heights. Knight had recorded Sidney Simien's "My Toot Toot" (another Crescent City copyright) with producer Isaac Bolden, only to find herself competing with a version by Denise LaSalle, co-produced by Couch. Knight won the race at home, but not abroad: LaSalle's Malaco-made "Toot Toot" strutted all the way into the British top 10 in 1985. The Chimneyville Express was right on time.

109

HOT PANTS (SHE GOT TO USE WHAT SHE GOT TO GET WHAT SHE WANTS) (PART 1)

James Brown

PEOPLE 2501
WRITERS: JAMES BROWN, FRED WESLEY
PRODUCER: JAMES BROWN
August 7, 1971 (1 week)

In the summer of '71, James Brown left King Records. The Cincinnati independent had been his home since the night in January 1956 when Ralph Bass signed up the Flames for $200.

The label had put a staggering 64 of his singles on the *Billboard* charts, 38 of them in the top ten. Now, Soul Brother No. 1 was joining Polydor, the company that had distributed his records abroad for the previous three years. In its July 24, 1971, edition, *Billboard* reported, "The five-year contract includes all James Brown product except for two current singles, 'Escape-ism' and 'Hot Pants,' which will remain in the King catalog. The deal also includes publishing."

"Hot Pants," then, was JB's last recording for King, and the second release on his newly established custom label, People. When Brown switched to Polydor on July 1, King kept the record for a sell-off period—long enough to hit Number One and an impressive number 15 on the pop charts.

The year not only marked a new record deal for Brown, but also a new band—the J.B.'s, including Bootsy and Catfish Collins, split in March—and the homecoming of a veteran, Fred Wesley.

A fertile trombonist and budding arranger, Wesley had returned from an 18-month self-imposed exile to become bandleader and an important fixture in

Brown's '70s fortunes. He originally joined the James Brown Band in 1968, recommended by trumpeter Waymon Reed, a credible jazz musician who was also the magnet for Pee Wee Ellis.

Wesley often clashed with Brown, and left about a year later. He returned in January 1971, before the demise of the Bootsy/Catfish J.B.'s. "When I was offered the job, I grabbed it, because I had matured," Wesley admits. "I understood James Brown better."

"Hot Pants" was recorded on May 13 at the Starday/King studios in Nashville. With Wesley on trombone, the band included veterans Jabo Starks (drums), Bobby Byrd (organ), and St. Clair Pinckney (tenor), with new guitarists Hearlon "Cheese" Martin and Robert Coleman, and Fred Thomas (bass). Also, Johnny Griggs (congas) and Jimmy Parker (alto) were in on the session.

The tune is quintessential '70s James Brown. Clearly, the original J.B.'s style—simple groove, guitars up front, Jabo locked in—proved the right formula. Wesley stayed with it, perhaps because he had no choice. What else could he do with new players? In time, he improved on and jazzed up the prescription, but this track is almost textbook.

"I went in to a rehearsal or a writing session with a basic idea from James," explains Wesley. "I'd go in and get it together, then James would come in and fine-tune it, give it the spice. His vocal really made the arrangement.

"It was always a show atmosphere, no matter where we were. Generally, whenever we recorded, everybody could see him. The first rule you'd learn in working with James Brown: *watch* James Brown. Because going in, you never knew who was going to solo."

110

MERCY MERCY ME (THE ECOLOGY)

Marvin Gaye

TAMLA 54207
WRITER: MARVIN GAYE
PRODUCER: MARVIN GAYE
August 14, 1971 (2 weeks)

Mercy Mercy Me (The Ecology)" was the second 45 from Marvin Gaye's landmark album, *What's Going On*. Motown founder Berry Gordy Jr. hadn't much cared for the first single, the LP's title track, and doubted its suitability for release. But by the middle of 1971, Gaye's creative instincts were validated: *What's Going On* crashed on the soul album charts in the top five, and began charging up the pop rankings.

Motown released "Mercy Mercy Me (The Ecology)" in June, and *Billboard* called the record a "super original rhythm number with a strong lyric line and vocal workout." Its strength did, indeed, lie in the lyrics; Gaye's environmental concern contrasted with the content of most pop and R&B songs of the day. And as the late Earl Van Dyke, leader of Motown's incandescent studio band, said later, "Berry Gordy didn't understand the world 'ecology.' It had to be explained to him."

In fact, much of *What's Going On* demonstrated Gaye's emerging social awareness. To help execute his masterwork, the singer had used an unusual blend of musicians. They included members of Earl Van Dyke's regular cadre—guitarists Joe Messina and Robert White, bassists James Jamerson and Bob Babitt, percussionists Jack Brokensha and Jack Ashford—together with a number of players recruited by arranger David Van DePitte. Among these were Chet Forest on drums and sax soloists Eli Fountain (alto) and Bill Moore (tenor). Gaye himself played piano.

"Marvin wanted somebody other than the normal drummers who worked at Motown," says Van DePitte. "Chet was coming from a little different place: He was a white guy, and he had done a great deal of studying in the classical vein. He was also one of the best jazz drummers I ever worked with. When this guy locked into a groove, you couldn't shift him."

For Van Dyke and his regular session players, the project was musically closer to home than most of their Motown work. "Basically, all the staff musicians were jazz musicians," he said. "They had left Detroit in the '50s, and Berry got them all back together. Everybody came from a different place or a different group. They were hand-picked. So *What's Going On* was very, very simple—too simple."

The string section on the album, led by concert master Gordon Staples, came from the Detroit Symphony Orchestra. The strings and horns were recorded at what had been the Golden World studios in Detroit, the rhythm tracks at Motown's old studio on West Grand Boulevard.

As an experienced arranger, Van DePitte knew how to handle his assignment. Handling Gaye was another matter. "It was a prolonged process only because Marvin didn't show up half the time," he says. "We were working at his home, and I would go and sit for hours. He would have an afternoon or evening appointment, and he'd not show—so I would just go home and try for another day.

"The actual time we spent working at the album probably wasn't any longer than a week, but I think it ended up going over a period of three to four months all told, because of trying to hook up with Marvin."

At the time, Van DePitte notes, Gaye was preoccupied with tryouts for the Detroit Lions, the result of a friendship with several of the players. Ultimately, it was a fruitless exercise, but "so much on his mind that the album was almost secondary," according to Van DePitte.

"When the Lions refused him—it wasn't his athletic abilities, they just didn't want to be obligated to him for any injuries that might happen—then he turned to the album all of a sudden, and it was time to start writing."

111

SPANISH HARLEM

Aretha Franklin

ATLANTIC 2817
WRITERS: JERRY LEIBER, PHIL SPECTOR
PRODUCERS: JERRY WEXLER, TOM DOWD, ARIF MARDIN
August 28, 1971 (3 weeks)

As the pages on the calendar flip backwards to October 27, 1960, Arif Mardin can picture it: "Ben E. King in the booth," he says. "Leiber and Stoller in the control room, strings and guitars, the rhythm section, all at the same time."

King cut "Spanish Harlem" on that date, and—although originally planned as a B side—it would become the first elegant gem of his cluster of solo hits. On February 16, 1971, Aretha Franklin added new luster to the song, and it would become her highest-charted pop hit since 1968's "Chain Of Fools."

"That was part of a group of songs that were recorded for the *Young, Gifted and Black* album," explains Mardin, who co-produced them with Jerry Wexler and Tom Dowd. Then, he says, "Spanish Harlem" was withheld and put into *Aretha's Greatest Hits*.

Franklin was working at Miami's Criteria studios, and those February '71 sessions produced some of her most confident—and most personal—recordings: not only "Spanish Harlem," but also "Rock Steady," "Day Dreaming" and "All the King's Horses."

The rhythm section featured Donny Hathaway on electric piano and organ, Cornell Dupree on guitar, Chuck Rainey on bass, and Bernard Purdie on drums. Sisters Carolyn and Erma Franklin sang background, with Carolyn's group, the Sweethearts of Soul: Ann Clark, Pat Smith, and Margaret Branch.

"I remember putting this Spanish guitar on 'Spanish Harlem,' " says Mardin, identifying the player as Don Arnone. "It wasn't Cornell Dupree," he adds, refuting information published elsewhere. "Cornell doesn't play acoustic.

"Aretha's [piano] solo was very long on the original version, so I had to make a copy of Aretha's last word and when she ended the phrase [before the bridge], cut the tape physically and put that last word onto where the piano solo starts in order to make the edit sound natural."

After the track was cut in Miami, Mardin added sweetening in New York, including flute ("always Hubert Laws") and congas ("could have been Ralph MacDonald"), as well as cellos. For strings, he favored Gene Orloff as concert master, with a 10- or 11-piece section: four first violins, three second violins, two violas, and one or two cellos.

"I always used the same people since the '60s, from the [New York] Philharmonic," Mardin notes. "I saw Gene's name somewhere, I said, 'I want this guy.' Why? Because I remembered he was one of the violin players who played on *Charlie Parker and Strings*. As a jazz fan, I thought if anyone can play for Bird, he's good enough for me."

112

STICK-UP

The Honey Cone

HOT WAX 7106
WRITERS: GENERAL JOHNSON, ANGELO BOND, GREG PERRY
PRODUCERS: GREG PERRY, GENERAL JOHNSON
September 18, 1971 (2 weeks)

The Motown connection was etched into every groove at Hot Wax Records, label home of the Honey Cone. After all, the proprietors were Holland/Dozier/Holland.

"They were pretty good teachers—they knew what they wanted," agrees Edna Wright, who was lead singer of the 'Cone. "What I loved about working with Eddie Holland, and especially Greg Perry and Norman Johnson, was that they were perfectionists. They wouldn't let a song go until it was right. They would re-cut and re-cut, and I would re-sing and re-sing. I'd re-sing 'til I dropped!"

Johnson and Perry were key creative players at Hot Wax and Invictus, its sister label. They were responsible for the Honey Cone's "Want Ads" [see 106] and "Stick-Up," as well as for hits by Freda Payne, 100 Proof Aged in Soul, and the 8th Day. Johnson doubled as lead singer of Chairmen of the Board, just as he had fronted the Showmen ("It Will Stand") during his high school years.

Perry got his start at Chess Records, woodshedding in a back-room studio with the encouragement of A&R director Billy Davis. Turning down a Motown publishing deal because of dubious contract terms, he joined Holland/Dozier/Holland at their new venture.

Perry was 17 at the time. "They signed me to do album projects," he says. "They didn't think there were going to be any singles or anything like that.

The Honey Cone

Then we started competing: I got with General Johnson and we just started cranking material out.

"I would come up with an idea and maybe the chorus line. General was a lot better lyrically [than I was] in those days, and we had another guy who was phenomenal with lyrics, Angelo Bond. We were trying, I guess, to resemble the Holland/Dozier/Holland team, where Brian and Lamont would come up with the chorus lines and melody, then they'd just turn the lyrics over to Eddie.

"Believe it or not, 'Stick-Up' was written the same day we wrote 'Want Ads,' which was about a year before it came out. Actually, we wrote six or seven tunes which were started at the same time—and about five became hits. We got together one night and it was instant: Everything we did was like magic."

Most of the Hot Wax/Invictus hotshots recorded at Holland/Dozier/Holland's own studio, a converted theater on Detroit's Grand River Avenue. "Bob Babbitt played bass," recalls Perry. "Zachary Slater was the drummer. Dennis Coffey was one of the guitar players; Ray Monette, who went on to work with Rare Earth, was our first guitar player."

Others included Sylvester Rivers and Johnny Griffith on keyboards, Eddie Willis and Ray Parker Jr. on guitars, and Jack Ashford and Eddie "Bongo" Brown on percussion. McKinley Jackson was the primary rhythm arranger; Tony Camillo, H. B. Barnum, and Paul Riser also arranged. "Most of the things we just mouthed," Perry concludes. "We'd tell [the musicians] what we wanted, and then they'd play 'em."

113

MAKE IT FUNKY (PART 1)

James Brown

POLYDOR 14088
WRITERS: JAMES BROWN, CHARLES BOBBITT
PRODUCER: JAMES BROWN
October 2, 1971 (2 weeks)

James Brown's first recording for Polydor, "Make It Funky," was a party groove, a largely-instrumental jam with members of his band and entourage chipping in background vocals and chants.

The week after the single hit Number One, the label threw its own party in the pages of *Billboard*: a special supplement to celebrate the signing of James Brown. "It takes plenty to be Soul Brother No. 1," advised the lead article, prefacing pages of copy about JB's extraordinary industry and achievements.

His concert schedule, the supplement reported, was an annual 335 performances. His stage show featured a troupe of dancers, a 21-piece orchestra with four drummers (two working and two standing by), a male singer, a female singer, and a backup trio. His business interests included JB Broadcasting, with radio stations in Augusta, Baltimore, and Knoxville, Tennessee.

Among his overseas excursions, *Billboard* reported, was a trip to Africa the previous December. "We'd stop the plane at some remote town to refuel, and I'd be aroused from my sleep by hundreds of people trying to break into the aircraft to see me," Brown was quoted as saying. "So I had to get out of the plane into an open car and wave as we drove through the crowds."

In another part of the supplement, Polydor president Jerry Schoenbaum declared, "It is of notable importance that Brown is sincere in his empathy with the black people, and his records and his image reflect this. He constantly advises all young people to stay in school and away from drugs...but there's no stopping anyone getting into this man's music."

While the record company was cooking up this spread, Bobby Byrd, his voice drenched in Southern grit, had a simple query for his boss on "Make It Funky": *What you gon' play now?* To which Brown responded, *Bobby, I don't know, but whats'n'ever I play, it's got to be* funky. Affirms Byrd: *Yeah.*

This funkin' session took place at Rodel Studios in the nation's capital—Brown's only Number One recorded there—on July 13, 1971. The rhythm section was Jabo Starks (of course) on drums; Fred Thomas, bass; and Robert Coleman and Hearlon Martin, guitars. The horns were bandleader Fred Wesley on trombone; Jerone Sanford and Russell Crimes, trumpets; Jimmy Parker, alto sax; and St. Clair Pinckney, tenor sax. JB himself played organ.

In keeping with the party mood near the end of "Part 1" of "Make It Funky," James throws out various soul food favorites. He trips over "smothered steak," but quickly corrects himself with a laugh. Then Fred Wesley yells, "Pass the peas," and JB is amused again. "I see you're up on your thing, brother," he approves. The new J.B.'s had cut their single, "Pass the Peas," just two weeks earlier.

114

THIN LINE BETWEEN LOVE & HATE

The Persuaders

ATCO 6822
WRITERS: RICHARD AND ROBERT POINDEXTER, JACKIE MEMBERS
PRODUCER: RICHARD AND ROBERT POINDEXTER
October 16, 1971 (2 weeks)

"Very modern, those guys," recalls Arif Mardin, "very fresh. There was R&B at the time like that. Not perfect vocals, but..."

Atlantic Records' linchpin arranger of the '60s and '70s is talking about the Persuaders, whose "Thin Line Between Love & Hate" was blessed with his poignant string charts and the impassioned vocal leadership of Douglas "Smokey" Scott.

The record was acquired by Atlantic via songwriters Richard and Robert Poindexter, who had their own production company, Win Or Lose. They cut it with Richard's arrangement and the Persuaders' own band, Young, Gifted & Bad, featuring Angel Luis Paniagua (guitar), Paul Young (vibes), Leroy Quick (drums), and Harry Giscombe (bass).

"Smokey" Scott, James Barnes, Willie Holland, and Charles Stodghill were the Persuaders—and before that, crossing the thin line between showbiz and deceit, the Showstoppers. In the late '60s, the quartet was one of a number of American R&B acts tempted across the Atlantic by an unscrupulous British concert promoter. He would contract the performers, then hand them another, better-known name when they stepped off the plane, figuring European audiences wouldn't detect the fiction.

At the time, Scott and his group were known as the Internationals. Disembarking in the U.K., they became the Showstoppers, to capitalize on the local hit ("Ain't Nothing But a Houseparty") enjoyed by the latter group—wherever they were. The deception sobered the Internationals, however, and Scott told *Blues & Soul* that they disbanded for about a year. "Then we decided we wanted to try it again. But first we had to come up with a new name because our previous manager owned the name of the Internationals."

And so they became the Persuaders, subsequently hooking up with the Poindexters and waxing what may have been the first chart-topping domestic-violence song, "Thin Line Between Love & Hate." It became a certified gold record, followed by another hit, "Love Gonna Pack Up (And Walk Out)." In 1973, the group—after some membership changes—returned to the top ten with "Some Guys Have All the Luck."

Guitarist Ronny Drayton, who played in the Persuaders' band for a couple of years, recalls, "They were very good live: the R&B–type dancing and singing group, with polished suits and all. We were on those crazy bus tours, doing the chitlin circuit with everyone from the O'Jays to the Platters. It was the heyday of that vocal group thing."

Personality-wise, Drayton affirms, Douglas Scott was the man. "He had the *savoir faire*." But there was also internal bickering and, the guitarist adds, "some really big fights. One night, one of the guys got hit in the head with a microphone—and that ended it all."

For the Persuaders, perhaps, but not for their songs. Rod Stewart turned "Some Guys Have All The Luck" into a transatlantic pop smash in 1984, the same year that the Pretenders walked "Thin Line Between Love & Hate" into the U.K. top 50.

115

TRAPPED BY A THING CALLED LOVE

Denise LaSalle

WESTBOUND 182

WRITER: DENISE LASALLE

PRODUCERS: BILL JONES, DENISE LASALLE

October 30, 1971 (1 week)

Just before Al, there was LaSalle. "Trapped by a Thing Called Love" sprinkled Willie Mitchell's magic dust over the top of the charts two months before Al Green's first Number One, "Let's Stay Together."

Mitchell arranged and recorded the song at the Royal Recording Studios in Memphis, deploying many of the same God-gifted musicians he used with Al Green. But it took some persuading to convince both Denise LaSalle and Armen Boladian, the head of Westbound Records, that "Trapped by a Thing Called Love" had hit potential. "There was a big fight over that song," recalls Mitchell.

LaSalle was Chicago-based, but one of her solo sides ("Hung Up, Strung Out") was leased by Detroit's Westbound. "They did a little bit of success with that record," the singer told journalist David Nelson, "enough to make them want to go on. They sent me $15,000 to go back to the studio and produce another session."

That was at Royal, where Willie Mitchell had been recording another Westbound act, the Detroit Emeralds. "Denise came down," he says, "she had a song called 'Keep It Coming,' it was really hot. She said, 'I just wrote another song.' I said, 'What is it?' I go to the piano—she didn't play piano—and she started singing it. Mm-mmm!"

When the session was over, LaSalle was sure "Keep It Coming" was *the* one. Mitchell disagreed. "I said, 'Nope, but you just cut a hit: "Trapped by a Thing Called Love." In fact, you just cut a million-seller.' She said, 'Oh, no, that's no good.' "

Judgment calls aside, the production credits for the recording went to Crajon Enterprises, the company formed by LaSalle (whose real name was Denise Craig) and husband Bill Jones. "They were married, but Bill wasn't around when I cut that record," declares Mitchell. "Denise flew down, we cut the tracks, she went back, I finished the record. The vocals were one take in the studio."

Among the players on the date were Howard Grimes on drums, Leroy Hodges on bass, Marvell Thomas on keyboards, and Rhodes/Chalmers/Rhodes on backup vocals. The horn section included Andrew Love (alto), Wayne Jackson (trumpet), and James Mitchell (baritone sax). "Denise went back to

Chicago," Mitchell states, "I put the Rhodes on it and the horns."

Three months later, according to Mitchell, Westbound's Boladian called. "He said, 'I understand you like this "Trapped by a Thing Called Love." Why don't you go and finish it?' So I sweetened it up and sent this tape to him.

"He called back and said, 'Man, the bass is too heavy on here, the drums don't sound good. Send me the tape and we'll send it up to Canada and have it mixed again.' So he got it mixed and sent it back to me. I said, 'You already got a hit, I don't know why you keep mixing this thing.' It went around for about six months. He finally put it out [with the original mix] and the thing exploded. I think Chicago ordered 75,000 records the first week alone."

116

INNER CITY BLUES (MAKE ME WANNA HOLLER)

Marvin Gaye

TAMLA 54209
WRITERS: MARVIN GAYE, JAMES NYX
PRODUCER: MARVIN GAYE
November 6, 1971 (2 weeks)

"Inner City Blues (Make Me Wanna Holler)" was one of three songs on Marvin Gaye's *What's Going On* album to credit James Nyx as co-author. Although one ex-Motown executive claims that Nyx was nothing more than a janitor, he had previously written with Gaye (for the Originals) and used to work with Harvey Fuqua, Gaye's mentor, before Fuqua joined Motown.

"Marvin couldn't read or write music per se," says David Van DePitte, who received front-cover billing on the album for arranging and conducting the orchestra. "He needed not only a musical secretary, but somebody who knew how to organize the stuff and get it down on tape in an appropriate style."

The singer had "an elaborate setup in his living room," according to Van DePitte, "where he could sit down at the piano anytime he wanted, throw a couple of switches and record everything he did."

"Inner City Blues" was released in September 1971. By then, *What's Going On* had become a music industry sensation, vying for the top of the pop album charts with the Rolling Stones' *Sticky Fingers* and Carole King's *Tapestry*. The title track was the singer's biggest pop single since 1968, and both "Mercy Mercy Me" and "Inner City Blues" followed it into the top ten.

Yet David Van DePitte recalls that Motown wasn't even going to release *What's Going On* at first. "Which I felt was a shame, after all the work that went into it and the money spent on it. Motown thought Marvin was absolutely insane, and that I had lost my marbles, too. This was going to be the biggest fiasco that ever happened. Nobody believed in it at all."

Given his involvement, Van DePitte obviously

Marvin Gaye (left) accepts the Key to the City in Detroit

felt otherwise. "I thought it was just different enough that it might hit with the general public. Of course, his messages were rather timely. They may have been a little strong, but not necessarily when you compare them with what some other artists of the day were doing.

"It was just that it hadn't been done in that format before. People didn't get up and start screaming and hollering about dope and ghettos and things. But I did think that if it saw the light of day, the general public would probably at least give it a tumble. They'd have to say, 'Gee, that's different.' "

Barney Ales, who was president of Motown Records in 1971, says it's not true that the label didn't want to release the LP. After the title tune was a smash, he contends, "there was no way we wouldn't cash in, and put the album out as soon as possible."

But Ales confirms that Berry Gordy didn't like Gaye's handiwork. After "What's Going On" came out as a single, "Berry called me in and said, 'How could you release that? It's the worst record I've ever heard.' He had me on the coals."

117

HAVE YOU SEEN HER

The Chi-Lites

BRUNSWICK 55462
WRITERS: EUGENE RECORD, BARBARA ACKLIN
PRODUCER: EUGENE RECORD
November 20, 1971 (2 weeks)

Eugene Record was a gifted writer, singer and producer, whose work illuminated Chicago—and then the nation—during the late '60s and early '70s. His songs have also stood time's test, as M.C. Hammer, Paul Young, UB40, Glenn Jones, and Swing Out Sister, among others, have proved in the '80s and '90s.

Record had some help from Panasonic: "A little bitty tape recorder, like a small briefcase," he says. "It had a nice sound." The music he recorded on it filled the basement apartment where he lived in the Windy City, together with "my guitar and a lot of odds and ends, a drum set and all that kind of stuff." He laughs at the memory of "trying to get everything on one track."

Record's career around that time was on two tracks: He was a member of the Chi-Lites and a writer for Carl Davis's Jalynne Music outfit. He and Barbara Acklin, a fellow writer who initially worked as a receptionist at Brunswick Records, became a successful team. Among their hit 1967–69 copyrights were "Two Little Kids" for Peaches & Herb, "Love Makes a Woman" and "Am I the Same Girl" for Acklin herself, and "Soulful Strut" for Young-Holt Unlimited.

Then Record's other career advanced, as the Chi-Lites—comprising himself, Marshall Thompson, Creadel "Red" Jones, and Robert "Squirrel" Lester—cracked the *Billboard* charts for the first time in 1969.

Two years and nine hits later, the group harmonized all the way to Number One with the melancholy grace of "Have You Seen Her"—thanks to a little groundwork by Isaac Hayes. "I had written the song about five years before," says Record. "I used to carry it around with me, with all my other stuff. The reason I didn't do anything with it at the time was because nobody was making anything over three minutes."

Hayes deep-sixed that tradition with symphony-length songs and opened the door for Record. "When Isaac came out with *Hot Buttered Soul*, nobody had done anything like that. So I said, 'Well, we've got this song that's five minutes long, why don't we use this?' That was the last tune we put on the album, 'cause we had space for it."

Record cut the basic track with drummer Quinton Joseph, one of Chicago's leading studio musicians. "It was just me and him," he says. "I was on organ and guitar and bass, he played drums and something else. We were doing a demo. And so Carl heard it, he liked it, and said, 'Let's put the group on.' " The session was done at Sound Market Recording on North Michigan Avenue; Quinton and Willie Henderson shared the arranger chores.

Even then, it took R&B radio—and a number of cover versions—to force "Have You Seen Her" onto the market. Soul jocks nationwide began jamming the tune as a track from the Chi-Lites' *(For God's Sake) Give More Power to the People* album in October 1971, even as Brunswick was working another single by the group.

Baltimore combo Frankie and the Spindles were just one of seven acts around the country who recognized a hit—and rushed a cover of "Have You Seen Her" into stores while Brunswick slept. Two weeks later, Brunswick figured out what Frankie and the others knew, and shipped the original version as a 45.

118

FAMILY AFFAIR

Sly & the Family Stone

EPIC 10805
WRITER: SYLVESTER STEWART
PRODUCER: SLY STONE
December 4, 1971 (5 weeks)

Music, motorcycles, automobiles, dogs. Truly, a family affair: Sly Stone, his brother Freddie and sister Rose, Larry Graham, Cynthia Robinson,

Jerry Martini, Greg Errico. "A lot of things we used to do together," remembers Graham, the bass player. "For example, when we got into motorcycles, we *all* got into motorcycles. We had Hondas and Triumphs, and we'd go riding at the beach together.

"When we got cars, we all got T-birds. Freddie had a pink T-bird, Sly had a purple one, and mine was turquoise. We had psychedelic tops put on 'em, and we would drive into Las Vegas in these T-birds with psychedelic colors, and folks would go, 'Like, wow, who is this?' "

"Then we got into dogs: the fastest, the tallest, the meanest, everything. You name it, we had it. Freddie had the tallest, an Irish wolfhound. I had the fastest, a pair of salukis. Rose had the only dog in the world with a black tongue, a chow chow. Greg and Jerry had the biggest—Greg had a St. Bernard, Jerry had a great puli." And Sly? "He had the meanest," says Graham. "Pit bulls."

Columbia Records president Clive Davis had cause to be mean himself by mid-1971: More than two years had passed since the band's last album of new material. Sly was preoccupied with an exotic lifestyle; his credibility had been damaged by canceled concerts, drugs, and a succession of managers.

Davis wanted a new album, and refused to pay any royalty advances until completion. That fall, Sly finally delivered. *There's a Riot Goin' On* was a hugely personal, subversive work—"a departure that worried me at first," wrote Davis in his autobiography. "But, as always, Sly knew what he was doing musically."

Despite its title, "Family Affair" was driven by Sly's demons, not those of the band. Larry Graham, for one, affirms that he wasn't involved. "When you listen to it, you can tell it's not thumping and plucking," he says, referring to his distinctive, influential bass style—it was Sly himself on bass. "He used to play with a pick."

The rest of the Family Stone hadn't anticipated fracture and divorce, according to Graham. "To everyone, it seemed like, 'Well, this is a family that's going to be together.' We'd just be old men playing together."

That's the spirit that gave the band its unique drive, he declares. "The joy was reflected in the music. As long as we were getting along and we were happy and there was that harmony, you could feel it in the music. When we lost that, you could also hear it in the music."

"Family Affair" was certainly the Family Stone's last mass-appeal smash. Their name graced the top 10 of the R&B charts once more, in 1973, but never again the upper reaches of the Hot 100. Sly's last gold-certified studio LP was 1974's *Small Talk*, featuring a different family on the cover: Sly, his wife Silva, and baby Sylvester. Soon after, Silva filed for divorce.

119

LET'S STAY TOGETHER

Al Green

HI 2202
WRITERS: WILLIE MITCHELL, AL GREEN, AL JACKSON
PRODUCER: WILLIE MITCHELL
January 8, 1972 (9 weeks)

Al Green didn't like "Let's Stay Together," according to Willie Mitchell, the man who produced it. "The only fight I ever had with him," Mitchell says, "was about 'Let's Stay Together,' because he thought 'Let's Stay Together' was not a hit."

Green's falsetto would sell a reported 30 million records by 1976. Like Sam Cooke before him and Luther Vandross still to come, it would make him *the* R&B love man of his time. But Mitchell recalls that "Al didn't like his voice. He said, 'I sound too thin. I want to open up...'

"In fact, the record almost didn't come out [because] he didn't like his voice on it. I said, 'Man, this is the way it is, and the record is going out.' The record came out Monday and went gold on Thursday, and after that there were no more fights."

Mitchell was a session player and instrumentalist turned producer, then president of Hi Records. Green was a gospel singer turned one-hit wonder (1968's "Back Up Train") who Mitchell had rescued from obscurity at a now-legendary club date in Odessa, Texas. With Booker T. and the MGs' drummer, Al Jackson Jr., the pair was already responsible for one gold single, "Tired of Being Alone," and would pound out seven more between 1971 and 1974.

"I used to be a jazz player," explains Mitchell, "and I always said that if I got a guy who had a really silky voice...we could make the rhythm section really strong and let that be the roughness of the take. I didn't want to use chords that everybody else used. I used a lot of jazz [chords]...and that was the difference for him. It created a style of being [silky] on top and rough on the bottom...That's why his records went pop."

To concoct that sort of steel-belted smoothness, "I had to tone [Al] down," Mitchell says. In his first days at Hi, Green was still making deep soul records, scoring a minor R&B hit on Junior Parker's "Driving Wheel" and a bigger hit with a cover of "I Can't Get Next to You."

Besides steering Green away from the blues, writer Peter Guralnick notes, Mitchell smoothed out Green's look, cutting his afro and putting him in a business suit.

Then there was the matter of Green's vocal style. "I wanted more magic in his voice," Mitchell remembers. "I would tell him to sing softer because he was singing too loud. It took from 'Tired of Being Alone' to 'Let's Stay Together' to perfect that feeling I wanted."

Five months passed between "Tired of Being Alone" and "Let's Stay Together," but only a few minutes of that actually went into the writing. Mitchell and Jackson started while Green was on tour in England. "Al got his sticks and I got to the piano and figured out the changes," Mitchell relates. When Green came back, Mitchell gave him the demo. "I said, 'This song, man, who do you hear?' He said, 'Just give me 15 minutes,' and he wrote 'Let's Stay Together.' "

120

TALKING LOUD AND SAYING NOTHING (PART 1)

James Brown

POLYDOR 14109
WRITER: JAMES BROWN, BOBBY BYRD
PRODUCER: JAMES BROWN
March 11, 1972 (1 week)

Take a breath, get a scorecard. "Talking Loud and Saying Nothing," one of James Brown's vibrant, political, truthful, and richly funky jams, took a twisting path to get made properly, let alone released. When it finally hit the street, sixteen months after it was (re-)recorded, the record streaked to Number One.

Often interpreted, or used, as a response to white-on-black maneuvering, "Talking Loud and Saying Nothing" was a platform for JB's anger at...many things. "James was mad when he wrote the words, mad when we cut it," says co-writer and co-vocalist Bobby Byrd. "Mad at everything from his business relationships to his old lady. And some of it was the 'man' thing—he was letting everybody know he was a *man*. The boss."

The song was originally essayed as a fuzz-rock experiment with local Cincinnati studio musicians headed by Dave Matthews, at the King studios on February 24, 1970. It was another critical in-between period for Brown: his classic band was a shell, and the shell would leave a few weeks later [see 95—"Super Bad"]. "Talking Loud" didn't seem significant. Same lyrics, but no bite, no blood. Nevertheless, King scheduled it for single release—then cancelled.

Cut to seven months and one week later, October 1: JB was back in the groove with Bootsy Collins and the J.B.'s. Alan Leeds, working for James at the time, recalls, "Brown wanted to use Capricorn Studios in Macon, Georgia, but it was booked. James was upset that Phil Walden didn't throw out whoever was occupying the room, because our only alternative in town was to go to Bobby Smith's studios. JB was uncomfortable there, and for this session kept coming in and out of the room."

When the monstrous remake was in the can, King scheduled *both* versions for simultaneous release, as the follow-up to "Get Up, Get Into It, Get Involved." King 6359'S' was the new version, to send to the "soul" radio stations, and King 6359'P' was the earlier, rock treatment, reactivated to service the "pop" stations. For reasons unknown, only the pop version was pressed. Then the whole release was cancelled. Instead, "Soul Power" was the next single.

Yet "Talking Loud and Saying Nothing" wouldn't rest. It finally appeared in two parts as Brown's fourth 45 for his new label, Polydor, in February 1972—when most of the track's personnel were long gone.

Here's the twist: the original "pop" version on King appeared in a few stores when the company's owners cleared some warehouse inventory in the early 1970s. While the snafu confused some consumers looking for the funk, not the fuzz, it apparently inspired one Harlem youngster: Brown's fleeting rock experiment began with a chant of "How ya like me now," a challenging line appropriated by Kool Moe Dee for his 1987 hit of that name.

121

I GOTCHA

Joe Tex

DIAL 1010
WRITER: JOE TEX
PRODUCER: BUDDY KILLEN
March 18, 1972 (1 week)

The largest-selling single of Joe Tex's career didn't get off to a promising start. "I Gotcha" was recorded at Nashville's Sound Shop toward the end of 1971, according to producer Buddy Killen. "It just seemed like the musicians were totally bored with it. It was a real ho-hum session. For one thing, the intro was too long."

Killen ran the tape through one more time. "I started listening to it, mixing it down, and thought, 'I know what's wrong with this record: There's too much stuff going on.' So I took something out of the middle, took some off the front, made it shorter—and it absolutely exploded."

The song itself may have been written years earlier. Tex told journalist Bob Gallagher that he originally composed "I Gotcha" for King Floyd [see 98—"Groove Me"] around 1967–68, but couldn't

Joe Tex with producer Buddy Killen

make a deal for it. Then he recorded the song himself, but shelved the results until later.

Even then, Tex didn't share his producer's enthusiasm for the new, improved version. To complicate matters, it was the other side of the single ("Mother's Prayer") that drew an initial response from radio in the closing weeks of 1971. "That started taking off," says Killen, "then all of a sudden they caught onto 'I Gotcha.' "

"They" were Atlanta, Birmingham, Miami, New York, and other urban centers. "You could just feel it when those big cities kicked in," Killen explains. "I remember when 'I Gotcha' was at number two on the pop charts, and it was only kept out of the top by 'The First Time Ever I Saw Your Face.' "

(There was other soulful competition that week in May 1972. Aside from Roberta Flack and Joe Tex, the top five featured the Stylistics, Michael Jackson, and Aretha Franklin. The top five of the *pop* charts, that is.)

"I Gotcha" went on to sell 3 million copies, by Killen's estimate. Yet within weeks of its chart peak, Tex quit music to follow the Black Muslims and preach their faith. "I was having problems with my label," he told *Billboard* several years later.

"In the period between 1972 and mid-1975, I went on a lecture tour across the country, and I devoted time to the nation of Islam. I spoke in all the cities where I previously performed, and the same people who came to see my show came to hear me speak."

Tex eventually returned to music—his last major hit was 1977's "Ain't Gonna Bump No More (With No Big Fat Woman)"—but succumbed to a heart attack on August 13, 1982. "He died [because of] the government," concludes Buddy Killen. "He'd spend a lot of money, and the government would take his homes and stuff because he never paid his income tax. Joe just wasn't a businessman."

122

IN THE RAIN

The Dramatics

VOLT 4075
WRITER: TONY HESTER
PRODUCER: TONY HESTER
March 25, 1972 (4 weeks)

In Detroit, Motown Records cast a long shadow. Any number of local artists *not* affiliated with the company fought to avoid being compared to—or influenced by—the titans of Berry Gordy's empire.

"You have to remember that any group coming out of Detroit was looked upon as an offshoot of the Temptations," states Don Davis, who was one of the city's most successful non-Motown producers, and the man who helped launch the Dramatics onto the national scene in 1971.

Davis wanted to differentiate the group by emphasizing the tenor of Ron Banks at least as much as the David Ruffin–styled vocals of William (Wee Gee) Howard. "We were trying to get Wee Gee to sound more and more like himself, rather than like Ruffin," he says. "On the very first record he made with us, 'Your Love Was Strange,' he came off sounding so much like David that we said, 'We've got to get away from that,' and get a lot of that tenor sound into this thing and set the mood of the group."

The Dramatics—Banks, Howard, Larry Demps, Willie Ford, Elbert Wilkins—had been around the Motor City since 1964. They recorded for the Golden World label, connecting there with Davis, a one-time session guitarist who had begun to make a name for himself in production. "Your Love Was Strange" was leased to Stax/Volt, but then the label dropped the group for lack of original material.

Their salvation was the late Tony Hester, a local writer who had peddled some copyrights to Motown and Golden World. "Tony had a creative thing for the Dramatics," says Davis. "I re-signed the group because of the songs Tony presented to me. When we got together with him, 'In the Rain' stuck out as one of the songs we could rebuild the Dramatics with.

"Tony was an extremely bright writer, and he worked in minor keys. He used his major chords inside his songs to bring alarm and attention, but he was always a minor-key writer." In 1971, Hester authored and produced the Dramatics' first top 20 hits, "Whatcha See Is Whatcha Get" and "Get Up and Get Down," both rhythmic tunes.

The hat trick came with "In the Rain," a ballad featuring Banks's tremulous lead and the group's mellifluous harmonies, dramatized by a sound-effects downpour. The song was cut at United Sound in Detroit. "At that particular time, there was another generation of [local] musicians coming up," explains Davis.

"There was Michael Henderson, the bassist on that record, and Dennis Coffey on guitar—he had not gone to the Motown fold yet." Also playing, according to Davis, were Johnny Griffith (piano) and Uriel Jones (drums), well-known for their Motown work.

"In the Rain," the Dramatics' biggest hit, was also the high point of Tony Hester's career—before drug addiction took its toll. "Unfortunately, he was hooked early on," says Davis, "and his writing was seriously impaired once he really got afflicted." Even so, Hester was not afraid to tackle the subject in song, recording the Dramatics on such polemics as "The Devil Is Dope" and "Beware of the Man with the Candy in His Hand."

123

DAY DREAMING

Aretha Franklin

ATLANTIC 2866
WRITER: ARETHA FRANKLIN
PRODUCERS: JERRY WEXLER, TOM DOWD, ARIF MARDIN
April 22, 1972 (2 weeks)

Lady Soul prized her privacy, always deflecting those who wanted a glimpse—or more—of the inner Aretha. "Our Lady of Mysterious Sorrows," Jerry Wexler called her.

Sometimes, those sorrows became public. A 1968 cover story in *Time* magazine was especially candid, quoting Cecil Franklin as saying, "For the last few years, Aretha is simply not Aretha. You see flashes of her, and then she's back in her shell." In particular, the singer's travails with spouse Ted White were identified.

Wexler says today that "It's not politically correct that grief and submission and being dominated can result in anything good, but it sure comes out in some great music. That's what the blues are all about, and it's also in gospel.

"Because of her personal angst, there were problems, marriages, relationships. Sometimes, she would be very moody and very depressed, almost morbidly unhappy. Sometimes, it would be difficult. But once she got in the studio...I never recall any problem in the studio."

And sometimes—just sometimes—a brighter, extroverted Aretha would be apparent. " 'Day Dreaming' was rather personal," she told biographer Mark

Bego. "And I was thinking about someone who used to be a friend of mine. I'll give you a hint. Used to be with one of the hottest groups in the country, tall, dark and fine!"

At the time, the smart money was on Dennis Edwards of the Temptations. Aretha even recorded a song he wrote ("You and Me") at Miami's Criteria studios in March 1970. Eleven months later, she was back there "day dreaming" about him—if Edwards it was.

"The timing of the introduction was very tricky," says co-producer Arif Mardin about "Day Dreaming." "You can't keep time [to the meter], but it's great. The drumming and the track are fabulous. That's Donny Hathaway on electric piano; Aretha's background vocal arrangement was great."

Bernard Purdie coaxed the drums and Chuck Rainey fingered bass, while Cornell Dupree and Don Arnone played electric and acoustic guitars, respectively. Hubert Laws was the flautist. "Alto flute would sometimes be more sensual," Mardin comments.

Material from that session in February 1971 formed much of *Young, Gifted and Black*, which became Aretha's first gold-certified studio album since 1968's *Aretha Now*. "That period, from then on, Jerry [Wexler] and Tom [Dowd] had moved to Miami," explains Mardin, "and I was in New York and Aretha was living in New York, so I mixed [the recordings] all by myself.

"I used to send mixes to Jerry by courier. He would listen and give me his approval—it was a great period for me—and I used to play with the tapes, like the cat [who had] the cream."

124

I'LL TAKE YOU THERE

The Staple Singers

STAX 0125
WRITER: ALVERTIS ISBELL
PRODUCER: AL BELL
May 6, 1972 (4 weeks)

At home in Chicago, America's torch-bearer of civil rights, Jesse Jackson, was receiving a visit from the president of Stax Records, Al Bell. Ministers both, they spoke about black business, black music, black resources.

"Jesse said to me, 'One of the greatest black acts in America is the Staple Singers,' " recalls Bell. " 'They're on your label, and you're sitting there, allowing them to graze. Can't nobody produce Mavis, Pops, Cleo, Pervis, and Yvonne but you. And if you don't do that, you will have denied our culture the opportunity to hear the Staple Singers the way they should be heard.' "

Bell, of course, acceded. The year was 1970, and America's first family of gospel had already been together for two decades. They had joined Stax two years earlier, but not reached their full potential. "The involvement became spiritual," Bell says, "because I knew the Staples going back to my days in radio in Arkansas. They became my pulpit."

"I'll Take You There" was a highly personal sermon. Bell's younger brother had died, his third sibling to perish by the gun, and the Stax chief went home to Little Rock. Last respects paid, the casket buried, Bell returned to his parents' house and walked to the back yard. "My father had a yellow school bus he used to use to haul cotton choppers and cotton pickers in his younger years, and it was his little keepsake.

"I went back and sat on the front fender, and as I was sitting there, in my mind I heard bass, piano, guitar, and I heard: *I know a place/Ain't nobody worried/Ain't nobody crying/Ain't no smiling faces/Lying to the races*. All of that came at one time, sitting there on that bus. And I proceeded to cry."

By his own admission, Bell became obsessed with making the song work. He turned first to musicians at the Muscle Shoals Sound studios, his team for the Staples sessions: Barry Beckett on keyboards, David Hood on bass, Roger Hawkins on drums, Jimmy Johnson on guitar. "I sat there with Barry and all of the guys, and hummed out these parts. We ended up with about 30 minutes on tape."

Next, the Stax chief traveled to Chicago to see Mavis Staples. "We sat on her living room floor, with me pounding out, showing her where that beat was and where I was phrasing it. She started doing it, and adding her bits as it evolved.

"We went in the studio and put it down with her, then used Cleotha, Yvonne and Mavis to do the background, and Mavis did Pops's part in the background." Later, too, the elder Staples's tremulous guitar solo was overdubbed, together with the stacked horns of Ben Cauley and the Barkays. "And Terry Manning put harmonica down from beginning to end," Bell notes, "but we just used that little taste in there."

The author of "I'll Take You There" remains convinced that it was written through him, not by him. "If you play that record," declares Bell, "stand and look out your window. Look at the trees blowing and the birds and life moving. You'll find that everything's in time with it, and it's in time with everything. Strike a match and watch—it's all in time."

Ninteen years later, in December 1991, Mavis Staples returned, figuratively, to the place where Al Bell received his inspiration. She was guest vocalist on a new version of "I'll Take You There" by BeBe & CeCe Winans, from America's newest family of gospel music. Strike another match.

125

OH GIRL

The Chi-Lites

BRUNSWICK 55471
WRITER: EUGENE RECORD
PRODUCER: EUGENE RECORD
June 3, 1972 (2 weeks)

A little taste of country corn, courtesy of harmonica player Cy Touff, and a whole barrel of Chicago soul gave the Chi-Lites the prize denied to many of their vocal-group peers: a crossover smash that spun all the way to the top of both the R&B and pop charts.

"Oh Girl" was the quartet's most successful single, although it took the seasoned ears of producer Carl Davis to convince lead singer Eugene Record of its potential. "I had some songs on a tape," Record explains, "about seven songs. So I gave them to Carl one day, and he called me that night. 'Man, you've got a tune on this tape, I swear, it's a Number One tune.'

"I said, 'Carl, which one?' He said, '*You* give me the title.' So I named all of them except 'Oh Girl,' and asked him again, 'Which one, man, which one?' He said, 'There's only one left.' I said, 'You've got to be kidding.' He said, 'Man, I'm telling you, that's a Number One hit.' "

Record should have known. The Chi-Lites' previous hit [see 117—"Have You Seen Her"] had just affirmed his composing and vocal skills, honed during more than 10 years on the Chicago music scene. As a writer, Record found that the night time was the right time. "No telephones, it's quiet, you can work. I worked mostly at night. Sometimes I would have an idea, get up, put it down on tape, then go back to bed."

As a musician in the studio, Record found an able partner in drummer Quinton Joseph. "He was bad, man, he could lock a groove and keep it. He was fast, too, plus he stood up and played. All his drums were on long legs. He was short, but he'd kick up so much fuss over there in the corner. He and I would be dust when we'd get through—a big cloud of dust."

They worked mostly at Brunswick's own studios in Chicago, with Bruce Swedien as engineer. For "Oh Girl," the session featured Record himself on bass and guitar, Tom Tom Washington on piano, and Quinton Joseph on drums, with Touff on harmonica. "It came off good," says Record, "but we hadn't done the strings yet. All we had was the rhythm and the harmonica."

Armed with a tape of "Oh Girl," the Chi-Lites prepared for their March 1972 appearance on Flip Wilson's top-rated television show. "They wanted us to do 'Have You Seen Her' and another tune. Carl [Davis] said, 'See if they'll let you do this.' We were in the dressing room, the people from the show came in. I said, 'We don't know what second tune you want us to do, but "Oh Girl" is what we're working on now. It's not quite finished, but our manager wants us to play it for you.'

"Shoot, man, they heard the first sixteen bars...and forget it! 'Yes,' they said, 'yes, yes.' Even though we didn't have strings, just rhythm and harmonica. We did the tune, and it took off. It was Number One behind that show. Everything was right on time!"

126

WOMAN'S GOTTA HAVE IT

Bobby Womack

UNITED ARTISTS 50902
WRITERS: BOBBY WOMACK,
LINDA WOMACK, DARRYL CARTER
PRODUCER: BOBBY WOMACK
June 17, 1972 (1 week)

"Woman's Gotta Have It" was written as a message to a husband who was neglecting his wife. Unfortunately, it was based on a real couple that songwriter Darryl Carter knew. "It was a nice way of trying to tell him that his wife was about to do something shady," Carter says.

Bobby Womack and Darryl Carter first met at American Sound Studios in Memphis in the '60s, where Carter was working as an engineer for producer Chips Moman and Womack was playing guitar and writing songs for Wilson Pickett. "I told Chips at the time, 'I think we ought to cut Bobby ourselves,' because we had one of the hottest rhythm sections in the country."

They wrote "Woman's Gotta Have It" with Linda Cooke Womack in the '60s, intending it for Jackie Wilson. But the song wasn't recorded until Womack returned to American Sound in 1972 to complete his *Understanding* album, which he had begun at Rick Hall's Muscle Shoals studio in Alabama.

Carter recalls how the song was written: "With Bobby Womack, you don't have to worry about melodies. He's an instant melody. He's a heck of a guitar player...The melody might come from either one of us. In fact, we wrote songs line by line. Each line grew as we progressed. We didn't just do lyrics to a melody. We would sit down and write the song together."

It was very difficult to record, according to Carter. "The song didn't have a basic beat. It was peculiar because it had a bassline that just kept turning after completion. It wasn't broken down into a 4/4 or a 3/4 situation. It was almost like a calypso song without the rhythm. I eventually came back and overdubbed some congas to hold it together because we didn't have a basic backbeat on it...I don't think the band even understood it at first. Most of the time they would let you know what they thought—and they didn't know what to think because it was an absolute new song. I don't know if anything has been done like 'Woman's Gotta Have It' since then. I don't know another rhythm pattern like that."

Personnel on the track included Mike Leech on bass, Reggie Young on guitar, Bobby Emmons on organ, Hayward Bishop on drums and percussion, and Bobby Wood on electric and acoustic piano. Womack and Leech did the string arrangements.

Carter says that he completed four tracks with Womack at American Sound. "He had already cut five or six things in Muscle Shoals. We gave him the tapes and he left. The next thing I know, the song is on the street."

"Woman's Gotta Have It" was Womack's first Number One single, a great reward for an artist who had first charted in *Billboard* 10 years earlier with "Lookin' for a Love" by the Valentinos [see 167]. As a solo artist, his first chart entry was "What Is This" on Minit. In 1970, Minit was absorbed by its parent company, Liberty, and Womack was switched over to that label. In 1971, Liberty was shuttered by its owner, TransAmerica, and the roster was shifted to United Artists, which became Womack's new home.

"Woman's Gotta Have It" also registered on the pop chart, peaking at number 60. James Taylor recorded a cover version in 1976 for his final Warner Brothers studio album, *In the Pocket.*

127

LEAN ON ME

Bill Withers

SUSSEX 235
WRITER: BILL WITHERS
PRODUCER: BILL WITHERS
June 24, 1972 (1 week)

"I don't know if I would write anything like that now, because it was a more innocent time for me," Bill Withers replies when asked about "Lean on Me." "I'm from West Virginia and that's how everybody had to live. Nobody had very much. Everybody I knew worked in the coal mines."

Withers explains that when people needed goods or services beyond their normal incomes, they bonded together and chipped in. "So I came from a help-each-other-out kind of environment...That song for me is reflective of being in close contact with grow-

Bill Withers

ing up where people really existed by doing things for each other. We judged a person on whether he was a good person or not by how willing they were to help somebody."

"Lean on Me" was Withers's third chart single, following "Ain't No Sunshine" and "Grandma's Hands." The latter two songs appeared on his debut album, *Just as I Am,* and were produced by Booker T. Jones. Withers came to the music business later than most. He ended his Navy career after nine years and moved to Los Angeles at age 32 to follow his interest in music. By day, he worked for different aircraft companies; at night he recorded his own demos. Eventually, a friend introduced him to Clarence Avant of Sussex Records.

When he wrote "Lean on Me," it wasn't meant specifically for any particular album. "I was writing because there was some creative urge to say things that I would like to hear somebody say," Withers explains. "I hadn't been around long enough for albums to become projects or songs to become material or music to become product. I hadn't been tainted by the nomenclature. So nothing was written for anything. It was just written because that's the way I felt. Those were my values."

Withers remembers writing "Lean on Me" the very first time he sat down at his newly unpacked Wurlitzer piano. "I had no idea what the notes were. I found these spaces on the keys and liked that sound. So I was going up and down with it and it sounded like some of those hymns that I grew up with. It was in that same genre. So I kept doing it because I liked it. It's probably why I never learned to play the piano, because I got a song out of the thing about five minutes after I got it. It was just luck."

Withers enjoyed recording the song. "I was recording with guys who were friends—the guys that had been the rhythm section for the Watts 103rd Street Rhythm Band. James Gadson was the drummer, Ray Jackson played the keyboards, Benorce Blackman was the guitar player, and Melvin Dunlap played the bass."

"Lean on Me" ended up on Withers's second album, *Still Bill*. The song has proven to be timeless—the British rock group Mud had a top 10 hit with it in the U.K. in 1976, and the R&B band Club Nouveau took it to number two in 1987. While many people have told him over the years how much "Lean on Me" has meant to them, Withers's favorite memory of the song is a personal one: "I was in a play at my kid's school. They gave me a little part in the play to sing it with them. I have to tell you, of all the situations I have been in in my life, and all the times when I was young and tall and slim and all the things that come at you—the women, the money, everything—the most deeply rewarding thing was for me to have my son graduating from the sixth grade...His class wanted me to be in their graduation play."

128

OUTA-SPACE

Billy Preston

A&M 1320
WRITERS: BILLY PRESTON, JOE GREENE
PRODUCER: BILLY PRESTON
July 1, 1972 (1 week)

Little Richard. Sam Cooke. Ray Charles. The Beatles. The Rolling Stones. They all had one thing in common: Their careers intersected with a musical prodigy who learned to play piano when he was three years old and became one of the most valued session musicians of the '60s before becoming a hit artist in his own right.

Billy Preston's mother played for the Voices of Victory at the Victory Baptist Church in Los Angeles. The young musician was 10 years old when he played the organ for Mahalia Jackson during an appearance at the church; a movie producer who came to hear Jackson cast the boy as W. C. Handy in the film *St. Louis Blues*. Billy was signed to Sam Cooke's label, Sar, and was 15 when he accompanied Cooke and Little Richard on a gospel tour. When they arrived in England in 1962, they discovered their young audiences wanted to hear pop music, and Billy found himself playing rock and roll for the first time.

During that tour, Preston met a couple of British bands that would have a profound impact on his life. He was introduced to the four lads from Liverpool known as the Beatles, who would later ask him to make a guest appearance on their song "Get Back." He also met the instrumental band Sounds Incorporated. When they were in New York in 1965, they introduced him to the producer of a new weekly ABC-TV musical series *Shindig*. Billy took Leon Russell's place as the resident keyboardist on the show, joining a company that included the Righteous Brothers, the Blossoms, and Glen Campbell. During one rehearsal, Billy sat in for a man who had been his neighbor when he was growing up. When Ray Charles arrived, everyone told him he had to hear Billy's impression of him. Charles was so impressed with the young musician, he asked him to play on his next album.

After his guest appearance with the Beatles in 1969, Billy signed with their Apple label and released two albums. But legal squabbles were tearing the company apart, and Billy thought it best to leave. It was an amicable parting, and Billy found a new home with A&M Records. It was convenient to be signed with a label based in his home town of Los Angeles, but Billy had another important reason for going with the label founded by Herb Alpert and Jerry Moss: "They allowed me the freedom to produce," says Preston.

Billy was teamed up with a "trainee engineer," Tommy Vicari. They went into A&M Studios in Hollywood with musicians like David T. Walker on guitar, Manuel Kellough on drums, and George Harrison on lead guitar. Quincy Jones arranged the strings and horns, and people like Bobby Womack and Sly Stone dropped by just to lend their support.

A&M found an obvious choice for a first single and title track for Billy's album debut on the label: "I Wrote a Simple Song." Billy preferred another cut, but the instrumental track was relegated to the B-side. "It was a song I made up in the studio," he explains. "It was the first time I'd played a clavinet. I rented one and brought it to the studio and made up this tune." Preston added a wah-wah pedal to the clavinet and started jamming in the studio, calling out changes to his band. "That was done in one take." He added an organ and handclaps to it later: "We really didn't do much overdubbing on it," he says. "I thought it was a hit...but evidently the company didn't." Billy wasn't sure what to call the track. "It sounded like something from outer space. The clavinet sound was new to me—really spacey, spaced out." That led Billy to call it "Outa-Space."

A&M executives warned him an instrumental would be difficult to break and proceeded to promote "I Wrote a Simple Song." But a DJ somewhere—Billy still isn't sure who—flipped it over and gave some airplay to "Outa-Space." After years of working on other artists' hits, Billy had a Number One single all to himself.

129

(IF LOVING YOU IS WRONG) I DON'T WANT TO BE RIGHT

Luther Ingram

KOKO 2111
WRITERS: HOMER BANKS, RAYMOND JACKSON, CARL HAMPTON
PRODUCER: JOHNNY BAYLOR
July 8, 1972 (4 weeks)

Call it the "power ballad" of 1972. Or the definitive "slipping around" saga. Or the zenith of Luther Ingram's career. Whatever the description, "(If Loving You Is Wrong) I Don't Want to Be Right" was a rhythm & blues milestone.

The song was composed around 1970 by Stax artisans Homer Banks, Carl Hampton, and Raymond Jackson in the hours after midnight, a collective effort of melody and lyrics. The trio decided to try their handiwork on the Emotions. "We cut a track with them," affirms Banks, "but at the time, I think everybody felt the song and the lyric were a little too mature for them. Everyone saw the Emotions as sweet young ladies—and that song was very, very bold."

Two years later, Luther Ingram, a Southern stylist with several R&B hits to his credit, happened to hear "(If Loving You Is Wrong) I Don't Want to Be Right" at the Stax HQ in Memphis. "I used to go into the studio maybe nine, ten o'clock, after everyone had gone," Ingram explains, "and I saw this tape on the shelf.

"It was a small reel, with a lot of dust on it. It was 'If Loving You Is Wrong' done by a woman. It was very up-tempo, and it was saying things that a woman would say about a married man. So I took it back home with me to Alton, Illinois, and my sister Jean and my brothers Jesse, Tommy, and Frank, we started experimenting with it.

"I remembered the song Gene Chandler had done, 'Man's Temptation,' and I asked my brother Jesse to play scales on a bass line, which was an octave on a guitar, and the song came more into a gospel feel. I thought that the minor key would make it a mournful type of happy-sad feeling, so I started to sing 'Man's Temptation.'

"We went to a club during the daytime when there was nobody there. We hooked up with my brother's group, and I played the up-tempo tune to them, so they would see what the changes were about. And then we just put the changes in a slow mood, and the track started happening."

To bottle the magic of "(If Loving You Is Wrong) I Don't Want to Be Right," Ingram went to the Muscle Shoals Sound studios in Alabama. The players were Barry Beckett, Shelton Clayton, Jimmy Johnson, Pete Carr, Roger Hawkins.

"We used a Wurlitzer with an Echoplex," recalls the singer, "to get the real shrill vibrations Aretha used in 'Bridge Over Troubled Water.' Jimmy Johnson was on rhythm guitar, he put his fills in. Shelton Clayton—Shell, we called him—he played the Wurlitzer, and Barry played the Hammond.

"With the guitar player [Pete Carr], I said, 'I need some tears,' so he got a crybaby wah-wah. And Roger played the drums. He had started it off a bit fast. It has a tempo in the introduction that is faster than when I come into it. 'Drop it back a little bit,' I said, and it fell just right in the pocket."

130

WHERE IS THE LOVE

Roberta Flack and Donny Hathaway

ATLANTIC 2879
WRITERS: RALPH MACDONALD, WILLIAM SALTER
PRODUCERS: JOEL DORN, ARIF MARDIN
August 5, 1972 (1 week)

Roberta Flack and Donny Hathaway, longtime friends and classmates at Howard University in Washington, D.C., earned their first Number One R&B single with a song originally composed for the 5th Dimension.

"We wrote it with them in mind," says one of the song's two authors, Ralph MacDonald. "They had a hit called 'Up-Up and Away' and my partner, William Salter, and I had an argument. I said it's a white group and he said it was a black group. We were both working for Harry Belafonte at the time and we felt that kind of song was right up our alley. We felt we could do something for this group, and we came up with 'Where Is the Love.' And we could never get it to them."

MacDonald, a percussionist, met Salter, a bass player, in 1953. In the '70s, MacDonald worked as a studio musician and was involved with solo sessions for Flack and Hathaway, both signed to Atlantic. Jerry Wexler decided the two artists should work together and suggested they cover Carole King's "You've Got a Friend." Their version was released simultaneously with a pop version by James Taylor, who had a hit with the song. Flack and Hathaway teamed up for another single, a cover of "You've Lost That Lovin' Feelin'," before releasing an entire album of duets.

"I don't think since Tammi Terrell and Marvin Gaye had there been two people who were more suitable for each other musically," Flack told Dick Clark. "When Donny and I went in the studio, we had not spent hours deciding what we were going to do, what we were going to sing...What we did was come up with the keys because our voices were very similar in terms of register and range. Donny had a wonderful tenor voice, but he could also sing some notes that were otherworldly and very high, and I had this ability, particularly then, to do those wonderful low-sounding notes as well as the natural high ones."

Flack and Hathaway had almost completed their first album together, but needed one more song. "I told her I had a tune I thought would be great for her and Donny," MacDonald recalls. "And she and Donny came over to my office at 1650 Broadway ...and they picked 'Where Is the Love.' "

Producer Arif Mardin remembers the two artists compromising on the key. "He tried a little bit, she tried a little bit. 'Let's cut it in E-flat. No, let's cut it in E'...and as they were doing it, it started to sound great. It was the stepchild of the album." MacDonald agrees: "It wasn't until they did the vocal that the song really began to come alive. As a musician, you lay down the track first and it's a nice track. [But] when Donny and Roberta started to sing, it really began to take shape. From the time that we heard them, we knew it was something special." MacDonald played percussion on the track, joined by Eric Gale on guitar, Chuck Rainey on electric bass, Bernard Purdie on drums, Jack Jennings on vibes, and Flack and Hathaway both on piano and electric piano.

"Donny Hathaway was one of the greatest artists I've ever met in my entire life...and Roberta Flack is my all-time favorite female artist in terms of vocals and performing," says MacDonald. "The two of them being together I think is one of the most fantastic experiences I have had in the music business so far."

131

I'M STILL IN LOVE WITH YOU

Al Green

HI 2216
WRITERS: AL GREEN, AL JACKSON, WILLIE MITCHELL
PRODUCER: WILLIE MITCHELL
August 12, 1972 (2 weeks)

For Al Green and producer Willie Mitchell, the hits just kept on comin' back in 1972, even when everybody went on vacation.

When the traffic through Royal Recording Studios in Memphis got to be too much, Green, Mitchell, and drummer/co-writer Al Jackson would head for a nearby Arkansas resort where they could work without interruptions.

"We used to go to Hot Springs on the lake and stay there for three or four days, and figure things out," Mitchell says, recalling those days. "The last time we went up there, we came up with 'Love and Happiness,' 'Still in Love with You,' and another song I can't remember."

The two songs Mitchell does remember are a study in contrasts. "Love and Happiness" is a gritty, churchy record that easily qualifies as one of Green's classics, but you won't find it described elsewhere in this book because it wasn't issued as a single until the late '70s, well after Green's hit streak had died down considerably.

"I'm Still in Love with You," even more than "Let's Stay Together," is the archetypal smooth Al Green record. So worried about not sounding gutsy just a few months before, Green barely breaks out of a falsetto this time. The lyrics drift in and out, almost as if Mitchell had released the demo instead of the finished record.

But "Still In Love" is the hardest-working laid-back record in show business. It's a showpiece for the team of musicians Mitchell assembled: the all-sibling rhythm section of bassist Leroy Hodges, keyboards player Charles Hodges and guitarist Mabon "Teenie" Hodges, percussionist (and sometimes drummer) Howard Grimes, and Al Jackson, the Booker T. and the MGs drummer who kept Green's records cooking and loping along simultaneously.

Mitchell made the switch from Grimes to Jackson on Green's singles after "Tired of Being Alone," when he decided to go for a softer sound. "Howard played too hard," Mitchell says. "He didn't float like Al. I think Al was one of the greatest drummers that ever was, because anything you heard, you could [explain] it to him and he would figure it out. Howard was a little bit stronger than I wanted on Al. Like 'Let's Stay Together,' he would have played really hard and the song wouldn't have floated."

Jackson himself would explain it this way at the time: "I believe in solid rhythm, whether I'm playing four-four accented or two-four accented. It's a syncopated rhythm with the bass drum and less emphasis on the left stick...It's a different groove from the Motown beat...I dig their sound, but they use the stomp rhythm practically in everything.

"The records they do are made from the switchboard and ours are natural...They use echo and we don't. We cut our drums flat. I don't use any muffling or anything. I just play the way I feel. I play with the butt end of my left stick. I developed that from playing hard on gigs."

132

POWER OF LOVE

Joe Simon

SPRING 128
WRITERS: KENNY GAMBLE, LEON HUFF, JOE SIMON
PRODUCER: BOBBY MARTIN
August 26, 1972 (2 weeks)

A collaboration with Philadelphia's wizards of soul, combined with a slot on one of 1972's hottest summer road shows, gave Joe Simon his second Number One hit, and his second certified-gold single.

"Power of Love" came from the singer's recording sessions with Kenny Gamble and Leon Huff, an alliance designed to refresh Joe's creative juices after a string of country-influenced hits produced by his manager, the late John Richbourg [see 73—"The Chokin' Kind"].

Richbourg moved Simon from Monument's Sound Stage 7 label to Polydor-distributed Spring Records in 1970. "I had a good contract to produce him, $25,000 up front, and the first thing we did on him, 'Your Turn to Cry,' did a million," Richbourg told British writer Barney Hoskyns. Indeed, "Your Turn to Cry" was Joe's biggest pop and R&B success since "The Chokin' Kind" in 1969. "After a year, however, I agreed to let [Spring] bring in some other producers."

Not just "some other producers," but the team who would turn out to be the hottest R&B alchemists since Motown's Holland/Dozier/Holland. When Kenny Gamble and Leon Huff began working with Simon in 1971, they already had a chart-topping track record with the Intruders [see 54—"Cowboys to Girls"] and Jerry Butler [see 64—"Hey, Western Union Man" and 71—"Only the Strong Survive"], although their Philadelphia International Records hadn't yet established itself as a major commercial force.

"I really like the set-up down there," Joe explained to *Blues & Soul* at the time. "I was able to communicate with the people...and we had a sort of 'together' relationship that made the whole thing very enjoyable for me."

And commercially successful, too. "Drowning in the Sea of Love" was Simon's first Gamble/Huff blockbuster, a moody milestone not unlike their productions with Jerry Butler. It reached the top three of the R&B charts, crossed to the Hot 100 (stopping only one slot short of the top 10), and sold a certified million copies. In addition, the album named after the single placed higher on the *Billboard* pop rankings than any other Simon LP before or since.

The singer followed up with another aquatic tale, "Pool of Bad Luck," then brightened the mood with "Power of Love," which he co-wrote with his Philly partners. Like its predecessors, the record was made at Sigma Sound with Gamble and Huff's regular crew of studio musicians, later known as MFSB, and arranger/producer Bobby Martin.

There's nothing in Simon's soulful performance to separate "Drowning in the Sea of Love" from "Power of Love," so it was probably Joe's spot on the "Soul Festival of Stars" tour that lofted the later release to the R&B summit. The package featured the Staple Singers, the Stylistics, and the Dramatics; it had "all the finger-snapping, hip-swaying color of a Harlem Baptist revival meeting," reported *Billboard*. Simon himself was notable for a "super-cool approach" onstage, enhanced by what the reviewer called a "bedazzling stage ensemble."

The nature of Joe's bedazzle became clearer the following January, when *Billboard* disclosed that he had recently acquired a $15,000 black diamond mink coat and a $15,000 imported sports car. Evidently, Simon had the power—and it wasn't just of love.

133

BACK STABBERS

The O'Jays

PHILADELPHIA INTERNATIONAL 3517
WRITERS: LEON HUFF, GENE McFADDEN, JOHN WHITEHEAD
PRODUCERS: KENNY GAMBLE, LEON HUFF
September 9, 1972 (1 week)

"Back Stabbers" was a breakthrough record not only for the O'Jays, but for producers Kenny Gamble and Leon Huff and their fledgling Philadelphia International Records. It was the first Number One single for the group as well as for the label, and it firmly established the Philly Sound as the beat of the '70s.

After recording "The Echo" as a member of the Epsilons, John Whitehead went to work for the new label. "While I was there I watched Gamble and Huff write songs, as well as the other songwriters who were working there at the time," says Whitehead. "I thought to myself, I could do that. And I went home and wrote my first song that I ever wrote in my life, which was 'Back Stabbers.' "

Whitehead was living on the fourth floor of the projects in Philadelphia at the time; his friend Gene McFadden, who was also in the Epsilons, lived on the 14th floor. "I called him up one night. I said, 'McFadden, you gotta come down to my apartment. I was watching Gamble and Huff write songs today. I think we can do that—it looked kind of easy.' " McFadden asked him how the producers worked: Whitehead

The O'Jays

told him that they come up with a title first. "At the time I was going through a couple of personal things with my family and outsiders who were trying to cause waves, and the words 'Back Stabbers' happened to come out." Both men thought that sounded like the title of a hit record. "And you gotta remember, at that time in 1972, records tended to be more on the fantasy side—'Jack went up the hill for Jill.' I think 'Back Stabbers' was the first song to actually tell it like it was. It was something you could put on and play for your friends if that's what you wanted to say to them."

Gene came down to the fourth floor with his guitar and played a simple melody "with a southern kind of lick" for John. "The lyrics came off the top of my head and I wrote them down on some paper," Whitehead continues. "I said, 'Tomorrow when I go to work, I'm gonna take this song and show it to Mr. Huff.' " Whitehead took the piece of notebook paper with the lyrics and folded it into his back pocket. The next day, as Huff wandered out of his office to get a soda, Whitehead ran up behind him and told his boss he had written a song the night before. Huff asked if it was strong. "So I pulled it out of my back pocket and started reciting the lyrics." Huff got his soda and walked back to his office. "By the time he got back to his door, something must have hit him, because he looked around at the lyric sheet in my hand and said, 'Let me see that.' " Huff asked Whitehead into his office. The writer had invited McFadden to the Philly International offices that day; he ran downstairs and told his partner to come to Leon's office. "We sat down at the piano with Mr. Huff, which was an honor because we weren't songwriters. This was our first attempt. And the magic, the chemistry came together sitting at that piano. Mr. Huff came up with the music and they loved my lyrics...They wanted the O'Jays to do it."

McFadden and Whitehead were still active with the Epsilons and thought their own group should have first crack at the song. "But the O'Jays were the first group that Philadelphia International signed and Mr. Gamble thought it would be a good song for them. They came in to hear the song. They hated it."

Eddie Levert, Walter Williams, and William Powell were persuaded by Gamble to record the song. The novice songwriters were invited to the recording session. "When I heard that track, I got goosebumps," says Whitehead. "I knew that I had never heard music like that before. I listened to the strings—they had a heavenly feel, against that funk...The most exciting thing was to see the O'Jays come in and interpret the song like I really felt it. And even more exciting was to open *Billboard* two weeks later and see it jump on the charts and rise that fast. Before that, I didn't know what *Billboard* was. Then it got to be my bible."

134

GET ON THE GOOD FOOT (PART 1)

James Brown

POLYDOR 14139
WRITERS: JAMES BROWN, FRED WESLEY, JOSEPH MIMS
PRODUCER: JAMES BROWN
September 16, 1972 (4 weeks)

It was a spring day at the Manhattan offices of James Brown Enterprises, where Bob Both—a junior staffer for Polydor Records, Brown's label—had a desk as A&R liaison. The year was 1972, and "I Got Ants In My Pants" was scheduled as JB's next single.

"He walked in with an eight-track master," Both recounts, "plopped it on my desk, and said, 'This is my next release.' It was 'Get on the Good Foot.' I said, 'I need a two-track stereo master.' He said, 'Do one.' "

Soon afterwards at radio station WDRW in Augusta, Georgia—Brown's dominion—a world premiere was in progress. "He was just off the plane from a mastering session," recalls former JB staffer Alan Leeds. "It was late at night and he called me up at home to tell me, 'Cancel all plans for "I Got Ants In My Pants," put on the radio, I'm going over to the station to play my new record.' I turned on the radio and there was James, making a grandiose introduction. And then he played 'Good Foot.' "

Brown's instincts were on the money. Released as a 45 that July, "Get on the Good Foot" locked up the summer summit for longer than any of his hits since "Say It Loud—I'm Black and I'm Proud" in 1968. (The listed co-writer of the song, Joseph Mims, was a young disc jockey at 'DRW.)

The recording session for "Get on the Good Foot" took place at Soundcraft Studios in North Augusta, South Carolina, on May 9, 1972. After Brown's explosive introduction ("Que pasa, people, que pasa?"), Bobby Roach underpins the tune with a powerful, protracted guitar riff, while bassman Fred Thomas and drummer John "Jabo" Starks bolt down the bottom. Brown exhorts, "C'mon! Git it!...Sharper now!!...Git it, Jab! Git it!!...Stop! Bass!" He's arranging the song on the fly—*from the organ chair.*

Also on the date: guitarist Hearlon "Cheese" Martin and the Fred Wesley-branded line of horns, featuring Wesley himself (trombone), Jimmy Parker (alto), St. Clair Pinckney (tenor), Ike Oakley and Russell Crimes (trumpets).

Gettin' on the *good*foot became as emblematic of JB as "Cold Sweat," "Papa's Got a Brand New Bag," or "I Got You (I Feel Good)." As usual, he not only picked up on and made music out of a few African-American catch phrases, but also coined a few himself.

Two decades later, one part of the lyric in "Get on the Good Foot" (about "the long-haired hippies and the Afro'ed blacks" getting together) has currency as Arrested Development's defining philosophy. Que pasa, Speech?

135

I'LL BE AROUND

Spinners

ATLANTIC 2904
WRITERS: THOM BELL, PHIL HURTT
PRODUCER: THOM BELL
October 14, 1972 (5 weeks)

The Spinners spent their first decade as a group in Detroit, where they managed to register in the top 10 three times. But even a hit like "It's a Shame," co-written and produced by Stevie Wonder, didn't advance them from being third-tier artists at Motown. Wisely, they moved on.

Thanks to some words from Aretha Franklin, the quintet was signed to Atlantic Records, where they were teamed up with another Motown expatriate, producer Jimmy Roach. He cut four sides on the group in early 1972, but those tracks were consigned to the shelf after label president Henry Allen was tipped off by his promotion staff that the group could do better.

Soon after, Thom Bell's phone rang in Philadelphia. It was Allen, offering the producer his choice of any act on the Atlantic roster to produce. Bell was concerned at being typecast for the sweet, sugar-coated hits he had produced for the Delfonics and the Stylistics. He asked Allen to show him a list of artists signed to Atlantic.

"They must have had 80, 90 artists. And at the bottom of the last page...I saw 'Spinn' and the rest of the word [wasn't printed] on the page." Bell asked if it was the Spinners, the group he had loved all the way back to their first hit on Tri-Phi, "That's What Girls Are Made For." When Atlantic confirmed they had signed the Spinners, Bell said he wanted to produce them and was asked if he would be interested in someone else. The producer declined and reaffirmed his decision. Jerry Greenberg and Ahmet Ertegun told Bell that if he could do something with the group, they were his.

Bell brought the Spinners to Sigma Sound Studios in Philadelphia on June 12, 1972. "Atlantic...could not afford to spend a lot of money on these guys, so they only wanted to do four songs," says Bell. The producer thought that was a mistake and wanted to record an entire album, but the label had already spent $20,000 on the Roach sessions and said no.

Spinners

When he was looking for material for the Spinners, Bell decided to write a song with three chords. He called in studio musicians like Roland Chambers, Norman Harris, and Bobby Eli on guitars, Ronnie Baker on bass, Earl Young on drums, Vince Montana on vibes and marimbas, and Larry Washington on congas and bongos. Don Renaldo directed the strings. The musicians laughed at the simple structure, but Bell told them to play it like he wrote it. "And they started feeling good about it...It only took 40 minutes."

Bell needed lyrics in a hurry: "My partner at the time, Linda Creed, was getting married...and it was impossible for her to do that and get her wedding together at the same time," the producer explains. Creed said she wouldn't mind if Bell worked with someone else. "I couldn't think of anybody, so I started knocking on doors in the office to see if I could find a lyricist. No one was there, because I'm an early bird...I found one room open, Bunny Sigler's room, but Bunny was not in there. A cat named Phil Hurtt was there." Bell had gone to high school with Hurtt. He asked the lyricist a question: "If I give you a melody, can you stick exactly to that melody...every ooh and every ahh that I want a lyric to, can you fit it in without changing it?" Hurtt took the challenge; Bell brought him back to his office and sang the melody for a song called "I'll Be Around." It didn't take long for the lyrics to be completed. "Next day, he came in with it. Bang! There it was!"

The Spinners recorded "I'll Be Around" as one of their four tracks, along with an Yvette Davis composition, "How Could I Let You Get Away." Atlantic released the latter as the group's label debut. Radio played it, but preferred the flip side. The week of October 14, 1972, "I'll Be Around" became the Spinners' first Number One hit.

136

IF YOU DON'T KNOW ME BY NOW

Harold Melvin & the Blue Notes

PHILADELPHIA INTERNATIONAL 3520
WRITERS: KENNY GAMBLE, LEON HUFF
PRODUCERS: KENNY GAMBLE, LEON HUFF
November 18, 1972 (2 weeks)

"I think 'If You Don't Know Me by Now' is the best ballad [Kenny] Gamble and [Leon] Huff ever wrote," says Joe Tarsia, founder of the famed Sigma Sound Studios in Philadelphia. "It just so happens that Gamble and Huff and Tarsia were all having marital problems at the same time...That song became my national anthem. Every married couple should listen to the words of that song."

Long before Harold Melvin ever knew that there was a man named Teddy Pendergrass, he and the Blue Notes hitched from Philadelphia to New York to compete at the Apollo Theater's amateur hour. After winning five weeks in a row, they were signed to Josie Records and recorded "If You Love Me" in 1957.

But it was a new group of Blue Notes who signed to Philadelphia International Records in 1971. Melvin had grown up with Gamble, so he wasn't surprised to hear from him while the group was playing at a hotel in Puerto Rico. Melvin accepted Gamble's invitation to join his new label, but had to complete a two-week contract before returning home. At this point in time, John Atkins was the lead singer of the group and Pendergrass was on drums.

"While we were in Puerto Rico, the club was so packed, [the owner] asked would we mind playing an extra set for the people to dance, so they could turn the people over who were waiting outside to get in," Melvin recalls. "I asked my musicians and they said they wouldn't mind. So I'm outside in the lobby and I hear this voice. I'm thinking maybe somebody walked up onstage. I had no idea that Teddy was singing...but I heard enough to know there was something there. I peeked back in and he was sitting back there. He had pulled the microphone back to the drums and was singing 'Hey There Lonely Girl.' And after that night, he said, 'I have something to say, and I can't say it on the drums.' "

So much to say, in fact, that Pendergrass replaced Atkins as lead singer. "I told Teddy I was going to see Gamble," Melvin continues, "I put some other guys together and built the group around Teddy. We were playing a club called the Living Room in Philadelphia and Huff came down. Teddy blew Huff's mind away when he heard him."

The new version of Harold Melvin & the Blue Notes peaked at number seven with their first Gamble-Huff release, "I Miss You." The follow-up was "If You Don't Know Me by Now." According to MFSB guitarist Bobby Eli, neither of those songs was written for Harold Melvin & the Blue Notes. "That batch was meant for the Dells," he reveals. "For some reason the deal didn't go through...But it worked and the rest is history. We all felt from day one that that was going to be a winning project. Sometimes I would go up to the studio when they were doing [Teddy's] vocals and I was floored. It was unbelievable."

Pendergrass's stunning rendition of "If You Don't Know Me by Now" captured the attention of R&B radio as well as pop radio. "The meaning of the song was so haunting and the melody was so beautiful and the story was so true," says Teddy. "The possibilities were there for it to be a big record, a huge record. At the time R&B music wasn't getting a fair shake on white radio and we didn't know for sure whether it would or not, but we thought it was the best candidate for a crossover. Our first record, 'I Miss You,' was the black national anthem but white radio told us it was too R&B." Three weeks after "If You Don't Know Me by Now" went to Number One on the R&B chart, it peaked at number three on the pop chart, the group's biggest success on the Hot 100.

137

YOU OUGHT TO BE WITH ME

Al Green

HI 2227
WRITERS: AL GREEN,
WILLIE MITCHELL, AL JACKSON
PRODUCER: WILLIE MITCHELL
December 2, 1972 (1 week)

Someone buying Al Green's records for the first time today might be forgiven for thinking he was a Motown artist. In the late '70s, Hi Records was absorbed by a small, Los Angeles–based label called Cream; several years later, Hi's biggest hits ended up being reissued on Motown, which is how you have to buy them now.

It wasn't such a bad fit. By reaching the soul market and the mainstream at the same time, Green's records with producer Willie Mitchell pulled off roughly the same trick as the Sound of Young America. In fact, given the success of this formula on "You Ought to Be with Me" and other hits, it's surprising that Mitchell continued to let Hi's other artists make such gritty records instead of trying for a whole assembly line full of Al Greens.

Mitchell's accomplishments with Green did not go unnoticed by the Motown folks. "I knew I hit the sound [I wanted]," Mitchell says, "because after we cut 'Let's Stay Together,' Motown wanted to rent the studio for a week." Motown brought 11 musicians down, but no vocalists. "They were checking how I miked the drums and what have you...They cut a week in here...no voices, just the musicians."

So what did the Motown people find? Well, when Mitchell took over the abandoned Royal movie theater in Memphis which served as Hi's studio, "I tore all the walls out...and took part of the floor out and slanted the floor to get the sound I wanted."

Mitchell didn't like the sound of the control board he inherited. To get more bottom, he made an eight-track recorder by taking four two-tracks, stacking them together, and putting them through a new mixer—at a total cost of $92. "Everything came through naturally," Mitchell says. "No EQ, just a little chamber echo."

On the Jackson/Green/Mitchell collaborations, Mitchell and Al Jackson would usually work songs out at the piano and snare drum, respectively, and then Green would add the lyrics.

Mitchell's dislike of studio gimmicks didn't stop him from making a record in pieces. "We never [recorded] the whole thing live," he says. "We would take the rhythm track down and Al would put his voice on it and I would figure out how I was going to color it. When Al put his voice on it, he was through...He never thought about the song anymore. He wouldn't hear it until I had mixed the song."

"You Ought to Be with Me" was the third single in a similar vein after "Let's Stay Together" (the others being "Look What You Done for Me" and "I'm Still in Love with You"), and with such a well-oiled machine, it's no surprise that Mitchell was sometimes accused of making the same record over and over.

Asked about this at the time, he told *Blues & Soul*, "I really believe that it's just a question of having a hit sound and Al Green is a hit sound...I think people misinterpret [his] style for Al Green sounding the same if they don't take the time to listen properly. How could he do six straight gold records sounding the same?"

138

ME AND MRS. JONES

Billy Paul

PHILADELPHIA INTERNATIONAL 3521
WRITERS: KENNY GAMBLE, LEON HUFF, CARY GILBERT
PRODUCERS: KENNY GAMBLE, LEON HUFF
December 9, 1972 (3 weeks)

The key to success for Billy Paul was blending his jazz style with a contemporary R&B sound, and producers Kenny Gamble and Leon Huff found the right balance with "Me and Mrs. Jones," a song that catapulted Billy to the top of *Billboard*'s R&B and pop charts.

Born Paul Williams in Philadelphia, Billy was one of the first artists signed to Gamble and Huff's Philadelphia International Records. Billy first met Kenny in 1967 at the Cadillac Club. The artist had already recorded some sides for an album, and Gamble worked with him on the final three tracks for *Feelin' Good at the Cadillac Club* and released it on his Gamble imprint. Very jazz-oriented, it wasn't a commercial success. When Gamble and Huff started up the Neptune label as a subsidiary of Chess Records, Paul went with them and released a version of Simon and Garfunkel's "Mrs. Robinson." When Leonard Chess died in 1969, Neptune was shuttered. Gamble and Huff then made a deal with CBS to start a new imprint, Philadelphia International.

Seeking to give Billy a big hit, Gamble and Huff joined with Cary Gilbert to write "Me and Mrs. Jones." But the vocalist wasn't enchanted with the song. "My first impression was that I didn't like it," says Billy. "It was a straight, straight song. It was the last song on the album, as a matter of fact, because we had to fill the album up." Billy took a break and travelled to St. Thomas for a vacation, but he brought "Me and Mrs. Jones" with him.

Billy Paul

"I rearranged the whole song," Paul remembers. "I worked it out in my head and listened thousands of times to see how I would improvise this and improvise that. So I made it my own. I came back and everybody I played it for swooned over it."

Billy loved working with Gamble and Huff and recording at Sigma Sound Studios. "The thing I miss most about it is the dedication that you had then that you don't have today. What I have against the electronic thing is the fact that you can sample a person that doesn't even have a voice. When you spend years and years in the business like I have, you get defensive sometimes. But the way [we did it] back then was the good way...If some background singers came in and sang the wrong note, they had to stay there all night and do it. It's not like running it through a machine now and putting them on pitch. And I loved that way."

The combination of Billy Paul and Gamble and Huff gelled with Billy's first release on Philadelphia International. "Kenny Gamble and Joe Tarsia would tell you they had a hard time...It took them two or three albums to really find my voice and to capture it. Because I have a low range and I have a high range and Joe used to always tell me that I'm singing low one minute and within seconds I'm in the red...Part of me being successful with Gamble and Huff and Sigma Sound was that they knew what to do with my voice. It was the same with the O'Jays. They knew how to cut each individual. It wasn't like you went in and sang with a track and that's it."

139

SUPERSTITION

Stevie Wonder

TAMLA 54226
WRITER: STEVIE WONDER
PRODUCER: STEVIE WONDER
January 6, 1973 (3 weeks)

For Stevie Wonder, freedom arrived on Thursday, May 13, 1971. Twenty-one on that date, he was liberated from all the recording and music publishing contracts signed with Motown when he was a minor.

Within three weeks, Wonder was making new music at Manhattan's Mediasound studios. Malcolm Cecil recalls that it was Memorial Day. "By the end of that Monday, it must have been two or three in the morning, we had 17 songs in the can," he says.

A onetime radar instructor, Cecil was engineering at Mediasound in 1971 and working with colleague Bob Margouleff, a photographer and musician. More than that, Margouleff was a man with a Moog, the ground-breaking synthesizer that Stevie Wonder first heard on an album by Tonto's Expanding Headband, *Zero Time*. The Headband was actually Cecil and Margouleff, whom Wonder spontaneously wanted to meet at Mediasound that Memorial Day weekend.

The result was a remarkable three-year union. Cecil and Margouleff helped Wonder maximize the Moog, programming it and recording all the music and songs he began to create. "We never stopped working from that moment, night and day," Margouleff remembers. "He'd do the playing, we'd do the programming, and we started to accumulate a huge library of songs."

Their first album together was *Music of My Mind*. Wonder had signed a lucrative new Motown contract by then, but the LP lacked a major hit single, so everyone was determined to avoid similar mistakes with the next project, *Talking Book*, for which Wonder began assembling songs in 1972.

One of them was "Superstition," initially earmarked for British rock guitarist Jeff Beck. Cecil explains, "Jeff heard this song Stevie wrote in London, called 'Maybe Your Baby.' Then Stevie invited him to New York to work on 'Lookin' for Another Pure Love.' " At the same time—and in the very same studio, New York's Electric Lady—Cecil and Margouleff were producing Beck's own album for Columbia Records. It was June 1972.

Beck wanted "Maybe Your Baby" for his project, according to Cecil, but Wonder wasn't keen. "So one day, Stevie says, 'OK, I'll write a song for you.' He asks, 'Mal, are the drums up?' He goes in, plays the drum track, then the clavinet tracks, and from that, he says, 'Let me have a mike,' and starts singing, 'Very superstitious...' "

Back in the control room, Beck asked if it was to be his song. Cecil says Wonder replied, " 'Song, not track. You're going to record this song.' Stevie wouldn't let him have the track, but let him have the song."

Yet it was "Superstition" without final lyrics. Cecil and Margouleff grew desperate, since the Beck album was due for delivery to Columbia's Clive Davis. Finally, Cecil says he sent Wonder to an Electric Lady anteroom with instructions to dictate lyrics to the secretary locked in with him.

That problem solved, there was another: Wonder asked to hear Beck's recording of the song—and changed his mind. Cecil recalls, "Stevie said, 'He can't have it, I'm going to keep it. It's too good.' "

What Wonder wanted, he got. "Clive Davis never forgave us," says Cecil. "We never got paid, the studio never got paid, and it broke up my relationship with Jeff." Meanwhile, Wonder finished his "Superstition" with the addition of vocals, plus sax and trumpet overdubs by Trevor Laurence and Steve Madaio, respectively. *Talking Book* was complete, and delivered to Motown.

140

WHY CAN'T WE LIVE TOGETHER

Timmy Thomas

GLADES 1703
WRITER: TIMMY THOMAS
PRODUCER: TIMMY THOMAS
January 27, 1973 (2 weeks)

A Lowrey organ. A timeless lyric. The son of a preacher man.

"Why Can't We Live Together" by Timmy Thomas was the first Number One for T.K. Productions of Hialeah, Florida. The company was an offshoot of Henry Stone's influential Tone Distributing, which handled most of the great independent labels—Atlantic, Motown, Chess, Roulette, Stax—in the sunshine state.

Stone also operated several of his own small labels through the '60s, but as industry changes affected Tone, he began emphasizing this side of the business.

Timmy Thomas

"Why Can't We Live Together" was one of the results.

"The T.K. studio was originally called Zoo," remembers Steve Alaimo, the former pop singer ("Every Day I Have to Cry" in 1963) who became right-hand man to Stone in Hialeah, a district of Miami. "King Sporty, who wrote 'Buffalo Soldier' for Bob Marley, brought Timmy Thomas in one day. He just had a Lowrey organ and a rhythm machine—and 'Why Can't We Live Together.'

"I was sitting there, thinking, 'We've got to make a demo [of this song], put some music on it,' when I realized: this is done, this *is* a record. We just transferred it to multi-track, and that was it."

It truly was. Recorded in Miami in August, "Why Can't We Live Together" hit the airwaves around October "and just kept on going," says Alaimo. Eventually, it sold two million copies.

"I had written the song out of frustration," Thomas told *Blues & Soul* in 1973. "It was written out of my concern for the world. Not a racial trouble, but a general problem of why we can't all live together—not necessarily black and white, but take a look around the world and see all the little problems that are being experienced. And all the big ones in places such as Israel and Egypt or Vietnam."

A minister's child, Indiana-born Thomas honed his musical skills during the '60s at Goldwax Records in Memphis, then relocated to Miami. He opened his own club there in 1972. "Timmy was always kind of a lounge artist," says Alaimo. "He played the organ, and sometimes wouldn't sing."

Thomas even tested "Why Can't We Live Together" in his nightspot. "It's almost a bossa nova beat, with a touch of Spanish in it," he said. "I was originally thinking of a different rhythm, although it was close to what we now have. But I tried it out in the lounge, and the people there loved it just this way so we settled on it this way."

Steve Alaimo reflects, "Timmy was never a hellacious vocalist, but he had a certain feel and believability, and he wrote some really nice lyrics. Plus, he was always very humble about his success—never a wise guy, never pushed himself forward. And the elation he felt when that record was a hit..."

141

COULD IT BE I'M FALLING IN LOVE

Spinners

ATLANTIC 2927
WRITERS: MERVIN STEALS, MELVIN STEALS
PRODUCER: THOM BELL
February 10, 1973 (1 week)

When I write things or when I come up with things and other writers write things, I know exactly what I want to hear for the artist," says producer Thom Bell, explaining how he found "Could It Be I'm Falling in Love" for the Spinners. "Trying to get James Brown to sing 'Ave Maria' doesn't particularly work because that's not his character. And Luciano Pavarotti, for him to sing 'Twist and Shout' is not in his character. So you find the material that fits the natural timbre...the natural rhythm of the artist. My job as a producer and a writer is to get what you have naturally and pull it out and cultivate it."

The group that Bell was cultivating first came together in 1955, when Billy Henderson, Bobbie Smith, Henry Fambrough, Pervis Jackson, and C.P. Spencer formed a group called the Domingos in Ferndale, Michigan. The name sounded too much like the Flamingos, so they rechristened themselves after the big chrome hubcaps on Bobbie's car. Spencer departed the Spinners; his place was taken by George Dixon. Harvey Fuqua signed them to his Tri-Phi label and sent them into the top 10 with "That's What Girls Are Made For." There were more personnel changes during the group's Motown years, and when they left the label, lead singer G. C. Cameron was replaced by a friend of his, Philip Walker, who changed his name to Phillippe Wynne.

"Could It Be I'm Falling in Love" was recorded at Sigma Sound Studios in Philadelphia on June 12, 1972, at the same four-song recording session that produced "I'll Be Around," the Spinners' first Number One hit [see 135]. Bell heard the song on a tape submitted by twin brothers, Melvin and Mervin Steals. They had sent him material previously, and he liked what he heard enough to encourage them to send more. "Could It Be I'm Falling in Love" was on the third tape they sent the producer. Bell thought it had a great melody but strange lyrics. "So we sat down and restructured the song," the producer recalls.

The track features Larry Washington on congas. "Sometimes the music gets a little herky-jerky, so in order to keep something uniform going...to keep a flow going, I used congas...There has to be some continuity there, so it doesn't throw people's ears off, it doesn't throw their rhythms off."

Although the Spinners excelled at background harmonies, female backing vocals are also featured prominently on the track. Carla Benson, Yvette Benton, and Barbara Ingram were singing behind the twin lead vocals of Bobbie Smith and Phillippe Wynne. "Men being what they are, they get bottom-heavy," Bell contends. "The human ear hears all ranges. They hear top, middle, and bottom, but when you get too bottom-heavy, you can't distinguish the words quite as well as you can with female vocals...And that's a problem we producers have in the studio of blending backgrounds with leads...You have to compromise between the two. I found the decibel level of the men, in order to accomplish what I was trying to accomplish, was above the decibel level of the leads and you lost the lead." The Spinners were used to having women singing in the background from their Motown days, according to Bell. "It didn't bother them at all. It got to the point where they said, 'Bell, anything you want to do. You gave us a Number One record when everyone else thought we were dead. Whatever you want to do is fine with us.' "

142

LOVE TRAIN

The O'Jays

PHILADELPHIA INTERNATIONAL 3524
WRITERS: KENNY GAMBLE, LEON HUFF
PRODUCERS: KENNY GAMBLE, LEON HUFF
February 17, 1973 (4 weeks)

Almost a decade after Martha & the Vandellas urged people to put aside their differences and go "Dancing in the Street," the O'Jays expanded on that theme and asked people all over the world to join a global "Love Train."

The second Number One hit for the O'Jays was fairly simple, and easily identified by Norman Harris's guitar lick. But had history taken a slightly different turn, the O'Jays might never have recorded "Love Train," "Back Stabbers," or any of their Number One hits.

The O'Jays first met Kenny Gamble and Leon Huff in New York City when the producers came to see the Intruders perform their Number One song [see 54—"Cowboys to Girls"]. Phil Terry, Eugene "Bird" Daughtry, and Robert "Big Sonny" Edwards of the Intruders told their bosses that they ought to take a closer look at the O'Jays with the idea of signing them to a label deal.

"We came home and we were playing a small club in Akron, Ohio," says Eddie Levert of the O'Jays. "At this time we were more pop-oriented than R&B. We had about 500 white people in there. This really floored Gamble and Huff. They didn't remember the early records like 'Lonely Drifter' and 'I Have Cried My Last Tear' that we did on Imperial." Gamble and Huff told the O'Jays that they wanted the group to come to Philadelphia and record. "We were in between contracts and looking for a deal," says Levert. "This is after Bell Records." The O'Jays signed with Gamble and Huff's Neptune label and recorded hits like "One Night Affair" and "Looky Looky (Look at Me Girl)."

Neptune was distributed by Chess Records, and when owner Leonard Chess died, the label shuttered. "Nobody got paid," says Levert. "We were very disappointed. We didn't know where we were going to go. Gamble and Huff didn't know what they were going to do either."

The O'Jays heard from the producers a couple of years later when they were starting up Philadelphia International, a new label to be distributed by a major company—CBS. "I was in Cleveland, they were in Philadelphia, and we were communicating," says Levert. "They said, 'Come back, it's going to be different. We're going to do some great stuff.' " Eddie told the other members of the O'Jays, but they still remembered the Neptune days and weren't so willing to take a chance again.

"Around this time, Gerald and Sean were born," says Eddie. "I had two kids and a wife to feed. Gamble and Huff kept calling me. I told the [other O'Jays], 'We're sitting here spinning our wheels. Nothing's happening. Nobody's calling. We need to go do something.' I went to Philadelphia by myself because Gamble and Huff talked me into coming up." The producers wanted to record Eddie as a solo artist, but Levert was still group-oriented. He listened to some of Gamble and Huff's new material and tried once more to get his fellow O'Jays to travel to Philadelphia.

Walter Williams and William Powell finally accepted his invitation; Bobby Massey did not. "He felt we would be better off if we wrote and produced our own stuff," says Levert. "But no one was clamoring to let the O'Jays produce."

143

NEITHER ONE OF US (WANTS TO BE THE FIRST TO SAY GOODBYE)

Gladys Knight & the Pips

SOUL 35098
WRITER: JIM WEATHERLY
PRODUCER: JOE PORTER
March 17, 1973 (4 weeks)

Gladys Knight & the Pips *wanted* to say 'bye as "Neither One of Us" glided up the charts. The clock was ticking on their Motown recording contract; midnight arrived on Friday, March 23, 1973. After that, their new deal with Buddah Records would take effect.

The quartet felt unfulfilled at Berry Gordy's shop, laboring in the shadow of stars he built from scratch, especially Diana Ross and the Supremes. "We weren't allowed to record with Holland/Dozier/Holland," Gladys told Steve Bloom of *Rolling Stone* years later. "It had to do with how you related to the family and how you got along with the upper-echelon acts: Smokey and Diana." Back in 1966, she had been against signing with Motown, but was outvoted by the Pips [see 46—"I Heard It Through the Grapevine"].

The group was democracy in action. "When they did their background vocals, she would sit in the booth and her brother, Bubba, would take charge in the studio," says Kenny Kerner, who co-produced two of their Number One hits for Buddah. "If they were off, she'd push the button: 'Bubba, you're flat here, you're sharp there.' They would listen to her.

"The opposite was true also. When she was in the studio, if she had trouble with a line or something, the Pips would be in the booth, saying, 'Gladys, I think that's not the right interpretation of the line.' It was never, 'I'm Gladys, you're the Pips, listen to what I say, I'm the boss.' "

Johnny Bristol, who wrote with the group and produced some of their best work at Motown, agrees. "When they were in the studio, Gladys became a Pip. She wouldn't let them do the harmony without her. They were a creative *team*."

Knight and the Pips recorded "Neither One of Us" in Los Angeles around mid-1972, in their first and only date with producer Joe Porter. Michael O'Martian and Artie Butler arranged the material, using their customary California session players at the Motown studios.

Porter handled a broader range of artists than most; his Motown credits included recordings by Lesley Gore, Bobby Darin, Diahann Carroll, and Thelma Houston. "Neither One of Us" was authored by Jim Weatherly, a college football whiz turned songwriter. Gladys, always on the lookout for powerful lyrics, had caressed country material before: Her recording of Kris Kristofferson's "Help Me Make It Through the Night" was a hit in the spring of 1972.

Coincidentally, Gladys and the Pips' "Neither One of Us" entered the *Billboard* soul charts during the same week in January 1973 that Bob Luman debuted on the country best-sellers with his version. The group's record reached Number One; Luman had to be content with a top ten berth in his field.

144

MASTERPIECE

The Temptations

GORDY 7126
WRITER: NORMAN WHITFIELD
PRODUCER: NORMAN WHITFIELD
April 14, 1973 (2 weeks)

Call it cinematic soul—music with the kind of vision and reality seldom seen in the "blaxploitation" movies of the early '70s. And consider the men responsible: Marvin Gaye ("Inner City Blues"), Stevie Wonder ("Living for the City"), and Norman Whitfield ("Papa Was a Rolling Stone"). They were more in touch with black America than a dozen new-wave film directors.

"I wanted to try some songs that had the scope and feeling of a movie," Whitfield told *Billboard* in 1973. He was talking about *Masterpiece*, the Temptations' album project that followed "Papa Was a Rolling Stone."

"The group had some skepticism about taking on the material," Whitfield admitted. "But their technique is so all-encompassing that once we had reached an understanding about what they were singing, the Temps were able to summon up the necessary extra energy the songs demanded."

Actually, *Masterpiece* demanded as much—if not more—from the musicians. The album tracks were lengthy and heavily instrumental; the full-length version of the title song featured the Temptations for less than half of its 14-minute running time. Even on the single, edited for airplay, a minute passed before the group began singing.

"I just wish we had had the opportunity to do more vocally on the album," Dennis Edwards told *Blues & Soul*. "I just don't think we did enough. It's really a question of time—we've never got two weeks to set aside for a recording or anything like that, so it's left up to Norman to work out the tracks for us and we add the vocals wherever possible."

It was all part of Whitfield's increasing musical sophistication, according to Paul Riser, who arranged "Papa Was a Rolling Stone" and the entire *Masterpiece* album. "First of all," he says, "we'd start it with eight tracks. He would, of course, lay as much as he could there. He always filled his tracks up, especially guitar overdubs, although his bass thing was pretty much worked out. It was mostly guitar stuff, keyboard overdubs and things."

The producer's choice of guitarists—he was still recording in Detroit at this time—included Joe Messina, Melvin "Wah Wah" Watson, Robert White, Robert Ward, and Eddie Willis. On keyboards for the *Masterpiece* sessions were Earl Van Dyke and Johnny Griffith; on bass were Leroy Taylor, Bob Babbitt, and Eddie Watkins; on drums were Richard "Pistol" Allen, Uriel Jones, Andrew Smith, and Aaron Smith; percussionists included Eddie "Bongo" Brown, Jack Ashford, and Jack Brokensha.

"Norman was persistent in what he wanted," Riser explains, "but very, very good-natured—probably the most good-natured of all of them. He was not a tense person, he'd keep it loose, but always work it how he wanted. He would work the rhythm section until he got it, and they enjoyed it."

Judging by Dennis Edwards's comments, Whitfield's recording process wasn't so enjoyable for the Temptations. "Look, trends were changing and I was only interested in keeping them on top and in keeping them current," the producer said a few years later. "A transition was needed, but I admit I never really confided in them as to what I was doing."

Sylvia

145

PILLOW TALK

Sylvia

VIBRATION 521
WRITERS: SYLVIA ROBINSON, MICHAEL BURTON
PRODUCERS: SYLVIA ROBINSON, MICHAEL BURTON
April 28, 1973 (2 weeks)

One summer's day in 1968, Sylvia Robinson proudly showed King Coleman around her eight-track Soul Sound Studios in Englewood, New Jersey. "Coleman is promotion chief for Miss Robinson's new label, All Platinum Records," *Billboard* reported. "Mickey and Sylvia's recording of 'Love Is Strange' was a best-seller a few years ago."

Flash back to 1956. Sylvia Vanderpool, just turned 21, walks into a New York studio and meets RCA Records producer Bob Rolontz, who's heard about her and partner Mickey Baker. "I said I was interested in signing them to a contract, and told her to call me," recalls Rolontz. "She never did. She told me later, 'I didn't like you.' "

Nevertheless, Rolontz *did* put Robinson and Baker under contract. "I liked their blend, I liked the sound," he says. "The rest was good fortune and hard work." On October 17 of that year, he produced "Love Is Strange"—and delivered Sylvia's first Number One record.

Fast-forward to 1973. Sylvia, now 36, is running All Platinum Records in Englewood with husband Joe Robinson. She has a song, composed at home some 18 months earlier. Initially, though, it seemed more suitable for another artist. "I wrote 'Pillow Talk' for Al Green," admits Robinson, but Green rejected it." So Sylvia recorded her own version and—presto!—it was her second Number One record.

Seventeen years may separate the two chart-toppers, but both are hallmarked by Robinson's quirky vocals. And where Mickey Baker played guitar on "Love Is Strange," Sylvia strummed (acoustic) on "Pillow Talk." Behind her was Yogi Horton on drums, Frank Pescod on bass, Sammy Lowe on keyboards, Walter Morris on lead and rhythm guitar, and Craig Derry on congas.

Like Motown and Stax, the Robinsons built their company and their sound with an in-house studio and in-house musicians. "Because the acts are able to stay in the studio all night if they want to get what they want," Joe Robinson told *Blues & Soul* in 1973. "And it's cheaper to fly in from anywhere than to record locally at high studio rates. Not only that, but artists get familiar with the way the studio operates and the way the producers work."

Horton, the drummer, was a vital part of the team for a while. (Later he played behind Nick Ashford and Valerie Simpson, Diana Ross, and Luther Vandross, among others.) So was the late Sammy Lowe, who arranged many of the sessions, writing charts and bringing in such elements as horns and strings. "It was kind of like a family there for a long time," Lowe said.

"Pillow Talk" proved to be All Platinum's most successful single, certified gold and a top three pop smash. It was also the first release on a new imprint, Vibration, created for Johnny Halonka's Beta Record Distributors. "They offered us a good deal for exclusivity," says Sylvia Robinson.

Flash forward again, this time to 1979. At the Robinsons' new business venture, Sugarhill Records, Sylvia produces a 12-inch single that helps ignite a new music trend: "Rapper's Delight" by the Sugarhill Gang. Good fortune and persistence pay off once more.

146

FUNKY WORM

Ohio Players

WESTBOUND 214
WRITERS: OHIO PLAYERS
PRODUCERS: OHIO PLAYERS
May 12, 1973 (1 week)

The history of the Ohio Players begins in 1959 when Robert Ward formed a group called the Ohio Untouchables that included Ralph "Pee Wee" Middlebrook, Marshall Jones, and Clarence Satchell. Ward was related to the founder of Detroit's LuPine Records, and the Untouchables were asked to back up the Falcons and their new lead singer, Wilson Pickett, on "I Found a Love," a number six hit in 1962.

The Ohio Untouchables backed up other Lupine artists and recorded their own single, "Love Is Amazing," that sold well locally. But by 1964 Ward was recording as a solo artist (he would ultimately re-record "Love Is Amazing" on his 1991 comeback album, *Fear No Evil*) and the other Ohio Untouchables were home in Dayton. They reformed as an octet called the Ohio Players and signed with Compass Records, breaking into the R&B chart for the first time in 1968 with "Trespassin'," which peaked at number 50. The follow-up, "It's a Cryin' Shame," failed to chart and Compass lost its direction. So the Ohio Players headed west to the California-based Capitol label, and released one album, *Observations in Time.*

By 1971, there was something new happening in R&B music. Sly Stone had been fusing progressive rock music with soul, and the new lineup of the Ohio Players followed the same path.

They recorded "Pain" for an independent Dayton label, Top Hit. The funky workout was picked up by Detroit's Westbound label and transformed into a minor national hit, reaching number 35 on the *Billboard* R&B chart. The Ohio Players at this time consisted of the three original Untouchables— Middlebrook (trumpet), Jones (bass), and Satchell (saxophone, flute)—plus Greg Webster (drums), Leroy "Sugarfoot" Bonner (guitar, vocals), Walter "Junie" Morrison (piano, vocals), Bruce Napier (trumpet, vocals), and Marvin Pierce (trombone, vocals).

The Players had newfound freedom on Westbound. "They had George Clinton and a group called Parliament on their roster," says Marshall Jones. "They had suits and ties and they were doing steps like the Temptations. We got on the label and had a funk/street sound and the next thing we knew, they had a funk sound and were calling themselves Parliament/Funkadelic."

The "Pain" single led to an album of the same name, most notable for the cover image of a bald dominatrix with a leather G-string preparing to crack her whip over a submissive male. It was only the first in a series of S&M images that adorned the covers of the Ohio Players albums. The series continued with *Pleasure,* which contained an unlikely novelty song called "Funky Worm."

"I don't know how we came up with that," Jones marvels. "We were in the studio and we thought about doing something we thought was funky. And we did 'Funky Worm' not realizing it was going to be a major record."

Morrison provided the voice of an aged Granny, singing about a graveyard worm. "When it came out, we would do shows and these people would bring their kids," says Jones. "They would put them up on the stage and they were little kids, eight, nine, 10 years old. I guess it caught the imagination of the youth of that time."

147

LEAVING ME

The Independents

WAND 11252
WRITERS: CHUCK JACKSON, MARVIN YANCY
PRODUCERS: CHUCK JACKSON, MARVIN YANCY
May 19, 1973 (1 week)

Only the smart survive. When Jerry Butler's partnership with Kenny Gamble and Leon Huff dissolved in 1970, the singer needed new song sources. His solution: a writers' workshop, formed in Chicago with financing from Chappell Music. "One of my arguments," Butler declares, "was that there were lots of talented young writers around, but they were so busy working, trying to make ends meet, that they couldn't really apply the time to their craft."

Chuck Jackson was one of those talents whom the workshop helped. "I had always written songs," he says, "through my high school years and grammar school years." Sometimes he sought inspiration in letters penned by his teenage brother and a buddy. "I used to spend hours trying to think of things to say, and when they would leave the room, they'd leave all that stuff lying around. I would go in there and read it." That teenage brother knew the power of prose; he would grow up to be a civil rights leader and U.S. presidential candidate, Jesse Jackson.

Later, at one of Jesse's black enterprise events in Chicago, Chuck met Marvin Yancy, a minister who also played piano for a number of gospel artists. The two men became fast friends, writing together for the Butler workshop. One song, "Just As Long As You Need Me," caught the ear of Eddie Thomas, former manager of the Impressions. Jackson recalls, "The way it came off, Eddie said, 'Man, you have got to sing this yourself.' "

And so the Independents were formed, with Jackson as lead vocalist. "I never really wanted to be a singer," he says. "Eddie talked me into it." Thomas also secured the group a deal with Scepter/Wand Records, while Jackson and Yancy recruited Helen Curry and Maurice Jackson (no relation) to complete the line-up.

"Just As Long As You Need Me" was an R&B smash in 1972; "Leaving Me" followed. It was, according to Jackson, just one more of their spontaneous ideas. "Marvin and I were together so much at the time," he says, and they were writing constantly. They also used pseudonyms—Marvin Barge and Jimmy Jiles—for those first few records, a ploy Jackson now attributes to bad legal advice and financial wranglings.

The material was cut at Chicago's Paul Serrano Recording, with Chess musicians and arrangers Gene Barge and Tom Tom Washington. "We were all buddies on the corner," explains Jackson. "There were the guys who were doing Earth, Wind & Fire. Gene Record of the Chi-Lites gave us little hints and pointers, and the Emotions were all friends of ours. We all used to hang together, eight or nine groups out of that one scene."

A certified million-seller, "Leaving Me" was one of seven R&B top 10 hits for the Independents during 1972–74. But the best was yet to come, thanks to a chance meeting involving Jackson, Yancy, and the daughter of one of America's most celebrated singers [see 222—"This Will Be"].

148

I'M GONNA LOVE YOU JUST A LITTLE MORE BABY

Barry White

20TH CENTURY 2018
WRITER: BARRY WHITE
PRODUCER: BARRY WHITE
May 26, 1973 (2 weeks)

I never wanted to sing professionally," confides Barry White. "My interest was arranging, writing, and producing. When I first stepped up to the mike in 1960, that was probably the greatest thrill of my life in this business. It was even more overwhelming than my first gold album."

Born in Galveston, Texas, and raised in Watts, California, Barry White went to jail when he was 15 for stealing tires off Cadillacs. He was released on August 28, 1960, and on September 4 some friends he had known since his days in John Adams Junior High asked him to record a song with them. Barry sang bass on "Little Girl" for the Upfronts. The record failed, but Barry caught the fire. "I knew what I was going to be in this world."

Barry went to work for Bob Keene, whose labels included Del-Fi, Mustang, and Bronco. In 1967, Barry wrote and produced "It May Be Winter Outside (But in My Heart It's Spring)," a Supremes soundalike by Felice Taylor. The single peaked at number 42. Two years later, Barry met the three women who would become Love Unlimited, his girl group. He took them to Uni Records in 1972, and they hit with "Walkin' in the Rain with the One I Love." When Russ Regan left the label to head up 20th Century Records, White got the trio out of its contract and brought them to Regan.

Barry kept a small office at the corner of Sunset and LaBrea in Los Angeles, where he loved to write songs and sleep on the floor. His plan was to find a male singer for his artists' roster, and he was writing songs accordingly. One night he composed the music for "I'm Gonna Love You Just a Little More Baby." "I sung it on a little reel-to-reel tape recorder. I knew as a producer that [I] was the voice for that song." The idea terrified him.

Barry was so opposed to recording himself, he told his first and only lie to his business partner and friend, Larry Nunes. Nunes asked White if he had written any new material, and the answer was no. "I told him that for almost 30 days and then finally told him, 'I had it when you asked me. I didn't want to play it for you.' "

By this time, Barry had written an entire album. Nunes listened to the demos and the two men fought for two and a half months about who was going to record the material. "What I was doing was fighting my destiny," Barry admits. "So I gave in to him. I cut the album. Russ Regan gave us a contract. I went in the studio and cut 'I'm Gonna Love You Just a Little More Baby.' All the masters were at that session: Wah Wah Watson, Ray Parker, Dean Parks, David T. [Walker], Wilton Felder, Ed Greene, Nathan East, Gary Coleman on vibes. I'm on piano."

Barry refers to the song as his "national anthem." But it wasn't universally accepted by his label. "That was the first big fight we had," says Barry. "There were some people at 20th Century Records who didn't like the album. They said the album was nothing. There wasn't but five songs on it. The songs were too long. And this is black and white [people] who told me this." Clive Davis almost picked up the album for Columbia Records, according to Barry, but someone else championed his cause at 20th Century. "Elton John heard a dub of my album and he stole it. He took it to London and he took it home with him to convince some people that this might be the thing. And 'I'm Gonna Love You' took about six months to break."

149

ONE OF A KIND (LOVE AFFAIR)

Spinners

ATLANTIC 2962
WRITER: JOSEPH B. JEFFERSON
PRODUCER: THOM BELL
June 9, 1973 (4 weeks)

Growing up in Richmond, Virginia, Joseph B. Jefferson not only listened to his mother's record albums, he read the liner notes. "I always wanted to know about the people behind the scenes," he explains. Jefferson taught himself to play drums, and after a stint in the Army, decided to follow his dream. "I always wanted to be a writer, as far back as I can remember, because I thought these were the mysterious people. You saw the stars all the time but you never saw the writers [or] the producers."

Jefferson was touring with the Manhattans when he met Tony Bell, who offered to introduce Jefferson to his brother. Thom Bell remembers his impression of the man from Richmond: "He was energetic. He was a clean cat and he knew what he wanted to do and I felt he had something to offer...I gave him an office and a piano. I said 'Go to town.' "

Jefferson received some unexpected inspiration when his relationship with a young lady suddenly ended. "We were living together and she walked out," he says. "I came home off the road and she had taken all her stuff. I went in the kitchen and turned the light on and she had written on the wall...'I'm in love with you. I can't stay with you.' " Two days later, Thom called and asked if he had any songs. Joseph replied in the affirmative and Bell asked what he had. "I said, 'It's called "One Of A Kind (Love Affair)." ' And I hadn't written the song. I was sulking over the fact this lady had left me. He said, 'That's a great title. Let me hear it.' So I had to buckle down and try to write a song."

The two men met the following Saturday and Jefferson played a couple of verses. "[Thom] said, 'Let me ask you something. Is this the best that you can really do with this song?' I said, 'Maybe not.' My pride was hurt." Bell said he liked the song but wanted Jefferson to work on it some more. They met again two weeks later. Jefferson describes that meeting: "I played it for him. Once I got to the first chorus, he [said], 'You don't have to play any more. It's a great song. It's a Number One record.' And I said, 'Get out of here!' "

Bell thought it would be a perfect tune for Bobbie Smith and Phillippe Wynne to share lead vocal duties. "Bobbie was a light voice and Phillippe was the one that took you to the gospel, took you to church and made you hear it. He made you move. One was pop, one was R&B. One was rural, one was urban."

Bell says he knew how Wynne would sing it: "1-2-3, boom, 1-2-3, boom...because he's got a lot of rhythm, that down-home old gospel way of doing things." The studio musicians resisted the beat Bell heard but the producer insisted they record it his way: "I said, 'Close your ears and read the music. Don't try to create it. I know exactly what it's going to sound like.' They still didn't particularly knock the knot about that 1-2-3-kick business, but they went along with the program and that's exactly how Phillippe and Bobbie sang it."

Phillippe's ad-lib vocals at the end weren't planned, according to Bell. "That was an accident...If you look at the three [songs] previous to that, you won't hear Phillippe as prominently. When we got near the end of the song we kept going and going. I said, 'Everybody does endings like this and this is boring.' " Bell thought he would try something different. "I got an idea to create a brand-new ending, and to make people think the record's over, all of a sudden it's going to come back again."

150

DOING IT TO DEATH

Fred Wesley and the J.B.'s

PEOPLE 621
WRITER: JAMES BROWN
PRODUCER: JAMES BROWN
July 7, 1973 (2 weeks)

James Brown's tour director, Alan Leeds, was in Pittsburgh on personal business in January 1973, when the phone rang. "It was Buddy Nolan from JB's office," he remembers. "He said three words: 'Guess who's back?' "

Maceo! The signature of passion in most Brown classics was the tenor sax of Maceo Parker, who blew his first such solo on 1965's "Papa's Got a Brand New Bag" [see 9]. Save for an Army stint, he spent the rest of the decade in that capacity, then departed with the core of Brown's '60s band in a March '70 mutiny.

"I left to see how it would be on my own," Parker told *Blues & Soul*. "And I found out that I didn't know anything about the business like I thought I did. Recognizing this after two years of scuffling, I had to look upon [James] to help me."

Back on the bus with Parker in '73 were guitarist Jimmy Nolen, tenor player Eldee Williams (Maceo was featured on alto for this period), and trumpeters Darryl "Hasaan" Jamison and Jerone "Jasaan" Sanford, two of the original teenaged J.B.'s.

"Doing It to Death" was the free-form funk jam that celebrated Maceo's return. Brown kidded him during the tune's opening ad-libs: "How you feel, Mace?" After Parker's affirmative reply, Brown cracked, "Can't call your name—I don't want people to know you're in here."

Others were paged, too. "Hey, Jab! Sure gettin' down," Brown called to his cornerstone drummer, John "Jabo" Starks. " 'Doing It to Death' was like an old-style shuffle groove," Starks says. "I played that like a Bobby 'Blue' Bland song.

"A lot of guys cannot do a shuffle—take that bass drum and double it and walk it through a song. A lot of guys used to tell me [when I played] it sounded like a rumbie. I would say, 'It's a beat, it's a groove, it's a *stomp* that you get. You don't just hear it, it *moves* you. And I know how to do it so it moves you."

Another cornerstone was Fred Wesley, who received top billing on "Doing It to Death" even though Brown called the shots. Wesley blew a few trombone choruses, waved in by his boss ("Fred! Can you take us higher?") and counterpointed by blasts from the other horn players.

The full lineup on this session: Parker, Wesley, Nolen, Williams, Starks, Jamison, Sanford, Fred Thomas (bass), Hearlon "Cheese" Martin (guitar), St. Clair Pinckney (tenor), and Ike Oakley (trumpet). The date was January 29, 1973; the venue was International Studios in Augusta, Georgia.

"Doing It to Death" was to have been incorporated into a two-LP package called *James & Lyn Get Down with*

The J. B.'s

the J.B.'s, Live at the Apollo. The complete version, clocking in at just over 12 minutes, was mastered, but edited into a single in April 1973 when the set was cancelled. The band's credit was reinforced by a spliced-on intro, in which longtime Brown emcee Danny Ray tags the J.B.'s as "the eighth wonder of the world."

151

I BELIEVE IN YOU (YOU BELIEVE IN ME)

Johnnie Taylor

STAX 0161
WRITER: DON DAVIS
PRODUCER: DON DAVIS
July 21, 1973 (2 weeks)

When *Billboard* reported in 1973 that Johnnie Taylor was being considered for the lead role in a movie about the late Sam Cooke, it was hardly a surprise.

After all, Taylor was his replacement in gospel music's celebrated Soul Stirrers, and later recorded for the Sar/Derby labels owned by Cooke and his manager, J. W. Alexander. Also, Taylor's longtime producer at Stax Records, Don Davis, remembers the singer repeating career advice given to him by Alexander: "Take it slow, take it slow."

When J.T. took it slow—exemplified by "I Believe in You"—he sounded rather like Cooke: sweet and soulful, cool and contemplative. Don Davis says he composed that song eight years before it was recorded, and even then it "incubated" for another four years.

"It was [originally] a song called 'Tomorrow,' and I kept wanting to cut it. I went to Muscle Shoals, but I didn't like the old groove I had. I changed the groove, and then the song didn't fit, so it stayed in my attache case for about four years."

During the first half of 1973, Davis was in California, working on material for Johnnie Taylor's *Taylored in Silk* LP. "We had two songs to do before we had the album finished—and I didn't have two songs. So I pulled out 'I Believe in You.'

"I knew what I wanted to call it: a couple of years after the track was recorded, I kept saying, 'Well, I don't want to talk about love and love and love, I just want to talk about something else. How 'bout believing in somebody?' "

Davis was booked for an 11:00 A.M. recording session at the A&M studios in Los Angeles, he remembers. "I got up about seven o'clock and put that sucker down. It was wonderful—a song that incubated for a long time."

Finally finished with "I Believe in You" and ready to record, Davis journeyed to Muscle Shoals to cut the track for Taylor. The musicians were the storied team from that Alabama site: Barry Beckett on keyboards, David Hood on bass, Roger Hawkins on drums, and Jimmy Johnson on guitar.

Later, Davis overdubbed strings at United Sound in Detroit, as well as the flute that reinforces the song's hook. "I was going flute-crazy then," he says. "I always liked those long oboe and lonely flute sounds. It was an alto flute that time, I think."

Released in May 1973, "I Believe in You" went on to become a certified-gold single and Johnnie Taylor's biggest crossover hit since "Who's Making Love." He told *Blues & Soul*, "I remember way back when I first started out, people said I was just like Sam Cooke—and he was one of my greatest influences, even though I didn't realize it totally myself...Then after years of practice, you find yourself developing your own thing."

152

ANGEL

Aretha Franklin

ATLANTIC 2969
WRITERS: CAROLYN FRANKLIN,
SONNY SAUNDERS
PRODUCERS: QUINCY JONES, ARETHA FRANKLIN
August 4, 1973 (2 weeks)

In the Queen of Soul's crown, some of the most precious jewels ("Baby, Baby, Baby," "Ain't No Way," "Angel") were created by her younger sister, Carolyn Franklin. "She was a very talented writer and singer," says Erma Franklin, whose own gem, "Piece of My Heart," featured background vocal arrangements by Carolyn. "It was just innate, a natural part of her."

William "Sonny" Saunders, who co-wrote "Angel," has vivid memories of the youngest Franklin sister from their days in Detroit. "Carolyn was driven, she lived and breathed music," he says. "She loved the business. It really hurt me that she never attained the stature that some others attained. Because she wanted it so much."

Saunders belonged to one of Motown's first groups, the Satintones, and later became a leading arranger in the music communities of Detroit and Chicago [see 44—"Higher And Higher"]. He says "Angel" was his first collaboration with Carolyn Franklin. "We were very close friends. We lived about three blocks apart, and just being in the same business, we just sort of hung out together. Some of the guys in the Four Tops lived not far from her, so we all kind of congregated in that same area."

For "Angel," Franklin had a melody and some lyrics. "She fooled around with the piano a little bit," explains Saunders, "but she couldn't come up with anything she felt was really happening with the song. So I happened to be over one day and she said, 'Sonny, let's write it together.'

"I said, 'Hey, no big deal,' so I sat down at the piano and we fooled around for maybe about 20 minutes." Then a musical motif from Burt Bacharach clicked with Saunders, "and there it was. The rest of the song just came from there."

This exquisite "Angel" wasn't composed specifically for Aretha. "The song felt so great to us after we had finished it," remembers Saunders. " 'I'm going to give this to sister 'Ree,' " Carolyn said. "Aretha liked it right away. It wasn't long after that she recorded it."

Franklin did so in April 1972, during sessions with producer Quincy Jones at The Record Plant in Los Angeles. Aside from tenor sax soloist Joe Farrell, the musicians were uncredited, although they probably included Eric Gale, Wah-Wah Watson, and David T. Walker (guitars), Chuck Rainey (bass), James Gadson or Paul Humphries (drums), and Joe Sample, Richard Tee, or Billy Preston (keyboards), all of whom played for Quincy in the '70s.

The outcome was *Hey Now Hey (The Other Side Of The Sky)*, Aretha's first Atlantic album without the customary production team of Jerry Wexler, Arif Mardin and Tom Dowd. It was issued in June 1973, preceded by "Angel." The single became Aretha's thirteenth R&B Number One, but the LP charted lower than any of her previous Atlantic releases.

Carolyn Franklin made records of her own in the '70s, appeared with Aretha in John Belushi and Dan Aykroyd's *The Blues Brothers* movie, and sang background vocals into the '80s. On April 25, 1988, she died of cancer at age 44.

153

LET'S GET IT ON

Marvin Gaye

TAMLA 54234
WRITERS: ED TOWNSEND, MARVIN GAYE
PRODUCERS: MARVIN GAYE, ED TOWNSEND
August 18, 1973 (6 weeks)

"I bet you I'm the most cooperative artist you ever had."

Marvin Gaye made that claim after finishing work on "Let's Get It On," according to Ed Townsend, who played a leading role in the album's songwriting and production. And Townsend's verdict? "He certainly was."

Gaye *could* go to the other extreme, judging by arranger David Van DePitte's experiences a couple of years earlier [see 103—"What's Going On"]. So before beginning the project, Townsend negotiated with Motown and Jobete Music, its publishing division. "We had a few problems getting what I wanted," he says, "because I wanted to own part of the publishing."

Clearly, Townsend was no music biz novice. After hitting the charts as a singer ("For Your Love") in 1958, he began creating for others. Among his credits are two of soul music's most compelling moments: "The Love of My Man" by Theola Kilgore and "Foolish Fool" by Dee Dee Warwick, both of which he wrote and produced.

Visiting Los Angeles around late 1972, Townsend was told by a colleague that Gaye had been asking about him. "So I went to his apartment," he recalls, "and while at the piano, played a few tunes I had written. Marvin said to me, 'I will record them if you produce them.' I said, 'I'll produce them, provided you get up now and call Berry, and tell him that you want me to.' "

Gaye apparently did telephone Gordy, and a deal began to take shape. Townsend secured his 50-percent publishing stake, and got down to work at Motown's studios in Hollywood, with the help of his longtime arranger, Rene Hall.

When released in July 1973, "Let's Get It On" caused a stir for its explicit, carnal message. Yet Townsend contends that it began as a song not about sex, but about overcoming addiction. It also mirrored personal experience, from the time the producer was at an alcohol rehabilitation center in upstate New York. "I had worked to help build one, up near Monticello, and while doing that project, I wrote the tune about the business of life. You know, 'Life is life, and let's get on with it.' "

The tracks were cut with a seasoned crew of musicians, including the Crusaders' Joe Sample (keyboards) and Wilton Felder (bass), drummer Eddie "Bongo" Brown, guitarists David T. Walker and "Wah-Wah" Watson, and Gaye himself on piano.

The singer layered his lead and backup vocals over the instrumentation—and Townsend remembers making fun of Gaye's fondness for studio tricks. "I came along during that era when you didn't have a lot of overdubbing. You started with two tracks, then four tracks, and when you went in, you had to cut the mustard.

"I stopped him one day, stopped the session, and said, 'Marvin, I understand why you don't go on tour, because you can't take this studio with you and stop and overdub at Madison Square Garden. You have to start at the beginning and go to the end.'

"That pissed him off really bad, you know, and he took off his shirt, went and got on the microphone and sang 'Let's Get It On' for ten minutes. When he was finished, he put his shirt back on and said, 'Now what do you think?' And it came out wonderful."

154

HIGHER GROUND

Stevie Wonder

TAMLA 54235
WRITER: STEVIE WONDER
PRODUCER: STEVIE WONDER
September 29, 1973 (1 week)

On August 6, 1973, just days after his path breaking *Innervisions* album was released, Stevie Wonder almost reached a higher ground.

The car taking him to a concert in Durham, South Carolina, collided with a logging truck on Route 85. Wonder's skull was broken, his brain bruised, and he was in a coma for days at the North Carolina Baptist Hospital in Winston-Salem.

"They wouldn't let us go to see him in hospital," recalls Malcolm Cecil, the British musician and engineer who helped Wonder create his *Talking Book* and *Innervisions* albums. "We wanted to. There were probably a lot of people who did. We wanted to play some of his music to him when he came around."

Wonder's road manager, Ira Tucker Jr., apparently had the same thought. "I had told the doctor that Stevie lives and breathes music, and that this might be a way of getting him back to consciousness," Tucker explained to Constanze Elsner, author of *Stevie Wonder* (Popular Library, 1977).

Stevie Wonder

"When I first tried, I didn't get any response from Stevie. But the next day I went back and very loudly I sang 'Higher Ground' directly into his ear, while I had taken his hand." Tucker had the right idea. "After a while Stevie's fingers started going in time with the song. Then I knew it, that he was going to make it!"

Wonder had composed the song three months earlier, on May 11. "The song just came to me, the words, the music, it all happened within a few hours and I recorded it at once," he said later. "I didn't know what it was all about, but it was almost as if I had to get it done. As if something was going to happen, some change would come up."

Malcolm Cecil remembers "Higher Ground" being cut at New York's Mediasound studios, with Wonder on ARP and Moog synthesizers and all other instruments. "That was like a shuffle blues when it started," he says. "Most of that stuff was recorded in the same way: Stevie playing clavinet and singing at the same time, usually 'la la la' for the words that were not written yet.

"Then he would usually go over and put on a bassline next; sometimes it was drums. On 'Higher Ground,' I think it was bass, then the drums came after that. It was built up in that fashion."

Cecil and partner Bob Margouleff programmed all the synthesizers Wonder used on *Innervisions*, and served as associate producers. "We used the filtration part of the ARP to modify the clavinet," adds Margouleff. "And we set up the studio in such a way that Stevie knew how to get around.

"Malcolm and I would arrange the studio with all the various keyboard instruments: synthesizer, grand piano, Fender Rhodes, drums, and any other specialized instrument. They would all be in a big circle, and they'd all be [switched] on at the same time. Stevie could walk from one to the other."

155

KEEP ON TRUCKIN' (PART 1)

Eddie Kendricks

TAMLA 54238
WRITERS: FRANK WILSON, ANITA POREE, LEONARD CASTON
PRODUCERS: FRANK WILSON, LEONARD CASTON
October 6, 1973 (2 weeks)

Eddie Kendricks's crystal falsetto was the light of the Temptations, just as David Ruffin's sandpaper tenor was the shade. Their exit—Ruffin in July 1968, Kendricks in March 1971—robbed the group of its original equilibrium, of the calibrated contrast between their styles.

That said, Kendricks took two years to find his own commercial balance as a solo artist. "Keep on Truckin' " was his seventh Tamla single; none of the previous six reached the R&B top 10 or the pop top 40.

Songwriter/producer Frank Wilson recalls that Kendricks was scouting solo album possibilities while still recording with the Temptations. "Motown sort of gave him the green light, because he asked if I would be his producer." He agreed, after checking with label executives "to make sure they were actually going to promote it."

Wilson continues, "We just decided we would try and do something to show Eddie's versatility as a vocalist, and try and do an interesting album—which meant I had to convince him to do stuff in his lower register as well as his falsetto."

Among the album's songs was one ("This Used to Be the Home Of Johnnie Mae") co-written by Leonard Caston. "I was just beginning the project and not certain what I wanted to do with Eddie," says Wilson. "There was this writer who was sitting out in the hallway, trying to get on with Motown. And Motown had decided he was not going to be useful."

It was Caston, who already had a track record as an author of hits for Chess Records and as a member of the Radiants. He convinced Wilson to audition "Johnnie Mae," and a partnership was forged.

By the time of Kendricks's third album in 1973, the two writers had honed their skills. "When Leonard and I would get together," explains Wilson, "we would look at just different pieces of grooves. Things would start musically, and if we really liked it, we'd work at coming up with the melody and the structure. Then we'd get with Anita Poree. She'd come up with the basic lyric idea, and we'd work together to completion."

Thus, "Keep on Truckin' " was crafted. "We'd cut the tracks first," says Wilson, "and then get with Eddie and rehearse. Both Leonard and I could sing falsetto, so we could actually select a key and everything without him." They worked in Los Angeles at the Motown studios and Crystal Sound Recording. Players included Ed Greene on drums, Dean Parks and Greg Poree on guitars, Gary Coleman on vibes, and King Errisson on congas. Motor City magician James Jamerson was on bass, Jerry Peters on organ, and Caston on piano.

Yet "Keep on Truckin' " was not the first choice as a single. "I remember having [Capitol Records executive] Larkin Arnold come by the house to listen," says Wilson, "and the song we were really high on was 'Darling Come Back Home.' He said, 'That's a Number One record,' and we loved it. But I guess somehow we lost it in the mix." The next release was "Keep on Truckin' "...and Eddie's solo career was aloft.

156

MIDNIGHT TRAIN TO GEORGIA

Gladys Knight & the Pips

BUDDAH 383

WRITER: JIM WEATHERLY

PRODUCER: TONY CAMILLO

October 20, 1973 (4 weeks)

Cissy Houston, mother of Whitney, was the first aboard that midnight train, at least 12 months before Gladys Knight & the Pips.

The onetime background singer and leader of the Sweet Inspirations cut Jim Weatherly's song in 1972 for Janus Records. By coincidence, it was originally called "Midnight Plane to Houston." Weatherly had recorded a version himself. "It was based on a conversation I had with somebody...about taking a midnight plane to Houston," the songwriter once said.

"I wrote it as kind of a country song. Then we sent the song to a guy named Sonny Limbo in Atlanta, and he wanted to cut it on Cissy Houston...He asked if I minded if he changed the title to 'Midnight Train to Georgia.' And I said, 'No, I don't mind. Just don't change the rest of the song.' " Limbo produced Houston's version, although the lyric adaptation didn't help her record become a hit.

Meanwhile, Gladys Knight & the Pips—after more than six years at Motown—were making a career move. Switching to Buddah Records in 1973, they began working right away with producer Tony Camillo. "I had signed a girl, Sandra Richardson, to Buddah," Camillo explains. "We recorded 'I Feel a Song' on her and they released it, but the record died in the excitement of signing Gladys. Sandra was my artist, but [Buddah executive] Neil Bogart got me involved with Gladys."

Their first Buddah single was "Where Peaceful Waters Flow," another Jim Weatherly ballad, which the group co-produced with Camillo. For their second, Gladys and the Pips bought train tickets. "Everyone was excited when we cut the song—it seemed to want to be a hit by itself," says Camillo, who had not heard Cissy Houston's version.

The instrumental track was done at his studio in Somerville, New Jersey, with Andrew Smith on drums, Bob Babbitt on bass, Barry Miles on acoustic piano, and Camillo himself on electric piano and organ. The group added their vocals at Artie Fields's studio in Detroit.

At Motown, Gladys and the Pips were given little say in song selection; at Buddah, things were different. Producer Kenny Kerner [see 162—"I've Got to Use My Imagination"] explains, "They took every single song that they got, sat around in a circle, the

Gladys Knight & the Pips

four of them and their producers, and played every one from beginning to end. They all had paper and pencil in their hands, and as the song went by, they took notes.

"When the song ended, they went around the circle and each person talked about the song. Gladys would say, 'I really like the lyrics, but the tempo was too fast,' for example. Everyone commented, then they added up the good and bad comments. If it was mediocre or poor, they'd just discard the song. They did that for 40, 50 songs, however many they had, until they whittled it down to eight or ten songs to use on the album."

"Midnight Train to Georgia" was a great vehicle for Gladys and the Pips, garnering them a 1973 Grammy for best R&B vocal group performance. They won another Grammy that year, too, when "Neither One of Us" [see 143] triumphed in the pop vocal group category. Singing R&B or pop, this quartet was trained well.

157

SPACE RACE

Billy Preston

A&M 1463
WRITER: BILLY PRESTON
PRODUCER: BILLY PRESTON
November 17, 1973 (1 week)

The third instrumental Number One single of the modern R&B era was by the same artist who recorded the second instrumental Number One hit since *Billboard* reactivated the R&B chart in 1965. Billy Preston, who says he was too busy touring to watch *Star Trek* on a regular basis, did it the first time with "Outa-Space" [see 128] and the second time with "Space Race."

Like its predecessor, "Space Race" was recorded at A&M Studios in Hollywood, and marked a new first for Billy in the studio. When he recorded "Outa-Space," it was the first time he had played a clavinet; on "Space Race," it was the first time he had played an aarp synthesizer. "We had rented an aarp Pro-Soloist for the session," Preston recalls. "I was experimenting with the Pro-Soloist and came up with 'Space Race.' "

Preston had seen synthesizers before—when he recorded "Get Back" and other songs for *Let It Be*. The Beatles had used a Moog Synthesizer—now considered an antique. "It had big modules and all the wires, but I had never played one that was compact like the Pro-Soloist," says Billy. "It was great—it had a lot of different sounds. I found one setting that gave me this high-pitched growl sound I like a lot, which I seldom hear on synthesizers today."

Preston played keyboards and used his regular band of musicians on the track, including Manuel Kellough on drums and David T. Walker on guitar. He originally planned to call the track "Funky Thing in A," but eventually awarded that title to another song. He explains why he came up with the title "Space Race": "It was a conscious [effort] to make it relate to the last instrumental. There was a lot of space exploration going on at that time, so it was appropriate." Preston contemplated adding lyrics and recording a vocal track, but ultimately decided to leave the song an instrumental. He knew he would have less resistance from his record label this time, having proven himself with an earlier instrumental hit. He was right; A&M had enough confidence in "Space Race" to release it as the follow-up to "Will It Go Round in Circles," a single that went Number One pop and number 10 R&B.

"Space Race" achieved an immortality of sorts when producer Larry Klein selected Billy's instrumental track as background music for ABC-TV's long-running *American Bandstand*. Preston made several appearances on the weekly series. "We had many, many guests appear on the show during its run," says Klein. "Every so often one of the guest stars was more like a member of the family, and that was the case with Billy." Shortly after Preston performed "Space Race" on *Bandstand*, Klein was looking for an instrumental piece of music to play while host Dick Clark sat in the audience bleachers with the kids who danced on the show. "I listened to a lot of different candidates and Billy's recording was the obvious choice." Because it had a great beat and was easy to dance to? "It *did* have a great beat, but we needed something where the kids could move in their seats without actually dancing." Klein continued to use "Space Race" through all of *Bandstand*'s incarnations—on ABC, in syndication, and on the USA Network—until the show completed its run in 1989.

Preston remained with A&M through 1978, but ultimately felt creatively confined and left for Motown. Songwriter Carol Connors asked him to record a song for the soundtrack of the Gabe Kaplan basketball comedy, *Fast Break*. Motown executive Suzanne de Passe, who managed Preston as well as Syreeta ("Harbour Love"), put her two clients together and had them record a duet for the film. "With You I'm Born Again" was a major pop hit, peaking at number four. It only managed to reach number 86 on the R&B chart.

158

THE LOVE I LOST (PART 1)

Harold Melvin & the Blue Notes

PHILADELPHIA INTERNATIONAL 3533
WRITERS: KENNY GAMBLE, LEON HUFF
PRODUCERS: KENNY GAMBLE, LEON HUFF
November 24, 1973 (2 weeks)

"The Love I Lost" was a rousing, get-'em-on-the-dance-floor hit, but it didn't start off that way, according to Bobby Eli, lead guitarist for the MFSB musicians who played on the song. "When the song was originally counted off in the studio, it was a ballad. We played it and it loped along and nobody really liked it," Eli recalls. "Kenny Gamble at that time was feeling a little rambunctious and all of a sudden he said, 'The hell with it, man, let's count it off.' He picked the tempo up...so it actually was a ballad [that] evolved into a disco song."

Joe Tarsia, who engineered the song at his Sigma Sound Studios in Philadelphia, reacts immediately when he's asked about "The Love I Lost": "When you say those words to me, I think of the epitome of dance music. Gamble and Huff did not set out to make dance music per se. They set out to make music...I don't even know if they knew what the word disco was. Their music came from their pores. They never followed or copied anyone that I know of. People always say, 'What's the Philly sound?' My answer to that is they put those lush arrangements and big orchestrations to street corner music, to doo-wop harmonizing."

Harold Melvin calls "The Love I Lost" a "true" song, as opposed to being just a little pop song. "Every song we recorded was true. These things happened in somebody's life." Melvin says recording Teddy Pendergrass's vocals took a couple of days. "We'd take him in and put the vocals down and then after I'd get back to my home, I'd sit down and listen to them. It seemed like I could hear things being said in my head that weren't on the tape. Then I would take Teddy back in and put the ad-libs on and mix the harmony."

Pendergrass says that the "sing-along" element of "The Love I Lost" was the key to its success. "It's about what people are concerned about—love—and the production was undeniable," the vocalist comments. "It was a song that had meaning and substance and it was real."

Pendergrass, originally recruited from a singing group called the Cadillacs to be the Blue Notes' drummer, played his first set of drums to stay out of his mother's hair. "She worked at a club and drums were the only thing the musicians left," says Teddy, who started singing in church when he was three. "I recorded a [song] when I was 16. The record didn't work and I went back to playing drums."

Teddy didn't spend a lot of time worrying about whether pop radio would accept his gospel-influenced style. "I was more concerned with pop radio, white radio—whatever you want to call it—recognizing that a song is a song. I don't care what color you are singing it. That to me was the issue, because pop radio wasn't playing a lot of black music unless it sounded white...What I was proud of most of all was that pop radio started recognizing that you can't deny this music because music is what it's all about."

159

IF YOU'RE READY (COME GO WITH ME)

The Staple Singers

STAX 0179
WRITERS: HOMER BANKS, RAYMOND JACKSON, CARL HAMPTON
PRODUCER: AL BELL
December 8, 1973 (3 weeks)

The family that starts together...charts together. Twenty years after they began making records, the Staple Singers hit a commercial streak that carried eight of their soulful sermons into *Billboard*'s R&B top 10 between 1971 and 1973.

The producer of those hits was Al Bell, president of Stax Records, who also authored their first Number One [see 124—"I'll Take You There"]. A towering figure in the black music industry of the time, Bell is modest today about those achievements. "I can't sing, I can't dance, I can't carry a tune at all," he says. "I don't know when something is sharp or flat, I don't know a C from a B. I know when it's right, I know when it's wrong, I know when it feels good."

It felt best when Bell took the Chicago-bred Staples clan to the Muscle Shoals Sound studios in Alabama. There, they forged a high-voltage surge of power from the southern grid: Jimmy Johnson on rhythm guitar, Barry Beckett on keyboards, David Hood on bass, and Roger Hawkins on drums.

"We sang our earlier pop releases over prerecorded instrumental tracks," Cleo Staples told *Billboard* in 1973. "But it just didn't have the same feeling as recording with live musicians in the studio. We can really cook with musicians that we feel loose with, and who can follow us as we change things during a take."

Cooking was on Raymond Jackson's mind when he called across to fellow writers Homer Banks and Carl Hampton at Stax one day. "We were getting ready to eat lunch at the 4-Way Grill, a restaurant not too far from Stax," says Banks. "They had good, home-cooked food. Raymond called out, 'If you're ready, come go with me.'

"Carl said, 'That's a nice title.' We knew we were getting ready to go into the studio with the Staples. It didn't take us long to write the song, we did it overnight, and went into studio C and put down a demo."

Those sessions were "complex, deep, involved, with an inordinate amount of time spent on them," declares Al Bell. "I would go to Muscle Shoals and do the basic rhythm [tracks] with Mavis and the Staples, so she could sing while they were performing.

"Then I'd come back to Memphis, put down a rough vocal on Mavis, get my background voices and then let them go, and come back and work on Mavis's vocal until we got that like we wanted it. Then we'd let her go, and build from that point forward." The guitar overdubs would often feature Terry Manning, a versatile musician and engineer at Ardent Recordings in Memphis. Horns and strings were frequently done in Detroit, with the help of arranger Johnny Allen.

"I captured a lot of things the Staples would throw away, or thought they had thrown away," Bell states. "I had a track running—I never told them this—and I had it down on tape. 'No, we don't like that,' they'd say. I said, 'Keep it on tape, Terry.' Then we'd come back and mix it in."

160

LIVING FOR THE CITY

Stevie Wonder

TAMLA 54242
WRITER: STEVIE WONDER
PRODUCER: STEVIE WONDER
December 29, 1973 (2 weeks)

With "Living for the City," Stevie Wonder's vision became wide-screen. While Hollywood was pumping out *Shaft*, *Superfly*, and *Slaughter's Big Rip-Off*, Wonder was offering a different, authentic perspective of Black America.

"Cinematic—that's the way Stevie perceives the world," says Bob Margouleff, the Moog synthesizer master who, with Malcolm Cecil, helped Wonder focus his creative energy. "I came from the film business, so it was a synergistic thing. Stevie, Malcolm and I put all of our experiences together, and adjusted them 'til they all worked."

Of course, neither Margouleff nor Cecil pretends that the creativity came from anyone but Wonder. "He'd do the playing, we'd do the programming," affirms Margouleff. "Sometimes he'd just go into the studio and work on a groove—and four weeks later, it was a song."

On "Living for the City," Wonder played every instrument. It was the second 45 from his innovative *Innervisions*, the third of four albums he made with Cecil and Margouleff between 1971 and 1974. Where the first single [see 154—"Higher Ground"] was metaphoric and spiritual, "Living for the City" was literal, earthbound—and quite graphic.

In fact, Margouleff's movie experience may have helped perfect the "sonic snapshots" that embellish the song's narrative: the arrival of the singer in New York, the street-hustle that gets him arrested, his imprisonment.

More helpful, though, was the fact that Margouleff's father was the mayor of Great Neck, New York. It was there, he says, that some of the vignettes were captured. "I remember running around on a rainy afternoon, recording the village with a Nagra [portable tape machine]. We took a policeman, and actually staged the 'bust' at the village park."

Back in Manhattan, Margouleff and Cecil recruited the driver of an oil truck—who was eating at a cafe near the Mediasound studios on West 57th Street—to rev up his rig for the bus sounds, at 3:00 A.M. "It was one take, and he drove off," says Cecil.

The other bit players in "Living for the City" were Wonder associates: his brother, Calvin, as the victim; road manager Ira Tucker Jr. as the street hustler; and attorney Johanan Vigoda as the judge ("Ten years!").

Margouleff and Cecil played bad guys, too, as the latter explains: "When we were doing Stevie's vocal, we had him in the studio all day. The quality changes from that very simple voice at the beginning to the angry, hardened criminal-type at the end. To get the anger, we would do things purposely to make Stevie mad.

"Bob and I had him out in the studio, and Stevie asked, 'What do you think?' We said, 'Hey, man, it sounds out of tune.' Stevie said, 'What do you mean, it's out of tune? You must be deaf, what's in between your ears?'

"So we started insulting him, getting him really angry. One of the things he hates most is in the middle of a [vocal] phrase, you stop the tape. So we did this purposely to get him riled up—and then we got the feel of the end of the record. We got him shouting, so that he was literally hoarse. And it was one of the best tracks we ever did."

161

UNTIL YOU COME BACK TO ME (THAT'S WHAT I'M GONNA DO)

Aretha Franklin

ATLANTIC 2995
WRITERS: STEVIE WONDER, CLARENCE PAUL, MORRIS BROADNAX
PRODUCERS: ARETHA FRANKLIN, ARIF MARDIN, JERRY WEXLER
January 12, 1974 (1 week)

Both were both raised in the Motor City; both blossomed young—he first recorded at age 11, she at 14—and both came to play towering roles in popular music, defining the form as much as reflecting it.

Stevie Wonder and Aretha Franklin shared an eventful year in 1973. His ground-breaking album *Innervisions* was released then, just days before he nearly died in an auto accident; her bold experiment with producer Quincy Jones, *Hey Now Hey (The Other Side Of The Sky)*, was greeted with the lowest chart position of any of her Atlantic albums to date, just as her contract with the label was expiring.

The song that was to connect the two artists was cut by Wonder in 1967. "First, I recorded it on Stevie," explains Clarence Paul, the Motown A&R stalwart who helped develop the youngster's talent [see 24—"Blowin' in the Wind"]. He says co-author Morris Broadnax may have played it to Aretha Franklin around that time. "Later, four or five years later, Stevie played it for her."

Wonder wrote the melody of the song's chorus, according to Paul. "He would always start [compositions] and get almost through with them, then leave them alone," he says. "Then I put a bridge in it, and did some of the lyrics; a lot of the lyrics were written by Morris. I did the structures and everything—whatever was missing, I put in." Broadnax, Wonder, and Paul had previously collaborated; one of their hits was the Contours' "Just a Little Misunderstanding."

Aretha Franklin taped her interpretation of "Until You Come Back to Me" on September 7, 1973. It was the one song she recorded that Friday in Atlantic's Manhattan studios, setting a melancholy mood with the piano introduction. The rest of the track featured the usual top-notch musicians, including Hugh McCracken on guitar, Donny Hathaway on electric piano, Richard Tee on organ, Chuck Rainey on bass, Bernard Purdie on drums, and Ken Bichel on synthesizer. Background vocalists were Ann Clark, Pat Smith, and Margaret Branch.

Later, co-producer Arif Mardin overdubbed strings, horns, and Joe Farrell's flute solo. "I had a lot

Aretha Franklin

to do with that record," Mardin observes, "from Cornell's guitar hooks to the orchestral arrangement—of which I'm really proud. The harmonic structure of the song is jazzy; I don't even know whether Stevie sang it."

Wonder had indeed done so, although four years passed before the recording was released commercially (as part of his long-delayed *Anthology* set). "I love Aretha's version," says Clarence Paul, who also cites the tune's staying power through versions by Deniece Williams and Johnny Mathis, Miki Howard, and Basia, among others. "I always figured it was a good song."

And perhaps even a deal-closer. As "Until You Come Back to Me" climbed the pop and R&B charts towards the end of 1973, Aretha re-signed with Atlantic Records.

162

I'VE GOT TO USE MY IMAGINATION

Gladys Knight & the Pips

BUDDAH 393
WRITERS: GERRY GOFFIN, BARRY GOLDBERG
PRODUCERS: KENNY KERNER, RICHIE WISE
January 19, 1974 (1 week)

Kenny Kerner still remembers the phone call from Neil Bogart of Buddah Records. The label was hot with the Stories' "Brother Louie," which Kerner and colleague Richie Wise had produced. "I'm sitting at my desk at *Cash Box*, where I worked at the time, the phone rings, and it was Neil. He goes, 'Come up to the office after work, Gladys Knight & the Pips want you to produce them.'

"I say, 'Neil, gimme a break. They've been around 20 years, they've had more hits than we can count; we've had, what, maybe two or three.' He goes, 'I'm serious, come over.' And I say, 'Do they know we're white?' Just like that.

"Neil cracks up. 'Yes,' he laughs, 'they know you're white, they know you're Jewish, they know all the records you've made. They just got through listening to "Brother Louie," and they want you to produce a couple of tracks on their next album.' "

Gladys Knight, of course, knew how to break the ice. "Richie and I go over," continues Kerner, "and there was the group, sitting in Neil's office, all four of them. Gladys looks at me, and goes, 'You're white!' " The room dissolved into laughter.

Yet when the time came, the group was consummately serious. "I've Got to Use My Imagination" was selected from "boxes of songs that we all went over," says Kerner. To record the instrumental track, Wise and Kerner booked time at Bell Sound, New York. "At that time, the demos were on acetate," recalls Wise. "We would listen to those, and cut the tracks. In the case of 'Imagination,' I think the demo was the same kind of thing with the tom-tom groove, and we just changed it slightly to give a little more room to delineate the verses and chorus."

Al Green

With the help of engineer Warren Dewey, Wise and Kerner assembled a team of musicians who had played with David Bromberg: Hugh McDonald on bass, Steve Burgh on guitar, Steve Mosley on drums, Jeff Gutcheon on piano. Later, arranger Larry Wilcox handled sweetening chores.

For reference vocals, the producers used session singer Tasha Thomas. "We used to send Gladys a track with and without the reference vocal," says Wise, "so she'd be able to hear it the way we had it down, and learn it." Then he and Kerner flew to Detroit—although the downtown studio employed for "I've Got to Use My Imagination" was, in Wise's words, "a total piece of shit."

Regardless, the group was ready. "You have to remember that by this time," says Wise, "Gladys had already done her own reference vocal and spent time working with the Pips on background. She's four hours into the song—she knows just what she's doing, just where she's at. So when she goes out there to sing...goodnight!"

163

LIVIN' FOR YOU

Al Green

HI 2257
WRITERS: AL GREEN, WILLIE MITCHELL
PRODUCER: WILLIE MITCHELL
January 26, 1974 (1 week)

"On Thanksgiving Day, we were going to dinner at my house. I went by Al's office and said, 'Man, I've got an idea for a song.' So we sat there and wrote the song in about an hour. Then we went on to dinner."

That's producer Willie Mitchell describing how he and Al Green wrote "Livin' for You." It's a great story, but things may not have happened exactly as Mitchell recalls. "Livin' for You" actually hit the charts a few days before Thanksgiving, 1973. The record business moved fast in those days, but not *that* fast.

But there's no sense in making a meal of this, even if Green and Mitchell did. The point is that "Livin' for You" marked a pretty significant turning point for the singer. It was the first of his Number One hits on which funky drummer Al Jackson wasn't the co-writer, and it marked a change in Green's sound.

Jackson was key in bringing Al to Hi Records in Memphis, and a major part of the Green team, but he never severed his ties with Hi's crosstown rival label, Stax. "Al had gotten so involved in Stax at this time," explains Mitchell, "that when you wanted him, you couldn't get him because he was out...most times with Booker T. and the MGs, or what have you."

While Green and Mitchell wrote "Livin' for You" on their own, guitarist Mabon Hodges had already stepped in to fill Jackson's shoes as co-writer on the previous single, "Here I Am (Come and Take Me)," and would often do so through the mid-'70s.

From then on, the signature sound established with "Let's Stay Together" [see 119] and "I'm Still in Love with You" [see 131] gave way to a tougher, deep-soul groove with more obvious gospel overtones, especially as religion began occupying a greater place in Green's life.

Most of the band was the same, though, with Howard Grimes on drums when Al Jackson wasn't available, and the Hodges brothers: Leroy on bass, Teenie on guitar, and Charles on keyboards. The horn section featured trumpeter Wayne Jackson, tenor sax men Andrew Love and Ed Logan, baritone sax player James Mitchell, and trombonist Jack Hale.

Singing background vocals were Charles Chalmers and Donna and Sandra Rhodes; Chalmers handled many of the string arrangements, too, with James Mitchell. The venue was constant, of course: Royal Recording Studios on South Lauderdale in Memphis.

Some of the songs from 1973–74, especially "Here I Am" and "Sha La La (Make Me Happy)," are classics on a par with any of Green's work. But it was ironic that after bringing their jazzy, more sophisticated sound to '70s R&B, Mitchell and Green headed back toward what they'd abandoned.

It was a gutsy move, and it may have cost Al his crossover audience. While the *Livin' for You* album went gold, the single was Green's first hit not to do so since "Tired of Being Alone" in 1971. Not coincidentally, it was also his first record since then to miss the pop top ten.

164

LET YOUR HAIR DOWN

The Temptations

GORDY 7133
WRITER: NORMAN WHITFIELD
PRODUCER: NORMAN WHITFIELD
February 2, 1974 (1 week)

For his last album with the Temptations, Norman Whitfield had his eye on the future. The project was called *1990*, and songs such as "Let Your Hair Down," "Ain't No Justice," and the title track created a musical mood almost as desolate as Ridley Scott's *Blade Runner*. So did the sci-fi cover art, that was light years away from, say, 1965's *The Temptations Sing Smokey*.

The group rose to the challenge: Dennis Edwards may never have been in stronger voice than on "Let Your Hair Down," a crunching, up-tempo plea to "Mr. Businessman" to loosen his tie—and his attitude. But there was the underlying suspicion that Norman Whitfield's partnership with the Temptations was almost out of fuel, and that the producer was looking elsewhere for creative opportunities.

"The last album I did for Motown was *1990*," confirms Whitfield. "My leaving was strictly a decision that I had a lot more to offer, and Motown was going through an organizational revamping. Berry was gracious enough to let me go, but asked me to stay for [a further] six months. I personally was geared up and ready to go. Anticipating my leaving, I started working on a few little groups in my house, Rose Royce being one of them."

In fact, Whitfield had already deployed that group on *1990*. The album featured, in addition to various Motown session regulars, rhythm and horn contributions by Kenji Brown on guitar, Lequeint "Duke" Jobe on bass, Henry Garner Jr. on drums, Victor Nix on keyboards, Michael Moore on tenor sax, Terral Santiel on congas, and Kenny Copeland and Fred Dunn on trumpets. This was almost the entire lineup of what would become Rose Royce [see 261—"Car Wash"].

The group originated from California, where Whitfield recorded much of *1990* during 1973. "He would leave the session open to us, well, to anybody," Kenji Brown told *Black Music*. "We'd go down and watch and learn how to stay in the pocket, learn how not to get wild and not play too much jazz and so forth, because, you know, he grumbles."

Whitfield knew exactly what he wanted, Brown said. "He'll probably mess around for 45 minutes and the last 15 minutes of that hour, he just gets like *that*. He'll do whatever it takes to get the bottom line done."

True enough, says the producer. "I was always the guy who had the highest cutting percentage in the world, mainly because I would go after that hit record. If I could get that hit in 45 minutes or maybe an hour and a half, I would just let the musicians go.

"Once I got the hit—and maybe eight times out of 10 I did have it—I was satisfied, so I would just devote my time to making sure I got the hit. I could always fill the album with different types of songs and stuff, but that hit record was the key. It was the vehicle in terms of selling the album, and selling the act."

By recording *1990* and other projects in Los Angeles, Norman Whitfield had finally bid farewell to Detroit. "I wasn't that thrilled with California the couple of times I had come out here," says the producer, but he knew that eventually he would have to join the rest of Motown in Hollywood. "We as people outgrew Michigan, and were looking for more in terms of our personal lives." Letting their hair down, perhaps.

165

BOOGIE DOWN

Eddie Kendricks

TAMLA 54243
WRITERS: FRANK WILSON,
LEONARD CASTON, ANITA POREE
PRODUCERS: FRANK WILSON, LEONARD CASTON
February 9, 1974 (3 weeks)

For Eddie Kendricks, life after the Temptations was tough for the first couple of years. "It was a very depressing period," he confided to *Billboard* in 1973, although quitting was not a consideration. "No, my mind told me I needed to stop, but my heart told me I couldn't."

Motown's Frank Wilson also persevered, producing Kendricks from the moment he left the group and eventually striking gold [see 155—"Keep On Truckin' "]. "Having sung with a group for all those years," says Wilson, "Eddie [as a solo artist] really had to be produced—especially when it came to convincing him about the lower register.

"I thought to listen to falsetto all the way through an album might be somewhat boring. Just getting his confidence up, number one, was the key thing, so he would actually try it. But he was very good to work with."

As it turned out, of course, both of Kendricks's back-to-back Number One singles, "Keep on Truckin' " and "Boogie Down," featured his moonshot falsetto. Both were also the highest-charted R&B and pop hits for any former member of the Temptations.

About "Boogie Down," Wilson comments, "We were basically interested in making sure we did not lose what we had gained with 'Keep on Truckin'.' We knew that they were both club records. They were groove tracks with a gospel, churchy kind of background feel. We did an awful lot in terms of just letting the background ride over the vamp, so most of those songs were half-background grooves and the other half, of course, were leads."

Wilson's co-writer and co-producer, Leonard Caston, was among the musicians who fired up those locomotive instrumental tracks. "Leonard played on all of the things that he participated in as a writer. He would play acoustic piano, and if I remember correctly, Jerry Peters played organ."

They worked in Los Angeles at the Motown studios and at Crystal Sound Recording. The musicians included bass players James Jamerson on Fender and Darrell Clayborne on standup, drummers Ed Greene

Eddie Kendricks

and Kenny Rice, guitarists Dean Parks and Greg Poree, percussionists Gary Coleman on vibes and King Errisson on congas. Arrangements were done by Wilson, Caston, and David Van DePitte.

"When you had a guy like Leonard coming over to play you the tunes or make a demo," says Van DePitte, "you couldn't miss—the guy was an impeccable player. I loved his powerful touch, he really beat the hell out of a piano. A lot of times, Leonard left out a third of the chords and was just using open fifths and sevenths and things like that. I wondered what happened to the thirds, and I would call him up, and he'd say, 'No, leave all the thirds out.' It was a piece of cake."

Wilson was equally professional, but tough. "The rhythm section guys hated him," says Van DePitte, "because Frank believed that the tune was made in the rhythm section, and he would work them to death down to the last detail."

166

MIGHTY LOVE—PART 1

Spinners

ATLANTIC 3006
WRITERS: CHARLES SIMMONS, JOSEPH B. JEFFERSON, BRUCE HAWES
PRODUCER: THOM BELL
March 2, 1974 (2 weeks)

Joseph B. Jefferson remembers the day he first realized he might make it as a songwriter. It was a few months after his first hit, the Spinners' "One of a Kind (Love Affair)" [see 149]. "I ran downstairs to pick up the mail. There was a letter from BMI [with] a check in there. One quick look at it and I said, 'They sent me $20.' My lady Rosa came in. She was looking through the mail and ran in and said, 'Joe, did you look at this check?' 'Yeah, BMI sent me 20 bucks.' 'Are you crazy? This is $20,000.' That's when it really dawned on me that I had something here."

Soon after "One of a Kind (Love Affair)" hit Number One, Jefferson acquired two new writing partners, Bruce Hawes and Charles Simmons. "Tommy [Bell] orchestrated that because they had been coming in individually," Jefferson recalls. "These two guys had been showing Tommy songs, trying to get things on albums. Tommy thought they were talented and had something. He didn't put me with both of them at the same time. I met Bruce Hawes first. [Thom] would tell me, 'You should sit down with Bruce Hawes and maybe you guys can come up with something.' And then when he got with Bruce, he said, 'This Jefferson guy is really talented. Maybe you should sit down with him.' And we did. We got together in a little room and Bruce and I started writing. He's a great writer—he's a great keyboard player, so that made the team even stronger, because we both do lyrics and melody."

After Jefferson and Hawes had been working together for awhile, Bell introduced them to a third writer. "[Thom] said, 'I'm going to send a guy to you. He doesn't play anything, but he's a great melody man and he comes up with some great ideas.' So [Charles Simmons] came down...Our first collaboration together was 'Mighty Love.' "

Jefferson wrote the first two verses and started the chorus. "I showed it to Charlie and Bruce. I had the lyrics...but I never had a title. Bruce came up with the title and in an hour's time, we had the tune done."

By the time the three writers penned "Mighty Love," they Spinners' sound was well established. "After we wrote a few things, we recognized that we had something special," Jefferson acknowledges. "These guys, especially Phillippe Wynne, could take anything and run with it. They could really breathe life into it and it gives a writer as well as a producer more incentive when you know you have that kind of vehicle. There was no limit to what these guys could have done when we were writing. Anything we brought, they could do it."

Jefferson, Hawes, and Simmons introduced "Mighty Love" to Bell the way they played him all of their songs. "We had a little four-track," Jefferson describes. "There weren't any computers, no high-tech stuff. We used to pound on the side of the piano and stomp our feet for the foot drum. We'd make a little four-track demo with piano and vocals with us singing. We created our own harmonies and backgrounds. We created the background we wanted to hear in the song. We'd set up a meeting with [Bell]. Even though we had it on tape, he would say, 'I want to hear you guys do it live. I want to know if you're shucking me or not.' He would make us gather around the piano and do it a cappella. And he'd jump right in the middle because if you play something for him once, he's got it. The guy is a genius."

167

LOOKIN' FOR A LOVE

Bobby Womack

UNITED ARTISTS 375
WRITERS: J. W. ALEXANDER, ZELDA SAMUELS
PRODUCER: BOBBY WOMACK
March 16, 1974 (3 weeks)

Bobby Womack first met Sam Cooke when the Womack Brothers opened for the Soul Stirrers, the gospel group that featured Cooke as lead singer.

One night, when Cooke's bass player split after an argument, 16-year-old Bobby said he could fill in for the missing musician. A doubtful Cooke asked Womack if he knew how to play the songs. The youngster impressed Cooke by playing the bass as well as both lead guitar parts—impressed him so much, in fact, that Cooke fired his two guitar players and replaced them with Womack.

As he became established as a secular star, Cooke started his own record labels, Derby and Sar, and signed the five Womack Brothers to the latter. Cooke thought their name sounded too religious and suggested a "flashier" name, the Valentinos.

"I was running Sam Cooke's label at the time and with everything I wrote, they included something of mine on every session for all his artists on Sar and Derby," says Zelda Samuels. She had worked for Decca Records and Fred Fisher music and was inspired by Marvin Fisher to start writing songs. "Somehow when he was writing music, it sounded like words to me," she explains. "I heard words with his beautiful music...so I just started writing. And eventually I had songs recorded. I always did the lyric in its entirety and in some instances added music to it myself, just singing in my head, and copyists would take it down."

After stints on Tin Pan Alley and in the Brill Building, Samuels landed at Cooke's company. "At Sam's office, I was writing almost every day," she says. She took the gospel melody "Couldn't Hear Nobody Pray" and sat down to write new lyrics to it. "That's what Sam used to do. He used to write to gospel melodies." Samuels wrote all of the lyrics and handed them to J. W. Alexander so he could write the music. "I think what really made it a hit is Sam Cooke produced it for the Valentinos," says Zelda. "He put in that 'Lookin', lookin', lookin'.' I only had two of them and he put in lots of them. He made the song—arrangers will make or break a song."

Released on Sar in 1962, "Lookin' for a Love" by the Valentinos peaked at number eight on the R&B chart and number 72 pop. Two years later, the Valentinos had their last chart entry with "It's All Over Now," a song covered that same year by the Rolling Stones.

In 1971, "Lookin' for a Love" became the first chart hit for the Boston-based J. Geils Band. The rock outfit took the song to number 39 on the pop chart. Womack didn't care for the J. Geils version, claiming the band discarded the melody of the song. Two years later, Womack was in the studio warming up to record a new album for United Artists. He had a batch of original songs, but wanted to get loose with something familiar. He decided to take a dry run with the song that first put the Valentinos on the chart. He took two passes on the song while tape was rolling. It was just a rhythm track—Womack didn't add any horns, as he would usually do. Then he forgot all about the track and ran through the 14 new songs he wanted to record.

Later, at home, Womack listened to his material and was struck by the version of "Lookin' for a Love" he had used to warm up. Everybody who heard it agreed it would be a hit single, so Womack called his album *Lookin' for a Love Again* and released the title track as the first single. In March of 1974 he had his second Number One on the R&B chart.

168

BEST THING THAT EVER HAPPENED TO ME

Gladys Knight & the Pips

BUDDAH 403

WRITER: JIM WEATHERLY

PRODUCERS: KENNY KERNER, RICHIE WISE

April 6, 1974 (2 weeks)

There's not an obvious connection between show-biz veteran Danny Thomas and soul queen Gladys Knight, but songwriter Jim Weatherly drew it.

Thomas, father-in-law of Weatherly's manager in the early '70s, was the first to cut "Best Thing That Ever Happened to Me"—and that was the version Richie Wise heard when considering material for Knight. "Danny was like singing it to his mother, or something," Wise says. (In fact, Thomas did the song as a Christmas present to his wife.)

Weatherly often looked for an everyday phrase to underpin his stately but down-to-earth ballads. "Just like I always do when I write, I tried to come up with an idea for a title," he told author Tom Roland in *The Billboard Book of Number One Country Hits*, "and it dawned on me that I'd never heard a song called 'You're the Best Thing That Ever Happened to Me.' And yet it was something that you heard people say about five or six times a week, either on television, or in movies, or people you're talking to."

The song took shape in 1971, Weatherly explains: "I basically wrote it in a very short period of time, probably 30 minutes or an hour." Two years later, a version by Ray Price topped the *Billboard* country charts.

Then came Gladys and the Pips. "Jim Weatherly was already hot from previous hits they had," says Kenny Kerner, who co-produced the quartet with Richie Wise. "They very much liked his lyrics. Country and rhythm & blues are very similar—and they loved the line, 'the best thing that ever happened to me.' "

Kerner and Wise cut their instrumental tracks at New York's Bell Sound during August and September 1973, with guitarist Steve Burgh, keyboardist Jeff Gutcheon, drummer Steve Mosley, and bassist Hugh

McDonald. Burgh and Gutcheon had recorded with David Bromberg on his *Demon in Disguise* album; that also featured session singer Tasha Thomas, whom Kerner and Wise used to provide a guide vocal on "Best Thing That Ever Happened to Me."

Later, the producers flew to Detroit to record Gladys and the Pips. "We found a studio out in Warren, Michigan, called Pampa," says Wise. "It was a new 24-track that had opened up about 14 miles out of Detroit. The owner's name was Jim Bruzzese, a 350-pound Italian guy, and the studio was in the back of a bowling alley. The first question he asked was, 'Are you hungry?' The bowling alley had a killer restaurant! The waitresses from the bowling alley would bring pizzas, fried chicken, hamburgers. It was unbelievable.

"From then on when we went to Pampa, the first thing that the guys from the Pips wanted to do was order food. And Gladys used to bring her bowling ball. Once I think she brought her daughter, and went bowling during the recording session."

169

TSOP (THE SOUND OF PHILADELPHIA)

MFSB featuring the Three Degrees

PHILADELPHIA INTERNATIONAL 3540
WRITERS: KENNY GAMBLE, LEON HUFF
PRODUCERS: KENNY GAMBLE, LEON HUFF
April 20, 1974 (1 week)

"There was no MFSB as such until 1973," says guitarist Bobby Eli. "We were doing sessions way before then. We were just the boys in the rhythm section from Sigma Sound and we would work with everyone—it wasn't just [Kenny] Gamble and [Leon] Huff. We went in the studio and did a remake of 'Family Affair' by Sly Stone. And when that came out they called the entity 'The Family.' And then when they compiled the tunes for the first MFSB album, that's when that name came about."

No one is certain when the aggregation known as MFSB first came together, mainly because the lineup of musicians was fluid. People came and went as they were available, but the nucleus of the group formed in the Cameo/Parkway days of the early '60s. Some of the musicians played with Huff on Swan Records' "Little Eva" by the Locomotions and a single called "The Spy" by the Men from U.N.C.L.E. Some historians consider "The Horse" by Cliff Nobles and Co. to be the first true MFSB record. That 1968 instrumental was a B-side that accidentally became a hit. Also in 1968, Bernie Binnick recorded a funky sitar instrumental, "Keem-O-Sabe," on United Artists that featured many of the MFSB musicians. Two years later, those same musicians played on "Overture from Tommy" by the Assembled Multitude.

The core of the group consisted of Ronnie Baker, Norman Harris, Earl Young, and Bobby Eli. Baker and Harris were rhythm guitarists and Young, the bass singer for Kenny Gamble's group, the Romeos, became a drummer when he filled in for a missing band member on a Barbara Mason session. Huff described Eli to Gamble as a "bad white boy who plays guitar" and recommended him as a session musician. "The rhythm section became so tight," says Eli. "The more we played together, the tighter we got and it just kind of worked. It was really accidental, but everybody played so well together and knew each other's next moves that it was magic. At first there wasn't a lot of session work and then it got better as time went by."

After recording the instrumental cover of "Family Affair," the Sigma Sound musicians heard that television producer Don Cornelius was looking for a new theme song for his weekly *Soul Train* series. "It had an old theme song but he wasn't happy with it," says Eli. That "old theme" was "Hot Potatoes" by King Curtis, a track Cornelius had been using as a personal theme song even before *Soul Train* premiered as a local show in Chicago on August 17, 1970. When the series became nationally syndicated, Cornelius wanted to buy the rights to the song, but negotiations with Curtis's heirs fell through. When Cornelius bumped into Gamble in New York, he told the producer he was looking for a new theme.

"Some of the writers and producers, Thom Bell and Norman Harris and myself and different people, came up with ideas for songs, all of which were recorded at the session that 'TSOP' was recorded at," says Eli. Obviously, the one that Gamble and Huff wrote was the one they used. I guess it happened to work politically and that's the one that was picked for the *Soul Train* theme." Eli says "TSOP" was clearly the best choice, although all were up-tempo. "One of them might have been a little too jazzy. But the one that became known as 'TSOP' really stood out. And that's when they wrote the [lyrics] to the track and got the Three Degrees to do the backing vocals. Bobby Martin did the horn and string arrangements on it."

The success of "TSOP" transformed MFSB from a group of studio musicians to "real" recording artists with name recognition. "Technically, although there are 28 or 30 musicians, there were 11 charter members of MFSB who were royalty participants," Eli explains. It was too large a group to consider any kind of extended tour, Eli says. "We did do gigs here and there. We did a CBS convention. It sounded just like the studio—everybody was amazed how close to the studio it sounded."

170

THE PAYBACK (PART 1)

James Brown

POLYDOR 14223
WRITERS: JAMES BROWN,
FRED WESLEY, JOHN STARKS
PRODUCER: JAMES BROWN
April 27, 1974 (2 weeks)

James Brown will compose the score to the sequel to *Black Caesar* now before the cameras," *Billboard* reported in April 1973. "Brown will appear in the sequel as a private detective—his acting debut."

This was the era that movies like *Shaft* and *Superfly* were hot at the box office, and their soundtrack albums were going gold. No surprise, then, that AIP producer/director Larry Cohen should want Brown to score his blaxploitation pictures.

The first two were *Black Caesar* and *Slaughter's Big Rip-Off*; both yielded top 20 singles for JB. The third had a working title of *Black Caesar's Revenge*.

Three Brown employees—music director Fred Wesley, drummer John "Jabo" Starks, and front-office staffer Bob Both—each recall watching a rough cut on a movieola in mid-1973. For the theme song, Wesley had already written lyrics and music. But when JB came to the recording session with something else on his mind, says Wesley, "he tore up the paper with the words I had written. He just tore the whole thing apart."

John Starks adds, "We sat and watched the movie, wrote it out. Fred had the words...and James completely changed everything. We got caught in the middle of an ocean without a paddle. It was do or die—James had to make the record *then*. All we had was the rhythm. I just tried to hold it and make it *solid*."

Bob Both, director of A&R for James Brown Enterprises, recollects, "The words to 'The Payback' describe exactly what was going on in the [picture's] opening scene. This was going to be the theme for the movie. James was in one of his moods that day. He kept saying the word 'damn' throughout the track, and I had to go back and where I could, punch them out."

Brown had cause to be moody. His relentless concert schedule was affecting his health; a couple of recent records had failed to reach the top 10; and, more profoundly, his son Teddy had been killed in an auto crash in June.

The basic rhythm track for "The Payback" was cut August 4 at International Studios in Augusta, Georgia. The musicians were Starks (drums), Wesley (trombone), Jimmy Nolen and Hearlon "Cheese" Martin (guitars), Fred Thomas (bass), and John Morgan (tambourine). About a month later in New York, Wesley and Both overdubbed background vocals and horn parts by members of Brown's road band.

Wesley flew to Los Angeles to deliver the tapes to Cohen. " 'It's not funky enough, *babe*,' " Fred recalls being told. The musician advised the movie maker to deliver the message personally. "I could hear James through the phone yelling at Larry, who handed the phone over. James said, 'Mr. Wesley, bring the tapes back to Augusta right now!' "

With his film finally titled *Hell up in Harlem*, Cohen bought a new score by Motown's Freddie Perren and Fonce Mizell, and a theme song by Edwin Starr. Single and soundtrack album sank without trace.

"The Payback," meanwhile, went to Number One. Call it the Godfather of Soul's revenge.

171

DANCING MACHINE

The Jackson 5

MOTOWN 1286
WRITERS: HAL DAVIS,
DON FLETCHER, WELDON DEAN PARKS
PRODUCER: HAL DAVIS
May 11, 1974 (1 week)

In his book *Moonwalk* (Doubleday, 1988), Michael Jackson suggests that when his brother, Jermaine, married Berry Gordy's daughter, Hazel, the Motown founder regained his enthusiasm for the Jackson 5. So was it coincidence that "Dancing Machine," their first single release after the wedding, became the group's biggest hit in almost three years?

"Dancing Machine" began life as the last track on side two of the Jacksons' 1973 album, *Get It Together*, produced by Hal Davis. He remembers being inspired to write the song. "I had a girl who liked me a lot. Those were the days when I drank: I wasn't an alcoholic, but I liked to drink, especially Remy Martin. This girl would come in and say, 'You got a drink? I'm gonna dance for you.'

"And she danced to every damn thing! She even jumped up on my desk, so I told Don Fletcher, 'Man, she's a dancing machine.' I didn't realize what I'd said. He said, 'Hey, man, that's the title.' "

Davis, Fletcher, and guitarist Dean Parks put the song together, and the track was cut at the Sound Factory in Los Angeles. "The bass player was William Salter," says Davis, "Joe Sample was on keyboards, and the drummer was James Gadson. Nobody can play that foot like him."

Gadson's hard-hitting footwork and Sample's synthesizer evidently appealed to Michael Jackson. "I loved 'Dancing Machine,' loved the groove and the feel of that song," he wrote in his autobiography. "Disco music had its detractors, but to us it seemed our rite of passage into the adult world."

The record's instrumental and vocal arrangements were handled, respectively, by Arthur Wright and James Carmichael, who had worked together six years earlier on another R&B smash [see 40—"Make Me Yours"]. Wright remembers Dean Parks ("an excellent guitar player") at the "Dancing Machine" session, and thinks that Louis Shelton could have been on the date, too. "At the time, we'd use two and three guitar players."

Michael Jackson sang lead on "Dancing Machine," of course, with Jermaine as the second voice. For backup singers, Davis employed the Waters and Oma Heard, among others. "You knew when the Jacksons were singing," says Wright. "They did their harmonies and so forth, and you knew when there were professional harmonies to be done—but only to enhance, never to substitute."

When "Dancing Machine" appeared on the *Get It Together* album, it featured space-travel sound effects and a woman's voice, mostly inaudible. "The lady talks to him," says Davis. "She comes down and you can hear the spaceship, and she says, 'What can I do for you, master?' He says, 'I want you to dance for me.' "

172

I'M IN LOVE

Aretha Franklin

ATLANTIC 2999
WRITER: BOBBY WOMACK
PRODUCERS: JERRY WEXLER, ARIF MARDIN, ARETHA FRANKLIN
May 18, 1974 (2 weeks)

The soulful sound of the South—muddy, dirty, gritty—permeates every groove of the first recording of "I'm in Love," by Wilson Pickett, as well as the second, by Bobby Womack.

It figures. Both were made at the same Memphis studio, Pickett's version in July 1967, Womack's a year or so later. Both also featured Womack and Reggie Young on guitars, Bobby Wood on piano, Gene Chrisman on drums, and Bobby Emmons on organ.

By contrast, Aretha Franklin's "I'm in Love" is crisp, clear, glistening—like a digital recording, except that digital wasn't possible when she cut it, in April of 1973. New York's finest are behind her: Stanley Clarke on bass, Bob James on keyboards, Rick Marotta on drums, David Spinozza and Cornell Dupree on guitars.

Of course, Manhattan and Memphis combined aren't roomy enough for Aretha's vocal power. Polite and restrained for the song's first half, she surrenders to love's euphoria after the bridge and—with Jerry Wexler and Arif Mardin punching in the echo—wails like a banshee. This woman is *in love*.

When recording in New York, Lady Soul mostly worked at Atlantic, but "I'm in Love" was cut at A&R Studios. Arif Mardin, who co-produced the session with Wexler and Franklin, recalls, "Wexler said, 'You know, we've done so many things with her, let's do something else. Let's do some of the old standards, too.'

"And this time, instead of the old team, we had Billy Eaton doing orchestral arrangements. So it was a live date, and it was wonderful. Stanley on bass, Rick on drums, for example. It was obvious we wanted to have a slightly different sound." Background vocalists were Cissy Houston, Judy Clay, Gwen Guthrie, and Deidre Tuck.

The originator of "I'm in Love" knew Aretha, of course: Bobby Womack had played guitar on much of her classic *Lady Soul* album in 1967. Yet when he created the song—for Wilson Pickett—it was a difficult time. Womack's considerable talents were being obscured by the fallout from his marriage to Barbara Cooke, widow of his mentor, Sam Cooke.

"I was getting static from all around the world," he told music archivist and producer Leo Sacks. "It was devastating. Radio people were throwing my records in the garbage. I started wearing shades just to hide my pain. I didn't want you to look into my eyes, that's how hurt I was. But, I wanted everyone to know how I felt. That I loved Barbara. That Sam was my partner. That I was in living hell.

"Then someone said, 'Pickett's your ticket. Channel your energies through him, and so I wrote 'I'm in Love.' "

Pickett's performance—a top five R&B hit in 1968—captured the ballad's most joyful and painfully tragic aspects. Womack says, "When I played him the demo, Pickett ran around the room screaming, 'Womack! You're crazy! All this hurt comin' out of you! *I'm gonna tell this story!*' He sang it with the feeling I wanted, of someone who was crying out, because he knew my situation."

173

BE THANKFUL FOR WHAT YOU GOT

William DeVaughn

ROXBURY 0236
WRITER: WILLIAM DEVAUGHN
PRODUCERS: FRANK FIORAVANTI, JOHN DAVIS
June 1, 1974 (1 week)

A Jehovah's Witness from Washington, D.C., spent $900 to touch thousands—if not millions—of lives with the coolest lyric this side of

William DeVaughn

Christendom and the coolest groove since Al Green's "Let's Stay Together."

It was William DeVaughn who paid to cut "Be Thankful for What You Got" for a Philadelphia company called Omega Sound Inc. "It was sort of a shady outfit," says John Davis, who worked for Omega and co-produced the record. "They used to advertise, 'Send us your songs, we'll record them, and make you a star,' that kind of thing." The catch: to be "discovered," would-be stars had to pay Omega up-front.

"They offered me a job as an arranger," Davis recollects, "and it was an opportunity to stop playing in bar bands and get into the studio. I thought, 'I'll stay with these guys and learn what I can learn.' "

In 1973, DeVaughn answered an Omega advertisement in *Billboard*. "So they sent a guy down to Washington to hear my tapes and audition," the singer later explained, "and they liked what they heard and sent me to Philadelphia for another audition. They said that they would record me if I could find $1,400. So I went back to Washington and managed to raise $900."

Davis remembers, "From time to time, Omega would actually take somebody into the studio and record their songs legitimately—and they decided they would do it with William. I was told to hire some guys and put a session together."

The studio was Sigma Sound, the guys were Philadelphia's finest: Earl Young on drums, Norman Harris on guitar, Ron Baker on bass, Larry Washington on congas, Vince Montana on vibes. Vocalizing in back were Nadine Felder and Gwen Oliver.

"Technically, there are two chord changes in the whole song," Davis says, "so there wasn't much to have arranged. I was playing organ, with the other guys facing me. We just started playing the two chord changes, William got in the middle of the room, they baffled him up, and he started to sing.

"He had a real silky voice and, obviously, he knew the song well. There's a great guitar line where Norman Harris was answering him. That was one of those sessions where it was good to have the singer there as the musicians juiced it up."

When "Be Thankful for What You Got" was finished, Omega vice president Frank Fioravanti shopped the master around New York. "And he was turned down by some of the most-respected A&R people in the business," Davis declares. "They told him it was the worst record they'd heard.

"Frank got kinda upset and, on a whim, flew out to L.A. to do the same there, hoping there'd be a different attitude. And in one day, he had three offers! The best was from Wes Farrell of Chelsea Records."

Yet even when "Be Thankful for What You Got" was a hit for Chelsea's Roxbury label, life didn't change for William DeVaughn. "The record was at Number One," Davis concludes, "and he was still going door-to-door in Washington as a Jehovah's Witness."

174

HOLLYWOOD SWINGING

Kool & the Gang

DE-LITE 561
WRITERS: RICKY WEST, KOOL & THE GANG
PRODUCERS: KOOL & THE GANG
June 8, 1974 (1 week)

Call it Hollywood-*quelque chose*. Kool & the Gang's first Number One was indirectly indebted to a French-speaking, African-born sax player known as Manu Dibango.

The group's label, De-Lite Records, was certainly aware of Dibango—who called his music Afro-*quelque chose* (which literally translates to "Afro-something")—in the spring of '73. The saxman's exotic "Soul Makossa" track was the hottest record in Harlem: Imported copies from France were changing hands to the tune of $2 to $3 apiece, and several American record companies were anxious to cut cover versions.

De-Lite was one of them. Khalis Bayyan, who (as Ronald Bell) was Kool & the Gang's music director, and younger brother of Robert "Kool" Bell, explains, "We'd just finished the *Good Times* album, and the record company wanted something more commercial."

The remake of "Soul Makossa" was suggested. "We thought, 'If that's what it is, we can do that, *easy*.' " Instead of covering Dibango, says Bayyan, "We all met for rehearsal at 11 A.M. the next morning, and made up 'Funky Stuff,' 'Jungle Boogie,' and 'Hollywood Swinging' right there. We recorded them that night at Mediasound on 57th Street—studio B, downstairs in what used to be the old church morgue. It had a great sound."

So did Kool & the Gang, who began as the Jazziacs around 1964 with Robert (bass), Ronald (trumpet, sax), Dennis Thomas (sax, flute), George Brown (drums), Charles Smith (guitar), Robert Mickens (trumpet), and Ricky Westfield (keyboards). Also a regular: guitarist Woody Sparrow. The group lived in Jersey City then, but aspired to play across the Hudson River.

Gigging around New York and toiling through several identities—the Soul Town Revue, the New Dimensions—the band was seen by producer Gene Redd and signed to De-Lite in 1969. Over the next four years, their jazz-based, horn-driven, post-Sly funk yielded a number of influential singles ("Kool & the Gang," "Let the Music Take Your Mind") and albums (*Live at the Sex Machine, Live at P.J.'s*).

In "Hollywood Swinging," which came from 1973's *Wild and Peaceful*, keyboardist Westfield had a starring role, instrumentally and vocally. Bayyan says, "Ricky wrote the verses, and it's a true story. We did play in Hollywood [to record *Live At P.J.s.*] and he was taken by it.

"But while it was a true story, it was really for everybody. As kids, Kool and I used to go see John Coltrane, Hank Mobley, Art Blakey, all the jazz greats. We looked up to them and wanted to 'get into a band.' "

"Hollywood Swinging" also borrowed from Mandrill, the Brooklyn jazz rockers whose "Fencewalk" strutted into the top 20 in June 1973. "One of their songs had a rhythm in threes," says Bayyan. "I 'heard' that, and made it the bassline."

The Gang probably heard "Fencewalk" and "Soul Makossa" in the same place: New York station WBLS-FM, where cool 'n' natty DJ Frankie Crocker nicknamed himself "Hollywood." Playing Manu, Mandrill, *and* Kool & the Gang, Hollywood was swinging all right.

Kool & the Gang

Blue Magic

175

SIDESHOW

Blue Magic

ATCO 6961
WRITERS: VINNIE BARRETT, BOBBY ELI
PRODUCER: NORMAN HARRIS
June 15, 1974 (1 week)

In the great workshops of rhythm & blues—Chess, Atlantic, Motown, Stax, Philadelphia International—the atmosphere was *family*. True, the passage of time has jaundiced that view, and for many of the artists and musicians, the rewards weren't shared as they should have been in a family. But the sense of bonding among them was powerful, and productive.

The focal point of the Philadelphia family in the '70s was Sigma Sound, running 24 hours a day, seven days a week. "You always felt at home," says songwriter Gwen Woolfolk, "and [studio boss] Joe Tarsia always welcomed you." She adds, "We'd practically want to sleep there. And he gave you sessions to do when you didn't have any money. There was never a problem."

With partner Bobby Eli, Woolfolk was writing then under the name Vinnie Barrett. Together, they created a pair of the Philadelphia era's gold-certified classics, "Sideshow" by Blue Magic and "Love Won't Let Me Wait" by Major Harris [see 208].

"Sideshow" introduced Blue Magic to the top of the charts, a year after their 1973 debut, "Spell." The group, signed to WMOT Productions and placed with Atco Records, comprised lead singer Ted Mills, tenors Vernon Sawyer and Keith Beaton, baritone Wendell Sawyer, and bass Richard Pratt. "Ted was like Smokey Robinson," says Woolfolk. "He wasn't a great singer, but he was a great expressionist.

"Actually, Ted never thought he was going to turn out to be an artist. He was a songwriter; he was wandering around Philly, competing with us. Every time there was a session in town, there he was with his songs."

Mills, who had been in a local group, the Topics, caught the attention of WMOT executives. They put him with another act, the Shades of Love, and renamed the outcome Blue Magic. The quintet began recording at Sigma in 1973; the late Norman Harris was producer. Later that year, "Sideshow" was cut with the musicians of MFSB, who included Harris and Bobby Eli (guitars), Ron Baker (bass), Ron Kersey (piano), Earl Young (drums), Vince Montana (vibes), and concertmaster Don Renaldo.

The "Sideshow" metaphor came from a real circus visit by Woolfolk and Eli. "One day, I said to Bobby, 'Hey, let's stop writing, let's go out and have some life.' We went from there to an antique museum that had all the old circus toys. Then we started work on the song later that night."

The Impressions

The chorus was complete in a few days, recalls Woolfolk, but the verses took four months. "I didn't want to present the story as a happy thing. People who work for the circus are very hard-working, very strong—and sad things have happened to them. So I wanted that idea—when the sideshow is gone, the singer is still an unhappy person."

After it was finished, Woolfolk remembers she and Eli sitting in his Philly apartment at midnight, eating cookies and listening to music or the TV. "Norman Harris came over, but we couldn't hear the doorbell, so he had to throw a stone at the window. 'What are you doing,' he asked. We said we'd just finished writing this song, 'Sideshow.' He thought it was great, and told us he wanted to cut it on Blue Magic."

The group followed up with another big-top tune, "Three Ring Circus," which performed strongly for R&B and pop crowds alike during the fall of 1974.

176

FINALLY GOT MYSELF TOGETHER (I'M A CHANGED MAN)

The Impressions

CURTOM 1997
WRITER: ED TOWNSEND
PRODUCER: ED TOWNSEND
June 22, 1974 (2 weeks)

The Impressions without Curtis Mayfield—like the Miracles minus Smokey Robinson—were facing a career crunch in 1973. Their record sales were in a tailspin, and their lead singer, Leroy Hutson, was not working out.

Mayfield had quit the group in 1970, encouraged by Marv Stuart, his manager and partner in Curtom

Records. Hutson took Mayfield's place for three years. When he left, longtime Impressions Fred Cash and Sam Gooden decided to draft not one new member, but two: Reggie Torian and Ralph Johnson. At the same time, Curtom recruited music veteran Ed Townsend to help out.

"Marv Stuart was in New York," explains Townsend. "We met accidentally at the Queens booking agency, and he asked me to come to Chicago to do the Impressions. I had known the guys, because 'For Your Love' was a hit for me at the same time as their first hit, 'For Your Precious Love' with Jerry Butler. We made a deal, and I went out there."

While in Chicago, the producer took part in a testimonial dinner for WVON disc jockey E. Rodney Jones, paying tribute to him with a speech about self-help. "It was during the time when I was getting myself together," admits Townsend, who had wrestled with alcoholism. "Those lyrics were pretty right on: *a little smoke and a little drink/Kept my head bad so I couldn't think*. And that was generally what the song was about."

Townsend did some recording with the Impressions in the Windy City, but says that "Finally Got Myself Together (I'm a Changed Man)" was cut in Los Angeles. "It wasn't until the next album that I worked at Curtom [in Chicago]," he explains. "I did it at the RCA studios in Hollywood, and used Rene Hall on that date and a couple of others."

The session featured some of the same musicians who played on Marvin Gaye's *Let's Get It On* album, which Townsend co-produced. Among them: David T. Walker and Melvin "Wah-Wah" Watson on guitars, Eddie "Bongo" Brown on drums, Wilton Felder on bass, and Joe Sample on keyboards.

"I brought the Impressions to California to do the overdubs," Townsend recounts. "They had to get accustomed to singing with an orchestra. We did everything simultaneously. I liked that because musicians have a tendency to become a little more understanding about what they're doing when they hear the lyrics and hear things, rather than looking at a cold, written track. The feeling can be passed on to the musicians as they play."

Townsend affirms that Ralph Johnson and Reggie Torian were new to the Impressions at the time, and that "Finally Got Myself Together" sported Johnson's tenor and lead vocals. "I know he had just come in from down south," he says.

On December 17, 1973, the new, four-man Impressions made their first public performance, at Mister Kelly's in Chicago. Six months later, "Finally Got Myself Together" was at Number One. "It's been a little rough," admitted Fred Cash at the time, "switching around the harmonies and the stage show. But there is no doubt in my mind that it's worth it." Changes often make the best impression.

177

ROCK YOUR BABY

George McCrae

T.K. 1004

WRITERS/PRODUCERS: HARRY WAYNE CASEY, RICHARD FINCH

July 6, 1974 (2 weeks)

From the clubs to the charts, popular music's hottest trend was highlighted in a front-page *Billboard* report during the same week that George McCrae and the Hues Corporation arrested the peak positions of the Hot Soul Singles and the Hot 100, respectively, with "Rock Your Baby" and "Rock The Boat."

"Don't write off discotheques to the nostalgia files of the '60s quite yet," declared the magazine's cover story. "With a new look and a strong flavoring of R&B music, they're part of the in-scene once again in major markets, and record promotion men are pulling out all the stops to tap the dance clubs' resources for breaking new product."

Just three months earlier, Harry (KC) Casey and Rick Finch had created the basics of "Rock Your Baby" in the attic studio of Henry Stone's TK Records in Hialeah, Florida. "It took us about 45 minutes to get the keyboard, bass and drum track down," Casey told *Billboard*.

"We used scrap tape and only had to pay Jerome Smith, the guitarist. I did keyboard and Rick was on bass and drums. When George got the tune, it only took two takes for him to get it down."

George McCrae was lucky to get the song at all. Casey and Finch initially felt "Rock Your Baby" was best suited for a female singer. They thought of his wife, Gwen McCrae, who at least had a couple of T.K.-tooled hits to her credit, or Betty Wright, who had helped grow the company with 1971's "Clean Up Woman." Coincidentally, it was Wright and her producer, Willie Clarke, who had seen George and Gwen perform in Florida as part of the Jiving Jets, and advised T.K. boss Henry Stone of their talent.

George McCrae confirmed that Casey and Finch wanted Wright, Latimore or Timmy Thomas to record "Rock Your Baby" at first. "But," he explained, "they were all busy doing their own thing and no one wanted it. I was so desperate at that point, I would have sung anything to get a record out."

Even so, he asked his mother, sister, and "lady friends" for their opinion on how he should cut the song. "They all told me to sing it soft and dreamy, and not to emulate the hard, loud funk music that was so popular at the time."

The emerging wave of discos, rather than R&B radio, gave "Rock Your Baby" its first public exposure.

"Unlike the white, Top 40-oriented clubs of the early '60s, today's discotheques are more representative of musical trends in the black community," reported *Billboard*. "Funky music is in, and the average discotheque customer is more than willing to pay to dance to his/her R&B favorite."

For all his desperation to get a record out, George McCrae was surprised at the outcome. "I wasn't prepared at the time to handle such a monster record," he said. "Only way I could begin to understand was to go out on my own initiative and overcome my fears. I was used to performing in front of 200 people. When 'Rock Your Baby' broke, I'd find myself in front of 5,000, 10,000 people. It's a frightening situation, really, and I wasn't prepared."

178

MY THANG

James Brown

POLYDOR 14244
WRITER: JAMES BROWN
PRODUCER: JAMES BROWN
July 20, 1974 (2 weeks)

A brand new ministry, a brand new funk. "My Thang" was James Brown's only Number One where he wasn't in the studio with the band as the track was being recorded. It was only his second Number One to feature sessions musicians, not his regular players (the first was "It's a Man's Man's Man's World," cut seven years earlier). And it's one of the few studio-crew funk records that *worked*—a sign that not only was JB's road band losing a bit of steam, but also that the professionals were waking up to the man's formula.

When he signed with Polydor Records in 1971, Brown had the resources of larger recording budgets and the services of production associates Dave Matthews, Fred Wesley, and Bob Both. Matthews, who had worked at King Records years before, was neither in Brown's band nor on his staff, but he served as arranger/conductor whenever JB recorded in New York during the early '70s.

By the time "My Thang" was recorded in late 1973, Wesley had picked up the bandleading baton. He continued to use the powerful cadre of jazz-funk players recruited by Matthews, and cultivated some of his own. The session took place at A&R Studios in New York on November 27, 1973, with guitarists Joe Beck and Sam Brown, tenor saxmen Joe Farrell and Frank Vicari, bassist Gordon Edwards, and trombonist Michael Gipson, who also blew alto sax.

Ex-JB bandleader Pee Wee Ellis made an appearance on the date, playing baritone sax. He, too, worked the New York studio circuit, thanks to Dave Matthews. So did drummer Jimmy Madison, one of the Cincinnati bar band musicians used semi-regularly by Brown and Matthews at King Records.

James Brown

In the control booth for "My Thang" was Bob Both. The session tape reveals him coaching and tightening up a horn part. "Play it the way Fred sang it," he advised. Lead and background vocals were done the day after the track was laid down; percussion overdubs by sessioneer Sue Evans were added later.

"I'd mixed the track and Brown liked it," remarks Both. "He said, 'I don't want to lose it, I don't want to lose that groove. But I want to add something.' To accomplish that, I copied the stereo master over to a four-track tape, and added the percussion overdubs to the original mix."

"My Thang" was the follow-up to "The Payback," and the second of three consecutive Number One hits for JB in 1974. That was his best-ever chart showing in a single year, although Brown wrote in his autobiography that Polydor Records "destroyed my sound."

In the opening lines of "My Thang," Brown announced a fresh take on his music ("A brand new funk!"), with Fred Wesley chanting "Tell us about it" in response. It gave birth to the new title "Minister of New New Super Heavy Funk," which JB subsequently had printed on the label of each one of his releases.

A brand new ministry, a brand new funk.

179

FEEL LIKE MAKIN' LOVE

Roberta Flack

ATLANTIC 3025
WRITER: EUGENE MCDANIELS
PRODUCER: RUBINA FLAKE
August 3, 1974 (5 weeks)

Gene McDaniels invited his assistant, Morgan Ames, to spend a relaxing weekend with his family at his in-laws' cabin at Lake Arrowhead, California. She arrived on a Friday, and Saturday morning Gene was surprised to find his guest heading for her car with her bag packed. "I said, 'Where are you going? We're getting ready to go out on the lake and have some fun.' She said, 'Gotta get back to town. I feel like makin' love.' I said, 'See ya!' and wrote the song. It took me 25 minutes."

McDaniels, who had hits of his own in 1961–62 ("A Hundred Pounds of Clay," "Tower of Strength"), composed the song on his Yamaha guitar and called Roberta Flack as soon as it was completed. "I said, 'I've got a Number One song for you.' She said, 'What's the name?' I said, 'Feel Like Makin' Love' and she said, 'I'm on my way.' "

McDaniels and Flack had been working together ever since jazz keyboardist Les McCann introduced them. Flack recorded McDaniels's "Compared to What" on her debut album for Atlantic, *First Take*, and continued to record his compositions, like "Reverend Lee" and "Sunday and Sister Jones." Responding to his call, Roberta landed at LAX and Gene drove her up to his place in Lake Arrowhead. She stayed for a few days and they ran through the song. A couple of weeks later, they were at Bell Sound Studios in New York, ready to record. "I called up Leon Pendarvis, who had been working with me at the time. I asked him to give me a hand because it was Roberta Flack, and I didn't want to stumble," says McDaniels. "Leon didn't play but he sat with me behind the controls. He made alterations in the arrangements and put pushes in a couple of spots." Gene put together a team of studio musicians: Bob James on piano, Idris Muhammad on drums, Gary King on bass, and Richie Resnicoff and Hugh McCracken on guitars.

The session took about three hours. "Roberta likes to work slow," says McDaniels. "I like to work fast. If you've got it right, why mess around? You put the music in front of these [sessions musicians], they run through it twice and bingo, they've got it. We're talking 10 minutes here. By the time an hour goes by and the engineer makes his adjustments, the tune logically should have been nailed...because these people are really, really good. They're the cream of the crop in New York City. We were waiting for Roberta to be satisfied...She took her time and more power to her. She knows how she likes to work and that works for her."

The release date for the single came and went—but there was no product on the street. McDaniels ran into Joel Dorn, who had produced Flack's earlier albums, at Atlantic Recording Studios in New York. Dorn told McDaniels that he had just done a remix of "Feel Like Makin' Love" and invited him to hear it. "It blew my socks off," says McDaniels. "It was so cool—the man has genius...I'm good but he's better. I was ecstatic with it." But Joel's mix never saw the light of day. "Roberta rejected the mix. She did a mix herself with some other people I don't even know, and that's the one that made it to the street. I never really liked the mix. I didn't think it was good. Joel's is the one that should have been put in the street; it would have been twice the hit."

Flack is still McDaniels's favorite singer. "I respect her tremendously. She's a powerful woman—I would love to cut an album on her today."

180

CAN'T GET ENOUGH OF YOUR LOVE, BABE

Barry White

20TH CENTURY 2120
WRITER: BARRY WHITE
PRODUCER: BARRY WHITE
September 7, 1974 (3 weeks)

Barry White has written a lot of love songs, but "Can't Get Enough of Your Love, Babe" is very special to him. "That's the only song I wrote about my experience with my wife. The only song," he emphasizes. "I'll write from your experience. I'll hear [someone] talk about his lady in a negative way, I'll turn it around into a positive story. I'll hear you talk positive, turn yours into a negative. That's what I [usually] do."

White felt some extra pressure while recording "Can't Get Enough of Your Love, Babe" for his third album. His first two albums for 20th Century were proven winners. He had even beaten the sophomore jinx. But he considered his third effort to be the "album of proof."

White was no longer sleeping on the floor and writing songs at his small office at Sunset and LaBrea. Now he had two homes in the hills overlooking the San Fernando Valley. He was recording at Whitney

Studios in the city of Glendale, a suburb nestled between Burbank and Pasadena. "Nobody black, nobody in the record business [who was] white went to that studio," Barry laughs. "Only the Mormon Tabernacle Choir used it to cut their Christmas carols. I found it one Saturday. I said that I got to find a studio and I don't want it in Hollywood."

White remembers recording "Can't Get Enough of Your Love, Babe" at Whitney. "We're sitting in the studio. It's all cut. Everybody's listening and it's near break time, an hour break. Everybody's jumping up and down over this song. Everybody but me. And I'm sitting in this booth, Wah Wah [Watson] on one side, Ray Parker on the other, David T. [Walker] in the back, Wilton [Felder] sitting over in the corner. 'It's a smash, B.W., what's wrong?' I said, 'You guys go take your break. When you come back, we're gonna fix this song.' "

Long before he recorded "I'm Gonna Love You Just a Little More Baby," Barry had a reputation in the industry for being able to tell people what was wrong with their tracks. "People used to invite me to their sessions to fix their basslines, their drums, the guitar. I knew these things," says the man who to this day cannot read music, but hears it in his heart.

Barry didn't tell the musicians at Whitney Studios that day what was wrong with "Can't Get Enough of Your Love, Babe." He just let them take their break. When they returned, he told them they were going to cut the track again. "I said, 'Wilton, come here. I'm gonna change your bassline. Ed Greene, I want to change your foot.' When that changed and we recorded it, they looked at each other. That's when they really knew where Barry White was on a spiritual level. Nobody knew the bassline and the foot was missing until they heard the right one on it...If that song had gone out the way it was, the way they liked it, it would have never been the hit that it was."

And how big a hit was it? "Can't Get Enough of Your Love, Babe" was Barry's second Number One single on the R&B chart and his first on the Hot 100.

181

YOU HAVEN'T DONE NOTHIN'

Stevie Wonder

TAMLA 54252
WRITER: STEVIE WONDER
PRODUCER: STEVIE WONDER
September 28, 1974 (2 weeks)

Stevie Wonder's work was often a bill of writes: songs with a political message, songs that spoke for millions of African-Americans, songs about empowerment—or the lack of it.

"You Haven't Done Nothin' " was typical. "Everybody promises you everything," declared Wonder at the time of the record's release, "but in the end, nothing comes out of it. I don't vote for anybody until after they have really done something that I know about. I want to see them *do* something first.

"The only trouble is that you always hear the President or people say that they are doing all they can. And they feed you with hopes for years and years. But that is probably typical of most people in very important positions who have a lot of power. I'm sick and tired of listening to all their lies."

Wonder was smart enough, of course, to make his political indictments radio-friendly. "The best way to get an important and heavy message across is to wrap it up nicely," he declared. "With songs, I've found out, it's better to try and level out the weight of the lyrics by making the melody lighter.

"After all, people want to be entertained, which is all right with me. So if you have a catchy melody instead of making the whole song sound like a lesson, people are more likely to play the tune. They can dance to it and still listen to the lyrics, and hopefully think about them."

"You Haven't Done Nothin,' " released two weeks before Richard Nixon resigned the Presidency, topped the R&B charts *and* become Stevie Wonder's first Number One on the Hot 100 since "You Are the Sunshine of My Life," 18 months earlier.

It was the lead-off single from *Fulfillingness' First Finale*, the album intended to mirror and summarize the superstar's creative achievements to date. That Wonder was in reflective mood was clear in March 1974, when he announced his intention to quit the music business two years later.

Even so, he spent much of '74 on the material that comprised *Fulfillingness*, recording at Electric Lady and Mediasound in New York, and at Record Plant and Westlake in Los Angeles. "He is very straight to the point, very clear on what he wants," comments Malcolm Cecil, who was associate producer of the album with Bob Margouleff. "You can also tell him the truth [about his work], you could tell him what you really thought. That's what he wanted, and he would listen to us."

In addition to Wonder's instrumental and vocal parts on "You Haven't Done Nothin'," the record featured Reggie McBride (bass) and the Jackson 5 (background vocals). Margouleff remembers the group's contribution, including Michael's arrival at Record Plant with his tutor. "It was done in Studio B, and there was a party-like atmosphere. Everyone was so blown away with the harmonies they did."

Fulfillingness' First Finale earned Stevie five Grammy awards, and helped contain an outbreak of vanilla in the 1974 honors—Marvin Hamlisch won four, and Olivia Newton-John took the prize for record of the year.

182

PAPA DON'T TAKE NO MESS (PART 1)

James Brown

POLYDOR 14255
WRITERS: JAMES BROWN, FRED WESLEY,
JOHN STARKS, CHARLES BOBBIT
PRODUCER: JAMES BROWN
October 12, 1974 (1 week)

During a very busy 1973, in the midst of summertime concerts, TV dates, and several different recording sessions for a movie soundtrack [see 170—"The Payback"], James Brown stopped back home. On August 23 at Augusta's International Studios, he cut three long grooves: "Papa Don't Take No Mess," "Time Is Running Out," and "Shoot Your Shot."

When the soundtrack was rejected, by the movie's producer, JB assembled the music into *The Payback*. But "Papa Don't Take No Mess" didn't surface until August 1974, when its unedited 14 minutes filled the fourth side of *Hell*, Brown's second two-LP set that year.

Hell was idiosyncratic: gothic cover, remakes of "Please Please Please" (in Spanish) and "I Can't Stand Myself," and a version of "When the Saints Go Marching In." A single released ahead of the album was a hit [see 178—"My Thang"] and another track, "Cold-blooded," made some noise. But it was "Papa" that really caught radio's attention, forcing a seven-inch edit into the market within days. For James, it was one of the few times that a single broke out of an album.

"Papa Don't Take No Mess" showcased the J.B.'s in a compelling ambience: Fred Wesley's horn arrangement, Brown's ad-libbed rhymes and screams, the combination of hooks like Maceo Parker's alto sax, guitarist Jimmy Nolen's delicate rhythm strokes, and drummer John "Jabo" Starks's rock-steady beat, snare pops and jazzy riffs that follow the leader.

Also on the session: Hearlon "Cheese" Martin (guitar), Fred Thomas or Charles Sherrell (bass), St. Clair Pinckney (tenor sax), Ike Oakley (trumpet), and either John Morgan or Johnny Griggs (percussion).

"We had a few days off," explains Starks, "and the way James worked was that if you didn't take off for home right away, he found out and kept you around. James always wanted to rehearse and try stuff out.

"We'd go into the studio and didn't always know what we were supposed to play. So we would groove, and if he came in and heard something he liked, he'd have us go back and try it out—his way. Turn it around, add some licks."

"Papa" was one of those, Starks affirms. "James had us stay on that vamp, until he figured out where he wanted to go. For my part, I heard it as a semi-jazz thing, but I knew no way in the world that James would go for that. It was too hip.

"So I went back to a rhythm I used to try with Bobby Bland, but never recorded—one of those things I always heard in my mind. James came over to the kit and said, 'Let me show you what I mean.' Now, he couldn't really play, but I said, 'OK, uh-huh,' and went back to what I was doing. James said, '*That's* what I want!' "

Starks also tips his hat to Fred Wesley, who himself acknowledges Jabo as the glue that kept the J.B.'s in the groove. "We had a good collaboration," Starks concludes. "Fred would say, 'Just play you.' He gave me that freedom, but always within the arrangement he had written for us."

183

DO IT ('TIL YOU'RE SATISFIED)

B.T. Express

ROADSHOW 12395
WRITER: BILLY NICHOLS
PRODUCER: JEFF LANE
October 19, 1974 (1 week)

The nucleus of the New York–based group B.T. Express was created when saxophonist Bill Risbrook and guitarist Richard Thompson were recruited by manager King Davis to form the King Davis House Rockers. They played gigs in New York and recorded a single for Columbia, "Rum Punch." When it didn't sell, they changed the name of the band to Madison Street Express, after the boulevard where their rehearsal hall was located in Brooklyn. Risbrook added more permanent members to the group, including his brother Louis, and in 1973 they had a third name: the Brooklyn Trucking Express.

Billy Nichols, a saxophonist and guitarist who travelled with Marvin Gaye and the Spinners, was in a band called the Invaders when they shared a bill with the King David House Rockers. After that initial meeting, Nichols was playing guitar in the house band for a Broadway musical version of *Two Gentlemen of Verona*. The bass player was Louis Risbrook. "When the play closed, he told me that someone wanted to record his group," says Nichols. Risbrook knew that Nichols had written songs for artists like Millie Jackson and suggested he might want to compose something for B.T. Express.

" 'Do It ('Til You're Satisfied)' was a tune written to motivate me," says Nichols. "I wanted anytime in my life to look at that and say, 'How could I not be motivated?' " Nichols came up with the groove first, inspired by a drum machine he had just purchased.

B. T. Express

"It had that beat on it. It was that and the experience of songs that I liked, James Brown's music and other people—the Isley Brothers. All the funk that I liked, the Ohio Players—people like that."

At first, Billy just wanted to use the title of the song as the complete lyric, chanted over the track. "The lyrics that I used, I didn't want to give them to Louis the day he came over to get the song. I felt like they weren't necessary. I felt like 'Do it 'til you're satisfied' was complete."

Billy made a home demo on a two-track machine. After producer Jeff Lane heard it, he told Nichols he loved the song and wanted B.T. Express to record it. "They wanted me to play on it, because I had put down all the parts, to make sure it was just like I'd put it down," says the songwriter.

The recording was completed in two takes. Bill Risbrook played sax and flute, Louis Risbrook played bass and organ, Richard Thompson was on guitar, Terrell Woods played drums, and Barbara Joyce Lomas provided vocals. "They asked me to join the group," says Nichols, "but I didn't want to because I wanted to establish myself as a producer and a songwriter—to stay put instead of travelling around. I had travelled around years ago with Marvin Gaye...I had my fill of it when I came to New York. I wanted to settle down and do my thing here."

Nichols was very fond of B.T. Express. "I thought they were an exceptionally good band, especially at playing other people's material. To me they were a rhythm and blues band and I think you judge those bands by the way they play somebody else's songs. B.T. was one of those groups that could play anybody's song and sound just like them...I think that was one of their greatest assets."

184

HIGHER PLANE

Kool & the Gang

DE-LITE 1562

WRITERS: RONALD BELL, KOOL & THE GANG

PRODUCERS: KOOL & THE GANG

October 26, 1974 (1 week)

We thought we were real good," declares James "J.T." Taylor, "and then *they* came out that night and..."

Taylor smiles. The man who sang on a half-dozen Number One hits is describing the time when he fronted a band called the Filet of Soul, opening for a transcendent Kool & the Gang at a college somewhere in New Jersey. "I remember trying to get backstage, but someone wouldn't let me in. I just wanted to say hello."

Six years later, J.T. did more than get backstage; he took center stage as the band's lead singer [see 320—"Ladies Night"] and gave voice to their platinum era. "As a music listener," he says, "we had Kool & the Gang from Jersey City, the Isley Brothers from T-Neck, the Moments from Englewood. That was our East coast connection in music.

"Our band used to mimic Kool & the Gang, so when I saw them, they were everything that I imagined and more. They didn't have a singer per se, but the songs, they played them so well."

Kool's gang did so in the musical hothouse that was the early '70s. "There was something in the air then," says Khalis Bayyan (a/k/a Ronald Bell), the band's sax player and sibling to leader Robert "Kool" Bell. "Stevie Wonder had 'Higher Ground,' Earth, Wind & Fire had 'Head to the Sky' and *Open Our Eyes*. We were all tapping into it."

A few years earlier, that arresting fusion of jazz and funk had landed Kool & the Gang a contract with De-Lite Records. After several modest-selling albums, they hit their commercial stride in 1973–74: a trio of singles from *Wild and Peaceful* breached the top 10, two turned gold, and one claimed the summit [see 174—"Hollywood Swinging"]. The LP was certified gold, too, and spent 60 weeks on the pop charts.

"Higher Plane" was the reconnaissance mission from the band's next album, *Light of Worlds*. "This song came after *success*—gold records, the accolades," says Bayyan. "The lyric is self-explanatory. For me, it was an offering for people to reach for higher things in life, to strive for excellence. That was the energy behind it."

Like its predecessor, *Light of Worlds* was recorded at Mediasound, the midtown Manhattan studio where Stevie Wonder also worked at the time. (Sometimes, he and Kool & the Gang even shared horn player Larry Gittens.) "We like to think of ourselves as scientists of sound," Robert Bell said soon after the LP's release. "We are always seeking knowledge that will improve our musical ability, and we spend most of our time experimenting with ideas. Some come off, some don't, but we never tire of looking. That's why I feel that *Light of Worlds* is our best album to date. At least, it's our best album artistically, shall we say."

Kool & the Gang

185

LET'S STRAIGHTEN IT OUT

Latimore

GLADES 1722
WRITER: BENNY LATIMORE
PRODUCER: STEVE ALAIMO
November 2, 1974 (2 weeks)

When Benny Latimore hit the top of the charts in November 1974 with "Let's Straighten It Out," the producer of the record, Steve Alaimo, was criss-crossing the home of kings.

"I was in England with KC and the Sunshine Band," he explains, "and we spent 30 days playing all the pubs around London." The KC crew was capitalizing on "Queen of Clubs," a top 10 smash in Britain six months before the band broke onto the American pop charts.

"I called back to the studio," Alaimo recounts, "and found out that Latimore was at Number One and Little Beaver was at number two [with "Party Down"]. I was the hottest R&B producer in America with the top two records, and there I was in London."

Alaimo had journeyed long and hard to get to the summit. For the first half of the '60s, he was a singer, making records for Chess, touring the nation. "And Benny Latimore was the organ player in my band," he says.

When Alaimo switched to producing in the second half of the '60s, he recorded Tennessee-born, blues-leaning Latimore for Henry Stone's various Florida labels. "We did a bunch of things through the years, with no great success." That changed in 1973 when Latimore's remake of "Stormy Monday" cracked the R&B charts. "The world had recorded this song," Alaimo concedes. "I never thought it would be a hit." When it was, Latimore's career began to lift off.

"Benny had never really written any songs [until then]," the producer adds. "He was always very shy. He was also very much of a perfectionist." When the singer wrote "Let's Straighten It Out" and brought the song to Alaimo, for example, "we must have spent two days on the piano intro until he got it the way he wanted."

Moreover, Latimore's Fender electric piano was one of only three instruments on the track. The rich bass of Ron Bogdon and the moody drums of Robert Furgeson were the others. A couple of Alaimo's colleagues even laughed at the record's sparse sound, he recalls. "They said, 'How can you make an R&B record without a guitar?' "

Apparently, Benny and Steve could. "We were in there for days 'til five or six in the morning. When people asked what we were working on, I'd say, 'Well, we've got the intro.' " The recording session took place in Hialeah, Florida, at the four-track studio that was part of Henry Stone's emerging T.K. group of labels.

Latimore

For his part, Latimore attributed the success of "Let's Straighten It Out" to the lyric. "A woman will feel things much deeper, much more quickly and much more accurately than a man," he told *Black Music* some years later. "But if something's bothering her, she might not say anything about it.

"And if she doesn't, then she'll sit around and go the opposite way...she'll be feeling it but not saying it. And so the man'll be wondering, 'What's wrong with her? What has she found out now?' He's gotta get it straightened out."

186

WOMAN TO WOMAN

Shirley Brown

TRUTH 3206

WRITERS: JAMES BANKS, EDDIE MARION, HENDERSON THIGPEN

PRODUCERS: AL JACKSON, JIM STEWART

November 16, 1974 (2 weeks)

The competition from Philadelphia, Miami, New York, and Los Angeles was intense, but the top of the *Billboard* charts belonged to Memphis this week in November 1974.

More significantly, Shirley Brown's "Woman to Woman" was a swan song for Memphis-based Stax Records. After this hit, the once-mighty home of Otis Redding, Johnnie Taylor, and the Staple Singers never again claimed the top of the charts.

In the fall of '74, when "Woman to Woman" was released on a new Stax imprint, Truth, times were truly tough—but not hopeless. Taylor and the Staples were about to defect, yet the Memphis machine still proved capable of taking Brown's soap opera to Number One.

And a soap opera it certainly was: an arresting tale of man's infidelity to woman—and how Brown dealt with it—rapped (for the most part) in a "telephone call" to "Barbara." During the conversation, Shirley left no pocket unexplored, no secret untold, no possessions unclaimed.

"We had gone into the demo studio and cut a rhythm track, and it laid around for probably a couple of weeks," explains James Banks, one of the song's three writers and brother of another Stax author, Homer Banks. "One night, we were just sitting in the office and put the track on to try to come up with some [lyrics] for it.

"We started out with a rap, because we knew raps were limited at that time. We were kinda in doubt about having a rap that long on the front [of the song], but decided to keep it because we needed it long to say the things we wanted to say."

The basic concept of "Woman to Woman" was in the rap portion, Banks adds, "so that inspired us to come up with the title and the melody." He says he and partners Henderson Thigpen and Eddie Marion each helped the music and lyrics take shape. "We wrote together as a team, and the contributions were equal."

The song was offered to Inez ("Mockingbird") Foxx, but she passed, suggesting the rap made it more suitable for Isaac Hayes. Meanwhile, Banks and his co-writers went to Detroit to handle another assignment. Returning to Memphis, they found that Stax producers Jim Stewart and Al Jackson had cut a rhythm track for "Woman to Woman." It was intended for Shirley Brown, whom bluesman Albert King had previously brought to the company.

"She went in and got that song down in a couple of takes," recalls Banks. "She has a church background and the melody's not too far from that feel, so she kinda brought it home. All the chemistry was right."

Stax's rhythm alchemist, Al Jackson, played drums on "Woman to Woman," with Lester Snell on organ, Marvell Thomas on piano, and (by Banks's recollection) Michael Toles on guitar. When the record took off, "it kinda lifted everybody's spirits," says the songwriter. "They thought, 'Maybe this will pull Stax out of the hole.' A lot of people had hopes right up until the end, 'til they closed the doors on them."

187

I FEEL A SONG (IN MY HEART)

Gladys Knight & the Pips

BUDDAH 433

WRITERS: TONY CAMILLO, MARY SAWYER

PRODUCERS: TONY CAMILLO, GLADYS KNIGHT & THE PIPS

November 30, 1974 (2 weeks)

Perseverance pays. Producer Tony Camillo recorded three interpretations of "I Feel a Song (In My Heart)" before batting a home run with Gladys Knight and the Pips.

One was the squeaky flip of a midchart Stairsteps single in 1972; another was a shrill reading by pop-soul stylist Linda Carr that same year. With Gladys and the Pips, however, the song acquired warmth and depth—and became their sixth Number One in four years.

In 1973, Camillo was involved in producing "Where Peaceful Waters Flow" and "Midnight Train to Georgia," the group's first successes after they left Motown for Buddah Records. His return engagement came in '74, following their soundtrack package with Curtis Mayfield, *Claudine*.

"I would reach out to various publishers and ask them to submit material," says Camillo. "Then I'd put a tape together for the artists to hear." On this occasion, he added one of his own compositions with co-lyricist Mary Sawyer: "I Feel a Song."

Camillo's preferred singer on the demos was Sandra Richardson, "because she sounded like Gladys." In fact, he says Buddah even issued Richardson's version of "I Feel a Song" as a single, in vain.

"After I presented the songs to Gladys," Camillo continues, "she'd go, 'Love that, like this,' and so on. It was Sandra's version of 'I Feel a Song' on the tape, and Gladys thought it was good to do."

Camillo arranged and laid down the track in his Venture Sound studio in Somerville, New Jersey. The rhythm section included Andrew Smith on drums, Barry Miles on acoustic piano, Bob Babbitt on bass, and Camillo on organ and electric piano. "I often used the same core of musicians," he says. Those players were on Gladys Knight & the Pips' first Number One for Buddah [see 156—"Midnight Train To Georgia"], and much else. Miles, for instance, played behind Jimmy McGriff and Esther Phillips; Babbitt was on numerous Detroit sessions, including Marvin Gaye's *What's Going On*.

To cut Gladys and the Pips' vocals, Camillo flew to Detroit, where they were living, and set to work at Artie Fields Productions. "She's a real professional," he says. "She was very quick in recording, she'd often get the take on the second or third go."

The Pips were equally skilled, and a favorite technique for a full harmony sound was to double their vocals. "Doubling was always very important to them," says Richie Wise, who co-produced their other Number One hits at Buddah. "Sometimes when you double it, it just gets right in the cracks, and makes for this beautiful bed.

"The Pips really sounded great double. What sounded thin as one set [of vocals] sounded just gorgeous when they sang it again. Then Gladys would do her lead. You'd sit there and, oh boy, it was just the greatest thing in the world."

188

YOU GOT THE LOVE

Rufus featuring Chaka Khan

ABC 12032
WRITERS: CHAKA KHAN, RAY PARKER JR.
PRODUCERS: BOB MONACO, RUFUS
December 14, 1974 (1 week)

Ray Parker Jr. vividly remembers the first time he talked to Chaka Khan. "I met her backstage at a Stevie Wonder concert when we were younger. I actually had other ideas for her and she kept saying, 'Oh, I can sing, me and my little sister. I can sing'...and when I came to California and met her and the band, she reminded me of that." He may not have appreciated her vocal ability the first time he met her, but times change. "In my opinion, she's the most talented singer in the world. I love her voice. Today, she is still my favorite singer."

Parker and Khan were destined to cross paths again after their fateful introduction. Shortly after relocating to Los Angeles, 18-year-old studio guitar whiz Ray Parker Jr. walked into a studio where Barry White was recording. "A session was going on and I pushed stop on the tape recorder and told him that his song needed a little of my guitar playing on it," Parker recalls, "and he gave me a shot. He said. 'You can get out there right now and let's hear it.' "

Parker made the grade and started a long association with White. Ray even wrote a song for him, carefully imitating Barry's unique style. "He didn't like it, and Andre Fischer of Rufus did," says Parker. The song ended up on *Rags to Rufus*. "At the time, they were a new band and I was pretty disappointed," Parker admits. "I wanted Barry White or Stevie Wonder to do it."

Parker recorded the song on a four-channel tape recorder, where he could do some slight overdubbing, but nothing fancy. He explains how Chaka Khan contributed to the song: "She wrote some of the lyrics. We weren't actually in the same room. I put the music down and we went in the studio and cut the track. I had some of the lyrics done and I guess they couldn't find me, or we got lost and they couldn't get the rest of the lyrics, so she finished writing it." Chaka came up with the title, "You Got the Love."

Parker was certain he had the strongest song on Rufus's second album and that he would get the first single, until the group recorded Stevie Wonder's "Tell Me Something Good." Suddenly, he was in second place. The Wonder song was the initial single released from *Rags to Rufus*, but it peaked at number three. "You Got the Love" was the follow-up, and it became the first of the group's five Number One hits.

Did having a hit song by Rufus help Parker's career? "Are you kidding? I was overwhelmed. I had written a lot of songs before and some of them had come out, but nothing to mention on the radio in a big way. So that song for me was like the highlight of my life. I'd drive down Sunset Boulevard and it would be playing on the radio and you couldn't tell me anything!" Parker says he made a mistake when he was asked to become a part of Rufus. "I should have joined the band. At the time they wanted me to, but I was busy. I thought I was busy in the studio playing the guitar."

189

SHE'S GONE

Tavares

CAPITOL 3957
WRITERS: DARYL HALL, JOHN OATES
PRODUCERS: DENNIS LAMBERT, BRIAN POTTER
December 21, 1974 (1 week)

Daryl Hall and John Oates were still relative unknowns when the five Tavares brothers recorded a version of the duo's Atlantic single "She's

Gone" and took it to the top of the R&B chart. Two years later, Hall and Oates finally had a pop hit with the same tune.

"Some songs take a long time to write, some songs don't," says Hall. "That one was a really fast one. John and I were both going through the same experiences and we put them down as fast as we could think of them. That's where the words come from. And John had been playing the pattern on an acoustic guitar, and I changed it to a keyboard. By changing it, I changed the whole feel of the thing. And then I added a lot of different chords."

"She's Gone" features a beautiful vocal arrangement, which Hall credits to the duo's Philadelphia upbringing. "We both came from street-corner singing, real doo-wop harmonies, the real traditional place that Philadelphia music comes from." Hall was the one who usually worked out the vocal arrangements. "The interesting thing was the octave lead, which not too many people had done before," Daryl points out. "That had to do with the sound of John's voice and my voice and we decided that instead of trying to sing a normal duo thing—singing in two-part harmony—we decided to try octaves instead."

Hall and Oates recorded "She's Gone" for their *Abandoned Luncheonette* album, released on Atlantic in early 1974. Issued as a single, "She's Gone" was the first Hall and Oates record to chart on the Hot 100. It peaked at number 60. That might have been the end of the story, if not for producers Dennis Lambert and Brian Potter.

Ralph, Antone ("Chubby"), Feliciano ("Butch"), Arthur ("Pooch"), and Perry Lee ("Tiny") Tavares, all from New Bedford, Massachusetts, had already recorded one single for Capitol, "Check It Out," before they were teamed with Lambert and Potter. "They were a fabulous vocal group, in the tradition of vocal groups that had come before them, like the Temptations and the Four Tops," says Lambert. "They were younger and we felt we could capture the spirit of the market at that time and incorporate some of the classic characteristics of earlier R&B records, [and] have something both contemporary and classic at the same time."

The first songs Lambert and Potter recorded with Tavares were ballads, "She's Gone" among them. "I knew that song from Hall and Oates' first album," says Lambert. "I always thought that that was a fabulous song that would be very adaptable to an R&B version. So I introduced it to the group and they loved it. They thought it was a little adventurous. That was what I thought was the charm of the song."

The Tavares recording differed only slightly from the original. "We stayed fairly true to the original record," Lambert maintains. "We introduced more full harmony singing and we tried to make the track a little funkier. But basically it's fairly close in structure to the original."

Lambert remembers being as elated as the group when "She's Gone" went to Number One. Daryl Hall was happy, too: "I thought it was great, because my first records were played on the R&B stations in Philadelphia and I had a hard time getting on pop radio. So I looked at it as an early indication of something that seems to have continued."

190

BOOGIE ON REGGAE WOMAN

Stevie Wonder

TAMLA 54254
WRITER: STEVIE WONDER
PRODUCER: STEVIE WONDER
December 28, 1974 (2 weeks)

As the first and second singles, respectively, from Stevie Wonder's *Fulfillingness' First Finale* album, the polemics of "You Haven't Done Nothin' " gave way to the carefree celebration of "Boogie on Reggae Woman."

Both were huge hits on the Hot 100 and R&B charts, helping the album to become Wonder's first Number One pop LP since *Recorded Live! The 12 Year Old Genius* in 1963. It was fitting that the cover of *Fulfillingness* featured illustrations of Dr. Martin Luther King and JFK—symbols of '63—alongside depictions of gold discs, Grammy awards, and a Motortown Revue tour bus.

Judging by the logsheets kept by Wonder's associate producers, Malcolm Cecil and Bob Margouleff, he got started on "Boogie on Reggae Woman" in 1973, around the same time as "Jesus Children of America," which appeared on his previous album, *Innervisions*.

"Three new tunes (untitled)," declares the Cecil/Margouleff log, identifying them as "jazz tune," "words unheard," and "Hello Jesus," plus a fourth, "Bogey [*sic*] on Reggae Woman."

Wonder was so prolific, of course, that "Hello Jesus" could have been an entirely different song from "Jesus Children of America." Cecil says, "We didn't record albums, we recorded songs. When it was time to put an album out, it was, 'What songs have we got?'

"We spent a lot of time figuring out what would work after which song, what tempos would work, blending them together. We would argue and push and say, 'You've got to have this one,' and so on, but Stevie had the final say."

Margouleff agrees. "He never really worked toward creating an album project, he'd just write for a library, for a body of work, then we'd draw from the library. We'd go to [attorney] Johanan Vigoda's office—I remember he had three or four dead plants on his desk—and pick songs. No bodyguards, no business people, no one hovering. It was very quiet—and very musical."

Margouleff calls "Boogie on Reggae Woman" one of his favorite songs. "It was supposed to go on *Innervisions*," he says, "it was created at that time. That was a library pull: I argued to get it on *Fulfillingness*."

Wonder was constantly creating, whether at Mediasound or Electric Lady in New York, or at Record Plant in Los Angeles. So Cecil and Margouleff were constantly on call. "It would be whatever Stevie felt like working on that day or that night," says Cecil. "We would go in and if Stevie wasn't around, that's when Bob and I would mix. He [Stevie] would say, 'I can't get in [to the studio], I'm in Detroit and I'm with this lady. Why don't you mix so-and-so?' "

Wonder's extraordinary four-year, four-album partnership with his two studio wizards ended with *Fulfillingness' First Finale*. "The only contract we ever had with Stevie was the one to stop working with him," says Cecil. And as a curtain-closer, the LP took the 1974 Grammy as Album of the Year—-just as *Innervisions* had taken the 1973 prize.

191

KUNG FU FIGHTING

Carl Douglas

20TH CENTURY 2140
WRITER: CARL DOUGLAS
PRODUCER: BIDDU
January 11, 1975 (1 week)

The first British-based singer to top the R&B charts, Carl Douglas, had a connection to the first British soul band to have hits in America, the Foundations.

Both acts were signed to Pye Records, the U.K. label associated with other black acts in that country—Geno Washington, Jimmy James, the Real Thing—and with multi-million-selling novelties, such as "Kung Fu Fighting."

"People loved that record and hated it, too," admits Peter Summerfield, who was then on the A&R staff of the British company and worked with Douglas. "At Pye, we had a lot of those."

"Kung Fu Fighting" came to the label in 1974 via independent producer Biddu. "I had met him a year or two before that," says Summerfield, "and I think his first production through Pye was with a group called the Playthings."

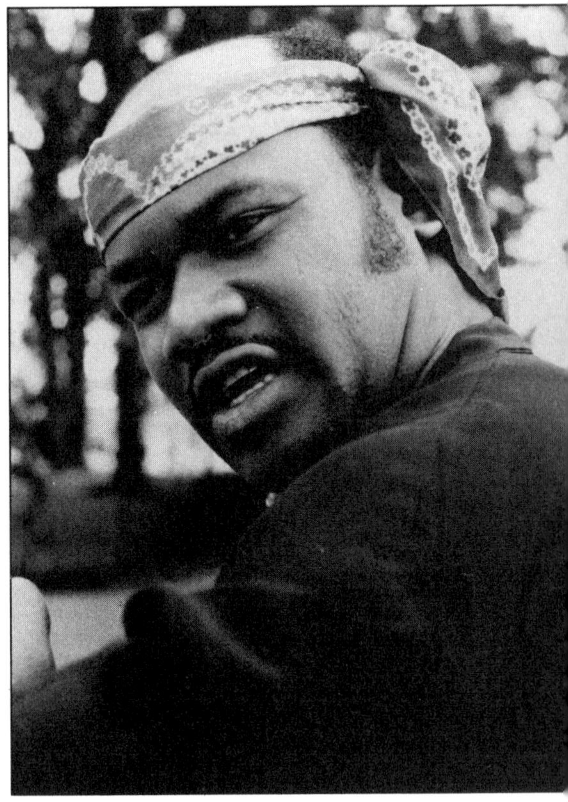

Carl Douglas

When Biddu submitted some material by Douglas, Summerfield and other members of the company's A&R team, Robin Blanchflower and Peter Prince, opted for a novelty song instead of "I Want to Give You My Everything," a more straightforward tune. "We thought the B-side was better than the A-side," he recalls. That was "Kung Fu Fighting."

For his part, Jamaican-born Carl Douglas lived on and off in Britain, playing in bands that opened for visiting U.S. soul stars. "What I could see as successful ingredients for a British [R&B] sound were a commercial thing, with some heavy American rhythms wrapped around it," Douglas told *Black Music* in the mid-'70s. "Some people had tried it, but they hadn't got it together in the right way."

Douglas, who hung out with musician friends in London, remembered leaving one Soho night spot in May 1974 and passing a pinball alley. "There was some record playing, I don't remember which, but there were quite a few young kids in there who were having a kind of mock fight in time to the music. I turned to the guy I was with and said, 'Damn, looks like everybody's kung fu fighting,' and at that moment, I heard it all in my head, melody line as well, so I had to rush home and write it down."

He recorded the song with Biddu at London's Nova Studios. Working to an arrangement by the late Gerry Shury were Chris Rae (guitar), Barry De Souza (drums), and Frank McDonald (bass), with Shury on keyboards and backup vocals provided by Bones.

After a few cautionary weeks when it seemed as if Pye's success with home-grown soul might not extend to "Kung Fu Fighting," the record began to take off in Britain—and eventually chopped its way to Number One there in September 1974.

Then Pye chieftain Louis Benjamin placed a call to 20th Century Records president Russ Regan in Los Angeles. The two men knew each other: some years earlier, Regan had been a senior executive at Uni Records, the label that acquired U.S. release rights from Pye for...the Foundations.

"I remember taking the Carl Douglas record to Los Angeles," concludes Peter Summerfield. "Russ, who was one of my idols as a record man, said, 'It could happen here—I'll take a chance.' " And happen it did.

192

YOU'RE THE FIRST, THE LAST, MY EVERYTHING

Barry White

20TH CENTURY 2133
WRITERS: BARRY WHITE, TONY SEPE, P. STERLING RADCLIFFE
PRODUCER: BARRY WHITE
January 18, 1975 (1 week)

Sterling Radcliffe wrote a country & western song called "You're the First, the Last, the In-Between" and tried to get someone to record it. He tried for 21 years. The demo that he recorded himself even featured the clop of horses' hooves to keep rhythm, but no one was interested.

Barry White knew Sterling Radcliffe through his friend and arranger, Gene Page. "One Christmas, I didn't have any money. Sterling went and got my children some toys," Barry recalls. "I never forgot that. When I became successful, he said, 'I got a song, Barry. I want you to listen to it.' 'Bring the song over, Sterling, because I owe you a big one.' He brought the song. I listened to the damn thing. Tony Sepe, the other name on the record, started laughing, because he knew that song was nothing. When he got through playing it, I said, 'Sterling, that song is a smash.' Tony's face actually changed. I said, 'Sterling, I want you to stay out of my face for the next two or three weeks. When you come back, you're going to be part of a smash.' "

White admits he asked Sterling, who is still a friend today, to stay away because he had a habit of getting on people's nerves. "You can't hang around him too long." But he wasn't kidding about the song's potential. "I heard what was inside that song," he says. "Took it, rewrote it, kept the chord changes, kept part of his melody, added my new melody to it and all new lyrics except for 'You're the first, my last' from 'In-Between.' When Sterling heard that song, he cried. Right in front of me, and everybody was looking at him. It was me and Sterling who wrote that song, but there's three names on the record. Tony bought into Sterling's piece."

"You're the First, the Last, My Everything" became Barry's third Number One single. Even though he knew it would be big when he finished it, he wasn't so sure along the way. Barry had worked on Sterling's song in the recording studio located in one of his two adjoining San Fernando Valley homes. He loved the words and melody by the time he arrived at Whitney Studios in Glendale to record the track. He sang it one time, went in the booth to listen to it, and knew he was in trouble. "It didn't work. And I didn't have time to figure out why. Frank [Kejmar], my engineer, was scared to death...I said, 'Don't worry about it, Frank. You play the track.' I went into the studio and made up my own melody all the way through. Half of the words in it I changed right in front of the microphone. 'We gotta keep that! We gotta keep that!'—they were going crazy in that booth. 'Don't stop to tell me that! Let's get it finished because I'm coming off the top of my head,' like the lyrics, rapping...now I got a whole new thing."

193

FIRE

Ohio Players

MERCURY 73643
WRITERS: OHIO PLAYERS
PRODUCERS: OHIO PLAYERS
January 25, 1975 (2 weeks)

After hitting Number One with a novelty song [see 146—"Funky Worm"], the Ohio Players shifted gears, changed some members of the group, and signed with a new label, Mercury.

They left behind Walter "Junie" Morrison, the voice of the "Funky Worm," who elected to remain with Westbound and join the label's other big group, Parliament/Funkadelic. Billy Beck took over the keyboards and Jimmy "Diamond" Williams came on board as the new drummer.

Williams explains how the Ohio Players sound continued to evolve: "Back then—and I don't want to

Ohio Players

sound like we're talking about prehistoric times—it was a time where musicians would go in the studio and play. We didn't carry our instruments in a briefcase and they weren't set up in a box or programmed at home. Sometimes we'd be out on the road practicing and sometimes we would try certain grooves after a song just to see if the audience had a vibe with it. And if they did, this is something we'd take immediately into the studio and incorporate into a song. We would play a lot and practice a lot and make it happen in the studio."

Leroy "Sugarfoot" Bonner recalls how "Fire" got started: "We were in the studio making tracks and all of a sudden, it leaped out." The group told Bonner they thought the song should be called "Fire." He explains, "They come with the names and I have to write to them. If the music is good, it doesn't take long to get inspired. To use all the effects one could use on a track like that, the fire engines and all that, seemed very apropos to what was going on on the albums of that era. Other people were using babies crying and kids singing and street sounds. A lot of people were using sound effects of various natures, so we thought about that also."

After the rhythm track for "Fire" was recorded, the group was in California to play some dates. "*Skin Tight* was out and doing real well and we were staying at a motel Stevie Wonder owned on Sunset," says Williams. "He was staying at the motel and he was playing us his rhythm tracks for *Songs in the Key of Life* and we were playing him the rhythm tracks for 'Fire.' He heard it and knew it was a smash. Just like before we even said any words on the track, we knew it was a smash. There was nothing that was going to stop this hit."

Having another Number One song made a big impact on the Ohio Players, explains Williams: "Change is a part of life. It did change and for a lot of reasons, it changed for the better. 'Fire' was a very positive tune. We were on top of the charts and we were on top of the world."

But there was one unfortunate side effect to having a hit single called "Fire," Williams points out. Some people apparently thought it was amusing to set fires in hotel rooms, especially when the Ohio Players were staying in those hotels. "They kicked us out of the Hyatt House on Sunset [Boulevard] in California when somebody started a fire on the floor and burned a bed because we were staying there. We had to leave."

194
HAPPY PEOPLE
The Temptations

GORDY 7138
WRITERS: JEFFREY BOWEN,
DONALD BALDWIN, LIONEL RICHIE
PRODUCERS: JEFFREY BOWEN, BERRY GORDY JR.
February 8, 1975 (1 week)

The Temptations opened 1975 just like '74: at the top of the charts.

But "Happy People" meant more. It marked the group's separation from producer Norman Whitfield, the mastermind who gave them 25 top ten R&B records (including ten Number Ones) during 1966–74.

Whitfield's last album project before leaving Motown was the Temptations' *1990* [see 164—"Let Your Hair Down"]. Despite their extraordinary success under his tutelage, the group found the producer hard-going towards the end. "Working with Norman was always a strain," said lead singer Dennis Edwards a couple of years later, "there was very little freedom."

The man tasked with following Whitfield's act was Jeffrey Bowen, an assistant to onetime Motown A&R chief Mickey Stevenson in the mid-'60s. He co-produced the Temptations' *In a Mellow Mood* album in 1967. Later, he joined Holland/Dozier/Holland's Invictus/Hot Wax labels, and produced the Chairmen of the Board's final hits. By 1974, Bowen was back at Motown.

The other chairman of the board, Berry Gordy, took charge of the Temptations' recording plans after Whitfield quit. In doing so, he recruited Stevie Wonder (whose tracks went unreleased) and James Carmichael. Gordy had Carmichael cut a song called "Glasshouse" with the group, then challenged Jeffrey Bowen to create a better version. He did—and got the assignment to produce the LP that became *A Song For You*.

Sessions took place at Motown's Hollywood studios, with Melvin "Wah-Wah" Ragin and Eddie Hazel (guitars), James Gadson and Zachary Frazier (drums), William Nelson (bass), and Donald Baldwin (keyboards, sax, clarinet). Carmichael arranged horns and strings.

At the same time and in the same studios, Bowen and Carmichael were recording tracks with the Commodores, whose sax and piano player, Lionel Richie, helped write "Happy People." Another member of that band, William King, told *Blues & Soul*, "At first, we thought of doing 'Happy People' for ourselves, but we decided against it."

Nevertheless, several of the Commodores' instrumental parts were used on the Temptations' version of the song, according to King. "Lionel plays piano, Walter Orange plays drums, and Thomas McClary plays guitar," he said. "And the horn parts are the same, except that...they have added a lot more to give a bigger production sound. I know that they have changed the bass track, and that a new guitar track was added to our original."

The result was a bold, brassy "Happy People," which pulled the Temps back from Norman Whitfield's overproduced quirks towards the progressive funk of the Ohio Players and Earth, Wind & Fire. As a single, it surged up the charts in the opening weeks of 1975 and laid the groundwork for *A Song for You* to become the Temptations' 15th album to occupy the R&B summit.

Furthermore, "Happy People" was the second of two hits that January to combine Jeffrey Bowen's creative skills and the Commodores' musicianship. First was "I Feel Sanctified," co-written and produced by Bowen, and the band's follow-up to their chart debut, "Machine Gun."

195
I BELONG TO YOU
Love Unlimited

20TH CENTURY 2141
WRITER: BARRY WHITE
PRODUCER: BARRY WHITE
February 15, 1975 (1 week)

"We know who daddy is," Glodean White, Love Unlimited's lead vocalist, told *Billboard* in 1979. "We're the babies and he's the daddy."

In truth, Glodean was talking about her husband, Barry White, who fathered the idea of Love Unlimited. "It's always been like a family affair," she said. "The first thing an artist would want to have is a well-known and qualified producer, and we have one built-in. We have no reason to feel in the shadow."

Love Unlimited was Glodean, her younger sister Linda James, and Diane Taylor. The group met their future daddy—uh, producer—through another singer; he liked their sound, and suggested cutting a record with him. The upshot was "Walkin' in the Rain with the One I Love," a top ten R&B hit for the trio in 1972. "I would say Barry was the fourth member of Love Unlimited," declared Glodean. "He tailor-made all our songs for us."

White had experience tailoring for women. While at Bob Keene's Bronco/Mustang labels in the mid-'60s, he made records with the likes of Viola Wills and Felice Taylor. One of Wills's near-hits was "Lost

Labelle

Without the Love of My Guy," a shuffle ballad arranged and co-written by White. "I had an intro on that song which Glodean loved," he says. "Out of all the people in the world who bought that song, when I met my wife, it was in her record stack.

"I said, 'What is this doing here?' She said, 'You know about Viola Wills?' I said, 'Read the label: produced and written by Barry White.' Blew her mind. She always loved the intro to that song, the piano thing."

So Glodean urged her future spouse to write a fresh song featuring the same introduction. "And I looked at her," he recalls. "I said, 'Glo, I don't want to do anything I've done already.' She said, 'Please, please, honey, please. Just put that intro and write me a new song.' "

White surrendered, and "I Belong to You" was the outcome. With Gene Page as arranger, White cut the tune at the Whitney Recording Studios in Glendale and deployed it in Love Unlimited's *In Heat* LP. "That whole album was exciting," he says. The musicians were many of the same players who were on Barry's own hits, such as David T. Walker, Dean Parks, and Melvin Ragin on guitars, Wilton Felder on bass, and Ed Greene on drums. White himself played piano.

"The strings on that record killed them," Barry declares. "The melody threw them, the rhythm stopping, and it had everything to make a ballad the hottest-selling music in the world. And ballads are the worst [type of] records in the world to try to sell."

196

LADY MARMALADE

Labelle

EPIC 50048
WRITERS: BOB CREWE, KENNY NOLAN
PRODUCER: ALLEN TOUSSAINT
February 22, 1975 (1 week)

Patti LaBelle says she had no idea what *"Voulez-vous couchez avec moi ce soir?"* meant when she recorded "Lady Marmalade." "We just knew that it sounded like a hit," she professes. "We didn't know it was about a hooker and 'Will you sleep with me tonight?' But after we recorded it and found out what it was, we said, 'Well, a hooker has to make a living, too.' "

Patti first heard the song while she was on the way to Los Angeles International Airport with Sarah Dash and Nona Hendryx from Labelle. They were headed to New Orleans to record with producer Allen Toussaint when Bob Crewe asked them to come by and listen to something. They stopped at his apartment and heard "Lady Marmalade," a song he had written with Kenny Nolan. Convinced that it was a hit, the trio brought it to Toussaint, who recorded it for Labelle's first Epic album, *Nightbirds*.

Nolan had already written some segments of "Lady Marmalade," including the "*Voulez-vous...*" hook, before he met Crewe. The two of them were scheduled to produce a song for Bobby Darin. After Darin died, however, they hooked up in 1974 to write songs together. They completed "Lady Marmalade" and recorded it on an obscure 20th Century Records album by a group called the Eleventh Hour that featured Nolan as lead vocalist. "I sounded like Frankie Valli on acid," Nolan suggests.

Toussaint's version was very different from the Eleventh Hour recording, according to Nolan. "They changed the rhythm around greatly. It was never that up and fiery. When I wrote it with Crewe, it was a little more laid-back." Nolan first heard the song when Toussaint sent him a copy of the single. "I had heard a lot of talk about it from the people at CBS," says the songwriter. "I put it on the record player—I didn't believe it. It was 10 times as fast in tempo. I could never have in a million years conceived the way they had done it."

Patti says she was thrilled to work with Toussaint, one of the most influential New Orleans musicians in the '60s. His production credits included "Ooh Poo Pah Do" for Jesse Hill, "Mother-in-Law" for Ernie K-Doe, "It Will Stand" for the Showmen, "I Like It Like That" for Chris Kenner, "Working in the Coal Mine" for Lee Dorsey, and "Sophisticated Cissy" for the Meters. Patti found she only had one major difference with Toussaint. "He works at a very slow pace and I'm a Gemini and I work very fast. But he said, 'Everything takes time,' and he took time and he was right. It took time to get that hit. He just works a little differently than I'm used to."

Nightbirds revealed a whole new look and name for the three women in Labelle, who were known as Patti LaBelle and the Bluebelles when they recorded songs like "Down The Aisle" and "You'll Never Walk Alone." A quartet before the departure of Cindy Birdsong for the Supremes in 1967, LaBelle emerged from London as silver-suited space divas. "We came back to the States and we knew we had to have a gimmick and the gimmick was the clothes," Patti explains. "We had a lot to say, but three black women were definitely not going to get too much attention coming back looking ordinary. So we came back with a crazy look. And after they finished looking, they started listening...I hate using gimmicks, but we had to and it worked. Then it stuck with us for awhile, so the fans were looking for it. So we kept doing it for their sake, and after that we calmed down a bit."

197

SHAME, SHAME, SHAME

Shirley & Company

VIBRATION 532
WRITER: SYLVIA ROBINSON
PRODUCER: SYLVIA ROBINSON
March 1, 1975 (1 week)

In the mid-1950s, Shirley & Lee crossed paths with Mickey & Sylvia on the road, somewhere in America. Two decades later, by way of a Playboy phone call, Shirley and Sylvia were reunited.

Shirley Goodman's "Let the Good Times Roll" with Leonard Lee went to Number One in September 1956, followed six months later by Sylvia Vanderpool's "Love Is Strange" with Mickey Baker. Eighteen years to the month after that, "Shame, Shame, Shame" took over at the top.

"We'd been good friends and kept in touch over the years," Goodman explained to *Black Music* in 1975. "Then last December, she called me while I was working at Playboy Records and said that if I was ready to record again, she had a song for me."

At the time, Sylvia was married to Joe Robinson and the couple was operating All Platinum Records out of Englewood, New Jersey [see 145—"Pillow Talk"]. She was thinking of "Shame, Shame, Shame" for Shirley, but the song already had a history.

Drummer Clarence Oliver and guitarist Walter Morris, members of All Platinum's studio band, both remember Donnie Elbert working with them on "Shame, Shame, Shame" in 1974. "We played that initially with Donnie," says Oliver. "The track was done first; Shirley was put on much later."

Singer/songwriter Elbert had been in and out of the R&B charts since the late '50s, but his biggest hit was for All Platinum: a 1971 remake of the Supremes' "Where Did Our Love Go." He left the label soon afterwards, only to rejoin three years later.

"Donnie was the main person we were dealing with when we cut the track [for "Shame, Shame, Shame"]," affirms Walter Morris. "Sylvia had a lot to do with it after we laid the foundation. She produced all the rest."

Aside from Morris's relentless riffing and Oliver's propulsive hi-hat, the record featured Jonathan Williams on bass, Bernadette Randle on piano, and Seldon Powell's wailing alto sax throughout the second half. The "zing" heard at the song's hook was a sitar, played by Morris.

Shirley

"When I got to town, we went right to the studio," Shirley outlined to *Black Music*. "It was amazing, everything was ready. They'd already cut the track and even the key was just right, only [Sylvia] wasn't sure who to put on the record with me.

"We tried it several ways, including a version with Hank Ballard, but it was Jesus who really knew the song, and when he and I tried it together, it hit just right. And we cut it that same night."

Shirley's arresting male company on "Shame, Shame, Shame" is, indeed, Jesus Alvarez, who had joined All Platinum some months before. Coincidentally or not, her vocal on the record closely resembles Elbert's style on his earlier sides, such as "A Little Piece of Leather."

Clarence Oliver says there was "friction" between Elbert and All Platinum over "Shame, Shame, Shame." Joe Robinson confirms the dispute, while noting that Elbert recorded a song in England in 1975 ("You're Gonna Cry When I'm Gone") with the same melody as Shirley's hit. "We bought the master out," he concludes.

198

EXPRESS

B.T. Express

ROADSHOW 7001

WRITERS: LOUIS RISBROOK, BARBARA J. LOMAS, WILLIAM RISBROOK, ORLANDO TERRELL WOODS, RICHARD THOMPSON, CARLOS WARD, DENNIS E. ROWE

PRODUCER: JEFF LANE

March 8, 1975 (1 week)

The three Risbrook brothers were born into a musical family. Their mother played violin and piano, and their father excelled at trombone. Jamal Risbrook (née Louis), took up the clarinet when he was eight, moved over to trumpet, and then as a teenager became interested in guitar and bass. At the age of 15, he was touring with Wilson Pickett.

Jamal's brother Bill played in a Brooklyn-based band called King Davis and the House Rockers, while his brother Bob was in another local group, the Revets. Jamal joined that band for a couple of years before switching over to the House Rockers, the band that evolved into B.T. Express. The group's first Number One single, "Do It ('Til You're Satisfied)" [see 183], was written by a friend of Jamal's, Billy Nichols. Drummer Terrell Woods suggested to Jamal that they should come up with some original material. Terrell played a bassline for Jamal that was the basis of their second Number One single, "Express."

"That's all it was," says Risbrook, "just that one line. We started playing it and then we started adding stuff to it, adding guitar lines and so forth, and then Carlos Ward, who played alto sax with us, wrote the horn line. In no time at all, that song was put together."

"Express" featured repetitive lines, which made it an outstanding choice for getting people to dance when it was played live. "It was just a groove, really," says Risbrook. "That's what we used to do a lot in terms of playing at those dances. That's why we were very popular as a [live] band, because we knew how to lay a groove and set the tone and let the people dance, rather than do a lot of stuff that we might like as musicians but the people wouldn't be getting into. We were really a groove band and that's what kept us working on the dance circuit, playing dances for years."

The string arrangements on "Express" were by Randy Muller, who was handed the assignment by producer Jeff Lane. "That was my first studio job writing for strings and orchestra," says Muller. "I never did that before. Jeff said, 'Muller, I need an arrangement. You're a genius, right? Go and give me some violins.' I never did any stuff with violins. I was a horn guy. So I went and asked a teacher of mine, 'Tell me something about strings.' And I got a book and I read. I had to do it in two days. The reason the parts are so simple is that Jeff came to pick me up to take me to the studio...I sat at my dinner table. My grandmother was there and the car horn is blowing. And I said, 'I've got to get this thing done!' I put the tape on and wrote out the parts...I learned a lot about deliberating over tracks, wanting to make them so perfect—and the things that [took me] 15, 20 minutes end up being the biggest hits."

Years later, Jamal was surprised to learn that Randy had not arranged strings before. "It sounded good to us when we heard the demos...It was the combination of the funk underneath and the strings on top. If that's his first thing, it was great."

199

SUPERNATURAL THING (PART 1)

Ben E. King

ATLANTIC 3241
WRITERS: PAT GRANT, GWEN GUTHRIE
PRODUCERS: BERT DECOUTEAUX,
TONY SILVESTER
March 15, 1975 (1 week)

The voice of Ben E. King drifted across the airwaves in the opening weeks of 1975, as "Supernatural Thing" refuted the maxim that you can never go home again.

For King, home was Atlantic Records. There, he fronted the Drifters during 1959–60 (his was the signature lead on "There Goes My Baby" and "Save the Last Dance for Me") and then enjoyed a string of successful solo sides.

In 1974, several years after King had left the label, Atlantic co-founder Ahmet Ertegun was in Miami and caught his act at a local nightspot. A reunion was suggested. "One of the things about Ahmet," says the singer, "is that he's one of the nicest men in the business. I know things the public doesn't know; he's a dear friend forever."

So King set out to work for Atlantic at Mediasound, the Manhattan church-turned-studio, with producers Bert deCouteaux and Tony Silvester. "Originally, 'Supernatural Thing' was supposed to be the old classic 'Fever,' " he explains. The track was cut, but it soon became apparent that another song was in the making. "We changed the bassline, put a chorus on the track, and gave it to some writers," Silvester told *Billboard* a few months after the session.

Those writers were Gwen Guthrie [see 435—"Ain't Nothin' Goin' On but the Rent"] and Pat Grant, signed to a publishing deal with deCouteaux and Silvester. Just months earlier, the same team had created "Love Don't You Go Through No Changes on Me," the first hit for Sister Sledge.

As Grant and Guthrie shaped "Supernatural Thing," Silvester and deCouteaux redefined Ben E. King's sound. The singer recalls, "Bert said, 'What's your range?' I said, 'Well, basically I sing baritone.' He said, 'But no, what else can you do?'

"So he started playing the piano and going at different levels. Finally he got up to the high pitch of my voice, and said, 'Let's do it there.' I said, 'OK, you'll have to make sure it's a clear day. That's really not my favorite thing to do.' It was the top of my range, not straining, but it was like, you have to stay there and not try to push it too much higher then. But he found it."

DeCouteaux and partner Silvester also found a hypnotic, fractured rhythm track to attach to King's higher-pitched vocals. Musicians on the date included guitarists Carlos Alomar, Jeff Mironov and Jerry Friedman, Bob Babbitt on bass, Jimmy Young on drums, and Ricky Williams, Derek Smith, and deCouteaux on keyboards.

Among those whose fluid percussion work underpinned the groove was conga player Carlos Martin; backup singers included writer Guthrie and Lani Groves. And the main attraction, Ben E. King, cut his vocal in one take, reading the lyrics from a piece of paper.

An R&B *and* pop chartbuster, "Supernatural Thing" stands as King's most popular solo side, bar one—the immortal "Stand By Me." That was a top 10 pop record twice—and on both occasions, it was released through Atlantic Records. You *can* go home again.

200

SHINING STAR

Earth, Wind & Fire

COLUMBIA 10090
WRITERS: MAURICE WHITE, PHILIP BAILEY, LARRY DUNN
PRODUCER: MAURICE WHITE
March 22, 1975 (2 weeks)

Only John Denver was supposed to be getting his ideas this way, but the ugly truth is that a lot of artists were sitting in the Rocky Mountains in the mid-'70s waiting for their muse to show up. Even respectable musicians like Earth, Wind & Fire's Maurice White, who had gone there to write the soundtrack for a new movie, *That's the Way of the World*, from the director of *Superfly*.

"That was an inspirational time," White says of the nine months it took to make *That's the Way of the World*. "We recorded the album in Nederland, Colorado, which is right outside Boulder, up in the mountains at the Caribou Ranch...I wrote 'Shining Star' one night after walking about and looking at the skies and seeing a shining star, so then we directed it towards a positive image."

That's the Way of the World was director Sig Shore's attempt to blow the lid off the music business, back in the days of the mid-'70s payola scandals. EW&F didn't just write the soundtrack for Shore, they actually played "The Group," the credible R&B act that A&R man Harvey Keitel wanted to sign instead of the candy-assed family bubblegum act that his bosses were foisting on him.

Going into that movie, EW&F were certainly well cast as a cult act. Since the early '70s, when White made the transition from producer/studio musician (and former Ramsey Lewis Trio member) to leader of an R&B/jazz group, his band had been through two names (the first was the Salty Peppers), several line-ups, and three labels.

By 1974, Earth, Wind & Fire had racked up a handful of medium-sized soul hits, building themselves a sizable following. The band at that point included leader White, handling vocals, drums, and kalimba; Philip Bailey, vocals, congas, and percussion; Verdine White, bass; Larry Dunn, keyboards; Al McKay and Johnny Graham, guitars and percussion; Ralph Johnson, drums; and Andrew Woolfolk, saxophones, flute, and percussion.

During this period, they were R&B's most eclectic band; by the end of the '70s, they would also be one of the poppiest. "A lot of black groups are now more interested in making music that will appeal to everyone," Maurice White told *Billboard* in 1975, "than only making what used to be called soul music, and things are changing. It was simply our goal to reach everybody."

They would eventually become one of the few R&B–based acts to find a home at FM rock radio. The group, said Maurice White, had toured with "everyone from Uriah Heep to Santana to Weather Report" by 1975. And when drummer Fred White joined the line-up that year, he had worked for both Donny Hathaway and Little Feat.

"Shining Star," cut at Caribou at the tail end of '74, proved to be the record to appeal to Earth, Wind & Fire's R&B base, its FM rock cult, and—as White had hoped—everybody in between. A gold single from a double-platinum album, it was the band's only Number One pop hit; it would also make them the first R&B group to top the pop albums and singles charts simultaneously.

As for *That's the Way of the World*, the movie, it disappeared quickly. Fearing that people would see the album as a side project, not an EW&F album, White wisely had made a point of not allowing it to be labeled as a soundtrack. Eventually, however, once the record came out and did better than the movie, Sig Shore would reverse things—and retitle his picture *Shining Star*.

201

SHOESHINE BOY

Eddie Kendricks

TAMLA 54257
WRITERS: HARRY BOOKER, LINDA ALLEN
PRODUCERS: FRANK WILSON, LEONARD CASTON
April 5, 1975 (1 week)

With "Shoeshine Boy," as with so many Motown releases, the opinion of Berry Gordy made the difference.

When Eddie Kendricks's recording was first released, according to composer Linda Allen, another senior Motown executive didn't like the lyrics—arguing that they demeaned black people—and wanted the record killed. "But Berry believed in the song so much," Allen remembers. "He said a shoeshine boy could be anybody, that he didn't have to be black."

Given its chance by the boss, "Shoeshine Boy" developed into one of Kendricks's biggest hits. It was a professional milestone for Allen as well: her first published song. "It opened so many doors for me," she says. "To even have a song out as a single, a writer had to be signed exclusively to Motown. I wanted to be independent, I did not sign."

Allen worked for producer Frank Wilson, who had successfully handled Kendricks's segue from the

Eddie Kendricks

Temptations to a solo career. "I remember when Eddie first came to Frank in Detroit. He wanted to be by himself, and he wanted Frank to produce him. He was taking a risk."

It was a risk that paid off, with the singer's popularity exploding in 1973 [see 155—"Keep On Truckin'," 165—"Boogie Down"]. When time came to record his fifth album, Frank Wilson selected "Shoeshine Boy," authored by Allen with Harry Booker, a singer turned writer.

"Harry was a shoeshine boy once," she says, "and he came up with the idea. We took it from there. It was a song to encourage people, to say that no matter what you do, do the best you can. At that time, Harry and I were trying to be like Nick Ashford and Valerie Simpson as writers; I remember working on the song in an apartment in Hollywood."

Allen says Frank Wilson would have heard "Shoeshine Boy" in demo form, sung by Booker or by Wayne Cooper. "Frank would give Eddie the demo to study, then they'd record." Booker and Cooper sang backup on the session, done at Motown's studios in Hollywood. The musicians were James Jamerson or Henry Davis on bass, Ed Greene or James Gadson on drums, Melvin "Wah-Wah" Watson, Jay Graydon and Ray Parker Jr. on guitars, and Wilson's co-producer, Leonard Caston, on piano. Jerry Long and Sanford Shire were the arrangers.

"I know Eddie didn't particularly like 'Shoeshine Boy' [at first]," says Wilson, "but we convinced him it was really a good song, that it had a lot of potential as a crossover record. We basically were interested in taking him just a little bit more pop, but try and maintain enough of the soul to go up the R&B charts."

"I liked Eddie, sweet Eddie," concludes Allen. "He liked people, he spoke his mind—and he had a sense of humor. But he was like the wind, here one minute, gone the next."

202

L-O-V-E (LOVE)

Al Green

HI 2282
WRITERS: AL GREEN,
WILLIE MITCHELL, MABON HODGES
PRODUCER: WILLIE MITCHELL
April 12, 1975 (2 weeks)

Critics tend to look at Al Green's journey from sex to salvation as having happened one of two ways.

Some say there was a constant struggle for Green's soul taking place—the one that began with dad kicking him out of the house for singing secular music—that was present on all his records. Others think Green was born again after a brush with death in October 1974 when his ex-girlfriend Mary Woodson scalded him with a pot of grits, then fatally shot herself.

Green was never much help on the matter. He told Geoffrey Himes of *Musician* in the early '80s that he was born again in 1973, before the Woodson tragedy, and that no specific incident set things off.

But in 1975 the singer told Denise Hall of *Black Music* that his conversion did take place after Woodson's death (he also told Hall that after receiving Christ, he suddenly noticed flowers growing again). And there's an early-'80s label bio that attributes everything to a fall from the stage during a 1979 concert in Cincinnati.

However much of the gospel influence you find in Green's early successes, you'll find much more as things progress, especially on "L-O-V-E (Love)," the first post-Woodson single and the fifth of Green's six Number One R&B hits. Here Green sings of salvation

Al Green

and the heavens. If "Love And Happiness" was the first stylistic sighting of Rev. Al, "L-O-V-E (Love)" was the hit where Green started going about the Lord's work.

The record was also the second of his hits where guitarist Mabon "Teenie" Hodges replaced Al Jackson as co-writer. As in the past, writing was an informal affair. "Me and Al had written the song and Teenie came by," Mitchell remembers. "He said, 'Man, I like this song,' so I said, 'Well, take it home and write me...eight bars [for the middle],' so when he brought it back, we inserted that into 'L-O-V-E' and that was it."

The record is more conventionally structured than Green's earlier successes. On those, the instruments seemed to dart in and out, as if somebody had left the room to get a soda. Here, the horns are where you expect them; Howard Grimes's drums kick in at the end of the bridge to propel you back to the fade; and there are actual Philly-style strings starting the whole thing off.

As with Al's conversion, whether Willie Mitchell meant to acknowledge the sound of Philadelphia is hard to pin down. Back then, he told an interviewer that he couldn't let himself be influenced by others' success. These days, Mitchell allows that "I really admired Gamble & Huff, and Thom Bell. We used to listen to each other a lot. I really liked the smoothness they had."

203

SHAKEY GROUND

The Temptations

GORDY 7142
WRITERS: JEFFREY BOWEN, EDDIE HAZEL, AL BOYD
PRODUCERS: JEFFREY BOWEN, BERRY GORDY JR.
April 26, 1975 (1 week)

The man who produced two Number One hits for the Temptations, a couple more top ten records, *and* a Number One album, was surprisingly unpopular with members of the group.

"He saw artists as a six-pack of beer," comments Melvin Franklin about Jeffrey Bowen, meaning they were disposable after use. "He was a spaceman," says Richard Street, "from another planet." And Otis Williams, writing in his autobiography of the Temptations, said Bowen had "fine ideas," but couldn't handle people.

For all the reputed conflicts with the quintet, Bowen gave the Temps in 1975 what they'd not had since 1968: back-to-back Number One records, "Happy People" and "Shakey Ground." Furthermore, the LP that spawned those singles, *A Song for You*, is one of their most enduring—notable for such finely honed ballads as "Memories" and the title track as well as the chart-toppers.

The funk of "Shakey Ground" not only reflected Bowen's debt to the Commodores and horn arranger James Carmichael [see 194—"Happy People"], but also mirrored the background of guitarist Eddie Hazel, the song's co-writer and a member of George Clinton's Funkadelic.

Like other tracks on *A Song for You*, "Shakey Ground" was cut during 1974 at the Motown studios in Los Angeles. To get the rock-solid rhythms he wanted for the album, Bowen employed three drummers, including Zachary Frazier and California stalwart James Gadson. "He's an anchor," says Melvin Franklin of Gadson. "One of the greatest drummers."

Eddie Hazel and Melvin "Wah Wah" Ragin were guitarists on the sessions, while William (Billy Bass) Nelson fingered the bass and Donald Baldwin played all the keyboards (clavinet, piano, Moog), as well as sax and clarinet.

The Temptations at this time comprised Richard Street, Melvin Franklin, Otis Williams, Damon Harris, and lead singer Dennis Edwards. During the recording of the album, however, frictions began to develop between Harris and other members. Later, he was fired and replaced by Glenn Leonard. "We were sorry to have to drop him," commented Williams, "but, again, no one man is greater than the group."

In 1976, the Temps cut another album with Jeffrey Bowen, entitled *Wings of Love*. The experience was apparently no happier than for *A Song for You*. Melvin Franklin contends that the producer used session singers for much of the group harmony work behind Dennis Edwards.

"We were on a flight one day, and a guy turned to me and said, 'I sang bass for you on such-and-such,' " explains Franklin, still angry at the recollection. "I do my own singing! For *Wings of Love*, we were on one or two songs on that LP. [Bowen] used Dennis and that was it."

204
WHAT AM I GONNA DO WITH YOU
Barry White

20TH CENTURY 2177
WRITER: BARRY WHITE
PRODUCER: BARRY WHITE
May 3, 1975 (1 week)

I always told my lady before she became my wife, 'I have two wives, and one of them came before you did,' " says Barry White. His first "wife" was, of course, his music. Glodean understood. Music was her life, too, as the lead singer for Love Unlimited. "[She's] got two husbands. I've got two wives." When Glodean wanted to find out what was new with Barry's music, she'd ask, "What you got for your lady this time, Barry?" The maestro's fourth Number One R&B single was an ode to his first wife.

"My success was so high," Barry says when asked about "What Am I Gonna Do with You." "You ever had somebody be so good to you, you say, 'Man, what am I gonna do with you?' That's what I was saying to that lady called music. I'm sitting there with *I've Got So Much to Give* on the charts, *Stone Gon'* was still on the charts, *Can't Get Enough* was on the charts. Now here comes *Just Another Way to Say I Love You*...Love Unlimited's *Under the Influence of...* was on the charts. [Their] *In Heat* was coming out. *Rhapsody in White* is on the chart and *White Gold* is on the chart. Now what else can I say but, 'What am I gonna do with you? We've been making love for hours, for years, and baby we're still going strong.' That was my way of telling her thank you for so much. To be that young and have all of that from a person who came from nothing."

The "rup-dup-de-dup" trill at the end of the song was inspired by a number seven hit from 1966. "I got that from Billy Stewart, who did a song called 'Summertime,' " Barry reveals. "All the things that you hear in your life can appear again, and because it's old, it becomes new. I use Nat King Cole tricks, a lot of Jesse Belvin tricks, Marvin Gaye tricks, Billy Stewart tricks, [and] my own."

"What Am I Gonna Do with You" was recorded at the studio Barry loved to use in Glendale, California: Whitney Studios. The rhythm section consisted of Don Peake, David T. Walker, Ray Parker, Wah Wah Watson, Ed Greene, Wilton Felder, and Gary Coleman. The song was arranged by the man who did all of Barry's arrangements, Gene Page.

"I've admired him since 1961, when I heard he was working with Phil Spector," Barry says of his friend. "His strings always spoke in a certain way. His rhythms spoke a certain way...One day I got to meet him, the day they were arranging 'Harlem Shuffle' [by Bob and Earl]. Gene Page walked in that room ...I was honored to meet him. I didn't say much to him, I respected who he was and he was busy. In 1966, I had my first A&R job. Forty dollars a week for Mustang/Bronco. And [Bob Keene] was going to let me record. First one I hired was Gene Page."

When the Mustang/Bronco labels folded, Barry had a family to support, and no job. "Gene Page used to feed my family, pay my rent, give me gas money, food money for my children. I never had to pay him back. Tried many times...he'd never take it. When my ship came in, why would I use anybody else? When you say Barry White, Love Unlimited Orchestra, whatever else you say, always mention his name."

205
GET DOWN, GET DOWN (GET ON THE FLOOR)
Joe Simon

SPRING 156
WRITERS: RAEFORD GERALD, JOE SIMON
PRODUCERS: RAEFORD GERALD, JOE SIMON
May 10, 1975 (2 weeks)

Here's the irony of "Get Down, Get Down (Get on the Floor)": A singer who spent most of his recording career fusing country music with rhythm & blues to fine effect gained his biggest hit with a disco tune.

Coincidentally, the writer/producer who helped Joe Simon do that, Raeford Gerald, did the same for another R&B traditionalist. The very week that "Get Down" spun to the top, Garland ("Jealous Kind of Fella") Green returned to the charts with a disco workout, "Bumpin' and Stompin'," also co-written by Gerald.

Simon's label, Spring, must have wondered why it hadn't gotten him on the dance floor sooner. Just a couple of years before "Get Down," the company had been employing freelance country promotion staff to augment its pop marketing muscle on behalf of *Simon*

Country. That made-in-Nashville package—including songs by Freddy Fender and Eddy Arnold—never even charted.

The singer had tried other experiments: the 1973 theme tune from the blaxploitation movie *Cleopatra Jones*, kept Simon's name on the best-seller lists, even if it didn't exactly enhance his soul/country reputation.

Roy Rifkind, who was one of the principals at Spring, says it was the label's idea to match Simon with Raeford Gerald. Most of Joe's earlier work for Spring was produced by his manager, John Richbourg. When Richbourg fell ill, Simon tried producing himself and also worked with Brad Shapiro.

Joe Simon

Gerald was signed to Spring as a writer/producer and worked with Simon on his very first chart single for the label, "Your Time to Cry," as well as on hits like "Ask Me What You Want" and "My Man, A Sweet Man" for the company's other leading R&B artist, Millie Jackson. Gerald was also signed to Spring as an artist. As Ray Godfrey, he charted in 1970 with "I Gotta Get Away (From My Own Self)." Four years later, he had a number 40 hit in England with a dance-oriented song called "Tom the Peeper," under the name Act One.

"Joe used to hang out at the office and Rae used to write in the office," Rifkind remembers. He suggested they go in the studio and see what results they would get. "They would record practically all night and then the next morning they would bring in a dub and we would listen to it," says the label founder.

One morning Simon and Gerald brought in the rhythm tracks to the song that would become "Get Down, Get Down (Get on the Floor)." Rifkind recalls, "When we heard the rhythm tracks we realized there was a certain feel there; we knew it would be a smash."

The song also fulfilled one particular wish that Rifkind had for Joe Simon. "I really wanted him to cross over. 'Get Down, Get Down' was the record that did it." Indeed, it was Simon's first and only top 10 hit on the pop chart. He had come close three times—"The Chokin' Kind" peaked at number 13 and both "Drowning in the Sea of Love" and "The Power of Love" reached number 11. Shortly after "Get Down, Get Down (Get on the Floor)" reached the summit of the R&B chart, Simon finally made the pop top 10, as the tune went to number eight on the Hot 100 the week of June 21, 1975.

206

BABY THAT'S BACKATCHA

Smokey Robinson

TAMLA 54258
WRITER: WILLIAM "SMOKEY" ROBINSON
PRODUCER: WILLIAM "SMOKEY" ROBINSON
May 24, 1975 (1 week)

As Fred Smith's flute cuts through the breeze, shadowed by Wayne Tweed's bass, a quiet storm blows over the horizon. That's Smokey Robinson, and "Baby That's Backatcha."

When he left the Miracles in 1972, Motown's premier poet gained the freedom to test the creative climate around him. "During the time I've been off the road," Robinson told *Black Music*, "I've been doing a lot of listening to other groups, something I never had too much opportunity to do before.

"There was one thing that really struck me the more I listened, and that was the growing emphasis on the funky thing, heavy brass, that type of thing. It seemed like that's where just about everybody was coming from."

True enough. Even Smokey's erstwhile troubadours, the Temptations, were funkin' around. Their "Happy People," featuring a rhythm track by the Commodores [see 194], was at Number One the week before Motown released "Baby That's Backatcha."

"So I decided to concentrate on another direction," Robinson said, "and go completely away from that particular sound. I figured there were enough people into that bag already without me adding my two cents' worth. Without the pressures involved in running a group, I've been able to spend more time in the studios, and experiment 'til I could come up with a sound that satisfied my ear and my soul."

The satisfying result was *A Quiet Storm*, the third solo album of Smokey's career, preceded by "Baby That's Backatcha," the first Number One of that solo career.

To further make his point, Robinson cut his vocals in a lower key. "There are so many artists singing in a higher key," he said. "I knew that I had to change my style to get where I want to go. So now my sound appears softer and my voice clearer."

Swirling around *A Quiet Storm* were the woodwinds of Fred Smith, the electric cello of Michael Jacobsen, the keyboards of Russ Turner, and, of course, the exquisite guitar of Robinson's lifetime collaborator, Marv Tarplin. The arrangements were done by Turner and Robinson.

Other vital contributors were Joseph Brown on drums, Wayne Tweed on bass, and James "Alibe" Sledge on bongos and congas. Singing background were Sledge, Turner, Melba Bradford, and Carmen Bryant. The album was recorded at Motown's Hollywood studios.

"I owe an awful lot to the musicians who were involved, they really got the feel exactly how I visualized it," said Robinson at the time. "I just hope other people, the public, feel the same way about it as I do. I hope with this album I've found a corner in the music world that's for me, my place, you know?"

He did, of course. In addition to its R&B impact, "Baby That's Backatcha" did better on the pop charts than any previous Robinson release. Likewise, *A Quiet Storm* ranked as his top-selling solo album until 1979's *Where There's Smoke* blew into town.

207

SPIRIT OF THE BOOGIE

Kool & the Gang

DE-LITE 1567
WRITERS: RONALD BELL, DONAL BOYCE, KOOL & THE GANG
PRODUCERS: RONALD BELL, KOOL & THE GANG
May 31, 1975 (1 week)

One weekend in New York, Robert Bell asked to borrow a bass guitar. It was around 1964 and he was at the celebrated Cafe Wha' in Greenwich Village. "Every Sunday," Bell explained, "they had a hootenanny with Richie Havens, some country and western people, and an Afro ensemble playing percussion...us."

Fingering the borrowed bass, Bell essayed "Comin' Home Baby," Mel Torme's hit of a year earlier, "which you can play on one string. That was the beginning of my becoming a bass player."

The "us" in Bell's tale were the musicians who became known as Kool & the Gang five years later, anchored by his bass dexterity. "We depend on those bass riffs and most of our hits started out from the bassline," Bell's brother, Ronald, told *Blues & Soul* in 1975. "I'm so brainwashed to thinking of the bassline that I even start off with a bassline when I'm writing material.

"On the up-tempo things, that bassline is probably even more important. Listen to 'Funky Stuff,' 'Jungle Boogie,' or 'Hollywood Swinging'—they all had the bassline to start with. And they were all recorded within hours of each other."

On "Spirit of the Boogie," according to Bayyan, "we were trying to get a harder sound, using a double bass—synthesizer bass and Kool's bass. It was also an experimentation with close harmonies on the horns. And that's [the group's alto sax player] Dee Tee singing 'Yeah, yeah, yeah.' "

"Spirit of the Boogie" was a clever, albeit more spiritual, nod to the group's first certified-gold single, "Jungle Boogie." Says Bayyan, "I was coming out of Mediasound and it hit me—I heard the melody in my head, with the chord changes on top.

"The hook came to me right then, too: *It's the spirit of the Boogie/The baddest little boogie in the land*. Sometimes song ideas, melodies, or hooks float out there. I just heard this one, picked it up, moved on it, and started playing."

Another hook repeated from "Jungle Boogie" was the vocal effects of Donal Boyce, who was part of Kool & the Gang's technical crew, working sound and lights. "But he had a voice that could do anything," Bayyan recalls. "We'd be working and he'd make all these different voices. I said, 'Hey, set up the mike and let's go.' Live, he'd do his bit during those songs, then go back to the tech side."

This "Spirit" had an afterlife, too. Its B-side was "Summer Madness," a cool Kool instrumental that reached the R&B top 40 in its own right during 1975, then came back in Sylvester Stallone's *Rocky* two years later.

"Nobody had told us," remembers Cleveland Brown, a key member of Kool & the Gang's staff. "We were watching this movie about a white boxer. When it came to the scene where Stallone dropped the needle on the record, and 'Summer Madness' started playing. I can tell you we got pretty loud in the theater."

208

LOVE WON'T LET ME WAIT

Major Harris

ATLANTIC 3248
WRITERS: BOBBY ELI, VINNIE BARRETT
PRODUCER: BOBBY ELI
June 7, 1975 (1 week)

Sure, "Love Won't Let Me Wait" was an above-average Philly soul ballad, from a town where even average was better than most records from elsewhere. But what really promoted Major Harris to the top of his rank was the, uh, climax.

"We cut the thing in such a way that it would bring out the sexy atmosphere of the song," the singer explained to *Black Music* in 1975. "The session was on a summer day, so we turned the lights down in the studio to get the right kinda atmosphere...We were gonna put some rain noises in there, too, 'cause folk seem to dig making love on rainy days. We shelved that idea, but we kept the sexy lady."

That would be Barbara Ingram, part of a trio of Philadelphia background singers (her partners were Carla Benton and Yvette Benson) heard behind the Spinners and the Stylistics, among many others. The session took place at Sigma Sound.

"Yes, Barbara did the moans," says Gwen Woolfolk, co-author of "Love Won't Let Me Wait" under her writing name of Vinnie Barrett. "We had to lock the doors to keep the guys from getting to her! All the lights were off in the studio—except Major had a little light on his lyric stand."

Woolfolk and partner Bobby Eli had composed the song in about 20 minutes flat, at three o'clock one morning in Eli's Philadelphia apartment. "We had just come from an MFSB session," she says. "Bobby played guitar for them from day one. We were working on another song, and this title came up because we were talking about always having to wait. But love won't let you wait!"

Later, the song was chosen for Major Harris's debut Atlantic album, soon after he had signed with the independent Philly production firm known as WMOT. "What happened the night it was recorded was Bobby's idea," says Woolfolk. "He said, 'Why don't we do an interlude, where you really have some exaggeration about what's going on?' " She says they learned to create an atmosphere in the studio from producer Kenny Gamble. "He was a great one for doing that."

Eli, who arranged and produced the record, also played the track's distinctive guitar. With him were bassist Ron Baker, drummer Earl Shelton, pianist Ron Kersey, percussionist Larry Washington, and another guitarist, Norman Harris. Strings and horns were directed by Don Renaldo.

Major Harris himself had hooked up with the WMOT (We Men of Talent) team while a member of the Delfonics, the archetypal '70s falsetto soulsters from the City of Brotherly Love. Earlier, he was produced by Stan Watson, who recorded the Delfonics for his Philly Groove label.

"Love Won't Let Me Wait" appeared first as a five-minute track on Harris's *My Way*, while another song slugged it out as a 45. When radio got the album, however, their turntables cued up Major's "interlude" with Barbara Ingram. "I got a call from Ron Sutton at WHUR Washington," says Gwen Woolfolk. "He said, 'I *insist* on playing this ballad.' "

209

ROCKIN' CHAIR

Gwen McCrae

CAT 1996
WRITERS: CLARENCE REID, WILLIE CLARKE
PRODUCERS: STEVE ALAIMO,
WILLIE CLARKE, CLARENCE REID
June 14, 1975 (1 week)

Using one of the oldest metaphors in rhythm & blues, "Rockin' Chair" was originally earmarked for Betty Wright, first lady of song at Henry Stone's T.K. Productions. When she declined to rock it, the tune went to Gwen McCrae, the company's second distaff star.

"Rockin' Chair" was written by Clarence Reid and Willie Clarke, who had been part of Stone's creative team since the mid-'60s. Their big break came in 1968 with Wright's "Girls Can't Do What the Guys Do," a top 20 hit.

Reid, Wright, and Clarke hung out together. "I had a car at the time, because I was teaching school," remembers Clarke. "We would go from place to place, and wherever they had a piano, that's where we would work. The three of us would be together from sun-up 'til sundown and then some. We would put these songs together."

Meanwhile, Henry Stone's shop had also signed Gwen McCrae and husband George. They began recording together with producers Steve Alaimo and Brad Shapiro, but couldn't cut a hit. "Then George decided to manage Gwen," says Alaimo. "She was a brilliant singer, and since the duet things weren't happening, I decided to work with her." In 1970, he produced Gwen's first success, "Lead Me On."

As the '70s advanced, Stone's company became progressively hotter with Betty Wright ("Clean Up Woman"), Timmy Thomas [see 140—"Why Can't We Live Together"], and Latimore [see 185—"Let's Straighten It Out"], among others.

In 1974, George McCrae got his turn at Number One [see 177—"Rock Your Baby"] with a song originally written for Gwen. And so, says Alaimo, "there was a problem. George had already resigned himself to being her manager, but then he got the big hit. So the heat was on, because I had to cut a record on Gwen. I went to Clarence Reid and said, 'We gotta come up with something.' "

By this time, Betty Wright had passed on "Rockin' Chair," and a version by Reid himself was on the shelf. "Clarence was never a great singer," comments Alaimo, "but we made records on him 'cause he wanted to sing." (He was also money in the bank for T.K. as Blowfly, purveyor of porno records.)

The "Rockin' Chair" track was already cut, declares Willie Clarke. "All they had to do was put it on the machine and put the vocals on." The musicians were Ron Bogdon on bass, Robert Furgeson on drums, and "the keyboard player probably had to be Timmy Thomas," according to Clarke, who says that George McCrae and his wife did the background vocals. "George was a very creative person. When he put that little 'Rock Your Baby' chant into 'Rockin' Chair,' that really set it off."

True enough. Like a southern Motown, the T.K. labels benefited from an open creative atmosphere—and an open door. "People just walked in off the street, over the railroad tracks," says Steve Alaimo. "We never turned anybody away, never recorded anybody who people had already heard of. We were eager to be successful, and worked hard."

"It was like a family-type situation," agrees Willie Clarke. "Betty [Wright] sang on most of the stuff that came out of there. So did Gwen, George, KC. Most of the singers would do the vocalizing for each other.

"It was exciting—and I don't think there was another record company who offered people the opportunities Henry Stone did. Whatever [music fans] wanted at that time, Henry would say, 'Let 'em have it.' "

210

GIVE THE PEOPLE WHAT THEY WANT

The O'Jays

PHILADELPHIA INTERNATIONAL 3565
WRITERS: KENNY GAMBLE, LEON HUFF
PRODUCERS: KENNY GAMBLE, LEON HUFF
June 21, 1975 (1 week)

"Was that a Number One record?" Eddie Levert says with some surprise in his voice when asked about "Give the People What They Want."

He shouldn't be expected to have kept tabs, especially when you consider that the O'Jays have 10 Number One hits. And it's not as if he doesn't remember the tune. The first thing that comes to mind when he hears the title is the unusual high-hat rhythm in the song. "[Kenny] Gamble was able to set it so far out in the track. It was basically the thing that carried that whole track, and everything else moved along with it. It was our very first funky-bluesy kind of thing. I didn't realize that was Number One—*that's* why it still survives today. Every once in a while we do it in its entirety, but mostly we do it in medley form."

But not always. Walter Williams mentions that the song was only recently removed from medley status. " 'Give the People What They Want' was another one of those message songs that I thought was hardcore but true," Walter comments about the musical plea for "freedom, justice, and equality." He adds, "I think it was a message that Gamble wanted to get out. He had some messages that he wanted to get out to the people and he used the O'Jays to do that." Williams makes it clear he doesn't think that Gamble was misusing the O'Jays and that they were a proper vehicle for the songwriter's messages.

While the O'Jays still include major hits like "Back Stabbers" and "Love Train" in their act, Williams isn't sure the messages are listened to as closely today as they were in the '70s. "I think people hear them and don't hear them," he says on a break from recording in the O'Jays' studio in Ohio. "They were good messages. I don't know if they're depressing today or if time has moved somewhere else. Things haven't changed that much. People have changed and probably do not want to hear as many messages as we did in those days."

Williams reflects on the fact that the O'Jays are still together, more than 40 years after he first met Eddie Levert. "I met Eddie when I was six and he was seven. He had two brothers, Andrew and Tommy, and we used to sing spiritual songs together in church on Sunday. We met in the neighborhood one summer when Eddie moved in. We discovered we could sing, clowned around doing it, and then got serious."

Walter was 15 and Eddie was 16 when they turned professional. "I had a dream I would probably retire from this when I was 30," laughs Williams, who was 31 when "Back Stabbers" became the O'Jays first Number One song. "At one point I wanted to get out of it and perhaps manage some other singers or get into producing or writing a little more. But it didn't happen that way and I don't regret it. I'm starting to venture into it now, and a lot more successfully."

211

LOOK AT ME (I'M IN LOVE)

The Moments

STANG 5060
WRITERS: AL GOODMAN, HARRY RAY, WALTER MORRIS
PRODUCERS: AL GOODMAN, HARRY RAY, WALTER MORRIS
June 28, 1975 (1 week)

Like other songs recorded by the Moments, "Look at Me (I'm in Love)" began life around Al Goodman's kitchen table in his Hackensack, New Jersey, home. Goodman and the group's Harry Ray often worked in that informal setting, according to their longtime guitarist, Walter Morris. "That's basically where all our songs started," he explains.

The Moments had been to the top of the charts before [see 89—"Love on a Two-Way Street"], and were comfortable with the creative process. From Hackensack, they'd motor to Joe and Sylvia Robinson's All Platinum Records in nearby Englewood, where a second-floor studio played host to the next stage.

"We had Bernadette Randle on keyboards, just messing around with the song then, before we put it together," says Morris. "From there, Sammy Lowe charted the arrangement and we went downstairs and recorded it."

Upstairs was an eight-track studio for woodshedding; below was the 16-track for serious recording. "We never had the luxuries of the big studios of that time," comments Clarence Oliver, who played drums on "Look at Me" as part of the All Platinum house band, "but we had a lot of groove and raw talent. And we had good people."

One of them was the late Sammy Lowe. "Look how he would do those string arrangements," says Oliver. "Guys would come in and hum the strings, and Sam wrote it all down. It made everyone look like geniuses.

The Moments

The Commodores

"But the environment was very loose. It wasn't by the clock, 'cause we weren't on the clock. It wasn't like New York, across the bridge there. We could do as many takes as we wanted, although we played so well together that they started calling us 'one-take.'"

Oliver, Morris, Randle, and bass player Jonathan Williams were that rhythm section, which powered other All Platinum milestones, including Shirley & Company's "Shame, Shame, Shame" [see 197]. "At first, we were a band that played on the road a lot with the Moments," says the drummer. "But after they found out how well we worked together, we started to do things with Sylvia. And it just snowballed from her to all the artists."

The exquisite, full-harmony sound of the Moments, as popular as that of the Delfonics, Blue Magic, the Stylistics, and other '70s vocal groups, was All Platinum at its most up-market, and the string sound played a major role. "It was a pretty good studio," said Sammy Lowe some years later, "large enough for that whole string section. I've used as many as 12 violins. We would make the track first, then I'd write for the strings. If we wanted somebody on another instrument, like an oboe, we'd dub it on."

Most of the other All Platinum releases were no-frills and funky—as much because of studio limitations as anything else. "We got as high as 24-track," explained Lowe, "but we started off with two." Frequently, the Moments' Al Goodman would double as an engineer. "He and I were in the studio late at night because we had to do this whole album in one week," the arranger recalled. "Al and I were real tight."

212

SLIPPERY WHEN WET

Commodores

MOTOWN 1338
WRITER: THOMAS McCLARY
PRODUCER: JAMES ANTHONY CARMICHAEL, THE COMMODORES
July 5, 1975 (1 week)

Patience wasn't a virtue for the Commodores—it was a necessity. The group joined Motown Records in July 1971, becoming one of the first signings to the company's freshly minted MoWest label. They opened for the Jackson 5 at Madison Square Garden that same month, but three years passed before their first chart entry, "Machine Gun."

Another 14 months elapsed before the group's' first R&B chart-topper, "Slippery When Wet," and it was three years more before their first pop Number One, "Three Times a Lady."

"The talent was always there," says Gloria Jones, the singer/songwriter [see 99—"If I Were Your Woman"] who co-authored and co-produced "The Zoo (The Human Zoo)," the Commodores' first release on MoWest. "They were from the South and here they were in Hollywood—they had this rawness, this freshness and energy, that was just amazing."

The group comprised Walter Orange on drums, Ronald LaPread on bass, Thomas McClary on guitar, William King on trumpet, Milan Williams on keyboards, and Lionel Richie on sax. "Walter was doing all of the lead vocals," recalls Jones. "I suggested to [Motown's] Suzanne dePasse that I wanted to change the sound. I said, 'I'd like to put Lionel behind the microphone.' "

Richie certainly handled lead lines on "The Zoo," but it was mostly a group effort—as were "Machine Gun" and "I Feel Sanctified," the Commodores' first pair of hits in 1974. "They were actually a band that could perform right there in the studio," says Jones.

"Slippery When Wet" was their third chart success, a skin tight fusion of rhythm 'n' horns arranged and produced by James Carmichael at Motown's Hollywood studios. Significantly, it was the company's first Number One to feature the kind of ensemble funk being popularized in 1974–75 by the Ohio Players, Kool & and the Gang, and Earth, Wind & Fire.

The song was composed by guitarist Thomas McClary, founder member of the Commodores. "I always considered myself primarily a guitarist, then a songwriter," he said. "Music is about having strong lyrics, great melodies and arrangements that are there for a purpose, and not just haphazardly thrown together. Everything really has to go toward that one theme."

McClary purposefully formed the group at college, Alabama's Tuskegee Institute. "There was a freshman talent show and I decided to get a group together," he told *Billboard*. "I had learned the ukulele, so I switched to guitar pretty easily.

"I was walking around on campus and bumped into Lionel Richie. We talked about playing together and went down into his grandmother's basement, where he blew my mind by playing Herbie Hancock's 'Maiden Voyage' note for note."

McClary, Richie, and trumpeter William King teamed up for the talent show, recognizing they were onto something as they prepared tunes by James Brown ("Cold Sweat") and Lou Rawls. "We rehearsed for about 30 minutes," said McClary, "and everyone in the room got a feeling that we could all be big together, because there was such a perfect chemistry there."

213

THE HUSTLE

Van McCoy & The Soul City Symphony

AVCO 4653

WRITER: VAN MCCOY

PRODUCERS: HUGO PERETTI, LUIGI CREATORE

July 12, 1975 (1 week)

The *real* McCoy was responsible for such superior rhythm & blues as "Getting Mighty Crowded" by Betty Everett, "The Sweetest Thing This Side of Heaven" by Chris Bartley, "Right on the Tip of My Tongue" by Brenda and the Tabulations, and "Giving Up" by Gladys Knight & the Pips.

The McCoy most will remember was responsible for "The Hustle."

In truth, the origins of "The Hustle" can be traced to others: to producers Hugo and Luigi, to disco DJ David Todd, and to Charles Kipps Jr., who was McCoy's business partner at the time [see 233—"Walk Away from Love"].

"Van was working on an album for Hugo and Luigi," says Kipps, "which came about because he had been doing arrangements for the Stylistics. In discussions with Hugo and Luigi, they were convinced—or agreed—to do an instrumental album with Van.

"He always wanted to be a vocalist, they wanted to do an instrumental album. We were in New York and Van was busy writing arrangements for the album. The session was the next morning, and he was busy finishing something. He'd been invited by a disc jockey at a club called the Adam's Apple. He was busy, so I went. That was one of the pluses of not being an arranger: You could do whatever you wanted the night before a session.

"So I saw this dance [at the club], the hustle, and it was an amazing thing. Up until that time, people in discos and clubs weren't touching—and all of a sudden, there was this elaborate kind of hand-holding and dancing and that kind of thing.

"I came back about midnight and told Van about it, and he said, 'What do you think about a song called "The Hustle"?' I tried to describe the dance the best I could, and he wrote 'The Hustle' literally then: He wrote it, arranged it, and went into the session the next day, and recorded it as kind of the eleventh song."

This was early 1975, and McCoy was working at Mediasound in Manhattan, gainfully employing his favorite highly skilled musicians: Gordon Edwards on bass, Steve Gadd and Rick Marotta on drums, Richard Tee on electric piano, Eric Gale and John Tropea on guitars, plus horn and string sections directed by Gene Orloff. McCoy himself played acoustic piano.

As "The Hustle" was being tracked, co-producer Hugo Peretti suggested using a piccolo—played by Philip Bodner—for the tune's instrumental motif, rather than the guitar that had originally been deployed by McCoy.

"Once 'The Hustle' became a hit," explains Kipps, "the dance took off, and it became kind of a different dance. The hustle I saw was a Latin hustle. When 'The Hustle' came out and it was much more soaring strings and pop and piccolo and all that stuff, people started doing a different kind of hustle spontaneously—which was more like a ballroom dance. So that extent, the record did create a different dance."

Van McCoy

214

FIGHT THE POWER (PART 1)

The Isley Brothers

T-NECK 2256
WRITERS: ERNIE ISLEY, MARVIN ISLEY, CHRIS JASPER, RUDOLPH ISLEY, O'KELLY ISLEY, RONALD ISLEY
PRODUCERS: THE ISLEY BROTHERS
July 19, 1975 (3 weeks)

If the Isley Brothers had recorded a song with lyrics like "Fight the Power" in 1956, the authorities would have come calling. During those Eisenhower days, as Ronald, Rudolph, and O'Kelly Isley began their career [see 72—"It's Your Thing"], black musicians didn't make records about "all that bullshit going down."

Fast-forward to 1975: A younger brother, Ernie Isley, hops into the shower just before his first visit to Disneyland. "I turned on the water," he recalls, "and started singing, *Time is truly wasting/There's no guarantee/ Smiles in the making/Fight the Powers that be*. The idea came like a bolt of lightning. I jumped out of the shower and wrote that down!"

"Fight the Power" became the lead-off single for *The Heat Is On*, the first Isleys' LP to go all the way to the pop chart peak. It was also their biggest success since 1973's *3 + 3*, the album that formally introduced younger brothers Ernie and Marvin Isley and cousin Chris Jasper.

"We'd been in the studio and touring [with Ron, Rudy, and O'Kelly] for a couple of years before *3 + 3*," explains Jasper, who was the group's keyboard player. "But that was the first time we all appeared on the cover of an album."

By then, the Isleys were well and truly rejuvenated. Guitarist Ernie, who also played drums on their records, explains, "The sound essentially changed—although there was no plan for it to change—from like a horn-group thing to more of a hard rhythm section. 'It's Your Thing' was one kind of sound, 'Work to Do' was another, which was basically stripped down. We started to incorporate more of the drums/bass/keyboards/guitar thing, and the vocals became much more identifiable."

The Heat Is On was cut early in 1975 at Kendun Recorders, Los Angeles. Explaining the song's provocative lyrics, Ernie says that, originally, "instead of singing 'bullshit,' I had said 'nonsense.' When Ronald started singing it, he used the BS word, and I thought, 'Oh yeah, we're going to change that' [on the album], I didn't know it was going to be permanent.

"When it came time to remix it, I said, 'You're going to have grandmothers and kids listening. You're the Isley Brothers and here you start getting a little street, a little vulgar—somebody's going to say something.' " The others disagreed. "They said, 'Look, the lyrical direction of the song is such that it merits this, Ernie. Let's stand up and say what we're talking about, as opposed to trying to be PG about it.' And, of course, when it was put that way, that was the way it was taken."

Still, Ernie Isley laughs at the memory of playing "Fight the Power" in concert, "and when we'd get to the bridge, we had 18,000 people singing 'bullshit going down!' "

215

HOPE THAT WE CAN BE TOGETHER SOON

Sharon Paige and Harold Melvin & the Blue Notes

PHILADELPHIA INTERNATIONAL 3569
WRITERS: KENNY GAMBLE, LEON HUFF
PRODUCERS: KENNY GAMBLE, LEON HUFF, HAROLD MELVIN
August 9, 1975 (1 week)

When Dusty Springfield recorded the follow-up to her acclaimed 1969 *Dusty in Memphis* album, some said she should have called it *Dusty in Philadelphia*. That's because the British singer's *A Brand New Me* was written and produced by Kenny Gamble and Leon Huff at Sigma Sound Studios. One of the songs on side one was "Let's Get Together Soon." While it didn't make any noise for Dusty, it was reworked five years later by Gamble and Huff and released under the title "Hope That We Can Be Together Soon" as a duet featuring Sharon Paige and Teddy Pendergrass.

Philadelphia-born Paige had appeared at some local talent shows before crossing paths with Gamble and Huff. Eventually she managed to get an office job at Philadelphia International. "Gamble and Huff didn't think I could sing and I spent a year just working in the office," she told a journalist.

Harold Melvin disagreed with Gamble and Huff. "She had a hell of a sound," he opines. He gave her a chance to perform with the Blue Notes on stage at the Mark IV club in Washington, D.C. "I always felt [the Dusty Springfield song] was a smash...That was the first song I showed [Sharon]. I went in to Sigma Sound and took my musicians that played with me on the road. I cut the track and Gamble didn't even know."

Bobby Eli, lead guitarist for MFSB, joined Melvin and his musicians in the studio. "I played all the guitars on that because I was the only [guitar player] who showed up that day. Harold put the rhythm track together—I don't remember Gamble being there. I would do a lot of sessions just with Harold, without Gamble. Of course, looking on the record, it says produced by Gamble and Huff...I guess Gamble and Huff finished it up. But that was Harold's baby. I remember putting the vocal down with Sharon—I liked it right away. I thought it was different and thought it was going to be humongous."

Engineer Joe Tarsia notified Kenny that something was happening in the studio, according to Harold. "Joe called him and said, 'Did you hear there's something that Harold's cutting down here? You should hear this song!' And then Gamble called in Bobby Martin, the master arranger, and we cut the track. Gamble listened to the track and we brought Teddy and Sharon in and myself, and we put the vocals on."

Pendergrass, who would later record chart duets with Stephanie Mills ("Two Hearts") and Whitney Houston ("Hold Me"), went to Number One with his first duet partner, Sharon Paige. "It was a pleasure to have our little angel sing on the song with us," Teddy says. "We all wanted her to have a record. It was her chance to shine."

216

DREAM MERCHANT

New Birth

BUDDAH 470
WRITERS: LARRY WEISS, JERRY ROSS
PRODUCERS: JAMES BAKER, MELVIN WILSON
August 16, 1975 (1 week)

New Birth's "fast-paced, well coordinated act...brings the audience to its feet in a bacchanalian burst of revelry," declared *Billboard* in 1973, apparently unafraid of hyperbole.

New Birth

"I had a concept that I wanted to try out with New Birth," explained the bacchanalia's originator, Harvey Fuqua, better known as a Motown songwriter and producer. "It's so hard for an act to get work without a hit record, and there were so many people involved in New Birth and the band and everything—about 17 people altogether—that I was gonna make it four acts in one. Then if one guy got a hit, the complete package could still work: 'If you wanna see so-and-so, then you gotta take everybody else,' that kind of deal."

The four acts in New Birth's carnival were the Nite-Lighters, the Mint Juleps, the New Sound, and Alan Frye. Fuqua launched them from his Louisville hometown—where he settled after leaving Motown—and snared an RCA recording contract.

In 1973, the band's multi-textured, high-concept R&B pulled off a top 40 pop album, *Birth Day*, fueled by "It's Impossible," their first hit single. Yes, that's the Perry Como "It's Impossible," stripped and resprayed with the help of Londee Loren's industrial-strength voice.

A couple of years later, a leaner New Birth—down to a mere 12 musicians—had split from Fuqua and RCA and joined Buddah Records. For good measure, though, lead singer Loren still popped out of a four-by-eight-foot "egg" on stage.

Their Buddah debut, *Blind Baby*, featured Londee, Alan Frye, and brothers Melvin and Leslie Wilson as vocalists, backed by James Baker (keyboards), Robin Russell (drums), Carl McDaniel and Charlie Hearndon (guitars), Leroy Taylor (bass), Robert Jackson (trumpet), Austin Lander (baritone sax), and Tony Churchill (tenor).

The album, recorded at Sunwest Recording Studios in Hollywood, featured 11 New Birth originals and "Dream Merchant," a remake. "I don't know why, but we have always been more successful on singles with other people's songs," Frye told *Blues & Soul*. "Our biggest hit has been 'I Can Understand It,' and that was written by Bobby Womack. Then there was 'Wildflower,' and that wasn't our own. And [neither] was 'Until It's Time for You to Go.' "

With "Dream Merchant," New Birth revived a song originally written for Jerry Butler by Jerry Ross and Larry Weiss. Ross was A&R director for Mercury Records, "and Jerry was one of my favorite R&B balladeers," he says. "The first thing I cut with him from my 'A' file [of songs] was 'I Dig You Baby,' and that turned his career around.

"I was friendly at that time with Larry Weiss, and we came up with the idea of a song about hope, faith and someone who would make a wish come true—a dream merchant."

Ross says he was pleased and surprised at New Birth's remake, which outsold the 1967 original. "They took it in a different direction—kind of funky—but it's the type of song where the poetry of the lyric tells the story."

217

GET DOWN TONIGHT

KC and the Sunshine Band

T.K. 1009
WRITERS: HARRY WAYNE CASEY, RICHARD FINCH
PRODUCERS: HARRY WAYNE CASEY, RICHARD FINCH
August 23, 1975 (1 week)

Harry Wayne Casey, better known as KC, grew up in Hialeah, Florida, in a musical family that enjoyed singing gospel songs. His mother and her sisters sang on commercials produced in Miami. "So I was always around the business in a way, not pop at that time, but the gospel part of it. I was one of the lucky ones gifted with playing the keyboards."

At 16, KC was in a band called Five Doors Down. "I didn't play the keyboards. I just sang. When I played the piano, I played privately at the house. When I recorded the first [KC and the Sunshine Band] record, it wasn't until I went to England on a tour that I realized, 'Oh my God, I've got to play and sing at the same time.' "

A big fan of Motown, Atlantic, and Stax, KC also worked in a Hialeah record store. Picking up records at Tone Distributors, he was invited to visit the T.K. recording studios owned by the company. "Right then, there was a feeling that, 'I want to be around here,' " he remembers. "So I used to hang out there every day after work. I'd sit around for hours and hours. Finally they gave me a key to the door." KC did odd jobs for free until he was allowed to play keyboards on some sessions, which led to producing T.K. artists like Betty Wright, Jimmy (Bo) Horne, and George McCrae [see 177—"Rock Your Baby"].

About a year after KC went to work at T.K., Indianapolis-born Rick Finch was hired to work in the studio for $46 a week. "He was very electronically inclined," says KC. "He loved to tear things apart and fix them. We both seemed like underdogs [at the company] and I had some insight there was something greater there." After the success of "Rock Your Baby" and some early hits by the studio aggregation known as "KC and the Sunshine Junkanoo Band" in Great Britain, KC decided it was time to put something permanent together. "I went to the three musicians who played with me, Robert [Johnson] on drums, Rick [Finch] on bass, Jerome [Smith] played guitar and I said, 'I think there's something happening here. Why don't we become a group?' "

After "Queen of Clubs" and "Sound Your Funky Horn" made the top 20 in the U.K., KC and the Sunshine Band returned from a British tour to record their second album in Florida. One of the songs they cut for that sophomore disc was a Casey-Finch song called "Get Down Tonight." KC didn't realize at first that the rush of notes in the intro was a technique once used by Les Paul. "It was a slowing down of the track and putting a guitar on slow and then speeding the track back up to its original speed," says KC, who loved the final result. "I remember there being a kind of euphoria, something strange. It's something I can't really explain. I must have played it a hundred times and I knew something special had happened."

"Get Down Tonight" entered the R&B chart on April 12, 1975, and the pop chart exactly three months later on July 12. "I remember it going on the *Billboard* charts and falling down and I went to [T.K. founder] Henry [Stone] and said, 'Henry, "Get Down Tonight" is a smash. What's going on?' We then left for Europe and by the time we came back, it was Number One on the charts."

KC's critics must have been surprised. "They said I would never make it: 'You sound black, and white people don't make it doing that.' I wasn't copying anyone...I do what comes from my soul."

Graham Central Station

218
YOUR LOVE
Graham Central Station

WARNER BROS. 8105
WRITER/PRODUCER: LARRY GRAHAM
August 30, 1975 (1 week)

Sly Stone was the engine of the Family Stone, but the greater his speed, the greater the risk of derailment. In 1970, the group missed almost a third of its scheduled concert stops; the following year, Stone was late delivering new material to Columbia Records [see 118—"Family Affair"].

Bass player Larry Graham disembarked from the Family Stone in 1972. "When I left," he says, "I didn't have plans on starting my own band. There was the group of musicians called Hot Chocolate, and I was going to be their producer and songwriter.

"After a lot of rehearsing and things to get the band together, one night we played a club called Bimbo's in San Francisco. The place was packed, and on the last song, I sat in. Something clicked—and the whole place went nuts. It was obvious to all of us that something had just happened. And it was obvious that I had to be in this band."

Hot Chocolate became Graham Central Station, and opened for business in 1973. Warner Bros. Records came calling, and soon the group was steaming ahead with a hit single ("Can You Handle It?") and a pair of well-received albums.

Then "Your Love" arrived. "It felt like a good record," declares Graham, "but I can't say it was obviously a hit song, because a lot of the things we were doing were unique to Warner Bros. There was no other group on the label that had that kind of sound. It was like, 'What do we do with this?' It had that kind of hit feel to it, but we just had to wait and see what the company would get behind."

In fact, "Your Love" turned into black gold and the Burbank label's first R&B Number One. "Everybody was really excited about that," recalls Graham, "and it was also the first hit I'd ever had singing falsetto. It just fit the song in my mind when I created it. That was just the way it should go, and then later dropping to my natural voice."

The recording was done around spring 1975 at the Wally Heider studios in San Francisco, as part of the Station's third album, *Ain't No 'Bout-A-Doubt It*. On synthesizer and vocals was Patryce "Chocolate" Banks, with Robert Sam on organ, David Vega on guitar, Manuel Kellough on drums, and Hershall Kennedy on clavinet. Lending support were the Tower of Power horns.

"I was looking for uniqueness," says Graham, "which I found in David Vega—he was a unique guitar player. I found it in Chocolate—she was very different from other female vocalists. That was the ingredient I was looking for in the original Hot Chocolate. The band had everything except the bass player. He wasn't very unique, and I guess that's why when I sat in with the band, it clicked."

219

HOW LONG (BETCHA' GOT A CHICK ON THE SIDE)

Pointer Sisters

ABC/BLUE THUMB 265

WRITERS: ANITA POINTER, RUTH POINTER, JUNE POINTER, BONNIE POINTER, DAVID RUBINSON

PRODUCER: DAVID RUBINSON

September 6, 1975 (2 weeks)

Producer David Rubinson, a partner in Bill Graham's Fillmore Corporation, first heard the Pointer Sisters when they sang backing vocals on demos recorded by songwriter Michael Takemitsu. Rubinson asked the four siblings from Oakland, California, to sing background vocals for Cold Blood and Tower of Power. When the Pointers received an offer from Zebra Records, they flew to Texas to record their own album. "Next thing I know, I got a call [at] two o'clock in the morning from Anita," says Rubinson. She was crying in her hotel room in Austin. "This guy brought them out there, stranded them in a hotel, obviously had no record company and no plans to record them. I don't know what his plans were, but they weren't recording."

Rubinson drove to the airport, plunked down his American Express card and paid for their return airfare to San Francisco. "As soon as they got home, I said, 'You guys are too good to go through this. Let's make records.' " He signed them to the Fillmore Corporation with plans to record an album. Then Jerry Wexler of Atlantic Records saw them singing backing vocals for Elvin Bishop at the Whisky on the Sunset Strip in Los Angeles and signed them to the label.

Wexler sent them to Malaco Studios in Jackson, Mississippi, to work with Wardell Quezerque, the man who produced "Mr. Big Stuff" for Jean Knight. "We did five or six songs," Anita recalls. "We brought the songs back to San Francisco and David Rubinson literally had a fit. He threw his briefcase around the office. He started screaming and hollering, 'How could they do that to you? You're not just an R&B group!' We had songs that we had written, songs that were funky, really innovative. They turned them into R&B songs—put that R&B groove under everything we did."

Rubinson elaborates, "They weren't the typical black women singers. They were very independent-minded and they shopped at thrift shops and had a whole '40s look...Atlantic made these generic R&B records. They were horrible." Rubinson and Graham dissolved their partnership; Rubinson didn't care what Graham kept, except for the Pointer Sisters contract. "We got out of Atlantic. I brought them to Blue Thumb—[label founder] Bob Krasnow heard them and loved them."

Ruth, Anita, Bonnie, and June had a hit off their first Blue Thumb album: "Yes We Can Can" went number 12 R&B and number 11 pop in 1973. Two years later, the quartet had a Number One single with "How Long (Betcha' Got a Chick on the Side)" from the *Steppin'* album. "I came in with a country song that I had written called 'How Long,' " Anita remembers. "David had come up with this hook, 'Betcha' got a chick on the side.' At first I said, 'Wait a minute, the guys are gonna get mad at us for singing something like that.' "

David explains where the hook came from: "I had done a record for Taj Mahal. I was producing him for many years and he had a syncopated way of singing. And he was doing a song called 'Stealing,' an old blues song. One day I was playing the tape and started riffing off the syncopation and came up with 'Betcha' got a chick on the side.' "

The Pointer Sisters were on the road when David and Anita melded the two songs, and they rehearsed it immediately. "We got the band that was working with them live and I started on a little bit of a rhythm track," Rubinson says. He notes that the idea for the rhythm track came from "Homework," a John Lee Hooker song from the album *Free Beer and Chicken*. "On the record is a groove Hooker did with Wah Wah Watson. Ruth played me the record and I heard this groove. I called Wah Wah Watson up, which is the first time I think I ever worked with him...and we cut the track and then put their vocals on."

Rubinson is still enthusiastic about the Pointer Sisters. "Their sense of phrasing and syncopation is perfect...their vowel sounds are perfectly matched...their time and rhythm is perfect...They're just naturals. They were from the very first time I recorded them with Elvin Bishop."

220

IT ONLY TAKES A MINUTE

Tavares

CAPITOL 4111
WRITERS: DENNIS LAMBERT, BRIAN POTTER
PRODUCERS: DENNIS LAMBERT, BRIAN POTTER
September 20, 1975 (1 week)

When Dennis Lambert and Brian Potter first worked with the Tavares brothers, they produced ballads like "She's Gone" [see 189]. "I always thought they were a great ballad group," Lambert confirms. "They liked to do both up-tempo songs and ballads. I think they do both things well. It just worked out that the up-tempo songs were a little bit more accessible to the mainstream."

Lambert and Potter had a purpose in mind when they wrote "It Only Takes a Minute." "We were trying to come up with something that would give them that real big crossover hit that they had lacked up to that point," says Lambert. "At the time, Capitol Records' R&B department was relatively new. The feeling was if we could make a record that would sit right on the fence, they'd be able to do well with it in the R&B area and on the pop side. Al Coury and his whole team of pop promotion people would have something that would meet with little or no resistance at top 40 radio. And that seemed to do the job."

The galloping rhythms of "It Only Takes a Minute" were built into the song as it was written, according to Lambert. "The exciting thing about working in that time was that a lot of the songs that we wrote were created on the piano and much of what happened in the studio was a product of the inspiration of the moment." Lambert credits arranger and keyboard player Michael Omartian and the rhythm section with contributing to the success of

Tavares

the song. For most of their work with Tavares, Lambert and Potter used the same coterie of musicians: Larry Carlton and Dean Parks on guitar, Ed Greene on drums, and Wilton Felder of the Crusaders on bass.

Lambert describes the recording process he and Potter employed with Tavares: "We used to do a guide lead vocal first. Then we would concentrate on doing all the background parts before we went back to do a complete finished lead. Sometimes in the process of doing that guide lead, we got a very inspired and no-pressure performance that we wound up keeping, if not all, at least a good part of it. But we used to work very carefully on putting together all the background parts, because that was their real strength, and we tried to exploit their really great harmony singing.

"We did a lot of experimentation and tried to push the envelope a little bit on that song, because it was rather a long record and one of the first associated with the dance music/disco era. We were trying to do something that would work in that new genre."

"It Only Takes a Minute" was revived in 1993 by Take That, a British quintet of teenagers who took the song into the top 10 of the U.K. chart.

221

DO IT ANY WAY YOU WANNA

People's Choice

TSOP 4769
WRITER: LEON HUFF
PRODUCER: LEON HUFF
September 27, 1975 (1 week)

The locomotive funk and minimalist vocals of "Do It Anyway You Wanna" were not only the people's choice for Number One during September '75, but also the sole Number One enjoyed by the TSOP (The Sound of Philadelphia) label, an offshoot of almighty Philadelphia International Records.

The founding father of People's Choice was diminutive Frankie Brunson, who recorded for various labels in the '60s and sang with a band fronted by jazz saxman Lynn Hope. The musicians included pianist Bobby Martin, who became a vital player in the studio team assembled by Kenny Gamble and Leon Huff at Philadelphia International.

Later still, Brunson connected with a Philly combo called the Fashions, featuring bassist Roger Andrews and drummer Dave Thompson. When the three fell out of the Fashions, they formed People's Choice, together with guitarist Stanley Burton and percussionist Leon Lee.

"This independent producer called Bill Perry decided to record us in 1971," said Brunson. "We did a session with him at Frank Virtue's studio. And he got the record placed with Phil-L.A. of Soul. That was 'I Likes to Do It.' "

The tune was the group's national breakthrough, an R&B success that also crossed to the pop charts. "The Staple Singers recommended us to do the Al Green show at the Apollo," explained Brunson, "and that was held over one week. Kenny Gamble came over to see us there and he said he was sorry to have let our first single get away from him. He said, 'As soon as you're free of your contractual obligations, you come and look us up.' "

Brunson, Thompson and Andrews selected their future in 1974, signing People's Choice to the Gamble & Huff camp. "Leon [Huff] listened to us and suggested we needed to make it just a little less raw," said Brunson. "Like he really dug our sound, but he thought we needed to give it a little bit more production. The disco thing was really starting to happen, so we started cutting things that were in that kind of general direction."

Huff wrote and produced "Do It Any Way You Wanna," one of the last tracks recorded for the People's Choice debut TSOP album, *Boogie Down U.S.A.* He and Bobby Eli played on the Sigma Sound sessions—keyboards and guitar, respectively—with the group.

Released in June 1975 as the album's third single, "Do It Any Way You Wanna" hustled up the charts and sold a million—Philadelphia International's only single to be certified gold that year.

"I can't tell you what funk is," Brunson admitted, "an' I don't know who started it. Somebody said it was James Brown, but it was going before him. It's just the hard beat, the beat that makes you move. When you hear it, you wanna shake your stick or whatever you do...but you just *can't* sit still."

222

THIS WILL BE

Natalie Cole

CAPITOL 4109
WRITERS: CHUCK JACKSON, MARVIN YANCY
PRODUCERS: CHUCK JACKSON, MARVIN YANCY
October 4, 1975 (2 weeks)

Unforgettable: the high-voltage surge of "This Will Be," heralding a newcomer with the electricity of Aretha, the bloodlines of a "King," and a minister at the piano.

Natalie Cole lit up the music business in the summer of '75, and the sound and sass of "This Will Be" made comparisons with Franklin inevitable. Coincidentally, the Queen of Soul was in a slump that year—the first since 1967 during which she failed to crown the top of the R&B singles charts.

A minister, Marvin Yancy, played a key part in Cole's debut, just as Aretha's father, Reverend C. L. Franklin, was at the center of her musical upbringing in church. Yancy and partner Charles (Chuck) Jackson had been the creative core of the Independents, Chicago chartmakers in the early '70s [see 147—"Leaving Me"]. They were to become the architects of Cole's breakthrough.

When the Independents dissolved, the pair continued to write, looking to place songs with other artists. Through manager Bob Schwaid, Jackson and Yancy met Cole in New York in October 1974. "We were walking down somewhere in Times Square," Jackson recounts, "and Kevin Hunter and Natalie were walking the opposite way." Hunter, who was Cole's manager, and Schwaid knew each other from past experience.

"Kevin said, 'This is Nat Cole's daughter, she's just come in from Toronto,' " explains Jackson, recalling that the five of them went to a local rehearsal room right there and then. "We laughed, it was like we had known each other for years. Natalie was looking so cute, and Marvin and I were trying to get an act." The impromptu session went well, he says. "Marvin got to play piano...he was just banging it out like he was in church."

Natalie Cole

The chemistry proved perfect, and Cole began working with Jackson and Yancy at Curtis Mayfield's Curtom studios in Chicago toward the end of 1974. They deployed an experienced session crew, including Quinton Joseph on drums, Joseph Scott on bass, Tennyson Stephens on organ and, of course, Marvin Yancy on piano.

Cole had been aching for a label contract for some time. Jackson says, "Natalie had been to pretty well every company in the country because of her daddy." No one was interested, including her late father's home, Capitol Records. That was because "she was singing rock and roll," Jackson says—but when the Jackson/Yancy material came to the attention of Capitol's Larkin Arnold, a deal was struck.

"This Will Be" was created at the end of a particular Chicago session, just 48 hours before Arnold and Cole were due to leave town. Jackson remembers, "Larkin said, 'Chuck, we've got some great stuff, man, but I still don't hear the single.' So they went back to their hotel—and we wrote 'This Will Be'! We finished it that night, and I put it in my pocket, like a school paper."

223

(THEY JUST CAN'T STOP IT THE) GAMES PEOPLE PLAY

Spinners

ATLANTIC 3284
WRITERS: JOSEPH B. JEFFERSON, BRUCE HAWES, CHARLES SIMMONS
PRODUCER: THOM BELL
October 18, 1975 (1 week)

The Spinners' fourth Number One single resulted from producer Thom Bell's attempt to blend the music of the '30s, '40s, '50s, '60s, and '70s into one production. "Ragtime, Mills Brothers, Ink Spots, Django Reinhardt," Bell elaborates. "I was trying to get into the old Tin Pan Alley thing and create it in '70s terminology. If you listen to the harmonies and go back to the Mills Brothers and the Ink Spots, you'll see that's what I was trying to create."

Released first as "Games People Play," the song underwent a title change when staffers at the performing rights society BMI suggested royalties from the song might get mixed up with those from "Games People Play" by Joe South. Atlantic reissued the single with awkward punctuation: "(They Just Can't Stop It The) Games People Play." The song gives all five of the Spinners a turn at singing lead. "That's right," Bell confirms. "That used Pervis, the bass. Finally, I noticed that basses are just basses. They never get the same accolades as lead singers. Like in a band, the piano player never gets the same response as those cats out front like the guitar players and bass players and the drummers. Poor piano players like me get to sit in the background...and [people] think we wear thick glasses and we're nerds."

In "Games People Play," Bell actually gave the bass something to sing. "Basses are not usually designed to do anything but hold the root...in order to hold it all together. He's the bottom and they're not really known for being soloists...It's so low and so deep that most people never want to hear a bass, [or] so they think." Being kept in the background affects bass singers, the producer believes. "You don't feel that you're a real asset to a group, because you aren't out front. So I said I'm going to come up with something for that guy. And from the moment I gave him that part, his whole personality, his whole persona, his whole everything changed. He's known for that one thing, but that one thing changed his life: 'Twelve forty-five.' Then came Bobbie, the regular lead singer: 'So I felt so all alone.' Then came Phillippe: 'Games people play.' He didn't have a whole lot because I was trying to give everyone a little shot. And if you can do it, that cements a totally different sound...and that's how that came about, because I wanted the old barbershop quartet sound. And I was trying to mix barbershop with...'Go little glowworm, glimmer, glimmer.' "

"Games People Play" was the third Number One hit for the Spinners written by Joseph B. Jefferson and the second by Bruce Hawes and Charles Simmons. "After we wrote a few things, we recognized that, 'Wait a minute, we've got something real special here,' " Jefferson recalls. "These guys, especially Phillippe Wynne, [could] take anything and run with it. They can really breathe life into it and it gives a writer as well as a producer more of an incentive to write when you know you've got that kind of vehicle. There's no limit to what these guys could have done when we were writing. Anything we brought [to them], they could do it and it was great."

224

TO EACH HIS OWN

Faith, Hope & Charity

RCA 10343
WRITER: VAN MCCOY
PRODUCER: VAN MCCOY
October 25, 1975 (1 week)

At the midpoint of the 1970s, business was booming for Van McCoy, the former psychology major who became one of pop music's most versatile songwriters, arrangers, and producers. Three of his 1975 projects grabbed the peak of the R&B charts; two of them also claimed slots in the top ten of the Hot 100 [see 213—"The Hustle," 233—"Walk Away from Love"].

The record that *didn't* cross to the pop market for McCoy featured a soulful trio from Tampa, Florida, who were dubbed Faith, Hope & Charity by another ace producer, Bob Crewe. The group comprised Zulema Cusseaux, Albert Bailey, and Brenda Hilliard.

McCoy's first productions with the group charted in 1970, and he also used them extensively as backup singers. After Cusseaux went solo, Hilliard and Bailey worked as a duo. In 1975, they found a new recruit, Diane Destry, and reconnected with McCoy.

"Van wanted the group back as a trio," Bailey told *Blues & Soul*, "and we ran across Diane, who [fit] the bill exactly. So within a short period of time, we had arranged to do a singles date with RCA. They were very pleased with the result, and decided that we should go for an album."

"To Each His Own" came from those sessions, done at the RCA studios in New York. Charles Kipps Jr., who was McCoy's business partner and also wrote for Faith, Hope & Charity, remembers the trio as strong background vocalists, fast and proficient, who made the transition to frontline performers without difficulty. As her vocals attest, Hilliard was the most obvious talent and, he says, "probably the backbone of the group."

Even so, Van McCoy left nothing to chance in the recording process. "He was an arranger at heart," says Kipps, "and he loved writing string lines, loved that big kind of sound. For example, he would listen to classical music at home, as opposed to R&B or pop. I think if he had been born 100 years earlier, Van would have been a composer."

Among the musicians behind Faith, Hope & Charity were Steve Gadd on drums, Gordon Edwards on bass, Eric Gale and David Spinozza on guitars, Richard Tee and Leon Pendarvis on keyboards, and Arthur Jenkins and George Devens on various percussion instruments. The horn and string sections were directed by Gene Orloff.

Devens was part of McCoy's signature sound, playing orchestra bells, vibes and koboso. "I usually use orchestra bells as a highlight," the producer explained to *Black Music* in 1975, "or like icing on the cake for the strings if it's a ballad, or on the melody. It's very ethereal. It's kind of different also on up things like 'To Each His Own.' "

The record may have been FH&C's commercial zenith, but not their creative peak. The 1978 album, *Faith, Hope & Charity*, was filled with rich, mellifluous songs, mostly penned by Van McCoy. "The producer flaunts his formula so superbly," gushed a *Billboard* reviewer, "that any future modifications surely seem superfluous. This is the real McCoy."

225

SWEET STICKY THING

Ohio Players

MERCURY 73713
WRITERS: OHIO PLAYERS
PRODUCERS: OHIO PLAYERS
November 1, 1975 (1 week)

The most difficult part of making "Sweet Sticky Thing" wasn't recording the song, according to Ohio Players drummer Jimmy "Diamond" Williams. It was photographing the cover of the album it was on, *Honey*.

"After we did the album, we thought the music was good, but the photo session..." Williams pauses for a moment. "You would have had to have been there. And I wish you well when you come home to your wife and say, 'This is what I had to do. They made me, honey. I didn't want to do it, but somebody's got to do this dirty job.' "

The Ohio Players couldn't release an album with a pastoral mountain scene, not after the S&M antics featured on *Pain, Pleasure, Ecstasy, Climax, Skin Tight,* and *Fire*. In comparison, *Honey* was mild. The cover featured a model tasting some honey right out of the jar, wearing nothing but...well, wearing nothing, actually. On the inside cover, she was wearing nothin' but honey.

At least Williams didn't have to explain the recording session to anyone. "Most of the tracks we did at the time were seven to nine minutes long," he says. "That's like playing seven to nine minutes without making mistakes so obvious or evident to the point where you've got to say, 'Take it back to the top!' And then we've got to get through nine more minutes of this. You're on edge trying to keep everything together, playing in time, on time."

One of those long tracks was "Sweet Sticky Thing," the third Ohio Players single to reach the Number One position on *Billboard's* R&B singles chart. "It goes through a lot of changes, not only musically but rhythmically," Williams explains. "Vocally there's a lot of parts and there are solos and then there's a big ending where chords change and it goes off into cymbal crashes and rolls. Musically it encompassed everything that I could probably hope to play that I've learned in the years of being a student of this craft. Everything that I knew how to play, I played on that record."

"Sweet Sticky Thing" is softer and jazzier than most of the Ohio Players' other hits. "But there's still a drive to it," Williams points out. "That's part of my business, to keep the drive up and keep it happening rhythmically."

Ohio Players

The title of "Sweet Sticky Thing" was a direct outgrowth from the title track of the *Honey* album, according to Williams. "A lot of the songs of that era were playoffs of [other] titles. Like with 'Fire,' we had 'Smoke.' This was a play off the title 'Honey.' [We asked ourselves], 'What can we say besides "Honey"? Oh, look at that girl! You're a sweet, sticky thing!' If that ain't a play off the title 'Honey,' I don't know what is."

Williams vividly remembers Leroy "Sugarfoot" Bonner recording the vocals on "Sweet Sticky Thing." The drummer says, "We are all perfectionists to a point and you're in the studio to perfect what you're doing...Sugarfoot is one of those guys who can go over a lead vocal and a whole verse with all the inflections that he's done [before]...I've caught myself onstage watching this guy instead of performing myself because that's how good he is."

226

LOW RIDER

War

UNITED ARTISTS 706
WRITERS: S. ALLEN, HAROLD BROWN, MORRIS DICKERSON, JERRY GOLDSTEIN, LONNIE JORDAN, CHARLES MILLER, LEE OSKAR, HOWARD SCOTT
PRODUCERS: JERRY GOLDSTEIN, LONNIE JORDAN, HOWARD SCOTT
November 8, 1975 (1 week)

"We came from that whole culture of low riders," says Howard Scott, one of the founders of War. "We went to school with all the low riders and it seemed like a natural thing to write a song about the low riders."

Scott was born and raised in San Pedro, California, where he was friends with Harold Brown from nearby Long Beach, B. B. Dickerson from Harbor City, and Lonnie Jordan from Compton. Just out of high school, they started a band called the Creators. They recorded some tracks for a local label and, with the addition of Charles Miller, evolved into an outfit called Nite Shift. They had about a dozen members when they played a club called the Rag Doll in North Hollywood. British rock star Eric Burdon (who had a Number One pop hit, "The House of the Rising Sun," when he was a member of the Animals), Danish musician Lee Oskar, and producer Jerry Goldstein dropped in while Nite Shift was there to back up football player Deacon Jones, but the vocalist hadn't shown up that evening. Oskar jumped up on stage to jam with the group. After the performance, Goldstein went backstage and invited the group to his home the next day.

He offered them the opportunity to record and tour as Burdon's backing band. Rechristened War by manager Steve Gold, they reduced themselves to seven players—Scott on guitar and vocals, Brown on drums and percussion, Dickerson on bass and vocals, Miller on saxophone and clarinet, Oskar on harmonica, Jordan on keyboards and vocals, and "Papa Dee" Allen on keyboards and vocals. The group recorded two albums with Eric Burdon and had a number three pop hit with "Spill the Wine" from their first collaboration, *Eric Burdon Declares War.*

"After Eric left, it was War all by itself and we had to get out there and jump in that deep water and see what it was like, and believe me, it was deep," says Scott. "Eric was always a shield between us and the real world. When he left, we took the responsibility." The band signed with United Artists and developed their own Latin-tinged sound, scoring top 10 hits like "The World Is a Ghetto,"and "The Cisco Kid."

Scott describes the origin of their one and only Number One hit: "Charles Miller started singing a line about low riders, and we jumped on it. Charles had a '48 Chevy at the time, and it was quite natural. He was low riding real tough in the van." Scott also remembers the recording session: "We got into a jam...Charles was off on his tenor saxophone and he started singing the 'Low Rider' thing...We had the groove, so we just kept playing that groove until we had about a couple of minutes of it that we knew were solid...And we went back and listened to it, cut, got the best parts where Charles was singing, and then came back and as a group wrote it. And then Lee Oskar and Charles put the horn line [in]."

War continued to have hits on United Artists for another year, but by 1976 the label and group cited "philosophical differences" and went their separate ways. War delivered one final album, for the Blue Note subsidiary, and then signed with MCA.

227

FLY, ROBIN, FLY

Silver Convention

MIDLAND INTERNATIONAL 10339
WRITERS: SILVESTER LEVAY, STEPHAN PRAGER
PRODUCER: MICHAEL KUNZE
November 15, 1975 (1 week)

"It's the bassline, stupid." All right, so record producer Michael Kunze and arranger/composer Silvester Levay didn't exchange exactly those words after they'd checked out German discotheques to see—and hear—what patrons were dancing to. But they *did* recognize that it was the bottom of the records, the sonorous bass grooves, that propelled people onto the floor in '74.

"So," recalls Kunze, "I told Silvester, 'All we have to do is find some nice bass rhythms and illustrate them a little.' " From that piece of market research was born Silver Convention.

"Fly, Robin, Fly" was recorded for the group's debut album by Kunze and Levay at the Union studios in Munich, Germany. The musicians were Gary Unwin (bass), Keith Forsey (drums), and Levay (keyboards). The string section—drawn from the Munich Philharmonic Orchestra—was conducted by Fritz Sonnleithner.

Levay and Kunze had previously collaborated on various projects. "I found out that the way Silvester played piano was very creative," says the producer. "He played a lot of melodies while he was doing chords, so I asked him if he would be interested in handling arrangements for my artists."

After one such session—for a singer competing in the Eurovision Song Contest—Kunze and Levay used the remaining studio time to cut an instrumental Levay had just written. But the tune needed a vocal hook, and session singers were drafted.

When Ralph Siegel of Jupiter Records heard the result ("Save Me"), he suggested taking it to MIDEM, the annual music industry convention held in the South of France. It was January 1975. "Ralph got back a week later," explains Kunze, "and called us to say 'You must do an album, because we've had a lot of interest in the single.' "

As "Save Me" began breaking in the U.K., Siegel wanted a group to promote the song. The original session vocalists weren't interested, so a couple of singers from the Jupiter roster (Ramona Wolf, Linda Thompson) and a Kunze acquaintance (Penny McLean) became Silver Convention.

To prepare for the album, the producer and the arranger undertook their first-hand club research. "At that time, a lot of disco music featured brass," says

Silver Convention

Kunze. "We knew we had a problem there, because there were no suitable brass players in Munich, but we had a very strong string section. I told Silvester, 'You write for bass, but we'll do it with strings.' That's how the distinctive string sound was developed."

"Fly, Robin, Fly" itself was penned by Levay and Stephan Prager, who originally called the song "Run, Rabbit, Run." It was released as a single in America by Midland International Records, whose Bob Reno had acquired the rights from Ralph Siegel at MIDEM '75. "The whole disco scene had just started in the States," says Kunze, "and the record pools had become very influential."

Independent labels like Midland serviced the pool DJs, gaining enough exposure for their records to turn them into national hits. "It was a series of happy coincidences for us," Kunze concludes, "and I doubt if there was a better time for small record companies."

LET'S DO IT AGAIN

The Staple Singers

CURTOM 0109
WRITER: CURTIS MAYFIELD
PRODUCER: CURTIS MAYFIELD
November 22, 1975 (2 weeks)

Curtis Mayfield never traded the chill of lakeside Chicago for the warmth of oceanside Los Angeles, but he wrote for Hollywood, all the same.

Superfly was Mayfield's first movie score—and a gold-plated smash, at that. The 1972 soundtrack album sold a million, topped the pop charts, and spun off a couple of gold singles. His next was successful, too: the *Claudine* score with Gladys Knight & the Pips.

No surprise, then, that Mayfield should be tapped to write the music for 1975's *Let's Do It Again*, a comedy starring Sidney Poitier (who also directed) and Bill Cosby. "Having had some experience with *Superfly* and *Claudine*, I was totally ready to lock in for a movie like that," he says. "Of course, the whole idea was to save the movie people a lot of money by not only having a score, but also a soundtrack LP out on the street prior to the movie."

In addition, the project gave Mayfield a chance to work with the Staple Singers—after his Curtom label lost out to Warner Bros. Records in a contest to sign the group. "We bid on the Staples and lost," said Marv Stuart at the time, "and ended up producing them." Stuart was Mayfield's manager and partner in Curtom Records, which was then distributed by Warner Bros.

And so Curtis traveled to Hollywood for the makers of *Let's Do It Again*. He recalls, "They had me come out and showed me their first film, which was *Uptown Saturday Night*. This was to be the sequel, but it was different enough where you could come totally with your music and create something different.

Mavis Staples

"I felt very good with Mavis and Pops and the Staples. You could bring in the love and the feelings and all the sweet things that I knew they would be introducing. It would be something nice they could do, and still have it blend into parts of the movie."

After their gospel-rooted years at Stax Records, the Staples appeared ready to stretch out. The sisters "had become women," says Mayfield, "and we could speak totally on the love side. But Pops was always leery as to what type of music and lyrics should be a part for his girls. They being totally brought up in the church, you could understand that. So he was always there. I even wrote a [vocal] part for him."

The group recorded "Let's Do It Again" at Curtom's Chicago studios, with a rhythm section comprising Phil Upchurch and Gary Thompson on guitars, Joseph Scott on bass, Quinton Joseph on drums, and Floyd Morris on keyboards. Mayfield played guitar, too, and the sessions were arranged by Gil Askey, a former Motown stalwart, and Rich Tufo, A&R director at Curtom.

"Let's Do It Again" proved to be "just perfect" for the Staples, according to Mayfield, and for the film. The single soared to the summit of both the R&B and pop charts in '75, and went gold. Did Mayfield expect such a sizable success? "I loved it so much, I didn't care," he says. "Sometimes you just feel that way."

229

THAT'S THE WAY (I LIKE IT)

KC and the Sunshine Band

T.K. 1015
WRITERS: HARRY WAYNE CASEY, RICHARD FINCH
PRODUCERS: HARRY WAYNE CASEY, RICHARD FINCH
November 29, 1975 (1 week)

When KC and the Sunshine Band first recorded "That's the Way (I Like It)," it sounded like it could have been rated X. KC says with regret, "I had to cool it down. The 'uh-huh, uh-huh's were more like a moaning and groaning, and I had to clean that up considerably. It was 1975 and I just thought it was a little too risqué. And I thought, 'Boy, wait 'til my mother hears this one!' "

KC's mother, who was a singer herself, had a strong influence on her son. "My mother was into rhythm & blues music and [the first song I heard] must have been a Jerry Butler record. She loved Jerry Butler, Nat King Cole, and of course, the Flamingos. I've always loved to dance. My mother has always been a dancer and loves to dance. She gets all the credit for that part." KC had another role model for his outgoing stage persona. "Diana Ross had a lot to do with my influence as far as my attitude and the smile and to always be up and happy. When you saw Diana Ross and the Supremes, they made you happy when you looked at them. And of course, when I'd get on the stage even before we were successful, when I'd perform locally, I wanted to do as much as I could to excite the crowd—that was important to me. That's when I'm happy, up there onstage...It's like you go into a trance, a spiritual thing—it just becomes uncontrollable."

Critics were loud in their praise of KC and the Sunshine Band's live performances. Steve Ditlea wrote in the *New York Times*: "In person, they are one of the most exciting groups performing today. On stage KC becomes truly possessed by his rhythms, happily rocking from side to side as he stands over his electric piano, skipping across the floor, proselytizing his listeners to give in to the spirit of his fervent sound. This is no insecure Caucasian kid mimicking black inflections, exhorting a crowd to 'put your hands together.' Raised in the Pentecostal Church, KC has assimilated black music as if he were born to it. Like Elvis Presley a generation ago, KC has the stage presence and the musical ability to bridge the cultural chasm separating white performers and black listeners as well as between black music and white audiences."

KC of KC and the Sunshine Band

"That's the Way (I Like It)" featured the horns that became a prominent trademark of the Sunshine Band's sound. "I think it was because there were horns in a lot of things I listened to," says KC. "I always loved anything with piano, horns, and percussion. And of course, the group I was in before that actually became part of the Sunshine Band had four horns in the front. I guess it was because of Blood, Sweat & Tears, Chicago, and Tower of Power that horns really became prevalent. I knew that's what I wanted to be about, also." Also prominent in "That's the Way (I Like It)" were the female background vocals. "People have always used background vocals and I think female vocals were added to attract the male sector," says KC, who did a fine job attracting the "female sector" himself.

"That's the Way (I Like It)" had a second life when Dead or Alive, a pop band from Liverpool, covered it. It was their first U.K. chart single, peaking at number 22 in 1984.

230

I LOVE MUSIC (PART 1)

The O'Jays

PHILADELPHIA INTERNATIONAL 3577
WRITERS: KENNY GAMBLE, LEON HUFF
PRODUCERS: KENNY GAMBLE, LEON HUFF
December 6, 1975 (1 week)

I Love Music" was the fourth O'Jays Number One single in just over three years. "That was one of the longest tracks we recorded back then," recalls MFSB guitarist Bobby Eli. "I remember Norman Harris had an exceptional guitar solo on there—he was the other guitar player along with me and he was also the arranger of the strings on that one. The rhythm track in the studio really kicked that particular day."

Normally, the O'Jays recorded their vocals with Gamble and Huff very quickly. "If we didn't get it in three takes, it wasn't going to be done," says Eddie Levert, who explains that on the first take, the artists did what they wanted to do. On the second take, they did it Gamble and Huff's way. "Then you do the take where you do what both of you want." More time was spent completing the background vocals: "Because all of those had to be thought up [in the studio]."

"I Love Music" took a little longer, according to Levert. "That was a song they had to cut a few times to get the right feeling to it. I think Gamble wrote all the words right there in the studio. We really put the song together in the studio—it was one of the songs we took two days to record. It was a disco classic."

Sigma Sound Studios founder Joe Tarsia played an important part in "I Love Music" beyond his regular role as engineer. "I mixed that song," he explains. "As Gamble and Huff got more confidence in their engineer, they used to spend less and less time in the mixing room. Sometimes they would show up and say, 'Change this a little bit. Change that a little bit.' And ["I Love Music"] is one of the tunes I would take credit for mixing solo."

Tarsia especially enjoyed working with the O'Jays. "Walt [Williams] was so laid back," says the engineer. "Eddie sang 10 decibels louder and I had to put a pad in one microphone. Walt used to lean back and sing and Eddie used to climb into the microphone—I mean, literally put the microphone in his mouth."

Eli describes the O'Jays as a producer's dream. "They would always be at the session, usually at the rhythm date sitting on stools singing the song to give us an idea of how the songs went. Just having them there was an inspiration to help us come up with different licks. It really was amazing."

Tarsia also gives high marks to his two most important clients, Gamble and Huff. Kenny talked about their songwriting craft to Tom Vickers in *Rolling Stone*: "We write a lot of titles down and we just start talking and put a tape recorder on and just start singing and playing till we come up with something that sounds original to us," the Philadelphia International founder said. "We try to find out what direction we want the artist to go into and why certain albums are successful. And where did it leave the people that buy those albums; what do they want next from this particular artist? If you're going to be a loudspeaker at all, you've gotta say something. Instead of just giving them a beat, we try and deliver a message that will uplift their minds and will get them away from all the evil that's instilled in the world."

231

FULL OF FIRE

Al Green

HI 2300
WRITERS: MABON HODGES, WILLIE MITCHELL, AL GREEN
PRODUCER: WILLIE MITCHELL
December 20, 1975 (1 week)

I can dance! Dance! Dance! Dance! Dance! Dance! Those were pretty typical lyrics for an R&B hit in the fall of '75. Eighteen months after "Rock the Boat" and "Rock Your Baby," strings and syncopation were the order of the day—even for veteran artists—as one soul stalwart after another felt the disco beat seeping into their records.

But Al Green, R&B's love man, turned boogie man?

Well, it was true. "Full of Fire" was Green's most overt foray into boogie wonderland: chugging disco with a noticeable debt to the percolating Miami sound of KC and the Sunshine Band. Like more than one of Al's mid-'70s records, it was launched with trade ads promising a dynamic new sound for the singer. More than ever, it was proof that Green and his producer, Willie Mitchell, were suddenly letting others set their agenda, instead of vice versa.

But it worked. "Full of Fire" went to Number One for Green, even though Mitchell had to leave the confines of Royal Recording at 1320 South Lauderdale to get there. He remembers that the Memphis Horns were working with the Doobie Brothers, and that Rhodes, Chalmers & Rhodes were backing Paul Anka. "So I recorded part of it in Vegas and part of it in Chicago," he recalls. "The sound changed ...because it was a different studio."

That wasn't the only change. Green's transformation from the ladies' pal to Rev. Al was becoming increasingly clear. In one verse of the song, Green referred to "a power" guiding him; elsewhere, he declared that he was over 21 and that his life had just begun. Since the singer had been over 21 for a decade, one can only assume that he was affirming a different sort of new life.

Green and Mitchell would have one last hit with 1976's spunky, underrated "Keep Me Cryin'." A year later, Mitchell was out of the picture and Green was producing himself. His final major R&B hit, "Belle," was about a preacher confronted with a non-spiritual love, a barely disguised rewrite of Green's own confusion at the time. By decade's end, his records were all gospel, his chart presence was negligible, and author Peter Guralnick would soon comment that Green himself, "generally does not seem to be of this world."

Mitchell admits to being "very disappointed" when Al turned to gospel. "He came to me and told me [what] he wanted to do...I said I really don't know anything about gospel and I am really not interested in trying to do a gospel record, and I just gave him my blessing and said go make some gospel records."

The two men, who did in fact work together again in the '80s, remain friends to this day. "He's always at my house at Christmas or Thanksgiving," says Mitchell. And if Al keeps coming over, there's always the chance of new Green/Mitchell delights.

232

LOVE ROLLERCOASTER

Ohio Players

MERCURY 73734
WRITERS: OHIO PLAYERS
PRODUCERS: OHIO PLAYERS
December 27, 1975 (1 week)

Jimmy "Diamond" Williams sets the scene for the creation of the Ohio Players' fourth Number One hit: "We were on a twin engine Navajo. We were flying. The skies were rough. We were in a thunderstorm. This little plane was getting tossed around like God is smacking us himself. And we were hitting air pockets that dropped us four, five hundred feet. Now I know, because I was in the co-pilot's seat. I took lessons; Marvin [Pierce] and myself took lessons. We were flying so much we said, 'We're going to fly ourselves.' I was looking at the altimeter. I know how far we're dropping. People's hands were on the ceiling of this plane. You were lifted up out of your seat. And we said, 'We have got to love what we're doing, because this is a love rollercoaster.' "

"Somebody said the words and I wrote to them," says lead singer Leroy "Sugarfoot" Bonner, who earned his nickname before he became an Ohio Player. "I was the youngest guy in an old blues band," he explains. "Instead of calling me 'Tenderfoot,' a little girl said, 'Don't call him Tenderfoot. He's a sugar.' So they started saying, 'He's a Sugarfoot.' It stuck with me, and now I prefer to be called Sugar."

Bonner wasn't fond of "Love Rollercoaster." "That's one song I personally never did think was going to be a hit," he says. "It sounds kind of corny to me. I wrote it, but to this day I don't know what I wrote. The words didn't really make any sense to me. But it was a hit." The vocals didn't sound like anything else on the radio in the mid-'70s. "A lot of the stuff we do is very experimental," Bonner agrees. "We wanted to do what nobody else wanted to do. We don't ever want to do what other people do. I personally live my life like that. I don't care what the industry says or what people do in the business. It's not important to me. It's what I do that's important. That's the way you get to be your own individual and have your own style."

"Love Rollercoaster" became controversial after a DJ in California with a twisted sense of humor started a rumor that a woman had been killed in the studio while the track was being recorded. Her "screams" were audible, according to the jock. "There is a part in the song where there's a breakdown," Williams acknowledges. "It's just guitars and it's right before the second verse and Billy Beck does one of those inhaling-type screeches like Minnie Riperton did to reach her high note or Mariah Carey does to go octaves above. The DJ made this crack and it swept the country. People were asking us, 'Did you kill this chick in the studio?' The band took a vow of silence because that makes you sell more records."

Williams says that "Sugarfoot" always had fun recording the vocals for the Ohio Players. "He can express himself," says the drummer. "He's got that character voice. It's just like a person having a radio voice. Whatever he says is going to be alright."

"Love Rollercoaster," the Players' second Number One on the pop chart, broadened the group's audience, says Williams. "We saw numbers changing. By the *Honey* album, we had three platinum albums in a row. And we had two singles off that album that were big hits. So you start to see the general public is coming out to see you. That's reflected in the Spanish community and the Mexican community. You start to do shows like *The Midnight Special* and you're on *Soul Train* and Dick Clark."

Williams says the group's unique style of producing themselves worked to the Ohio Players' advantage. Often the band went into the studio without any preconceived notions of what they were going to come up with, or any material prepared in advance. Sometimes the magic didn't work, so the musicians would talk, have a cigarette, and go home. "It worked out real well," says Williams. "We didn't have anybody bothering us [or] pressuring us to do what we knew we had to do."

233

WALK AWAY FROM LOVE

David Ruffin

MOTOWN 1376
WRITER: CHARLES KIPPS JR.
PRODUCER: VAN MCCOY
January 3, 1976 (1 week)

In the 1970 race to vote the Presidents into the charts, Van McCoy and Charles Kipps were a winning ticket. In this election, the Presidents were a vocal trio from the nation's capital, managed by Kipps and produced by McCoy.

"One of the group knew Van, who had a house in Washington," explains Kipps, "and that's how we met." A partnership was created—which was even called White House Productions—and the outcome was several hits for the Presidents, including "For You" and "5-10-15-20 (25-30 Years of Love)."

The group left the charts after 1971, but the White House team stayed together. While one partner covered the creative angles, the other had the business smarts. "Van had been producing, writing and arranging for a long time," says Kipps, "and had a great many contacts in the business. I immediately started renewing those contacts for him."

The pair's link to David Ruffin came about during one of those renewal phone calls. "Suzanne de Passe at Motown was looking for someone to produce David," Kipps recalls. "She knew Van from the past, we met with her, and a deal was made."

Seven years after leaving the Temptations [see 59—"I Could Never Love Another"], Ruffin was in dire straits. "It was a comedown," the singer told journalist Bob Fukuyama in 1975. "I started out hot and cooled off. It's been hard getting gigs the last few years."

Kipps already had "Walk Away from Love" in hand. "I had written it just prior to making the deal to produce David," he says. "Van and I discussed it, and played it for David. He immediately loved it, so that was a good sign."

An even better sign was that Ruffin perfected the song in the studio on the first take. "Everyone was so knocked out, especially when David went up to the high note. He did it so effortlessly. What was funny was that we were all saying, 'That's it, that's it,' and David was saying, 'No, I can do better.' So he did

David Ruffin

another seven or eight takes, and then finally came out and said, 'You're right, that's it.' "

The session was done at New York's Mediasound, with McCoy—as arranger and producer—using his favored crew of top-rated players, including Gordon Edwards on bass, Richard Tee and Paul Griffin on keyboards, Steve Gadd on drums, Ken Bichel on synthesizer, and guitarists Eric Gale, John Tropea, and Hugh McCracken. McCoy himself played piano, and Gene Orloff put together the string and horn sections. Faith, Hope & Charity [see 224—"To Each His Own"] contributed backup vocals.

"We never did a head session," says Kipps. "Everything was arranged from the percussion to every single drumbeat, every single lick." Given the caliber of the musicians, however, McCoy and Kipps did not discourage on-the-spot suggestions. "We had absolute musical literacy from everyone, and everyone knew exactly what they could do. It was more like a party than a session."

234

SING A SONG

Earth, Wind & Fire

COLUMBIA 10251
WRITERS: MAURICE WHITE, AL MCKAY
PRODUCERS: MAURICE WHITE, CHARLES STEPNEY
January 10, 1976 (2 weeks)

The leader of Earth, Wind & Fire, Maurice White, once told *Musician* magazine that he wanted to liberate R&B stage shows from the "drill team" precision of the '60s. But down inside, that was part of EW&F, too. It was, after all, seeing a drum and bugle corps on the streets of his Memphis hometown that lured White into showbiz—and seems to have determined the size of future EW&F line-ups: asked by label owner Leonard Chess to bring a few buddies for a session, White once showed up with his entire college band.

More importantly, "Sing a Song," the studio success from Earth, Wind & Fire's live LP, *Gratitude*, is the band's hit that most recalls the sweet, snappy Chicago R&B records that White and partner Charles Stepney helped craft through the mid- to late '60s [see 11—"Rescue Me"]. Slow down the tempo a tick and you can easily imagine the Esquires or the Radiants stepping smartly to it.

Authored by White and EW&F guitarist Al McKay, "Sing a Song" was committed to tape at Hollywood's Wally Heider Recording on August 14, 1975. Released a couple of months later, it quickly reached gold, as *Gratitude*—a Number One album—raced towards double-platinum. The LP would go on to be nominated for three Grammys, and win one.

Impressive feats all. Especially when you consider that a live set released nine months after a band's big break [see 200—"Shining Star"] would usually have been just a stopgap project until they got a real album finished. Some historians will tell you that *Frampton Comes Alive* was the record that made live albums a serious business, but Earth, Wind & Fire's accomplishments here edge Frampton's by several months, and they had a career before and after.

White's band also made R&B concerts a serious event. Pianos floated. Bassist Verdine White would be engulfed by a box lowered from the ceiling, but Maurice White would be the one who emerged from it—a stunt developed for the group by Broadway magician Doug Henning. The band would enter from an oversized movie screen, or in front of a giant pyramid. One tour would be designed by Stig Edgren, the man responsible for the 1984 Los Angeles Olympics finale and Pope John Paul II's Dodger Stadium mass.

"To me, the music business should be glamorous," Verdine White told an interviewer in the mid-'70s. "People do want to be entertained, they don't want you being heavy all the time; cats like Elton John know that, too. That's why we go in for theatrics on stage, we take the attitude that we can entertain you and tell you something, too."

Earth, Wind & Fire had spent the fall preceding the release of *Gratitude* opening for Santana across Europe and usually upstaging the more established band. Certainly the only R&B act that could step in the arena with them at the time was Parliament/Funkadelic. George Clinton's records were as loopy as Maurice White's were smooth, but both men came off the R&B assembly line of the '60s.

Both had a strong sense of the cosmic; both sang about dancing your way out of your restrictions; and, ultimately, White's doctrine of keeping your head to the sky wasn't so different from Clinton's mantra of freeing your mind so your ass could follow.

235

WAKE UP EVERYBODY (PART 1)

Harold Melvin & the Blue Notes

PHILADELPHIA INTERNATIONAL 3579
WRITERS: JOHN WHITEHEAD, GENE MCFADDEN, VICTOR CARSTARPHEN
PRODUCERS: KENNY GAMBLE, LEON HUFF
January 17, 1976 (2 weeks)

After Gene McFadden and John Whitehead scored a Number One hit for the O'Jays with the first song they ever wrote [see 133—"Back Stabbers"], they were assigned to work with another Philadelphia International Records group, Harold

Melvin & the Blue Notes. "The first song that we wrote for them was 'Bad Luck,' " says Whitehead, pointing out it was written while Richard Nixon was President of the United States. "It felt like since he was the President, the poorer people, the underprivileged, the minority people were catching a bad break. It was worse than the Reagan era to us at that time. So I felt compelled to write something that had to do with social consciousness and I did 'Bad Luck.' "

Whitehead enjoyed writing for the Blue Notes because he had a similar vocal tone to the group's lead singer, Teddy Pendergrass. They attended the same school together, Thomas Edison, and were friends when they were 15 years old. Whitehead knew that Pendergrass could play the drums and that he wanted to be a singer. When John was a member of a local singing group, the Epsilons, Teddy would often ask to join them but never quite made it into the ranks. John says now it was a mistake not to invite Teddy in. But fate has a way of working things out. "I think things happen the way they were meant to happen. I still ended up writing and producing his songs."

Whitehead says it was easy to write for Harold Melvin & the Blue Notes. "Easier than it was for the O'Jays," he adds. In late 1975, McFadden and Whitehead teamed up with Victor Carstarphen to write another socially conscious song for Melvin and the Blue Notes. " 'Wake Up Everybody,' I felt, was really needed...It wasn't a dance tune, it was a tune that people had to listen to."

Carstarphen played piano while the three collaborators were working on the song. "He was playing 'Wake Up' before we even wrote the lyrics," recalls Whitehead. "The lyrics just came out as they did in 'Back Stabbers.' They flowed out of my mouth as if God was telegraphing what he wanted me to say. It didn't take any thought because in my mind I knew the problem. The only problem was saying it the right way in song format." Whitehead waited until all the lyrics were written down on paper before he read them back. "It's not like I think about them first and write them down. I sing them. With 'Ain't No Stoppin' Us Now' [see 313] and a lot of songs I recorded, I made it up as I went along in the studio."

Whitehead is candid about his experience in the studio with Harold Melvin & the Blue Notes. "Working with them was a challenge because most of the Blue Notes couldn't sing...When we cut a record, me and McFadden and Gamble and Huff would be the Blue Notes. We would sing all the backgrounds in the studio like a Milli Vanilli kind of a thing. But you gotta remember at that time, this was acceptable. Teddy and Harold could sing all their own parts."

The writer recalls the first time he heard the completed version of "Wake Up Everybody," a song whose album version runs seven minutes and 30 seconds. "I said, 'This song says so much, but I don't know if people are gonna like it because it's not a danceable tune...It starts off slow and builds and builds and at the end, you feel like you're in church, in a Baptist church. I think that is one of the key points that attracted black people to this song, because it had that spiritual vibe...And Teddy is a master coming across like that. He was an ordained minister at 10 years old. So he had that gospel tone in his voice anyway, and all it did was help the song."

236

TURNING POINT

Tyrone Davis

DAKAR 4550
WRITER: LEO GRAHAM
PRODUCER: LEO GRAHAM
February 7, 1976 (1 week)

Chicago's finest gathered once more: Quinton Joseph on drums, Phil Upchurch on guitar, Bernard Reed on bass, Tennyson Stephens on piano, the Kitty Haywood Singers on backup vocals.

This time, it was the fall of 1975 at Paragon Studios, with arranger James Mack and producer Leo Graham. The team was there to cut a new song for Tyrone Davis, which would turn out to be his biggest success since "Turn Back the Hands of Time" six years earlier.

Graham had already co-written a couple of hits for Davis, namely 1973's "Without You in My Life" and 1974's "I Wish It Was Me." He recalls how "Turning Point" came about. "I play guitar, and I was sitting around at home one day, watching a movie on TV. Someone said 'turning point' in the movie, and that started me off playing a little riff."

With assistance from Upchurch, the riff developed. "Phil had a studio," Graham explains, "and I played the idea to him to lay it on tape. He added a few lines; guys like that are so talented." The outcome was "a nice groove," according to the songwriter, who played it for Davis. "He said, 'Well, I don't know.' "

So Graham kept "Turning Point" for a while, then offered it to local R&B stylist Bobby Jones. "Bobby liked the song, but when I talked about it with my wife, she said, 'Maybe you better let Tyrone hear it one more time.' I called him and said I wanted to come by and play it again. That time, the song clicked with him."

With Davis agreeing to record it, Graham worked on the instrumental track at Paragon with James Mack and the musicians. "I would always sing a guide vocal first," he says. "In my earlier years, I was a singer around the Chicago area."

Tyrone, meanwhile, got cracking with his part of the equation. "He's not a singer who takes a lot of time to record," states Graham. "He does his homework, he knows what he has to do. And by him knowing that, he made my job much easier. I've cut three songs with Tyrone in a couple of hours. His part goes faster than any other part of a record!"

The sessions were also fun. "Tyrone is a great storyteller," Graham remembers. "He's had so many experiences in the business. You could sit down and listen to him for hours—and that's what we often did after the end of the session."

"Turning Point" was just that for the singer, too. Although it was a Number One single, Davis soon afterwards left the independent Dakar label for giant Columbia Records. Leo Graham continued as the singer's creative force, however, writing and producing a series of smashes over the next six years, including "Give It Up (Turn It Loose)," "This I Swear," "In the Mood," and "Are You Serious."

237

INSEPARABLE

Natalie Cole

CAPITOL 4193
WRITERS: CHUCK JACKSON, MARVIN YANCY
PRODUCERS: CHUCK JACKSON, MARVIN YANCY
February 14, 1976 (1 week)

The singer *Billboard* described as "a young, personable lady who moves well and works hard" in 1973 was moving and working like none other in 1976. The year was barely eight weeks old when Natalie Cole won the first two Grammys of her career—including the prize for best female R&B vocal performance, which Aretha Franklin had owned for the previous *eight* years—and achieved her second Number One single.

A timeless ballad, "Inseparable" was both the title track and the second hit from Cole's debut album on Capitol Records. By February of '76, the LP had already topped the R&B charts and spent six months among the pop best-sellers. The tune was intended "as a bridge between her dad and herself," according to Chuck Jackson, who co-wrote and co-produced (with Marvin Yancy) the entire contents of the *Inseparable* album.

"In fact, the song is only some two minutes and 30 seconds long," lyricist Jackson explains. "Marvin picked me up at my apartment [in Chicago], and I wrote it from the North side to the South side in the car! When we got to Marvin's house, we did two minutes, 30 seconds of it and never had a bridge. It was just a spontaneous thing.

"I wanted to get Nat Cole involved with his daughter, and I wanted to bring out the love between Marvin, myself, and Natalie. She could really sing these kinds of songs, because she had been singing them all the time. They set her apart from the everyday artist."

By then, Natalie had been laying claim to her parent's songbook for several years. "She touchingly remembered her father with 'Mona Lisa,' " *Billboard* noted in its June 1973 notice of her opening slot—for Cornelius Brothers & Sister Rose—at New York's Copacabana. "If her singing style wasn't quite as marked as her father's was, she easily makes up for it by the zeal of her performance," wrote the reviewer. Other numbers in her repertoire then: "Respect" and "Killing Me Softly with His Song."

"Inseparable" was recorded at Chicago's Curtom and Universal studios in 1975 by Jackson and Yancy, working with Richard Evans. Evans, a seasoned Windy City arranger with jazz in his background, favored such musicians as Tennyson Stephens on keyboards, Morris Jennings or Quinton Joseph on drums, Joseph Scott or Bernard Reed on bass, Phil Upchurch on guitar, and Henry Gibson on percussion. Marvin Yancy himself played piano behind Natalie, just as he had done behind Oscar Brown (with Evans arranging) the year before.

"Everyone was live," says Jackson. "We used three pieces [for the basic tracks] and after we got the three pieces down, we would from there put everything on top—with live strings—and then Natalie would come in and overdub her lead vocals."

238

SWEET THING

Rufus Featuring Chaka Khan

ABC 12149
WRITERS: TONY MAIDEN, CHAKA KHAN
PRODUCER: RUFUS
February 21, 1976 (2 weeks)

Tony Maiden, a Los Angeles–born guitarist who played for Billy Preston, was in a band called High Voltage with bass player Bobby Watson when that outfit played a club date with Rufus in Chicago. Maiden knew Rufus drummer Andre Fischer from high school, and while he didn't think anything special would come from that gig, he was soon proven wrong.

Rufus moved on to Los Angeles and Maiden got a call from Fischer, asking him and Watson to join the group. "Bobby was getting ready to leave for Europe to play with a band, the Stu Garden Trio. So I told him not [to go]. I felt like something was getting

Chaka Khan

ready to happen." Still, Maiden wasn't sure if he would accept the offer. "I wasn't all that excited to get in another band at the time because I was tired of being in groups and breaking up." But he trusted Fischer, and after meeting with him and lead vocalist Chaka Khan, Maiden thought this experience might be different. "We talked and jammed for a couple weeks...and we wrote a couple of songs. Everything we used to do was so spontaneous and I loved that. So I said, 'I think this is going to be the one.' "

Maiden's first Number One single as a writer was also spontaneous. "We wrote that in the studio," says Chaka. "Tony had a track and I sat down and scribbled the words while they were tracking it." Maiden says it took only half an hour to compose the tune. "We needed one more song. I had a few chords and Chaka always hums stuff when I play the guitar. She gets up and walks to the booth to sing. And we were ready to go. We just [did] a scratch thing and 'Sweet Thing' was born. It was very simple. Chaka always liked to do jazz. Andre liked strings and stuff. But I said, 'No strings. Chaka's voice and the band.' "

Maiden feels that one of Rufus's strongest attributes was the communication between everyone in the group. "Chaka, when she's into it, when we're into it, we had like a communication. I can't even explain it. It's just a certain kind of groove thing."

Tony says having a Number One single was not that important to him. "I didn't really concern myself with it. I was mostly concerned about getting the group off the ground and keeping my eyes focused on our destiny and where we were going with our music...I'd been in a lot of bands that lose the magic and I tried to keep that."

"Sweet Thing," the second Number One single for Rufus and Chaka Khan, was a hit again in March, 1993, when Mary J. Blige took it to number 16. "They pretty much did it like the way we did it," says Maiden. "Note for note and the changes and everything, so I respected that." Before Blige took a crack at it, the song had been covered by a couple of rappers. "It was out there. It was because all the kids are into rap, but it still didn't work. But I think that song is such a great song and like I was saying to Andre, if you do too much to it, it'll be distorted. And she did it just like Chaka did it, but it was Mary J. Blige's voice on there, like Whitney [Houston] did 'I'm Every Woman.' "

239

BOOGIE FEVER

The Sylvers

CAPITOL 4179
WRITERS: KENI ST. LEWIS, FREDDIE PERREN
PRODUCER: FREDDIE PERREN
March 6, 1976 (1 week)

Working with the Sylvers was a very special project for producer Freddie Perren. "It was the first one after spending six years at Motown and working with the Jackson 5. The last thing I did at Motown was 'Love Machine' with the Miracles. I really wasn't sure what I was going to do. I had spoken with them about resigning."

While considering that option, Perren talked with a friend from his college days, Larkin Arnold. The Capitol Records vice president asked Perren what he thought about working with the Sylvers—nine brothers and sisters who grew up in Los Angeles. Perren, aware of the Sylvers since their days on MGM's Pride subsidiary, met with the group and heard them sing. "They really blew me away with their rendition of 'Time After Time' in a very soft Vegas style. Not something you would want to put out to hit the R&B chart, but something that would show their versatility onstage. I said, 'Boy, this is really a great group.' "

Perren also noticed that the Sylvers family had something in common with the Jackson family. "I've been blessed to work with families," the producer comments. "There seems to be a thread that holds families together musically. There's usually a low singer, a middle singer, and a high singer. God seems to have made a person for each part that needs to be sung. The Sylvers were pure singers—they had been singing since they were little kids."

The four oldest Sylvers—Olympia, Leon, Charmaine, and James—performed as the Little Angels when they were small children. It wasn't until they signed with Capitol that the group expanded to nine, including Edmund, Ricky, Angie, Pat, and Foster. Right after they signed with the label, Perren was reunited with an old friend, Keni St. Lewis, and they decided to write together. "At that time, everyone was using the word 'Boogie,' " says Keni. "It was 'Boogie Down' and 'Boogie This' and 'Boogie That.' So I kept trying to think of how I could make the word effective. At first I had 'Epidemic' but that didn't sing too well. As I thought about it, it came out 'Boogie Fever.' "

The Sylvers rehearsed some of the tunes Perren and St. Lewis had written at Freddie's house. "Larkin was there and he listened," says Perren. "He likes to get involved; he's not a pencil-pusher. He likes to hear the material [and] screen it. For some reason, I never got a chance to play 'Boogie Fever' for him. We were recording at the Total Experience recording studio, which was behind Capitol. He dropped over on the day we were cutting the tracks to 'Boogie Fever.' He walked in and said, 'What's that?' I said, 'You didn't hear that [earlier]. It's called "Boogie Fever." ' He nodded his head, moved along to it, and by the end of the song he was saying, 'Yeah, that's good,' so we started off on the right foot with him."

Perren had to choose one of the nine Sylvers siblings to sing lead vocals on "Boogie Fever." "He went around the room finding voices and he wound up saying I was the one," Edmund recalls. "Any one of my family members could have sung lead. We've always been a total group where there wasn't any lead singer."

Perren remembers that "Edmund was perfect at the time because he was beginning to mature, yet he still had a youthful flavor to his voice. It appealed to kids and to young adults as well."

Johnnie Taylor

240

DISCO LADY

Johnnie Taylor

COLUMBIA 10281
WRITERS: HARVEY SCALES, AL VANCE, DON DAVIS
PRODUCER: DON DAVIS
March 13, 1976 (6 weeks)

To the list of his talents as a singer, add Johnnie Taylor: soul psychic.

"With two hundred million people in this country," he told *Billboard* in 1973, "[selling] a million records is not a lot of records by comparison. I think when we're heard on the Top 40 stations without having to sell a million records on the R&B stations...then I think we'll start seeing sales like five million, and more."

Two-and-a-half years later, "Disco Lady" became the first certified-platinum single in the history of the recording industry, selling more than two million copies. What's more, it raced up the Hot 100 and the

R&B charts simultaneously, as radio stations in both music formats reacted immediately to an obvious blockbuster.

Producer Don Davis says he realized the record wasn't just another soul smash while visiting "some real sophisticated part of L.A. where they wouldn't normally be playing any black records. I walked into this discotheque: 'Disco Lady' was spinning and they were dancing. I said, '*This* is going to be big.' "

Like an earlier Taylor hit [see 151—"I Believe in You"], "Disco Lady" began life as another song. "Harvey Scales had brought it to me," explains Davis, "and I liked certain parts of the groove. One day, we were in the studio with Bootsy Collins, Bernie Worrell, and a drummer who couldn't play. We started grooving—and nobody wanted to stop. It was infectious, contaminating, the whole place was..."

The sentence dangles as Davis recalls a track so hot that even George Clinton—with whom bassmaster Collins and keyboard whiz Worrell usually played—was upset. "It was the first time I had ever recorded with George's people," Davis declares. "He got so pissed at the end of that, he wouldn't let me record with them anymore."

The session took place at the producer's customary haunt, United Sound in Detroit. Armed with the track, he began shaping the lyrics, drawing inspiration from a vintage Curtis Mayfield song about a campfire siren ("Gypsy Woman") and from the memory of an African dancer he'd seen on vacation in Spain.

"When this woman got up on the floor, everybody else would sit down because she would just take the whole place. I'm thinking that Curtis had written 'Gypsy Woman,' I gotta write this. This is going to be 'Disco Lady.' I didn't plagiarize his lyrics, but I sure plagiarized his thought."

Later, Davis added Johnnie Taylor's lead vocals, and horns arranged by David Van DePitte. "Some girl walked in and said '[Don] wants you to do something with this,' " remembers Van DePitte, who was midway through another Davis project at United. "She literally threw it across the desk. We ran downstairs before the [other] date was over and put some horns on—and the next thing I knew, here comes 'Disco Lady.' "

Background vocals were done by studio group Brandy, plus Dawn's Telma Hopkins, herself a former sessioneer in Detroit. "She was in town and just begged me to sing on a Johnnie Taylor record," says Davis.

When "Disco Lady" was finally finished, Johnnie Taylor phoned the producer. "He said, 'Pete'—he called everybody Pete—'my voice is too low, the record doesn't suit me, and I think we need to go with something else.' " Fortunately, the singer was open to persuasion. Turns out Don Davis had some psychic powers of his own.

241

LIVIN' FOR THE WEEKEND

The O'Jays

PHILADELPHIA INTERNATIONAL 3587
WRITERS: KENNY GAMBLE, LEON HUFF, CARY GILBERT
PRODUCERS: KENNY GAMBLE, LEON HUFF
April 24, 1976 (2 weeks)

In other words, Thank God It's Friday. "The thing about 'Livin' for the Weekend' that really blew my mind was the two tempos," says the founder of Sigma Sound Studios, Joe Tarsia. "I think when I got into the business I was snobby. I used to like jazz and all of a sudden the major part of what I was doing was urban or black music. I learned to appreciate it. But once in a while I said, 'This record will never [make it]. I thought ["Livin' for the Weekend"] was really bizarre. But I also thought Billy Paul was out of tune on 'Me and Mrs. Jones' and it would never be a hit."

The two tempos on the album version of "Livin' for the Weekend" also intrigued Eddie Levert. "The song starts off in a slower tempo and then goes to the up-tempo, so we got a chance to go back through our musical history and use some of the things that were used by earlier people like the Isley Brothers when they sang 'Shout.' "

Levert says he also liked "Livin' for the Weekend" because "It had jazz, blues overtones, an up-tempo thing to it—this was another chance to flaunt our stuff, to show that we were well-seasoned performers and there were no limits to what we could do."

"Livin' for the Weekend" was the fifth O'Jays single to top the R&B chart. It fell two-thirds of the way into the '70s, in the middle of Gamble and Huff's domination of the charts. The producers' enormous success didn't change the way they operated at Philadelphia International Records, according to MFSB guitarist Bobby Eli.

"It was still relatively loose, the way records were made," says Eli. "The best way to get hits is to have a loose atmosphere...There were jokes flying everywhere. You have to keep the musicians happy. It should be a party atmosphere and you can't be too tense or too strict...The Gamble and Huff tracks probably had a lot more energy in them because they weren't rigid." Eli says that producer Thom Bell ran a much tighter ship. "All the music was written out. There weren't just basic chord charts. Everything was notated and he wanted everything a certain way. It was good because we got paid accordingly and he kept us working a lot. It was so rigid, one time a fly got on Earl Young's drum music and [he thought it was a note printed on the music, so] he played it."

Brass Construction

"Livin' for the Weekend" was the first O'Jays single to be released after a change in personnel. Original member William Powell stopped touring in January, 1976, due to illness. Eddie and Walter conducted an extensive search to find a replacement for the road and came up with Sammy Strain, who had been with Little Anthony & the Imperials since 1964. The O'Jays had been looking for a younger man to take Powell's place, but Strain's experience put him in good stead. Within three weeks, he had learned all of the group's routines and took his place alongside the other members.

Powell continued to record with the O'Jays up until his death on May 26, 1977. Strain then became a full-fledged O'Jay, joining Eddie and Walter in the studio as well as on the road.

242

MOVIN'

Brass Construction

UNITED ARTISTS 775
WRITERS: RANDY MULLER, WADE WILLAMSTON
PRODUCER: JEFF LANE
May 8, 1976 (1 week)

Before they cut "Movin,' " Brass Construction recorded a number of tracks that featured a jazzy, big band sound. "It wasn't really hitting commercially," admits group founder Randy Muller. "You know, nine black guys doing this kind of stuff. It wasn't working. So they said, 'Randy, write some words and put something on top of this stuff and make it a little more commercial.' That's why you notice there's very [few] words on the first album. Just a couple of chants and that's it."

Muller, born in Guyana on the northeast coast of South America, wasn't born into a family that was particularly musical. His sister played a little piano and his brother experimented with a saxophone before deciding to play basketball. Randy wrote some Latin-influeced songs when he was seven. He was sent by his family to live with his grandmother in Brooklyn in 1963. Attending George Gershwin Junior High School, he met Wade Williamston (bass) and Larry Payton (drums). "We came together for a talent show and then we decided to continue playing," Muller explains. "It was like an after-school project. Some guys played basketball; we did music." With Jesse Ward (sax), they put together a rhythm section in 1967 called the Dynamic Souls. Joseph Arthur-Wong (guitar), Morris Price (trumpet, percussion), and Wayne Parris (trumpet) were added, followed by Mickey Grudge (saxophone, clarinet) and Sandy Billups (percussion). They won a Battle of the Bands in Manhattan in 1969 and met up with producer Jeff Lane. With some of the band members still in school, they recorded a single called "Two Timin' Woman," which Lane released on his own label, Dock Records.

Muller was surprised when Lane asked him to do the string arrangements for a group he had signed to Scepter, B.T. Express [see 183—"Do It ('Til You're Satisfied)"]. He learned everything he could about violins in two days so he could work with the group. He arranged "No Charge" for Shirley Caesar and then Brass Construction got a label deal with United Artists. The first album was recorded over a three-month period at two New York studios, Ultra-Sonic and Groove Sound.

"Movin' " was constructed while the band was laying down some tracks in the studio. "I had this groove and we jammed for 16 minutes," says Muller. "I think that's the maximum time the tape could have recorded. I put some words to it, basic chants, did the arrangement—it was one of those instant things." On the original track, Muller recorded drums, bass, guitar, and keyboards. Horns and vocals were added later. The title came from the sound of the track, according to Muller. "It just sounded that way. During that time, we wanted to make positive songs; most of the Brass songs were like that."

The group was surprised by the album's success; they went from playing regular gigs at New York discos to touring with Rufus. Muller found it hard to believe he had a Number One single until the group played the Just Jazz club in Philadelphia. "To see the turnout, it was unbelievable. I said, 'Maybe there's some substance to this rumor that we had a hit record.' "

243

LOVE HANGOVER

Diana Ross

MOTOWN 1392
WRITERS: PAM SAWYER, MARILYN MCLEOD
PRODUCER: HAL DAVIS
May 15, 1976 (1 week)

A dram of brandy, a splash of vodka, and—presto!—Hal Davis mixed Diana Ross's most successful R&B cocktail since "Ain't No Mountain High Enough."

Motown producer Davis was thirsting for a hit as 1975 drew to a close. "I needed a smash right away," he recalls, "because the Jacksons had left and everybody said, 'Well, it's over, Hal doesn't have the group, what's he going to do?' "

Hearing a demo of "Love Hangover" in a colleague's office, Davis learned that Marilyn McLeod was its co-author. "I called Marilyn and said, 'Hey, I like the tune, I want to cut it tonight.' "

Davis recorded the track at the Paramount studios in Los Angeles. "I went in, two o'clock in the morning, and bought everyone a shot of Remy Martin," he says. Shaking (not stirring) the twin-tempo groove were Joe Sample on keyboards, James Gadson on drums, and Henry Davis on bass. Dave Blumberg and Clay Drayton handled the arrangement.

Even so, some of the musicians didn't taste the spirit. "They didn't want to up-tempo it, I had to fight," Davis contends. "Joe didn't like the idea when I broke it up with the vamp there and went into the disco thing." The distinctive guitar run that pumped the tune's up-tempo segment was overdubbed later by Art Wright, who would perform similar services on a later Hal Davis project [see 264—"Don't Leave Me This Way"].

It was Motown *capo* Berry Gordy who thought "Love Hangover" suitable for Diana Ross, but she was cool. "She said she didn't want to do it, she didn't like disco," remembers Davis. "She had just had her baby, she came in moody, and didn't really want to get into anything. So we got her a little taste of vodka—she's a vodka drinker—and she sat back, kicked her shoes off, and said, 'Well, I'll go out and give it a try.' "

Earlier, Davis had instructed engineer Russ Terrana to set up a strobe light in the studio. "You see, I play with the mind, set the mood. Diana got in there, started singing. She said, 'It sounds pretty good.'

"She got into it: Her eyes were flashing, the strobe was flashing, the vodka was tasting better, the engineer was popping. There were only three of us sitting there, but you would have sworn there was a party going on! That's why it was a smash."

But only after the discos—and a cover version by the 5th Dimension—forced Motown's hand. The label was promoting another track from the singer's *Diana Ross* album, and Berry Gordy wanted to stay the course. Then the 5th Dimension single hit the market. Gordy capitulated, his staff scrambled—one executive remembers the hastily-called Saturday promotion meeting—and the Ross single was rush-released, quickly drowning the competition.

244

KISS AND SAY GOODBYE

The Manhattans

COLUMBIA 10310
WRITER: WINFRED "BLUE" LOVETT
PRODUCERS: THE MANHATTANS, BOBBY MARTIN
May 22, 1976 (1 week)

"Kiss and Say Goodbye" might have been a country music blockbuster for Glen Campbell, and the Manhattans might have been the biggest black group in country music. Instead...

A long way from Nashville, Winfred "Blue" Lovett was a founder member of the Manhattans. They coalesced in the early '60s around Jersey City, then advanced across the Hudson River and into show-business by winning third place in an Apollo Theater talent contest.

Signing in 1964 with Carnival Records, the group gained their first national chart success with "I Wanna Be (Your Everything)," written by Lovett. He sang bass; the other members were Edward "Sonny" Bivins and Kenneth "Wally" Kelly (both tenors), Richard "Ricky" Taylor (baritone), and the late George "Smitty" Smith (lead).

For the next eight years, the Manhattans produced a steady stream of midsize R&B hits for Carnival, then for King's DeLuxe Records imprint. Smith died in 1970, to be replaced as lead vocalist by Gerald Alston. Two years later, the quintet joined Columbia Records and started recording with Philadelphia producer Bobby Martin.

"Things really began to take a turn for the better when we signed with Columbia...and we began to see what was possible for us," Lovett told *Black Music*. "I'd

The Manhattans

been doing a lot of songwriting, mostly on planes, and I got lucky with 'Kiss and Say Goodbye.'

"I'd never thought of it as a number for the Manhattans to record, to me it was a Glen Campbell tune. We recorded it at the same time as 'Hurt' [in early 1975] but a year went by before Columbia decided to release it. I think they were waiting for the right time: the disco thing was firmly established when we came right in there with something totally different from everything people were hearing."

The Manhattans would often prepare material with their own band, Little Harlem, then give the tapes to producer Martin. He would write arrangements for the musicians of Philadelphia's MFSB session team, and cut the tracks and vocals at Sigma Sound.

"Kiss and Say Goodbye" was released in March 1976, as Lovett explained. "It had nearly sold a million in [the black] market before it crossed over." He added, "We had two versions of the record played: the white stations didn't like the rap, the black stations did. We didn't care just as long as the record kept selling."

It did that—to become the second single in music industry history to acquire a platinum certification for sales of two million. The Manhattans gained the accolade in August '76, just a few months after fellow Columbia artist Johnnie Taylor collected the first platinum single award [see 240—"Disco Lady"].

As for the Manhattans' broader aspirations in music, "Blue" Lovett told *Billboard* a few years after "Kiss and Say Goodbye" that a black country group ("something that maybe sounds like the Oak Ridge Boys") was just around the corner.

"Gospel...R&B...country, they tell true stories. That's what the people want right now," he said. "Whoever ventures over, if there ever is a black country group, it's got to be big—if the record company is willing to venture out and let it happen."

245

I WANT YOU

Marvin Gaye

TAMLA 54264

WRITERS: LEON WARE, T-BOY ROSS

PRODUCER: LEON WARE

May 29, 1976 (1 week)

The man who helped create a couple of Motown milestones in the '70s boasts a lifetime's connection with Berry Gordy. "He was my first producer when I was 17," says Leon Ware, who later shaped Marvin Gaye's *I Want You* album and authored its songs. "Berry was producing me, a group called the Gaylords, and Jackie Wilson. But I wasn't a patient teenager, and he was very busy with Jackie and this other group—so I walked off."

Ware worked sporadically at Motown over the next 20 years, making a significant splash in 1972 with Michael Jackson's "I Wanna Be Where You Are." He wrote that song with Diana Ross's brother, Arthur, better known as T-Boy. "He was on the staff at Jobete Music," explains Ware. "I liked him immediately, and he had some great ideas."

A couple of years later, according to Ware, he composed "I Want You" and shared the credit with T-Boy to advance the latter's career. Soon afterwards, Berry Gordy "was walking through the studio," says Ware, "he heard the song and fell in love with it."

The Motown boss thought "I Want You" would be ideal for Marvin Gaye, who hadn't made a studio album since 1973's *Let's Get It On*. "He had his religious retreats and different difficulties," comments Ware. "But this was the first thing that had interested him for over two years, and he came into the studio and started working on that song."

Coincidentally, Ware had been recording his own project for Motown. "I actually had finished the album, strings, my vocals, and everything," he says. "In the process of working on 'I Want You,' I was at Marvin's ranch. He was someplace else in the house, and I was playing a piece of my album. He came in and said, 'What's that?' I said, 'This is an album I'm just about finished with.' "

Captivated by Ware's music, Gaye proposed a different plan. " 'Leon,' he says, 'how about me and you working on my whole album?' At first I didn't believe him, because nobody had ever really had a whole album on Marvin Gaye. We had to do it for me to believe it! For him to do that many songs of mine, hey, I didn't care about me not putting my album out."

And so *I Want You* took shape, with Marvin using the arrangements and instrumental tracks already recorded by Ware. He had employed the best California musicians available anyway, including drummer James Gadson, bass players Chuck Rainey and Wilton Felder, and guitarists Dennis Coffey, Melvin "Wah-Wah" Ragin, and Ray Parker Jr.

On keyboards were Sonny Burke, Jerry Peters, and John Barnes; the conga/bongo players were Bobbye Jean Hall and Eddie "Bongo" Brown. The horns and strings were arranged by Coleridge Taylor Perkinson.

"The music is all mine," affirms Ware. "All we did was rewrite [the lyrics of] every song on the album. The attitude and the feeling and the lust and the sensuality—our thinking processes were very similar."

The vocals were cut at Motown's Hollywood facilities and Gaye's own studio nearby. "Marvin and I freaked each other out on many, many occasions as to how closely we thought alike, musically and vocally and backgroundwise," declares Ware. "We were spiritually one, for a long time."

246
YOUNG HEARTS RUN FREE
Candi Staton

WARNER BROS. 8181
WRITER: DAVE CRAWFORD
PRODUCER: DAVE CRAWFORD
June 5, 1976 (1 week)

Alabama's Candi Staton was the first lady of southern soul, whose 13 R&B top 20 hits gave her the chart edge over Georgia's Millie Jackson (11), Tennessee's Carla Thomas (10) and Florida's Betty Wright (also 10).

Candi Staton

Yet her most successful single was not made in Muscle Shoals or Memphis, but in Los Angeles. And when Staton first arrived at the Los Angeles studio where she was to make "Young Hearts Run Free," producer Dave Crawford was so busy with the instrumental tracks that he paid the singer no mind. "I said, 'David, I'm here,' " recalls Staton. "He said, 'Yeah, yeah, sure—OK, do that guitar lick again.' I had to yell, 'David, I'm *here!*' "

Crawford was "the total producer," according to Staton. "I asked him what he was playing, and he replied, 'You'll love it.' That's all he said. I told him I'd appreciate it if he'd give me a track so I could go home and learn the lyrics."

Staton was in a hurry to record her vocals, anyway. "I was on the road. I had a gig to do in South Carolina, so David got me into the studio that morning. We started at eight o'clock, and I did the whole album in one day. My voice was in perfect condition. We went through everything, and I got on the plane that night at eleven o'clock and did the gig the next day."

Crawford had written "Young Hearts Run Free" and four more of the album's eight songs, cutting the tracks at Sound City Studios with Ray Parker Jr. and Jay Graydon on guitars, Ollie Brown on drums, and Scotty Edwards on bass. Motown alumni Jack Ashford handled percussion, and there were three keyboard players: Sonny Burke, Sylvester Rivers (who also did the arrangements), and Michael Boddicker. Among the backup vocalists were Deniece Williams and Rochelle Runnells.

The Los Angeles sessions marked the first time Staton teamed up with Crawford. Previously, she and Muscle Shoals maestro Rick Hall had crafted a 1969–74 sequence of bold, brassy and *southern* soul sides, including "I'd Rather Be a Young Man's Sweetheart," "Stand by Your Man," and "As Long as He Takes Care of Home."

Hall signed Staton on the advice of singer Clarence Carter, who also negotiated the singer's contractual release from a local label, Unity Records. "I was stuck with this little United something in Birmingham," recalls Staton, "Clarence said, 'Uh-oh, I can't tell Rick, but we're going to have to get you out of this some kinda way.' "

Carter's choice was a $1,500 payoff, bargained down from the $2,000 that Unity sought. Six months later, "I'd Rather Be an Old Man's Sweetheart" became a hit—and a year after that, Candi and Clarence were married.

Staton later turned to the gospel music she sang as a youngster in Alabama, preaching as a minister and no longer suggesting that "Young Hearts Run Free." She says, "That song was encouraging young women not to get married, but to shack up. I just don't endorse that now."

The Brothers Johnson

247

I'LL BE GOOD TO YOU

The Brothers Johnson

A&M 1806
WRITERS: GEORGE JOHNSON, LOUIS JOHNSON, SENORA SAM
PRODUCER: QUINCY JONES
June 12, 1976 (1 week)

George and Louis Johnson were already veteran session players for artists like Billy Preston, Bill Withers, Bobby Womack, and many others the day they were in Studio B at the Record Plant to audition for Stevie Wonder. The funk coming out of the studio was so strong, the producer in Studio C had to stop by and find out who was making all of those sounds. The visitor was Quincy Jones, who was very impressed. "The next thing we knew," says George, "we were in the studio with Quincy, cutting some tracks."

The tracks were for Quincy's *Mellow Madness* album. The Johnsons wrote four songs for the album, toured Japan with Quincy, and were signed to A&M Records to record their own material. "We had about 200 tunes," George explains. "We would go to Quincy's house. We'd bring tapes in paper bags—cassettes, reel to reels. We went through each and every one of them. Quincy had a little note pad. He would take notes on things we were doing and titles." Together, they selected 20 songs that could be recorded for their debut album, and narrowed the list down to 10.

George details his inspiration for one of those 10 songs: "At the time I was seeing three young ladies. It got to the point where things were a little hectic, especially around Thanksgiving and Christmas time. I did the whole scenario of hopping from here to there and it got a little rough on me. I decided to write a song called 'I'll Be Good to You.' It was a commitment I decided to make for myself to one lady in particular—the lady that I wound up marrying, Debbie Johnson. I wrote it for her, 'I'd be good to you.'"

Sharing writing credit with George and Louis on the song is a woman named Senora Sam, a friend of the brothers. "The day I was writing 'I'll Be Good to You,' she happened to come over to the house," says George. He was in his room recording a demo and Sam suggested a line, "the way we stand and the way we lie."

The demo tape of the song had one bassline, a drum machine, and nine guitars layered on top of each other. "At that point I was working on my arranging skills and Quincy tweaked that for me." In the studio, Quincy assigned the different guitar parts to keyboards, horns, and guitars. George, a reluctant vocalist, sang lead. "I never really claimed to be a singer," he confesses. "Quincy *made* me sing on his *Mellow Madness* album, on a song entitled 'Is It Love That We're Missin',' a tune we'd written while in Japan on tour with Quincy."

George acknowledges Jones's role as the brothers' mentor. "Quincy taught me the order and the way we did things. By him making me double or triple my vocals, he taught me to sing with myself, he taught me to lock my vocals with myself...It was a learning experience for all of us. It felt like being in school the whole time."

The ascension of "I'll Be Good to You" to Number One didn't have a major impact on the brothers. "It didn't really hit us," George admits. "My brother and I were more excited about being in the studio and recording...We had no experience in the record business so we didn't have any ideas as far as marketing strategy or how people would choose our first single or what they would like the first single to be, to represent us as the Brothers Johnson. I guess it was so obvious with the contagious hook that it just stood out on its own."

248

SOPHISTICATED LADY (SHE'S A DIFFERENT LADY)

Natalie Cole

CAPITOL 4259
WRITERS: CHUCK JACKSON, MARVIN YANCY, NATALIE COLE
PRODUCERS: CHUCK JACKSON, MARVIN YANCY, GENE BARGE, RICHARD EVANS
June 19, 1976 (1 week)

In the summer of '76, Natalie Cole did what Hollywood wisdom used to advise against: She married her producer. The singer and Marvin Yancy were wed on July 31 in Chicago, soon after "Sophisticated Lady (She's a Different Lady)" became her third Number One.

And soon after that, Cole made it clear she was searching for creative growth to match her changing personal horizons. "I don't want to get too commercial," she told *Billboard*. "I am heading in the same direction as [Stevie] Wonder. All of his songs have messages. He is very much into himself and his music relates to people. This is where I am going."

Marvin Yancy also knew about messages, having backed some of gospel music's great names. "I started playing the piano 'round the age of 13 for my father's church," he said in 1977, "and from there I ventured out into playing for some of the major gospel groups, people like Jessy Dixon, Rev. James Cleveland, Albertina Walker, and Inez Andrews."

But it was the music of jazz giant Duke Ellington that inspired Yancy and partner Charles (Chuck) Jackson to write "Sophisticated Lady (She's a Different Lady)." Explains Jackson, "My mother used to talk about [Ellington's] 'Take The "A" Train' and 'Sophisticated Lady' when we were kids. So I would think about a sophisticated lady—what she was doing onstage, how she would handle her crowd.

"I would go to Natalie's show, sit all the way in the back, and look at the people. I said, 'Boy, this chick is really sophisticated in that she knows what to say, she has the gift of charisma. Black people, white people, everybody loves Natalie. She is sophisticated, doing her own thing.'

"Marvin said, 'That's a title for a song.' I said, 'Man, Ellington already has 'Sophisticated Lady.' He said, 'Well, yes, but he never did it like we're going to do it!' So that kind of influenced what our next project was going to be, based on that character. You know, we tried to keep [our music] on the move."

"Sophisticated Lady" was recorded for Cole's second album, *Natalie*, at Curtom Studios in Chicago, where Yancy and Jackson employed arrangers Gene Barge and Richard Evans. Barge, whose wailing sax once powered the garage R&B of Gary U.S. Bonds, had been on staff at Chess Records in the late '60s. So had Evans, who arranged for the likes of Marlena Shaw, Ramsey Lewis, and other jazz artists.

For *Natalie*, they recruited the cream of the Windy City, including Tennyson Stephens on keyboards, Phil Upchurch and Cash McCall on guitars, Joseph Scott on bass, Quinton Joseph on drums, and "Master" Henry Gibson on congas. Marvin Yancy played piano, Chuck Jackson handled percussion, and Natalie herself sang all the backing vocals. Sophisticated players for a sophisticated lady.

Cole had a hell of a pedigree, of course, even if her parents didn't approve of rock and roll. "Once my father noticed that I had an interest in music," she told *Rolling Stone*, "they tried to train me on what they thought was the right stuff." Later, when the young Cole essayed an Ella Fitzgerald song a capella for her father, she recalls, "He said, 'By gosh, you've got it.' "

249

SOMETHING HE CAN FEEL

Aretha Franklin

ATLANTIC 3326
WRITER: CURTIS MAYFIELD
PRODUCER: CURTIS MAYFIELD
June 26, 1976 (4 weeks)

Never mind *Dreamgirls*—what about *Sparkle*? Years before Michael Bennett's Broadway extravaganza about a black female group called the Dreams [see 362—"And I'm Telling You I'm Not Going"], there was this modest little movie about a black female group called the Sisters.

Set in Harlem at the cusp of the '60s, *Sparkle* starred Lonette McKee, Irene Cara, and Dwan Smith as an aspiring vocal trio, with Philip Michael Thomas (pre-*Miami Vice*) playing their manager. The Warner Bros. film was flawed—by stereotypical characters, mostly—but it did offer a grainy realism, a thoughtful outlook, and a score by Curtis Mayfield.

"Something He Can Feel" was one of the Sisters' signature songs in the movie, performed during a nightclub sequence with an undulating sexiness that must have inspired En Vogue's 1991 remake. "I had written all of those songs for the youngsters who were acting in *Sparkle*," confirms Mayfield, who at the time was riding high with his soundtrack music for another Warner Bros. picture, "Let's Do It Again" [see 228]. "What is funny is how the depth of my writing made me think of Aretha."

The youngsters in *Sparkle* were not so amused—they had hoped and expected that their recordings of Mayfield's songs would be released as the movie's soundtrack. Lonette McKee, for one, voiced her disappointment publicly while trying to maintain a dual career as singer and actress.

Mayfield admits, "I should have actually released it with the kids, but I was out trying to find somebody to do an album with. Somehow Aretha heard the tunes and fell in love with them, and asked if she could do them."

Franklin recorded the material with Mayfield and arranger Rich Tufo in Chicago during April 1976. They worked at the Curtom studios with the house rhythm section: Mayfield himself on lead guitar, Tufo on keyboards, Gary Thompson on rhythm guitar, Joseph Scott on bass, Donnell Hagan on drums, and "Master" Henry Gibson on congas. Leading the horns was Lennie Druss; directing the string section was Sol Bobrov; vocalizing in back were the Kitty Haywood Singers.

As a song, "Something He Can Feel" was based on "how I thought a woman might feel when she was to love a man," Mayfield explains. He says producing Aretha was quite different to working on "Let's Do It Again" with the Staple Singers. "Here's an act who, totally within her own ability, could produce herself. I wanted it to be something, you know, respectful from both ends."

At the time, there were reports that Mayfield and Franklin clashed in the studio. "It wasn't hard at all," he maintains, "because she loved the tunes. She had her ways, but I had my ways, and found the way to make it work."

Even with their original of "Something He Can Feel" confined to a Warner Bros. vault, Irene Cara and Lonette McKee found their way, too: Cara connected to hit movies and smash songs in the '80s ("Fame," "Flashdance...What A Feeling"); McKee won leading roles in such pictures as *Which Way Is Up*, *'Round Midnight*, and *Jungle Fever*, and recorded for Spike Lee's 40 Acres & A Mule Musicworks.

250

YOU'LL NEVER FIND ANOTHER LOVE LIKE MINE

Lou Rawls

PHILADELPHIA INTERNATIONAL 3592
WRITERS: KENNY GAMBLE, LEON HUFF
PRODUCERS: KENNY GAMBLE, LEON HUFF
July 24, 1976 (2 weeks)

After a long association with Capitol Records, Lou Rawls moved to MGM. Under the stewardship of label president Mike Curb, Rawls had a top 20 hit with "A Natural Man," produced by Michael Lloyd. "Michael and I hit it off right away," says Rawls. "Then Mike Curb threw his hat in the political ring and that's when the label started to tremble. I said, 'I don't play political games.' " Rawls also didn't care to be cast in a bubble-gum image, and left the label for Larry Uttal's Bell Records.

He stayed "for a minute...I did one album. That was when Clive Davis took over Bell. While I was in the studio, they changed the name to Arista." Rawls says his one album for the label was very middle-of-the-road. The title track was released as a single. Unfortunately, Tavares released the same song and a cover battle ensued. Rawls took Daryl Hall and John Oates's "She's Gone" to number 81 while Tavares had a Number One hit [see 189].

In 1976, Rawls found a new label to call home, almost 3,000 miles away from his base in Southern California. The Chicago-born artist took up residence at Philadelphia International, the label founded by Kenny Gamble and Leon Huff.

Lou Rawls

"I met them when they were producing Nancy Wilson for Capitol back in the '60s," says Rawls. "We had talked about getting together one day and trying something out. At the time I was with Capitol working with David Axelrod and Nick Venet."

Rawls was friendly with some of the artists on Philadelphia International, including the O'Jays and Harold Melvin. Rawls first met the O'Jays when they opened for him at Leo's Casino in Cleveland, before they signed with Philadelphia International. When several people suggested that Rawls get in touch with Gamble and Huff to see if they had any songs for him, Rawls did so and received a positive response. "They said, 'We've been thinking about you, wondering what you were doing,' because I hadn't recorded anything for awhile. They said, 'Why don't you come [over]. Let's work something out,' so I went back to Philadelphia and they wrote 'You'll Never Find Another Love Like Mine.' After we talked they did some research and listened to all my old stuff that they could find. It was really right on because they had done the research as far as my vocal dexterity was concerned. It was really tailor-made."

Rawls says he knew "You'll Never Find Another Love Like Mine" was a smash from the first time Gamble sang it for him while Huff played the piano. He didn't know if the song was written from personal experience, but he knew that Gamble was going through a divorce at the time from Dee Dee Sharp.

Rawls says he recorded the song the way that suits him best—live. "When you're recording to tracks, you don't get the same input that you get when you're in the studio with the musicians, feeding off each other. It gives me a little more impetus to be creative as far as the vocals are concerned. When you cut to a track, you're stuck with that."

251
GETAWAY
Earth, Wind & Fire

COLUMBIA 10373
WRITERS: BELOYD TAYLOR, PETER COR
PRODUCERS: MAURICE WHITE, CHARLES STEPNEY
August 7, 1976 (2 weeks)

"We started a lot of stuff together, chess, yoga. And we all began to learn about the Creator."

That's how Earth, Wind & Fire opened Al McKay's eyes, according to a mid-'70s interview with the group's guitarist and sometime co-writer. EW&F typified '70s spirituality where the scriptural met the more generally cosmic. God, chess, and yoga weren't such a strange mix, and leader Maurice White wasn't averse to throwing astrology, Buddhism, or vegetarianism in there either.

So it was no surprise that White had announced his intention to do a spiritual album almost as soon as EW&F had broken through commercially. Or that the group's first full studio LP after *That's the Way of the World* was, indeed, called *Spirit*. Or that he might, by one account, record a hit single about meditating.

It's never really spelled out, but one late-'70s rock encyclopedia swears the lyrics of "Getaway" are "relating to transcendental meditation, which all the group members practice." EW&F wouldn't have been the only band celebrating TM back then; the Beach Boys' "TM Song" came out at virtually the same time. But as was usually the case with a group that wanted to make musical and spiritual experimentation palatable for the masses, EW&F was much more mantra-of-fact about its beliefs.

Also, unlike the now-obscure "TM Song," "Getaway" was hardly a record to which one could actually practice transcendental meditation. It features the most explosive drumming of any Earth, Wind & Fire record, which is saying a lot for a band led by a drummer. Listen to it enough times and you might eventually achieve inner peace, but total relaxation is definitely out.

"Getaway" was recorded at Wally Heider's studio in Hollywood in April 1976, as part of *Spirit*. It was the first album made under the auspices of White's newly formed Kalimba Productions, named for the African thumb piano that would become his onstage trademark. Sadly, it was also the last LP White crafted with co-writer/producer Charles Stepney, who died of a heart attack on May 17, 1976, at age 45.

Stepney's experience as an in-house producer/arranger at Chess Records went back to the time when Muddy Waters and Howlin' Wolf were the label's big acts. Through Earth, Wind & Fire's glory days, he was really the only person who White would accept as a full partner. Even today, Stepney is still the topic about which White becomes most animated. "He was a guy who knew it all," he says. "He had the classical background, he had the gospel background, the blues background, he had played with almost everybody.

"Charles used to experiment in the studio. He had a studio in his basement, he was into electronics and synthesizers and all that, long before we knew what they were...[To us] he was just a guy down there in his basement making funny sounds like a scientist.

"We learned a lot from Charles, and he made a tremendous contribution to Earth, Wind & Fire after I got it together. After I brought him in, he just brought something with him...All the musicians in the band learned and benefited tremendously from his presence," White adds. And although "Getaway" was EW&F's first big hit written outside the group, White says it was one of several songs that "wouldn't have existed" without Stepney's contributions as an arranger.

252

WHO'D SHE COO?

Ohio Players

MERCURY 73814
WRITERS: OHIO PLAYERS
PRODUCERS: OHIO PLAYERS
August 21, 1976 (1 week)

Don't feel too bad if you didn't understand the Ohio Players' "Who'd She Coo?" Some members of the group didn't get it either.

"That's another one that didn't make any sense to me," declares lead singer Leroy "Sugarfoot" Bonner. "Titles like 'Who'd She Coo?'—what does that mean? You have a great track. And if you can't find anything to do with it, you just do something stupid. But you know it's going to be a hit because the track is so great and people don't care. And usually if it's something that's crazy, they'll love it even more."

Trumpet player Ralph "Pee Wee" Middlebrook will never forget recording "Who'd She Coo?" He was lucky to be at the session. Actually, he was lucky to be alive.

"When we did that [song] I was still healing," he remembers. "I had an accident. A head-on collision. I had all my teeth knocked out, so I had a plate. We did the tune and it sounded kind of backwards to me. But we had to change around—we had to do something different. We were mixing jazz with rock and it was working the first 15 years. But we had to do something real weird. And this is what came out of that [*Contradiction*] album. We were trying to be something else. We didn't want to go into the studio and come out with the same type of album we had been coming out with. We were mostly a jazz group [in the beginning]. So we were like on one side of the street. By playing jazz, we were doing albums but they weren't selling. So we decided to take rock and meet in the middle of the street with the rock and the jazz, and then we started selling both." As it turned out, "Who'd She Coo?" returned the Players to their jazz roots. "We came on the other side of the street a little deeper than we were on the rock side," Middlebrook agrees.

Drummer Jimmy "Diamond" Williams says "Who'd She Coo?" was a relatively easy song to record. "That wasn't a heavy tune at all—a little lyric thing that went back, around and about, a little bass-part breakdown and that was it. You didn't have to go to Music School 101. You didn't have to take a thousand tries to get this one down."

Middlebrook describes how the Ohio Players usually wrote their songs: "Everybody had an open mind. We were always open for suggestions. Everybody had to write each tune, which gave everybody the right to collect royalties. Like I would have an idea—I could feel it. We would try it, and if it worked, we used it. And if it didn't work, everybody would have a suggestion. We all tried to contribute to the songs."

The horn player, who retired from the group in 1980 when he was 41, is happy when he hears contemporary musicians who have been influenced by the sound of the Ohio Players. "I listen to them and I love it. I'm glad I did something in this world that would [make] other people stop and listen and say, 'Hey, let's do this.' That's the greatest thing I wanted to achieve."

253

(SHAKE, SHAKE, SHAKE) SHAKE YOUR BOOTY

KC and the Sunshine Band

T.K. 1019
WRITERS: HARRY WAYNE CASEY, RICHARD FINCH
PRODUCERS: HARRY WAYNE CASEY, RICHARD FINCH
August 28, 1976 (4 weeks)

Exactly one year after their first Number One single topped the *Billboard* chart, KC and the Sunshine Band returned to the chart summit with their third Number One hit, "(Shake, Shake, Shake)

KC and the Sunshine Band

Shake Your Booty." No one was more surprised than the group's founder. KC confesses, "I didn't think that was going to be a hit."

He wrote the song after being on the road. He noticed that at most performances, there would be one or two people in an audience who wouldn't stand up and participate because their friends were watching them. "I wrote that about doing your own thing. Don't fight the feeling. If you feel it, get up and feel it. Don't feel insecure. You're the best—the best in the world. I tried to put some self-confidence in people. 'Shake Your Booty' was just another way of saying 'Get Down Tonight' or 'Blow Your Whistle' or 'Sound Your Funky Horn.' "

KC disagrees with those who dismissed "Shake Your Booty" as another piece of disco fluff. "To some it was a nonsense song, but it had a lot more meaning and depth...There were several connotations to 'Shake Your Booty.' It could mean to get off your can and get out there and do it, in every area, not necessarily dancing—in your whole life."

At the same time, KC and the Sunshine Band were more interested in audiences having fun then in dispensing social commentary. "I wanted things to be up," KC agrees. "I guess a lot of times when I write, it's the lowest point in my life. I'm probably in a semi-depressed mode. And I think I would write things to bring me up. I remember in college, if I had a problem with a girl or something, I would write. Instead of talking to someone, I would write it and put it in words, and mentally that would satisfy me. It was like I was going to my own psychiatrist...by writing it down, it helped me get through it. And it helped me explain, at least to myself, how I felt and I'd know I'd written down how I felt and there was no need to tell anyone."

"Shake Your Booty" featured the sound of a clavinet, mistaken by some as a guitar. "I went up an octave higher on the clavinet," KC explains. "It's actually the clavinet giving it that higher sound."

KC's writing and producing partner was Rick Finch. KC explains his contribution: "He was the engineer and we both shared ideas. I was the last set of ears. And we worked very well together. Neither of us interfered with the other—we both had equal input. He was very talented. It worked very well for us. We both were able to do things and so many times, you go in the studio and people get into an argument...but we never had that situation."

While enjoying great success, KC also experienced some low moments. "We were so huge and sometimes it would get very frightening and sometimes it would get very lonely. I can remember looking out at the crowd from my hotel room and wishing I could be on that side of it sometimes. A lot of times, as a matter of fact." Still, KC says it was "all wonderful. When we went out, we went to work and that's what we did. We did our show, came back to the hotel, and went to sleep, woke up, and we left for another city."

254
PLAY THAT FUNKY MUSIC
Wild Cherry

EPIC 50225
WRITER: ROBERT PARISSI
PRODUCER: ROBERT PARISSI
September 4, 1976 (2 weeks)

When Robert Parissi was four years old, his 14-year-old sister started buying records by artists like Little Richard and Bill Haley & His Comets. "These high school girls were going wild and I was just a little kid, but the guitar was fascinating to me," says Parissi. "So I would look at her records and I couldn't read, but I would memorize the way the label looked." Years later, when Parissi did get into the music business, he already knew information like who Sam Phillips of Sun Records was. "I had this history in my brain and I didn't realize it until I thought, 'My God, it was because of those [records].' "

Parissi first considered playing music when he was in fifth grade. Faced with a choice between playing football and playing in the school band, he picked the latter—a more intelligent choice, he figured, as it was less likely to produce broken bones.

Parissi grew up loving R&B, especially Motown, as well as the Beatles. By the time he was playing in a rock band in 1976, the disco era was getting underway and patrons at clubs like the 2001 disco in Pittsburgh didn't want to hear the aggressive rock played by Wild Cherry.

"I went into the dressing room one night and told the guys, 'We are not going to be able to exist without putting out a local record.' " Parissi suggested to lead guitarist Bryan Bassett, keyboard player Mark Avsec, bassist Allen Wentz, and drummer Ron Beitle that they cover the Commodores' "I Feel Sanctified" and write their own song for the B-side. Beitle suggested they simply follow the orders of the customers who would shout, "Play that funky music, white boy." Parissi grabbed a bar order pad and wrote down the words for the song that would overpower the Commodores' song to become the A-side and a Number One hit for Wild Cherry.

"Play That Funky Music" was cut at Cleveland Recording, the same studio where rock bands like Grand Funk, the James Gang, and the Outsiders created some of their biggest hits. "They were used to cutting rock and roll and when I came in to cut this stuff, it was more of a dance thing," says Parissi. "But the engineer, Ken Hammond, was in tune to what needed to happen to the song." That included having the drums out front, something rock artists like Paul McCartney and David Bowie were doing in records like "Silly Love Songs" and "Fame." "All the rock people were just starting to put the drums and bass out front," says Parissi. "That's what the disco records were doing. The dance records had breakdowns. The breakdown in that tune...was like 'Honky Tonk Women.' Because we were a club band, and I knew that when we played that song, the breakdown with the drums did something to people on the dance floor."

It wasn't Parissi who picked "Play That Funky Music" to be the hit side of the Wild Cherry single. Carl Maduri and Mike Belkin, owners of the Sweet City Records label, made a deal with Epic Records and decided to push "Play That Funky Music" as an A-side. But the artist was thrilled to have a Number One song. "I was the happiest puppy that ever lived...I got a chance to meet the Beatles and people I never thought I was going to meet in my life, and they all knew what I had done. Plus, people accepted what I had done and liked it."

255
JUST TO BE CLOSE TO YOU
Commodores

MOTOWN 1402
WRITER: LIONEL RICHIE
PRODUCERS: JAMES ANTHONY CARMICHAEL, THE COMMODORES
October 9, 1976 (2 weeks)

After scoring their first Number One single with an ensemble funk song [see 212—"Slippery When Wet"], the Commodores returned to the top of the R&B chart with a soft, sweet ballad penned by Lionel Richie. It would set the tone for the group's fortunes through the next five years.

One of the first things Richie learned after the Commodores achieved chart success with "Machine Gun" in 1974 was how to sustain a career. When he told Motown producer Hal Davis that the group had their first hit, the producer said that was history and asked what Richie was planning for a follow-up. "Davis then gave me some words of wisdom: 'The key to this business is year after year. Not a hit record. The only way you take money out of the record business is year after year.' That's when I went

The Commodores

back in my house and began seriously writing some songs," Richie told Nelson George.

The direction his writing would take was apparent when the Commodores had a number two single in early 1976 with Lionel's mid-tempo ballad, "Sweet Love." It was also their first top 10 pop hit, peaking at number five. The group followed "Sweet Love" with "Just to Be Close to You" and was surprised to find resistance from pop radio.

"Certain stations considered our music too black for listeners. 'Just to Be Close to You' was one [example]," Milan Williams told Sharon Davis. "But if that tune was too black to be played on a pop station, then how the hell did it get to number seven in the national charts!"

Thomas McClary added, "Statements about music being too black are hindering the people that are listening to the music and they are also hindering the artist. Whatever we create should be accepted and rejected by people as a whole. Why should we have to sell 800,000 copies at Number One in the R&B chart before we get accepted as pop?"

Richie concluded, "What we're dealing with is that age-old problem of people's hang-ups. In the music business you'll find that musicians are universal people. We can go to Japan, Colombia, South Carolina, and I can meet someone I've never seen before in my life and immediately we have something we can identify with, and that's music. The problem is musicians are very open-minded people dealing with a very closed-minded society!"

The success of "Just to Be Close to You" helped bring the Commodores to the forefront of the Motown roster in the second half of the '70s. The group was used to hearing manager Benny Ashburn say terrible things about the company, but they knew it was just his way of doing business. On the other hand, drummer Walter "Clyde" Orange says the group never felt like they were part of the Motown family.

"I felt they had their little clique and there were certain groups that would always be part of that clique that was the original Motown." But Orange has nothing bad to say about the label. "We wouldn't have been able to do what we did if there hadn't been a Motown for the Commodores. I love what Berry Gordy did...We had our ups and downs with them, but Motown will still be Number One with me."

256
THE RUBBERBAND MAN
Spinners

ATLANTIC 3355
WRITERS: THOM BELL, LINDA CREED
PRODUCER: THOM BELL
October 23, 1976 (1 week)

"The Rubberband Man," the sixth Number One by the Spinners, was originally written about Thom Bell's son, Mark. "It was called 'The Fat Man' because my boy was a chunky fellow all the time he was growing up," the producer explains. "In fact, he's a big guy today and I'm glad I was nice to him, because he can step on me now...He's a huge guy, six-foot-seven, 375 [pounds], and looks exactly like a Samoan."

As a first-grader, Mark already weighed 150 pounds, according to his father. "Each one of my children, I wrote them a song to make them feel part of something...His was 'The Fat Man.' After he got to be eight or nine, the kids were picking on him so much, calling him 'the fat man.' So I said, 'We're going to change this around. We can't call him 'the fat man' anymore, because that sounds derogatory. So we're going to call him 'Big Man.' "

By the time the Spinners got hold of the song, it had metamorphosed into "The Rubberband Man." "Did you ever go to a party and the party is a drag?" Bell asks. "Everyone's waiting for something or someone and that person never gets there, or that thing never gets there that makes the party jump. Well, I depicted the idea of everyone waiting for this someone to come...When he does, he gets down. He does it. I mean, he makes them jump! It was about a big guy who could really out-dance [everyone]. Most large people are assumed to be slow, lumbersome, clumsy...but some big guys and big women can do these things. So that was written for big people who were hip, to change the whole idea of a person being large being sloppy, slow."

Bell wrote the song with his longtime collaborator, Linda Creed. "Creed was very much like me," Bell remembers. "I wanted to be a singer at one time and she wanted to be a singer, but neither one of us had it." Bell met Creed through Randy Cain of the Delfonics, and soon learned she wrote poetry. Bell asked if she could write to a melody and Creed said she'd give it a try. Their first song was "Free Girl," recorded by Dusty Springfield, then came "Stop, Look, Listen (To Your Heart)" for the Stylistics. Bell recalls fondly how he used to argue with Creed, who passed away at the age of 37 on April 10, 1986. "Just like I'm particular about a melody, she was extremely particular about the lyric. 'Rubberband Man' never knocked her out because she said it was ignorant. Anybody could write that. I said, 'Too bad. That's the way I like it.' She and I used to fight tooth and nail...but in a friendly fight."

"The Rubberband Man" was the only song written about one of Bell's children that was actually recorded. The producer thought of a unique way to illustrate his song. "I got hold of a company and begged them to come out with these [giant] rubber bands because I designed a whole dance and the Spinners...even to this day, they still have those huge elastic rubber bands when they do the dance."

The track was recorded at Bell's regular base of operations, Sigma Sound Studios in Philadelphia. Bell's brother Tony played guitar along with Bobby Eli. Larry Washington was featured on percussion, Andrew Smith played drums, Bell was on keyboards, and Carla Benson, Yvette Benton, and Barbara Ingram sang backing vocals. The unusual bass sounds on "The Rubberband Man" came not only from bassist Bob Babbitt, but an instrument called a "funk box." "[Babbitt] would always come in with all kinds of different gadgets. Bobby Eli...was hooked to a funk box also."

257
MESSAGE IN OUR MUSIC
The O'Jays

PHILADELPHIA INTERNATIONAL 3601
WRITERS: KENNY GAMBLE, LEON HUFF
PRODUCERS: KENNY GAMBLE, LEON HUFF
October 30, 1976 (1 week)

When he was growing up in Canton, Ohio, Eddie Levert of the O'Jays heard many different kinds of music.

"We were exposed to 'Randy's Record Shop' out of Nashville late at night—we could only get the station from 10 o'clock at night until three or four in the morning and then it would fade out. We would listen to WHLO, which was our parents' station, out of Akron. They played the top 40 format. They played a lot of black records, because they were crossing over. We heard the Frank Sinatras, the Barbra Streisands, the Spinners, Howling Wolf—we heard all of it. I think this has a lot to do with the longevity of the group. It didn't narrow the scope of the kind of music we could do."

Levert believes that "Message in Our Music" is one of the songs that benefited the most from the O'Jays' diverse musical tastes. "It had a Latin feel," the lead singer says. "We got a chance to venture off into the calypso thing, reflecting our background. 'Message in Our Music' had all types of music—the shoobydooby-doos, some jazz overtones." Levert adds that Kenny Gamble and Leon Huff were also able to marry the easy listening sound of the day with contemporary R&B, which added to the success of "Message in Our Music."

Gamble talked about writing message songs as well as love songs with Dede Dabney around the time that "Message in Our Music" went to Number One. "We're starting to write some good love songs," he said modestly. "We're writing some message songs. We switch back and forth, so we can keep ourselves doing something fresh...You go by different experiences that you see people go through. All you do is put them into words and music."

Like all of the O'Jays songs on Philadelphia International, "Message in Our Music" was recorded at Sigma Sound Studios. Founder Joe Tarsia recalls the role the studio played in the O'Jays' sixth Number One hit: "Sigma Sound was one of the first studios in the world to successfully use console automation. The first working system was produced by Alison Research and I bought it. The owner came and installed it. There were other systems—there was an Olive console that didn't work and Quad A had a system they couldn't get off the ground. So to the best of my knowledge, we were the first to use console automation, but it wasn't bug-free when I was using it.

"To this day, Kenny says, 'Someday I'm going to remix "Message in Our Music," ' because toward the end of the recording, the automation collapsed and the horns are doing a little staccato thing. There is a gross malfunction in the final mix. Gamble would let certain things slide because if they felt right, he didn't care if it was technically right. If the singer got the feeling and he was a little off-key, that was more important than it was to be technically correct, which I appreciate. But my computer system fouling up—that he's never forgotten." Was there anything Tarsia could have done to correct the problem? "Yes, remix it," he replies. "Somehow it got past both of us. Sometimes we used to work all night, into the next day, no big thing."

The Sigma Sound Studios were founded in 1968 when Tarsia, the engineer for Cameo/Parkway Records, decided to put up his house, his car, and all of the money he had in the bank to finance his own studio. "It was perfect timing," Tarsia says. "I opened the doors and all my friends—Gamble and Huff, Thom Bell, Madara and White—they all came to Sigma. All of a sudden I was working day and night."

Tarsia came up with the studio name while eating in a Greek restaurant. "The placemat had the Greek alphabet and I said, 'The Greek alphabet invokes precision and is used in science.' I almost made my assistants wear white lab coats...In some ways I kept a prissy place and that's the way people treated it."

258

LOVE BALLAD

L.T.D.

A&M 1847
WRITER: SKIP SCARBOROUGH
PRODUCERS: LARRY MIZELL, FONCE MIZELL, C. DAVIS
November 6, 1976 (2 weeks)

In the week that Jimmy Carter edged out Gerald Ford for the presidency, there were a lot of people asking for the new single by Jeffrey Osborne and L.T.D. But probably not a lot who knew how to ask for it.

Did they want "Much More Than They Can See"? "Hold Me and Say You Care"? "Lovers Come, Lovers Go"?

Eventually, they figured it out. Which is good, because writer Skip Scarborough wasn't too hung up about the title. "I had this melody and I didn't have a title for a long time because it didn't have a hook," he says, "so I just called it 'Love Ballad.' "

Scarborough was musical director for Creative Source, a five-person attempt at a 5th Dimension for the funk era—assembled, in fact, by that quintet's Ron Townson. One night, the group was playing a hotel in Bermuda, but Scarborough's body was still on West Coast time. So he got the security guards to let him into the lounge downstairs where, he says, it took him about 20 minutes to write "Love Ballad."

Scarborough didn't have any artist in mind, he notes. In fact, he had both a male and female demo cut. And a lot of artists, including Tavares, passed on the song initially. In an era when even instrumentals managed to work the title a few dozen times—think of "The Hustle" or "Do It Any Way You Wanna"—the lack of an obvious hook scared people, Scarborough recalls.

That "Love Ballad" would eventually be a hit for L.T.D. was underpinned by coincidence: lead singer/drummer Jeffrey Osborne had done a week's fill-in with Creative Source several years earlier. The night he went to see Love Men Ltd. (their name before L.T.D.) perform, "their drummer was hauled off to jail for fighting outside the club," he says. "I went up and played with them, sang a few songs, and they asked me to join."

The group signed to A&M in 1972 via Jerry Butler's Fountain Records. Their lineup changed several times, but core members included Osborne, his brother Billy (co-lead vocals, keyboards), Henry Davis (bass), Jimmie Davis (keyboards), John McGhee (guitar), and a versatile horn section comprising Jake Riley, Abraham Miller, Lorenzo Carnegie, and Carle Vickers.

"Love Ballad" was on L.T.D.'s third album, *Love to the World*, cut at the A&M studios in Los Angeles with

L.T.D.

producers Fonce and Larry Mizell. Incidentally, the vocal for that song—which was used as a last-minute replacement for another tune—was the product of a second all-nighter.

Jeffrey Osborne remembers that the Mizells showed up at the studio in the early hours. "I had been sitting there since about 11 that night," he says, "so I was determined to sing. I did that vocal at six o'clock in the morning."

259

YOU DON'T HAVE TO BE A STAR (TO BE IN MY SHOW)

Marilyn McCoo & Billy Davis, Jr.

ABC 12208
WRITERS: JAMES DEAN, JOHN GLOVER
PRODUCER: DON DAVIS
November 20, 1976 (1 week)

You didn't have to be in Detroit to capture the Motown sound.

For "You Don't Have to Be a Star," producer Don Davis journeyed west. "With that record," he explains, "I felt I could create the old Motown feeling. There was something in me like a homing pigeon. I went off to L.A. to get Jamerson."

James Jamerson, that is, whose basslines were the foundation of almost every great Motown record of the '60s. He had moved to California in 1973. Detroit-based Davis also recruited a couple of other West Coast musicians "who I was crazy about," including drummer James Gadson. "I knew if I could get Jamerson on bass and Gadson on drums, I would see the whole picture, clear as could be."

Marilyn McCoo and Billy Davis, Jr., founding members of the 5th Dimension, had left that group in November 1975. Under individual contract to ABC Records, they cut some solo sides: Billy with McKinley Jackson ("Three Steps from True Love"), Marilyn with Don Davis ("Time Is a Restless Old Man").

"ABC was getting ready to release my single," McCoo told an interviewer in 1977, "when Billy and I decided that with this new act we were going to have [as a duo], it wasn't a good idea to start coming out with solo records. We went back to them and said we'd really like to record together."

They cut an initial three songs with Davis, and one of them, "I Hope We Get to Love in Time," became the couple's first top 40 R&B hit. It was composed by James Dean and John Glover, who were signed to Davis's Groovesville publishing arm. Dean was previously best-known as co-author of Jimmy Ruffin's "What Becomes of the Brokenhearted."

"James Dean was the ghost writer of many of the Motown hits," says the producer. "He writes exactly like Brian Holland, and they're all in the same family. This guy was born writing. He brought 'You Don't Have to Be a Star' to me, along with some other songs, and I said, 'Man, this is a smash.'

"We cut the basic track in L.A. at the ABC studios. I gave Jamerson an idea of the licks I wanted, the song started off, and it took about two takes—it just fell in place like it should." Strings and horns were done in New York with arranger Horace Ott; McCoo and Davis cut their vocals in Los Angeles during the first few months of 1976.

ABC Records shipped the couple's *I Hope We Get to Love in Time* debut album mid-year, lifting "You Don't

Marilyn McCoo & Billy Davis, Jr.

Have to Be a Star" as a single in August. Don Davis reflects, "It was probably one of the only songs I ever zeroed in on and said, 'This is the way it ought to sound, this is the way it ought to feel,' and had it come off like that."

DAZZ

Brick

BANG 727
WRITERS: RAY RANSOM, REGGIE HARGIS, EDDIE IRONS
PRODUCERS: JIM HEALY, JOHNNY DUNCAN, ROBERT LEE, BRICK
November 27, 1976 (4 weeks)

Every Wednesday, from noon 'til six, five musicians would show up to jam at Southside Sound on Main Street, in Atlanta's College Park suburb. The second-floor eight-track studio wasn't top-drawer: The roof leaked when it rained, and there was no air-conditioning. But a year's worth of Wednesdays there delivered one of the biggest hits of 1976.

That smash was "Dazz," and the musicians were Brick: Reggie Hargis (guitar), Jimmy Brown (horns), Donald Nevins (keyboards), Eddie Irons (drums), and Ray Ransom (bass). "We were right out of college," recalls Hargis, who went to Morris Brown in Atlanta with Ransom and Nevins.

The three played together in a band called Hellaphanalia ("one of those college names," says the guitarist) and even cut a single, "Ain't Nothin' Superstar 'Bout Me," released on Tangerine Records.

After Hellaphanalia broke up, Hargis, Nevins and Ransom connected with Brown and Irons. "I remember seeing Eddie at this club called the Crow's Nest on Huntom Street in Atlanta," says Hargis. "He had this heavy definition of snare and foot, constantly on time."

The new group's name originated at Irons's home. "We were in Eddie's back yard," Hargis recounts, "and his father was building a swimming pool. That's why I thought of Brick. I said, 'I don't want no space names, let me come up with something *solid*. Brick sounds good, and if it sticks by tomorrow, let's use it.' "

"We started playing together, and we would go to the studio one day a week, Wednesdays. By the time we got in, we had to hurry up and come with ideas. Each member would color each other member's ideas with instruments. We had to have it all down by six [o'clock], because the engineer had to be somewhere at seven to play."

Twelve months of one-day sessions in 1975 produced an album's worth of material as well as a single, "Music Matic." The latter came out through a local independent label, Main Street, affiliated with the eight-track where Brick recorded. The studio president was Johnny Duncan; he and colleagues Bob Lee and the late Jim Healy got Atlanta's Bang Records interested in the band.

Hargis explains, "We were playing at this club, the Golden Horn, where [Bang president] Eddie Biscoe saw us and liked us. Things happened so fast—we signed the contract right there in the dressing room." That was in January 1976; the band's debut album, *Good High*, was issued in July.

"Dazz," a tale of disco jazz fronted by Jimmy Brown's exuberant sax and flute work, followed as a single. "We had this track," says Hargis, "it was drums, bass, and guitar, just a rhythm ride. We broke it up into different segments, different patterns, guitar solos. But Jimmy was a jazz soloist, and the undercurrent of 'Dazz' was like a soft funk. He had the flute experience from jazz, and put it on top." Brown was "really talented," adds Hargis. "He played sax, trumpet, trombone, flute, clarinet—a total of 14 woodwind instruments!"

261

CAR WASH

Rose Royce

MCA 40615
WRITER: NORMAN WHITFIELD
PRODUCER: NORMAN WHITFIELD
December 25, 1976 (2 weeks)

The fact that the lyrics of "Car Wash," the hit record, were originally written on a Kentucky Fried Chicken bag is as improbable as the genesis of *Car Wash*, the movie.

Film producer Art Linson recalled how he was taken with the notion of doing a stage musical built around the life of a car wash. "You had to be young, completely reckless, and desperate for money to go to [Universal Pictures] and say, 'I've got this idea, ya know, guys in orange suits, and we're gonna put it to music.' " he told Peter Biskind in *Premiere* magazine. Universal chief Ned Tanen, by Linson's account, said, "This is the worst idea for a play I've ever heard. I think we should just make a movie out of it right away."

Record producer Norman Whitfield wasn't crazy about the idea of *Car Wash* as a movie, either—at least, not as one featuring his music. But director Michael Schultz really wanted him, and kept up the pressure. "Norman saw dollar signs," says Gwen Dickey, the former lead singer of the band who recorded the soundtrack, Rose Royce.

Whitfield also saw something else: the opportunity to use *Car Wash* as a vehicle to launch the career of Rose Royce, his latest proteges. The group had already played behind the Temptations [see 164—"Let Your Hair Down"], and the producer had cut an album's worth of material with them. "We were recording that when Norman was offered the *Car Wash* soundtrack," affirms Dickey. "They wanted him to use the Temptations or the Undisputed Truth, but he wanted to break us."

Coincidentally, it was one of the Truth's vocalists, Joe Harris, who had introduced Dickey to Whitfield. "I was working with a group in Miami, the Jewels, when I was discovered by Joe," she explains. "They flew me to L.A. to audition for the Truth, but Norman decided it would be best for me to go with Rose Royce."

Renamed Rose Norwalt for that purpose, Dickey joined a lineup comprising Kenji Brown (guitar), Lequeint "Duke" Jobe (bass), Henry Garner (drums), Victor Nix (keyboards), Terry Santiel (percussion), and a horn section: trumpeters Kenny Copeland and Freddie Dunn, saxman Michael Moore.

MCA Records had the rights to the *Car Wash* soundtrack. Having successfully argued with the label about using a brand-new group for the music, Whitfield and Rose Royce got down to work. "We rehearsed at Norman's house, then went into the studio to record the tracks," says Gwen. "Once the instrumentation was put down, it was just so electric. Norman said, 'This is going to be a major hit.' "

Dickey recalls Whitfield writing the lyrics of "Car Wash" after a basketball game, on the fried chicken wrap. "He said, 'I want you to sing this for me.' I said, 'I'm not singing this song, it's crazy.' Norman replied, 'Believe me, this song is going to make you rich.' I told him, 'Yeah, right.' "

Cutting the tune with the band at Sound Factory West in Los Angeles, Dickey labored over one of the quirkier lyric lines, about an Indian chief. "Norman told me, 'You're not singing "chief," you're singing "sheep." ' I told him, 'I'm not,' but we fought over it. I must have sung that line 60 times."

Rose Royce also saw the making of *Car Wash*, the movie. Whitfield was scoring it as Michael Schultz rolled the cameras. "We would go each day to watch the filming so Norman would know what to come up with for that segment," says Dickey.

Movie and music came up trumps. Michael Schultz's handiwork, which cost Universal less than $2 million to make, collected $20 million at the box office. Norman Whitfield's labors delivered a gold soundtrack album for MCA and, as planned, broke Rose Royce. After *Car Wash* yielded two other top 10 R&B singles, he signed the band to his own Whitfield Records and produced more hits—although probably without the help of KFC bags.

262

DARLIN' DARLIN' BABY (SWEET, TENDER, LOVE)

The O'Jays

PHILADELPHIA INTERNATIONAL 3610
WRITERS: KENNY GAMBLE, LEON HUFF
PRODUCERS: KENNY GAMBLE, LEON HUFF
January 8, 1977 (1 week)

"I think 'Darlin' Darlin' Baby' is part of the saga of [Kenny] Gamble and [Leon] Huff's ups and downs in their personal relationships," suggests Walter Williams of the O'Jays.

Eddie Levert backs up Walter's opinion. "At this time, Gamble was going through a lot of things with his marriage. This song represented how he truly felt about his wife. It was a very tender song and represented the way a man felt about a woman and that was how Kenny Gamble felt about Dee Dee Sharp. Gamble was a very romantic guy—he did some things I thought I would never do for my wife," Eddie says with the kind of laugh that lets you know he probably *did* do some of those very same romantic things after all.

If there is any doubt that the O'Jays' seventh Number One reflected what was happening in the lives of the two men who wrote and produced most of the group's hits, Sigma Sound engineer Joe Tarsia lends credence to Levert and Williams's accounts. "Kenny and Leon's song titles are the story of their life, absolutely," Tarsia comments. "You could tell when [Gamble] was having trouble."

Williams remembers a time when someone mentioned an impending marriage to Kenny. "[Gamble] said, 'You'll really be able to write songs now,' which meant to me that things he was dealing with on a day-to-day basis would influence him to write more realistic material. I think that was the key to [Gamble and Huff's] success. They wrote about things that were real and true and very relevant to people. They happened to be gifted with melodies and the ability to put tracks together. We learned a great deal from them."

"Darlin' Darlin' Baby (Sweet, Tender, Love)" differed from many of the O'Jays' previous hits in that it was a romantic song instead of a message song like "Back Stabbers" or "Give the People What They Want." At first, the group enjoyed recording the message songs, says Eddie. "I loved having something to say," he reports. "I loved doing songs like 'Ship Ahoy.' I loved the fact that we were doing songs like 'Rich Get Richer,' letting you know about society and raising questions." It also raised the consciousness of the

O'Jays, explains Levert: "All of these things we were recording were things that we would sit down and talk about with Gamble and Huff. Gamble was more the talker and had profound things to say."

But by the time the O'Jays recorded "Darlin' Darlin' Baby," they were happy to be free from playing the role of Gamble and Huff's messengers. "We got to the point where we were tired of doing the message [songs] because we felt we had taken it as far as we could go without being redundant," says Levert. "You don't want to keep banging people across the head. We said, 'What is the ultimate message that you give in music—or anything?' The ultimate message is love.' "

263

I WISH

Stevie Wonder

TAMLA 54274
WRITER: STEVIE WONDER
PRODUCER: STEVIE WONDER
January 15, 1977 (5 weeks)

By 1976, Stevie Wonder was accustomed to landmarks. He was the first artist to reach Number One on three *Billboard* charts simultaneously; he had won ten Grammy awards, including the Best Album prize for two consecutive years. And he had signed the music industry's most lucrative contract to date, a seven-year arrangement with Motown Records said to be worth $13 million.

When the megadeal was inked on Friday, April 9, 1976, Wonder referred to a partially completed album. "The most important thing in my mind is that if it takes two years or seven years [to complete an LP], I must be satisfied when it's done."

In fact, the double-LP album *Songs in the Key of Life* took the lesser of those time periods: it was released in September of 1976, only two years after *Fulfillingness' First Finale*, his previous album. And to judge from an interview Wonder later gave to *Musician* magazine's David Breskin, "I Wish" was one of the last songs created for the project.

"The day I wrote it was a Saturday, the day of a Motown picnic in the summer of '76," he recounted. "God, I remember that because I was having this really bad toothache. It was ridiculous. I had such a good time at the picnic that I went to Crystal Recording Studio right afterward and the vibe came right to my mind: running at the picnic, the contests, we all participated.

"It was a lot of fun, even though I couldn't eat the hot dogs—that was around the time of the creation of those chicken hot dogs. And from that came the 'I Wish' vibe. And I started talking to Gary [Olazabel] and we were talking about spiritual movements, 'The Wheel of '84,' and when you go off to war and all that stuff." Yet Wonder realized that cosmic lyrics weren't appropriate: "The music was too much fun," he said, "the words didn't have the *fun* of the track."

To record "I Wish," Wonder enlisted drummer Raymond Pounds and bassist Nathan Watts, plus a horn section featuring Hank Redd (alto sax), Ray Maldonado and Steve Madaio (trumpets), and Trevor Lawrence (tenor sax). Four years earlier, Madaio and Lawrence had provided the boost to another Wonder chart-topper, "Superstition" [see 139].

When time came to promote *Songs in the Key of Life*, Motown's summer picnic must have stayed in Stevie's thoughts. The album was launched with an all-day outing for the media at Longview Farm in rural Worcester, Massachusetts. Wonder even donned a cowboy outfit, complete with cardboard gun holsters featuring the *Songs* cover design, to stroll around the farm grounds.

Fortunately, the album's artistic stature exceeded the hype. "Stevie's a perfectionist," observes Bob Margouleff, who worked on Wonder's earlier milestone LPs. "He's one of the greatest masters of the pop vocal that I know. In the years [since then], my many experiences have never even come close to his musicality, his inventiveness. Sometimes you reach up and touch the sun."

264

DON'T LEAVE ME THIS WAY

Thelma Houston

TAMLA 54278
WRITERS: KENNY GAMBLE,
LEON HUFF, CARY GILBERT
PRODUCER: HAL DAVIS
February 19, 1977 (1 week)

She recorded gospel music with Art Reynolds. She worked with the composer of "Wichita Lineman" and "MacArthur Park," Jimmy Webb. She interpreted the songs of Laura Nyro, Kris Kristofferson, Mick Jagger and Keith Richards, and Sammy Cahn.

She made a live, direct-to-disc album before most people knew what that was. She was produced by Jimmy Jam and Terry Lewis before most people knew who they were. And she received a Grammy nomination before most people knew who *she* was.

Thelma Houston's calling card has always been her versatility—and in 1976, that was a problem. "Everybody in the world had produced her," remembers Hal Davis, the man who did finally crack the case, "and nobody could come up with a hit. We needed to bring Thelma home."

Talk about understatement. Between 1971, when Houston was signed to MoWest Records, and late 1976, when "Don't Leave Me This Way" was released, she'd hit the charts just once. That was with 1974's "You've Been Doin' So Wrong for So Long," nominated for a Grammy award.

"Don't Leave Me This Way" was originally recorded by Harold Melvin and the Bluenotes, featuring Teddy Pendergrass. Hal Davis thought the song strong enough to stand another version, and laid the basics in late 1975, during the same period he created a smash for Diana Ross [see 243—"Love Hangover"]. Both tracks were done at the Paramount studios in Los Angeles; Davis used the same core of musicians, including Art Wright on guitar, Henry Davis on bass, and James Gadson on drums, with the Waters on backup.

Instrumentally, Wright's propulsive lead guitar is the signature sound of "Don't Leave Me This Way" and "Love Hangover." He also arranged the Houston track, and recalls that its keyboards would have been in the hands of John Barnes, Greg Phillinganes, or Sonny Burke.

Both records exploded out of the discos, hungry for diva-fronted tracks with enough length (and beats-per-minute) to jam the dance floor. But when Davis was cutting "Don't Leave Me This Way," a local AFM official complained about the running time. "We were seven minutes into the tune," he tells, "and the guy walked in from the union, saying, 'Hey, we've been hearing that you're cutting these long versions. You can't keep doing that, we're going to have to start charging extra.'

"I think it was three minutes to six, and when it hit six o'clock, he says, 'You can't keep going.' We were jamming: we had a vamp going, the cats were playing, and this crazy joker from the union said, 'Well, I'm going to stop the date.'

"I jumped out of my chair. 'If you go out there,' I said, 'it'll be the first time you've been

Thelma Houston

knocked out.' I knew I had a beautiful masterpiece, and he had no feeling. But by that time, it was five minutes past six, and the guys had quit playing. They came in [to the control room] and said, 'We did this for Hal, and he don't have to pay nothing for the union.' Now, how many guys can you get to do that?"

265
I'VE GOT LOVE ON MY MIND
Natalie Cole

CAPITOL 4360
WRITERS: CHUCK JACKSON, MARVIN YANCY
PRODUCERS: CHUCK JACKSON, MARVIN YANCY
February 26, 1977 (5 weeks)

During her first few years in the limelight, Natalie Cole sang in the shadow of two giants: her father, and Aretha Franklin. "The early stages of my career were difficult," she admitted to *Billboard* in 1976, "because people wanted to stereotype me. They were saying, 'Hey, kid, you'll get over much faster if you stick to the way your father sang. Go with ballads with a smooth, soft style.' I couldn't do that because it was not me."

"She had a lot of confidence," says Chuck Jackson, one-half of the writing and production team that masterminded her breakthrough. "She came from a different background [than other R&B singers], from a more jazzy thing with her dad. And in Canada, she was doing rock and roll."

Canadian promoter Kevin Hunter played a key managerial role in Cole's career, through whom she met Chuck Jackson and Marvin Yancy [see 222—"This Will Be"]. "We just kind of helped her bring out the soul, the spirit, the R&B sound," says Jackson. "I sang the demos and was right there in the studio, and Marvin gave her that gospel feel on the piano. We just kind of coached her through the whole thing."

Cole herself explained to *Black Music* in 1978, "I've never tried to be like Aretha or my dad or anybody. Of course, Aretha was an influence, she was the essence of R&B to me, but I've never consciously tried to copy her on my records. It's funny, as soon as I got with Capitol [Records], my manager told me to drop her songs from my act. And I did. But because I have such an admiration for Aretha, people can still hear a similarity. And you can't blame them sometimes."

In April 1976, the connection extended beyond the two singers' vocal styles. That was the month Aretha Franklin dropped into Chicago, to record Curtis Mayfield's songs from the *Sparkle* movie soundtrack. Logically, she used the Curtom studios—the very site where Natalie Cole had recorded the demos that convinced Capitol Records to sign her.

Later the same year, Cole cut "I've Got Love on My Mind" at Paul Serrano's studio in the Windy City. She employed several of the same musicians who were on the Aretha date, including guitarists Phil Upchurch and drummer Donnell Hagan. Other players were Tennyson Stephens and Marvin Yancy on keyboards, Criss Johnson on guitar, Larry Ball on bass, Terry Fryer on synthesizer, and Derf Recklaw on percussion. Gene Barge arranged the rhythm track and Richard Evans did the horn and string charts.

"I've Got Love on My Mind" was Cole's fourth record to reach Number One, which did so during the month that she disclosed her July 1976 marriage to Marvin Yancy and announced that she was pregnant. The singer also collected a Grammy (her third) for "Sophisticated Lady (She's a Different Lady)" and her first platinum award for the album *Unpredictable*.

266
TRYIN' TO LOVE TWO
William Bell

MERCURY 73839
WRITERS: WILLIAM BELL, PAUL MITCHELL
PRODUCERS: WILLIAM BELL, PAUL MITCHELL
April 2, 1977 (1 week)

There *was* life after Stax. William Bell was one of several artists who enjoyed their biggest hits—in his case, "Tryin' to Love Two"—after disembarking from Jim Stewart's Memphis train.

When Stax began losing its creative and financial footing during 1973–74, the result was depressing, "especially for the artists who were there from the beginning," says Bell, citing the likes of David Porter, Isaac Hayes, and Rufus and Carla Thomas. "It was like a family dying, a home being destroyed."

Bell himself had been part of that family for more than 10 years, crafting such quietly soulful classics as "You Don't Miss Your Water" and "Tribute to a King." He left the label (and Memphis) before it crashed, taking a three-year sabbatical from recording. "I had to clear my head and regroup," he says. "I was one of the lucky ones at Stax, because I did have some outside business interests. And rather than just sit around and vegetate, I said to myself, 'Well, I'll just get involved in acting, and see if I like that.' "

Based in Atlanta, Bell worked with a repertory group there and even appeared in a movie. He also got to know Paul Mitchell, who was playing in a jazz trio at Dante's, a local club. "We got to talking and became good friends," the singer recounts. "He's a wonderful pianist and arranger, and I'd go and listen to him play."

William Bell

In 1976, Charlie Fach of Mercury Records—which had been distributing Bell's Peachtree label—tried to persuade him to return to recording. "In the initial deal, I was just going to do a single for them," he explains.

"Tryin' to Love Two" was an idea Bell had "partly through personal experience, partly through observation," which had been kicking around in his head for several years. "I had basically all of the lyrical content and just a sketch of melody," he says, "so Paul and sat down and completed it."

The rhythm track was cut at Allen Toussaint's Sea-saint studio in New Orleans. "Allen and I had been friends for a long time," Bell declares. "On my first trip to New Orleans, he came by and caught one of the shows, and he and I just kinda hit it off."

The musicians on the session were Chocolate Milk, a Toussaint-favored Memphis band whose members included Robert Dabon (keyboards), Dwight Richards (drums), and Mario Tio (guitar). Bell's vocal, plus horn and string parts arranged by Mitchell, were added at Atlanta's Sound Pit.

"It's a song about life and something which most people who have been involved in more than one relationship can identify with," Bell summarizes, "but I was totally surprised it sold at the magnitude it did."

"Tryin' to Love Two" crossed to the top 10 of the pop charts, and went gold. "I had been with Stax for 13 years," says Bell, "and had some hits and stuff, but this was a monumental pop hit—and the first record I did after getting back to recording!"

267

AT MIDNIGHT (MY LOVE WILL LIFT YOU UP)

Rufus featuring Chaka Khan

ABC 12239

WRITERS: TONY MAIDEN, LALOMIE WASHBURN

PRODUCER: RUFUS

April 9, 1977 (2 weeks)

Before they joined Rufus, guitarist Tony Maiden and bassist Bobby Watson were in High Voltage, a group that included Memphis-born Lalomie Washburn. She had started singing with her mother, sisters, and brothers in church and moved to California to pursue her dreams of being a singer. She was living in San Francisco's Fillmore district when she auditioned for the band, which signed with Columbia in the early '70s.

After Maiden and Watson joined Rufus, Washburn stayed in touch with them. She was at Tony's home in Topanga Canyon while it was being renovated. "We were writing this song in the middle of a little room downstairs near the fireplace with everything in the world surrounding us," she recalls. "Furniture and everything out of place. And he had put this track together a couple of weeks prior to this. We had a bottle of wine and a fire and I sat there and repeatedly brainwashed myself with the track."

It was around midnight when the words were actually written. Washburn calls the song a gift. "I'm a cliché queen," she laughs. "Now in the '90s, I call myself respectfully a 'hooker'—a woman who has the hooks. It has become a gift that immediately the thing to say comes to mind."

Washburn accompanied Maiden to the studio to record a demo. "I usually put the lead on and the backgrounds and stack them up," she says. "This particular time, me and a couple of other friends put the backgrounds on." Washburn's voice remained on the track. "Yes, I'm still stuck on there. Chaka said, 'It stays if it works. There's no need to go back in and redo the backing [vocals] if it's already working.' "

The co-writer suspected the song was a hit right from the beginning. "When [the words] hit you and they're really right and you don't take earthly credibility, you do take it as from a higher source," she explains. "You know when they're a hit because I

Rufus featuring Chaka Khan

shudder. I tremor like I got a chill from the inside out. It rises up on you and then it lets go."

Maiden explains that it was not difficult to structure a song for Rufus that allowed Chaka to show off her vocal ability. "Nothing was hard. Everything really flowed well with us back then. I mean, God was there with us. Everybody was communicating. I'd play a lick and Bobby would automatically go there, and [drummer] Andre [Fischer] would feel it and then Chaka was like an instrument herself. And everything just kind of flowed."

Washburn enjoyed working with Rufus and Chaka Khan because of her friendship with Maiden and Watson. Having a Number One single was an extra thrill. "I can't describe it," she says. "It's like the happiest feeling in the world when you finally relate to most of the people that are on the American side of the Earth and they say, 'Yes, right. Thumbs-up.' It's the best feeling in the world. You've said something that so many people agree with, it makes you feel wonderful."

268

THE PRIDE (PART 1)

The Isley Brothers

T-NECK 2262
WRITERS: RUDOLPH ISLEY, O'KELLY ISLEY, RONALD ISLEY, CHRIS JASPER, ERNIE ISLEY, MARVIN ISLEY
PRODUCERS: THE ISLEY BROTHERS
April 23, 1977 (1 week)

Although the Isley Brothers shared writing credits equally during the '70s, much of their material originated with a single member—often one of the younger players. In the case of "The Pride," it was Chris Jasper.

He explains, "I usually think from the standpoint of music first, the total sound, rather than just a lyric. So with 'The Pride,' I wanted to try to make to make it funky: a lot of counterpoint happening, but solid basslines and whatnot.

The Isley Brothers

"I had four basic parts first, then I started thinking about the lyric. And it's funny how that came: I had this dream, and this guy in the dream said to me, 'Have you heard "The Politician," that new song by the Isley Brothers?' I don't know what my response was, but when I woke up, I thought, '"The Politician"? Hey, maybe I can make a political statement.' So that's when I wrote 'The Pride.' "

Ernie Isley dates the song to November 1976. "That's when we began doing the basic track, which was an idea that started with Chris. Particularly coming out of the bridge, it had some very funkily voiced chords. The hardest thing was coming up with a melody and lyric. Ronald suggested something melodywise. And there had just been an election after the Watergate thing, so that's what the song was about."

As part of the Isleys' *Go For Your Guns* album, "The Pride" was recorded in upstate New York at Bearsville Sound Studio, near Woodstock. As usual, the rhythm track featured Jasper on keyboards, Marvin Isley on bass, and Ernie doubling on guitar and drums.

"If I had an idea," Jasper elaborates, "I would say to Ernie, 'I'd like the drums to do this rhythm or that rhythm.' He'd play the drum part, while I was playing one of the keyboard parts. I would put the rest of the keyboards on, and he would add his guitar. Then we might do the bass part with Marvin, or if there was a synthesizer bass, I'd do that. At that point, we'd usually do a guide vocal in the studio—me or Ernie would do that—then the other guys would get involved."

Ernie adds, "On a couple of records, that same guide track may be along with Ronald's lead vocal. Or if we were putting down a harmony part—and if I was trying an idea for layers of harmony or something—we would go in and put that down. If it worked, we'd keep it. If not, we would do it over.

"When we began putting something together, it was really raw. It was kind of scary, too, because that was the first time we went into a 24-track studio without Kelly, Rudolph, or Ronald present. It just so happened that the idea we tried was 'The Pride.' In hindsight, what were we intimidated about?"

269

GOT TO GIVE IT UP (PART 1)

Marvin Gaye

TAMLA 54280
WRITER: MARVIN GAYE
PRODUCER: ART STEWART
April 30, 1977 (5 weeks)

Disco? In his mind, Marvin Gaye was quite clear about it.

"To me, there are two types of dance tunes, disco and funk," he told *Black Music* in 1977, "and 'Give It Up' is a funk tune, meaning it's got a chant to it, it's got a round type of overplay—like at the end it's got two chants going simultaneously, and the bassline is hypnotic. Disco is more monotonous."

Settling that issue, Marvin moved on: "I'm a little mischievous in my music. If you notice, I like to play. I want everybody, as long as I'm here, to say, 'I wonder what Marvin Gaye is going to do.' I don't know what I'm going to do. I know what I ain't gonna do, and what I ain't gonna do is come back with something pretty much like what I have done already."

No argument there: "Got to Give It Up," a tribal chant embellished with Gaye's transcendent falsetto, was quite different than his previous blockbuster, "I Want You" [see 245]. And, as with much of his work, he was indebted to another musician for its creation.

"Marv used to fool with this thing called 'Life's Opera,' " recording engineer Art Stewart told author David Ritz, echoing the recollections of an earlier Motowner, Sylvia Moy [see 12—"Ain't That Peculiar"]. "Absolutely brilliant reflections on his life. Genius stuff. He'd do it in between his other projects. I'd urge him to keep working on it, but he'd say, 'Oh, Art, that thing ain't about nothing.' He said the same about 'Got to Give It Up,' only I was more insistent on that one.

"He had this riff that seemed very danceable. He was doing crazy things like banging on a half-filled grapefruit juice bottle for rhythm. Well, I kept stuff like that on the track. Also people talking in the studio—that loose feeling."

Stewart and Gaye cut the song during the fall of 1976 in Los Angeles, with Bugsy Wilcox on drums, Johnny (J.T.) McGhee on guitar, and Jack Ashford on hotel sheet (a styrene board that produced a "wobble" sound) and tambourine. Marvin's brother Frankie and wife-to-be Jan Hunter contributed background vocals.

Ashford, a jazz vibes player and percussionist whom Gaye had introduced to Motown in 1962, recalls the session at the singer's own Hollywood studio. "I'd seen him in the early days, but he had changed so drastically that by the time he got his own thing going—after *What's Going On*—he overdubbed [vocals] sitting right at the recording console.

"He didn't go out into the studio. He would sit at one end of the console, Art Stewart would sit at the other, and he'd sing about two lines at a time. He'd say, 'OK, run that back.' Then they'd punch the whole thing in. It was really weird, because they had the [microphone] boom coming right over the top of the console, and he would just sit and sing there. Marvin was so creative."

270

WHODUNIT

Tavares

CAPITOL 4398
WRITERS: KENI ST. LEWIS, FREDDIE PERREN
PRODUCER: FREDDIE PERREN
May 21, 1977 (1 week)

Keni St. Lewis always loved detective stories, and was a particular fan of movies like *The Thin Man* and *Mr. and Mrs. North*, as well as anything featuring Sherlock Holmes and Charlie Chan. So it wasn't a surprise that he came up with a song for Tavares called "Whodunit."

St. Lewis was born and raised in Washington, D.C., where he met Howard University student Freddie Perren at a talent show on campus. They liked each other's work and decided to team up, although not much came of their efforts while they lived in the District. Perren moved west, where he hooked up with Motown and produced the earliest hits for the Jackson 5 [see 83—"I Want You Back"].

St. Lewis eventually came to California and reunited with Perren. Keni wrote "Farewell My Summer Love," produced by Freddie for Michael Jackson in 1974 but not released until 1984. Perren and St. Lewis had their first big hit together with "Boogie Fever," a Number One hit for the Sylvers [see 239]. That cemented their relationship with Capitol Records executive Larkin Arnold, who told Perren that he was being considered to produce one of the label's hottest acts, Tavares.

"The manager and the group were throwing three names around and it was Norman Harris, Van McCoy, and myself," says Perren, who informed St. Lewis they might be working with the five brothers from New Bedford, Massachusetts. Perren and St. Lewis retreated to the four-track studio Freddie had in his home and came up with "Heaven Must Be Missing an Angel." Perren was hired to produce the group based on that song, which peaked at number three.

Perren remembers the first time St. Lewis sang "Whodunit" for him. "Everything to that point had been disco. This was a little slower. I thought it was catchy, but I wasn't 100 percent sold on the song because I was still into the up-tempo, disco thing." When Perren met with Larkin Arnold and Tavares manager Brian Panella to present songs for a new Tavares album, he saved "Whodunit" for last. "They went crazy," says Perren. "They started grooving off of it...They got really carried away with it. That's how it ended up on the album."

Perren rehearsed the song by playing the "Dragnet" intro at the beginning, but not wanting to risk a lawsuit he reversed the notes, still giving the intro a "Dragnet" feeling. Perren put together a band that included James Gadson on drums, Bob Bowles on guitar, Scott Edwards on bass, John Barnes and Sonny Burke on keyboards, Bob Zimitti on percussion, and Paulinho da Costa on congas. "The guys in the band really liked it because everything they were doing around town was disco and they thought it was a nice change," says Perren. "They put their hearts into it."

The producer remembers how excited his writing partner was at the session. "When we were out there working with the band, Keni was singing the whole time, as if he were onstage and this was his backup band. I remember him sweating because he was getting so excited—that was one of those special moments. There are a lot of songs I've recorded over the years [for which] I don't remember the individual rhythm sessions, but that one sticks out in particular, even to where everybody was standing and sitting."

271

SIR DUKE

Stevie Wonder

TAMLA 54281
WRITER: STEVIE WONDER
PRODUCER: STEVIE WONDER
May 28, 1977 (1 week)

When the National Academy of Recording Arts & Sciences honored Duke Ellington in 1966 with a Lifetime Achievement Award, the citation could have applied to Stevie Wonder—and someday probably will.

It praised Ellington's "tremendously high standards of musicianship and creativity maintained throughout his entire career," and recognized "his artistic integrity and dedication to the music that has influenced and inspired countless peoples throughout the world."

Wonder paid his own tribute to the Duke 10 years later, as part of his ambitious *Songs in the Key of Life*. (What Ellington would have said about spending $600,000 to record an album—even a two-LP set—is something else.)

"With 'Sir Duke,' I knew the title from the beginning but wanted it to be about the musicians who did something for us," Wonder told a *Billboard* college symposium in 1977. "So soon they are forgotten. I wanted to show my appreciation. They gave us something that is supposed to be forever. That's the basic idea of what we do and how we hook it up."

Wonder has been showing appreciation of other musicians throughout his career, starting with 1963's *Tribute to Uncle Ray* album. Five years after that, his instrumental *Eivets Rednow* LP included a salute to jazz great Wes Montgomery.

"I wrote 'Bye Bye World'...for Wes," Wonder said. "I told him about the song and then, not long after, there was his tragic death." Stevie paid even more direct homage to Montgomery by writing "We All Remember Wes," which was recorded by George Benson in 1977 on his *Weekend in L.A.* album.

"Sir Duke," honoring Count Basie, Glenn Miller, Louis Armstrong, and Ella Fitzgerald as well as Ellington, featured Wonder's musicianship—especially on the Yamaha GX10 synthesizer he called his "dream machine"—and that of eight sessioneers: Raymond Pounds (drums), Nathan Watts (bass), Mike Sembello (lead guitar), Ben Bridges (rhythm guitar), Hank Redd (alto sax), Trevor Lawrence (tenor sax), and Ray Maldonado and Steve Madaio (trumpet).

The material on *Songs in the Key of Life* was cut during 1975–76 at four studios: Crystal in Hollywood, Hit Factory in New York, Record Plant in Los Angeles, and Record Plant in Sausalito. "There were times," bass player Nathan Watts told author James Haskins, "when he'd stay in the studio 48 hours straight. You couldn't even get the cat to stop and eat."

It was an intense, if exhilarating, experience for everyone involved. Ironically, Wonder's warp-speed surge into self-possessed creativity at age 21 had happened because he sought less dependence on others. Malcolm Cecil, who helped enfranchise Stevie with the Moog synthesizer [see 139—"Superstition"], recalls, "[He said], 'Gene Kee is my musical director, but I really want to get away from the band thing. Because I have to play to Gene, Gene has to write it down, then he has to tell a player, then I have to correct the whole thing. It's too far away from my original idea.' "

And he was seldom short of original ideas. Bob Margouleff, who was Malcolm Cecil's partner in Wonderland, calls popular music the "pagan ritual" of our day and Stevie one of "the great witch doctors." Adds Margouleff, "He brought some real truths [to music]. And although we used synthesizers, there were no samples, no preconceived things. Stevie created his own world, reflecting his time."

272

BREAK IT TO ME GENTLY

Aretha Franklin

ATLANTIC 3393
WRITERS: MARVIN HAMLISCH, CAROLE BAYER SAGER
PRODUCERS: MARVIN HAMLISCH, CAROLE BAYER SAGER
June 18, 1977 (1 week)

Shortly after Marvin Hamlisch and Carole Bayer Sager played "Break It to Me Gently" for Aretha Franklin at her home in Encino, California, Marvin received a phone call on his answering machine from the artist. She left a message that said, "Hello, Marvin, this is Aretha..."—long pause—"...*Franklin*." Hamlisch thought to himself, who else named Aretha would be calling?

Sager and Hamlisch were introduced to each other by a mutual acquaintance who thought they should write together. Sager had a number of hits to her credit ("A Groovy Kind of Love," "When I Need You"). Hamlisch had also dabbled in pop songs ("Sunshine, Lollipops and Rainbows"), but was better known for his movie work ("The Way We Were") and theatrical composing (*A Chorus Line*). When they met, Hamlisch had just written the score for a television pilot. "He played me this thing and I didn't particularly like it," Sager recalls. "I said, 'I don't think that's something I could do very well, but if you want to write a pop song with me, I have this title, "Break It to Me Gently." ' "

They collaborated on the song in Marvin's New York apartment, without any particular artist in mind. "When we finished, we were thinking of ideal casting. I think [Aretha] is the very first person we thought of," says Carole. In California, they called Aretha and she invited them to come right over and play the song for her. It was the first time that Carole had met the First Lady of Soul. "I was stunned that I was sitting in Aretha Franklin's living room, at her piano, with a big chandelier in the room, playing this song." Aretha started to sing along; fortunately, Carole's tape recorder was running. "I taped that meeting when she was singing. I played it in my car every day for probably months until she actually made the record."

The song was recorded at a studio in the San Fernando Valley on a hot, sweltering day. "Aretha doesn't like air conditioning because of her voice, but none of this mattered," Carole remembers. "There are people I hold sacrosanct—it's almost a religious experience. If they ever sing your songs, you can genuinely call yourself a songwriter, and she was right up there on the list. It's Aretha singing your song that makes it an unbelievable thrill."

Marty Paich arranged the strings for the session and his son, David Paich, played keyboards. Also on the session were Sylvester Rivers on keyboards, Lee Ritenour and Ray Parker Jr. on guitars, Chuck Rainey on bass, Harold Mason on drums, and Joe Clayton on conga drums.

Sager and Hamlisch were both surprised that the song went to Number One on the R&B chart. "I thought sure it would be a huge pop hit because it was me and Marvin," Carole professes. "It wasn't exactly Jam and Lewis." Nevertheless, the song stalled on the Hot 100, peaking at number 85. It was Aretha's final pop chart single on Atlantic before her move to Arista. Fifteen years would pass before Sager would work with Aretha again. Along with Burt Bacharach, she wrote and produced "Ever Changing Times" and "Someone Else's Eyes" on Aretha's *What You See Is What You Sweat.*

273

BEST OF MY LOVE

The Emotions

COLUMBIA 10544
WRITERS: MAURICE WHITE, AL MCKAY
PRODUCER: MAURICE WHITE
June 25, 1977 (4 weeks)

"When you become aware of the tools you're dealing with, you hear certain things," says Maurice White, explaining that by "tools," he means the human voice. "When you become aware of the sounds of the voice, you can almost re-create that voice in your head."

The producer of "Best of My Love" had the use of the finest tools: the harmonic sound of Wanda, Sheila, and Pamela Hutchinson—the Emotions. When White signed the Chicago sisters (including founding member Jeanette Hutchinson) to his Kalimba production company in 1975, they had already honed their skills through years of singing in church, on the gospel road (as the Hutchinson Sunbeams) with Mahalia Jackson, and on a series of hits for Stax Records.

The first of those was "So I Can Love You," a soulful side that reached the R&B top three in 1969 and even cracked the pop top 40. The Emotions scored another dozen chart entries at Stax, but suffered from the company's eventual demise.

At which point Maurice White stepped in. He had actually known the girls since the early '60s, when he played in a Chi-town music revue that also featured the Hutchinson siblings. "They were incredible," he says, "and you know, they were great a cappella, too. They could walk in this room and just light it up."

Flowers was the Emotions' first album for Kalimba, released on Columbia Records in 1976 through White's CBS deal. "Best of My Love" was part of their second LP, *Rejoice*, made in March and April of '77.

"We arrived in Los Angeles with a bunch of songs we'd written, ready to show Maurice," explained Wanda to authors Bob Gilbert and Gary Theroux in *The Top Ten* (Fireside, 1982). "He had a few of his own, including 'Best of My Love,' which he had not yet completed. He had the rhythm down and had sung the song on a demo tape, even though the words weren't all finished."

White affirms the tale, saying he had the Emotions in mind when he and Earth, Wind & Fire's Al McKay authored the tune. "If I was going to write a song for a certain voice," he comments, "then I would look for certain chords and certain melodies that make you feel certain things. That's the way 'Best of My Love' was created, primarily for them."

The *Rejoice* sessions took place at the Wally Heider, Hollywood Sound, and Sunset Sound studios, with White and co-producer Clarence McDonald, plus arranger Tom Tom Washington. McDonald played piano and clavinet on "Best of My Love," with guitarist McKay and other members of Earth, Wind & Fire: Verdine White (bass), Fred White (drums), and Larry Dunn (synthesizer). The EW&F horns were on the date, too, as was percussionist Paulinha DaCosta.

"I learned the song off [Maurice's] demo and practiced singing it in the same register that he had," said Wanda Hutchinson. "Well, the day we went to rehearse the song in the studio, he said, 'No, Wanda, I mean for you to sing it an octave higher.' So I said, 'Maurice, I've never sung that high in that range.' And he said, 'Well, you don't know if you don't try it.' So we did it, but I was still pretty doubtful."

Wanda said she still wasn't used to it the first time she heard "Best of My Love" on the radio. "But what happened was that when my range got higher, the intensity of my vibrato sharpened a little. It got a cut on it, and people like it. And I've got to say, I've come to like it myself, now."

The sun beamed on the Hutchinsons when "Best of My Love" was released in May 1977. The single became a gold-certified crossover smash, with four weeks at the R&B summit and five weeks atop the Hot 100. It also powered *Rejoice* to platinum, with seven weeks at Number One on the R&B album charts and a top 10 berth in the nation's pop listings.

A couple of years later, the Emotions returned Maurice White's favor, adding golden harmonies to Earth, Wind & Fire's "Boogie Wonderland." That record—also a crossover monster—earned the sisters another spell in the chart sun.

274

EASY

Commodores

MOTOWN 1418
WRITER: LIONEL RICHIE
PRODUCERS: JAMES ANTHONY CARMICHAEL, THE COMMODORES
July 16, 1977 (1 week)

Stung by charges that his song "Just to Be Close to You" was "too black" to be played on pop radio, Lionel Richie wrote a song that he thought could easily be played on R&B, pop, and country stations. Did he succeed? "Easy" went to Number One on the R&B chart and became the Commodores' biggest pop hit at the time by peaking at number four on the Hot 100. While the Commodores' version didn't cross over to country, versions by John Wesley Ryles, Barry Kaye, Bobby Hood, and Jimmie Rodgers & Michele made the country chart in 1978–79.

Looking at their roots, it isn't surprising that the Commodores could hit all of *Billboard*'s charts. "We're country boys from Tuskegee, Alabama," says drummer Walter "Clyde" Orange, pointing out that bass player Ronnie LaPread had family that lived on a farm and once wrote a song called "Gimme My Mule."

Richie's ballads brought the Commodores to the top of the chart, but Orange also credits producer James Anthony Carmichael with playing a valuable role in the success of the group.

"It was James Carmichael who brought our music to fruition," says the drummer. "The Commodores, before we hit Number One, played everything from Jimi Hendrix to Three Dog Night...We opened up the Jackson 5 tour doing 'Liar' and got over because of our arrangement. Those were the kinds of songs we did. Tunes by Chase, tunes that were hard rock. We did those kind of songs and we did our R&B too. When we wrote music, we used a screaming guitar. At Motown, they didn't know how to record that. It wasn't until James Carmichael came into focus—along with Cal Harris, the engineer—and said, 'If you want to put a screaming guitar in the middle of something, this is how we do it.' "

Orange says the Commodores first learned of Carmichael when they watched him work with the Jackson 5 and other Motown artists. "We said, 'If we just had this guy, our problems would be over.' We weren't thinking about having a hit record. Our music wasn't straight, that's the only thing we were concerned about. He consented to work with us and when he came in, it was great. He taught us a lot."

Orange also gives due to his fellow group member. "God bless Lionel Richie, wherever he is and whatever he's doing," says the man who now sings some lead vocals for the Commodores. "We realized back then [that ballads were] our strength. I learned somewhere back then that the real meat and potatoes is in the writing, writing songs that are going to be around for years to come."

Orange admits at the time he didn't understand where Richie was coming from. "I didn't come up listening to Elton John. If Elton was around, he was in the mix with James Brown, Otis Redding, Wilson Pickett, Sam Cooke, and the Motown sound. I came from the black side of things. I'm from Jacksonville, Florida, and at the time there was a station called WOBS. They played everything from country to blues to pop to R&B, and I was well versed. But it was basically black music. That's the craft I wanted to bring to this group."

275

SLIDE

Slave

COTILLION 44218
WRITERS: STEPHEN WASHINGTON, MARK HICKS, MARK ADAMS, DANIEL WEBSTER, TIMOTHY DOZIER, FLOYD MILLER, THOMAS LOCKETT, ORION WILHOITE, CARTER BRADLEY
PRODUCER: JEFF DIXON
July 30, 1977 (1 week)

The nine members of Slave began their chart career in a big way—with a Number One song their first time out.

Like the Ohio Players [see 146—"Funky Worm"], Slave began in Dayton. Founding member Steve Washington was even related to that band—he was the nephew of Ohio Player Ralph "Pee Wee" Middlebrook. Washington was from East Orange, New Jersey, but moved to Dayton in 1975 to live with his uncle and finish high school. During that summer, he formed a band called Black Satin Soul that included Mark Hicks and Tim Dozier. Hicks had been playing rock and roll guitar in the style of Grand Funk Railroad and Black Sabbath, but decided to join an R&B band anyway. When another local group, the Mystics, broke up, three of its members—Mark Adams, Thomas Lockett, and Floyd Miller—were added to Washington's group. In October of 1975, Danny Webster and Carter Bradley came on board and the group expanded to nine with the addition of Orion Wilhoite.

Adams was the youngest person in the group—he was still in grade school while the others were in high school. He remembers how the nine-man aggregation got its name: "We were at a rehearsal and Floyd Miller came in the room with a T-shirt that said 'Slave' and we said, 'Hmmm, something about that name.' We wanted to take that and make a 180-degree turn—a positive instead of a negative. We're all slaves to the universe and to God and just to life. We're not slaves amongst ourselves and to each other. And that is our concept behind the name."

The group travelled to Washington's home in New Jersey where they met Jeff Dixon, program director for WNJR, a powerhouse R&B station in Newark. "Jeff heard us and liked us," says Adams. "He took us in the studio and let us record and produce ourselves."

Adams remembers how the group's first hit was the last song written for the album. "It was about three o'clock in the morning. We were in New Jersey. Mark Hicks, Steve Washington, and I were the only ones up. We started hitting that groove and the whole house got up. We added to it and went in the studio the next morning and recorded it live. And 'Slide' was really the first take. The lyrics came from Mark Hicks, and the actual groove came from myself."

After Slave completed "Slide," Dixon took the material to Henry Allen, head of Atlantic Records' Cotillion label. "He signed us right there," says Adams. "It happened so fast, I almost didn't believe it."

Adams remembers how excited the group was to hit Number One with their first single. "It was an experience I'll never forget. I really cannot describe the feeling, because it was constant energy. We were busy as I don't know what. We were playing every night for almost a year straight. 'Slide' was one of those songs that hung around for months."

The membership of Slave changed several times; the most significant addition was when vocalists Steve Arrington and Starleana Young came on board in 1978. "Slave was more or less a university of great talent and we had a lot of people come through and a lot of people graduate," says Adams. "It's hard to harness people when they're talented."

276

STRAWBERRY LETTER 23

The Brothers Johnson

A&M 1949
WRITER: SHUGGIE OTIS
PRODUCER: QUINCY JONES
August 6, 1977 (1 week)

Johnny Otis was a legendary figure in R&B music before George and Louis Johnson were born. Otis, the son of Greek immigrants, was born in Vallejo, California, on December 28, 1921. After finishing high school in 1939, he saw Count Basie perform at the World's Fair in San Francisco and decided he wanted to be a musician. He worked in various bands in the early '40s and opened his own nightclub in south central Los Angeles in 1948. He formed the Johnny Otis Rhythm & Blues Caravan and wrote and produced hits for artists like Little Esther, Jackie Wilson, Johnny Ace, and Big Mama Thornton. He discovered artists like Etta James, Little Esther Phillips, Hank Ballard & the Midnighters, and Little Willie John, and had his own top 10 hit in 1958 with "Willie and the Hand Jive."

In 1968 Otis recorded the album *Cold Shot* featuring his teen-aged son Shuggie on guitar. Two years later, Shuggie recorded his own debut album, *Here Comes Shuggie Otis.*

The Brothers Johnson hung out with Shuggie in Los Angeles. "He was this incredible musician who played everything from drum to bass to guitar to keyboards, and he'd write songs," says George, who at one time dated one of Shuggie's cousins. She gave George a copy of Shuggie's 1971 album, *Freedom Flight,* and George fell in love with the first two songs: "Ice Cold Daydream" and "Strawberry Letter 23."

The latter song was heard at Louis Johnson's wedding; he decided to march down the aisle to Shuggie's version. "Around that time we were working on our second album and Louis had a meeting with Quincy Jones and mentioned to him that we'd love to do that on our album," George remembers. "Quincy had never heard the song—that's what I dig about Quincy, he's very open to every suggestion. He knew we were young enough to have our ears tuned into things we liked."

Shuggie had composed the song for his girlfriend, who wrote him strawberry-scented letters. "He would answer her back," explains George. "They had written back and forth 22 letters with this strawberry scent." For the 23rd letter, Shuggie wrote a song—which is why the lyrics refer to "Strawberry Letter 22." The song itself was "Strawberry Letter 23."

When the Brothers Johnson went into the studio with Quincy to record the song, the producer brought in guitar veteran Lee Ritenour to play the complex solo. "I learned to play the solo part after he put it on record for me," says George. The bell heard on the track was like one heard in the original version. "The only thing we didn't duplicate was...an organ sound in the B-section of the song," says George. "We used something else."

George's vocal interpretation was dead-on to Shuggie's. "It had to be, because the song was so melodic," says the older Johnson brother. "I put a couple of little twists in here and there. I did alter it slightly. I don't think Shuggie realized how huge that song was when he did it [originally]."

George still loves Shuggie's version and plays it often. "My kids will say, 'OK, dad, let's hear *your* version!' "

277

FLOAT ON

The Floaters

ABC 12284
WRITERS: ARNOLD INGRAM, JAMES MITCHELL JR., MARVIN WILLIS
PRODUCER: WOODY WILSON
August 13, 1977 (6 weeks)

The song "Float On" floated into James Mitchell Jr.'s dreams one night. "I was in bed, and my wife must have thought I was crazy when I jumped up," he remembers. "I jumped up because I usually keep a recorder to hum ideas [into]...I might hum out a bassline, the whole melody all the way through a tune...So I hummed it down, and came up with how I wanted the chords to go. I came up with the break on each one of the guys saying something. The next morning, I called Marvin [Willis]. He thought I was crazy...I woke him up about seven."

Along with brothers Abe and Ivory Tilmon, Mitchell was a member of the Detroit Emeralds, a Motor City–based group that had top 10 hits on the Westbound label in 1971–72 with "Do Me Right," "You Want It, You Got It," and "Baby Let Me Take You (In My Arms)." Mitchell explains, "Abe and myself always said that if we ever had any kind of success, we would put something back into the community and help other young artists trying to make it." With their earnings, they purchased a bar called the Emerald Lounge. Mitchell's parents managed the club while the Detroit Emeralds were on tour, and Sunday afternoons were reserved for younger talent to perform. One of the groups featured on Sundays was the Junior Floaters, an outfit that included James's younger brother, Paul, along with Larry Cunningham, Charles Clark, Jonathan Murray, and Ralph Mitchell (no relation to James and Paul), who joined the group in September of 1976.

Mitchell teamed up with Marvin Willis and Arnold Ingram to write material for the group. "We went to work for about half a year, putting different songs together," Mitchell recalls. " 'Float On' was the last tune done for the album. I was trying to get a theme for the album...Their whole thing was dancing more than being singers...They were like young Temptations." Mitchell noticed how young women reacted to the individual Floaters and came up with the idea of each member introducing himself by name and astrological sign in "Float On."

The song's layered harmonies were inspired by a number of different sources, Wilson notes: "I think the combination of what Smokey did with the Miracles as well as the Four Tops with 'Still Water

The Floaters

(Love)'...and an old tune by the Manhattans, 'Follow Your Heart'...The Dramatics were on the same label [as the Floaters] and they had a song called '(I'm Going By) The Stars in Your Eyes.' Just different thoughts, different things that jumped in my head came together to make it happen."

The Floaters were signed to Woody Wilson's Fee Records. Their first single, "I Am So Glad I Took My Time," was released on Fee before Wilson signed a deal with ABC Records. "Float On" was recorded at Pac 3, a Detroit studio located in a garage. It was the same facility the Detroit Emeralds used to record their hits. Motown session guitarist Dennis Coffey, famous for his "Scorpio" instrumental from 1971, played on the session, as did Mitchell's cousin Kenny Goodman on guitar, Guy Hutson on bass, Arthur "Buster" Marbury on drums, Lorenzo Brown on percussion, Jack Brokensha on vibes, Larry Nazero on flute, and Gary Schunk on clarinet and synthesizers. Co-writers Ingram and Willis played piano and trumpet, respectively.

"Float On" was an international hit; it went to Number One in Great Britain a month before topping the *Billboard* R&B chart in America. "They were very hard-working young guys and there was a magic about them," Mitchell concludes. "Each one had something special going on. They were entertainers...It was a real joy working with them and seeing things happen to people you love."

278

KEEP IT COMIN' LOVE

KC and the Sunshine Band

T.K. 1023
WRITERS: HARRY WAYNE CASEY, RICHARD FINCH
PRODUCERS: HARRY WAYNE CASEY, RICHARD FINCH
September 24, 1977 (1 week)

Like many of KC and the Sunshine Band's hits, "Keep It Comin' Love" employed a lot of repetition of the lyrical hooks. "We were writing commercial songs," KC concedes. "I remember working in the [record] stores and the reason we would always use so much repetition was because I didn't want anyone not to know the name of the song once they heard it on the radio. When they went into the store, I wanted them to know it was 'Keep It Comin' Love,' or whatever."

"Keep It Comin' Love" is the final track on the *Part 3* album. It's connected directly to the song that precedes it, "I'm Your Boogie Man," which preceded "Keep It Comin' Love" as a single and peaked at number three on *Billboard*'s R&B chart. "They were both recorded at the same time," KC explains. "I was sitting there waiting for them to roll back [the tape] and I came up with the [horn part] and it seemed to all fit. Rick [Finch] and I decided we should put the two songs together nonstop on the album."

"Keep It Comin' Love" was the fourth and final Number One hit for KC and the Sunshine Band in the '70s. They didn't even return to the top 10 until "Do You Wanna Go Party" peaked at number eight in 1979. On the pop chart, they had the first Number One single of the '80s, "Please Don't Go," but it failed to chart R&B. The flip side, "I Betcha Didn't Know That," went to number 25 on the R&B chart.

KC's career was suddenly interrupted on January 15, 1982. The artist was seven blocks from his home in Hialeah, Florida, when the car he was driving was hit head-on by another vehicle. He suffered a concussion and pinched a nerve on the right side of his

KC and the Sunshine Band

body, causing him to lose all feeling in that area. Confined to a wheelchair, he had to learn to walk all over again. He endured a difficult year of recuperation, and still endured pain on a daily basis as long as two years later.

With the passing of the disco era, T.K. Records filed for bankruptcy and the Sunshine Band dissolved. KC signed with Epic and released a couple of albums under the group name and one as a solo effort. "Give It Up" from *All in a Night's Work* became his first Number One hit in the U.K., but Epic's U.S. operation declined to release it and KC won his release from the label. He started his own independent label and released "Give It Up" on his own.

The end of the disco era was clearly not the end of KC. "I had always planned on having a long-range career," he attests, "and never thought of being here today and gone tomorrow. I think dance or rhythm music never dies; I think a name [disco] died." KC thinks the name was inappropriate, "because the type of music that was being played in the clubs was actually rhythm & blues music, and not disco or any other form. I had always been a little upset because the credit had not been given to rhythm & blues."

279

IT'S ECSTASY WHEN YOU LAY DOWN NEXT TO ME

Barry White

20TH CENTURY 2350
WRITERS: NELSON PIGFORD, EKUNDAYO PARIS
PRODUCER: BARRY WHITE
October 1, 1977 (5 weeks)

"It's Ecstasy When You Lay Down Next to Me" returned Barry White to the top 10 after an absence of almost two years. With a five-week run at Number One, it's the most successful of all his R&B chart singles, and his only top 10 hit not to include the name Barry White in the writing credits. "It's very difficult to write for Barry White," the artist concedes, "because his voice is so low."

"Ecstasy" was written by Ekundayo Paris and Nelson Pigford. Ekundayo and his brother Adeneyi, both born in Los Angeles, wrote songs in high school. "I started off as a singer doing background sessions with people like Neil Diamond and B.B. King," says Ekundayo. He and his brother were two of five writers on "Sooner or Later," a top 10 pop hit for the Grass Roots in 1971. Through a co-writer, they met New Jersey transplant Nelson Pigford soon after he moved to California in 1973. "I got into songwriting by accident," says Pigford. "The Paris brothers wrote some music and it seemed we were able to write some lyrics to a lot of things they already had on tape." After working together for some time, Ekundayo and Nelson parted temporarily.

Paris was attending Los Angeles City College as a music student when he came up with a piece of music and decided Pigford should write the lyrics. But he no longer had Pigford's telephone number, so he went to the residential hotel in Hollywood where Nelson was living and played the track for him. "We both started bouncing ideas, trying to get something uplifting, something positive, something to bring two people together and take it to the ultimate," says Paris. "There was no particular idea that set me off," Pigford adds. "I remember what we first thought about was 'Ecstasy,' and as the song developed we decided to give it more of a title." The song was completed that same afternoon. They used some friends' equipment to record a four-track demo with an out-of-tune piano. They hadn't written the song with any particular artist in mind, but fate intervened. "We took it to a mastering place and tweaked the tape some," says Paris. "We ran into Billy Page, Gene's brother, and Billy said Barry was looking for material. So thanks to Billy—he got it to Barry."

White received the tape before leaving for a tour of Europe. "I take all my stuff on the road," Barry says. "I'm not only there to do concerts. I'm going to write, too." Barry heard the demo for the first time while staying at a hotel in France. "Everybody in my crew was going up and down the hall laughing at that song. I said, 'This is a smash, man!' " White's version ultimately sounded very different from the demo. "The next time they heard it, they could not believe it was the same song."

Barry confirmed the song was a hit after he recorded the instrumental track. "That's when everybody knows we got one. It's there before they hear the lyric, and they say, 'You shouldn't put lyrics on that, B. W., that's an instrumental!' That's when I know I got the stuff. It's gotta be great as music before anybody does anything else to it."

Paris and Pigford didn't hear what Barry had done to their song until it was released. "It was Barry's style," Paris notes. "I think I would have cut it perhaps more up-tempo...but he had his audience in mind." Pigford elaborates, "It was a bit different. He took an approach to it and stayed with the melody, but he changed some of the other things to make it truly be his."

Both writers were thrilled to have a Number One song. "This song went far beyond what we could have ever expected of it," says a grateful Nelson.

And if you thought the nine words "It's Ecstasy When You Lay Down Next to Me" made for a long title, it was replaced at Number One by an even *longer* nine-word title.

280

(EVERY TIME I TURN AROUND) BACK IN LOVE AGAIN

L.T.D.

A&M 1974
WRITERS: LEN RON HANKS, ZANE GREY
PRODUCER: BOBBY MARTIN
November 5, 1977 (2 weeks)

It took L.T.D. eight years of hard traveling to break through with "Love Ballad" [see 258]. But the Love, Togetherness & Devotion crew nearly celebrated by breaking up.

One mid-'70s article reported that the band found themselves plagued by business problems and a lack of internal communication in the wake of "Love Ballad." But they muddled through, bringing in a new management company and, through them, veteran Philly producer Bobby Martin.

The result? A year to the day after their first Number One, L.T.D. were back at the summit with "Back in Love Again," the song that would also become their only top 10 pop hit and gold single.

Even with the success of "Love Ballad," the 10-piece had decided to leave producers Larry and Fonce Mizell, whose background was with jazz artists, in favor of someone with greater pop sensibilities. Lead singer Jeffrey Osborne, who calls Martin "one of the tastiest producers I've ever met," adds, "He really knew how to get the most out of just simplicity. He would listen to what was there and just reinforce it."

Besides arranging Carle Vickers's distinctive trumpet solo, Osborne says, "Bobby would take melodies that were already within the piano and write the string arrangement from it. He tied everything together very well."

Osborne remembers that it was Martin who brought in songwriters Len Ron Hanks and Zane Grey although, coincidentally, the pair had also worked with L.T.D. mentor Jerry Butler several years earlier. (Grey and Hanks would go on to several R&B hits of their own in 1978–79 with the similarly peppy "You Fooled Me" and "Dancin'.")

It was Osborne who found the female backup vocalist heard on several L.T.D. hits. "For the very pretty things, the airy things on the top, we always called a girl in," he says. "And it was Angela Winbush who sang on most of them." Still four years away from her own hits as half of Rene & Angela, Winbush "sang a demo on a couple of things I was writing," according to Osborne. "I asked her at that point if she'd be interested in doing some background vocals."

"Back in Love Again" came from L.T.D.'s fourth album for A&M Records, *Something to Love*, laid down at Lonnie Simmons's Total Experience studios in Los Angeles. "Immediately when we started recording that song, it just had a magic about it," says Osborne.

In fact, it's hard to imagine there's a sad note to anything as relentlessly upbeat as "Back in Love Again," but there is. Drummer Melvin Webb, known to the group as "Big Mel" and praised by Osborne for his "incredible left hand," died shortly after the record was finished.

281

SERPENTINE FIRE

Earth, Wind & Fire

COLUMBIA 10625
WRITERS: MAURICE WHITE, VERDINE WHITE, SONNY BURKE
PRODUCER: MAURICE WHITE
November 19, 1977 (7 weeks)

Maurice White once said it was *That's the Way of the World* that gave Earth, Wind & Fire "universal acceptance," adding, "That's when we knew our message was not just for black people." But it was 1977's *All 'N All*, he declared, that "just solidified the whole thing. Just solidified the whole world vibration."

It's a little odd that White should single out that album. *All 'N All* was plenty successful—double platinum, number three on the pop LP chart, winner of three Grammys—but neither of its classic hits, "Serpentine Fire" or "Fantasy," were pop smashes.

On the R&B charts, "Serpentine Fire" spent seven weeks at Number One—the longest run since Al Green's "Let's Stay Together" in 1972—and was Earth, Wind & Fire's second-biggest hit. On the Hot 100, it only went to number 13.

Even if the record had gotten closer to the top, it would have been resisted by Debby Boone's "You Light up My Life," the song that held Number One hostage through the fall of '77. It was as if the band played by EW&F in the movie *That's the Way of the World* really had been shunted aside for a family bubble-gum act.

So if Maurice White perceives *All 'N All* as his band's pop breakthrough, it may be because after the death of longtime partner Charles Stepney, he turned frequently to the pop side for collaborators like David Foster or Allee Willis [see 305—"September"].

Recorded in June 1977 at Hollywood Sound, *All 'N All* was co-produced by Joe Wissert, the ex–Mickey Mouse Club dancer who had guided EW&F in their early days at Columbia Records. Eumir Deodato, who would soon utilize White's techniques to revitalize Kool & the Gang, was one of the arrangers, as was Tom Tom Washington.

"I went to Brazil for a vacation," Maurice White told journalist David Nathan. "When I came back, I was fresh and ready to start writing. I was affected by what I'd heard there. I think of that album as a turning point in our maturity musically. That record got everyone's attention."

Earth, Wind & Fire bassist Verdine White explained, "That was one of the hardest records I ever worked on. We were all in there sweating ourselves into the ground. Maurice was singing, playing drums, producing. And it was one of the best albums we ever did."

The band's leader said "Serpentine Fire" reflected his belief that it's "up to each individual to do what is right for them." He continued, "Sure, a lot of people don't know what 'Serpentine Fire' means. In many cases, they pronounce it wrongly [it's "ser-pen-TEEN"]. But they can dance to it, so they go 'head on! It actually comes from India, and deals with a form of yoga.

"It's the magic fluid in your spine and it is actually the energy that runs from your gonads and runs up into your brain. And it is the energy that runs around your whole body."

FFUN

Con Funk Shun

MERCURY 73959
WRITER: MICHAEL COOPER
PRODUCER: SKIP SCARBOROUGH
January 7, 1978 (2 weeks)

Even in an era of large-ensemble pop-funk bands with broad sensibilities, Con Funk Shun's influences were pretty diverse. As lead singer Michael Cooper told writer Harry Weinger, "We were into Wes Montgomery *and* the Archies."

The chorus of "Ffun" cannibalizes both the Beach Boys, who had also been known to have some fun-fun-fun, and Bachman-Turner Overdrive, whose "b-b-b-baby" had helped popularize the stuttering hook back in the days when you could do that without seeming insensitive toward people with speech disabilities.

Con Funk Shun

The structure of "Ffun," by Cooper's own admission, came from a funky, flute-driven record that spent a month at Number One around the time Con Funk Shun's major label debut, "Sho' Feels Good to Me," was stalling at number 68.

"We had to analyze what people wanted," Cooper explained. "We used that criteria after our first album didn't sell. We were into 'Dazz' by Brick and we modeled ourselves after them. We had the same instrumentation.

"We were on our way to Club Nairobi in Little Rock, Arkansas. I had a little four-track recorder. I beat out the pattern to 'Ffun' on my lap, and played the bass and guitar parts into the machine. I used the hi-hat cymbals where the vocal was supposed to go."

Then Cooper added one more touch of Dazz because, he notes, back then "everything had to have a flute solo."

Con Funk Shun was originally Project Soul from Vallejo, California, comprising Cooper and drummer Louis McCall. The band expanded in 1969 with Felton Pilate (keyboards, horns), Karl Fuller (trumpet), Paul Harrell (sax), Cedric Martin (bass), and Danny Thomas (keyboards). At this point, the band relocated to Memphis, where they appeared in the concert film *Wattstax* and played behind both the Soul Children and Rufus Thomas—some of whose sense of humor often seemed to rub off on the group.

After a spell at Stax founder Estelle Axton's Fretone label, the seven-piece joined Mercury Records in July 1976. While their first album was a pickup of Fretone material, the second was *Secrets*, featuring "Ffun." It was recorded with producer Skip Scarborough at the CBS studios in San Francisco during March and April 1976.

Scarborough remembers Con Fun Shun as writing eight-minute songs, another distinguishing characteristic of '70s funk bands. Once they got past that, however, he says they were "pretty easy to work with," although fostering harmony among them was another issue.

"On 'Ffun' everybody sings 'la-la-la-la' in unison, but when they tried to go into the harmonies, they couldn't hear it," Scarborough explains. "So I would have them sing all the 'fun-fun-fun' on one track, and overdub that, then come back and just sing the lead line, so they wouldn't have to try and figure out, 'Well, I gotta jump a ninth from this point, and jump back.' "

Con Funk Shun would remain consistently successful until their mid-'80s breakup, when Michael Cooper continued as a solo artist, too legit to quit. No quitter, either, was Con Funk Shun's other songwriter, Felton Pilate, who became the producer/musical director for (M.C.) Hammer and his stable of artists.

283

OUR LOVE

Natalie Cole

CAPITOL 4509
WRITERS: CHUCK JACKSON, MARVIN YANCY
PRODUCERS: CHUCK JACKSON, MARVIN YANCY
January 21, 1978 (2 weeks)

In retrospect, irony resonates through "Our Love," from the poignant piano played by Natalie Cole's husband, Marvin Yancy, to the lyrical declarations of mountain-moving, everlasting love penned by Yancy's partner in music, Chuck Jackson.

The song was Cole's last Number One of the '70s. Within a couple of years of its release, she had separated from Yancy—a fracture fueled by her cocaine dependency—and watched her career decline from chart-topping records to the point where she routinely struggled to reach the top 20.

Later, the singer admitted to *Newsweek* that she was using drugs "to put a huge Band-Aid on a woman who as a little girl had problems with self-esteem...I was running away from the fact that I didn't feel I was worthy."

"Our Love" originated with Chuck Jackson and Marvin Yancy, the team responsible for all of Cole's previous hits. "Marv and I had laid it out so well that when we gave her a demo, she would keep it for a week or two [and then record the song]," explains Jackson. She lived and breathed music, he says.

The partnership was professional *and* personal. "We were together every day, anyhow, because Marv and she became lovers. And every day we were together, we were in the studio, always thinking about hit records. So it was a marriage that I thought was made in heaven, we got along so well together. Natalie and Marvin were so tight...that when we wrote a record, when we wrote a hit, she was the first to hear it, and she'd say, 'I want it.' "

"Our Love," like Cole's first four Number One hits, featured Yancy on piano. "He didn't read music, but he was going on feel," affirms Jackson. "That's why it was so raw and natural and original. Because everything Marvin played, he played it differently. When you get [musicians who work from written arrangements], they play basically what is Americanized, approved through society. But when you find a Marvin Yancy, who goes against the rules, it comes out real well."

The Windy City was part of that chemistry, too. Even after Yancy and Jackson moved to Cole's Los Angeles hometown, they kept the Chicago connection. "We never recorded [in Los Angeles], we didn't like it in terms of the musicians," says Jackson.

In fact, Natalie's *Thankful* album, which contained "Our Love," employed studio players from Chicago (Donnell Hagan on drums, Larry Ball on bass, Yancy on keyboards) and from Los Angeles (Ray Parker Jr. and Lee Ritenour on guitars, Sonny Burke on organ, Michael Boddicker on synthesizer). Cole cut her vocals at the ABC Recording Studios, Los Angeles.

After the singer and her husband split, Yancy returned to live and work in Chicago, maintaining his late father's church and making gospel records. In 1985, he died of a heart attack, at age 34.

284

THEME SONG FROM "WHICH WAY IS UP"

Stargard

MCA 40825
WRITER: NORMAN WHITFIELD
PRODUCER: MARK DAVIS
February 4, 1978 (2 weeks)

The undisputed truth: "Theme Song from 'Which Way Is Up' " was the second movie-music smash for Rose Royce, Norman Whitfield, and Michael Schultz. "Car Wash" [see 261] was the first.

Also accurate: "Theme Song from 'Which Way Is Up' " was sung by a group whose driving force, Rochelle Runnells, owed her lucky break to...the Undisputed Truth. The lead singer of that Motown act, Joe Harris, brought her to the attention of producer Whitfield in 1973. Later, Runnells wrote a couple of tunes on the Truth's *Method to the Madness* album, released on Whitfield Records in 1976.

Stargard was formed the following year by Runnells, Janice Williams, and Debra Anderson. Rochelle and Debra had sung together on tour with Anthony Newley; Janice was Debra's replacement in that revue. Runnells had also voiced backgrounds on Candi Staton's biggest hit [see 246—"Young Hearts Run Free"].

As Stargard, the three women were signed to Dr. Rock Productions, a company operated by Mark Davis and Walter Ainsworth, two longtime associates of Norman Whitfield. Davis had played keyboards on many of the producer's Motown recordings; Ainsworth had been general manager of Whitfield Records.

Dr. Rock cut a production deal with MCA Records, gaining rights to release the theme song from *Which Way Is Up*, a Richard Pryor movie directed by Michael Schultz for MCA's Universal Pictures. Earlier, Schultz had made *Car Wash* for Universal, with a music soundtrack produced by Whitfield and performed by Rose Royce.

And so, for his Stargard project, Mark Davis was able to use those very same musicians, recording at Sound Factory West in Los Angeles. "Like it's no secret that Mark and Norman have known each other for quite a while," Rochelle Runnells explained to *Black Music*. "They go back ten years with Motown. Mark basically knows Norman's style and Norman knows Mark's style...Norman wrote the song and handed it to Mark and said, '*Go!*.'

"Rose Royce offered to do the tracks; that was a compliment from one group of artists to another, everyone does it. And Rose Royce have a style of playing, they're not a studio band. It's like if we sang background for another artist, you would instantly recognize us because we have a certain style. And yet, *some* people have actually asked if Rose Royce sang on 'Which Way Is Up' and not us."

Later, Stargard might have been glad to be mistaken for another group: The trio was featured in Michael Schultz's cinematic version of *Sgt. Pepper's Lonely Hearts Club Band*. They played the Diamonds, as in "Lucy and the Diamonds," who tried to lure Peter Frampton (as Billy Shears) into signing with Big Deal Records. As a movie, it was no big deal. Later still, Runnells and Mark Davis had a hand in the soundtrack to *Cheech & Chong's Next Movie*. You remember that one too, no doubt.

Nevertheless, Norman Whitfield stayed loyal to Stargard. He wrote their second R&B top ten hit, "What You Waitin' For," deployed them as background singers on a number of his own label's subsequent album projects, and used Runnells's skills as a songwriter, too. When you're up, you're up.

285

TOO HOT TA TROT

Commodores

MOTOWN 1432
WRITERS: THOMAS MCCLARY, MILAN WILLIAMS, WALTER ORANGE, LIONEL RICHIE, RONALD LAPREAD, WILLIAM KING
PRODUCERS: JAMES ANTHONY CARMICHAEL, THE COMMODORES
February 18, 1978 (1 week)

Neil Bogart, founder of Casablanca Records and executive producer of the motion picture *Thank God It's Friday*, didn't bother to screen the 1978 Columbia Pictures release for critics. "This is definitely *not* a critics' film," he said in the *San Francisco Examiner*. "I don't think we made a critics' picture, therefore there was nothing to gain by screening it for the critics."

That didn't stop movie reviewers from seeing the film and writing their comments, of course. Ben Fong-Torres dubbed the movie *Saturday Night Earache* in *Rolling Stone*, and called it a "plotless, pointless

The Commodores

derivative of *Car Wash*." He said, "The music just keeps droning, wiping out what dialogue there is."

The film, a Motown-Casablanca FilmWorks Production, boasted artists from both labels' rosters on the soundtrack. Donna Summer led the Casablanca charge with "Last Dance," which won an Oscar for songwriter Paul Jabara. Motown lent three of its top acts: Diana Ross, Thelma Houston, and the Commodores, who actually were given the opportunity to appear in the film.

The group contributed "Too Hot Ta Trot," a song written by all six Commodores. "We were forced to put it together in one day," complains drummer Walter Orange. They were on tour when manager Benny Ashburn told them to fly to Los Angeles, where they would spend three days making their motion picture debut. The Commodores arrived in Hollywood ready for their close-up when they were told to come up with a song for the movie. "They said, 'You're going into the studio, gentlemen. You're going to write, make up something and put words to it,' " Orange recalls.

The Commodores requested information about the storyline and a description of some key scenes. "It was about this chick. She liked to get high and boozed up and she was 'Too Hot Ta Trot.' It was one of those old sayings," Orange explains. "We were very good at making up tracks. We could write a track in a couple of hours." Orange came up with some lyrics based on the movie's plot; the rest of the group wasn't impressed. "But everybody was really excited about going back on tour," says Walter. "They weren't thinking about writing lyrics and getting deep and heavy. So at the end of the day we had no choice but to go with my lyrics. And [Lionel] Richie said, 'You're writing it, you sing it.' "

Orange handled lead vocals while the rest of the group sang the chant "Too Hot Ta Trot." Orange is candid in his assessment of the song: "If you listen to it, it's not one of those that we put a whole hell of a lot of thought into. It was one of those sing-along chants, but the group was hot. It was our time. It was one of those songs that was surrounded by a great product, a movie. All these things helped. Nobody's going to go back and record 'Too Hot Ta Trot' or any of those funk songs, because they come and they go. They're not like ballads that people can hold onto. They're just fad songs, and that's the way I wrote."

286

IT'S YOU THAT I NEED

Enchantment

ROADSHOW 1124
WRITERS: MICHAEL STOKES, VERDELL LANIER
PRODUCER: MICHAEL STOKES
February 25, 1978 (1 week)

The enchanted frog? It must be something in Detroit's drinking water. Like George Clinton and his Sir Nose D'VoidofFunk, Enchantment chose a mascot for their stage antics—in this case, a frog emblazoned on the back of their floor-length green capes (with Mandrake-the-Magician collars).

With capes, canes and top hats, Enchantment had a routine beyond unison-stepping in the Motown mold. "We want to get even more involved in staging as opposed to five men prancing in time with each other," group member Bobby Green had explained to *Billboard*.

Discussing the, uh, frog and the group's act, the onetime head of Roadshow Records, Fred Frank, says, "It was the removal of the capes and so forth: the transitions into their dance steps. That gave the illusion of magic. The enchanted frog was just something we came up with in their album artwork, and they just took it a step further."

Spawned in Detroit in 1966, Enchantment was Emanuel (E.J.) Johnson, Bobby Green, Joe Thomas, David Banks, and Ed "Mickey" Clanton. For years, they gigged around the city in the shadow of Motown Records and its stars. Johnson told an interviewer that his childhood best friend was Stevie Wonder (both men are blind). Clanton claimed he was given his nickname by Smokey Robinson. And Thomas reported that a vocal group that rehearsed in his living room went on to become the Temptations.

In the mid-1970s, the quintet was introduced by producer Michael Stokes to Fred Frank, who was directing the careers of B.T. Express and Brass Construction. "I was looking for a third act," he says, "and Michael was telling me about this group he was developing in Detroit. It was exactly what I wanted: a doo-wop kind of soulful group."

A doo-wop kind of soulful ballad, "Gloria," was Enchantment's first top 10 hit, followed by "Sunshine" and "It's You That I Need." Michael Stokes co-wrote all three songs. "He used to put a group of writers together," says Frank. "He would get four, five people and throw them into a think tank, and he would come up with some music.

"He and E.J. would do like Stevie Wonder; they would just goof and track. Michael would do this in his basement, sit and play, and get onto something." The most promising results would be put on tape at Detroit's Sound Suite studios, with some of the city's key session players.

Enchantment's lead vocalist Johnson was "one of the greatest singers I ever heard," Frank remarks. "E.J. could do vocal acrobatics, he was just incredible—for somebody who was blind, it just never held him back. Onstage, he just lit up. And then you'd let him loose in the studio and let him do his thing.

"I'd have to say that the group's harmonies and Emanuel's lead vocals were what people put their money down to see," concludes Frank. "And when it got down to closing the show, it was Emanuel." And let's not forget that frog.

287

FLASH LIGHT

Parliament

CASABLANCA 909
WRITERS: GEORGE CLINTON, BERNIE WORRELL, WILLIAM "BOOTSY" COLLINS
PRODUCER: GEORGE CLINTON
March 4, 1978 (3 weeks)

P-Funk bassist Bootsy Collins remembered "Flash Light" this way in a mid-'70s interview: "I cut that for Bootsy's Rubber Band. And 'Funkentelechy.' Those are the first two tunes I cut for my first album, but George [Clinton], uh, needed two tunes, two smash tunes, two instant tunes that would be played, so we got together. It was cool, because I knew I had a bunch more tunes I could cut."

Keyboard player Bernie Worrell remembers it differently. He agrees that "Flash Light" started off as a song for Collins and his Bootsy's Rubber Band. But he says that after Bootsy cut it as a demo with drums and guitars, he decided he didn't like it, so the song ended up with Parliament—and the bass part was not Collins, but Worrell playing a keyboard bass, something he had done for years as a studio musician.

Of course, both these stories—and any more you may hear about P-Funk in these pages—are subject to George Clinton's own caveat: "Fantasy is reality." Besides, things were happening fast in the Parliament/Funkadelic camp in those days, and nobody can really be expected to have all the events straight.

For one thing, the musicians—dozens of them—were all over the lot (which, for recording purposes, was often Detroit's United Sound). Aside from Bootsy, Cordell (Boogie) Mosson, and several other bass variables, there were guitarists Eddie Hazel, Garry Shider, Michael Hampton, Glenn Goins, Phelps (Catfish) Collins, and more.

On keyboards and synthesizers, count in Worrell, Walter (Junie) Morrison, and David Lee Chong. Behind the drums, add up Gary Bronson, Jerome Brailey, Larry Fratangelo, Tiki Fulwood, and Bootsy again, to name a few. The horn section was gifted with such James Brown alumni as Fred Wesley, Maceo Parker, and Richard (Kush) Griffith, among other Clinton regulars and top session players.

Much of P-Funk's legend derived from its stage show. The group's *Mothership Connection* album was the story of "afro nauts" who, having stashed the secret of the true funk in the pyramids, came back to free the world from mental slavery. The mothership was a $250,000 set and one of the few things that could upstage the rest of a P-Funk show: Clinton in a shoulder-length, platinum fright wig, guys in diapers, women with large, padded bottoms pre-Sir-Mix-A-Lot.

It was on Parliament's albums that Clinton's elaborate tales could best play themselves out—if you cared about hearing the story. "Flash Light" pounds along nicely on pure demented energy, but it only makes sense if you know about Sir Nose D'Voidof-Funk, the villain of *Funkentelechy vs. the Placebo Syndrome*. Sir Nose began life with Bootsy's contention (on his own "The Pinnochio Theory") that "if you fake the funk, your nose is going to grow."

Fortunately, nobody much cared whether "Flash Light" made sense. It wasn't the first single from *Funkentelechy*, but it quickly emerged from the album through airplay. Once it hit, less than a year after the success of *Star Wars*, fans began bringing flashlights to the show and brandishing them like light sabers. When the band finally manufactured their own, they would sell 2,000 to 3,0000 flashlights a night.

William "Bootsy" Collins

288
BOOTZILLA
Bootsy's Rubber Band

WARNER BROS. 8512
WRITERS: GEORGE CLINTON, WILLIAM "BOOTSY" COLLINS
PRODUCERS: GEORGE CLINTON, WILLIAM "BOOTSY" COLLINS
March 25, 1978 (1 week)

Dr. Funkenstein created a monster. The doctor, a/k/a George Clinton, didn't just have two groups making records at once—Parliament and Funkadelic—he eventually had so many spin-off acts that one of them, Bootsy's Rubber Band, was able to occupy the Number One spot a week after Parliament.

Two different sets of P-Funk backup singers got groups: Parlet and the Brides of Funkenstein. Horn player Maceo Parker and the Horny Horns got a solo record. So did keyboard player Bernie Worrell and guitarist Eddie Hazel. Quazar, Zapp, Xavion, the Sweat Band, and, later, Jimmy G and the Tackheads all had some connection to the Clinton mothership.

But the P-Funk all-star with the longest run of solo successes was clearly bassist William "Bootsy" Collins, whose chart action began in '76 with "Stretchin' Out (In a Rubber Band)," even as he contributed to the Parliament/Funkadelic hits. Former P-Funk staffer Tom Vickers remembers the Funk Mobsters walking around saying "Bootsy's a monster" to each other. And what monster would he have been but the rhinestone rock star, Bootzilla?

Without the solo hits, Collins would have gone down not only as George Clinton's secret weapon, but also as the bass player on James Brown's "Get Up (I Feel Like Being A) Sex Machine" and "Super Bad" [see 95]. He worked in a Cincinnati-area band, too, with one Philippe Wynne, who, after serving as the Spinners' defining voice, performed with Clinton and crew on an ad hoc basis. And Collins had two different stints with Parliament/Funkadelic.

When Clinton brought Bootsy back into the fold for that second tour of duty, he did so with plans for him to have his own group, initially called Bootsy's Early Sunn. When Funkadelic jumped from Westbound to Warner Brothers, Bootsy was signed sight unseen as part of the package. "George knew [Warner Brothers A&R executive] Bob Krasnow, and that's how it happened," he said at the time.

"Bootzilla," co-authored by Clinton, was the major hit from the second of Collins's back-to-back gold solo albums, *Ahh...The Name Is Bootsy, Baby!* and *Bootsy? Player of the Year*. Both topped the R&B album rankings and breached the top 20 of the pop charts.

While one can hardly accuse George Clinton of a lack of imagination, Collins's contributions to P-Funkdom—beyond the atomic-weight basslines—seemed to include a good helping of humor. Bootsy's solo projects didn't have much of the cosmic ambitiousness of P-Funk, but seemed more intended for sheer enjoyment. In fact, so much of his humor would stem from cartoons that there would eventually be a cartoon film of Bootsy done for his "Player of the Year?" tour.

289

THE CLOSER I GET TO YOU

Roberta Flack with Donny Hathaway

ATLANTIC 3463
WRITERS: REGGIE LUCAS, JAMES MTUME
PRODUCERS: JOE FERLA, ROBERTA FLACK, EUGENE McDANIELS
April 1, 1978 (2 weeks)

Reggie Lucas and James Mtume met while they were playing in Miles Davis's band. Lucas played guitar and Mtume played percussion from 1971 to 1975. "We both had an interest in producing and writing commercial R&B music, different than the progressive jazz we were doing with Miles," says Lucas. "So we started doing it together on the road. We had an aborted attempt when we left Miles to enter into the record industry—we found out we had to pay a lot of dues. People wouldn't accept us on face value being able to play commercial music after playing with Miles. So we wound up back in Roberta Flack's band as touring musicians."

In between tours with Flack, Lucas and Mtume worked on their songwriting. "We were constantly writing songs, submitting demos to people, doing the whole nine yards," says Lucas. They came up with a song Mtume titled "The Closer I Get to You." "I played the guitar and Mtume played the keyboards and we used to sit around in each other's houses. We'd work on things on a little sketchpad, write the lyrics, and play it into what would be primitive by today's standards—a little beat box that recorded."

They were working on the sessions for Flack's *Blue Lights in the Basement* album when they told producer/engineer Joe Ferla about "The Closer I Get to You." "We did a real quick track of it, and she came down and heard it and liked it. Then it went through a long process of being produced by other people and ultimately got on the record."

Lucas and Mtume didn't come up with the idea of having the song recorded as a duet. Flack was being managed at the time by David Franklin, who also managed Donny Hathaway. Six years had passed since the two artists had a Number One single with "Where Is the Love" [see 130].

The song was recorded in segments. "We had the track and Roberta spent a lot of time on the vocals," Lucas remembers. "Donny on the other hand was hospitalized...They had to get special permission to get him out of the hospital. It was a big deal. And they were able to do that. They pulled him out of the hospital and had him come in for a few minutes to sing and then flew him back...Donny was medicated and ill. He wasn't in very good shape."

As the writers, Lucas and Mtume were invited to the recording session. They were grateful for the opportunity and found the finished product to be very close to their original demo. "It's a very simple song," says Lucas. "It was just a melody, chords, and a little rhythm. It was a perfect song for them."

The initial single from the album was the Christmas-themed "25th of Last December." Released just a few weeks before the holiday, the single peaked at number 52, Flack's lowest-charted single to this date. As 1978 rolled in, Atlantic released "The Closer I Get to You" as the follow-up.

"Roberta is one of the great voices of all time," Lucas comments. "She's got a beautiful instrument. It's so pure and crystal-clear...and Donny was so brilliant...Even though he was not well at the time, the one thing that was amazing was when he sat down and played the piano and sang, you could see what a genius he was. It was a really inspiring experience to be around the guy just a little bit."

290

TOO MUCH, TOO LITTLE, TOO LATE

Johnny Mathis & Deniece Williams

COLUMBIA 10693
WRITERS: NAT KIPNER, JOHN VALLINS
PRODUCER: JACK GOLD
April 15, 1978 (4 weeks)

When Johnny Mathis was climbing the *Billboard* pop charts in March of 1963 with "What Will Mary Say"—his last top 10 hit until "Too Much, Too Little, Too Late"—the Bee Gees were newly signed to Australia's Festival Records.

That's not just a way of putting things into chronological perspective—there is a connection, and that's Nat Kipner. He managed the teenage Bee Gees brothers in the early '60s, before they left Australia for Britain and began making a string of international hits.

Johnny Mathis

Fifteen years later, Kipner's name could be found on "Too Much, Too Little, Too Late," the first Number One hit (pop *and* R&B) of Johnny Mathis's long career. Coincidentally, two hot Bee Gees singles were moving up the R&B charts as Mathis and partner Deniece Williams reached the summit.

The quintessential pop balladeer known for such smooth sides as "Chances Are" and "The Twelfth of Never," Mathis wanted a new twist on his recording formula in the fall of 1977. Jack Gold, his producer, and Mike Dilbeck, an A&R man at CBS Records, thought of recruiting Deniece Williams to pair up with Mathis.

"They discussed it and came to my managers to enquire as to whether we'd like to do it," said Williams in a *Blues & Soul* interview at the time. "They asked me on a Wednesday. I said 'yes,' and on the Thursday, Johnny and I were in the studio recording the song!"

Deniece did that during a break in her tour with Earth, Wind & Fire, whose leader, Maurice White, had signed her to Kalimba Productions in 1976. Williams's first hit, "Free," reached number two on the soul charts early the next year.

"Too Much, Too Little, Too Late" almost didn't reach Williams and Mathis. Nat Kipner had composed the song in London with partner John Vallins. "We wrote it and he just forgot about it," explains Kipner. "He went off on his own situation and, without reference to him, I went and demo'd it."

The result was "a pretty good demo," by Kipner's account, which garnered some interest from Polydor Records. In fact, he says the U.K. label was close to releasing a version of "Too Much, Too Little, Too Late" by an English pop duo. "In the meantime," says the songwriter, "I went to visit America to visit my son Steve, who was working there."

At his offspring's recommendation, Kipner connected with an American publisher. "I took it to them amongst a lot of other songs," he explains. "They called me [about it] in due course when I was back in England." Mathis was interested in "Too Much, Too Little, Too Late." And so the Polydor popsters lost out.

According to Kipner, the hit version faithfully duplicated the arrangement of his original demo. Mathis and Williams cut the song at the A&M studios in Los Angeles, with arranger Gene Page recruiting his customary California sessioneers, including guitarists David T. Walker and Melvin "Wah-Wah" Ragin, bassist Scott Edwards, drummer Ed Greene, and keyboard players Michel Rubini and Sylvester Rivers.

Deniece Williams said she and Mathis "felt really relaxed around each other—the vibes were great. It was particularly interesting because it was a first for both of us. Neither had ever done a 'duet' per se, and it seemed like we just fell right into the groove."

291

TAKE ME TO THE NEXT PHASE (PART 1)

The Isley Brothers

T-NECK 2272
WRITERS: ERNIE ISLEY, MARVIN ISLEY,
CHRIS JASPER, RUDOLPH ISLEY,
O'KELLY ISLEY, RONALD ISLEY
PRODUCER: THE ISLEY BROTHERS
May 13, 1978 (2 weeks)

By the middle of 1978, the Isley Brothers were toasting five years with mighty CBS Records, which marketed and distributed their T-Neck label. It was a productive partnership, typified that year by the success of *Showdown*, the group's fourth consecutive release to reach the top 10 of the pop album chart.

"The years '75 and '77 to '78 were particularly exciting," agrees Ernie Isley. "*We* didn't know what we would be doing next! When somebody would have an idea and I might get excited, we'd play it for Ronald and he got excited, then play it for another brother and they'd get excited. From a creative point of view, it was something where we kept feeding off each other."

"Take Me to the Next Phase," released as a single from *Showdown*, was one of Ernie's ideas that took shape in the studio at Bearsville, New York. "It's funny, it was going a little differently to how it ended up," recollects keyboards whiz Chris Jasper. "Musically, it wasn't working, so I suggested to Ernie that he play the drums, because he was trying to do it a different way.

"I said, 'Go out into the booth and play drums, and I'll play the synthesizer bass, let's just work from that.' That's when it happened—those were the first two parts that went on the song, then we built from there."

Ernie confirms, "There were two different versions of the song originally: One I had vocally which I had recorded and played for Chris first, and there was one he had heard and said, 'Nah, it can't go like that.' Then we got into the studio and I played the drumbeat, and we knew what the guitar would be doing.

"Chris played a somewhat different bassline on synth, as opposed to the original bassline. The melody was alright, it was just the bassline that wasn't fitting. So it was really exciting to change it—and for it to work."

Part of the excitement, says Ernie, also came from the three musicians—himself, Jasper, and bass player Marvin—doing "the stomps and stuff on 24 separate tracks, and blending it in with a live thing. That just happened to work very well. Between the song, all the performances, the lyric and all that, yeah, it blended itself."

Ironically, the *Showdown* album achieved its pop chart action and platinum sales without a crossover single. "Take Me to the Next Phase" was the Isleys' first R&B Number One that couldn't crack the Hot 100 at all. Pop radio apparently preferred the blue-eyed fever of another set of brothers that spring: the Bee Gees.

292

USE TA BE MY GIRL

The O'Jays

PHILADELPHIA INTERNATIONAL 3642
WRITERS: KENNY GAMBLE, LEON HUFF
PRODUCERS: KENNY GAMBLE, LEON HUFF
May 27, 1978 (5 weeks)

If someone were to ask you to name the O'Jays' most successful song on the R&B chart, you'd probably answer "Back Stabbers" or "Love Train" or maybe even "I Love Music." But all three of those would be wrong. The trio's biggest hit in the history of the R&B chart is "Use Ta Be My Girl," which stayed on top for five weeks and remained on the chart for 21 weeks, longer than any other O'Jays single.

That doesn't mean anyone at Philadelphia International thought the song was going to be big. "No one, including the O'Jays or [Kenny] Gamble and [Leon] Huff, thought that was a Number One record until it came out and we heard it on the radio," says lead singer Eddie Levert.

"Use Ta Be My Girl" had a retro sound that paid homage to some of the great doo-wop singers of the past. "*Animal House* was out around that time and I was a great fan of John Belushi," says Levert. "There was a group in the film named Otis Day and the Knights and they were doing this 'shama-lama-ding-dong' song. So we thought, let's do some of this old stuff on our record. We put the 'shoop-shoop's in so everyone could relate to it."

The O'Jays and their producers weren't the only ones who had doubts about "Use Ta Be My Girl" before it was released. "I hated that record," bemoans Joe Tarsia, head of Sigma Sound Studios in Philadelphia and the man who engineered the single. "Technically, from an engineering standpoint, I didn't like the sound of the record. I thought it sounded muddy. Today, I would say it's a great record."

MFSB guitarist Bobby Eli played on the track and had a different opinion. "That one sounded like a hit right away," he says. "As soon as we got onto the rhythm chart, it sounded like it had that Number One vibe. The guys were sitting there on stools as usual, singing the song, and it just flowed. That whole group of sessions stood out and felt like they

The O'Jays

were going to be some of the biggest records they had."

During the time that the O'Jays recorded "Use Ta Be My Girl," the Sigma Sound Studios were a 24-hour-a-day operation, says Eli. "If I would get three or four hours sleep, I was lucky," the guitarist says. "Sometimes I'd actually sleep in the studio in the vocal booth. I'd tell the guys, 'Lock the studio up and leave me here.' By that time I lived out in New Jersey. It was far to drive and if I was too tired, I just stayed there. And then a janitor would come in and wake me up...The more I did it, the better I felt. The hell with sleep, let me be creative."

Eli, who became a record producer himself, describes Gamble and Huff's typical regimen for an O'Jays album: "They would record all the rhythm tracks in one five-day period. Then they would do the vocals later. While they were doing their vocals in one studio, that gave me time to start production on my rhythm tracks because we would use the same musicians...We kept the place hopping bigtime."

293

STUFF LIKE THAT

Quincy Jones

A&M 2043

WRITERS: QUINCY JONES, NICKOLAS ASHFORD, VALERIE SIMPSON, ERIC GALE, STEVE GADD, RICHARD TEE, RALPH MACDONALD

PRODUCER: QUINCY JONES

July 1, 1978 (1 week)

He was one of the first people we met in New York," explains Valerie Simpson, "when we were songwriters in the Flomar days. He was an executive at Mercury or something. He liked us and always remembered us."

Simpson is discussing the middle '60s, when she and partner Nick Ashford had just started out on the yellow brick road [see 23—"Let's Go Get Stoned"]. And when the "he" in question was, indeed, a vice president at Mercury Records, as well as one of

America's most formidable musicians, composers and producers: Quincy Jones.

A decade later, Ashford, Simpson, and Jones were caught up in a whirlwind of projects together which were to spin magic into the airwaves and onto the charts. It was 1978, and Quincy was working on his own album, *Sounds...and Stuff Like That*, as well as the third LP by the Brothers Johnson (*Blam!*) and the soundtrack of one of Hollywood's most extravagant movies, *The Wiz*, starring Diana Ross and Michael Jackson.

Sounds...and Stuff Like That featured some of the top session singers of the day—Patti Austin, Gwen Guthrie, Luther Vandross—and the finest studio musicians. "Quincy called us," says Nick Ashford, "and he said he had this track that he wanted us to listen to, and if we felt anything, to write something on it." They did just that.

Meanwhile, Jones was toiling at Cherokee Recording and Westlake Audio in Los Angeles. "When we went out there," Ashford continues, "I don't know what he expected, but he was so shocked and so happy. 'Oh, you did it,' he said. 'I love it, I love it, you wrote the hell out of it.' "

Quincy Jones

In fact, the songwriter says the assignment was easy. "The track was there, and Val and I just gave it some thought." The music on Quincy's tape showcased the hot rhythms of Eric Gale (guitar), Steve Gadd (drums), Richard Tee (keyboards), and Ralph MacDonald (percussion).

"All the guys on the track are the writers," says Simpson. "It feels like they went in with a title and said, 'Let's just mess around 'til we get something, some stuff like that.' It's just one big mishmash." Adds Ashford, "Right: one big mishmash hit."

"Stuff Like That" featured the additional skills of Anthony Jackson (bass), David T. Walker (guitar), and George Young (sax), and the rambunctious vocals of Ashford, Simpson, and Chaka Khan. "The energy that pops out of that lady when she sings," says Simpson about Chaka. "Oooh, goose bump time!"

Khan had just interpreted another Ashford/ Simpson song [see 302—"I'm Every Woman"] for her first solo album, but the couple weren't at the session. " 'Stuff Like That' was the first time we were in a recording situation together," reports Valerie. "She comes in full of bubbles," comments Nick. "Makes you wanna do more than you intended to do!"

294

CLOSE THE DOOR

Teddy Pendergrass

PHILADELPHIA INTERNATIONAL 3733
WRITERS: KENNY GAMBLE, LEON HUFF
PRODUCERS: KENNY GAMBLE, LEON HUFF
July 8, 1978 (2 weeks)

By the end of 1975, *Billboard* had reported several times on the split of Harold Melvin & the Blue Notes, with lead singer Teddy Pendergrass supposedly ready to head up the Blue Notes while Melvin maintained a group of his own under the same name. When the legal dust settled, Harold Melvin & the Blue Notes pacted with the ABC label while Teddy Pendergrass signed a new solo deal with Kenny Gamble and Leon Huff's Philadelphia International Records.

Pendergrass's first chart single on his own was "I Don't Love You Anymore," a top five hit in 1977. A year later, "Close the Door" returned him to the top of the R&B singles chart for the first time since his lead vocal on "Wake Up Everybody (Part 1)" [see 235]. The transition from lead singer to solo star appeared seamless, but not everything was the same. "It made a difference because I had gotten accustomed to having four other guys up there with me," says Teddy. "But I quickly realized I knew what my job

Teddy Pendergrass

was and knew what my objectives were and realized that's why I had left, to do it by myself. I adjusted to it fast—real fast. And with the backing of Gamble and Huff...it continued to be a great marriage."

"Close the Door" was a benchmark release, according to Pendergrass. "That song helped establish the concept people had about me, who they felt I really was, and what they felt I was really about. I guess that's where they get the expression that, 'When you think of romantic songs, you think of Teddy. When you think of lovemaking, you think of Teddy.' And I don't say that facetiously. I say that because it was those kind of songs back then that I did that started people thinking of me in that fashion. It was a very natural evolution—Gamble and Huff started writing those songs because they watched the way people were reacting."

The strongest reactions were from female fans who were interested in Teddy—and not just for his voice. The physical attraction factor was so strong that Pendergrass performed concerts designated "for ladies only." When asked if he had a sense of humor about such events, he replies, "That wasn't done for a joke. That was a very serious approach to doing concerts...I wasn't there to play. I was there to make sure that I locked in to my audience, my female audience, and gave them a show they wouldn't forget without having to do what Madonna does, without having to go to extremes."

The man with the sensual baritone voice says he didn't have one particular person in mind when he was singing romantic tunes. "It was the situation I had in mind. You put yourself in the situation—like an actor gets into character, you get into that character. I guess I didn't have to go too far to get into the character because everything I've ever sung and anything I sing is what I believe. I don't compromise anything. So if it's not something that I already feel natural about, I don't do it. I feel very comfortable about anything that I sing—any subject matter or any melody...Whatever I do is me. So songs like ["Close the Door"] are not hard for me to get in character about, because it's a part of Teddy."

295

YOU AND I

Rick James

GORDY 7156
WRITER: RICK JAMES
PRODUCERS: RICK JAMES, ART STEWART
July 22, 1978 (2 weeks)

Growing up in Buffalo, New York, Rick James wanted to be an athlete like Jim Brown. Good but not great at sports, Rick turned his attention to music and took up an instrument when he was nine years old. "I had the ability to play drums—I don't know where that came from," he says.

He became serious about music while living in Canada. As Ricky James Matthews, he joined the Mynah Birds, a band that included Neil Young and Bruce Palmer. "It wasn't really rock," James says of their music. "It was a combination of folk, R&B, blues. We did a lot of original stuff." Rick learned a lot about songwriting and guitar playing from Neil, although the band didn't stay together long. "We signed with Motown, but I was AWOL from the Navy," Rick says. "Once Motown found out, they told me to go back and face the music and then I could come back. I did, and by that time Neil and Bruce had sold all the equipment in Canada, went to California, and formed Buffalo Springfield. I went back to Motown as a writer/producer."

Rick worked with Motown artists like Bobby Taylor, the Spinners, and the Marvelettes, but wasn't thinking about a career as a solo artist at this point. "I never thought I had a great voice," says Rick, who had a high, Frankie Lymon–type singing voice as a youngster. "I was always very shy with my voice—I still am. I don't consider myself a singer at all. But after Neil started making records and I started hearing other groups, I decided, 'If they can do it, I can do it.' " He was especially convinced after hearing Bootsy Collins sing. "After I heard Bootsy, I said, 'Oh my god, if this guy can be a star, I know I can do it.' "

After taking a break in London, Rick returned to America in 1977. He financed the recording of an album in a small eight-track studio in Buffalo, then went to California to find a label deal. "I didn't really want to be with Motown," he confides. "But I was in the building to see record companies. A guy named Jeffrey Bowen stopped me and asked what I was doing." Rick said he had an album of original material and Bowen suggested let Motown hear it. "So he took 'You and I' to Berry Gordy [and] Suzanne de Passe and they all liked it and released it." The record became his chart debut.

"I never ever thought that record was going to be a hit," he confesses. "It was written about my wife. After [we] separated, that's when I finally decided I could write love songs. It was an up-tempo love song...The disco era was happening and I didn't want to do Van McCoy–type stuff...I'm really into simplicity. I came up with it from a bassline."

The song was replete with sexual double entendres like, "We'll be together until six is nine." James agrees: "Definitely a sexual entendre. I was into Bob Dylan and Holland/Dozier/Holland and Smokey Robinson. Those are some of the greatest lyricists. I always felt the things I could say, I could use entendres and innuendoes to say them. And when I wrote music, I wanted to write and be able to say sexual things, but not blatantly."

James was taken by surprise when "You and I" went to Number One. "I had been in the business since the '60s, so you can imagine how long I'd been trying to make records...and when it happened, I was totally dazed...I said once I got one hit, once I got one foot in the door, then I would be unstoppable. And 'You and I' gave me that foot in the door."

296

BOOGIE OOGIE OOGIE

A Taste of Honey

CAPITOL 4565

WRITERS: JANICE MARIE JOHNSON, PERRY KIBBLE

PRODUCERS: FONCE MIZELL, LARRY MIZELL

August 5, 1978 (1 week)

Janice Marie Johnson was in a girl group called the Quniques (the Uniques was already taken) when the members went to audition for Princess Cruises in 1970. Another band called the Exits was at the audition, and Janice met their keyboardist, Perry Kibble. The Quniques didn't have a steady band, so Janice invited Perry's group to back them up at important engagements.

Janice was playing bass at various showcases in Hollywood and asked Perry to accompany her on piano. Janice thought of adding a female guitarist, and the trio called itself A Taste of Honey. When their guitar player opted for a more domestic life, Janice went to an audition for an all-female band—not to join, but to seek out other female guitar players. She recruited Hazel Payne at the end of 1976.

They were playing the Etc. Club in Hollywood, where they were seen by executives from local record labels. Harold Childs, then at A&M, passed on signing them. Janice and company were asked to play at the last minute for the wedding of Smokey Robinson's bass player, Wayne Tweed. Larry and Fonce Mizell, who had produced tracks for the Jackson 5 and L.T.D., were there and arranged for the group to audition for Larkin Arnold, then with Capitol Records. He signed A Taste of Honey to the label.

Soon after getting a record deal, the group was playing Norton Air Force Base in San Bernardino, California. It was the first gig to feature Hazel. "People were mesmerized by the fact there were two girls playing [instruments], and they wouldn't get on the dance floor," says Janice Marie. So she came up with a chant to motivate people to dance: "If you're thinking that you're too cool to boogie, we've got news for you. Everyone here tonight must boogie and you are no exception to the rule." Janice happened to tape the band's performance that night. "When I got back to the hotel, I said, 'That sounds like a pretty good lyric for a song.' Took my bass out, came up with the bassline, and went to Perry and said, 'Help me put this together.' Some songs come very quickly. Other ones you have to work at. That song was not one I had to work at too hard."

The bass solo at the beginning of the track came about while the group was warming up to record in the studio. "I just started playing a solo," says Janice Marie. "I didn't even know they were recording it. The next thing I knew that was the intro of the song."

Arnold thought the title "Boogie Oogie Oogie" was too simple and urged Johnson to change it. "But he also suggested that I take those African braids out of my hair because it was too ethnic and so I listened to no one," she says.

Janice Marie was driving her 1967 Volvo the first time she heard "Boogie Oogie Oogie" on the radio. "I almost had an accident. I ran a red light, I was so excited. I was trying to pull over but I didn't realize the light was red and should have stayed where I was."

The group was too busy touring to worry about how "Boogie Oogie Oogie" was doing on the *Billboard* charts, according to Janice Marie. "We started off with the Commodores tour, then went to the Isley Brothers, and ended up with Betty Wright," says Johnson. "Larkin Arnold called us on the road and told us it was Number One."

The success of the song was a double-edged sword. "I still have a problem that we were labelled a disco group," says Janice Marie. "We were not disco. 'Boogie Oogie Oogie' had a groove to it. Anything at that time that was up-tempo was considered disco...If [people] had listened to that album, we had ballads and cha-cha type tempo songs...but it was a great energy for that time period. In fact, [dance songs] are coming back, so it can't be all wrong."

297

THREE TIMES A LADY

Commodores

MOTOWN 1443
WRITER: LIONEL RICHIE
PRODUCERS: JAMES ANTHONY CARMICHAEL, THE COMMODORES
August 12, 1978 (2 weeks)

Sometimes it might have seemed like there was only one member of the Commodores, but in truth there were six men in the group, and all of them had an opportunity to contribute songs to the group's albums.

"We had a system where each one of us was pushed to have a song on an album," says drummer Walter "Clyde" Orange. "That was our security—thanks to our manager, Benjamin [Benny] Ashburn, and to [producer] James Anthony Carmichael, who saw that everybody had something to offer."

Most of the Commodores' Motown albums featured eight songs apiece. "Unless you came in with nothing, you were going to have a song on the album," Orange explains. "The thing was to pick the best songs from each person that would make that album stand up and be real strong when you put the whole package together. It was always a fight, but the fight came for the seventh song and the eighth song, because that meant somebody was going to have two songs on the album. And it kept you razor-sharp. It kept you thinking, it kept you writing, it kept you aggressive. It was a competition. We never worried about other groups in terms of what they're going to have on their album, where they're coming from. It was about where each of us in the group was coming from. So it was a healthy thing."

Orange remembers the group' reaction when they first heard a song Lionel Richie submitted for inclusion on their *Natural High* album. It was called "Three Times a Lady." The drummer says, "That's one song we didn't have to argue about. Richie sang the first 16 bars and we said, 'That goes on the album,' and that was it. That was the only song we never argued about."

Richie was inspired to write "Three Times a Lady" after he attended a party celebrating his parents' 37th wedding anniversary. "My father stood up and gave this wonderful speech about how he had been around my mother and spent years of ups and downs...and he's probably never taken the time to say, 'Thank you, Alberta, for all the years that you've spent with me and struggled with me,' and I said, 'My goodness, I'm in the same situation,' " Lionel told Dick Clark. "I haven't taken the time to tell my wife thank you. How many other guys are in the same position?"

"Three Times a Lady," the first single released from *Natural High*, became the Commodores' fourth Number One R&B hit and first Number One pop hit. It is the song most identified with the group, but Richie was amazed that it became such a big hit, considering the timing.

"Right in the middle of disco, we came out with 'Three Times a Lady,' which people wondered about," he said in *Billboard*. "The time to make a statement is when everyone is looking at you. I've seen some artists try to make a statement when their careers were over. As a group, we've never been satisfied with one category and being on one level. 'Three Times a Lady' did something for the Commodores and Lionel Richie. We were a nice group until that song put us in another league."

GET OFF

Foxy

DASH 5046
WRITERS: CARL DRIGGS, ISH LEDESMA
PRODUCER: CORY WADE
August 26, 1978 (2 weeks)

Ish Ledesma and his Miami-based dance band, Foxy, were playing to a packed house at a club in Ocean City, Maryland, when they let loose with a disco chant that was popular in Florida. "And the owner of the club ran up onstage, made the band stop, and said, 'Don't do that,' " says Ledesma. "I said, 'What are you talking about? All the people in the audience are doing it. They're having a great time.' " But the owner was not to be swayed. "He got very ornery and said, 'I forbid you to do that. If you do that one more time, I'm going to throw you in the bay and choke you and your amps will be in the water'...So we played it tame for the rest of the night."

But not for long. "I had every intention of going home that night and writing something to come back the next day with to hit him over the head so he couldn't take it anymore." Ish and Carl Driggs decided to write some raunchy lyrics. "Everybody used to say, 'Get off' all the time...so I thought that would be a good title to use because it was a little offensive." Ish started the song with a series of "Ooh-wa"s and wanted to put "a really big one at the end to make this guy's hair stand on his head. And the drummer, who was always the safe guy, said, 'Let's not do that. We're going to get fired.' And I said, 'Forget this guy. Who wants to work for a tyrant?'...So we get in there and play the first set. We're playing it real nice, real cool." They were one song into their second set when Ish signalled the band to play "Get Off."

"We didn't even finish the first 'Ooh-wa' chant because six bouncers rushed onstage, pulled all our plugs, took all our equipment and literally threw it outside." The members of Foxy weren't choked or thrown in the bay, but they were out in the street a mere five minutes after they started to play "Get Off." The rest of the band was angry at Ish, but he offered to rent a van and pay their way home.

Back in Miami, Ish went to Henry Stone, the founder of T.K. Records, where Foxy had been acting as the house band since KC & the Sunshine Band had become too popular to stay at home. Ledesma told Stone about "Get Off" and said, 'It's either so annoying because this one guy couldn't stand it, [or] there's gotta be something in it." Stone told him to go in the studio and cut the track. "It took us an hour to record it," says Ish. "It's only three pieces with a piano bridge."

The other members of Foxy playing on the track are Arnold Paseiro (bass), Richie Puente Jr. (percussion), Charlie Murciano (keyboards), and Joe Galdo (drums). Ish and Carl double-tracked their vocals. The bridge was too high and their falsettos didn't work, so they used female singers. "We brought it back to Henry...and he flipped out. He said, 'This is a Number One song.' A week later it came out and it was the biggest thing in the world. So from two weeks from the time that we got kicked out of the place, we had a hit on our hands."

Foxy followed "Get Off" with the similar "Hot Number" and then "Rrrrrrock." They toured as the opening act for Sister Sledge and the Jacksons, and Ish got to sing "Shake Your Body (Down to the Ground)" with Michael. After Foxy broke up, Ish started a band called Oxo. They had a top 30 pop hit on Geffen with "Whirly Girl" in 1983. Ish went on to record a solo album for Geffen, and in 1987 he put together a female trio called Company B and produced a top 30 hit for them, "Fascinated."

299

HOLDING ON (WHEN LOVE IS GONE)

L.T.D.

A&M 2057

WRITERS: JEFFREY OSBORNE, J.T. MCGHEE

PRODUCER: BOBBY MARTIN

September 9, 1978 (2 weeks)

"This time, it's personal." That's not really what L.T.D. frontman/drummer Jeffrey Osborne and guitarist Johnnie McGhee said before releasing "Holding On (When Love Is Gone)." But it could have been.

Like Earth, Wind & Fire, another rhythm & blues band with pop aspirations, L.T.D. had never been shy about sending out for material, first to R&B songwriters Skip Scarborough [see 258—"Love Ballad"] and Grey & Hanks [see 280—"Back in Love Again"], then even to Richard Kerr, who had penned hits for Barry Manilow and Dionne Warwick. By the time Osborne went solo, his writers included Michael Sembello, Chicago's David Wolinski, and Barry Mann and Cynthia Weil.

But "Holding On" was more than the first Number One written inside L.T.D. It was therapy for both its authors. "It was very ironic with that song, because we were both going through the same thing, which was divorce," Osborne recalls. "That song was definitely written from experience."

McGhee, who had played on Marvin Gaye's "Got to Give It Up" before joining L.T.D., "was a very incredible, funky guitar player, and I wish he'd done more writing with the group," Osborne declares.

"He gave me just a guitar track of just him playing. I kind of searched through all of it and came up with the melody and everything else." Even without its emotional subtext, "Holding On" was "one of the tougher ones to put together," the singer affirms, "because there really wasn't much there when he gave it to me."

"Holding On" was featured in L.T.D.'s *Togetherness* album, recorded—like their previous release—at the Total Experience studios in Los Angeles. Philadelphia's Bobby Martin produced, and handled horn and string arrangements, while McGhee did the rhythm arrangements.

For this album, the band's lineup comprised Osborne and his keyboard-playing brother, Billy, as well as McGhee, Henry Davis on bass, Jimmie Davis on keyboards, and a horn section staffed by Lorenzo Carnegie (tenor and alto sax), Abraham Miller (tenor), Jake Riley (trombone), and Carle Vickers (trumpet, soprano sax).

L.T.D. would hold on until 1983, although Osborne went solo after 1980's *Shine On*, taking Billy with him. Jeffrey left L.T.D. *before* Lionel Richie departed the Commodores, but he used his last days in roughly the same way: by honing his chops on some increasingly MOR-ish ballads.

"You have to understand the makeup of L.T.D.," Osborne says of those last days. "There were 10 members and there was a power struggle within the group, which made it hard. The saxophone player wanted to be the leader, and then I had a brother in the group who wanted to be the leader. Everybody wanted to battle to do different things."

300

GOT TO GET YOU INTO MY LIFE

Earth, Wind & Fire

COLUMBIA 10796
WRITERS: JOHN LENNON, PAUL MCCARTNEY
PRODUCER: MAURICE WHITE
September 23, 1978 (1 week)

It's a real late-night movie. And I'm acting, of all things, in the movie. Please don't see it."

We're cheating a little here. Maurice White of Earth, Wind & Fire is, in fact, talking about another film that his group acted in, 1975's *That's the Way of the World*. But there are actually people who consider that movie to be underrated—especially record biz folks, some of whom call it the most accurate music business flick ever made.

Anyway, "please don't see it" is a fair summary of *Sgt. Pepper's Lonely Hearts Club Band*. Producer/record mogul Robert Stigwood's 1978 cinematic fiasco ended the acting careers of Peter Frampton and the Bee Gees before they began, and severely damaged the fortunes of Michael Schultz, until then one of the few black directors making Hollywood studio movies.

It couldn't even yield a successful soundtrack: the double album gave the music industry its longstanding joke about the release that "shipped gold and returned platinum."

To the extent that Stigwood's film has a plot, it concerns the small town of Heartland, where Frampton and the Bee Gees play Beatles songs in the town bandstand until they're lured to an evil metropolis. The group's instruments are stolen by a punk band, played by those inveterate new wavers, Aerosmith. In a movie where scenes and character names seem to have been chosen primarily as segues to certain songs, Earth, Wind & Fire are the entertainment at the benefit for Mr. Kite, who, in this case, is George Burns as the Mayor of Heartland.

Maurice White's musicians somehow managed to come through *Sgt. Pepper* with their dignity intact, and "Got to Get You into My Life" was the movie's biggest hit—a top 10 pop success as well as an R&B chart-topper.

It was also the most distinctive reworking of a Lennon/McCartney song in the movie. The Beatles' 1966 original was a tribute to show-band R&B, so it was an obvious cover for a band known for its horn section. But where Lennon and McCartney brought the horns in right away, as if to prove they could, White held them back for a minute, to show he didn't have to.

"Got to Get You into My Life," complete with guitar solo by Al McKay, was cut in October 1977 at Northstar Studios in Boulder, Colorado. Earth, Wind & Fire's involvement in *Sgt. Pepper* came about, Maurice White says, because "I'd always respected the Beatles, we all respected their songs, so it was an opportunity to do something with [them].

"I wasn't even trying to get a hit. We were given three songs to choose from. I chose 'Got to Get You into My Life' because that felt right to me...And, you know, that song has probably sold more singles for us than anything else."

301

ONE NATION UNDER A GROOVE (PART 1)

Funkadelic

WARNER BROS. 8618
WRITERS: GEORGE CLINTON,
WALTER "JUNIE" MORRISON, GARRY SHIDER
PRODUCER: GEORGE CLINTON
September 30, 1978 (6 weeks)

George Clinton had two groups, so the fact that he had two girlfriends should hardly be surprising. He must have gotten away with it by telling one that she was dating the leader of Parliament, and the other that she was seeing the leader of Funkadelic.

It was in 1978, with his two girlfriends in tow, that the P-Funkers went to shoot a movie, according to Tom Vickers, Clinton's onetime "minister of information." George had earlier told an interviewer that there were plans for *two* movies: one tied to Parliament's *Motor Booty Affair* album, the other a quasi-documentary that would show the Mothership landing in New York.

Filming did actually take place for the latter opus in Times Square and at the United Nations Plaza. As the sun came up in front of the U.N. the next morning, Vickers remembers, a worker was hoisting the 80 or so flags of the U.N. and Clinton asked one of his two girlfriends what she thought. "One nation under a groove," she responded.

It wasn't the first time a P-Funk title had been as much a comment on the state of the group as anything else. As keyboard player Bernie Worrell notes, "Up for the Down Stroke" could be about anybody, including tax accountants, but it was also meant to motivate the band internally. So were "Standing on the Verge of Getting It On," "Let's Take It to the Stage," and "Tear The Roof off the Sucker."

Clinton conceived Funkadelic during the late '60s when true hipsters considered albums important and singles crassly commercial. So until Parliament resurfaced in the mid-'70s, Funkadelic had been only modestly successful as a singles act. Parliament, after all, was by design the hit machine [see 287—"Flash Light"].

"We didn't know who was going to do it," Clinton told *Blues & Soul* just a few weeks after "One Nation under a Groove" hit the top. "We knew it was going to be a smash for whoever did it. Timing was so important."

He continued, "We really wanted it to be a hit so we really made it more commercial and more straightforward than I like to do. The band were even singing, 'Corny or not, here we come!' It's corny but it's clever and the time is right for it. It's something we hadn't done since our Motown days.

"At one time, we were gonna do it much harsher, but it didn't suit the vibration of the song. We don't want people to think of us as being political—although we were political but from a mental standpoint. Burn down the ghettos in your head and trespass in your own mind, that's what we are trying to say."

Clinton also affirmed that a smash single for Funkadelic meant more "than if Parliament has ten hits." He explained, "Funkadelic is such a movement that when it has a hit, it helps everybody. I know it's unlikely that we'll ever get another hit single like this again, but we'll always sell a lot of albums."

302

I'M EVERY WOMAN

Chaka Khan

WARNER BROS./TATTOO 8683
WRITERS: NICKOLAS ASHFORD, VALERIE SIMPSON
PRODUCER: ARIF MARDIN
November 11, 1978 (3 weeks)

With the help of producer Arif Mardin and songwriters Nick Ashford and Valerie Simpson, Chaka Khan *arrived* in 1978 with "I'm Every Woman," her solo debut.

Admittedly, Rufus—with Chaka at the lead microphone—had already made a splash that decade. "Tell Me Something Good" was an R&B and pop giant in 1974, and the band enhanced their status with 1975's "Sweet Thing" [see 238] and 1977's "At Midnight" [267], among other hits.

But "I'm Every Woman" was a declaration of particular independence and strength. It was forged with Mardin, a producer who had 10 years' studio experience of another formidable lady, Aretha Franklin. "Chaka's then-manager called me and said, 'Would you like to...' and I said, 'Are you kidding?' "

Mardin flew to Los Angeles to meet Khan and to discuss possible recording schedules. "We really hit it off because she's a wonderful lady," he declares, "and also a modernist, very avant garde thinking."

As it turned out, the singer was looking to New York for her first solo project. "She wanted to get away from her entourage, get into a new scene," recalls Mardin, "and we recorded at Atlantic [in Manhattan].

"We had some good songs but one day, in the middle of the session, Valerie Simpson calls me up and says, 'We've got a song for Chaka.' I said, 'Great, send it over.' I believe it wasn't even a cassette, it was an acetate or some really old form or something. We played it, we immediately took down the chords and recorded it. It was 'I'm Every Woman.' A gift from Valerie."

Simpson's husband and songwriter partner, Nick Ashford, remembers that Mardin had asked for any songs suitable for Chaka. "Val had already started that melody on the piano," he says. "I think it had been hanging around."

His collaborator agrees. "I had a hard time with 'I'm Every Woman,' because the whole woman thing took a long time to come through," laughs Simpson—and then laughs again as Ashford deadpans, "It's hard when you have to assume the role of the woman."

Khan recorded vocals for the song "in maybe an hour or something," recalls Mardin. "She has this crystal-clear voice, and total creativity. You don't even tell her what to do, she does it."

The band for the session included Steve Ferrone on drums, Anthony Jackson on bass, Richard Tee on piano, and Hamish Stuart, Phil Upchurch, and Onnie McIntyre on guitars. Says Mardin, "We literally took down the chords [from the Ashford/Simpson acetate] and assigned them, 'You play this, you play that.' Then I believe I wrote the strings after the vocal was done."

The producer is unstinting in praise for Khan: She knows instinctively how to approach a song. " 'OK,' she says, 'this is how I'm going to sing this.' And it's perfect. For example, if she had sung *I'm every woman* short, I would have objected. But [the way she stretches the first line of the chorus] is exactly ideal. It doesn't need producing, it doesn't need correction. If it's good, don't change it."

303

LE FREAK

Chic

ATLANTIC 3519
WRITERS: NILE RODGERS, BERNARD EDWARDS
PRODUCERS: BERNARD EDWARDS, NILE RODGERS
December 2, 1978 (5 weeks)

When Chic's "Dance, Dance, Dance" was played at the *Billboard* disco convention in 1977, claims Nile Rodgers, "no one had ever heard bass like that. We were blowing speakers."

Rodgers, a founding member of the band, is honest enough to point out that their distinctive sound wasn't planned. "Chic accidentally became something we didn't even know we had," he says, verbalizing the explosive technique of the band's drummer, Tony Thompson: "Frap! Scoot! Bam!"

"We do that because once we were auditioning for a production job with Ashford & Simpson. They wanted Tony to play something like that—and he couldn't. So he made it his duty to learn."

As a result, says Rodgers, Thompson hits the drums harder than anyone he's ever seen. "Whenever we did our records, we would have all this low-end and big snare drums and stuff. For dance records, we had a lot of snare and handclaps, big backbeats and big low end."

That was, of course, after Rodgers's woodshedding days as a guitarist with a "Sesame Street" touring band, and after he and partner Bernard Edwards (who played bass) had toiled together in a black rock outfit, Allah and the Knife-Wielding Punks.

Chic took shape in 1977 when a club DJ at New York's Night Owl began playing dance tracks by the two musicians. Then their recording of "Dance, Dance, Dance" (made with drummer Thompson) graduated into a massive disco, R&B, and pop hit after it was picked up by Atlantic Records.

One year later came "Le Freak," written to capitalize on the dance of the same name, just as "Dance, Dance, Dance" was tailored to exploit the popularity of the hustle. "We thought about the dance

Chic

marathons in the '20s," says Rodgers. "People would go to these things just to earn five dollars. We'd seen the movie *They Shoot Horses, Don't They?* We made the association between those dance marathons and when we'd go to a club, seeing kids who would never leave the floor."

Rodgers, Edwards, and Thompson cut "Le Freak" at the Power Station in New York, with Alfa Anderson and Luci Martin as featured singers. Raymond Jones and Robert Sabino played keyboards, Sammy Figueroa handled percussion, and Cheryl Hong, Karen Milne, and Marianne Carroll were the distinctive "Chic strings" directed by Gene Orloff.

"In a strange way," Rodgers declares, "when we were looking for the identity of Chic, we were trying to take a point in black history where there was class and a signature and an identity. We tried to update that, using all of the vibe, and sort of superimpose that on new people.

"We think of ourselves as real musicians, fairly sophisticated, so I didn't want my music not to reflect that knowledge. I wanted to orchestrate—in fact, I actually did that as a job, just doing orchestration without even playing or working."

By contrast, Rodgers says, "Bernard wasn't classically trained like that. He started playing by ear. That's a good thing about collaboration: You have your set of rules, they have their set. I always wanted to over-intellectualize everything, Bernard always wanted to get down to the grass roots. So we balanced our respective personalities, and we had Chic."

304

GOT TO BE REAL

Cheryl Lynn

COLUMBIA 10808

WRITERS: CHERYL LYNN, DAVID PAICH, DAVID FOSTER

PRODUCERS: DAVID PAICH, MARTY PAICH

January 6, 1979 (1 week)

Did any contestant ever go on to have a successful career after competing on *The Gong Show*? Los Angeles–born Cheryl Lynn did, after singing Billy Preston and Bruce Fisher's "You Are So Beautiful" on the tacky talent show hosted by Chuck Barris. "It was the only song I knew besides a lot of hymns and gospel songs," says the artist, who was very involved in the Church of the Living God, where her mother was Minister of Music. "And if you were to watch the video...I was such a little, plain church girl."

Cheryl Lynn enjoyed singing in the church choir, but was too shy to be a featured soloist. Her boyfriend at the time convinced her to audition for *The Gong Show*. Cheryl recalls her appearance: "I went down there one Thursday morning to do the show...We taped in June and the show did not air until September 14th, so I had completely forgotten about it." In fact, she missed seeing the show on the air because she had her first professional job: performing in *The Wiz* in San Francisco.

The reaction to her *Gong Show* appearance was swift. Barris predicted she would be an overnight star and record companies started calling. "Ahmet Ertegun, Jerry Greenberg, Bob Krasnow, Bruce Lundvall, Walter Yetnikoff," Cheryl Lynn ticks off. "I had a list of names...and when they would call, I would...sit there in amazement, because I honestly didn't know who these people were and I was amazed at the response I was getting." Cheryl Lynn met with executives from different labels and found herself most comfortable with Lundvall and Yetnikoff at CBS Records.

Cheryl Lynn was teamed up with executive producer Bruce Johnston at Columbia. He introduced her to Marty and David Paich. "David and I really clicked well together," says the singer. "He'd play the piano and I would sing. And I would make up stuff as he would play. I would sing what I felt, and that was the basis of my first album...That's how we came up with 'Got to Be Real,' in his back house. The music was written by David [with David Foster], but the melody line and the lyrics were written by me."

Cheryl Lynn explains how she came up with the title: "I'm a real romantic person because I always think about love...With 'Got to Be Real,' I was thinking about real love, real affection. If you just be true, everything will be alright for you."

She found it exciting to be in the studio with the musicians assembled by her producers. Ray Parker Jr. played guitar, James Gadson was on drums, David Shields played bass, and David Paich was on keyboards. "David [Paich] and I created a lot of energy in that back room and a lot of what was felt in that room was carried to the studio," Cheryl Lynn says. "All of the vocals on that first album were the first rundown. I sang while the musicians played in the studio. So the vocals were done live."

The formerly shy choir singer adapted well to the studio. "I think it was because I was enjoying so much what I was doing. And I think success comes from being able to do something that you really like, to have a job that you really enjoy doing. It wasn't like a job to me, it was like, 'I'm having fun.' The atmosphere that was created in the studio for me was 'Be yourself.' All I did was express myself."

Cheryl recalls listening to all of the songs cut for her first album and deciding with David Paich that "Got to Be Real" was the best candidate for a debut single, although she enjoyed all of the songs she had recorded. "I had a copy of all five of the up-tempo songs and I would ride around in the car and listen to those five songs over and over and over again. And I would never get tired of them. It seemed like they had so much energy and being my first album, I felt that this was such a special time for me."

305

SEPTEMBER

Earth, Wind & Fire

ARC 10854
WRITERS: MAURICE WHITE,
AL MCKAY, ALLEE WILLIS
PRODUCER: MAURICE WHITE
January 13, 1979 (1 week)

How far ahead of his time was Earth, Wind & Fire's Maurice White? About 13 years in one case.

In the summer of 1979, during the last big days of the disco boom, White told *Billboard* that group harmony was poised for a comeback. "My principle for producing," he said, "is to pay attention to the roots of America, which is doo-wop music. No matter what we do, we always get back to doo-wop."

White was early on a lot of things. He'd been sneaking world-beat music onto EW&F's records long before Paul Simon decided to make an African-influenced album, but somehow that didn't get as much attention coming from an R&B artist. As for his prediction about street corner harmonies, that came true also, but not until the early '90s, when groups like Boyz II Men and Shai scored a cappella hits.

Even before that *Billboard* interview, White had been carrying a torch for doo-wop. EW&F's 1977 *All 'N All* album had one cut, "Brazilian Rhyme," with a refrain you can still hear guys singing a cappella on street corners now: *Bow dee ow/bow dee ow/bow dee ow dee ow dee ow/bow do bow bow bow*. A year later, White would shorten that refrain a little—to *bow dee ow dee ow dee ow*—and make it the centerpiece of "September," the gold single from Earth, Wind & Fire's first greatest hits album.

It was the first of several EW&F songs created with the help of California songsmiths Allee Willis (who also co-authored "Boogie Wonderland") and David Foster (who co-wrote "After the Love Has Gone"). All were recorded at Hollywood Sound in Los Angeles during August and September 1978.

"David Foster is a guy we've been knowing for some time," Verdine White told David Nathan of *Blues & Soul*. "He used to be a member of Skylark, and he's worked with all manner of people, including Hall & Oates. And Allee Willis is a songwriter who first came to our attention through one of the ladies in our office and one of the Harlettes."

This outside collaboration was relatively unusual; most of Earth, Wind & Fire's prior hits had been composed within the band. Yet their lineup was fairly constant during this time, with Maurice White and Philip Bailey handling lead vocals; Verdine White on bass; Larry Dunn on keyboards; Al McKay and Johnny Graham on guitars; Fred White and Ralph Johnson on drums; and Andrew Woolfolk on saxophone, flute, and percussion.

The group's signature horn section, the Phenix Horns, featured Michael Harris and Rahmlee Michael Davis (both on trumpet and flugelhorn), Louis Satterfield (trombone), and Don Myrick (saxophones).

"September" was the first single to appear under White's own American Recording Corporation (ARC) imprint, which would also house future releases by his stable of production acts, including the Emotions, Deniece Williams, and D. J. Rogers.

306

AQUA BOOGIE

Parliament

CASABLANCA 950
WRITERS: GEORGE CLINTON,
WILLIAM "BOOTSY" COLLINS, BERNIE WORRELL
PRODUCER: GEORGE CLINTON
January 20, 1979 (4 weeks)

Pity George Clinton and the guys of P-Funk. By the time Parliament's "Aqua Boogie" reached Number One, it had been a little more than two months since any of their projects had been in the top slot. Unaccustomed to such lean times, George must have been ready to hock the Mothership by then.

Well, perhaps not. But "Aqua Boogie" was the keystone of a new P-Funk tour where Clinton made a quixotic attempt to top the spectacle of his "Mothership Connection" road show. He'd keep Sir Nose D'VoidofFunk, the arch enemy of funk who was too cool to dance and never learned to swim either. But instead of disembarking from the Mothership, the guys in the P-Funk mob were now supposed to give the illusion that they were playing underwater.

Tom Vickers, the so-called minister of information in the P-Funk army then, remembers the initial plan was to create the underwater effect by having the band behind a gauzy screen at first, but that cut off the artists' sight lines and didn't give them as much of a chance to interact with each other. Later, Vickers says, they tried using fans to blow streamers that

Parliament

looked like sea-grass, and deployed a lot of green and turquoise onstage.

Clinton even had ambitions to commit some of his frivolity to film: "We were holding this [tour] back for the movie to come first, but we couldn't wait," he told *Blues & Soul*. "The movie will be called *Motor Booty Affair*...We have been trying to get this one together for years, but we had a lot of trouble getting the business thing together. We're not going to do it 'till it can be done just right. I'd rather never do it and keep the dream than do it wrongly."

Vickers emphasizes that the "Motor Booty Affair" tour didn't flop; it was just something of an anti-climax after the Mothership. But that and the constant buzz of activity for the last two years did have the effect of wearing the group down, and both Vickers and keyboard player Bernie Worrell agree that things were never entirely the same afterwards. Things, in one of George Clinton's descriptive phrases, tended to "de-loop" after this.

As for another of Clinton's words—"psychoalphadiscobetabioaquadoloop," the one that makes up most of the chorus of "Aqua Boogie"—Vickers says that the P-Funk commander was always fascinated with *Mary Poppins*, and that George had been looking for his own "supercalifragalisticexpialidocious" long before settling on this one. One early attempt from a previous Funkadelic album was a reference to the "promentaldiscobackwashenemasquad."

"Aqua Boogie" was the last we'd hear of Sir Nose for four years, by the way. He reappeared then in a top 10 R&B hit by another P-Funk spin-off, Xavion's "Work That Sucker to Death." No water wings in sight.

307

BUSTIN' LOOSE PART 1

Chuck Brown & the Soul Searchers

SOURCE 40967
WRITER: CHUCK BROWN
PRODUCER: JAMES PURDIE
February 17, 1979 (4 weeks)

"Listen," Chuck Brown commands, "I had to fire guys to get guys to play this thing like I wanted."

Brown's talking about "Bustin' Loose," of course, the go-go groove thing that thrust the veteran Washington, D.C., bandleader into the national spotlight after 10 years of satisfying audiences in and around the nation's capital. "I had to find a certain drummer to find that certain beat I wanted," says Brown. "I'd been trying to get drummers to play that particular groove for the longest time. The beat is so simple, most drummers don't like to play it."

Brown put together the Soul Searchers in D.C. in 1968, with a core that included Frank Wellman on drums, John Ewell on bass, and himself on guitar. They expanded the lineup—and their audience—in 1972, fueled by a top 40 R&B hit, "We the People." That was made for Clarence Avant's Sussex Records, whose biggest star, Bill Withers, had turned the label on to the Soul Searchers.

Brown originated "Bustin' Loose" around 1976. "It was just an idea that came to me," he recalls. "A syncopation idea, a funky rhythm idea, and I kept hearing it, like an engine turning over in my head. It stayed with me, so finally I wrote a song out of that particular groove."

The Soul Searchers, who put "Bustin' Loose" into their show repertoire that year, were a *working* band. "We did a lot around the East coast: seven nights a week and double, triple gigs on weekends," Brown says. "We could easily do ten gigs a weekend."

The bandleader contends he knew "Bustin' Loose" was a smash from its concert reaction. "Anytime you play a tune for two years and people keep requesting it, that tells you. When I wrote the song, I just had that feeling: Ain't nothing out there like this, it's got to be accepted."

Even so, it took a fellow musician, James Purdie, to convince Brown that he should put "Bustin' Loose" on disc. "I was sick of records. I didn't make money off records [but] I could play seven nights a week. James talked me into recording one more time."

The Soul Searchers went to Sigma Sound in Philadelphia, where "Bustin' Loose" was "the first track we laid," according to Brown. Aside from his lead vocals and guitar work, the band featured Ricky Wellman (drums), Jerry Wilder (bass), Curtis Johnson (organ), John Buchanan (synthesizer), Gregory Gerran (congas), Leroy Fleming (sax), and Donald Tillery (trumpet).

The record's heartbeat was the responsibility of Ricky Wellman, son of Brown's first drummer. "I fired three drummers before I got to Ricky," he states. "I knew what I wanted. We laid the [rhythm] track, and I went back and laid the horns. The next week, we brought in some girls and a crowd, and had the whole band and all repeat 'Bustin' Loose' after me.

"We were married to the tune when we cut it. It was just so tight we couldn't make any mistakes. And that's the one that opened the door to the go-go sound, and got musicians to understand its simplicity, its effectiveness."

308

I GOT MY MIND MADE UP (YOU CAN GET IT GIRL)

Instant Funk

SALSOUL 2078
WRITERS: KIM MILLER,
SCOTTY MILLER, RAYMOND EARL
PRODUCER: BUNNY SIGLER
March 17, 1979 (3 weeks)

Raymond Earl and Scotty Miller first met when they attended junior high school together in Trenton, New Jersey. They formed a two-piece band, Raymond on guitar and Scotty on drums, and then teamed up with five singers who called themselves the T.N.J.'s—T for Trenton, NJ for New Jersey. Together, they appeared at local dances and venues, performing Motown hits and other R&B songs. Raymond moved over to bass and Scotty's younger brother Kim came in as guitarist. They split into two units—a vocal group called the T.N.J.'s and a backup band called Instant Funk. A fateful meeting with Philadelphia artist/writer/producer Bunny Sigler led to a recording contract and, ultimately, a Number One single.

Sigler's friend Jackie Ellis introduced him to the T.N.J.'s. Sigler, a staff producer for Philadelphia International at the time, liked their music and invited them to play on a session for the O'Jays and tour with him. "It was like a small little revue," says Raymond Earl. "We did two or three years of working the chitlin' circuit, working extremely hard...Once we got back to Philly, Bunny felt strongly enough about the band to take them into the studio and that's when we started writing."

"They could play anything," Sigler enthuses. "At Gamble/Huff...I was recording everybody and it was easier for me if I had my own band who could play rather than going in and having charts written up."

Scotty Miller came up with the idea for "I Got My Mind Made Up (You Can Get It Girl)." "He came up with the hook line and the idea...We rehearsed it a couple of times [and] showed it to Bunny," Earl remembers. "He fine-tuned it." Sigler had earned some money from an album titled *Let Me Party with You* and invested it in a recording session for Instant Funk. He booked them into an eight-track studio that normally recorded commercials. "They had some nice equipment," says Sigler.

Earl recalls the recording session: "It was like someone came up with a rough idea and we would get the feel of it playing it live and [we] let it flow. Things would more or less happen on their own. That tune sort of wrote itself." James Carmichael, a vocalist introduced to the group by Sigler, sang lead.

Sigler picks up the story of the track: "I cut a demo...and after a few people liked it, I took it down to Alpha. I had the guys that had the eight-track bring their tape down and we transferred that to 24-track." Sigler worked on the track at Alpha, Sigma Sound, and Blank Tapes in New York. "Bob Black mixed it and we didn't have computers at the time," says Sigler. "There's a sound the bass makes that goes, 'Duuup.' That sound was made by him fading the bass and taking it in and out." Sigler brought in a female vocalist just to add the 'Say what?' line and wasn't sure he would include it in the final mix. "It ended up working, so we put it on the tape," says Sigler.

Reaction to the song was tepid. "We went to all the labels and they told us, 'The hook's not strong. It sounds incomplete,' " says Earl. But Sigler moved from Philadelphia International to Salsoul Records, and Instant Funk was signed to the label. Still, no one predicted "I Got My Mind Made Up" would be a hit.

"It wasn't supposed to be the single," Sigler reports. "There was another song I wrote called 'Cool Aid,' and that was supposed to be the name of the album." Although "I Got My Mind Made Up" wasn't specifically a "disco" song it was categorized as one. "We were writing what felt good to us," says Earl. "We never claimed to be a disco band." Sigler concurs: "This group was a funk group and they got accepted by disco. I think one reason [was that] disco [artists] always made long records and me and Instant Funk could make some of the longest."

"I Got My Mind Made Up (You Can Get It Girl)" was not only Instant Funk's first chart single—it was their only pop hit, peaking at number 20 on the Hot 100. Although the group placed eight more singles on the R&B chart, all on Salsoul, they never made the top 30 again. "No Stoppin' That Rockin' " was their second-biggest R&B hit; it peaked at number 32 in 1983.

309

HE'S THE GREATEST DANCER

Sister Sledge

COTILLION 44245

WRITERS: NILE RODGERS, BERNARD EDWARDS

PRODUCERS: BERNARD EDWARDS, NILE RODGERS

March 31, 1979 (1 week)

Nile Rodgers and Bernard Edwards, the writer/producer team behind Chic, had scored just a couple of hits when their bosses at Atlantic Records said they could produce anybody on the label they wanted. That meant the Rolling Stones. Or Yes. Or Bette Midler. But Nile and 'nard chose Sister Sledge.

Rodgers now says they shied away from an established act because it gave them a better shot at recognition. "If we do the Stones and we come up with 'Jumpin' Jack Flash,' they're just going to think it's the Stones again." And while the pair would eventually become very good at adapting to the styles of other artists, they wanted one without a signature sound.

That would be the Sledges, four sisters who had joined Atlantic in 1973 when they were between ages 14 and 18. They had bounced from producer to producer, scoring only one medium-sized hit, "Love Don't Go Through No Changes on Me," in 1975. Feeling robbed of a normal adolescence, the quartet had given themselves only until the end of the decade to score before returning to civilian life.

Atlantic chief Jerry Greenberg had made it clear that Sister Sledge were a priority. " 'These girls are really like family to us,' " he told Rodgers, somewhat presciently. Rodgers also liked the fact that "they could really sing...To me, [lead vocalist] Kathy is just like Aretha Franklin, really unbelievable and the only person in the world who sings like that."

Sledge's *We Are Family* album and Chic's second LP, *C'est Chic*, were recorded simultaneously in late 1978 at New York's Power Station. Rodgers and Edwards played guitar and bass, respectively, with Tony Thompson (drums), Robert Sabino and Andy Schwartz (piano), Raymond Jones (Fender Rhodes), and Sammy Figueroa (percussion). Behind them were the Chic strings: Karen Milne, Cheryl Hong, and Marianne Carroll.

Kathy Sledge remembers that the original strategy was for Sister Sledge to record "I Want Your Love" and for Chic to cut "He's the Greatest Dancer." Rodgers, however, says his game plan was to lead off with "We Are Family" [see 314], but that the Atlantic folks didn't like that song, which left him scrambling.

"We had this other song for Chic called 'He's the Greatest Dancer,' and it was going to be our lead-off single. We hadn't even written 'Le Freak.' Then, all of a sudden, we didn't have a record for Sledge, so we gave them that song, because it wasn't a song yet, it was just a groove."

For the Sisters, "He's the Greatest Dancer" wasn't even a song when they cut it. "When I recorded the lead, there wasn't really even a melody," Kathy says. "They would never let you hear a song before you were ready to record it. I learned that song through the board. Nile would punch the button and give me [the lyrics] line for line. It was kind of like having to make your own melody up."

310

DISCO NIGHTS (ROCK-FREAK)

GQ

ARISTA 0388
WRITER: E. RAHIEM LEBLANC
PRODUCERS: JIMMY SIMPSON, BEAU RAY FLEMING
April 14, 1979 (2 weeks)

Before Emmanuel Rahiem LeBlanc, Keith "Sabu" Crier, Herb Lane, and Paul Service formed GQ, they recorded an earlier version of the song "Disco Nights (Rock-Freak)" as the Rhythm Makers. But there was an even earlier incarnation of the song, when it was titled "Soul on Your Side" and recorded in the early '70s.

LeBlanc grew up in the Bronx, where he became interested in music while he was in the third grade. "I taught some other musicians and made a band because I was versed in a lot of different instruments," he recalls. LeBlanc was 13 when he recorded "Solid" with the Sons of Darkness for an independent label.

Music was a way to stay off the streets, according to LeBlanc, and he found a kindred spirit in bass player Keith "Sabu" Crier. "We decided to hook up and started doings gigs at school and school parties, anywhere we could get some exposure."

The Rhythm Makers were renamed GQ by their manager, Tony Lopez, who thought the group should have a new image. "And as GQ [was] affiliated with *Gentlemen's Quarterly,* we figured GQ had a good quality," says LeBlanc. GQ was a club band at first, playing an average of five nights a week at various clubs around New York City. "Being a self-contained group—we were only four pieces—when we went out, it blew a lot of minds that our sound was bigger than they expected. They were looking for people behind the curtain because we were known as 'the little orchestra.' We always captured the nuances of recording even though we [had] minimal instrumentation."

GQ

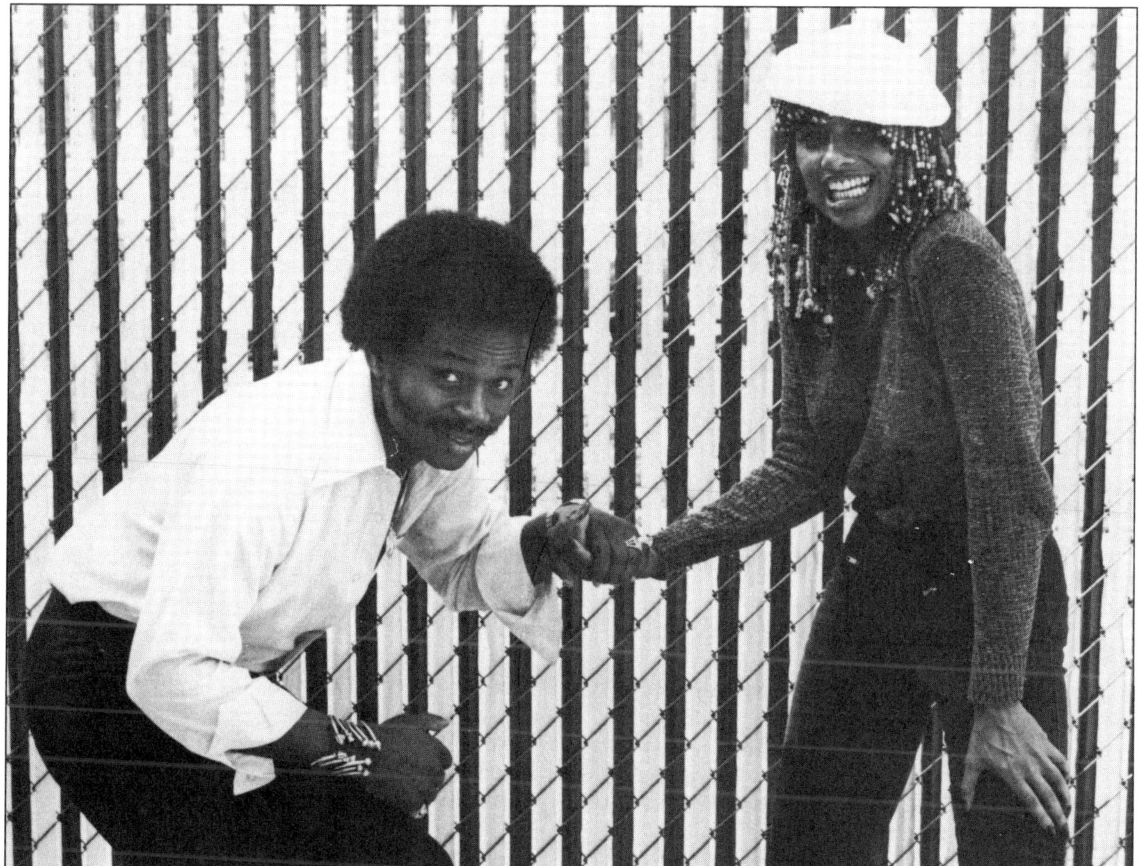

Peaches & Herb

Producer Beau Ray Fleming caught the attention of Arista vice president Larkin Arnold by playing a tape of GQ for him over a car stereo. "We were auditioning and Arista Records was the only one to really take a chance and come down," says LeBlanc. Arnold liked "Disco Nights" and asked them to play it again—and again. "A week later, we had a deal," LeBlanc adds.

The song "Disco Nights" resulted from the experience the band gathered playing live gigs. "We tried to incorporate all those feelings that we had performing and listening to the charts at the time, the way music was changing," says LeBlanc. " 'Rock-Freak' was a chant that came very naturally. The music broke down, so we rocked low and freaked high. That was the dance. There was a 'Rock' dance where you would sway your knees back and forth, and the 'Freak' was, you would point your hands up in the sky like John Travolta. So rock low and freak high. It became a call-and-response thing."

The band had been playing the song for so long that recording it was easy. "We had it together because we'd been playing that song from conception," says LeBlanc. "We'd been playing it not only those years before it became 'Disco Nights,' we tested it a couple times in our live gigs and we developed it and changed it according to the reactions of the crowd."

311

REUNITED

Peaches and Herb

POLYDOR 14547

WRITERS: DINO FEKARIS, FREDDIE PERREN

PRODUCER: FREDDIE PERREN

April 28, 1979 (4 weeks)

Freddie Perren was working at Sabin's Records at 9th and U in Washington, D.C., while he was a student at Howard University. Right around the corner, his friend Herb Feemster worked at another record store. In January of 1965, producer Van McCoy walked into Herb's store to promote a girl group he was working with, the Sweet Things. Herb convinced McCoy to give him an audition as an artist, and a week later Feemster had a record deal. During a recording session in New York, McCoy had some extra studio time and decided to record a duet with Herb and the lead singer of the Sweet Things, Francine Barker. Their first single, "Let's Fall in Love," established the duo of Peaches and Herb in early 1966.

Herb and Francine had more hits, including "Close Your Eyes" and "For Your Love," until Francine took a break and was replaced temporarily by Marlene Mack. In 1970, Herb took an exam for the Washington, D.C., Police Department. On July 20 of that year he quit the music business and went to work for the city. But he missed singing, and in 1976 decided Peaches and Herb should be reunited.

Former model Linda Greene met Herb through Van McCoy and became the third Peaches. After one album on MCA produced by McCoy, the duo signed with Freddie Perren's production company and Polydor Records.

Teamed with another former Motown writer, Dino Fekaris, Freddie planned to record four songs in May of 1978, another four in August, and have the album ready for release in October. One of the songs in the initial batch was "Reunited." Perren remembers writing it with Fekaris: "We were working on another song. I was sitting at the piano in Studio B, which was our little writing room. And I said, 'We probably ought to have one of these,' so I started playing it. We both got enamored with the groove and the idea. Dino went home to work on it." He came back the next day with the title. "Peaches was there and we played it for her and she started to cry. From then on, we discovered if she didn't cry, then we didn't have a hit. Every time she cried, something good happened."

For the session at his Mom and Pop's Company Store in Studio City, California, Perren's regular keyboard player John Barnes was away in San Francisco, so the producer brought in Larry Farrell. James Gadson played drums, Bob Bowles, Melvin "Wah Wah" Ragin, and David T. Walker were on guitars, and Bob Zimitti and Paulinho da Costa handled percussion.

The vocal sessions were rough, as Perren recalls. "We had a specific way we wanted it sung. There wasn't a lot of room for ad-libs. It took a lot of time and they were tired. When we finished, they said, 'Whew! We're glad we don't have to do that one again!"

When Perren brought the duo back to the studio in August to record four more songs, they cut a disco-oriented track called "Shake Your Groove Thing." Polydor executives decided to go with the disco song first. "Shake Your Groove Thing" peaked at number four and then radio stations jumped on "Reunited," forcing an early release.

"When I met Kenny Gamble a few years later, he said, 'I want to compliment you on "Reunited." That's a beautiful song,' " Perren recalls. "He said, 'I got the album and when I heard "Reunited" I said, "Oh man, that's the hit right there." ' "

312

I WANNA BE WITH YOU (PART 1)

The Isley Brothers

T-NECK 2279
WRITERS: ERNIE ISLEY, MARVIN ISLEY, CHRIS JASPER, RUDOLPH ISLEY, O'KELLY ISLEY, RONALD ISLEY
PRODUCERS: THE ISLEY BROTHERS
May 26, 1979 (1 week)

I Wanna Be with You" was "just another slapping kind of funk tune that kind of came together as we went," according to Chris Jasper, one-third of the second generation of Isley Brothers.

The younger men augmented the group's distinctive vocals—especially those of leader Ron Isley—with instrumental power. Guitarist Ernie Isley was one of the most formidable axemen in rock and soul.

"Jimi Hendrix was supposed to be giving me guitar lessons," says Ernie. "But one day I wanted to be a guitar player, and the next I wanted to be a fireman or a baseball player."

Since Ernie was about 12 years old when Hendrix belonged to the Isley Brothers' band, such indifference to his would-be tutor is understandable. "A lot of people get confused," he declares. "They say, 'Didn't Jimi teach Ernie how to play?' "

By the time the youngster *was* interested, Hendrix had moved on. But there was no shortage of other role models. "A lot of musicians were back and forth throughout the house," says Ernie. "It's just that of all of them, [Jimi] is the one who went on to make it in his own right."

He admits to being influenced by Sly & the Family Stone ("their songs and the way they presented them"). And, he says, "there were three, maybe four guys I've got to mention. One was a left-handed guitar player who slept in the house for about six weeks, when I was 12 or 13."

The others were Jose Feliciano, Jimmy Reed ("my brother Kelly had these blues records in his closet"), and Charles Pitts Jr., a member of the Midnight Movers and the guitarist on the Isleys Brothers' 1969 blockbuster "It's Your Thing" [see 72].

From those influences, Ernie developed his own "first-take" skill in playing solos for the group's records. Bass player and percussionist Marvin Isley explains, "Because [the solos] were done so quickly, he would maybe say, 'No, I don't like that, I really know what I want to play now.' But we'd tell him, 'No, no, we're keeping that one.' "

Marvin was Ernie's sounding board for "I Wanna Be with You," as they worked at upstate New York's Bearsville studios. "He and I were debating what the next song should be," Ernie recalls, "and I said, 'Try this.' "

Marvin's enthusiasm firmed up the idea, although "it was hard coming up with the melody because the track was such a killer," he says. "For three or four days, we couldn't come up with anything. Once we did and Ronald sang it, that was it. Kelly went downtown [to CBS Records] right after it was mixed. 'Have them put this out, tell them this is the single,' we said. And they did."

313

AIN'T NO STOPPIN' US NOW

McFadden & Whitehead

PHILADELPHIA INTERNATIONAL 3681
WRITERS: JOHN WHITEHEAD, GENE MCFADDEN, JERRY COHEN
PRODUCERS: JOHN WHITEHEAD, GENE McFADDEN, JERRY COHEN
June 2, 1979 (1 week)

"That song has so much power in the words, so much magic in the melody," asserts John Whitehead, one half of hitmakers McFadden & Whitehead. "It demands to be heard."

He's not talking about "Ain't No Stopping Us Now"—although the description would fit—but about another, earlier work with a positive message: "A Change Is Gonna Come" by Sam Cooke. "If you put that song on right now," says Whitehead, "even though it was recorded way back when, you still hope a change is gonna come."

True enough. Cooke's anthem and "Ain't No Stopping Us Now" stand together as timeless declarations of optimism and purpose, alongside, say, Curtis Mayfield's "Keep on Pushing" and Otis Redding's "Respect."

In the case of Redding, McFadden and Whitehead knew about him first-hand. Their group, the Epsilons, had toured with the singer for two years; later, they recorded for Stax, then Philadelphia International Records.

Lacking dependable income as artists, the pair turned to writing songs in 1972, with Leon Huff's help. Their debut: "Back Stabbers," a Number One for the O'Jays [see 133].

"As our first song put us on a successful road," says Whitehead, "we kind of got out of sync with singing. It was like putting gas in all these other artists' rockets: standing on the platform here on earth, watching them shoot to the moon. Eventually I said to Gene, 'We need to give ourselves one of these hits.' "

Leon Huff and his Philly International co-pilot, Kenny Gamble, weren't keen. "They rejected the idea, because they thought we were happy as writers and producers," explains Whitehead.

"So they fought us and fought us until finally they said, 'OK, go into the studio and do one song. We respect you as writers, let's see if y'all got what it takes to be artists.' The first thing that came into our minds was, 'They're letting us go in the studio: ain't no stopping us now!' "

With their keyboard player, Jerry Cohen, and arranger Jack Faith, the duo worked up the instrumental track for the song. The musicians included James Williams on bass, Keith Benson on drums, and Dennis Harris and Bobby Eli on guitars. The strings and horns were directed by Don Renaldo; the background singers were Barbara Ingram, Yvette Benson, and Carla Benton.

"The day we were supposed to cut the vocal," says Whitehead, "I'd stayed up the night before, partying or whatever. I got to the session the next day and Gene said, 'John, do you have the lyrics?' I said, 'Sure, I got 'em,' when the reality was I didn't have anything except for the title.

"So when we went in the studio and they put that mike on, I started making up words that instant. It all just came out in one take, like a godsend. It was so exciting that we just let the song keep playing, for like 10, 15 minutes.

"The lyrics pertained to our situation at Philadelphia International, but they also lent themselves to a whole lot of other people's situations. Everyone adopted that song—colleges, football teams, even races and countries—because it was a song of motivation, of determination. It fitted in with what a couple of million other people wanted to say!"

314

WE ARE FAMILY

Sister Sledge

COTILLION 44251
WRITERS: NILE RODGERS, BERNARD EDWARDS
PRODUCERS: BERNARD EDWARDS, NILE RODGERS
June 9, 1979 (1 week)

Nile Rodgers and Bernard Edwards really can't claim divine intervention for the instantly recognizable guitar riff that drives "We Are Family." But the guys from Chic do have the children of God to thank for Sister Sledge's signature hit and only gold single—the '70s band led by Martha Velez called the Children of God, that is.

"When I was a kid," Rodgers says, "I was a hippie and I used to go up to [Woodstock] and check these guys out...Martha would sing this song called 'Do What You Wanna Do' and I used to love this [riff]...I said one day I'm gonna put that in a song, one day I'm gonna find the right cut."

The right cut turned out to be Sister Sledge's "We Are Family," a lyric Rodgers and Edwards had come up with after meeting the sister act. Once they threw in the riff from "Do What You Wanna Do," Rodgers says, "it was just like...all this chromatic movement, this disco vamp, wow! Bernard got into it, started doing his thing, next thing you know, we had the track."

The session was done at the Power Station in New York [see 309—"He's The Greatest Dancer"]. Yet when the Chic team played "We Are Family" for Atlantic Records, "[they] didn't hear it," Rodgers reports. "Don't hear this? 'Nah, don't hear it.' "

Eager to please with their first major outside project, Chic cannibalized their own album for "He's the Greatest Dancer." But "We Are Family" garnered tremendous play both in the clubs and on the radio as an album cut. Well before "Greatest Dancer" had run its course, the runaway success of "Family" was undeniable.

"We Are Family" was cut in one take, with Rodgers and Edwards feeding lead singer Kathy Sledge her lines one at a time because, she says, "they wanted the spontaneity. That song had so much energy...and my sisters and Nile and Bernard were there pushing me on when I did the ad lib track" that takes the song over the top at its conclusion.

Like "Ain't No Stoppin' Us Now," "We Are Family" became a civil rights anthem as well as a feminist anthem, a gay rights anthem, the theme of family reunions, and the rallying cry of the 1979 World Series champion Pittsburgh Pirates.

Singing background on both "He's the Greatest Dancer" and "We Are Family" was another Cotillion Records artist who'd labored for years without a hit: Luther Vandross. Hearing the playback of "We Are Family" and knowing it was somebody else's career record, Kathy Sledge recalls, was a bittersweet experience for Vandross. "There was an almost frustrated look on his face," she says. "Now I know why: You never know the frustration of different artists until you've been there."

For the Sledges, "We Are Family" would prove a hard act to follow. "There was some magic to that song," Kathy states. "Even to this day when I speak at different schools for Career Day, I'll get first graders who know 'We Are Family.' It's almost like it's passed down [through the generations] because it's such a strong song."

315

RING MY BELL

Anita Ward

JUANA 3422
WRITER: FREDERICK KNIGHT
PRODUCER: FREDERICK KNIGHT
June 16, 1979 (5 weeks)

Disco was at its frenzied peak in the summer of '79, and for a couple of minutes, Anita Ward was queen. The 21-year-old from Memphis even showed up at *Billboard*'s disco convention in New York that July, performing "Ring My Bell" at the Roseland Ballroom as if there were no tomorrow. Her timing was exquisite: The next disco convention was canceled, for lack of interest.

The instigator of Ward's success was Frederick Knight, an R&B journeyman with hits to his credit before *and* after "Ring My Bell." He reached the top 10 as a singer in 1972 with "I've Been Lonely Too Long" for Stax Records, then placed his songs with the likes of Shirley Brown, Lloyd Price, Dorothy Moore, and Marlena Shaw.

Knight also set up Juana Records in his hometown of Birmingham, Alabama, and launched the chart career of the Controllers. Their mellow soul harmonies ("Somebody's Gotta Win, Somebody's Gotta Lose") were the label's calling card until "Ring My Bell."

Anita Ward, who sang gospel and classical music while at college, met Knight in late 1977 through manager Chuck Holmes. She told writer Paul Sexton, "Frederick and I just sat and talked about what he could do for me." She admitted being influenced by Aretha Franklin and Diana Ross, "but I never tried to copy them."

After her graduation the following May, Ward joined Juana and began recording. "Ring My Bell" was originally intended for Stacy Lattisaw [see 553—"Where Do We Go from Here"], but Knight rewrote his song after Lattisaw signed to another label. "It was the last number we did on the album," admitted Ward, "so it came close to not being done at all."

In fact, she said, "We took the song very lightly, we were working much harder to promote the album." Knight cut the tracks at the Malaco studios in Jackson, Mississippi, with himself and Carson Whitsett on keyboards, Ray Griffin on bass, James Stroud on drums, and Michael Toles and Michael Ward among the guitarists.

The synthesized drum that gave "Ring My Bell" its hook was also played by Knight. "The syndrum was one of the last things we put on the record," said Ward. "Frederick just asked me what I thought of the sound...It wasn't supposed to be a gimmick. We didn't realize we'd started a whole craze with it."

The song had another advantage: Frederick Knight's Juana label was distributed at the time by T.K. Records, an R&B force that developed into a disco epicenter during the second half of the '70s. With T.K.'s clout, "Ring My Bell" resonated to the summit in six chart weeks—and Anita Ward got her invitation to Roseland.

316
BAD GIRLS
Donna Summer

CASABLANCA 988
WRITERS: DONNA SUMMER, BRUCE SUDANO, EDDIE HOKENSON, JOE ESPOSITO
PRODUCERS: GIORGIO MORODER, PETE BELLOTTE
July 21, 1979 (1 week)

"Bad Girls" was in the can for two years before Casablanca Records released the Donna Summer song. When they did, it became her only single to go to Number One on both the R&B and pop charts.

Summer played the song for label founder Neil Bogart when she first conceived of it with the members of the vocal group Brooklyn Dreams—her husband Bruce Sudano, Eddie Hokenson, and Joe Esposito. "We had written it in the studio and then I took it to Neil and played it for him and I was extremely ecstatic about it," Donna relates. "He felt that it was too rock and roll for me at the time. [He said] I should give it to Cher. And I really got upset with that! It had nothing to do with Cher. I felt that it could be a hit record for me and I wasn't giving it to anybody. So I took it and put it away and it kind of got stored."

Two years later, Steve Smith was putting up some tapes for producer Giorgio Moroder so he could find some blank space to record some new masters. "He stumbled across the song," says Donna. "But by then, I'd forgotten it." Smith told her she should listen to the song again, and he had to sing it to her to remind her what it sounded like. "He played it for Giorgio and Giorgio liked the song. Afterward I said, 'Giorgio, go in and reproduce the song.' "

The version the producer came up with didn't have any of the famous "toot-toots" or "beep-beeps" on it. "I kept feeling there was an emptiness in the beginning and I said, 'Let me go in and ad-lib something.' So I came up with the toot-toots and the beep-beeps, which actually were the catchy part of the song."

Donna Summer

The original idea for the song had been Donna's. "One of my secretaries at the time when I was working at Casablanca had gone out onto Sunset Boulevard. Certain parts of Sunset were notoriously a girly-type place for picking up girls and the police were always chasing them away. I guess because [my secretary] was black, they accosted her and harassed her...it really upset me. And because of that, this song came about. I started ad-libbing with Brooklyn Dreams in the studio and the song just popped into my head."

Critics credited Summer and Moroder for bringing rock and roll and disco music together on *Bad Girls*. "We did it deliberately," Donna says. "We thought it was time to incorporate some other elements into the music. It was getting a little bit boring, with the strings and all that. I've always liked rock and roll music, so I wanted to give it a little bit of an edge."

The Summer-Moroder team was a perfect match. "In a strange way, he's a mentor to me and he's like my big brother," says the artist. "He's a very gentle-spirited person...He's very serious about his music, but he has a real egoless kind of personality...and I appreciate that as a singer. When he needs me to do something in a certain way, he allows me to sing it the way I feel it. And if he feels it's too one-way or the other, he'll talk to me...And he has a lot of respect for women, and I think that helps when you're working with a man."

317

GOOD TIMES

Chic

ATLANTIC 3584
WRITERS: NILE RODGERS, BERNARD EDWARDS
PRODUCERS: BERNARD EDWARDS, NILE RODGERS
July 28, 1979 (6 weeks)

During the spring of 1979, the members of Chic were in New York's Power Station studios, preparing their third album. "That's usually when your brain is wide open," declares Nile Rodgers, the group's guitarist and co-founder. "That's usually the best album, because it sums up where you've come from and where you're going."

Where Chic had come from was "Le Freak" [see 303], the biggest-selling single in the history of Atlantic Records. It also ruled the Hot 100 on *three* separate occasions, reaching Number One in December 1978, then returning after hits by Barbra Streisand & Neil Diamond and the Bee Gees took their turns at the top.

Where Chic was *going*, on the other hand, was "the biggest mistake of our entire careers," according to Rodgers. The lead-off single for their third album, *Risque*, was to be "My Feet Keep Dancing," a hot-shoc shuffle that featured live tap dancing by Fayard Nicholas of the Nicholas Brothers and Eugene Jackson of Our Gang.

"The whole thing of putting the tap dancers on the record—there was no sampling in those days—to us was just brilliant," says Rodgers, "and we knew that was our big hit. Atlantic had singles pressed and ready to go. Then for two days, Bernard and I stopped talking to each other."

Despite their gold-and-platinum track record, the men of Chic were unsettled. "We were both sitting around and were very hostile with each other, so I

Chic

said, 'Man, come on back here, I've got to talk to you.' Bernard said, 'Yeah, I've got to talk to you, too.' "

What followed was the realization that neither actually wanted "My Feet Keep Dancing" as their new single—and that both felt "Good Times" was a better choice. They also recognized that it was Atlantic's enthusiasm for "My Feet Keep Dancing" that had kept the pair from voicing their true feelings. And so the record company released "Good Times" as the opening 45 from *Risque*.

"Good Times" itself was "our reaction to the press," reports Rodgers. "These people started criticizing us, talking about Chic as escapist music. Well, they got that right! And even the worst person you can think of—whoever that person is—still sits back and sings a tune. Even that person has a concept of having a good time."

The record also helped fuel another music trend. Its central riff was sampled by the Sugarhill Gang for their path-breaking "Rapper's Delight." Says Rodgers, "As soon as we released it, the whole hip-hop thing developed and the rappers in the clubs were rapping over our record."

It took legal moves by the Chic chiefs to secure a share in the composer credits for "Rapper's Delight." Says Rodgers, "There was rapping over a lot of other records, too, but they used 'Good Times' because it was so popular and became so big so quick."

Five months later, incidentally, "My Feet Keep Dancing" *was* released as a single. It tap-danced to a halt outside the R&B top 40—and also became Chic's first single to miss the Hot 100 entirely.

318

DON'T STOP 'TIL YOU GET ENOUGH

Michael Jackson

EPIC 50742
WRITER: MICHAEL JACKSON
PRODUCER: QUINCY JONES
September 8, 1979 (5 weeks)

Although he released a number of solo singles while still signed to Motown, Michael Jackson didn't have a Number One hit of his own on the R&B chart until "Don't Stop 'Til You Get Enough," the first single from *Off the Wall*.

After a long string of chart hits on Berry Gordy's label, the Jackson 5 left for Epic—without their name and without Jermaine. Motown had a registered trademark on "Jackson 5" and Jermaine had married Hazel Gordy and become Berry's son-in-law. Youngest brother Randy joined the group, renamed the Jacksons, and the brothers finally had the opportunity to write and produce their own material.

Michael's first Epic solo single was "You Can't Win (Part 1)," from the soundtrack of *The Wiz*. Like the movie, it was not well received, peaking at number 42 on the R&B chart. But starring as the Scarecrow in the film version of the Broadway play did have a strong impact on Michael's recording career—he found the perfect producer for his first solo Epic album in the man who produced the soundtrack of *The Wiz*..

"One day I called Quincy [Jones] up to ask if he could suggest some great people who might want to do my album," Michael said in *Melody Maker*. "It was the first time I fully wrote and produced my songs, and I was looking for somebody who would give me that freedom, plus somebody who's unlimited musically. Quincy calls me 'Smelly,' and said, 'Well, Smelly, why don't you let me do it?' I said, 'That's a great idea!' It sounded phony, like I was trying to hint to that, but I wasn't. I didn't even think of that. But Quincy does jazz, he does movie scores, rock 'n' roll, funk, pop—he's all colors and that's the kind of people I like to work with. I went over to his house about every other day and we just put it together."

Michael wrote "Don't Stop 'Til You Get Enough" at his home in Encino, California. Walking around the house, he found himself singing about forces and the power of love, inspired by his mother's faith—she is a Jehovah's Witness. Michael played percussion and piano in his own 24-track studio and asked brother Randy to play piano on the demo.

" 'Don't Stop 'Til You Get Enough' had a spoken intro over bass, partly to build up tension and surprise people with the swirling strings and percussion," Michael wrote in his autobiography, *Moonwalk*. "It was also unusual because of my vocal arrangement. On that cut I sing in overdubs as a kind of group. I wrote myself a high part, one that my solo voice couldn't carry on its own, to fit in with the music I was hearing in my head, so I let the arrangement take over from the singing. Q's fade at the end was amazing, with guitars chopping like kalimbas, the African thumb pianos. That song means a lot to me because it was the first song I wrote as a whole."

Michael and Randy played percussion on the actual track. Quincy put together an impressive list of musicians to join them: Louis Johnson (bass), John Robinson (drums), Greg Phillinganes (electric piano), David Williams (guitar), Marlo Henderson (guitar), Richard Heath (percussion), Paulinho da Costa (percussion), and the Seawind Horns: Jerry Hey (trumpet and flugelhorn), Larry Williams (tenor and alto saxes and flute), Kim Hutchcroft (baritone and tenor saxes and flute), William Reichenbach (trombone), and Gary Grant (trumpet). Background vocals were provided by Michael as well as Jim Gilstrap, Augie Johnson, Mortonette Jenkins, Paulette McWilliams, and Zedric Williams.

319

(NOT JUST) KNEE DEEP (PART 1)

Funkadelic

WARNER BROS. 49040
WRITER: GEORGE CLINTON
PRODUCER: GEORGE CLINTON
October 13, 1979 (3 weeks)

"George [Clinton] would talk in this dialect. If you weren't versed in it, you wouldn't know what he was talking about."

Tom Vickers, who served as Parliament/ Funkadelic's press secretary during the band's glory years of 1976-80, says the lingo the P-Funk mob used on their records or on those loopy liner notes was also the way they talked on the bus between shows. Members of the ensemble would talk about "geepies" (Bootsy fans) or something "having a 3 on it" (a drug reference to one that had been cut three times, but ultimately meaning anything watered down). Clinton, says Vickers, served as the "referee," deciding which terms would stay or go.

When the references weren't pharmaceutical, they were often just cosmic. Clinton was always fond of the word "deep," Vickers remembers. There was a song called "Deep" on one of Parliament's albums. Then there was the original name of what became the *Motor Booty Affair* album, *Music For The Deep*. Finally, Clinton got to show off his depth on "(not just) Knee Deep."

The record—made in Detroit with his usual gang [see 287—"Flash Light"]—may be the most straightforward P-Funk hit since "(I Wanna Testify)," or at least "Up for the Down Stroke." Like "One Nation Under a Groove," its references to "happy feet" show Clinton at least glancing sideways at disco, something he reportedly viewed as both silly (like P-Funk) and trifling (unlike his own work).

By scoring a Number One hit in October 1979, P-Funk had all but outlasted disco, which was already experiencing a backlash at summer's end. Nevertheless, "(not just) Knee Deep" represented the beginning of the end for the P-Funk dynasty. The conservatism of the Reagan/Bush era was but a year away. Prince, who'd been a mid-chart artist with one good song just a year earlier, was four weeks from the top. And as Funkadelic reached the summit, a record by the Sugarhill Gang called "Rapper's Delight" hit the R&B charts en route to the top five.

"(not just) Knee Deep" would eventually prove itself more enduring than "Rapper's Delight" (in 1993, for example, its track would appear in only slightly altered form as Bobby Brown's "Get Away"). But that didn't mean that Clinton—who had anticipated rap on cuts like "P-Funk" and "Take Your Dead Ass Home"—would know how to handle the hip-hop era. Tom Vickers recalls playing Grandmaster Flash for some of the group and being told "this shit will never happen." He adds, "George saw rap coming and tried to deny it."

Eventually, Clinton would try to co-opt hip-hop, at least somewhat. On "Loopzilla," his first single under his own name and the one before "Atomic Dog" [see 370], he name-checked Afrika Bambaataa's pioneering "Planet Rock." P-Funk had always taken its reference points from the outside world, but this was the first sign of hip-hop sneaking into the Clinton camp's glossary. And that was deep.

320

LADIES NIGHT

Kool & the Gang

DE-LITE 801
WRITERS: GEORGE BROWN, KOOL & THE GANG
PRODUCER: EUMIR DEODATO
November 3, 1979 (3 weeks)

As the sun rose on 1979, Kool & the Gang were *cold*. Sure, they enjoyed a moment of glory when the *Saturday Night Fever* soundtrack—containing their "Open Sesame"—danced off with the top album award at the Grammy ceremonies on February 15.

Yet "Open Sesame" was a 1976 recording, and the band hadn't been in the top 10 since then. Founder member Khalis Bayyan (Ronald Bell) was even thinking of leaving in '79. "But we decided to give it one more shot," he says. "We consciously changed our musical structure to make pop records."

The gang recruited a jazz-oriented producer with pop aspirations of his own: Eumir Deodato. "He was in the process of going more commercial and doing dance music," says Jim Bonnefond, who was an engineer at the House of Music in West Orange, New Jersey, where the producer often recorded.

"The band came to look at the studio while Deodato was working on his album, *Knights of Fantasy*. One thing led to another, and they decided to give him a try. They had pretty much of a jazz background, so they knew about Deo and respected him."

One further change was necessary for Kool & the Gang's rebirth: a lead singer. "We interviewed a couple of people, but when J.T. came in, I *knew* he was the right one," comments Bayyan. "There was a Nat 'King' Cole vibe about him, a smooth texture in his voice that fitted right with the group."

J.T. was James Taylor, a vocalist who had previously fronted a couple of area bands, including the Filet of Soul. He knew House of Music co-owner

The Commodores

Stephan Galfas, and learned that Kool & the Gang needed a singer. "I went there and met the guys," says Taylor, "and halfway through the day, they just asked me to sit by the piano and start singing. Two weeks after that, I did my first concert with them."

Taylor also got busy on the band's new album, as Bayyan, their music director, began assembling the components. "I was at home, working on the chords for 'Celebration,' " Bayyan says. "It wasn't finished, it was just an idea. Kool walked in and said two things: 'Ladies Night' and 'Hangin' Out.' "

Bayyan didn't need more than the title ideas. "To me, they were immediate," he says. " 'Ladies Night' was already sold. It was *destined* to win. I mean, there were ladies nights everywhere."

The band's drummer, George Brown, wanted to develop the idea further. "He came back with a musical foundation for 'Ladies Night,' " recalls Bayyan, "and then we all collaborated on putting together the pieces. But we didn't have a hook. Deo suggested we needed one, so I came up with *Oh yes, it's ladies night/And the feeling's right/Oh yes, it's ladies night/Oh what a night.*

"My mother, Aminah, had a hand in that one. Because she would say to me, 'Always give the people nursery rhymes. Give them something they remember.' She liked the Dells' song, 'Oh, What a Nite,' so I put that in. When we were finished, we were all in tune that this was *it*. We just didn't know *how* big!"

321

STILL

Commodores

MOTOWN 1474
WRITER: LIONEL RICHIE
PRODUCERS: JAMES ANTHONY CARMICHAEL, THE COMMODORES
November 24, 1979 (1 week)

The Commodores had two big hits in 1979. Both were inspired by the breakup of married couples.

"Sail On," the first single from *Midnight Magic*, was written about the failing marriage of William "Smitty" Smith, a boyhood chum of Lionel Richie. Smith, who calls Richie "Skeet," talked to his pal from nine o'clock one night until sunrise. "Skeet mostly just listened," Smith related to Roberta Plutzik, author of a biography on Richie. "We cried, and when I walked out in the morning, I knew he was the old Skeet, and that he cared. Six months later, he sent me the song, with the message that he'd written it with me in mind, and every line in 'Sail On' refers to something we talked over."

"Sail On" was still enjoying its chart run when Motown rush-released a second single from *Midnight Magic*. " 'Still' was the other side of the coin from 'Sail On,' " Richie told Dick Clark. The song was written about another couple that was in the process of breaking up. Both the husband and the wife were good friends with Lionel. "I admired their strength," Richie said. "They decided their marriage was not the thing for them and they were probably destroying what they had in the first place, which was friendship...They both sat down and said, 'Listen, we want to be friends, we said some things wrong. Let's get a divorce and that way [we] can still be in love and still love [each other] as friends.' "

That last bit of wisdom might have applied to Lionel Richie and the Commodores as well. It was Lionel's songwriting success that eventually led him to split from the group.

The beginning of the end came when the Commodores were planning a 96-date concert tour. Drummer Walter Orange had a motorcycle accident, postponing the tour by several weeks. That gave Richie time to respond to overtures from country-oriented pop star Kenny Rogers, who was impressed with songs like "Sail On" and "Still." Rogers contacted Motown's publishing arm, Jobete, about the possibility of working with Richie. While Orange recuperated, the Commodores' star songwriter flew to Las Vegas to confer with Rogers.

"The idea was that Lionel would come from R&B and I'd come from country, and we'd meet somewhere in pop," Rogers told Paul Grein in *Billboard*. "I needed new input and that's where Lionel came in."

During their first meeting, Lionel played two songs for Kenny: "Lady" and "Goin' Back to Alabama." Rogers liked them both and recorded the pair in one session that lasted over eight hours. "Lady" went to Number One on the pop chart and stayed there for six weeks. It was Richie's first production work outside of the Commodores, and the success of "Lady," combined with Lionel's duet with Diana Ross [see 348—"Endless Love"], hastened his exit from the group.

Unable to resist the inevitable, a group meeting was called in Tuskegee. It was an emotional gathering, with some of the Commodores moved to tears as Lionel announced he would be leaving his friends and co-workers for a solo career.

322

I WANNA BE YOUR LOVER

Prince

WARNER BROS. 49050
WRITER: PRINCE
PRODUCER: PRINCE
December 1, 1979 (2 weeks)

Prince Rogers Nelson was born June 7, 1958, to John and Mattie Nelson. His father was a bandleader who earned a living working for Honeywell Computers; his mother had sung with his father's jazz trio. Prince was 10 when his father left the family. Mattie remarried, but her new husband Hayward Baker didn't care much for his stepson's interest in playing the piano (although he did take the youngster to see a James Brown concert, a defining moment for the future star). When he was 14, Prince left home.

"I went to live with my real father, but that didn't last too long because he's as stubborn as I am," Prince said. "I lived with my aunt for a while. I was constantly running from family to family." He ended up living in the basement of Bernadette Anderson, mother of his friend Andre. Prince decorated his new living quarters in rabbit fur and mirrors and wrote songs there—sometimes three or four a day. Some of his lyrics were inspired by his sexual imagination. "All fantasies," he told Barbara Graustark in *Musician*. "Because I didn't have anything around me...there were no people. No anything. When I started writing, I cut myself off from relationships with women."

He taught himself to play guitar, keyboards, drums, and many other instruments—more than 27, he counted—until he was a one-man band able to single-handedly record his own demo tapes. He also had a group called Grand Central, featuring his friend Andre Anderson (later known as Andre Cymone) on bass guitar, Andre's sister Linda on keyboards, and Prince's cousin Charles Smith on drums. Smith was replaced by Morris Day [see 480—"Fishnet"] and the band name was changed to Champagne.

In 1976, Prince took off for New York to secure a recording contract. Meanwhile, a demo tape recorded with British engineer Chris Moon caught the ear of Owen Husney, an advertising agent in Minneapolis. When Prince returned to his home city, Husney and attorney Gary Levinson financed the recording of demos that sounded more professional. In March of 1977 Husney and Levinson began negotiations with various record companies with one stipulation: The unproven artist would be able to produce himself.

It was unusual for an untested talent to win that point, but Warner Brothers agreed and offered Prince a long-term contract.

Prince

It took five months to record *For You,* not to mention twice the advance money Warner Brothers had offered for Prince's first *three* albums.

The title of Prince's first single didn't endear him to many radio program directors. "Soft and Wet" only managed to reach number 92 on the Hot 100, but achieved a respectable number 12 position on the R&B chart. The follow-up, "Just As Long As We're Together," didn't chart pop and squeaked in at number 91 R&B.

In June of 1979 Prince went back into the studio to record his sophomore album. *Prince* was completed in six weeks and the initial single established him as someone to keep an eye on in the '80s. "I Wanna Be Your Lover" peaked at number 11 pop, and would remain his biggest Hot 100 hit until "Little Red Corvette" cracked the top 10 in 1983. It also became his first R&B Number One, and would remain his biggest R&B hit until the release of "When Doves Cry" in 1984.

323

DO YOU LOVE WHAT YOU FEEL

Rufus and Chaka

MCA 41131
WRITER: DAVID "HAWK" WOLINSKI
PRODUCER: QUINCY JONES
December 15, 1979 (3 weeks)

After three self-produced Number One hits, Rufus turned to one of the hottest producers in the business. But working with the group was no picnic for Quincy Jones. "I was always late to the studio," Chaka Khan confesses. "Once Quincy had to wrestle me, physically wrestle me down to the floor and make me commit to being on time. And it's something I think he needed to do...The album went smoothly after that."

"Do You Love What You Feel" was written by Chicago-born David "Hawk" Wolinski, who grew up loving jazz. Influenced by Dave Brubeck, he started playing when he was 14. While in a band called Madura, he was managed and produced by James Guercio, who would later produce Chicago and Blood, Sweat & Tears. Wolinski also played bass for Ted Nugent and worked with the Shadows of Knight ("Gloria"). Faced with a choice of playing with the Buckinghams or the Shadows, he chose the latter, because "they got more chicks."

Wolinski moved to San Francisco and then transplanted himself to Los Angeles. There he played behind Minnie Riperton, but when the singer fell ill she had to dismiss her musicians. "The day that I got the notice I was going to be off retainer from Minnie, [Kevin Murphy] calls up." The keyboard player for Rufus offered Wolinski a job with the band.

"Hawk" had already been working on his songwriting, but not in a commercial vein. "I never wrote with the intention of writing a single," he says. "Or anything that was three minutes. I never thought about time. And back in the days I'm talking about, you didn't need to have a hit single to have a hit band—[like] Emerson, Lake, and Palmer. So I never wrote anything with verses and choruses. And when I got with Rufus, because of their commercial success my writing had to be a lot more disciplined, which was really great. It helped me out a lot."

Wolinski wrote "Do You Love What You Feel" in his home studio and took it to his producer. "Quincy didn't like the bridge of the song...To his credit, he was trying to push me to see if there was anything better there. So we had our one and only confrontation. Everything I tried to write after this original idea, he didn't like and I didn't either. And I got to the point where after writing three or four different things, I said, 'We're going to do it with this bridge the way it is.' And he said, 'I don't think so.' " Wolinski held his ground and said he would withdraw the song. "So it ended up getting done my way. It ended up being a nice song."

Wolinski remembers the recording session being a quick one. "Chaka was so fast...she would come in and [say], 'OK, let me sing that.' Boom, it would be done." The writer believes "Do You Love What You Feel" was the simplest, most straightforward dance tune on the *Masterjam* album, "which is what I think Quincy wanted to concentrate on." He believes the key to the producer's success is his ability to pick the right person to play the right part. "And when you look at the personnel, they changed a lot. He kept certain people in and then he would bring certain people around and they always were the right person. That's a tremendous ability, to be able to recognize talent."

While working on *Masterjam,* Quincy was also busy producing an album called *Off the Wall.* He invited Wolinski and Watson to contribute to Michael Jackson's album, and they played on the track "Rock with You."

324

ROCK WITH YOU

Michael Jackson

EPIC 50797
WRITER: ROD TEMPERTON
PRODUCER: QUINCY JONES
January 5, 1980 (6 weeks)

Quincy Jones had the distinction of producing the last Number One single of the '70s [see 323—"Do You Love What You Feel"] as well as the first Number One single of the '80s, Michael Jackson's "Rock with You."

But Quincy almost didn't produce the *Off the Wall* album. "I perceived him as a bubble-gum singer," he said in a BBC interview on Radio 1 in October, 1992. "A good one," Jones added. "An enormous talent." One of the contributions Quincy made to Jackson's career was bringing him out of adolescence. "I love *Off the Wall,*" the producer said. "I loved making it and the feeling of discovering a [new] part of Michael. I dropped a lot of his keys way down so he wouldn't be singing so high all the time...so you could feel some of his maturity."

Once Jones accepted Jackson's invitation to produce the album, the producer knew what his first job was. "I started to try to find a collection of songs I thought would be good for Michael." Jackson wrote three songs on the album: "Don't Stop 'Til You Get Enough," "Get on the Floor" (with Louis Johnson of the Brothers Johnson), and "Working Day and

Shalamar

Night." For the other songs on the album, Quincy called up writers he already knew well. One of them was Rod Temperton, a founding member of the Anglo-American band Heatwave. Temperton wrote their three biggest hits, "Boogie Nights," "Always and Forever," and "The Groove Line."

"Rod came to me after he cut the second album with Heatwave," Quincy said on the BBC. "Rod told me he was a big fan of my movie scores and we got to talk and hit the piano together...I heard an incredible songwriter-arranger at work, no matter how [the music] was played. [Heatwave were] not the greatest musicians. They made wonderful records—the structure and the words." Quincy was certain that if he called Rod and asked him to compose some material for *Off the Wall*, the writer would come through.

While Jones was producing much of *Off the Wall*, Michael was on the road with his brothers for the *Destiny* tour. "He didn't even know we were recording the tracks with Rod Temperton," Quincy said. Jones spent a weekend cutting the tracks for "Rock with You" and two other Temperton songs, "Burn This Disco Out" and what became the title track of the album, "Off the Wall." The musicians on duty that weekend were Bobby Watson (bass), John Robinson (drums), David Williams and Marlo Henderson (guitars), Greg Phillinganes and Michael Boddicker (synthesizers), Rufus's David "Hawk" Wolinski (electric piano), Jerry Hey (trumpet and flugelhorn), Larry Williams (flute and tenor and alto sax), Kim Hutchcroft (flute and baritone and tenor sax), William Reichenbach (trombone), and Gary Grant (trumpet).

Michael arrived at the studio on Monday to hear what the musicians had cooked up over the weekend. He didn't know who Rod was, according to Quincy, but he loved the songs.

Michael wrote in *Moonwalk* that "Rock with You" was exactly the kind of song he wanted for the album. "It was perfect for me to sing and move to," he stated. "Rod...had written the song with a more relentless, get-down arrangement in mind, but Quincy softened the attack and slipped in a synthesizer that sounded like a conch shell's insides on a beach."

325
THE SECOND TIME AROUND
Shalamar

SOLAR 11709
WRITERS: LEON SYLVERS, WILLIAM SHELBY
PRODUCER: LEON SYLVERS
February 16, 1980 (1 week)

When Jody Watley's parents divorced, she moved with her mother from Kansas City, Missouri, to Southern California. "It was exciting for me, thinking I was going to end up living in Los Angeles, because the first thing I wanted to do was to get on *Soul Train*," she remembers.

Watley wrote to the show asking to audition as a dancer, but never heard back. "Ironically, a young man in church approached me about being his partner on *Soul Train* because his partner was out of town and he thought I had a cool look." That was good for one taping, and then Watley tried sneaking in. "This went on for months until I started getting recognized and eventually I became a regular dancer on the show," Watley explains. With her partner Jeffrey Daniels, Watley traveled as a *Soul Train* dancer and appeared in a Wolfman Jack revue.

There was also a Soul Train label, which issued a medley of Motown songs under the title "Uptown Festival." The artist credited on the label was Shalamar, but there was no Shalamar—only a group of studio musicians. One of the vocalists on "Uptown Festival" was Gary Mumford, who was asked to join a real Shalamar along with Watley and Daniels. Mumford was replaced by Gerald Brown by the time the trio recorded "Take That to the Bank." Watley says, "Gerald was a lot older than the two of us and it didn't work out. We had known Howard [Hewett] from performing at a popular club called Maverick's Flats. We were on the road when Gerald left us and it was like an emergency...Jeffrey and I thought of Howard Hewett and we told Dick Griffey."

The first hit for the newly revised Shalamar was "The Second Time Around." It was also the first hit for producer Leon Sylvers, who credits Freddie Perren with teaching him the essentials of production when they worked together on Sylvers' hits like "Boogie Fever" [see 239].

Sylvers teamed up with William Shelby, whose brother Thomas was a member of Lakeside [see 338—"Fantastic Voyage"]. Shelby, who did odd jobs for label president Dick Griffey, had already written a song for Solar artist Carrie Lucas, but didn't care for the way it was produced. Griffey told Shelby to go in the studio with Sylvers and work on "The Second Time Around" for Shalamar.

Shelby was glad to work with the trio, especially since he liked Hewett's voice. "I said, 'If anybody's going to sing my songs, he'll be the one who can sing them'...and Jeffrey and Jody were young, innocent kids. They were more dancers than singers at that time. Jody could sing...It was an experience writing for her because I had to write for somebody who wasn't like an Anita Baker."

Shelby came up with the chords for the verses of the song and Sylvers added a melody and a bassline. "We just started singing 'The Second Time Around' and I said, 'Yeah, that'll work,' " Shelby recalls, adding that the lyric was inspired by a girl he left behind in Dayton, Ohio. He thought that when he returned as a successful musician, things would be different the second time around.

Sylvers recalls that Griffey liked the song the first time he heard it. "After he heard the hook he said, 'You can cut that tomorrow.' I didn't know it was going to be a Number One record, but I knew I had something."

326

SPECIAL LADY

Ray, Goodman & Brown

POLYDOR 2033
WRITERS: HARRY RAY,
AL GOODMAN, LEE WALTER
PRODUCER: VINCENT CASTELLANO
February 23, 1980 (1 week)

The first top 20 hit by Ray, Goodman & Brown was, in fact, the tenth top 20 hit by Ray, Goodman & Brown. There was almost a decade between them—and a matter of identity.

In 1970, Harry Ray, Al Goodman, and Billy Brown were the Moments, basking in the glow of the group's first Number One, "Love on a Two-Way Street" [see 89]. That was recorded by Goodman, Brown, and Johnny Morgan; when founding member Morgan left shortly afterwards, Harry Ray took his place.

For the next seven years, the trio was a constant R&B chart presence with such hits as "If I Didn't Care," "Sexy Mama," "Girls," and "I Don't Wanna Go." Then their relationship with All Platinum Records soured. "There was a legal hassle that prevented us from using the name the Moments," Harry Ray told a reporter in 1979. "But Ray is my daddy's name and no one can take that away from me."

Today, All Platinum co-founder Joe Robinson says the dispute wasn't over the name, but over a particular tune, "I Guarantee." He doesn't elaborate, but suggests the song was the original idea for "Special Lady," which brought Harry, Al, and Billy—rechristened Ray, Goodman & Brown—back into the gold circle.

Walter Lee Morris, who co-wrote "Special Lady," remembers specifically when it was created. "Harry came in [the studio] with the lyrics one day when they had left All Platinum. He was showing the producer the song.

"But it wasn't structured too well, so I got the guitar and we just messed around with it. I was putting it together the way it should go, chord-wise, while he was singing it. And then we pieced it together like that."

As the group's longtime guitarist [see 211—"Look at Me"], Morris also played on the record. It was

Ray, Goodman & Brown

arranged by Lou Toby, who handled keyboards alongside drummer Richard Crooks and bassist Bob Babbitt. The producer was Vince Castellano. "I wanted to keep the guys in the same basic format as when they were the Moments," Castellano told *Billboard*. "They are basically a woman's group, but we wanted to go a step farther."

"There were times we went onstage and we couldn't even sing because of the girls rushing the stage and that sort of thing," said Billy Brown some years later, affirming the trio's place in the rich R&B tradition of falsetto performers who magnetized the female audience.

Crisp and clean, "Special Lady" was cut at Hugo Peretti and Luigi Creatore's studio at Englewood Cliffs, New Jersey—a stone's throw from the Englewood headquarters of All Platinum. The H&L room was better-equipped, although Ray, Goodman and Brown *always* made the most of what they had.

"All Platinum didn't have the [best] quality of sound," reflects Walter Morris, "but they had the sound that people liked. It had a lot to do with the musicians and singers, who could take the little they had and make it sound good. We only had a little bit, but we made it work. And it sold."

327

AND THE BEAT GOES ON

The Whispers

SOLAR 11894

WRITERS: LEON SYLVERS III, STEPHEN SHOCKLEY, WILLIAM SHELBY

PRODUCERS: DICK GRIFFEY, LEON SYLVERS III, THE WHISPERS

March 1, 1980 (5 weeks)

Twin brothers Walter and Wallace Scott were five years old when they made their first professional appearance, singing "Me and My Shadow" onstage. They were seasoned veterans by the time they formed the first incarnation of the Whispers as high school students in the '60s.

Walter and Wallace were performing as the Scott Twins when they entered a talent show and became friendly backstage with the Eden Trio: Nicholas Caldwell, Marcus Hutson, and Gordy Harmon. "While waiting to go on, we were doo-wopping, the five of us," Walter recalls. "We decided after the talent show we had a pretty good sound and we decided to put the group together."

The Whispers

Harmon introduced them to Lew Bedell, owner of Dore Records. He liked their smooth vocalizing and told them their harmonies sounded like a whisper. The group was named and signed to Dore. "The Dip" was a regional hit in Los Angeles in 1964 but failed to chart in *Billboard*.

In 1968, Walter Scott attended a Curtis Mayfield concert and met Dick Griffey, who said he wanted the opportunity to make the Whispers the biggest group in the business by managing them. "All our career we heard people say how great they thought we were...so I thought, here was another guy giving me the spiel, and I paid him no attention." After six months of phone calls, Walter set up a meeting between Griffey and the Whispers. "He had a conversation with the guys and they were impressed. That's how he became our manager," says Walter.

The Whispers charted on the Soul Clock label in 1969 and switched over to Chess's Janus subsidiary in 1970. In 1973 Harmon split and was replaced by Leaveil Degree, and two years later Griffey started his own label, Soul Train. The Whispers became one of the company's mainstays.

By 1979, the label name had changed to Solar and the Whispers were joined on the roster by Dynasty, a group formed by Leon Sylvers. "We were singing a lot of his songs," says Walter. "He was producing us as well as Shalamar [see 325—"The Second Time Around"]. Leon liked our vocal ability very much...He liked our ability to sing his songs better than his own group could. We had a great rapport with him."

But disco was in its heyday, and artists like Donna Summer were having hits, not vocal quintets like the Whispers. Ballads like "Olivia (Lost and Turned Out)" failed to make the top 10, and album sales were faltering. "It left us...caught in a trap because we weren't prepared," says Walter. "And it almost put us out of business...We thought about having to go back and get jobs again because we had not been successful."

The group was at its lowest point as 1979 was coming to a close. Then Sylvers brought them a new song he had co-written. "When we heard 'And the Beat Goes On,' we had no doubt that was a hit record...The hook, that was the key."

Walter has a vivid memory of the recording session. "What I remember most is how difficult it was to get drum sounds...[Leon] would be in there for two or three hours just putting a bass drum down. He would do it with his two hands."

As much as they believed in the song, the Whispers still had some doubts about their chances for chart success. "We had really gotten very discouraged," Walter says. "We said, 'This is probably another [failure] and we're going to have to forget about it. We gave it a good try.' " "And the Beat Goes On" entered the R&B chart on January 19, 1980, and was Number One six weeks later. "It taught us a lot...You suffer for a long time trying to be successful and it can change with one record....For the next five years we established our reputation and our uniqueness was seen by a lot of people because of one record, 'And the Beat Goes On.' "

328

STOMP!

The Brothers Johnson

A&M 2216
WRITERS: LOUIS JOHNSON, GEORGE JOHNSON, VALERIE JOHNSON, ROD TEMPERTON
PRODUCER: QUINCY JONES
April 5, 1980 (2 weeks)

Quincy Jones gave the Brothers Johnson a title to work with and told them to come up with a song.

"He said, 'George, why don't you write this song and call it "Stomp!" ' He would do that to me; he did that with 'Get the Funk Out Ma Face.' He threw that title at me and I went home and wrote that song in about 15 minutes, the fastest song for the Brothers Johnson."

"Stomp!" took a little longer. George recalls the process: "I wrote 'Stomp!' on this piece of paper. I drew a picture of this big old foot, this big shoe, everything I could think of. It was like, 'What in the hell can I write "Stomp!" about?' " George stared at the piece of paper. "It's a challenge coming from Quincy to me, is how I looked at it. He's asking me to do this. I am the lyricist. I went home and stayed up for 18 hours. I had papers all over my desk, papers all over my studio, trash cans full. I would write, throw stuff away, go back." He uncrumpled pieces of paper from the trash, switched lines around and finally dragged himself back to the studio at 2:00 the next afternoon without getting any sleep. "I told him I had the song. If I was smart, I would have told him that I needed to go back home and go to bed and come back the next day. But knowing how we all worked, I was so into it, we rolled tape and I sang it and it was a keeper."

The Brothers Johnson collaborated on the song with British writer Rod Temperton, one of the founding members of the group Heatwave ("Boogie Nights"). George first met Rod in Louis's kitchen: "I was leery about him...It was like, 'How do you fit in with our funk?' I respected his presence because of Quincy. I knew that he had done work with Heatwave. I knew he was a great writer. But I wanted to bust him. I really wanted to find out the truth. I said, 'You tell me to my face right now that you did not get all those concepts of writing from the Stylistics, the Dramatics'—I named all of the great artists—and he told me, 'George, you're totally right. That's where I got all of my music.' He had been listening to all these soulful R&B groups out of Philadelphia, the West Coast, the East Coast. I wasn't going to feel right with him unless he confessed to me."

Perhaps George didn't realize at that first meeting how self-effacing Temperton could be. When accepting a British award for international achievement, Temperton quipped that his credibility was blown. "People think I'm black and from Atlanta," he told the crowd. "But now my publisher will have to admit I'm this white chap from Grimsby."

George is the first to admit that his own style owed a lot to those who came before him. "The truth of my funk is it definitely comes from Sly and the Family Stone, period. If it hadn't been for Sly and the Family Stone...the closest thing to funk would have been James Brown. It was two different types of funk. I will always give Sly Stone that credit, which a lot of people don't. Between him and Jimi Hendrix and Quincy Jones and the whole Motown thing and rock and roll, that's where it comes from."

329

DON'T SAY GOODNIGHT (IT'S TIME FOR LOVE) (PARTS 1 & 2)

The Isley Brothers

T-NECK 2290
WRITERS: ERNIE ISLEY, MARVIN ISLEY, CHRIS JASPER, RUDOLPH ISLEY, O'KELLY ISLEY, RONALD ISLEY
PRODUCERS: THE ISLEY BROTHERS
April 19, 1980 (4 weeks)

"Don't Say Goodnight," the first Isley Brothers ballad to reach Number One, might have been their last, since half the group's members were eyeing the door marked "Exit."

"The three of us were going to do Isley/Jasper/Isley before we actually did," claims Chris Jasper. "That whole album, *Go All the Way*, was intended to be an I/J/I record, and the songs on there were for that."

The fault line matched the Isleys' generational line-up. The three who thought about going—all the way—were Jasper (keyboards), Ernie Isley (guitar, drums), and Marvin Isley (bass, percussion). They had joined their elders 10 years earlier, creating the "3 + 3" combination that revolutionized the group's sound—and their demographic appeal.

In any event, Jasper and his Isley cousins delayed their departure [see 417—"Caravan of Love"]. As if to affirm that decision, "Don't Say Goodnight" became the group's longest-running Number One since "It's Your Thing." It even cracked the top 40 of the pop charts, which the Isleys hadn't reached since 1977.

The song, recorded at the Bearsville Sound Studio near Woodstock, took shape through Chris Jasper. "I was thinking about the stage performance, the different rhythmic breaks in the song and everything," he says. "It was approached in that direction, a slow song to get a stage reaction."

Comments Ernie Isley, "The decision to do the song that particular way was obviously fruitful. [For ideas], we listened to a lot of different records, a ton of stuff." That included the music coming out of Kenny Gamble and Leon Huff's Philadelphia International workshop, he says.

"As a matter of fact, 'Don't Say Goodnight' was one of the first records we did using a string sound, a string synthesizer. So along with it being a down-tempo song, it was a radical move. It was, like, 'Hey, the Isley Brothers, yeah, we know what it's going to be—an up-tempo thing, bang the walls out.'

"Then this came in and it was, like, 'Wait a minute, it's got this whole sultry, sensuous kind of an intro before it even gets to the vocal part.' And I remember CBS Records being floored by that just as a track, before the vocals were added."

Malcolm Cecil, who engineered the Isleys' *3 + 3* and *The Heat Is On* albums with Bob Margouleff, remembers the younger members as "beautiful, beautiful people"—and very organized. "Their trip was that they would come in totally rehearsed, knowing exactly what they wanted. Ernie and Marvin and Chris were like a little unit, they worked together really well. From the time they walked in to the studio to the time they walked out, it was 14 days. That was it."

330

LET'S GET SERIOUS

Jermaine Jackson

MOTOWN 1469
WRITERS: STEVIE WONDER, LEE GARRETT
PRODUCER: STEVIE WONDER
May 17, 1980 (6 weeks)

Stevie Wonder monopolized the chart summit for 25 percent of 1980, with Jermaine Jackson's persuasive "Let's Get Serious" in the spring and Wonder's own exuberant "Master Blaster (Jammin')" in the fall.

"Serious" was also the longest-running Number One involving Wonder since "Signed, Sealed, Delivered, I'm Yours" a decade earlier [see 91]. Coincidentally, he wrote both songs with Lee Garrett, the onetime music director of Philadelphia's soul-formatted WHAT and a former nightclub singer.

Garrett recalls, "[Stevie] said, 'I've got this thing that I'm gonna produce for Jermaine, and I really don't have anything for him.' I think it was almost completely on deadline."

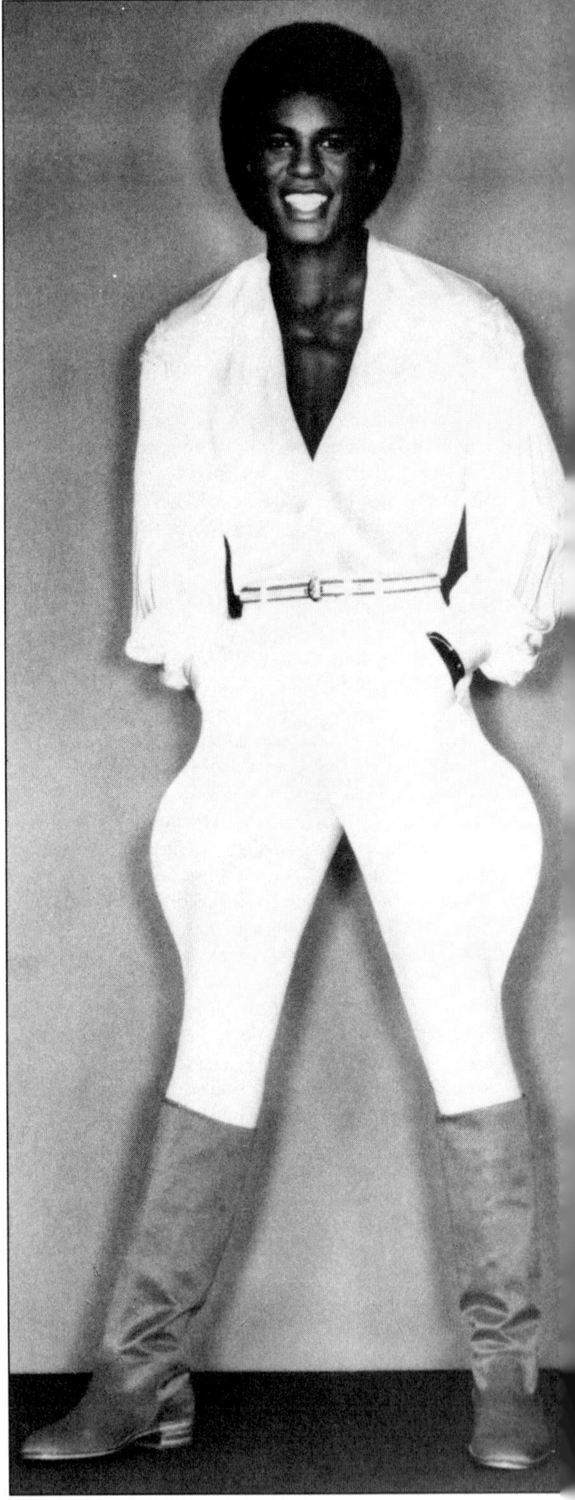

Jermaine Jackson

Wonder—who was seldom introduced to a deadline he didn't miss—had "this track, nothing else, just a track," according to Garrett. "He said, 'What do you hear?' I listened and listened, and all of a sudden it hit me, and I started jumping up and down, singing 'let's get serious.' That's it. He wrote most of the words and stuff. I just kind of did the track and the melody. I felt particularly proud of that, because it was only our two names on it."

Jermaine Jackson had been cutting solo records since 1972, when he was still one of the Jackson 5. His '73 update of "Daddy's Home" was the biggest pop hit for anyone in the Jacksons—together or separately—that year. When the group signed to Epic Records in March of 1976, Jermaine stayed "home" at Motown with his daddy-in-law, Berry Gordy, and dutifully cranked out an album a year: *My Name Is Jermaine* (1976), *Feel the Fire* (1977), and *Frontiers* (1978).

Frontiers included a faithful cover by Jackson of Stevie Wonder's "Isn't She Lovely." Two years later, they teamed up for "Let's Get Serious." Commented Jackson at the time, "That record, I still ask myself, 'How did he come up with certain grooves and certain feels and stuff?' "

The Wonder groove was certainly etched deeply on "Let's Get Serious." Jackson said, "Stevie wrote it for me, but when he dubbed me in on the song, we did it 15 times. I'm pretty sure I got it pretty close to how he wanted it, but still it's not how he would sing the song."

Of course, Wonder *did* sing on the record, as well as playing drums, piano, guitar, and synthesizer. "We recorded it here, there, and everywhere," said Jermaine. That included Motown's own Hollywood studios, and such other Los Angeles facilities as Crystal, Whitney, and Kendun.

Additional musicians on the sessions included Nathan Watts on bass, Ben Bridges and Rick Zunigar on guitars, and Larry Gittens on trumpet. Backup vocals were performed by Angela Winbush, Alexandra Brown, and Marva Holcolm, as well as by Jackson and Wonder.

"You know how you feel, you know what you're capable of doing," said Jackson, "whereas when [Stevie] produces, he gives you freedom but he knows how he wants everything."

Jermaine followed "Let's Get Serious" with another Wonder-produced opus, "You're Supposed to Keep Your Love for Me." He also maintained the collaborative habit for later projects. His 1982 hit, "Let Me Tickle Your Fancy," featured background vocals by Devo, Akron's favorite sons.

Two years later, Jackson's first album for Arista Records included a duet with labelmate Whitney Houston, who was barely known at the time. And in 1985, he teamed up with Pia Zadora for "When the Rain Begins to Fall," from a movie entitled *Voyage of the Rock Aliens*.

331

TAKE YOUR TIME (DO IT RIGHT)

The S.O.S. Band

TABU 5522
WRITERS: HAROLD CLAYTON, SIGIDI ABDALLAH
PRODUCER: SIGIDI ABDALLAH
June 28, 1980 (5 weeks)

When he was 16 years old, Sigidi Abdallah dreamt that he was in a recording studio where lights were flashing on a console and a string section was present. "I had a score in front of me and I was changing bars, and at that point I did not know music," he recalls. He woke up from that dream knowing he would produce records. Years later, when he was recording the strings for "Take Your Time (Do It Right)," he looked around and realized it was the moment from his dream. Clairvoyance or self-fulfilling prophecy? Abdallah isn't sure, but he did produce a Number One single for the Atlanta-based S.O.S. Band.

Chicago-born Abdallah moved to Los Angeles with his family when he was nine. He collected records and took note of the names and producers credited on the labels, especially Motown. He joined a vocal group, and started to write songs. He recorded a wine commercial produced by Warren Zevon and came under the tutelage of record producer Bones Howe (the 5th Dimension, the Association).

As a copyist, he wrote lead sheets for Motown and Almo/Irving Music, where he met Clarence Avant, head of Tabu Records. "He liked me and wanted to give me a shot," says Abdallah. "He had a group in Atlanta called Santa Monica and I went down to see them. I was impressed with the musicianship and Mary Davis's voice." Abdallah told Avant he wanted to produce the group, and the label head told him to find a hit record and give him a call. Abdallah was fooling around with some basslines when a friend he had known since junior high, Harold Clayton, dropped by. Clayton had a title for a song, "Show You Right," which mutated into "Do It Right" and then became "Take Your Time (Do It Right)."

"In that one session we wrote the chorus...I wrote the verses over the next couple weeks." But Abdallah didn't wait to have the verses—he went to Avant the day after the chorus was written and told him he had a hit song for Santa Monica. Avant advised him not to cut a disco record, as the disco era was over. "And I told him, 'I don't know if it's going to be a disco record, but it's going to be a record you can dance all night to.' "

Abdallah returned to Atlanta to record the song. He used the band to cut the track: Jason Bryant on keyboards, Bruno Speight on guitar, John Simpson on bass, Willie "Sonny" Killebrew on saxophone, James Earl Jones III on drums, and Davis on vocals and keyboards. The intricate percussion track was embellished by layering patterns over it, including the sound of five skillets on the floor.

Davis's vocals were androgynous enough to make people wonder if the lead vocalist was male or female. "Mary Davis has one of the most unusual voices," Abdallah acknowledges. "Like they say the camera loves some people, the microphone loves her. The sound of her voice is so incredible, which I think is the key factor in their whole string of hits." Abdallah adds that 70 percent of the vocal track was Davis's first take. "I didn't have the second verse completed. So I had her sing the first verse twice and then a few days later I finished the second verse. I tried to have her do the whole thing over. She never duplicated and definitely never topped that performance. So we ended up keeping most of that and putting in the verse and patching up a couple of spots."

Abdallah asked Jason Bryant why the band was named Santa Monica and the keyboardist replied he had once played a gig in that California beach city. Back in Los Angeles, Abdallah went to the beach to think of a new concept and logo for the group. He came up with the S.O.S. Band, inspired by a song he had written called "News" that incorporated Morse Code.

332

ONE IN A MILLION YOU

Larry Graham

WARNER BROS. 49221
WRITER: SAM DEES
PRODUCER: LARRY GRAHAM
August 2, 1980 (2 weeks)

To the dark velvet of "One in a Million You" from the liquid funk of Sly & the Family Stone sounds like a long-distance migration, but for Larry Graham, it was a journey home.

"I got into ballads when my mother and I were working together," Graham explains, recollecting the time before he became the bass-playing foundation for Sly Stone's innovative band [see 68—"Everyday People"]. "She would always make me sing ballads."

Mother and son formed two-thirds of the Dell Graham Trio, a nightclub attraction around California's Bay Area during the early '60s. "She tried to please all the customers," says Larry. "Whatever they asked for, we wanted to be able to play it: country & western, blues, jazz, whatever. So she would have me singing things like 'Ebb Tide' and 'The Shadow of Your Smile.' "

Larry Graham

Even after joining the Family Stone, the bassist retained elements of that style. "The first thing I ever cut with them," he says, "was really a ballad, 'Let Me Hear It from You.' That was on the very first album."

Thirteen years later, however, Warner Brothers Records wasn't exactly expecting a ballad as the hallmark of Graham's first solo album, *One in a Million You*, in 1980. He says, "It was like 'What do we do with this?' Because I had been giving them this funk all those years. Then to come with this record..."

His '70s exponents of that funk, Graham Central Station, had separated by this time. "There were members of the group who wanted to go on and do their own thing," he says, "so I continued on and just used a solo thing, thinking that eventually I might go back and make some Graham Central Station records, too."

Graham recorded the *One in a Million You* album at his home studio in the Hollywood Hills, playing various instruments, including bass and drums. "Eric Daniels was on keyboards," he notes, "and Wilton Rabb was on guitar." The musician's wife, Tina Graham, added background vocals.

The author of the title track was Sam Dees, a respected writer whose work had been recorded by

Frederick Knight ("I Betcha Didn't Know That"), Loleatta Holloway ("Cry to Me"), Dorothy Moore ("Special Occasion") and himself, among others.

"One in a Million You" still needed mixing, Graham recalls, when he heard the song in his head while out driving with his wife. "We rushed home, fired up the board and put the tape on. It was, 'OK, you take that half of the board, and I'll take this half,' and we just mixed it ourselves, without an engineer. It was human automation!"

The smash that "One in a Million You" became—Larry Graham's biggest R&B and pop success since his days with Sly Stone—also affirmed the lessons Dell Graham taught her son. "She passed on a couple of years ago," he tells, "and when she died in my arms, I was singing that song to her.

"It was very touching. To her, it was kind of like, 'I told you, I told you to sing those ballads.' That's what the record was to her. My grandmother, though, she kinda liked the funky stuff!"

333

UPSIDE DOWN

Diana Ross

MOTOWN 1494
WRITERS: BERNARD EDWARDS, NILE RODGERS
PRODUCERS: BERNARD EDWARDS, NILE RODGERS
August 16, 1980 (4 weeks)

"Upside Down" was Diana Ross's most successful single since leaving the Supremes, and she owed it partly to her children. Moreover, the song powered the singer's *Diana* album to number two on the pop charts, her first to reach the top since 1972's *Lady Sings the Blues* soundtrack.

The team responsible for this success, Nile Rodgers and Bernard Edwards, were at their peak in 1979. Their own band, Chic, was hot with a gold single [see 317—"Good Times"] and back-to-back platinum albums. And their Sister Sledge productions were hugely popular, too [see 309—"He's the Greatest Dancer," 314—"We Are Family"].

Rodgers remembers Ross showing up to see Chic at the Santa Monica Civic Auditorium in California. "Diana couldn't believe the crowd reaction. She said, 'I haven't seen this since the Jackson 5.' She was backstage, dancing and into it. 'My kids made me come and see this show, all they were talking about was Chic, Chic, Chic. That's what I want my record to sound like.' "

Rodgers and Edwards accepted the challenge. "We went to visit her," Rodgers says, "and told what we always tell people: 'We'll just sit down and talk with you for a couple of hours, then go home and write the album.' "

Spending that time with Ross, the pair learned she wanted nothing like her previous Motown records. "She said, 'I don't want this to sound like L.A. at all. I left California, I'm in New York, I've got a whole new life here.' "

The producers obliged, applying their rhythm-heavy Chic sound to the singer's sharp, angular voice. The album was largely done at New York's Power Station and Electric Lady studios, with Rodgers on guitar, Edwards on bass, Tony Thompson on drums, and Raymond Jones and Andy Schwartz on keyboards. Chic's Alfa Anderson and Luci Martin sang background, and what Rodgers calls "the funky Chic strings" were played by Karen Milne, Cheryl Hong, and Valerie Heywood, under concertmaster Gene Orloff.

The lyrics of "Upside Down" personified the changes Ross was making to her life and career. "Only she knew this was her last record on Motown," says Rodgers. "We had no idea." Nor had they realized how much diplomacy was necessary. "We had to learn that with certain artists, if you tell them they're singing flat, they might look at you and say, 'What?' "

That happened during the making of *Diana*, and the candor wasn't appreciated. "She went to the South of France for two or three months," says Rodgers. "but we worked it all out."

Well, perhaps not *all* of it. After finishing the album, the producers heard from Motown. "They called us up," explains Rodgers, "and said, 'Guys, we really have a problem with this mix.' Then Diana calls us up and says, 'I don't know why you have my voice so low.' You know what the problem was? We had more bass than they ever had on records before!"

Ross and Motown engineer Russ Terrana remixed the album to the singer's taste, but they couldn't upstage the Chic groove—and *Diana* hit the album charts even before "Upside Down" was shipped as a single.

334

GIVE ME THE NIGHT

George Benson

WARNER BROS. 49505
WRITER: ROD TEMPERTON
PRODUCER: QUINCY JONES
September 13, 1980 (3 weeks)

George Benson says it was very exciting to record "Give Me the Night," his first Number One single, "because I've always had a great respect for Quincy Jones, and he had just produced an incredible album for Michael Jackson called *Off the Wall*. He had broken some serious ice and I knew I was in a good position to come up with a chartbuster with the album that we eventually called *Give Me the Night.*"

The title song was the last one recorded for the project, according to Benson. "We were searching for that one pop thing that had danceability and R&B and pop and everything in it. We had done some really nice songs. We had recorded 'Love X Love' and 'Moody's Mood,' so we had a variety of things for the album. But we hadn't found that one pop thing we were looking for."

Quincy told George he had one more song he wanted him to consider. "He said, 'We have the tracks but we need your input.' So we got to the studio that night and he played it for me. Instantly, I had a feeling for the song so I started creating the signature thing on the guitar. And I put on the vocal with Rod Temperton's direction. He's very good—he knows what he wants. That's why he and Q really work well together. He comes in with solid ideas and they already have built-in hooks, which is the thing that makes his stuff interesting in addition to good lyrics and easy-to-sing melodic lines."

There was no demo—Rod sang "Give Me the Night" over the track for George. "I learn very fast," says the artist, "so after I heard it a couple of times, I knew it. But he was still looking for certain phrases and certain ways of singing the song that I wasn't familiar with. We hung in there. We finally got it on tape. We knew we had something special, but the thing that made me know I had a hit was when Quincy sent me a copy of the song. I was in Hawaii with my family and played the song and my kids came back to me 10 or 15 minutes later and said, 'Dad, play that song again.' I said, 'What song?' because they'd never asked me that before. So I knew that I had a song that was going to be successful, but how successful was hard to predict."

Benson thought that part of the song's charm was centered in the backing vocals by Patti Austin. "She and Quincy made a good team because Quincy makes you work and he looks for the hook and then he wants it to sound like it was made for the song." Benson also thought engineer Bruce Swedien and Quincy were a great combination. "He had plenty of tracks," George says of the engineer. "They believe in keeping the music clean. They never liked to run the same tape over the recording heads or playback heads at any time. Once they filled a tape up, they would take that tape off and leave it up until the final mix came along. And that made for some excellent sonics at mix time. So I had never worked like that before, but it's something Quincy Jones still does to this day."

Benson had his commercial breakthrough with "This Masquerade," a number three hit in 1976. Many people assume that was the first vocal recorded by the artist best known for his jazz guitar playing, but in fact, "I was a singer first," George clarifies. "I made records when I was 10 years old as a vocalist. And I sang before I started playing the ukulele, which I started playing at seven. The guitar was always a backup instrument for me until I was 19 years old. I started going to jam sessions when I was 17 or 18 and when I was 19 I went on the road with Jack McDuff, the organist. Jack did not like singing...so I didn't sing for the three years I was with him. That's why I became known outside of my home town as a guitar player."

335

FUNKIN' FOR JAMAICA (N.Y.)

Tom Browne

GRP 2506

WRITERS: TOM BROWNE, TONI SMITH

PRODUCERS: DAVE GRUSIN, LARRY ROSEN

October 4, 1980 (4 weeks)

Probably the only commercial pilot to navigate the R&B charts, Tom Browne touched down at the top with a tribute to his Jamaica home in Queens, New York. "It was a funky tune," he says, "but a very jazz-oriented city."

When Browne wasn't flying for Executive Air Charter in the '70s, he was playing trumpet with Weldon Irvine, Sonny Fortune, and Lonnie Liston Smith. In 1979, he took a solo trip with *Browne Sugar*, a powerful jazz-fusion album on GRP Records.

The label's principals, Dave Grusin and Larry Rosen, knew how to foster new talent. "One of the nice things about GRP," Browne comments, "was that you could go into the studio and have a trial-and-error session."

And so it was a relaxed environment which produced "Funkin' for Jamaica (N.Y.)" while Browne was cutting his second album, *Love Approach*. "We didn't go into the session pre-planned," affirms co-producer Larry Rosen. "We just had the basic track down, and wanted to see what developed." A&R Studios in New York was the recording site.

The track started at the home of Browne's parents. "I remember being upstairs and writing the bassline," he says. "Then when I gave Bernard [Wright] the idea in the studio, his eyes just lit up. Once he got the groove, it was, 'Let me go, leave me alone, I've got it.' From that point, it became more of a jam session: 'You add the jelly, I'll bring the peanut butter.' "

Behind Browne's incisive trumpet and Toni Smith's fierce vocals, Wright played synthesizer and electric piano on "Funkin' for Jamaica (N.Y.)," alongside Grusin (acoustic piano), Marcus Miller (bass), Bobby

Broom (guitar), Buddy Williams (drums), and Crusher Bennett (percussion). "Everyone brought their own signature to it," comments the trumpeter. "There's no one particular style.

"Toni was dating one of the keyboard players who used to be in my band," says Browne. "I was introduced to her, and she became our featured vocalist. She has a style similar to Chaka Khan's and, in fact, there was a lot of confusion over whether 'Funkin' for Jamaica' was Chaka's new record."

"It was unlike anything else on *Love Approach*," admits Larry Rosen, who also remembers cutting the tune's street-party sounds with "a whole bunch of guys from Queens" in one take.

Browne adds, "Just about all the musicians involved—Bernard, Omar Hakim [who played drums elsewhere on *Love Approach*], Marcus—were from Jamaica. Some of the musicians just came into the geographic area by osmosis. It had several jazz clubs very conducive for young players coming up."

As for his record's Number One success, the high-flyin' trumpeter says, "We had no idea it was going to do what it did." Browne also didn't expect pop success—and he didn't get it: "Funkin' for Jamaica (N.Y.)" was one of the few R&B chart-toppers of its time to miss the Hot 100 entirely.

336

MASTER BLASTER (JAMMIN')

Stevie Wonder

TAMLA 54317
WRITER: STEVIE WONDER
PRODUCER: STEVIE WONDER
November 1, 1980 (7 weeks)

As Stevie Wonder recovered from his near-fatal auto accident in August 1973, Bob Marley's Wailers embarked on their first major U.S. tour, opening for (and upstaging) Sly Stone.

"Reggae reflects what goes on around us, right or wrong," Marley advised a *Billboard* interviewer who asked how he reconciled songs like "I Shot the Sheriff" with his religious views. "We don't tell people to shoot anybody, we just say it happens."

Wonder harmonized with Marley on "I Shot the Sheriff" two years later, during a boisterous October 1975 concert at the National Stadium in Kingston, Jamaica, while the Wailers jammed with Stevie's

Stevie Wonder and Bob Marley

band. The two titans performed together again at the inaugural conference of the Black Music Association in Philadelphia in June 1979.

"Their relationship was kind of renewed then," says Keith Harris, a longtime Wonder associate who took him onstage during Marley's Philadelphia set that night. Later, when Stevie spontaneously created lyrics for "Master Blaster (Jammin')," Harris was the one scribbling them down, "to make sure he didn't forget them."

Wonder had been listening to "a lot of reggae records," Harris mentions, some from the latter's own collection, shipped over from England. "I remember playing 'Revolution Dub' by Lee Perry, which was actually quite an old record by then. Stevie was really interested in the different sounds and the scratching styles that Perry was doing."

At the time, Wonder was still putting final touches to his *Journey Through the Secret Life of Plants* soundtrack album, released in November 1979. Only about a year later—the blink of an eye, based on Stevie's usual delivery schedule—he came out with *Hotter Than July*, which contained "Master Blaster (Jammin')."

"It just felt right then for someone like him to do a reggae-type track," says Harris. "Especially in America, where the music had never really been accepted in the mainstream. People like the Police were coming out with what was overtly reggae material, but nobody was recognizing its roots. Stevie felt if he did a song attributing things to artists like Bob Marley, it would make people recognize reggae's influence."

Hotter Than July was recorded in Los Angeles. "It actually came together quite quickly," Harris notes. "He'd had quite a lot of ideas for songs while working on *Secret Life of Plants*, which didn't fit on that. The album was cut at the new Wonderland studio, which he'd just bought."

Wonder played electric piano and clavinet on "Master Blaster (Jammin')," backed by Nathan Watts (bass), Dennis Davis (drums), Ben Bridges and Rick Zunigar (guitars), Isaiah Sanders (organ), Earl DeRouen (percussion), Hank Redd (sax), and Larry Gittens (trumpet). Angela Winbush, Marva Holcolm, Shirley Brewer, and Alexandra Brown Evans did background vocals.

In October 1980, shortly after "Master Blaster (Jammin')" was released, Bob Marley collapsed in New York. His illness, diagnosed as cancer, scuttled plans for a tour with Wonder, and Marley was admitted to a European treatment clinic.

"I remember Stevie calling Bob in Germany from a pay phone somewhere on the East Coast," says Keith Harris. "We were on tour and the tour bus pulled over at this truck stop for him to phone." On May 13, 1981, performing in Stockholm, Wonder dedicated his birthday show to reggae's emperor—who had died two days earlier.

337

CELEBRATION

Kool & the Gang

DE-LITE 807
WRITERS: RONALD BELL, KOOL & THE GANG
PRODUCER: EUMIR DEODATO
December 20, 1980 (6 weeks)

Restored to creative and commercial vitality with the *Ladies Night* album, Kool & the Gang returned to New Jersey's House of Music to work with producer Eumir Deodato. The result was an anthem.

"Celebration"? Ask James Taylor about the song, and he laughs. "My mother told me when she heard it, 'You're gonna play this song for the rest of your life—so get ready!' "

Ask Khalis Bayyan, the Gang's music director, and he pinpoints the closing lines of their previous Number One. "You know at the end of 'Ladies Night,' there's a line that goes, *Come on, let's all celebrate...*? That was the key to finishing 'Celebration.'"

On the record, that line was sung by Cynthia Huggins, Joan "Samiah" Motley, and Kelly Barretto, the gang's background vocalists (they sang on "Ladies Night," too) who were known as Something Sweet.

In Bayyan's mind, the "celebration" motif had taken shape some two years earlier. "The initial idea came from the Qur'an," he says. "I was reading the passage where God was creating Adam, and the angels were celebrating and singing praises. That inspired me to write the basic chords and the line, *Everyone around the world, come on, celebration*."

The final song was a true collaboration, with lyric parts from Imani Smith (formerly Donna Johnson), who had sung with the band in the past; from lead singer Taylor; and from the band's keyboard player, Earl Toon, who had joined at the same time as J.T.

When the time came to cut "Celebration," Kool & the Gang were in fine form. There was the signature guitar of Charles Smith, the foundation stones of Robert "Kool" Bell (bass) and George Brown (drums), the keyboards of Amir Bayyan, the tenor sax and keyboards of Khalis Bayyan, and the punchy horns of Dennis Thomas on alto sax, Robert Mickens and Michael Ray on trumpets, and Clifford Adams on trombone.

"We finished the rehearsal track in Miami," recalls Cleveland Brown, a longtime associate of the band. "Khalis was in a trance. It was the first time he had listened to a track from beginning to end with an aerial view, without trying to perfect it piece by piece.

"He looked me right in the eye and said, 'Do you realize what we've just done? We've created a monster.

This is it. This is going to be an international anthem, this is going to be played at weddings, bar mitzvahs, and all joyous occasions beyond our time on Earth! This is going to change us.'

"It was the first time I had ever seen him get outside of himself and be objective about a Kool & the Gang song. He kept jumping in front of me, excited. It was an overwhelming moment."

Released in September 1980, "Celebration" became Kool & the Gang's longest-running Number One, a certified-platinum smash that also crossed to the top of the Hot 100. The song was featured during the 1981 Super Bowl festivities and, more poignantly, in homecoming ceremonies for American hostages released from Iran on January 26, 1981. The predictions of Khalis Bayyan (and J.T.'s mother) about an international anthem came true.

338

FANTASTIC VOYAGE

Lakeside

SOLAR 12129

WRITERS: FRED ALEXANDER, JR., NORMAN BEAVERS, MARVIN CRAIG, FRED LEWIS, TIEMEYER MCCAIN, THOMAS SHELBY, STEPHEN SHOCKLEY, OTIS STOKES, MARK WOOD, JR.

PRODUCERS: LAKESIDE

January 31, 1981 (2 weeks)

Thomas Shelby says that when he and the other members of Lakeside were growing up in Dayton, Ohio, "There were only three things for you to

Lakeside

do if you were a black man: be in a band, be an athlete, or be in the street life—a criminal. I took the athlete and the band."

Shelby and Otis Stokes were in a band called the Bad Bunch, but they felt the other members weren't serious about their music, so they quit. Mark Wood, who was in an outfit called the Young Underground, was looking for two new members for his group. The merged unit signed with a Chicago label and changed their name to Ohio Lakeside Express, which got shortened to Lakeside.

In the summer of '72, Shelby rented a U-Haul and moved the band to California. They played at the Club Citadel in Hollywood for a month, then were seen at the Crenshaw Palace nightclub by Motown producer Frank Wilson.

He signed the group to the label, and after one album both producer and band moved to ABC Records. When that company was sold to MCA, the nine-member group received an offer from Norman Whitfield to sign with his label. They were about to accept when Dick Griffey asked them to join the roster at Solar Records, home of the Whispers, Carrie Lucas, and Shalamar. When he said they could write their own material, that sealed the deal.

Lakeside, a self-contained band, played a lot of sessions for Solar artists, but they also charted on their own with "It's All the Way Live (Part 1)" in 1978. Exactly two years later, "Fantastic Voyage" entered the chart.

"At that time, we had our own rehearsal hall," Shelby says. "We'd get grooves together first and put lyrics to them later. Everybody would take [the grooves] home and if somebody worked on it, that's how it would go. We had nine people and they were trying to do their own thing. But we always said we're going to have at least one song on every album that everybody wrote together."

Lakeside had all of the songs written for their third Solar album except for one. "I went to the studio and the track was playing...I was just being silly and I happened to have my captain's hat on," recalls Shelby, who loves the ocean. While the track played, he sang, "I'm the captain of this vessel. We want to take you on a cruise." Steve Shockley liked what he heard, and soon all nine of them had dived into writing the song.

Shelby says the lyrics were finished in one day and the rap part was completed the next. He remembers enjoying the recording session. "At that time, all of the Solar acts recorded in the same studio. We had Ping-Pong tables in there. We had a small boxing gym. It was a bunch of guys, so we had a lot of fun."

Shelby credits Dick Griffey with picking "Fantastic Voyage" for single release. "It was a mutual agreement...It was different, especially with what you would call the chant in there. It was what you might call 'polished funk.' I guess they would call it pop today."

339

BURN RUBBER (WHY YOU WANNA HURT ME)

The Gap Band

MERCURY 76091
WRITERS: LONNIE SIMMONS, CHARLIE WILSON, RUDY TAYLOR
PRODUCER: LONNIE SIMMONS
February 14, 1981 (2 weeks)

Shhh. The audience is listening. It may not have been in THX, but the sound effect of a car screeching its tires at the beginning of "Burn Rubber (Why You Wanna Hurt Me)" was created in the parking lot of the Hollywood studio where the song was recorded. "Cavin Yarbrough had a Volkswagen and it would make the 'Ruum, ruum, ruum' noise, but it wouldn't burn rubber because it wouldn't take off fast enough," explains producer Lonnie Simmons. "So we had to have two cars. One car would make the roaring noise and we had another car that took off, 'Eeeerh,' and we recorded that and put it on the front of the record."

Simmons received a phone call from a top executive at Polygram who asked him to remove the sound effect because he thought radio stations wouldn't play it. "I took the front end off, the burning rubber noise, and shipped it to Polygram," says Simmons. "And Polygram called and said, 'We're sorry, but we have a problem. We sent some of the records out with the noise on and the public accepted it. Now they don't want this version.' So they went back to the original cut."

Simmons recalls how he came up with the song "Burn Rubber" in the first place. "When I was a young guy living in Dallas, I was going to college and experienced what the song is saying. It could have been a love story if you slowed the track down, because it talked about this girl leaving this guy and running home to mother, and burning rubber out the back door and taking all of her clothes and leaving only hangers and bows in the closet. Part of that was a true story." Simmons combined his own personal memories with the tale of a Gap Band roadie who went to get his girlfriend something from the store, only to return and discover she had moved out.

"We were on tour and [Lonnie] brought the idea to us," says Rudy Taylor, who mixed sound for the Gap Band and was also a songwriter. "I had been watching *Smokey and the Bandit* the night before. I remember the guy who drove the truck with Burt Reynolds had told him, 'Let's put the pedal to the metal and burn rubber.' So that line stuck with me."

The Gap Band

The Gap Band was formed in the early '70s by three brothers from Tulsa, Oklahoma. Ronnie (trumpets and keyboards), Charles (lead vocals and keyboards), and Robert (bass) first sang in their father's church. They named their group after three of Tulsa's main streets: Greenwood, Archer, and Pine.

Leon Russell hired them to be his opening act in 1973 and they recorded an album for his Shelter label. They were backing D.J. Rogers ("Love Brought Me Back") when they met Simmons. "I noticed that Charlie Wilson was very talented," says the producer, "and I approached him right before I bought the [Total Experience] recording studio. And he said, 'I'm signed right now to someone and as soon as my deal is up, we can talk.' "

Wilson became a free agent right after Simmons closed the deal for the studio. Simmons proposed a group that would include Charlie's brothers, à la an R&B version of the Bee Gees. "Because at that time, there were 14 members or something like that in the entire Gap Band and I thought that would be a problem later on, so I suggested we take the three main guys and make a group out of them."

340

DON'T STOP THE MUSIC

Yarbrough & Peoples

MERCURY 76085
WRITERS: JONAH ELLIS, ALISA PEOPLES, LONNIE SIMMONS
PRODUCERS: JONAH ELLIS, LONNIE SIMMONS
February 28, 1981 (5 weeks)

During the week, Lonnie Simmons was busy running his Total Experience record label. But on the weekends, he'd catch up with his main attraction, the Gap Band, on the road. One Friday night he headed to Dallas, where the Gap Band was appearing. He was sleeping comfortably in his hotel room when someone pounded on the door just after four o'clock in the morning.

It was Charles Wilson of the Gap Band. He had a tape in his hand and he told Simmons he had to listen to it. "I said, 'OK, give me the tape. I'll listen to it in the morning when I get up.' He said, 'No, no. You've got to listen to it now.' It was a tape of

Yarbrough and Peoples and they were standing behind him." Cavin Yarbrough and Alisa Peoples came in and sat down in Simmons's hotel room as he listened to their tape. After an exchange of phone numbers, the couple left with Wilson.

Simmons, who had to bring another act to Polygram under his contract, thought Yarbrough had a voice that sounded like Donny Hathaway. "I don't know what I thought about the tape, but I knew I liked the two people I was talking to," Simmons recalls. "Their attitudes were good. When I got back to Los Angeles, I didn't call them. And all of a sudden one day they were in my lobby and I went out and talked to them." They were still looking for a label deal. "They were such good people and very humble," says Simmons. He offered them a chance to record a demo and teamed them up with a producer signed to Total Experience, Jonah Ellis.

The musician from Wilson, North Carolina, had come to Simmons's company in hopes of being a recording artist. He was introduced to Yarbrough and Peoples at SIR Studios, and then headed out to their home in Sun Valley, California, to rehearse some material.

Ellis came up with seven songs for the couple to record. The last of the seven was a song called "When the Music Stops." Ellis was living in the Oakwood Garden apartments on Barham Boulevard between Burbank and Hollywood when he sat down with a drum machine and wrote the song. "I had a little CR78 and an acoustic guitar and I was thinking when people go to a dance and it's over, my idea was that a guy wants to take this girl home and turn her on again. It was like a throwaway song. We were gonna do it if we could get it in; if not, we were gonna just leave it out."

Yarbrough wanted to do the song, so Ellis laid down a track with a drum machine and Jonathan Moffett on drums. "It had an unusual beat," Jonah says. "The strong beat was on the up rather than the down." Ellis brought in the Waters to sing backing vocals. He had trouble with Cavin's voice, because it was more suited to a Peabo Bryson–type song than the harder funk of "When the Music Stops."

After listening to all of the material Ellis recorded with the group, Simmons went back in the studio to make some alterations on "When the Music Stops." "We changed the vocals," he says. "I came up with, 'Don't you stop it.' We changed the bass. We changed the keyboards. In the end, we had about a hundred mixes on the song. Everyone was getting batty in the studio, like, 'Why does he keep mixing this song over and over?' We went back and used the first mix."

Ellis told Simmons there was no point calling the song "When the Music Stops" when the phrase "Don't stop the music" was so prominent. The retitled single raced up the *Billboard* chart, neck and neck with another Total Experience act. "Burn Rubber (Why You Wanna Hurt Me)" by the Gap Band passed "Don't Stop the Music" and hit Number One. "I got the advance numbers through the computer before the chart was printed," says Simmons. "I went by Yarbrough's house and said, 'Next week your record will be Number One' and his lip dropped. He couldn't believe it. I said, 'Watch it. It'll be out next week. You'll see.' " When Yarbrough picked up his copy of *Billboard* the following week, he found out that Simmons was correct: the Gap Band had fallen to number two and Yarbrough and Peoples's very first single had gone to Number One.

341

BEING WITH YOU

Smokey Robinson

TAMLA 54321
WRITER: WILLIAM ROBINSON, JR.
PRODUCER: GEORGE TOBIN
April 4, 1981 (5 weeks)

The woman with "Bette Davis Eyes," Kim Carnes, was indirectly responsible for the biggest hit of Smokey Robinson's solo recording career. If Kim and producer George Tobin hadn't fallen out, she might have cut "Being with You" instead of Smokey.

Tobin had produced Carnes's remake of the Miracles' "More Love," which Robinson wrote, and it was a top 10 pop hit in August of 1980. The next month, Smokey called Tobin at his Los Angeles office. "He said he had another great song for Kim," Tobin recalls. "I didn't want to tell him that she and I had this major fight over 'Bette Davis Eyes' and a bunch of other songs that I didn't think were particularly worth recording, and she did.

"So I just didn't tell Smokey that I wasn't producing Kim anymore. I said, 'Come on over,' and when he did, he played 'Being with You' for me on a Fender Rhodes in my office. He's pitching it to me for Kim, and I'm saying, 'No, no, this is great for you, you ought to do it.' "

Tobin admits Robinson might have thought he didn't like the song, and was being diplomatic about it. "I said, 'Look, I'll make the record with you, I'll pay for it, and if you don't like it, it can be your demo so you won't have to go sing it live for anybody.' Smokey replied, 'Well, no one has ever produced me [as a solo artist] before.' So I said, 'Well, I'll do it.' "

Robinson thought about this idea, by Tobin's account, and called him a couple of hours later to agree. "So we went in that night at seven o'clock, and by about four o'clock the next afternoon, we had it done."

Smokey Robinson

Always a fast worker, Tobin arranged and cut "Being with You" at his own 24-track Studio Sound Recorders in North Hollywood. "I put a band together that night," he says. The rhythm section featured Mike Piccirillo (guitar, synthesizer, organ), Scott Edwards (bass), Ed Greene (drums), and Bill Cuomo (keyboards). Cuomo also played for Kim Carnes, and it was his arrangement that gave "Bette Davis Eyes" its signature synthesizer sound.

Robinson, Piccirillo, and another Tobin associate, singer Robert John, did background vocals on "Being with You," with Robinson and his wife, Claudette. "Smokey was just incredible to work with," says the producer, "he's such a natural singer. I think we did two or three takes, and I combined the best of them."

At first, Motown founder Berry Gordy wasn't impressed with the record ("His quote was, 'I don't hear no hit,' " according to Tobin), and neither were others at the company. Yet within a few weeks of its January 1981 release, "Being with You" reacted at R&B *and* pop radio, and began to sell.

Aside from its R&B impact, "Being with You" turned into Smokey Robinson's highest-charting solo hit on the pop charts, reaching number two in May. The ultimate irony: The song that kept him from the Hot 100 summit was "Bette Davis Eyes."

342

SUKIYAKI

A Taste of Honey

CAPITOL 4953
WRITERS: ROKUSUKE EI, HACHIDAI NAKAMURA
PRODUCER: GEORGE DUKE
May 9, 1981 (1 week)

"Sukiyaki' is a song I used to sing back in 1963," says Janice Marie Johnson. "I used to know all the words in Japanese and I had no idea what I was singing." The bass guitarist for A Taste of Honey learned the song "just by listening to the original record by Kyu Sakamoto."

A Taste of Honey were well-known in Japan even before they signed with Capitol Records in America. The group was a fivesome in 1974 when they entered the Yamaha Song Festival. Janice Marie wasn't the regular lead singer, but she happened to sing the number they entered in the festival. Unfortunately, they lost.

Janice Marie got the idea for A Taste of Honey to record "Sukiyaki" while driving around Los Angeles. "I heard a version of 'Ooh Baby Baby' by Linda Ronstadt and I said, 'God, that's what we need...an old song like that.' Because at the time we were labelled disco and disco was already dead."

Janice Marie thought of writing new lyrics in English for the song and asked her Japanese subpublisher to contact one of the original writers and get permission to update the song. She asked three different people to translate the original lyrics and got three very different interpretations. One person told her it was a death march that described a man holding his head up on the way to being executed. Another said it was about life in general, with a man walking with his head up to keep his tears from falling down. And a third said it was about a love gone bad. "Me being the hopeless romantic that I am, I decided to write about a love gone bad," says Janice Marie.

Coming up with new English lyrics took about two weeks. Janice Marie thought her first set of lyrics were too elementary and tried to write something more profound. "I ran the lyrics by George Duke, who was the producer, and he said, 'Janice, go with your instinct. Don't worry about it being too simple.' So we went back to the original lyrics."

A Taste of Honey was reduced to a duo by the time "Sukiyaki" was recorded—Janice Marie on bass and Hazel Payne on guitar. Janice Marie loved working with Duke in the studio: "That was the first time I was able to play bass with very qualified musicians. I was scared to death. I had never played with musicians of the caliber of George Duke and Roland

A Taste of Honey

Bautista. It was a great session." She did change Duke's mind about one thing. "George added a little disco thing at the end where it would go up-tempo, and I begged him, 'George, no! Leave it a ballad.' I didn't have any problems convincing him. He put a beautiful arrangement to it."

A contractual dispute almost kept the track from being released. After recording the song, Janice Marie discovered the original writer who gave permission for her to record the song had given the rights away years before. Janice had to give up any claim to the song before the publisher would allow it to be placed on an album. "I put them to the test and they were really going to take the song off the album," she remembers. "I knew in my heart it was the only song that would take us out of the disco category."

Capitol Records didn't favor the song, and Marvin Isley of the Isley Brothers discouraged Janice from doing a Japanese fan dance to the song onstage. But again, she followed her instincts. "Rescue Me" was the first single released from the *Twice as Sweet* album, and the label promised Janice Marie that "Sukiyaki" would be next. Instead, "I'm Talkin' 'Bout You" was issued. " 'Sukiyaki' ended up being the third single and I believe they put that out just to shut me up. But radio had started playing the song, so they were forced to put it out."

After "Sukiyaki" was a hit, the band returned to Japan and Janice Marie had the opportunity to perform the song with Kyu Sakamoto. "When we first started in Japan, we were struggling. We played the smaller clubs and the U.S.O., but when we toured with Kyu Sakamoto we got to see what first-class was all about...The most fun I had in Japan was to tour with Kyu Sakamoto and my grandmother being there."

343

A WOMAN NEEDS LOVE (JUST LIKE YOU DO)

Ray Parker Jr. and Raydio

ARISTA 0592
WRITER: RAY PARKER JR.
PRODUCER: RAY PARKER JR.
May 16, 1981 (2 weeks)

"Boy, do I remember that song," Ray Parker Jr. replies when asked about "A Woman Needs Love (Just Like You Do)," his first Number One hit. "It took me a month to get the vocal down. It was the first song that I ever sang all the way through that was going to be released on record, and I was a nervous wreck."

Parker says he tried recording the song in several different keys. "For some reason I couldn't get used to the sound of my voice. On a lot of other records, there were pieces of me and pieces of [Raydio members] Arnell [Carmichael] and Jerry [Knight] giving me some relief and singing other sections. It was very difficult for me to carry the song all the way from the beginning to the end."

Regarding his vocals, Parker comments, "I wish I had the control of a Luther Vandross. He's my favorite male singer. He just has unbelievable control. It looks like he should knock out his vocal in half an hour and mine should take me a week, trying all day. I don't think I have the Johnny Mathis voice—mine is somewhere between Luther Vandross and Bob Dylan. I'm in the middle somewhere, so people are listening for the sincerity of the voice and am I going to be believable with what it is that I'm saying."

Parker has a clear memory of what inspired him to write "A Woman Needs Love (Just Like You Do)": "I had a bunch of girls in the studio one day and they were discussing guys. And to be honest and truthful, everything they said [I put in] the song...I was taking it all in, being the fly on the wall, and I came up with a song about it. That is probably the only song I ever wrote in my entire life that I felt was going to be a hit. That was the only song that when I finished it, I said, 'We can go to the bank now.' "

Parker first established his name in Detroit, where at age 15 he was playing sessions for artists signed to Holland/Dozier/Holland's Hot Wax and Invictus labels, including Freda Payne, the Chairmen of the Board, Laura Lee, and the Honey Cone. His first session for the labels was for 100 Proof's "Everything Good Is Bad." He also was a backing musician at Detroit's 20 Grand club, where he played live for Gladys Knight & the Pips, the Temptations, the Spinners, and Stevie Wonder.

Wonder called one day in 1972 and asked Parker to join him on a Rolling Stones tour. Parker didn't believe it was Stevie and hung up the phone, but the persistent Motown star called back and sang "Superstition" over the phone to convince Parker. After playing on the *Talking Book* and *Innervisions* sessions, Parker packed up the car and headed for Los Angeles.

"It was like starting over when I got here," Parker says from his home in the Southern California mountains. "About the only thing I could bring with me was my knowledge of how to play the guitar. And California was actually a little easier to get in the clique than Detroit."

Parker played on some Leon Haywood sessions, had a small part in the Bill Cosby film *Uptown Saturday Night*, and had his first success as a songwriter when Rufus and Chaka Khan recorded "You Got the Love" [see 188]. For his first releases on Arista, he put together a band called Raydio with Carmichael and

Knight, as well as Larry Tolbert, Darren Carmichael, and Charles Fearing. Why didn't he start out as a solo artist? "Because I didn't think I could sing that well. I couldn't sing on pitch, so for me to think about carrying the whole album with just my voice would be overextending my ego."

344

WHAT CHA' GONNA DO FOR ME

Chaka Khan

WARNER BROS. 49692
WRITERS: NED DOHENY, HAMISH STUART
PRODUCER: ARIF MARDIN
May 30, 1981 (2 weeks)

When Chaka Khan signed as a solo artist with Warner Brothers, her manager suggested she listen to some artists she liked when she was growing up in order to choose a producer. "Arif [Mardin] was one of the people I came up with, as I loved Aretha Franklin," says Khan, who had lunch meetings with three or four producers. "Arif was the one who I felt was the warmest, most human person—the most unpretentious and the most dedicated to the art form. I instinctively sensed that and that's how I chose him. And it was one of those instances where you make a quick decision and it turns out to be a great one for you for a long period of time."

Chaka's third album for Warner Brothers was named after a Ned Dohney–Hamish Stuart song, "What Cha' Gonna Do for Me." Doheny, a Los Angeles–born musician, met Stuart in 1974 when his group, the Average White Band, came to town and played the popular Troubadour club. They became friends and decided to collaborate on songs. "The first time we ever got together to write something, we wrote a tune called 'A Love of Your Own,' which startled us so thoroughly that we didn't write again for quite a while after that," says Doheny.

Stuart continued to look Doheny up whenever he was in Los Angeles, and they eventually wrote a second song. Doheny had the basic framework but still needed a bridge. "All I really had were the original couple of lines, 'All night and day, just chipping away.' We started horsing around on guitar and piano. I wrote all the words except for 'What Cha' Gonna Do for Me,' which he wrote. It came together quickly and we were pretty excited about it."

Doheny and Stuart did not have any particular artist in mind when they wrote the song. "We assumed that both of us would record it, which is what usually happened to our stuff at that point," says Doheny. The Average White Band tried cutting it and asked Doheny to sing a guide vocal. "I got into the booth and I was trying to hit all the notes and not do anything particularly fancy. So I look into the control booth and there's Chaka Khan. I don't care how well you sing or don't...the presence of Chaka Khan is enough to unnerve just about anyone. And she heard it and really liked it. She poked her head into the vocal booth and asked if she could sing with me. And of course, that made me all gooey."

Chaka thought enough of the song to tell Arif about it. "But it wasn't until he heard the somewhat simpler vocal that I did that he actually wanted to do the tune," says Doheny.

"We recorded the track in Switzerland," recalls Mardin. "She did her vocals in Montreux." Doheny agrees the song was mixed strangely, with Chaka's voice way down there with the instruments. "Arif has a knack for doing that," Khan confirms. "He treated my voice in the mix like I was an instrument. He's a musical arranger and he is also a musician himself, a piano player. And he always thought that I was an instrument that he could play anything he wanted to on, in a way. [It was] like a vicarious situation, but a good one for me. Someone once called him Svengali, but I don't think it was that deep."

345

GIVE IT TO ME BABY

Rick James

GORDY 7197
WRITER: RICK JAMES
PRODUCER: RICK JAMES
June 13, 1981 (5 weeks)

Rick James is the person who first called his music "Punk Funk," but he meant it as a joke.

"Punk rock was going on, the Sex Pistols and what not, and they were all rebellious, young, poor Cockney British kids who were really speaking their minds," the artist explains. "And I was a poor black kid and I mentioned it as a joke once. White people have always taken black music and labelled it—blues, R&B—and I wanted to label my [music] before a white person took it and labelled it something. So I said, 'I call it "Punk Funk." ' [It] was a word I used to describe freedom—that I could sing about anything, the government, policemen killing friends of mine, sex, or whatever...So people started to take [Punk Funk] seriously. I knew that would happen."

James's 1981 *Street Songs* album put his career into overdrive. As the decade started, he was well-established not only as an artist, but as a writer/producer for Teena Marie and his backing group, the Stone City Band. Then he decided to do what he wanted to do—record a ballad-oriented album. He took off for the

Rick James

islands and created *Garden of Love.* "People kept telling me, 'Rick, you've got to go back to the street. Dump the ballads...get back to the roots.' I went back home and I went back to the ghetto and I went back to the streets and I went back to the prostitutes––the whole thing. I went back to the slum and wrote about what was real. And I had a vengeance in my heart to come back. Before *Garden of Love,* every album had gone platinum...*Garden of Love* barely went gold. I was determined to do the greatest album that was inside of me."

The first single from *Street Songs* was "Give It to Me Baby." James recalls, "I wrote it because I had come home one night and my old lady was in bed and I wanted to mess around, but I was too drunk. So I sat at the piano and wrote the song." James, who never studied music in school, says he doesn't know where the rolling bassline came from, but it felt right to him. "The part I really liked in it was the horns. I was really into that. But I'm really into rolling basslines, basslines that move. I was quite complimented when Quincy Jones kind of took that line and put it on the song 'Thriller.' "

James knocked out the vocal for "Give It to Me Baby" in two or three takes. "It was another one of those songs where I couldn't take my voice seriously. I mean, how do you sing a song about coming home and not being able to get any?...It seemed like all the songs I was writing real serious and trying to sing real serious, they never [became] hits—'Fire and Desire,' 'Ebony Eyes,' stuff like that. But most of the stuff I did that the kids liked had all this weird vocal attitude."

Why did Rick release "Give It to Me Baby" as a single before "Super Freak"? He explains, "I had a long talk with my band. I thought I had so many singles on that album, I didn't know what to release." The band members and Rick's friends voted for "Give It to Me Baby." Rick wasn't surprised: " 'Super Freak' I never thought would be a single in my life." While "Give It to Me Baby" was the bigger R&B hit, "Super Freak (Part 1)" became Rick's second-biggest hit on the pop chart, peaking at number 16. Only "You and I" at number 13 went higher.

346

DOUBLE DUTCH BUS

Frankie Smith

WMOT 5356
WRITERS: FRANKIE SMITH, BILL BLOOM
PRODUCERS: FRANKIE SMITH, BILL BLOOM
August 18, 1981 (4 weeks)

Frankie Smith was born in Philadelphia, PA, but discovered his destiny in Tennessee while he was majoring in elementary education in college.

Entertaining was in his blood—his uncle was famed comedian Pigmeat Markham ("Here Comes the Judge"). Smith's minor subjects were history and music. "I wandered into a room one day. It had a piano in it, and I watched another piano player execute various chords and I got hooked. I started patterning chords behind this piano player until I eventually learned how to play. I was self-taught—I played by ear. I said to myself, 'I want to be a songwriter. I want to play piano.' "

Returning home, Smith boldly ventured into the offices of Philadelphia International Records and told Kenny Gamble and Leon Huff he wanted to start a career as a songwriter. "Gamble and Huff actually taught me the formula," says Smith. His first song to be recorded was "Hard Not to Like You," cut by Archie Bell & the Drells. While working at Philadelphia International, he met another songwriter, Bill Bloom, who had written for Melba Moore, Jean Carne, and the Futures. Smith and Bloom collaborated, and when the label became inactive, the two men decided to remain a team. They signed with another Philadelphia-based record company, WMOT, but not before Frankie looked for other employment.

"I had to work while we were waiting for a record deal to be consummated," he explains. "I applied for a job as a bus driver in Philadelphia. I passed the physical. They told me I was hired and would start in two weeks. Told me what my salary would be. They said, 'You'll be hearing from us,' and I never heard from them."

Under the name Franklin Franklin, Smith had recorded a song for Paramount Records in 1971 called "Double Dutch," based on the popular urban jump-rope game. The single wasn't a hit, but Smith believed in the concept.

WMOT gave Smith and Bloom 15 minutes of studio time at the end of a recording session for Fat Larry's Band. "All we did was lay down a drum track and Fat Larry was the drummer for us," says Bloom. "We didn't have any more time, so we took the drum track home and I listened to that and came up with a little keyboard part for it. The next week I did the keyboard track and that's all we had time for." In a couple of weeks they added a bass track and decided they had a nice groove. The WMOT executives were impressed enough to give them studio time of their own. The incident with the bus company inspired Frankie to complete the track. "I caught myself being a little upset and I told the engineers, 'Drop my voice, the lead voice. Bring up the rhythm track.' And I started making stuff up about double dutch bus and I started cursing. They laughed and said, 'We can't put this on the record.' " Frankie laughed too and had them run the tape back so he could record a version that would be radio-friendly.

It was after 2:00 A.M. and Frankie used a gravelly, froggy voice. "He kept sort of the same idea that he had originally. It was really about playing rope," says Bloom. "At that time, Kurtis Blow was popular. 'The Breaks' was the first popular rap song...and Frankie thought it would be a good idea if we competed with that a little bit, with the rap. But the other thing that was happening in Philadelphia at that time, the kids in school were using this contemporary Pig Latin...so we thought it would be a great idea to use some of that because it was geared toward kids."

Frankie taped a bus horn at a local terminal to use in the intro and invited some local kids to come in to add their Pig Latin slang. "Originally we had one long song called 'Double Dutch,' " says Bloom. "And then we decided to cut it in half because there were two different characters. There was a female vocalist on it also."

Her name was Beverly Johnson, and her half was called "Double Dutch." Bloom and Smith assumed that would be the A-side. "But the record company liked the 'Double Dutch Bus' side...and what was ironic, we wrote it for kids but it broke in the adult discos because of the dance beat. It was hard to get some stations to play it, but once they played it, it sort of sold itself."

347

I'M IN LOVE

Evelyn King

RCA 12243
WRITER: KASHIF
PRODUCER: MORRIE BROWN
August 15, 1981 (1 week)

Evelyn King was working at Sigma Sound Studios, but not as a recording artist. Her father, an R&B performer who had been with the Harptones and the Orioles, handled maintenance and her mother Johnniea did cleaning work and was a part-time receptionist. Evelyn accompanied her mother one night to Sigma Sound Studios to help her out. "I started cleaning and she told me to sing for her," says the Bronx-born star who moved to Philadelphia in 1970. "I was vacuum cleaning at the time, and as soon as I started singing Sam Cooke's song, 'A Change Is Gonna Come,' a tall thin guy came out of the blue, because we didn't expect anyone to be there. He said, 'One day I'm going to make you a star.' " The teenager thought to herself, "Yeah, right!" But the producer who called himself T. Life was true to his word.

Her parents already knew she was talented and gave her strong support. "[My father] knew a lot about the record business," says Evelyn. "We used to do amateur hour when we were kids. It was always,

Evelyn King

'Don't be afraid. Do what you gotta do and if it's good talent, we'll let you know.' I was never shy." Evelyn loved the song "Hypnotized" by Linda Jones and sang it "like crazy," she says. At 14 she was in a local band, Volume One, which evolved into Mirage. T. Life, who said Evelyn had "very big pipes for a kid," worked with her on tracks for *Smooth Talk,* her debut album on RCA. Her first single, "Shame," was a big disco hit and peaked at number seven in 1978, making a name for Evelyn "Champagne" King.

For her fourth RCA album, King was teamed up with Morrie Brown, Kashif, and Paul Lawrence Jones III. Kashif remembers meeting Evelyn for the first time: "She was unbelievable...The first thing we noticed, Evelyn always travels with this huge entourage, her family and people who are very festive and willing and ready to have a good time. She came to the studio and she had a wonderful voice....The first thing we wanted to do was make her sing higher, because she liked to sing in the lower registers, an alto tone for a woman. And that tended to make her sound a little older. We wanted to make her more youthful and bring a more vibrant sound to her. She was a little reluctant and we hadn't gained her trust yet. We pushed and prodded and then she finally sang a little higher and it came out great."

"I'm in Love," the last song written for the album, was composed specifically for King. According to the singer, "The only thing that really shocked [the producers] was that Evelyn goes in ready to go. I already knew what I had to do."

Kashif was thrilled to get his first Number One song. "It was a new style for the time. The production of the song was ground-breaking in that it was one of the first—if not the first—all-synthesized R&B/pop hits. We were like the first of the one-man-band producer types. After that came one-man-band producers where one guy played all the instruments, did all the background vocals, [and] the arrangements....I think that was a pivotal point in both music and certainly in my career, because it sounded so different from everything else on the radio."

Radio played an integral part in making the record a hit. "RCA did a very clever thing," Kashif acknowledges. "The stations in New York were very competitive at the time. There was BLS, KTU, and KISS. RCA sent three messengers with synchronized watches to those stations. They were to hand [the single] to the program directors at the same exact time. They were all R&B dance stations and they were successful...My friends started calling me, 'Hey, your song is on BLS.' And I turned on BLS...Then somebody would call, 'Hey, your song is on KTU.' This is like within the same minute...I turned to KTU. It was on KTU. And then someone called to say, 'Hey, your song is on KISS'...and then I turned to KISS and it was on all three stations at the same time in New York. Not bad for a guy who had never had a hit record before!"

348

ENDLESS LOVE

Diana Ross & Lionel Richie

MOTOWN 1519
WRITER: LIONEL RICHIE
PRODUCER: LIONEL RICHIE
August 22, 1981 (7 weeks)

Long after people have forgotten the film *Endless Love,* starring Brooke Shields—a point that perhaps has already been reached—they will still recall the romantic ballad from the film, which paired up two of Motown's most popular artists in one of the most successful duets ever recorded.

Actually, Diana Ross was no longer a Motown artist when she recorded "Endless Love" with Lionel Richie. She had already split from Berry Gordy's label when film director Franco Zeffirelli suggested that Richie record his title song with a female artist, namely Diana. The former lead singer of the

Diana Ross and Lionel Richie

Supremes had signed with RCA Records for North America and hadn't recorded any material for her new bosses, but they graciously consented to let her record one last time for her former label.

Richie had not yet departed the Commodores for a solo career when he was asked to meet with Zeffirelli and producer Jon Peters. They asked the Motown star if he would compose an instrumental theme for *Endless Love,* something on the order of Francis Lai's music for *Love Story.* Lionel played them some music that hadn't yet been recorded by the Commodores. Then the director changed his mind and decided he wanted a title theme with lyrics. Lionel agreed to write some, and then Zeffirelli made the request for Lionel to team up with Diana Ross.

Two busy stars with too busy schedules—it didn't look like Richie and Ross would ever be together in the same room to record the song. Lionel was occupied recording the next Commodores album and producing Kenny Rogers in Los Angeles and Diana's schedule didn't bring her near Southern California. A compromise was reached when Diana was booked to appear in a hotel located on the California/Nevada border in Lake Tahoe. Richie agreed to meet her in Reno, about an hour away by car. Time was booked at a recording studio at three in the morning, giving Diana time to drive there after her late show at 1:00 A.M. and Lionel time to get there after a recording session.

Diana was given the melody prior to the recording session, but not the lyrics. Lionel said he would bring them with him. Recording commenced at 3:30 in the morning, and by 5:00 A.M. "Endless Love" was committed to tape.

The superstar duet gave Motown one of the biggest hits in the company's history. "Endless Love" was Number One for seven weeks, matching "I Heard It Through the Grapevine" by Marvin Gaye. At the time of "Endless Love," only "I Can't Help Myself" by the Four Tops (nine weeks) and "Ain't Too Proud to Beg" by the Temptations (eight weeks) had been Number One longer.

Diana and Lionel never had a follow-up to "Endless Love," although the soundtrack featured another duet by the two artists. "Dreaming of You" was a more upbeat song and remains available only on the soundtrack album.

349

WHEN SHE WAS MY GIRL

The Four Tops

CASABLANCA 2338
WRITERS: MARC BLATTE, LARRY GOTTLIEB
PRODUCER: DAVID WOLFERT
October 10, 1981 (2 weeks)

What becomes a legend most? A Number One hit, of course, especially when it features the same four guys who have been singing together since 1954. How long ago is that? So long ago that Berry Gordy was running the 3-D Record Mart in Detroit.

The Four Tops—Levi Stubbs, Obie Benson, Lawrence Payton, Duke Fakir—didn't have a recording contract at the beginning of the '80s, but they were working steadily and they did have a manager, Ron Strasner.

When producer David Wolfert's wife, Laurie, met Strasner in Los Angeles sometime in 1981, she called her spouse at the recording studio right away. "She said, 'You've got to come over and meet this guy,' " recalls Wolfert. She knew that Levi Stubbs was her husband's idol.

"Ron and I hit it off really well," says the producer, and the Tops signed to Casablanca Records via The Entertainment Company, where Wolfert was a staff producer. "I set about hunting for songs," he reports. "When you produce a band that doesn't write, why should you have the job if you don't have the songs?"

Wolfert found "When She Was My Girl" through producer Rick Chertoff, a friend. "He may not have shown me the song, but he told me about these two writers, Larry Gottlieb and Marc Blatte." The tune came in the form of "a little synthesizer demo," says Wolfert, "which Larry sang.

"It didn't have a bridge, which we had to write. And then I got a bunch of other material together—some of which I wrote—and got on a plane to meet the Four Tops for the first time, cold, in a hotel room in Detroit."

Once acquainted, they got down to the recording sessions that produced the Tops' Casablanca debut album, *Tonight!*. With rhythm arranger Bill Meyers, Wolfert cut the tracks at the Cherokee studios in Los Angeles. The musicians included Meyers on piano, Nathan East on bass, the late Jeff Porcaro on drums, and David Williams, Carlos Rios, and Wolfert himself on guitars. The melodica solo on "When She Was My Girl," a key to the record's nostalgic charm, was played by Ralph Schuckett.

The Tops cut their vocals at the RCA studios in New York. "They were an absolute blast," Wolfert

The Four Tops

declares. "It's funny—when you're a producer and arranger, you make your living telling people what to do. With the Tops, it was kind of daunting. Levi's my idol and I'm telling him how to phrase a song, how to sing it."

With "When She Was My Girl," Stubbs didn't need much coaching. "Of all the songs, that was absolutely the one I had to direct least," says Wolfert. "I'm pretty sure that's mostly the live vocal he sang with the band, unrehearsed."

The record's "boom-be-boom-boom" hook featured the Tops' Obie Benson, whose idea it was. "Originally, we only had that once," explains Wolfert. "Charles Koppelman, head of The Entertainment Company, heard it, and suggested we bring it back at the end."

350

NEVER TOO MUCH

Luther Vandross

EPIC 02409
WRITER: LUTHER VANDROSS
PRODUCER: LUTHER VANDROSS
October 24, 1981 (2 weeks)

Luther Vandross grew up surrounded by music. He was four years old when his sister Patricia joined the Crests, the New York City group that rehearsed in his family's apartment before they recorded "16 Candles." Luther loved girl groups, especially the Shirelles, and when he was a teenager, his mother knew the worst punishment she could give her son was to forbid him from watching the Supremes on *The Ed Sullivan Show*.

With his friend Fonzi Thornton, Luther was always forming this group or that group, with names like Shades of Jade. He moved away to attend Western Michigan College, but left to follow his musical vision. He earned money taking back defective merchandise for S&H Green Stamps, and his first big break was singing backup and arranging vocals on David Bowie's *Young Americans* album. That led to sessions with Carly Simon, Ringo Starr, Chaka Khan, Bette Midler, Donna Summer, and Barbra Streisand. As a session backing vocalist, he met bass player Marcus Miller, and they decided to write together.

Vandross put a group together and was signed to Atlantic's Cotillion label. They were called Luther, and they lasted about a year. He found lucrative work as a jingle singer, crooning ditties like "Proud as a Peacock" for NBC and "Reach Out and Touch" for AT&T. He continued working for artists like Nile Rodgers and Bernard Edwards, singing on Chic's "Dance, Dance, Dance (Yowsah, Yowsah, Yowsah)" and "Le Freak." Later, he was hired to sing backing vocals for Change, a European/American group founded by Italian producer Jacques Fred Petrus.

Luther Vandross

"They heard me in the context of being a background singer and said, 'Oh, can we get you to sing lead vocal on a song?' And I said, 'As long as two things are understood.' See, I was making a lot of money as a jingle and background singer. So to take me out of that, you had to be talking some mighty, mighty stuff. I told them if I didn't like my performance, I was to be able to stand there and erase it myself. And they said fine. And I said also that my name is printed as lead vocalist. Well, radio, particularly black radio, took to Change and started calling my name...'That was Luther Vandross with Change...Gosh, does this guy need to make an album.' So that's what made me make my demo."

Luther saved his jingle money to finance a two-song demo. Larkin Arnold and Jerome Gasper at Epic were interested enough to listen to "Sugar and Spice" and "Never Too Much."

"I loved 'Sugar and Spice' because it was bouncier," Luther reveals. "It had more ear candy. It reminded me of 'Give Me the Night' by George Benson. And

'Never Too Much' was the underdog song in my mind. When I took it to the company, they heard 'Sugar and Spice' first. They said, 'Oh, that's nice.' And when they heard 'Never Too Much,' they started groovin' and the deal was done after that."

Luther explains the genesis of "Never Too Much": "As a background singer and background vocal arranger, I always had ideas for background parts. So I was learning whatever I was learning about chords. 'Never Too Much' had a lot of eleventh chords in it...against that I kept singing, 'Never too much, never too much' in two-part harmony and that stuck in my mind. The next thing that happened was the 'Oh my love' section and then the guitar part...and I put those three elements together and the song was easy to form."

It was more than a love song, according to Luther. "The song was more and more interesting with each line. The first half of the song is about me...and then the second verse is about me waking up. It's all about my introspection and then the second verse is about the action of living that out."

351

I HEARD IT THROUGH THE GRAPEVINE (PART 1)

Roger

WARNER BROS. 49786
WRITERS: NORMAN WHITFIELD, BARRETT STRONG
PRODUCER: ROGER TROUTMAN
November 7, 1981 (2 weeks)

"Marvin Gaye made 'Heard It Through the Grapevine' and it was Number One," says Roger Troutman. "Gladys Knight & the Pips made 'Grapevine' and it was Number One. Creedence Clearwater Revival made 'Grapevine'...so a song that had been [a hit] three times by three different kinds of artists—a black male, a black female, and a rock and roll group—was like a no-miss situation in my mind."

Roger was right. His recording of the Norman Whitfield/Barrett Strong classic returned "I Heard It Through the Grapevine" to the top of the *Billboard* R&B chart, making it the only song to be Number One by three different artists.

Roger, born in Hamilton, Ohio, started thinking about recording "Grapevine" after the success of 1980's "More Bounce to the Ounce," a number two single by his funk group, Zapp, that featured the Vocoder voice box. Troutman became interested in the device after seeing Stevie Wonder work with it on a television program and after hearing Peter Frampton use it on *Frampton Comes Alive!* "People seemed to like the voice box, but it seemed as if people couldn't understand what I was saying," Roger elaborates. "So I wanted to prove to people that I could say anything with the voice box. I said to myself, 'The best way to prove this is to take a song everybody knows and do a remake...If they think they can't understand the words through the voice box, they'll know the words because whoever made the song before me would have planted those lyrics in the listener's mind."

Roger was absolutely certain that "I Heard It Through the Grapevine" was the song he was going to cover. "Nobody was going to change my mind," he attests. "I was on a mission. No question." His production work for his version of "Grapevine" was inspired by Cameo and Weather Report. "I lifted a little piece from them...and Norman Whitfield, the way he was dealing with basslines and drummers and saxophones with 'Papa Was a Rollin' Stone.' I threw all those ideas in a pot [and] stirred it up."

Roger's next step was to bring his brother Lester in the studio to lay down the drum track. "Once I was watching *The Making of Star Wars* and the director and producers were talking about how they had to explain

Roger

to the actors that they had to play to something that wasn't there...something was going to be superimposed later. I always had to talk to Lester and say, 'Right here I'm going to have something else come in. It's not there.' And Lester would say, 'How do you expect me to emphasize something that's not there?' It was very difficult and I really had to work with Lester and coax him and make him show emotion in certain areas of the song where there was nothing recorded except me standing there saying, 'Yeah, Yeah. Boom, boom. More of this, more of that!' "

Roger remembers that Warner Brothers executives were willing to support any decision he made about which track should be released as the first single from *The Many Facets of Roger*. He found it difficult to choose between "So Ruff, So Tuff," a soundalike for "More Bounce to the Ounce," and "Grapevine."

"When black radio got hold of the album, DJs couldn't make up their minds either," he says. But with some encouragement from his brother Larry, "Grapevine" won out and Roger found it thrilling to watch it move up the chart. "I've never experienced any feeling like having a Number One record. It is the ultimate in acceptance and it was amazing."

352

TAKE MY HEART (YOU CAN HAVE IT IF YOU WANT IT)

Kool & the Gang

DE-LITE 815
WRITERS: CHARLES SMITH, JAMES TAYLOR, GEORGE BROWN, KOOL & THE GANG
PRODUCERS: EUMIR DEODATO, KOOL & THE GANG
November 21, 1981 (1 week)

The percolating guitar introduction on "Take My Heart" belongs to Charles Smith, a founder member of Kool & the Gang [see 174—"Hollywood Swinging"].

"That's Charles's calling card from way back," declares James "J.T." Taylor, lead singer of the group for most of the '80s. "He would have all those rhythms, and play 'em only the way Charles could play."

Smith devised the groove for "Take My Heart," the lead-off single for the *Something Special* album. "What was also happening," adds Taylor, "was that Ronald was experimenting with a little reggae, while George wrote a lot of the song's melody and lyrics."

Ronald Bell (a/k/a Khalis Bayyan) was the group's music director and reggae-taster, George Brown was the drummer, who also played keyboards. "Ronald, Charles, and George were really good writers," says Taylor, "so they had most of [the song] ready.

"But we would still collaborate. They were very fair with that part—sometimes too fair. They'd give people credit who didn't do too much. It was just their spirit, which was nice."

The *Something Special* sessions took place during 1981 at Kool & the Gang's customary haunt, the House of Music in West Orange, New Jersey. "There was a lot of jamming in the studio," remembers Jim Bonnefond, the studio's engineer at the time. "They'd work out a chord progression, sit and jam with that for a while, get ideas."

The recording process was protracted, too, because producer Eumir Deodato was a perfectionist. "Getting tracks that held together feel-wise and tempo-wise was pretty important to us," says Bonnefond. "Sometimes it meant editing takes together, so we spent quite a bit of time on the tracks."

Deodato wanted "a really tight, clean sound," according to Bonnefond. "The House of Music had pretty good noise reduction, and good monitoring so that the bottom end could be dealt with properly. That was one of the primary things for us and the band, too. It was a good, tight sound, nice and clean."

Comments James Taylor, "There was no guessing with Deodato, musically or technically. He felt the band used to overproduce themselves: too many horns and too much arranging. With his jazz background, he kept the flavor of what the group had been into long before I was there. That still satisfied the guys to a point."

Taylor attributes the Marvin Gaye influence in "Take My Heart" to the gang's drummer, George Brown. "He was in the control room, just partying—everyone was in there. I said, 'George, like Marvin, huh?' He said, 'Yeah, yeah!' We were having a good time."

Something Special turned out to be the last album Deodato produced for Kool & the Gang. Their third consecutive platinum release, it surrendered four top ten R&B hits during 1981–82, including "Take My Heart" and "Get Down on It."

Both of those songs crossed to the top 20 of the Hot 100, while "Get Down on It" also became the group's first major U.K. success. In appreciation, they crossed the Atlantic in October 1982 and took the hearts of Britons in London, Manchester, and Birmingham.

The Gang maintained their Anglophile connection with another tour in 1984, which happened to coincide with Bob Geldof's fundraising efforts for Ethiopian famine relief. As a result, Kool (Robert Bell), James Taylor, and Dennis "Dee Tee" Thomas were among the 36 artists who recorded "Do They Know It's Christmas?" in London that November.

The all-star charity release, billed as Band Aid, went on to become a U.K. Number One, a U.S. top 20 hit, and the inspiration for an American equivalent [see 405—"We Are the World"].

353

LET'S GROOVE

Earth, Wind & Fire

ARC 02536
WRITERS: MAURICE WHITE,
WAYNE VAUGHAN, WANDA VAUGHAN
PRODUCER: MAURICE WHITE
November 28, 1981 (8 weeks)

It's hard to believe, but less than two years after "Boogie Wonderland" and "After the Love Has Gone," Maurice White and Earth, Wind & Fire were, according to an account in *Musician*, "personae non grata" at Columbia Records.

EW&F had followed the double-platinum impact of *I Am* with 1980's double LP, *Faces*. On it, White backed away from the poppy outside collaborations that had made *I Am* so successful, producing an album that wasn't really embraced by either pop or R&B audiences.

Columbia had obviously hoped for something more commercial. White, for his part, wasn't shy about complaining in public when he felt his records weren't promoted enough. By early '81, *Musician* says, "The [label's] message was muted but clear: 'If your music won't sell itself, we certainly won't sell it for you. Better luck next album.' "

White's response was to go back into his newly built Los Angeles studio complex right away. He replaced longtime guitarist Al McKay with Roland Bautista. He enlisted the Emotions' Wanda Hutchinson and her husband, Wayne Vaughan, as co-writers. And on the vocoderized opening of "Let's Groove"—the first single from *Raise!*—White served notice that this was a new, improved EW&F. If the trademark horns and harmonies were still there, this time some grit was added to the mix.

While he was recording *Raise!* in May 1981, White would go as far as admitting to Pablo Guzman of *Musician* that his records were becoming too clean. "A lot of times I might be guilty of trying to perfect what I'm doing, instead of enhancing it. You try to do better each time around..."

This time, the jagged edges were proudly displayed. Guzman described *Raise!* this way: "Scronch punk guitars shatter mixes, synthesizer notes meander out of tonality, Brecker Brothers horn lines attack the listener from blistering percussive textures...The transformation is genuinely startling, the more so because so much of the familiar elements of the band's sound are intact."

Earth, Wind & Fire

The writer called "Let's Groove" the record that would "definitely establish" EW&F's "escape from the museum of the '70s." It's hard to imagine now, but the song would also threaten the crossover base that White had worked so hard to build. The funkier EW&F was unleashed at a time when Top 40 radio was wary of anything to the left of, say, "He's So Shy" by the Pointer Sisters. "Let's Groove" would go top five pop on the basis of sales from E&B radio, but a number of key top 40 stations never played it.

Listeners, however, weren't similarly hung up. "Let's Groove" went gold and became the band's longest-running Number One single, spending eight weeks atop the R&B charts. *Raise!* went platinum and brought in Grammy nominations for two consecutive years, including a 1982 win for best R&B vocal performance.

354

TURN YOUR LOVE AROUND

George Benson

WARNER BROS. 49846
WRITERS: JAY GRAYDON,
STEVE LUKATHER, BILL CHAMPLIN
PRODUCER: JAY GRAYDON
January 23, 1982 (1 week)

In 1981, Lenny Waronker and Tommy LiPuma of Warner Brothers Records wanted to put out a greatest-hits collection on George Benson with two new songs. They asked producer Jay Graydon to come up with some material. "So for days I'm trying to come up with a song," says Graydon. "I'm not coming up with anything great. Finally, two days before George gets here, I come up with a chorus. I was eating dinner with Steve Lukather that night. I said, 'Listen to this chorus. See if you can come up with a verse while I finish getting ready.' " Within 20 minutes, Lukather had a verse and the two men went out to dinner.

"Everything was great except now we needed a bridge," Graydon continues. "So we called Bill Champlin and said, 'Get on over here. We need lyrics and a bridge to this song.' This song was one of the fastest-written songs I've ever been involved in. [We] did the demo that night and George came in town the next day."

Benson arrived and met Graydon for the first time. "I liked him instantly," says the artist. "He had his own recording studio in his house, the best home recording studio I have ever seen, because it was professionally built with a lot of good equipment. He and I got along very well because we're both guitar players."

Benson and Graydon formed a mutual admiration society in the studio. "I really appreciated his input on this," says the producer. "The first couple of days we did the vocal, he was singing the tune too light. I said, 'You gotta dig in more.' He said, 'I can't dig in. This is the way it is.' I said, 'Go out there one more time and dig in as hard as you can. Give me all you got,' and he did. That was the key to the whole thing. I think that his aggressiveness in the vocal was a major turning point for me, thinking of the song now as really a complete song with a great performance. Bill Champlin sang background vocals on it. We really worked hard on those to make them just as great as we could. And if you listen to the record now, they still sound incredible."

Benson acknowledges that his singing voice is soft. "It's one of those things I'm not able to escape from...It's like Nat Cole singing an up-tempo song. He still sounds smooth. I'm not putting myself in Nat's category, but that's the only explanation I can give." Still, he loved "Turn Your Love Around." "I thought it had a great hook in it. I don't like to create the hook, but if I can find a song that already has one built in and sounds natural, that's perfect."

The track was one of the first to use a drum machine, according to Graydon. "One of the first Linn drum machines that was made ended up on the record. Tried to replace it with real drums, but it didn't feel right. Jeff Porcaro was the drum programmer...David Paich of Toto played synthesizer bass."

Although Benson is known for his guitar virtuosity, it was Graydon who played the instrument for this song. "George's style of guitar playing didn't lend [itself] to the type of part that needed to be on this record," says the producer. "We let him take a shot at playing, but stylistically it didn't fit the song."

Benson believes the song went to Number One because "it had everything. There was nothing like it on the radio. You can dance to it; you can listen to it. It worked real well."

355

I CAN'T GO FOR THAT (NO CAN DO)

Daryl Hall and John Oates

RCA 12361
WRITERS: DARYL HALL,
JOHN OATES, SARA ALLEN
PRODUCERS: DARYL HALL, JOHN OATES
January 30, 1982 (1 week)

Daryl Hall and John Oates were bona fide pop stars by the time they secured a Number One hit on the R&B charts, although Daryl was no stranger to soul music. The first record he ever bought was "It's Gonna Work Out Fine" by Ike & Tina Turner, and as a teenager he was singing backing vocals for groups like the Miracles and the Temptations when they played the Uptown Theater in Philadelphia. His first experience in the studio was playing at a session for Kenny Gamble and the Romeos, led by one of the men who would put the Philly Sound on the map in the 1970s.

Daryl met John in a service elevator at the Adelphi Ballroom in Philadelphia. They were both leading their own groups (Daryl's was the Temptones and John's was the Masters) and were trying to get away from a fight between rival gangs. Two years after that initial meeting, they teamed up professionally. Three more years passed before they released their debut album, *Whole Oates,* on Atlantic Records.

Daryl's first R&B Number One hit came in the form of a cover version. Tavares topped the *Billboard* chart with their remake of Hall and Oates's "She's Gone" [see 189].

The duo first charted R&B with "Alone Too Long," number 98 in 1975. They achieved platinum status with the *Voices* album in 1980. It was during the recording of that album that Daryl first worked on the song that would become "I Can't Go For That (No Can Do)."

"I had this chorus and I had never finished the verse," says Daryl. "It was just one of those extra songs I had laying around." After recording a track for the *Private Eyes* album, Daryl remained in the studio when the session ended and turned on a drum machine. "It was one of those really simple ones and I got that really simple beat and started playing around with it. I put an organ sound on the synthesizer and started playing the bassline and created the song on the spot. Then I played all of the instruments myself and sang that 'dut-dut-dut-da' part to John and he went in the studio and played what I told him on the guitar. So it was pretty much a one-man band thing with John playing the guitar. Then I started singing some scat melodies and created a verse on the spot and then we wrote the words a couple days later and had a song."

A sax solo by Charlie DeChant was added later. "He played a great sax part on that," Daryl acknowledges. "He comes up with great melodies."

Daryl added the parenthetical "No Can Do" to the title because it "kept happening through the whole song," he says. "It was almost like a double chorus, so I figured we'd use both. I still call it 'No Can Do.' I don't think of it as 'I Can't Go For That.' " Along with Hall and Oates, Sara Allen is credited as a writer on the song. "She's been writing lyrics with John and me for years and years," Daryl explains. "I wrote most of the lyrics and on this particular song, used Sara and John as sounding boards. But they were there and were throwing ideas out."

After "I Can't Go for That (No Can Do)" topped the R&B chart, Hall and Oates continued to rack up R&B hits like "One on One," which peaked at number eight in 1983. A year later, Daryl scored a number three hit with "Swept Away," a song he wrote and produced for Diana Ross.

356

CALL ME

Skyy

SALSOUL 2152
WRITER: RANDY MULLER
PRODUCERS: RANDY MULLER, SOLOMON ROBERTS JR.
February 6, 1982 (2 weeks)

The Manhattan-based octet known as Skyy reached the upper portion of the *Billboard* chart in 1980–81 with "Here's to You" and "High," two positive, upbeat songs that reflected the great relationship the group had with their label, Salsoul. "And then Ken Cayre, the head of the company then, said, 'Randy, your songs are so nice and beautiful. We want some controversy. Come on, let's get nasty! Look at a soap opera and come up with something,' " says producer Randy Muller, one of the founders of Brass Construction [see 242—"Movin' "].

Muller promised Cayre he would write a "crazy song," one that wasn't about an ideal relationship. The idea came to Muller while he was on an airplane travelling to New York from the West Coast. He scribbled it down on a napkin, and wrote the bassline on his way home in a taxi.

Muller and co-producer Solomon Roberts, Jr., the leader of Skyy, came up with the idea of using a telephone conversation while they were in the studio recording the song. "We did that in the mix at the end of the session," Randy explains. "I usually listen to a record to see if it's complete. I listen as if I'm listening to the radio and I said, 'We need something else.' It just evolved—as a matter of fact, I was making a call and said, 'That's it! That sound!' "

"These kinds of things weren't in records at that time," says Roberts. "We winged it and came up with a conversation on the phone and everybody loved it. We used an actual touch-tone phone to make that dialing sound."

Skyy and Brass Construction hailed from the same neighborhood in Brooklyn. "First it was B.T. Express, then Brass Construction, and we were the last people that were sort of left over," Roberts says. "Randy and myself put together a production company called Alligator Bit Him." Muller and Roberts were working with a trio of sisters—Denise Dunning Crawford,

Skyy

Dolores Dunning-Milligan, and Bonne Dunning Bario, who performed as Dilara. The producers also had a male R&B funk band signed to their company. They decided to combine the two acts. It's no longer clear just who named the group, but Roberts remembers they were all into astrology and wanted a name that would show how they felt about their music and their live stage performance.

" 'Sky' [evokes] all sorts of moods," he believes. "It can be cloudy. It can be stormy. It can be sunny. It can be calm, and it described everything we felt about ourselves conceptually. Then we decided that we wanted to give it a little something extra, so we stuck an extra 'y' on it."

Muller appreciated moving from Brass Construction to Skyy. "One of the problems of working with a group with a certain name and style is that your universe of songs is limited," he feels. "You have to get a 'Brass' song...so it gave me an outlet for other types of ideas that I had. And I needed that latitude...that range of expression. It really allowed for different types of writing styles for me."

357

THAT GIRL

Stevie Wonder

TAMLA 1602
WRITER: STEVIE WONDER
PRODUCER: STEVIE WONDER
February 20, 1982 (9 weeks)

"That Girl" spent more weeks at Number One than any record since Al Green's "Let's Stay Together," ten years earlier. The late Jay Lasker, president of Motown Records at the time, couldn't have wished for a bigger hit from one of his biggest stars.

Then again, Lasker had devised an entire strategy around Wonder to boost the company's business in 1982. To him, "That Girl" was the linchpin of that strategy.

Motown was platinum-powered in '81, with Rick James's *Street Songs* and Wonder's *Hotter Than July*, as well as "Endless Love," the Diana Ross/Lionel Richie soap opera that sold close to three million singles.

But the outlook for 1982 was uncertain: Ross and Marvin Gaye had left the company, the Commodores had peaked, and—based on his previous delivery schedule—Stevie Wonder wasn't likely to turn in a new album much before 1984.

Hotter Than July had been a substantial success, selling two million copies and riding the charts for almost twice as long as its predecessor, *Journey through the Secret Life of Plants*.

Yet Lasker judged that Wonder was in financial trouble: His Los Angeles radio station, KJLH, was losing money, other business interests were a cash drain, and "he didn't know the value of a dollar," according to the Motown president. "He told me many times that he never worried about money."

With Berry Gordy's approval, Lasker offered Stevie $2 million to allow Motown to compile a greatest-hits album for 1982 release. It was to feature his post-1971 work, over which Wonder had more contractual control than his earlier Motown recordings. The singer responded by upping the ante to $3 million, insisting that the package should be a double album, *Original Musiquarium I*, and include four new songs.

"That Girl" was one of the four, recorded at the Wonderland Studios in Los Angeles. A solo tour de force, it showcased Stevie playing drums, harmonica, Fender Rhodes, piano, and synthesizers. "For something like 'Sir Duke,' I saw musicians and I just went about getting them," he told an interviewer, "but for something like 'That Girl,' you just basically do it yourself."

Stevie Wonder

Although Lasker preferred the commercial certainty of a single album and only a couple of new songs, he consented to Wonder's *Musiquarium* wishes—but didn't reckon on his artist's celebrated tardiness. Stevie delivered "That Girl" in December 1981, saying he would complete the other new songs and the album (only he had the master recordings of his '70s hits) by the end of the following month.

January came and went without Wonder's work. So did February, March, and April. "That Girl" arrested the R&B summit and peaked in the pop charts during March, but Lasker fretted over the lack of an album in the stores while the single was on the radio.

Motown finally got *Musiquarium* in May, and rushed the 16-track set to market. "I'd lay odds that Stevie and Motown lost sales of a million albums by releasing it so long after the single," Lasker lamented. "We'd wasted a whole hit."

358

IF IT AIN'T ONE THING...IT'S ANOTHER

Richard "Dimples" Fields

BOARDWALK 139
WRITERS: RICHARD "DIMPLES" FIELDS, BELINDA WILSON
PRODUCERS: RICHARD "DIMPLES" FIELDS, BELINDA WILSON
April 24, 1982 (3 weeks)

Long before he signed with Neil Bogart's Boardwalk Records, Richard "Dimples" Fields wrote down his feelings about the way things were in the world when he was in high school. The result was a song called "If It Ain't One Thing...It's Another," which Fields released on *Spoiled Rotten*, the third of his five locally issued albums in San Francisco.

After he gained some notoriety with a song called "She's Got Papers on Me," Fields was in a Bay Area car dealership getting his Mercedes repainted when he ran into an old friend from high school named Gwendolyn. "We went to lunch," Fields explains, "and during the course of the meal, she said, 'I've been following your career, and every time people come to my house, they ask, "Play that song by that guy." ' I named a variety of songs and she said, 'Nah, I'm talking about that great one, "If It Ain't One Thing...It's Another." ' " Fields mentioned he was thinking of re-recording it someday, and Gwendolyn asked what he was waiting for. "For world conditions

Richard "Dimples" Fields

to get worse," he told her. She responded, "What do you want it to do, explode?"

The next day, Fields and his arranger went into the studio and cut a new version of the song. The original was a slow ballad. With co-writer and co-producer Belinda Wilson, Fields added "a little bounce to it." The vocal was difficult to complete, the artist says. "Normally, I can do my vocals inside of six hours. My average is three hours. That vocal took 75 hours. When I finished, I started clowning. And then I mellowed it down and put that dialogue in, straight off the top of my head. And then I gave it to Neil [Bogart]. He said, 'I only have one problem. The talking part.' I said, 'Neil, I didn't make that song for anybody else. I made that song for me. If you don't take it in its entirety, you can't have it.' Bogart called the next day and said, 'We're going with it.' "

Fields, who might have been a professional baseball player if not for a leg injury, attributes the song to his Christian upbringing. "My thinking has been rather sound throughout my life, and that's because of the good people that have been in my life. My mother is great. My stepmother is great. My father was just one of those people that knew things. When I made 'If It Ain't One Thing...It's Another,' I said, 'Well, let me look at everything I heard on the news and see what people complain about.' "

The song addressed some serious issues. "Everybody seems to be getting divorced," he says. "Relationships are getting worse. Black people are still complaining [about] what their lives are like. Although Martin Luther King's [birthday] is a holiday now, justice and fair play and equality, all that is still on the back burner."

Still, Fields didn't simply view these issues as problems. "I think what we call problems are situations that have to be resolved, and there's an answer to anything. I was showing people what I believe is the answer to all their confusion."

359

IT'S GONNA TAKE A MIRACLE

Deniece Williams

ARC 02812
WRITERS: TEDDY RANDAZZO,
BOBBY WEINSTEIN, LOU STALLMAN
PRODUCERS: THOM BELL, DENIECE WILLIAMS
May 15, 1982 (2 weeks)

Teddy Randazzo's chart career began in 1955 when he recorded "Times Two, I Love You" as a member of the Three Chuckles. Later he recorded on his own, hitting the *Billboard* Hot 100 with songs like "Little Serenade" and "The Way of a Clown." In 1964 he was back on the charts as the writer and producer of "I'm on the Outside (Looking In)" and "Goin' Out of My Head," big hits for Little Anthony & the Imperials. A few months later he scored again as the writer and producer of "It's Gonna Take a Miracle," the chart debut of the Royalettes.

As an artist for ABC-Paramount, Teddy had visited Baltimore several times, where he was taken to local radio stations by Harold Berkman, who handled promotion for the label. Berkman was handling similar chores for MGM Records when he asked Randazzo to produce material for four young girls who had won a statewide televised talent contest. Berkman thought the Royalettes should record a new version of "He's Gone," the first charted single by the Bronx girl group the Chantels in 1957.

"I went in the studio and recorded that, but I wasn't thrilled with it," says Randazzo. "I didn't think it was a hit. I wanted to come up with something that was better for them...I knew where their keys were...It wasn't a difficult thing to figure out what they needed."

Along with Bobby Weinstein and Lou Stallman, Randazzo wrote "It's Gonna Take a Miracle" expressly for the Royalettes. The arrangements were written the following day and Randazzo went back to the studio the following night to record the tracks. Then the Royalettes recorded their vocals, and Randazzo hooked together two four-track machines to give the recording more depth. "When I listened to the finished tape, I knew the song was a smash," the producer adds. On August 7, 1965, "It's Gonna Take a Miracle" by the Royalettes entered the *Billboard* R&B singles chart, eventually peaking at number 28.

Two decades later, producer Thom Bell hooked up with Deniece Williams at the suggestion of a friend, Don Taylor. Deniece had already scored a Number One hit with Johnny Mathis [see 290—"Too Much, Too Little, Too Late"] and wanted more pop success. The first thing they needed was material. "Songs are the master key that open any door," the producer told Williams. They collaborated and Bell was impressed. "We started writing and she was a fantastic lyricist and a fantastic singer. She knows as an artist and as a creative entity and as a human being how to sing and how to relay a song to the civilian in the street."

When it came to finding outside material to cover, a little E.S.P. came in handy. "She must have been reading my mind or I was reading hers. She said, 'There was a song I always wanted to do.' I said, 'What song was that?' 'A song by the Royalettes.' I said, ' "It's Gonna Take a Miracle." ' She said, 'Yeah, how did you know?' I said, 'That's a song I always wanted to do, too.' But she was the one who brought it to my attention. [It] was on my mind too, but she didn't know it. So we got the record and we got the sheet music and I got a key on her and away we went. I changed a few things around but it's basically the same song."

Bell and Williams produced "It's Gonna Take a Miracle" at the famed Sigma Sound Studios in Philadelphia. working with chief engineer Joe Tarsia. Bill Neale and Bobby Eli played guitars, George Merrill programmed the synthesizer, Bob Babbitt played bass and piccolo bass, Charles Collins was on drums, Larry Washington and Ed Shay handled percussion, Don Renaldo was responsible for strings and horns, and George Merrill, Joseph B. Jefferson, and Bell sang backing vocals.

360

LET IT WHIP

The Dazz Band

MOTOWN 1609
WRITERS: REGGIE ANDREWS, NDUGU CHANCLER
PRODUCER: REGGIE ANDREWS
May 29, 1982 (5 weeks)

Motown's 92nd Number One R&B single was by the Dazz Band, an eight-man outfit from Cleveland that had already registered some chart entries on the 20th Century label under the name Kinsman Dazz. The "Kinsman" came from the Kinsman Grill in East Cleveland, owned by Sonny Jones. When Jones became involved with the band, he asked them to include the "Kinsman" in their name. The "Dazz" came from a contraction of "danceable jazz," an appropriate choice for the horn and keyboard—dominated funk fusion group.

There were a lot of jazz clubs in Cleveland in the late '60s and early '70s. As soon as he graduated from high school, Bobby Harris knew he wanted to be a jazz saxophonist and had no interest in rock and roll. That changed when he was walking down Euclid Avenue and found himself in a club called Le Cav. There he heard the hybrid sounds of a band with a pop format that played a lot of jazz. Harris thought it was a "compromise" that worked, and was inspired by the group—Blood, Sweat & Tears—to form his own outfit.

He called his group Bell Telefunk, and they eventually merged with Pierre DeMudd's group, Brain Tree. Kinsman Dazz released two albums on 20th Century before changing their name to the Dazz Band and signing with Motown.

Ndugu Chancler had co-produced George Duke's first R&B chart single, "Reach for It," in 1977. Then Chancler teamed up with Reggie Andrews, a student teacher from the high school he had attended, to write songs. "We had some bands together—the Ujima Ensemble and a group called Comma," says Chancler. "Reggie and I remained friends from school and kept our musical association." Chancler attended Locke High School in Dominguez Hills, a facility that counts Patrice Rushen, Gerald Albright, and a great number of session musicians among its graduates.

Chancler recorded some solo efforts for Epic in 1979 and reconnected with Andrews, who was then an A&R staffer for Motown. They wrote some songs for Switch, and Andrews invited Chancler to play on various Motown sessions. "We started stockpiling a bunch of music and then he got involved with the Dazz Band as a producer," says Chancler. They collaborated on a song for *Let the Music Play*, the Dazz Band's first album for Motown. For the second album, *Keep It Live,* Andrews and Chancler wrote "Let It Whip."

"We wanted to create a song that they could make a dance out of," says Chancler. "A song that was different in that it would be something that no one had ever really talked about on a record." First, they came up with the track. "That was the premiere stage of a lot of the drum machines. At that time we were using the Roland 808. Reggie had the 808 and I had the Linn Drum, and we used a mini-Moog bass...and we put this track together and started thinking, 'What kind of lyric content could we talk about that could end up being a dance?' And Reggie came up with the idea of a whip."

The Dazz Band

It took about a month to finish the song, according to Chancler, as he and Andrews were working on a number of other tracks at the same time. "We called our working process a song factory. We were mass-producing."

The Dazz Band liked the song. "Surprisingly, they didn't turn down any of our music," says Chancler. "I think part of that was we knew all the guys, and we knew what they could do and how they would do it. They really knew where they wanted to go, so it was a just a matter of molding the songs to a 'T' for them. They were good players, and there was a mesh of technology and the players. They played on the records along with the drum machine, so it is all of them [on the record]." In addition to Harris on sax and DeMudd on trumpet and lead vocals, the Dazz Band consisted of Keith Harrison (keyboards), Sennie "Skip" Martin III (trumpet), Eric Fearman (guitar), Marion McClain (guitar), Kevin Kendrick (keyboards), Kenny Pettus (percussion), Issac Wiley Jr. (drums), Michael Wiley (bass), and Juan Lively (lead vocals).

Motown wanted to release a ballad as the initial single from the second album, according to Chancler, but finally went with "Let It Whip." "It had the right stuff at the right time," says a grateful Bobby Harris, who watched the song climb to number five pop and Number One R&B.

361

EARLY IN THE MORNING

The Gap Band

TOTAL EXPERIENCE 8201
WRITERS: LONNIE SIMMONS, CHARLIE WILSON, RUDY TAYLOR
PRODUCER: LONNIE SIMMONS
June 26, 1982 (3 weeks)

"Early in the Morning' was an answer to 'Burn Rubber,' a follow-up, a continuation of the story," says writer/producer Lonnie Simmons. "It says in the song, *I gotta get up early in the morning/Go out and find me another lover just like the other lover/One that won't run to mother/One that won't burn rubber.*"

Rudy Taylor, who contributed a line about the early bird catching the worm, remembers that there was a lot of pressure on the Gap Band to come up with another hit as big as "Burn Rubber (Why You Wanna Hurt Me)" [see 339]. "We worked to the point where one night, Charlie [Wilson] was doing vocals and he walked out because it was [too much] stress and the pressure of trying to get a hit record." Taylor explains the ulterior motive behind the song's title: "Most [radio] program directors worked morning drive shifts. So we were trying to come up with a record that could catch them, something we knew they would want to play the first thing in the morning."

Simmons recalls how difficult it was to record the song. "Everything we did was a marathon," he says. "It had to be perfect. And back then, a lot of things came out better after they were mixed...I used to be really creative along with my engineer at that time. I used to be real creative at putting something together better than we already had. Some of the songs were good just like they came out of the studio, but 'Burn Rubber' and 'Early in the Morning' were mixed and mixed and mixed and edited and edited and edited. It went on for days."

Taylor corroborates, "I think the way you'd know the record was ready to go was you were tired of it. It got on your nerves. You didn't want to hear it anymore, then you knew it was ready for the streets...For 'Early in the Morning' I must have rolled tape on that at least 5,000 times. I'm serious—5,000 times I heard that song over and over. By the time we finished it, I was dead tired of it. When it came on the radio, I used to turn the radio off. But I had a young daughter and she loved it. Every time it came on, she'd turn it up loud."

Taylor may have grown tired of the Gap Band version, but he enjoyed the 1988 cover version by British singer Robert Palmer. It made the top 20 of the pop chart. "I liked it a lot," Taylor says. "He did it justice."

The Gap Band weren't known only for their funk, but also for their stylish image, sort of a cowboy chic. "I started D.J. Rogers off with that look, and when he left the organization, I carried it over to the Gap Band," says Simmons. "If you go back and look at any of his early albums, you'll see a cowboy hat on his head and a western-type suit. And [the Gap Band] are from Tulsa, so it made it real easy to adapt to it, to look the part. Plus back then, it was hard for an act to crossover and I was trying to use every bit of ammunition. I felt if they had an across-the-board look, where maybe a country person in a store saw this picture of the Gap Band, they'd probably say, 'I wonder if this is country music. What is this?' "

362

AND I AM TELLING YOU I'M NOT GOING

Jennifer Holliday

GEFFEN 29983
WRITERS: TOM EYEN, HENRY KRIEGER
PRODUCER: DAVID FOSTER
July 24, 1982 (4 weeks)

"I've always been fascinated by top-harmony trios," the late Tom Eyen once said in *Saturday Review*. "To me, three-girl harmony *is* music."

Eyen and Henry Krieger first collaborated on *The Dirtiest Musical*, a musical version of Eyen's *The Dirtiest Show in Town*, an off-Broadway hit in 1971. "Nell Carter was in *The Dirtiest Musical*, and we'd written a showstopping song ["Can You See?"] for her and the theater shook for like five, six minutes with applause," says Krieger. "And we realized if we could do that, maybe we could do a whole show like that. Not that it would constantly stop, but it would be full of emotional songs."

In 1979, Eyen and Krieger received approval from Joe Papp to do a workshop production based on their idea about a frustrated backup singer elevated to stardom. "We did a summer workshop and then Nell got the show *Gimme a Break*," Krieger recalls. "So she got busy and we waited for about a year...I called Nell and said, 'What about working together?' She said, 'We'll talk about it.' So we decided it would probably be best to face reality and let her be."

Eyen and Krieger approached *A Chorus Line* director Michael Bennett about directing *Dreamgirls*. Sheryl Lee Ralph and Loretta Devine had already been cast in the workshop production; Jennifer Holliday was discovered in *Your Arms Too Short to Box with God*. "She was a very young, raw talent, but very strong," says Krieger. "She came in and sang for us and we hired her."

Holliday was cast as Effie White, lead singer of a black female vocal trio who is fired from the group

Jennifer Holliday (left)

and replaced by one of the background singers. Her Act I finish came into being late in the first workshop production of *Dreamgirls.*

"Tom was directing the actors and I was directing the musicians," Krieger remembers. "I was writing by the seat of my pants. Every day it was something new. Every night I'd have to write for the next day. Tom said, 'Here's a lyric. Please make this into a song. Go off by yourself today because we need it really soon.' And so I went into a room with a piano." Krieger was working at Bennett's studios at 19th and Broadway, while the movie version of *Annie* was filming on the same floor. Krieger felt frustrated and couldn't come up with any music. *Annie* producer Ray Stark popped in and asked if he could use the phone. "He called Switzerland and this place and that place...and when he left, the song came right out. I wrote the whole thing." Krieger immediately brought it to the rehearsal room, stopped the actors, and played it for Jennifer Holliday, who sang it back. They knew instantaneously that they had their show-stopping song.

Holliday won rave reviews as soon as *Dreamgirls* opened at the Imperial Theatre on December 20, 1981. "Maria Callas herself would have admired this devastating fusion of singing and acting," Jack Kroll wrote in *Newsweek* of Holliday's Act I closer. She performed the gut-wrenching number eight times a week onstage and had no problem recording the song in one take for the cast album. "But then they were disappointed because they wanted me to tone it down," she says. "They wanted me to make it more 'pop.' David Foster was very upset and had David Geffen call me personally to go back in the studio to redo it. And I wouldn't...because I felt I had done a good job and so they threatened me and told me they were going to get Gladys Knight to sing it. They said that the song stuck out like a sore thumb. They were going for a new sound, a different sound and mine was too emotional and it would never get airplay. Of course, they were wrong. It didn't matter to them, both of them are very wealthy, but at that point, if I hadn't stuck to my gut feelings, I really don't know what would have happened...People would have thought that I sold out. So I'm glad I didn't and I'm glad I didn't listen to them."

363

DANCE FLOOR (PART I)

Zapp

WARNER BROS. 29961
WRITERS: ROGER TROUTMAN, LARRY TROUTMAN
PRODUCERS: ROGER TROUTMAN, ZAPP TROUTMAN
August 21, 1982 (2 weeks)

"It was so unorthodox, such a bizarre, insane way of making a record," Roger Troutman muses about Zapp's Number One single. "I never knew exactly what I was going to do next.

"I was putting one thing down and shifting through that and listening to the next thing. It was very, I guess you could say, helter-skelter. The only thing I was sure about was that I wanted to call the song 'Dance Floor,' because I was imagining a guy at a discotheque who's a bit bashful. But he knew if [he] went to a discotheque that he could watch pretty girls dance and shake and wiggle on the dance floor and all he had to do was stand in the corner because he was too shy to dance or ask for dates...And no one would ever know what he was feeling. So those kind of crazy ideas were always floating in the back of my mind while I was putting the track together. When I saw an opportunity to record a verse or if I felt inspired...I would run in the studio and set everything up and record a verse and listen to it. Then maybe I would stop for that day and come back the next day or two days later and try to do another verse."

It was a very different way of recording for Roger, totally opposite to his carefully detailed plan when he recorded his first Number One hit [see 351—"I Heard It Through the Grapevine"]. Without a road map, Roger couldn't even be sure of when he reached the end of his journey. "My family was asking me, 'How much longer are you going to be in there?' " he laughs. "I finally finished when my brother Larry said to me, 'You got this great thing down here two minutes in. You should take that out of the ending and put that in the beginning and then halfway through

Zapp

the song, take that beginning and start the whole song over again.' After having it all together, he listened to what I called the finished [master] and then he tweaked that. He was very helpful in helping me edit what I had put together. Without his input, I think the song wouldn't have been as exciting as it was. I had a lot of things in the wrong place."

Warner Brothers Records was anxiously awaiting Zapp's second album, a virtual follow-up to Roger's solo effort, *The Many Facets of Roger*. The group consisted of Roger and his brothers, Larry, Lester, and Terry (nicknamed "Zapp" because when he was a baby he couldn't pronounce the name of his brothers' elementary school principal, Elza Sapp). Roger had no doubts that "Dance Floor" should be the first single. "I sent a cassette copy of the final mix to a DJ in Cleveland. I told him, 'Please, whatever you do, don't put this on the air. Just play it and tell me what you think.' " The DJ called Roger back and praised the song up and down. "A couple weeks later," Roger continues, "I was at the mall in Dayton and saw a kid with a boom box and 'Dance Floor' was playing. I ran up to the kid and said, 'How did you get that?' He said, 'I was in Cleveland and taped it off the radio. Ain't that a bad jam? Ain't nobody got that jam but me!' " Roger called the DJ to see what had happened. "He said, 'I couldn't help it, man. It's a great song!' A couple of days later, some Warner Brothers executives called, upset because competing radio stations in Cleveland wanted the record. To calm everybody down, the execs proposed releasing a different track. "I protested," says Roger. "I said, 'No, no. The problem is a DJ/record company problem. The problem isn't the record. The record needs to be released. We're going to release "Dance Floor" first.' "

364

JUMP TO IT

Aretha Franklin

ARISTA 0699
WRITERS: LUTHER VANDROSS, MARCUS MILLER
PRODUCER: LUTHER VANDROSS
September 4, 1982 (4 weeks)

After 17 Number One R&B singles on Atlantic, Aretha Franklin scored her first Number One hit on Arista with a song produced by a man who called "I Never Loved A Man (The Way I Love You)" a high point in his street education.

Shortly after his first Number One single was released [see 350—"Never Too Much"], Luther Vandross did an interview with *Rolling Stone*. "The last question the interviewer asked me was, 'Now that you have your first album having gone gold, what would you want to do next? How would you follow this up?' And my quote was, 'I'd wrestle Bruno Sammartino for a chance to produce Aretha Franklin,' and [Arista label president] Clive Davis read that and called me up and said, 'You really want to do that?' and gave Aretha my number."

Aretha Franklin

Aretha called Luther and asked what he had in mind. "I said, 'I just love you so much and I have some ideas that I think would work on you, that I think you would wear well.' She said, 'Well, I love "Never Too Much," and when I heard "A House Is Not a Home," I thought you had lost your mind.' That was her quote...and she says, 'Do your thing and send it to me.' "

Vandross was guest starring on *Saturday Night Live*. His writing partner Marcus Miller had been in the show's band and was back that week to play behind Luther. "During a break, I said, 'You'll never believe it! I spoke to Aretha Franklin today and we need a song.' And there was a piano that was going to be moved soon sitting in the hallway and we sat down and started. Marcus went home and worked on a track...and then I worked on the chorus and the hook and...sent it to Aretha with me singing it, and she loved it. And then I got to do the whole album."

Jump to It was Aretha's third album for Arista. The first two had yielded singles like "United Together," "What a Fool Believes" and "Love All the Hurt Away," a duet with George Benson. Arif Mardin and Chuck

Jackson were the only producers to work with Aretha on her Arista material until Luther was called in. "The thing about her that's so incredible is that she comes to the studio so prepared," says Vandross. "If you are ever witness to a recording session, you'll notice that an artist will step up to the microphone and a couple of hours later they start to sound like who you know them to be. Aretha Franklin becomes Aretha Franklin immediately. She gets to the essence of her talent very quickly. It's startling...anybody that records her should know to have the microphone on even for the sound check, even for the first take. Because 'Jump to It' was basically the first take."

Vandross employed his familiar crew on the session. Nat Adderley Jr. played keyboards, Doc Powell was on guitar, Yogi Horton played the drums, Crusher Bennett was on congas and co-writer Miller played bass and programed the synthesizer. Backing vocals were provided by Luther's longtime favorite, Cissy Houston, and Tawatha Agee, Phillip Ballou, Brenda White, Michelle Cobbs, Fonzi Thornton, and Vandross himself.

"That recording session was heaven from the time the song was written," Luther professes, while pointing out the song has more depth to it than just being a joyous romp. "It also has a very sinister quality to it too when you have those guitars staying on those same notes against different chords. It doesn't move, so that creates a lot of tension. It's very, very soulful."

365

LOVE COME DOWN

Evelyn King

RCA 13273
WRITER: KASHIF
PRODUCER: MORRIE BROWN
October 2, 1982 (5 weeks)

After writing and producing one Number One song for Evelyn King [see 347—"I'm in Love"], the team of Morrie Brown, Kashif, and Paul Lawrence Jones III was asked to produce the artist's next album. "The chemistry was right," Kashif believes. "They asked us to do it again and we got lucky again. My style had developed a little bit more and there's a little more orchestration and a little more layering. I had really begun to understand and

Evelyn King (right), with Kashif

develop that stacked vocal sound, a very close kind of harmony background...It got easier the second time around. She had just come off a hit...People were willing to play it, the disc jockeys and folks were willing to hear it, and they liked the song."

The song was "Love Come Down." Kashif was influenced by the work of Leon Sylvers. "He had come off such a long list of hits, beautiful songs, and great orchestrations. We took some of what he was doing and took it a little bit to the next level." Kashif recalls writing the hit. "I wanted to write a song where the verses were in contrast with the chorus. Because the chorus is in a major key in B-flat major and the verses are in D-minor...I used to write my basslines in a different key than the song...so I was able to capture a sound and people couldn't figure out what it was. Even inside the verse, we did the same thing. I remember those shiftings and the high bell sounds...It was like a carnival to me."

The producer had a great time working with Evelyn in the studio. "She was fantastic—she could sing so well. Double herself and sing backgrounds, and she did it so effortlessly...It would just flow out of her mouth." Kashif played all of the instruments but one—Ira Siegal was on guitar.

Kashif remembers the first time he heard the song on the radio. "One of the things that used to strike me about songs when I was a kid was when I could hear the song from way off, like on the radio if you were outside. You may have been a block or two away...you could hear certain parts of it...that signature you recognized and something just lodged in your subconscious. You had to hear but one or two notes of it and you knew exactly what it was. I began to incorporate different things like that into my music. So I put that bell thing in there. And I remember being in Central Park and there was a guy skating. I could see [him] from a long way off...I could hear the music and it was a very sunny day and this guy was turning and doing all kinds of tricks and having the time of his life on those skates and it was to my song. It made a great impression on me and I appreciated his enthusiasm and excitement about the music."

As had been the case for "I'm in Love," the name on the label for "Love Come Down" was Evelyn King, minus the "Champagne" in the middle. "It was taken away from me," the singer complains. "RCA took it out...They told me it was too 'old' of a name. They wanted to change it and see what happened...I didn't even know they were taking it out." King was on tour and wasn't aware of the change until she returned home and saw the record. "['Champagne'] was a great name for the stage. My mom chose it...and it worked for me...It was very important to me and I kept it. I just said, 'You cannot do that'...It's still there."

366

SEXUAL HEALING

Marvin Gaye

COLUMBIA 03302
WRITERS: MARVIN GAYE, ODELL BROWN, DAVID RITZ
PRODUCER: MARVIN GAYE
November 6, 1982 (10 weeks)

If he had to go, Marvin Gaye may as well have left after "Sexual Healing."

It was a song that perfectly summarized the contradictions of his life—deeply spiritual, profoundly carnal—and his art. It also proved he *could* succeed beyond the recording empire that gave him fame: Motown.

In 1980, a tax exile living in Europe, Gaye wanted out of that empire. The late Jay Lasker, newly installed as Motown's president, took a phone call to that effect. Checking with Berry Gordy, Lasker was told, "If you can make a deal, let him go."

In February of 1981, Marvin's attorney, Curtis Shaw, advised Larkin Arnold at CBS Records of Gaye's availability. "Motown had agreed with Curtis on a figure for which they'd be willing to let Marvin go," Arnold said later. That sum was $2 million.

"The first album will be a single-disk set produced by Gaye," reported *Billboard* soon after the singer's CBS deal was done. "All the songs are identified and rough tracks have been cut on three or four of them."

In April 1982, author David Ritz traveled to Belgium to see Gaye. "I was writing Marvin's autobiography," he says. It was to be an "as-told-to" tome that Ritz had been working on for a couple of years. Relaxing in Gaye's apartment, Ritz noticed a book of pornographic cartoons, which included depictions of women being violated. "This was all under the guise of avant-garde Parisian art," says Ritz. "I told Marvin, 'This is some really sick shit here. You don't need that, you need sexual healing.'

"He said, 'I love that concept, why don't you put some words to it?' Odell Brown's track was playing in the background, and I wrote the first chorus in four minutes. Marvin took it and changed some of the words, made an arrangement out of it, and said, 'This is a hit.' "

Soon afterwards, Larkin Arnold visited Belgium to check on Gaye's progress. "So we go to Brussels with a home-made demo tape of 'Sexual Healing,' " says Ritz. "We ping-ponged it off two tape-recorders for Larkin, and he loved it."

The singer cut most of his CBS debut album, *Midnight Love*, at Studio Katy in Ohaine, Belgium, with the assistance from his pre-Motown mentor from the

Marvin Gaye

Moonglows, Harvey Fuqua. On "Sexual Healing," Gaye played drums, electric piano, synthesizer, organ, congas, and percussion. Guitar parts were added by Gordon Banks, who also sang background with Fuqua and Gaye.

"We tried at first to use European musicians, but I couldn't get quite the feeling I wanted," Marvin told *Blues & Soul* after the album's release. "I was also under a lot of emotional and economic pressures. So I abandoned the idea of doing it with musicians and started in with the synthesizers."

When "Sexual Healing" was released in October of 1982, David Ritz received no composing credit, to his distress. He explains that when he challenged Gaye, "Marvin said, 'I put your name on the album.' I told him, 'I want a taste.' " In other words, a royalty-earning co-authorship.

Gaye's reluctance to agree to that forced Ritz to sue him in 1983. After Marvin's death the following year, his estate took over defense of the lawsuit; a settlement was reached in 1988. Since then, Ritz has received co-writer credits for "Sexual Healing," and a share in the royalties.

367

THE GIRL IS MINE

Michael Jackson and Paul McCartney

EPIC 03288
WRITER: MICHAEL JACKSON
PRODUCER: QUINCY JONES
January 15, 1983 (3 weeks)

Michael Jackson and Paul McCartney, the only Beatle to appear on the R&B chart, tell different stories about how they met.

"Michael originally rang me up on Christmas day...and I didn't believe it was him," the former Beatle said in an interview recorded for a three-hour radio special, *Paul McCartney: The Beatles and Beyond*. "Eventually I said, 'Is that really you?' He was laughing on the phone and he said, 'You don't believe me, do you?' " Paul says Michael convinced him and told him why he was calling: "It turned out that he...fancied coming over to England. I think he had some time off, and he fancied trying to write some stuff with me. I said well, you know, great. Let me think about it...and I thought about it and thought well, why not? I admire him a lot, I really like his singing and his dancing and his musical abilities."

Michael wrote about meeting Paul in his *Moonwalk* autobiography: "I saw Paul for the first time at a party on the Queen Mary, which is docked in Long Beach. His daughter Heather got my number from someone and gave me a call to invite me to this big party. She liked our music and we got to talking. Much later, when his *Wings Over America* tour was completed, Paul and his family were in Los Angeles. They invited me to a party at the Harold Lloyd estate. Paul McCartney and I first met at that party. We shook hands amid a huge crowd of people, and he said, 'You know, I've written a song for you.' I was very surprised and thanked him. And he started singing 'Girlfriend' to me at the party."

But both artists were busy with their own careers and lives, and two years passed before they spoke again. Paul recorded "Girlfriend" for his *London Town* album and Michael didn't think about the song again until Quincy Jones suggested he record it for *Off the Wall* without realizing it had been written with Jackson in mind.

When Michael was ready to record the follow-up to *Off the Wall*, he did ring Paul up and suggested they write some songs together. That resulted in "The Girl Is Mine" and "Say, Say, Say."

"When I approached Paul, I wanted to repay the favor he had done me in contributing 'Girlfriend' to *Off the Wall*," Michael stated in *Moonwalk*. "I wrote 'The Girl Is Mine,' which I knew would be right for his voice and mine working together, and we also did work on 'Say, Say, Say,' which we wound up finishing later with George Martin, the great Beatles producer."

Greg Phillinganes, David Foster, and Steve Porcaro played synthesizers on "The Girl Is Mine." David Paich was on piano, Louis Johnson of the Brothers Johnson played bass, Dean Parks and Steve Lukather played guitars, and Jeff Porcaro was on drums.

"Quincy and I eventually chose 'The Girl Is Mine' as the obvious first single from *Thriller*," Michael wrote in his book. "We really didn't have much choice. When you have two strong names like that together on a song, it has to come out first or it gets played to death and overexposed. We had to get it out of the way."

"The Girl Is Mine" is Paul McCartney's only Number One R&B single as an artist, but he had been to the top of the R&B chart once before as a songwriter—Earth, Wind & Fire covered the Beatles' "Got to Get You into My Life" [see 300], penned by McCartney and John Lennon.

368
OUTSTANDING
The Gap Band

TOTAL EXPERIENCE 8205
WRITERS: RAYMOND CALHOUN, LONNIE SIMMONS, CHARLIE WILSON
PRODUCER: LONNIE SIMMONS
February 5, 1983 (1 week)

Raymond Calhoun remembers the day he was inspired to write his first song, "Outstanding." He was home with his one-year-old daughter, sitting at his brand-new piano. "It just came to me, believe it or not," he says. "You know how you sit at the piano and twiddle around? All of a sudden I noticed I was coming up with something. I didn't really think much of it at the time."

He credits his daughter for giving him the idea for the song. "She was sitting there and I was happy that she was born. I got inspired and came up with the hook while I was playing the chords, saying, 'She's outstanding.' "

Calhoun grew up in Washington, D.C., and got his first break in 1976 as a back-up musician for the Manhattans [see 244—"Kiss and Say Goodbye"]. After a seven-month interim period working with Peaches and Herb [see 311—"Reunited"], he was hired as percussionist/drummer for the Gap Band in 1979.

"I was with them for four years before I wrote anything for them," says Calhoun, who took "Outstanding" to the group and producer Lonnie Simmons. "I played it for them on the piano and they said, 'Go ahead and cut it.' " I played all the instruments on it and Charlie [Wilson] came in and I sang the vocal for him. He sang it just like I did and it ended up on the [*Gap Band IV*] album. I didn't know it was going to be a hit."

Although the song was written about his daughter, Calhoun wasn't averse to Simmons's suggestion that the song could also be about a woman. Lonnie remembers the first time he heard the song: "He handed me the lyrics and Charlie and I went in the studio and started putting the vocal on and when we got through with the song, [Calhoun] said, 'Wait! The second verse should be the first verse and the first verse should be the second verse.' And I said, 'That's not the way you've got it written on this paper.' He said, 'I made a mistake. You gotta change it.' I said, 'No, it sounds alright to me like it is. Trust me. It'll be fine.' And that's the way you hear it now."

Calhoun says the song was recorded in one take. "That's how they used to do most of their songs. They would go in the studio and say, 'This is wrong' and Lonnie would say, 'Let's not change it. Let's leave it like it is and leave the rawness to it.' " Calhoun also says the session was very relaxed, especially after being with other artists who had intense recording sessions. "But Charlie, Ronnie, and [the band] did it like, 'OK, let's cut this. Let's go get some pizza.' It wasn't stressful at all. I learned a lot from the guys through the years, how to record and how to develop my craft."

Rudy Taylor, the group's engineer, also remembers the "Outstanding" session. "Lonnie likes to play percussion. He had this little off-beat he was playing. We worked on that and it really paid off. I was talking to Ice Cube. He said that was his favorite part in the whole record, that little percussion thing. And he said that's what makes it happen for them now, for the rappers. I think like eight rap groups have redone 'Outstanding.' It's still got that flavor ten years later, so it must be happening."

Michael Jackson

369

BILLIE JEAN

Michael Jackson

EPIC 03509
WRITER: MICHAEL JACKSON
PRODUCER: QUINCY JONES
February 12, 1983 (9 weeks)

"Not My Lover' was a title we almost used for 'Billie Jean' because Q had some objections to calling the song 'Billie Jean,' my original title," Michael Jackson wrote in his *Moonwalk* autobiography. "He felt people might immediately think of Billie Jean King, the tennis player."

If they did, it didn't stop them from buying the second single issued from *Thriller.* "Billie Jean" went to Number One and stayed there for nine weeks, the longest-running Number One hit of Michael's career.

"A lot of people have asked me about that song, and the answer is very simple," Michael stated in his book. "It's just a case of a girl who says that I'm the father of her child and I'm pleading innocence because 'the kid is not my son.' There never was a real 'Billie Jean' (except for the ones who came after the song). The girl in the song is a composite of people we've been plagued by over the years. This kind of thing has happened to some of my brothers and I used to be really amazed by it. I couldn't understand how these girls could say they were carrying someone's child when it wasn't true."

Michael states that while writing the song, he was totally absorbed by it, to the exclusion of everything else. Taking a break from a recording session, he was riding down the Ventura Freeway in California's San Fernando Valley with one of his employees, Nelson Hayes. As they turned onto an off-ramp, a kid on a motorcycle pulled up to their car and told them it was on fire. They noticed the smoke and pulled the Rolls over to the side of the ramp. "I was so absorbed by this tune floating in my head that I didn't even focus on the awful possibilities until later," Michael commented.

Working with Quincy and Michael on the track were Dean Parks (guitar), Louis Johnson (bass), Leon Ndugu Chancler (drums), Michael Boddicker (emulator), and Greg Phillinganes, Greg Smith, and Bill Wolfer (synthesizers). Johnson, who played the dominant bassline suggested by Michael, talked about the session in *Musician*: "[Michael] had me bring all my guitars to see how they sounded playing the part. I tried three or four basses before we settled on the Yamaha. It's really live, with a lot of power and guts." Although Tom Scott wasn't credited in the liner notes, he played a lyricon solo in the background of the mix. Engineer Bruce Swedien said in *Musician*, "It was Quincy's idea to weave this thread into the thing. It was a last-minute overdub thing. Quincy calls it 'ear candy.' It's just a subliminal element that works well."

Chancler joined the recording process late in the game to enhance the "punch" of the song. He added his comments in *Musician*: "I was placed in a room by myself, so there was no [sound] leakage. Both Michael and Quincy came in to suggest things for the two or three hours it took to cut the track. I played through it about eight to 10 times."

Michael's vocal on "Billie Jean" was completed in one amazing take. Even more amazing was his performance of the song on the television special marking Motown's 25th anniversary. The night before the taping, he still didn't know how he was going to perform the song. Alone in his kitchen, he played it very loud and let the music tell him what to do. And that's when he decided he would perform the Moonwalk for the very first time in public when he sang "Billie Jean" on *Motown 25*.

370

ATOMIC DOG

George Clinton

CAPITOL 5201
WRITERS: GEORGE CLINTON, GARRY SHIDER, DAVID SPRADLEY
PRODUCERS: GEORGE CLINTON, TED CURRIER
April 16, 1983 (4 weeks)

The scene: George Clinton is awaiting his turn at the top of the *Billboard* charts. Ahead of him is romance (Lionel Richie's "You Are") and a paternity dispute (Michael Jackson's "Billie Jean"). It's April Fool's Day, 1983—the kind of day that suits Clinton best. Woof, woof.

Actually, "Atomic Dog" had to stay at heel for a few more weeks before getting into the Number One pound. But George was used to adversity. "I told them point-blank it's gonna get rough and it would be hard to stay together," he explained to *Billboard* that April. "They said they wouldn't leave, but when things did get tight, many did leave—but that was cool." He added, "Lawyers and wives make it a bitch to keep any band together."

"They" were the funky mongrels Clinton had steered to fame and notoriety as Funkadelic [see 301—"One Nation Under a Groove"] and Parliament [see 287—"Flash Light"]. But the pioneering band(s) disassembled in the early '80s, thanks to attorneys, spouses, and probably spouses' attorneys, too.

So Clinton decided to go it alone, signing to Capitol Records as a solo artist—the first time that had happened in the 20-plus years of his career. However, his first album for the label, *Computer Games*, rounded up many of his favorite hounds for musical support. Among them were Bernie Worrell, Junie Morrison, Eddie Hazel, Garry Shider, Fred Wesley, and Richard "Kush" Griffith. Recording was done at Detroit's United Sound and The Disc studios.

"This album is the funkentelechy of the '80s," Clinton commented upon its release in November 1982. "We had a lot more time to work on this one than usual, and all that last-minute tinkering paid off." The lead-off single, "Loopzilla," spun into the top 20, but it was "Atomic Dog" that returned Dr. Funkenstein to the summit for the first time since "(not just) Knee Deep Part 1" in 1979. "We had to have a few puppies runnin' around this album 'cause we were underdoggin' when we started it," said Clinton. "Besides, a lot of the material was written during the Chinese Year of the Dog."

"Atomic Dog" itself was a strange record, he confirmed to a *Blues & Soul* reporter later. "I walked in the studio blind as a bat and out of my head, and I didn't

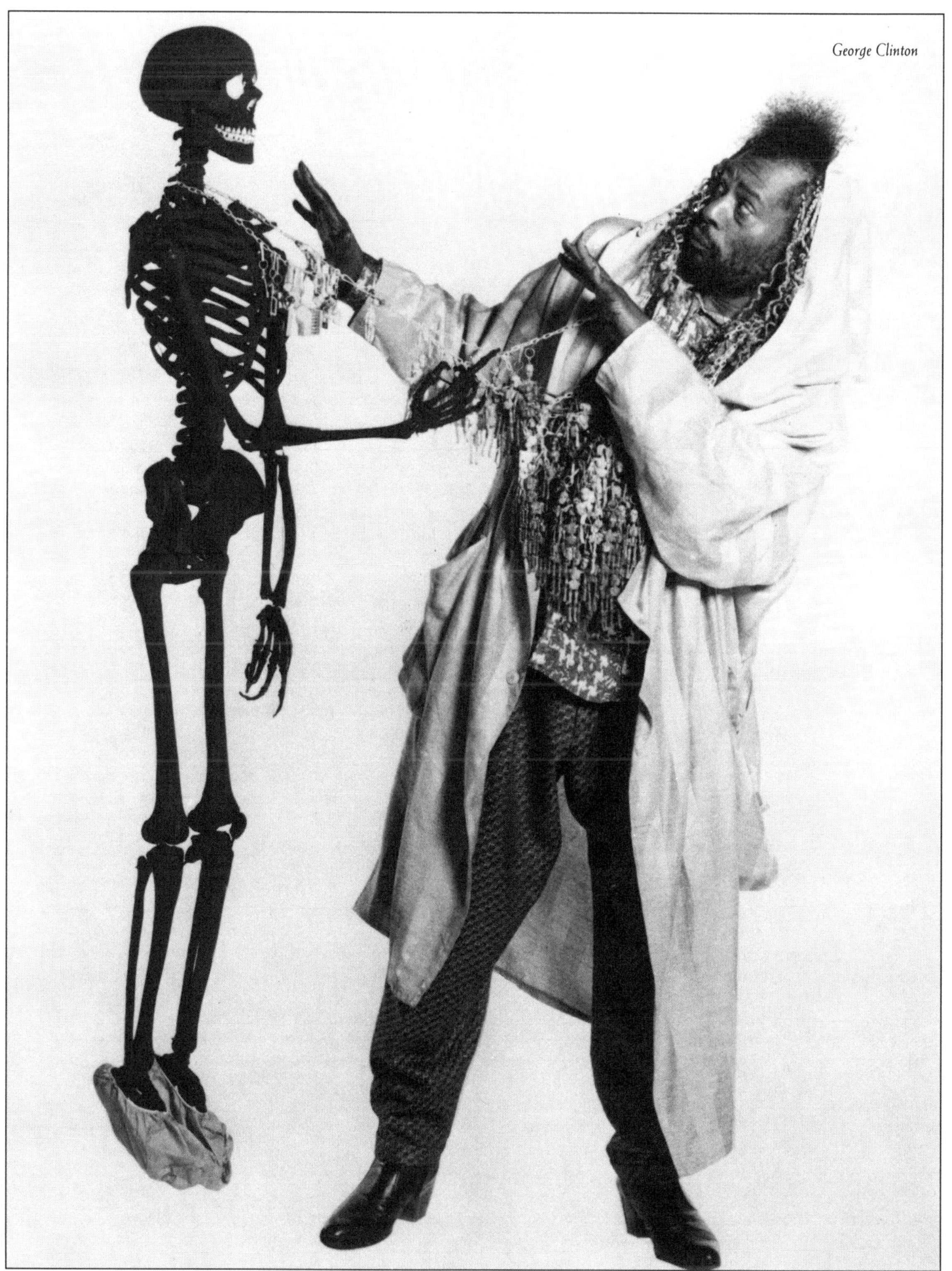

George Clinton

realize the track was backwards so I just started singing. I just made up something in my head, till I could figure out what the track was. So I started from the top with 'This is the story of a famous dog.' I ad-libbed the entire song.

"I didn't feel good until I said [the] 'Do the dog catcher/bow wow' bit," Clinton continued. "I was just changing, then suddenly the hook hit me like 'Whoff! Why must I chase the cat? It's nuthin' but the dog in me.' I thought, 'Oh shit! I've got a hook and a half here,' and from then on, I *knew* I had a song." Helping out with the project were Garry Shider and David Spradley, with Shider and David Lee Chong as arrangers.

To make sure his fans hadn't forgotten the funk, George took his show on the road as "Atomic Dog" was unleashed. "They had a loyalty to me and what we can do together," he declared about the Parlia-funkadelicament members who joined him. "I've always said it's everybody and nobody who makes the music.

"People started saying it's this guy or it's that one, and they started believing it was just them. People told me it was just me, [that] I didn't need anybody else. But I couldn't do it alone, and neither could they."

371

CANDY GIRL

New Edition

STREETWISE 1108
WRITERS: MAURICE STARR, MICHAEL JONZUN
PRODUCERS: MAURICE STARR, MICHAEL JONZUN
May 14, 1983 (1 week)

When the five original members of New Edition first got together, they didn't have very big dreams. Forming a group seemed like a good way to earn enough change to go to the movies, and entering a local talent show was one way of becoming known as the best group in Boston. What they got was enough change to buy their own chain of movie theaters, and they went way beyond Boston in terms of international recognition.

Bobby Brown grew up in Roxbury, Massachusetts, where his family lived in the Orchard Park projects. His mother was a schoolteacher who liked James Brown and his father was a construction worker who enjoyed listening to the blues. Being poor didn't stop Bobby from wanting expensive things. "I always wanted the $100 sneakers. I always wanted the better things in life," he said in *Rolling Stone*. "If I seen anything, a sweatsuit I wanted in the store, I'd have to get some money to get that suit. I had to get mine the way I knew how to get it—stealing and whatever I had to do. A lot of my friends, either they're passed away, in jail, or on drugs."

Bobby was just 11 when he witnessed the murder of his best friend. The incident was traumatic enough for his mother to seek out a therapy program for her son. "I knew exactly what I wanted after that," Bobby said in *Musician*. "I asked Mike Bivins, Ricky Bell, and Ralph Tresvant—we was all pals—if they wanted to get serious and they said, 'Sure.' There was a show comin' up in two days and we wanted to get in it. Got the kind of steps the Temptations had, picked the song—'Ain't No Stoppin' Us Now'—and we were gone."

They were choreographed by Brook Payne, whose nephew Ronnie DeVoe became the fifth member of New Edition, an amalgamation of two names picked out of a hat. In 1981 the group competed in the Hollywood Talent Night contest at the Strand Theater in Boston. They came in second, but sponsor Maurice Starr liked Tresvant's high-pitched voice and told the youngsters he wanted to produce them anyway.

Starr signed New Edition to the New York–based Streetwise label. Along with his brother Michael Jonzun, he wrote and produced a Jackson 5–styled song called "Candy Girl." In May of 1983, the single went to Number One on the American R&B chart and the British pop chart. That's when Ronnie DeVoe first realized he might have a musical career ahead of him. " 'Candy Girl' was Number One and Michael Jackson's 'Beat It' was number two. That was amazing to me because I had been watching the Jacksons and Michael Jackson's success for most of my life. At that point I realized we had something going for us and as long as we stayed together and focused...we could last for a long time."

Bobby Brown didn't mind the tag the critics pegged on the group because of "Candy Girl," he said in *Musician*. "Bubblegum? Yeah, it *was* in a way. But I don't think that's a negative term necessarily. The Jacksons were deemed the same thing; the press just gave it to us. We were just being what we were: kids. We might've grown up in a bad neighborhood, but there was still some sweetness there."

The association with Starr didn't last long. There were two more singles on Streetwise—"Is This the End" and "Popcorn Love." In 1984 the group severed ties with Starr and signed with MCA. The producer carried through with his promise to the group to find five white boys and start over. The ultimate result was New Kids on the Block. Starr's writing and production work won his new group a place on the R&B chart, as "I'll Be Loving You (Forever)" managed to peak at number 12.

372
BEAT IT
Michael Jackson

EPIC 03759
WRITER: MICHAEL JACKSON
PRODUCER: QUINCY JONES
May 21, 1983 (1 week)

Michael Jackson credited his manager at the time, Frank DiLeo, with having a brilliant understanding of the record industry. Jackson cited an example in his *Moonwalk* autobiography: "We released 'Beat It' as a single while 'Billie Jean' was still at Number One. CBS screamed, 'You're crazy. This will kill "Billie Jean." ' But Frank told them not to worry, that both songs would be Number One and both would be in the top 10 at the same time. They were."

Elsewhere in *Moonwalk,* Jackson detailed the origin of the third Number One single from *Thriller.* "Before I wrote 'Beat It,' I had been thinking I wanted to write the type of rock song that I would go out and buy, but also something totally different from the rock music I was hearing on top 40 radio at the time. 'Beat It' was written with school kids in mind. I've always loved creating pieces that will appeal to kids. It's fun to write for them and know what they like because they're a very demanding audience."

Jackson pointed out that the lyrics to "Beat It" described what he would do if he were in trouble. "Its message—that we should abhor violence—is something I believe deeply. It tells kids to be smart and avoid trouble. I don't mean to say you should turn the other cheek while someone kicks in your teeth, but, unless your back is against the wall and you have absolutely no choice, just get away before violence breaks out. If you fight and get killed, you've gained nothing and lost everything. You're the loser, and so are the people who love you. That's what 'Beat It' is supposed to get across."

Jackson was credited as "drum case beater" on the song. He was supported in the studio by Greg Phillinganes and Steve Porcaro (synthesizers), Bill Wolfer (keyboards), Tom Bahler (synclaver), Steve Lukather (guitars, electric bass), Paul Jackson (guitar), Jeff Porcaro (drums), and special guest star Eddie Van Halen (guitar solo).

Van Halen almost missed his chance to work with Jackson. Eddie's telephone wasn't working properly and he received two phone calls in a row where he couldn't hear the party who was calling. When the phone rang a third time, Eddie let loose with a string of expletives. The rock guitarist told *Musician* that he then heard a voice say: "This is Quincy, Quincy Jones." A surprised Van Halen replied, "I'm sorry, I get so many crank calls that I didn't know." Quincy asked Eddie if he was up for recording a song with Michael.

Van Halen was so up for it, he refused to accept any pay for his work. "I didn't care," he said. "I did it as a favor." Jackson's vocals were as intense as Van Halen's guitar playing. Engineer Bruce Swedien talked about Michael's rigorous vocal training during the *Thriller* sessions: "During that period, every day—I don't mean one day a week or something—every day that Michael records vocals, he's at his vocal coach's place at 8:30 in the morning. So when he comes in, he's ready to go."

Michael Jackson

373

SAVE THE OVERTIME (FOR ME)

Gladys Knight & the Pips

COLUMBIA 03761
WRITERS: RICKEY SMITH, JOEY GALLO,
BUBBA KNIGHT, GLADYS KNIGHT, SAM DEES
PRODUCER: RICKEY SMITH
May 28, 1983 (1 week)

Twenty-two years to the week after they made their chart debut with "Every Beat of My Heart," Gladys Knight & the Pips were back on top of the *Billboard* R&B chart with "Save the Overtime (For Me)," their first Number One single on Columbia Records.

Sam Dees first met Gladys through Jack Gold, who produced the artist's Columbia debut, a solo album titled *Gladys Knight*. Dees, who recorded for Atlantic in the early '70s, had written songs for Ben E. King, Margie Joseph, and the Persuaders by the time he submitted "My World" to Gladys in 1978. Three years later, Dees formed a writing partnership with Gladys and her brother Bubba and went to work on the group's third Columbia album, *Visions*.

The Knight/Dees/Knight team produced half the album and Leon Sylvers took responsibility for the other half. "Leon came in with this track that they didn't have a lyric for," Gladys recalls. "It was really a hot track and he said, 'We're getting close to the wire. If you guys want to take this track and see what you can do with it, be our guest.' So we took the track home and worked on it for a little while and just loved it. And we stayed up until the wee hours—Sam in particular was working overtime that night."

Dees was staying in the guest house at Gladys's home in Las Vegas, and the three writers worked out of his bungalow. "Sam had an inspiration as to where to go with the song and he got up in the middle of the night," Gladys adds. "When Bubba and I got up the next morning, he showed us what he had done and where he was going with it."

Dees remembers the writing process: "We had aimed the storyline at a person giving his all for his boss, but remembering there's someone else at home that could use some loving." The three collaborators worked on the demo together. "She would sing a little bit, I would sing a little bit," says Dees. "The song was very easy to do after we got it into the studio."

With the Pips, Gladys recorded at Sylvers's home studio. "They would be in there doing tracks and I'd be in the kitchen cooking," Gladys recalls. "Everybody would eat, then we'd get over to the studio and make the music."

Gladys Knight & the Pips

After 22 years of recording, Gladys had her first self-penned hit. Dees remembers how great he felt when "Save the Overtime" went to Number One. "I've had several songs done by different recording artists, but Gladys has a way of doing something to a lyric, especially to a lyric that she liked. We had a good feeling about the record and the record company had a real good feeling and we really didn't know what we were into until we saw the first chart action on it." Actually, there was some foreshadowing that the song would be a hit, according to Dees: "There were several people in town that had their own personal copies and we had gone to a party and someone had a tape of the song. It was playing there before it was released, and they were really jammin' to it, so we had a reasonably good feeling about it. But we really and truly didn't know. We just did our best effort and left it at that."

374

JUICY FRUIT

Mtume

EPIC 03578

WRITER: JAMES MTUME

PRODUCER: JAMES MTUME

June 4, 1983 (8 weeks)

Jazz musician James Mtume crossed over to pop when he co-wrote "The Closer I Get to You" for Roberta Flack and Donny Hathaway [see 289]. After that success, James was recruited to write and produce for Stephanie Mills, Phyllis Hyman, Lou Rawls, and the Spinners. "Having been fortunate with those records, I thought it was time to see what would happen if I put the same energy into the group that I was putting into those other acts," says the man who lent his name to Mtume.

"I wanted to do some things not necessarily using full orchestration, which is what the production sound had been on all those records. So I broke it down to what I call neosymbolism, and 'Juicy Fruit' was the first [song] in that direction. I had done band albums under the name of Mtume before, but they were always sandwiched in between the next Stephanie Mills [record]—nothing that required a great deal of focus."

The keyboardist who once worked with jazz greats like Miles Davis, Freddie Hubbard, Joe Henderson, and Sonny Rollins put together his own group and signed with Epic. Mtume consisted of Ed "Tree" Moore on lead and rhythm guitar, Philip Fields on keyboards, Raymond Jackson on bass, Tawatha Agee on lead vocals and percussion, and James on lead vocals and keyboards.

"Juicy Fruit" was part of a series that included "You, Me and He," a number two single. "I wanted to try dealing with some songs from what I call the female perspective, but written by a man," says Mtume. "I always felt that women were much more descriptive and imaginative. Most male records, when it came to sensuality, were like, 'Do it to me baby.' "

The title came to Mtume before the lyrics. "I do the music first, lay the rhythm track down. And as I'm listening, the titles always come. It just felt like 'Juicy Fruit.' It wasn't about the candy, but that was a metaphor. I didn't write the lyrics until the day of the vocals. I never write lyrics until the day when we're actually cutting the vocals for the song."

So Mtume works best under pressure? "Love it, love it," he affirms. "Pressure makes diamonds and breaks glass. As Tawatha finished the first verse, I'm writing the second. It's pressure and it's also the excitement of capturing a moment. Maybe that's part of my jazz background—I have to have something that lends itself to absolute spontaneity. When you're recording a song, the vocals are the last opportunity to be absolutely spontaneous and I choose to do it like that."

Mtume credits Marvin Gaye's "Sexual Healing" with opening the door for a song like "Juicy Fruit." The lyrics to "Juicy Fruit" did cause some controversy, and Mtume was told by one Epic executive that radio wouldn't play it. "It was sensual," the writer/producer acknowledges, while still pointing out that "it was not obscene in any sense of the word."

Nine days after the single was released, Mtume received a phone call from the head of Epic's promotion department to tell him the record was exploding all over the country. "It busted wide out of Houston," says Mtume. "It was a much more creative time for sounds and experiments. I don't know if a record like that would work now, because everything sounds so much the same."

375

SHE WORKS HARD FOR THE MONEY

Donna Summer

MERCURY 812 370

WRITERS: DONNA SUMMER, MICHAEL OMARTIAN

PRODUCER: MICHAEL OMARTIAN

July 30, 1983 (3 weeks)

Donna Summer and her manager Susan Munao were attending a party at Chasen's, a fashionable restaurant right on the border of Beverly Hills, when Donna excused herself to go to the ladies' room. She walked in and found an elderly female bathroom attendant asleep on a couch. "She was

Donna Summer

perched in the corner," Donna recalls, "and there was a teenie TV set on and people were coming in and out of the bathroom, spraying perfume [and] putting makeup on and I thought to myself, 'God, she works hard for the money.' And the minute I said it, it was like a bell went off in my head."

Donna asked for a paper and pen and sat down on a bench in the ladies' room. "I started scribbling 'She Works Hard for the Money,' the title. And I started writing down what I had seen in that room so I wouldn't forget it."

Summer rushed back to her table to tell Munao that she had just come up with a hit. "I was so excited. The song wasn't even written yet. I already knew. I walked around in a glow all night because I couldn't wait to get to the studio the next day to tell Michael [Omartian]."

"She Works Hard for the Money" became the title track for Summer's one and only album for Mercury Records. After reigning as the queen of disco for five years on Casablanca [see 316—"Bad Girls"], Summer sued manager Joyce Bogart and the label itself, founded by Neil Bogart, for $10 million, claiming "undue influence, misrepresentation, and fraud." Released from her contract with the company, Summer was the first artist signed to David Geffen's new label on June 19, 1980.

Summer still owed Casablanca one more album when she signed with Geffen. Her new label wasn't too thrilled that she was going to work with Omartian, fearing the two born-again Christians might produce a gospel album. They allowed Donna to fulfill her Casablanca contract with the album that Omartian was going to produce. Because Casablanca had been purchased and folded into Polygram, *She Works Hard for the Money* was issued on the corporation's Mercury label.

Summer became interested in working with Omartian after she heard his work with pop artist Christopher Cross, particularly his hit "Sailing." "Michael was a godsend," says Donna. "He was like Giorgio [Moroder]. Mild-tempered, incredibly creative. I mean, the guy could play his bazookas off...He does whatever he does to perfection."

"She Works Hard for the Money" was the last song written for the album, according to Omartian. "We sat down and I started playing that little groove and she came out to the studio and in about 10 minutes we're flowing with it. She finished it in a day or so and then we recorded it. It was a quick one, done in a couple of days. That turned out to be the single that really drove the album."

376

GET IT RIGHT

Aretha Franklin

ARISTA 9043
WRITERS: LUTHER VANDROSS, MARCUS MILLER
PRODUCER: LUTHER VANDROSS
August 20, 1983 (2 weeks)

"I thought 'Jump to It' should have done better on the pop side of town," says the man who wrote and produced Aretha's first Number One on Arista, Luther Vandross. "Jump to It" peaked at number 24 on the *Billboard* Hot 100. "I remember being anxious and honored to be asked to do 'Get It Right.' You know how you feel after you do a successful project and you go back in for the second one, the follow-up. You feel very stoked. You feel very encouraged and very positive. That's the way I felt then...I wouldn't give up that experience for anything."

Luther Vandross actually met Aretha Franklin before they worked together in the studio. He was 15 years old when she experienced her first success on Atlantic Records with "I Never Loved a Man (The Way I Love You)," and he idolized her from that point on. A year prior to producing her for Arista, he opened for Lady Soul in Washington, D.C. "I remember being brought to her room to meet her ...She was standing there and she had on a dress that reminded me of something out of *The King and I*...and I knew nothing about her manner. I didn't know she was slightly shy, a little quiet in countenance and texture. And so I walked into the room and she said, 'Hmmm, "Never Too Much" '...and later she told me, 'I had never heard [it] when I said that to you. I just knew it was the title of your song'...I found that to be the cutest thing in the world."

"Get It Right" was recorded in New York. "At that point she was singing in a slightly lower register and so I got to write a lot of things where she was digging down into that really soulful area of her voice. That was fun. And she had plenty of high A's and high F-sharps...There was a lot of that, but she also was enjoying singing some of the alto registers as well. The writing of the songs was catering to that. The musicians were all tremendous. There were no machines back then, so all of that was live." That came as a surprise to some. Another Arista artist, Kashif, asked drummer Yogi Horton if he was upset that Luther was using a drum machine. Vandross laughs, "Yogi took so much pride in saying, 'That ain't no damn drum machine. That's me!' "

After admiring Aretha from afar for so many years, how did Luther feel about working with her in the studio? "I figured that because so much of what I loved was inspired by this person that she would understand me, and I was absolutely right. I was not speaking a different language...Aretha always sings in tune. So those values, I sort of subconsciously assimilated. I mean, the people that I love always sing in tune."

Vandross also had to deal with the potentially uncomfortable position of being an authority figure to one of his idols: "In terms of telling Aretha what to do, I had to confront myself and say, 'OK, it's fine to be a fan, but you're going to blow this gig if you go in there as a fan.' You have to put that on the back burner and go in there authoritatively and gently tell her what you'd like to accomplish with this and get her through it, because she's looking to you for direction and for some guidance."

Aretha let her producer know how she felt about the outcome. Luther describes the scene: "She came and sat in the control room and closed her eyes and every once in a while, she'd lift her hand up and point her index finger toward the ceiling [as if to say], 'I like this.' "

377

COLD BLOODED

Rick James

GORDY 1687
WRITER: RICK JAMES
PRODUCER: RICK JAMES
September 3, 1983 (6 weeks)

Rick James, the king of Punk Funk, had a very strong image: long braided hair, outrageous clothing, beautiful women wrapped around him. There was no mistaking him for someone tender and romantic like Luther Vandross or Lionel Richie. James wore his sexuality on his sleeve and didn't care what anyone thought about it. But was that the real Rick James?

"The whole Rick James persona was a creation," he reveals. "My real name is James A. Johnson. But there's a craziness and lunacy in everyone. I wanted to create an image [so] I could live my fantasies of lunacy legitimately. Not to say Rick James is insane or anything like that—quite the contrary. He knew what he was doing when he was doing it."

"Cold Blooded," Rick's most successful R&B hit, continued his fascination with bold, sexy women. He remembers what inspired its creation: "At the Grammy Awards, Quincy Jones talked to me and said, 'Rick, we've got your groove.' If you listen to 'Thriller,' it's really like 'Give It to Me Baby.' He explained it to me and said, 'Rick, you gotta change up...because we got you,' and he did."

Rick was working out of his home studio in Buffalo, New York at the time and decided to heed Quincy's advice. "I said, 'I'm going to change. I would start giving my music more air, more space.' " Rick was seeing actress Linda Blair during this period and wrote "Cold Blooded" about her. Wait, it's not as bad as it sounds. "She loved it, because 'Cold Blooded' is a very positive word," Rick clarifies. "The line she really loved was, 'In my dic-tionary' because I kind of got away with that one. I didn't get away with 'In My House' [by the Mary Jane Girls]. I mean, 'In My House' went to number [three] before they found out I was actually talking about a vagina."

Rick and Linda were in the studio together when he wrote the song. "I started playing synthesizer because she wanted to learn how to write music. I told her anything you play is correct no matter what keys you touch...So I started playing this lick, 'Doom doom doom doom doom, doom de doom,' and that's how the song transpired."

Rick played all of the instruments on "Cold Blooded," using mostly synthesizers. It marked a distinct change from his previous guitar-laden material. "No horns, no moving basslines, none of that...Just turn it around and create something fresh, and 'Cold Blooded' is what I came up with." The vocal featured an attitude much like his hit "Super Freak." Rick says, "I was making fun of me and talking about her. I didn't want to be too explicit about who she was."

"Cold Blooded" was Rick's last Number One hit for Motown. Although he left the label for the Warner Brothers family [see 496—"Loosey's Rap"], he'll always remember one of the highlights of his Gordy years—working with the Temptations.

"Having the only record in history with all of them on it," he specifies. "When I did 'Super Freak' and I said, 'Temptations sing,' there were four Temptations singing background. It started a Temptations revival...They ended up getting back together and they did a reunion album, but all seven of them weren't [together] on any of the tracks. So I wrote a song called 'Standing on the Top' and it's the only song [with all of them]." During the session, Rick turned to a friend of his in the studio and said, "I can't believe we're sitting here with the Temptations and I'm actually telling Eddie Kendricks and David Ruffin what to sing."

378

AIN'T NOBODY

Rufus and Chaka Khan

WARNER BROS. 29555
WRITER: DAVID "HAWK" WOLINSKI
PRODUCER: RUSS TITELMAN
October 15, 1983 (1 week)

Roger Linn, a guitar player who worked with Leon Russell, almost joined Rufus, according to keyboard player David "Hawk" Wolinski. "He didn't sing, and that's why we didn't get him. But he had this drum machine invention that he wanted a lot of people to invest in, and we didn't, being the visionaries that we were." Although Linn didn't become part of the group, he did contribute to Rufus's fourth Number One single, "Ain't Nobody."

Before he played keyboards for Rufus, Wolinski was working with singer Minnie Riperton ("Lovin' You"). While playing a gig in Philadelphia opening for Stevie Wonder, "Hawk" met guitarist Michael Sembello ("Maniac"). "We had always threatened to write something together. We tried and nothing happened," says Wolinski. "I always liked his style. It was right around that period of time that I was working with Sembello that I sat down in my studio, and by this time I had a 24-track studio. I came up with this goofy, little stupid beginning idea, a crazy thing. And then all of a sudden I attached a sequencer to it. If you recall, at that time there were no sequencers. I had serial number 11 Roger Linn Drum Machine. I sat down with this drum machine [and] had this little groove. I wanted to write a song." Not happy with the straight 4/4 dance music that was predominant at the time, Wolinski wanted to write a song people could dance to that didn't follow the pack. "I didn't want the bass to hit at the same time as the bass drum. And I tried to write this really weird thing...As soon as I came up with the idea, the rest of the song fell down immediately."

Wolinski played the finished song for his friend Glenn Frey. The former Eagle, a big R&B fan, proclaimed it a Number One record. "Quincy [Jones] heard that record and wanted to do it on *Thriller* with Michael Jackson," says Wolinski. "Except that I promised [Russ] Titelman, who produced it, that I would keep it for Rufus. I could have been greedy, but I wasn't. Which is probably why I'm not living in Beverly Hills."

Not everyone in Rufus appreciated the new technology Wolinski was applying to the song. "I thought it got a little bit out of hand," says guitarist Tony Maiden, "because I'm from the old school." Maiden agreed to experiment with the drum machine as long as the recording process didn't take an extraordinarily long time. Although he pioneered the use of computers in the group, Wolinski agrees with Maiden. "He's absolutely right. It's kind of ironic...I never realized it would take over so completely, that you'd get people who don't know how to play...that instead of the exception, it would become the rule...And my feelings about R&B have completely changed. It's a tragedy what's happened to music."

Despite Maiden's feelings, the band decided to record "Ain't Nobody." "We did a democratic vote like we did on every song," recalls Chaka Khan. The group decided "it should be part of our album repertoire. It was a lot different when we finished it than it was when he presented it to us. It wasn't as funky as it is now."

"Ain't Nobody" was one of the new studio recordings included on Rufus's first album for Warner Brothers, *Live—Stompin' at the Savoy*. But label executives wanted to release a different cut as a single. Wolinski went against his belief that the record company should select the singles and spoke up. "I said, 'If you don't release that song, it's off the record. And I will give that thing to Quincy for Michael and retire.' So they released it and it was the most successful song I've ever written and probably very influential...It had that funky kind of dance rhythm that really hadn't been done before."

Rufus followed "Ain't Nobody" with their final R&B chart single, "One Million Kisses," which peaked at number 37, while Khan continued her success with another Number One hit [see 395—"I Feel for You"].

379

ALL NIGHT LONG (ALL NIGHT)

Lionel Richie

MOTOWN 1698
WRITER: LIONEL RICHIE
PRODUCERS: LIONEL RICHIE, JAMES ANTHONY CARMICHAEL
October 22, 1983 (7 weeks)

It wasn't difficult to see that Lionel Richie and the Commodores were coming to a parting of the ways. It was Richie's songwriting that had propelled the group to the top of the charts, and the spotlight continued to shine brighter on him as he stepped away from the group to write and produce Kenny Rogers's "Lady" and a duet for himself and Diana Ross, the title tune from the soundtrack to *Endless Love*.

"Kenny Rogers just *sang* 'Lady,' " Lionel said in 1982. "I just wrote it and stayed over in the wings. [With] 'Endless Love,' I was in front of 361 million people at the Oscars, singing live, *close-up*...after that evening, life changed."

A group meeting was held and the issue finally resolved: Richie would leave the Commodores and pursue his own career. Over a nine-month period, Lionel recorded his first solo album for Motown. Although he didn't achieve any R&B Number One singles from that album, he did reach the top 10 three times: "Truly" was number two for an amazing nine weeks; "You Are" was number two for three weeks, and "My Love" peaked at number six.

A year later, Lionel explored new territory on his second solo effort, *Can't Slow Down*. The first single was a joyous celebration with Caribbean influences and the sounds of partying. Paul Sexton of *Record Mirror* asked Richie about the words in "All Night Long (All Night)." Discussing the refrain, "Tom bo li de say di moi ya, yeah, jambo, jumbo," Richie said, "If you go back and try to find out what it means, it's like most of [Bob] Marley's chants, they don't really mean anything, but you know what they mean—you know what I'm saying? It's an old Jamaican chant."

Richie explained in *USA Today* how he perfected the pronunciation of the Jamaican words: "I was worried about getting the right words and about pronouncing them right. My wife's gynecologist is Jamaican, so for a week I was after him. Finally he said, 'Look, Lionel, I'm right in the middle of an appointment, can we talk later?' "

"All Night Long (All Night)" was recorded at Ocean Way Studios on Sunset Boulevard in Hollywood. Richie and Greg Phillinganes were credited with playing synthesizers. Abraham Laboriel was on

Lionel Richie

bass guitar, Darrell Jones and Tim May played guitars, John Robinson was behind the drums, and Paulinho da Costa was responsible for percussion. Background vocals were sung by Richie along with Deborah Thomas, Richard Marx (almost four years before he had his first pop hit, "Don't Mean Nothing"), David Cochrane, Kin Vassy, Calvin Harris, and James Anthony Carmichael. Melinda Joyce Chatman provided vocal sound effects.

In early 1984, Richie was asked if he would perform at the closing ceremonies of the Olympic Games to be held in Los Angeles that summer. His televised appearance would be seen by more than 2.6 billion people in 120 countries. Richie didn't say yes right away—he consulted with his friend Kenny Rogers. When Lionel told David Wolper he would do it, the producer asked him to sing "All Night Long (All Night)." Richie was joined by 200 breakdancers and athletes from all over the globe for the spectacular number, as he sang an extended version of his Number One hit with a new verse written especially for the Olympics.

380

TIME WILL REVEAL

DeBarge

GORDY 1705
WRITERS: BUNNY DEBARGE, ELDRA DEBARGE
PRODUCER: ELDRA DEBARGE
December 10, 1983 (5 weeks)

Jermaine Jackson and his wife, Hazel Gordy Jackson, were in an elevator in the Hollywood office building that is home to Motown Records when they met two musicians who wanted to sign with the label. Greg Williams and Jody Sims handed their tape to the Jacksons, and the next day Jermaine called to offer their group First Class a deal. The agreement was finalized in the hospital where Hazel gave birth to the couple's first son, Jermaine Jr. In May of 1977, the group was signed to Motown and their name was changed to Switch.

Bobby and Tommy DeBarge, two siblings from a Grand Rapids, Michigan, family of 10 children, were part of Switch. Robert and Etterlene DeBarge's other children were musical, too, and Bobby helped five of them get their start in the business. "It was always his dream to have a family group," says El DeBarge. "So he introduced us to Jermaine, knowing that Jermaine could get us to the right people."

El, Mark, James, Randy, and their sister Bunny signed with Motown in 1982. The first DeBarge single, "Stop! Don't Tease Me," only reached number 46, but they struck pay dirt with their next two singles, "I Like It" (number two for four weeks) and "All This Love" (number five).

The first single from their second album was "Time Will Reveal." "I had written that song before 'All This Love' and I had never finished it," says El. "Like a lot of my songs, it's timeless. Sometimes I'll write one verse to a song, leave it alone for about four or five years, and the Lord won't give me the rest of the song until it's ready. And by the time we had finished our first album and were ready for a second album, somehow I was able to complete that song. I guess it was its time."

El explains his sister's contribution to the song: "Bunny I used a lot to help me bring my ideas home. She would put on a lot of finishing touches. Sometimes she didn't do anything but give me two words. She always had a major contribution, even if it was only two words. And so I would always make sure that people knew. I would put her name on so people knew she made a great contribution."

El wrote "Time Will Reveal" in his usual way, sitting at a piano. "The title just came to me. The first words that actually came to me were, 'What can I do to make you feel secure?' and nothing else. I sat on that and said, 'This must be what the song's going to be about.' Later on, the Lord just gave it to me. I hadn't had that experience with anybody, but I felt that somebody out there needed to hear that. I needed to tell someone a story."

El put the track together himself. "The group always depended on me to put all the music together," he explains. "My family does play instruments, but they would bring all the songs to me and have me arrange them." El followed his heart with the track. "I made sure everything I did from the verse to the bridge to the hook kept on feeling good. If I felt any dead spot, I would have to sit and think. I didn't want to start off good and then the next part I go to be boring. So I made sure the song stayed interesting from beginning to end."

It took El two weeks to finish the vocal. "I had to live with it and feel it. I'd sing it and take a break from it for a few days and go back to it." He took care of his voice by drinking a lot of tea, without sugar or honey. "When you sing in the studio, honey tends to coat your throat and soothe it and you'll oversing something because you don't feel the strain. And the next day, you'll feel worse off. So I would drink tea, straight up with no sugar, and try to concentrate."

381

JOANNA

Kool & the Gang

DE-LITE 829
WRITERS: CHARLES SMITH,
JAMES TAYLOR, KOOL & THE GANG
PRODUCERS: RONALD BELL, JIM BONNEFOND,
KOOL & THE GANG
January 14, 1984 (2 weeks)

Above all, Kool & the Gang were a *working* band. And in the fall of 1983, they were scheduled to play three nights at New York's Radio City Music Hall. It was just days before the release of their *In the Heart* album.

"Either 'In the Heart' or 'Straight Ahead' was going to be the first single from the album," explains veteran Gang associate Cleveland Brown. "They were the lead track on side one and side two, respectively."

In rehearsal, guitarist Charles Smith wanted to try out "Joanna," one of his songs from the album. "It went so well, the group decided to fit it into the show," says Brown. "This was a pretty big experiment, since it was Kool & the Gang policy never to play an untested song onstage.

"Well, the Radio City crowd got so frenzied by the chorus and horn break—people jumping up and down as if it were a hit anthem—that the group was taken by surprise. They were looking at each other, wondering what was up. But they tried it again the next night, and the next. And I remember Khalis [Bayyan] came backstage and said, 'They went berserk! I guess it's the first single.' "

Recorded at the House of Music in West Orange, New Jersey, and released in November 1983, "Joanna" cruised up the *Billboard* R&B and pop charts as the year turned. Later, it was certified gold.

The song was "a natural," observes Khalis Bayyan, the Gang's music director and brother of leader Robert "Kool" Bell. "It just shone and sparkled, even during the demo stages. When Charles brought it to us, it was called 'Dear Mom.' I suggested he change a few chords. He came in the next day with the foundation for a good song."

And, he says, they wanted to have a "name" song like Toto's "Rosanna," a huge hit the previous year. Lending it added sparkle was: the trombone solo by Clifford Adams, who had joined the band in 1976. "We used tenor sax solos all the time, so this was different," comments Bayyan.

In the Heart was different, too: the first Kool & the Gang album since 1979 without producer Eumir Deodato, who was a key player in their commercial renaissance [see 320—"Ladies Night"]. "We worked by committee this time," Robert "Kool" Bell said when the album was issued. "It's hard for 10 people to come to a decision together, but we managed remarkably well. My brother, Ronald Bell, headed the committee and he helped us come to a sound we were all happy with."

Jim Bonnefond assumed Deodato's duties, co-producing with Ronald (Khalis) and the rest of the band. He had engineered all the albums at the House of Music since *Ladies Night*, and knew the musicians' skills and shortcomings. In particular, he pays tribute to Bayyan's direction and focus, calling him "very fluent" musically. "If anything," suggests Bonnefond, "I just loosened up the sound a little bit."

Patti LaBelle

382

IF ONLY YOU KNEW

Patti LaBelle

PHILADELPHIA INTERNATIONAL 04248
WRITERS: CYNTHIA BIGGS, KENNY GAMBLE, DEXTER WANSEL
PRODUCERS: KENNY GAMBLE, DEXTER WANSEL
January 28, 1984 (4 weeks)

Dexter Wansel was 12 years old when he got a job as a "go-fer" at the Uptown Theater in Philadelphia. For five years, he went for sandwiches and coffee or ran to the laundry to pick up clothes for the artists who played the theater—people like Martha Reeves, Stevie Wonder, and Patti LaBelle.

Wansel and LaBelle were reunited years later when she signed with Philadelphia International to record a solo album and Wansel was working for Kenny Gamble and Leon Huff as a writer/producer. After the breakup of Labelle [see 196—"Lady Marmalade"], Patti recorded several albums for Epic without achieving any major hits. Moving to Philadelphia International Records made sense for the hometown girl. "When I left Epic I had a lot of decisions to make regarding my career. I decided that what I really want most is a hit record, and I believe Kenny and Leon can deliver that for me," she said in *Billboard*. "I actually grew up with Kenny. When he became successful he asked me to come to PIR. But I wasn't ready...I decided that now is the time."

Wansel connected with the Philly duo in 1975, when he was playing in a band called Yellow Sunshine that included guitarist Roland Chambers, a regular player on many Philadelphia sessions. Soon after they met, Gamble asked Wansel if he had written any songs that MFSB could record. "I played him something and he liked it, and that's when it started," Wansel recalls.

The first Wansel song that Patti recorded was intended for someone else. "I had written a song for Jackson Browne called 'Shoot Him on Sight.' I had just finished demoing it up to send out to him and Patti said, 'Why can't I sing that? I want a rock and roll song like that.' " Patti recorded it for her first Philadelphia International album, *The Spirit's in It*, released in 1981. *I'm in Love Again*, released in 1984, contained another Wansel song, "If Only You Knew," co-written with Cynthia Biggs and Kenny Gamble.

"I had written all the music—all I had was melody and music," says Wansel. "When I played it for Cynthia Biggs, she came up with the idea of 'If Only You Knew.' " The song was almost complete when Wansel and Biggs had a difference of opinion over a couple of lines. Unable to settle it themselves, they approached Gamble, who agreed to listen to what they had written. He came up with a suggestion that worked. "That was his contribution as a writer, helping us to complete and realize the song," says Wansel.

Gamble said the song would be good for Patti. "She thought it was beautiful," says Wansel. "I didn't really think too much of the song...it wasn't my favorite...but she loved it from the very beginning and saw the potential, that there were a lot of lonely people out there who loved other people and didn't really know how to say it. She felt that she could say it for them."

Wansel says that Patti is "a producer's dream come true." He produced the song with Gamble, recording the rhythm track with him. Then Wansel supervised the recording of the lead vocals, Gamble did the backgrounds and the strings, and Wansel mixed it. Patti did six takes on the lead vocals and she and Wansel couldn't decide which one they liked best. "There were some takes where she was mulching the words a little bit. When she used to sing with Labelle, there were a lot of words you couldn't quite understand, even on 'Lady Marmalade.' I said, 'Patti, when you're smiling and singing, it seems that the words come out so clear.' So I asked her to smile when she sang a couple of takes, which she did and the words came out clear as a bell. So we mixed some of the better performances from some of the other takes together with those two takes to make one."

383

ENCORE

Cheryl Lynn

COLUMBIA 04256
WRITERS: TERRY LEWIS, JAMES HARRIS III
PRODUCERS: CHERYL LYNN,
TERRY LEWIS, JAMES HARRIS III
February 25, 1984 (1 week)

Jimmy Jam and Terry Lewis were the keyboardist and bass player for the Time [see 571—"Jerk Out"], a band from Minneapolis that found a mentor in Prince. He helped them secure a record contract with the same label he was signed to, Warner Brothers, and took artistic control of the group. Jam and Lewis were late for a gig one night because they were delayed by a snowstorm in Atlanta, where they were producing a session for the S.O.S. Band [see 331—"Take Your Time (Do It Right)"], an offense for which Prince fined Jam and Lewis $900 each and, a few days later, fired them. They were devastated—not so much at the loss of money and fame, but at the thought of not working with their friends in the Time anymore. It also affected their attitude about producing other artists. While they were touring with the Time, it was something to do for fun. Forced out on their own, they had to take it more seriously.

Jam and Lewis were still in the Time when they first met Cheryl Lynn. They were on tour with the group, appearing in Long Beach, California, when they took time out to meet the woman who had scored a Number One hit with "Got to Be Real" [see 304]. "I don't think they were supposed to be there," Cheryl Lynn remembers. "I think they snuck in from doing the show with Prince that night."

Jimmy recalls that evening, too. "We tried to come up with a song on the spot in the studio. That didn't work out because we were trying to do double duty. So we told her when we got the next break in the tour, we would come back to Los Angeles and try to come up with a song for her."

During their next break, they followed through on their promise. "It started out as just a drum machine," Jimmy recalls. "Some songs we write on the piano and the chords come first. That was a song where the beat actually came first. We had an apartment in L.A. and we were sitting around with a drum machine and came up with this funky beat. We were trying to come up with a beat that was so funky that even if we didn't put music to it, it would still be cool."

Cheryl Lynn thought the track, called "Encore," was "really special—it had a nice dance groove. By that time, I was known as 'the club person' or 'the dance person.' So they were trying to bring me a strong R&B groove." She enjoyed working with Jam and Lewis, just as she had enjoyed working with David Paich on her first Number One song. "They allowed me to be me," she says. "They give you the ground work, the foundation that you need to walk on and then they let you build from there and create or do whatever it is you want."

"Encore" wasn't the first single released. "[Label executive] Larkin Arnold liked this other song," says Cheryl Lynn. It was called "Preppie." "It's much more pop-oriented than 'Encore,' " she says. "And me being a black artist, I definitely have to go up the urban chart before you can think about crossing over. So the song was excellent but it wasn't accepted on the urban charts. I think it would have been a huge hit on the pop charts. It wasn't getting the response from radio when we initially put it out...so we didn't wait on it. We pulled it immediately...What we needed was the strong urban hit, which was 'Encore.' "

"Preppie" pooped out at number 85 on the *Billboard* R&B chart. " 'Encore' gave Jimmy and Terry their very first Number One R&B [hit]," Cheryl Lynn says proudly. "I've been fortunate enough to not necessarily say, 'I'm going with the big, big guys.' A lot of times the people that I was working with, this was their beginning...but there was something we had to offer each other then...Their talent was there."

384

SOMEBODY'S WATCHING ME

Rockwell

MOTOWN 1702
WRITER: ROCKWELL
PRODUCERS: CURTIS ANTHONY NOLEN, ROCKWELL
March 3, 1984 (5 weeks)

Kennedy Gordy couldn't get anyone at his publishing company interested in a song he had written. Curtis Anthony Nolen, a staff writer at Jobete, remembers when Gordy, the son of company founder Berry Gordy, dropped by one of the weekly staff meetings: "He wanted to present a song. No one in the meeting was interested in the song at all. No one wanted to hear it."

Nolen, who was also a staff producer for Motown, listened to Gordy's demo. "He presented it to me in its roughest form. He had a small sideways arrangement of it on a little four-track. He sang the lyrics to me over the demo. That's the way he presented the song to everybody. No one could hear it. I was the only person who could hear the hit potential in the song."

Nolen maintained a recording studio at his home and invited Gordy to work on the track there. Nolen

Rockwell

suggested they rearrange the music and record it again. Armed with a new demo, they might be able to coax enough financing from Motown to get Gordy into a professional studio.

Nolen wasn't just trying to be kind—he really believed the song about paranoia could be a hit. "It was the year of big brother [1984]. I knew the lyrics were timely."

Nolen and Gordy managed to get financing from Motown to go into a real studio. They recorded the song with Jim Felber on bass synthesizer, Nolen on all of the other synthesizers, and Gordy doing the drum programming.

They realized they needed to add another voice on the chorus. A famous voice, if they could get one. "We figured, 'Who's the most famous person in the world right now? Michael Jackson.' " How could they get through to Michael? Easy: His brother Jermaine was married to Kennedy's sister Hazel.

Nolen and Gordy took a 24-track demo to Michael at his parents' home in Encino. Kennedy was singing lead and Curtis put his voice in the places he wanted Michael to add vocals. "He loved it," says Nolen. "He called his family downstairs to hear it." They scheduled studio time for Michael, but he didn't show up. The producers discovered he was at an amusement park with Donny Osmond that night. An apologetic Michael rescheduled for the following weekend, and Nolen and Gordy picked him up themselves and drove him to the studio. "He heard the song. He said, 'Turn on the tape. Turn off the lights and let's go for it,' " Nolen remembers. "It took him all of an hour and 15 minutes to complete his portion of the song."

Having Michael Jackson on the track wasn't the end of the story. "We were still in the prove-ourselves-to-Mr. Gordy mode," says Nolen. He and Kennedy drove to Berry's Bel Air mansion one weekend morning while he was entertaining Chuck Connors and other celebrities at breakfast. The producers handed the tape to Berry and left the room. They heard cheering and knew they were home free. "Then [Berry] told us, 'Don't expect too much R&B play out of this. It'll probably go pretty good on the pop chart.' I figured, little does he know, I designed this to be a Number One record all the way around. So here's the Chairman of the Board of Motown telling us we're not going to get that much R&B play. Well, it winds up being Number One R&B."

The single wasn't issued under Kennedy's real name. They were looking for something like 'Prince' when they were inspired by a Norman Rockwell photograph. They thought about spelling it "Roqwell," but figured Kennedy knew how to "rock well" and left it at that.

385

SHE'S STRANGE

Cameo

ATLANTA ARTISTS 818 384
WRITERS: LARRY BLACKMON,
CHARLIE SINGLETON, NATHAN LEFTENANT,
TOMI JENKINS
PRODUCER: LARRY BLACKMON
April 7, 1984 (4 weeks)

Larry Blackmon grew up not far from the Apollo Theater in Harlem. He was just four years old when his aunt began taking him to see the great stars of the day, including Sam Cooke, Jackie Wilson, and James Brown. "I don't know if I was taken with the excitement of it all, the lights, the precision of the performance, the organization, or the manipulation of the audience...I dreamed a great deal and I think that planted the seeds. It wasn't until I was 14 that I started lip synching songs at home. In junior high school I joined the band and learned to play drums formally. I started my first band at the age of 14, an all-acoustic band [with] drums and horns. We did shows for the Board of Education around different schools."

In the early '70s, Blackmon played drums on sessions for groups like Black Ivory ("Don't Turn Around," "You and I") before joining a group called East Coast. That outfit evolved into the New York City Players. They recorded a disco song called "Find My Way" that found its way to Neil Bogart at Casablanca, who "happened to like the song and signed the group, not knowing we were a black group," says Blackmon. Bogart released the single on Chocolate City, a label helmed by Cecil Holmes. After it bombed, Holmes came to New York to hear new material by the band, rechristened Cameo, and released a new single, "Rigor Mortis," at the end of 1976.

Blackmon was attending Juilliard and working part-time in a clothing store. He was fitting a customer one day when WBLS played "Rigor Mortis." "I was so elated," he recalls, "I asked one of my coworkers to take over and I went down to my locker and cleaned it out and never looked back."

Cameo had 18 chart singles on Chocolate City through 1982. The following year, Blackmon formed his own label, Atlanta Artists, distributed by Polygram. The third Cameo single released on the new label was "She's Strange."

Blackmon says that tune was "a very unique song for the time because rap had just started to come in very strong and be accepted by a wide commercial market. 'She's Strange' was a thinking man's rap...The whole Cameo concept dealt with a character and that character was Larry Blackmon. A lot of the episodes and escapades of this particular character made it easy to write for that character." Blackmon describes the character: "I took a little from the volatile behavior of some actors and their characters, such as Al Pacino, the coolness of a Marlon Brando, the intelligence and persona of a Sidney Poitier...so it gave a cutting edge to this character."

Blackmon had a 16-track studio in the basement of his Atlanta home and wrote "She's Strange" around the time he was experimenting with playing the drums and bass himself. "I felt that I had a good musical track and I wanted to write about something I could relate to. I use a lot of my past experiences and then I imagine and create a scenario from the experiences of others as well as an interesting ending."

Blackmon didn't play all of the instruments on the actual track. "What I would do is use musicians that we had working with us because they were better musicians than I. And it left room for me to do other things in the way of production that I enjoyed a great deal."

386

HELLO

Lionel Richie

MOTOWN 1722
WRITER: LIONEL RICHIE
PRODUCERS: LIONEL RICHIE,
JAMES ANTHONY CARMICHAEL
May 5, 1984 (3 weeks)

Lionel Richie wrote "Hello" for his first solo album, but rejected the ballad over the protests of his wife Brenda and the assistant to producer James Carmichael, Rita Leigh. When Lionel said he was also thinking of passing over "Hello" for his second album, *Can't Slow Down*, Brenda insisted it be included.

Richie developed into a ballad writer of the first order during his days with the Commodores. He told a reporter in 1982 how he came to specialize in sweet, romantic songs: "If you can imagine a Commodores album session and every guy brings in 10 songs. Somebody's got to be first and somebody's got to be last. Over the years, I made myself the last person to present the songs. Normally, everybody would bring in an up-tempo song and I'd always say, 'This album needs one slow song.' That's how slow songs came into play."

"Hello," the third single from *Can't Slow Down*, was recorded at Ocean Way Studios in Hollywood. Richie did the vocal arrangements and played piano. Reginald "Sonny" Burke was on the Fender Rhodes, Michael Boddicker programmed the synthesizers, Tim May played acoustic guitar, Darrell Jones provided electric guitar, Paul Leim handled the drums, Joe Chemay was featured on bass guitar and Louie Shelton was also given credit for his guitar work.

While Richie's string of hit singles didn't need much assistance from extraneous sources, the video for "Hello" surely boosted its chart fortunes. Lionel's manager Ken Kragen contacted television commercial wizard Bob Giraldi, the director of videos for Michael Jackson's "Beat It," Pat Benatar's "Love Is a Battlefield," and Paul McCartney and Michael Jackson's "Say, Say, Say." Giraldi had previously directed the video of "Running With the Night" for Richie, which had whetted the artist's desire to act.

It was fitting then that he played a drama teacher, Mr. Reynolds, in the video for "Hello." He falls in love with a student he sees in class, but can only love her from a distance. When he drops in on a sculpture class, he discovers his secret love has sculpted a bust of him as she sees him—in her mind's eye, for she is blind.

While "Hello" was Richie's only Number One single of 1984, he did collect four top 10 singles that year. There were other financial rewards in 1984: Richie signed what was reputed to be an $8.5 million contract with the soft drink corporation Pepsico. As his part of the deal, Lionel wrote songs and performed in TV commercials for Pepsi. When the deal was negotiated, the company promised to join the artist in making charitable contributions. As Richie said in *Ebony*, "I want to make more than music. I want to make statements and I also want to make changes in areas such as minority education. For a long time, I have had an interest in talented kids with no opportunities. Unlike a lot of corporations that merely pay lip service, Pepsi has signed on the dotted line to do something about it."

387

DON'T WASTE YOUR TIME

Yarbrough & Peoples

TOTAL EXPERIENCE 2400
WRITER: JONAH ELLIS
PRODUCER: JONAH ELLIS
May 26, 1984 (1 week)

When Jonah Ellis was a 19-year-old college student, he returned home to Washington, D.C., and discovered his girlfriend had been stepping out on him. "I caught her messing around with this other guy. I think she was sad that she had gotten caught like that, and there was nothing she could do about it at that point. She cared about me and I cared about her...It was unfortunate. We broke up." A mutual friend from high school had broken the bad news to Jonah, and after the breakup, he started dating her. Years later, that collegiate love triangle inspired Jonah to write "Don't Waste Your Time" for Yarbrough & Peoples.

"We couldn't get Cavin [Yarbrough's] voice on it," says the producer. Ellis was at a Beverly Hills club one night when a friend made some suggestions of how to change the song. "He didn't give me the exact words, but it kind of rung a bell." Ellis worked on some new vocal parts for Cavin and Alisa Peoples and went back into the studio. "We didn't use a live drummer. I always thought it wasn't as big a song as 'Don't Stop the Music' [because] it didn't have the same feel to me ...We couldn't get the up beat as strongly as in 'Don't Stop the Music.' The bass drum kick pattern was the same, but the way the drum machine was built at that time...I couldn't get the strong beat on the up beat. I put down a click track with the drum track in case we wanted to come back and lock up something else. And then I used the click track to trigger a synthesizer."

Lonnie Simmons, the head of Total Experience, suggested that Ellis take the track to Philadelphia and have Nick Martinelli and David Todd mix it. "We had gone to 48 tracks on this particular song," says Ellis. "They brought up all of these tracks we weren't even planning to use. They listened to the mix I had done in Los Angeles and asked me what I wanted in. I made some suggestions but they put in some things I wouldn't have put in, like the click track. They brought up whatever sounded good to them, because they were used to it in the clubs, whatever they thought was hip at the time...but it worked."

Ellis's opinion of Yarbrough & Peoples remains strong. "I thought they were really great. [Alisa's] voice wasn't that high, but she had sort of a Gladys Knight–type voice, more low and very rich and stunning. Cavin, his voice was kind of high, and I think that's what sometimes caused a problem trying to get them to match. A lot of times you hear a girl singing and she sings a part on top of a guy singing and it's not too much of a problem. But in this case, her voice was lower than his."

Ellis also enjoyed working with the couple on a personal level. "They were very highly spiritual—I mean people with good hearts, especially [Alisa]. Her father was a preacher in Texas."

Success had its ups and downs for the couple who met through their piano teacher when they were children. "It was very scary for Cavin and myself," Peoples said in *Blues & Soul*. "We underwent some drastic changes in a very short time...But for all of that, I really wouldn't change a thing about the way it's all gone down."

Yarbrough & Peoples

388

LET'S HEAR IT FOR THE BOY

Deniece Williams

COLUMBIA 04417
WRITERS: TOM SNOW, DEAN PITCHFORD
PRODUCER: GEORGE DUKE
June 2, 1984 (3 weeks)

Dean Pitchford and Tom Snow wrote a song to underscore the scene in the motion picture *Footloose* where Kevin Bacon teaches an awkward Christopher Penn how to dance. Everyone connected with the film loved the tune, but as production continued, they heard it over and over and over again. "Like any hit song played for eight months, we all grew tired of it and wanted new blood," says Pitchford. "I went back to Tom Snow and said, 'Tom, we have to do it again.' One night I went to his house for dinner and we worked late. I said I wanted something uplifting, a girl singing about how good her boyfriend is, even though he trips over his own two feet, and she gets to the point where she says, 'Let's hear it for the boy!' "

As soon as they came up with that phrase, the two writers knew they had something and worked late into the night completing the song. Pitchford invited Deniece Williams and producer George Duke to consider recording the number for the movie. "We heard the song and liked it," Deniece remembers. "Everyone else had seen the film. They explained the storyline to me, and we did it."

Deniece Williams

Pitchford explains why the first recording session in Los Angeles didn't work out: "Deniece sang it very girlish. I think she took the 'boy' very seriously. I called her and said, 'Deniece, this is not a girl, this is a woman!' " But Deniece was now back in New York. She agreed to return to Los Angeles and record the song again. With a deadline approaching, she was rushed from the airport to the studio without even stopping to pick up her luggage. It was 11:00 P.M. on the West Coast, but Deniece was still on Eastern time. Joining her in the studio were Paul Jackson on guitar, Paulinho da Costa on percussion, and producer Duke programming the Linn drums and synthesizers. Songwriters George Merrill and Shannon Rubicam [see 422—"How Will I Know"] provided backing vocals. "In 20 minutes, she recut it brilliantly," Pitchford says. "When she finished we all looked at each other, and knew this is what it was meant to be."

Deniece was nervous when she attended the *Footloose* premiere. "I sat there the whole time on pins and needles. By the time they got to my song, I thought it was incredible. If I had come to the film without the music in and they asked me what segment I wanted my song to be in, I would have chosen that segment."

Deniece relates to the film's premise of a rural, midwestern town that bans dancing. "I'm a product of that same type of environment. *Footloose* is really a story closely knitted to my growing up in Indiana in a very religious environment and wanting to do something different. I had had a couple of successes and still didn't know whether or not I wanted this career. It came from thinking I was doing something wrong against God." Deniece finally realized that "He had given me this talent to do exactly what I'm doing. It's a gift, and I think it would be worse if I weren't using it."

389

LOVELITE

O'Bryan

CAPITOL 5329
WRITERS: O'BRYAN BURNETTE II, DON CORNELIUS
PRODUCERS: O'BRYAN, FRIENDSHIP PRODUCERS
June 23, 1984 (1 week)

For two decades after October 2, 1971, almost every artist who topped the *Billboard* charts owed a debt of gratitude to Don Cornelius, the one-time insurance salesman and "swing man" at radio station WVON in Chicago. That's because almost every one of them appeared on *Soul Train*, the trend-setting television showcase for black music—and dancing—that Cornelius launched into syndication on that date.

In the case of O'Bryan Burnett II from Sneads Ferry, North Carolina, the gratitude may have been greater. Discovered by Philadelphia producer Ron ("Have Mercy") Kersey, the young singer was introduced to Cornelius in 1982 and signed to a management contract within a couple of weeks.

With the *Soul Train* driver to guide him, O'Bryan was on track. His debut album for Capitol Records, *Doin' Alright*, yielded a top five single, "The Gigolo," and a chart-riding remake of the Four Tops' "Still Water (Love)."

Crediting his mentor, O'Bryan told *Blues & Soul*, "[Don] has had a great deal of influence on me and he's constantly behind me in everything I try to do. He also stays on top of me and that's very important, because otherwise I might tend to relax."

Cornelius went further on the singer's second LP, co-writing "Soul Train's A-Comin' " *and* featuring the song as the theme to his hour of TV soul power. (An earlier signature tune for the show, "TSOP (The Sound Of Philadelphia)" by MFSB featuring the Three Degrees, was an R&B and pop smash in 1974.)

O'Bryan

"Soul Train's A-Comin' " wasn't issued as a single, but two other tracks from the album, "I'm Freaky" and a version of Stevie Wonder's "You And I," were top 20 hits during 1983.

The following year, O'Bryan turned on "Lovelite" as the first single from his new Capitol LP, *Be My Lover*. "The biggest difference between this album and the one before is in the actual sound of the music," O'Bryan explained at the time. "It represents a big step forward for me. We used a lot more synthesizers this time.

"I played most keyboard parts and came up with a wide variety of sounds—for example, the horns, the bass and some of the guitar licks were actually done on a synthesizer. I played acoustic piano separately, of course, and I had to call in someone to play the acoustic guitar. But it's very much my own work and of that I'm proud."

The synthesizer-heavy "Lovelite" also brings to mind the bright funk of Leon Sylvers's work at Solar Records—the label co-founded by Don Cornelius with his onetime talent coordinator at *Soul Train*, Dick Griffey.

O'Bryan's style resembled Prince's, too, he admitted. "But you know that vocal sound is my natural voice. In fact, until we moved to California from the East, that was the way I always used to sing."

390

WHEN DOVES CRY

Prince

WARNER BROS. 29286
WRITER: PRINCE
PRODUCER: PRINCE
June 30, 1984 (8 weeks)

"It was fabulous to watch him work," says an admiring Peggy McCreary, Prince's engineer on his second Number One and most successful R&B chart hit, "When Doves Cry," the lead-off single from the soundtrack of *Purple Rain*.

"He was a genius and it was amazing to watch this kind of talent," she enthuses. "He was real spontaneous and sometimes he'd dream about a song and he'd call up and come in and we'd do it start to finish. It didn't matter how long it took. Sometimes he'd go home and he'd leave it up on the board and come back but most of the time it was a one-day thing and then he might come back and remix it. Or however long it took, that's how long we were there.

"The thing I remember about 'When Doves Cry' is that we cut it and when he was playing with it before he did the vocals, he took the bass out and he said, 'There's nobody that's going to have the guts to do this.' And he was smiling from ear to ear. He felt this was the best and he knew he had a hit song...so he decided to do something really daring. That's what Prince was all about."

McCreary, a former waitress at the Roxy on the Sunset Strip, loved working around music and became interested in setting up live sound at the nightclub during the day. That led to a job as a gofer at Sunset Sound in Hollywood; she says it was the first time they had hired a woman, and they did so reluctantly at that. Three months later she was asked to work on a Kris Kristofferson project and she eventually quit her job at the Roxy to engineer full-time.

She remembers the first time she met Prince. He had been working at another studio but the equipment broke down and they sent him over to Sunset Sound. "The girl who worked the desk was really scared for me, because it was a Saturday, which meant no one was around. I expected this big, huge, Barry White–kind of guy because they said, 'He writes these really sexy songs' and I thought, 'Oh, no!' I went in there and here was this really polite, very shy man. He'd mumble something and I'd say, 'Excuse me? You're going to have to talk to me, because I don't understand what you want at all.' So we started working together and then he came back and always requested me, and it just became a relationship."

A *working* relationship. Peggy is now married to David Leonard, who was her boyfriend during the time of "When Doves Cry." Leonard also worked on the song. "Prince wanted me to cut the master and I was really nervous, so I asked David if he'd come in to help me. So David and I worked as a team on *Purple Rain.* That movie just kind of came about. Maybe Prince knew what was going on, but we certainly weren't clued in until later."

McCreary says she would work with Prince for months at a time on various projects, including Vanity 6, the Time, and Sheila E. "All of a sudden he'd just leave. He'd come to work one day and he was sick of L.A. and he'd go back to Minneapolis. And he'd just reappear the same way."

The engineer, nicknamed Peggy Mac by Prince, recalls how the artist usually worked: "He would run through [a song] with just a piano and a vocal. And sometimes he'd do the drums and then the bass...The room was always set up and you had to be ready to do whatever he felt like doing. It was real spontaneous. You had to be there with him, which was the hard part and the exciting part. But when you're exhausted, it's hard to be excited. It was the longest I ever worked with anybody in my life. I worked around the clock, 24 hours. He said sometimes the only reason he went home was so I could sleep."

391

GHOSTBUSTERS

Ray Parker Jr.

ARISTA 9212
WRITER: RAY PARKER JR.
PRODUCER: RAY PARKER JR.
August 25, 1984 (2 weeks)

Imagine someone just asked you to write the title song of an upcoming big-budget movie starring Bill Murray, Dan Aykroyd, Harold Ramis, and Ernie Hudson. The only problem is, you have to find a word that rhymes with "Ghostbusters."

"If you were starting from scratch and somebody said, 'We want you to include the name "Ghostbusters" a lot of times,' it was a horrible word," says the man who wrote the title song, Ray Parker Jr.

"It really started out to be just a track in a movie," he explains. "There were not going to be any records or videos or albums or any of the rest of it. [Director] Ivan Reitman heard the song and thought it should be a record and I thought he was a little bit crazy, because I never really sang about a ghost. I always sang about girls. I heard the song—it sounded nice to me. I had no idea that it was going to blow up as big as it did."

It was big all right, as big as the Sta-Puff Marshmallow Man. Parker recalls how the song was recorded: "It happened very fast because I didn't have any time. In order to get paid, if I didn't have it in a few days, that was the end of that. They were going to use source music." Parker screened the film to get his creative juices flowing. "There was a part in the movie where they showed the four ghostbusters and they had the telephone number. It occurred to me that the word 'Ghostbuster' is such an awkward, uneasy name to put to music. And when I saw that part of the film, I knew to make it a commercial...that was the only way I could get it in the song, and I felt really silly saying the word 'Ghostbusters,' so I never said it. I got other people to say it. So not once in the song do I ever say it."

Parker details how he produced the prominent horn sound in the song: "That's one saxophone coupled with a guitar and a synthesizer. It sounds like a big brass section but it's only one saxophone. We got lucky there—I don't have any clue as to why it sounds like that. But it was just the right blend of a guitar, one synthesizer playing one note, and a saxophone. And for some reason, the wave forms made it sound large."

It was the sound of "Ghostbusters" that attracted the attention of Huey Lewis, who thought the song sounded too close to his own 1984 hit, "I Want a New Drug." Lewis said in *Rock Express,* "We had a legitimate complaint and that was settled out of court—very handsomely, I might add...When I heard the song, I thought, well that's a neat rip-off, but it was kinda cool." Huey's manager Bob Brown thought otherwise and initiated the legal action.

Parker had two more R&B chart singles on Arista after "Ghostbusters" went to Number One. He then signed with Geffen for one album, and subsequently moved to MCA. He was happiest on Arista, and returned to the label in 1993. "For me, [Arista label head] Clive Davis is my saving grace," says the artist. He introduced me to the record business...and it was a mistake to have ever left his label in the first place. But through strange negotiations and lack of communications and one of my best friends being at another record company, it was too late for me to turn back and I had to go to the other record company." Parker says Geffen wasn't that interested in R&B and MCA was too big of a machine. "The sensitive part of Arista is [that] Clive Davis really likes the songs. He likes the music."

As for *Ghostbusters II,* some were surprised that Parker wasn't asked to write a sequel to his Number One song. The big hit tune from the second film was Bobby Brown's "On Our Own" [see 531]. "With *Ghostbusters,* they never wanted to see me again," Parker laments. "To me, that's strange. [But] that's not strange in the record business."

392

CARIBBEAN QUEEN (NO MORE LOVE ON THE RUN)

Billy Ocean

JIVE 9199
WRITERS: KEITH DIAMOND, BILLY OCEAN
PRODUCER: KEITH DIAMOND
September 8, 1984 (4 weeks)

Billy Ocean first made a name in America with a 1976 pop hit on Ariola, "Love Really Hurts Without You," and a top 10 R&B and dance club hit, "Night (Feel Like Getting Down)," released on Epic in 1981. When Billy parted company with that label, his manager, Laurie Jay, introduced him to Clive Calder, head of Jive Records. "I liked the way he was speaking," Ocean says. "I liked the plans and ideas that he had."

It was Calder who teamed Billy with Keith Diamond. "They get up-and-coming talent coming through the record company all the time, and they look for budding talent," Billy explains. "They put different people together if they think you're suited to one another or you can bring out the best in each other. And I'm always open for any sort of experiments like that, because I find them very interesting."

Billy and Keith went to work in a small studio at Ocean's home in London. Keith played the piano while Billy worked out melodies. "You get a word here and a little melody here and you just keep going...All the initial stages of any song are based so much on inspiration."

Ocean and Diamond came up with a song called "European Queen." "It was the first time I'd been in the studio in three or four years," says Billy, who crossed the pond to record the song. "What really brought out the tempo to that song was going to America and using American musicians," he acknowledges. "There are brilliant musicians in America. It's almost like a nation of music...We can't say there aren't good musicians over here [in London] and good songwriters...but we're talking about individual talented musicians, like great drummers, great bass players, great guitarists, great piano players, great singers. The list is endless." Playing on the Diamond-produced tracks for the *Suddenly* album were Barry Eastmond on keyboards and synthesizers, Clarence "Blinky" Brice, Eddie Martinez, Vic Linton, and Geoff Whitehorn on guitars; Timmy Allen on bass; Tony Maroni on percussion; and Jeff Smith on sax. Ocean and Diamond programmed the Linn and Simmons drums.

It was Calder who suggested recording alternatives to "European Queen," featuring different geographic locations. A 12-inch single released in the U.K. included "African Queen" and "Caribbean Queen." Billy simply plugged in his vocals for the new versions. "I think if I had to sing the whole thing over again, I probably wouldn't have bothered," he says. "You dish out that first flow of inspiration, and sometimes it's very hard to do it again. Not in the sense of singing it live—I'm talking about when you record something, you want to hear it a certain way. And once you're happy and satisfied with that, it doesn't matter if you do it again, there'll always be something somewhere in there that you think, 'I wish I had that the way it was in the original.' "

When Jive released the single in America, they passed on "European Queen," which failed to catch on in Europe, in favor of "Caribbean Queen."

The decision proved wise; "Caribbean Queen (No More Love on the Run)" gave Billy his first Number One hit in America on the R&B chart as well as the pop chart.

393

LET'S GO CRAZY

Prince and the Revolution

WARNER BROS. 29216
WRITERS: PRINCE AND THE REVOLUTION
PRODUCERS: PRINCE AND THE REVOLUTION
October 6, 1984 (1 week)

In the days of *Purple Rain*, Prince had two methods for recording songs, according to Susan Rogers, one of his engineers at the time.

"He would either work all by himself and play all the instruments in the studio—that's how it was done most of the time—[or] occasionally he would work with his band. He always had a warehouse set up for rehearsals. Unless we were out on the road, the instruments were always set up...No isolation, no headphones, no nothing. It was just right smack in the middle of this warehouse with rust falling from the ceiling and a little piece of carpet on the floor. That was how we recorded 'Let's Go Crazy.' "

Rogers, originally hired to keep Prince's home studio equipment in good running order, found herself also working as an engineer—which suited her fine, because that's exactly what she wanted to do. She vividly remembers when Prince recorded "Let's Go Crazy," his second Number One single from the *Purple Rain* soundtrack.

"He had come down [to the warehouse] with the song already written and what he would do on these occasions is he would teach it to the band. Because his band members knew him and knew what he liked, it was pretty easy. He usually had the drum beat. Some of the band members came up with their own parts. Mark Brown was a very funky bass player. Once Prince taught him the basic part, Mark was free to expand on that if he wanted to. Wendy Melvoin and Lisa Coleman particularly had their own musical sensibility that was different from Prince's, which he liked very much." Wendy and Lisa were able to put their own stamp on some songs, according to Rogers, but not "Let's Go Crazy," which, Rogers says, "was more up-tempo, so they had their parts that they played. The fun part of that recording was Matt Fink doing that piano solo. There were a few different takes, but Prince gave Matt the basic idea and Matt, knowing Prince so well and knowing what he liked, got that solo on the third take and we kept replaying it over and over again, because it was just great to listen to."

Rogers recalls that Prince cut his lead vocal live. "I think all we overdubbed after that was when Prince put on a couple of additional guitar parts," she says. The sound of audience applause was also overdubbed for the opening concert scene in *Purple Rain* where Prince sings "Let's Go Crazy." Rogers says the songs were transferred to a quarter-inch playback machine called a Nagra. "When we shot those concert scenes at First Avenue, we would take the Nagra down there and that would provide the playback for the audience. And then in the movie, it's the album track with the audience added onto it."

Was Prince concerned about how the public would receive his film and the soundtrack? Rogers says that right after production on the movie was completed, Prince told her and some members of Vanity 6 about a dream he had the night before. "I remember Prince saying, 'I had a dream last night that *Purple Rain* came out and those two guys on TV, the fat guy and the skinny guy, were reviewing the movie and that fat guy was just tearing me up.' It was really funny because Siskel and Ebert actually liked the film a lot."

394

I JUST CALLED TO SAY I LOVE YOU

Stevie Wonder

MOTOWN 1745
WRITER: STEVIE WONDER
PRODUCER: STEVIE WONDER
October 13, 1984 (3 weeks)

"There are people who think Stevie Wonder's a villain," declares Lee Garrett, "and there are people who think I'm the villain. Really, there are no villains in this whole thing."

Songwriter and recording artist Garrett is discussing the legally entangled tale of "I Just Called to Say I Love You." The song became the biggest hit single of Wonder's career, with worldwide sales exceeding four million. It also sparked a $10 million lawsuit and a fuss with those Oscar folks, the Academy of Motion Picture Arts & Sciences.

Stevie Wonder

Garrett knows about Stevie Wonder—together, they authored a pair of Number One hits [see 91—"Signed, Sealed, Delivered, I'm Yours," 330—"Let's Get Serious"]. They had met years earlier at the Michigan School for the Blind, and their lives crisscrossed through the '60s and '70s.

"I Just Called to Say I Love You" started as a melody composed by Wonder, years before he penned the lyrics. He wrote those as the song was earmarked for use in the soundtrack of *The Woman in Red*, a 1984 comedy starring and directed by Gene Wilder.

Brought into the project by Dionne Warwick, Wonder put the music together in a fraction of the time he took for a "normal" studio album. When Motown president Jay Lasker first heard the material, he refused to release it. When Stevie later played him an additional song, "I Just Called to Say I Love You," Lasker relented.

Much of the soundtrack was recorded at Stevie's Wonderland studios in Los Angeles. On "I Just Called to Say I Love You," he played all the instruments, including vocoder, synthesizers, and drums.

Shipped as a single in August 1984, the song exploded to the peak of the pop and R&B charts within eight weeks. By contrast, *The Woman in Red* was a box office disappointment, but it did win Wonder an Academy Award for best original movie song that year.

Next came the lawsuit. Lee Garrett and another writer, Lloyd Chiate, claimed in October 1985 that Wonder's song had infringed one of theirs, "I Just Called to Say," authored seven years earlier. The pair sought $10 million in damages. In May 1986, however, Garrett pulled out of the lawsuit, apparently satisfied that no theft was involved. "We had agreed we had two songs with the same title," he says, "but they were nothing alike."

Wonder's assertion that his "I Just Called to Say I Love You" was written years before caused a temporary fuss under Oscar rules, which state that an eligible song must have been written specifically for a film, but the superstar got to keep his award anyway.

Garrett's friendship with him survived, too. "We're still cool," Lee says. "We haven't talked in a while, but I got a message the other day that I'd better call his ass, because it's been too long. People stuck wedges between us, but we always kind of laughed it off. Some of the things hurt, but we were man enough to admit they hurt, and dealt with it."

395

I FEEL FOR YOU

Chaka Khan

WARNER BROS. 29195
WRITER: PRINCE
PRODUCER: ARIF MARDIN
November 3, 1984 (3 weeks)

One of the most unforgettable introductions ever recorded must be Melle Mel's rap at the beginning of Chaka Khan's "I Feel for You." But Chaka Khan wasn't exactly thrilled with it: "I recorded the song one night and came back the next evening prepared to start on another track and Arif [Mardin] said he had a surprise for me. He played this guy repeating my name over and over again. I was so embarrassed. I thought it was horrible. And he said I have to trust him on this one, that he knew it would be a big hit. So I washed my hands of it and said, 'OK...go ahead.' "

Arif Mardin had produced Chaka's first two solo albums for Warner Brothers and had specific instructions from the label to head in a more commercial direction for the third. "They said, 'You're not listening to the pulse of America and the industry,' " Khan said in a 1984 *Billboard* interview. "So Arif and I had to make a conscious effort to do that. 'I Feel for You' is obviously a song that appeals to a lot of younger

Chaka Khan

kids. And the stuff Arif and I have been doing for the past five years hasn't. We've been Michelangelo-ing out. We've...been doing a lot of jazz and having a good time doing what we wanted to do. We didn't really have an ear tuned in to the rest of the world or the market. With this album, Warner Brothers did say, 'We'd like to sell some albums now, guys, if you don't mind.' " Khan says she consented because she was afraid if she said no, the label would insist on finding a different producer.

While looking for material, Mardin received a cassette of "I Feel for You" from Dale Kawashima at Prince's publishing company. Kawashima told the producer the song was from Prince's second album, but he thought it would be great for Chaka. "A lot of people didn't like that song," Arif says. "The only people who did were Chaka and me."

The track was cut in New York with Reggie Griffin handling the arrangements. Chaka "needed a little coaching...because she wanted to outdo Prince and be better than Prince," Mardin says. The producer's dream was that Prince would play guitar on the track and Stevie Wonder would add harmonica. "I had this scenario of a lot of different people being involved. Prince [had] schedule problems, couldn't do it; Stevie Wonder said yes." Mardin flew to Los Angeles to record Stevie and discovered the session was scheduled the same day as Marvin Gaye's funeral. "Sure enough, [Stevie] showed up; he's a professional, and he played beautifully. Then I said I really need a love rap on this. Chaka's brother and I were always joking...you've got two sisters and they sound like drumbeats: Chaka Khan/Chaka Khan, Taka Boom/Taka Boom." Mardin asked Griffin if he could find Melle Mel of Grandmaster Flash fame to record the words "Chaka Khan/Chaka Khan" like a drumbeat. Mardin told the arranger: "I don't want a regular rap, I want it very short, about eight lines." Mel recorded his lines at the Sugarhill Studios.

Mardin remembers how upset the singer was when she heard the intro. "She told me she never liked the idea of hearing her name on record. It was very alien to her, she had to get used to it." Mardin previewed the song for friends at parties. "The rap at one point was a centerpiece, in the middle...My engineer, Lou Hahn, [said], 'I think you should really put this earlier.' Then it became like a bookend."

In the end, "I Feel for You" cost around $30,000 to record—more expensive than any other track on the album, and more expensive than most individual songs in 1984. Chaka grew to like the introduction enough to include it in live appearances—her brother Mark Stevens or keyboard player Michael Duff substituted for Melle Mel—but still has one problem with the song. "It is difficult to live with because everyone does it to me. Today, they still come up with this opening rap and somehow think they're doing something vivid and real and fresh and cool and it's like, *'Really.'* "

396

COOL IT NOW

New Edition

MCA 52455
WRITERS: VINCENT BRANTLEY, RICK TIMAS
PRODUCERS: VINCENT BRANTLEY, RICK TIMAS
November 24, 1984 (1 week)

Vincent Brantley and Rick Timas had a song they thought would be great for MCA's new signing, the teenaged New Edition, but they couldn't get through to label vice president Jheryl Busby on the phone and were feeling frustrated. They went ahead and recorded "Cool It Now" with an older, unknown group, but the song didn't really fit them. Finding themselves back at square one, they were working late in their home studio in South Central Los Angeles when they decided to head to their local AM-PM to get some snacks. "It was about two in the morning," Brantley recalls. "We were riding down Crenshaw Boulevard and we spotted Jheryl Busby going in the opposite direction."

They made a sudden U-turn and followed the executive to a neighborhood chicken diner. "We pulled in right behind him and I jumped out of the car and called out his name," Brantley continues. "He was a little startled at first and then he recognized me." Brantley expressed his frustrations about trying

New Edition

to get in touch with Busby and told him about the song. "We had the tape right there...I began to sing the song over the tape while the cassette played. He liked the energy and he asked us to come by Ray Parker Jr.'s studio the next day to play the same song for [New Edition's] manager, Bill Dern."

Brantley and Timas arrived early and found New Edition in the studio recording "Mr. Telephone Man" [see 400]. The writers waited outside at the hardware store next to the studio, set their boom box on a washing machine, and played the song for Dern when he came out.

"He liked it instantly," says Brantley. "He made a phone call to Jheryl and they decided they would let us produce the song on the group because we were both young and the group was young and most of the other producers were older."

Brantley and Timas had actually written a few songs for the group already. They had purchased a copy of *Candy Girl*, the group's debut album on the Streetwise label, and crafted material they thought would be suitable for the five teenagers. "We had a drum machine and two keyboards," says Brantley. They hooked them up and Timas laid down a beat and a bassline while Brantley put down the chords and then wrote the lyrics and a melody. "[The title] 'Cool It Now' just popped up in my head and I started singing it and we liked it instantly," Brantley recalls. Brantley and Timas played all of the instruments themselves.

Working with New Edition was like a "big party," according to the writer/producer. "We were like kids at heart and we were able to do our responsibilities and at the same time [have] fun. The guys were hyper and girls were constantly calling...Bobby [Brown] was rolling around on the floor breakdancing. They were a bundle of energy."

"Cool It Now" was one of the very first commercial R&B hits to include a rap interlude. "They were listening to Run-D.M.C. and all these rappers," Brantley explains. "They were trying to imitate other rappers. We decided [to] put a little rap thing in the song, which wasn't a thing then—it was a pioneering move."

Brantley became close friends with lead singer Ralph Tresvant. "He was like my little buddy...We would hang out and go eat when we were done working. We finished up the last song and Jheryl came down to the studio with a bottle of champagne. He toasted to the work that we had done." Brantley later heard that "Mr. Telephone Man" was being considered as the first MCA single, but Busby's instincts were to go with "Cool It Now" first.

Hitting Number One was "sensational," says the writer/producer. "For a whole year, I walked around on a cloud. That stroke of fortune that night to run into Jheryl was truly the break we needed."

397

SOLID

Ashford & Simpson

CAPITOL 5397
WRITERS: NICKOLAS ASHFORD, VALERIE SIMPSON
PRODUCERS: NICKOLAS ASHFORD, VALERIE SIMPSON
December 1, 1984 (3 weeks)

Nine years of small print were enough for Nick Ashford and Valerie Simpson. After writing and producing hits for Ray Charles, Marvin Gaye and Tammi Terrell, Diana Ross, and others, they wanted to become artists in their own right.

This meant leaving Motown. Valerie's two solo albums for the label hadn't sold, and a duet album (*Nick and Val*) had been recorded but never released. "Motown thought of us as house producers and writers," Ashford said later, "and we wanted to break out of that." So in 1973, Ashford & Simpson signed with Warner Brothers Records.

It turned out to be a productive eight-year partnership, marked by 22 R&B hit singles (including "It Seems to Hang On" and "Found a Cure") and three gold albums. Nick and Val also developed relationships with other Warner Brothers artists; for instance, they composed Chaka Khan's first solo smash [see 302—"I'm Every Woman"] and her third, "Clouds."

What Warner didn't deliver for Ashford & Simpson was a crossover smash. For that, the couple needed the help of another label, Capitol, and their most bankable record of the '80s, "Solid."

"The song came about from the streets," recounts Ashford, "because at that time, I was walking around New York and the brothers had an expression, 'Yo, solid,' you know. I came home and said [to Val], 'That kinda applies to something about us.' It happened spontaneously."

"Solid" was the lead-off single for the couple's third album for Capitol, recorded during 1984 at New York's 39th Street Music and Blank Tapes studios. Reflecting their skill and experience, Nick and Val not only wrote and produced the material, but also handled the vocal, rhythm, and horn arrangements.

Simpson played synthesizers on "Solid," while the balance of the rhythm crew featured bass player Francisco Centeno, drummer Chris Parker, guitarist Sid McGinnis, and percussionist Jimmy Simpson. The horn players were Joe Mosello (trumpet) and Vinnie Della-Rocca (sax). Joining Ashford & Simpson on background vocals were Ullanda McCullough and Ray Simpson.

Francois Kevorkian and Ron St. Germain mixed the single to its reverberating peak, with Kevorkian suggesting the use of an a capella introduction drawn from one of the song's middle verses. "That was his idea," Simpson confirms. Ashford adds, "The simplicity of [the song] seemed to appeal to the kids," says Ashford, "but you don't always know what you're doing when you're doing it."

Were the lyrics of "Solid" intended to be perceived as an in-depth portrait of the couple's marriage? "No," says Simpson, "but it sounded good...It's funny, I think you write in the third person, and people always want to [read something into lyrics]. I can't take the weight of all these songs, hundreds of songs. To think I could have been all of those...I'd be so old and tired!"

Ashford & Simpson

398

OPERATOR

Midnight Star

SOLAR 69684
WRITERS: BO WATSON, REGGIE CALLOWAY, BELINDA LIPSCOMB
PRODUCER: REGGIE CALLOWAY
December 22, 1984 (5 weeks)

Reggie and Vincent Calloway were born into a musical family. "My father played trumpet, our aunt was an opera singer, and our uncle was a keyboardist, so it was in the blood," says brother Reggie.

There were early signs that Reggie was going to be a musician. "My grandmother had a piano in the house and we used to go there and bang out tunes. I wouldn't call it writing songs, but somewhere around high school I actually started writing my first compositions."

Reggie formed his first bands while in high school—first there was the Motown Masters, then the Mad Dog Fire Department. He formed his next group, Sunchild, while he was in college.

"It was a jazz fusion–type group. That's when my roots started steering strictly toward jazz and I was only going to be a jazz musician. When it came time for that group to make the big step, some of the members weren't ready to make the sacrifice. So I disbanded that group and went back to my college, Kentucky State University, and decided I was going to put together what I called a supergroup. I went through the university and hand-picked the members to form Midnight Star."

Reggie played trumpet, flute, and percussion while Vincent was on trombone, trumpet, and percussion. The other members of the band chosen by Reggie were Melvin Gantry (lead vocals), Bo Watson (lead vocals and keyboards), Jeffrey Cooper (lead guitar and keyboards), Kenneth Gant (bass and vocals), Bobby Lovelace (drums), Walter Simmons (saxophone, keyboards, and percussion), and Belinda Lipscomb (lead vocals).

Midnight Star played a lot of gigs in the Ohio-Kentucky area until they were given the opportunity to perform in New York. "We packed up everything that we owned...A few people heard us there and started passing the word," says Reggie. Dick Griffey of Solar Records expressed an interest in the group, and they signed with the label.

Reggie explains how he came up with the idea for "Operator": "We often look around for concepts that relate to day-to-day life and figure out how we can make a twist on it...Almost every day you're talking to an operator or you get disconnected or you dial a wrong number. It was before sampling, so we recorded an actual operator and used it in the record."

Calloway details how the group worked in the studio: "That was a time we were using a lot of the DMX drum machine and we'd play all the parts live to that particular beat. We didn't do a lot of sequencing back then. It was mostly live, unless it was some of the percolating parts like the ones in 'Operator.' For the most part, the bass and all the rhythms were live and we'd overdub and lay in the parts. Vocals were the most fun—we had quite a few lead vocalists back then and we'd distribute those parts pretty well to keep a good flow."

Having a large group was sometimes a hindrance, according to Calloway. "When your sound is too disperse, people have a hard time picking out who the group is when they hear lead vocals here and lead vocals there. So it was important to get a group sound."

The Calloways left Midnight Star after getting a taste of outside production work. They produced "Meeting in the Ladies Room" for Klymaxx, as well as material for the Whispers and the Deele. "After a while we got bit by the production bug and wanted to spread out and do more things. It's hard to stay in a large group when you're doing other things. So it was a sacrifice to break off and get into more songwriting, more production. We also wanted to do some things on our own...it's just self-expression," says Reggie, who had a hit in 1990 with "I Wanna Be Rich," recorded with his brother and released under the group name Calloway.

399

GOTTA GET YOU HOME TONIGHT

Eugene Wilde

PHILLY WORLD 99710
WRITERS: RONALD BROOMFIELD, MCKINLEY HORTON
PRODUCERS: MICHAEL FORTE, DONALD ROBINSON
January 26, 1985 (1 week)

Ronald Broomfield grew up in Miami in a very musical family. His father sang and his mother was a keyboard player, so it wasn't surprising the youngster learned to sing at age five and then joined his brothers professionally when he was 12. That happened soon after Ronald received a cherished Christmas present from his parents: a Fender Rhodes piano. Broomfield, who changed his name to Eugene Wilde after seeing an advertisement for a nightclub called Wilde Flowers, performed with his family under several different group names, including the

Broomfields, Broomfield Corporate Jam, La Voyage, and Simplicious. At one family appearance, a man named Bedrock saw Wilde perform and offered to manage him. With support from his family, Wilde went out on his own and Bedrock secured a deal with a Philadelphia-based label, Philly World.

Wilde recalls his first meeting at Philly World: "I walked in the studio and shook everybody's hand and McKinley Horton said, 'Let's go to the piano and write music.' " Although their styles were different, they quickly blended them. "Bedrock said, 'Think music. Think hit records. Let's pack up and go to England and give you guys a chance to be in new surroundings.' "

Being in London had an immediate impact. "We started kicking around a whole lot of ideas. We were coming up with some interesting things but decided to take a break. We went to a club and started cooling out, because we had been working all day." The place was filled with beautiful women. "I was in heaven. The guys were walking around in a daze and I could see it in every guy's eye—they were thinking, 'Hmmm, do I want her?' And a thought just came into my mind, 'Gotta Get You Home Tonight.' And I went and found McKinley and said, 'I know you're having a great time, but guess what? Party's over. We have to go and work.' He looked at me like I was crazy. I said, 'I got a great idea in my head and we gotta go.' So we hopped in a cab and went back to the hotel and I think it took maybe all of 10 minutes to write the song."

During his 10-week visit to the U.K., Wilde captured "Gotta Get You Home Tonight" on a small cassette recorder, along with seven other songs written with Horton. "Prior to going in to record at Philly World, we had 'Studio C' for demoing records and we went in there. The demo was basically the finished product, which was very similar to what we came up with in England," says Wilde. "When I started practicing the background vocals, the producer said, 'You sound great. Why don't you sing all the background parts?' So I did."

But "Gotta Get You Home Tonight" was not the obvious single, according to Eugene. "It wasn't even supposed to be the single. The first one that came out was 'Let Her Feel It,' a song I had done previously with Simplicious." But friends told him that the hit single was the one that had a Marvin Gaye feel to it. "The idea that it sounded like Marvin never crossed my mind. What really gave it the Marvin Gaye sound was the drum track. I was writing on a machine that had a built-in drum sound and we used it."

"Gotta Get You Home Tonight" moved slowly up the chart. "Just as it was getting ready to die, it picked up momentum. Philly World didn't have 25 or 30 acts, so they could keep pushing it. They never gave up on the record."

400

MR. TELEPHONE MAN

New Edition

MCA 52484
WRITER: RAY PARKER JR.
PRODUCER: RAY PARKER JR.
February 2, 1985 (3 weeks)

Sheryl Busby, head of black music for MCA Records at the time, invited Ray Parker Jr. to fly to the Bahamas and meet the members of New Edition. Parker liked the West Indies, but wasn't sure why he was there. "I had not any clue of what he wanted me to do or what he was talking about," Parker remembers. "And he said, 'The group is going to do your song' and I really thought they were going to do something else. So they started playing this song that I hadn't heard in who-knows-when that they dug up from somewhere."

The song was "Mr. Telephone Man," which Parker had written back in the days of his 1977 debut hit, "Jack and Jill." Dale Kawashima had turned Busby on to the song. "It was the strangest thing because they wanted me to produce a song that I didn't particularly like for myself," Parker says. "I had canned the song and never recorded it for myself. They thought it was a hit."

Parker found it somewhat frightening that he was asked to record the song in the same style as the original demo. His suggestion to update the sound was turned down. "They wanted to use real drums and no computers," Parker explains.

"Mr. Telephone Man" was different than previous New Edition singles. "Believe it or not, Bobby Brown is singing the lead," Parker reveals. "Ralph [Tresvant] is singing the parts in the verse, the lower, smoother parts. From what I understand from Bobby, that's his first [lead] vocal on a record. They really didn't think that he could sing that well, but he was the only one who could hit the 'Mr. Telephone Man' line up high because it was in another register, a strange register." Parker allows that Brown wasn't the first choice to sing lead on the track. "At the time, Ralph was the lead singer and he sang the verses great. But when we got to the chorus, he couldn't sing it. And so to make it happen, we had to get Bobby. He was the only one who got it."

Parker recorded the song at his own studios in North Hollywood, California. He explains that he needs his own studio because of his one-man-band style. "Playing all the instruments was always such a long tedious process that I would have been broke in [someone else's] studio. And nobody ever got the sounds that I was trying to get and so I had to learn to engineer and work the boards, otherwise I would have been lost." As an example, Parker describes how he plays and records himself: "I put the fuzztone on the record button and then I run into the next room, hit it, and then run back. And there's a little more work to that, [it's] a little more time-consuming."

Parker recalls that when he turned in the finished version of "Mr. Telephone Man," he had doubts about it. "I was still a little scared because I said, 'It sounds just like I thought it was gonna sound.' It sounded just like if I had done it years ago. And everybody liked it."

He still has fond memories of working with New Edition. "Those are the only guys I ever wrote a hit record for that called me back. I'll never forget that...They're very talented guys and they were the only ones to say, 'Thank you for writing us a hit and please come write us another one.'"

401

MISSING YOU

Diana Ross

RCA 13966
WRITER: LIONEL RICHIE
PRODUCERS: LIONEL RICHIE,
JAMES ANTHONY CARMICHAEL
February 23, 1985 (3 weeks)

The late Jay Lasker, only weeks after his November 1980 appointment as president of Motown Records, was called into a meeting with Berry Gordy and Diana Ross. The subject was her Motown contract, which was about to expire.

"Berry tried to orchestrate it like a movie," Lasker recalled of the discussions. "But Diana was no slouch. She curled up in Berry's chair and played her recording of 'It's My Turn'—prophetic, I thought."

Then Gordy took Ross's hand, according to Lasker, "and lured her into a slow, slow dance—smack in the middle of this meeting—to the chagrin of Diana's adviser, who paled at the idea of her blowing his whole big deal for sentimental reasons."

Diana's head evidently overruled her heart, because she quit Gordy's company for RCA Records in 1981. Yet in her music, the past was often present: for instance, the singer's only Number One for RCA, "Missing You," involved three legends of Motown—Marvin Gaye, Smokey Robinson, and Lionel Richie—not long after Gaye's death in April 1984.

"It actually came out of a conversation that Smokey Robinson and I had one evening about how we were missing Marvin," Ross later explained, "and what he meant to us, as well as to music. Then Lionel and I got to talking about how we need to tell people

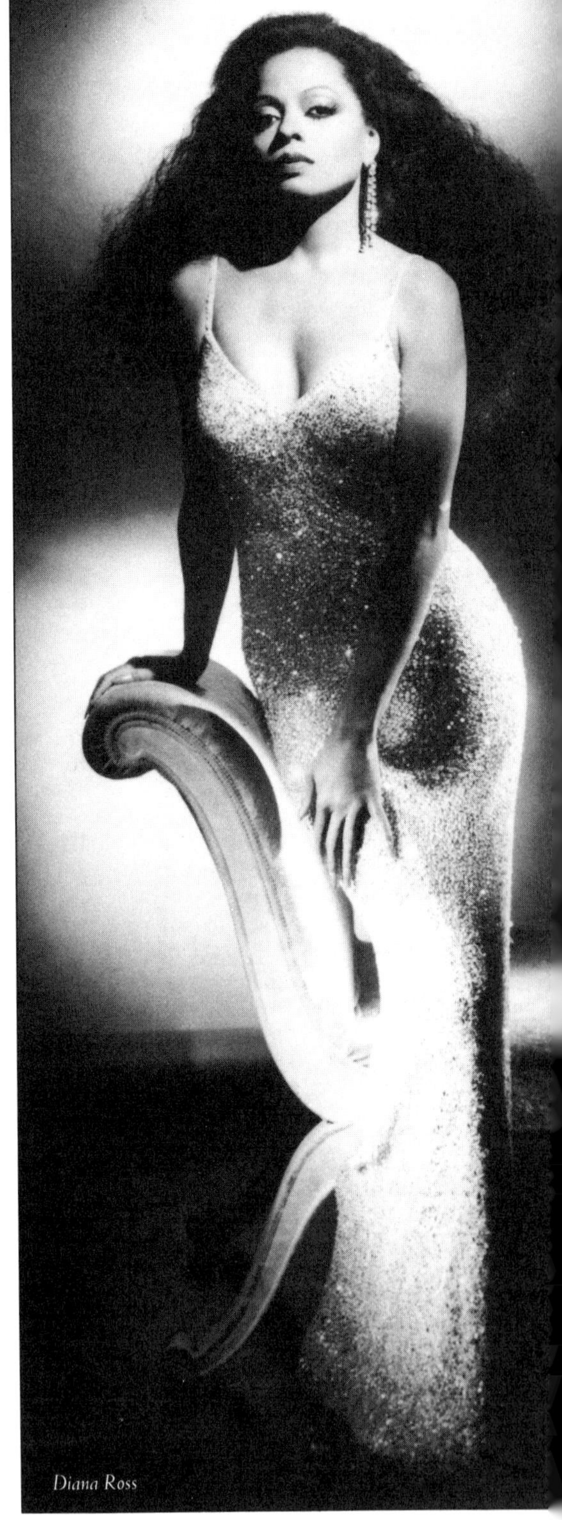

Diana Ross

that we love them while they're still alive. Lionel used all this to write that beautiful and special song."

Richie and Ross had collaborated before, of course [see 348—"Endless Love"], and the result was the biggest-selling single in Motown's history. Lionel had also gained insights into Diana's work through observing Berry Gordy, who let him into the studio while he oversaw the *Diana & Marvin* album. (Later, Richie confirmed that the two stars didn't cut their vocals together.)

Diana recorded "Missing You" in mid-1984 for her fourth RCA album, *Swept Away*, released that September. Richie played keyboards on the session, arranging and producing the song with James Carmichael, his longtime Commodores collaborator.

The promotional video clip for "Missing You" maintained Ross's links with her past. It not only featured footage of Marvin Gaye, but also images of other fallen stars of Motown, including the Supremes' Florence Ballard and the Temptations' Paul Williams.

The death of Marvin Gaye affected many musicians and performers. Lionel Richie's former colleague in the Commodores, Walter Orange, was moved to song [see 402—"Nightshift"]. So was Stevie Wonder, who sang "Lighting up the Candles" at Gaye's funeral on April 5, 1984, and later included it in his *Jungle Fever* album.

Teena Marie composed and recorded "My Dear Mr. Gaye" with Leon Ware, co-writer of Marvin Gaye's "I Want You." Another former Motown artist, Edwin Starr, paid tribute with "Marvin," which was a British release. And Frankie Beverly & Maze—who had received Gaye's help with their career in the '70s—paid tribute to him in "Silky Soul," a top five R&B hit in January 1990. They all missed Marvin.

402

NIGHTSHIFT

Commodores

MOTOWN 1773
WRITERS: WALTER ORANGE, DENNIS LAMBERT, FRANNE GOLDE
PRODUCER: DENNIS LAMBERT
March 16, 1985 (4 weeks)

And so "Nightshift" displaced "Missing You" at Number One, paying back-to-back tribute to the late, great Marvin Gaye. At the same time, the Commodores regained—for a moment—the chart stature they used to enjoy when the author of "Missing You" was their lead singer.

The Commodores *knew* about loss. Their collective heart was broken when manager Benny Ashburn, the wizard who transported them, in Lionel Richie's words, "from the ground floor to the top of the world," died in 1982. The following year, Richie quit the group, and their longtime producer, James Carmichael, went with him. And in 1984, guitarist and founder member Thomas McClary left.

To recover, the Commodores reached out, first to singer J. D. Nicholas, then to producer Dennis Lambert. Nicholas joined the band after working as a session singer (behind Diana Ross, among others) and, before that, as a member of Heatwave, the British soul combo.

Lambert, meanwhile, had begun to move in Motown circles through his prior acquaintance with company president Jay Lasker. The co-author of "Nightshift," Franne Golde, explains, "The band had approached Dennis to work with them. Of course, Lionel had left and they really hadn't had any success.

"Each member wanted to write, so they each submitted ideas. One of them, by Walter Orange, was this little groove he had going, which was the bass line to 'Nightshift.'

"Dennis played me a few things, and then he played me that. The only thing in the song was, 'Marvin, he was a friend of mine.' That was all he had. I said, 'This is fabulous, I love it.' When Dennis said, 'We need to make this like 'Rock and Roll Heaven,' I said, 'Great, let's do it.' "

"Rock and Roll Heaven" was the 1974 pop drama by the Righteous Brothers, which Lambert co-produced, about rock's fallen heroes: Otis Redding, Janis Joplin, Jim Morrison, and more. Lambert suggested the idea of the update soon after Golde happened to see the 1982 Henry Winkler/Michael Keaton movie *Night Shift* on TV.

In her mind's eye, Golde now admits with a laugh, she pictured singers on the nightshift in heaven, "coming out and giving their concert. And right when I explained that, Dennis said, 'Gonna be some sweet sounds comin' down on the nightshift.' "

The song "wrote itself" from then on, says Golde. "It took two mornings in the studio, while Dennis was in with the Commodores. We got *The Billboard Book of Top 40 Hits* and looked up Marvin Gaye and Jackie Wilson. I wrote down all the titles of their songs, and we incorporated that into the lyric."

Lambert recorded the Commodores in Los Angeles at Soundcastle Studio Center, augmenting the group's instrumental skills with such session professionals as Peter Wolf (keyboards) and Paul Jackson (guitar). Wolf also did the arrangement.

Singing lead on "Nightshift" was the song's creator, Walter Orange, who had vocally co-fronted the Commodores in their early days [see 212—"Slippery When Wet"]. Says Golde, "Originally, Walter had sung the whole song. But then it was so great when Dennis decided to put J. D. in the second verse. It just worked so wonderfully."

403
BACK IN STRIDE
Maze featuring Frankie Beverly

CAPITOL 5431
WRITER: FRANKIE BEVERLY
PRODUCER: FRANKIE BEVERLY
April 13, 1985 (2 weeks)

Frankie Beverly was born and raised in Philadelphia, where he was one of the earliest proponents of the Philly Sound. First he was in a doo-wop group called the Blenders when he was 17. Then he became one of the Butlers, a five-man group similar to the Temptations, with local hits like "She Tried to Kiss Me" and "The Sun's Message." Then he was in Raw Soul, a group that worked with producers like Kenny Gamble and Leon Huff while recording material for RCA. In 1972, just as Gamble and Huff were beginning the golden period of Philadelphia International Records, Raw Soul headed west to San Francisco, drawn by the success of Sly & the Family Stone and Santana.

The sister of Jan Gaye saw the group perform in San Francisco. Word got to Jan's husband, Marvin, who invited Frankie to visit him in Los Angeles. Gaye championed the band to Larkin Arnold at Capitol Records and also suggested a name change. The group came up with five new monikers, including Karma, Charisma, Caravan, and even San Francisco. They chose Maze.

Marvin Gaye was "a big influence" on the life of Frankie Beverly. "To meet the cat was nothing I ever imagined, and then to befriend him was just too much. What a great man. He liked me I think because I reminded him of him in my commitment to my thing. Not wanting to sell out, to...have the integrity to do something that may not be the hot thing. The man took care of us for over a year. The band wasn't doing well at all and he literally helped us pay our rent."

Gaye saw them through a rough period, but then the band signed with Capitol in 1976. The line-up at the time included Beverly and Ronald Lowry on vocals and congas, McKinley "Bug" Williams on vocals and percussion, Sam Porter on keyboards, Robin Duhe on bass guitar, Joe Provost on drums, and Wayne (a.k.a. Wuane) Thomas on lead guitar. Provost was replaced by Ahaguna G. Sun in 1977. Sun and Thomas departed, and three new members joined: Ron Smith, Billy Johnson, and Philip Woo. The latter three left Maze just before the group

Maze featuring Frankie Beverly

recorded its first Number One hit, "Back in Stride" and Thomas returned. As a result of the changes, "Word was out that Maze is breaking up, Maze is not going to be the same, and [the song] was our way of saying, 'We are not only still here, we're back in stride again,' " Beverly professes. "It was like a statement from the band saying that no two or three people are going to change the essence of what this band is about. So that was a very exciting time for me."

Recalling how "Back in Stride" was constructed, Beverly says that the groove came first. "It's very rare that it's story or lyrics first on anything that's fast," he explains. "Some of the ballads on the other hand, I might very well have some great lyrics that after a while I put music to, but most of the time it's the groove first."

Recording the song was not easy, according to the group's leader. "I do remember it was very hard. We recorded it when we were on the road playing, so I recorded it in a few cities. [We] went in a few recording studios in different cities and finally wound up getting what I needed home in San Francisco."

404

RHYTHM OF THE NIGHT

DeBarge

GORDY 1770
WRITER: DIANE WARREN
PRODUCER: RICHARD PERRY
April 27, 1985 (1 week)

"I don't even know how to spell the word 'rhythm.' I don't really have a lot of rhythm. And I wrote 'Rhythm of the Night,' " laughs Diane Warren.

While she has since been named *Billboard*'s pop songwriter of the year and ASCAP's songwriter of the year, she was a relative unknown when Suzanne Coston, music supervisor for the martial arts film *The Last Dragon*, asked her to contribute to the soundtrack of the movie that starred Taimak, Julius J. Carry III, Faith Prince, and Vanity. Coston described the scene in the film to Warren. "I was told about the movie, and I'd started the song anyway. It turned out that the song really worked out," says the composer.

Although Warren had previously concentrated on ballads, the up-tempo "Rhythm of the Night" was one of the first songs she wrote with a drum machine. A demo was recorded with Tommy Funderbrook singing lead. "There was one part in the demo where the guitar player hit a wrong note," says Warren. "To this day, when I hear that record, I keep thinking it's going to hit that wrong note."

Suzanne de Passe at Motown asked Richard Perry to produce the song for DeBarge. "I loved their previous work," says Perry. "I thought that 'All This Love' and 'Time Will Reveal' were real classics. This [song] was very different for them, being up-tempo. But I loved the song. I immediately heard it as a potential hit and felt it would be great for them."

Perry appreciated the demo, but wanted to put more funk in the final version. "I tried to make it have not only more of a street feeling, but a street atmosphere. I overdubbed the sounds of street [noises]." The members of DeBarge provided the street sounds, "to create the actual happening on the record, as opposed to just singing the song," Perry explains.

The producer chose to record the track with live musicians. "I'm sure people were using drum machines, but not to the degree they do today. Plus, I've always loved to cut live."

The inspiration for the party atmosphere of the song, says Perry, was Lionel Richie's "All Night Long (All Night)" [see 379]. "That was a natural influence for this song," he explains, adding that lead singer El Debarge "is really a gem to work with. He couldn't be a nicer guy. He's a delight...I never had any problems at all, and the group was fine, too. They were really nice and cooperative." Warren is equally enthusiastic about El: "I love his voice. That song has a special place in my heart, because it was the first song I wrote on my own that was a big hit."

"Rhythm of the Night" went to Number One on the R&B chart and number three on the pop chart. It raised Warren's stature in the music industry. "People took my calls a little quicker," she says. "One hit doesn't completely open the world to you, but it opens the door a crack more if you have the goods to get in there even more than that."

405

WE ARE THE WORLD

USA for Africa

COLUMBIA 04389
WRITERS: MICHAEL JACKSON, LIONEL RICHIE
PRODUCER: QUINCY JONES
May 4, 1985 (2 weeks)

Harry Belafonte called artist manager and television producer Ken Kragen and suggested staging a concert featuring black performers to raise money for Africa. Kragen countered that a single concert wouldn't raise the kind of funds Belafonte was talking about, and came up with an alternative idea: an American version of Band Aid, the effort organized by Bob Geldof in the U.K. to raise money for the starving people of Africa that resulted in the song "Do They Know It's Christmas?"

Kragen called one of his clients, Lionel Richie, to discuss the idea. He also asked Quincy Jones to pro-

USA for Africa

duce a recording and Michael Jackson to contribute. Kragen says his most important decision was to reserve time at A&M Studios in Hollywood on January 28, 1985, the night of the American Music Awards. "It was a perfect way to make sure that I could get the maximum number of artists to take part," Kragen said in *Billboard*. "I knew that a number of key artists would be at the American Music Awards. I also knew that there were certain artists who would attract the others into the project: Michael, Lionel, Stevie [Wonder], Bruce Springsteen."

Richie and Jackson knew they had to write something special, considering the artists involved and the importance of the project. "I can't really say how the song came about," Richie admitted in *Billboard*. "Neither one of us saw the other put his hands on the keyboard. That's how we write. He brought in an idea, I brought in an idea; we went back, we listened, and then we smashed both ideas together. The music came first. As for the lyrics...it just kind of flowed...I'd throw out a line, Michael would come back with a greater line—the same one, with the words changed around differently—and I'd change his line...And it actually only took us about two-and-a-half hours to nail it, after three days of preparation."

Quincy recorded the instrumental tracks first and sent demo tapes to all of the artists involved with a note to "check your egos at the door." Jones said in *Billboard*, "I put that line in a letter I sent to all the artists before they got there, and everybody understood...Oh, there were little murmurs beforehand that the song 'is not rock 'n' roll'...but once we got to the session, I was sure everything would totally even itself out and bring everyone into a euphoric state, and that's what happened."

The artists began arriving at 10:00 P.M., following the awards ceremony and party. Each soloist found his or her name taped on the floor. Six microphones were arranged in a semi-circle. The chorus, featuring all of the artists, was recorded first, then soloists added their parts. By 8:00 A.M., Lionel and Quincy were the only musicians left in the studio.

The single arrived in stores March 7. Over 800,000 copies were shipped, and all were sold out by the weekend. Less than a year after its release, the total estimated worldwide sales of singles, albums, videos and related products added up to $44 million.

406

FRESH

Kool & the Gang

DE-LITE 880 623
WRITERS: JAMES TAYLOR, SANDY LINZER, KOOL & THE GANG
PRODUCERS: JIM BONNEFOND, RONALD BELL, KOOL & THE GANG
May 18, 1985 (1 week)

They called their 27th album *Emergency*, but there was no crisis in the Kool & the Gang camp in 1984. Or was there?

After recruiting lead singer James "J.T." Taylor and outside producer Eumir Deodato, the band soared to new commercial heights. They cut three consecutive platinum albums, and another two that went gold. As well as a clutch of R&B Number Ones, they scored 10 top 40 pop hits between 1979 and 1984, including five that reached the top 10.

Taylor recalls, "We started getting a lot of flak from music industry people—about radio, R&B charts, stuff like that—saying we were selling out, trying to be white, or trying to sound white or pop.

"We took offense, because first of all, we were very active in our neighborhood, very active with charities. We donated quite a bit. Still, we saw our black audience decline to 15% and then 10%. Yet as much as they criticized us, every top 10 pop hit we had was a Number One R&B smash." (Well, almost: in *Billboard*, some of their crossover successes, such as "Too Hot" and "Get Down on It," didn't go all the way on the R&B charts.)

When *Emergency* rang the release bell in November 1984, however, critics couldn't label the album pure pop. Some cuts recalled the band's jazz origins, while the first single, "Misled," was black rock—*before* Living Colour. And the set's Number One single, "Fresh," was a crisp R&B sound from James Taylor's past.

"That was a song from the band I had prior to joining Kool & the Gang," he says, "but it was a totally different groove. When I played it for [Gang drummer] George Brown, he changed it." Leader Robert "Kool" Bell suggested a more syncopated bassline, too. "He put a repetitive thing in there, and made it commercially sound."

Finally, producer Jim Bonnefond tapped songwriter Sandy Linzer for some lyrics. The two had previously collaborated on Dr. Buzzard's Original "Savannah" Band. "When Kool & the Gang were cutting this album," says Linzer, "they were behind schedule, they needed some work done. I was leaving for Los Angeles in a couple of days, so I didn't have much more than a night to work on the material."

"Fresh" was the song Linzer chose. "They had a title, and they wanted a lyric about all the fresh things that were going on in the world. I just changed it to 'She's fresh,' wrote the lyrics to the verses, and submitted it."

"Sandy really finished it off for us," agrees the band's Khalis Bayyan, who also remembers the good feeling of "Fresh," before it was even released. "It was the fall when we finally finished the mix. We brought it outside [at the House of Music] and listened to it on a boom box.

Kool & the Gang

"We were looking out over the trees in the back yard of the studio, and as soon as the music came on, a breeze came up and leaves started falling." Bayyan sighs. "The changing colors, leaves floating by, the music playing...'Fresh' was a nice experience."

407

YOU GIVE GOOD LOVE

Whitney Houston

ARISTA 9274
WRITER: LALA
PRODUCER: KASHIF
May 25, 1985 (1 week)

Who would have guessed that while Cissy Houston was recording hits with the Sweet Inspirations and singing back-up for Elvis Presley and Aretha Franklin, she was also raising a daughter who would one day conquer the R&B chart in spectacular fashion.

Whitney Houston began her solo career on Arista Records the right way: with a Number One song. "You Give Good Love" was the first single released from her debut album. Kashif, who produced the track, first heard Whitney sing when she showcased at Sweetwater's in New York. Later, he was shown a video of her performance on *The Merv Griffin Show*. That's when he said yes to a request that he produce some tracks for her first album. Kashif wasn't sure of the proper direction for Whitney until he heard a song composed by a friend of his from his days playing in a Brooklyn band. LaLa had been in a rival group, although they had worked together on free-lance gigs. Later, he signed her to his publishing company, and was surprised one day when she showed up at his house in tears.

LaLa had written a song she really believed in and had sent it out to a popular female recording artist. "I was a big Roberta Flack fan," LaLa explains. "I had an opportunity to meet her. Kashif was on tour with her and she surprised me because she was so friendly." LaLa had already written top 10 hits for Glenn Jones ("Show Me") and Melba Moore ("Livin' for Your Love"), and says that Flack expressed familiarity with her work and told LaLa she had to write a song for her. "I was totally excited and said I would get on it right away. She said, 'When you finish it, you can come to my house and have tea.' " LaLa was excited about the invitation and a chance to see inside the famous Dakota apartment building. "I wrote the song while I was in class," says LaLa. "It served a dual purpose. I used it as a class assignment—I was at Juilliard at the time. I also decided to demo it and submit it to her."

It was snowing in Manhattan and LaLa was under the weather the day she brought her tape to the Dakota. The security guard asked her to wait a moment while he called up. But LaLa wasn't invited up for tea. She was told to leave the package and wait for a phone call the next day. "I was very anxious to hear from her," says the songwriter. "I called her and once again her assistant kind of snubbed me and said, 'Don't call us, we'll call you.' " When LaLa spilled out her frustration to Kashif, the producer asked to hear the song. LaLa played him "You Give Good Love" and he pronounced it a smash. Kashif had been recording on Arista since 1983, and he played LaLa's tune for label president Clive Davis, who loved it.

Whitney came to Kashif's studio to hear the song, but LaLa didn't have her demo tape with her, so she performed it live. "Before I ended the song, she picked up on the lyrics and was singing it along with me," says a surprised LaLa.

Kashif asked his best friend, Bashiri Johnson, to play percussion on the track. J.T. Lewis played some of the drum parts, Roy Wooten also played drums, Ira Siegal was on guitar, and LaLa and Yogi Lee sang backing vocals. Kashif played many instruments himself, including the bass marimba. "It's huge," he describes, "at least six feet tall, and you have to stand on a chair to play it. [It gives] a very deep, woody, Africany ethnic sound, and I used that on the bridge of the song playing along with the bassline. Whitney was unbelievable in the studio. What you hear on that record is her singing the song for the first time, and we punched in a few notes."

The song was mixed by Michael O'Reilly at Atlantic Studios. "We finished on a Tuesday," says Kashif. "I remember saying, 'God, this song sounds so great...something's going to happen with this song.' When we finished it, we rushed it to Clive. The very next day, it was on the radio."

408

ROCK ME TONIGHT (FOR OLD TIMES SAKE)

Freddie Jackson

CAPITOL 5459
WRITER: PAUL LAURENCE
PRODUCER: PAUL LAURENCE
June 1, 1985 (6 weeks)

But for Harlem's White Rock Baptist Church, the people responsible for a few Number One records might never have become acquainted.

In the '60s, it was where Nick Ashford caught first sight of Valerie Simpson, and decided to get to know her; in the '70s, it was where Freddie Jackson met Laurence Jones, kindling the friendship that eventually

Freddie Jackson

produced "Rock Me Tonight" and ignited Jackson's career.

"Valerie taught Paul to play piano, actually," explains Jackson, who attended a neighboring church until he heard about the contemporary music featured at the White Rock Baptist. "I joined and I met Paul. We just hit it off real well—he loved my voice."

Years later, "Rock Me Tonight" would make that apparent. By then, Freddie had put in time singing background for Melba Moore and even co-authoring her 1983 hit, "Keepin' My Lover Satisfied." Laurence Jones (otherwise known as Paul Laurence) was also in the Moore camp (otherwise known as Hush Productions) by this time, having crafted her '82 success, "Love's Comin' at Ya."

Hush executives installed Jackson in the recording studio on his birthday—October 2, 1984—to begin work on his debut album "as a gift," says the singer. Barry Eastmond wrote and produced six of the eight tunes, but Paul Laurence's "Rock Me Tonight" was the breakthrough.

That track was recorded at Digital By Dickinson in Bloomfield, New Jersey, with Laurence handling keyboards, synthesizer, and drum programs, Timmy Allen on bass, and Mike Campbell on guitar. Laurence and Reggie King sang background vocals.

"Paul wrote that especially for me," says Jackson, who had previously done reference vocals of Laurence's songs for other artists. "But it was the last song I did for the album.

"When you get down to the last song, you should know pretty much what your first single is. At that point, we didn't. So 'Rock Me Tonight' comes along and I'm like, 'Oh, that's good.' But everybody who heard it said, 'This is a *great* song.' I was listening to other songs to come out as the first single, possibly 'I Wanna Say I Love You' or 'Good Morning Heartache,' but they all liked 'Rock Me Tonight.' "

Meanwhile, Charles Huggins of Hush Productions had pitched Jackson's project to Capitol Records after turndowns by Motown, and RCA. Capitol was Melba Moore's label and, coincidentally, where Freddie was under contract in 1981–82 as a member of a band called Mystic Merlin. "The strangest thing," he says, "is that Capitol wasn't aware that it was me in that group when I made the *Rock Me Tonight* album."

The single came out in March 1985 and "took people by storm," according to the singer. "Retailers were calling up the company saying, like, 'This song is phenomenal, where are the records, what's going on?' They had to put [extra] people to work in the pressing plants to press up the album."

409

HANGIN' ON A STRING (CONTEMPLATING)

Loose Ends

MCA 52570
WRITERS: CARL MCINTOSH, JANE EUGENE, STEVE NICHOL
PRODUCER: NICK MARTINELLI
July 13, 1985 (1 week)

In the middle of a chart year dominated by top-drawer American names—Diana Ross, Maze, Kool & the Gang, Aretha Franklin, the USA for Africa cabal—there was a little bit of England: Loose Ends.

Carl McIntosh, Jane Eugene, and Steve Nichol formed the group as Loose End in London during the early '80s. Two of them, Nichol and Eugene, had met at the Guildhall School of Music and Drama; session bassist McIntosh joined later. Their debut single on Virgin Records, "In the Sky," was written by two members of the biggest British black band of the previous decade, the Real Thing.

As Loose Ends, the trio breached the U.K. charts for the first time in 1984 with three hits, including "Tell Me What You Want," produced by Philadelphia's Nick Martinelli. The following year, "Hangin' on a String (Contemplating)" became their first major British hit—and first American success.

"The song was written in England," explains Carl McIntosh, "and I think we were in a little studio in London somewhere. We went to America, and Nick Martinelli changed it around a bit. We didn't mind at the time, because we had a lot of respect for him."

"Hangin' on a String" was originally part of Loose Ends' second U.K. album, *So Where Are You*, recorded with Martinelli at Sigma Sound, Philadelphia. "We had sent the songs over to him," says McIntosh, "and normally he'd throw out one or two, or make a few suggestions of songs we should do. But on this occasion, after the first album, he agreed to all the tunes, and he liked what we were doing anyway."

Not everyone in the studio concurred. "The engineer didn't really like my guitar playing," McIntosh chuckles. "He was a guitar player, too. I was a London musician—a guitarist, but very unorthodox. I did the guitar solo on the tune, and the engineer kind of laughed afterwards. But Nick told him, 'Make that sound great, OK, 'cause I think it's happening.' He did, and it came out great."

For American release, Virgin had placed Loose Ends with MCA Records. The U.S. label combined songs from *So Where Are You* with selections from the group's U.K. debut album to make *A Little Spice*, which featured "Hangin' on a String." Says McIntosh, "The MCA deal didn't even involve us. We were just a little jazz band at the time on Virgin."

All three members of Loose Ends played and sang on "Hangin' on a String," the song opening with Jane Eugene's cool, contemplating tones. "Jane would normally sing the lead vocal," says McIntosh, "but that tune was so funky that I just jumped in there with my verse. We used to bounce off each other like that, anyway. It was kind of a natural thing."

410

SAVE YOUR LOVE (FOR #1)

René & Angela

MERCURY 880 731

WRITERS: RENÉ MOORE, ANGELA WINBUSH

PRODUCERS: BOBBY WATSON, BRUCE SWEDIEN, RENÉ MOORE, ANGELA WINBUSH

July 20, 1985 (2 weeks)

René Moore and Angela Winbush had separate careers before they teamed up for a series of albums on Capitol and Mercury, and after six years of chart hits they went their separate ways again.

Moore, born in Los Angeles, was a high school friend of George and Louis Johnson and performed in various bands with them before they became well-known as the Brothers Johnson [see 247—"I'll Be Good to You"]. Moore's brother, Bobby Watson, experienced chart success in the '70s as the bass player for Rufus [see 188—"You Got the Love"]. Before recording with Winbush, Moore worked with Motown producer Mickey Stevenson and his wife, Kim Weston.

Winbush hails from St. Louis, where her family was very involved in the church and gospel music. She learned to play piano when she was very young, but didn't feel her musical talent was recognized until she attended Howard University in Washington, D.C. "Then I started taking it more seriously," she says. She formed a trio that opened for artists like Al Jarreau and Van McCoy, and after graduation she worked for a few months as a backup singer for Jean Carne [see 432—"Closer Than Close"].

That led to singing backing vocals for Stevie Wonder in his group Wonderlove. In the fall of 1977, singer Carolyn Dennis introduced René and Angela at a rehearsal of the Terry Lynn Community Choir. René credits Angela with the idea of working together. "We were both pursuing individual interests musically, and she came up with the idea of writing songs together and [forming] the duo."

By February of the following year they recorded a demo tape. The first song they wrote together was "Changes," recorded by Lenny Williams. But not everyone liked their demo reel. "We had a lot of rejections when we first started," Angela remembers. René adds, "Jerry Wexler [of Atlantic Records] said, 'My grandmother could do this.' "

Through mutual friends, René and Angela met Dr. Cecil Hale, then an executive with Capitol Records. He was taken with the song "Do You Really Love Me" and signed the duo to the label. That song became their first single to chart, although they never cracked the R&B top 10 during their four-year stint with the label.

In 1985 René and Angela were pacted to Polygram and released an album titled *Street Called Desire* on the Mercury label. The first single was "Save Your Love (For #1)."

Moore remembers, "Originally it was 'Save Some Love,' and the engineer/producer we worked with, Bruce Swedien, came up with 'Save Your Love.' It was recorded completely at my house. I've always had my own studio. It went from a four-track to an eight-track to a 16-track to a 24-track. It was just so I could work on my craft more."

When "Save Your Love (For #1)" was first recorded, René did the rap in the song. But through Mercury's A&R staff, René and Angela asked labelmate Kurtis Blow to handle the rap. The single's Number One status changed their lives. "When that record went to Number One," says Moore, "it actually brought tears to my eyes. To work so hard on a career and then have that success, it's definitely a feat."

411

FREEWAY OF LOVE

Aretha Franklin

ARISTA 9354
WRITERS: NARADA MICHAEL WALDEN, JEFFREY COHEN
PRODUCER: NARADA MICHAEL WALDEN
August 3, 1985 (5 weeks)

Producer Narada Michael Walden was asked by Arista Records President Clive Davis if he would like to work with one of the label's main attractions, Dionne Warwick, and Walden said yes. He came up with some songs for Warwick, but says the chemistry wasn't right at the time, and the project didn't go forward.

"So Clive said how would I feel about working with Aretha, and I said, 'Yeah,' because I had just been to the Grammys and I'd seen Aretha win a Grammy for 'Hold On I'm Comin',' and I realized the whole community really liked her. I mean, of course people like Aretha Franklin, but people want to give her awards, want to do things for her, want to see her win stuff. So I felt if I came with the right songs that she'd have a shot at winning a Grammy again and strong success."

The initial Franklin-Walden team-up produced two songs, "Who's Zoomin' Who" and "Until You Say You Love Me." Aretha inspired the former title during a telephone conversation with Narada, and the producer co-wrote the latter with Preston Glass. "Then there was a track called 'Freeway of Love' that I had in the can," says Walden. "I was going to use it on my album and decided not to and Preston suggested I use it for Aretha."

"Freeway of Love" was composed in Walden's living room on a big black Yamaha piano. "I was pounding away and the chorus came to me and I broke a sweat playing it," Narada remembers. "I had 'pink Cadillac,' but I couldn't find the right rhyme scheme. Jeffrey Cohen came over with 'Wind's against my back.' " Walden gave Cohen a cassette of the track and Cohen wrote a lyric for the verse. "I knew I wanted it cut in that old Motown style," says Walden, who recorded it himself a year and a half

Aretha Franklin, with producer Narada Michael Walden

before giving it to Franklin. Narada didn't play his own unreleased version for Aretha. "I completely changed it for her. I cut it in her key and had a girl named Kitty Beethoven demo it."

The producer remembers the first time he walked into the studio in Detroit to work with Lady Soul. "She wore jeans. She wore her fur coat and a T-shirt underneath it, and she had her Kool cigarettes and her hair was kind of pouffy, kind of nice...We met at this place called United Sound Studios." They recorded "Who's Zoomin' Who." "But it wasn't in their good room," says Walden. "It was in their bad room downstairs—old, beat-up, junky room."

For "Freeway of Love," they moved to United's best studio. "The board was in front of me but to look at her, I had to look over my right shoulder," says the producer. "[After] those first two or three takes, I knew we had a smash because her vibe was so strong."

Walden lists the musicians he used on the session: "Preston Glass played the vibes. Of course, I played the drums. Randy Jackson played Moog bass. A fabulous player, Corrado Rustici, played guitar." Walter Afanasieff, who would later become a producer in his own right, played keyboards. Greg Gonaway was on tambourine and background vocals were provided by Aretha's sister Carolyn, Sylvester, Jeanie Tracy, Vicki Randle, Jim Gilstrap, Preston Glass, Kitty Beethoven, and Laundon Von Kendricks. The sax solo was by Clarence Clemons. "I had just gone to see Bruce Springsteen live," says Walden. "We brought Clarence to the studio...He blew that solo at nine in the morning. That's early for a rock and roll musician."

"Freeway of Love" was Aretha's 20th Number One hit. Walden has no regrets that his own version didn't see the light of day. "It wouldn't have been a hit like that. I respect myself as an artist, but nothing that I would have done could have been as big and as powerful as Aretha Franklin and what she did with that record."

412

SAVING ALL MY LOVE FOR YOU

Whitney Houston

ARISTA 9381
WRITERS: MICHAEL MASSER, GERRY GOFFIN
PRODUCER: MICHAEL MASSER
September 7, 1985 (1 week)

Michael Masser will never forget the moment he first saw Whitney Houston.

His good friend Clive Davis, head of Arista Records, invited him to hear a new, young female singer at Sweetwater's in New York. "As I walked in, I thought I heard 'Greatest Love of All,' " Masser recalls. He was right—Whitney Houston was singing the song Masser had written with Linda Creed. "I was stunned," says Masser. "And then I heard her sing and it was incredible. That stuck with me forever."

Masser met Houston as well as her family and manager that night. Whitney's mother, Cissy Houston, told Masser that "Greatest Love of All" was one of the first songs Whitney had learned how to sing and was one of her daughter's personal favorites.

Around this time, Masser was scheduled to work with Teddy Pendergrass, but the singer's automobile accident intervened and years would pass before they would come together in the studio. Masser wanted to record a song he had written with Creed as a duet between Pendergrass and a female vocalist. "There were a lot of singers who wanted to be a part of that song, whether for the song or to be a part of Teddy's comeback," says Michael, who decided Whitney should be the one. "I had this gut feeling and I had to fight very hard for her. It was a major battle and I stuck to my guns." The result was "Hold Me," a top five single for Pendergrass in 1984 and Houston's chart debut.

Masser was invited to be one of the producers of Houston's first album for Arista. In addition to "Greatest Love of All," he had her record "Saving All My Love for You," a song Masser had written in the '70s with Gerry Goffin in his New York apartment overlooking Central Park. "I did the song on Marilyn McCoo and it definitely had a different production flavor and a different structure," says Masser. He had some new ideas when he decided to produce the torch song for Houston. "I told Whitney, 'This is going to make the women cry. It's a woman's song.' "

Houston was confident and tough when she first sang the song, according to Masser. Eventually Masser elicited a more vulnerable performance. "It was suggested that I try some fancy things at the end, more R&B-ish moves, and I couldn't make that work. So I kept it simple...and then I experimented with that sax part. I had Tom Scott [record] a couple dozen takes and I was thrilled with the song. I felt that should be the single."

Masser discovered that Clive Davis was leaning toward "All at Once" as the follow-up to "You Give Good Love." While working on a film set with Gene Wilder in Santa Fe, New Mexico, Masser heard that Houston was opening at the Roxy in Los Angeles. "I told Whitney, when you sing this song, say, 'The women will understand it.' And I made a side bet with Clive. I said, 'Clive, if all the women jump up for this song, you know it should be the single.' So we made a foolish bet and she sang it and I guess that's how it happened—but maybe they just liked it anyway."

Masser concludes, "I totally fell in love with Whitney on that song...When I first recorded her, she was excited and it was a real charge for me because this was a new talent and someone I liked a lot. She was always a nice girl, always a sweetheart. And I said, 'Imagine if you make it. I mean, really imagine it, Whitney!' "

413

CHERISH

Kool & the Gang

DE-LITE 880 869
WRITERS: RONALD BELL,
JAMES TAYLOR, KOOL & THE GANG
PRODUCERS: JIM BONNEFOND, RONALD BELL,
KOOL & THE GANG
September 14, 1985 (1 week)

After years of recording in the New Jersey woodlands at the House of Music, Kool & the Gang made a switch to the oceanside rhythms of the Bahamas. There, at the famed Compass Point studios in Nassau, they worked on tracks for the 1984 album that would become *Emergency*.

"The idea of being in the sun, by the beach, was very attractive," says producer Jim Bonnefond. "We thought it would be good to get away, so that everybody's head was in a different place."

The change in environment paid off: Three of the four top 10 hits out of *Emergency* got started in Nassau, including "Fresh" and "Cherish." The latter also developed into the band's biggest pop single since "Joanna."

The album was notable for another reason: Kool & the Gang's music director, Khalis Bayyan, elected to use a drum machine with the band. "He had been working on some songs and buying lots of equipment," says Bonnefond. "We were experimenting and it sounded good. So we said, 'Why don't we use drum machines?' "

With "Cherish," as with other Gang songs, Bayyan focused on the track, lead vocalist James Taylor on the lyrics. "I knew it was a hit the minute I heard it inside of me," says Khalis. "I kept it around for a couple of years before we did anything with it. But the intro alone told me it was gonna *go*. This was a song that was gonna take you there."

After the Gang had furnished the track, Bayyan handed it to J.T. "That was the first song I had ever lyrically written in one sitting, and it wasn't changed," says Taylor, who made his contribution

Kool & the Gang

while still in the Bahamas. "Some of the guys had their families there, their children.

"I remember one morning walking to the beach before we started studio work, and I saw the kids playing—everyone was out there having fun. I thought, 'Man, we're really blessed. To think where I grew up, South Carolina, eight sisters, two brothers, pretty poor.' I reflected on that, what God has given us, and I said, 'We really should cherish this.'

"I went to my room that night, and wrote the lyrics. I knocked on Kool's door the next morning—his wife was with him—and I said, 'Just come on over and check this out.' And they read it, and told me, 'This is great.' "

With tracks for several of the *Emergency* songs laid down at Compass Point, Kool & the Gang returned to the House of Music to cut vocals and finish up. In the process, Jim Bonnefond called in writer Sandy Linzer to help out with some lyrics [see 406—"Fresh"].

"Jim wanted me to rewrite the lyrics to 'Cherish,' but I told him they were great," says Linzer. "They used maybe a couple of lines in the chorus that I gave them *gratis*, but I thought the song was perfect."

So perfect, in fact, that it met with the approval of Bobby Bell, father of Khalis and Kool. "He was ill when this song became a hit," says Bayyan. "My uncle told me that my dad was listening to it on the radio on the night he passed away [in October 1985]. I always think, he must have heard that line, *Help me make it through the night...*"

414

OH SHEILA

Ready for the World

MCA 52636
WRITERS: MELVIN RILEY JR., GORDON STROZIER, GERALD VALENTINE
PRODUCERS: READY FOR THE WORLD
September 21, 1985 (2 weeks)

A house for his parents, a Porsche for himself. Melvin Riley Jr. gained the trappings of success fast, thanks to natural talent and a helping hand from one of Detroit's most influential radio jocks, the Electrifying Mojo.

Riley was the leader of Ready for the World, whose Prince-ly "Oh Sheila" was one of 1985's crossover giants: a Number One on *Billboard*'s R&B and Hot 100 charts. "Melvin was definitely the talent [of the group]," says Gary Spaniola, who co-produced Ready for the World's second chart-topper [see 442—"Love You Down"] in 1986. "He's a natural-born singer: he just opens his mouth and it sounds great."

The band came from Flint, Michigan, brought together by Riley (who played rhythm guitar and piano, as well as handling lead vocals) and schoolmate Gordon Strozier (lead guitar). Gerald Valentine was on drums, Gregory Potts on keyboards, John Eaton on bass, and Willie Triplett on percussion.

"Oh Sheila" was Ready for the World's third single for MCA Records, following a pair of successful, group-composed ballads ("Tonight," "Deep Inside Your Love") which had reached the R&B top 10 in 1985.

Their earliest recordings were made at Bernard Terry's Silver Sun studio in Flint, shopped around to various labels (including MCA) but rejected. So the group recut "Tonight" with Terry for their own imprint, Blue Lake Records, and released it locally. Melvin Riley told *Rock Scene*, "We brought the record to the Electrifying Mojo and he played it on his show. That was our big break." The WJLB airplay turned "Tonight" into a Detroit-area smash—and MCA signed Ready for the World.

"I didn't think success would happen this fast," said Riley. "Everybody kept warning me that it would be hard and take a long time. I was going to college, studying to be a teacher. My parents told me to have a skill. They said we'd be struggling for a long time."

As Ready for the World's pop breakthrough, "Oh Sheila" made the difference. "I used to feel like I was gonna wake up in the morning and say, 'Damn, this was a dream,' " Riley commented a couple of years later. "But I know it's reality. I bought my parents a house. My fans helped me buy it. I got a Porsche now. I went to the American Music Awards and was sitting next to all these celebrities—Smokey Robinson, Lionel Richie, and Huey Lewis were there...We weren't used to that."

415

YOU ARE MY LADY

Freddie Jackson

CAPITOL 5495
WRITER: BARRY J. EASTMOND
PRODUCER: BARRY J. EASTMOND
October 5, 1985 (2 weeks)

That's the biggest pop song I've had," declares Freddie Jackson, contemplating the fact that "You Are My Lady" climbed higher on the Hot 100 in *Billboard* than his blockbuster debut [see 408—"Rock Me Tonight"] or any of his subsequent hits.

"Most people, black or white, will come up to me and cite 'You Are My Lady.' They remember 'Rock Me Tonight,' but there's something about 'You Are My Lady' that is a classic."

Dolly Eastmond certainly has cause to cite the song: It was composed about her by writer/producer Barry Eastmond, her husband. "At the time, we had a small, one-bedroom apartment in Brooklyn," says Barry, "and off in the corner of my living room, I had a little four-track set up with a couple of synths and drum machines. I'd wake up in the morning at eight or nine, and write 'til six or seven at night."

Eastmond was musical director for Melba Moore then; her husband, Charles Huggins, was a principal in Hush Productions, which managed Moore and Freddie Jackson, among others. "I had known Freddie for about a year," Eastmond says. "I met him through Paul Laurence, and had used him on some background for a couple of songs I had arranged on one of Melba's albums."

In the fall of 1984, Hush bankrolled the recording of Jackson's debut LP. "Paul was busy on another project and only had time to do one or two songs [for Freddie], and he recommended me for the majority of the album," remembers Eastmond. "So Freddie and I got together."

"You Are My Lady" was the first song he penned for the project. "I wasn't really sure if Freddie would like it. He came over to my house and I put up a rough demo. I had to sing the song to him, and I don't have the best voice in the world. So I sang, and Freddie said, 'Even with your voice, I can tell this is a great song!'

"He went ahead and recorded the demo, took it back to his management—and they loved it, they were thrilled. It really amazed me, 'cause it was the kind of song I wrote in an hour. It just came to me like that."

Together with the five other numbers Eastmond wrote and produced for the *Rock Me Tonight* album, "You Are My Lady" was recorded at Celestial Sounds in New York. The musicians on the track were Wayne Brathwaite (bass) and Ira Siegal (guitar), with Eastmond himself on keyboards, synthesizer, and drum programs. B. J. (Brenda) Nelson, Audrey Wheeler, and Melba Moore were background vocalists.

As a single, the paean to Dolly Eastmond reached its R&B peak in October. A month later, it cruised to number 12 on the pop charts, six slots higher than "Rock Me Tonight" had attained. "To this day," Barry Eastmond comments, "I'm still shocked at the success it's had, and how much it has done for Freddie's career."

Eastmond says he had more modest ambitions for the project. "We were hoping that some people would hear it, because we felt it was a great album. But I wasn't aware of what Paul [Laurence] was cutting, so when you're involved with three or more producers, you wonder if it's going to work. When I got a [final] copy of the album, I was really amazed at how well it did work."

416

PART-TIME LOVER

Stevie Wonder

TAMLA 1808
WRITER: STEVIE WONDER
PRODUCER: STEVIE WONDER
October 19, 1985 (6 weeks)

"It could not have happened at a more appropriate time," the essay began. "The glow of the full moon had bathed them in a circle of energy. The four walls of the room had expanded to include the four corners of the earth. Their hearts were recalling the cycles of love, while their minds were exploring the square root of the universe."

Who said liner notes were dead?

Stevie Wonder's *In Square Circle*, the album that gave birth to "Part-Time Lover," came complete with an essay from which the above is excerpted. The central character appeared to be "Songlife" (the Cosmic Carrier), but the thousand words or so—signed by Stevland Morris (i.e., Wonder) and Theresa Cropper—didn't throw much light upon the album contents.

More specific were the performance credits, which showed that Wonder played drums and synthesizers on "Part-Time Lover" and that Luther Vandross shared the lead vocal. Among those singing backup were Stevie's former wife, Syreeta Wright, and Philip Bailey of Earth, Wind & Fire. It was digitally recorded at Stevie's own Los Angeles studio, Wonderland.

"It just took me a long time to get the songs I wanted," Wonder explained to *USA Today* upon the September 1985 release of *In Square Circle*. "I usually come up with the music first and then come up with an idea about the song. I sing a lyric out loud and change it right away if it sounds like too many words. I practice piano every day and sing other people's songs when I do."

Wonder added, "The album represents who I am in this decade, but it also represents what I'm seeing in a lot of situations with a lot of people. The theme...is that life and love are beautiful, but people have to work at making things happen all the time."

Motown wanted to make things happen for its premier artist, who had been teasing president Jay Lasker in 1983–84 with previews from *In Square Circle*. In mid-'84, Lasker heard from Wonder's attorney, Johanan Vigoda, about a change in plan: The singer wanted the company to release a soundtrack collaboration with Dionne Warwick, *The Woman in Red*, ahead of his promised studio set.

The Motown chieftain was not thrilled, agreeing only if Wonder would enhance the soundtrack album's commercial clout by adding a song entitled "I Just

Called to Say I Love You" [see 394]. And so *In Square Circle* was deferred again, until after *The Woman in Red*.

When Wonder finally did finish *In Square Circle*, he lifted Jay Lasker's spirits by showcasing it for hundreds of the nation's record retailers at their annual convention in Florida in March of 1985. Released six months later, the album sold more than a million copies and produced the ninth Number One pop single of Stevie's career, "Part-Time Lover."

"It could not have happened at a more appropriate time. The glow of the full moon..."

417

CARAVAN OF LOVE

Isley/Jasper/Isley

CBS ASSOCIATED 05611
WRITERS: ERNIE ISLEY, CHRIS JASPER, MARVIN ISLEY
PRODUCERS: CHRIS JASPER, ERNIE ISLEY, MARVIN ISLEY
November 30, 1985 (3 weeks)

Echoing the theme of Curtis Mayfield's "People Get Ready" from 20 years earlier, Isley/Jasper/Isley urged people to board the "Caravan of Love" to find equality and deliverance.

"I had been looking at the world scene quite a bit," says Chris Jasper, explaining the song, "and wasn't pleased with what I was seeing. I just felt that we all needed a positive message."

The music came before the lyrics, he admits. "I had the musical track and part of the melody. In fact, I had been walking around humming the melody for maybe a month or so. Then one afternoon I was just sitting in the office, with a note pad. Those lyrics just kind of poured out. It was one of those things that had to be inspired: I wrote it in about 20 minutes."

Isley/Jasper/Isley was the breakaway rhythm section of the Isley Brothers [see 329—"Don't Say Goodnight"], and "Caravan of Love" was the title track and lead-off single from their second album. "We were kind of looking for musical ideas that really reflected a little more soul than the previous album," says Jasper.

Where the earlier project was recorded at the Bearsville studios near Woodstock, New York—where many of the Isley Brothers albums were made—the trio switched to Eastern Artists Recording Studio (EARS) in East Orange, New Jersey, for the new sessions.

Jasper played piano and synthesizers, and sang the lead vocals of "Caravan of Love." Ernie Isley handled lead and rhythm guitar, and drums. Marvin Isley played bass and bass synthesizer. "As we were doing the song and I would hear the playbacks, it just came

Isley/Jasper/Isley

together," says Jasper. "It sounded like a film score in sections. I knew 'Caravan' was going to be a hit, I just didn't know how big it was going to be."

The single was on the R&B charts for almost six months, and the album reached the top three. A year later, an a capella remake of "Caravan of Love" by the Housemartins hit Number One in the U.K. "I was kind of surprised at first," says Jasper, "because I was expecting to hear some music at some point. I would never have thought to do an a capella version, so I was really kind of thrilled about that."

Isley/Jasper/Isley couldn't repeat the impact of "Caravan of Love," but Chris Jasper doesn't appear to regret the trio's departure from the Isley Brothers. "Even though it was something that was unnecessary, some good things came from it, too. The three of us actually got to do what we wanted to do."

418

DON'T SAY NO TONIGHT

Eugene Wilde

PHILLY WORLD 99608
WRITERS: RONALD BROOMFIELD, MCKINLEY HORTON
PRODUCER: DONALD ROBINSON
December 21, 1985 (3 weeks)

Eugene Wilde was ecstatic when his first single went to Number One [see 399—"Gotta Get You Home Tonight"]. He remembers being in Los Angeles at a taping of *American Bandstand* when his manager gave him the news over the telephone. "I put the phone down and kept pinching myself. I said, 'I gotta be dreaming.' It was really an achievement for me." But immediately after having his first chart entry hit the top, Wilde heard from people in the music business who told him it was a once-in-a-lifetime thing. "They said, 'You'll never get another Number One record. How can you top "Gotta Get You Home Tonight"?' "

Determined to prove them all wrong, Wilde and co-writer McKinley Horton sequestered themselves inside Philly World's Studio B. "We came up with idea after idea and scrapped them. Finally, I said, 'We need to put a "Tonight" record out. It worked great once, so let's try it again.' So instead of 'Gotta Get You Home Tonight,' we said, 'What would happen if you got home and you wouldn't want her to say no?' We came up with the concept, threw on the drum machine and got a beat happening and started playing some chords, and then the hook just popped into my mind."

Wilde was ready to record the song, but his manager Bedrock was out of the country. "We said, 'Hey man, get back here. We have to get back in the studio.' He said, 'Why don't you go home for a week or two, and I'll be back in two weeks. I want to see what you guys are doing.' He came back and heard us, and in a week, we were back in the studio cutting the album."

Unlike "Gotta Get You Home Tonight," which wasn't even considered for single release when it was first recorded, Wilde knew from the beginning that "Don't Say No Tonight" would be a hit. "We knew that was going to be the first single without a doubt."

Still, Wilde admits it was nerve-wracking watching "Don't Say No Tonight" move up the *Billboard* chart. "There was a lot of pressure on me because people were saying, 'I don't think it can happen again.' There was also a lot of pressure on the staff at Philly World to do it again."

After scoring two Number One singles with "Tonight" in the title, Wilde knew he had a good thing going. His next album included the title track "I Choose You (Tonight)." In 1993, he recorded "How About Tonight." "I think that's going to wind it up," he says with a laugh.

Wilde followed "Don't Say No Tonight" with "Diana," which reached number 10. That was his last single on Philly World; the label closed down and Wilde signed to MCA and then was switched to the Magnolia subsidiary.

Eugene Wilde

419

SAY YOU, SAY ME

Lionel Richie

MOTOWN 1819
WRITER: LIONEL RICHIE
PRODUCERS: LIONEL RICHIE,
JAMES ANTHONY CARMICHAEL
January 11, 1986 (2 weeks)

Although British pop vocalist Phil Collins had top 10 R&B hits with songs like "Easy Lover" (a duet with Philip Bailey) and "Sussudio," he failed to chart with "Separate Lives," a duet with Marilyn Martin that was the first single from the Taylor Hackford film *White Nights*. Lionel Richie had no such problem with his contribution to the soundtrack of that film. "Say You, Say Me" became his third solo Number One and the 10th of his career. It also won him an Oscar for Best Original Song.

Director Hackford originally asked Richie to write a title song for his film, which starred Mikhail Baryshnikov as a Russian defector who happens to be the world's greatest ballet star and Gregory Hines as an American soldier who has defected to the Soviet Union.

"We showed [Lionel] the film and he loved it," says Gary LeMel, who at the time headed the music department at Columbia Pictures. "He definitely wanted to write a title song. A couple of weeks later I heard back from [Lionel's manager] Ken Kragen [who] said, 'Look, he can't seem to write anything called "White Nights," but he's written something that he thinks is one of the better things he's written and it fits the picture perfectly.' " Hackford and LeMel listened to the demo of "Say You, Say Me" and agreed that it was perfect for the movie.

They did have one problem: They weren't allowed to include one of the biggest songs from the film on the soundtrack. Atlantic had the rights to release the album and Lionel was signed to Motown. Ordinarily, that would be no problem—companies frequently give artists permission to guest-star on projects being released by other companies, especially since they may need a return favor one day.

"Lionel was supposed to deliver his [new] solo album to Motown on a certain date," LeMel explains. "Motown would not allow us to have 'Say You, Say Me' on the soundtrack but they agreed to release it as a single in time to promote the picture...As things turned out, Lionel [didn't] finish his album for almost a year...The movie didn't suffer...[but] the soundtrack album would have sold more had [the song] been on [it]."

Richie's album was going to be called *Say You, Say Me*, but too much time elapsed between the single hitting Number One and the album's release. When it finally hit the stores in August, 1986, it was titled *Dancing on the Ceiling*. The title track was released as a single a month prior to the album; it went to number six on the R&B chart. The next two singles were bigger hits: "Love Will Conquer All" spent two weeks at number two and "Ballerina Girl" peaked at number five. The next single, the reggae-influenced "Se La," faltered at number 12 and broke Lionel's top 10 streak after 13 consecutive top 10 hits, stretching back to another soundtrack single, "Endless Love," his duet with Diana Ross [see 348].

420

THAT'S WHAT FRIENDS ARE FOR

Dionne and Friends

ARISTA 9422
WRITERS: BURT BACHARACH,
CAROLE BAYER SAGER
PRODUCERS: BURT BACHARACH,
CAROLE BAYER SAGER
January 25, 1986 (3 weeks)

Four years before "That's What Friends Are For" became an anthem for AIDS research, it was a little-noticed song in the film *Night Shift*, which starred Henry Winkler, Michael Keaton, and Shelley Long.

Rod Stewart sang the Burt Bacharach–Carole Bayer Sager tune in the film. The composers were disappointed he didn't give the song more of an edge. "Burt and I were not very happy with the record," Sager confirms. "The record company didn't want to consider it as a single for Rod because they thought it was too soft. The song quietly disappeared into oblivion."

And stayed there until the husband-and-wife team of Bacharach and Sager were scheduled to produce material for Dionne Warwick in 1985. Bacharach and Warwick had been estranged for 10 years after Burt split with longtime writing partner Hal David and Warwick sued them for not fulfilling a contractual obligation. Producer Aaron Spelling helped reunite Burt and Dionne after Bacharach and Sager wrote the theme song for Spelling's *Finder of Lost Loves* television series. Spelling asked Burt to have Warwick record the song.

Carole remembered the number they had written for *Night Shift* and asked Burt to play it for Dionne. Warwick thought it might make a good duet with Stevie Wonder, with whom she had recently worked on the soundtrack for *The Woman in Red*. "We cut the track and Dionne sounded wonderful on it," says Sager. "The day that Stevie came in to do his vocal, Elizabeth Taylor came down to the studio with our

Dionne and Friends, from left: Carole Bayer Sager, Burt Bacharach, Clive Davis, Elizabeth Taylor, Dionne Warwick, Stevie Wonder, and Gladys Knight

friend Neil Simon. They were just mesmerized by the performance."

Seeing Taylor in the studio gave Sager an idea. "I'm a friend of Elizabeth and I know how active she is in AIDS research. It just hit me that this song was so poignant, and wouldn't it be incredible if we donated the proceeds to AmFar [American Foundation for AIDS Research]."

Taylor was overwhelmed by the idea, and Bacharach, Warwick, and Wonder were all equally supportive. When they decided to add another voice to the track, Dionne requested Gladys Knight. "It still needed one more singer, one more punch at the end," says Sager. "It was [Arista label president] Clive Davis who suggested Elton John. Clive had become very involved with the record by then." Davis agreed to add Arista's proceeds to the AmFar donation.

Elton, who had appeared on the R&B chart with "Bennie and the Jets" (number 15), "Philadelphia Freedom" (number 32) and "Mama Can't Buy You Love" (number 36), received a copy of the work-in-progress and flew to Los Angeles to complete the track. The final version gave Dionne her first Number One single; her previous chart peak had been "Then Came You" with the Spinners, which went to number two in the summer of 1974.

421

DO ME BABY

Meli'sa Morgan

CAPITOL 5523
WRITER: PRINCE
PRODUCER: PAUL LAURENCE
February 15, 1986 (3 weeks)

Newly signed to Capitol Records, Meli'sa Morgan had a meeting with label executive Don Grierson, who said he had the perfect song for her to record on her solo album debut. "I said, 'If you say so, you're the boss.' And he sent me this demo of 'Do Me Baby.' At that time I was 21 years old. [I said] 'What is this song? I'm not singing this. My parents will never forgive me if I sing this song,' because Prince's version was so erotic. I called Don Grierson and said, 'I don't care if you're the boss. I'm not singing this.'

"He said, 'Meli'sa, trust me. If you do this song, this will be the beginning of a very great career for you. I wouldn't steer you wrong. You don't have to sing it quite as sensual as he's singing it. Sing it your way.' With the help of Paul Laurence, we went in and changed it a little bit. I sang it in one day—I didn't have to go back in. He said, 'That's it. I've got everything I need.' And the next time I heard it, it was on the radio."

Meli'sa Morgan

Morgan grew up in Queens, New York, where she sang at home for her mother and joined a gospel group when she was eight. In high school, Meli'sa fronted some local R&B bands, performing cover versions of hits by artists like Aretha Franklin and the Ohio Players. In 1982 she was in a trio called High Fashion that was signed to Capitol, but her big break came when she was singing background vocals for Kashif. "He would call me in to do the sessions and he would stack my voices in harmony and I would do the sessions by myself. I got to sing on his album, on Melba Moore's album, on Whitney Houston's first album." While touring with Kashif, Meli'sa was signed to Hush Productions, a management company that secured the deal with Capitol.

That same management company handled Paul Laurence, who was producing Freddie Jackson [see 408—"Rock Me Tonight (For Old Times Sake)"] for Capitol. Meli'sa was told she would be Laurence's next project. "When you're new, you don't have very much say-so," she points out. "But I was very lucky to work with him, because he's a very talented producer."

"Do Me Baby," originally recorded by Prince on his *Controversy* album, was the last song Meli'sa recorded for her debut album. "Everybody was in agreement that that was the one," says Meli'sa. She says she didn't realize how big the song was in the R&B community until she performed it live. "When the band played the first note, everybody would go crazy. I said, 'What did I do?' I didn't realize they were going crazy because they really loved the song."

Meli'sa eventually was introduced to Prince. "The first time I met him, he said, 'Thank you for such a great song.' And I said, 'No, you wrote the song. Thank *you* for such a great song.' He said, 'No, you made it happen. Thank *you*.' So that was a real compliment."

422

HOW WILL I KNOW

Whitney Houston

ARISTA 9434
WRITERS: GEORGE MERRILL,
SHANNON RUBICAM,
NARADA MICHAEL WALDEN
PRODUCER: NARADA MICHAEL WALDEN
March 8, 1986 (1 week)

"How Will I Know" was written because the husband-and-wife team of George Merrill and Shannon Rubicam, signed to A&M Records as Boy Meets Girl ("Waiting for a Star to Fall"), were asked by label executive John McClain to write some songs for Janet Jackson. Janet and her management passed on "How Will I Know," which upset the songwriters. "We thought it was perfect for her at the time. We had written it completely with her in mind," says Merrill.

Brenda Andrews of Almo/Irving Music played the song for Gerry Griffith, then director of R&B music in the A&R department at Arista. He was on the lookout for material for a new Arista artist, Whitney Houston. "We had a lot of R&B-based tunes, we had a few ballads, but we didn't have a pop crossover song," Griffith notes. "So when I heard 'How Will I Know,' I said this is absolutely perfect. I played it for Clive [and] he fell in love with it."

Merrill and Rubicam heard from Andrews that Griffith wanted the song for Whitney. "I wasn't very familiar with her family background," Merrill admits. "I didn't even realize at that time there was a pretty big industry buzz about her future."

Producer Narada Michael Walden was too busy working with Aretha Franklin on the *Who's Zoomin' Who* album to be thinking about a new artist like Houston. "Gerry called and begged me to produce this song," Walden says. "I had no idea who Whitney Houston was...I explained to Gerry the Aretha record was a very important album...and it wasn't the kind of thing we wanted to take time out of. He persuaded me to listen to the song and give it serious thought."

Walden wanted to make some radical changes from George and Shannon's demo, but the songwriters said no. The producer called Griffith back and told him the project wasn't going to happen. "First of all, the songwriters don't want me to touch their song, and second of all, I don't know who Whitney Houston is. I don't have time to mess with her," Walden told Griffith. A second phone call to the composers with a request for them to write additional lyrics to a verse Walden had composed met with a favorable response. "It turned out fine," says Rubicam. "The reason we balked at first was that we hadn't ever co-written with anybody...We didn't know Narada and we had never spoken with him before. We weren't used to the idea of someone changing [our] song...Now it's easier to let go, but at that time it was hard to be flexible."

The instrumental tracks were completed by Walden at his Tarpan Studios in San Rafael, California. He flew to New York and recorded Whitney's vocals in one day. Then he invited her mother, Cissy Houston, to sing background vocals. "I asked Whitney to sing on the background session," Walden says. "She was reluctant because she wanted to enjoy hearing her mother sing. I said, 'No, get out there and sing,' so she did. The background sounds incredible...Clive Davis heard the mix and immediately proclaimed it a '10,' which is outrageous for him, because he doesn't like anything!"

423

YOUR SMILE

René & Angela

MERCURY 884 271
WRITERS: RENÉ MOORE, ANGELA WINBUSH
PRODUCERS: BOBBY WATSON, BRUCE SWEDIEN, RENÉ MOORE, ANGELA WINBUSH
March 15, 1986 (1 week)

After being shut out of the R&B top 10 for four years in a row while signed with Capitol, René Moore and Angela Winbush hit paydirt with an album for Mercury. The first single from *Street Called Desire* went to Number One [see 410—"Save Your Love (For #1)"]. The follow-up, "I'll Be Good," peaked at number two. And the third single, "Your Smile," returned the duo to the top of the R&B chart.

"We wrote that together," Moore says of their second chart-topper, acknowledging it was inspired by Winbush's grandmother. He explains the method the two songwriters usually employed to come up with new material: "We would just sit in a room and toss ideas back and forth and then we would play them for Bobby Watson and he would work on them with us." Watson was the bass player for Rufus [see 188—"You Got the Love"] as well as Moore's brother. "Then we would play them for Bruce Swedien and he'd work on them." Moore is lavish with praise for Swedien, who engineered many of Michael Jackson's albums. "It was one of the best experiences I've ever had because I learned so much from him," says Moore, who worked with Swedien on the "Jam" track from Jackson's *Dangerous.*

Watson and Swedien put together an impressive roster of musicians to play on René & Angela's Mercury album. Leon Ndugu Chancler, Rayford Griffin, John Robinson, and André Fischer were on drums. Paul Pesco, Michael McGloiry, Tony Maiden (of Rufus), Paul Jackson, and Donald Griffin played guitars. Paulinho da Costa handled percussion. Watson played bass, Moore was responsible for synth bass, and the synthesizers were programmed by Ramsey Embick, Jeff Lorber, and René & Angela, who also played keyboards.

René & Angela's Mercury debut was also their last album together for the label. The duo broke up, and Winbush recorded a solo album, *Sharp,* which yielded a Number One hit [see 471—"Angel"].

In a *Billboard* interview, Moore described what it was like to suddenly be a solo act after a decade of being paired with Winbush: "It felt really strange at first, but the acceptance has been really positive." In the same interview, Moore claimed that Winbush's relationship with manager Ronald Isley was the main reason for the breakup of the act. "[Isley] felt that the group was going nowhere and that he could do better," Moore maintained. "But I wasn't interested in what they were interested in, so I walked away." After the split, lawsuits were filed by both parties regarding royalties and copyright credits. While Winbush hit the top of the chart with "Angel," Moore also stayed in the Polygram family, issuing an album titled *Destination Love* on the Polydor label. His first two singles, "All or Nothing" and "Never Say Goodbye to Love," both went top 20 R&B.

424

WHAT HAVE YOU DONE FOR ME LATELY

Janet Jackson

A&M 2812
WRITERS: JAMES HARRIS III, TERRY LEWIS, JANET JACKSON
PRODUCERS: JIMMY JAM, TERRY LEWIS
March 22, 1986 (2 weeks)

After recording a couple of dreamy-teen albums for A&M, Janet Jackson took a quick left turn and released *Control,* a mature and confident album produced by Flyte Tyme masters Jimmy Jam and Terry Lewis.

"What Have You Done for Me Lately" was the last song recorded for the album. John McClain, the A&M executive who brought Jackson and the Jam/Lewis team together, heard the cuts "Nasty" and "Control" and asked the producers to come up with another up-tempo funky song in the same vein. Jackson had already returned to Los Angeles after working on the album and had to fly back to Flyte Tyme Studios to record the song McClain requested. "When she came back to Minneapolis, the day she came in the studio, we were playing that track really loud," Jimmy Jam remembers. "She was sitting outside in the lounge and said, 'Man, that's a funky track. Who's that for?' And we said, 'It's for you' and she said, 'Oh, cool.' I think she was very pleased when she heard the track."

Jimmy was familiar with Janet's first two A&M albums before he and Lewis took the assignment of working with the young star. "My background is [as] a DJ, so I played Janet's early records," the producer says. "I could look at it from a fan's perspective and say, 'I'm a fan. Now if I could hear them do a song, this is the kind of song they should be doing.' " Jam and Lewis felt that with the right songs and the right approach, Janet was "a superstar in the making." Jimmy adds, "I think that's the reason why we were so excited about doing the record and the reason we wanted to do the whole record rather than two or three songs."

Janet Jackson

Like many of the other songs on the album, "What Have You Done for Me Lately" resulted from Jam and Lewis getting to know Jackson on a personal level. "We interpreted a lot of her thoughts at that time because she had just broken up with her husband and had gone through a lot of changes. So everything was directly inspired by her even if it wasn't [sitting down with her] and actually writing lyrics. It was basically her thoughts and we interpreted them and put them down."

Jimmy recalls how the song was written: "The bassline happened by accident...A lot of things happen like that. I was playing another song for Terry that I had thought of a track for, and the change in the song is the bassline you hear in 'What Have You Done for Me Lately.' And while I was playing the song, Terry said, 'What's that bassline?' " Jimmy told him it was the change but Lewis liked what he was hearing and turned his drum machine on. "He said, 'Play that bass line along with this beat,' and that's how the track for the song evolved. That's the nice thing about having a partner—things you don't notice, he picks up. [With] him being a bass player, that makes it easier for him to hear basslines and he heard that one."

Jam and Lewis were responsible for all of the instrumentation on the tracks. Jimmy handled synthesizers, digital sampling, percussion, acoustic piano, and background vocals, while Terry was credited with drum programming, percussion, and background vocals. Janet also provided backing vocals, as did her friend Melanie Andrews.

The producers picked "What Have You Done for Me Lately" to be the first single from *Control*. "We felt really strongly about it being the introduction to what we obviously hoped would be a good album that everybody would enjoy," says Jimmy Jam. "I think it was very representative of the sparseness and the funkiness that the rest of the album had and the attitude Janet had about being in control, being...mature to the point where she had definite opinions about what she wanted to say."

425

KISS

Prince and the Revolution

PAISLEY PARK 28751
WRITERS: PRINCE AND THE REVOLUTION
PRODUCERS: PRINCE AND THE REVOLUTION
April 5, 1986 (4 weeks)

Prince was constantly playing or recording something, so how could one tell when he was moving on from one album to the next?

Engineer Susan Rogers knew to look for certain clues, such as a change in what kind of music he was listening to at home, or a change in his look. After playing the last show of a tour at the Orange Bowl in Miami, Rogers went to California with Prince and the Revolution to record the *Parade* album, an unofficial soundtrack for the film *Under the Cherry Moon*. "Prince had changed his clothes and changed his hair," says Rogers. "He had a new haircut and a new look to match."

While Prince was in Studio 3 at Sunset Sound in Hollywood recording songs like "Under the Cherry Moon" and "Anotherloverholeinyohead," bass player Mark Brown was next door in Studio 2 with producer David Z. "They were working on a group called Mazarati, a band of Mark Brown's that was signed to Paisley Park," according to Rogers. Mark and David gave periodic progress reports to Prince. "At one point they came over and said they needed another song," Rogers recalls. "Prince was in the middle of something. He said, 'Alright, as soon as I can get to it, I'll write you something.' So he took a few minutes. He took an acoustic guitar and he had one of those little portable cassette recorders, with the built-in microphone...[He] pressed 'record' on the little

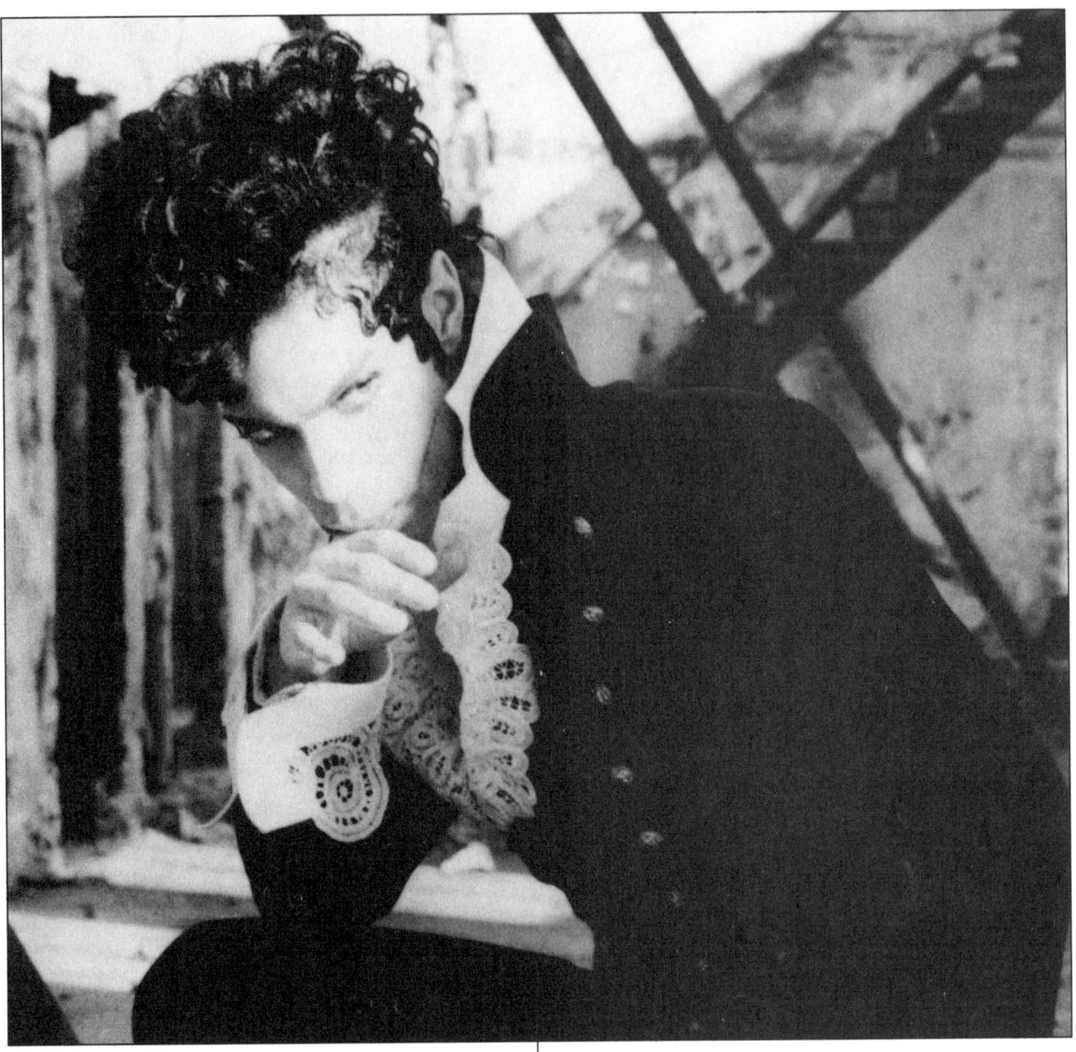

Prince

cassette recorder and came up with 'Kiss.' He played the part and wrote the words very quickly and sang it into the mike. He gave these guys a little demo cassette and said, 'Go to work on that.'

"They took it next door and came up with a drum program," Rogers continues. David Z. came up with the keyboard part, triggered by the high-hat pattern. The lead singer of Mazarati, Sir Casey Terry, added his vocal and the rest of the band provided backgrounds.

A day or two later, with the track about three-fourths completed, Mark and David returned to Studio 3 and asked Prince to check out what they had. "We played the cassette and we all flipped," says Rogers. "I was in the room with Prince and Peggy McCreary, another engineer, and we all looked at each other and said, 'Man, this is a hit!' And Prince laughed and said, 'I'm taking this back.' He looked a little funny about it because he knew they had put a lot of hard work into it."

Prince recorded his lead vocal over the track. "The leader of Mazarati had never gotten it," Rogers maintains. "[He] didn't do a great lead vocal. They did great backgrounds, but they never nailed the lead vocal." In addition to a new vocal, Prince added Wendy Melvoin's wah-wah guitar part.

Rogers says it did not take very long for Prince to complete "Kiss." "When that was done, we knew we had a great song. I think he always felt a little awkward about taking the song back from Mazarati...I think David Z. was really happy that it turned into a Prince song instead of a Mazarati song. I think Mazarati felt a little bad about it, but I don't think it would have saved their career."

426

I HAVE LEARNED TO RESPECT THE POWER OF LOVE

Stephanie Mills

MCA 52731
WRITERS: RENÉ MOORE, ANGELA WINBUSH
PRODUCER: RON KERSEY
May 3, 1986 (2 weeks)

After stints with Dunhill, Motown, 20th Century, and Casablanca, Stephanie Mills joined MCA Records at the personal invitation of label chief Irving Azoff. But she almost missed out on her first Number One single when the label released "I Have Learned to Respect the Power of Love" as the B-side of a dance-flavored track.

"I can laugh about it now," says producer Ron Kersey. "They put the song out with 'Stand Back' as the A-side and the disc jockeys automatically flipped it on their own. And Jheryl [Busby, head of black music at MCA Records] said, 'You know how much money you cost me? I've got to bring all that product back.' "

"Stand Back" reached number 15 on its own, then "I Have Learned to Respect the Power of Love" was reissued with a new catalog number as an A-side. The song, composed by Angela Winbush and René Moore [see 410—"Save Your Love (For #1)"], was originally recorded by the female trio Alton McClain & Destiny, who were signed to Polydor in 1979.

Mills heard a demo of the tune and was immediately attracted to it. "It was originally a gospel song," she says. "I love that song because my core audience loves to hear me sing songs that relate to love—and women just love that kind of stuff."

Stephanie's version differed from the demo. "Mine was tailored to my voice and my style of singing," says the Broadway star. "Angela later recorded the song herself and it was a little more churchy."

Producer Kersey knew Winbush and says he was trying to do a good job with the new version, "so I wouldn't screw up her song." He says he listened to the demo very carefully to capture the feeling that Winbush and Moore wanted for their composition. "I don't know how to put this into words," Kersey says when trying to describe how he wanted the song to feel. "I like to work in the middle of the night and I worked on it until it made me feel like I was lying on a cloud. I used sounds to make it really soothing to the ear, to the soul, so to speak."

Mills says she spent a long time working with Kersey on the production. "I was just beginning to express myself vocally the way I wanted to. A lot of times, you get songs that writers want you to sing note-for-note and want you to express the way they would sing it if they were singing it. This was my chance to sing the song the way I really felt it. He was a good producer for me."

Kersey returns the compliment. "She's very cooperative, very professional," he offers. "She made mention in an interview that she really appreciated me helping her, especially in her ad-libs. I can sing a little bit, and I have a feeling for where a song has to go at a certain point in time. And she was like clay—she let me mold her."

427

ON MY OWN

Patti LaBelle and Michael McDonald

MCA 52770
WRITERS: BURT BACHARACH, CAROLE BAYER SAGER
PRODUCERS: BURT BACHARACH, CAROLE BAYER SAGER
May 17, 1986 (4 weeks)

"On My Own," Patti LaBelle's third Number One hit, was discarded after the first attempt to record it, but Patti rescued it from oblivion with some help from Burt Bacharach and Carole Bayer Sager.

"We wrote it slowly, very slowly," Sager remembers. "Burt had the melody for a while. I had a hard time putting lyrics to it. We played it for Patti in various stages of writing it. She loved it. She said, 'When it's finished, I'll cut it.' " Bacharach and Sager wanted to produce the session themselves, but Patti was already working with producer Richard Perry (DeBarge, the Pointer Sisters) and he wanted to cut it himself. Burt and Carole dropped by the studio and were disappointed with what they heard. "We didn't think he had a handle on it," Sager notes. "I think Richard tried to cut the track twice...he finally decided he loved the song but [it] wasn't coming together for him. So he was going to dump it."

Patti confirms Carole's account: "We literally threw it out. And I was saying, '...no way can we throw this song away.' So I said to Richard, 'We have to call Burt and we have to get somebody to maybe do a duet with it.' "

Bacharach and Sager asked Sandy Gallin, Patti's manager and a good friend of theirs, if they could take a shot at recording the song. They cut the track with a live band, added Patti's vocal, and then decided something was missing. "It was crying out for a male voice," says Carole.

Patti returned home to Philadelphia while Carole contacted Michael McDonald, the former lead singer of the Doobie Brothers ("What a Fool Believes"), to see if he'd be interested in singing on two different tracks that she and Burt were producing for Patti. McDonald listened to "On My Own" as well as "Sleep with Me Tonight" and chose the former because he thought he would do his best job on it. He was also assured it wouldn't be a single, as he had already done a number of projects outside his contract with Warner Brothers. His label agreed to let him guest star with Patti on the song as long as it would only be an album track.

McDonald added his vocals in a Los Angeles recording studio while LaBelle was home in Philadelphia. The first time around, McDonald's contributions were considered a cameo performance. "It certainly couldn't be considered a duet," says Sager. "His entrance wasn't until three-quarters through the record. He didn't come in until after the bridge." People heard the song and told the producers they were crazy not to take more advantage of McDonald's talent. So they persuaded the artist to come back and record a larger part that would make the song a full-fledged duet.

"I sang to Patti's voice on tape," McDonald commented to Mary Campbell of the Associated Press. "When you're together, live, there's a certain energy you can attain. But there's a tendency to just move ahead and not spend time with details. Everybody is going with the performance. Here, I got to go in and fix some lines, and she did, too. I think it's cheating, in one respect, but it can only make it better."

A video for the song was created by filming Patti and Michael separately—she was in New York and he was in Los Angeles. They finally met for the first time at the NBC studios in Burbank when they performed the song on *The Tonight Show Starring Johnny Carson*.

428

NASTY

Janet Jackson

A&M 2830
WRITERS: JAMES HARRIS III, TERRY LEWIS, JANET JACKSON
PRODUCERS: JIMMY JAM, TERRY LEWIS
June 14, 1986 (2 weeks)

Jimmy Jam particularly remembers one review of "Nasty," the second single and the second Number One hit from Janet Jackson's *Control*. "[The reviewer] said, 'One minute she's singing, "Let's wait awhile" and the next minute she's talking about, "Let's get nasty." ' And I wrote him back and said, 'You're a reviewer. Have you ever listened to the lyrics of the song? She's saying, "I don't like nasty boys." That's what the song is saying.' And of course he printed in the paper that I'd written him back...Now he gives us good reviews."

The song "Nasty" was written after Jimmy bought a new keyboard called a Mirage. "It [had] a factory sound that was in there...more of a sound-effect type of sound," he describes. "I've always been—probably from being around Prince—interested in using unorthodox types of things to get melodies and sounds. That was a very unmelodic type of sound, but we found a way to build a melody around it."

The lyric for the song came from conversations between the writing/producing team and the artist. "It's not like a big light goes off [or] someone says, 'Wow, that would make a great song.' You just listen to what people say and then try to interpret it. I can't remember a moment that we thought it would be cool to do a song called 'Nasty'; it just happened."

Janet recorded "Nasty" and the other tracks for *Control* in Minneapolis, because Jam and Lewis insisted she record at their Flyte Tyme studios. It wasn't just because it was their home base—they knew that being away from her family in Encino, California, would force Jackson to fend for herself. Before they went to work in the studio, Jam and Lewis spent a week getting to know Janet on a personal level. "I told them my whole story, what I wanted to do," Janet told Anthony DeCurtis in *Rolling Stone*. "I told them about things that happened in my life and what I really wanted this album to be about. I said, 'I need you guys to help me express how I feel, to help me put my feelings out.' "

The producers noticed Janet's creativity blossoming as she realized—about halfway through the project—that they were incorporating her input into their songs. Jimmy Jam elaborates, "At one point, I remember her saying, 'Are you guys taping my conversations?' We said, 'No, we're just listening to you. We're trying to make an album about you.' When you do a whole album on somebody like Alexander O'Neal, you get a chance to really know them, and we're always interested in having the input of the artist, because it's ultimately the artist's album and our job is to bring out the best in them. What we were doing for Janet was nothing that we hadn't done before. We just had a little more time. It was the first project where we had our own studio, so it was a very comfortable, relaxed atmosphere...and [we didn't have to worry] the time clock was ticking and we're paying for studio time."

Janet played keyboards and provided backing vocals for the song, along with the "Nasty Boy" vocalists: Jam and Lewis, along with fellow Time comrades Jerome Benton and Jellybean Johnson. Jimmy played keyboards and percussion, and was responsible for the drum programming, while Terry played percussion.

429

THERE'LL BE SAD SONGS (TO MAKE YOU CRY)

Billy Ocean

JIVE 9465
WRITERS: WAYNE BRATHWAITE, BARRY J. EASTMOND, BILLY OCEAN
PRODUCERS: BARRY J. EASTMOND, WAYNE BRATHWAITE
June 28, 1986 (2 weeks)

Barry Eastmond had been hired by producer Keith Diamond to play keyboards and do the string arrangements for Billy Ocean's first Jive album, *Suddenly*, which included the Number One single "Caribbean Queen (No More Love on the Run)" [see 392]. When it came time to record Ocean's second album for Jive, label president Clive Calder asked Eastmond to move up to the producer's chair, along with Wayne Brathwaite.

One of the first tracks written for *Love Zone* was "There'll Be Sad Songs (To Make You Cry)," according to Eastmond. "I had the music in my head for a little while. It seemed perfect for Billy. The lyrics came out of a story my wife told me about a friend of hers. She had just broken up with the fellow she had been going out with for years. There was a particular song that always made her think of her boyfriend. She was at a party given by her new boyfriend and the song came on and reminded her of the old boyfriend. She broke down...We thought that was an interesting story so we wrote the song about it." The sad song that made her cry was, strangely enough, another Billy Ocean song—"Suddenly."

"A lot of the *Love Zone* album was written in London over at Battery Studios in Willesden," says Eastmond. "We cut basic tracks in London and then flew to New York and did guitar overdubs and background vocals. For a couple of tracks, we used a live rhythm section—'Sad Songs' was one. Then we would fly back to London and Billy would do all the vocals in London."

"It was a change of environment for them. It wasn't a change for me, because I live here," Ocean says from his London home. Eastmond adds, "I wasn't exposed to the radio over there, so I wasn't really conscious of what was happening on radio while I was writing—which was probably a good thing."

Eastmond loved working with Ocean, but found it difficult to adjust to his schedule. "The hardest thing for me working with Billy is that he loves late, late hours, and there were times he'd be doing a lead vocal at three or four in the morning and I'm literally falling asleep at the console. Once he gets going, he doesn't want to stop 'til it gets done. Wayne and I took turns with the tea to stay awake."

For *Love Zone*, Eastmond relied on a core of musicians that he loved to work with, including Buddy Williams on drums, Bashiri Johnson on percussion, and Eric Rehl on synthesizer. Brathwaite played bass and Eastmond did all the keyboard work.

Ocean recorded his vocals in his usual fashion. "I don't have any formulas," he explains. "I sing and then maybe I sing again and warm up and then maybe the producer says, 'Let's try one'...and it might not be the right one...Then I'd have a listen and think, 'Maybe I can get it better.' But once I get that feeling flowing through it, that's the one." Ocean doesn't listen to the track too much before taking to the microphone. "Because by the time you go in the studio, it becomes a stale track. [I] listen enough so that I know where the breaks and the stops come and to run it through your mind and work out your own little things. But not really listening and trying to sing to the track. You save that for the studio."

430

WHO'S JOHNNY

El DeBarge

GORDY 1842
WRITERS: PETER WOLF, INA WOLF
PRODUCER: PETER WOLF
July 12, 1986 (1 week)

I really didn't want to move away from my family," says El DeBarge, who had experienced great success with his siblings in DeBarge [see 380—"Time Will Reveal"]. "I was scared, but I thought I'd try it. I had a lot of people telling me, 'Go ahead, do it.' And before I knew it, I was doing it."

The separation came in stages. First, Motown released a couple of singles from the *Rhythm of the Night* album by "El DeBarge featuring DeBarge." In 1986, he recorded an album on his own. "The solo album came about from me being the focal point," says El.

El worked with a number of different producers on that first solo project. "It was very interesting experiencing the different approaches, the different psyches of each producer," he comments. One of those producers was Peter Wolf, who had helmed projects for Starship, Go West, and the Commodores [see 402—"Nightshift"], and had been an artist himself for Motown, recording an album with his wife Ina for the company's rock label, Morocco.

The DeBarge/Wolf team-up originated when the production company behind the film *Short Circuit*

El DeBarge

asked Wolf to write and produce a song for the movie about a cute little runaway robot named Number Five. "I had just come off the *Top Gun* thing with Kenny Loggins ["Playing with the Boys"] and they said, 'We loved your track on *Top Gun*,' " Wolf explains. "They showed me the movie and we started talking artists and then all of a sudden somebody had the glorious idea—El DeBarge. We met with El and he was into it. At the same time, Motown approached me—if I do that one song, why don't I immediately do a few more for El's album? So I did three songs and one was this track that was for the movie."

Peter and Ina tossed ideas around and came up with "Who's Johnny" as the song's title. "I was lying in bed and the song came to me," Peter says. "I wrote the song one morning, literally lying in bed. I woke up and I was toying with the idea and the whole thing was right there, chorus and all."

The producers of *Short Circuit* fell in love with the song, says Wolf. "At the end of the movie, they changed a scene where Number Five says, 'I'm tired of being called Number Five. I should get a real name.' And somebody says, 'How about Johnny?' "

El's reaction was more muted. "I thought it was a bit different from where I was at musically. But it was for a movie. They had convinced me that it would open a whole lot of ears to El DeBarge. 'Well,' I said, 'that's a good thing.' "

El says that he and Wolf worked well together in the studio. "Peter was a good producer because he knew how to make you feel relaxed as an artist, but not too relaxed. He also knew how to put you on the edge so he can get the best out of you. And he didn't overwork you. He had a good vibe, a spirit about him that I always look for."

El explains why his vocal on the song was so energetic: "We knew how we had to approach that song. He told me, 'El, this is a song with a lot of energy. The music has a lot of energy. We want the vocal to feel like that too. So when you sing it, remember to get that in your mind.' "

Wolf was impressed with DeBarge: "He was absolutely phenomenal—one of the most talented vocalists I've ever worked with." One morning Wolf arrived at the studio, "and I hear some furious be-bop piano. I walked in and El DeBarge is sitting at the piano playing some serious bop. I couldn't believe that this kid could play piano like that. El DeBarge is a serious, serious musician."

431

RUMORS

The Timex Social Club

JAY 7001
WRITERS: MARCUS THOMPSON, MICHAEL MARSHALL, ALEX HILL
PRODUCERS: JAY KING, DENZIL FOSTER
July 19, 1986 (2 weeks)

For a couple of weeks in 1986, a former break-dancer and small-time concert promoter broke the major labels' grip on the R&B summit. Jay King's tiny Jay Records from Sacramento produced the only independently distributed single to reach Number One that year.

The Timex Social Club's "Rumors" was a Caribbean-cool, rap-influenced song created by a former Berkeley High School student, Michael Marshall, and a couple of friends. "You know how people talk too much and spread rumors," Marshall explained. "We used to hear them all the time and got inspired to write it.

"Most of the people in the song are from the high school. I've always been a fan of Michael Jackson and, back then, there were always rumors about him. Then there were people at the school like Tina, [the girl in the song]. It's a true, down-to-earth thing."

With buddies Marcus Thompson and Alex Hill, Marshall performed "Rumors" at a school function in the spring of 1984. Then they put the song on tape, gaining some local airplay on college station KALX-FM in Berkeley.

Enter Jay King, a resident of Vallejo, California, the hometown of funkmasters Con Funk Shun [see 282—"Ffun"]. In the studio of Con Funk Shun's Felton Pilate, King got to know Denzil Foster and Thomas McElroy and started scouting for talent.

"This guy gave me a four-track of a song called 'Rumors,' " King said. "Everyone thought it sucked except me. I could hear what was happening, and I could hear it being a hit with some changes. We wanted to do it on Con Funk Shun, but [leader] Michael Cooper turned it down. So we called the guys who did the original and said they should record it."

The session took place in January 1986 at Starlight Studios in Richmond, California. Marshall took the lead vocals, with Thompson and Hill handling keyboards, drum programming, and background vocals.

"We made a lot of changes in the record," said King, to the concern of Marcus Thompson. "I told Marcus, 'I'm spending the money, I'm the producer, I'm the record company. I'm not going to do anything to hurt your song, we're just trying to make it better. If it's a bomb, we'll take the blame; if it's a hit, we'll take the credit.' "

After failing to interest major labels in his project, King turned to Don Macmillan ("He fronted me everything") of indie Macola Records in Hollywood. Released on the Jay label in February of '86, "Rumors" began to break as the weather warmed nationwide.

For the Timex Social Club, the record represented their 15 minutes in the spotlight—they had a couple of smaller hits on another label, then disappeared.

For Jay King, the million-seller led to a deal with Warner Bros. for a new group, Club Nouveau, featuring himself, fellow producers Denzil Foster and Thomas McElroy, Samuelle Prater, and Valerie Watson. During 1986–87, the Club created four top 10 R&B hits, including a remake of "Lean on Me," which topped the pop charts.

432

CLOSER THAN CLOSE

Jean Carne

OMNI 99531
WRITERS: TERRY PRICE, BRANDI WELLS
PRODUCER: GROVER WASHINGTON, JR.
August 2, 1986 (2 weeks)

"Working with Grover Washington Jr. was one of the most wonderful experiences of my life," Jean Carne enthuses. "It came about as a result of a suggestion made by a reporter in Philadelphia. His name is Vernon Odom and he mentioned years ago, "You and Grover should have a collaboration of some sort. You should just get together because I can feel that you're kindred spirits."

Carne signed with the Philly-based Omni label after stints with Philadelphia International and Motown, and her manager asked if she would like to work with Washington. She told him it would be a dream come true.

Songwriter Terry Price grew up in Philadelphia, in the same neighborhood as John Whitehead [see 313—"Ain't No Stoppin' Us Now"] and Teddy Pendergrass. Signed at first to Philadelphia International as part of a group called the Futures, Price then tried to sell himself to the label as a songwriter, but was told he needed more experience.

"I had the knack for writing songs," says Price. "Philly International finally hired me as an exclusive writer, where I made a hundred dollars a week." Working with other staff writers at the label run by Kenny Gamble and Leon Huff, Price wrote songs for Archie Bell & the Drells, the Jones Girls, and Jean Carne. Price left the label for another local company, WMOT, where he met artist Brandi Wells. They became romantically involved. Meanwhile, WMOT merged with another company and became Omni Records. Price was named head of A&R and continued to write and produce.

He and Wells lived in an apartment building owned by the company. "We had them move a piano in the basement," he recalls. "I would sit at the piano with a tape player and just put down music...I didn't have an eight-track or a four-track...so I would put the music on one tape recorder. Then I would set the other tape recorder up...and sing it." In this fashion, Price wrote a song called "Closer Than Close." The lyrics were inspired by his relationship with Wells. "Brandi and I were going through some changes at the time and I kept telling her if we could just be closer..." Price says that Wells's friends were telling her she was going to be a star and didn't need him. "I kept trying to tell her if we could be closer than close, in other words, closer than they think we are, then it would work out."

Jean Carne

Price asked Wells to sing on the demo and added her name to the writing credits. He took the song to the president of the label, Steve Bernstein. According to Price, the executive said the song was too old-fashioned. But one of the artists signed to Omni felt differently.

"Jean Carne was on the record label. As head of A&R, part of my job was getting songs together for her. Being head of A&R didn't mean she had to accept my song, but she loved it even with Steve saying it was dated." Price has high praise for Carne. "I like her range and I like her as a person. She was very sweet. She would listen to what you said and she would do it."

Carne was visiting a friend in Philadelphia when she heard a blood-curdling cry. Thinking a burglar had broken in through the fourth-story window, Carne ran up the stairs two at a time to find her friend screaming, "On the radio!" Although her single hadn't been released yet, WDAS was playing a test pressing. "That was how I heard it the first time," says Carne. "I heard it again while I was driving and I wanted to put my car in park, jump out and stop all the traffic around me and tell them, 'Turn your radio on! You've got to hear my record!' "

433

DO YOU GET ENOUGH LOVE

Shirley Jones

PHILADELPHIA INTERNATIONAL 50034
WRITER: BUNNY SIGLER
PRODUCERS: KENNY GAMBLE, BUNNY SIGLER
August 16, 1986 (2 weeks)

Bunny Sigler was in his office at Philadelphia International Records, putting down the track for a song he was writing for the O'Jays, when he heard a knock on his door. It was Shirley Jones, who was working in the next office with Dexter Wansel. She told Sigler she wanted to record the song she heard through the wall. He told her, "You can't. It's for the O'Jays." But Sigler talked to label co-founder Kenny Gamble, who told him that if Jones liked the song that much, Sigler should produce it for her. And

Shirley Jones

that's how she came to record "Do You Get Enough Love."

Jones was born and raised in Detroit. Her mother, Mary Frazier Jones, was one of the first gospel artists signed to RCA. Shirley and her middle sister Brenda sang with their mother, and when youngest sister Valerie was old enough, she joined them.

The sisters were 12, 13, and 14 years old when they turned to secular music. They met manager Dick Scott, who had them open for acts like the Four Tops and Little Richard when they came to Detroit. Eventually the Jones Girls recorded for Paramount and Curtom Records before touring with Diana Ross as backing singers from 1976 to early 1979.

"She gave us our own spot where we sang, 'If I Ever Lose This Heaven,' " Shirley remembers. "She told us we were ready to break out on our own and she was going to do everything she could to help us." When Kenny Gamble and Patti LaBelle were in the audience one night, Diana arranged for them to meet the Jones Girls. "As soon as I got back to the hotel, Kenny Gamble called me and wanted to know if we would be interested in talking," says Shirley.

The Jones Girls signed with Philadelphia International and recorded their own albums. They also did backing sessions for many of the artists on the label's roster. They eventually recorded one album for RCA, but then Shirley's sisters wanted to take a break.

Brenda got married and Valerie decided to attend college. "Kenny Gamble called me and asked me if I was going to take a break, too," says Shirley. "I said no. I wanted to keep singing. He said, 'Let's do a solo thing.' "

Sigler played piano and bass on the track. Larry Davis played guitar, programmed the drums, and joined Sigler on bass. Jack Faith played flute and horn. The vocal session went quickly. "One thing I found out about Shirley," says Sigler, "if you give her a song, she comes in and she knows it."

The artist explains why: "I usually do everything in a couple of takes because I will take the song and I will rehearse, rehearse, rehearse in my hotel room or my home, and I live with it. I like to get into the lyrics and have the song become a part of me. I'll pull out some sort of experience pertaining to the song, so I can relate to it and I'll go in there and knock it out."

Jones had no problem relating to the lyrics of "Do You Get Enough Love." She was two weeks into recording her *Always in the Mood* album when she met Harold Hubbard of the Harlem Globetrotters, who was staying at the same hotel in Philadelphia. They fell in love and he called her every night while he was travelling with the Globetrotters. She would sing him each new song on the album when he phoned. "I remember singing 'Do You Get Enough Love' about 20 times for him and he said, 'That's gonna be a hit.' I think because I was so much in love, where prior to that I had some on-again, off-again relationships, the lyrics pertained to my situation because I felt like, 'Yeah, I am finally getting enough love.' " Hubbard and Jones were married on September 5, 1986, just two weeks after "Do You Get Enough Love" fell from Number One.

434

LOVE ZONE

Billy Ocean

JIVE 9510
WRITERS: WAYNE BRATHWAITE, BARRY J. EASTMOND, BILLY OCEAN
PRODUCERS: BARRY J. EASTMOND, WAYNE BRATHWAITE
August 30, 1986 (1 week)

Billy Ocean and Barry Eastmond both credit their late partner, Wayne Brathwaite, for coming up with the bassline that turned into Ocean's third Number One single, "Love Zone."

"For 'Love Zone,' I came up with the drumbeat and told [Wayne] to 'play anything you hear over this.' He came up with this killer bassline," says Eastmond. "The whole idea and inspiration and vibe to that really came from Wayne," Ocean concurs. As Wayne played his bass, Billy sang whatever came into his head and hit upon the word "zone." Ocean remembers, "That's how the ideas come. I was singing 'zone' and thinking, 'Well, zone—zone.' Sometimes you don't see certain things, and Wayne just said, 'Love Zone,' which to me at first sounded strange." Billy wondered what direction the song would follow after Wayne's suggestion. "But as you listen to it and throw ideas about and you mellow out on it, you try new melodies. While you're doing that, the story's building."

Ocean says he doesn't write by formula. "Maybe the more literate you are, the more well-educated you are, the more you can look at the lyric and be able to do tricks with it. For me, the whole thing comes from how it feels and the words—words with rhythm. You've written about love so many times, but love in itself is such a wide topic. You can write a whole song saying 'I love you' without mentioning the word 'love' once. Fortunately, I love playing with words...searching for words, which is a pain at most times, but the joy is when suddenly what you've been troubling over for days or hours, you put it down and come back and look at it and suddenly, it makes sense."

Eastmond recalls how the song was completed after Wayne came up with the title: "Billy started singing melodies to the track right there and then. He was there in the studio, he heard the groove Wayne was playing on bass, he sang melodies over it. He'd sing around different hooks."

Billy Ocean was born in Trinidad as Leslie Sebastian Charles. When he was four, a friend of the family gave him a toy ukulele for Christmas and ignited his interest in music. He was seven when his family moved to the East End of London. There were six children in all, crowded into two bedrooms while their parents slept downstairs. Young Leslie still loved the calypso music of his home country, but living in Britain exposed him to new musical influences.

His parents wanted him to attend college like his siblings, but he preferred the life of a professional musician. He compromised by taking a course in tailoring and working on Savile Row during the day while singing at night. After a year he was fired from the tailoring job and focused exclusively on his music.

He used several stage names while singing in London pubs, including Joshua, Big Ben, and Sam Spade. He finally settled on Billy Ocean, remembering later that there was a football team in his village called Ocean 11, named after the film *Oceans 11* that starred Frank Sinatra and Sammy Davis Jr.

Teamed with producer Ben Findon, Billy signed with GTO Records. He was still installing windshield wipers at a Ford plant in 1976 when he heard his first single, "Love Really Hurts Without You," on Radio Luxembourg. He knew he was suddenly free to leave that job—and he did.

435

AIN'T NOTHIN' GOIN' ON BUT THE RENT

Gwen Guthrie

POLYDOR 885 106
WRITER: GWEN GUTHRIE
PRODUCERS: GWEN GUTHRIE, DAVID "PIC" CONLEY
September 6, 1986 (1 week)

Gwen Guthrie was aiming for a musical career even in high school, when she was in the Ebonettes, a four-member girl group with matching gowns, shoes, earrings, and elbow-length gloves. "It was a hobby for me," she says. "Two of us became professional. The other one is Brenda White King. She's a noted session singer." Later, while working as a first grade teacher in the New York City school system, Gwen got a call from one of her high school friends asking if she could fill in on a recording session for a backing singer who was ill. Gwen showed up and found out she would be working with producer Arif Mardin, backing Aretha Franklin on "I'm in Love" [see 172]. "This is how I made my big break into the business," Gwen reports. "Right at the top."

Six months later, Gwen signed with producer Bert DeCoteaux as a staff writer. One of her earliest hits was the comeback song for Ben E. King, "Supernatural Thing" [see 199]. A call to work on a Peter Tosh session in 1978 introduced her to reggae stars Sly Dunbar and Robbie Shakespeare. When they signed with Island Records, they invited Gwen to come to Nassau and record all the lead vocals for one of their albums. Island founder Chris Blackwell heard the finished product and signed Gwen to his label.

After four chart hits on Island and two on the Garage label, Guthrie signed to Polydor and went to work on her *Good to Go Lover* album. "I was sitting at my kitchen table and I started humming this melody," says Gwen, who remembered the phrase "ain't nothin' goin' on but the rent," which is what her South Carolina–born grandfather used to say when someone asked him "What's goin' on?"

"I'm a mother of two, so I'm an authority where certain things are concerned!" Gwen exclaims. "The two biggest arguments in relationships are usually money and children. So I think people just related to it. And it had a good beat."

Guthrie produced her debut album in conjunction with David "Pic" Conley of the New Jersey group Surface. Guthrie had told Conley about the song she wanted to record. "We'd always laugh every time she'd say 'ain't nothin' goin' on but the rent,' " he says. "So we ended up in the studio one day—myself and Sly Dunbar. Sly put together this beat off the drum machine. I picked up the bass synthesizer and started playing this line that I styled from 'White Lines' [by] Grandmaster Flash. We put the track together in minutes and then Gwen started singing on top of it. It magically came together." Later, Conley added some guitar licks from Ira Siegal. "I didn't know this was going to be a huge record...It was just fun to me," the producer says. "Out of nowhere, this was the first [Polydor] single."

Gwen Guthrie

Gwen noticed interesting reactions to the song. "I would get mixed reactions from the men. Some guys would tease me, 'You're causing me to break up with my girl.' A couple of guys were really upset." Most women loved the song, but some thought she was in favor of living with a man because of his money; she told them that wasn't the point. "I was just saying it takes two. That both parties should be productive." A British magazine called to find out how she felt about women becoming prostitutes to pay the rent. "I said, 'That's a bit heavy for me.' I had my assistant tell them that Miss Guthrie won't be available. But it's funny how people take things to the extreme. I didn't mean it that way at all."

436

(POP, POP, POP, POP) GOES MY MIND

Levert

ATLANTIC 89389
WRITERS: GERALD LEVERT, MARC GORDON
PRODUCERS: KEG JOHNSON, WILMER RAGLIN
September 13, 1986 (1 week)

Gerald and Sean Levert grew up in Cleveland listening to the music of the O'Jays. That's no surprise, as their dad Eddie was one of the founding members of that classic R&B group.

"I went on tour from the age of 11 until I was 16 or 17," Gerald explains. "I would meet a lot of people and learn from that experience. It taught me what I wanted to be and I knew what direction I wanted to go in. I wanted to be a professional and I wanted to be around for awhile." Among the artists Gerald saw up-close and personal were Gladys Knight & the Pips, the Temptations, and Marvin Gaye.

One of the things Eddie told his older son was to write his own songs. "My father bought me a grand piano when I was about nine. I was writing at the age of 10. I used to write my little songs from that—I think that's what made me become a good writer. I learned about song structure and I learned about writing with substance...I like the songs that will be here forever."

Sean Levert is clear about how he got into the group: "Gerald pulled me into this. Because he was always singing all the time and he was a little older, so my father could take him on the road during the summers. He would love to see my father do his thing. He would come back and tell me [about it]."

The third member of Levert came from outside the family. Marc Gordon's mother took him over to the Levert house to play, and the three boys became friends during their elementary school years. Marc started playing the piano in junior high school. Inspired by George Clinton, the Isley Brothers, Marvin Gaye, and Earth, Wind & Fire, Marc wrote his first song in high school.

The trio recorded some demos in the Levert basement, but couldn't get any record labels interested. "We got discouraged, but it made us better," Gerald concedes. "It made us work harder...to prove people wrong...and whenever people told me 'no,' that made me go back and write another [song]."

Levert recorded for the Tempre label, owned by former Philadelphia International executive Harry Coombs. They charted with "I'm Still" in March of 1985, and then signed with Atlantic Records.

For the first single on their new label, Levert relied on a track recorded years before in the basement. "Marc had [the track] for a long time and we could never figure out a name for it," says Gerald. "My mother was making popcorn and I just sat there. 'Pop, pop, pop, pop, pop, pop, pop,' and I turned it into a song. I had to make it make sense." It didn't occur to Gerald at first that it might be a love song. "You start thinking, OK, 'Pop goes the weasel,' 'Pop goes my head,' 'Pop goes whatever.' So it was 'Pop goes my mind' and I figured it was a love song. Make it a love song about [losing] your mind."

Marc was 22, Gerald was 20, and Sean was 18 when Levert's Atlantic debut became their first Number One single. "I didn't have any expectations of going Number One," says Marc. "It's a great feeling to be Number One," Gerald adds. "There are songs that don't even enter the charts, and to be Number One is great."

437

THE RAIN

Oran "Juice" Jones

DEF JAM 06209
WRITER: VINCENT BELL
PRODUCERS: VINCENT BELL, RUSSELL SIMMONS
September 20, 1986 (2 weeks)

Oran "Juice" Jones is candid about why he wanted to sing: "Money," he replies. The Houston-born, Harlem-raised Jones is equally candid about how he met Russell Simmons of Def Jam Records: "Hustling, man. We were selling jewelry and stuff, and Russell was putting together shows with Kurtis [Blow]. He had this group, Run-D.M.C., that he wanted to produce and I was going to give him some money to produce them." When that didn't happen right away, Simmons asked Jones if he'd be interested in making a record. He said yes, even though he'd never sung before.

Jones remembers his reaction the first time he walked into a recording studio: "It was like *Star Trek*. It was like we were on a spaceship...I had brought some cats down with me to hang out and it was brand new for them, too. They were scared to touch things. But after a while they started touching everything."

Vincent Bell wrote "The Rain" for Jones. Three weeks before it was scheduled to be released, Jones listened to the finished track. "The song didn't really hit me. I said, 'Man, there's something missing. So I wrote this little monologue on the end of it—the talking part. I spent my own money and booked the time and tagged that on the end of it. Originally it was just a song. When the song stopped, that's where [the record] stopped." Jones says the monologue was

Oran "Juice" Jones

inspired by real life. "I saw cats around me hanging out with their girlfriends. Their girlfriends were jerking them. [The guys] were beating them up, man, and that seemed primitive to me...so I thought, 'Let me not leave [the song] normal. Let me throw a little added twist on it and have it come from a different perspective...take a bad situation and put a little humor on it.' "

At first, Bell didn't take kindly to the added rap, according to Jones. "He got kind of critical. He said I shouldn't have put that on the record. But it's good that it happened, because that's what actually sold the record. That's what made it sell. It wasn't about me as a singer or Vinnie as a producer or Russell as a manager. What it was about was the art. If we're not going to stimulate, then why do it at all? If you're going to make an average record, then why do this at all? So the bottom line was I wanted to sell the record, regardless of what anybody thought."

"The Rain" wasn't the first single released from Jones's eponymous debut album. A ballad, "You Can't Hide from Love," was issued, and peaked at number 75 on the *Billboard* chart. Jones credits an independent promoter named Eddie Pugh with discovering "The Rain" and taking it to radio. "That's when the record exploded," Jones says. "Nobody knew. Not Russell. Not the record company, not even me. Nobody knew but Eddie Pugh. And then there was another cat, Ruben Rodriguez. He wasn't at Columbia at the time...but he also jumped on the record. He started working it...Those are the two cats who really knew."

438

WORD UP

Cameo

ATLANTA ARTISTS 884 933
WRITERS: LARRY BLACKMON, TOMI JENKINS
PRODUCER: LARRY BLACKMON
October 4, 1986 (3 weeks)

From their Chocolate City days through their time on Larry Blackmon's Atlanta Artists label, Cameo was known for their hard funk. "I think it was a combination of maturing in music in the '70s and having the advantage of more of an eclectic style combining the dynamics of rock and the rhythm of funk," Blackmon replies when asked how he created the group's sound. "And it developed from there. What we tried to do was create whatever we wanted to do rather than what the trend was."

Cameo has been as large as 13 people and as small as a trio. "I started Cameo and brought in other members as the group evolved," explains Blackmon. "I was pretty tired touring with temperamental lead singers who would decide on any given day, depending on what side of the bed they got up on, if they felt like working or not. Everyone's livelihood depended on the unit, [so] I wanted a concept that had individual members that were strong. I looked for instrumentalists who could sing and do more than just one thing. Which is how I came up with the name Cameo: a cameo performance by individuals making the whole."

In May of 1986, Blackmon reduced Cameo down to a core of three people: himself, Tomi Jenkins and Nathan Leftenant, with other musicians coming in as needed. Blackmon describes how their biggest hit was recorded: "With 'Word Up,' as with a lot of the Cameo material, I might record and do pre-production on a third of the songs that you might hear on an album. Then the other two-thirds are ideas from myself or other individuals working with me that we spontaneously complete in the studio...'Word Up' was created right there in the studio, having pieces of the idea before going in. I like experimenting with sounds and I think 'Word Up' had a lot to do with that. That whole album, I experimented with a lot of different sounds. It was quite an exhilarating experience."

Blackmon had been hearing the expression 'word up' at parties; one British fan shouted it to him as he was leaving BBC's White City studios after appearing on the weekly British TV chart show, *Top of the Pops*.

Blackmon, who considers himself more a song stylist than a vocalist, recorded his vocals with a filter to thin his voice. "Then I put that through a transistor radio speaker. So I had multiple sounds that I combined to make that particular character come alive. Cameo's music has always been to me like an ongoing Broadway musical with the theme changing with each album."

"Word Up" established Cameo on the pop chart as well as internationally. If the phrase hadn't been in the universal vernacular before, it was now. "We felt very good about that," Blackmon reports. "We felt as if it was due. We enjoyed the international success of that record and we appreciated having been a part of that whole movement."

439

SHAKE YOU DOWN

Gregory Abbott

COLUMBIA 06191
WRITER: GREGORY ABBOTT
PRODUCER: GREGORY ABBOTT
October 25, 1986 (2 weeks)

The song was my attempt to express how men feel when they see a woman they like," says Gregory Abbott of his first single, "Shake You Down." "Emotionally, the phrase 'Shake you down' made sense to me, and when I repeated it to a lady friend of mine, she definitely understood what I was saying. So that became the hook of the song."

Abbott started working on the demo of "Shake You Down" at his own Grabbitt Studios. "I work up a drum track and some chord changes and a general theme of the song and then put a lyric to it, sing down a vocal track. Once I have that structured the way I really want it, I bring in my musician friends. In this case, it was T. M. Stevens on bass, Alan Palanker on keyboards, Marlon Graves on guitar, and Dave Beal on drums. I let them do their interpretation of what I've laid down, then sing a final vocal. In the case of 'Shake You Down,' the vocal melody was a lot different from what it ended up being. I originally had a melodic line going through the chorus. When I finally laid down the backgrounds, I found the melody going over those backgrounds didn't work, so I just did a call-and-response thing where I answered the backgrounds." The midsection wasn't written until Abbott recorded his final vocal. He let the spirit hit him and improvised on the spot.

"Shake You Down" was one of three songs on a demo tape that helped Abbott secure a deal with Columbia Records. He was introduced to the label through the efforts of his uncle, Mike Abbott, who told people at Charles Koppelman's The Entertainment Company about his nephew. CBS agreed to let Abbott produce himself, an unusual arrangement for a new artist. But Abbott knew his way around a studio. After securing his undergraduate degree in psychology at Boston University and his Master's at California State University at San Francisco, he did graduate work in literature at Stanford. He taught various courses at UC Berkeley and interrupted his doctorate studies to pursue a career in music. He met Marvin Gaye, who had a 24-track studio, and learned at the hands of a master.

Abbott moved to Los Angeles, where he met and married Freda Payne ("Band of Gold"). She recorded four of his songs on her *Stares and Whispers* and *Supernatural High* albums. Abbott returned to Manhattan and worked as a researcher for a Wall Street brokerage. At night, he worked on his music at a recording studio. When some investment bankers noticed him listening to his Walkman during the day, they were curious to hear his music and took an interest in Abbott's career. They financed a studio in his home as well as a label, Gramercy Park Records.

After producing other artists for the label, Abbott decided to turn his attention to himself. "People would often ask who was singing on the demos I'd worked on," Abbott told David Nathan. "I figured it couldn't hurt to produce myself. After all, I know the artist in question pretty well—and I think he knows how to take direction."

Abbott spent three years writing songs for himself. "I was determined not to go rushing out there with any old kind of stuff. So I waited 'til I had three songs that I felt really represented me in the way I wanted to be heard." He recorded 40 songs and selected the three best to submit to CBS. His first choice for a single was "I Got the Feelin' (It's Over)," but that turned out to be the follow-up to "Shake You Down."

440

A LITTLE BIT MORE

Melba Moore with Freddie Jackson

CAPITOL 5632
WRITERS: GENE MCFADDEN, LINDA VITALI, JAMES MCKINNEY
PRODUCER: GENE MCFADDEN
November 8, 1986 (1 week)

"I love duets because two voices immediately add a completely different perspective to a song," proclaimed Melba Moore a few years ago.

"A duet immediately adds another dimension to a song—it almost becomes like a one-act play, two actors playing roles. It's like eavesdropping on a couple's very emotional, private moments. Duets can be very powerful."

Judging by the charts in the '80s, you'd have needed a crowbar to tear Melba from her love of pairing up. In 1984, she got together with Lillo Thomas for "(Can't Take Half) All of You." In '86, she teamed with Kashif for "Love the One I'm With," a top five R&B hit.

The following year, there was Dennis Collins and "It's Been So Long," another top 10 success. In 1988, Moore was back with Kashif for "I'm in Love." And that's to say nothing of Freddie Jackson.

"The magic is together, looking face-to-face," agrees Jackson, although he may not have taken the duet habit quite as seriously as Melba. Cutting "A Little Bit More" with her was, well, fun. "We laughed the majority of the session," he says. "Gene McFadden was, like, 'Are we ever going to get any work done?' Melba and I are a riot together—we call each other boyfriend and girlfriend, you know. Charles [Huggins, a principal in Hush Productions, the company that managed Jackson and Moore] is like, 'What's going on? That's my wife.' "

Melba recorded "A Little Bit More" for her Capitol album, *A Lot of Love*. "That was a very special song, written by Gene McFadden," says Jackson. "I had been working with Melba, singing background for her, so I knew her tones, she knew my tones. It was very easy for both of us to go into the studio and sing that song."

McFadden wrote "A Little Bit More" with Linda Vitali and James McKinney, cutting it at Unique Recording, Celestial, and the Hit Factory. McKinney handled keyboards and drum programming, with Timmy Allen on bass and Mike Campbell on guitar.

While Melba and Freddie were doing "A Little Bit More," Jackson was also sweating—New York burned in the summer of '86—over *Just Like the First Time*, the follow-up to his breakthrough *Rock Me Tonight* album. And he spent two back-to-back days filming video clips for "A Little Bit More" and the song that was to displace it on the charts, "Tasty Love."

"[Melba and I] do a lot of private things together," Jackson concludes. "We did another duet after that, 'I Can't Complain,' but it wasn't as successful as 'A Little Bit More.' Patti LaBelle has threatened me—says I'd better not sing with anybody else!" Jackson laughs. "I did a duet with Natalie Cole, then Irene Cara. Patti says, 'What is this, is there something wrong with me?' "

441

TASTY LOVE

Freddie Jackson

CAPITOL 5616
WRITERS: PAUL LAURENCE, FREDDIE JACKSON
PRODUCER: PAUL LAURENCE
November 15, 1986 (4 weeks)

When "Tasty Love" displaced "A Little Bit More," Freddie Jackson entered the history books. As *Billboard* columnist Paul Grein reported that week, Jackson became the first artist to succeed himself at Number One on the magazine's R&B charts since Dinah Washington in July 1960.

"To give you an idea of how long ago that was," wrote Grein, "Eisenhower was president, Connie Francis was the hottest singer on wax, and Freddie Jackson was a nine-month-old baby in Harlem."

Jackson had already entered the Capitol Records history books in 1985, when his "Rock Me Tonight" [see 408] became the label's longest-running Number One since Nat Cole's "Straighten up and Fly Right" in 1944. (Don't *ask* who was president then.)

"Tasty Love" was composed by Jackson and Paul Laurence, the writer/producer of "Rock Me Tonight" who knew the singer from their collective school days. "We go back to playing at Paul's mother's project apartment in New York," he says.

"Paul always challenges me, because he knows me from singing way back. So he's very hard on me and, for some reason, I feel like he doesn't want me to think things are easy. And he does that quite well!"

Jackson also draws a sharp contrast between Laurence and Barry Eastmond, the writer/producer of "You Are My Lady," which followed "Rock Me Tonight" to Number One. "They have two totally different styles," he says. "Barry gives me the orchestration part of the music that I like, where Paul will give me the more *soul*ful—maybe street—sound.

"There are certain words Barry won't use, like 'Y'all,' where Paul might. Barry won't use 'ain't' too much, where Paul will. So both give me two totally different types of music, but I think they're both sophisticated."

And where Eastmond is a relatively fast worker, Laurence is not. Jackson explains, "[Paul says] 'OK, it's time to make an album, so what are we going to record, what are we going to write about?' He works like that, so sometimes I could strangle him 'cause he takes so long. But then the end result is really worth the wait."

The four weeks that "Tasty Love" spent at Number One offered proof of that. It was the lead-off single from Jackson's second album, *Just Like the First Time*. Laurence recorded the song at his favored New Jersey studio, Digital By Dickinson, in Bloomfield, and at New York's Soundworks. The track featured Laurence himself on keyboards, with bassist Timmy Allen and guitarist Mike "Dino" Campbell. Jackson sang background vocals.

"I feel a good ballad will stand the test of time," Freddie summarizes. "There are so many up-tempo songs that just happen and you dance off of them, you know. After a certain amount of time, the new dance that goes with that particular record has faded—so the song fades out. A good ballad is going to do just what it's supposed to: live. You feel the emotion, you'll remember it."

442

LOVE YOU DOWN

Ready for the World

MCA 52947

WRITER: MELVIN RILEY JR.

PRODUCERS: READY FOR THE WORLD, GARY SPANIOLA

December 13, 1986 (2 weeks)

Ready for the World were ready for another smash in the fall of 1986, to match their first Number One [see 414—"Oh Sheila"] a year earlier. This time, Detroit's Gary Spaniola was enlisted to help the sextet with production.

A musician with a local pedigree in a band called Bitter Sweet Alley, Spaniola owned the 24-track Seller Sound Studio in Sterling Heights. Ready for the World moved in to cut their second MCA album, *Long Time Coming*. Which it was, according to the producer. "They wrote probably three-quarters of the tunes in the studio," he says. "They were pretty slow. They had just come off a platinum record, so they were on a cloud."

Nonetheless, Spaniola was impressed by Ready for the World's lead singer and chief lyricist, Melvin Riley. "He is one of those people you don't have to worry about recording over and over to get him in tune and all that. He's there. And he writes with feel, he doesn't just think technical."

Riley himself explained to *Rock Scene*, "I don't fully work out songs, I just come up with ideas. When I get off the road, I can think clearly enough to develop them into full pieces. I have bags of tapes when I get off the road. So I just reach into a bag, pull out a tape, listen to it and work out an idea until it's developed."

With Riley (who also plays rhythm guitar and piano) in Ready for the World were Gordon Strozier (lead guitar), Gregory Potts (keyboards), John Eaton (bass), Gerald Valentine (drums), and Willie Triplett (percussion). Strozier, Potts and Triplett sang backing vocals.

Ironically, "Love You Down" almost didn't make it out of the Seller Sound sessions. Spaniola recalls, "It was a song that Melvin and myself really liked and everyone else was, 'Naah, it's just another slow, sap song.' He originally sang, 'Let me lay you down.' I kept telling him, 'Melvin, this isn't going to go anywhere [with those lyrics].'

"So after coming up with 'Love You Down,' we finished it relatively quickly—it wasn't that important on the list. Then we sent rough mixes of all the tunes to Louil Silas at MCA, who flipped over this tune. He said, 'This is coming out first, this is a smash.'

"So I ended up mixing the single at my studio, probably in about an hour, an hour-and-a-half at the most. Louil had called to say, 'This thing's got to be here.' I had to jump on a plane that was leaving Detroit at six o'clock for L.A. I finished the mix at five and made it to the airport as they were closing the jet door. It was that close."

443

GIRLFRIEND

Bobby Brown

MCA 52866
WRITERS: LARRY WHITE,
LEE PETERS, KIRK CRUMPLER
PRODUCER: LARRY WHITE
December 27, 1986 (2 weeks)

Bobby Baresford Brown was just 14 years old when he experienced his first Number One hit as part of New Edition [see 371—"Candy Girl"]. Three and a half years later, he had left the teen quintet and was back on top of the *Billboard* R&B chart with his first solo single, "Girlfriend." You'd think he'd be happy with *King of Stage,* his first album away from New Edition, but it didn't represent the direction Brown wanted to follow.

"It was really a solo New Edition album," Bobby complains. "The voice was there, the voice they remember from 'Candy Girl.' It didn't work out for me. We had to regroup and find out what my identity was as a singer."

Despite Bobby's disappointment with the album, "Girlfriend" kept his name high on the chart. It was recorded at Michael Denten's Infinite Studios in Alameda, California. Denten had worked on a couple of projects with Collage ("Get in Touch with Me"), an outfit signed to Solar Records. Group members Larry White, Lee Peters, and Kirk Crumpler had written the song "Girlfriend" for another Solar group, the Whispers [see 327—"And the Beat Goes On"]. "They hadn't finished it and then [they] hooked up with Bobby and at that point they got the song together for him," says Denten.

Denten recalls a Bobby Brown very different from the public image the artist presented in the '90s. "Bobby was very quiet, very mellow at the time," the studio owner says. "Even more on the timid side...He was very to himself." Denten adds that Brown was very easy to work with. "He was coming into his own as far as getting into his vocals and doing a solo project. He was open to a lot of suggestions that Larry was throwing out to him for doing vocals for the song."

White, who had been the lead vocalist for Collage, produced the track and played guitar, bass, and percussion and sang backing vocals. He also sang on the demo, which was forwarded to Louil Silas at MCA Records so Bobby could hear it and have some rehearsal time before recording his own vocal. Crumpler was responsible for the bass synthesizer and keyboards and Peters was one of the background singers.

Bobby Brown

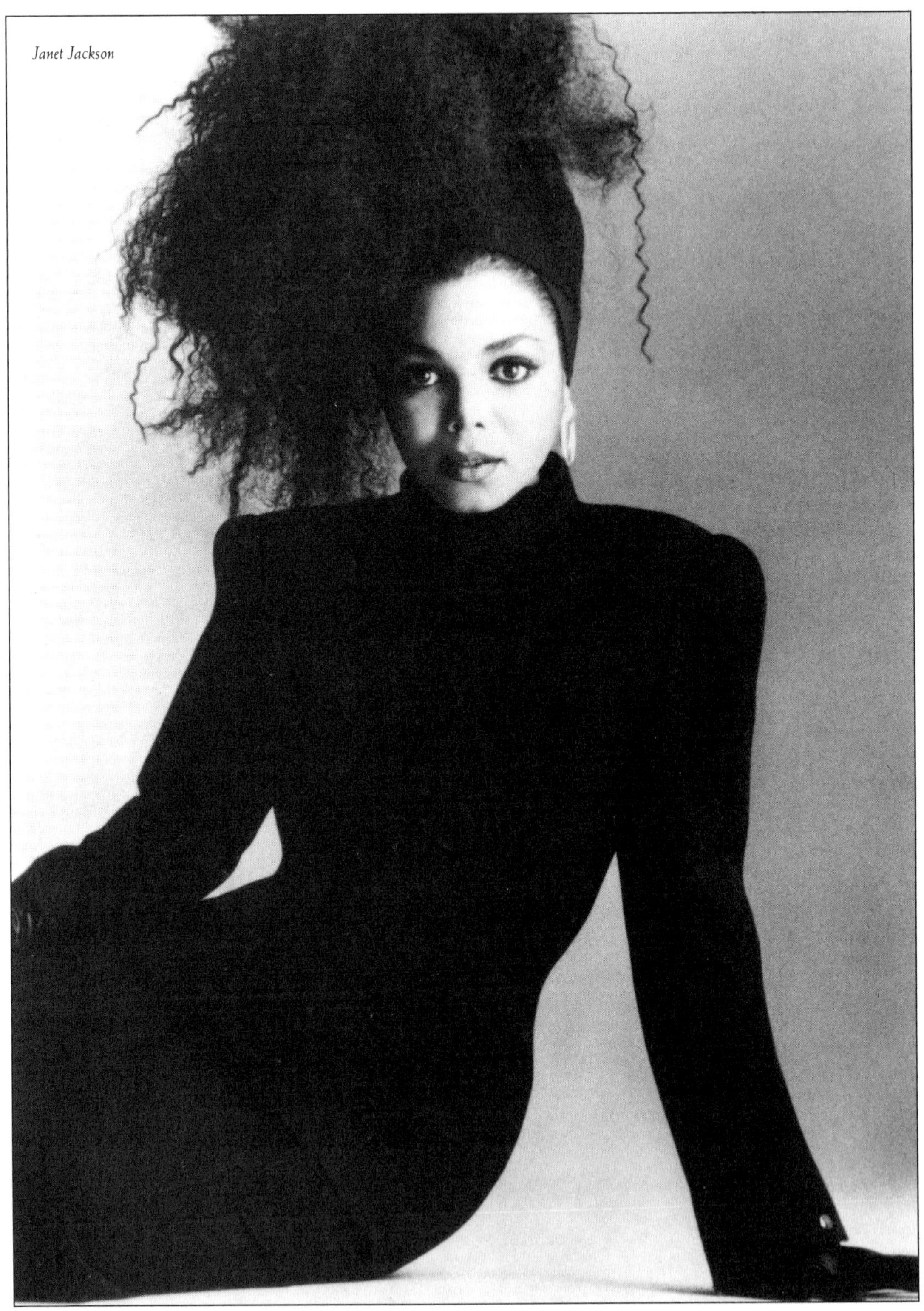

Janet Jackson

Melicio Magdaluyo was the soprano saxophone player who contributed all of the horn parts on the track. Emilio Conesa also played guitar, and the keyboard section also included Jay Logan and Grady Wilkins. The other background singers were Richard Aquon, Olie Bowlds, and Wilkins.

Denten recalls the recording process: "We did a lot of sequencing. We were using a Yamaha sequencer, I think it was the Q-1, and also the Linn Drum. I think it was the Linn 9000 that was new at the time. Then a lot of tracks we redid live afterward. Once we got the basic tracks finished, Bobby came into town with his brother and we spent about two days working on vocal parts, getting them together with the background vocalists and Bobby."

Silas came up to Infinite Studios the day Denten was mixing the track with White and stayed until it was finished. "[It was a] normal routine with Larry White," says Denten. "We spent pretty much all day and all night working on the track, tweaking it up. And when we finished and sent it down there, I think they made a decision within a couple of weeks. They wanted to release it as a single."

444

CONTROL

Janet Jackson

A&M 2877

WRITERS: JAMES HARRIS III, TERRY LEWIS, JANET JACKSON

PRODUCERS: JIMMY JAM, TERRY LEWIS

January 10, 1987 (1 week)

The title track from Janet Jackson's third A&M album summed up what was going on in her life: "The fact that she had moved out, that she had decided to make singing her career," says producer Jimmy Jam. "When she first started singing and got a record deal, it was more or less her dad's idea, because she had the talent to do it but she was not 100 percent confident in her abilities to do that as a full-time career, so she was acting and doing other things. I think with the *Control* album, we were very fortunate that she had decided that the music side of things was what she was going to concentrate on. We wanted a song that represented all the things she was feeling, and we felt like 'Control' was the song."

" 'Control' came from the heart," Janet affirmed to Robert Hilburn in the *Los Angeles Times*. "It was all about stepping out, taking control of your life...A certain point in your life when you ask yourself who you are and what you want to do."

The distinctive break in "Control" came about by accident, the producer reveals. "When you program drum machines, you program a lot of different patterns in. But the way we do it, we never put the programs in a sequence. We play and change the sequences by hand. So at one point in 'Nasty,' I changed to the wrong sequence and it made this weird drum break. A lot of times when that happens, we leave it and figure out what to do with it musically later. That's what happened on 'Control.' There are two or three breaks where it stops and there's a little 'do-do-do-do-do-do,' and that was the creation of hitting the wrong drum program at the wrong time. But it worked."

The two producers were personally responsible for most of the music heard on "Control." Jimmy handled drum and synthesizer programming, digital sampling, and percussion, and Terry played percussion. Janet contributed on keyboards and sang backing vocals along with Melanie Andrews, Hami Wave, and Lewis.

Like the other Number One singles on the *Control* album, the title track sported a video that showed off Janet's dancing ability. Mary Lambert, who directed "Control" as well as "Nasty," told Hilburn, "She is really driven to be—I don't want to say better than Michael—but to create her own image. And it was a time of independence and growth for her."

Jimmy Jam allows that he was "blown away" by Janet's videos. "That's the great thing about working with Janet," he enthuses. "Besides what she brings to you in the studio, when it comes time to do the videos and the whole thing, she pulls off that aspect of it so well...As writers, you hope the singer enhances whatever ideas you put down on a page and brings them to life. That's what Janet does better than anybody else and probably the reason we've had the most success with her, [is] her ability to bring it home after the studio work is done. She does such a great job after that."

445

STOP TO LOVE

Luther Vandross

EPIC 06523

WRITERS: LUTHER VANDROSS, NAT ADDERLEY JR.

PRODUCERS: LUTHER VANDROSS, MARCUS MILLER

January 17, 1987 (2 weeks)

'Stop to Love' was the first song we ever wrote on the spot," says Luther Vandross. "We were in a place called Montserrat, which is the little island off of Antigua at a studio called Air Studios." Beatles producer George Martin owned Air Studios, with facilities in London as well as Montserrat. "We were there and we had written 'Give Me the Reason' in L.A., Nat [Adderley Jr.] and I. And I said, 'Nat, we need one other up-tempo song, but not exactly a dance song. I don't want to compete with KC and the Sunshine Band, I don't want to take over that slot. We just need something with energy but not a dance number.'

"And so we sat at the piano as Marcus [Miller] was working on something else that he had written...and started with that sort of boogie-woogie. It all started with one note. One bass note that just went on forever, and then we changed the syncopation and finally the chords came, and after that I went back to the hotel. Went to the little house where we were staying and finished it."

Luther describes the process of writing the lyrics: "As a man writing the song, I wanted to talk about a woman who worked and a woman who was motivated, was a bit overly motivated by career...You work a lot and you never stop to love. That's a lyric that a woman would traditionally sing, and I thought it was interesting that I would sing it."

The song was recorded one track at a time at Air. "That was the first time we were starting to use machines," says Vandross. "It was a very interesting process. The layering of it took more time, but the result is great."

"We knew it was good," Macus Miller agrees, "[but] you never know if it's going to fit in with what's going with radio at the time. 'Stop to Love' was interesting because of the sounds. We had Jason Miles doing some sound programming and he came up with some really interesting stuff."

One of the reasons Luther loves "Stop to Love" is the voice in the background—the voice of one of his longtime idols, Cissy Houston. "It's so amazing that my perspective for liking certain records is the background vocals," he says. "I know that my favorite records through the years have been the records with the best background vocals, in addition to the best lead vocals, of course. Cissy Houston...had the best background vocals, and when [Nick] Ashford and [Valerie] Simpson produced Diana Ross, they had Joshie Armstead and Ashford and Simpson singing the background vocals. That was just incredible."

In a *Rolling Stone* interview with David Ritz, Luther mentioned that Cissy Houston and the other Sweet Inspirations "taught me what thick, luscious harmony was all about." He talked about being depressed during his last two semesters at Western Michigan College. "My only consolations were the Sweet Inspirations and Aretha. That was 1970 when Aretha's *This Girl's in Love with You* album with 'Eleanor Rigby' came out. Each morning I'd listen to her while waiting for the college cafeteria to open."

446

CANDY

Cameo

ATLANTA ARTISTS 888 193
WRITERS: LARRY BLACKMON, TOMI JENKINS
PRODUCER: LARRY BLACKMON
January 31, 1987 (2 weeks)

Cameo followed their second Number One single, "Word Up" [see 438] with their third chart-topper, "Candy."

Larry Blackmon recalls how "Candy" came to life: "Tomi [Jenkins] had a bassline that was very interesting. We were staying at the Mayflower Hotel in New York and he came to my room and said, 'I've been messing around with this bassline. I don't know—let me play it for you.' He played it for me and I put the drums to it and we went from there. I wanted the vocal to be different coming in and out, letting the groove itself be the main lead, and I also wanted influences of a rock nature going through it. Not because it was rock, but because the transitions felt right. And I loved ad-libbing on it."

The origin of the title is simple to explain: "It was about a love being so sweet and complete, you just could not get enough of it," says Blackmon. "We related it to a kid in a candy store."

"Candy" was included on the *Word Up* album. "What was unique for that album was I invented a snare sound that became standard in the industry and is still used today," Blackmon says. "The exciting thing is to hear your snare sound duplicated on some of the biggest hits and watching Sunday football and Monday night football and to hear it in the commercials. I'm not going to divulge exactly how I did it, but I used a real different technique with recording. Actually, the snare wasn't a snare. It was a clap sound that I recorded in a special way, which gave off that percussive hit that became standard. You can remember certain drum sounds through the years that people used and they would relate to them by giving them a certain name...The Cameo snare was always related to as 'Cameo snare.' We developed that for 'Word Up' and used it again in 'Candy.' "

Perhaps as memorable as the sound Cameo made in the studio was the image they presented to the public. The cover of the *Word Up* album featured the group in Jean-Paul Gaultier outfits and way-out hair styles, a fashion statement that Madonna would also employ. "Jean-Paul was a Cameo fan, and we had arranged through our clothing designer at that time, Twice Anderson, to obtain his new spring collection," Blackmon explains. "It had to be returned immediately, of course, and we were very fortunate to get it,

Cameo

because it was a first. And those were the clothes we wore on the album cover. While we were doing a show at Wembley, Jean-Paul was there and he came backstage and I had bought one of his leather jackets from Barney's. I mean, I liked his stuff before meeting him. And he said, 'Larry, you don't need to wear clothes from [the] store. Everyone has that. You come to Paris. You come and I can make something special for you.' So our trip took us back to Paris. We did a concert at the Zenith and we sat in on his big introduction of his spring collection at one of his runway shows. The next day he took us over to his boutique and gave us so many clothes, then he took us to his workroom and gave us a bunch of stuff."

Blackmon says he was excited to come in contact with someone who had vibrant, creative energy like Gaultier. "Spending a lot of time in Europe really put me in touch with the fact that I was an artist. When you come up in the music business here in the States, the whole commercial thing is embedded so much in your artistry...But I never felt as if I was an artist until traveling in other circles and getting in touch with the feeling of being creative, and Paris is a city that inspires you so much."

Melba Moore

447

FALLING

Melba Moore

CAPITOL 5651
WRITERS: FRANNE GOLDE, GENE MCFADDEN
PRODUCER: GENE MCFADDEN
February 14, 1987 (1 week)

For someone so steeped in Broadway—from *Hair* to *Timbuktu*—Melba Moore sure knew how to make a decent R&B record.

In 1969, for example, she did just that with "Don't Stop, Sing Along with the Music," a quasi-Motown bouncer that was later popular on Britain's "northern soul" circuit. She did it again in 1976 with the turbo-driven "This Is It," produced by Van McCoy. And in 1982, she customized the zippy "Love's Comin' at Ya," written by Paul Laurence Jones, who sang gospel with Freddie Jackson before Jackson became Melba's protege.

Moore arrived on the Great White Way during the late '60s in *Hair,* then advanced to *Purlie,* another successful musical. In 1971, a *Billboard* reviewer declared that she had "an extraordinary voice that combined the feel of opera, gospel, and good ole downhome blues."

But those four-octave pipes had to wait until 1987 to top the charts, and that was with the decidedly mellow "Falling." The song was composed by Franne Golde, who had helped craft the Commodores' "Nightshift" [see 402], and Gene McFadden, who was half of the team responsible for such Philadelphia gems as "Back Stabbers" [see 133] and "Ain't No Stoppin' Us Now" [see 313].

"I absolutely loved 'Ain't No Stoppin' Us Now,' " explains Golde, "and I had been working at a studio in L.A. called Suma. The owner was Rick Stevens, who at the time had started a publishing company and signed McFadden and [John] Whitehead. So one day I met them and said, 'You know, I gotta write with you guys sometime.' "

The time came soon. "I was in the studio one day," Golde recalls, "playing around on the keyboards, and Gene came in. He just started singing a melody. He's the only person I've ever met—other than maybe Albert Hammond—who you can literally play one or two chords to, and he can come up with this gorgeous melody out of the air.

"That's what he did: He sang down this beautiful melody and sang down some lyrics along with it, just off the top of his head. And within a few days, we had 'Falling.' That was it."

By this time, Moore's credits included a couple more Broadway shows (*Timbuktu, Inacent Black*), multiple

TV appearances, several movie roles, and a selection of hit records. In fact, Gene McFadden and John Whitehead had produced her version of the Bee Gees' "You Stepped into My Life," a top 20 R&B success in 1978.

Eight years after that, McFadden served as one of the producers of Melba's *A Lot of Love* album, recording "Falling" at New York's Celestial and Unique studios with Timmy Allen (bass), Jimmy McKinney (keyboards) and Mike "Dino" Campbell (guitar), among others.

"My favorite version of the song is actually the demo, which Gene sang," says Franne Golde. "And I got the sax player [Phil Kenzie] who did 'Year of the Cat' with Al Stewart to do almost like a duet thing with Gene, and it's just classic. But they didn't cut it like that with Melba."

448

HAVE YOU EVER LOVED SOMEBODY

Freddie Jackson

CAPITOL 5661
WRITERS: BARRY J. EASTMOND, JOLYON SKINNER
PRODUCER: BARRY J. EASTMOND
February 21, 1987 (2 weeks)

To those who say Freddie Jackson's career reads like a soap opera—from computer-punching clerical worker to background vocalist for a Broadway diva, then platinum sales with his debut album—the singer might reply that there's only one life to live. Or that he's one of the young and the restless.

After all, what else is there to do in 89 cities across America while waiting to put on a show? Not a lot, Jackson admitted after his first nationwide tour (with Melba Moore) in 1985. And so he became an enthusiastic fan of television soaps.

To feed that appetite, the chart-topper also appeared on *One Life to Live*, following in the footsteps of such other mid-'80s guests as Rick James, Starpoint, Patti Austin, and Kool & the Gang. "I saw the others perform," Jackson said at the time, "and thought, 'Hey, I have a record out, too. And it's double-platinum. When can *I* get on?' "

Jackson's been getting on the charts since 1985's "Rock Me Tonight" and the million-selling album of the same name. For the follow-up, he reconnected with the songwriter and producer responsible for most of the first LP, Barry Eastmond.

This was '86, and Eastmond, for his part, had hooked up with fellow songwriter Jolyon Skinner. "Keith Diamond had recommended that I get together with Jolyon on a Controllers project," he says. "We hit it off and decided to keep writing together.

"We would both come up with the hook [for a song], then come up with the track. Or I'd get together with Jolyon and figure out a hook, then he'd take it from there. We would do it pretty quickly: the process only used to take a couple of hours." Jackson agrees. "Barry does a lot of pre-production in his home, he'll give me the tapes to live with, and then we'll go into the studio to finish the work."

"Have You Ever Loved Somebody" was composed for Jackson's second album, *Just Like the First Time*. Eastmond explains, "That was a song we wrote and said, 'Well, *we* like it, but we wonder if it's something people will get into.' "

It was cut at New York's Unique Recording and Celestial Sounds. "That track was mostly me," says the producer, "with keyboards, a drum machine, and synth bass. Eric Rehl did some synth, too, and Ira Siegal played guitar." Background vocalists were Jackson, Vaneese Thomas (daughter of Rufus) and Curtis King.

To support the release of *Just Like the First Time*, Freddie went on the road again. "You step on the stage, feel the tension and excitement, see people actually running to the stage, and know that they want *you* to make them happy. Once I feel the intensity, I come alive."

And, in between, there are always the soaps.

449

SLOW DOWN

Loose Ends

MCA 52976
WRITERS: CARL MCINTOSH,
JANE EUGENE, STEVE NICHOL
PRODUCER: NICK MARTINELLI
March 7, 1987 (1 week)

Loose Ends did more than become the first British band to top the U.S. rhythm & blues charts—they did it *twice*.

In 1987, the trio of Carl McIntosh, Jane Eugene, and Steve Nichol got serious about America: embarking on a 42-date tour with Freddie Jackson. Two years earlier, Jackson's six weeks at Number One with "Rock Me Tonight" was terminated by Loose Ends' first summit-seeker [see 409—"Hangin' on a String"].

Jackson obviously held no grudges. "We had real good fun on that tour," says McIntosh. "We did uptempo stuff and Freddie did smooth-tempo stuff, so when we'd go onstage, it would be all funky, and when he came on, it'd be all cool."

It was also Loose Ends' first U.S. excursion as a playing band. "We hadn't toured live with a group before, the three of us had only done track dates," recalls McIntosh. "And that's kind of boring after a while." Musical director for the tour was Lesette Wilson, who worked for Freddie Jackson's management/ production team, Hush.

For "Slow Down," Loose Ends again collaborated with producer Nick Martinelli and recorded in Philadelphia. "We were working with a new team Nick had put together on that album," says McIntosh, "and a lot of the tunes we did then were recorded through the Fairlight. But I didn't like it; it made the music sound mechanical."

Midway through cutting the album at Sigma Sound, McIntosh and the other group members "came back to London [for a break] and got together some new ideas." One of them was "Slow Down."

McIntosh explains, "I had a reggae tune, which was real roots reggae, and I went back to Philadelphia and played it for Nick. He said, 'That's not reggae.' I said, 'What do you mean, that's not reggae? I'm Jamaican.' "

Martinelli was comparing the groove to Lionel Richie's "All Night Long (All Night)," which is "a bassline type of tune," says McIntosh. "I think he kind of saw that as reggae-ish basslines in soul music. So we made a move to make the bassline have that type of effect in 'Slow Down,' and I think it worked. Although he didn't agree with me about what reggae was, we came out with something."

Loose Ends sang and played on "Slow Down," according to McIntosh. "That was the only track on the album that didn't have Fairlight or any sequencing. It was just a drum machine and everything else was live."

Including saxman Sam Peake. "Me and Nicky disagreed on that," says McIntosh. "He wanted a smooth-type sound, but I heard more of a Maceo Parker type of sax. Sam's a friend of mine, so when I didn't like the solo, Nicky just got up and left the room. He knew if I didn't like it, we'd have to do something. So I spoke to Sam, and he came up with this solo, which was amazing—a real Maceo vibe."

450

LET'S WAIT AWHILE

Janet Jackson

A&M 2906
WRITERS: JAMES HARRIS III, TERRY LEWIS, JANET JACKSON, MELANIE ANDREWS
PRODUCERS: JIMMY JAM, TERRY LEWIS, JANET JACKSON
March 14, 1987 (1 week)

When John McClain of A&M Records suggested working with producers Jimmy Jam and Terry Lewis to Janet Jackson, she loved the idea because she wanted the same funky sound they had produced for artists like the S.O.S. Band, Cherrelle, and Alexander O'Neal. But based on the first two songs recorded for *Control*, she might have wondered where the funk went.

"The first few songs we did with her weren't what would be considered the funkier songs on the album, like 'Control,' 'Nasty,' and 'What Have You Done for Me Lately,' " says Jimmy Jam. "We actually started out doing 'Let's Wait Awhile' and 'Funny How Time Flies.' "

"Let's Wait Awhile" was written by the producers along with Jackson and her best friend at the time, Melanie Andrews, who accompanied Janet to Minneapolis for the sessions at Flyte Tyme. The lyrics were already written when Jam and Lewis sat down at a piano to compose the music. "I didn't think at the time we were sending out any kind of significant message," says Jimmy. "For us it was more like a love song. It got interpreted as maybe more of a statement than it was intended to be. It's a very simple love song and it was just saying, 'Let's wait. I'm not going anywhere, so let's just take our time.' Lyrically, that was Janet's concept and we shaped the music to fit." After the album was released, Jam and Lewis had feedback from teachers that they used the song to illustrate for their students that they didn't have to be forced into having sex. "Sometimes music reaches a broader meaning and it's fantastic to be associated with something like that," Jimmy acknowledges.

Although *Control* is known for its up-tempo, funky songs, Jam and Lewis enjoyed producing ballads for Janet. "She's a great melody singer," Jimmy offers. "Almost like the way a sax or a flute can play a melody, she has one of those voices that's really conducive to singing melodies, so we always try to write strong melodies on all her songs." The producer adds that "Let's Wait Awhile" was an example of a "really nice melody and harmony, and she ends up doing all the vocals. She does almost all the backgrounds herself...She has incredible range; she can sing parts like a man would sing them and then go all the way up and sing all the high parts too."

In addition to providing lead and backing vocals, Janet played digital bells on the track. Jimmy Jam handled drum programming, digital keyboards, acoustic piano, and percussion. Terry Lewis also played percussion. O'Nicholas Raths played six and 12-string acoustic guitar, and Melanie Andrews added some backing vocals.

"Let's Wait Awhile" was the fourth Number One single from *Control*. "People look at it like a growing part of Janet's career," says Jimmy Jam. "It was definitely a growing part of our career, because we felt like we could work the way that we wanted to work. And even though we had hit records up to that point, they had always been recorded [elsewhere]—some in Atlanta, some in Los Angeles...It was a new beginning for us to be in control of the products we recorded."

451

LOOKING FOR A NEW LOVE

Jody Watley

MCA 52956
WRITERS: ANDRE CYMONE, JODY WATLEY
PRODUCERS: ANDRE CYMONE, DAVID Z.
March 21, 1987 (3 weeks)

After seven years in Shalamar [see 325—"The Second Time Around"], Jody Watley opted to take more control of her career. "When you're in a group it's like a democracy," she points out. "Majority rules. And I was ready to move on."

The former *Soul Train* dancer didn't rush into being a solo artist. She shifted into low gear and moved to England, where she recorded some miscellaneous tracks with groups like the Art of Noise. After two and a half years in the U.K., she was more certain of the direction she wanted to follow and returned to Los Angeles, where she met Andre Cymone in a club. "I recognized him from being in the original Prince lineup and he recognized me from Shalamar, so we struck up a conversation." Watley told him she was working on material for a solo debut album. "He said he had all this music, tons of music, and he needed lyrics for a lot of these songs. And my contribution to my songs is usually melody and lyrics."

Watley got commitments from other producers as well, including Bernard Edwards and Patrick Leonard. She also garnered a promise from George Michael to record a duet before she signed with a record label. "When I presented myself to the various record companies, they pretty much had a complete package," she explains. "They had demos and the whole bit. Although I had been a member of a singing group, I was very wary of that being important. Though it was something I was proud of, I really played that down."

The last song recorded for Watley's first MCA album was "Looking for a New Love." Jody recalls how the song was written: "Andre gave me a cassette of various musical tracks and I picked the ones I thought suited me the best. It was ironic because I was going through a breakup at the time and when I heard the music, the title came into my head immediately. Sometimes you hear the music and the ideas start to flow. I was really angry when I wrote the lyrics and I meant every word...When it came out, it was like an anthem because everybody at some point goes through a breakup and that feeling of 'You'll see' and 'I'm going to get over you.' It was almost as if I was writing in a diary."

One line in the song became a catch phrase, and its popularity increased when it was uttered by one of the world's greatest box office attractions. "The phrase that became so popular, 'Hasta la vista, baby,' I just thought of it. People had it on their answering machines and then Arnold Schwarzenegger made it famous again in *Terminator 2*."

Like all of the songs on her first album, "Looking for a New Love" remained true to its demo form, Watley says. "We did the demos on eight-track and I wanted to keep the raw essence of the demo." Cymone was responsible for all of the music; Watley completed her vocals quickly. "I find the first or second take is always the best," she maintains. "All the producers I've worked with are always pleasantly surprised that I work as quickly as I do. I think part of it is because I co-write. I've done the lyrics, so it's not like I'm learning the song. When I go in to sing it, it's instantly from the heart because I've written it."

452

SIGN 'O' THE TIMES

Prince

PAISLEY PARK 28399
WRITER: PRINCE
PRODUCER: PRINCE
April 11, 1987 (3 weeks)

Once again, Prince changed his look and engineer Susan Rogers knew it was time to start recording a new album. With new hair and new clothes, Prince was at Sunset Sound in Hollywood to record "Sign 'O' the Times," "The Cross," and "Adore." The Paisley Park studios were being built at this time, and Prince hated the winters in Minnesota. "It was a luxury to be able to work in Los Angeles when it was 40-below back home," says Rogers.

Prince did not bother with demos for his own recordings, according to his engineer. "He always recorded everything directly from his head right up to the master. There were certain songs I used to call 'Sunday songs.' It always seemed on Sunday his songs were a little more profound, and 'Sign 'O' the Times' was one of them. On Sunday, we would sometimes start a little bit later in the day." On a typical Sunday, the studio was quiet and Prince was the only client in the building.

Rogers remembers the Sunday Prince arrived at Sunset Sound to record "Sign 'O' the Times." "He came right in and went to work. He had a Fairlight synthesizer...that's where the drums came from, and almost all the sounds on that [song] were Fairlight." Programmer Todd Harriman accompanied Prince; according to Rogers, the artist didn't program or create his own sounds but simply used the stock sounds that were already built into the synthesizer. "Like he did everything, he just walked in and started recording it, from his head right to the tape. He did the drum pattern very quickly and did all the overdubs and then the vocals. I remember being very impressed with it—I didn't know then that it was going to be the title song on the album. But when he was recording an album, he had the whole album in mind as he was doing it and he would go somewhat in order. I think at that time he must have had a concept for the album. He would do a song that was the signature song of the album, and when he recorded that, he knew that was going to be the cornerstone of the album."

Prince recorded his vocal for the socially relevant "Sign 'O' the Times" in the same fashion as his other songs, according to Rogers. "He always recorded his vocals by himself, which other artists don't do. We'd get the track halfway or three-quarters of the way there and then set him up with a microphone in the control room. He'd have certain tracks on the multi-track that he would use and he'd do the vocal completely alone. I think that was the only way he could really get the performance."

Some critics charged that *Sign 'O' the Times* was less polished than Prince's earlier albums, especially its predecessor. "*Parade* is where he first started making use of strings," says Rogers. "And on *Sign 'O' the Times* he got away from that a little bit. Maybe that's what made it sound a little less polished." Rogers acknowledges that *Sign 'O' the Times* was recorded during a more difficult period in Prince's life. "He was coming down from the headiness of his huge success and he was aware that his audience was changing and things were changing for him. So it may have been a little bit darker in that respect. But we spent more time and money on 'Sign 'O' the Times' than on anything he'd ever done. Much more work went into it."

453

DON'T DISTURB THIS GROOVE

The System

ATLANTIC 89320
WRITERS: DAVID FRANK, MIC MURPHY
PRODUCERS: THE SYSTEM
May 2, 1987 (1 week)

David Frank's future was set when he won a contest in the fifth grade for composing a song. "I don't even know if I was the absolute winner," he confesses. "A lot of people won the contest, but my mother made such a big fuss about how great it was, it convinced me I could write music as well as play it."

Growing up outside of Boston, Frank was a classically trained musician studying piano. In high school

The System

he played in various rock and R&B bands, and while attending the Berklee College of Music developed a love for jazz. He continued to write songs, record demos, and send them off to record companies with little results. Then he decided to move to New York City and make a living in the music business—which proved very difficult.

Once in the Big Apple, he met Mic Murphy. With some free studio time coming his way in exchange for his services as a musician, Frank asked Murphy to join him at a session. They recorded a track, added the vocals, mixed it that night, and had a completed recording by six o'clock the following morning. Murphy took the master tape to a friend who was an engineer and had a 12-inch lacquer made. They took it to the A&R department of Mirage Records, an Atlantic subsidiary run by Jerry Greenberg, former president of Atlantic. Mirage signed the duo on the spot, and the track, "It's Passion," was included in their debut album, *Sweat*, along with their first single, "You Are in My System," which peaked at number 10 on the R&B chart.

Murphy was responsible for naming the duo, according to Frank. "Mic heard it on a TV show, 'Honey, you just can't get him out of your system.' and said we should write a song called 'You Are in My System.' "

"Don't Disturb This Groove," the title track of their third album, literally started as a groove. "I worked on a musical track for two or three days, and I remember thinking, 'Why am I spending so much time on this? I don't know whether it's going to be good, it's a little bit too jazzy, and I'm probably making a mistake,' " Frank relates. "But I couldn't stop myself. I kept working on this track. I had the verse and the chorus of the song. I had all the parts you hear on the record." Frank asked his partner to come over and help him. "He came over and said the bridge should be the chorus, have it go 'round twice. So I did and gave it to him and he came back with the title and the idea for the melody of 'Don't Disturb This Groove.' We added a bridge a couple of weeks later [and] added a counter-melody."

Frank and Murphy went into the studio a couple of months later to record the song. "I remember when we did the album, we did four songs initially. 'Don't Disturb This Groove' was part of the first four. We remixed it—we didn't rest until it sounded the way we wanted it to sound. I definitely had the feeling people were going to love it. I wasn't sure it was going to be Number One—I just thought it was a song that people would fall in love with."

Released on Atlantic after the Mirage label was folded into its parent logo, "Don't Disturb This Groove" went to number four on the pop chart and became the System's one and only chart-topper on the R&B chart.

454

THERE'S NOTHING BETTER THAN LOVE

Luther Vandross with Gregory Hines

EPIC 06978
WRITERS: LUTHER VANDROSS, JOHN "SKIP" ANDERSON
PRODUCERS: LUTHER VANDROSS, MARCUS MILLER
May 9, 1987 (1 week)

Luther Vandross was watching *Saturday Night Live* the night Gregory Hines performed a blues song, "I Got the Lowest of the Lowdown Blues," with Eubie Blake on piano. "I was blown away by his voice," Luther enthuses. "All my favorite singers were always female singers...with the exception of Eddie

Gregory Hines

Kendricks, and Peabo Bryson's voice is just beautiful...but I loved Gregory." Luther had never met the actor, but he called and asked Hines if he would be interested in recording something together.

"He said, 'Of course I would.' I sent him songs and he loved them, and we called each other. We actually first met in Venice Beach [California] at a little restaurant there, to talk about the project."

The next step was to book studio time. "It was interesting putting it together with someone who sings in approximately the same range as I do," says Luther. "It would seem that since I'm a second tenor, I would automatically want a first tenor to do a duet with me. Since I cover the middle-low part, I would want someone who would cover the middle-high. But Gregory was also a second tenor covering middle-low, so that pushed me up. I had to cover the middle-high...[It was] a little challenging for me."

Luther wrote "There's Nothing Better Than Love" with the synthesizer player from his band, John "Skip" Anderson. "He did the chord changes and I loved them, and I wrote a melody and the lyric. It just happened—when you put H_2 and O in a test tube, water happens. There's really no particular thing other than the chemistry and the propelling of the process going on."

While recording with Hines was fun, Vandross also found some of it to be a difficult process. "He was not a recording artist. The experience was very new to him, especially the experience as it pertained to pop radio. He had a semi-Broadwayish tone in his voice, which we spent every waking hour trying to sidestep. After a while he really started to get it, and it was great.

"On the songs that came after that, it was much easier. The tendency [is] to overpronounce words...I suppose it's like a stage actor, when you're trying to reach the last row. It's when a stage actor transforms himself into a screen actor, then the gestures and the facial expressions have to be reduced by a large percentage, because the camera will pick up that eyebrow that raises, whereas the person in the next-to-last row can't see it unless you really raise it. And the same thing applies vocally. If you're saying the word 'love,' you have to really emphasize that *v* when you're onstage trying to reach the last row. But on a record, the microphone picks up your lips parting to say the word 'love,' so all you have to do is think the *v* and it comes out."

"There's Nothing Better Than Love" was the third Number One hit for Vandross. Hines, who broke into show business with a family act called Hines, Hines, and Dad, returned to the top 10 a little more than a year later with a solo recording, "That Girl Wants to Dance with Me." In 1992, he won a Tony Award for playing Jelly Roll Morton in the Broadway production of *Jelly's Last Jam*.

455

ALWAYS

Atlantic Starr

WARNER BROS. 28455
WRITERS: JONATHAN LEWIS, DAVID LEWIS, WAYNE LEWIS
PRODUCERS: DAVID LEWIS, WAYNE LEWIS
May 16, 1987 (2 weeks)

Atlantic Starr would have recorded "Always" in 1982 if their producer at the time, James Anthony Carmichael, hadn't objected. "He decided that it wasn't the right time," says Wayne Lewis, who wrote the song with his brothers Jonathan and David. "He wanted us to hold on to it. We ended up never using it with him...It worked out perfectly. I guess there is a time for everything.

"My brother Jonathan came up with a chord progression that was kind of hymnal, but with a country-western edge and also an R&B edge—a mixture of all three," Wayne elaborates. David continues the story: "There's a little writing room at A&M Records and we went over there and played around with it and finished the music. Then we went to a little studio we had in Mount Vernon and laid down the track, and we all played it together. Wayne would play keyboards and drums and I would play keyboards and Jonathan would play keyboards. Just different parts, because that's all we had at the time, a drum machine and a keyboard. That's how we put it together on a four-track. And then Wayne took it home and did the lyrics." The song was written as a duet. "That's exactly what we had in mind," David confirms. "When Wayne first wrote the lyrics, there was a girl's part and a guy's part to the song. It's a love song between a woman and a man."

Wayne says the inspiration for the lyrics came from wanting to write a love song. "I think at the time nature was a big thing, so I tried to relate a love song to nature with the sun and the rain, all the beautiful things—because it's all related. Natural or pure love is related with nature." Wayne also came up with the title. "At the end of the phrases, I kept coming up with 'Always,' so I said, 'Why not just call it "Always"?' And I was not into naming songs with 30-word titles."

"Always" was finally recorded for *All in the Name of Love*, the group's first album for Warner Brothers after a long spell with A&M. The vocals were recorded in two different sessions. Wayne produced the New York session where Barbara Weathers laid down her lead vocals and then David recorded his part in Los Angeles. Weathers replaced the group's previous female vocalist, Sharon Bryant, after a conflict divided the group during the recording of their 1983 album, *Yours Forever.* The new Atlantic Starr consisted of the three Lewis Brothers, percussionist Joe Phillips, and Weathers. "She had a clear sweet voice that sat right out in front," says Wayne. "Sometimes people have voices that sit right in your ear like they're there with you."

The Lewis brothers weren't convinced "Always" should be their first single for their new label. "We wanted to have a dance song first," says Wayne. "Benny Medina from Warner Brothers convinced us it should be our first single. We went along with him for a lot of different reasons, and it turned out to be the perfect single."

"It was a fresh relationship," David says of the band being new to Warner Brothers. "We came in with a Number One record. And [Chairman of the Board] Mo Ostin was saying, 'Who could ask for more?' He was so proud of us. We were everything he could ask an artist to be."

456

HEAD TO TOE

Lisa Lisa and Cult Jam

COLUMBIA 07008
WRITERS: FULL FORCE
PRODUCERS: FULL FORCE
May 30, 1987 (2 weeks)

The six members of Brooklyn's Full Force were looking for a girl group to produce when their former roadie Mike Hughes, the drummer of Cult Jam, brought them 16-year-old Lisa Velez. The youngest of 10 children, the teenager was employed at Benetton, where she was kept busy folding sweaters. At night, she would sneak out of her family's apartment to go to the Fun House, a New York City night spot popular with rappers and break-dancers. "I was gonna do anything possible to get discovered," she said in *Spin.*

Lisa Lisa and Cult Jam

She auditioned at the East Flatbush home of the three George brothers in Full Force—Bowlegged Lou, Paul Anthony, and B-Fine. "Lisa came walking in the basement all nervous, 'cause the six of us are pretty big guys," says Bowlegged Lou. Paul Anthony told her how pretty she was, which helped ease the tension. She sat on a stool and performed two songs written by Hughes and the other half of Cult Jam, Spanador (Alex Mosely).

"She was singing so off-key, because the song was kind of corny," says Bowlegged Lou, who hid in the bathroom of his East Flatbush home so the others wouldn't see him laughing. "If we had to judge on those two songs, we wouldn't have brought in Lisa." But Paul Anthony asked if she could sing something more familiar. Once they heard her vocalize on Sheena Easton's "For Your Eyes Only," the members of Full Force knew their search was over.

"We weren't looking for a Patti LaBelle–type singer," Lou explains. "We were looking for a young singer all the kids could identify with. Lisa had a pretty good voice. She wasn't spectacular, but she [had] the type of voice that when it came on the radio, girls could emulate [it]. And there was no female singer at the time [who was] Puerto Rican, Spanish like Lisa."

Paul Anthony was inspired to write "Head to Toe" by his girlfriend Sharon. "She said that to me quite a number of times. I'm a bodybuilder and I'm always working out. When we're alone together, she'd say, 'Baby, I just love you from head to toe.' " Paul was looking for a song that could tell a story in 10 words or less. "It was about 6:30 in the morning and I was looking for that kind of simplistic melody that could tell the story from the moment you hear it. And I'm a big fanatic about Motown, so I used those influences in terms of flavoring the melody."

Paul knew right away the song had potential. "Sometimes you have a magical song that you know is a hit from the moment you do it. And the moment I made up the bassline, I knew it was going to be catchy."

While Paul was responsible for the track, the writing and producing credits go to Full Force. "Nine times out of 10, whoever spearheaded the song, we'll look for them to be in the studio, because only they can feel the feeling," Paul says. "Lots of times you may have had two people spearhead it or one or all and we'll all be in there. It works well that way. Full Force is a total democracy, so it's always divided by six. It doesn't matter who did what. We all share in it equally. As far as the studio chores, everybody will come in and put in their element. Vocals are something I really forge ahead on, so I'm usually there. If it's something on the funky tip and the beats, I'll look for [Baby] Gerry or Curt-t-t [Curtis Bedeau] to be there."

457

ROCK STEADY

The Whispers

SOLAR 70006

WRITERS: L.A. REID, BABYFACE, BO WATSON, DWAYNE LADD

PRODUCERS: L.A. REID, BABYFACE

June 13, 1987 (1 week)

Walter Scott first met L.A. Reid and Babyface in Atlanta at a Kool Jazz Festival. "They were very young—Kenny Edmonds and L.A. Reid, as we knew them then. They were trying to get songs to us when we met Kenny; he said we were very much instrumental in how he felt about all the songs that he wrote, because as a kid in Indianapolis he had heard 'Lady' and all of the early ballads that we did."

L.A. Reid and Babyface came to the attention of Solar Records founder Dick Griffey through Midnight Star [see 398—"Operator"]. The writers/producers were part of the Cincinnati group the Deele, signed to Solar in 1983.

Babyface was living in Los Angeles when Midnight Star played the Universal Amphitheater. Bo Watson of Midnight Star dropped by Babyface's apartment for a visit. "We started to write a couple of things together," says Babyface. "He put an idea down on a Linn 9000...It sat for a little while and then I picked it up again and then went in and finished the song. The title of the song came from a keyboard stand that was called 'Rok Steady.' I looked at that and said, 'Let me try and make that the hook.' It all came together after that."

Babyface met up with the Whispers again while they were recording an album produced by Reggie Calloway of Midnight Star. "They said they liked my writing. L.A. and I were talking to them and they said, 'If you want to, the next record we'll do something with you guys as producers. Just write it and produce it.' And they were really giving us a shot, from us not having any real experience...It was really them that gave us the chance."

The Whispers were impressed with the novice producers. "They knew what they were doing," says Walter. "It was a perfect situation. You had two guys learning their craft with a group that had learned quite a bit and both sides were willing to give, and that's the best atmosphere you can have. They respected us for what we had done. We respected them for what we knew they could do...Kenny and L.A. were hungry at that period of their career and they were eager like we were. We lived and ate and slept in the studio. That's all we thought of."

Walter remembers hearing "Rock Steady" for the first time: "Their demos were like records. Kenny did all the vocals. But once we put our vocal to it, that was the finishing touch." The Whispers brought in some friends while recording the song. "We wanted it to have a party atmosphere and they agreed to do that."

L.A. and Babyface appreciated the opportunity to work with the group. "It was unbelievable, that you're actually in there working with the Whispers," Babyface recalls. "We were really happy to be there working, period."

The album the Whispers were working on wasn't entirely produced by the men from the Deele. "We recorded a bunch of songs, but the two that ended up on the album were 'In the Mood' and 'Rock Steady,' " says Walter. "The only reason we didn't do more of their songs was because Mr. Griffey, who had a label to run, felt that with this kind of talent, you should spread the wealth around. So he really prevented them from giving us any more songs. They wanted to—we had a great relationship—but we ended up with those two."

Scott credits label head Griffey with picking "Rock Steady" as the single. "We wanted to come with 'In the Mood'...he was trying to go with another 'And the Beat Goes On,' and we have to give credit that he was right."

458

DIAMONDS

Herb Alpert

A&M 2929

WRITERS: JIMMY JAM, TERRY LEWIS

PRODUCERS: JIMMY JAM, TERRY LEWIS

June 20, 1987 (2 weeks)

It was Carol Channing who first expressed the thought that "Diamonds Are a Girl's Best Friend" when she sang Leo Robin and Jule Styne's song in the 1949 Broadway production of *Gentlemen Prefer Blondes*. In 1953, Marilyn Monroe sang the same tune in the film version. Another three decades would pass before Janet Jackson and Lisa Keith would vocalize the same sentiment in a song written and produced by Jimmy Jam and Terry Lewis for one of the owners of A&M Records, Herb Alpert.

Jimmy Jam came up with the idea to do the song. "As I do with most ideas I have, I give them to Terry and I say, 'I've got this concept, "Diamonds are a girl's best friend." ' And he said, 'Oh, is that original? You came up with that?' And I said, 'Yeah, but in a different way. It's a different song'...and then he fleshed it out."

In 1986, John McClain of A&M's urban department suggested to Phil Oakey of the British pop group the Human League that Jam and Lewis produce the band's next album. During the sessions for *Human*, the Flyte Tyme duo cut the instrumental track that would become "Diamonds." "It wasn't for the Human League, but it was something that got cut in that time period," Jimmy Jam explains. McClain heard the track and insisted that the producers save it for a project that he would give them later.

When Jam and Lewis completed the Human League project, they took a vacation. Easing back into work, they hooked up with Alpert. "It wasn't a project with any pressure attached to it, because he's the boss," says Jimmy. "He's not going to fire himself if he doesn't have a hit. And we felt it was a great learning experience working with Herb, because of his business obviously with A&M and also as a musician."

While they were producing several tracks for Alpert's *Keep Your Eye on Me* album, Janet Jackson returned to Minneapolis to work on a re-mix of the song "Control" for a video. "She heard we were doing the Herb Alpert track and were planning on using Lisa Keith, who had done a lot of backgrounds for us and did the lead on 'Making Love in the Rain,' another Herb Alpert track," says Jimmy Jam. "Janet heard the track and said, 'Oh, I gotta sing on that!' " Jam and Lewis were happy to have Jackson sing with Keith. "Both her and Lisa sing in unison on the whole track, but the voice you recognize is Janet's because you're familiar with it," Jimmy says. "Both voices are neck and neck with each other volumewise."

The rise of "Diamonds" to the top of the chart coincided with the 25th anniversary of A&M Records, the label Alpert began with Jerry Moss in Los Angeles in 1962. Alpert became an avid record buyer after he heard Ray Anthony's "Young Man with a Horn." After serving in the Army, Alpert became a staff writer for Keen Records, where he co-wrote Sam Cooke's "Wonderful World." Alpert kept crossing paths with Moss, an expert in record promotion, and they formed Carnival Records. It turned out that the name was already taken, so they renamed the label using their initials.

"It's very pleasing to get a hit for the boss," Jimmy Jam acknowledges. The single's success perhaps made up for the damage Alpert wreaked on another front while he was in Minneapolis. "He cleaned us off the ping-pong table," Jimmy complains. "Terry was the defending champion of Flyte Tyme at that point, and Herb came in and messed us up." Revenge, however, was sweet. "We got him back. He came up and did trumpet on a song called 'Someday Is Tonight' on the *Rhythm Nation* album and we returned the favor. We have a $10 bill framed in our game room and he's got a $5 bill framed in his office that he took from Terry. We're up on him five bucks now."

459

I FEEL GOOD ALL OVER

Stephanie Mills

MCA 53056
WRITERS: ANNETTE HARDEMAN, GABRIEL HARDEMAN
PRODUCER: NICK MARTINELLI
July 4, 1987 (3 weeks)

Songwriters Gabriel and Annette Hardeman thought "I Feel Good All Over" would be a perfect song for Patti Labelle and sent it to her in hopes she would record it. "But I heard it first," says Stephanie Mills, who, like Patti, recorded for MCA.

The Hardemans had both been in singing groups before they met in Philadelphia. Gabriel, from Atlanta, headed up the Gabriel Hardeman Delegation on Savoy Records while Annette, from North Carolina, was in First Choice ("Armed and Extremely Dangerous") on Philly Groove.

Gabriel had originally written "I Feel Good All Over" in 1980. His wife took the song and "dressed it up a little bit." When they didn't hear back from Labelle, they submitted it to producer Nick Martinelli. "Annette and I wanted to write a positive love song," says Gabriel, "and you can tell the gospel influence and the soul influence in the writing. We tried to put ourselves in the situation of someone meeting and looking at a person inside and growing in experience."

"I had a good time recording that song," says Mills. "When you record with Nick, he's Italian so he cooks a lot of pasta and has a lot of Italian food in the studio." Martinelli remembers the session as being very interesting: "We cut it live. I used Donald Robinson [on piano], Daryl Burgee on drums, Doug Grigsby on bass, and Randy Bowland on guitar. That was my basic rhythm section in Philadelphia that I cut a lot of my songs with."

Gabriel and Annette were also at the session. "We were at a studio that right now is a rehearsal hall here in Philadelphia," he says. "It was called Alpha International Studio. It's closed, but sometimes I go in rehearsal room number six—I will never forget it...I told Nick I could write the charts for the song...I wrote the tracks down, the lead sheets for the instruments...and while we were laying it down, Cassandra and Stephanie Mills were there. Stephanie came in and did a reference vocal. After the music tracks were laid down, my wife and I and a few other singers in the [Gabriel Hardeman Delegation] laid the background vocals."

Stephanie's final vocal matched her reference vocal so closely that Martinelli almost couldn't tell them apart. "I do my homework and then I lay down a rough vocal...They could print it like that," says Mills. "But then I sleep on it and come back and really nail what I did the day before. I try to record my songs like I would do them live. For a long time I didn't do that but when I would perform live, many people would say that my live rendition was so much better. They felt I was holding back on record. So now when I record, I try to do what I would do if I was standing in front of an audience."

The Hardemans were at a rehearsal at Drexel University, where Annette worked in the music department, when a student told them she heard "I Feel Good All Over" on the radio. The songwriters rushed out to buy a copy of *Billboard* and discovered their song had been released as a single. They kept watching the charts for its progress. "We got a call from Nick Martinelli and he said, 'It's number two. It's expected to be Number One next week.' Sure enough, that following week it hit Number One. It was something we had never experienced in our lives and it was the first song we had ever gotten to an artist."

460

FAKE

Alexander O'Neal

TABU 07100
WRITERS: JAMES HARRIS III, TERRY LEWIS
PRODUCERS: JIMMY JAM, TERRY LEWIS
July 25, 1987 (2 weeks)

Fake" was a mistake. "In those days there were digital samples of drums and you could tune them up or down and you could switch cards and have different drums," explains writer/producer Jimmy Jam. "The drum pattern that became 'Fake' was actually for a different song, but the sounds that were in there were the wrong sounds for the drum pattern. They were all very low, rumbly sounds and they should have been more high-pitched sounds. I turned it on by mistake and liked the way it sounded. I put a bassline with it and the next day Terry came in and I said, 'I got this track. It's kind of cool.' I played it for him and he loved it."

Jam and Lewis already had the concept of the *Hearsay* album for Alexander O'Neal. "*Hearsay* is like Alexander's *Control* if you will," Jam explains. "It's really an album that was autobiographical in a way. So when we did 'Fake,' I came up with the concept and Terry wrote the lyrics for it. We knew Alex so well at that point because it was the second album we had done with him, plus we had played in bands with him for 10 years before that. We just knew the things he

Alexander O'Neal

would say and the kind of attitude he'd have toward the song."

O'Neal was born in Natchez, Mississippi, but moved to Minneapolis when he was 20. He joined a group called the Mystics and played the local cover-band circuit. He departed for New Orleans, then Los Angeles and Las Vegas before returning to Minneapolis in 1977. He met Jam and Lewis as well as Prince and was encouraged to use his natural gift. "Singing was one of the talents I knew I had," he told Vivien Goldman, "but I didn't deal with it. I recognize all my strongest attributes, and I put them in a little chest over there. But never in my fondest dreams did I imagine singing would be my professional calling or my claim to fame."

O'Neal spent a short time in a group called Enterprise before being recruited into Flyte Tyme, a band that included Jam and Lewis as well as Monte Moir. A disagreement with Prince led Alexander to leave the band. After being replaced as lead vocalist by Morris Day, he formed a rock and roll band called Alexander. "Can you imagine a black rock and roll band in the Twin Cities?" he asks. "We did Rolling Stones and Def Leppard songs. I always felt that black artists created rock and roll. We gave it away, and they took it. But if you really listen, you realize that the original rock and roll was just stepped-up blues."

After his rock and roll experience, O'Neal recorded a 12-inch single, "Playroom," for a Chicago-based independent label. He signed with Tabu Records in 1984 and teamed up with Jam and Lewis (who became independent producers after the Time broke up) as well as Moir for his label debut.

"One of the nice things about working with Alex is that he is one of the few male singers who can do up-tempo songs as well as the ballads," says Jimmy Jam. "He's had some great ballads, but 'Fake' is a real funky, gritty song. He can handle that as well as he can handle a ballad—that makes it easy to write for him."

461

THE PLEASURE PRINCIPLE

Janet Jackson

A&M 2927
WRITER: MONTE MOIR
PRODUCER: MONTE MOIR
August 8, 1987 (1 week)

How did writer/producer Monte Moir learn that the one track he had created for Janet Jackson's *Control* would be released as a single? "I found out through *Billboard*," he reveals. "It was a year and a half after the album had been out. I had been working with Terry Lewis and Jimmy Jam and by then we had parted ways. I didn't realize it was going to be coming out as a single at all, although I had known it was getting a lot of airplay and the clubs had been playing it a lot. The next thing I knew, it was a single. I didn't expect much at that point because usually radio's pretty much played the album out by then."

But radio wasn't tired of Janet, and neither was the listening or buying public. "The Pleasure Principle," the sixth single from *Control*, was the fifth to go to number one on the R&B chart. It was the first time in chart history that one artist had five Number One R&B hits from the same album.

Moir, a former member of the Time [see 571—"Jerk Out"] along with Jam and Lewis, wrote "The Pleasure Principle" specifically for Jackson when he heard the project was coming up at Flyte Tyme Studios. He created the song before Jam and Lewis determined what direction the album would take. "At that point, it hadn't been totally understood. I think ideas were being kicked around. I came in with a couple of song ideas and that one seemed to fit in real well."

Moir describes how he wrote the song: "I do the music first. I had the beat and the basic chord structure. What I'll do is put a cassette on, maybe with the drum machine going, and play along with it. I might play through a whole side of the tape and sing along or play some different parts. And that's what I did with that one to come up with a certain bridge part and certain little lines that come in toward the end of the song. You can go back and listen to the cassette later and find out some interesting things that you may have forgotten if you had been doing it without a tape."

After he wrote the music, Moir worked on the lyrics. "That came about a little backward because I ended up writing all the verse stuff first. A lot of people come up with the title first and write a concept or something around that and this was really the opposite. I had to figure out what I was talking about and come up with some sort of title. It's about getting out of a situation that you don't want to be in."

Moir cut the track and sang a rough lead over the top of it to give Jackson an idea of where it was going. "She went home and came back and did her thing—like the next night," says Moir, who enjoyed working with the artist. "She came in and knew the song pretty much inside out. A lot of singers will come in and they don't study too much or do their homework or really get to know the song, and they'll be reading everything off the sheet. You tend to take a longer time because you're not only focusing on the performance, but they're trying to remember lyrics and everything else."

The Flyte Tyme facility in Minneapolis was still fairly new when Moir produced "The Pleasure Principle." "I remember it being very busy and everybody having a hard time getting in to do their work, because there were so many things going on at the time. It seemed like the track came together fairly quickly, because we didn't have much time to get everything done, which I think can bring something out in a song that may not be there if you have too much time. Jimmy's always [said] a lot of the biggest hits have not been perfect recordings, but there's something about them, something you can't really explain."

462

JAM TONIGHT

Freddie Jackson

CAPITOL 44037

WRITERS: FREDDIE JACKSON, PAUL LAURENCE

PRODUCER: PAUL LAURENCE

August 15, 1987 (1 week)

"Jam Tonight," Freddie Jackson's fifth solo Number One, sweetened the top of the charts two summers after his arresting debut, "Rock Me Tonight (For Old Times Sake)." But the song was born much earlier.

In fact, "Jam Tonight" dates back to the period when school (and church) buddies Jackson and Paul Laurence Jones were part of the latter's group, Laurence Jones Ensemble, gigging around New York.

Jackson's Big Apple day job was as a clerk/typist, pounding out 100 words a minute on a word processor. In between the labor, he wrote song lyrics such as "Jam Tonight." He recalls, "I was sitting at my terminal, typing that song, and this melody came. All day, it had been in my mind, and we were just about to do a gig—this group, L.J.E.—and Paul was, like, 'Everybody [in the group] should write a song.' My deadline was that week. So I came up with this melody and the next thing you know, I'm sitting downtown [typing in "Jam Tonight"]. And my boss is standing behind me, saying, 'No, that is not a job.' I'd been caught quite a few times for doing things like that." So Jackson was fired.

Music, not typing, was in Jackson's blood, of course. "When I was growing up, I used to listen to Nat 'King' Cole, a lot of Sam Cooke, Donny Hathaway," he tells. "I used to be at the Apollo Theater every Saturday, so I had the opportunity to see Otis Redding, Sam & Dave, the real legendary performers. I guess I got the end of that stuff, but I'm glad to have been able to experience that, not just hear about it or read about it. [I saw] Martha Reeves and the Vandellas, Diana Ross and the Supremes, the Jackson 5."

Jackson's influences—especially Cole and Hathaway—seeped through his debut album (which also contained a version of Billie Holiday's "Good Morning Heartache") and the follow-up, *Just Like the First Time*.

"Jam Tonight," the third single from that second album, was recorded at three studios—New Jersey's Digital By Dickinson in Bloomfield and New York's Quadrasonic and Electric Lady—by producer Paul Laurence. He did the rhythm and vocal arrangements, also playing keyboards. The other keyboard musician was Eric Rehl, while Leslie Ming was the drummer; Audrey Wheeler, Cindy Mizell, and Yoland Lee were background vocalists.

Four years earlier, "Jam Tonight" had played a part in captivating Melba Moore, who helped develop Jackson's career [see 408—"Rock Me Tonight"]. The song was part of his set at the New York club where Moore first saw him. "It was just a three-piece combo," he says. "I was singing Natalie Cole's 'Lovers,' Luther Vandross's 'A House Is Not a Home,' some Jeffrey Osborne songs, a few of mine—and 'Jam Tonight.' "

Today, how does Jackson communicate onstage and on disc? "I think about that lady who's just over a relationship and needs to be comforted, or the lady who's just got married...If her guy can't tell her certain things like how he feels, I can tell her, on his behalf, through my music."

Levert

463
CASANOVA
Levert

ATLANTIC 89217
WRITER: REGGIE CALLOWAY
PRODUCER: REGGIE CALLOWAY
August 22, 1987 (2 weeks)

Reggie Calloway [see 398—"Operator"] wrote "Casanova" two years before it was recorded by Levert. "Sometimes you write a song and you have no purpose for it," Calloway explains. "It's just for your own enjoyment. I came up with that song while on tour, riding down the highway on a tour bus. There are a lot of points where you don't see any houses. You don't see anything but road. I guess I have some country-western roots in me and 'Casanova' started out as one of my country-western songs."

After their debut album performed well, Gerald Levert and Marc Gordon of Levert expected to write all of the songs for their sophomore effort. They completed 10 numbers and played them for label executives at Atlantic, who only liked seven. The record company wanted Levert to move in a funkier direction, and suggested an outside producer—Calloway. At first the trio was upset, but after giving it some thought, decided it might be a good idea.

During a phone conversation with Reggie, Gerald mentioned what he was looking for: "At that time, Club Noveau had a record out called 'Lean on Me' and I said, 'Man, if we can get a song with that kind of melody and that kind of beat, then I think we can have a smash.' Calloway remembered "Casanova" but was unsure how to give it a funkier groove. "The lyrics were real simple, straight ahead, no curves, no trick words, just like a conversation," he says. "I had to think of where it would fit on radio. I had to study what was going on at the time, what kind of beats were happening. That was one of those cases where at three o'clock in the morning you have a choice of either getting up and going to the tape recorder or sleep, saying you'll remember it tomorrow. Luckily I got up and ran to my little tape recorder, put the beat down, went back to sleep, woke up, and finished it."

Gerald loved "Casanova" the first time he heard it. "I thought it was a smash from the beginning, the end, the middle, whatever. That was just a smash...no one could tell me anything different."

But they tried. "Nobody was with me," Gerald laments. "I was the only one who thought this was a smash record. And when we finally did it, everybody [said], 'Yeah, it's a smash.' "

Working on the song in the studio proved difficult for the trio. "It was rough," Gerald admits. "It was the longest time it's ever taken me to do a performance on a song, and that frustrated me. There was a certain way Reggie wanted it delivered and I didn't really see how he wanted me to deliver it. It frustrated me a lot, but I did it, and we worked it out."

Levert recorded several songs with Calloway before choosing two to complete their album. "They were looking for that one smash that would bring the whole picture across and we were lucky enough to come up with that," says Reggie, who still has plans for "Casanova." "I'm going to release it sometime in the near future in that [country-western] version."

464

LOVE IS A HOUSE

The Force M.D.'s

TOMMY BOY 28300
WRITERS: MARTIN LASCELLES, GEOFF GURD, GINA FOSTER
PRODUCERS: GEOFF GURD, MARTIN LASCELLES
September 5, 1987 (2 weeks)

The Material Girl was sitting by herself one evening in 1987 at the Cadillac Bar in New York, just after the movie premiere of *Who's That Girl*. OK, not *completely* by herself: "Well, she had a couple of bodyguards around," admitted Antoine Maurice Lundy (otherwise known as T.C.D. of the Force M.D.'s), "but no one else. So we went up to one of the guys and he told Madonna who we were. Then we broke into an a cappella version of one of our songs, 'Forgive Me Girl,' but using the words, 'Who's That Girl?' "

Madonna was "kinda impressed," Lundy claimed in a *Blues & Soul* interview. "She said she knew our records and then told us to 'stay right there,' while she got her managers and all to come over while we did it again. About a week later, her managers were speaking to ours and next thing we knew, we were on her tour!"

Bold and brassy gets results, just as they did in the early '80s when the Force M.D.'s took their act onto New York's Staten Island ferry or down to the streets of Greenwich Village. The result: an average $400 a day in tips.

The rap-cum-harmony-vocals group, which comprised Lundy and his brother Stevie, Jesse Lee Daniels, Trisco Pearson, and Charles Nelson, were called Dr. Rock and the M.C.'s back then. They had changed that to the Force M.D.'s (standing for "musical diversity") by the time of their first single, "Let Me Love You," for New York independent label Tommy Boy in April 1984. Their second release, "Tears," was a national top five R&B success and stayed on the charts for 21 weeks; the song was written by the quintet with label founder Tom Silverman.

The record that took the Force M.D.'s all the way to Number One, "Love Is a House," opened for business almost three years later. British writers Martin Lascelles and Geoff Gurd were inspired by the group's 1986 smash, "Tender Love," to send them the song.

"The original demo had a female vocalist on it," explained Stevie Lundy (who goes by the stage name Stevie D.) to journalist David Nathan, "but we knew right away that it was the perfect song for us." That vocalist was Gina Foster, co-author of "Love Is a House" with Lascelles and Gurd. Her own version, produced by Leon Sylvers, was issued by Britain's deConstruction label in 1989.

"We figured we'd give some new people a shot, rather than just going along with the predictable names," said Stevie D. "We felt having some young, new teams to work with would be good for us, too." The recording was done by Gurd and Lascelles at London's Red Shop Recorders, and at New York's Shelton Leigh Palmer studio. Foster, Derek Green, and Morris Michael contributed additional vocal arrangements.

"Love Is a House" formed part of the third Force M.D.'s album, *Touch and Go*, released in July 1987. "Our vocals have evolved, but they are not over-polished harmonies," remarked T.C.D. at the time. "We grew up singing together, and we never had a vocal teacher telling us, 'Sing this or that.' Ours is a natural harmony that comes from inside.

"Ken Webb of WBLS New York said he thought we sound like we sing from jail, which gives you an idea of how much feeling we do put into our songs. Like Ben E. King said, 'Singing with a group is unexplainable.' It's like everyone has the same heartbeat, and together we've created another being."

465

I JUST CAN'T STOP LOVING YOU

Michael Jackson and Siedah Garrett

EPIC 07253
WRITER: MICHAEL JACKSON
PRODUCER: QUINCY JONES
September 19, 1987 (1 week)

Michael Jackson and Barbra Streisand? Michael Jackson and Whitney Houston?

It might have been. Barbra Streisand was Michael's first choice as a singing partner on "I Just Can't Stop Loving You," according to his manager at the time, Frank Dileo. Streisand didn't like the tune, said Dileo, who commented in *Rolling Stone*: "I knew the song was a hit—with or without Barbra." Houston was then considered, but that partnership didn't work out either.

The ultimate choice was a young singer from North Hollywood who had been the guest vocalist on Dennis Edwards's "Don't Look Any Further," a number two single in 1984. Siedah Garrett first met

Quincy Jones when she auditioned for a vocal group he was putting together. She and four male singers were chosen out of 800 candidates to become Deco. The group worked with Quincy on the *Fast Forward* soundtrack, and after they dissolved Siedah was signed to a solo recording deal with Quincy's label, Qwest.

Garrett wrote her first song while in Deco. "The guys in the group wanted a publishing deal along with their recording contract. I'd never written a song before in my life!" she exclaims with a laugh. "So I was sort of pushed into writing." In May of 1987 she was invited to Quincy's home along with other songwriters and was told that the producer was looking for songs for Michael Jackson's next album. The next day, Siedah met with one of her writing partners, Glen Ballard, to work on songs for her own album. She told Ballard about Quincy's request, and her partner suggested they try and write something for Michael. The result was "Man in the Mirror" [see 481]. Siedah was invited to sing backing vocals on the track.

"Then a few days later I got another call from Quincy. I was called back [to the studio] and I thought we were gonna finish," Siedah explains. In the meantime, Jones sent her a tape of another song. "It's not unusual for me to get a tape from Quincy's office, because people send him songs for me to sing. The only thing different about this demo that didn't register at the time is that it was Michael Jackson singing."

Siedah arrived at the studio, expecting to find the Winans gospel group and Andrae Crouch's choir from the "Man in the Mirror" sessions, but the only people present were Quincy, Michael, engineer Bruce Swedien, and Siedah. She assumed she was early and the others would be arriving soon. Quincy asked if she received the tape. "I got the tape." He asked if she'd listened to the song. "I listened to the song." He asked if she could sing the song. "I can sing the song." Quincy told her to go sing it.

"I walked over to the other side of the studio, where there's two mike stands, music on either side. Michael Jackson on this end of the microphone, me on the other end, and *that's* when I knew we were going to do a duet."

"I Just Can't Stop Loving You" was the first single released from *Bad.* Like the first singles from *Off the Wall* and *Thriller,* it went to Number One. Listening to the final version, it's difficult to distinguish Michael's vocals from Siedah's. "When we were doing it, I didn't realize how much we were sounding alike," she confides. "Michael is a vocal chameleon; he can sound like anybody. I think he was trying to blend with me. Quincy sat back, closed his eyes and said he'd be damned if he could tell which one of us was which."

466

I NEED LOVE

L.L. Cool J

DEF JAM 07350
WRITERS: JAMES TODD SMITH, BOBBY ERVING, DARRYL PIERCE, DWAYNE SIMON
PRODUCERS: L.L. COOL J, L.A. POSSE
September 26, 1987 (1 week)

James Todd Smith was listening to underground rappers like Cold Crush 4, Double Trouble, and the Fantastic Romantic 5 when he was a nine-year-old in Queens, New York. He was 11 when "Rapper's Delight" by the Sugarhill Gang went to number four on the *Billboard* chart, and by the time he was 13 he was making his own demo tapes in his basement and sending them out to record companies that specialized in rap. At 19, as an artist on Def Jam, he went against the advice of his friends and released "I Need Love," the first successful rap ballad. It crossed over to the pop chart and helped popularize rap beyond the urban market.

James was raised by his maternal grandparents after his parents divorced when he was four. Music ran in his blood: His mother, Ondrea Smith, played the accordion and wrote poetry. His father, James Nunya, ran a trucking company but also recorded some material in the Barry White/Marvin Gaye vein. One day James came home from school and discovered a gift from his grandfather: two turntables and a mixer. He adopted his stage name after he told a young girl who questioned his sex appeal, "Ladies love cool James."

L.L. Cool J was 16 when he sent a demo off to Rick Rubin, who owned Def Jam along with Russell Simmons. L.L. called every day to see if Rubin had received the tape; finally, the 22-year-old New York University student called back and left a message with Cool J's grandmother. As a result, the young rapper recorded "I Need a Beat," Def Jam's first 12-inch single. When Def Jam signed with CBS for distribution a year later, L.L.'s *Radio* was the first album to be released. He performed the song "I Can't Live Without My Radio" in the movie *Krush Groove;* it was the first L.L. Cool J single to make the R&B chart, peaking at number 15 in early 1986.

For his second album, *Bigger and Deffer,* the rapper went in the studio with DJ Bobcat (Bobby Erving), a member of the L.A. Posse along with Darryl Pierce and Dwayne Simon. L.L. wrote the lyrics to "I Need Love" in the basement of his grandmother's house. It took him less than half an hour. "I was talking about a true spiritual love, and romantic love also," he explains. "Just true love, companionship. That's

LL Cool J

something I wanted." He did not have a relationship at the time, he says. "I was only 18, so there wasn't too much happening in my life."

Within two days, the recording process was underway. "The song didn't go through any changes," says Cool J. "The only thing we did was put a keyboard on it, a few strings, and the chorus. We didn't know how to fix it," he laughs. "We made the track, rapped to it, and mixed it. That was it."

L.L. didn't have a lot of support from his friends. "A lot of guys said, 'You shouldn't do that. It sounds like Christmas music. It's terrible. It's the worst song.'" Cool J talked it over with Bobcat and they decided to go ahead with the song despite the opposition. After recording the track with engineer Steve Ett, L.L. took the tape home and listened to it. "It was really emotional...I really needed love and wrote it from the heart."

L.L. says he was not wise enough in the ways of the record business at that point to record the song as a marketing ploy. "It was spontaneous. No one sat down and said, 'We need a ballad,' because there were no rap ballads...It wasn't contrived. I didn't have all that industry know-how, like SoundScan...I didn't know anything."

467

LOST IN EMOTION

Lisa Lisa and Cult Jam

COLUMBIA 07267
WRITERS: FULL FORCE
PRODUCERS: FULL FORCE
October 3, 1987 (1 week)

L. L. Cool J lost his place at Number One to a group that sported his initials—Lisa Lisa and Cult Jam.

B-Fine, one of the three George brothers in Full Force, is a big music fan whose collection includes a surprising variety of artists. "I buy all those 'Greatest Hits' of everybody, from Stax to the Carpenters. The Carpenters had great melodies. Chicago, groups that were way before me, I buy them to hear because it always comes back to that. I would buy the greatest-hits on CD collections [like] the Motown artists to get a flavor."

It was the Motown flavor that influenced B-Fine when he wrote "Lost in Emotion," the second Number One single for Lisa Lisa and Cult Jam. "I wanted to do something real Motown-sounding," says B-Fine.

"Lisa's voice always reminded me of Martha & the Vandellas and the Supremes." B-Fine worked at home on the song. "I wrote the whole song, lyrics and all the music, inside my head. And the first time I got to hear all of the music and everything was when I got in the studio. I even did the sax solo in my head. I knew it was going to sound like the way it did. It was just one of those simple Motown-sounding types of songs."

B-Fine's brother, Bowlegged Lou, says the song was inspired by one of Motown's outstanding female artists, Mary Wells. He was listening to a greatest hits album one day. "[The song] playing was 'Two Lovers.' And right after 'Two Lovers' came 'You Beat Me to the Punch.' So what we did is made ["Lost in Emotion"] a combination of 'Two Lovers' and 'You Beat Me to the Punch.' We didn't steal the riffs; all we did was get the flavoring of it."

B-Fine doesn't credit any particular song with forming the genesis of "Lost in Emotion." "It wasn't a song I took as seriously as everybody else did," B-Fine admits. "I just did it thinking it would be good for Lisa. I didn't think it was going to be a Number One record. I just thought it was a good song. The company heard it and freaked."

B-Fine eschewed synthesized sounds in favor of real bells and xylophones on the track. "I wanted to create the [old] sound, because the cassettes of greatest hits I was listening to were live. And if you don't play bass guitar or some of the instruments, you're not going to capture [that sound]. You just can't capture expression and feelings. By playing the bass and the xylophones and different things, it will work on people's subconscious minds and make them say, 'Damn, I like this. This reminds me of...' rather than let it be electronic. And when you hear that song, it feels different."

Like his brothers and the other members of Full Force, B-Fine enjoyed working with Lisa. "It was a lot of fun. Lisa was just a year out of high school. At the time we went around playing her tape for people, a lot of record companies didn't like her voice. They loved the songs but they wanted to change it. But I always wanted to capture something that I felt if the average young girl would sing, they would sound like Lisa and I thought that was definitely appealing. In actuality, that's what happened, because right after Lisa, there were 20 other girls who came out sounding like that."

One of B-Fine's brothers, Paul Anthony, agrees it was fun to work with Lisa. "It was family. Lisa was always a hard worker and a trooper and Cult Jam was like, 'Hey, I'm down, let's go'...We believed in one another and they believed in the formula that Full Force had for them and it worked. Lisa's solo now, but we're still very much friends. It was definitely magical."

468

(YOU'RE PUTTIN') A RUSH ON ME

Stephanie Mills

MCA 53151

WRITERS: TIMMY ALLEN, PAUL LAURENCE

PRODUCER: PAUL LAURENCE

October 10, 1987 (1 week)

If you dropped by the Cellar restaurant at 95th and Columbus in New York City in the early '80s, you might have heard a band called Kinky Fox that featured among its members vocalist Johnny Kemp [see 488—"Just Got Paid"]. The bassist in the group was a musician from Philadelphia, Timmy Allen.

Allen had a number of fans, including Larry Blackmon of Cameo and a producer named Paul Laurence, who was working with Freddie Jackson [see 408—"Rock Me Tonight (For Old Times Sake)"]. Laurence invited Allen to play on some tracks for Jackson, and Allen mentioned that he did some songwriting. "I let him hear some things and he liked the tracks, so we started collaborating on lyrics," Allen says.

Allen was home one day working on a track when he thought of the title "Puttin' a Rush on Me." He's not sure where the inspiration came from. "I get a rhythm of a melody and then it just comes out. I can't even tell you [where it comes from] because I'm not thinking of anything in particular."

Allen told Laurence he had a "hell of a track." At the time, the producer was working with Stephanie Mills. "He came and listened to it and said, 'Man, this is a smash.' And he wrote the verses but he loved the concept of the hook that I had," Allen says.

Allen recorded a demo with his own vocal and gave it to Laurence. But that wasn't the version Stephanie heard.

"That song was quite interesting," Mills responds when the title is mentioned. "They sent a tape to me that wasn't done. But I knew I liked it because it was real simple and I liked what it said, especially in that time—the middle '80s."

The artist recalls hearing a demo: "It was Paul singing on it and Paul really can't sing. You just have to listen to it and read between the lines. But he just sang a little part of it. What was good about working with Paul is that I like producers who know what they want to hear. Because I can sing anything and I can sing any way you want me to. So sometimes I like for producers to give me directions. In that song, he was very good at giving me directions [about] how he wanted it so I wouldn't sing it too much so that it would stay a real hooky kind of song."

Like many of Stephanie's hits, "(You're Puttin') A Rush on Me" had a memorable title and hook. "I think that's what makes a good song," Mills ventures, "a song you can sing along with and you remember it. The hook has to be strong and the title is also very important."

"(You're Puttin') A Rush on Me" was the third Number One hit for Mills. They were all from different producers; she enjoys the challenge of working with various creative people. "I think it keeps it fresh and you learn which producers really work for you," she comments. "Being that I'm a real singer, I need producers who really know how to produce singers and not just produce grooves, who concentrate more on the musician side of it. I try to use producers who are used to working with singers."

469

BAD

Michael Jackson

EPIC 07418
WRITER: MICHAEL JACKSON
PRODUCER: QUINCY JONES
October 17, 1987 (3 weeks)

"Why did it take so long to make *Bad?*" Michael Jackson asked in *Moonwalk*. "The answer is that Quincy [Jones] and I decided that this album should be as close to perfect as humanly possible. A perfectionist has to take his time; he shapes and he molds and he sculpts that thing until it's perfect. He can't let it go before he's satisfied; he can't.

"If it's not right, you throw it away and do it over. You work that thing till it's just right. When it's as perfect as you can make it, you put it out there. Really, you've got to get it to where it's just right; that's the secret. That's the difference between a number 30 record and a Number One record that stays Number One for weeks. It's got to be good."

Of course, there was also the pressure of following the most successful album of all time—*Thriller*, with more than 40 million copies sold worldwide. "There was a lot of tension because we felt we were competing with ourselves," Michael stated in his book. "It's very hard to create something when you feel like you're in competition with yourself because no matter how you look at it, people are always going to compare *Bad* to *Thriller*. You can always say, 'Aw, forget *Thriller*,' but no one ever will."

The title song of Michael's third solo album for Epic was first heard by the world on August 31, 1987, when CBS broadcast a half-hour special that included the 18-minute Martin Scorsese–directed "Bad" video.

" 'Bad' is a song about the street," Michael wrote. "It's about this kid from a bad neighborhood who gets to go away to a private school. He comes back to the old neighborhood when he's on a break from school and the kids from the neighborhood start giving him trouble. He sings, 'I'm bad, you're bad, who's bad, who's the best?' He's saying when you're strong and good, *then* you're bad."

Working with Quincy and Michael in the studio on "Bad" were Greg Phillinganes, John Barnes, and Michael Boddicker (synthesizers), John Robinson (drums), Douglas Getschal (drum programming), David Williams (guitar), Kim Hutchcroft and Larry Williams (saxophones), Gary Grant and Jerry Hey (trumpets), Paulinho da Costa (percussion), and Christopher Currell (synclaver keyboards and digital guitar). The Hammond B3 Midi organ solo was played by a special guest star, jazz organist Jimmy Smith.

There was one person missing from the "Bad" session. The song was originally written for Michael to sing as a duet with Prince. "We never told anybody about that because we didn't want to jinx the record at first," Quincy told Alan DiPerna. "It took a long time to convince Michael to do a record with Prince. He finally said, 'OK, let's give it a shot,' and he wrote this song for him. Then we had this meeting...The upshot of it was that Prince didn't do the record."

470

LOVIN' YOU

The O'Jays

PHILADELPHIA INTERNATIONAL 50084
WRITERS: KENNY GAMBLE, LEON HUFF
PRODUCERS: KENNY GAMBLE, LEON HUFF
November 7, 1987 (1 week)

The '80s looked like a pretty bleak decade for the O'Jays.

When the group first came together, the '50s were almost over. Eddie Levert and Walter Williams were performing as the Levert Brothers in their hometown of Canton, Ohio. William Powell, Bobby Massey, and Bill Isles joined them and formed the Mascots. Cleveland DJ Eddie O'Jay became their manager and lent them his name.

In the '60s, the O'Jays had their earliest chart hits. They signed with Los Angeles–based Imperial Records in 1963 and went in the studio with H.B. Barnum. "Lonely Drifter" was their first single to chart, followed by "Lipstick Traces (On a Cigarette)" and "Let It All Out." After a brief deal with Bell Records, the O'Jays met Kenny Gamble and Leon Huff and signed with their Neptune logo.

That paved the way for the '70s, when the O'Jays were among the brightest stars in the Philadelphia International firmament. By the time the decade ended, they had amassed eight Number One hits, spending a total of 16 weeks atop the *Billboard* R&B singles chart.

Then came the drought. "You have those moments where you feel it could be over," founding member Eddie Levert admits. "The only time I truly thought it was over was the period from 1980 to 1987, where it was very dry."

The O'Jays didn't suddenly run out of gas. There was a specific reason for their lack of hits, Eddie believes. "We'd gone to South Africa and made people mad," he says without rancor. "They were boycotting our gigs and it was hard to get airplay. We [realized] going to South Africa was the worst thing we could have ever done in our lives."

The trio went with good intentions. "We did not play to any segregated audiences," Eddie relates. "We made it a requirement that they must be able to let black and white in. We didn't say we only want to play for blacks." The controversy began as soon as the O'Jays landed at the airport, where the press had gathered to question the group. The problem was

Angela Winbush

resolved later when the O'Jays apologized and were removed from the United Nations list of performers who violated the cultural boycott of South Africa.

"I know we have people who hate certain people and certain ethnic groups," Eddie says. "But I always thought it was on a very small scale. Going to South Africa let me know that it's a very large thing. I thought [humanity] had grown mentally, past all of the petty things. I thought we were bigger than that as people, as human beings."

By 1987, Eddie was thinking about calling it a day. He thought he could write and produce, or find something outside of the music business. "And along comes 'Lovin' You' to say, 'No, we think you have a few more in you.' "

Gamble and Huff moved their Philadelphia International Records from CBS to EMI in the '80s, but the O'Jays comeback record wasn't a contemporary song. " 'Lovin' You' was written in the '70s," says Eddie. "We should have recorded it then."

It was the final O'Jays Number One single to be written and produced by Gamble and Huff. "They were having their problems getting along with each other, which affected the music," Eddie says. "You knew they would never part company, but they were going through a rough time with each other. We were happy to get away from that and do our own music. We needed to be away from there at that time because they were not in harmony and all we could do was hurt each other. By doing the songs they were [writing], we probably would have hurt ourselves along with them too."

471

ANGEL

Angela Winbush

MERCURY 888 831
WRITER: ANGELA WINBUSH
PRODUCER: ANGELA WINBUSH
November 14, 1987 (2 weeks)

When the duo of René Moore and Angela Winbush broke up after two Number One singles, both artists remained in the PolyGram family as solo performers. Moore recorded for Polydor while Winbush remained on Mercury and scored a chart-topping hit of her own, "Angel."

"I wasn't surprised that people would like it, but I was surprised it went Number One," she says. "You never know what's going to happen with a record when you put it out. You don't assume."

Winbush assessed the difference between her 10-year collaboration with Moore and having a career of her own: "I think my music as a solo artist is a little freer and happier, only because there was less tension in the recording and I could paint the pictures of the music the way I saw them. I think the René & Angela music had a darker color to it. I see music in colors, so I think 'I'll Be Good' may have had a darker color than 'C'est Toi,' which could be a continuance of 'I'll Be Good,' except it has a brighter, poppier color.

"I know this doesn't make sense," Angela stops to almost apologize, "but I see songs in colors, like 'I'll Be Good' is very, very dark blue to me. 'C'est Toi' is blue but a different blue, more like an aquamarine. And 'Angel' and 'Your Smile' are very similar—I did that purposely, to show that this is the same girl that came from the duo and the same person who wrote those songs is writing these songs, but it's a different color to the production and the presence of the song."

Another advantage in being on her own, she says, is that she gets to show off more vocally. "Obviously you don't have to split the song in half, whereas you have to compensate and make allowances for songs when you're working with other people."

Angela says that many people assumed she had a romantic relationship with René, but claims that wasn't so. "They would either assume we were married or we were cousins or we were sister and brother...None of the above is true. We were working together."

No one had to make any assumptions about Angela's relationship with her manager, Ronald Isley of the Isley Brothers. She recalls how they met: "Ron said he wanted to work with the people who did 'Your Smile.' " Warner Brothers executive Benny Medina arranged for them to get together over a lunch. Angela told Ronald she was a fan of the Isley Brothers, had all of their albums, and had written some songs that would be perfect for the group. "It was a big thing for me, having a song that a singer of that caliber would perform," she says.

On June 26, 1993, Ronald Isley and Angela Winbush were married in Los Angeles. They interrupted their professional careers long enough to honeymoon in Hawaii on the island of Maui.

472

SKELETONS

Stevie Wonder

MOTOWN 1907
WRITER: STEVIE WONDER
PRODUCER: STEVIE WONDER
November 28, 1987 (2 weeks)

In the mid-1970s, the two years between Stevie Wonder's *Fulfillingness' First Finale* and *Songs in the Key of Life* seemed like a lifetime—especially when compared to the prolific output of, say, Elton John or Chicago in the same decade.

But by the mid-'80s, two years between superstar albums seemed like the industry norm. In fact, the interval between Wonder's *In Square Circle* in 1985 and *Characters* in 1987 was short by some artists' standards.

Stevie also knew that times—and his audience's anticipation—had changed. No more languid picnics at farms in New England [see 263—"I Wish"]. To help promote *Characters*, he covered all the bases, including an appearance at a radio industry convention early in 1988.

There, in a Dallas hotel ballroom crammed with station program directors and record label promotion staff, Stevie sang "Skeletons" and another of the album's songs, "Get It." (He also excused himself from playing a longer set with the quintessential alibi of the '80s: One of his synthesizer programs, on a computer disc, was missing.)

"Skeletons" was vintage Wonder, an astringent sideswipe at politicians and other public figures that recalled his 1974 Number One, "You Haven't Done Nothin'." Discussing the song at the time, he explained that it "started about 4:30 to 5:00 in the afternoon. I went home and I was just working on a riff, a bass riff, and after I came up with *nah nah nah nah nah*, I then came up with the *what did your mama tell you...*

"I just started singing *skeletons in the closet...* I was just singing that, you know, *nah nah nah nah nah—skeletons in your closet*, and from that came the song. It kinda just fell out, kind of similarly to when I did 'Superstition'...It just kinda *came*, just kinda came out," he explained.

Wonder recorded most of *Characters* at his own Wonderland studios in Los Angeles, with longtime associate Gary Olazabel engineering and mixing. The computer and synthesizer programming on "Skeletons" was done by Robert Arbittier; the track featured no other musicians. The background vocalists included the son of the late Little Willie John, Keith John, who in 1982 had signed with Stevie's WonDirection Records.

The album was "about many characters, not one particular character," Wonder declared upon its release in November 1987. "Characters in politics, the character of people in relationships...the different *moods* of people, bringing out their character."

Characters is "actually broken up into two parts," he added. "These are the first 12 songs...There are twelve more songs that will happen in another few months from now."

As usual, Wonder stretched the meaning of time and space—almost four years passed before his next album, and that was the movie soundtrack of Spike Lee's *Jungle Fever*.

473

SYSTEM OF SURVIVAL

Earth, Wind & Fire

COLUMBIA 07608
WRITER: SKYLARK
PRODUCERS: MAURICE WHITE, PRESTON GLASS
December 12, 1987 (1 week)

It sounds like something a press agent would have concocted, but it's Maurice White's story and, six years later, he's sticking to it. The Earth, Wind & Fire chief swears that the lead-off single from EW&F's reunion album, *Touch the World*, came from an unknown named Skylark who submitted it as follows:

"Philip [Bailey] and I were in San Francisco ...recording some of the earlier songs from 'Touch the World'...and most days we stayed at the same hotel. We were walking to the car, and we saw all of a sudden this box taped to the car. I thought it was a bomb. I didn't know what it was. It had 'Maurice' written across it.

"We put the tape in the tape recorder and 'System of Survival' came on in its present state, like bam! We looked at each other like, 'This is it, this is it!' So immediately when I got to the studio, I called [Skylark] up, he's about six-foot-seven, a big guy, and I got him to work on the song with us."

It's hardly surprising that Skylark knew how to find White's car; the pair obviously thought a lot alike already. "System of Survival" crosses EW&F's earlier voice-of-the-people hit, "Let Me Talk," with the dancing-for-inner-peace lyric of "Let's Groove."

Skylark did, indeed, get to appear on the record, handling the drums and synthesizer programming, and contributing background vocals. It was recorded in July 1987 at Studio D in Sausalito, California. Co-producer Preston Glass played guitar and synthesizer, and did additional drum programming; Jerry Hey wrote the horn arrangement. And if you closed your eyes in listening to "System of Survival," it was almost as if time had stood still since EW&F's last album in late '83.

It hadn't, of course. White had spent his time off scoring a movie and expanding his production roster to include such unlikely clients as Barbra Streisand and Neil Diamond. White's 1985 solo remake of

Earth, Wind & Fire

"Stand By Me" went top ten R&B, but he hadn't crossed pop, or followed it up.

Philip Bailey had fared somewhat better. Having borrowed the Earth, Wind & Fire horns for several of his own projects, Genesis leader Phil Collins popped in to duet on Bailey's "Easy Lover," giving him a gold single and two Grammy nominations in the process.

During the EW&F hiatus, Bailey responded to the inevitable question about a reunion by telling an interviewer, "I don't know. Go ask Maurice. If anybody knows, he does." But it was Bailey who, according to a group bio, initiated the reunion by "hounding" White until the group finally went back into the studio in late '86. The outcome was *Touch the World,* and, with the help of Skylark's Scotch-taped smash-in-a-box, their last Number One hit.

474

I WANT TO BE YOUR MAN

Roger

REPRISE 28229
WRITERS: ROGER TROUTMAN, LARRY TROUTMAN
PRODUCER: ROGER TROUTMAN
December 19, 1987 (1 week)

When Roger Troutman wrote "I Want to Be Your Man," he was looking to make a statement. "Guys have trouble committing and women want us to commit," he suggests. "Women want us to admit that we don't want to commit."

Roger developed that idea into a song with the help of his brother Larry, who heard him working on a track in the style of "Computer Love," a top 10 hit in 1986 for their group Zapp. "I was playing in Dallas and [Larry] flew out. We sat in the hotel room one day and wrote the song. I talked to him about what I was trying to say and one thing led to another...We came back and recorded a vocal."

Like "Computer Love," "I Want to Be Your Man" was a ballad featuring Roger's vocals filtered through the Vocoder voice box. "It was a mixture of my human voice and the voice box. I had never done that before," says Roger. "I have a keen understanding of harmony and music and I have a very good understanding of layering...so it would always take a lot of time [to record] because with the voice box, I can only play one note at a time." After he finished layering tracks, if he didn't like the result he would have to go back to the beginning and layer six or seven harmony parts, which took additional time.

Roger credits background singer Nicole Cottom with being a great inspiration during the long hours it took to complete the song. "She graduated the same day as Larry's daughter. Larry heard Nicole singing at her graduation, and mentioned her to me...so I had her come in and she would work in the afternoons helping me do background parts." Cottom was in the studio the day Roger was recording his vocals for "I Want to Be Your Man." Roger recalls, "There was a spot in the song where there was a hole and I asked her to do something. It was so good, there was no need to take it out."

Despite all of his hard work on the song, Roger says he hated "I Want to Be Your Man" when it was completed. He thought it was suitable album filler, but got a different reaction when he played it for executives at his label, Warner Brothers.

"[Label president] Lenny Waronker called and said, 'This song is so great...we want you to leave Warner Brothers Records and put you over on Reprise.' " Waronker, along with label chairman Mo Ostin, were ready to reactivate Warner's sister label, which had been dormant for several years. They told Roger they felt "I Want to Be Your Man" would be a "perfect opening act" to bring the label back. Troutman found the idea frightening, because he already knew the Warners staff and didn't want to start working with new personnel. He was told that while there would be a new promotion department for pop music, he would be working with the same R&B promotion people he already knew. "It showed a compassion and belief in 'I Want to Be Your Man' from the record company, and of course I agreed," Roger says. "Lenny wanted to launch the record in a big way. He and Benny Medina took a hands-on approach to marketing...and I have to say it was a great success. It was Number One black and number three pop." Because of the record's crossover success, Roger was invited to perform at a rodeo in Texas before a crowd of 20,000, in addition to a six-night stand at Disneyland.

475

THE WAY YOU MAKE ME FEEL

Michael Jackson

EPIC 07645
WRITER: MICHAEL JACKSON
PRODUCER: QUINCY JONES
December 26, 1987 (4 weeks)

Just like he did with *Thriller,* Michael Jackson pulled a hat trick with *Bad.* Both albums gave the King of Pop three Number One singles in a row.

"The Way You Make Me Feel" was the third single issued from *Bad,* after "I Just Can't Stop Loving You" [see 465] and the title tune [see 469]. The fact that it even appeared on the album proved that it was one of Jackson's favorite tracks, for it survived an elimination process that wiped out more than 50 compositions.

"Michael initially had about 66 songs," producer Quincy Jones told Alan DiPerna in *Music & Sound Output*. "But by the time I came in, it had been narrowed down to somewhere between 33 and 36 songs, which in many ways is like having nothing. Too much can be the same as too little. I had my eye on 10, maybe 12, of those 33 songs."

Jones explained how he thought *Bad* differed from *Thriller*: "It's all about contrasts, you know. We had a lot of highly textured, very sophisticated harmonic structures on a lot of the songs on *Thriller*. So it was fun to go the other way. And I'm sure we had that in mind when we were selecting the final songs we were going to use. 'Let's really get raw,' we thought, 'and make Michael dig into another side of himself.' On 'The Way You Make Me Feel' he sounds like..." Engineer Bruce Swedien interrupted Jones at that point to say, "Oh those vocal licks...that's Jimmy Reed!"

Swedien offered his own comments about *Bad*, including the fact that he doesn't have to perform any magic on Michael's vocals. "All those doubles on his vocal aren't trick electronics. He sings them, and all the backgrounds too."

"The Way You Make Me Feel" helped Michael to continue to make chart history. It was his eighth Number One solo hit and the 14th of his career, including his six chart-toppers with the Jackson 5. It was his seventh Number One single of the '80s, more than anyone else had amassed in the decade. And during its four-week run at the top, it extended his chart span to 18 years—not bad for someone under 30.

Quincy used his regular band of musicians on "The Way You Make Me Feel." The lineup included John Robinson (drums), Douglas Getschal (drum programming), Eric Gale and David Williams (guitars), Kim Hutchcroft and Larry Williams (saxophones), Gary Grant and Jerry Hey (trumpets), Ollie E. Brown and Paulinho da Costa (percussion), Christopher Currell (synclavier and finger snaps), and John Barnes, Michael Boddicker, and Greg Phillinganes (synthesizers).

476

LOVE OVERBOARD

Gladys Knight & the Pips

MCA 53210

WRITER: REGGIE CALLOWAY

PRODUCERS: REGGIE CALLOWAY, VINCENT CALLOWAY

January 23, 1988 (1 week)

Between 1967 and 1985, Gladys Knight & the Pips had 49 entries on the R&B chart, divided almost evenly between three labels—Motown's Soul imprint, Buddah, and Columbia. In 1986, the group signed with MCA. "Jheryl [Busby] had wooed us and we had known him for many years, when he was at A&M," Gladys explains. "He finally got us to come over and sign with MCA. And Jheryl was like the A&R person for our recording project, which we were very happy about. That was the understanding when we went over there, that we would have that kind of relationship."

The group began recording songs for their first MCA album, but Busby felt they didn't have a hit single yet. "He told everybody, 'We're not doing it until we get it.' I loved that," Gladys says. "That's what I miss about Jheryl not being there now."

Louil Silas of MCA asked Reggie and Vincent Calloway [see 398—"Operator"] to come up with some songs for Gladys and the Pips. "Generally we try to write a song for a particular artist," says Reggie. "We try to get a feel for what their life has been about, what they would feel good saying, and what comes well through them."

Reggie focused on personal relationships to create a song for Gladys. "You know, how a person can love someone so much that it hurts," he elaborates. "You do all the wrong things for all the right reasons. I had that concept and said, 'That works for Gladys really well,' because I knew that everybody has relationship problems and no one is immune to that. [I wrote] from a woman's point of view, because women are usually unfortunately the ones who seem to love too hard. Men are a little bit more immune. From time to time, it goes both ways—but it fit her like a glove."

Calloway came up with the hook first and then the beat. "I worked with the Linn 9000 on that and wanted a big beat that her voice could ride on top of—a track that was real open, but had a good melody and enough room for her to be Gladys and be expressive."

The track was recorded at QCA Studios in Cincinnati. George Duke played acoustic piano, Joel Davis and David Ervin played keyboards, Gene Robinson was on guitar, and Freddie "Ready" Washington handled bass guitar. At this point, the Calloways had no personal contact with Knight. "We didn't know if she liked the song," says Reggie. "We sent her a demo of the hook, the groove, and I think I was humming—the words weren't finished." The group was touring, so if they liked the song, the Calloways were going to have to meet them on the road to record the vocals. "I said, 'If she doesn't call, I don't think I'll be leaving,' because you can be a little intimidated by working with a star that big if you don't know what they're feeling."

Finally, Reggie got the call. "I'll never forget, he came to Denver," Gladys says. "We found this little recording studio. It was somebody's house and we went in there and took a few hours." Reggie recalls

Gladys Knight & the Pips

the session: "It was one of those all-nighters. Working with her was a real dream because I had never worked with a person who's had that much experience who says to you, 'Take your time. Don't rush. Let's just get it right.' "

Gladys concludes, "We felt when we left that we had something. And we did. We had a Number One record."

477

I WANT HER

Keith Sweat

VINTERTAINMENT 69431
WRITERS: TEDDY RILEY, KEITH SWEAT
PRODUCERS: KEITH SWEAT, TEDDY RILEY
January 30, 1988 (3 weeks)

Teddy Riley and Keith Sweat teamed up to create "I Want Her," the single that led the way for the sound of traditional R&B music married to a harder, hip-hop beat. The amalgamation was dubbed New Jack Swing by Barry Cooper, who later wrote the film *New Jack City*. "He gave me the name this music should be called," Riley acknowledges. "He said, 'I want you to take this name and roll with it.' "

Keith Sweat—his real name—was the third of five children in his family. He grew up in the Grant Projects in Harlem, not far from the Apollo Theater. He saw the Jacksons perform when he was 14 and knew music would be his life. While attending City College to study communications and child psychology in 1984, he was asked to be the lead vocalist of Jamilah. The New York funk band played music in the fashion of Slave and Parliament, and opened for artists like Teddy Pendergrass, the Whispers, and the Delfonics. "I was only in the band a short time because I didn't like their concept," Sweat told Alex Henderson. "I wanted to do my own thing, write my own music, and find my own direction."

After graduating from college, Sweat found work on Wall Street. While working during the day as a commodities broker for Paine Webber, he devoted his nights to music, cutting demos, and looking for a recording contract. He met E. Rahiem LeBlanc and Herb Lane of the group GQ [see 310—"Disco Nights (Rock-Freak)"], and they offered him the opportunity to record at their studio in the Bronx. Through a friend named Judy Hutson, Sweat met Vincent Davis, owner of the independent Vintertainment label. Davis played Sweat's demos for executives at Elektra and secured a deal that gave Keith a chance to produce himself.

While working on material at Power Play studios in Queens, Sweat ran into an old friend who was in the next room working with Heavy D. "I knew him through Jamilah and I was in a group called Total Climax," says Teddy Riley. "He was working on his album and he didn't have enough tunes...so I said, 'Why don't you let me do something with you?' That's how we got together."

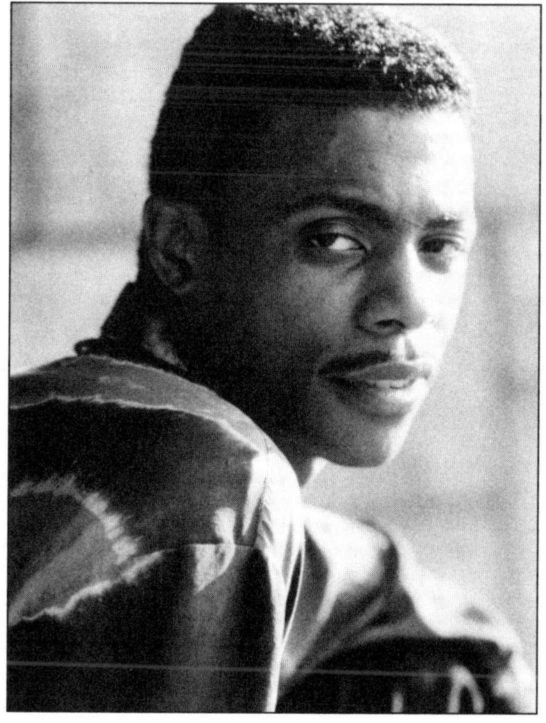

Keith Sweat

Sweat kept his day job while he and Riley collaborated. "He was at home working on the music," says Keith. "We were working it out over the phone. Then we made arrangements to get together right after I got off work." Teddy recalls creating "I Want Her": "I wrote that in my home and we came up with the words on my four-track...I came up with the beat. I came up with the hook. I came up with all the background parts and part of the lead." This all happened in one day. "I make the beat first and then I will also come up with a melody...Always with my grooves, I have to have a melody with them...then I started putting background stuff, the 'I Want Her' parts on top of it, and started building the tune."

The lyrics weren't inspired by any particular woman. "It's inspired by the guys beings in clubs and they see a girl that they want and they don't know how to approach [her]," Teddy explains.

Riley and Sweat were at similar points in their careers at that time, according to Keith. "We wanted to make it...establish ourselves in the music business. We both had the same craving, the same hunger.

Our wants and desires were pretty much the same. We wanted to be successful in what we were doing." Keith was thrilled that his first single was a smash. "I just wanted to hear myself on the radio. I really wasn't thinking about whether it was going to be a hit...I was overwhelmed that people accepted the song."

The song was not only accepted, it paved the way for the New Jack Swing movement. And when it went to Number One, Keith felt secure enough to leave his job on Wall Street. He told Alan Light in *Rolling Stone*, "That's when I knew I could definitely do this for a living."

478

GIRLFRIEND

Pebbles

MCA 53185
WRITERS: L.A. REID, BABYFACE
PRODUCERS: L.A. REID, BABYFACE
February 20, 1988 (2 weeks)

"When I first saw Pebbles, I thought that she was such a clever artist," says writer/producer Antonio "L.A." Reid, who fell in love with Pebbles and later married her. "I walked in the studio and she was producing her record herself. She was sitting there with an engineer and I said, 'Where's the producer? And she said, 'Well, I guess it's me.' "

Aside from experiencing love at first sight, Reid was impressed with Pebbles's knowledge of music and the music business. "That helped her create her vision for what she wanted with her career. I was fascinated by the fact that an artist could have so much control over their career. I was very impressed with that. When I heard her voice, I thought there was something there. I pride myself on being able to spot stars. And when I heard her sing I said to myself, 'OK, here's one. This girl's gonna be major.' And I was glad to see I was correct."

Reid and his partner Kenny "Babyface" Edmonds were latecomers to Pebbles's debut album. They were so late, in fact, that they almost missed it completely. Pebbles had almost finished her first record for MCA when Reid and Babyface met with label executive Cheryl Dickerson. She invited the producers to peruse a list of MCA artists to see who they would like to work with. Reid and Babyface expressed interest in the Mac Band [see 493—"Roses Are Red"], Bobby Brown [see 494—"Don't Be Cruel"], the Boys [see 507—"Dial My Heart"], and Pebbles.

Dickerson invited them to meet Pebbles at the studio but warned them, "The project isn't available. You can't do that one. There's no room—she's about through with the record." Reid and Babyface dropped by the studio where Pebbles was working anyway.

After they met her, they thought a song they had written for Vanessa Williams's first album would be perfect for Pebbles. Negotiations for Williams to record "Girlfriend" were dragging, so the producers let Pebbles listen to it. "When I heard Pebbles sing the record, I felt it fit her perfectly and I wanted the record to happen with her," says Babyface.

"I wanted the song because it touches on a real subject that I've been through," says the artist. The song was written from a woman's point of view, something Reid and Babyface also did for Karyn White [see 520—"Love Saw It"]. "That's the angle that I've always written from," says Babyface, "knowing how men are and knowing how women think at times and putting that into words."

And very clever words at that. "I thought it was very close to the street," Reid says. "At the time, rap music, which is sort of the storybook of ghetto life, didn't have such an appeal. So the little things that we used that were sort of street at the time seemed to be so hip."

Babyface suggests that the recording session might have gone faster if Reid hadn't been falling in love with their artist. "That might be true," Reid concedes. "I definitely fell deeply in love...It was one of those inevitable things. I think it worked out for the best. Here we are six years [later] and we're still together."

479

YOU WILL KNOW

Stevie Wonder

MOTOWN 1919
WRITER: STEVIE WONDER
PRODUCER: STEVIE WONDER
March 5, 1988 (1 week)

For a quarter-century, Stevie Wonder—man and boy—couldn't reach the chart summit with a ballad.

It wasn't for the lack of trying, both as a boy ("With a Child's Heart," for example) and as a man ("Send One Your Love," "Ribbon in the Sky"). Finally, "You Will Know" did the trick in 1988, almost 25 years after his very first Number One, "Fingertips."

The second single from Wonder's *Characters* album, "You Will Know" was, of course, self-composed, self-arranged, self-produced, and emphatically a ballad. On it, Stevie sang and played synthesizers, percussion, drums, synclavier, Moog bass, and Fairlight.

" 'You Will Know' originally started off as a love song that turned into a song dealing with another form of love," explained Wonder when the record was released. "And that is the most important form of love of all, the force of God."

The lyrics, he continued, were about "a person who has lost their way in life...feeling that they have no purpose in life, no reason for life. [That person] is saved. As they get down on their knees and start to pray and look up to heaven for the answer, they hear a voice that says, *You will know/Troubled heart you'll know/Problems have solutions/Trust and I will show*.

"That voice," said Wonder, "is the Almighty, God, or Allah, whomever one believes in."

"You Will Know" and the rest of *Characters* was recorded at the singer's Wonderland studios in Los Angeles. His longtime engineer Gary Olazabel was associate producer; Rob Arbittier helped program the synthesizers and the Synclavier. "The technology we have used is a technology that is being used a lot," Wonder remarked. "The *way* in which we are using this technology is what I think makes it unique.

"The Synclavier is a very current, a very much used instrument, or computer synthesizer, in a lot of today's music. So, too, is the Fairlight, and other such synthesizers and computers have now become the marriage of the technology of computer, keyboards and synthesizers."

Wonder was constantly looking for unusual sounds, and ways to get them. Malcolm Cecil, who worked with him on *Music of My Mind* through *Fulfillingness' First Finale* and then renewed the relationship with 1991's *Jungle Fever*, recalls, "With all the mixes, starting with 'Superstition,' I bought a little radio transmitter, a signal generator. We hooked up to the AM modulation and did an AM transmission of the mix to car radios in the car park.

"I would put the signal generator on the bonnet of the car and wind the aerial around the car aerial, so it wasn't transmitted generally—it was just straight radio-to-radio. Then we would listen and adjust the mix according to what we were hearing, so that it sounded really good in the car. And Stevie does that to this day."

480

FISHNET

Morris Day

WARNER BROS. 28201
WRITERS: MORRIS DAY,
JAMES HARRIS III, TERRY LEWIS
PRODUCERS: JIMMY JAM, TERRY LEWIS
March 12, 1988 (2 weeks)

Jimmy Jam remembers the night in Minneapolis when the song "Fishnet" was born. "We used to go to First Avenue late, at closing time. We actually wouldn't go in the club. We'd hang out outside as people were coming out. There was this girl sitting in a car and she had fishnet pantyhose on. One of the guys [Popeye Grier] who worked for Flyte Tyme who now manages Mint Condition said, 'Man, look at those fishnet black pantyhose,' and we thought that would be a good song."

The track was created when Jam and partner Terry Lewis started to work on a new album for Morris Day, one of their ex-Time mates. "Morris is a great drummer, which a lot of people don't know," says Jimmy Jam. "We set up a drum set, Terry picked up the bass, and I picked up the keyboard. We stuck a cassette in the machine and we played for however long the cassette was, 90 minutes. We each took a copy of the cassette, went home, and listened to the whole thing. There was one point in the 90 minutes where we really caught this groove, where Terry started playing this bass part that was really funky and I started playing chords that really worked and we all agreed to make a song out of that. I reminded Terry about the 'Fishnet black pantyhose' concept and that that would work for this song, and we gave the concept to Morris and he wrote the lyrics."

Morris Day didn't always plan to be a lead singer, let alone a soloist. "I had to be talked into becoming the lead singer for the Time," he reveals. "I was perfectly happy being a drummer. It was sort of a security blanket."

Jimmy Jam corroborates this: "He was always a behind-the-scenes guy. In the old days we used to call him Morris 'Too Hot' Day." The nickname came from the Kool & the Gang hit. "It was a hard song to sing because it had a lot of chord changes in it," says Jimmy Jam. But while drumming for a group called Enterprise Band of Pleasure, the female lead singer spelled Day on drums while he stepped out front to sing "Too Hot." Jam continues: "We'd be impressed...so we always knew he could sing."

Day says his over-the-top image started out as a way to have fun. "I think everybody acts kind of crazy when they're in their circle or element. I think the laugh and the whole way of talking developed and then we started pursuing a record deal. I was living [this image] because I was always with my band...so I was more on than not. It became a thing for me where I would talk on a more intense level like I do with the laugh."

Jimmy Jam explains how Morris comes up with his well-known ad-libs. "Most of them he comes up with on the spot. He comes up with a lot more stuff than we can actually use. So he usually talks and then we'll take the ones that we like. He's very witty."

Day says he acts differently when working on his own. "If I'm producing a vocal myself, then I think it out. I may have two tracks to choose from, but the way Jimmy and Terry like to work, they'll turn on the mike and have me go in there and I go into a thing and keep going and going and they'll say, 'Let's do it again.' I'll keep going until we end up with three or four tracks and they're able to sort through and make composites. I can't work like that personally, but I am able to keep coming up with the goods."

481

MAN IN THE MIRROR

Michael Jackson

EPIC 07668

WRITERS: SIEDAH GARRETT, GLEN BALLARD

PRODUCER: QUINCY JONES

March 26, 1988 (1 week)

Siedah Garrett had never written a song in her life until she became the only female singer in the Quincy Jones–produced quintet Deco. "The guys in the group wanted a publishing deal along with their recording contract," she explains. "So I was sort of pushed into writing."

In May of 1987, while Michael Jackson was working on *Bad* with Quincy, Garrett was invited along with other songwriters to attend a meeting at the producer's home. "The meeting was at 11 o'clock and I didn't get there 'til 12 because I got lost," Siedah remembers. "So I take my notes as to...what he wants in this next song for Michael, because he hasn't found all the songs yet. He said, 'We need another smash for Michael's album. I just want hits, that's all I want.' "

Siedah had an appointment the next day with one of her writing partners, Glen Ballard, to work on material for her own album. She told him about Quincy's request and Glen suggested they work on something for Michael. "I gave him this 'I'm really disappointed' look. But I said OK."

Ballard recalled the day in *SongTalk*: "I started singing a verse idea melodically. I heard her singing something about 'a man in the mirror,' and I said, 'That's great. I love that.' So the first time I heard the title it was actually in the song."

They completed the demo on a Friday night. An inner voice told Siedah to call Quincy immediately and tell him about the song. She told the producer that irregular though it may be, she couldn't wait until Monday for him to hear "Man in the Mirror." Quincy told her to come over right away.

"The front door opens and there's 12 guys sitting at his dining room table in business suits with clipboards...They're having this big meeting about some movie Q's gonna do." Siedah handed him the demo and asked him to call her back as soon as possible.

Four hours later she heard from Quincy. "Uhh, I don't know," he said over the phone. Then he laughed and told her the song was incredible. But he gave her a warning: "He said, 'I've been playing Michael songs for two years. We've been in the studio for 11 months. I don't know if he's going to take this song. But don't worry, if he doesn't do it on this record, we'll do it on yours.' "

It only took a few days for Quincy to tell Siedah that Michael was going to record her song. A week later, another call from the studio informed Siedah that Michael wanted to make the bridge longer. Quincy planned to bring in the Winans and the Andrae Crouch Choir to sing backing vocals—and Quincy wanted Siedah to join them.

"On the day of the session, just before the Winans left and before the choir came in, Michael came in...and I extended my hand to shake Michael's hand, and...he pulls me to him and kisses me on the cheek, and of course externally I'm very cool, and my heart's going, 'Oh my God! Oh my God! I've just been kissed by Michael Jackson!' "

482

WISHING WELL

Terence Trent D'Arby

COLUMBIA 07675

WRITERS: TERENCE TRENT D'ARBY, SEAN OLIVER

PRODUCERS: MARTYN WARE, TERENCE TRENT D'ARBY

April 2, 1988 (1 week)

Terence Trent D'Arby didn't hit it off too well with the British press after he was signed to CBS Records in the U.K. Perhaps it was because he said his first disc was "the most brilliant debut album from any artist this decade." Perhaps it was because he claimed it was a better work than *Sgt. Pepper's Lonely Hearts Club Band*.

Whatever the reason, the native New Yorker had to explain himself and his clippings when he arrived in America. He told Robert Hilburn of the *Los Angeles Times*: "You've got to realize that I said a lot of [outrageous] things in England. A lot of it was what I truly believed, but a lot was exaggerated to make a point. You have to hit people over the head to make them notice, and I did it. I know how to play the game. But now I'm worried that a lot of people in America think I am some kind of hype because of all that has been written in England—and I'm very serious about my music and my career. I don't want to be just the latest curiosity."

The British arm of CBS Records teamed up D'Arby with producer Howard Gray, who had worked with the Cure and Scritti Politti. A couple of tracks were recorded, including an initial single, "If You Let Me

Stay." Then Martyn Ware of Heaven 17 was brought in to record nine tracks, enough to complete a debut album.

" 'Wishing Well' was written when I was in a half-asleep, half-awake state of mind," D'Arby told Robin Smith in *Record Mirror*. "I like the feel of the words on the song. Actually, most of my lyrics are written in about 10 minutes."

"If You Let Me Stay" peaked at number 19; "Wishing Well" was the follow-up. Both tracks were included on *Introducing the Hardline According to Terence Trent D'Arby*. "I want this album to leave a taste in your mouth that's as wholesome as your mum's best apple pie," the artist told Smith.

D'Arby was an unlikely person to have a Number One hit; he grew up in a strict Pentecostal family, forbidden to listen to any music except for gospel. A friend's mother used to buy her son a new single each week, and one day seven-year-old Terence was mesmerized by a single from a group he had never heard of. The song was "I Want You Back" by the Jackson 5.

"You can't believe how much those [Jackson 5] records meant to me," D'Arby told Hilburn. "I had been singing in church and there was something about singing that made me know it was what I was meant to do. But I kept thinking, even as a child, that there was something else, besides gospel, to sing and then I heard the Jackson 5 and it was like a whole new world opening up for me. It was like I had found my own world."

Teena Marie

483

OOO LA LA LA

Teena Marie

EPIC 07708
WRITERS: TEENA MARIE, ALLEN MCGRIER
PRODUCER: TEENA MARIE
April 9, 1988 (1 week)

Rick James remembers the first time he met Teena Marie. "I was walking around the Motown office and I heard this girl singing her ass off," he says. "I walked in and here's this little short munchkin white girl. I said, 'Wow, you're really great. Are you on Motown?' "

Mary Christine Brockert, raised in Venice, California, was indeed on the Motown roster. She had formed her own band at age 13. "I used to listen to all the early Tamla things like Stevie [Wonder] and Marvin [Gaye]," Teena told Sharon Davis. "I was introduced to Howard Davis, who got me an audition with Berry Gordy. Berry wanted me for a movie he was planning at the time...The project got shelved but he still wanted me on the label."

Teena was in the Motown family for three years without much success. Her manager at the time, Winnie Martin, suggested she let Rick James produce her, but Teena was resistant. "I was really fed up all the way around," she said. "Why should Rick be able to work with me after everyone else had failed?"

But Rick James felt there was kismet between them and wanted to produce Teena Marie. "Working with her was my first chance to teach someone all the things I knew," says James. "I taught her guitar. I taught her bass and piano and I taught her how to produce. Showed her how to carry her vocals where she wouldn't exploit the song too fast, using her range."

The Rick James/Teena Marie collaboration resulted in *Wild and Peaceful*, an album that contained the dance club hit "I'm a Sucker for Your Love." Richard Rudolph, widower of Minnie Riperton, produced Teena's second album for Motown, *Lady T*.

"After I taught her everything I could—I was like her mentor—that's when I let her go," James says. "It was probably the greatest experience I've ever had working with a vocalist, because as I watched her grow into a great producer and a great writer...in my heart I always felt responsible for bringing this out."

Teena described how she felt about Rick to Sharon Davis: "Rick knew there were feelings in my heart and songs upon my lips. He didn't say, 'This is a white girl, I can't produce her' because he doesn't think in those terms. Our relationship grew into something really beautiful."

Teena's relationship with Motown did not grow in the same direction. After three years of chart hits on the Gordy label, she sued the company for nonpayment of royalties and signed a deal with Epic. There was a countersuit, but Teena felt vindicated by an out-of-court settlement.

"Every good artist needs a lawsuit," she told Rob Hoerburger in *Billboard*. "At the time it was going on I was very bitter and frightened, and when I won the suit there was no great euphoria. I'm just really sorry it had to happen. I still have a lot of friends at Motown." Now I don't think about it on an everyday basis—I try to look at the good things and not trip on the bad, otherwise I might really trip."

Teena scored her first pop success on Epic when "Lovergirl" went to number four on the Hot 100. It was number nine R&B. Three years later, Teena Marie was sitting on top of the R&B chart, as "Ooo La La La" became her first Number One single.

It proved to be the biggest R&B hit of her career. The follow-up, "Work It," peaked at number 10. She charted again in 1990 with "Here's Looking at You," a number 11 hit, and "If I Were a Bell," which returned her to the top 10 by peaking at number eight.

484

GET OUTTA MY DREAMS, GET INTO MY CAR

Billy Ocean

JIVE 9678

WRITERS: ROBERT JOHN "MUTT" LANGE, BILLY OCEAN

PRODUCER: ROBERT JOHN "MUTT" LANGE

April 16, 1988 (1 week)

The "Loverboy" succeeded the "Lovergirl" at Number One when Billy Ocean's "Get Outta My Dreams, Get into My Car" followed Teena Marie's "Ooo La La" at the top of the *Billboard* R&B chart.

Billy Ocean credits producer Robert John "Mutt" Lange with the idea for his fourth Number One hit. "I like to think he works pretty much the same [as I do]. He plays with words and things and suddenly one day it makes sense to him and he takes it further. 'Get outta my dreams, get into my car' is a very clever lyric. He had most of the chorus of that, lyrically and everything...Most of the verse and everything else had a lot of my contribution. But when you're dealing with a song...the song is only as good as the chorus."

Lange was better known for working with hard rock acts like the Cars and AC/DC than an R&B singer like Billy Ocean. "Working with him is like working with nobody else, because he is the hardest person I've worked with," says Billy. "I don't mean that in a derogatory sense at all. I say it with a lot of respect...He was very fussy to work with, but he knows exactly what he wants. So he'd make you do a line or a word over and over. Ninety-nine percent of the song is there, right? But if there's one thing somewhere in the middle, even a breath that he thinks should go in there, he'd put it in."

The lead-off single from the *Tear Down These Walls* album ran into trouble in England, where the song was recorded. "They thought 'Get outta My Dreams, Get into My Car' would encourage little children to be kidnapped, to get into strangers' cars," says Ocean. "I suppose it's something that you can't really argue with." Some of the grunts and groans from the intro were edited out.

Ocean thought the song sounded like a hit single as soon as Lange told him about the idea. "When you listen to some of the things he did with the Cars and a lot of other people, AC/DC and all the others, you know you're in safe hands. Mutt's not one of the easiest producers, but he gets results."

Ocean has learned to be more serious about the recording process as the years have gone by. "I remember I used to drink in the studio. Not like I was a drunkard or anything like that, but I'd be encouraged by the producers I was working with...They'll think it's cool to go into the studio with a few bottles of wine and they'll treat the whole thing as a party. I find that over the years, I've gotten a lot more disciplined in the studio. I find the studio a very creative place to be. I can actually go in there and from scratch write and produce a track. I also find that once you go into the studio and discipline yourself enough to know the purpose you're in there for, invariably you never waste any time. You always come out with something."

485

DA'BUTT

E.U.

EMI MANHATTAN 50115
WRITERS: MARCUS MILLER, MARK STEVENS
PRODUCER: MARCUS MILLER
April 23, 1988 (1 week)

Finally, a dance everyone could get behind. When director Spike Lee needed a song for his movie *School Daze,* he called Luther Vandross's co-writer and co-producer, bassist Marcus Miller. "He said there was going to be a party and the dancers were going to be doing this dance called 'Da'Butt' and he needed a song called 'Da'Butt,' " Miller remembers. Of course, there was no dance called "Da'Butt." Not yet. "He figured that everyone would come up with their own version of it. So it was my job to realize this thing. And it was tricky, because the butt—what are you going to write about?"

Miller knew the song had to be humorous, yet still have credibility. He called up a friend of his, Mark Stevens, who is Chaka Khan's brother. Along with Lenny White, Miller and Stevens had been in a group called the Jamaica Boys. "I had a good framework and I asked Mark to come in and scat a lead vocal so I could hear what was going on," Miller continues. "Mark got into it and started coming up with his own lyrics. Once he said, 'Backfield in motion,' I said, 'Let's finish this because it's going to be funny. It's going to be good.' "

Miller sent the finished demo to the director, and Lee requested some minor changes. Then Miller called in E.U., also known as Experience Unlimited. The nine-piece outfit from Washington, D.C., had a regional hit in 1980 with a song called "Rock Yer Butt." "It was a little tricky, because the normal E.U. go-go sound had a slower tempo than the one we had for 'Da'Butt,' so they had to adjust to a faster beat. But the drummer Ju Ju House played such a thick beat that everybody fell in," says Miller.

Although the producer had studied their music, the band was leery of him. "After the first day I took them to the side and said, 'Look, guys, this is going to be your record. It's going to say "E.U." on it. After it's done, I'm going home and that's it. You guys have to live with this, so if there are any suggestions you want to make, you should make them.' When they realized I wanted their input, they were cool. All of a sudden, stuff started flowing and they were coming up with ideas. Sugar Bear, the lead singer...started calling girls' names and talking about how they had a big ol' butt...It was a pretty spontaneous thing. They came up with some interesting overdubs I wouldn't have thought of. And I added a horn section that they normally wouldn't use and it worked with their sound."

Miller considers "Da'Butt" the "least self-conscious" record he has ever produced. "Spike brought everybody from the cast down to the studio and I put out some potato chips. We had an actual party along with the track and recorded that. Everything you hear on that record is genuine, and you can hear me laughing at the funny stuff the lead singer's saying because I'm standing right next to him."

Miller loved how the song was used in the film. "It was exactly how Spike had described it to me. I think it was one of the best things in the movie." The producer was surprised at the nationwide reaction to the song and the dance. "The guys from E.U. told me they'd go on the road and play the song, and women would jump up on the stage and start taking their clothes off." He thought they were kidding until the drummer showed him photographic evidence. "He said, 'I bring my camera to the stage with me now.' "

486

NITE AND DAY

Al B. Sure!

WARNER BROS. 28192
WRITERS: AL B. SURE!, KYLE WEST
PRODUCER: KYLE WEST
April 30, 1988 (3 weeks)

Born in Boston and raised in Mount Vernon, New York, Al B. Sure! grew up listening to the music of Marvin Gaye, Johnny Mathis, and "whatever else came on the radio that mom had on," says the singer who won't reveal his real surname (but whose parents are Al and Cassandra Brown).

Al broke into the music business at the young age of 10. He was living in New Jersey then, and had a friend whose mother knew songwriter Ellie Greenwich. "Ellie heard us all singing one day and was in the middle of doing a soundtrack for the 'Sesame

Street' parks," Al says. She had us sing on it and do the video, which I never got to see. I would love to see it."

The experience of being in a recording studio stayed with him, although football, baseball, and basketball took precedence. Still, he found time for music. "My cousin Kyle [West] and I would go over to his house after school and we had my Uncle Nick's organ in the basement and a little tape recorder. We'd write and record our little songs. But it was just for fun."

A star quarterback at Mount Vernon High School, Al was best friends with Eddie F., who was working with a rapper named Heavy D.

"Heavy D. wanted to make a record," he recalls. "Eddie was the DJ and I was the engineer, and Heavy would come over and record. I was into rapping, but then I would sing on a few of the tracks and Eddie pushed me into singing."

Al turned down a football scholarship to the University of Iowa to attend the Center for the Media Arts in New York. Eddie F. introduced Al to Heavy D.'s manager, Andre Harrell, a former account executive at a New York gospel radio station, WWRL. Heavy D. was signed to MCA, and Al provided vocals for some of his tracks, including "Money Earning Mount Vernon." Harrell brought Al to the attention of Benny Medina, vice president of A&R, black music, at Warner Brothers.

As a new artist at the company, Al was entered in the Sony Innovators Award competition by Karen Jones, a Warners A&R manager. From a field of 51, the panel of judges picked Al as the winner. The judges included Quincy Jones and Herbie Hancock. The demo tape submitted to the contest included a song Al had written as a tenth grader, "Nite and Day." "I wrote it in the lunchroom eating a cheeseburger," Al confides. He and Kyle recorded a demo but discarded it.

One of the tracks on Al's *In Effect Mode,* his debut album for Warner Brothers, "Nite and Day" was recorded in the same basement where Al and Kyle had recorded their grammar school efforts. The duo spent six months recording the album, and Al and Kyle played all the instruments.

Al recorded French and Spanish versions of "Nite and Day," as well as a longer, extended version. Medina praised the song in a *Billboard* interview: "[It] was a very well-written song and [had] a sexy mood. That's something that transcends color and chart category. Al has a sexy, falsetto texture to his voice and very obvious good looks, which were major attractions from a marketing standpoint."

It was Warner Brothers executives Medina and Jones who came up with the idea of ending Al's name with an exclamation point—as a symbol of his positive personality, according to the artist.

487

MERCEDES BOY

Pebbles

MCA 53279
WRITER: PEBBLES
PRODUCER: CHARLIE WILSON
May 21, 1988 (1 week)

Yes, Pebbles is named after *that* Pebbles. When she was 10, Perri McKissack was nicknamed by her godfather after Fred and Wilma Flintstone's daughter. "I think it was the way I wore my hair or something that made him think of that," says the Oakland-born singer. "And then that was my nickname all my life, so it's still with me today."

Pebbles

Pebbles says her initial breakthrough came about as a result of a lot of hard work, strategy, and marketing, not to mention some good music. "I did lots of demos, but demos are demos," she says. "Everybody has a demo. I did a videotape version of 'Mercedes Boy,' and that's what [MCA executives] saw first and they really liked it." Marvin Robinson, a program director for an Oakland radio station, introduced Pebbles to label personnel, and Louil Silas Jr. and Jheryl Busby soon signed her to MCA.

Pebbles wasn't surprised that she got her big breakin the industry. "From birth I've always believed in myself. That sounds funny, but I've always known I was going to be in entertainment. I didn't know if people were going to like me or not, but I knew this was where I was going."

Pebbles's first Number One song [see 478—"Girlfriend"] ended up as a last-minute addition to her first album, thanks to a meeting with the writer/producer team of L.A. Reid and Babyface. By that time, she already had the song "Mercedes Boy" ready for her MCA debut.

" 'Mercedes Boy' is about a guy I fell in love with," Pebbles reveals. "The real story is that I used to see him around for years and we would have eye contact and we would have mutual friends but we would never speak to each other. It was like we were scared of each other and we both had different relationships at the time. And it wasn't until five years later that we finally met each other and had a relationship and fell in love."

Pebbles would see her paramour at a local club called The Dock of the Bay, which she frequented on Thursday nights. "It was so strange, because all during high school he went with this girl at my school but I never thought about him so much. And then years later I would see him all the time and we'd still never talk. We'd wave from a distance because we had gotten used to seeing each other all the time. And one day, while I was very deeply in love with this guy, I wrote a song."

The reference to the German luxury automobile came from the fact that both Pebbles and her would-be boyfriend drove Mercedes. "So he was my 'Mercedes Boy.' It's funny, I'm saying, 'Do you want to ride in my Mercedes, boy?' instead of the guy. The girl's being real up-front and aggressive."

Even though the song, produced by Charlie Wilson of the Gap Band [see 339—"Burn Rubber (Why You Wanna Hurt Me)"], gave Pebbles her second Number One hit on the R&B chart, she still had reservations about the overall quality of her debut album. "I didn't concentrate as hard as I should have vocally on this album," she confessed at the time. "I had too many business things I was doing...But I'm happy that everybody is liking what I did. I think I'll be better next time."

488

JUST GOT PAID

Johnny Kemp

COLUMBIA 07744
WRITERS: JOHNNY KEMP, GENE GRIFFIN
PRODUCERS: TEDDY RILEY, JOHNNY KEMP
May 28, 1988 (2 weeks)

Teddy Riley didn't write "Just Got Paid" with any particular artist in mind. "We didn't even know we were going to give it to Johnny Kemp," the producer explains. "We thought it was going to go on the Keith Sweat album. I don't write songs for a certain artist. I just write, and whoever comes to get it, then we go with that person."

Born in Nassau in the Bahamas, Kemp started singing in church and school. By the time he was 13, he was playing in clubs around the island. After being featured as a singer in a casino at age 15, Kemp met the members of a band called Foxfire. They invited him to visit them in New York. When the female lead singer of Foxfire disappeared in 1979, they sent Kemp a ticket to the Big Apple. To avoid a conflict with a country band, the group changed its name to Kinky Fox.

Kemp was in Kinky Fox when he met Keith Sweat, who was in a group called Jamilah, and Teddy Riley, who was in an outfit called Total Climax. "It was like a clique back then," says Kemp. "It was like a group of bands and we all played in the same clubs, haunted the same dives."

Kemp left Kinky Fox in 1982 and concentrated on his songwriting. He continued to play solo dates in clubs, and almost signed a recording deal with Polygram. About a year and a half later, Kemp was signed to Columbia with the help of another friend, Kashif.

Kemp details the origin of "Just Got Paid": "I was walking down the street minding my own business and ran into Keith on the street right around the corner from my house, right around the corner from Teddy's house. Keith was working on his record with Teddy." Sweat suggested Kemp listen to some of the material that Riley was writing. "Keith took me over to Teddy's house and he didn't stay very long. I hung out with Teddy...That very day, he gave me the track for 'Just Got Paid' and I completed the lyrics. The chorus was already done and the basic premise of the song was already there. It was just a matter of completing the verses. I was trying to incorporate some of the contemporary language that was going on at the time, 'lookin' fly' and 'the posse' and all that. It was something he was working on with Keith and apparently Keith didn't like it enough to put it on his record. I liked it enough to put it on mine."

Kashif had purchased Jackie Robinson's former home in Connecticut, and the song was recorded in the home studio he had built. "I had the track," says Kemp. "I had a tape of it and [Teddy] had a tape of it and both of us forgot to bring it. So we didn't have the demo. So he said, 'I remember what I did. I can do it again. I can reprogram it, no problem.' He reprogrammed the whole thing. It took him a few hours and he did the whole thing from scratch. And I said, 'I don't need the tape because I know what I want to do.' He did all the tracks and then we did backgrounds." Riley brought Aaron Hall of Guy [see 535—"My Fantasy"] to join in on the background vocals.

"At the end of the night, we were getting ready to turn in. We were all beat. And I said, 'Let me put a scratch vocal down before we split.' I went in and did one take and that's what you hear on the record...One take and it's beautiful. We didn't touch a thing."

489

LITTLE WALTER

Tony! Toni! Toné!

WING 887 385
WRITERS: DENZIL FOSTER,
THOMAS MCELROY, TONY! TONI! TONÉ!
PRODUCERS: DENZIL FOSTER,
THOMAS MCELROY
June 11, 1988 (1 week)

"Little Walter" is the son of "Wade in the Water." Raphael Wiggins, founder of Tony! Toni! Toné! along with his older brother Dwayne and their cousin Timothy Christian, had been listening to the Chambers Brothers' version of "Wade in the Water" while working on their first album with producers Denzil Foster and Thomas McElroy. "I started joking around, singing, 'Hey, little Walter,' Raphael recalls. Foster picks up the story: "It was kind of funky. We [said], 'We can't do "Wade in the Water" over again. We went to find out who wrote the record and it had no writer. So the record was just one of those things that was passed down. I said, 'Cool. We won't get in trouble. Let's change the name to "Little Walter." ' "

Raphael calls it "a message song." Although it wasn't directly stated, Little Walter was rather shady; he was the kind of drug dealer who might sell to children. Foster describes him as "that type of character that you didn't know about...your best friend could be a dope dealer and you might not know it."

Foster, McElroy and the Tonys pictured the comedian Sinbad playing the role of Little Walter in the video as they wrote the song, and eventually cast him in the part. "We were saying he'd be a perfect roommate for somebody," says Foster. In the storyline, lead singer Raphael had a roommate who seemed to be perfect but was actually selling drugs. Raphael "is a little young, he has this kid voice," says Foster. "We felt like that would get to kids and tell them a little story at the same time."

"Little Walter," recorded at McElroy's house, marked Raphael's singing debut. "I'm not a singer," he professes. "I've only been singing since I started on that album. So it was weird hearing my voice back on the record. I didn't like it."

Growing up in Oakland, Raphael and Dwayne had strong musical influences in their family. Their father played different instruments, and their uncle had a local gospel choir called the Holy Messengers. Raphael sang with that group and picked up the guitar and bass at an early age. He admired Parliament, and while still performing gospel, played for some groups that opened for the P-Funk All Stars when they played Oakland. Raphael was in a group with his cousin Timothy when Dwayne joined them. "We weren't really into being a group [that would be] making records," says Raphael. "We were too young. But Dwayne was thinking about trying to get a deal." It took them a while to find their niche, but eventually a tape was sent to Ed Eckstine, who was helming the new Wing subsidiary at Polygram. "They passed on it," says Raphael.

But then Foster and McElroy met with Eckstine to discuss a production deal. Foster hadn't heard Tony! Toni! Tone! yet, but McElroy, who went to school with Raphael, assured his partner the group sounded great. "So I went in there and started selling the Tonys like they were the next coming of Earth, Wind & Fire," says Foster. Eckstine remembered his reaction to the tape, but took the producers' word and signed the group. "We kept saying, 'We'll take care of the rest. Everything else will fall in line,' " says Foster. The Tonys rewarded their producers' faith in them by giving Eckstine his first Number One single on the Wing label.

490

ONE MORE TRY

George Michael

COLUMBIA 07773
WRITER: GEORGE MICHAEL
PRODUCER: GEORGE MICHAEL
June 18, 1988 (1 week)

"With *Faith* I was not trying to make black music or white music," George Michael said in *The Beat*. "I was just trying to make good music." The British pop star had already scored three R&B hits while paired with Andrew Ridgeley in Wham!, and had a number five R&B hit with "I Knew You Were Waiting (For Me)," a duet with Aretha Franklin.

"In terms of music, any definition of soul is something that comes from the heart to the mouth and bypasses the head," Michael said. "I never thought I sounded black. When people ask why I have a black following, and how come I've had that much support from R&B, I think it's because I've progressed as a singer with each album. I try to say what I feel and make that jump from the heart to the mouth, and pretend there's no thought process in between. Every time I go back into the studio I get closer to doing that. I've still got a way to go, but that is soul singing to me. It has nothing to do with what color you are, it's really got to do with expressing yourself without any kind of blockage."

Georgios Kyriacos Panayiotou was born in Bushey, near the North London suburb of Watford. He met Ridgeley in school, and they shared a love for music. After nine months of unemployment, they wrote "Wham Rap," inspired by the Sugarhill Gang's "Rapper's Delight." They were signed to the independent Innervision label in Great Britain before being wooed away by CBS Records.

Ater a much-publicized split that included allegations of Ridgeley's minimal contributions to Wham!, George achieved even greater success as a solo artist. His album *Faith* yielded a number of hit singles, including "One More Try." In an interview with Chris Heath, George called the song, "the best thing I've ever done. [It's] about my attitude coming out of my last relationship and into this new one when I was pretty unwilling to be open to anything."

George also spoke about the song in a Columbia biography: "The best songs are my ballads. I will probably be remembered for my ballads over the next five or 10 years. While 'Careless Whisper' was loved by many, it did nothing for me emotionally. Most likely because it seems like it's from another lifetime. On the other hand, 'One More Try' is a ballad very close to my heart. Many people compare the two. But for me, there is no comparison."

The pop star not only recorded a duet with Aretha Franklin, he also teamed up with Jody Watley and sang with Smokey Robinson and Stevie Wonder on a Motown TV special. Bob Sherwood, a Columbia Records vice president, told *Rolling Stone* that George wanted to be kept fully informed of his progress on the R&B chart. "He's taken great pride in the accomplishment. George shows as much enthusiasm about reaching the pinnacle in the black-urban market as he does about the pop market—if not more."

George confirmed that with Gary Graff of the Knight-Ridder newspaper chain. "I was much happier with [*Faith*] being the Number One black album than I was when it became the Number One pop album. There was much more of a sense of achievement."

491

JOY

Teddy Pendergrass

ASYLUM 69401
WRITERS: REGGIE CALLOWAY, JOEL DAVIS, VINCENT CALLOWAY
PRODUCERS: REGGIE CALLOWAY, VINCENT CALLOWAY
June 25, 1988 (2 weeks)

Reggie Calloway and Teddy Pendergrass both had the same manager, Shep Gordon of Alive Enterprises. "Teddy's album was just about finished and they needed a hit," Calloway recalls. "We were on a real good run and Shep said, 'Do him a favor,' not knowing that we'd be happy to work with Teddy anyway."

The first thing Reggie wanted to do was meet the artist, who had been involved in a terrible automobile accident on March 18, 1982, that left him a quadriplegic. "I wanted to see what his life was all about," says Reggie. "What changes he was going through, how he was adjusting, how much power for singing did he actually have." Calloway found his usual optimism challenged when he arrived in Philadelphia.

"I saw the chair and the van and all the hook-ups. I realized this is real. This is the situation he is actually dealing with. This is not something you read about in a magazine, and how do we convey this to the world? How is he dealing with this? What gives a person the will to go on, knowing they have a handicap they were not born with but that came up later in their lives? What we found was a person who had a lot of drive and a lot of positive thoughts. Even though he had one handicap, he was very free in most other ways and in his mind. There was a lot of joy in his life. He has a great family and he still has his voice, a wonderful home, a wonderful wife, so I wanted to write about that. And I came up with the concept of 'Joy.' "

Calloway returned home to write the song. "I didn't get the concept right away when I went back, because I was still searching. I had to register everything I had learned to put it into one word. I think the music came first." Calloway collaborated with co-writer Joel Davis, who had one groove with a chord progression. "We took that little progression out of the tune he was working on and began to write a song around it. We had to redo the beat and we finished the music without a concept and did all of the chord changes and some of the basic melodies. We took a break and when I came back, I had the concept. At that point, it was pretty easy to finish."

Gordon didn't hear the song as a big hit, according to Calloway. But the writer/producer assured him the magic was in the lyrics. "You had to get inside of it and live with it to get the whole meaning," Calloway suggests. "It's one of those songs that grow on you."

Reggie didn't want Teddy to over-rehearse the tune. "He had a rough demo, but I didn't want him to work too hard. We let him do his own demo, so to speak. We taught it to him line by line, and once he got the feel of it, then he could go back and correct it, rather than trying to deal with my voice and my interpretation." Calloway also didn't want to alter the melody, so he thought it best that Pendergrass not be too familiar with the song before recording it.

"Joy" was Teddy's first Number One in almost 10 years [see 294—"Close the Door"] and the first since his accident. "Without his music, he'd be a different person," Calloway believes. "He'd still be who he is but that would be taking a large part of his life away."

492

PARADISE

Sade

EPIC 07904

WRITERS: HELEN FOLASADE ADU, ANDREW HALE, STUART MATTHEWMAN, PAUL S DENMAN

PRODUCER: SADE

July 9, 1988 (1 week)

Is Sade a band or a female vocalist? And how do you pronounce Sade anyway?

By the time "Paradise" went to Number One, those questions were long answered. Sade is a band *and* a female vocalist. Helen Folasade Adu, born in Nigeria and raised in England from the age of four, is known as Sade and she lent her name to her group as well. And no, it doesn't rhyme with Jade. "In Nigeria, you don't have S-H to make a *sh*," she explains. "You just have a little mark on the 'S,' so it's completely different...pronounced SHA-day."

She started listening to American soul and jazz music when she was 13. Her favorites included Nina Simone, Ray Charles, Al Green, and Aretha Franklin. "I didn't ever have a burning desire to be a singer," she confesses. "I just fell into it by accident." She studied fashion design at St. Martin's School of Art in London and then designed men's clothing while doing some singing and modeling. "The only thing that was actually paying anything was the modeling," she says. "It wasn't serious. I didn't have a portfolio."

In 1980 she was asked to sing harmony for Arriva, a Latin-funk group. One of their most popular live numbers was a song she wrote with band member Ray St. John, "Smooth Operator." It would later become her first hit in the States. In 1981, she joined the eight-piece funk band known as Pride as one of two female backing vocalists. Stuart Matthewman was the sax player and Paul Denman played bass. "The idea was you could have the main group, then other people could do little offshoots within the group," Matthewman explains. "Barbara, the other backing singer, would do a little set. Sade would do a little set. When Sade [sang], it was me on sax, Paul on bass, and the drummer. We used to open up for the main group. We did a lot of gigs around London...The [record] companies all came down, were very interested...They were more interested in Sade than the main group. But we really wanted to sign the whole thing. So we stuck with it for about a year...and eventually the whole group came to us and said, 'Look, this is stupid. We're holding you back. You should go ahead and sign.' " With Andrew Hale on keyboards, they pacted with Epic Records in the U.K.

Sade

The group first worked on "Paradise" while touring Europe. They were preparing material for their second album, *Promise*. "We were in Barcelona and hired some equipment and put it in the hotel room," says Matthewman. The four musicians had a song they had been trying to write since 1982—and it still isn't finished to this day. "Whenever we're about to start recording, we always start trying to do this song and we never finish it, but we always get ideas from it to do other songs. And some ideas came from that, lyricwise," Matthewman says. The band resumed working on "Paradise" in Holland. "We started jamming around again and worked a bit more on the song," Stuart recalls. "And then we forgot about it until we went in to do the *Stronger Than Pride* album...We were sitting out on a jetty in Nassau. We were listening to a tape of us playing in the studio and a big airplane came over, a 747, and Sade says, 'I want it to sound like that...like a motor chugging on without changing'...and she said, 'Paradise' and we rushed back to the studio and did it."

493

ROSES ARE RED

Mac Band featuring the McCampbell Brothers

MCA 53177
WRITERS: BABYFACE, L.A. REID
PRODUCERS: L.A. REID, BABYFACE
July 16, 1988 (1 week)

L.A. Reid and Babyface took a simple rhyme known by every school child and turned it into a Number One hit for Charles, Derrick, Kelvin, and Ray McCampbell—four brothers from Flint, Michigan, who moved to Dallas and formed the Mac Band.

"Roses Are Red" wasn't written for the McCampbell brothers originally, according to Babyface. "We gave the Whispers the choice of having 'Rock Steady' [see 457] or 'Roses Are Red,' " says the writer/producer. "They made the decision. I think it was a budget decision—they wanted to take just one of the records. They passed on 'Roses Are Red'...so that's how the Mac Band got the record."

How did L.A. and Babyface get the idea to do a song called "Roses Are Red"? "I wanted something simple," says Babyface. "That's one of my favorite hooks that I've written, but there's no real deep story about it."

Charles McCampbell remembers receiving a demo tape from Babyface with "Roses Are Red" on it and listening to it with his brothers. "The lyrics were good and the beat was real solid. The groove of the song was catchy and we knew the hook was one that would last for a long, long time. We could hear ourselves doing it and making it the Mac Band sound, because we do a lot of harmonies and Babyface is into good harmonies. So we came to the conclusion immediately that it was a strong song."

L.A. and Babyface cut the track in Los Angeles and then brought the brothers to Sunset-Bernet Sound Studios in Dallas to record the vocals. "Everything went so smoothly, it was as if we had worked together for years, even though we had just met," Charles reports. "We worked really hard on making sure we had the song nailed before they even got to town. So when we got to the studio, we knew it as well as they did and that was a big plus. We were able to go in there and knock down the parts and do all the harmonies. They were exciting and fun to work with—we spent a lot of time laughing and having a good time because the session was going so well."

Babyface concurs: "They could really sing, and they harmonized really well. It was quick. In the past, being in the studio wasn't always easy...Getting all the people [in a group] to blend used to take a long time and those guys went in there and did it in no time."

Charles believes one of the band's strong points is the brothers' ability to stay focused: "And being brothers, we have the ability to blend naturally without putting forth a whole lot of effort. We have the same kind of vocal chords, I guess you might say. I think each person has been established to sing his own part. I do the top note in most situations. Kelvin knows to get the bottom note and Ray knows how to get the middle note. So we go after it each time we do a song, [each of us singing] the note that [we] normally do."

L.A. Reid and Babyface wrote and produced just three of the nine songs on the brothers' debut album. "I think we like the 'hit-and-run,' " says Babyface. "We like to do maybe six songs at the most...and then we like for other people like Jimmy Jam and Terry Lewis or a Teddy Riley [to] deliver that other side."

Derrick handled lead vocal duties on "Roses Are Red," backed by his three brothers and Babyface. L.A. played drums and Babyface played keyboards.

494

DON'T BE CRUEL

Bobby Brown

MCA 53327
WRITERS: BABYFACE, L.A. REID, DARYL SIMMONS
PRODUCERS: L.A. REID, BABYFACE
July 23, 1988 (2 weeks)

If Bobby Brown had any doubts about leaving New Edition after recording his first solo album, *King of Stage*, they were erased by the enormous success of his second effort, *Don't Be Cruel*. The album sold more than six million copies and yielded three R&B Number One hits, beginning with the title track.

"I didn't have any idea it would have that kind of impact," producer L.A. Reid says candidly in retrospect. "But if there's any record that represents a time period, it's that one. What makes it special to me is that we had never heard anybody do rap music with R&B, ever. A lot of people get credit for it, but the first major hit that had rap and R&B combined was 'Don't Be Cruel.' "

When Reid and his partner Babyface went into the studio with Brown, the artist was still feeling the effects of his lackluster solo debut. "Bobby had a hunger," says Reid. "He had something to prove, because he had left New Edition and they were in the studio with Jimmy Jam and Terry Lewis working on the *Heart Break* album and he was in the studio with us. So it was sort of a quiet, playful competition. He was very determined that, 'I gotta show these guys I can make it on my own.' Face and I were with him and we said, 'We're going to help you. We know how important that is to you.' Did we know it was going to sell millions and millions? No. But we thought it was a hit."

Babyface recalls how the song "Don't Be Cruel" was written: "That song started off with a beat L.A. had done and I added on top of it. When it was first written, it wasn't for Bobby." Reid adds that the rap was there from the start. "It was a combination rap and vocal song from the very beginning. When there weren't even lyrics, we knew that, 'Right here is where the rap goes.' "

The producers enjoyed working with the former New Edition vocalist. "Bobby was a lot of fun," says Babyface. "When he would sing a record, it would become him. Some vocalists you work with, when they take hold of a record, it either works for them or it doesn't and Bobby is one of those kinds of people. When it works for them, it's totally their record. Nobody else could really do it...You couldn't give it to anybody else if you wanted to."

Reid and Babyface favored "Don't Be Cruel" as the lead-off single from Brown's second album. "I thought it was the perfect set-up for everything else he had done on the record," says L.A. "I thought it was one record that said, 'Here's a new style of music. Here's a new artist who has a certain presence that no one else has had in a long time.' I think it was a perfect combination of song and artist."

Brown was equally happy with his producers. "I put my music in their hands and they did the right thing with it," he told Jim Macnie in *Musician*. "I'd heard the Whispers stuff and Pebbles stuff and Deele stuff that they'd done...When they started doing the playback, they was killin'...and I was surprised, because they're a bit older, got suits on, and operate in a business mode. They're calm when they work. At Teddy [Riley's], everybody was energized; we were all young. But L.A. and Babyface cranked it, you can hear it."

495

OFF ON YOUR OWN (GIRL)

Al B. Sure!

WARNER BROS. 27870
WRITERS: AL B. SURE!, KYLE WEST
PRODUCER: KYLE WEST
August 6, 1988 (2 weeks)

Kyle West was interested in music when he was four years old, but by the time he was nine it seemed a little square in his neighborhood to be into that kind of thing. "It just didn't fit, a little black kid in the Bronx playing classical music, so I gave up music altogether," he explains. It wasn't until his sophomore year as a finance major at Louisiana State University that he returned to his first love, when his roommate bought a portable keyboard. "The only problem was, Al wasn't really into music then," Kyle says of his cousin. "He was a rapper. I said, 'Well, you're going to have to learn how to sing.' "

West recorded tapes of his music and left them with his cousin while he returned to school. "When I came back on break, he had written songs. It was amazing that a kid with no musical background, no writing talent...wrote great songs."

Kyle describes the music for "Off on Your Own (Girl)" as being "nothing special to me at all. I really wasn't that talented to make a song. I just made ideas. Al went through the tape and came up with something...the melody, the lyrics, everything."

The tape Al heard was recorded on a little four-track machine. "I would do the drums and then a piano chord–type track, not even the bassline first, and then I would hear a bassline and add [it]," West explains. "At that time I wasn't a producer, so I would keep bouncing tracks down and I would have like eight tracks of a lot of busy things going on. And then finally, when I got with Teddy [Riley], he said, 'You don't have to do all this...the simpler, the better.' "

Al B. Sure! remembers the inspiration for the lyrics to the song: "It was about a girl in high school who was a lesbian and I didn't know. I liked the girl and she wasn't checking for me, so I was trying to figure out what the problem was, and I found out she liked girls. She was real good looking...and I was pulling everything out of the bag to get her and she wasn't going for it. Then I found out she wasn't checking for the male species at all."

Recording the song took some time, according to West. "We did three different versions of that song. [DJ] Eddie F. helped us with one, and Teddy Riley helped us with one, but when we got into the studio we didn't know what we were doing," he candidly admits. "We learned a lot from Teddy," Al adds, "but then we figured out we can do this ourselves."

Executives at Warner Brothers were supportive of the young artist and his producer. "We'd send tapes back and forth to Benny [Medina, Warners Senior Vice President] and Benny would critique them and say, 'Maybe you guys should do this, maybe you guys should do that.' He gave us some constructive criticism, which was really good...We went from there and started to learn our own flavor of how we like to do things."

Kyle classifies Al's voice as a "gift." "I'm still amazed at what he hears [with] a nontrained ear," says West. "He's able to produce things vocally that are amazing to me."

496

LOOSEY'S RAP

Rick James featuring Roxanne Shante

REPRISE 27885
WRITER: RICK JAMES
PRODUCER: RICK JAMES
August 20, 1988 (1 week)

Ten years and one month after his first Number One hit, Rick James was back on top of the R&B singles chart, but this time he wasn't on Berry Gordy's label.

"I had a lawsuit with Motown, a very long, long suit," says James. "And after I got off Motown, I decided to shop a deal. So I met with a lot of people, Clive Davis...Mo Ostin...I met with three record companies in one day." Rick liked what Warner Brothers Records chairman Ostin had to say and signed with him, becoming one of the first artists to be released on the newly reactivated Reprise label. "Loosey's Rap" was the second Reprise single to hit Number One [see 474—"I Want to Be Your Man"] on the R&B chart.

"I was seeing a girl named Lucy," says James, "but I wasn't really talking about Lucy. It was a song about loose women. It was another one of those things where I played most of the instruments, and I wanted something really funky. 'Loosey's Rap' was really funky."

Label executives introduced Rick to rapper Roxanne Shante. "I didn't even know who she was," Rick says. "But I heard an album by her and rap was running real big. I was one of the first people to use rap with singing when I did 'P.I.M.P. the S.I.M.P.' with Grandmaster Flash. Nobody had applied vocals and rap together and I wanted to do something like that again. I heard Roxanne and really loved her voice." Shante, born Lolita Gooden in Long Island City, New York, was 15 when she first made the chart in 1985 with "Roxanne's Revenge." It was an answer record to UTFO's unkindly dissing of an "uncooperative" foxy female.

Shante met James at his studio in Buffalo to record "Loosey's Rap." "I didn't have a lot of respect for rappers until that happened—when they start rapping from the top of their heads, it's amazing...I told her to go for it and she did. She had a few things in it that I had to change, but [her part] was pretty well her."

James thought "Loosey's Rap" was the funkiest cut on the album and decided it should be the first single. "But I thought I had four singles on that album. That album was never promoted," he charges.

" 'Sexual Luv Affair' was my favorite song on that album. A song called 'Judy' about another girl I was seeing I thought was really great. I thought it was a real good album and I'm very very picky when it comes to my stuff. Every album that I've ever done, I've controlled the artwork and every song. I used to try and pick: 'This will do well and this will be the second release and this will be the third release.' 'Loosey' went Number One R&B with virtually no promotion."

497

NICE 'N' SLOW

Freddie Jackson

CAPITOL 44171
WRITERS: BARRY J. EASTMOND, JOLYON SKINNER
PRODUCER: BARRY J. EASTMOND
August 27, 1988 (3 weeks)

Freddie Jackson, protest singer? The same month that "Nice 'N' Slow" hit the streets, smooth 'n' soulful Freddie flew to London to perform at the Nelson Mandela 70th birthday celebrations. The Wembley Stadium super-concert on June 11 also featured Natalie Cole, Ashford & Simpson, and Al Green, as well as a slew of Anglo-American rock and pop acts.

"I believe in justice," Jackson told a British interviewer. "I have my freedom to go where I want to go, and I believe everyone else should also." He added, "I'm actually midway through rehearsals with my band in the States and coming here will drastically put back my schedules. But...*so what!*"

Those schedules were for Jackson's "Up Close and Personal" American tour, a summer itinerary to promote his third album, *Don't Let Love Slip Away*. "Nice 'N' Slow" was the lead-off single, co-authored by Barry Eastmond, the Juilliard graduate who crafted four of Freddie's first nine singles—every one a top 10 hit—between 1985 and 1987.

"Look Around," the 10th release, turned out to be Jackson's first miss—it could only climb to 69—but it was the *fifth* 45 extracted from his sophomore album, *Just Like the First Time*, which had gone platinum. Nevertheless, the folks at the singer's management firm, Hush Productions, took such matters seriously.

"It was an interesting predicament," says Eastmond, "because his management wanted to take Freddie in some other directions, but didn't want to lose his core audience. So we had to write songs his fans would love: nice grooves with some really strong, positive lyrics. Every album, it was a challenge."

Eastmond and lyricist Jolyon Skinner rose to it. They penned four of the 10 tunes on *Don't Let Love Slip Away*, including "Nice 'N' Slow" and the title track.

"Some songs would come right away," he says, "and there were some where we would challenge ourselves to come up with something a little different, like 'Crazy.' A lot of people didn't believe we did that."

Recorded at several studios around the New York area, "Nice 'N' Slow" saw Eastmond and Eric Rehl handle keyboards and related programming, with Barry also doing drum programming and writing the string arrangements. Mike "Dino" Campbell played guitar, and Freddie Jackson, Yolanda Lee, Curtis King, and Cindy Mizell sang background vocals.

The song's alto sax break was played by Najee. "It was the first time that I worked with him," explains Eastmond. "It was my idea—I loved his playing and, because he was managed by Hush, I knew it would be no problem to get him."

As for Eastmond's production style, slow it wasn't. "Barry is just so quick," affirms Freddie. "He'll just have four tracks done in a week like *that*. The next thing you know, you're coming in doing background vocals, and the next week I'm in doing leads. So five songs with Barry might take a month and you're done."

498

ANOTHER PART OF ME

Michael Jackson

EPIC 07962

WRITER: MICHAEL JACKSON

PRODUCER: QUINCY JONES

September 17, 1988 (1 week)

"Another Part of Me" was the sixth single released from Michael Jackson's *Bad*. Although it entered the chart almost a full year after the first single from the album [see 465—"I Just Can't Stop Loving You"], it was actually the first song anyone heard from Michael's long-awaited follow-up to *Thriller*.

"*Captain Eo* came about because the Disney Studios wanted me to come up with a new ride for the parks," Jackson wrote in *Moonwalk*, his 1988 autobiography. "They said they didn't care what I did, as long as it was something creative. I had this big meeting with them, and during the course of the afternoon I told them Walt Disney was a hero of mine and that I was very interested in Disney's history and philosophy. I wanted to do something with them that Mr. Disney himself would have approved. I had read a number of books about Walt Disney and his creative empire, and it was very important to me to do things as he would have."

The Disney folks finally asked Michael to star in a movie to be shown exclusively in the company's theme parks. The pop star agreed and said he would like to work with George Lucas and Steven Spielberg. The latter choice was busy with other projects, but producer Lucas found another partner—director Francis Ford Coppola.

Jackson met with Lucas at his Skywalker Ranch in Northern California and wrote a scenario for a short film that would feature the latest in 3-D technology. Lucas came up with the name Captain Eo, after the Greek word for "dawn."

"*Captain Eo* is about transformation and the way music can help change the world," Michael stated in his book. "...The story is about a young guy who goes on a mission to this miserable planet run by an evil queen. He is entrusted with the responsibility of bringing the inhabitants light and beauty. It's a great celebration of good over evil."

"Another Part of Me," one of the first songs written for *Bad*, appears at the end of *Captain Eo* after the evil queen, played by Angelica Houston, is transformed into a beautiful woman and Captain Eo and friends say their goodbyes.

The studio musicians included many of Quincy Jones's usual band of suspects: David Williams and Paul Jackson Jr. on guitars; Kim Hutchcroft and Larry Williams on saxophones; Gary Grant and Jerry Hey on trumpets; Christopher Currell on synclavier; and John Barnes and Rhett Lawrence on synthesizers.

Captain Eo premiered at DisneyWorld in Orlando, Florida, on September 12, 1986. Lucas, Coppola, and Houston attended the opening ceremonies, but was Michael there? If he was, he wasn't dressed as Michael Jackson. Manager Frank Dileo speculated the artist might have been present in one of the disguises he often uses to go out in public.

"Another Part of Me" was the fifth Number One R&B single from *Bad*. It was only the second time in chart history that an artist had five chart-topping hits from one album. The first person to accomplish this feat was Michael's sister, Janet [see 462—"The Pleasure Principle"].

499

SHE'S ON THE LEFT

Jeffrey Osborne

A&M 1227

WRITERS: ROBERT BROOKINS, JEFFREY OSBORNE, TONY HAYES, CLINTON BLANSON

PRODUCERS: JEFFREY OSBORNE, ROBERT BROOKINS

September 24, 1988 (1 week)

It's been just over 10 years since the last time that former L.T.D. lead singer Jeffrey Osborne figured in these pages, and a lot has happened.

Despite the warnings of record labels who, he says, told him that "after being with such a large band, my marketability was nil," Osborne has put together a successful solo career. He has racked up seven solo top ten R&B hits so far, among them "Don't You Get So Mad," "Stay with Me Tonight," and "You Should Be Mine (The Woo Woo Song)."

Osborne has also ventured into production, handling one side of an LP for Mother's Finest vocalist Joyce Kennedy, and material for Johnny Gill (never released, because Gill switched labels). He has also duetted with Kennedy on "The Last Time We Made Love," and with Dionne Warwick on "Love Power." Both have been top 10 hits.

Most notably, Osborne's collaborations with pop songwriters and producers have done a lot to define the smooth, medium-weight R&B of the mid-'80s. Despite this, the singer has never had a top 10 pop record—and until this month in 1988, never climbed all the way to the R&B summit.

"It was really quite a feat for me to finally get a Number One single in *Billboard*," says Osborne. "I've had a lot of releases and they usually get to number two!"

The runner-up habit was broken with the help of Robert Brookins, who, after a short-lived career as an MCA artist in the mid-'80s, became a ubiquitous writer/producer. "Robert and I were just hashing around ideas," explains Osborne, "and he had this groove that I was listening to. I asked, 'What are you doing with this?' He said, 'Well, I just started putting it together and it's kinda like here if you wanna work on it.' "

Jeffrey Osborne

Osborne's creative process was aided by a home studio. "There was a point when I was writing on four-track and then eight-track machines," he says, "and you always have to hope you can recapture what you wrote. When you're writing, there's magic that happens at that time—and sometimes you can't recreate it. If you go into the studio and try to get it down on 24-four track, sometimes you can lose the magic."

Evidently, Osborne and Brookins bottled the elixir of "She's on the Left," with some assistance. Tony Haynes was one of Brookins's co-lyricists, while Clinton Blanson helped come up with the track. The recording took place at Wings West in Los Angeles; Brookins handled synthesizer and Linn drum programming, and played keyboards.

Collaborators can provide impartial advice, too. Osborne says, "As a writer, you get to the point where you have to stop yourself, 'cause you can just keep adding and keep adding—and sometimes stray from the simple melodies that you want people to walk down the street and sing."

500

ADDICTED TO YOU

Levert

ATCO 99292
WRITERS: GERALD LEVERT, EDDIE LEVERT, MARC GORDON
PRODUCERS: GERALD LEVERT, MARC GORDON
October 1, 1988 (2 weeks)

Soundtracks from Eddie Murphy movies have provided hit singles for the pop chart as well as the R&B chart. *Beverly Hills Cop* included "The Heat Is On" by Glenn Frey, "Axel F" by Harold Faltermeyer, and "New Attitude" and "Stir It Up," both by Patti LaBelle. *Beverly Hills Cop II* contained "Shakedown" by Bob Seger as well as "I Want Your Sex" by George Michael. The soundtrack for *Coming to America* didn't contain any pop hits, but it did yield a Number One single to the R&B chart: "Addicted to You," the third chart-topper for Levert.

The John Landis–directed *Coming to America* starred Eddie Murphy as an African prince who comes to the United States to look for a wife in Queens. Arsenio Hall, James Earl Jones, and John Amos co-starred in the Paramount Pictures release.

The soundtrack was released on Atco, sister label to Atlantic, home of Levert. The group was asked to contribute a song to the film, which also included music by the System, the Cover Girls, Chico DeBarge, Mel and Kim, Sister Sledge, and Nona Hendryx.

Gerald details the evolution of the song: "Originally it was, 'I'm not into drinking, don't like the smell of smoke, I'm not into gambling, I'm afraid of being broke.' And I was trying to figure out a way to do it. And this girl who liked me, we were dating and she always used to say, 'I'm just addicted to you.' And I took that and made it into a song." Does the woman know? "She knows. She knows it's her song because she always says, 'I still want credit for that song.' "

The trio did not have a lot of time to complete the tune, with the deadline from the film company approaching. "That's why we had to do it while we were traveling," explains Marc Gordon. Co-writer Eddie Levert, lead singer of the O'Jays and father of Gerald and Sean Levert, explains why he collaborated with his son on the song: "My sons are my biggest fans. They are my biggest promoters, probably the best p.r. firm I could ever have. It's always been their dream to work together. We wrote this song on the bus coming from California to Florida. I was riding their bus, so Gerald and I wrote this song on the bus. This was the very first time we collaborated that the public was going to hear." The band stopped in Miami to record the song. They went into the studio without seeing any footage from the movie, but with a description of the story.

The three members of Levert were invited to a premiere of *Coming to America,* but were in for a surprise. "We thought we were going to the real [premiere]," says Sean Levert, "but they had [another] one in New York. And it was like a couple of people there, but Eddie [Murphy] wasn't there." Gerald was disappointed with the placement of the song in the movie. "It didn't get enough play. They didn't put it in a good spot. Like with *Boomerang,* I think all the songs in that movie were placed very well. But we got a Number One record out of it, so that was cool."

501

MY PREROGATIVE

Bobby Brown

MCA 53383
WRITERS: BOBBY BROWN, GENE GRIFFIN
PRODUCER: GENE GRIFFIN
October 15, 1988 (2 weeks)

Bobby Brown kept a careful watch on the charts when the second single from his *Don't Be Cruel* album was released. He was used to having Number One singles on the R&B chart—three with New Edition and two on his own, so far—but he very much wanted to cross over and have a Number One hit on the pop chart.

He was flipping through the pages of *Billboard* to check the progress of "My Prerogative" while talking to Jim Macnie of *Musician* magazine. "Lookit," he said,

"Phil Collins is sneakin' up on me. He's behind me, trying to get me. He's got enough Number Ones. See? Collins moved up again this week. I froze."

Manager George Smith pointed to another song on the chart, "Every Rose Has Its Thorn" by the rock group Poison. "It's this guy that's blocking us. He's been there too long." The very next day, Poison was gone and Bobby Brown was sitting atop the Hot 100 for the very first time.

"I just want to give my thanks to everyone who made me Number One pop," he later told Macnie, "and I also want to encourage people to listen to music that's labeled R&B, or street music—just give it a chance. I was never taught to look at a color. Music is music. You can't put a label on R&B or pop these days anyway, because you got guys like George Michael on the top of the black charts and you got me and Michael Jackson on the pop charts. People should hear all kinds of music."

"My Prerogative" hit Number One on the R&B chart, too—a full three months before it hit the top of the pop chart. It was a highly personal song for Brown, referring to his split from New Edition as well as dispelling rumors about drug use, rumors he vehemently denied. "I see what drugs can do to a person, so why would I be into 'em?" he asked in *Rolling Stone*. "Having the top male slot now, drugs would just bring me down, and down is not a place I want to go."

While the first single from *Don't Be Cruel*, the title track, was written and produced by L.A. Reid and Babyface, "My Prerogative" was helmed by the originator of new jack swing, Teddy Riley. "I'm actually the sole writer, along with Aaron Hall, who is one of the members of Guy," says Riley, discounting the writing and producing credit of Gene Griffin, his former manager. "We did it in my house on the four-track. And when we came up with that song, we thought of it for Bobby Brown because of all the situations he's been in—people saying he's on drugs...I feel it's Bobby's prerogative to do what he wants to do...It's cool for people to worry about Bobby and wonder what's going on, but that's his business."

Bobby talked about his contribution to the song in the March 1989 issue of *Musician*. "Teddy and I let a drumbeat play for about five minutes, added a bit of keys—not too much—put in the funky bassline, and brought the whole groove out. Teddy's one of the guys that's going to bring us into the '90s, with the heavy drum groove. When the bottom hits you like that, no way you're not going to like the song."

Don't Be Cruel proved to be a cornucopia of hit singles. After "My Prerogative" came "Roni," which peaked at number two. Then "Every Little Step" went to Number One [see 519]. Brown's next single was from *Ghostbusters II* [see 531—"On Our Own"]. Then it was back to the album for "Rock Wit'cha," which reached number three.

502

THE WAY YOU LOVE ME

Karyn White

WARNER BROS. 27773

WRITERS: BABYFACE, L.A. REID, DARYL SIMMONS

PRODUCERS: L.A. REID, BABYFACE

October 29, 1988 (1 week)

Karyn White still laughs when she recalls receiving the demo of "The Way You Love Me" from L.A. Reid and Babyface. "They were singing it, and at the beginning of the tape they said, 'Karyn White, welcome to the top.' "

Turns out they were right. "The Way You Love Me," the last song recorded for White's debut album on Warner Brothers, was the first song to be issued as a single and it carried her all the way to Number One on *Billboard's* R&B chart.

White had been aware of Reid and Babyface ever since they recorded as members of the Deele for Solar Records. The producers in turn had been aware of White since she recorded "Facts of Love" in 1986 with jazz fusion keyboardist Jeff Lorber. Reid elaborates on how he and Babyface were teamed up with White: "We went to Warner Brothers to talk to the vice president of A&R and he said, 'I'll tell you what, guys. We have Chaka Khan, we have Al Jarreau, we have Karyn White. Just tell us which one you want.' And I said, 'Clearly, Karyn White.' And everybody looked at me and said, 'Why?' "

Reid made his choice because he prefers working with new artists rather than established ones. In retrospect, he's happy he chose to work with White: "I like her a lot as an artist because her voice is so special to me. She truly has her own sound. Not that any of the [other] artists don't, but there's something about the sound of Karyn's voice that sends chills through me."

After seeing the video of "Facts of Love," Reid felt that White needed the right song to launch her solo career. "It was definitely a challenge because I thought 'Facts of Love' was the ultimate record for her. But once we started working with her, I think we probably worked closer with her than any of the other artists. We helped to develop her style. She helped us to hone in on what we thought we should be writing for her. And she was pretty clear about what she wanted."

"The Way You Love Me" is one of Reid's favorite songs. At first he places it in his top five, then admits it belongs in his top two. "That's one of my favorites, too," claims Babyface. "When I hear that on the radio, it still sounds like a hit today." Babyface recalls that someone at Warner Brothers didn't agree with that assessment. "I won't mention the name," he says generously. "Someone listened to it and said, 'That's not a hit. It's not happening.' And that was the first time I said, 'You are absolutely wrong. We're doing this record and you gotta go with this one.' " Reid, Babyface, and Warner Brothers vice president Benny Medina championed the song's release as a single.

Reid thinks the song was a hit because it blended hip-hop beats with elements of jazz. "And then it was a very funky song and she delivered it well. I remember she did it very quickly. She did it very confidently. When I think back to that time period, it's the one song that makes me think that we were smokin' at that point."

Babyface agrees. "It was a very L.A.-and-Babyface kind of record. It was pretty pop. It had one of our little hooks in it, the little string line that I used in 'Rock Steady.' If you want to ask, 'What's an L.A.-Babyface song?,' go to that one."

503
ANY LOVE
Luther Vandross

EPIC 08047

WRITERS: LUTHER VANDROSS, MARCUS MILLER

PRODUCERS: LUTHER VANDROSS, MARCUS MILLER

November 5, 1988 (1 week)

"If you italicize 'Any,' you'll get the point that I'm making," Luther Vandross comments when asked about his fourth Number One single.

" 'Any Love' is a song of encouragement," he says. "It's trying to tell you to hold it together, in spite of what you deem to be the missing piece in your life...That's a song just saying don't think that because one element of your life is missing that your life is totally worthless. A lot of people fly on empty, and that's what that song was trying to offer."

Luther adds that "Any Love" is one of the first autobiographical tunes he has composed. "I was feeling extraordinarily depressed when I wrote that song. And that's what came out. I didn't set out to write a song to depict all that I just told you. In retrospect, that's what the song did."

Vandross wrote the song with a man he had met years earlier when he was a background session singer. Marcus Miller was working sessions as a bass player. "We really got to be buddies when we both got into Roberta Flack's band," Miller says. "We were in the band for about a year and a half...and we realized we complemented each other musically."

Miller was responsible for the chords on "Any Love." "I wanted to do something that was bossa nova–ish," Miller explains. "Not that it would end up sounding like that, but I wanted to begin with that feeling." When he completed the track, he thought it sounded choppy and too complex, but he sent it to Luther anyway.

"I did the melody and the lyric," Luther recalls. The song did not take long to write. Luther says he can write quickly, "if the winds of creativity are blowing in my face—if they're tailwinds. But if they're headwinds, then it takes forever to write a song." After working on the song, Luther asked Marcus to meet him at the Right Track studio. When Marcus arrived, Luther asked him to go for a ride in his car. "That's where he does all his listening," Miller says. "So I go in his car and he's driving around New York singing me the song that he'd just written to this track. And he made the whole thing make so much sense. It tied all my loose ends together so well that I said, 'You're gonna make me look good.' He's not just a singer. Key changes don't intimidate him and complex harmonies don't intimidate him. He has a great ear and he can really make things work. From that point on, I realized I could get a little more complex with my writing and he'd stay right there. So 'Any Love' was a springboard for me."

"Any Love" is just one reason why Luther is often called the King of Romance, a title he disdains. "I think titles are limiting," he offers. "I think they pigeonhole you. Some people build careers on the similarity of one song to the next. In my opinion, the [first] three [Number One] songs have nothing in common other than my voice. They are not repeats of themselves." Pressed on the subject, Luther agrees that he writes about the joys as well as the problems of love. "And Picasso also used oil on canvas. That doesn't make all of his paintings the same. 'The King of Romance'...once that starts to get implanted, that means my up-tempo songs are going to get less of a canvas, and I don't particularly want that."

504
GIVING YOU THE BEST THAT I GOT
Anita Baker

ELEKTRA 69371

WRITERS: ANITA BAKER, SKIP SCARBOROUGH, RANDY HOLLAND

PRODUCER: MICHAEL J. POWELL

November 12, 1988 (2 weeks)

Songwriter/producer Skip Scarborough gave Anita Baker the best he had. But that wasn't what he originally planned.

Scarborough had first intended "Giving You the Best That I Got" for an Alabama-based act that, he

Anita Baker

says, never recorded. Then he sent it to Elektra Records for Baker's labelmate, Howard Hewett. One day, Baker heard the song in the halls, "and the next thing I knew, she was calling my service."

Scarborough says the singer told him, " 'This song really talks to me, but I want to make some lyric changes.' And I told her to go for it." Eventually, Baker made enough changes to become a co-writer with Scarborough and engineer/studio owner Randy Holland. It was also her idea to fashion the song's distinctive, scatted intro from a passage in the middle of Scarborough's demo.

Scarborough also notes that Baker actually picked up the tempo slightly from what he had submitted. That's a little hard to imagine, since "Giving You the Best" is one of the stateliest R&B hits ever. Baker had long straddled the line between R&B and jazz, but here the line is all but obliterated. (It is, in fact, jazz veteran Paulihno daCosta who serves as percussionist.)

She wasn't always so mellow. Her scorching versions of Gladys Knight's "Love Overboard" and Michael Jackson's "Another Part of Me" were often cited as the highlights of her national tour with Luther Vandross. But it was with ballads like 1983's "Angel" and 1986's "Sweet Love" that Baker made her reputation. By 1988, she and Vandross were queen and king of R&B radio's late-night "Quiet Storm" programs and could release whatever they liked.

Baker could also take as long as she wanted. Known as a control freak in the studio, the singer had turned down several well-known producers in favor of Michael Powell, the leader of her old R&B group, Chapter 8, because they were determined to remake her in their own image.

"Giving You the Best That I Got" features other alumni from post-Baker Chapter 8, namely Vernon Fails (keyboards) and Valerie Pinkston (background vocals). The track also has Nathan East on bass, Omar Hakim on drums, and Dean Gant on acoustic piano.

Baker had been engaged for two years when she recorded the song, but it was a celebration of wedded bliss of the sort usually found in country hits, not R&B. When British writer Dave Hill told her that it was unusual to hear R&B songs that "express well-being rather than pain," she was flattered.

"Thank you *very* much," Baker responded. "With rhythm & blues and soul, there is a tendency to have those tortured lyrics. My music does encompass that aspect, but in a different way, in the chord progressions of the songs I choose, which are on the minor side of the piano and which are usually pretty blue. They give a hint of sadness, but they have a happy lyric on top of them. I don't want to come home from a hard day of whatever and become depressed as a result of my selection of music."

505

THANKS FOR MY CHILD

Cheryl Pepsii Riley

COLUMBIA 07996
WRITERS: FULL FORCE
PRODUCERS: FULL FORCE
November 26, 1988 (1 week)

Cheryl Pepsii Riley was doing a radio interview when a female listener called in to thank her for writing a song about being a single parent. The caller added that men were dogs and no good. Bowlegged Lou of Full Force suddenly spoke up and told the caller: "Excuse me, sweetheart, but Full Force, which is six men, wrote that song. Cheryl didn't write a stitch of it." The listener was shocked, according to Lou. "Because when Cheryl sings it, you figure it's coming from a woman's point of view. There's no way you'd think a man wrote that."

It was an appropriate song for Riley to sing, considering that she was a licensed practical nurse who worked with handicapped children for 10 years. Despite stories to the contrary, it wasn't just Cheryl's work that inspired Bowlegged Lou to write the lyrics.

The inspiration for the lyrics came from one of the most difficult times in Lou's life. His wife was having trouble with her first pregnancy, and he came home one evening and discovered she had been taken to the hospital. He raced to see her and was dismayed at how she looked lying in a maternity-ward hospital bed, surrounded by the sound of crying babies. "Then you hear one mother disposed of her kid, or a lot of mothers having kids were single parents." The incident had a great impact on Lou, and he found himself thinking about it from a female perspective. "Throughout history, you could see a lot of times—especially in the black home—how the woman is the mother and the father. And I wanted to do a song about single parenthood...letting women know that not all men are insensitive to the situations of single parenthood."

Full Force keyboard player Baby Gerry came up with the music for the song. It wasn't the first composition that Full Force had offered to Cheryl. The Brooklyn-born singer met Bowlegged Lou when they were both acting in a community theater production of *To Kill an Angel.* Lou was already in Full Force and Cheryl was in a group called Stargaze. "The first time I heard her sing, it sent chills through my spine," says Lou. "I told her if anything ever happens where I get successful, I'll come back looking for her." Stargaze had just released a single called "You Can't Have It" when Lou called Cheryl and asked her to sing lead vocals on a song Full Force had written called "I Wonder If I Take You Home."

"At the time I didn't want to branch off into something else," says Riley. When the single was released a year later by Lisa Lisa and Cult Jam [see 456—"Head to Toe"], Lou called to tease her about the song she passed up. Stargaze had disbanded by this time. "I thought, 'Oh well, there was my chance to make it,' " says Cheryl. "But I did get a second chance."

She went in the studio with Full Force and Bowlegged Lou sang a reference vocal for her. It was the first time that anyone besides Lou and Baby Gerry had heard the sensitive song. "Everybody felt it was going to make some noise and that was really exciting," says Lou. At first there was only a piano on the track, but Lou's brother B-Fine of Full Force suggested adding drums. "It wasn't throughout the song, but in little spots that gave it the dynamic of drama," says Lou.

Cheryl was still working as a nurse when the single went to Number One. She and Lou were surprised at some of the negative publicity the song received. "Some of that controversy threw us for a loop," Lou admits. "The majority of people knew what the song was about, but then you get people [who said], 'That song's promoting teenage sex and we shouldn't be [doing that].' And if you listen to the lyrics, it ain't about that!"

506

HEY LOVER

Freddie Jackson

CAPITOL 44208
WRITERS: SONNY MOORE, KEITH WASHINGTON
PRODUCER: PAUL LAURENCE
December 3, 1988 (1 week)

Freddie Jackson's eighth Number One, "Hey Lover," connected to his past, when he and buddy Paul Laurence were in Paul's group, the Laurence Jones Ensemble, playing gigs around New York with an eye on the main chance. "Sonny Moore used to be the manager for L.J.E.," says Jackson. "The manager, the drummer, the roadie—he was everything for us."

Years later, Moore hooked up with singer/songwriter Keith Washington and, together, they penned "Hey Lover" in Charlotte, North Carolina. Washington told *Blues & Soul* he was there "for a different atmosphere, to get away from the fast line for a while."

The pair would "literally write every day," continued Washington. "Sonny knew Paul Laurence and we sent him some songs for an album he was doing with Freddie Jackson. When we submitted the tune 'Hey Lover,' Freddie really liked it but he wanted some of the lyrics to be changed.

"We rewrote the song on the phone and the next time I heard it, I was in a nightclub and I couldn't believe one of my songs had been recorded!" Later still, Washington had another cause for disbelief: His own recording of "Missing You" became a Number One single in 1991.

"Hey Lover" was part of Freddie Jackson's third album, *Don't Let Love Slip Away*, and recorded at Sound Ideas, New York. Producer Paul Laurence arranged the track and played all the instruments, with programming done by Darryl Shepard. Background vocalists were Audrey Wheeler, Cindy Mizell, and Yolanda Lee.

Jackson's relationship with Paul Laurence—who wrote and produced his debut hit [see 408—"Rock Me Tonight"]—was strengthened by the bonding of youth. "We partied at each other's houses, knew each other's families, enjoyed music and went to church together, and trusted each other," Jackson proclaims.

Church played a significant role. "I think it did a lot for us," the singer continues. "It united us, and keeps us together still, like brothers. It also did a lot for us musically; it instilled a lot of strength and body in my voice, I think. A lot of soul."

Perhaps because of that relationship, Laurence can be a hard taskmaster. "Paul is just like a tyrant sometimes," says Jackson, laughing. "We don't like each other in the studio sometimes! He might spend half an hour on a line and I'm like, 'Oh no, I can't believe I'm doing this, I can't sing anymore, do I have the chops anymore?'

"Paul may be looking for that word 'it' to really sound [right]. He'll say, 'I want people to believe that word 'it.' My God, how many ways are there to say the word?" Yet Laurence's drive for feeling paid off: *Don't Let Love Slip Away* became Jackson's third consecutive gold album and third Number One in the fall of 1988.

507

DIAL MY HEART

The Boys

MOTOWN 53301
WRITERS: L.A. REID, BABYFACE, DARYL SIMMONS
PRODUCERS: L.A. REID, BABYFACE
December 10, 1988 (1 week)

Khiry, Hakeem, Tajh, and Bilal Abdul-Samad ranged in age from six to 11 when they decided to raise some funds to buy their dad a Father's Day present. Their mom suggested they could earn money by performing at the beach. "So we took our jambox and started performing some songs," Tajh remembers. "And we made $56. Instead of us taking my father out to dinner, he took us, because he was so proud of us."

The brothers continued to sing at the beach for the next 18 months, then recorded a demo. Their parents took the tape to Motown, MCA, and Solar Records. All three companies expressed interest, but the Boys pacted with MCA. When that company purchased Motown from Berry Gordy, MCA executive Jheryl Busby was named president of Motown, and he took the Boys with him.

The quartet was almost finished recording their *Messages from the Boys* album when they met L.A. Reid and Babyface, two members of the Deele—the group that had a top 10 hit with "Two Occasions" in early 1988. L.A. and Babyface were introduced to the Boys by Greg Scelsa, who Babyface met when he first moved to Los Angeles in 1985.

L.A. and Babyface submitted "Lucky Charm" and "A Little Romance" to the Boys, then came back later with a third song, "Dial My Heart." "Babyface played it for my mom and Hakeem and they said they didn't like it," Khiry recalls. "My dad called Babyface and L.A. and told them to come over to the house [because] he wanted to hear it. So they came over and sung it for us, and we liked it."

Babyface thought the song was great right from the beginning. "That was one we were real crazy about," he confirms. "I like the hook on it, the whole telephone thing. I think the neat thing about that one [was] it was still 'kiddie.' It kind of had a 'candy' feel, but it also had a little edge to it. And that's what made it a better record than 'Lucky Charm,' because 'Lucky Charm' was so bubble-gum. 'Dial My Heart' at least was bubble-yum." Babyface remembers the initial reaction to the song: "Everybody didn't hear it immediately because it's a long hook...That hook came at the very end...If you don't get the hook in a couple phrases, nobody will remember it. I think it was one of those records that have to grow on you. And it certainly had to grow on them—we forced the issue on that one."

The producers looked on the Abdul-Samad brothers more as their chance to do New Edition than the Jackson 5, even though the label was Motown and many people thought of the group as an '80s version of the Jacksons.

"It was great working with them," Tajh says of the two producers. "We learned so much...Those guys are perfectionists when they do vocals. They like to get everything perfect." Babyface returns the compliment: "That was the first time they were in the studio and it took a little bit of time because they were very young and hadn't gotten quite there yet. But they grew immediately. Hakeem [is] really good. A great writer...We knew at that point his future in terms of writing and producing was going to definitely grow."

508

EVERYTHING I MISS AT HOME

Cherrelle

TABU 08052
WRITERS: JAMES HARRIS III, TERRY LEWIS
PRODUCERS: JIMMY JAM, TERRY LEWIS
December 17, 1988 (1 week)

Cheryl Norton was born in Los Angeles, where her family spent the winters. Her father was an attorney and his work also took him to Detroit, where the family would go for the summer. But when they decided to live in Detroit full time, she resisted, not wanting to endure the cold weather. She eventually joined her parents anyway, and met their neighbor, musician Michael Henderson. He invited her to the studio while he was recording his *In the Night Time* album.

Cherrelle

Cheryl found a job in Detroit at a bank, where she worked nine to five and then spent the evenings in the studio. But the bank did pay off in one aspect—it's where she found her stage name. "I never got to work on time, and my boss was so mad, she would scream out, 'Cher-elle, you are late again! Cher-elle, can you get to work on time? Cher-elle, would you get off of that telephone?' She screamed at me 24 hours a day. It got to the point where I just loved to hear her call me Cherrelle! The name stuck."

After touring with Henderson, Cherrelle went out on her own. She recorded a demo that found its way to Tabu Records. Her father negotiated a contract with the label, and the artist came under the guidance of the writing and producing team of Jimmy Jam and Terry Lewis. In 1984, she had a top 10 hit with "I Didn't Mean to Turn You On," later a pop hit for Robert Palmer. In 1986 she recorded a duet with Alexander O'Neal, "Saturday Love," which peaked at number two. Two years later, another duet with O'Neal, "Never Knew Love Like This," also peaked at number two.

For her third Tabu album, Jam and Lewis wanted to do more than record a collection of songs. Like O'Neal's *Hearsay* album, they wanted to employ a theme. "It was called *Affair* and was about a relationship that went sour," Jimmy Jam explains. " 'Everything I Miss at Home' was the centerpiece, the song that explained what the album was about...It turned out exactly the way we wanted it to turn out. We wanted a nightclubby piano jazz lounge type of feel to the song, where you can almost see the woman at the bar having a drink, contemplating what her next move is. She's at the crossroads. Is she going to her husband or is she going to have the affair, or maybe someone's having an affair behind her back."

Jam and Lewis were especially happy to produce a Number One hit for Cherrelle after enduring some difficult times during the recording of "Saturday Love." "We had an engineer walk out on us after we had just built the studio and we didn't know how to run it," Jam reminisces. "The client we had in town at the time was Cherrelle. We were blowing speakers [and] plugging in patch cords wrong because we didn't know what to do." The artist kept her cool. "This was an artist with [her] career on the line and a couple of producers who didn't have it together. Cherrelle was so understanding and made us feel so at home. We called her the guinea pig of the studio. Everybody after that benefited from the mistakes we made on Cherrelle. 'Saturday Love' was the record that launched her career, so it worked out OK. She was so understanding about everything that we were glad by the time we got to 'Everything I Miss at Home,' she got to work in a studio where we knew what we were doing."

509

TUMBLIN' DOWN

Ziggy Marley & the Melody Makers

VIRGIN 99299
WRITERS: ZIGGY MARLEY, TYRONE DOWNIE
PRODUCERS: CHRIS FRANTZ, TINA WEYMOUTH
December 24, 1988 (2 weeks)

Bob Marley once said of his children, "Them grow up and play music, as a natural thing."

Ziggy (née David) Marley was the second child and first son born to Bob and Rita Marley in Trench Town, Kingston, Jamaica. Ziggy started banging on drums when he was very young. After a month of guitar lessons, he taught himself to play from a book. At the age of 10, Ziggy made his professional debut when he recorded "Children Playing in the Streets" with the Melody Makers—his sisters Sharon and Cedella and his brother Stephen. The song had been written for them by their father. Ziggy was 13 when Bob Marley died of brain cancer.

The son of Jamaica's most famous Rastafarian made his first public appearance as one of the Melody Makers at the fourth annual Reggae Sunsplash Festival in Montego Bay on August 6, 1981. The event was billed as a tribute to the late icon.

Ziggy was still a skinny teenager when he signed with EMI Records. Nancy Jeffries of Virgin's A&R staff saw Ziggy and the Melody Makers perform at the Ritz in New York right after the EMI deal ended. "I made contact with them and went down to Jamaica to visit and talk about their recording career," she says. "I remember how young Ziggy looked...In the time we worked together, he absolutely changed from young boy to young man. You wouldn't recognize him from one [time] to the next. He didn't have dreads yet—he was just out of school and wasn't allowed to grow dreads in school."

The Virgin folks were going to have Alex Sadkin produce Ziggy's label debut, but he was involved in a fatal automobile crash. "It was very hard to think of who would be good for this," Jeffries admits. "Someone suggested Chris [Frantz] and Tina [Weymouth], who had never made a record yet as producers. I knew of their ongoing interest in reggae and how they kept in contact with that world and their love of Bob Marley's music."

The drummer and bassist of Talking Heads, who also founded the spin-off Tom Tom Club, made a world-class album, according to Jeffries, but not necessarily a Jamaican record with the rough edges left in. "The music was still roots," the A&R woman says. "A lot of times...those things get tossed out the window."

Virgin staffers felt there were two or three obvious choices for singles and went with "Tomorrow People"

Ziggy Marley & the Melody Makers

first. "It sounded really pop and it was very important to Ziggy and his brothers and sisters that they have acceptance in the area of black music." So Jeffries contacted Hank Shocklee, best known for producing Public Enemy, to do a remix of "Tumblin' Down" for single release.

"He was great," Jeffries says. "He really understood what it was about. I remember him talking with his hands about what he does when he remixes something. He said, 'I take one style and another and I moosh 'em together,' which is what he did." Shocklee mixed in bits of "Genius of Love," a 1982 dance club hit by Tom Tom Club.

"Tumblin' Down" took Ziggy to chart heights that his father never reached. "Exodus" was Bob Marley's biggest R&B hit, peaking at number 19 in 1977. Ziggy was aware that while he was following in his father's footsteps, he also needed to forge his own identity. "Whenever people say to me that he sounds like his father, I find that hard to believe," says Jeffries. "There's quite a big difference. His voice is huskier. People always draw comparisons but to Ziggy, it was very important that he made his own music...So there's similarities because they're both roots but [Ziggy] was always very strong about having his own sound and his own world."

510

OASIS

Roberta Flack

ATLANTIC 88996
WRITERS: MARCUS MILLER, MARK STEVENS
PRODUCER: MARCUS MILLER
January 7, 1989 (1 week)

Roberta Flack's fourth Number One single arrived almost 11 years after her third chart-topper [see 289—"The Closer I Get to You"]. Appropriately, it was titled "Oasis."

Oddly, the beautiful, African-inspired melody had something in common with a completely different Number One hit—"Da'Butt" by E.U. [see 485]. Both were written by Marcus Miller and Mark Stevens and produced by Miller, a former member of Flack's band.

Along with his writing partner, Luther Vandross, Miller had appeared on Roberta Flack albums and toured with the singer. Flack called Miller around the time that "Da'Butt" was shaking and said she was looking for a producer. "She confided to me later that she was a little intimidated because I work with Luther," says Miller. "And I said, 'Roberta, we both were in your band. Why are you intimidated by us? This is me, Marcus!' And she said, 'I know, but you guys are different guys now.' And I appreciated the respect she

Roberta Flack

had for us. I said, 'OK, none of that, though.' She eventually got real comfortable. If you hear 'Oasis,' she's just going for it and it's really good."

Miller and Stevens took the same approach with "Oasis" that they took with "Da'Butt," even though the project differed greatly. Miller explains: "I had a melody and I wanted Mark to scat it. He started coming up with lyrics and we eventually finished it that way." Marcus thought up the title. "I had the track, and you sit around and listen to it and if you're open to your thoughts, it'll come to you. You have to not be self-conscious about it. You say, ' "Oasis," great, now what do I write about an oasis?' Finishing it was the difficult part. That's where Mark came in handy, because he threw things out and a lot of them were really good."

Miller sent the track off to Flack. "She loved it, and it was real exciting because it had an African feeling to it and there wasn't any of that happening on the radio. Her voice seemed to fit in perfectly with it. An African girl came up with some chant lyrics for Roberta to sing. I think Roberta loved the way it came out."

The song "Oasis" was one of three Miller/Stevens numbers on the *Oasis* album. The title song was recorded at three New York studios: Right Track, Skyline, and Master Sound Astoria. David Sanborn played the alto saxophone solo, Buddy Williams was on drums, Steve Thornton handled percussion, Jason Miller programmed the synthesizers, and Miller took care of bass and keyboards. In addition to Miller, Stevens, and Flack, the background singers were Lani Groves, Chude Mondlane, Brenda White-King, and Dennis Collins.

Miller considers Flack to be a perfectionist. Working with her, he says, is a special experience: "The trip is the first time you record [a classic artist], to see the voice that's so familiar coming out of an actual person. You want to say, 'You sound just like Roberta Flack,' and trying to verbalize that, you always sound silly. To stand in front of Miles Davis or Roberta Flack or Luther and hearing [the voice] come out of a normal person who walks and talks and just happens to be able to make this great music—it's always a trip to me and it always makes me realize how blessed I am."

511

SUPERWOMAN

Karyn White

WARNER BROS. 27783
WRITERS: L.A. REID, BABYFACE, DARYL SIMMONS
PRODUCERS: L.A. REID, BABYFACE
January 14, 1989 (3 weeks)

"I don't want to sound cocky, but it's the perfect lyric," Antonio "L.A." Reid says of "Superwoman," Karyn White's second Number One single. "There's nothing on it that I would change, ever."

His partner reveals that the song owes something to a 5th Dimension hit from 1971. "The inspiration came from wanting to write a woman's anthem," says Kenny "Babyface" Edmonds, "and part of the idea of the lyrics came from 'One Less Bell to Answer.' The whole idea of the hook, 'One less bell to answer, one less egg to fry, one less man to pick up after,' how simple that was. It was straight to the core of something you do everyday. That's how [we came up with] the lyrics to 'Superwoman,' trying to get those simple, not normal words that would go in a song."

Babyface adds that he loves White's vocal performance. "She really delivered the record. We worked a little bit on that record. It took us a little while to get that one. We weren't exactly sure where we wanted her to come from on it, but we found it."

Reid shares his memories of the session: "What I remember most about 'Superwoman' was Face being in the studio with Karyn and just working her over. 'Again, please. Again. Again. Again.' And Face really pulled the performance out of her on that record. On some of the other records, I think I probably worked a lot closer to her, like 'The Way You Love Me,' but on 'Superwoman' I really have to give credit to Kenny because he really brought it out of her. He made her deliver that record."

White's assessment matches her producers' sentiments. "They really brought a lot out of me that I didn't know I could do," she says. "I was used to producing my own vocals. As far as singing, I went and did my own thing. But they were really picky—emotion was so important to them. They feel that sells records. Michael Jackson has a lot of [emotion] and I really admire that. At first, I was just singing. I wasn't really thinking about what I was actually doing."

One of the prominent features of "Superwoman" is that White's voice is out in front. "When you have a really great voice, you want that to be heard," Babyface explains. "You need that voice in order to feel the emotion from it. I think the main thing we push for is at least the best emotional performance that you can get from any of the singers. In some cases it's a little more and in some cases it's not as much. It's as much as the person can give—but even when it's as much as a person can give, if you can feel that they're giving all they got, then that's all that matters."

"Superwoman" was recorded at Studio Masters in Los Angeles. Babyface played keyboards, Reid provided drums and percussion, and Kayo was on bass. White and Babyface sang background vocals along with Bunny Hull and Carmen Carter.

512

CAN YOU STAND THE RAIN

New Edition

MCA 53464
WRITERS: JAMES HARRIS III, TERRY LEWIS
PRODUCERS: JIMMY JAM, TERRY LEWIS
February 4, 1989 (2 weeks)

Jimmy Jam and Terry Lewis were asked to contribute a couple of songs to the Dan Aykroyd/Tom Hanks film version of *Dragnet* and were told they could work with any artist on the MCA roster. "We picked Patti LaBelle and New Edition," says Jimmy Jam. "This was a chance to get to know the New Edition, because there had been some talk about us getting involved with them. They were at a career crossroads where they had done a couple of successful albums and a couple of successful tours but were in the place where you have to grow up—and how do you make that transition? I think we had a reputation in the industry at the time of being able to give everybody a unique sound, listen to the artist, and bring the best of them out. I think that's one of the reasons they were interested in us."

Recording the song "Helplessly in Love" for the soundtrack gave Jam and Lewis the opportunity to know the five members of New Edition personally. Based on their experience with that one song, they knew they wanted to work with the group on a bigger project.

Heart Break was the first New Edition album without Bobby Brown. He exited in 1986 to record a solo album [see 443—"Girlfriend"]. "They were really happy for Bobby," says Jimmy Jam. "His first album wasn't big by any stretch of the imagination and a lot of people were telling him, 'Oh, you made a mistake.' [New Edition] never told him that. They said, 'So what? "Girlfriend" was a Number One record, so you're cool. Now do your next record.' "

Bobby's replacement in the quintet was Johnny Gill, a singer from Washington, D.C., who had recorded for Atlantic, both on his own and with Stacy Lattisaw. "We wanted to have a song that introduced Johnny Gill as part of the New Edition and then have Ralph [Tresvant], who was the familiar voice, take the song home, and also use Ricky [Bell], who at that time hadn't done a lot of lead vocals. We even used Michael Bivins on a little piece where he says, 'Come on, baby, let's go get wet.' So we tried to utilize all the guys in the group and introduce Johnny Gill. We wanted to have a song in the mode of the Stylistics' 'You Make Me Feel Brand New,' where the low voice comes in and then the high voice takes over."

The lyrics were inspired by the five members of New Edition. "They're always on tour and a lot of them are leaving women behind when they go on tour and a lot of times they would talk about how hard it was and how women don't trust them...In Minneapolis we're familiar with weather. We have snow storms and we made an analogy to weather, 'Sunny days, everybody loves them, but can you stand the rain?'—can you stand it when I'm not around?"

Jam and Lewis wondered if there would be any friction between New Edition and the new addition, who already had an established solo career. "But it became a mutual admiration society. When Johnny would sing, Ralph would always sit in the studio next to me and watch him and say, 'Oh, he can sing.' And then when Ralph would sing, Johnny would sit next to me and say, 'Oh man, Ralph can sing.' So they both got really close during the project and any thought that we had that there might be jealousy got erased. They were both very professional and very respectful of each other's talents, and that made the recording very easy."

"Can You Stand the Rain" was the third single released from *Heart Break*. It's Number One status "was a good sign that people were accepting New Edition at that point," says Jimmy Jam. The producer was pleased to be able to assist in the group's transition from, as the final song on the album says, "Boys to Men."

513

DREAMIN'

Vanessa Williams

WING 871 078

WRITERS: LISA MONTEGOMARY, GENEVA PASCHAL

PRODUCER: DONALD ROBINSON

February 18, 1989 (2 weeks)

Vanessa Williams heard the original version of the song "Dreamin' " and liked it so much, she asked Donald Robinson, the man who produced it for the Guinn family on Motown, to helm a remake for *The Right Stuff*, her first album on Mercury's Wing subsidiary.

Famous for being a deposed Miss America before the album was released, Vanessa's reputation quickly changed when people heard how talented she was. Those who only knew her for her photographs in *Penthouse* didn't realize the Tarrytown, New York, native was the daughter of two music teachers, and that by age five she could play the piano, violin, and flute.

Philadelphia-based Donald Robinson signed with Motown's publishing arm, Jobete, after a stint with the Philly World label. That's where he first met the Guinn family, who recorded for Philly World as New Experience before they made a pact with Motown. Randy, Michael, Skip, Bonnie, Earl, and Marjorie Guinn teamed with Lori Fulton to record "Dreamin,' " a song written by Lisa Montegomary and Geneva Paschal.

The Guinn version received a lot of airplay on radio stations that featured the Quiet Storm format, but the song never made the *Billboard* chart. Holly Greene, a staffer at Jobete, sent the song to Wing Records chief Ed Eckstine when she heard he was looking for material for his new signing, Vanessa Williams. Greene put Eckstine in touch with Robinson and the label president asked him to record a new version of "Dreamin' " for Williams. Robinson was not surprised that the song was getting a second chance. "There was something magical about that hook and the chord progressions that went with it and the lyrics matched so well. I think that's what really made it for that song—the simplicity of it."

Robinson recorded the new version at the legendary Sigma Sound Studios in Philadelphia. "[For] the original, we used mostly sequencers," Robinson recalls. "I think the Fairlight was the big instrument around at that time. I decided I was going to mix live musicians with the sequenced parts. I used live guitar, which I didn't do on the original. I used live percussion and added more colors to it. I played it for Ed, and he loved it. Then he flew Vanessa in and we worked on it for about three days. [The original] was a half-step higher than the key Vanessa sang it in. It was a little faster, also. We slowed it down. I think the original version didn't have a saxophone, which gave it more soulfulness. I remember changing the bridge section. In the original, the bridge was maybe a little too jazzy and we made it more pop on the version Vanessa did." Lori Fulton, who sang on the Guinn version, did background vocals along with Carol Coleman and Rochelle Farrell.

Robinson had an intuitive feeling that Vanessa's version would be a hit, but was still leery. "I had no idea it would go that far, mainly because of the Guinn family not taking off," he says. The song established Williams as a pop contender as well as an R&B star. "She's a very hard worker," Robinson acknowledges. "She gave me 100 percent. We were only supposed to be [in the studio] for six hours and we ended up there for three days. But we came out with something great. [She's] very easy to work with, a very nice woman."

Vanessa Williams

514

JUST BECAUSE

Anita Baker

ELEKTRA 69327
WRITERS: MICHAEL O'HARA,
SAMMY MCKINNEY, ALEX BROWN
PRODUCER: MICHAEL J. POWELL
March 4, 1989 (1 week)

About a year after songwriters Michael O'Hara and Sammy McKinney were introduced to each other through their publishing company, McKinney called O'Hara on the phone with an idea for a song he wanted to place on Anita Baker's next album. O'Hara asked what the title was. "He said, 'Just Because,' " O'Hara recalls. "And I said, 'Just because *what?*' I didn't get it. It went over my head."

McKinney explained, "When you love someone, it could be something as simple as their eyes, their soul, their face, anything, but you really can't explain it. It's just because." O'Hara suddenly understood, and could hear the music in his head. "I sat at the piano and started writing it. It was like taking dictation from God. It came right through me."

O'Hara called McKinney back at work. McKinney was so excited about what his partner had written, he called it a day and met up with O'Hara so they could finish the song. With some help from lyricist Alex Brown, they completed "Just Because."

It was actually the second song they submitted to Baker. McKinney, a hair stylist with many celebrity clients, was determined to place a song with Anita after his friend and client Lori Perri told him the songstress was looking for new material. McKinney and O'Hara wrote their first song together, "Feel So Good," and sent it to Baker. She hesitated and the song found its way to Patti LaBelle, who liked it but didn't record it. It ended up on the soundtrack of *Do the Right Thing*, recorded by Lori and her sisters, whose group was called Perri.

McKinney asked Lori to sing on the demo of "Just Because," and explains that Anita passed on the song the first time she heard it. "At the time, I was doing Miki Howard's hair. She was looking for songs too, so I played it for her. One thing I used to say, because of inexperience, was, 'I wrote this song just for you.' I told that to Miki and she loved the song and put it on hold."

Meanwhile, Anita went to work on her new album. Angry at her producer one day, she asked Lori to take her for a drive so she could cool off. "She got in the car and as fate would have it, the song was just coming on," says McKinney. Lori asked Anita why she didn't like "Just Because." "Anita didn't answer," says McKinney. "Lori looks over at her and her eyes were closed. She was swaying from side to side, And after the song was over, Anita said, 'This is my song. I'm doing this song.' " Lori called McKinney and told him to meet Anita at the studio with a lyric sheet. "I said, 'But Lori, Miki Howard has that song on hold.' She said, 'And I just told you that Anita Baker who sold five million records is on her way over here to pick up your song. You better get over here.' "

McKinney admits he didn't love Baker's version the first time he heard it. "There were some things that Lori had done melodically that I was married to. But after I got used to it, I loved it. After I started hearing it on the radio all the time, I really loved it." O'Hara found the final version faithful to the demo. "It's the same key, the same arrangement, everything." He credits producer Michael J. Powell. "He recognized that the demo was the heart of the song as far as the production was concerned...I'm really grateful for what they did for the song."

515

JUST COOLIN'

Levert featuring Heavy D.

ATLANTIC 88959
WRITERS: GERALD LEVERT, MARC GORDON
PRODUCERS: GERALD LEVERT, MARC GORDON
March 11, 1989 (1 week)

"Just Coolin' ' was a concept I had for an album," Gerald Levert explains. "Everybody was saying it. 'What you been doin'?' 'Coolin', I'm just coolin' out,' so I said, 'Let's cut the album *Just Coolin'*,' and I came up with an idea for a song called 'Just Coolin'.' I hummed it on tape and it had the same bassline it has now but I had it as a mellower groove."

Meanwhile, Gerald told his writing partner, Marc Gordon, about the song. "Without any idea of what the music would sound like, I started working on it," says Marc. "When I finished it and came back, it was totally different than what he thought it would be. I think he thought it would be a little slower...It had this hard edge on it." Marc came up with the track by starting with a drum beat, then working on the bass.

Gerald didn't mind that Marc had changed the groove, because he liked the direction the song was taking. The next step was to add a guest star: New York rapper Heavy D. The three members of Levert often ran into the rap star. "At first we would always see each other and say, 'We're going to work together,' " says Gerald. "Finally, when there came time [to do] a song, he called me and said, 'Come on man, we got to work together.' Finally his people called and they wanted too much. We couldn't work it out." Gerald

Surface

decided to forgo the idea of working with Heavy D., and proceeded to record "Just Coolin' " without him. "We had mixed the song; it was done and we ended up talking to Heavy again," says Marc. "We were in Philadelphia [at Sigma Sound] and he had called. He ended up coming down and we mixed it again."

By the time "Just Coolin' " became their fourth Number One single, Levert had expanded their horizons and were producing other artists as well, including Troop, Stephanie Mills, Jennifer Holliday, the Rude Boys, Miki Howard, and even the O'Jays, with Gerald and Sean Levert's father, Eddie.

But working with other artists didn't affect Levert's style, according to Gerald. "When you work with other people, they want your style. They want your influence and I think we've done enough stuff that people know where our sound is and that we give good quality music. I just finished [working with] Teddy Pendergrass. We worked with the O'Jays. I'm working with Barry White. I'm about to do some things with Aretha Franklin and Gladys Knight...They want what we do and they like what we do."

With all of Levert's success, it's not surprising that some people think the three members are older than they are. "A lot of people think I'm in my 30s," says Gerald. "We've been doing this for a long time, and I think people, when they look at us, think, 'Wow, you guys are old and you've been here for a long time,' and we're just getting started...Because of the kind of music we are capable of writing, we can write the young stuff and we can write the more mature songs, and it's a trip to them when they hear we're able to do that."

Still, Gerald considers the highlight of his career "being able to work with all the people I admired in the past that influenced me, like Barry, Teddy, the O'Jays, Gladys, the Winans, Aretha, James Ingram, Stephanie, Anita Baker...all these people that I love...That is probably the best reward in the world, that you can give back to people who have given you so much in your career. That is the greatest thing you could ask for."

516

CLOSER THAN FRIENDS

Surface

COLUMBIA 08537
WRITERS: BERNARD JACKSON, DAVID TOWNSEND
PRODUCERS: DAVID "PIC" CONLEY, DAVID TOWNSEND, BERNARD JACKSON
March 18, 1989 (2 weeks)

David Townsend's father told his son that when he finished college, he would help him do whatever he wanted to do. Fortunately for David, his father was Ed Townsend, who had his own top 10 single in 1958 with "For Your Love," and then wrote a Number One hit for Marvin Gaye [see 153—"Let's Get It On"].

"I was instrumental in getting the contract with Columbia," says the senior member of the Townsend family. "But as far as hands-on in the studio...my son is responsible for that." Ed was in Mississippi building a recording studio for the black community when David flew down from New York, depressed that things weren't going well. "After about eight weeks, he said, 'What am I going to do?' I said, 'You're going to get your butt back on a plane, you're going back to New York, and you're going to try again.' And after that, the first project that came up was successful...I was sort of flipped out about the style they had. It was purely theirs, and some was influenced by things I had done with him in the studio." Indeed, Ed's son even told him that when he and David "Pic" Conley are in the studio, they often look at each other and say, "That's what Pops would do."

Surface first hit the top 10 in 1987 with "Happy," a song that spent two weeks at number two. Two years later, they scored their first Number One hit with "Closer Than Friends." Bernard Jackson recalls: "Townsend sent the track to me. I was in California...staying out there with friends for months...Most of the tracks that Townsend send to me, I love them...I love what he does and I write as I normally write. That [lyric] just came out naturally. When you're a songwriter/artist, you just do what you do, you don't really know how it's done. I guess it's from a higher state somewhere. But I remember sitting in this small room, putting down this idea, and I even sung it on a little four-track from the track that he sent me, and I played it over the phone for him. He loved it right away."

The title came about while looking for another way to say "I love you," according to Jackson. The song was recorded in what Surface calls "the Lab"—a 24-track studio in Conley's living room in New Jersey. "All I can remember is the mascot cat laying down on the little seat next to me while I'm singing this song on the microphone," Bernard laughs. Like most Surface songs, the vocals for "Closer Than Friends" were recorded in one day. "That's the way I like to work," Jackson confirms. "Do one song and get the lead first. Take my time and get it 'til I like it and then I do the backgrounds, and I'm through."

Townsend played electric piano on the track and was responsible for synthesizer and drum programming. Conley played the synth bass and also did drum programming. Vassal Benford played acoustic piano and synthesizers.

Conley considers "Closer Than Friends" to be one of the group's best songs, although he didn't think so when he first heard it. "I wasn't too sure about it, because it was in demo form. But after we finished producing it, it came to life. It was good enough for me to like it for the album. We actually decide on every song that goes on the album. We call it 'giggling.' If I'm giggling, Dave's giggling, and Bernard's giggling, then it goes on the album. And we try to do it fairly. We try to make sure everybody's got a strong portion of the writership."

517
LUCKY CHARM
The Boys

MOTOWN 1952
WRITERS: BABYFACE, L.A. REID, GREG SCELSA, DARYL SIMMONS
PRODUCERS: L.A. REID, BABYFACE
April 1, 1989 (1 week)

When Babyface moved to Los Angeles in 1985, he stayed at the home of a friend, Greg Scelsa. "We did a little bit of co-writing together," says Babyface. "Greg knew the Boys because he does kids' albums...He used to have the Boys perform at some of the functions they used to do. When he found out we were going to work with them, he said, 'We should write something for them.' "

Working with L.A. Reid and Daryl Simmons, they came up with "Lucky Charm," which sounded "extremely youthful," according to Babyface. "They had demoed it already," Tajh Abdul-Samad recalls. "They had the music and Face sung the track to us, and we liked it."

L.A. and Babyface played all of the instruments on the track. They received some assistance from Pebbles [see 478—"Girlfriend"]. "She helped produce the vocals and sung some background vocals along with Kevon [Edmonds] of After 7 [see 558—"Ready or Not"]," says Khiry Abdul-Samad. The four brothers paid close attention to how L.A. and Babyface worked in the studio. "That's where we learned how to produce," Khiry acknowledges. And they learned a lot: "Placement as far as doing vocals. Melodies. We learned a lot of different melody tactics...how important melody is. How important lyrics are."

"Lucky Charm" was the second consecutive Number One single from the brothers' debut, *Messages from the Boys*. It was the first time since Stevie Wonder's *Characters* in 1987 that Motown had scored two consecutive Number One singles from the same album. Did the Boys feel any pressure, being the label's first new success under the administration of Jheryl Busby? "We were a little naïve to the situation," Khiry admits. "We were just little kids, happy to be out there, finally getting a chance. We'd been performing on the beach for four years, so this was our dream...It all happened so fast. Before we knew it, we had a Number One single. [There] wasn't that much pressure because we didn't expect it. I guess there was more pressure for all the executives behind the scenes to perform, to bring home a Number one, a debut platinum artist in their new venture."

The benefits of having two Number One singles were many. "We got to see the world," says Khiry. "We're constantly traveling and we always meet new people. We get to see what's out there...because if you don't know what's out there, then you won't reach for anything."

The Abdul-Samad brothers were living in Northridge, California, when they signed with Motown. The group was named after the youngsters were signed up for a local talent show. "We didn't have a name," Tajh explains. "So the people said, 'What's the name of the group that's going on next? What's the name?' and my mom said, 'Who, the boys?' and that's how we came up with the name. We've just kept it ever since." Khiry and Hakeem were the original members; they started off doing karate kicks to music. "I came in when Michael Jackson was real hot and I would do a little Michael Jackson routine," says Tajh. "And then Bilal [was] added when we were at the beach."

Today

518

GIRL I GOT MY EYES ON YOU

Today

MOTOWN 1954
WRITERS: LEE DRAKEFORD, LARRY SINGLETARY, WESLEY ADAMS, LARRY MCCAIN, GENE GRIFFIN
PRODUCER: GENE GRIFFIN
April 8, 1989 (1 week)

When he was five years old, Lee "Bubba" Drakeford's mother told him in church, "If you don't go up there and sing, Bub, God's gonna take your voice away." Terrified, he joined the choir at the Rock of Ages church.

Fortunately, the Englewood, New Jersey, youngster grew to like music and formed a group with some high school friends—Larry "Chief" Singletary, Wesley Adams, and Larry "Love" McCain. "We grew up together," Drakeford explains. "Chief and Wes were the rappers originally, and Love and I were the singers." They called themselves the Gents and had a fateful meeting in 1984 at an anti-drug benefit at the

Latin Quarter in New York. That's where they met André Harrell, who introduced them to Teddy Riley.

"We got together before he was *the* Teddy Riley," says Drakeford. It was Riley who came up with a new name for the quartet. "He said, 'Let's call you Today.' We were like, 'Today? Why Today?' He said, 'Think about it. Today!' Today means what's happening now. In effect, everything is Today."

Riley had a production deal with MCA Records and brought Today to the company. When label executive Jheryl Busby was named the president of Motown following Berry Gordy's sale of the corporation, he took Today with him. "We were very excited to be on Motown," says Drakeford.

The group loved working in the studio. "I wanted to go in there and learn everything quickly," Drakeford says. "When we went into the studio the first time, we weren't nervous because we used to save up all our money and go in studios around the local area. When we went in the studio with Teddy, it was, 'Oh man, we've got work to do.' It was something new for Teddy and something new for us. We were very comfortable."

Drakeford says the group knew that "Girl I Got My Eyes on You" was going to be a hit. "Teddy came up with the track and we came up with the melody and it hit so hard in the studio. We sat there for about two days and just listened to that track full blast."

When they were recording the song, Riley had the group lay down 20 tracks of vocals. "We were really busy in there," says Drakeford. "And Teddy is a perfectionist. He ain't having no flat notes. If he asks you for a straight note, he likes you to sing it straight, no vibrato. It was fun, because we were doing all different kinds of harmonies to make that blend. There was a certain way he wanted us to sing it. It took all night and Teddy did 10 different remixes. We said, 'Is that it?' and he said, 'No, I want you to do some more vocals on the song.' 'Oh my god, Teddy, you are crazy, man. What are you trying to do to us?' He said, 'You can do it. I believe in you all, Bub.' "

Today was on tour in Indianapolis with Guy and M.C. Hammer when Riley called them onstage and announced, "My first group that I produced, Today, went Number One in *Billboard* today." That's how Today found out that "Girl I Got My Eyes on You" had hit the top of the chart.

The group eventually left Motown and disbanded. "Motown was doing that old thing, 'Hey, you all be the Four Tops, the Boys will be the Jacksons, and the Good Girls will be the Supremes.' And we didn't want to go that way because that wasn't Today," says Drakeford. After the group split, he signed a solo deal with the EastWest label and returned to the chart as Big Bub with the singles "Tellin' Me Stories" and "24/7 (Good Lovin')."

519

EVERY LITTLE STEP

Bobby Brown

MCA 53618
WRITERS: L.A. REID, BABYFACE
PRODUCERS: L.A. REID, BABYFACE
April 15, 1989 (1 week)

A year after she hit the top of the chart with "Girlfriend" and "Mercedes Boy," Pebbles was responsible for another Number One hit—"Every Little Step." But she didn't record the song.

"I was riding in my car going to see my wife—who is my wife now but wasn't then—and I was so in love," says L.A. Reid. "And I remember pulling over to the side of the road and writing, 'I can't sleep at night, I toss and turn listening for the telephone.' And it was pure love that wrote those lyrics, believe me. My 50 percent of the song was written to my wife Pebbles."

"Every Little Step" wasn't written with Bobby Brown in mind. "I wrote it for myself," Kenny "Babyface" Edmonds reveals. "I was singing it really young, so I didn't care for it. Midnight Star [see 398—"Operator"] was working on an album. We tried to give it to them. And they'll hate me for this, but somebody in the group said it wasn't really happening. So we said, 'OK, if that's how you feel.' And we gave it to Bobby Brown. Bobby at that point wasn't a name as a solo artist. It was Bobby's energy that helped give that song life and that's the main thing about Bobby Brown—the energy he brings to records."

Reid remembers Babyface's original demo. "It sounded good," says L.A., "but it sounded a little too polite. When Bobby did it, it got raunchy. It had a little edge to it and that's what I liked about it."

Brown loved "Every Little Step" the first time he heard it, according to Babyface, who had to think twice before giving the song away. "Some people when they hear a song will say, 'Why don't you keep this for yourself?' But we don't all have the same vision and I think people think differently than L.A. and I do when it comes to a record that I might sing as to whether it's for me or not. In some cases, L.A. has felt I should have kept a song. But if I don't feel like it's me, I can't hold on to it. It's easier for me to let go, especially if I'm the writer. I have to lean pretty close to ballad-oriented things and things that feel right with my voice. I couldn't do anything real hard—it wouldn't be believable and I can't even sing hard enough to make it believable."

Reid sums up how he feels about Brown: "He laughs at me, because I'm very close to Bobby, and I always tell him he's like a television—you plug him in and he goes. He's a machine. And he doesn't get a lot of credit for being a great vocalist, but the energy level is just as special as someone who has a truly dynamic voice. I think they have equal importance in the marketplace."

Reid points out that while Brown was achieving multi-platinum success with *Don't Be Cruel*, other R&B artists who incorporated hip-hop sounds into their music were coming to the fore, including Al B. Sure!, Keith Sweat, Pebbles, Teddy Riley and Guy, and Johnny Gill. "That era was the most important era of black music that we had, in my opinion, since the earlier days of Motown or Philadelphia International."

520

LOVE SAW IT

Karyn White

WARNER BROS. 27538
WRITERS: L.A. REID, BABYFACE, DARYL SIMMONS
PRODUCERS: L.A. REID, BABYFACE
April 22, 1989 (2 weeks)

L.A. Reid credits engineer Jon Gass for helping to make "Love Saw It" a hit. "Jon had so much to do with the carving of our sound in general, but on that song, he nailed it. Sonically, 'Love Saw It' is the best-sounding record we have ever done—from a dynamic standpoint, from an EQing standpoint, which has nothing to do with the writing of the song. It's the best-sounding song I've ever heard on the radio."

The song was written as a duet, although Reid and his partner Babyface didn't know who would team up with Karyn White on the song. As it turned out, it was Babyface himself.

"That's probably my favorite duet of the ones I've done and I would love to do another duet with Karyn one day, because I felt we worked really well together," Babyface allows. "It was fun because it had a little bit of jazz to it and it was so laid back."

Reid says his partner enjoys recording duets. "I think Face likes to do it from a pure love of music. Whenever we get into a project and get really involved, the artist in him starts to come out. And he'll say, 'You know what? I'd like to try it.' And I'll say, 'You know what? It's a good idea.' There have been some times where we talked about it and decided against it. Especially recently because we've tried to carve out a niche, so that when his record came, it would be special. And he didn't want to get tagged as the guy who sings on every record he produces. But at that point he did duets with Karyn White and Pebbles. He did a duet with the lead singer of Damian Dame on his very first solo record called 'Haven't I Been Faithful.' That was the very first time we'd ever done it."

Babyface says the melody for "Love Saw It" came first and then the words fell into place. He acknowledges that his wife enjoys the fact that he can write a song from a woman's point of view. "She's pretty proud of the songs and I think she thinks there's a certain quality to them," says Babyface. "In terms of writing from a woman's point of view, I think part of it comes from [being] heartbroken or just being totally in love. It has more to do with me growing up and being in love and getting my heart broken again and again that allows me to be able to write sentimentally at times. Some feelings stick with you always."

"Love Saw It" was recorded at Silverlake Sound in Los Angeles. Babyface played guitar and keyboards while Reid was on drums and percussion. White and Babyface sang their own background vocals.

It was the third Number One single for White, who was born and raised in Los Angeles. Her course in life was set early, when she entered the Little Miss Ebony pageant at age five. Around the same time she saw Diana Ross in *Lady Sings the Blues* and told her mother she wanted to be a star. "She believed me," says Karyn.

She gave up cheerleading in high school because yelling was ruining her voice. At 16 she auditioned for *Dream Girls* but dropped out before she knew if she made it into the show because she was two years under the producers' age limit. White was 18 when she wrote "Automatic Passion," which was recorded by Stephanie Mills. She auditioned to replace Jody Watley in Shalamar but didn't get the job; she was briefly in a group called Legacy but was asked to leave because they didn't think she had a commercial sound.

Her big break came when she recorded a demo at Michael Jeffries's studio in San Francisco. That led to recording "Facts of Love" with Jeff Lorber and her own contract with Warner Brothers.

521

REAL LOVE

Jody Watley

MCA 53484
WRITERS: ANDRÉ CYMONE, JODY WATLEY
PRODUCER: ANDRÉ CYMONE
May 6, 1989 (1 week)

Jody Watley admits she felt the pressure of recording a second album after her first solo effort was so successful [see 451—"Looking for a New Love"]. "Inevitably you know you're going to be under a microscope," says the goddaughter of Jackie Wilson.

"How I put it in perspective is that each album should be like the first album...There's always room for growth. The most important thing is for you to

Jody Watley

know that you did the best you can do. I was definitely nervous about it because there's the whole 'sophomore jinx.' And I felt that because I won the Grammy for Best New Artist, a lot of people had terrible luck after they won it. So I put my nose to the grindstone and tried to come up with a wonderful second album."

As with "Looking for a New Love" on *Jody Watley,* the last song written for *Larger Than Life* was the first to be issued as a single and go to Number One on the R&B chart. "This was a case of the record company saying, 'We think you need one more song.' And that one more song was 'Real Love.' A lot of people thought it was the sequel to 'Looking for a New Love.' I wasn't thinking that when I did it."

Just as she did with her first album, Watley listened to a cassette of musical tracks composed by André Cymone and chose the ones she thought were best for her. When MCA asked for one more song, she listened to a track and the title "Real Love" came to her right away. "I keep notebooks all over my house [with] ideas, pieces of lyrics, song titles," she explains. "Usually when I hear a music track, the title is the first thing that comes to me. And it pays to be open because you can think, 'Well, I'm done. This is it,' but if someone [says], 'One more song,' one more song is easy to do."

Like many of her songs, "Real Love" portrays a strong, independent woman. "It comes across because I guess that's the essence of who I am," Watley says. "Having strength as a woman and conveying that in the songs, it just comes out. It is important to me to have that come across."

Watley vastly prefers her solo career to her days as part of Shalamar, and feels her success has prevented her from being merely an answer to a trivia question ("Who was the female member of Shalamar?"). "The best part is that I don't have to compromise with anyone," she elaborates. "Whatever my goals are with each project in terms of different styles of music or the style of singing that I'd like to do, it's really up to me. And I'm not the type of person who is content to rest upon what's done. I'm constantly looking to surprise myself as well as other people."

Watley mentions that she's willing to take risks. "That starts from being in a group and leaving at a time when you're having big success," she says, adding that she enjoys working with people who haven't established themselves yet. "Not necessarily the most obvious, most successful producers in an era of obvious choices in terms of [with] certain producers, it's almost guaranteed that you're going to have Number One records, and why not go that way? And I go against that. I like working with new people and people where I'm a fan of what they do."

522
START OF A ROMANCE
Skyy

ATLANTIC 88932
WRITERS: TOMMY MCCONNELL, JOE WILLIAMS
PRODUCERS: RANDY MULLER, SOLOMON ROBERTS JR.
May 13, 1989 (2 weeks)

Tommy McConnell hooked up with Skyy when he heard they were looking for a drummer. "I was one of those chronic audition guys," he says. "I went to this one audition in Brooklyn and it was downstairs in the basement. The guys were the first cats that I had met in a long time who were honest about their situation."

Born in Queens, McConnel first became interested in music when his parents took him to see shows at the Apollo Theater in the '60s. "I was always intrigued about the stage and performing," he says. "I got a summer job working for the Department of Parks and bought my first drum set, and the rest is history." McConnel decided to play drums because his was intrigued by R&B songs with heavy rhythms. In addition to playing the drums, he started writing songs. "I always had this creative thing going on. I was always trying to come up with new things. [Songwriting] happened after I fell in love with my girl...it was all from experience."

The members of Skyy didn't promise McConnell fame or fortune, but he took the gig anyway. The group was eventually rewarded with a Number One single [see 356—"Call Me"].

McConnell began working on "Start of a Romance" in 1987. "It was a low point for the group because we had been so active...I even had to take a job outside of music, which I really hated. It was in a salt factory and the work was grueling, both mentally and physically. I had worked up to foreman in a very short time and I realized I was unhappy and wanted to do music again." McConnell kept in touch with music through his side business—Culture Sound, a recording studio that he owned in Brooklyn. He was walking outside on a summer day, "and everybody was looking good and I had this great feeling. And the idea popped into my head, 'Start of a Romance.' " McConnell told himself he had to start working on the idea right away.

He had everything he needed to work on the song in his studio, including a drum machine and a computer. He worked on different rhythms and melodies until he got to a point where he felt stumped. He called an old friend, keyboardist Joe Williams. "I explained the concept and he had a smorgasbord of ideas to add. I wanted to stay true to what I originally felt. As the melody developed between the two of us, I said, 'I want to redo some parts. It sounds too [old-fashioned] R&B.' " To make the song contemporary, McConnell and Williams incorporated some rap elements into the song. The collaborators got some additional help from keyboardist Ricky Williams, and then called in Denise Dunning to lay down a lead vocal.

Hating his factory job as much as he did, McConnell counted on "Start of a Romance" being the comeback song for Skyy. "We got the demo from Tommy," remembers Randy Muller. "We heard it in very rough form and said it was a different kind of song...We wanted to keep it raw, just like [its] demo form...It needed some development in the tag. That's why we have that repeated vocal tag on there, to give it a little lift. We kept it basic, just added a little more percussion, some string things, what I call sweetening. It had that unique aspect that I think hits are made of."

Solomon Roberts Jr. credits the song with bringing Skyy back. "It was the first album and the first song on a new label and it was the 'start of a romance' for our public and for us. We felt that way after laying off for about three years."

523

MY FIRST LOVE

Atlantic Starr

WARNER BROS. 27525
WRITERS: DAVID LEWIS, WAYNE LEWIS
PRODUCERS: DAVID LEWIS, WAYNE LEWIS
May 27, 1989 (1 week)

When we write, lots of times we don't know where the inspiration comes from," says Wayne Lewis of Atlantic Starr. "It can come from yourself. It can come from somebody you're watching, just like 'Secret Lovers.' Or it can come from something you've seen in a movie and it just hits you to write about it...I must have seen something that had to do with my first love and so I thought 'My First Love' would be a great story to write about."

David Lewis is also not certain where he gets the inspiration for his music. "I might be looking outside my window and into the woods, looking at the birds, and whatever comes to my mind will happen. I try to stay in tune with my musical instruments so I can always capture the moment. That's what I think writing is all about. I think we're all writers or musicians, but you have to be there to catch the moment when it happens...and it's funny, because I don't think ideas really come from you. They just flow through you. Sometimes I'll be playing at the keyboard and it just happens. Those changes start coming alive. I don't sit down and say, 'This is the way I'm going to do it.' It just happens naturally."

For "My First Love," David had a track that reminded the brothers of the "great days of Thom Bell and the Stylistics," according to Wayne. "Our era," David interjects. "I started writing the lyrics," Wayne continues, "and it came together and we had another hit on our hands."

Jonathan describes how the group records its music: "We use live strings. We do most of the recording in Los Angeles...[but] not directly in the city—we record in Glendale, up in the hills, so we can have some seclusion and you don't have people dropping by unannounced, so we can really focus on what we've got to do."

"One thing we're glad about, because of our musical backgrounds, we're doing real music," Wayne adds. "We've studied classical. We came up with gospel in church. Most black singers come out of the church and we've been through Latin, reggae, every type of music that exists in our background and our career."

In Atlantic Starr, Wayne and David Lewis share the male lead vocal duties; for "My First Love," the honor fell to Wayne. "The first day, we went in and hit it," he recalls. "The rest of the time we were critiquing it and cleaning it up."

In addition to singing lead, Wayne played keyboards on the track. Jonathan also played keyboards, while David played keyboards and guitar. Joseph Phillips played percussion. "My First Love" was the initial single from *We're Movin' Up*, the group's second album for Warner Brothers. It was the first to feature Porscha Martin as female lead singer. The Lewis brothers went through 100 pictures and tapes searching for a replacement for Barbara Weathers, who in turn was a replacement for original female lead singer Sharon Bryant.

After four years with Atlantic Starr, Weathers decided to return to a solo career. She recorded an album for Warner Brothers that was produced by the Lewis brothers.

524

MISS YOU LIKE CRAZY

Natalie Cole

EMI 50185
WRITERS: MICHAEL MASSER, GERRY GOFFIN, PRESTON GLASS
PRODUCER: MICHAEL MASSER
June 3, 1989 (1 week)

When Michael Masser first worked with Natalie Cole, engineer Armen Steiner told the producer a story about a Nat King Cole recording session.

It seems that Nat had a few minutes left at the end of a recording session and they decided to do a quick first take on a song and then come back and do the real thing the next day. So Cole stepped up to the microphone and recorded "Mona Lisa."

"Everybody cried," says Masser, "and they spent the next few months trying to beat it and they never could. When I first met Natalie, she was going through personal changes in her life. And the first time I played her the song 'Someone That I Used to Love,' I had already put down three piano tracks myself. I chose one—didn't have time to hear it. She heard the song just a bit—enough to know it—sang it, and cried afterward." Later, Masser wanted to cut the song with Natalie singing live to an orchestra, but there was something about the first track that could never be matched, and that vocal was the one released to the public.

Natalie Cole

"So when I did 'Miss You Like Crazy,' I understood that about Natalie," says Masser, who also notes that Cole was concerned that her R&B audience wouldn't care for the song. "I felt, 'Let's just go for the song, and it will find its place,' because we can't predict these kinds of things...It's music for everyone. I was very surprised that it was her first Number One in [11] years. It also went Number One on the [Adult Contemporary] chart and it went top 10 in the pop chart and it went to the top in England."

Masser recalls how "Miss You Like Crazy" was written: "Preston Glass sent me different pieces of about 20 to 30 songs a few years before...There were a couple things [where] I said, 'Let me play with [this],' and he was considerate enough to let me do that. Then I brought in Gerry Goffin and worked with him on the words. Those two had not met. We all three had equal parts...but I had to make the song as I heard it and I felt comfortable working with Gerry...I had pretty clear views on how I'd like to hear [the song] so I put it together and waited for the right artist—and that right artist seemed to be Natalie."

Masser had lived with the song for two years by the time he recorded it with Natalie. "It's real important to me to make sure the song is right and there's nothing wrong with trying something a little bit different. Johnny Mercer, who was my mentor, said, 'Michael, just keep the little fragments and don't be afraid to experiment'...Sometimes it takes a little imagination to get the right version, to get the version of the hit that never was." To illustrate his point, Masser indicates that there were a number of ways to go with the ending of "Miss You Like Crazy."

"There's a little madness in there," he says. "I tried not to dilute it. I added a lot of music there, maybe extra parts it didn't need, but that's the way I heard it. I overloaded it with melody."

Masser remains fond of Cole and is proud of her continued success with albums like *Unforgettable* and *Take a Look*. He concludes, "I'm very pleased with her strength and the symbol she's become, with her bringing back all the good music, and I'd love to work with her over and over again."

525

ME MYSELF AND I

De la Soul

TOMMY BOY 7926
WRITERS: PAUL HOUSTON, KELVIN MERCER, DAVID JOLICOEUR, VINCENT MASON JR., PHILLIPPE WYNNE, GEORGE CLINTON
PRODUCER: PAUL HOUSTON
June 10, 1989 (1 week)

Flo and Eddie were not amused. The onetime members of the Turtles ("Happy Together") had recognized an unlicensed sample from one of their old records in "Transmitting Live from Mars," and placed a call to their attorneys. The result was a $1.7 million lawsuit.

The defendants in that action—the biggest anti-sampling case of the '80s, which was eventually settled out of court—were from the same flower-power mold as the Turtles: Kevin Mercer, David Jolicoeur, and Vincent Mason Jr.

Not literally, of course, but figuratively. They were the three members of De la Soul, whose first album, *3 Feet High and Rising*, featured "Transmitting Live from Mars" as well as an overall concept described as the "D.A.I.S.Y. Age," standing for Da Inner Sound, Y'all. Kind of hip-hop hippies.

Released in 1989, their album was widely considered a rap landmark for its loopy humor, melodic hooks, and quirky samples—and it was soon certified gold. "Transmitting Live from Mars" was one of the recording's many amusements, made up of a French-language instruction record superimposed over an organ loop.

"We've always been a little different from everyone else," Mercer (whose stage name is Posdnous) told *Blues & Soul*. "Even at school we'd wear '70s-type psychedelic clothes and borrow bell bottoms from our dads and stuff.

"I'd say the album is totally reflective of our personalities and upbringings. That's why it turned out the way it has and it's so original, because we didn't go out and copy anyone else."

Borrow, perhaps, but not copy. "Me Myself and I" was the breakout single from *3 Feet High and Rising*, a loopzilla hit that sampled the Parliafunkadelicament thang of George Clinton and Phillippe Wynne, late lead singer of the Spinners. Others sampled on the album were Hall & Oates, Steely Dan, Johnny Cash, Cymande, Sly Stone, and the Detroit Emeralds.

"Everything in our music is influenced from the '50s, '60s, and '70s," added Mercer, citing "De la Orgee" as another example. "We have a Barry White record, with him moaning on it, in the background, and we had a bunch of people come in and we started the beat and just all went crazy in the studio. That's how a lot of the album was actually conceived—very spontaneously."

De la Soul made their original rendezvous in high school in Amityville, New York. "Me and Dave [Jolicoeur] were in a group called Easy Street in Brooklyn, where I was a DJ," elaborated Mercer. "We wrote rhymes and found that we had pretty similar ideas. No one actually knew we could rap, but we decided to make some tapes—and came up with 'Plug Tunin',' and got Prince Paul [Houston] from Stetsasonic in our neighborhood to work with us."

In 1988, De la Soul were signed to Tommy Boy, the Manhattan independent label that was also home to Stetsasonic, and "Plug Tunin' " became their first single. "The response we've been getting speaks for itself," said Mercer then. "We've been getting played on the major radio stations such as [New York's] WBLS and KISS as well as on college and alternative music stations. The feedback from all circles has been great. It's opened rap out to people who wouldn't normally be into it."

Even Flo and Eddie?

526

HAVE YOU HAD YOUR LOVE TODAY

The O'Jays

EMI 50180
WRITERS: TERRY STUBBS, DERRICK PEARSON
PRODUCERS: WALTER WILLIAMS,
EDDIE LEVERT SR., TERRY STUBBS
June 17, 1989 (2 weeks)

Sixteen years and nine months after hitting Number One with "Back Stabbers," the O'Jays scored their 10th chart-topper. It was their first Number One hit that was not produced by Kenny Gamble and Leon Huff, and that did not appear on that duo's Philadelphia International Records.

While in high school, Terry Stubbs played in a Cleveland group called the Sly, Slick, and the Wicked, named for the Lost Generation hit from 1970. They opened one night for a local appearance by the O'Jays and were offered a management deal. After touring with the O'Jays, Stubbs became more interested in production and the Sly, Slick and the Wicked disbanded.

Stubbs was living in Washington, D.C., when he met Derrick Pearson at a recording studio in 1983. Pearson was writing songs for the go-go craze, and Stubbs wanted to incorporate that beat with some R&B sounds. Using a sequencer in his home studio, he came up with a track and played it for Stubbs, who took it to Cleveland so the O'Jays could hear it. "The track was in a raw stage at that point," says Stubbs. "So I ended up cutting the track again in Cleveland and then I wrote lyrics and a melody to it." At the time, Stubbs had taken a step back from music to spend time raising his son, and his inspiration for the lyrics were more spiritual then sensual. "I did that with that whole album. I said one thing, but inside I meant something else."

Gerald Levert, son of Eddie Levert of the O'Jays, and his partner in Levert, Marc Gordon, co-produced "Have You Had Your Love Today." A rapper named Jaz, who was signed to Capitol, contributed to the track. "We had a rap on there when I wrote it," says Stubbs. "It wasn't long enough, so we got Jaz to extend the part that we had already written. At that time, it was something different. We were like one of the pioneers of [recording] R&B with a rapper on it.

The O'Jays

We had just done it with Levert with "Just Coolin' " [see 515] and Heavy D and it worked out great, so we tried it with the O'Jays and it ended up with them getting a Number One record."

Playing keyboards on the track were Marc Gordon, Dwayne Mitchell, Dennis Williams, and Claude Gaudette, who also programmed the synthesizers. Rendal Bowland and Teddy Castellucci played guitars. John Robinson played drums while Jim Salamone took care of the drum programming. Lenny Castro was on percussion, Jimmy Williams and Freddie Washington played bass, and Ronald Kerden and David Boruff were on saxophone.

Stubbs notes that working with a veteran group like the O'Jays might be intimidating for other younger producers, but he had known the group since he was a teenager. "For me, it's a lot of fun. Because when I write with them, I'm the [fourth] O'Jay. We sing together all the time...I keep it very relaxed."

The O'Jays were very comfortable with the way Gamble and Huff produced records, but Stubbs had observed the legendary duo. "They used to go in one at a time. Eddie and Walter [Williams] did a lot of the leading, so they would put two booths in there and let them go at it, whereas it's a little different now. Soundwise, you don't want anybody leaking on the other track." Stubbs had Walter come in and record his part and then had Eddie arrive a few hours later. "They used to fight about who was going to go in first and get theirs done so they could go out at night."

527

SHOW & TELL

Peabo Bryson

CAPITOL 44347
WRITER: JERRY FULLER
PRODUCERS: SIR DEAN GANT, PEABO BRYSON
July 1, 1989 (1 week)

"I was a big fan of one particular record by Gladys Knight, 'Neither One of Us' [see 143], and so was Johnny [Mathis]," says songwriter Jerry Fuller. "He said we've got to have something like that." So Fuller wrote a song called "Show and Tell" and produced it for Mathis. It was released as a single on Columbia in 1973. "The record company really didn't get behind it and lost it," Fuller maintains. "I think they took it off the market after three weeks."

Fuller still believed in the song, and when Larry Uttal at Bell Records asked him to produce Al Wilson, Fuller decided to record the song with him. It was less than a year after the Mathis version failed. Fuller produced Wilson's version at Larrabee Studios in West Hollywood. "A man named Dennis Parker came up with that bass riff in there, which I think is the charm of that record," says Fuller. Wilson, who had already charted with "The Snake," took "Show and Tell" to number 10 on the R&B chart and to Number One on the Hot 100 in 1974.

In 1988, Fuller was invited to perform at the National Academy of Songwriters' annual Salute to the American Songwriter. He sang a medley of hits he had written for Ricky Nelson, as well as "Show and Tell." Sitting in the audience that night was Tom Vickers, then an A&R director for Capitol Records.

That same year, Peabo Bryson returned to Capitol Records after a stint with Elektra. His first album was underway when Vickers was assigned to the project. "I flew down to Atlanta and met with him and Dean Gant, who was the co-producer with Peabo," Vickers recalls. "I went over the material and they had a lot of good songs, but I felt they were lacking that one instant radio song to open the door and lead the way for the rest of the album to be discovered...Peabo and I were talking about the great vocalists that had influenced him and I said there are a lot of songs that seem to be resurfacing, like the Manhattans' [remake of] 'You Send Me.' "

Vickers asked Bryson if there were any Sam Cooke songs he wanted to remake and gave him a copy of Cooke's anthology album. "Peabo mentioned there was a song he always loved called 'Show and Tell,' " says Vickers, who remembered the Al Wilson version as well as Fuller's rendition at the NAS concert. Vickers found a copy and had it sent overnight to Bryson. Everyone agreed it would be the perfect song to cover.

"It's one of those rare occasions when an artist decides he's going to do something," Bryson says. "It's one of the songs that's touched my heart and become ingrained in my mind—I think probably because of what it meant to me when Al Wilson did it, remembering who I was, where I was, and what I was doing at that particular point. It held a personal kind of magic and emotional attachment."

Bryson credits Gant for coming up with an '80s version of the song. "You have to be very careful about doing a melody that is recognizable, in that you have to bring it into the '80s without compromising the quality or the content...We wanted to give it a hip kind of beat, but not take it someplace where you couldn't sing it and have it feel the same way, give you the same range of emotions, and have it build the way that it builds."

Bryson was not surprised it became his first Number One single. "The moment that Dean and I got together about the arrangement and the approach, we kind of knew. It's one of those rare occasions where you know you have something special. It was done very well and approached in a very smart and respectful manner. I think that great songs deserve that kind of consideration."

528

KEEP ON MOVIN'

Soul II Soul

VIRGIN 99205
WRITER: BERESFORD ROMEO
PRODUCERS: JAZZIE B, NELLEE HOOPER
July 8, 1989 (2 weeks)

By his own definition, Beresford Romeo, born in Britain of Antiguan parents, is not a musician. "I've never wanted anyone to spring me into that category," the man known better as Jazzie B told Paolo Hewitt in *Select.* "I'm a DJ and even my show is delivering the same vibes as being a DJ."

Jazzie B complains that many people take DJs for granted. "But they're probably as important as a record producer in terms of making a record happen," he believes. "It's almost like being a chemist or scientist where you put all the various elements together and come up with a formula."

Soul II Soul was born after Jazzie B completed high school and worked as a tape operator for a recording studio in London. In the evenings, he took his own sound system to West Indian house parties in London, where dancers paid admission to get in, and warehouse parties in London's East End. Jazzie B's partner, Philip "Daddae" Harvey, came up with the name Soul II Soul in order for them to market their services.

In 1985, Soul II Soul was hired by Nellee Hooper, a member of Bristol's Massive Attack, to bring their sound equipment to a London gig. Jazzie B thought he was being hired as a DJ, and the misunderstanding resulted in "a huge row" between Hooper and Jazzie B. Later, over a few drinks in a local pub, they became friends and Hooper was invited to join Soul II Soul.

Within a year, they gave up the underground scene for a more legal venture: playing music on Sunday nights at the Africa Centre in Covent Garden. That's where they met aspiring vocalists Rose Windross and Caron Wheeler. Given some free studio time in 1987, Jazzie B recorded a single, "Fairplay," and shopped it to 10 Records, a subsidiary of Virgin. Windross was the featured vocalist on the song, which peaked at number 63 in the U.K. "Feel Free," the follow-up, reached number 64. Meanwhile, the Soul II Soul collective expanded to sell popular fashions, including T-shirts, at their own shops in Camden Town and in the West End on Tottenham Court Road.

It was the third single, "Keep on Movin'," that took the group to number five in Great Britain. Jazzie B explains, "It started when I was running a nightclub in London and the police tried to close us down...[It] was a very big social event. We had to stand our ground and 'Keep on movin'.' "

Caron Wheeler was brought in as a backing vocalist for "Keep on Movin'." A singer since the age of 12, she had already done background vocals for Phil Collins, Erasure, and Elvis Costello when she was invited to work with Soul II Soul. Jazzie B loved her voice ("She's probably the most outstanding singer I've ever worked with") and promoted her to lead vocalist on "Keep on Movin.' "

The combination of reggae rhythm and dance shuffle propelled "Keep on Movin' " to the top of the American R&B chart, a rare feat for a British soul band. The track proved to be very influential on musicians on both sides of the pond. "A year later, everyone copied the record," says Jazzie B. "It's still quite flattering...Every day, you turn on the radio or MTV and someone's using the beats or someone's lifting this bit or the other."

529

TURNED AWAY

Chuckii Booker

ATLANTIC 88917
WRITERS: CHUCKII BOOKER,
DONNELL SPENCER, JR.
PRODUCER: CHUCKII BOOKER
July 22, 1989 (1 week)

Chuckii Booker was inspired to play piano at age seven by his mother, a gospel pianist. At 13, he became enamored of jazz, thanks to his Uncle Darnell, a jazz flautist who turned him on to Bob James, Hubert Laws, Richard Tee, Miles Davis, and Herbie Hancock. Barry White was also a major influence—and Booker's godfather.

Chuckii's best friend, Rex Salas, was a keyboard player for the group Tease ("Firestarter"), and when he left to tour with Jeffrey Osborne, he asked Booker to fill in for him. Chuckii played on their second and third albums, and wrote some songs for the group. Saxophonist Gerald Albright asked Booker to play on his album, and in November of 1988, Booker decided it was time to make his own statement. He submitted a tape of instrumental jams to Albright's manager, Raymond Shields, without realizing that the other side of the tape contained homemade demos of Booker singing his own material. Shields loved what he heard, agreed to manage Booker, and signed him to Atlantic Records.

Chuckii went to work on his first album. One of his collaborators was Donnell Spencer Jr., who had also played in Albright's band. "We hooked up and always used to joke about writing together," says Booker. "I was finishing up my album and came up with this track and Donnell came in and said, 'Man, this track is really serious. Do you have any lyrical ideas for it?' " Booker didn't, and Spencer came up with the words "Turned away" as the hook. Chuckii continues, "I took what he had and restructured it, focused it to put more emphasis on the person who we were talking to, rather than it being the story of a guy who was sulking all over the place and feeling bad. I changed it to where it didn't sound like he was drowning in his own tears."

Booker played all of the instruments on the track. "I cut it in one day," he says. "Earlier in my career, I would have these ideas and I would pay time to go into the studio and create a song right there on the spot. Sometimes when I go into the studio, I don't even know what I'm going to cut. I put a drum beat together and then I'll think of a bass line and then I'll start building the song. Before I know it, I have an actual track. Then I'll start thinking of different melodies and ideas for vocals."

Booker didn't expect "Turned Away" to be a hit, much less Number One. Sylvia Rhone, then in Atlantic's A&R department, picked the track as a single. "I knew it was such a different song at the time," says Chuckii. "It didn't sound like anything else. I figured no one would really accept it. But they did, and that made me feel good. And it made me continue to start thinking about doing different things, not always being the norm."

530

SHOWER ME WITH YOUR LOVE

Surface

COLUMBIA 68746
WRITER: BERNARD JACKSON
PRODUCERS: DAVID "PIC" CONLEY, DAVID TOWNSEND, BERNARD JACKSON
July 29, 1989 (1 week)

Bernard Jackson wrote "Shower Me with Your Love" not for his group Surface, but for a female singer signed to RCA. As he worked on the song, he said, "Wait a minute—this is sounding good. Change a lyric here, change a lyric there—I think maybe I could try this for me and see what happens."

He played it for the other two members of Surface over the telephone. David "Pic" Conley remembers his reaction: "I said, 'Bernard, do you know we're getting ready to do a Surface record?' He said, 'Yeah.' I said, 'Well, why are you doing something like this on her? Sorry, but I say we should be doing that one.' We ended up doing it because Dave [Townsend] felt the same way I did. We almost like cursed [Bernard] out. 'What are you doing? Are you crazy?' "

Jackson's position was understandable. "Shower Me with Your Love" was not a typical Surface song—not then. "Before 'Shower Me with Your Love,' there were no standard types of ballads that were on a Surface record,' Bernard points out. "And that one I knew without a doubt was a standard type of song."

The original tracks for "Shower Me with Your Love" were laid down in California, at the apartment of Jackson's friend Brian Simpson. A truck with a 24-track studio inside was parked in front of the building and all of the instruments were hooked up into the mobile recording unit. "Brian played all the basic tracks," Bernard remembers. "Then we sent the tape to New Jersey and Townsend put on a guitar. Pic put on a saxophone and I did the vocals, and Bobby Wooten put on string arrangements. Bob Brockman did some cymbal swells."

Jackson believes anyone can sing the song. "Male, female, it doesn't matter—the message is just as strong and you can reach a mass of people...It's colorless, it's ageless, and that's the type of thing I try to do with my writing anyway." Jackson had proof positive of the universal message of his song when it played a prominent role in the life of a comatose young girl with meningitis. "Her mother played 'Shower Me with Your Love' for her over and over and over and over, and she woke up...I don't think you can ask for a better reward, because I hope to write music that makes people happy, and that made me happy...I was even able to talk with the girl after. It was 6:30 in the morning and I had just gotten in around five. I was a mess, but I did get to speak to her, and I was glad she was alright. That's what music is about."

"Shower Me with Your Love" gave the trio a new image, but Conley says he doesn't mind people thinking of Surface as a group that specializes in ballads. "That's what made us famous," he says, attributing the success of the group to Bernard's voice. "We try to keep his voice very soft and sultry and kind of romantic. That's the way he is and we don't try to break him out of being what he is. We don't try to make a carburetor a gas tank."

531

ON OUR OWN

Bobby Brown

MCA 53662
WRITERS: L.A. REID, BABYFACE, DARYL SIMMONS
PRODUCERS: L.A. REID, BABYFACE
August 5, 1989 (1 week)

Ray Parker Jr. was certain he'd be asked to record the theme song for the sequel to *Ghostbusters*, and he planned to let the producers know he wanted a cameo role this time around. But the call to write the title tune for *Ghostbusters II* never came.

Bobby Brown

"It's kind of who's hot at the moment," explains Peter Afterman, one of the music supervisors for the follow-up movie. "With film companies, it's 'How do we get a hit single?' And obviously Bobby Brown at the time was very strong. If Bobby hadn't been willing to do it and we hadn't found somebody else who I felt was very strong, we would have definitely gone back to Ray. It's not that Ray was second-best or second-rate, it's just there's a thirst for the hot new thing."

Afterman had worked with director Ivan Reitman on a few other films, including *Twins,* and was asked what kind of music he thought would suit *Ghostbusters II.* "I suggested R&B, even though Ivan was not that familiar with any of these artists...Ivan was focusing on the rock stuff, but I felt that R&B was the way to go for this movie."

Afterman gave Reitman a copy of Brown's *Don't Be Cruel* album and the director agreed that the artist was a good choice. "We brought him to the set as we were starting to shoot the movie," Afterman recalls. "He was a very shy guy and loved the first *Ghostbusters* movie. He talked to Bill Murray and Dan Aykroyd...Bobby was wearing all kinds of chains around his neck and Bill made a comment, 'How do you hold your neck up with all those chains?' "

After reading the script, Brown said he would like to contribute a couple of songs to the movie. "He came back a second time, which is when he did his little cameo in the movie," says Afterman. "In the trailer, he and Ivan and I sat and talked about various ideas." After that session, Bobby wrote a song for the film called "We're Back." Afterman comments, "There wasn't really a great place for it in the film...[It] was not something Ivan felt was going to work in the movie. 'We're Back' had that funny sort of carnival line in it and I think Ivan may have felt it was funny over funny, as opposed to being a straight kind of R&B song."

The film's other music supervisor, Kathy Nelson, brought Peter a song written by L.A. Reid and Babyface. "I thought the song could really work for the movie," says Afterman. "I felt with a lyric change, it would be really great." Reid and Babyface wrote new lyrics to the song, changing the title from "On My Own" to "On Our Own."

It was a song that Babyface was originally going to record himself. "That was a difficult one, because we got the deal to do it and Bobby had written a song for *Ghostbusters* and he wanted his song to be the first single," Reid recalls. "So he was a little resistant about doing it. When he came to the studio, I detected a little bit of an attitude and I didn't know exactly where it was coming from at the time. I think it took him to get in the studio and get behind the mike and start singing to realize this was a major hit for him. I don't think he felt it at first, although we thought it was good from the very beginning."

532

BATDANCE

Prince

WARNER BROS. 22924
WRITER: PRINCE
PRODUCER: PRINCE
AUGUST 12, 1989 (1 week)

The Purple One had the Caped Crusader to thank for his sixth Number One single. It was a perfect match, as both were signed to Warner Brothers—Prince to the label, Batman to Warner subsidiary DC Comics in New York.

"We wanted to have a superstar artist and we wanted to keep it in the family, meaning the family of labels," says Gary LeMel, president of Warner Brothers Music. "We started seeing dailies, and it so happened that the Joker character was dressed in purple. The cars were purple. It started to point to Prince." LeMel approached Albert Magnoli, who was managing the artist at the time. Magnoli, who directed *Purple Rain* for the studio, loved the idea of his client being matched up with the Dark Knight, a character filled with conflict and haunted by his past.

Prince hopped on a Concorde in January 1989 to meet director Tim Burton on the set of *Batman* at Pinewood Studios, about 35 minutes outside of London. Burton was already using Prince's "1999" and "Baby I'm a Star" on a temporary soundtrack.

Prince met the actors playing Batman and Vicki Vale—Michael Keaton and Kim Basinger. He observed a scene being shot in the Batcave and watched about 40 minutes of rough footage. "He loved what he saw," LeMel reports. "He and Tim got along great. And there were three or four spots in the movie that were definitely song spots. They were written into the film—it wasn't like we were trying to jam anything in. One thing Tim would never do is put something in that wasn't part of the fabric."

Prince was supposed to continue on to Paris for a vacation, but was so enthused over the project, he flew home to Minneapolis to write songs. LeMel travelled to the Paisley Park complex and listened to the new material. "He had written songs that were in places that were really 'score' places, yet they were brilliantly done. But Tim wanted the big *Batman* score, and the songs to be where they were supposed to be."

A month later, Prince played eight songs for Burton. The director turned down three songs and asked for two additional tunes. The "Batdance" single, a pastiche of music, sounds, and dialogue featuring the voices of Keaton, Basinger, and Jack Nicholson, was not actually heard in the soundtrack. Prince put the track together overnight. LeMel continues: "He called us and said, 'You gotta hear this.' We heard it and flipped out. We knew it would never be in the movie but everyone thought, what a great marketing tool for giving the public an insight into the film. At that point, people had seen the teaser trailer, but hadn't heard any of the dialogue."

To illustrate the song, Prince filmed a video in which he played himself and Gemini, a half-Batman/half-Joker character.

After the success of "Batdance," Prince continued to mine the *Batman* soundtrack for more singles. "Partyman" peaked at number five, but "The Arms of Orion," a duet with Sheena Easton, failed to chart R&B. "Scandalous!," on the other hand, failed to make the pop chart, but sailed to number five R&B.

533

SOMETHING IN THE WAY (YOU MAKE ME FEEL)

Stephanie Mills

MCA 53624
WRITER: ANGELA WINBUSH
PRODUCER: ANGELA WINBUSH
August 19, 1989 (1 week)

Stephanie Mills was a mere child when she first sang in public, at the Cornerstone Baptist Church in Brooklyn. "I was baptized in church at seven years old," she says. "My mom took us to church every Sunday and to bible school, and then at the age of nine I auditioned for the musical play *Maggie Flynn*, and that's what really started my professional career."

At age 11 she competed and won in "The Amateur Hour" at the Apollo Theater in Harlem. That led to a six-week stint opening for the Isley Brothers. "I became really good friends with Ronnie [Isley]," says Stephanie. Years later, Ronnie became the manager of writer/producer/artist Angela Winbush, who co-wrote Stephanie's first Number One single [see 426—"I Have Learned to Respect the Power of Love"].

"I called him up and told him I really wanted to work with Angela," says Mills. "He made that possible and that's when we went in and did 'Something in the Way (You Make Me Feel).' I think Angela is an incredible and gifted songwriter and producer. I don't think she's had her due as a producer. She's wonderful to work with because she knows her work, she does her homework, and she knows how to tell you exactly what she wants, and then she allows you to deliver it with your own style."

The first time Mills took a Winbush song to Number One, it was a composition that had been written for someone else. This time, the song was written especially for Stephanie. "She played me a demo," Mills recalls. "She was singing and it was just her and a piano. But Angela can sing, so I got a very good idea of what the song was about and what direction she wanted to go with it."

Mills didn't find it difficult to sing the number in her own style, even though the songwriter was producing it. "She gives you so much freedom," Stephanie enthuses. "She's really accommodating. I know when I go into the studio, I work long hours because I like doing my own backgrounds and I like singing with myself and doing ad-libs with myself. So that takes up a lot of time. So you just have to be prepared, but she's very, very professional."

"Something in the Way (You Make Me Feel)" was the first single released from Stephanie's third MCA album, *Home*. The album featured Mills working with a number of different producers in addition to Winbush, including Teddy Riley, Nick Martinelli, LeMel Humes, Gerald Levert and Marc Gordon of Levert, Timmy Gatling, Wayne Brathwaite, and Barry Eastmond.

It was the *Home* album that helped Stephanie to define the type of songs she prefers to sing. "I came from *The Wiz* singing ballads, and when you think of my Number One R&B songs, most of them have been ballads. I think people expect me to sing ballads but they also like my mid-tempos like 'Something in the Way' and '(You're Puttin') A Rush on Me.' And at this time in my career, I've realized that 'Rush' and 'Something in the Way' are my up-tempos and I have to stick to my ballads. That's what my audience wants to hear."

534

IT'S NO CRIME

Babyface

SOLAR 68966
WRITERS: L.A. REID, BABYFACE, DARYL SIMMONS
PRODUCERS: L.A. REID, BABYFACE
August 26, 1989 (2 weeks)

It must have been difficult for Kenny Edmonds—nicknamed Babyface by Bootsy Collins to Kenny's initial chagrin—to gather enough songs for his second Solar album, *Tender Lover*. As fast as he could write them with his partner Antonio "L.A." Reid, he gave them away—to artists like Bobby Brown, Johnny Gill, the Mac Band, Karyn White, Pebbles, Paula Abdul, and a host of others.

Reid gives his partner Babyface the same consideration he gives any other performer. "I look at it from a producer's standpoint...I look at it as what's best for the artist. Whether it be Bobby Brown, Whitney Houston, or Toni Braxton. What song fits what artist? It's very easy for me. I'm usually correct when I say I think a song is for him or isn't. I usually base it on when [Babyface] performs it—if he goes in the studio and attempts to do a song, within the first five minutes I will know 'this is for him' or 'no, this isn't really for him.' And I'll be very honest and tell him."

The first single released from *Tender Lover* was "It's No Crime." The artist, who had already been in the top five in 1988 when he sang on "Two Occasions" by his group the Deele, says the song originated when he started humming something and it slipped out. "Usually when I start writing something, I hum words that aren't even words—maybe it sounded like 'It's No Crime' at the time. It was really different because it was something for my album and it wasn't something I would normally do."

Babyface

Babyface is credited with playing all of the instruments on the track, with a little help from his friends: the bass guitar and bass synth were provided by Kayo (who was also in the Deele), percussion was by De'Rock, and drums and percussion were courtesy of Reid. "The thing I remember about 'It's No Crime' was the industrial-sounding beat that we started with," says L.A. "That's how the song was creatively driven. I remember it translating into the video—we started doing the video in an industrial environment. For some reason, when I think of 'It's No Crime,' the first thing that comes to my mind is industrial noise."

Babyface didn't expect the song to reach Number One. "When we were recording it, we felt good about it but we weren't sure because it was different for us. We weren't sure what it was going to do. It wasn't a record you finished and said, 'OK, this is a Number One,' because it was questionable."

Edmonds had visited the Number One position several times as a writer and producer before "It's No Crime," notably with the Whispers, Pebbles, the Mac Band, Bobby Brown, Karyn White, and the Boys.

His first chart-topper as an artist didn't feel very different from his successes as a writer/producer. "I get as much gratification out of being a writer for someone else," he attests.

There was one difference working with Face as an artist as opposed to performers who weren't equal partners in writing and producing, says Reid. "If he makes a decision or a choice about something, I don't have to go along with it, but being that it's him, [he gets] 50 percent of the vote. [If it were] any other artist, it would just be their opinion."

MY FANTASY

Teddy Riley featuring Guy

MOTOWN 1968
WRITERS: TEDDY RILEY, GENE GRIFFIN
PRODUCERS: TEDDY RILEY, GENE GRIFFIN
September 9, 1989 (1 week)

When Spike Lee asked Teddy Riley to quickly come up with a song from Guy for the soundtrack of *Do the Right Thing,* the inventor of new jack swing had just the thing—a song he had written originally for someone else. "He always wanted to do something with us," Riley says of the director. "The song didn't really fit the concept of the movie, but it was a good song to put in there."

Riley wrote "My Fantasy" about "a girl that I would always dream about, so she's just a fantasy to me." It was intended for an artist named Zan, but Teddy took it back. "I said, 'No, you can't have that. I've got to have that song myself because I'm the only one who could bring that song across the way it's supposed to be,' " says Riley. "He tried to sing it [but] it didn't come out right. Aaron [Hall] tried to sing it. He's too strong for it. It needed somebody with an attitude, like Keith Sweat. Because I gave Keith Sweat his style of singing, I figured I can do that, too."

When Guy was formed, Riley had no intention of being the lead singer. "I never knew Aaron sang that well and when we finally got together he didn't want to be the lead singer," Riley told Jock Baird in *Musician.* "I said, 'No, you're the lead singer, we're going to put your voice out there. We're going to give this Guy group a style.' Which we did by using his voice with my new jack swing. We never thought it was going to be this big."

The man who instigated the group was Timmy Gatling, according to Teddy. The original lineup was Gatling, Riley, and Aaron Hall, who Riley had met at church. "Timmy didn't think we were going to make it, so he pursued another career," says Riley. "He left the group and we had to get Aaron's brother, Damian Hall."

Riley confirmed that he was happy to stay in the background. "I would never go out as a solo artist, even though so many people tell me to. I'm a little afraid of getting out onstage by myself. I'm the shy one in the group. I made a commitment not to deal with groups that didn't have the potential to *sing,* that didn't have a voice like Aaron or James Ingram or Johnny Kemp." Teddy compared his singing to Aaron's. "My style is more rappin' and more jumpity. Aaron's more soulful. I grew up with rap—and my way of making it make sense is with good music, with actual singing behind it."

Teddy became interested in music at a very early age, thanks to the support of his parents. "They brought a lot of instruments into the home and I was picking up on everything," he says. "I was one of those kids that pick up anything. I started writing my own songs at the age of 11 with a group by the name of Total Climax, and then I got into a group called Kids at Work."

Riley's uncle built a recording studio at a skating rink he owned on 155th Street, giving Teddy a chance to produce local New York artists like Heavy D. and the Boyz and Mr. Big Stuff.

536

REMEMBER (THE FIRST TIME)

Eric Gable

ORPHEUS 72663
WRITER: LAMONT COWARD
PRODUCER: DARRYL SHEPHERD
September 16, 1989 (1 week)

Eric Gable always thought about a singing career while growing up in New Orleans. A turning point occurred during his senior year in high school, when he won a talent contest by singing Stevie Wonder's "You and I." "One of the things I remember about winning is the response I got from the audience. People were going crazy, jumping up and down. It was really exciting for me, and that night I made up my mind that was what I wanted to do with my life."

Gable was cast in a musical, *Don't Get God Started,* and was seen by a longtime family friend, Willie Turpentine. Willie asked him to call Charles Huggins at Hush Productions, and Gable sang some Freddie Jackson and Luther Vandross songs for him over the phone, a cappella. "He asked me if I could be in New York the next day," Gable recounts. "I got together some funds, auditioned, and two days after I got there, they signed me to a management deal. The next week I was signed to Orpheus Records."

Gable was introduced to an in-house producer at Hush, Darryl Shepherd. Both artist and producer were roughly the same age. "Darryl was my first taskmaster," says the artist. "He worked me and whipped me into shape. It was a pleasure working with him, but he made me work very hard. We hung out together—he let me stay in his apartment for four-and-a-half months while we were recording the first half of the album."

One of the songs that found its way to Gable was "Remember (The First Time)," penned by a songwriter from Richmond, Virginia. Lamont Coward wrote the song while studying engineering in Philadelphia and missing his wife, Mary. "I was a little down and out. I was thinking about my wife often. And it was about four o'clock in the morning when the song came to my mind. I started composing it in the studio and we finished it that very same day and demoed it."

Coward's lawyer sent the demo to Mark Green at Capitol Records, who pitched it to Hush Productions. Gable's reaction: "When I first heard it, I didn't hear it. It had a very open feeling to it, more of a pop style. But once I got in and started singing it myself, I gave it my own thing. It really set a tone for all of the different music that I did on that first album. It had all of the right elements."

The song was the last one recorded for the album and the first one released as a single. Gable was in Tallahassee, Florida, when he received an important phone call. "I got a call about two o'clock in the morning telling me the record had gone to Number One. At the time I really didn't know the importance of having a Number One record, so it was no big deal to me. But now...I see how much work and how much luck it takes to have that happen. It was a wonderful catapult. That song is going to live with me forever."

537

CAN'T GET OVER YOU

Maze featuring Frankie Beverly

WARNER BROS. 22895
WRITER: FRANKIE BEVERLY
PRODUCER: FRANKIE BEVERLY
September 23, 1989 (2 weeks)

After 21 chart singles on Capitol, Maze took three years to regroup. The band members, famous for their live appearances, were exhausted. When Frankie Beverly and company resurfaced, they were signed to Warner Brothers. They came back strong with a new album, *Silky Soul*, and their second Number One hit, "Can't Get Over You."

Beverly believes the song will be considered as one of the group's "classics." "I'm not surprised it went all the way up to Number One, although I think I could have done a better recording of it. It's such a strong song that it overshadowed that." The song was inspired by a relationship that lasted almost eight years. "As in life, [sometimes] things don't work out. It's a song about a guy who can't get over this," Beverly explains. "It was very real, a real-life experience coming from the writer himself. I think that's one of the reasons why it was so strong." Beverly says the song poured out of him. He still talks to the woman it was written about, and although he didn't play it for her before it was released, she loves the song. Did she know it was written for her when she heard it? "I think so," says Beverly. "I never asked her, but it's kind of obvious."

Beverly called in some outside forces for the recording of "Can't Get Over You," including drummer Ricky Lawson and bass player Randy Jackson. "I wasn't quite getting what I wanted with my guys," Beverly says candidly. "The song was so important to me that I did everything I could do to get it exactly where I was trying to get it. So I reached out and grabbed some friends of mine that aren't in the band. Those same two were on 'Back in Stride,' too" [see 403].

"Can't Get Over You" was recorded in Beverly's 16-track home studio, which was new at the time. "I had some of the equipment and it was just a matter of expanding my house to incorporate a studio big enough," he told Ruth A. Robinson. "I brought the entire band in and we played." The line-up of Maze for the session included Vernon Black on lead and rhythm guitar, William Bryant on keyboards and synthesizers, Robin Duhe on bass, Wayne Lindsey on keyboards and synthesizers, Ronald "Roame" Lowry on congas and backing vocals, Ron Smith on lead and rhythm guitar, Michael White on drums, and McKinley "Bug" Williams on percussion and backing vocals. Having the studio in his home gave Beverly a lot of freedom: "I come in naked. You can get up any time of the night. From that point of view, it's been a godsend."

Reaction to "Can't Get Over You" was strong, according to the song's creator. "A lot of people [related to] the title and the intensity and I guess the spirit of it. People automatically knew it was [about] me. They kind of knew. 'Oh man, that must have been you, and I've been there before.' Women mostly, and mostly at the gigs, when I speak to people. That's what I heard a lot, how much people have been through the same thing."

Warner Brothers released the title track of Maze's label debut as the follow-up single. "Silky Soul" peaked at number four. "Love's on the Run" was the next single; it peaked at number 13, followed by "Songs of Love," which stopped at number 34.

538

BACK TO LIFE (HOWEVER DO YOU WANT ME)

Soul II Soul featuring Caron Wheeler

VIRGIN 99171
WRITER: BERESFORD ROMEO
PRODUCER: JAZZIE B
October 7, 1989 (1 week)

After the international success of his first Number One single, Jazzie B was not surprised that his record company wanted another Soul II Soul single featuring the same woman who had sung lead vocals on "Keep on Movin' " [see 528]. But Soul II Soul was less a group than a collective, featuring guest vocalists and musicians who would come and go, and Jazzie B and his partner Nellee Hooper had only one other track featuring Caron Wheeler's voice. "All we had were the a cappella vocals of Caron on 'Back to Life,' " says Jazzie B. "We had to put music to the vocals."

The record company's intent was clear: "What they were looking for was something to market," Jazzie B laughs. "We were quite renowned at that time for doing remixes, so it wasn't a problem for us to do that."

While "Keep on Movin' " was recorded specifically to be a single, "Back to Life" wasn't. As a result, people who bought the album *Keep on Movin'* may have been surprised to find the a cappella version of "Back to Life" rather than the fully produced single that came out later.

Caron Wheeler's success with Soul II Soul resulted in offers for her services as a solo artist. She signed with EMI for North America and RCA in the U.K. To many people who didn't understand that she was a guest vocalist and not a permanent fixture with the group, it appeared that she had split from Soul II Soul after having a couple of hit singles. "I think people misunderstand me moving on to express myself as a 'dis' against Soul II Soul," the singer said in *Blues & Soul*. "It *wasn't*. Basically I was invited to join the group and become a full-time member...If I'd stayed with Jazzie I don't think I'd have been given the space to express myself—not because nobody wanted me to, but basically because I'm a very outspoken person, and some of the things I wanted to say not everyone in the group may have agreed with. I felt it was time I actually started standing up for myself."

The influence Soul II Soul had on both British and American R&B was important to Jazzie B. "What we want to accomplish is for British black music to be taken more seriously," he told David Nathan in *Billboard*. "Being exposed to the British culture produces some different things and it's important for the world to realize that black people in Europe have something unique to offer with all the influences we've had—Caribbean, African, American, and European. We went to a major company like Virgin so we could penetrate the U.S. market and get some form of recognition for what we're doing. British companies hadn't been open to local black music until it became hip to be black. There were those who came before me, like Cymande, David Grant, Light of the World, and Beggar's Banquet, but British black music hasn't really been respected universally."

539

MISS YOU MUCH

Janet Jackson

A&M 1445
WRITERS: JAMES HARRIS III, TERRY LEWIS
PRODUCERS: JIMMY JAM, TERRY LEWIS
October 14, 1989 (2 weeks)

Just as her brother had to deal with the pressure of recording a follow-up to the best-selling album of all time, *Thriller*, Janet Jackson had to face a number of questions after she experienced multi-platinum success with *Control*, an album that gave her five Number One singles.

Would her next album do as well? Would it simply be *Control, Part 2*? Would she return to the Flyte Tyme studios in Minneapolis to work with producers Jimmy Jam and Terry Lewis again?

The answer to that last question might have been no if the lawyers had had their way. "It happens in sports, but after a very successful record or a very successful season, you renegotiate," Jimmy Jam suggests. Because Jam and Lewis and Jackson treated each other as friends, they preferred to let their lawyers and managers work out a new deal. But internal changes at A&M Records and a number of standstills frustrated the artist as well as the production team. "Then she called me one day and said, 'Look, do you want to do the record or not?' I said, 'Well, of course we want to do the record. Do you want us to do the record?' " Janet said yes and both parties directed their attorneys to make a deal. "Magically," Jimmy says, "in two weeks, there was a deal."

Janet arrived in Minneapolis in September of 1988, excited to go back to work. Jam and Lewis had several tracks ready for her to hear when she walked into Flyte Tyme. "I was working on the track to 'Miss You Much,' and she walked into the studio as I was putting down a keyboard part," says Jimmy Jam. "I pointed at the keyboard and gave her the key of the song, and she ended up doing the string part that actually made the record. That was the way we started off the album."

"Miss You Much" was the only track that Jam and Lewis already had a lyrical idea for, but Jackson didn't record her lead vocals during this visit. Jimmy explains: "The idea was to do the backgrounds first to get her voice back in tip-top singing shape, because she hadn't sung for probably two years."

Janet recorded the backing vocals for several tracks and then returned home to Los Angeles, where she stayed through the Christmas holiday season. During that period, Jam and Lewis continued their production work. Janet returned to Minneapolis in February of '89 and recording continued intensely for the next four months.

Jimmy Jam's girlfriend inspired the producer to write the lyric to "Miss You Much." "She wrote me a letter and said at the end of it, 'Miss you much,' and I thought that was a cool title." Jam and Lewis knew Janet liked the song by the smile on her face. "I think her strong point is doing melodies," the producer says. "We thought 'Miss You Much' had a real catchy melody. It made you feel good—it was a happy song."

540

BABY COME TO ME

Regina Belle

COLUMBIA 68969
WRITERS: NARADA MICHAEL WALDEN, JEFFREY COHEN
PRODUCER: NARADA MICHAEL WALDEN
October 28, 1989 (1 week)

Growing up in Englewood, New Jersey, Regina Belle was surrounded by music right from childhood. Her mother sang in a church choir, her father was in a professional singing group, and she was "glued to the TV" for the Grammys, *American Bandstand*, and *Soul Train*. She also remembers being "turned on to the Temptations" before she was five years old.

As a college student, she sang the black national anthem before an Mtume and Lisa Lisa concert. "Vaughn Harper, a radio personality in New York for the 'Quiet Storm,' heard me and asked me to give him a call," says Regina. "I didn't think anything of it...I never called him. He called me for some studio work and I blew him off. Then he called me again and asked if I was free to do [a session] the following weekend, so I said, 'Maybe he's serious.' "

Regina Belle

Regina ended up singing all of the background parts at the session and impressed Harper enough to have him recommend her to the Manhattans [see 244—"Kiss and Say Goodbye"] when they were auditioning female vocalists.

After touring with the Manhattans and working on their *Too Hot to Stop It* and *Back to Basics* albums, Regina signed to Columbia as a solo artist. For her first album, *All by Myself,* Regina worked with producer Nick Martinelli. For her second disc, *Stay with Me,* she re-teamed with Martinelli and also recorded with producers Barry Eastmond and Narada Michael Walden.

"Narada is an absolute angel," says Regina, recalling the sessions. "He's a hard worker, though. He pushes you a lot. It was a lot different working with him than Nick. He wants a thousand different versions so he can take that one part and say, 'OK, I'm going to use this.' "

Walden first met songwriter Jeffrey Cohen through producer David Rubinson at the Automat Studios in San Francisco. "I wasn't so into Jeff because I thought he was more of a country kind of cat," says Walden. "But when we got together I realized he could do everything I wanted him to do, and I aspired [for us] to be like the Burt Bacharach and Hal David of the '80s."

Walden and Cohen wrote "Baby Come to Me," the first track Walden produced for Belle. " 'Baby Come to Me' was done in my Tarpan Studios," says Walden. "I was at my keyboards. Walter Afanasieff helped me cut the tracks." Afanasieff played keyboards and bass and programmed the drums. Ren Klyce programmed the Fairlight CMI and Premik Russell Tubbs played the sax solo. Background vocals were provided by Kitty Beethoven, Claytoven Richardson, Melisa Kary, and Skyler Jett.

Walden brought Belle to Lahaina Sound on Maui in Hawaii to record her vocals. "I wanted her to experience and sound as romantic as possible," says the producer. "That really helped capture the mood." Belle did enjoy the ambience Walden created. "When you go in the studio, you have dim lights. You have candlelight. You have a beautiful bouquet of flowers. He tries to make a setting for you that's so wonderful that you don't have anything to concentrate on but singing."

"If you don't do the small things, you don't get the big things," Walden suggests. "I believe in comfort. I believe in luxury." He also believes in Regina Belle. "Regina is an unparalleled vocalist...When I first worked with her in Hawaii on those early sessions for 'Baby Come to Me,' I thought she was the reincarnation of Billie Holiday. I thought if Billie Holiday was alive now with her pipes and everything cool, it would be like Regina Belle. So I thought I was working with a modern-day Billie Holiday."

541

YOU ARE MY EVERYTHING

Surface

COLUMBIA 69016
WRITERS: DAVID "PIC" CONLEY, EVERETT COLLINS, DERRICK CULLER, DAVID TOWNSEND
PRODUCERS: DAVID "PIC" CONLEY, BERNARD JACKSON
November 4, 1989 (2 weeks)

Columbia Records continued to mine Surface's *2nd Wave* album for hits by releasing "You Are My Everything." A wise move—it was the third Number One single from the group's sophomore album.

The lyrics to "You Are My Everything" were at one time destined to be matched up with the music for Surface's first Number One hit, "Closer Than Friends." "Dave [Townsend] got a little angry at me because he had the original music to 'Closer Than Friends' and he thought I was going to put that hook [to "You Are My Everything"] on top of that music," explains David "Pic" Conley. "So everything happens for a reason. 'Closer Than Friends' went on to be a Number One song and 'You Are My Everything' went on this other music, which ended up to be a Number One song."

Conley and Townsend were working on fitting the lyrics to a new piece of music when the third member of Surface, Bernard Jackson, was out of town. So they called in their friend Derrick Culler to help them finish the lyrics. "We had Derrick do the demo for Bernard," Conley says. "I remember Bernard being very uncomfortable with the song. It was out of his key. But Dave convinced him the song was a hit. And he said, 'If we need to change the key for you, we will.' But at that point Bernard got stronger and said, 'Nah, don't change the key. Keep it like that.' So he stretched his voice to fit the song... Because he was so uncomfortable, I stayed out of the way. I showed Dave what to do, how to hit the buttons...so Dave actually engineered Bernard's lead vocal on that song. When I came downstairs and listened to it, it wasn't quite right for me. I pointed out a couple of different spots where I thought it could be improved upon, and that got Bernard even madder. But [he] wasn't mad because I was telling him. It was...'Damn, I tried so hard and still didn't get it right.' Bernard's a perfectionist, so he went after it very strong. The next thing you know he did it and didn't hear any difference, but there was a big difference. I felt like it was a hit song when it was completed, even before we put the arrangements on top, the flutes and all the pretty stuff."

Ironically, "You Are My Everything" knocked Regina Belle's "Baby Come to Me" out of Number One, but she couldn't have minded. She was featured as a guest vocalist on the Surface single. "She's a good friend of ours and we were labelmates," Conley relates. "As strong as she was and as wonderful a vocalist as she is, she would always call me up and say, 'Pic, I want to sing on a Surface album.' I never took her seriously. She called me once too many times and I said, 'We're working on the album right now. You want to sing on this record?' " Regina said yes, but Conley says he couldn't convince the other two members of Surface to have Regina sing a duet on the album. "We brought her down and once she got there she started to sing around on the song. We liked it so much, we wanted her to do another song. So we randomly dug in the barrel and pulled out a song, 'Hold On to Love,' and said, 'Do the same thing to this song.' "

Bernard says he enjoyed recording with Regina. "She's a Cancer girl and I'm a Cancer. She's crazy, I'm crazy," he says. "You don't even work with Regina. You just have fun."

542

DON'T TAKE IT PERSONAL

Jermaine Jackson

ARISTA 9875
WRITERS: DAVID CONLEY, DERRICK CULLER, DAVID TOWNSEND
PRODUCERS: DAVID TOWNSEND, DAVID "PIC" CONLEY
November 18, 1989 (1 week)

"That was a year I'll never forget," says David "Pic" Conley, speaking of 1989. "You see, L.A. [Reid] and Babyface and Terry [Lewis] and Jimmy Jam with two songs on the chart...I got an opportunity that's very rare...to have two songs go Number One back-to-back."

Conley really didn't mind if Jermaine Jackson knocked "You Are My Everything" by Surface off the top of the chart; sure, Conley was one-third of Surface, and he was one of the writers and producers of their third Number One hit, but he also co-wrote and produced Jermaine's second chart-topper of his career and his first for Arista, "Don't Take It Personal."

"I had been trying to get next to Clive Davis over at Arista for about two years," Conley reports. "We had been working on trying to get some songs over to Whitney and various artists, even Jermaine. We tried Jermaine countless times and ended up with zilch. He just didn't like our songs." Erik Nuri, who signed Surface to Columbia when he was with that label, moved to Arista's A&R department and called Conley.

Jermaine Jackson

"He said he was working on a project that was very very very very big and was getting ready to break all kinds of records. It was Milli Vanilli." Nuri wanted to know if Conley had any songs for the duo, and Conley offered a demo of one he had written with David Townsend of Surface and Derrick Culler. Conley heard back that Clive Davis liked "Don't Take It Personal," inspired by Culler's relationship with his ex-wife. The Arista label chief sent it to Milli Vanilli. "The next thing you know I'm getting calls from Germany from this producer Frank Farian, and he was trying to work it out so I could produce the music here and send the tapes to Germany and have them sing the song. I wasn't accustomed to doing things like that." Conley insisted on flying to Germany and says Farian insisted that he not.

Clive called Conley and David Townsend to his office to discuss the matter. According to Conley, he said, "I apologize for these guys not treating you properly and with respect because I know you need to be there...But this group is going to be so big that this is a financial decision...You make up your mind and tell me what you want to do and I'll respect it." Conley gave a final "no" to the Milli Vanilli deal, and Davis asked if he would be interested in cutting the song on another Arista artist—Jermaine Jackson.

Conley explains that Jackson, who could have cut the song anywhere, asked to use the same studio where Surface recorded their *2nd Wave* album. "He came to my house, [to] a raggedy little studio built in a dining room." Conley was impressed that Jackson already knew the song when he arrived. "He had all the lyrics memorized. He knew exactly how he wanted to do it," Conley recalls.

Conley admits that writing and producing "Don't Take It Personal" did a lot for his career. But if he could go back and change things, would he give the song to Milli Vanilli instead of Jackson? "Sure, we had a Number One with Jermaine, but it didn't sell a million records. Here comes Milli Vanilli with six million albums, right?" Conley thinks for a moment. "If I knew what I do now, of course I would! 'Bye, Jermaine!' "

HOME

Stephanie Mills

MCA 53712
WRITER: CHARLIE SMALLS
PRODUCER: NICK MARTINELLI
November 25, 1989 (1 week)

That song and *The Wiz* will stay with me forever," says Stephanie Mills, who was a 15-year-old from Brooklyn when she was cast as Dorothy in the black Broadway musical version of *The Wizard of Oz*.

"That song" is "Home," the show's emotional finale. There were different emotions associated with the song when Mills recorded it for her 1989 album *Home*. Ken Harper, producer of *The Wiz*, had passed away from complications associated with AIDS, and Charlie Smalls, composer and lyricist for the show, had died of kidney failure. "When they passed away, I felt that I wanted to sing that song in dedication to them," says Mills. "I also didn't want the world to lose sight of how talented Charlie Smalls and Ken Harper were. And I wanted to thank them for giving me my 'yellow brick road,' so to speak, because that's such a great song and Charlie Smalls was such a great writer. It was an emotional time for me in the studio—we had to stop a couple of times because as I was singing it, I would think of them and think of the time we had getting *The Wiz* off the ground back in '75 and no one thought we'd last through the years. We lasted five years after that. So there's a lot of emotional ties to that song."

After singing the song on stage several times a week for five years, Mills was happy to drop it from her solo act when *The Wiz* was over. "I started doing it again in concert because so many people asked for it," she says. "Everywhere I would go in concert, people would yell out, 'We want to hear "Home." ' I had stopped singing it because I was really tired of *The Wiz* and that whole image of me, and wanted to shed that. After talking to some friends in the business, I realized that being a part of *The Wiz* was actually a blessing and that I shouldn't try to rid myself of that."

The 1989 version differed only slightly from the 1975 original cast recording. "I wanted to update it a little, but not too much, because the song was so wonderful the way it was," Stephanie explains. "I wanted to sing it better than I sang it on the cast album, but I also wanted to make it a dedication to my friends. I wanted it to be produced really well and I knew Nick [Martinelli] would do a great job."

"Stephanie had an idea in mind for it and sent me a rough of it which had the talking in front," says

Stephanie Mills

Martinelli. "I had a programmer in Philadelphia named Jim Salamone. He came up with the basic arrangement and then I did a lot of live stuff on it too—strings and live guitar and bass and all that." The musical personnel included Douglas Grisby (bass), Randy Bowland (guitars), Donald Robinson (keyboards), and Curtis Dowd (synthesizers). The vocal group Take 6 sang backgrounds.

"We did a few takes the first time she was there," the producer recalls. "She wound up coming back again because neither of us was happy with it. And the second time we got it."

After "Home" became the second song from a Broadway musical to hit Number One on the R&B chart [see 362—"And I Am Telling You I'm Not Going"], Mills did something she never thought she would do—she agreed to play Dorothy again in a touring company of *The Wiz*. "Your audience really lets you know how they want to see you," she says. "On every plane I would be on, a stewardess or someone would ask me, 'When are you going to do *The Wiz* again?' And I would say, 'Don't you think I'm too old to do that?' 'Oh no, you don't look too old.' To be able to do it again at 36, I was thrilled and my reviews were quite kind. Outside of the original cast, the third cast of *The Wiz* for me was the best."

544
HERE AND NOW
Luther Vandross

EPIC 73029
WRITERS: TERRY STEELE, DAVID L. ELLIOTT
PRODUCERS: LUTHER VANDROSS, MARCUS MILLER
December 2, 1989 (2 weeks)

Luther Vandross was hanging out at the home of his friend Dionne Warwick, playing Pac-Man, when her son David Elliott walked in the room and offered to play his new demos for him. "He played a song and then he played 'Here and Now,' then he played another song and I said, 'Wait. Play that middle song again,' " Vandross recalls.

Elliott complied and Luther said, "Wait a minute. Wait a minute. Play that again." David played it again. "I said to myself, 'Am I hearing what I think I'm hearing?' " Vandross, who writes his own material except for cover versions of hits like "A House Is Not a Home" and "Superstar," loved David's song. "A song is like—even when I write them—an article of clothing. When Raquel Welch likes a dress, it's because she sees the dress and places herself in the dress in her mind and says, 'Oh yeah, this oughta work.' Now you get it on and you make a few adjustments here and there, and a few nips and tucks, but a song is very much the same. I wear it and I consider that I wear it and you nip it and tuck it to make it work for me. I kind of Lutherize it."

Vandross explains that the demo he heard was very different from his final version of the song. "It's similar to the way Aretha Franklin perceived 'I Say a Little Prayer' by Dionne." A lot of the song in the demo was implied, according to Luther. "You know, 'Here and now' and then that space right there before 'I promise...,' that's what appealed to me. Just the fact that someone had enough nerve to not fill in that space killed me. I said, 'That's me. I don't care who wrote this. I love this.' It didn't matter that I didn't write it."

"Here and Now" was recorded along with "Treat You Right" at the Hit Factory in New York and Westlake Studios in Hollywood. They were the two new songs added to *The Best of Luther Vandross...The Best of Love*, a double-CD compilation of greatest hits. "Nat's [Adderley Jr.] string arrangement, needless to say, was startling," Luther says with admiration. "It was gorgeous. I added the bridge. And the background vocals...wow. We went into New York and we got Cissy Houston and Tawatha Agee, Paulette McWilliams and Brenda White, and Lisa Fischer and Fonzi Thornton. So we got a major A-team thing happening."

"Here and Now" became Luther's fifth Number One single and a very popular song for weddings. "One of the biggest wedding songs, which is great," says the artist. "The other day, I had come from my dentist's office, and this was in a building where you park and you stop and pay the parking fee. And this girl comes running over...all out of breath. She says, 'I just wanted to ask you one question. I'm getting married in a month. How much do you charge to sing "Here and Now"?' It was the cutest thing I'd ever heard anybody ask me. So I just said, 'Wow, that song really works for weddings.' It really does. I definitely get requests to come and sing that song at weddings."

545
AIN'T NUTHIN' IN THE WORLD
Miki Howard

ATLANTIC 88826
WRITERS: JON NETTLESBY, TERRY COFFEY
PRODUCERS: JON NETTLESBY, TERRY COFFEY
December 16, 1989 (1 week)

Miki Howard was just shy of being eight months pregnant when she recorded "Ain't Nuthin' in the World" with writers/producers Jon Nettlesby and Terry Coffey for her third Atlantic album. "Every time the baby moves, you get a different sound out of her voice, because it's uncomfortable," explains

Nettlesby. "On some songs she was sitting in a chair bent over, holding her stomach, feet up, singing into a microphone, just blowing...and sometimes she would just be in the mood to go shopping, so we did a lot of shopping for baby clothes when we should have been in the studio recording. By the time we finished, the baby was ready to drop."

Howard, Nettlesby, and Coffey were all natives of Chicago. Miki's mother sang with the Gospel Caravan and her father was in the Pilgrim Jubilees. As a child, Miki sang gospel with the Rev. James Cleveland. She was nine when her family brought her to Los Angeles. At 15, she joined the group Side Effect, singing what she calls "R&Be-Bop."

Nettlesby and Coffey played in a Chicago band with a woman named Karen Mayo. When she became Miki's production coordinator, she asked her friends if they had any material for the singer.

Nettlesby remembers: "Terry had a melody [that] was like the hook 'Ain't Nuthin' in the World.' Usually when somebody sings a dummy melody idea, they're just singing anything so you can hear the melody. I liked 'Ain't Nuthin' in the World,' so I said, 'Why don't I keep that...and I'll make it make sense from there.' "

Miki Howard

Nettlesby and Coffey recorded a demo and gave the tape to their friend Karen, who handed it to Miki. Sylvia Rhone, then head of A&R for Atlantic Records, also heard the demo and a week later sent the same song to Howard. "I really liked the song and had never really done an up-tempo song that I thought was commercial," says Miki.

Nettlesby and Coffey used their own band, Truth Inc., on the session. Jon played drums and percussion, Terry was responsible for keyboards and synthesizer, and Horace "Bookie" Coleman handled rhythm and bass guitar. The backing vocals were provided by Miki and Bridgette Bryant.

"She does the part, 'Ain't nuthin' in the world,' because she has this really cool voice and I liked the way it sounded," says Miki, recalling the session. "She sang the background and I did all these double things, because at that time Chaka Khan had an album out that I really liked and she did this stuff that was great and I wanted to do it."

Miki was as surprised as her producers when "Ain't Nuthin' in the World" was chosen as the first single. "We were thinking 'If You Still Love Her,' because it's traditional Miki Howard, one of those torch songs that Miki's used to doing," says Nettlesby. "It shocked all of us."

The follow-up single, "Love Under New Management," spent two weeks at number two. Miki's next release was a cover of Stevie Wonder's "Until You Come Back to Me (That's What I'm Gonna Do)," originally a hit for Aretha Franklin. It peaked at number three. In 1990, Miki left Atlantic and was about to sign with another label when Cassandra Mills pacted his to Giant Records.

546

ALL OF MY LOVE

The Gap Band

CAPITOL 44418
WRITERS: RAYMOND CALHOUN, ALDYN ST. JON, RONNIE WILSON
PRODUCERS: CHARLES WILSON, RONNIE WILSON
December 23, 1989 (2 weeks)

After a seven-year gap between Number One hits, the Gap Band returned to the R&B chart summit with "All of My Love." Their four previous chart-toppers were all helmed by producer Lonnie Simmons for his Total Experience company, but now they were on Capitol, signed to the label by president David Berman. "At that point in time, Bobby Brown was having a lot of hits utilizing the Gap Band sound, so they were feeling like they wanted to get out there and show the world that the Gap Band still knew how to make great records," says Tom Vickers, who was part of Capitol's A&R staff at the time.

Although Simmons had produced a good number of hits for the Gap Band, in many ways they were grateful for the opportunity to take charge of their own album. "They were really looking forward to exercising their freedom and making what they considered a true Gap Band album, true to what the Gap Band was," says Vickers, who made many trips from the Capitol tower in Hollywood to Compton in South Central Los Angeles to work with Charlie, Ronnie, and Robert Wilson.

Raymond Calhoun, who wrote the Gap Band's final Number One hit on Total Experience [see 368—"Outstanding"], came up with "All of My Love."

"I initially came up with the track and the hook and the first verse," he remembers. "And then I had two other writers, Ronnie [Wilson] and Aldyn St. Jon, come up with the second verse with me." Calhoun says that "All of My Love" came about accidentally. "We had a little demo studio where we would try to come up with tunes. I was in the room one day while they were taking a break from writing and I wanted to get a song on the album. So I came up with a bassline and a drum track and then I told the guy who was engineering to put up a mike. I went in there and sung this little melody I had. That's all I had at first, so I went home and came back the next day with the lyrics to the first verse. And while [the Gap Band] was there, they realized, 'OK, he might have something here.' Then John and Ronnie helped me come up with the second verse of the song and we finished in two days."

Charlie Wilson felt "All of My Love" was a song he could really sink his teeth into, according to Vickers. Calhoun recalls how Charlie recorded it in the studio: "All the songs Charlie's ever done for me, he's always done them right away. Real easy, real quick, boom. He didn't have to think about it. He was inspired—he loved the track and it just came to him."

The Gap Band finished the *Round Trip* album in the Bahamas. "We recorded here [in Los Angeles], but went down there to do the vocals," says Calhoun.

Round Trip proved to be the end of the road for the Gap Band—their Capitol debut was their final album together. They didn't realize it at the time they were recording it, according to Calhoun. "I hoped that this album was going to hit and we were going to be doing another album." Contributing to the dissolution was Ronnie's desire to be a minister. "He was interested in Christian music a long time ago," says Calhoun. "We'd be on the road on the bus and he'd say, 'Man, I'm getting out of this and doing a gospel record.' "

547

TENDER LOVER

Babyface

SOLAR 74003

WRITERS: BABYFACE, L.A. REID, PERRI SMITH

PRODUCERS: L.A. REID, BABYFACE

January 6, 1990 (1 week)

"Tender Lover," the first Number One hit of the '90s, was a song Babyface tried to give away before he recorded it.

"That was a song we played for Lionel Richie," reveals Kenny Edmonds, best known as Babyface. "Lionel was putting a record together and at first he was interested and then somehow the business got kind of crazy, and so I ended up doing it [instead]." The song was also offered to the Jacksons, who recorded Reid and Babyface's "Nothin (That Compares 2 U)." The brothers turned it down, then changed their minds—but it was too late. By that time, Babyface had already decided to record it himself.

It became the title song for Babyface's second solo album and was written in much the same way as "It's No Crime," his first chart-topper. "We hummed the melody and it came together," Babyface explains. "The fun part about that song was 'Eleanor Rigby.' It started off with, 'Eleanor Rigby lived her life all alone,' and that was a fun line to throw in the beginning of it."

Hearing "Tender Lover" takes Babyface's partner, Antonio "L.A." Reid, back to a distinct period in time. "We wrote that song in '87 or '88, and it was a very special time for us. I think we wrote the most at that time. We spent more time writing then than we do today—life does change. We have a family. We have a record company. We have a business, and things have changed," says L.A., who was given those initials not because he dreamed of going to Los Angeles, but because he was fascinated with ants and ant hills when he was a child. L.A. stands for "Little Ant."

Reid describes his collaborator as a confident and creative vocalist. "When we go in [the studio] with some artists, they step behind the mike and sometimes they're really not sure what to do. When Face steps behind the mike, I think he's a little more confident of what he wants. Because he is a producer and a songwriter, I think he has a clue when he starts out. As for me, I'll just tell him, 'I think you're on course' or 'I think you're a little off course. I think you need a change in tone' or 'I think the tone you sang on the last pass was the better tone and you should try that more'...I'll give him guidance like that. But the licks that he chooses to sing, he creates them because he's a very creative artist."

Whether they are writing and producing themselves or supervising projects for other artists, Reid and Babyface work quickly. "It doesn't take long," Reid agrees. "The longest process is when we mix and I think that's true for most records. The actual recording process moves very quickly. We can go in and cut two or three songs in one day—the tracks—and then vocally we can usually get each song in about two sessions."

Working on the session for "Tender Lover" were Reid and Babyface's usual compatriots: former Deele member Kayo played bass guitar and bass synth, De'Rock handled percussion, and Reid was responsible for drums and percussion. Babyface played all of the other instruments, and background vocals were provided by Troop [see 557—"Spread My Wings"].

548

RHYTHM NATION

Janet Jackson

A&M 1455
WRITERS: JANET JACKSON, JAMES HARRIS III, TERRY LEWIS
PRODUCERS: JIMMY JAM, TERRY LEWIS
January 13, 1990 (1 week)

When Janet Jackson returned to Jimmy Jam and Terry Lewis's Flyte Tyme studios in Minneapolis to begin work on her follow-up album to *Control*, the first song she recorded was "Miss You Much" [see 539], but there was no unifying theme for the project—yet. At one point, she considered a suggestion from A&M's John McClain that she record a concept album about her family, but finally discarded that idea.

"We didn't have a clear picture of what we wanted the album to be conceptually," says producer Jimmy Jam. "We [weren't] even thinking along the lines of a concept, initially; all we wanted was not to do *Control, Part 2*. So I think we were intent on trying to find different sounding songs than the *Control* album."

Jackson came up with the concept of "Rhythm Nation," according to the producer. "A lot of it had to do with watching TV. We're avid TV watchers, and we would watch BET, MTV...then switch over to CNN, and there'd always be something messed-up happening. It was never good news, always bad news. I think the thing that really triggered it was the Stockton playground murders, which really hit Janet hard. She loves kids." That incident inspired Jackson, Jam, and Lewis to record "Livin' in a World (They Didn't Make)." Jam and Lewis already had the title but weren't planning to do anything with it. "It turned out to be the perfect song. But she couldn't write the lyrics to it...She couldn't put down what she wanted to say, and it ended up that Terry wrote the lyrics. It took him five minutes. She looked at them and said, 'This is perfect. This is exactly what I wanted to say.' From that point on we decided we should concentrate on doing some songs in that vein and we ended up with 'Rhythm Nation' and 'State of the World.'

"But the 'Rhythm Nation' concept was her idea. She said, 'Rhythm Nation,' and I immediately got an idea for the 'people of the world today,' that kind of chord, and then Terry said, 'We are part of the rhythm nation,' and the whole thing came together."

Janet elaborated on the concept in an interview with Robert Hilburn of the *Los Angeles Times*. She said the idea was based on reading about "nations" or clubs of young people, mostly black, in New York who came together seeking identity and support. "I thought it would be great if we could create our own nation...One that would have a positive message and that everyone would be free to join."

Jackson talked about the backlash from some critics to the "Rhythm Nation" concept with Hilburn: "I can just imagine what some people thought when they heard the album was going to be socially conscious...that I was trying to be Tracy Chapman. Well, I admire Tracy Chapman and bands like U2 a lot, but I am talking to a different audience...I wanted to take our message directly to the kids, and the way to do that is by making music you can really dance to. That was our whole goal: How can I get through to the kids with this?"

549

I'LL BE GOOD TO YOU

Quincy Jones featuring Ray Charles and Chaka Khan

QWEST 22697
WRITERS: GEORGE JOHNSON, LOUIS JOHNSON, SENORA SAM
PRODUCER: QUINCY JONES
January 20, 1990 (2 weeks)

After charting with a number of successful albums on A&M like *Body Heat* and *The Dude*, prolific producer Quincy Jones signed with Warner Brothers in 1981 and established his own label, Qwest. But it would take him almost a decade to record his own album for the label. "Somewhere along the way I got sidetracked," he wrote in *Billboard*, "with Michael Jackson's *Thriller*, Donna Summer, James Ingram, 'We Are the World,' *The Color Purple*...and then the *Bad* album."

Jones stated that he tried to start the *Back on the Block* album before he went to work on *The Color Purple* in 1985, but that project simply simmered while he was working on the film. "The longer it takes you, the stronger it has to be, and so it built up inside me. And it built to a point where I was determined not to compromise all the dreams I had for this record, as deadlines sometimes have a tendency to make you retreat from lofty concepts because of possibly not having the time to execute them."

George Johnson of the Brothers Johnson remembers getting a telephone call from Quincy sometime in 1989. "He asked for me to write another 'I'll Be Good to You' [see 247]. I said, 'No problem.' A week later he called back and said, 'I was thinking about taking "I'll Be Good to You" and just cutting it again.' I told him that would be a great idea, as opposed to duping something like it."

George joined Quincy and vocalists James Ingram and Chaka Khan in the studio. "They initially did all of the vocals and the lead parts. That same day Ray Charles happened to pop into the studio to drop in on Q. He hadn't seen him in a long time," says Johnson.

Quincy and Ray first met in Seattle, where Charles had relocated from Florida in 1948. Ready to leave the South behind, he had asked a friend to take a map and find the farthest point away from Florida that would still be in the United States. New York was five inches away on the map, but too intimidating. Los Angeles was seven inches away, and Seattle a full eight inches distant.

"He was only a couple of years younger than me," Charles said of Jones in *Billboard,* "and at that point he didn't really have his program together. He was just a teenager...Q was hungry for information, eager to learn anything he could. He was a sweet, likable dude...We've been partners ever since. Any time Quincy needs me, I'm there. And it works the other way around."

George Johnson had never met Ray Charles before, even though he lived around the corner from him while growing up in Los Angeles. "I didn't have any idea what Q was going to do. Ray was there while we were cutting the track. Quincy called me a week later and said, 'I had this great idea. I think I'll put Ray Charles on this,' and the next thing I knew Ray Charles was on the tune. He was the perfect person to do it. It was an honor for me to have this genius sing on the song. After I heard him, I didn't want to put my vocal on it again because it's a remake [and I wanted] to do something new."

Johnson says he wasn't surprised when Jones put some hip-hop drums under the vocals. "[Quincy] took the song I had written and did it his way. I really enjoyed watching how he personally interpreted it."

550

MAKE IT LIKE IT WAS

Regina Belle

COLUMBIA 73022
WRITER: CARVIN WINANS
PRODUCER: NICK MARTINELLI
February 3, 1990 (1 week)

"Carvin Winans wrote a hell of a tune," says Regina Belle of "Make It Like It Was," her second consecutive Number One single.

Fortunately for Belle, the rest of Carvin's family didn't agree with her. "I had originally written it for the Winans," says Carvin, "and they passed on it for the *Decisions* album." The Winans were a gospel quartet on Qwest Records consisting of Carvin, his twin brother Marvin, and their brothers Michael and Ronald, all older siblings to BeBe and CeCe Winans, a duo signed to Capitol.

Carvin made what he calls an "unexpensive demo" of the song and played it for his brothers. "I thought they would love it, and they passed," he says. Soon after, he was in New York to see a play, *Don't Get God Started,* that featured two of his brothers. Regina was in the audience that night and they exchanged phone numbers backstage.

Belle received Carvin's demo and loved it. "He sang it falsetto with a piano and it was really beautiful, just him singing," she recalls. " 'Make It Like It Was' was a beautiful tune from the first time I ever heard it."

Nick Martinelli, who produced Belle's first album for Columbia, helmed the tune. He first met Regina through Joe McEwen of CBS's A&R department. "He said they have a new artist and would I like to work with her," the producer remembers. He listened to a duet she recorded with the Manhattans. "They sent her down for me to meet her and hear her and I liked her, so we started working together."

"Nick Martinelli was largely responsible for a lot of what came out of that tune," Regina acknowledges. "It was just what he gives to me. Out of all the producers I've worked with, Nick is by far my favorite because we've developed such a friendship over the years. From a creative standpoint, I think Nick and I go a lot further because Nick likes to take those chances. He likes you to go ahead and try that note you've been wanting to try for about a year that you're scared to try in concert because you can't take it back if it doesn't work. He likes you to take your time and let everything you feel come out on the record. Then he tries to guide you as a result of that, as opposed to trying to set you on a trail and then you find your way down it. He likes to end up there with you."

Belle recorded "Make It Like It Was" live with the musicians at Sigma Sound in Philadelphia. Donald Robinson played piano, Randy Bowland played guitar, Curtis Dowd played the Rhodes, Mayra Casales was on percussion, and Daryl Burges handled the drums.

The vocal was an easy one to record, according to Belle. Carvin remembers the session: "She's a very hard worker and it doesn't take her long to do what she has to do. I think Nick took her through the lead vocals maybe three times...They made a composite of what they liked from each time and it was done." Even with a couple of Number One hits, Belle doesn't keep her eye on the charts. "I don't want to develop the expectation of having to chart Number One," she explains. "I always like to be within the top 20 or at least the top 10, and I'm blessed enough to do that. I feel grateful...It's great to know you have a Number One song, but if you concentrate on that too much, I think that affects what you're going to do when you go in the studio and what you're going to do onstage."

Winans, on the other hand, was thrilled when "Make It Like It Was" hit the top. "Somebody told me that we were number two," he recalls, "but had lost the bullet, and I said, 'Oh, no! Well, I guess two is better than three, but it's not Number One.' So I went and got *Billboard* anyway and I looked. We still had the bullet! And the week after we went to Number One."

551

REAL LOVE

Skyy

ATLANTIC 88816
WRITER: SOLOMON ROBERTS, JR.
PRODUCERS: RANDY MULLER, SOLOMON ROBERTS JR.
February 10, 1990 (1 week)

After registering 14 chart entries on the Salsoul label and one on Capitol between 1979 and 1986, including a Number One hit [see 356—"Call Me"], the Brooklyn-based octet known as Skyy took a three-year hiatus from recording. "We were changing record companies," explains lead singer Solomon Roberts, Jr. "For us, the record company is pretty much like a home, and you don't move into the first house you see. We had to talk to a few different companies and find out where their heads were at and let them know where we were at. Finally we settled on Atlantic Records. At that time they had just cleaned their roster and were starting to rebuild under Sylvia Rhone. She was into what the group was doing and they had nobody else on the label like us, so it was the perfect marriage at that time."

Working on the first album for their new label, Roberts wrote a song called "Real Love." "We were really looking for a ballad that was different from the other ballads we had," Roberts elaborates. "We wanted to expand the range of our group and of our lead vocalist, Denise Crawford. I sat down and thought of not a situation that I was going through, but a situation I know a lot of my friends go through, and how I would feel in that situation. I wrote about a guy who's afraid to commit, but the woman feels strongly and is not afraid to reassure him that this is it. It's not going to get any better, so let's get with it."

Producer Randy Muller acknowledges Roberts's writing skills: "I think he's the king of ballads. When we need a ballad, Solomon writes it. I guess we both know which hats we wear—I'm the up-tempo dance guy, the funk guy, and he's the ballad king."

Roberts wrote the song on a computer. "I was working on the song all day, just fiddling around because I don't really play keyboards that well. [I worked] six to eight hours to get down some of the parts to show the group how to do it. Right before I decided to save it, I said, 'This sequencer isn't sitting quite in the right spot. Let me move this out.' And I moved it and lost everything. At that point, I was too frustrated to do anything. I came back the next day and started all over again." In the end, Roberts was happy he had to write the song from scratch, because he believes it turned out better the second time.

"The demo sound was pretty good," Muller acknowledges. "We tried to match it up to the demo. Skyy was not known for ballads. We're known for up-tempo tracks [but] this one fit like a glove. The timing was right. It was the place the group should have been at, at that juncture in their career."

Roberts concludes, "It's an ongoing learning experience and we're learning every day."

552

IT'S GONNA BE ALRIGHT

Ruby Turner

JIVE 1317
WRITERS: LORIS HOLLAND, JOLYON SKINNER, RUBY TURNER
PRODUCERS: LORIS HOLLAND, JOLYON SKINNER
February 17, 1990 (1 week)

"For black Americans, [R&B] music is their roots," Jamaican native Ruby Turner, raised in Birmingham, England, told a London journalist. "They are born, bred, and raised on it. Here, we're not. It's something different altogether, and you either get into it or you don't. Well, I got into it. And I've spent most of my life apologizing for not being an American!"

American or not, Ruby topped the chart with the first single from her third album for Jive Records. Writer/producer Loris Holland deliberately went for an American sound while working with Ruby at Battery Studios in London. "The British vibe and the American vibe at the time were two different things," he contends. "Funky over [in England] is different than funky over here. Since they were releasing this in America, I was shooting for that."

Holland, born in Guyana, was a classically trained musician inspired to move into a jazzier groove when he met Marcus Miller [see 485—"Da'Butt"] while they attended school together. Signed to Zomba Music, he was sent to England to work with Turner on her second album, a songbook of Motown cover versions. Another writer/producer from Guyana, Jolyon Skinner, was working on some other tracks for Turner. When it came time to record her third album, Turner asked to work with the two producers again.

Clive Calder, head of Jive Records, asked Holland and Skinner to come up with a hit single for Turner. Influenced by what was happening in British soul music at the time with Jazzie B and his group Soul II Soul [see 538—"Back to Life"], Holland came up with some music. "I got the beat going and then I got the chords and the bassline. Jolyon came in and heard it, and then I didn't like the bassline anymore and changed it. Then Jolyon wrote a whole different song

Ruby Turner

off the music. We let Ruby listen to it. She was down, and I told her, 'Ruby, it's gonna be alright.' It was funny how the title came up from trying to encourage each other."

Turner had never written her own material before, but contributed to four songs on this third album, including the hit single. "Loris and Jolyon gave me the foundation and from there I was able to create," Ruby explains. She applies the same approach to her acting career. "The only way to [act] is to think like the characters think," she says. Ruby was inspired by a relationship she had at the time that was not going well. "I tend to create better from a broken heart," she laughs. "It was therapeutic. We're great friends now. It took a good three or four years before I weaned myself off this guy."

Holland, Skinner, and Turner worked on the song over a three-day period, rewriting and fine-tuning. Holland played bass and keyboards and did the drum programming. Jolyon played some guitar that was sampled in different parts of the song, and sang the main backing vocals. During the session, Loris and Jolyon were talking about music from back home and added some West Indian influences.

Ruby, who had sung backing vocals for Culture Club, Bryan Ferry, and UB40 before recording on her own, made a 23-state swing through the United States to help promote "It's Gonna Be Alright." It was still moving up the chart when she returned home. A week and a half later, her manager telephoned from New York to tell her the single was Number One. "I was on my own at the time—the realization was too much!" she exclaims.

553

WHERE DO WE GO FROM HERE

Stacy Lattisaw with Johnny Gill

MOTOWN 2026
WRITER: LEMEL HUMES
PRODUCER: LEMEL HUMES
February 24, 1990 (2 weeks)

Stacy Lattisaw and Johnny Gill were childhood friends in Washington, D.C. "We went to school together and he used to come over to my house every day," says Stacy. "I used to have talent shows in my basement." Johnny remembers them: "I would never participate in any of the shows. So one day she said, 'OK, everybody down here's got to do something,' and I had to do the only thing I knew how to do."

"I couldn't believe his voice and I told my mother, 'Come downstairs and hear him sing,' " Lattisaw recalls. They were 13-year-old junior high school

Stacy Lattisaw

students, but Stacy already had a contract with Atlantic Records and had hit the chart with "Let Me Be Your Angel" on the Cotillion subsidiary. Gill, who had been singing with the gospel group Wings of Faith since he was five, was recommended to Atlantic's Henry Allen by Lattisaw, and by the time he was 16 he was recording for Cotillion as well.

The label put the young singers together for an album of duets, resulting in a top 10 single, "Perfect Combination." "I've always wanted to do a duet," says Stacy. "Once I heard Johnny's voice, I wanted to sing with him." Gill likewise praises his singing partner: "She's always had such a pure voice and a very strong voice. I thought [it was like a] Marvin Gaye/Tammi Terrell kind of thing, and they were people we idolized."

Gill joined New Edition in 1988 and released a solo album on Motown in 1990. Lattisaw had signed with the company in 1986 and scored with a single, "Nail It to the Wall." Together again on the same label, they had the opportunity to record as a duo once more. Writer/producer LeMel Humes, who had just completed a project for Stephanie Mills on MCA, met with Stacy and her father Jerome in New York. Over a get-acquainted lunch, they agreed to work together.

Humes wrote "Where Do We Go from Here" based on Stacy and Johnny's personal and professional relationship. "They were looking for a duet from a lot of different writers, and I captured something they were right in the middle of." Humes wrote the song while sitting at his piano at home. "The melody just hit me and I started writing it. [The title] came right away."

Humes was scheduled to meet with Lattisaw in the studio the next day to work on another song. "I played it for her and the A&R director and they said it was perfect." Humes recorded a demo, which he shipped off to Gill. Meanwhile, Stacy played the song for Johnny over the phone and he agreed to record it with her.

Stacy's vocals were cut at Skyline in New York, while Johnny did his part at Cherokee Studios in Los Angeles. "That was a unique experience," says Gill. "That was the very first time I had recorded a song where she was in one place and I was in another. I had just come off a tour with the New Edition and they brought the tapes to me in order to put my part down." Stacy says it was easy to record, "because it reminded me of a gospel type song and that's something I always wanted to do."

Humes elaborates, "I wanted to [keep] them within the melody of the song without stretching it too much, but at the end let them go off like a church-ish vibe, to wail and sing back and forth, strong emotional singing, which brings it back to their roots."

554

ESCAPADE

Janet Jackson

A&M 1490
WRITERS: JANET JACKSON,
JAMES HARRIS III, TERRY LEWIS
PRODUCERS: JIMMY JAM, TERRY LEWIS
March 10, 1990 (1 week)

Janet Jackson's third Number One single from *Rhythm Nation 1814* might have been a remake of Martha & the Vandellas' top five hit from 1965, "Nowhere to Run."

"Janet's a big basketball fan, a big [Los Angeles] Lakers fan," producer Jimmy Jam explains, "and when she went to the games, they would always play one of the songs she liked, 'Nowhere to Run.' " Janet told Jimmy Jam and Terry Lewis that she wanted to record a new version of the Holland/Dozier/Holland classic. "I suggested that instead of doing a remake of 'Nowhere to Run,' let's do something with that kind of feel to it, but do our own song," says Jimmy Jam.

Jam and Lewis keep a book of titles, and they rummaged through it to find something appropriate. "Anytime we hear a phrase or a saying, we write it down as a title," says Jimmy. "We usually come up with the music first, then we try to think of a title that fits the way the music sounds. And 'Escapade' we thought was a cool word. It is kind of old-fashioned—people don't really say, 'Let's go on an escapade' anymore—but it really worked well with that track."

The instrumental track for "Escapade" was one of the first three recorded for the *Rhythm Nation 1814* album, along with "Miss You Much" [see 539] and "Love Will Never Do (Without You)." Jam continues outlining the genesis of the song: "While she was sitting in one room coming up with lyrics, I put it on the 24-track. We hooked the drum machine up. On my left hand I played the bass, on the right hand I played the chord. And it was just enough for her to sing to, which we do a lot. Because we like to let her sing to as minimum of a track as we can do, then fill in the track around her so that her part is the main part of the song. With 'Escapade,' she sang it and we kept saying we'll go back and redo the track...[But] we never redid the track.

"It's basically all drums. I don't even think there's a mix of the drums. I think all the drums are on one track. There's a keyboard bass and another thing, and that was it. All we added were the overdubs, little bells...because we'd gotten so used to the feel of the track, the mistakes and all, we ended up leaving it the way it was."

Jam programmed the drum and keyboards and played keyboards and percussion. Lewis played bass and percussion. They were joined by Dave Barry on guitars, and Johnny Gill provided the finger snaps.

As usual, Janet provided her own backing vocals. "Which is what we like to do with her," says Jimmy Jam, "because it's important for it to be a Janet Jackson record for her to sing all the parts."

A&M released four more singles from *Rhythm Nation 1814* after "Escapade," but none of them reached Number One on the R&B chart. "Alright" spent one week at number two, and then "Come Back to Me" had a two-week run at number two. The rock 'n' rollish "Black Cat" reached number 10 R&B and "Love Will Never Do (Without You)" peaked at number three.

555

THE SECRET GARDEN (SWEET SEDUCTION SUITE)

Quincy Jones featuring Al B. Sure!, James Ingram, El DeBarge, and Barry White

QWEST 19992
WRITERS: QUINCY JONES, ROD TEMPERTON, SIEDAH GARRETT, EL DEBARGE
PRODUCER: QUINCY JONES
March 17, 1990 (1 week)

Siedah Garrett remembers Quincy Jones describing his concept for "The Secret Garden." The producer told her, "I want this to be a love song about four men trying to court this woman and each of them bringing a different side of themselves to the party."

Quincy revealed the source of his idea in *Billboard*. "It was inspired by a book on women's sexual fantasies, *My Secret Garden* by Nancy Friday," he commented. "[The song is] moody, seductive, with a sexy rhythm section, synthesizers, and strings."

El DeBarge was in Detroit when Quincy called his manager to inquire if El would be interested in contributing vocals to *Back on the Block*, an album that Quincy said would combine "talented, young newcomers and first-team legends, pulling all the elements together in the family of sounds. It represents everything I have worked for after 40 years."

El said yes and flew to Los Angeles, where he met Quincy at Rod Temperton's home. Sleepless from the flight, he discovered that the song Jones wanted him to record wasn't finished. "He told me it was about a secret garden," says El. "He wanted it to be dreamy, pleasantly sexual. Not anything offensive, but he did want it to represent the feeling of the bedroom. And that was the hardest part, because we had to make it feel that way without using raunchy words. At the same time, we didn't want to get too philosophical—you know, the stars, the moon, and the sky and all that stuff. That's why it took us a day and a half. It's always easier if you can say, 'Well, baby, let me pull your panties down.' You have to be real careful how you deliver your message."

Garrett recalls how the four writers created the song at Temperton's house. "Rod had some chords that they'd started a basic track with. They were never happy with one part of the song or another, be it the melody or the lyrics. Finally I just said, 'What if the melody went like this?' and they agreed it was a good melody. When we started working on the lyrics we had four chefs and everyone was coming up with something to add. In this case, it was great, because we wound up complementing each other as opposed to one person getting their way throughout the whole song." Garrett says they worked on the song from 10:00 in the evening until 7:00 or 8:00 the next day.

Quincy's original lineup of vocalists for "The Secret Garden" included Stevie Wonder, Barry White, El DeBarge, and Al B. Sure! When Stevie couldn't make the session, James Ingram was called in. "They were all down at the studio," says Siedah, who sang background vocals with Al and El.

Barry White had also received a phone call from Quincy, inviting him to participate. "I heard it, I loved it. I called him back," says White. "I said, 'Q, I buy.' " White didn't know Jones wanted him to rap on the song until he got to the studio.

Garrett will never forget standing next to White as he recorded his part of the song. "I could feel his voice in my bones," she says. "It's the weirdest feeling. Everything he said you felt in your body, in the core of your being."

556

ALL AROUND THE WORLD

Lisa Stansfield

ARISTA 9928
WRITERS: LISA STANSFIELD, IAN DEVANEY, ANDY MORRIS
PRODUCERS: IAN DEVANEY, ANDY MORRIS
March 24, 1990 (2 weeks)

If you are a soul singer, you are a soul singer," Lisa Stansfield told Robert Hilburn in the *Los Angeles Times*. "If you are a heavy-metal singer, than you are a heavy-metal singer. What's color got to do with it? I don't go around thinking, 'I sing soul music and I'm white.' I just sing the way I feel."

Born in 1966 in Rochdale, England, Lisa made her career choice early. "This is what I've wanted to do since I was four years old, when me mum cleaned up the house and listened to Motown records all the time," she said in *USA Today*. "Diana Ross, Gladys Knight, and Aretha Franklin were me teachers." When she was six, she bought her first single, Donny Osmond's "Puppy Love." She was singing in a school musical when she met Ian Devaney, a guitarist playing in the band, and Andy Morris, a trumpet player from another school. Polydor Records in the U.K. released her first single, "The Only Way," when Lisa was 15. She calls that early work "a total embarrassment." She was hired to host *Razzamatazz*, a Saturday morning children's show in Britain. In one interview she says she fell over a child, in another she says she

Lisa Stansfield

kicked him. In either case, she quit the series without knowing what she would do next.

A chance reunion in a pub with Devaney and Morris led to a musical collaboration and a romantic relationship between Lisa and Ian. In 1984 the trio formed a group, Ede Bopp, but at their second gig changed the name to Blue Zone. They were signed to the independent Rocking Horse label. When that company was purchased by Arista, they were automatically added to that label's roster. An album was released in the United States and Europe, but not in the U.K. "The first couple of songs we wrote were quite heavily black-influenced," says Devaney. "And then when we first got involved with record companies, [we] came under all the pressures...so we drifted a little bit."

After Devaney and Morris persuaded Arista to let them produce one of their own tracks, they cut "Big Thing" for the B-side of one of their singles. Matt Black and Jonathan Moore, a pair of DJs who recorded as Coldcut, liked the track and wanted to collaborate. "People Hold On" was released by "Coldcut featuring Lisa Stansfield," and was a chart hit in the U.K. and a club hit in the States.

"All Around the World" was written while Lisa, Ian, and Andy were sitting around a piano. They came up with the chords and the Barry White–like talking intro at that first working session. "We started on a really rough demo," says Devaney. "It was literally done on an eight-track and the vocals were done in one take, straight away. It was done in a little studio behind Lisa's parents' house.

"When it came to making it into a record...we decided we couldn't touch the vocal because there was no point in trying to do it any better. The quality of the recording was quite poor...We transferred the vocal from the eight-track up to 24-track, took that into a big studio and put real strings on it, and then transferred for the third time back onto an eight-track and took it home and mixed it in a bedroom."

557

SPREAD MY WINGS

Troop

ATLANTIC 86244
WRITER: CHUCKII BOOKER
PRODUCER: CHUCKII BOOKER
April 7, 1990 (2 weeks)

The members of Troop didn't sing when they made their first public appearance. But there was no scandal—in fact, lip synching was the whole idea. Rodney Benford was a ninth grader in Pasadena, California, when his mother Shirley got the idea for her son to compete on the nationally syndicated television series *Puttin' on the Hits*.

"I came home from school and she said, 'Do you think you could get a group and go on *Puttin' on the Hits*?' I said sure, just to agree with her. The next day she made [an appointment for] the auditions." Realizing his mother was serious, Rodney asked his friends Steve Russell, Allen McNeil, John "Jon-Jon" Harreld, and Reggie Warren if they would go with him. "We practiced and practiced...and we went on and won. It was not our intention to win; we won by accident." The five students divided $1,000 for lip synching to the New Edition song "Cool It Now."

A producer named Greg Pare, impressed with their dancing and stage presence, contacted them to see if they could *really* sing. Up to the challenge, they rehearsed for two more weeks, this time actually vocalizing New Edition songs. "He came to see us and we blew him away," says Rodney. Sylvia Rhone of Atlantic's A&R department saw the group perform at a showcase in Los Angeles and signed them to the label. Their name was changed from Five of a Kind to Troop, and Atlantic labelmates Gerald Levert and Marc Gordon of the group Levert produced their first chart single, "Mamacita." Their debut album, which took eight months to record, also saw them working with producers like Brownmark at Paisley Park studios near Minneapolis and a new Atlantic artist, Chuckii Booker.

For Troop's second album, Booker offered them a song he had written for himself. It was a ballad similar to another one of his songs, "Turned Away" [see 529], and he didn't want to include both on the same album. "It was a toss-up," says Booker. "I said I'll save 'Spread My Wings.' Since I love Troop—they're like my little brothers—I felt this could help their career." Booker came up with the idea at home while noodling on his piano. "I hit a couple of chords, and I started humming the melody and went to grab some pen and paper real quick."

Steve Russell recalls the first time he heard the song: "I was sitting in my car and Chuckii sang it for me." Rusell loved "Turned Away" and wanted a song like that for Troop. He thought "Spread My Wings" was "the most beautiful song in the world."

Russell recorded his lead vocals in the studio just before leaving for the airport to sing with Keith Sweat in New York. "We work really well with Chuckii, so it's not hard recording. He knows how we sing and he knows exactly what to give each guy to get it done fast."

558

READY OR NOT

After 7

VIRGIN 98995
WRITERS: BABYFACE, L.A. REID
PRODUCERS: L.A. REID, BABYFACE
April 21, 1990 (2 weeks)

When red-hot producers Antonio "L.A." Reid and Kenny "Babyface" Edmonds made a production deal with Virgin Records, they promised label executives they would bring them one act.

"They signed the deal and they had no idea who the artist would be," says L.A. Reid. "And then we came up with After 7."

Reid and Babyface didn't have to look very far to find the three men who made up the group. Kevon and Melvin Edmonds are Babyface's brothers and Keith Mitchell is L.A.'s cousin. "We brought After 7 in and made a record on them and took it to Virgin and said, 'Here's your one record' and they said, 'Thank you!' and it worked out very well," Reid summarizes.

Mitchell started singing when he was seven years old and participated in young adult choirs at church for about seven years. At Indiana University, he pursued a business degree and found a home in the I.U. Soul Revue, an ensemble that performed top 40 soul music. Being part of the group meant attending a three-hour class that included information about the music business and the technical side of recording. "That's where I found my love for wanting to do the music continually," Keith says. In his second year with the I.U. Soul Revue he met another classmate, Kevon Edmonds. Mitchell found they had similar tastes in music, both being raised on Indianapolis AM radio in the late '60s and early '70s.

After college, they found 9-to-5 jobs. When it came time to record with their famous relatives, the members of After 7 learned the true meaning of patience. "We were working on a lot of projects at the time," Reid allows. "We were doing several records, and I think at one point they started to think we were giving them the runaround or they were not a priority to us, and actually it was quite the opposite. They were ultimately the priority but we didn't want to deal with it until we had the time to deal with it properly. It was a little frustrating for them but it went from one extreme to the other. They went from sitting around waiting to going to two or three sessions a day."

Mitchell remembers receiving an urgent call to rush to one of those sessions. "We were staying in the Oakwood Apartments in Burbank and Face called us early one Sunday morning and said, 'I think you guys need to get over here. I've got something special for you.' We threw our clothes on, ran straight over there, and he hit the sequencer. He had the music for 'Ready or Not' and he started singing the hook. It was a different harmony for us because we were used to singing just basic one-key harmony and he introduced us to some intricate, tricky harmony with 'Ready or Not.' But the song was very special...when he first called us, we all felt like it was going to be a strong song for the album. The words said everything you would want to tell a woman."

The first single released from After 7's debut album was "Heat of the Moment," which peaked at number five on the R&B chart. The follow-up was "Don't Cha' Think," which faltered at number 25. "Ready or Not," featuring Babyface on keyboards, Kayo on bass, and L.A. on drums, was the third single. "It's one of my favorite songs," enthuses L.A. "The tradeoff between the two lead vocalists [Kevon and Melvin] is what made the record."

559

POISON

Bell Biv DeVoe

MCA 53772
WRITER: ELLIOTT STRAITE
PRODUCER: DR. FREEZE
May 5, 1990 (2 weeks)

The origin of Bell Biv DeVoe can be traced to a backstage gathering in Los Angeles of producers Jimmy Jam and Terry Lewis and the members of New Edition at the last show of the *Heart Break* tour. "We were excited about the success of the record and kind of talking to everybody about what they were going to do in the future," Jimmy Jam recalls. "We had already been lined up to do the Johnny Gill album and some things on Ralph [Tresvant], and we asked the other three guys, 'What are you going to do?' "

Michael Bivins had already talked about getting into management. Ricky Bell replied that he might make a solo album or take some time off and relax. "They didn't really have a clear cut idea of what it was they wanted to do," says Jimmy, who suggested that Bell, Bivins, and Ronald DeVoe make an album together with Ricky singing and Michael and Ronald rapping. "I knew they could rap because we did a song called 'N.E. Heart Break' that was a rap song. I knew rhythmically they could pull it off and we knew that Ricky had a good enough voice to pull off lead singing and we just thought it would be a cool idea. We told them they should call it Bell, Bivins, & DeVoe, and they shortened it to Bell Biv DeVoe." Jam and Lewis called Louil Silas, who was in the A&R department at MCA Records at the time, and told him about the idea. Silas asked if Jam and Lewis would produce the album, but the Flyte Tyme duo suggested producers more into rap would be appropriate.

Bell, Bivins, and DeVoe didn't feel any particular pressure recording their own project, according to Ronnie. "Coming from New Edition, no one thought we were able to do anything, because we were in the background for the most part within that group. Everyone was looking to Ralph and Johnny to be the stars coming out of the group, so we kind of snuck up out of nowhere. As we were doing the album, everything came to us pretty quickly...Everything fell into place for us that first time around."

Bell Biv DeVoe worked with a number of producers on their first album, including Elliott Straite, better known as Dr. Freeze. "I had a track called 'Poison' five or six years ago that was supposed to be on my album," says Dr. Freeze, who played the track for the trio's manager, Hiram Hicks.

Dr. Freeze recounts how "Poison" came to be written: "You meet a girl and she might look really attractive, but you can never tell by the outside of a woman. It's always the inside...You don't know what her mind is. She could rob you. She could be a crook...Most of the girls out there with nice shapes, they take advantage of that and they take a lot of people's money. They use a lot of guys and that's why I called them 'Poison.' Poison might look like a piece of candy and look really good, and when you bite into it, you're dead."

Dr. Freeze wrote, produced, arranged, and played the instrumental track himself. He says Bell Biv DeVoe wanted their sound to differ from that of New Edition. "They were doing a lot of R&B and their stuff sounded great but they wanted more street this time and they wanted street producers and I happened to be one of them."

"Freeze was happy to be working with us because we were Ronnie, Ricky, and Michael of New Edition," says Bivins. "There was a good creative flow...He didn't really come in there and be hard on us. He came in with a New York vibe and it was cool...He had his dressing style and he was Dr. Freeze and we hadn't really heard of anybody like that."

560

RUB YOU THE RIGHT WAY

Johnny Gill

MOTOWN 1982

WRITERS: JAMES HARRIS III, TERRY LEWIS

PRODUCERS: JIMMY JAM, TERRY LEWIS

May 19, 1990 (1 week)

"We think of Johnny [Gill] as a 1990s version of a lot of classic singers," says producer Jimmy Jam. "I think he has some of the Stevie Wonder nuances, some of the Teddy Pendergrass aggressiveness, and some of the Donny Hathaway inflections in his voice. So when we write songs for him, we go back and borrow ingredients from the things that made those singers great. 'Rub You the Right Way' came about from that kind of thinking."

Jam and his partner Terry Lewis contributed songs to Gill's first album for Motown. Johnny had already recorded for Atlantic when he was 16 years old and for MCA as part of New Edition. "I think for a long time, Motown had trouble seeing Johnny as an up-tempo singer," Jimmy Jam assesses. "We always thought he'd be able to kill some up-tempo songs." Jam notes that the albums produced by Kenny Gamble and Leon Huff for Pendergrass in the '70s always included some aggressive, up-tempo cuts. " 'Rub You the Right Way' came from thinking, 'What would Teddy do if he were going to do an up-tempo, aggressive song?' "

The lyrical idea came from Lewis, inspired by seductive Pendergrass songs like "Close the Door" and "Turn off the Lights." "For us, Gamble and Huff are like the road map to success. Look at what they did as far as their productions and writing and the quality of their songs, and the fact that they wrote not only great love songs but socially significant songs, and how they parlayed that into a record label."

Gill is flattered by the comparisons to the great artists who came before him, but isn't sure they are accurate. "I don't put myself in Teddy's shoes because I think there will never be another Teddy. People with that kind of talent come only once in a million years. I've been such a big fan of Teddy's and Luther [Vandross] and on down the line. They're such an inspiration for me that you will hear the influences of not only Teddy but a lot of people in my vocal performances...You think of things they would do in the '90s and you try to recreate that along with being yourself."

As much as Gill loved working with Jam and Lewis, he had some doubts when he first met them. "In the beginning, it was really awkward. A lot of times, they don't demo the tapes. They show you how the song goes and let you interpret it right then and there, the way you choose to interpret it. That's why I think they've been so successful in working with people and people having their own sounds, because they make you interpret the song the way that you hear it once they tell you how it goes. You don't try to copy a demo tape; you sing what you feel."

Gill admits it takes him a long time to get ready to record in the studio. "I work whenever I feel like working. I've never been very fond of studios. I'm so used to singing and performing live that I hate going into the studio, because it is work. It's the same thing over and over and over again. If I feel like doing it, I will sing. And if I don't, I won't."

"It's like pulling teeth making records with Johnny," Jimmy Jam agrees, adding that it's not unpleasant. "He'll be in the studio for eight hours. If you get one hour of good work out of him, that's a good day. He covers it by being such a great singer, just so naturally gifted. So it's fun to work with him."

En Vogue

561

HOLD ON

En Vogue

ATLANTIC 87984
WRITERS: EN VOGUE, DENZIL FOSTER, THOMAS MCELROY
PRODUCERS: DENZIL FOSTER, THOMAS MCELROY
May 26, 1990 (2 weeks)

Denzil Foster and Thomas McElroy were still part of Club Nouveau ("Lean on Me") when they first thought about producing a female group. They also thought it would be difficult to find women willing to stay in a group rather than go on to solo careers. "We looked at the Supremes, the Emotions, the Pointer Sisters, Patti LaBelle and Labelle, even the Andrews Sisters—just saying what worked in those situations and what didn't," says Foster. They knew that men would be interested in sexy women, but they also wanted to find out what women wanted. "We took that into consideration, so we asked our mothers and friends and family."

They found out that women were interested in articulate, educated women who displayed class, and that black women didn't want to see women with long hair and light skin, but black women not trying to be anything else. "That was the key point," says Foster. "That really hit us hard. We wanted nice-looking women who had personalities and who could really sing. We didn't want everyone to sound alike, but we wanted the timbre to sound good."

They finally asked six women to audition. Five showed up. Foster and McElroy wanted to put together a trio, and were hoping one or two women from this first audition would qualify. The producers gave the candidates two-and-a-half hours to learn a new song, "Waitin' on You." The women sat in Foster's car, listening to it on his tape deck and then auditioned. Maxine Jones was first, followed by Dawn Robinson and Cindy Herron. Terry Ellis was late arriving from Texas and the fifth girl kept whining about when they were going to eat. Once they dismissed the hungry vocalist, they couldn't decide which of the other four to drop, so the group became a quartet.

Before recording as En Vogue, the four women lived together for a year. They sang backing vocals on other projects for Foster and McElroy and guest-starred on the *FM*^{2} album, a project designed to introduce the producers' roster. Dawn suggested they enter some talent contests and win some money, so Foster arranged an a cappella version of Smokey Robinson's "Who's Loving You" for them to sing.

"They were warming up to it one time and I accidentally hit the drum machine," says Foster. "I said, 'Wow, that's a funky intro, let's do that.' " The women suggested they could sing the old Motown tune to this new beat, but Foster thought it would be better to write a new song—an answer to "Who's Loving You." The result was "Hold On."

It wasn't an automatic choice for the first single. Foster and McElroy wanted it released, but say the folks at Atlantic Records thought it was too slow. The producers recognized that it was slower than most songs being played on the radio at the time. "But the hook was so strong," says Foster. "It set up the groove. You could say, 'Hey, these girls can sing.' En Vogue was different from other girl groups and we wanted that known."

Dawn elaborated on this very point in an interview with Paolo Hewitt of *Select*. "I think we're not as soft as you would think a girl group would be. We're not poppish or airish in that sense. We think about what we want to sing about and that's important to us."

562

THE BLUES

Tony! Toni! Toné!

WING 873 994

WRITERS: RAPHAEL WIGGINS, DWAYNE WIGGINS

PRODUCERS: TONY! TONI! TONÉ!

June 9, 1990 (1 week)

The three founding members of Tony! Toni! Toné! weren't sure what direction they wanted to take with their second album. "It was our first time producing our own album," says Dwayne Wiggins. "We had written a lot of songs on our first album, but we didn't get in any experience as producers. So we were going in with no tools at all to produce the album. It was a scary feeling—I guess they call it the sophomore jinx, and we definitely had it."

Producers Denzil Foster and Thomas McElroy had guided Tony! Toni! Toné! through their first album, *Who?*, and had helped them achieve a Number One single [see 489—"Little Walter"]. Raphael Wiggins, who had never been in a 24-track studio until he worked with Foster and McElroy, says the trio learned a lot from the producers, including that less is more. "We had to pull a lot of things back and make things a little simpler," he explains.

On their second album, the Tonys wanted to show their fans they were in charge of their own destiny. "That's why we called it *The Revival*...Like when I was over in London, I would sometimes leave our hotel in the middle of the night and go to a studio and sit in on somebody's session who I'd just met. And they were doing real percussion and real strings and I'd always wanted to get into that...I did a little bit on that [second] album and that's what *The Revival* was all about, having a good time."

On their first day of recording their second album, the Wiggins brothers took a break at an Oakland hamburger stand called Giant Burgers and started writing a song called "The Blues." Raphael recalls, "My brother was doing beats." The Tonys came up with a bassline and a drum part and hummed the rhythm all the way back to the studio. "I picked up the guitar and started playing this slow blues lick that runs consistently through the song. And then a buddy of mine, Carl Wheeler, came in and ripped some clavinet parts."

Dwayne adds to the story: "My father was a blues guitarist, so the first lick I learned was a blues lick. We decided we wanted to do something hip-hop bluesy. And that track just happened to come together."

Raphael refers to "The Blues" as "Parliament/ Charlie Brown" funk. "It had a little 'Charlie Brown' piano in it and some remnants of Parliament with a little kid singing with his high voice...That blues feeling [is] in there because when people sing about the blues, they're always down."

"The Blues" was a good choice for the first single from *The Revival*, according to Dwayne. "It was a good pacesetter. A lot of things that were out at that time had more of a [new jack] swing, and we didn't want to be put in that category. We wanted to do something that would open your ears up to something different. We liked the song ourselves."

Dwayne says it's important to the band to record songs that will also sound great when performed live. "That comes up a lot when we're writing songs," he explains. "We think of what song would I like to jam onstage, what kind of song would you like to open up with."

563

TOMORROW (A BETTER YOU, A BETTER ME)

Quincy Jones featuring Tevin Campbell

QWEST 19881
WRITERS: GEORGE JOHNSON, LOUIS JOHNSON, SIEDAH GARRETT
PRODUCER: QUINCY JONES
June 16, 1990 (1 week)

The third Number One single from Quincy Jones's multi-artist *Back on the Block* set was originally written by the Brothers Johnson [see 247—"I'll Be Good to You"] as an instrumental for their very first album, *Look Out for #1*.

"I was out with a friend of mine one sunny day in his MG with the top down, and I had already written I don't know how many songs," recalls George Johnson. "He brought me home one afternoon and I was parked in front of the house when I started whistling —and I was whistling the melody for 'Tomorrow.' "

George's *modus operandi* was to immediately capture the melodies that came into his head on a tape recorder so he wouldn't forget them. "After I put down the melody, I worked with the chord changes that accommodated the melody. Louis came downstairs and heard it and worked on the bassline."

Fourteen years after "Tomorrow" was released as an instrumental, Quincy called George to help out on the *Back on the Block* project [see 549—"I'll Be Good to You"]. "He was working with Siedah Garrett, who had already worked with Michael Jackson," says George. "She was coming up as a writer. He had Siedah write the lyrics to the melody and she came up with some incredible lyrics for 'Tomorrow.' I definitely approved of that."

Garrett, signed to Jones's publishing company, received a call from the producer asking her to write lyrics for the "Tomorrow" track. "I agonized over it for a couple of days, and so I finally called him," she remembers. "I said, 'Let me get a little more information.' Because I wasn't sure if he wanted the song to have the same melody or if he just wanted to give me a track. When I found out he wanted it to be called 'Tomorrow' and he wanted to use the melody that was already established, that made it a lot easier for me and I came up with a lyric at that point. I knew Tevin [Campbell] was going to sing it and I knew it had to be hopeful and youthful." Once she knew what Quincy wanted, Siedah completed the lyrics in a couple of days. "There are some songs that take a little longer. However, once I was put on the right track, this one was relatively easy."

Benny Medina of Warner Brothers Records had seen a video of Tevin singing and passed it along to Quincy. The producer flew the pre-teen newcomer to Los Angeles to record "Tomorrow." "I was very nervous," Tevin recalls. "Everyone was there. Siedah was there. The Crouches were there. Chaka was there. Ray [Charles] was there." It was the first time Tevin had met Quincy. The producer, who was in the middle of eating when Tevin arrived, asked him if he was ready to record. The young singer said yes and completed the song in one take. "Siedah sent me the lyrics," says Tevin, who was a fan of the Brothers Johnson. "I already knew the music. So I put the lyrics to the song the way I felt it."

Campbell loved working with Jones. "He's a genius. He lets you do what you feel...He doesn't hold you back. In the studio, he's no different than he is outside the studio. He's very down to earth, very warm, [and] has a great heart."

Tevin Campbell

M.C. Hammer

564

U CAN'T TOUCH THIS

M.C. Hammer

CAPITOL 15571
WRITERS: RICK JAMES, ALONZO MILLER, M.C. HAMMER
PRODUCER: M.C. HAMMER
June 23, 1990 (1 week)

Imagine Rick James's surprise the first time he heard "U Can't Touch This" on the radio.

"There were a lot of rappers doing my stuff," says James, who has four Number One hits of his own [see 295—"You and I"]. "I didn't appreciate at the time rappers sampling people's stuff. So I told my lawyers and my publishers, 'If any rappers want to use my stuff, I'm going to refuse. I don't [care] how much money because I don't want them doing it.' But they were making deals on the side with people because there was so much money going down and they didn't tell me about it. They made this deal with M.C. Hammer on 'Super Freak' and never told me. Had they told me, I would have refused."

James found out one day while riding in his car with a friend, who mentioned that a rapper had taken one of James's songs and was moving up the chart with it. It didn't take long for "U Can't Touch This" to come up on the radio. "I'm riding in the car and I hear the whole track of 'Super Freak.' They told me it was the Number One record in the country. So I called my lawyers and I was really pissed off and all of a sudden I found out how much money it was making. I said, 'OK.' But I never personally committed to M.C. Hammer doing 'Super Freak.' Had it been up to me, it wouldn't have been done."

Stanley Kirk Burrell was just three or four years old when he saw a televised performance featuring James Brown at the Apollo. He emulated the Godfather of Soul doing his "Please, Please, Please" routine, as his brother handed him a bedsheet to stand in for Brown's cape.

He wasn't thinking of a musical career, however. He was more interested in baseball and frequented the Oakland Coliseum, where he could watch the A's. Owner Charlie Finley spotted 11-year-old Burrell doing James Brown–type splits in the parking lot and hired him to work in the clubhouse. He was soon traveling with the team as a batboy, and was nicknamed Little Hammer because one player thought he bore a strong resemblance to Henry "Hammerin' Hank" Aaron.

His desire to become a professional ballplayer never panned out, so after high school Hammer joined the Navy. Following a three-year stint, he put together a Christian rap group called the Holy Ghost Boys.

Mike Davis and Dwayne Murphy of the A's backed him with a $20,000 investment and Hammer formed his own record company and sold his own single, "Ring 'Em," out of the trunk of his car. With Felton Pilate of Con Funk Shun [see 282—"Ffun"], he recorded an album called *Feel My Power.* Joy Bailey of Capitol's A&R department saw Hammer at the Oak Tree Cabaret in Oakland in May 1988 and arranged for the artist to meet label executives in Hollywood.

Capitol advanced Hammer $750,000, added some songs to his independently released debut album, and re-released it under the title *Let's Get It Started.* But it was his second Capitol release, *Please Hammer Don't Hurt 'Em,* that made the Oakland rapper a superstar. "U Can't Touch This" zoomed up the pop and R&B charts, peaking at number eight and Number One, respectively.

565

ALL I DO IS THINK OF YOU

Troop

ATLANTIC 87952
WRITERS: BRIAN HOLLAND, MICHAEL LOVESMITH
PRODUCER: CHUCKII BOOKER
June 30, 1990 (1 week)

Michael Lovesmith and his older brothers Danny and Louis were signed to Holland/Dozier/Holland's Music Merchant label as the Smith Connection. Michael wrote a song he felt was a hit and played it for his brothers; they thought "All I Do Is Think of You" was a nice song, but wanted something more up-tempo. They did record it, although it was never released. When Holland/Dozier/Holland returned to Motown in the mid-'70s, Michael came with them and the song was offered to the Jackson 5 for their *Moving Violation* album.

Released as the flip side of a remake of the Supremes' "Forever Came Today" and then as its own A-side, "All I Do Is Think of You" peaked at number 50. Thirteen years later, producer Chuckii Booker and Troop lead singer Steve Russell came up with the idea of covering the tune while hanging out at Booker's house. Chuckii explains, "He felt it would be a great song to cover and I told him, 'That's funny, because I was thinking about that for you guys, because you are like a '90s version of the Jacksons.' And Steve's a big fan of Michael Jackson's anyway. So we toyed with the idea and went for it. In the 'hood where all my buddies were, we used to love [that song]. Everybody used to play it and say, 'This is the cut. This should have been a big smash.' "

The fact that the song wasn't a huge success made it more attractive to Russell. "We wouldn't want to touch a big smash record and try to remake it, because then people are going to have their eyes on you...With 'All I Do Is Think of You,' a lot of people our age didn't even know the song and a lot of older people knew it and appreciated the fact that we would do a song like that. We wanted to make it a Troop record, and that's what we did."

Booker updated the song: "I put a lot of breaks in it, a lot of stops, things that a lot of people would do in concert, like a live version. I incorporated that style on tape so when the guys sing it live, people will remember all those big breaks."

Russell recalls recording the song: "I think that was a 10-hour session with backgrounds and lead vocals. I remember leaving the studio when it was time for Allen [McNeil] to sing his verse because he's the type of singer who is real original and likes to sing stuff his way. And I'm a big Michael Jackson fan. I was so sold on the way Michael sang it that I didn't want to interfere with how Alan sang it, so I left." When he heard the playback, Russell loved what his fellow Trooper had sung.

Russell had listened to the original version many, many times. "Before we did the song, on our first tour, that's all I listened to every day. I told everybody, 'Watch, we're going to do it.' Everybody was sick of the song." Russell finds it difficult to compare the Troop version to the Jackson 5 recording. "I was never satisfied with my performance on the song, ever. To this day when I hear it, I feel like I didn't touch the emotion that Michael had in the song."

When Lovesmith found out Troop was recording his song, he expected it to sound very different from the original. "I was flattered it was so close to Michael's version," he says. "Berry Gordy said it was a Number One record. He was right."

566

YOU CAN'T DENY IT

Lisa Stansfield

ARISTA 2024

WRITERS: LISA STANSFIELD, IAN DEVANEY, ANDY MORRIS

PRODUCERS: IAN DEVANEY, ANDY MORRIS

July 7, 1990 (1 week)

"I actually did the finished vocal to 'You Can't Deny It' in the toilet!" Lisa Stansfield exclaimed in *Blues & Soul*. "The worst thing with our toilet is that the flush on the loo went on for ages, so it would interfere with the recording, so we put up a sign saying, DO NOT FLUSH."

After Lisa's single "All Around the World" went to Number One in the U.K., Arista Records wanted an entire album from the artist. "So we delved back into everything we'd written in the previous year and got it going as soon as we could," says writer/producer Ian Devaney. "We were in between studios at the time, because the one where we did most of 'All Around the World' was burgled, so all of our gear was missing." That's why Lisa recorded at the home she shared with Devaney, and that's why her vocal was recorded in the bathroom.

"You Can't Deny It" started with Ian and Andy Morris writing the music and adding the flugel line. They were inspired by the sound of "Big Thing," a B-side they had recorded while they were still going by the group name Blue Zone. Andy played the horns on the track.

Devaney calls Stansfield a natural singer. "We generally don't mess about too much because the first or second performance of a song ends up being 99 percent of the thing that ends up on the record. She just goes in and that's it, really. We've always treated the song and the vocal as the foremost thing. We do like the beat to be heavy now and again, but we try never to let that spoil what the real meaning of the record is about."

When "You Can't Deny It" went to Number One, Stansfield became the first British female to have two consecutive chart-toppers on the *Billboard* R&B chart. "It's fantastic for us," Devaney acknowledges. "You know yourself what your influences are, but you don't really know if you're going to be accepted by the people who really know about that kind of music and really love that kind of music. So it's a thrill when you see a record go into the R&B chart. It's confirmation that you're doing something right."

Stansfield, who says she was strongly influenced by Marvin Gaye, Luther Vandross, Chaka Khan, Otis Redding, and Aretha Franklin, commented in the *New York Times*, "I've really found that white Americans have been more shocked than black Americans about what I'm doing and I don't know why that is. It just seems funny that the white population of America has such a hard time with it. This sort of borrowing in Europe is readily accepted. I think that if you hear music young, whatever music you hear influences you. I'm white, but I've been influenced by black music."

Lisa also attributes her success to listening to her heart. "I learned a lot of lessons from my experiences with Blue Zone," she said in BMI's quarterly *MusicWorld*. "One thing I've learned is that you should never compromise your convictions. When I was with Blue Zone, I did too much of that. We were all very naïve. Finally, when I recorded *Affection*, I promised myself that, first and foremost, I'd be true to my own heart. That I'd go with my gut instincts. It paid off."

567

MY, MY, MY

Johnny Gill

MOTOWN 2033
WRITERS: BABYFACE, DARYL SIMMONS
PRODUCERS: L.A. REID, BABYFACE
July 14, 1990 (2 weeks)

Johnny Gill worked with the two hottest writer/producer teams of the '90s when he recorded his debut album for Motown. Jimmy Jam and Terry Lewis produced his first Number One single [see 560—"Rub You the Right Way"] and L.A. Reid and Babyface produced the follow-up, the chart-topping "My, My, My."

"When I first heard 'My, My, My,' I played it for Jimmy and Terry and I played it for my godfather and I said, 'I don't know about this song.' It was a point where I was really close to the project and nothing was 'good enough,' " Johnny says. "When you're working with producers like Jam and Lewis and L.A. and Babyface, you're always looking for them to give you something that sounds like something they've done before. If you don't hear something that sounds like something they've done before, you think, 'Damn, I don't think they gave me their best stuff.' And what they've been so successful at doing is creating and giving everybody their own style and their own sound. And I didn't realize that that was the process."

Gill wasn't the first person to record "My, My, My." In fact, as Babyface explains, "That was one I originally cut for myself." I did an OK version of it, but Johnny turned it into his song. I'm really glad I'm not the kind of artist that feels like, 'I've got to have the song,' or 'I have to sing it, I know better.' I know when to let something go, rather than trying to hold onto something because I'm trying to build up my career."

Johnny Gill

When he wrote the song with Daryl Simmons, Babyface says he was looking for "something that was like the ultimate compliment, but in a more ethnic way." The original version he cut had as many "my"s in it as Johnny's. "The whole 'My, My, My' inspiration came from the Winans," Babyface acknowledges. "Because when Marvin Winans starts to sing, he sings, 'My, my, my, my, my.' I loved the way it sounded, so I started singing, 'My, my' when I would sing something, and it turned into a song."

Babyface's partner, L.A. Reid, liked the song when he heard it and called it "The My, My Song." "I didn't feel like I was soulful enough on it," Babyface admits. "I couldn't take it to the street, and Johnny could."

Gill explains how he approaches the recording of ballads like "My, My, My" as opposed to his uptempo material: "I like to learn the ballads—sing them down, listen to them, live with them for a day or so, learn the words so that I can come back in and perform them as opposed to singing off the paper. The ballads become so much more intimate and personal that you make sure you put yourself completely in that mood."

Gill was one of the first artists to give his label a pair of consecutive Number One hits after Jheryl Busby became president. The singer says he was happy "to be able to be part of the history of Motown, even though this is now called the new Motown. It's like we're carrying on the legacy. When you look at the people who have contributed to make Motown what it is today and be connected to it, it's an honor."

568

MAKE YOU SWEAT

Keith Sweat

VINTERTAINMENT 64961
WRITERS: KEITH SWEAT, TIMMY GATLING, BOBBY WOOTEN
PRODUCER: KEITH SWEAT
July 28, 1990 (1 week)

"I still wanted to be on the funky edge," Keith Sweat says about his second album, *I'll Give All My Love to You*. "Because I was established already, I wanted to give them something they could identify with me, so that's where 'Make You Sweat' came [from]...my last name played into the song so well."

Sweat was introduced to Chicago-born Bobby Wooten through a lawyer from the Windy City, Mel Reddick. Wooten had been the associate conductor of *Your Arms Too Short to Box with God* starring Jennifer Holliday [see 362—"And I Am Telling You I'm Not Going"], a keyboardist for Stephanie Mills [see 426—"I Have Learned to Respect the Power of Love"], and musical director for Phyllis Hyman. He started writing in earnest in 1983 while working with Hyman and two of her musicians, Barry Eastmond and Wayne Brathwaite [see 429—"There'll Be Sad Songs (To Make You Cry)"].

At their first meeting, Wooten and Sweat collaborated on a song titled "Come Back." "Then Keith went out on the road because at that time 'I Want Her' [see 477] was a hit," says Wooten. "He went out on tour and I didn't see him again for a year. So I was hoping that the tune would make it on the album. When he came back, he called me and we spent most of that year together working on the album. We did everything except for two songs on that album."

Wooten recalls how "Make You Sweat" came about: "Usually I would come prepared with a track already. I'd just make tracks. I work with drum machines and keyboards. I guess that's my major instrument, but I've learned to program drums. I would program drum, bass, and perhaps the keyboard sound and start off that way. We'd sit around and make up ideas. One of the gifts Keith has is that he stands up to a mike and just lets things come out...but the actual [song] came from an initial response to a particular track."

The original title Wooten and Sweat had for the track was "Rock This Girl Tonight." "Timmy Gatling was in the studio one day with us and started coming up with things," Wooten remembers. "The 'You say no, I say yes, girl I bet I'll make you sweat' came from Timmy. He had a lot to do with changing that hook."

The original track also went through some changes. "There were always adjustments being made, all the way up through the mix," Wooten says. "Since I was engineering most of it, it was pretty simple. Anytime we wanted to hear something different, we'd put it up. I think all the way up until the time the final mix was done, it was constantly changing, even to the point where Teddy Riley came in and did some drum programming pretty close to the end, which also served to enhance [the track]."

"Make You Sweat" was the first single issued from *I'll Give All My Love to You*. "I think 'Make You Sweat' was pretty timely when it happened because it further spurred on some of the 'New Jack' sound that was going on, although it's not really an authentic 'New Jack' tune," says Wooten. "I think that because Teddy had done the first album with Keith and with me appreciating and admiring the work he had done, I was pretty careful not to go back and rip off [Riley] and make that first album over again. The style is slightly different than all of the hip-hop or 'New Jack' elements of the first album. I think we were trying to prepare Keith for a more mature audience."

569
CAN'T STOP
After 7

VIRGIN 98961
WRITERS: BABYFACE, L.A. REID
PRODUCERS: L.A. REID, BABYFACE
August 4, 1990 (1 week)

"Can't Stop" was After 7's second consecutive Number One single. "I remember having a listening session for some of the people at Virgin and playing two or three songs," says writer/producer Antonio "L.A." Reid. "When that song came on, everybody's eyes lit up and they said, 'Yeah, this is the record.' I'm always motivated by how people respond to music and that one got the biggest response at that time, and I think that stuck with me."

The lyrics to "Can't Stop" were written on the spot at the control board in the studio, says After 7's Keith Mitchell, who is Reid's cousin. With the other two members of After 7 being Kenny "Babyface" Edmonds' brothers, it's not surprising there is an automatic bonding when they record together. "We know the perfection they strive for," Mitchell points out. "In working with them, we've learned that because that's what they go for, so we won't settle for less when we work with other producers. We listen to them, and then you have to listen to your heart and fine-tune both of those together. They know what works and what doesn't. To get the opportunity to work with them is a blessing and to have them as family is another blessing."

Mitchell remembers recording "Can't Stop." "It's one of the first songs that we sang down vocally, where we sang all the hooks of the song. With [current] technology, we can sing the hook one time and they have a sampler that can place your background vocals where they're supposed to be on a tape without you singing them over, but 'Can't Stop' was a song we sang all the way down."

Kevon Edmonds sang lead on "Can't Stop" while his brother Melvin joined him and Mitchell on background vocals. Babyface played keyboards and drums; Reid provided drums and percussion. The song was recorded at the Elumba studio in Hollywood.

Reid believes the single remix of the song was more appealing to a wider audience than the album version. "The original was very R&B and when we did the remix we were able to get some club play out of it and we really broadened the scope. We tailored it for a broader audience and gave it a better opportunity. Before I think the song was very urban. It was very black. I don't think that's a terrible thing, but for that time period, I think music that had a broader appeal did better whereas [in 1993] I think it's quite the opposite."

Mitchell says the pop remix was the trademark of LaFace productions. "They don't like to give you everything on the first go-round. They leave some things out, leave some things on the tape so they can come back and create a stronger song which is the same song. I think a lot of times the remixers are trying to change the song totally and they lose its feel."

570
VISION OF LOVE
Mariah Carey

COLUMBIA 73348
WRITERS: MARIAH CAREY, BEN MARGULIES
PRODUCERS: RHETT LAWRENCE, NARADA MICHAEL WALDEN
August 11, 1990 (2 weeks)

"They described her as a girl who was 18 and had the most incredible voice you've ever heard," says producer Rhett Lawrence. "I literally got goose bumps on my arms when I heard her sing. I couldn't believe the power and maturity in her voice."

Lawrence had already produced artists like Johnny Kemp and Earth, Wind & Fire for Columbia Records when he was asked to fly to New York and listen to a demo tape recorded by Mariah Carey. She had handed her demo tape personally to CBS Records Group president Tommy Mottola at a label party in Manhattan. Mottola listened to the tape during a limousine ride home from the party and was so impressed, he had the driver turn the car around so he could go back and find the singer. By the time he returned, she had left—and there was no phone number on the tape. Mottola spent the weekend trying to locate the talented unknown. She had been invited to the party by singer Brenda K. Starr, but Starr's managers didn't know who Carey was. On Monday, Mariah found a message from Tommy on her answering machine. "They wanted me to come to CBS Records, and I was so excited," she says.

After signing with the label, Carey flew to Los Angeles to work with Rhett Lawrence. The producer listened to a rough version of "Vision of Love," a song the artist had written with Ben Margulies. Mariah and Ben had written their first song together, the Motownish "Here We Go Round Again," when she was a high school student and he was a keyboard player who showed up for a session paid for by Mariah's older brother. "[Ben] can't really play keyboards very well—he's really more of a drummer—but after that day, we kept in touch, and we just sort of clicked as writers," Carey explains.

Lawrence describes the demo of "Vision of Love": "It was a different tempo at the time...a '50s sort of shuffle." Collaborating with Carey and Margulies, the producer altered the tempo and used Mariah's demo vocals as a second vocal in the tag of the song. It was recorded at Skyline Studios in New York with Margulies on drums, Ren Klyce programming the Linn drum, Jimmy Rip on guitars, Marcus Miller on bass, and Lawrence on keyboards.

The song was mixed by David Frazer at Tarpan Studios in San Rafael, California, the studio of producer Narada Michael Walden, who had also been called by Mottola to work with the newly discovered artist. "I was busy, didn't know if I had time to work with her," says Walden. But Mottola persisted, and the producer was impressed with his enthusiasm. "I promised when I was in New York, I would...sit down and meet with her...She was very shy." Walden enjoyed their working relationship: "Mariah is very astute in the studio....She likes to keep going at something for a long time before she's really satisfied. But I think a lot of that is what you experience when you're making your first album."

571

JERK OUT

The Time

PAISLEY PARK 19750
WRITERS/PRODUCERS: THE TIME
August 25, 1990 (1 week)

When Terry Lewis suggested that the seven members of the Time reunite, the first thing they did was call Prince, according to Jimmy Jam. "We said, 'If we do a reunion, it has to include you in some way behind the board or producing or helping us write songs,' because he was a big part of the Time. The live part of the Time was us, but the recording part, a lot of it was Prince's influences and songs. I think he was really surprised because there had been a lot of rumors that we didn't get along and because Prince had fired us. And we swept all that under the rug a long time ago."

In retrospect, Jam and Lewis consider being fired by Prince a tremendous favor. The Time was originally formed as an amalgamation of Flyte Time, a group that included Jam and Lewis as well as Jellybean Johnson and Monte Moir, and Grand Central, a band that featured Morris Day and Prince. When Prince signed with Warner Brothers, he combined Day with Flyte Time and developed the Time for the label. All went well until Jam and Lewis began moonlighting as producers and were caught in a snowstorm in Atlanta. They missed a Time concert in Texas and were dismissed by Prince. Moir left the group a month later and Johnson departed temporarily, returning to participate in the film *Purple Rain* along with new members Paul "St. Paul" Peterson and Jerome Benton, Lewis's brother. After *Purple Rain,* Day departed for a solo career and the Time was up.

"Jerk Out" was a song originally recorded for the third Time album, *Ice Cream Castle,* before Jam and Lewis were excused. "After we got kicked out, it languished on the shelf," says Jimmy Jam. "We always felt it was a great song, and rather than interpret what was going on in 1990, we wanted the [reunion] album to sound as if after 'Jungle Love' there would have been a next Time album in 1987." Jam recalls how "Jerk Out" was written by himself along with Prince, Jesse, and Terry. "Back in those days, Prince would come in with a lot of the ideas...and then we'd flesh them out. All the songs were written at rehearsal. It was always like a jam session. 'Jerk Out' was written like that. It was a drum machine groove that we filled in."

It wasn't easy for the seven Time members to get back into the group spirit at first, according to Day. "It was a great experience working with everyone. I think that was the best part. I think we found we had grown accustomed to making decisions on our own, so sometimes deciding on simple things proved to be a task. And it was difficult to function as a group."

Jimmy Jam agrees that it was tough bringing the band up to speed. "We were terrible the first day," he admits. "We started to play some of the songs like 'Get It Up' and 'Cool' and we were sloppy. Jellybean hadn't played drums for a long time because he plays guitar...Terry and I play in the studio all the time but that's a lot different than rehearsing every day or playing a live show every day. So we were lazy...Jesse sounded good because he had been doing solo albums. He plays guitar every single day, so he was probably in the best shape. The first day was scary...by the second day, we had it together and were really cooking and sounding good."

FEELS GOOD

Tony! Toni! Toné!

WING 877 436
WRITERS: TIM CHRISTIAN, CARL WHEELER, DWAYNE WIGGINS, RAPHAEL WIGGINS
PRODUCERS: TONY! TONI! TONÉ!
September 1, 1990 (2 weeks)

Dwayne Wiggins gives an accurate description of "Feels Good," the second consecutive Number One single from *The Revival.* He says it's like "Baptist shout music that makes you feel like moving."

His brother Raphael recalls, " 'Feels Good' is a song we didn't have any lyrics to. It was a nice track and we experimented with sampling—it's got a lot of sampling in it. I took a bit of 'Funky Drummer' that everybody and their mother used 50 times and I used it for the 51st time. But I changed it around—I think I used it [in a] way nobody ever used it before."

Raphael explains that a lot of rappers had sampled the song, but it hadn't been heard in an R&B number. "I sang it and did a real monsterish-type chord progression, going on through the song on the 'Feels Good' part—at the end it was more like testimony. I'm singing, 'I feel it all in my hands, I feel it all in my feet,' and I really felt that when I was singing it. I think that's why the record came off, because everything I was singing was so simple."

The younger Wiggins brother did hear people make fun of the song. "Like some of it was out of key...I sang it a couple of times and when I mixed it, I would bring another voice in and both of the voices would clash and it would be flat or sharp. Real singers were making jokes about it and I was laughing because I [replied], 'Maybe the key is a little flat and sharp these days. I hear a lot of people doing it.' But I didn't try to do it intentionally. It didn't matter because it was fun, it was energetic and it wasn't selling out. It wasn't meant to be poppy. It was just one of those soul-type things that anybody can get into because music to me is an international language and it speaks to all people if the right vibe is in the song."

Raphael is the first to admit he was not a veteran vocalist when Tony! Toni! Toné! signed their first record contract. "He didn't have a lot of singing experience when we started," his older brother Dwayne confirms. "He had experience playing behind other vocalists, but not as an up-front singer. We have a brother who sings a lot and we played behind a lot of acts that were vocal groups locally and we played behind a lot of choirs. We've had training in different areas—not what you would call classical training—[but with] jazz groups and different players."

Although the Tonys didn't originally consider themselves lead vocalists, they liked the way Raphael's voice came across. "He sounded so real and it brought the tracks together so well," Dwayne adds.

While "Feels Good" was a big hit, the trio prefers not to repeat old glories. "We like sitting in a room [with] guitar, drums, bass, and piano and just vibing—coming off the head with something that feels natural," says Dwayne. "On the second album, we used a banjo sound and a surangi. It's an Indian-style instrument. We like to try out new things."

Despite their success, Dwayne says he doesn't keep track of how the group is doing on the charts. "I picked up a *Billboard* and read this article we had in there, but that was the extent of it."

573

LIES

En Vogue

ATLANTIC 87893
WRITERS: EN VOGUE, DENZIL FOSTER, THOMAS MCELROY, KHAYREE SHAHEED
PRODUCERS: DENZIL FOSTER, THOMAS MCELROY
September 15, 1990 (1 week)

The four funky divas known as En Vogue were already tagged "the Supremes of the '90s" when they pulled off the Supremes-like feat of following their first Number One single [see 561—"Hold On"] with another.

" 'Lies' started off with that string intro," says writer/producer Denzil Foster. "We wanted to do this classical thing. At that time, we were influenced by Soul II Soul. It was like that feel, that little hip-hop smooth-tip thing. The intro was so strong, I was thinking, what could come after that and keep this smooth tip on this hard groove. I was just humming 'Lies.' 'Lies' felt like it. And we wanted to talk about something other than sex." Foster and McElroy both felt "Lies" was a very bold, strong title. "There's something about it. Like the word 'pain.' 'Lies' was a strong hook and we wrote about it and we were able to give the girls something to talk about other than a love song."

The rap on the politically themed song was written by Khayree Shaheed, a producer Foster and McElroy met while they were still in Club Nouveau. "He was always cool and he was a hip-hop producer in the Bay Area," says Foster. Debbie T performed the rap on the track.

Both Foster and McElroy knew that style would be an important element in the success of En Vogue. "I always had an eye for fashion and Tommy had an eye for fashion," says Foster. "And a few of the girls had pretty good eyes for fashion. So they went through *Vogue* magazines, *Mademoiselle,* and the European ones, because by the time it gets here, everybody's doing it. We felt by capturing the European look, we'd be more on the edge. They cut out things they liked and didn't like. When we finally knew what we wanted, we had to find people who could find those things."

The four women in En Vogue didn't all meet in one room until they auditioned for Foster and McElroy, but their lives had intersected in various combinations before that fateful day. Maxine Jones, originally from New Jersey, studied voice at Merritt College in Oakland. A few years before En Vogue became a reality, Maxine's hairdresser introduced her to a client who had relocated to the Bay Area from

Connecticut. Her name was Dawn Robinson, and the two women sang a few songs right there in the beauty salon to hear how they sounded together. Maxine met Cindy Herron in 1986 in San Francisco when they were both cast in a musical, *Green Christmas*. Cindy had encountered Terry Ellis in Houston, where they shared a pizza with a mutual friend.

Early in their career, the four members of En Vogue were warned they would end up hating each other, Maxine told Jeff Lorez in *Blues & Soul*. Dawn confirmed, "On the first promo tour we got over any strains and realized that we were all in this together, so we had to make it work for each other."

574

CRAZY

The Boys

MOTOWN 2053
WRITERS: HAKEEM ABDUL-SAMAD, KHIRY ABDUL-SAMAD, ASHLEY FEAZELL
PRODUCERS: HAKEEM ABDUL-SAMAD, KHIRY ABDUL-SAMAD
September 22, 1990 (1 week)

The four young Abdul-Samad brothers, better known as the Boys, composed a song for their first album, *Messages from the Boys*. "Be My Girl" was co-written with Craig Cooper. "And from there, we kept writing songs," says Khiry Abdul-Samad. The Boys did not meet too much resistance from executives at Motown Records when they let it be known they wanted to produce themselves as well as write their own material. "It wasn't that much of a fight because they believed in us a lot," says Tajh. "Enough for us to produce just about everything on the second album except for one song, which was done by L.A. and Babyface."

The first single from the Boys' second album was "Crazy," penned by Hakeem, Khiry, and their friend Ashley Feazell. Khiry Abdul-Samad recalls the origin of the song: "Hakeem came up with the music. I was in San Diego and went to a party with these girls. I was in a car with Ron DeVoe's girlfriend. She was giving me a lift to the party and they were playing the Gap Band's 'Humpin'' in the car. I said, 'Man, that is jammin'. I like that melody.' I went home and Hakeem had a track and I altered the melody a little bit and put it in that style." The song's hook line, "You've got me going crazy," came from the line in the Gap Band song, "You Got Me Humpin'."

The Boys had previously submitted a lot of their own material to Motown, but had always been turned down. "And then we came up with 'Crazy' and we walked into Jheryl [Busby]'s office and sung it to him right there in his ear and he went crazy," Khiry reports. "He said, 'We need to do this right now.' So we went ahead and did it and he told me to come up with a video concept...and we directed the video also."

After working with established, well-respected producers like L.A. Reid and Babyface, the young Abdul-Samad brothers were given the go-ahead to produce the track themselves. "It wasn't that hard," says Khiry. "Everybody made it seem like it was more than it was. But we were used to being in the studio."

"Crazy" was not only the third Number One single for the Boys, it was adapted into a commercial for Pepsi. It was a great accomplishment for the brothers who just a few years earlier had appeared on "Star Search," the weekly talent contest hosted by Ed McMahon. "They had an open tryout...'Junior Star Search,' " Tajh explains. "[There] were 4,000 people in the line and we were at the end of the line. The last people! Since we had been acting and had SAG and AFTRA cards, they let us come to the front of the line. So we got lucky and we got to the front and they let us on." The Boys performed "The Bird," a hit for the Minneapolis group known as the Time. "And then we lost," Tajh laments. "It was terrible."

Once they became successful, the Boys had to deal with being in the public eye. "It hasn't been as weird as you hear, like the Jackson stories," says Tajh. "We're just regular guys. We go out to the malls, hang out at clubs, all that stuff. We missed out on school, [but] we've got friends that keep us down to earth."

575

THIEVES IN THE TEMPLE

Prince

PAISLEY PARK 19751
WRITER: PRINCE
PRODUCER: PRINCE
September 29, 1990 (1 week)

Prince chose an interview in *Rolling Stone* to let the world know that he wouldn't be crushed if the critics didn't love his third film, *Graffiti Bridge*. "I can't please everybody," he said. "I didn't want to make *Die Hard 4*. But I'm also not looking to be Francis Ford Coppola. I see this more like those 1950s rock and roll movies."

As it turned out, the reviewers didn't care much for *Graffiti Bridge*, even though it was a sequel of sorts to Prince's much-heralded first film, *Purple Rain*. The music, however—that was another matter.

The soundtrack to *Graffiti Bridge* featured a variety of artists, including the Time, Mavis Staples, George Clinton, and Tevin Campbell, just 12 years old when he recorded his contribution. The first single released from the soundtrack was Prince's "Thieves in the Temple."

Tom Garneau, an engineer at Prince's Paisley Park complex, recalls, "They were shooting the film here, amongst other places in Minneapolis and that song was not in the movie—well, the song didn't exist. The song was actually recorded and mixed in one 30-hour session straight through and then was written into the movie because it came out so well."

Garneau, who lives just five miles away from Paisley Park, was hired to work at the studio in 1988 after he "got in the studio manager's face" at a trade show and asked if he could be an intern. The manager replied that Paisley Park didn't make use of interns, so they would have to hire him.

Garneau, who says the staff works very hard when Prince is in the studio, recalls how "Thieves in the Temple" was recorded: "He did all the instruments. We usually start with a drum machine and lay down a beat and then guitars. There's a lot of different instruments on it and some samples and things like that." Garneau explains that Prince doesn't follow one particular method. "But pretty early on, he got the vocals. When he does vocals, we set up his microphone for him in the control room and he operates the tape machine himself. We route the microphone to maybe half a dozen tracks and he sings all the lead vocals, all the harmonies, everything by himself. We disappear for about six hours and we come back and there are these full harmonies."

The mixing was done as they went along, says Garneau. "At that point we didn't know it was going to be the real thing. The mix evolves as you track songs and you add some effects, just to keep it pleasing to listen to while you're tracking. Mixes evolve that way. It was 90 percent there by the end of the day and it just took a little bit of extra tweaking to get something that we could actually put on tape that ended up being on the record."

Working side by side with Prince, Garneau has had the opportunity to know the real person, not just the media image. "A lot of people see him as real guarded and quiet," the engineer says. "When he's comfortable with you, he can be very warm and open and he has a really good sense of humor. That might be one unusual thing people might not think of."

The Boys

576
GIVING YOU THE BENEFIT
Pebbles

MCA 53891
WRITERS: L.A. REID, BABYFACE
PRODUCERS: L.A. REID, BABYFACE
October 6, 1990 (3 weeks)

After recording her debut album for MCA, Pebbles vowed she that would work even harder when making her next record. Writer/producer Antonio "L.A." Reid may not be the most objective observer available, especially since he is married to the artist, but in his opinion, Pebbles carried through on her promise.

"She did so much work on 'Giving You the Benefit,' " says Reid. "She did a lot of backgrounds. She made up a lot of parts and she was very instrumental in the success of that record. On that single, as well as the LP, we said, 'What we intend to accomplish with this next Pebbles record is for people to take her more seriously,' and I think we did it."

"Giving You the Benefit" is Reid's favorite Pebbles song of all the ones he and partner Kenny "Babyface" Edmonds have written and produced for the artist. "I remember mixing it so many times because I wanted it to be right," Reid declares. "At that time we had a studio in our home, so we had the luxury of doing it over and over. I remember doing it two or three different times and saying, 'This is important. We gotta make this great. Let's do it one more time, it's not quite right. And it was the first record we mixed in our own studio."

When Babyface hears the title "Giving You the Benefit," the first thing he remembers is where he was when he wrote it. "A lot of the songs were written in this apartment called the Terrace on Highland [in Hollywood]," he says, listing "Every Little Step," "Dial My Heart," and "Superwoman." Pebbles's first single from her sophomore album was written not too far away from that location. "I had graduated and started renting a house," he continues. "There was this little room like a guest room on a lower level, and I wrote 'Giving You the Benefit' there and 'On Our Own' and 'It's No Crime.' "

Babyface liked the track to "Giving You the Benefit." He remembers, "It felt very Pebbles to me when I finished it, and I remember calling up L.A. to tell him to come over and check this out. I had the melodies but not necessarily the hook yet." Babyface also credits Pebbles with adding the background parts once she got in the studio. "That's what's cool about Pebbles. When she makes a record, she helps make it her own, because she adds in all the little things that weren't necessarily part of the written song, extra things that add her flavor to it."

Pebbles

Babyface recalls who the musicians were on the session. "When it's bass guitar, it's always Kayo. He was the bass player of the Deele and he's been with us for a long time. He's the only one I ever want to play [bass]. He's always been there, so I'm hoping he will be there forever."

Reid is credited with drums and percussion and Babyface with keyboards and keyboard programming. Joining Pebbles on background vocals were Reid, Natisse "Bambi" Jones, and the members of After 7 [see 558—"Ready or Not"].

577

SO YOU LIKE WHAT YOU SEE

Samuelle

ATLANTIC 87864
WRITERS: DENZIL FOSTER, THOMAS McELROY, SAMUELLE
PRODUCERS: DENZIL FOSTER, THOMAS McELROY
October 27, 1990 (2 weeks)

Samuelle Prater was a freshman at Pinole Valley High School in Northern California when he met a senior named Denzil Foster. They played basketball together, and Foster talked about becoming a record producer. Prater said he wanted to be a recording artist, and the two students dreamed about working together someday.

"He graduated in '81 and I graduated in '84," Samuelle recalls. "Around July of '86, he gave me a call." Foster and his friend Thomas McElroy had been part of the Timex Social Club with Jay King. The group fractured over contractual differences after their first single went to Number One [see 431—"Rumors"]. Foster, McElroy, and King formed a new group, Club Nouveau, and wanted Samuelle to be their lead singer.

"Lean on Me," a remake of the Bill Withers song, spent three weeks at number two. Like the Timex Social Club, Club Nouveau also broke up; Samuelle attributes the split to bad business decisions. Foster and McElroy told him they were going to become producers, and he would be one of their solo artists. "We knew we were going to have to re-establish ourselves because Club Nouveau went on to get some more members in the group and were still out there," Samuelle explains. Foster and McElroy produced an album titled *FM*² that featured Samuelle and the four women who would later become En Vogue [see 561—"Hold On"] as vocalists.

"When we had a production deal at EastWest, we signed him as well as the girls," says Foster. The producer admits now that he wasn't sure what direction he wanted Samuelle to follow. "There were so many male artists out at the time, and we [said], 'Damn, where can you put Sam?' " The producers tried different approaches on various songs, including easy listening and strict R&B.

With production of the *Living in Black Paradise* album almost completed, Samuelle listened to the tapes and thought they were "nice." But "nice" wasn't what he wanted. "It was missing something that was me." The vocalist was in the studio with Foster and McElroy and heard a groove they were working on. "I said, 'That's it, right there.' " But the producers were working on a track for MC Lyte, who had guest-starred on the *FM*² project on a track called "Dr. Love." Foster asked Samuelle to say the word 'Delight' on the tape, still intending it for MC Lyte. "I said, 'Wait a minute. Time out! You've got to give me this track,' " Samuelle remembers. "I said, 'That's what I've been looking for. That's what I've been missing. Just roll the tape. I'm going under the headphones.' "

"Our artists will always outweigh somebody else's artists," says Foster, explaining why he decided to give Samuelle the track. "We said, 'If you like it that much, we'll do something with it.' And it became a hit."

578

LOVE TAKES TIME

Mariah Carey

COLUMBIA 73455
WRITERS: MARIAH CAREY, BEN MARGULIES
PRODUCER: WALTER AFANASIEFF
November 10, 1990 (1 week)

Anyone who purchased a copy of Mariah Carey's debut album when it was first released would not have known that "Love Takes Time" was included. It was such a last-minute addition that the title did not appear on the cover, the disc, or the enclosed booklet. It was more than a pleasant bonus for surprised listeners—it was Mariah's second Number One single out of two releases.

The album was already being mastered when Mariah and writing partner Ben Margulies composed "Love Takes Time," intending it for a second album sometime in the future. "It was sort of a gospelish thing I was improvising, then we began working on it," Margulies explains. "It was on a work tape that we had...and we recorded a very quick demo. It was just a piano vocal demo—I played live piano, and she sang it."

Mariah was on a mini-tour of 10 states, playing an acoustic set. While travelling on a CBS Records company plane, the vocalist played the demo of "Love Takes Time" for Columbia Records president Don Ienner, CBS Records Group president Tommy Mottola, and A&R honcho Bobby Colomby. They told Mariah the song was a "career-maker," and, despite her protests, had to be added to her debut album.

The demo was sent to producer Walter Afanasieff, an associate of producer Narada Michael Walden. Mottola and Ienner liked Afanasieff's work and had named him executive staff producer for the label.

"I guess to see if he made the right choice, [Tommy] called me up one day," Afanasieff recalls. "He said, 'We've got this Mariah Carey album done, but there's a song that she and Ben Margulies wrote that is phenomenal, and I want to try everything we can to put it on the album.' " Walter was willing, and was told he had two days to record the track. "I couldn't believe the opportunity that it was," he says. "I'd never produced anything by myself up until that time."

Mottola wanted the finished product to sound like the demo he loved so much. "We cut the song and the music and the basics in about a day," says Afanasieff. "The only reason is this deadline. It was do it or we were gonna miss out on the whole thing." With the deadline looming, he took the instrumental track to New York to cut Carey's vocals. "She did all the backgrounds, practically sang all night...We came back to the studio that afternoon, and we had to fix one line that we needed to get from Mariah. She fixed that one line very quickly, then [engineer] Dana [Jon Chappelle] and I got back on the plane with the tape, went back to the studio in Sausalito, and mixed it. So it was a three-day process: a day and a half for music, kind of like a day for vocals, and a day for mixing."

Columbia execs wanted Mariah's vocals a little louder, so a remix was completed quickly. Afanasieff asked if the song would make the album, and was told everyone at CBS would do their best to make it so. The presses were literally stopped, the original copies discarded, and with no time left to spare, "Love Takes Time" was included in Mariah Carey's stunning debut album.

579

B.B.D. (I THOUGHT IT WAS ME)?

Bell Biv DeVoe

MCA 53897
WRITERS: DARROL DURANT, RONEY HOOKS, ERIC SADLER, KEITH SHOCKLEE, PAUL STEWART
PRODUCERS: HANK SHOCKLEE, ERIC SADLER, KEITH SHOCKLEE
November 17, 1990 (1 week)

Of all the songs on Bell Biv DeVoe's first album, "B.B.D. (I Thought It Was Me)?" was one of the most difficult to record, according to Michael Bivins, who says that producer Hank Shocklee was a taskmaster. "He wanted it to be right. He [would say], 'Yo, your rapping needs to get better,' or 'Your singing needs to get better.' He was always on us. He worked us the most." The hard work paid off with a Number One single and the three members of Bell Biv DeVoe were grateful. "We learned a lot in the studio with him," Bivins allows. "Just how professional he is, and his vibe."

When Ricky Bell, Michael Bivins, and Ronnie DeVoe decided to record their own album away from New Edition, they looked for producers who were more in tune with the street. Talking about the producers of "B.B.D.," Ronnie says, "I had looked up to them for a while because they produced a lot of the rap songs that I was into at the time, from Public Enemy to a lot of other artists they were working with. So I was a little nervous, but the fact that they're kind of in our age range took a little bit of that nervousness out. But it was real cool working with them. They're in touch with the streets and they know what that side of life is all about."

"B.B.D. (I Thought It Was Me)?" was written specifically for the trio, although it didn't originally have that title. Writer/producer Eric Sadler says he and his partners were asked to submit some songs to the group, but "B.B.D." hadn't been written yet. "We worked on two songs and they liked the way we worked...They said, 'Can't you come up with another song?' So that's when we went back to the studio and said, 'What's going on now? Who's pretty hot?' Teddy Riley had been very, very hot and I said, 'Let me try to do a song in that sort of vein,' keeping my original style but incorporating some sort of 'new jack' feel to it and keeping it a little hip-hop. And I went back and wrote ["B.B.D."] in a day."

Sadler started the song by finding a groove on the keyboard, adding a bassline, and then working on the drumbeats. "And Roney Hooks worked on a melody and arrangement of strings to give it more of an R&B feel. He had originally come up with another chorus...The name of the song was going to be, 'She's a Freaky-Deaky Party Queen' and I didn't care for that." Sadler approached Paul Shebazz and asked him to come up with a new chorus. "Finally he came up with 'I Thought It Was Me,' " says Sadler. "So we combined what he had along with the verse and the rest of the song that Roney had."

Sadler says that Bell, Bivins, and DeVoe turned out to be more talented than he expected. "Most people thought that Bobby Brown or Ralph Tresvant were the most talented guys. I found out they all had the same talent. They were very talented and good singers and very good businessmen and easy to work with."

580

MISSUNDERSTANDING

Al B. Sure!

WARNER BROS. 19590
WRITERS: AL B. SURE!, DJ EDDIE F., NEVELLE
PRODUCERS: DJ EDDIE F., NEVELLE
November 24, 1990 (1 week)

I think Al is what you call a born star," offers DJ Eddie F., a friend of Al B. Sure! from their childhood days in Mount Vernon, New York. "He has that aura around him like he wants to be a celebrity or the center of attention. He has that charisma."

In return, Al gives Eddie the credit for pushing him to be a solo artist after they worked together on the first album by Heavy D. & the Boyz. "At one point he was rapping and I said, 'Why don't you sing?' because he had singing skills and he had rapping skills," says Eddie, who suggested that Al put some street flavor in his vocals. "That's the emergence of that whole sound, of mixing hip hop with R&B."

While Eddie F. didn't receive a specific producing credit on Al's first album, *In Effect Mode,* he did collaborate on ideas and tracks. "Everybody was learning from each other," says Eddie. "On the second album, after everyone had gotten a little more established and gotten their titles, they said, 'I'm a producer now' or 'I'm an artist now.' "

Eddie was working on a track at home one day when Al came over to hang out. "He heard it and said, 'Whose song is that?' " Eddie didn't have anyone particular in mind for the song, so Al asked for it on the spot.

They finished writing "Missunderstanding" that same day. "It had a real cool sound because it was like the next phase of whatever the new jack swing was at the time," says Al, who recalls how he came up with the lyrics: "I was upset with a woman at the time. I felt like I was being used and played with and I'd hooked up with the wrong person. That's what all my songs are about anyway—I write about an experience in my life. It's easiest to write about that." Does Al mind when people recognize themselves in his lyrics? "Not at all," he responds, "because maybe it will make them wake up."

Speaking as a producer, Eddie says he enjoys the time he spends in the studio with his friend. "Al is real good in the studio as far as putting backgrounds together and knowing what he wants to do and how he wants to do it. We've been working together for awhile, so to us it's like fun. It's just experimenting. It's not like being hired to do something."

Eddie says they didn't record "Missunderstanding" with the idea of making it a single. "We just made the record. When it came time to release the album, they said, 'This should be the single.' They did that without me."

"Missunderstanding" was the first single released from *Private Times...And the Whole 9!* The track was recorded at the Hit Factory in New York City. Al and his cousin Kyle West played keyboards. Background vocals were by Al and Craig Derry, Tabitha Brace, and Terri Robinson. The follow-up was "No Matter What You Do," a duet that demonstrated that Al B. Sure! had really arrived as a recording star. His partner for that track was none other than Diana Ross.

581

I'M YOUR BABY TONIGHT

Whitney Houston

ARISTA 2108
WRITERS: L.A. REID, BABYFACE
PRODUCERS: L.A. REID, BABYFACE
December 1, 1990 (2 weeks)

Clive Davis, president of Arista Records, asked writer/producers L.A. Reid and Babyface to work with Whitney Houston on her third album, which caused many to speculate that the label chief wanted to re-establish the pop diva's credibility with black audiences.

Houston gave her interpretation of the move to Tom Green in *USA Today:* "I would rather say to people that this new album is not different. It's just an extension of what Whitney has in store for them." As for the idea that she needed to regain credibility in the black community, Whitney said, "I get my flak like everybody else...but I'm just doing what I do best. I didn't plan on [selling 31 million albums]. It just happened. I would think black people would be proud...I don't sing music thinking this is black, or this is white...I sing songs that everybody's going to like."

Reid and Babyface had already produced 15 Number One hits for artists like the Whispers, Pebbles, Bobby Brown, Karyn White, the Boys, and Johnny Gill when they were hooked up with Houston for the first time. Reid explains their objective: "We wanted to come up with something that was different than anything Whitney had sung, so we approached it from that angle. We wanted to give her a new direction, and pick up where we felt she was lacking. We felt she needed more of a black base."

The producers wrote "I'm Your Baby Tonight" before they even met the artist. "When we had something, we asked her to come to Atlanta," Reid explains. "We met with her and had dinner; we had a ball, and played the song for her. She was very happy."

They gave her a tape of the demo, which Reid describes as a shuffle, "sort of a cross between something that's a little jazzy and a little funky." Two weeks later, Whitney was ready to record the song. Jon Gass and Barney Perkins engineered the track at Elumba Recording in Los Angeles. Donald Parks programmed the keyboards, Reid played drums and keyboards, and Babyface played bass and keyboards. Houston provided her own backing vocals.

Reid and Babyface discovered the song would be the album's title track "almost immediately after finishing," according to L.A. "Once all of the material

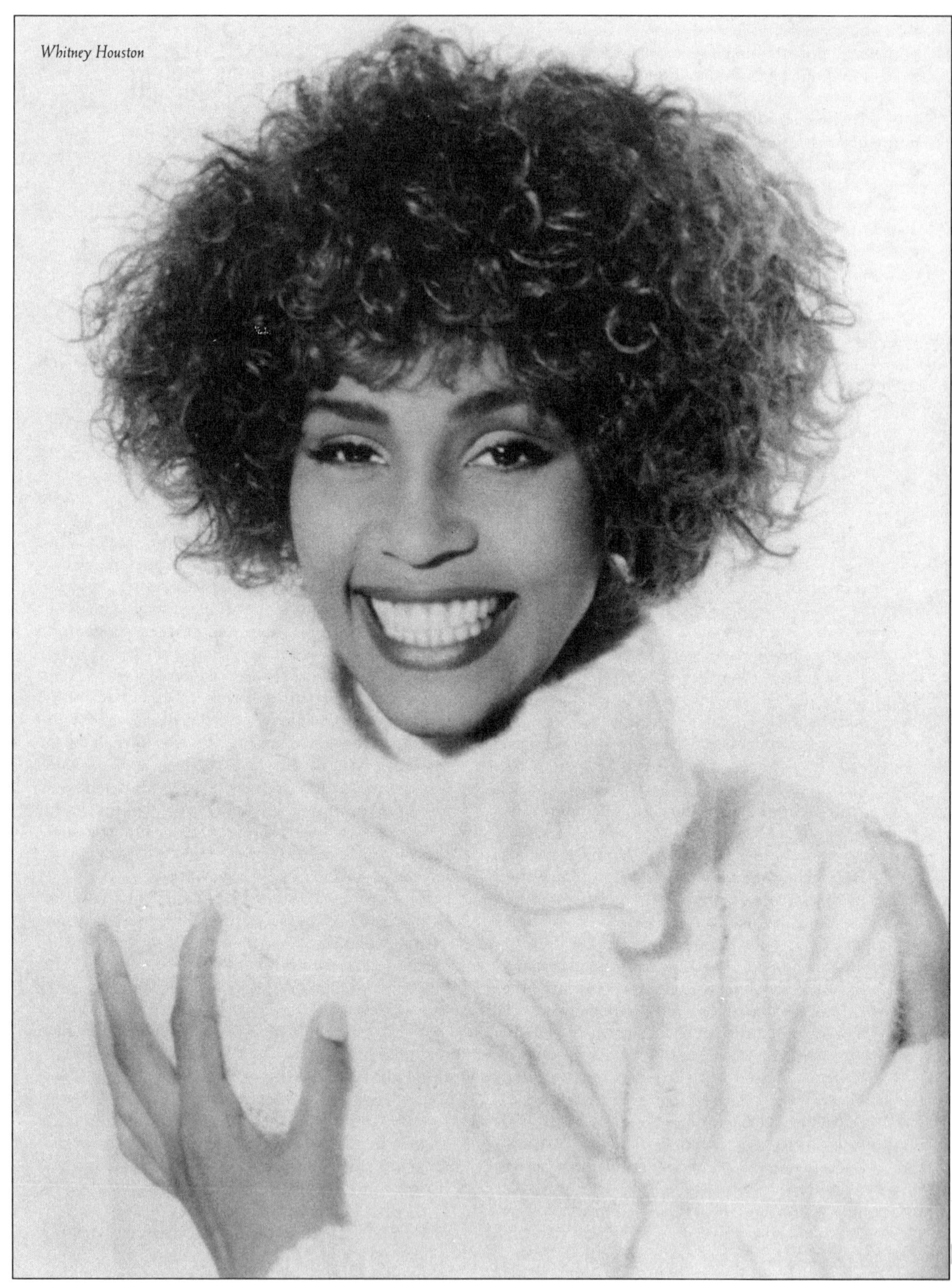
Whitney Houston

was recorded, it was pretty much decided then. We got a call that said, 'Guess what? You not only have the single, but you have the title track.' "

"I'm Your Baby Tonight" was Houston's fourth Number One single on the R&B chart. It also went to the summit of the Hot 100, where it gave L.A. Reid and Babyface their first-ever Number One pop hit.

582

SENSITIVITY

Ralph Tresvant

MCA 53932
WRITERS: JAMES HARRIS III, TERRY LEWIS
PRODUCERS: JIMMY JAM, TERRY LEWIS
December 15, 1990 (1 week)

When Ralph Tresvant released "Sensitivity," he was the only member of New Edition who hadn't had a Number One single outside of the group. Bobby Brown was the first New Edition alumnus to have his own chart-topping single [see 443—"Girlfriend"]. Ricky Bell, Michael Bivins and Ronald DeVoe scored as Bell Biv DeVoe [see 559—"Poison"], and Johnny Gill succeeded them [see 560—"Rub You the Right Way"]. The pressure was on Tresvant to prove himself with his first solo project. "My stomach was twisting up," he admitted to James T. Jones IV in *USA Today*. "I was scared. I didn't want to be the only one to put out something that didn't work."

Being the last member of New Edition to release his own project was an advantage for Tresvant, according to producer Jimmy Jam. "BBD had done their record, Johnny had done his record. Both were very successful, and that made it easy to see where Ralph should be. Ralph should be Ralph. He had already established himself as the voice of New Edition. Ralph falls into the category like Janet [Jackson] as a singer that can sing melody very well. So what we tried to do with Ralph was one of the same things we do with Janet, which is let him sing all the vocals, all the backgrounds, all the leads, to really make it his record."

For the first single, "Sensitivity," Jimmy says he and partner Terry Lewis "borrowed a page from Marvin Gaye, but even more than Marvin, a guy named Leon Ware, who produced and arranged a lot of the vocals on Marvin with a lot of layering."

Tresvant said in *Black Beat*, "That song, 'Sensitivity,' really *is* who I am." Jam agrees: "The artist really inspires the song. If we hadn't worked with Ralph, we probably never would have written 'Sensitivity' and if we hadn't worked with Johnny, we probably wouldn't have written 'Rub You the Right Way.' These songs are all products of how we interpret their personalities and the things they say to us. 'Sensitivity' was born out of the way we saw Ralph."

Tresvant was very comfortable working with Jam and Lewis at their Flyte Tyme Studios. "Their whole set-up in Minneapolis makes you feel really at home and comfortable," he said in *Blues & Soul*. "The whole atmosphere inspires nothing but creativity and great music." Jimmy Jam returns the compliment, calling Ralph "the hardest working person in the studio and easiest to record," along with Janet Jackson.

Jam played most of the instruments on the track himself. "I like tracks with atmosphere," he says. "I like tracks that have some depth to them and that take you some place and that's what we tried to do with 'Sensitivity,' make a bed for his voice to sleep on. It's a very soothing song but also a very funky song. It's very unorthodox in a way—it's not a standard verse-chorus-verse-second chorus type of song. It's a series of what we call B-sections, which are like sections that lead into the chorus...It's a unique structure."

Tresvant credits his producers with more than giving him a Number One hit: "Before I worked with Jimmy and Terry, I don't really think I knew where I was going," he said in *Blues & Soul*. "I had no real direction and was pretty unconfident. They helped me find the real me, and made me feel really strong about the songs I was singing, so that I couldn't wait for them to come out. The majority of things I did with them are melodic, soulful, and still hip—and I'm really comfortable with that."

583

IT NEVER RAINS (IN SOUTHERN CALIFORNIA)

Tony! Toni! Toné!

WING 879 068
WRITERS: TIM CHRISTIAN, RAPHAEL WIGGINS
PRODUCERS: TONY! TONI! TONÉ!
December 22, 1990 (2 weeks)

British pop composer Albert Hammond had an international hit in 1972 with "It Never Rains in Southern California," but the Northern California members of Tony! Toni! Toné! hadn't heard it. "We didn't find out until after our song was recorded and released, and someone told us," says Dwayne Wiggins.

"This wasn't a remake at all," he says, explaining how the group came up with the title. "One of our attorneys used to always say that whenever we came to Los Angeles from the cold. It would be raining in a different city or state or country, and we'd fly back for a meeting with him and it was hot. We'd be coming right from the plane with these big coats and he would say, 'Don't you know it never rains in Southern California?' He would always say that."

Tim Christian, the drummer and keyboard player for the trio and cousin to Dwayne and Raphael Wiggins, wrote the music for the third single from the second Tony! Toni! Toné! album, *The Revival*. "Tim can go in there and play every instrument and put the whole music track down and we might come in and color it with something and put a little guitar in there and put the vocals on top. And that track happened exactly like that—he played everything on it," says Dwayne.

Raphael adds, "[Tim] threw me this tape and went to the mall and I took the tape and started singing that hook, 'It Never Rains (In Southern California).' It fit so well, I wound up doing a verse to it and throwing some strings on the top."

How did Raphael develop a song from the attorney-inspired title? "I go back East a lot—New York, New Jersey," he responds. "I like being there. Sometimes when you're in New York, there's more of an overcast than there is in Southern California. Now I'm not from Los Angeles, I'm from Oakland. But Southern California is supposed to have the best weather. So I made up a story that I was in New York for awhile and my girl was in Southern California and I said, 'I can't wait until I get there to see you.' People feel like that sometimes when they're from Los Angeles and they're in New York. They want to come home to beautiful Southern California weather."

Raphael says that "It Never Rains (In Southern California)" was one of the songs on which he found himself becoming stronger vocally. "I went with the feeling," he comments. "We don't happen to be the greatest singers in the world, but we get the job done...There comes a point in time where you know if you're doing something right or wrong. I think at that time we started to notice that we have to deliver a certain way without trying to be all that, but just do the best we can. [On] any song that we sing, we approach the mike like men now."

Tony! Toni! Toné!

THE MOST NUMBER ONE R&B HITS . . .

BY ARTIST

1.	Aretha Franklin	20
2.	Stevie Wonder	18
3.	James Brown	16
4.	The Temptations	14
5.	Marvin Gaye	13
6.	Michael Jackson	10
	The O'Jays	10
8.	Kool & the Gang	9
	Gladys Knight & the Pips	9
10.	Earth, Wind & Fire	8
	Freddie Jackson	8
	Janet Jackson	8
13.	The Commodores	7
	Prince	7
15.	Natalie Cole	6
	Al Green	6
	The Isley Brothers	6
	The Jackson 5	6
	The Spinners	6
	The Supremes	6
21.	Stephanie Mills	5
	The Ohio Players	5
	Wilson Pickett	5
	Diana Ross	5
	Rufus	5
	Luther Vandross	5
	Barry White	5

BY WRITER

1.	Leon Huff	22
2.	Kenny Gamble	21
3.	Stevie Wonder	20
4.	Babyface	18
5.	James Brown	16
	Norman Whitfield	16
7.	James Harris III (Jimmy Jam)	15
	Terry Lewis	15
	L.A. Reid	15
10.	Lionel Richie	11
11.	Eddie Holland	10
	Barrett Strong	10
13.	Michael Jackson	9
	Kool & the Gang	9
	Prince	9
	Daryl Simmons	9
17.	Brian Holland	8
	William "Smokey" Robinson	8
19.	Nick Ashford	7
	George Clinton	7
	Lamont Dozier	7
	Marvin Gaye	7
	Valerie Simpson	7
24.	Al Green	6
	Ernie Isley	6
	Marvin Isley	6
	O'Kelly Isley	6
	Ronald Isley	6
	Rudolph Isley	6
	Chuck Jackson	6
	Janet Jackson	6
	Chris Jasper	6
	Willie Mitchell	6
	Freddie Perren	6
	Luther Vandross	6
	Maurice White	6
	Marvin Yancy	6
38.	Harry Wayne Casey (KC)	5
	Barry Eastmond	5
	Bernard Edwards	5
	Richard Finch	5
	Rick James	5
	Gene McFadden	5
	Marcus Miller	5

BY PRODUCER

1.	Kenny Gamble	22
2.	Leon Huff	21
	Quincy Jones	21
4.	Babyface	18
	L.A.Reid	18
	Jerry Wexler	18
7.	James Brown	17
8.	Jimmy Jam	15
	Terry Lewis	15
	Stevie Wonder	15
11.	Norman Whitfield	14
12.	Arif Mardin	13
13.	Maurice White	9
14.	James Anthony Carmichael	8
15.	Thom Bell	7
	Lamont Dozier	7
	Brian Holland	7
	Kool & the Gang	7
	Prince	7
	William "Smokey" Robinson	7
	Luther Vandross	7
22.	George Clinton	6
	Tom Dowd	6
	Marvin Gaye	6
	Berry Gordy Jr.	6
	Ernie Isley	6
	Marvin Isley	6
	O'Kelly Isley	6
	Ronald Isley	6
	Rudolph Isley	6
	Chuck Jackson	6
	Chris Jasper	6
	Paul Lawrence	6
	Marcus Miller	6
	Willie Mitchell	6
	Barry White	6
	Marvin Yancy	6
39.	Harry Wayne Casey (KC)	5
	David "Pic" Conley	5
	Don Davis	5
	Hal Davis	5
	Barry Eastmond	5
	Bernard Edwards	5
	Richard Finch	5
	Denzil Foster	5
	Nick Martinelli	5
	The Ohio Players	5
	Nile Rodgers	5

BY LABEL

1.	Atlantic	52
2.	Motown	43
3.	Tamla	35
4.	MCA	31
5.	Columbia	30
6.	Capitol	29
7.	Warner Brothers	28
8.	Epic	22
9.	Gordy	21
10.	Philadelphia International	20
11.	A&M	19
12.	Arista	14
13.	Mercury	13
14.	Stax	10
15.	De-Lite	9
	King	9
	Polydor	9
18.	ABC	8
19.	Solar	7
	20th Century	7
21.	Hi	6
	Soul	6
	T-Neck	6
24.	Buddah	5
	Jive	5
	RCA	5
	T.K.	5
	Virgin	5
	Wing	5

THE LONGEST-RUNNING NUMBER ONE R&B HITS

1.	"Sexual Healing," Marvin Gaye	10 weeks
2.	"I Can't Help Myself," The Four Tops	9 weeks
	"Let's Stay Together," Al Green	9 weeks
	"That Girl," Stevie Wonder	9 weeks
	"Billie Jean," Michael Jackson	9 weeks
6.	"Papa's Got a Brand New Bag," James Brown	8 weeks
	"Ain't Too Proud to Beg," The Temptations	8 weeks
	"Respect," Aretha Franklin	8 weeks
	"Let's Groove," Earth, Wind & Fire	8 weeks
	"Juicy Fruit," Mtume	8 weeks
	"When Doves Cry," Prince	8 weeks
12.	"634-5789 (Soulsville, USA)," Wilson Pickett	7 weeks
	"I Never Loved a Man," Aretha Franklin	7 weeks
	"Soul Man," Sam & Dave	7 weeks
	"I Heard It Through the Grapevine," Marvin Gaye	7 weeks
	"Serpentine Fire," Earth, Wind & Fire	7 weeks
	"Master Blaster (Jammin')," Stevie Wonder	7 weeks
	"Endless Love," Diana Ross & Lionel Richie	7 weeks
	"All Night Long (All Night)," Lionel Richie	7 weeks
20.	"My Girl," The Temptations	6 weeks
	"I Got You (I Feel Good)," James Brown	6 weeks
	"I Heard It Through the Grapevine," Gladys Knight & the Pips	6 weeks
	"Say It Loud—I'm Black and I'm Proud (Part 1)," James Brown	6 weeks
	"Too Busy Thinking About My Baby," Marvin Gaye	6 weeks
	"The Love You Save," The Jackson 5	6 weeks
	"Signed, Sealed, Delivered, I'm Yours," Stevie Wonder	6 weeks
	"I'll Be There," The Jackson 5	6 weeks
	"Let's Get It On," Marvin Gaye	6 weeks
	"Disco Lady," Johnnie Taylor	6 weeks
	"Float On," The Floaters	6 weeks

THE NUMBER ONE R&B HITS THAT ALSO TOPPED THE HOT 100

1965
"My Girl," The Temptations
"Back in My Arms Again," The Supremes
"I Can't Help Myself," The Four Tops

1966
"When a Man Loves a Woman," Percy Sledge
"You Can't Hurry Love," The Supremes
"Reach Out I'll Be There," The Four Tops
"You Keep Me Hangin' On," The Supremes

1967
"Love Is Here and Now You're Gone," The Supremes
"Respect," Aretha Franklin

1968
"(Sittin' On) The Dock of the Bay," Otis Redding
"Tighten Up," Archie Bell and the Drells
"Grazing in the Grass," Hugh Masekela
"I Heard It Through the Grapevine," Marvin Gaye

1969
"Everyday People," Sly & the Family Stone
"I Can't Get Next to You," The Temptations
"Someday We'll Be Together," Diana Ross and the Supremes

1970
"I Want You Back," The Jackson 5
"Thank You (Falettin Me Be Mice Elf Again)," Sly & the Family Stone
"ABC," The Jackson 5
"The Love You Save," The Jackson 5
"Ain't No Mountain High Enough," Diana Ross
"I'll Be There," The Jackson 5
"The Tears of a Clown," Smokey Robinson and the Miracles

1971
"Just My Imagination (Running Away with Me)," The Temptations
"Want Ads," The Honey Cone
"Family Affair," Sly & the Family Stone

1972
"Let's Stay Together," Al Green
"Oh Girl," The Chi-Lites
"I'll Take You There," The Staple Singers
"Lean on Me," Bill Withers
"Me and Mrs. Jones," Billy Paul

1973
"Superstition," Stevie Wonder
"Love Train," The O'Jays
"Let's Get It On," Marvin Gaye
"Midnight Train to Georgia," Gladys Knight & the Pips
"Keep On Truckin'," Eddie Kendricks

1974
"TSOP (The Sound of Philadelphia)," MFSB featuring the Three Degrees
"Rock Your Baby," George McCrae
"Feel Like Makin' Love," Roberta Flack
"Can't Get Enough of Your Love, Babe," Barry White
"You Haven't Done Nothin'," Stevie Wonder
"Kung Fu Fighting," Carl Douglas

1975
"Fire," The Ohio Players
"Lady Marmalade," LaBelle
"Shining Star," Earth, Wind & Fire
"The Hustle," Van McCoy and the Soul City Symphony
"Get Down Tonight," KC and the Sunshine Band
"That's the Way (I Like It)," KC and the Sunshine Band
"Fly, Robin, Fly," Silver Convention
"Let's Do It Again," The Staple Singers

1976
"Love Rollercoaster," The Ohio Players
"Disco Lady," Johnnie Taylor
"Boogie Fever," The Sylvers
"Love Hangover," Diana Ross
"Kiss and Say Goodbye," The Manhattans
"(Shake, Shake, Shake) Shake Your Booty," KC and the Sunshine Band
"Play That Funky Music," Wild Cherry

1977
"You Don't Have to Be a Star (To Be in My Show)," Marilyn McCoo and Billy Davis, Jr.
"I Wish," Stevie Wonder

"Car Wash," Rose Royce
"Don't Leave Me This Way," Thelma Houston
"Sir Duke," Stevie Wonder
"Got To Give It Up (Part 1)," Marvin Gaye
"Best of My Love," The Emotions

1978
"Too Much, Too Little, Too Late," Johnny Mathis and Deniece Williams
"Three Times a Lady," The Commodores
"Boogie Oogie Oogie," A Taste of Honey
"Le Freak," Chic

1979
"Reunited," Peaches & Herb
"Bad Girls," Donna Summer
"Ring My Bell," Anita Ward
"Good Times," Chic
"Don't Stop 'Til You Get Enough," Michael Jackson
"Still," The Commodores

1980
"Rock with You," Michael Jackson
"Upside Down," Diana Ross

1981
"Celebration," Kool & the Gang
"Endless Love," Diana Ross and Lionel Richie

1982
"I Can't Go for That (No Can Do)," Daryl Hall & John Oates

1983
"Billie Jean," Michael Jackson
"Beat It," Michael Jackson
"All Night Long (All Night)," Lionel Richie

1984
"Hello," Lionel Richie
"Let's Hear It for the Boy," Deniece Williams
"When Doves Cry," Prince
"Ghostbusters," Ray Parker Jr.
"Let's Go Crazy," Prince & the Revolution
"I Just Called to Say I Love You," Stevie Wonder
"Caribbean Queen (No More Love on the Run)," Billy Ocean

1985
"We Are the World," USA for Africa
"Saving All My Love for You," Whitney Houston
"Part-Time Lover," Stevie Wonder
"Say You, Say Me," Lionel Richie

1986
"That's What Friends Are For," Dionne & Friends
"How Will I Know," Whitney Houston
"Kiss," Prince & the Revolution
"On My Own," Patti LaBelle and Michael McDonald
"There'll Be Sad Songs (To Make You Cry)," Billy Ocean

1987
"Shake You Down," Gregory Abbott
"Always," Atlantic Starr
"Head to Toe," Lisa Lisa and Cult Jam
"I Just Can't Stop Loving You," Michael Jackson and Siedah Garrett
"Lost In Emotion," Lisa Lisa and Cult Jam
"Bad," Michael Jackson

1988
"The Way You Make Me Feel," Michael Jackson
"Man in the Mirror," Michael Jackson
"Get Outta My Dreams, Get into My Car," Billy Ocean
"Wishing Well," Terence Trent D'Arby
"One More Try," George Michael

1989
"My Prerogative," Bobby Brown
"Batdance," Prince
"Miss You Much," Janet Jackson

1990
"Escapade," Janet Jackson
"Vision of Love," Mariah Carey
"Love Takes Time," Mariah Carey
"I'm Your Baby Tonight," Whitney Houston

THE NUMBER ONE R&B HITS THAT DIDN'T REACH THE HOT 100

1976
"Turning Point," Tyrone Davis

1978
"Bootzilla," Bootsy's Rubber Band
"Take Me to the Next Phase (Part 1)," The Isley Brothers

1979
"I Wanna Be with You (Part 1)," The Isley Brothers

1980
"Funkin' for Jamaica (N.Y.)," Tom Browne

1982
"Dance Floor," Zapp

1983
"Atomic Dog," George Clinton

1984
"Lovelite," O'Bryan

1985
"Save Your Love (For #1)," Rene & Angela

1986
"I Have Learned to Respect the Power of Love," Stephanie Mills
"Closer Than Close," Jean Carne
"Do You Get Enough Love," Shirley Jones
"(Pop, Pop, Pop, Pop) Goes My Mind," Levert
"A Little Bit More," Melba Moore with Freddie Jackson

1987
"Falling," Melba Moore
"Slow Down," Loose Ends
"I Feel Good All Over," Stephanie Mills
"Lovin' You," The O'Jays
"Angel," Angela Winbush

1988
"Roses Are Red," The Mac Band featuring the McCampbell Brothers
"Loosey's Rap," Rick James featuring Roxanne Shante

ARTIST INDEX

Numerical references are to entry numbers, not page numbers.

172 I'm in Love
249 Something He Can Feel
272 Break It to Me Gently
364 Jump to It
376 Get It Right
411 Freeway of Love

Funkadelic
301 One Nation under a Groove (Part 1)
319 (not just) Knee Deep Part 1

Gable, Eric
536 Remember (The First Time)

Gap Band, The
339 Burn Rubber (Why You Wanna Hurt Me)
361 Early in the Morning
368 Outstanding
546 All of My Love

Gaye, Marvin
5 I'll Be Doggone
12 Ain't That Peculiar
66 I Heard It Through the Grapevine
74 Too Busy Thinking About My Baby
103 What's Going On
110 Mercy Mercy Me (The Ecology)
116 Inner City Blues (Make Me Wanna Holler)
153 Let's Get It On
245 I Want You
269 Got to Give It Up (Part 1)
366 Sexual Healing

Gaye, Marvin, and Tammi Terrell
57 Ain't Nothing Like the Real Thing
62 You're All I Need to Get By

Gill, Johnny
560 Rub You the Right Way
567 My, My, My

GQ
310 Disco Nights (Rock-Freak)

Graham Central Station
218 Your Love

Graham, Larry
332 One in a Million You

Green, Al
119 Let's Stay Together
131 I'm Still in Love with You
137 You Ought to Be with Me
163 Livin' for You
202 L-O-V-E (Love)
231 Full of Fire

Guthrie, Gwen
435 Ain't Nothin' Goin' On but the Rent

Hall, Daryl, and John Oates
355 I Can't Go for That (No Can Do)

Hammer, M.C.
564 U Can't Touch This

Harpo, Slim
16 Baby Scratch My Back

Harris, Major
208 Love Won't Let Me Wait

Holliday, Jennifer
362 And I Am Telling You I'm Not Going

Honey Cone, The
106 Want Ads
112 Stick-Up

Houston, Thelma
264 Don't Leave Me This Way

Houston, Whitney
407 You Give Good Love
412 Saving All My Love for You
422 How Will I Know
581 I'm Your Baby Tonight

Howard, Miki
545 Ain't Nuthin' in the World

Impressions, The
50 We're a Winner
77 Choice of Colors
176 Finally Got Myself Together (I'm a Changed Man)

Independents, The
147 Leaving Me

Ingram, Luther
129 (If Loving You Is Wrong) I Don't Want to Be Right

Instant Funk
308 I Got My Mind Made Up (You Can Get It Girl)

Intruders, The
54 Cowboys to Girls

Isley Brothers, The
72 It's Your Thing
214 Fight the Power (Part 1)
268 The Pride (Part 1)
291 Take Me to the Next Phase (Part 1)
312 I Wanna Be with You (Part 1)
329 Don't Say Goodnight (It's Time for Love) (Parts 1 & 2)

Isley/Jasper/Isley
417 Caravan of Love

Jackson 5, The
83 I Want You Back
87 ABC
90 The Love You Save
94 I'll Be There
104 Never Can Say Goodbye
171 Dancing Machine

Jackson, Freddie
408 Rock Me Tonight (For Old Times Sake)
415 You Are My Lady
441 Tasty Love
448 Have You Ever Loved Somebody
462 Jam Tonight
497 Nice 'N' Slow
506 Hey Lover

Jackson, Janet
424 What Have You Done for Me Lately
428 Nasty
444 Control
450 Let's Wait Awhile
461 The Pleasure Principle
539 Miss You Much
548 Rhythm Nation
554 Escapade

Jackson, Jermaine
330 Let's Get Serious
452 Don't Take It Personal

Jackson, Michael
318 Don't Stop 'Til You Get Enough
324 Rock With You
367 The Girl Is Mine*
369 Billie Jean
372 Beat It
465 I Just Can't Stop Loving You**
469 Bad
475 The Way You Make Me Feel
481 Man In The Mirror
498 Another Part Of Me

**Michael Jackson/Paul McCartney*
***Michael Jackson with Siedah Garrett*

James, Rick
295 You and I
345 Give It to Me Baby
377 Cold Blooded
496 Loosey's Rap*

**Rick James featuring Roxanne Shante*

Jones, Oran "Juice"
437 The Rain

Jones, Quincy
293 Stuff Like That
549 I'll Be Good To You*
555 The Secret Garden (Sweet Seduction Suite)**
563 Tomorrow (A Better You, A Better Me)***

**Quincy Jones featuring Ray Charles and Chaka Khan*
***Quincy Jones featuring Barry White, Al B. Sure!, James Ingram, and El DeBarge*
****Quincy Jones featuring Tevin Campbell*

Jones, Shirley
433 Do You Get Enough Love

KC and the Sunshine Band
217 Get Down Tonight
229 That's the Way (I Like It)
253 (Shake, Shake, Shake) Shake Your Booty
278 Keep It Comin' Love

Kemp, Johnny
488 Just Got Paid

Kendricks, Eddie
155 Keep on Truckin' (Part 1)
165 Boogie Down
201 Shoeshine Boy

Khan, Chaka
302 I'm Every Woman
344 What Cha' Gonna Do for Me
395 I Feel for You

King, Ben E.
199 Supernatural Thing (Part 1)

King, Evelyn
347 I'm in Love
365 Love Come Down

Knight, Gladys, & the Pips
46 I Heard It Through the Grapevine
99 If I Were Your Woman
143 Neither One of Us (Wants to Be the First to Say Goodbye)
156 Midnight Train to Georgia
162 I've Got to Use My Imagination
168 Best Thing That Ever Happened to Me
187 I Feel a Song (In My Heart)
373 Save The Overtime (For Me)
476 Love Overboard

Knight, Jean
108 Mr. Big Stuff

Kool & the Gang
174 Hollywood Swinging
184 Higher Plane
207 Spirit of the Boogie
320 Ladies Night
337 Celebration
352 Take My Heart (You Can Have It If You Want It)
381 Joanna
406 Fresh
413 Cherish

LaBelle
196 Lady Marmalade

LaBelle, Patti
382 If Only You Knew
427 On My Own*

**Patti LaBelle and Michael McDonald*

Lakeside
338 Fantastic Voyage

LaSalle, Denise
115 Trapped By a Thing Called Love

Latimore
185 Let's Straighten It Out

Lattisaw, Stacy, with Johnny Gill
553 Where Do We Go from Here

Levert
436 (Pop, Pop, Pop) Goes My Mind
463 Casanova
500 Addicted To You
515 Just Coolin'*

**Levert featuring Heavy D*

Lisa Lisa and Cult Jam
456 Head to Toe
467 Lost in Emotion

L.L. Cool J
466 I Need Love

Loose Ends
409 Hangin' on a String (Contemplating)
449 Slow Down

Love Unlimited
195 I Belong to You

L.T.D.
258 Love Ballad
280 (Every Time I Turn Around) Back in Love Again
299 Holding On (When Love Is Gone)

Lynn, Cheryl
304 Got to Be Real
383 Encore

Mac Band featuring the McCampbell Brothers, The
493 Roses Are Red

Manhattans, The
244 Kiss and Say Goodbye

Marie, Teena
483 Ooo La La La

TITLE INDEX

Numerical references are to entry numbers, not page numbers.

PHOTO CREDITS

The authors and editor gratefully acknowledge the following sources, who generously supplied the photographs appearing on the page numbers indicated:

Bob Fisher: 5, 13, 20, 36, 58, 64, 90, 97, 106, 110, 112, 115, 119, 124, 129, 137, 138, 146, 147, 154, 158, 162, 164, 171, 177, 179, 193, 219, 298, 356

Blues & Soul magazine: 25, 33, 43, 49, 56, 61, 69, 80, 81, 87, 101, 139, 148, 156, 168, 169, 173, 175, 182, 196, 201, 211, 218, 227, 228, 251

The Sharon Davis Collection: 82, 93, 122, 333

Redferns: 108, 128

A&M Records: 241, 361, 378, 423

Arista Records: 254, 306, 349, 357, 458, 490

Atlantic/EastWest Records: 18, 248, 260, 368, 386, 395, 432, 461, 473

CBS Records/Sony Music: 194, 198, 220, 292, 295, 309, 311, 315, 329, 344, 354, 373, 387, 389, 393, 398, 403, 411, 430, 437, 456

Capitol/EMI Records: 284, 313, 330, 337, 342, 347, 358, 382, 444, 446, 476

Elektra Records: 407, 427

Geffen Records: 304

Jive Records: 466

MCA Records: 335, 355, 377, 406, 414, 442, 450, 486, 459, 532

Motown Records: 3, 6, 7, 24, 31, 38, 41, 47, 54, 66, 73, 77, 84, 131, 161, 189, 208, 216, 234, 263, 272, 277, 283, 287, 290, 299, 302, 325, 366, 439, 467, 479, 485

Philadelphia International Records: 240, 242, 369

Polygram Records: 9, 44, 51, 142, 231, 255, 259, 269, 281, 291, 300, 328, 345, 351, 371, 381, 401, 435

RCA Records: 184, 289, 307, 340

Solar Records: 267, 270, 279, 452

T.K. Records: 206

Warner Bros. Records: 140, 200, 236, 265, 274, 293, 305, 334, 362

ABOUT THE AUTHORS

ADAM WHITE began reading *Billboard* in 1963—the same year that he bought his first Number One R&B hit, "Heat Wave," by Martha and the Vandellas, and ignited a lifelong passion for rhythm & blues.

White subsequently turned a hobby into a career when his articles began appearing in such British publications as *New Musical Express*, *Disc*, and *Melody Maker*. After working for the U.K. trade publication *Music Week*, he joined the editorial staff of *Billboard* in New York, where he rose through the ranks to become managing editor and, later, editor-in-chief. Today, he is *Billboard*'s international editor-in-chief, based in London.

In addition to interviewing hundreds of recording artists and music industry professionals over the past 25 years, White has compiled and annotated more than two dozen album reissues of historic R&B and rock and roll. He has scripted a six-hour, Grammy-nominated history of Motown Records for American radio, and he is the author of *The Billboard Book of Gold & Platinum Records*.

GARY NULL

FRED BRONSON is the author of two best-selling books, *The Billboard Book of Number One Hits*, now in its third edition, and *Billboard's Hottest Hot 100 Hits*. He also writes one of the most popular features in *Billboard* magazine, the "Chart Beat" column. In addition, he has co-written two episodes of *Star Trek: The Next Generation* and has written and produced various projects for Dick Clark, including ABC-TV's coverage of the Live Aid concert in Philadelphia and *America Picks the Number One Songs*, an ABC-TV two-hour special based on the *Number One Hits* book.

Bronson spent 12 years in the Media Relations Department at NBC-TV in Burbank, where he handled publicity for series, mini-series, and TV movies, including the Bob Hope specials, the *Tomorrow* show with Tom Snyder, and most of the network's science-fiction series, including *Man from Atlantis*, *Buck Rogers*, and *The Bionic Woman*.

Bronson has also produced segments for *2 on the Town*, which ran on the CBS affiliate in Los Angeles for many years, and is a frequent contributor to *Emmy*, the bi-monthly magazine published by the Academy of Television Arts and Sciences.

OTHER BOOKS BY ADAM WHITE AND FRED BRONSON

The Billboard Book of Gold & Platinum Records

BY ADAM WHITE

The ultimate measure of commercial success for a recording act is having a gold and platinum record awarded by the Recording Industry Association of America. Here is the complete guide to all the artists and records to win the industry's recognition of superior sales over the past 30 years. *The Billboard Book of Gold & Platinum Records* spans all music genres: pop, country, jazz, and even classical music. Organized in an easy-to-use alphabetical format, the book's entries include such information as writer and producer credits, the dates of a record's release and its gold and/or platinum certification, and its label and catalog number. The appendix contains separate listings of the most successful artists, writers, producers, and record labels.

416 pages. 7" x 9¼". 225 b&w illustrations. $19.95

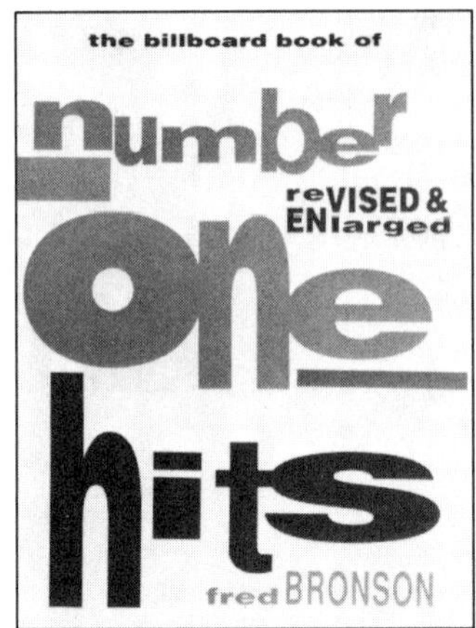

The Billboard Book of Number One Hits

REVISED & ENLARGED
3RD EDITION

BY FRED BRONSON

The trend-setting model on which all subsequent Billboard "hits" books have been based, *Number One Hits* looks behind the charts to tell the story behind every record to have topped the *Billboard* Hot 100 pop singles chart since 1955, offering an instructional and engaging overview of the rock era. In addition to featuring fresh quotes, stories, and anecdotes from the singers, writers, players, and producers behind the hits, each of the book's 806 entries includes songwriter and producer credits, the date and duration of the hit's Number One reign, and a look at the top five hits for the week that a given song nailed down the top spot on the Hot 100 chart. Hailed by the *New York Times* as "A treasure trove of pop lore."

848 pages. 7" x 9¼". 806 b&w illustrations. $21.95

Billboard's Hottest Hot 100 Hits

BY FRED BRONSON

This extremely entertaining volume puts a new spin on *Billboard*'s chart data by breaking down the top records from the Hot 100 pop singles chart into nearly 200 categories, including the top hits by major artists (the top 100 songs by the Beatles, the top 30 by Aretha Franklin, etc.), writers (the top 50 by Carole King, the top 30 by Prince), producers (the top 50 by Quincy Jones, the top 10 by Thom Bell), and labels (the top 100 on Arista, the top 30 on Chess). Other sections offer a wealth of trivia-rich information (the top 100 songs about animals, the top 100 by teenagers and pre-teens), and the book also offers year-by-year and decade-by-decade breakdowns of the top 100 songs from 1956 through 1990, as well as a newly computed list of the top 3,000 songs of the rock era. A must for music trivia fans.

416 pages. 7" x 9¼". 200 b&w illustrations. $19.95

BILLBOARD BOOKS **An imprint of Watson-Guptill Publications, Available From Your Bookstore**